Human Resource Management

GAINING A COMPETITIVE ADVANTAGE 10e

RAYMOND A. NOE
The Ohio State University

JOHN R. HOLLENBECK
Michigan State University

BARRY GERHART
University of Wisconsin–Madison

PATRICK M. WRIGHT
University of South Carolina

Mc
Graw
Hill
Education

HUMAN RESOURCE MANAGEMENT: GAINING A COMPETITIVE ADVANTAGE, TENTH EDITION

Published by McGraw-Hill Education, 2 Penn Plaza, New York, NY 10121. Copyright © 2017 by McGraw-Hill Education. All rights reserved. Printed in the United States of America. Previous editions © 2015, 2013, and 2010. No part of this publication may be reproduced or distributed in any form or by any means, or stored in a database or retrieval system, without the prior written consent of McGraw-Hill Education, including, but not limited to, in any network or other electronic storage or transmission, or broadcast for distance learning.

Some ancillaries, including electronic and print components, may not be available to customers outside the United States.

This book is printed on acid-free paper.

1 2 3 4 5 6 7 8 9 0 DOW/DOW 1 0 9 8 7 6

ISBN 978-1-259-57812-0
MHID 1-259-57812-7

Senior Vice President, Products & Markets: *Kurt L. Strand*
Vice President, General Manager, Products & Markets: *Michael Ryan*
Vice President, Content Design & Delivery: *Kimberly Meriwether David*
Managing Director: *Susan Gouijnstook*
Director: *Michael Ablassmeir*
Brand Manager: *Anke Weekes*
Director, Product Development: *Meghan Campbell*
Product Developer: *Michelle Houston*
Marketing Manager: *Michael Gedatus*
Market Development Specialist: *Sam Deffenbaugh*
Digital Product Analyst: *Kerry Shanahan*
Director, Content Design & Delivery: *Terri Schiest*
Program Manager: *Mary Conzachi*

Content Project Managers: *Mary E. Powers* (Core), *Evan Roberts* (Assessment)
Buyer: *Susan K. Culbertson*
Design: *Matt Backhaus*
Content Licensing Specialists: *Michelle D. Whitaker* (Image), *DeAnna Dausener* (Text)
Cover Image: © *Rawpixel Ltd/ Getty Images*
Compositor: *SPi Global*
Printer: *R. R. Donnelley*

Image Credit pages 2, 66, 100, 144, 182, 222, 262, 318, 376, 420, 456, 496, 534, 576, 628, 662): ©*g_studio/ GettyImages/©Andres Rodriguez/Alamy/©EdBockStock/ Alamy/©WavebreakMedialtd/Alamy/drbimages/ GettyImages*

All credits appearing on page or at the end of the book are considered to be an extension of the copyright page.

Library of Congress Cataloging-in-Publication Data

Noe, Raymond A.
   Human resource management : gaining a competitive advantage / Raymond A. Noe, The Ohio State University, John R. Hollenbeck, Michigan State University , Barry Gerhart, University of Wisconsin-Madison, Patrick M. Wright, University of South Carolina. —10 Edition.
      pages cm
   Revised edition of Human resource management, 2015.
   ISBN 978-1-259-57812-0 (alk. paper)
   1. Personnel management—United States. I. Title.
HF5549.2.U5N64 2016
658.3—dc23   2015035070

The Internet addresses listed in the text were accurate at the time of publication. The inclusion of a website does not indicate an endorsement by the authors or McGraw-Hill Education, and McGraw-Hill Education does not guarantee the accuracy of the information presented at these sites.

To my wife, Caroline, and my children, Ray, Tim,
and Melissa
—R. A. N.

To my parents, Harold and Elizabeth, my wife,
Patty, and my children, Jennifer, Marie, Timothy,
and Jeffrey
—J. R. H.

To my parents, Robert and Shirley, my wife,
Heather, and my children, Chris and Annie
—B. G.

To my parents, Patricia and Paul, my wife, Mary,
and my sons, Michael and Matthew
—P. M. W.

ABOUT THE AUTHORS

RAYMOND A. NOE is the Robert and Anne Hoyt Designated Professor of Management at The Ohio State University. He was previously a professor in the Department of Management at Michigan State University and the Industrial Relations Center of the Carlson School of Management, University of Minnesota. He received his BS in psychology from The Ohio State University and his MA and PhD in psychology from Michigan State University. Professor Noe conducts research and teaches undergraduate as well as MBA and PhD students in human resource management, managerial skills, quantitative methods, human resource information systems, training, employee development, and organizational behavior. He has published articles in the *Academy of Management Annals, Academy of Management Journal, Academy of Management Review, Journal of Applied Psychology, Journal of Vocational Behavior,* and *Personnel Psychology.* Professor Noe is currently on the editorial boards of several journals including *Personnel Psychology, Journal of Applied Psychology,* and *Journal of Management.* Professor Noe has received awards for his teaching and research excellence, including the Ernest J. McCormick Award for Distinguished Early Career Contribution from the Society for Industrial and Organizational Psychology. He is also a fellow of the Society of Industrial and Organizational Psychology.

JOHN R. HOLLENBECK holds the positions of University Distinguished Professor at Michigan State University and Eli Broad Professor of Management at the Eli Broad Graduate School of Business Administration. Dr. Hollenbeck received his PhD in Management from New York University in 1984. He served as the acting editor at *Organizational Behavior and Human Decision Processes* in 1995, the associate editor of *Decision Sciences* from 1999 to 2004, and the editor of *Personnel Psychology* from 1996 to 2002. He has published over 90 articles and book chapters on the topics of team decision making and work motivation. According to the Institute for Scientific Information, this body of work has been cited over 4,000 times by other researchers. Dr. Hollenbeck has been awarded fellowship status in both the Academy of Management and the American Psychological Association, and was recognized with the Career Achievement Award by the HR Division of the Academy of Management (2011), the Distinguished Service Contributions Award (2014), and the Early Career Award by the Society of Industrial and Organizational Psychology (1992). At Michigan State, Dr. Hollenbeck has won several teaching awards including the Michigan State Distinguished Faculty Award, the Michigan State Teacher-Scholar Award, and the Broad MBA Most Outstanding Faculty Member.

BARRY GERHART is Professor of Management and Human Resources and the Bruce R. Ellig Distinguished Chair in Pay and Organizational Effectiveness, Wisconsin School of Business, University of Wisconsin-Madison. He has also served as department chair or area coordinator at Cornell, Vanderbilt, and Wisconsin. His research interests include compensation, human resource strategy, international human resources, and employee retention. Professor Gerhart received his BS in psychology from Bowling Green State University and his PhD in industrial relations from the University of Wisconsin-Madison. He has co-authored two books in the area of compensation. He serves on the editorial boards of and has published in the *Academy of Management Journal, Industrial and Labor Relations Review, International Journal of Human Resource Management, Journal of Applied Psychology, Management and Organization Review,* and *Personnel Psychology.* Professor Gerhart is a past recipient of the Heneman Career Achievement Award, the Scholarly Achievement Award, and (twice) the International Human Resource Management Scholarly Research Award, all from the Human Resources Division, Academy of Management. He is a Fellow of the Academy of Management, the American Psychological Association, and the Society for Industrial and Organizational Psychology.

PATRICK M. WRIGHT is Thomas C. Vandiver Bicentennial Chair and the Director of the Center for Executive Succession in the Darla Moore School of Business at the University of South Carolina. Prior to joining USC, he served on the faculties at Cornell University, Texas A&M University, and the University of Notre Dame.

Professor Wright teaches, conducts research, and consults in the area of Strategic Human Resource Management (SHRM), particularly focusing on how firms use people as a source of competitive advantage and the changing nature of the Chief HR Officer role. He is the faculty leader for the Cornell ILR Executive Education/NAHR program, "The Chief HR Officer: Strategies for Success," aimed at developing potential successors to the CHRO role. He served as the lead editor on the recently released book, *The Chief HR Officer: Defining the New Role of Human Resource Leaders,* published by John Wiley and Sons.

He has published more than 60 research articles in journals as well as more than 20 chapters in books and edited volumes. He is the Editor at the *Journal of Management.* He has co-edited a special issue of *Research in Personnel and Human Resources Management* titled "Strategic Human Resource Management in the 21st Century" and guest edited a special issue of *Human Resource Management Review* titled "Research in Strategic HRM for the 21st Century."

He currently serves as a member on the Board of Directors for the Society for Human Resource Management and the National Academy of Human Resources (NAHR). He is a former board member of HRPS, SHRM Foundation, and World at Work (formerly American Compensation Association). From 2011 to 2015 he was named by *HRM Magazine* as one of the 20 "Most Influential Thought Leaders in HR."

The steady but slow recovery of the U.S. economy means that both consumers and businesses are carefully considering their spending patterns and investments. Both private-and public-sector employers are cautiously adding new employees if they see an increased demand for their products or services. Some companies are struggling to find qualified, talented, and skilled employees despite the many workers available. Also, they are continuing to examine how they can improve their "bottom line" while reducing costs. This has resulted in not only considering purchasing new technology and upgrading equipment, but putting a greater emphasis on ensuring that management practices and working conditions help employees work harder and smarter, and enhance their motivation, satisfaction, and commitment.

At the same time companies are taking steps to deal with the current economic conditions, they are also paying closer attention to how to engage in business practices that are economically sound but sustainable. That is, business practices that are ethical, protect the environment, and contribute to the communities from which the business draws the financial, physical, and human resources needed to provide its product and services. Consumers are demanding accountability in business practices: making money for shareholders should not involve abandoning ethics, ruining the environment, or taking advantage of employees from developing countries!

Regardless of whether a company's strategic direction involves downsizing, restructuring, growth, or a merger or acquisition, how human resources are managed is crucial for providing "value" to customers, shareholders, employees, and the community in which they are located. Our definition of "value" includes not only profits but also employee growth and satisfaction, additional employment opportunities, stewardship of the environment, and contributions to community programs. If a company fails to effectively use its financial capital, physical capital, and human capital to create "value," it will not survive. The way a company treats its employees (including those who are forced to leave their jobs) will influence the company's public reputation and brand as a responsible business, and its ability to attract talented employees. For example, the human resource practices at companies such as Google, SAS Institute, Quicken Loans, REI, and Wegmans Food Markets helped them earn recognition on *Fortune* magazine's recent list of the "The Top 100 Companies to Work For." This kind of publicity creates a positive image for these companies, helping them attract new employees, motivate and retain their current employees, and make their products and services more desirable to consumers.

We believe that all aspects of human resource management—including how companies interact with the environment; acquire, prepare, develop, and compensate employees; and design and evaluate work—can help companies meet their competitive challenges and create value. Meeting challenges is necessary to create value and to gain a competitive advantage.

The Competitive Challenges

The challenges that organizations face today can be grouped into three categories:

- **The sustainability challenge.** Sustainability refers to the ability of a company to survive and succeed in a dynamic competitive environment. Sustainability depends on how well a company meets the needs of those who have an interest in seeing that the company succeeds. Challenges to sustainability include the ability to deal with economic and social changes, engage in responsible and ethical business practices, efficiently use natural resources and protect the environment, provide high-quality products and services, and develop methods and measures (also known as metrics) to determine if the company is meeting stakeholder needs. To compete in today's economy companies use mergers and acquisitions, growth, and downsizing. Companies rely on skilled workers to be productive, creative, and innovative and to provide high-quality customer service; their work is demanding and companies cannot guarantee job security. One issue is how to attract and retain a committed, productive workforce in turbulent economic conditions that offer opportunity for financial success but can also turn sour, making every employee expendable. Forward-looking businesses are capitalizing on the strengths of a diverse multigenerational workforce. The experiences of Enron, *News of the World,* and Lehman Brothers provide vivid examples of how sustainability depends on ethical and responsible business practices, including the management of human resources. Another important issue is how to accomplish financial objectives through meeting both customer and employee needs. To meet the sustainability challenge companies must engage in human resource management practices that address short-term needs but help ensure the long-term success of the firm. The development and choice of human resource management practices should support business goals and strategy.

The role of ethical behavior in a company's sustainability has led us to include more discussion and examples of "integrity in action" in this edition. The actions of top executives and managers show employees how serious they are about human resource management practices. Also, employees look at their behaviors to determine if they are merely giving "lip service" to ethical behavior or if they genuinely care about creating an ethical workplace. As a result, in this edition of the book we include Integrity in Action boxes that highlight good (and bad) decisions about HR practices made by top executives, company leaders, and managers that either reinforce (or undermine) the importance of ethical behavior in the company.

- **The global challenge.** Companies must be prepared to compete with companies from around the world either in the United States or abroad. Companies must both defend their domestic markets from foreign competitors and broaden their scope to encompass global markets. Globalization is a continuing challenge as companies look to enter emerging markets in countries such as Brazil and China to provide their products and services.

- **The technology challenge.** Using new technologies such as computer-aided manufacturing, virtual reality, and social media can give companies an edge. New technologies can result in employees "working smarter" as well as provide higher-quality products and more efficient services to customers. Companies that have realized the greatest gains from new technology have human resource management practices that support the use of technology to create what is known as high-performance work systems. Work, training programs, and reward systems often need to be reconfigured to support employees' use of new technology. The three important aspects of high-performance work systems are (1) human resources and their capabilities, (2) new technology and its opportunities, and (3) efficient work structures and policies that allow employees and technology to interact. Companies are also using social media and e-HRM (electronic HRM) applications to give employees more ownership of the employment relationship through the ability to enroll in and participate in training programs, change benefits, communicate with co-workers and customers online, and work "virtually" with peers in geographically different locations.

We believe that organizations must successfully deal with these challenges to create and maintain value, and the key to facing these challenges is a motivated, well-trained, and committed workforce.

The Changing Role of the Human Resource Management Function

The human resource management (HRM) profession and practices have undergone substantial change and redefinition. Many articles written in both the academic and practitioner literature have been critical of the traditional HRM function. Unfortunately, in many organizations HRM services are not providing value but instead are mired down in managing trivial administrative tasks. Where this is true, HRM departments can be replaced with new technology or outsourced to a vendor who can provide higher-quality services at a lower cost. Although this recommendation is indeed somewhat extreme (and threatening to both HRM practitioners and those who teach human resource management!), it does demonstrate that companies need to ensure that their HRM functions are creating value for the firm.

Technology should be used where appropriate to automate routine activities, and managers should concentrate on HRM activities that can add substantial value to the company. Consider employee benefits: Technology is available to automate the process by which employees enroll in benefits programs and to keep detailed records of benefits usage. This use of technology frees up time for the manager to focus on activities that can create value for the firm (such as how to control health care costs and reduce workers' compensation claims).

Although the importance of some HRM departments is being debated, everyone agrees on the need to successfully manage human resources for a company to maximize its competitiveness. Several themes emerge from our conversations with managers and our review of research on HRM practices. First, in today's organizations, managers themselves are becoming more responsible for HRM practices and most believe that people issues are critical to business success. Second, most managers believe that their HRM departments are not well respected because of a perceived lack of competence, business sense, and contact with operations. A study by Deloitte consulting and *The Economist* Intelligence Unit found that only 23% of business executives believe that HR currently plays a significant role in strategy and operational results. Third, many managers believe that for HRM practices to be effective they need to be related to the strategic direction of the business. This text emphasizes how HRM practices can and should contribute to business goals and help to improve product and service quality and effectiveness. An important way, which we highlight throughout the text, is through using "Big Data" and evidence-based HR to demonstrate the value of HRM practices.

Our intent is to provide students with the background to be successful HRM professionals, to manage human resources effectively, and to be knowledgeable consumers of HRM products. Managers must be able to identify effective HRM practices to purchase these services from a consultant, to work with the HRM department, or to design and implement them personally. The text emphasizes how a manager can more effectively manage human resources and highlights important issues in current HRM practice.

This book represents a valuable approach to teaching human resource management for several reasons:

- The text draws from the diverse research, teaching, and consulting experiences of four authors who have taught human resource management to undergraduates, traditional day MBA students as a required and elective course, and more experienced managers and professional employees in weekend and evening MBA programs. The teamwork approach gives a depth and breadth to the coverage that is not found in other texts.

- Human resource management is viewed as critical to the success of a business. The text emphasizes how the HRM function, as well as the management of human resources, can help companies gain a competitive advantage.
- The book discusses current issues such as social networking, talent management, diversity, and employee engagement, all of which have a major impact on business and HRM practice.
- Strategic human resource management is introduced early in the book and integrated throughout the text.
- Examples of how new technologies are being used to improve the efficiency and effectiveness of HRM practices are provided throughout the text.
- We provide examples of how companies are evaluating HRM practices to determine their value.
- The Chapter openers, in-text boxes, and end-of-chapter materials provide questions that provide students the opportunity to discuss and apply HR concepts to a broad range of issues including strategic human resource management, HR in small businesses, ethics and HR's role in helping companies achieve sustainability, adopt and use technology, adapt to globalization, and practice integrity. This should make the HR classroom more interactive and increase students' understanding of the concepts and their application.

Organization

Human Resource Management: Gaining a Competitive Advantage includes an introductory chapter (Chapter 1) and five parts.

Chapter 1 provides a detailed discussion of the global, new economy, stakeholder, and work system challenges that influence companies' abilities to successfully meet the needs of shareholders, customers, employees, and other stakeholders. We discuss how the management of human resources can help companies meet the competitive challenges.

Part 1 includes a discussion of the environmental forces that companies face in attempting to capitalize on their human resources as a means to gain competitive advantage. The environmental forces include the strategic direction of the business, the legal environment, and the type of work performed and physical arrangement of the work.

A key focus of the strategic human resource management chapter is highlighting the role that staffing, performance management, training and development, and compensation play in different types of business strategies. A key focus of the legal chapter is enhancing managers' understanding of laws related to sexual harassment, affirmative action, and accommodations for disabled employees. The various types of discrimination and ways they have been interpreted by the courts are discussed. The chapter on analysis and design of work emphasizes how work systems can improve company competitiveness by alleviating job stress and by improving employees' motivation and satisfaction with their jobs.

Part 2 deals with the acquisition and preparation of human resources, including human resource planning and recruitment, selection, and training. The human resource planning chapter illustrates the process of developing a human resource plan. Also, the strengths and weaknesses of staffing options such as outsourcing, use of contingent workers, and downsizing are discussed. Strategies for recruiting talented employees are emphasized. The selection chapter emphasizes ways to minimize errors in employee selection and placement to improve the company's competitive position. Selection method standards such as validity and reliability are discussed in easily understandable terms without compromising the technical complexity of these issues. The chapter discusses selection methods such as interviews and various types of tests (including personality, honesty, and drug tests) and compares them on measures of validity, reliability, utility, and legality.

We discuss the components of effective training systems and the manager's role in determining employees' readiness for training, creating a positive learning environment, and ensuring that training is used on the job. The advantages and disadvantages of different training methods are described, such as e-learning and mobile training.

Part 3 explores how companies can determine the value of employees and capitalize on their talents through retention and development strategies. The performance management chapter examines the strengths and weaknesses of performance management methods that use ratings, objectives, or behaviors. The employee development chapter introduces the student to how assessment, job experiences, formal courses, and mentoring relationships are used to develop employees. The chapter on retention and separation discusses how managers can maximize employee productivity and satisfaction to avoid absenteeism and turnover. The use of employee surveys to monitor job and organizational characteristics that affect satisfaction and subsequently retention is emphasized.

Part 4 covers rewarding and compensating human resources, including designing pay structures, recognizing individual contributions, and providing benefits. Here we explore how managers should decide the pay rate for different jobs, given the company's compensation strategy and the worth of jobs. The advantages and disadvantages of merit pay, gainsharing, and skill-based pay are discussed. The benefits chapter highlights the different types of employer-provided benefits and discusses how benefit costs can be contained. International comparisons of compensation and benefit practices are provided.

Part 5 covers special topics in human resource management, including labor–management relations, international HRM, and managing the HRM function. The collective bargaining and labor relations chapter focuses on traditional issues in labor–management relations, such as union structure and membership, the organizing process, and contract negotiations; it also discusses new union agendas and less adversarial approaches to labor–management relations. Social and political changes, such as introduction of the euro currency in the European Community, are discussed in the chapter on global human resource management. Selecting, preparing, and rewarding employees for foreign assignments is also discussed. The text concludes with a chapter that emphasizes how HRM practices should be aligned to help the company meet its business objectives. The chapter emphasizes that the HRM function needs to have a customer focus to be effective.

New Feature and Content Changes in This Edition

All examples, figures, and statistics have been updated to incorporate the most recently published human resource data. Each chapter was revised to include current examples, research results, and relevant topical coverage. All of the Exercising Strategy, Managing People, and HR in Small Business end of chapter cases are either new or updated. Following are the highlights for each chapter.

Chapter 1

New Opening Vignette: How Marriott is using human resource practices to support expansion of its properties around the world and reinventing itself to appeal to millennial generation travelers' tastes and preferences.

New Boxes:
- Dow Chemical, Merck, and Novartis socially responsible programs help improve living conditions around the world.
- How the CEO of Gravity Payments introduced a new pay policy to help employees meet their expenses.
- Iberdrola USA, SAP, and Boeing efforts to prepare employees for global assignments.
- How General Cable used data to show the value of its high performance work practices.

New Text Material:
- HR in organizations: budgets, example of the role of HR in companies (Walgreens, Tesla Motors, Coeur Mining, and MGM International Resorts), managers expectations for the HR function, and the skills needed by HR professionals to contribute to the businesss.
- How companies are using big data and workforce analytics to understand turnover, talent, and sales performance (Intermountain Healthcare, Johnson Controls, SuccessFactors).
- Economy data, labor force statistics, occupational and job growth projections, skill shortages, working at home and flexible schedules.
- HR's role in insuring product quality and customer service including examples of HR practices of the 2014 Baldrige Award Winners (Asana, Unilever, Delaware North Companies, PricewaterhouseCoopers Public Sector Practice, Baylor Health Care System).
- Innotrac's and Dell's efforts to manage a multigenerational workforce and the value of hiring employees with disabilities.
- Ethics training used by Dimension Data and Xerox.
- Growth of world economy and global business for companies such as Gap, McDonald's, and Coca-Cola.
- Reshoring jobs in the United States (Hanesbrands, Peds Legware).
- Use of apps, robots, wearables, and mobile devices in the workplace.
- HindlePower's use of HR practices to support high performance work systems.

Chapter 2

New Opening Vignette: Changes in Southwest Airlines strategy as the company moves to "middle age."

New Boxes:
- Facebook's European privacy problem.
- Use of robots in China to lower labor costs.
- Practices that make 3M an admired, ethical company.
- Starbucks' college tuition program.

Chapter 3

New Opening Vignette: Sex discrimination at Kleiner Perkins.

New Boxes:
- Legal challenges Uber faces in the European Union.
- Satyam founder convicted of accounting scandal.
- Korn/Ferry executive inappropriate use of e-mail.
- Heineken's focus on sustainability through reducing water usage, carbon emissions, and promoting responsible drinking.

New Text Material:
- Frequency of discrimination cases.

Chapter 4

New Opening Vignette: The role of organizational and work design in the GM ignition switch debacle.

New Boxes:
- UPS's new technology for designing the safest and most efficient driving routes.
- How ISIS and other terrorist organizations structure themselves and why.
- Recent crackdowns in the manicure sweatshops in New York City.
- The new and controversial OSHA "name and shame" is working.
- Hospitals are using evidence-based management to improve cardiac care.

New Text Material:
- Poorly controlled menu design created work design problems at McDonald's.
- How to calculate "capital spending per worker," and what this metric means.
- The failed launch of the HealthCare.gov website was due to structural faults.
- Social network analysis is revolutionizing the use of informal structures.
- Ergonomic design related to sitting is being used to prevent inuries.

Chapter 5

New Opening Vignette: How Uber's business model that is centered around treating drivers as independent contractors is being challenged.

New Boxes:
- How companies that provide workers' smartphones balance work and privacy.
- The opening up of Cuba will lead to an increased supply of high-skill labor.
- The new nature of work is affecting the demand for a 4-year college degree.
- The failure to manage diversity at the CIA harms counterterrorism efforts.
- Increases in unemployment benefits result in higher unemployment.

New Text Material:
- Demand for workers in some industries is skyrocketing (elder care, welding).
- Labor shortages in the construction industry affecting the overall economy.
- Why companies often downsize their workforces even when business is good.
- Cuts to public health funding led to the Ebola breakouts in the United States.
- U.S. visa limits harm America's ability to compete in some high-tech fields.

Chapter 6

New Opening Vignette: How Abercrombie and Fitch was sued for religious discrimination when it failed to hire a young Muslim woman who wore a hijab.

New Boxes:
- Employers are collecting information on Facebook that would be illegal to ask in an interview.
- The crash of Germanwing's Flight 9525 could be traced to poor personnel selection processes.
- The use of criminal background checks is causing labor shortages in some industries.
- The fallout when a leader within the NAACP falsely claimed she was African American.
- The percentage of Hispanic Americans is changing due simply to reporting biases.

New Text Material:
- How "Big Data" applications are changing how personnel are selected.
- Game developers are building applications that can be used to simulate real jobs.
- The traditional belief that job performance is normally distributed may be false.
- Recent Supreme Court rulings make it more difficult to diversify the workforce.
- Scandals in the reporting of test scores from some foreign countries held up college selection decisions in 2014.

Chapter 7

New Opening Vignette: Highlighting how Keller Williams' commitment to training programs and training evaluation has contributed to the success of the business and its real estate agents.

New Boxes:
- STIHL's use training to help all of the company's stakeholders including consumers, distributors, and retailers work safely and productively.
- How Year Up trains low income youth for high demand jobs.
- Phillips, Accenture, and Etihad Airways are adapting their training practices to reach a global and cross-cultural workforce.
- Evans Analytical Group and Coca-Cola Bottling Company Consolidated use social media and apps to foster continuous learning.
- How Mountain American Credit demonstrated the effectiveness of its sales training for new employees.

New Text Material:
- Showing how KLA-Tencor conducted needs assessment for its service engineers.
- Highlighting how Mindtree Limited and Nemours create a positive learning environment using different training methods.
- Spectrum Health's use of a coaching guide to insure trained skills are reinforced by a manager.
- Companies such as Coca-Cola Sabo , SNI, and ADP are providing performance support using on-demand training materials such as YouTube videos.
- Examples of how companies including Greyhound Lines, CMS Energy, PPD, KLA-Tencor, Coca-Cola Bottling Company Consolidated, Farmers Insurance, and Sonic use different training methods including simulations, games, online learning, social media, blended learning, and action learning.
- Discussion of Massive Open Online Courses (MOOCs) for education and training including their advantages and disadvantages.
- How MasTec Utility Service Group uses a learning management system.

Chapter 8

New Opening Vignette: Adobe's performance management system that emphasizes ongoing feedback and eliminates annual ratings.

New Boxes:
- How Kaiser Permanente creates a culture of continuous improvement.
- The support Expedia provided its managers to use a new performance management system.
- How Connecticut Health uses business and employee goals to meet its mission of helping people gain access to affordable and high quality health care.
- Persistent Systems use of gamification for performance management.

New Text Material:
- How Texas Roadhouse revised its performance management system to focus on more frequent feedback and employee development.
- Key Performance Indicators (KPIs) and how Brinker International uses them.
- How Deloitte's performance management system for project teams meets the criteria for a good performance management system.
- Why Microsoft abandoned a forced ranking system.
- How to best use objectives or goals in performance management.
- Discussion of social performance management including peer-to-peer recognition, social media, and gamification.
- Examples of electronic monitoring in trucking industry, landscaping services, and health care.
- Examples of age discrimination lawsuits involving performance management.

Chapter 9

Revised Opening Vignette: ESPNs efforts in employee development.

New Boxes:
- How Genentech facilitates employee development career management through use of a virtual and physical development system.
- Sidley Austin's use of pro bono work to help less experienced lawyers develop their skills and benefit the community.
- SAP is demonstrating the value of its new employee mentoring program.
- How Dow Chemical develops global leaders and develops communities through local projects.

New Text Material:
- Job hopping and number of jobs employees have held in their careers.
- How companies (e.g., PEMCO Mutual Insurance Company, AT&T, Cartus, SAP, Mondelez, Airbnb, General Motors, Thomas Reuters, PwC, Valvoline, Paychex) use self-assessment, job rotation, customized courses and programs, 360-degree feedback, temporary assignments, mentoring, coaching, and succession planning.
- Stretch assignments and reverse mentoring.
- AstraZeneca and Johnson & Johnson's efforts to melt the glass ceiling women face in moving to top-level management positions.

Chapter 10

New Opening Vignette: The many reasons why working at the IRS is such a difficult job and what the agency is trying to do to shore up morale.

New Boxes:
- The use of wearable sensors creates opportunties and challenges for employers.
- How Chinese taxi drivers used wildcat strikes to drive Uber out of the country.
- The use of cell phones to do work at night is counterproductive.
- The lack of political correctness can get someone fired in the age of social media.
- New evidence supports the use of outplacement activities for promoting culture.

New Text Material:
- Failures within the Secret Service led to a wave of terminations.
- Social networking sites are being used to measure employee performance.
- No compete clauses are being increasingly used—even for low-skilled jobs.

- The use of alternative dispute resolution techniques can help or harm employee relations.
- Employers are using both rewards and punishments to improve employee health.

Chapter 11

New Opening Vignette: The role of labor market competition and business strategy in increasing wages and salary.

New Boxes:
- Zappos's and Amazon's pay to quit policy.
- Wage and overtime implications for independent contractors or full-time employees.
- Evidence that high wages reduce turnover costs for Walmart and Container Store.
- Where to manufacture products depends on labor costs.
- Providing higher wages for garment workers in Cambodia.

New Text Material:
- New salary test under the Fair Labor Standards Act (and the expected increase in the number of employees eligible for overtime premiums).
- How labor costs and other factors affect where new North American manufacturing plants are built.
- The distinction between equality and equity.

Chapter 12

New Opening Vignette: Employers raising pay but controlling fixed costs through profit sharing and reduced hiring of new employees.

New Boxes:
- Recruiting and retaining engineering talent in China.
- European banks use of bonus caps.
- Barclay's pay system holds employees accountable for ethical behavior.
- Tasty Catering open book management practices reduce costs and increase profit.

New Text Material:
- Effect pay plan has on workforce composition (sorting effect).
- Use of pay to differentiate between employees.
- Distribution of performance ratings and base pay increases in the United States.

Chapter 13

New Opening Vignette: Balancing work and family in Silicon Valley Companies.

New Boxes:
- Patagonia's use of benefits to sustain its business strategy.
- Microsoft requiring vendors to provide paid time off for their employees.
- Egg freezing: as a family-friendly benefit?
- The challenges of recruiting expatriates to Beijing because of its air quality.
- Evidence of outcomes of Sloan Valve's wellness program.

New Text Material:
- Number and percentage of people without health insurance in the United States.
- Use of big data to understand usage of health care coverage.
- Incentives and penalties employers can use under the Affordable Care Act to encourage healthy behavior.
- Employee preferences for how benefits are communicated.
- Decline in use of defined benefit plans.

Chapter 14

New Opening Vignette: Collective action by nonunion workers and supporters.

New Boxes:
- Alliance for Bangladesh Worker Safety.
- Using social media for union-related communications.
- Give and take of Boeing's contract negotiations.
- Evidence for high-performance work practice effectiveness across different countries.
- How differences in U.S. and German union strength influenced Amazon's strategy for dealing with unions.

New Text Material:
- Discussion of garment workers disaster in Bangladesh, employers responses, and potential role of labor unions in avoiding it.
- NLRB rules to streamline and speed up union representation elections.
- Companies use of managers to replace striking workers.
- Compensation rates for union and nonunion employees.

Chapter 15

New Opening Vignette: Walmart's global growth strategy.

New Boxes:
- How technology is changing the nature of work and blurring work and nonwork time.
- Risks and rewards of doing business in Africa.
- Airlines making money by charging fees which should not have been collected during the government shutdown.
- How changes in Vietnam's, China's, and India's economic systems have helped reduce poverty.

New Text Material:
- *Fortune* global companies and cost of living figures.
- Questions for assessing employees' suitability for overseas assignments.

Chapter 16

New Opening Vignette: The need for HR at tech start-ups.

New Boxes:
- How U.S. companies such as Otis are reshoring, i.e., bringing jobs back to the United States.
- IKEA's focus on efficient packaging and lower material costs contributes to sustainability.
- Humana's use of an app that helps improve customer health.
- AT&T misleads customers about their unlimited wireless data plan.

Acknowledgments

As this book enters its tenth edition, it is important to acknowledge those who started it all. The first edition of this book would not have been possible if not for the entrepreneurial spirit of two individuals. Bill Schoof, president of Austen Press, gave us the resources and had the confidence that four unproven textbook writers could provide a new perspective for teaching human resource management. John Weimeister, our former editor, provided us with valuable marketing information, helped us in making major decisions regarding the book, and made writing this book an enjoyable process. Anke Weekes, our current brand manager, continues to provide the same high-quality guidance and support we received from John. We also worked with an all-star development and project management team, including Heather Darr and Mary Powers. Their suggestions, patience, gentle prodding, and careful oversight kept the author team focused on providing a high-quality revision while meeting publication deadline. We would also like to thank Michael Gedatus for his marketing efforts for this new edition.

We would also like to thank the professors who gave of their time to review the text and attend focus groups. Their helpful comments and suggestions have greatly helped to enhance this learning program:

Vondra Armstrong
Pulaski Technical College

Richard Arvey
National University of Singapore

Steve Ash
University of Akron

Carlson Austin
South Carolina State University

Janice Baldwin
The University of Texas at Arlington

Alison Barber
Michigan State University

Kathleen Barnes
University of Wisconsin, Superior

Brian Bartel
Mid-State Technical College

James E. Bartlett, II
University of South Carolina–Columbia

Ron Beaulieu
Central Michigan University

Joan Benek-Rivera
University of Pennsylvania–Bloomsburg

Philip Benson
New Mexico State University

Nancy Bereman
Wichita State University

Chris Berger
Purdue University

Carol Bibly
Triton College

Angela Boston
The University of Texas at Arlington

Wendy Boswell
Texas A&M University

Sarah Bowman
Idaho State University

Charles Braun
University of Kentucky

James Browne
University of Southern Colorado

Ronald Brownie
Purdue University–North Central

Jon Bryan
Bridgewater State College

Gerald Calvasina
Southern Utah University

Stacy Campbell
Kennesaw State University

Martin Carrigan
University of Findlay

Georgia Chao
Michigan State University

Fay Cocchiara
Arkansas State University

LeAnne Coder
Western Kentucky University

Walter Coleman
Florida Southern College

Mary Connerley
Virginia Tech University

Donna Cooke
Florida Atlantic University–Davis

Craig Cowles
Bridgewater State College

Susie Cox
McNeese State University

Michael Crant
University of Notre Dame

Shaun W. Davenport
High Point University

Shannon Davis
North Carolina State University

Roger Dean
Washington & Lee University

John Delery
University of Arkansas

Fred Dorn
The University of Mississippi

Jennifer Dose
Messiah College

Tom Dougherty
University of Missouri

Berrin Erdogan
Portland State University

Angela Farrar
University of Nevada–Las Vegas

Dyanne Ferk
University of Illinois–Springfield

Robert Figler
University of Akron

Louis Firenze
Northwood University

Art Fischer
Pittsburgh State University

Barry Friedman
State University of New York at Oswego

Cynthia Fukami
University of Denver

Daniel J. Gallagher
University of Illinois–Springfield

Bonnie Fox Garrity
D'Youville College

Donald G. Gardner
University of Colorado at Colorado Springs

David Gerth
Nashville State Community College

Sonia Goltz
Michigan Technological University

Bob Graham
Sacred Heart University

Terri Griffith
Washington University

Ken Gross
University of Oklahoma–Norman

John Hannon
University at Buffalo

Bob Hatfield
Indiana University

Alan Heffner
James Monroe Center

Fred Heidrich
Black Hills State University

Rob Heneman
Ohio State University

Gary Hensel
McHenry County College

Kim Hester
Arkansas State University

Nancy Higgins
Montgomery College–Rockville

Wayne Hockwater
Florida State University

Fred Hughes
Faulkner University

Denise Tanguay Hoyer
Eastern Michigan University

Natalie J. Hunter
Portland State University

Julie Indvik
California State University, Chico

Sanford Jacoby
University of California, Los Angeles

Frank Jeffries
University of Alaska–Anchorage

Roy Johnson
Iowa State University

Gwen Jones
Fairleigh Dickinson University

Gwendolyn Jones
University of Akron

Hank Karp
Hampton University

Marianne Koch
University of Oregon

James Kolacek
Palm Beach Atlantic University

Tom Kolenko
Kennesaw State College

Elias Konwufine
Keiser University

Beth Koufteros
Texas A&M University

Ken Kovach
George Mason University

Chalmer Labig
Oklahoma State University

Patricia Lanier
University of Louisiana at Lafayette

Vonda Laughlin
Carson-Newman College

Helen LaVan
DePaul University

Renee Lerche
University of Michigan

Nancy Boyd Lillie
University of North Texas

Beth A. Livingston
Cornell University

Karen Locke
William & Mary

Michael Dane Loflin
York Technical College

Susan Madsen
Utah Valley University

Larry Mainstone
Valparaiso University

Ann-Marie Majeskey
Mount Olive College

Liz Malatestinic
Indiana University

Patricia Martina
University of Texas–San Antonio

Nicholas Mathys
DePaul University

Lisa McConnell
Oklahoma State University

Liliana Meneses
University of Maryland University College

Jessica Methot
Rutgers University

Angela Miles
North Carolina A&T State University

Stuart Milne
Georgia Institute of Technology

Barbara Minsky
Troy University

Kelly Mollica
University of Memphis

Jim Morgan
California State University–Chico

Pamela Mulvey
*Olney Central College
Lake Land College*

Gary Murray
Rose State College

David M. Nemi
Niagara County Community College

Nhung Nguyen
Towson University

Thomas J. Norman
California State University–Dominguez Hills

Millicent Nelson
Middle Tennessee State University

Lam Nguyen
Palm Beach State College

Cheri Ostroff
Teachers College Columbia

Teresa Palmer
Illinois State University

Robert Paul
Kansas State University

Tracy Porter
Cleveland State University

Gregory Quinet
Southern Polytechnic State University

Sam Rabinowitz
Rutgers University

David Rahn
California State University–Chico

Jude Rathburn
University of Wisconsin–Milwaukee

Katherine Ready
University of Wisconsin

Herbert Ricardo
Indian River State College

Mike Ritchie
University of South Carolina

Gwen Rivkin
Cardinal Stritch University

Mark Roehling
Michigan State University

Mary Ellen Rosetti
Hudson Valley Community College

Craig J. Russell
University of Oklahoma

Sarah Sanders-Smith
Purdue University–North Central

Miyako Schanely
Jefferson Community College

Robert Schappe
University of Michigan–Dearborn

Jack Schoenfelder
Ivy Tech Community College

Machelle K. Schroeder, PhD, SPHR
University of Wisconsin–Platteville

Joshua Schwarz
Miami University–Ohio

Pat Setlik
Harper College

Christina Shalley
Georgia Tech

Richard Shuey
Thomas More College

Richard Simpson
University of Utah

Romila Singh
University of Wisconsin–Milwaukee

Erika Engel Small
Coastal Carolina University

Mark Smith
Mississippi Gulf Coast Community College–Gulfport

Scott Snell
University of Virginia

Kris Sperstad
Chippewa Valley Technical College

Howard Stanger
Canisius College

Carol S. Steinhaus, PhD
Northern Michigan University

Gary Stroud
Franklin University

Cynthia Sutton
Indiana University–South Bend

Peg Thomas
Pennsylvania State University–Behrend

Steven L. Thomas
Missouri State University

Tom Timmerman
Tennessee Technology University

George Tompson
University of Tampa

J. Bruce Tracey
Cornell University

K. J. Tullis
University of Central Oklahoma

Dan Turban
University of Missouri–Columbia

Linda Turner
Morrisville State College

Linda Urbanski
University of Toledo

William Van Lente
Alliant International University

Charles Vance
Loyola Marymount University

Kim Wade
Washington State University

Sheng Wang
University of Nevada–Las Vegas

Renee Warning
University of Central Oklahoma

Lynn Wilson
Saint Leo University

Jenell Wittmer, PhD
University of Toledo

George Whaley
San Jose State University

Steve Woods
University of Baltimore

Daniel Yazak
Montana State University–Billings

Ryan D. Zimmerman
Texas A&M University

Raymond A. Noe
John R. Hollenbeck
Barry Gerhart
Patrick M. Wright

McGraw-Hill Connect®
Learn Without Limits

Connect is a teaching and learning platform that is proven to deliver better results for students and instructors.

Connect empowers students by continually adapting to deliver precisely what they need, when they need it, and how they need it, so your class time is more engaging and effective.

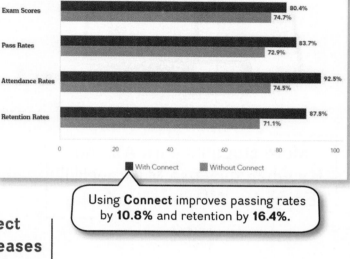

Course outcomes improve with Connect.

	With Connect	Without Connect
Exam Scores	80.4%	74.7%
Pass Rates	83.7%	72.9%
Attendance Rates	92.5%	74.5%
Retention Rates	87.5%	71.1%

Using **Connect** improves passing rates by **10.8%** and retention by **16.4%**.

88% of instructors who use Connect require it; instructor satisfaction increases by 38% when Connect is required.

Analytics

Connect Insight®

Connect Insight is Connect's new one-of-a-kind visual analytics dashboard—now available for both instructors and students—that provides at-a-glance information regarding student performance, which is immediately actionable. By presenting assignment, assessment, and topical performance results together with a time metric that is easily visible for aggregate or individual results, Connect Insight gives the user the ability to take a just-in-time approach to teaching and learning, which was never before available. Connect Insight presents data that empowers students and helps instructors improve class performance in a way that is efficient and effective.

Connect helps students achieve better grades

	A	B	C	D	F
With Connect	36%	29.5%	22%	4.3%	8.2%
Without Connect	22.2%	22.3%	25.6%	9.8%	20%

Based on McGraw-Hill Education Connect Effectiveness Study 2013

Students can view their results for any Connect course.

Mobile

Connect's new, intuitive mobile interface gives students and instructors flexible and convenient, anytime–anywhere access to all components of the Connect platform.

Adaptive

THE FIRST AND ONLY **ADAPTIVE READING EXPERIENCE** DESIGNED TO TRANSFORM THE WAY STUDENTS READ

> More students earn **A's** and **B's** when they use McGraw-Hill Education **Adaptive** products.

SmartBook®

Proven to help students improve grades and study more efficiently, SmartBook contains the same content within the print book, but actively tailors that content to the needs of the individual. SmartBook's adaptive technology provides precise, personalized instruction on what the student should do next, guiding the student to master and remember key concepts, targeting gaps in knowledge and offering customized feedback, and driving the student toward comprehension and retention of the subject matter. Available on smartphones and tablets, SmartBook puts learning at the student's fingertips—anywhere, anytime.

> Over **4 billion questions** have been answered, making McGraw-Hill Education products more intelligent, reliable, and precise.

STUDENTS WANT

SMARTBOOK®

95% of students reported **SmartBook** to be a more effective way of reading material

100% of students want to use the Practice Quiz feature available within **SmartBook** to help them study

100% of students reported having reliable access to off-campus wifi

90% of students say they would purchase **SmartBook** over print alone

95% reported that **SmartBook** would impact their study skills in a positive way

*Findings based on a 2015 focus group survey at Pellissippi State Community College administered by McGraw-Hill Education

INSTRUCTOR'S MANUAL

The Instructor's Manual contains notes, answers to the discussion questions, additional questions and exercises, teaching suggestions, and answers to the end-of-chapter case questions.

TEST BANK

The test bank has been revised and updated to reflect the content of the new edition of the book. Each chapter includes multiple-choice, true/false, and essay questions.

VIDEOS

Human Resource Management Videos offer clips on HRM issues for each chapter of this edition. You'll find a new video produced by the SHRM Foundation, entitled "Once the Deal Is Done: Making Mergers Work." Three new videos specifically address employee benefits: "GM Cuts Benefits and Pay," "Sulphur Springs Teachers," and "Google Employee Perks." Other new videos available for this edition include "E-Learning English" for the chapter on employee development and "Recession Job Growth" for the chapter on HR planning and recruitment.

POWERPOINT

This presentation program features detailed slides for each chapter.

MCGRAW-HILL CAMPUS

Campus McGraw-Hill Campus is a new one-stop teaching and learning experience available to users of any learning management system. This institutional service allows faculty and students to enjoy single sign-on (SSO) access to all McGraw-Hill Higher Education materials, including the award-winning McGraw-Hill Connect platform, from directly within the institution's website. With McGraw-Hill Campus, faculty receive instant access to teaching materials (e.g., eBooks, test banks, PowerPoint slides, animations, learning objects, etc.), allowing them to browse, search, and use any instructor ancillary content in our vast library at no additional cost to instructor or students.

MCGRAW-HILL AND BLACKBOARD

McGraw-Hill Higher Education and Blackboard have teamed up. What does this mean for you?

1. **Your life, simplified.** Now you and your students can access McGraw-Hill's Connect™ and Create™ right from within your Blackboard course—all with one single sign-on. Say good-bye to the days of logging in to multiple applications.

2. **Deep integration of content and tools.** Not only do you get single sign-on with Connect™ and Create™, you also get deep integration of McGraw-Hill content and content engines right in Blackboard. Whether you're choosing a book for your course or building Connect™ assignments, all the tools you need are right where you want them—inside Blackboard.

3. **Seamless gradebooks.** Are you tired of keeping multiple gradebooks and manually synchronizing grades into Blackboard? We thought so. When a student completes an integrated Connect™ assignment, the grade for that assignment automatically (and instantly) feeds your Blackboard grade center.

4. **A solution for everyone.** Whether your institution is already using Blackboard or you just want to try Blackboard on your own, we have a solution for you. McGraw-Hill and Blackboard can now offer you easy access to industry-leading technology and content, whether your campus hosts it, or we do. Be sure to ask your local McGraw-Hill representative for details.

MCGRAW-HILL CUSTOMER CARE CONTACT INFORMATION

At McGraw-Hill, we understand that getting the most from new technology can be challenging. That's why our services don't stop after you purchase our products. You can e-mail our product specialists 24 hours a day to get product-training online. Or you can search our knowledge bank of frequently asked questions on our support website. For customer support, call 800-331-5094 or visit www .mhhe.com/support. One of our technical support analysts will be able to assist you in a timely fashion.

BRIEF CONTENTS

CONTENTS

**PART 3
Assessment and
Development of HRM 318**

Human Resource Management

GAINING A COMPETITIVE ADVANTAGE

Human Resource Management: Gaining a Competitive Advantage

1

CHAPTER

Marriott: HR Practices Result in Engaged Employees and Satisfied Customers

If you have traveled, you probably have seen or stayed at a Marriott hotel. But did you know that Marriott owns few hotels? Most are owned by real estate partners, and Marriott manages or franchises them. Marriott is doing well in a competitive industry. Its 2014 revenue and net income ($13.8 billion, and $753 million, respectively) were at record levels. Financial analysts expect double digit growth in 2015 and the stock price hit a record high. In order to stay relevant in the hotel industry Marriott has added new properties around the world and is reinventing itself to appeal to tastes of the new Millennial generation of travelers. Marriott has added three new brands, Moxy Hotels, for budget-conscious travelers, and AC Hotels and Edition brand for more sophisticated travelers. Also, Marriott is changing room design to reflect Millennials' tastes and preferences: big comfortable beds, large televisions, large public lounges, and instead of traditional room service, online ordering and food delivery.

How Marriott manages its employees plays a key role in its financial performance and customer satisfaction. Its practices are based on the principle "Take care of associates and they will take care of customers." "We put people first" is one of Marriott's core values. Marriott has been on *Fortune* magazine's "Best Companies to Work For" list for all 18 years the list has been in existence, a distinction shared by only 11 other companies including Publix, Whole Foods, Nordstrom, and REI. The company has more than 200,000 employees, who work in hotel properties around the world. The work isn't necessarily sexy or sophisticated. Most employees, who are known as "associates," work helping guests, serving meals, and cleaning rooms. Housekeepers represent the largest category of associates. Eight-five percent of associates earn an hourly wage. Despite the routine nature of the work and demanding customers, associates often refer to their co-workers as "family," and many stay in their jobs for many years. Marriott's general manager tenure is 25 years—much greater than the industry average. More than 10,000 employees have worked at Marriott more than 20 years.

Marriott emphasizes hiring friendly people who can learn through training. For hourly associates the company screens for interpersonal skills, dependability, and positive disposition. Employees' opinions matter. At every hotel, each shift starts with a 15-minute meeting during which employees share updates and get motivated for the day's work. The meetings often include stretching, music, and dancing. Employee benefits also contribute to making it a desirable company to work for. The benefits include flexible scheduling, an employee assistance phone number, health care benefits for hourly employees if they work 30 hours a week, and discounts on room rates for employees, families, and friends. Employees working at company headquarters have access to a gym, dry cleaners, gift store, and day care. The company holds a celebration of excellence each year that recognizes outstanding employees who are flown in for the event. The best benefit may be the opportunity that all employees have to grow their careers.

Many top executives started as hourly employees working as housekeepers, waiters, sales people, or security guards. Employees are given opportunities to explore career paths and learn through job experiences. Mentoring from senior employees is common. Bill Marriott, the company's executive chairman and CEO for 40 years until stepping down, believes happy employees result in lower costs. Happy employees mean Mariott has lower turnover and less

CONTINUED

Introduction

Competitiveness
A company's ability to maintain and gain market share in its industry.

Marriott illustrates the key role that human resource management (HRM) plays in determining the survival, effectiveness, and competitiveness of U.S. businesses. **Competitiveness** refers to a company's ability to maintain and gain market share in its industry. Marriott's human resource management practices are helping support the company's business strategy and provide services the customer values. The value of a product or service is determined by its quality and how closely the product fits customer needs.

Competitiveness is related to company effectiveness, which is determined by whether the company satisfies the needs of stakeholders (groups affected by business practices). Important stakeholders include stockholders, who want a return on their investment; customers, who want a high-quality product or service; and employees, who desire interesting work and reasonable compensation for their services. The community, which wants the company to contribute to activities and projects and minimize pollution of the environment, is also an important stakeholder. Companies that do not meet stakeholders' needs are unlikely to have a competitive advantage over other firms in their industry.

Human Resource Management (HRM)
Policies, practices, and systems that influence employees' behavior, attitudes, and performance.

Human resource management (HRM) refers to the policies, practices, and systems that influence employees' behavior, attitudes, and performance. Many companies refer to HRM as involving "people practices." Figure 1.1 emphasizes that there are several important HRM practices. The strategy underlying these practices needs to be considered to maximize their influence on company performance. As the figure shows, HRM practices include analyzing and designing work, determining human resource needs (HR planning), attracting potential employees (recruiting), choosing employees (selection), teaching employees how to perform their jobs and preparing them for the future (training and development), rewarding employees (compensation), evaluating their performance (performance management), and creating a positive work environment (employee relations).

Figure 1.1

Human Resource Management Practices

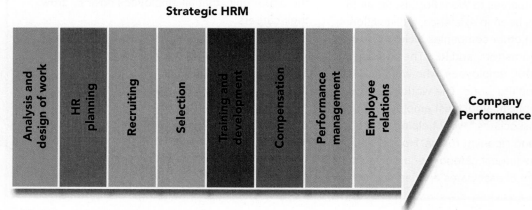

Strategic HRM

Analysis and design of work → HR planning → Recruiting → Selection → Training and development → Compensation → Performance management → Employee relations → **Company Performance**

The HRM practices discussed in this chapter's opening highlighted how effective HRM practices support business goals and objectives. That is, effective HRM practices are strategic! Effective HRM has been shown to enhance company performance by contributing to employee and customer satisfaction, innovation, productivity, and development of a favorable reputation in the firm's community.[1] The potential role of HRM in company performance has only recently been recognized.

We begin by discussing the roles and skills that a human resource management department and/or managers need for any company to be competitive. The second section of the chapter identifies the competitive challenges that U.S. companies currently face, which influence their ability to meet the needs of shareholders, customers, employees, and other stakeholders. We discuss how these competitive challenges are influencing HRM. The chapter concludes by highlighting the HRM practices covered in this book and the ways they help companies compete.

What Responsibilities and Roles Do HR Departments Perform?

Only recently have companies looked at HRM as a means to contribute to profitability, quality, and other business goals through enhancing and supporting business operations.

Table 1.1 shows the responsibilities of human resource departments. How much should companies budget for HR and how many HR professionals should a company

LO 1-1
Discuss the roles and activities of a company's human resource management function.

Table 1.1
Responsibilities of HR Departments

FUNCTION	RESPONSIBILITIES
Analysis and design of work	Job analysis, work analysis, job descriptions
Recruitment and selection	Recruiting, posting job descriptions, interviewing, testing, coordination use of temporary employees
Training and development	Orientation, skills training, development programs, career development
Performance management	Performance measures, preparation and administration of performance appraisals, feedback and coaching, discipline
Compensation and benefits	Wage and salary administration, incentive pay, insurance, vacation, retirement plans, profit sharing, health and wellness, stock plans
Employee relations/Labor relations	Attitude surveys, employee handbooks, labor law compliance, relocation and outplacement services
Personnel policies	Policy creation, policy communications
Employee data and information systems	Record keeping, HR information systems, workforce analytics, social media, Intranet and Internet access
Legal compliance	Policies to ensure lawful behavior; safety inspections, accessibility accommodations, privacy policies, ethics
Support for business strategy	Human resource planning and forecasting, talent management, change management, organization development

SOURCES: Based on Bureau of Labor Statistics, U.S. Department of Labor, *Occupational Outlook Handbook, 2012–13 Edition,* "Human Resources Specialists," on the Internet at www.bls.gov/ooh/business-and-financial/human-resources-specialists.htm, visited March 26, 2013; SHRM-BNA Survey no. 66, "Policy and Practice Forum: Human Resource Activities, Budgets, and Staffs, 2000–2001," *Bulletin to Management,* Bureau of National Affairs Policy and Practice Series (Washington, DC: Bureau of National Affairs, June 28, 2001).

employ? One study estimates that HR budgets on average are $2,936 per employee.[2] High-impact HR teams have one staff person per 64 employees, spend more than the average HR budget per employee ($4,434 on average per employee), and employ a higher percentage of HR specialists than more compliance-driven and basic HR organizations.

High-impact HR functions are more integrated with the business, skilled at helping managers in attracting, building, engaging, and retaining talented employees. They can adapt quickly to business needs and workforce changes, identify and promote talent from within the company, and are continuously trying to identify what motivates employees to help them grow and develop. Also, high-impact HR functions ensure that they are continuously building the talent and skills of HR professionals necessary to help the company meet new competitive challenges. The greater cost-per-employee of high-impact HR functions is offset by the greater savings resulting from reduced turnover and increased levels of employee engagement.

The HR department is solely responsible for outplacement, labor law compliance, record keeping, testing, unemployment compensation, and some aspects of benefits administration. The HR department is most likely to collaborate with other company functions on employment interviewing, performance management and discipline, and efforts to improve quality and productivity. Large companies are more likely than small ones to employ HR specialists, with benefits specialists being the most prevalent. Other common specializations include recruitment, compensation, and training and development.[3]

Many different roles and responsibilities can be performed by the HR department depending on the size of the company, the characteristics of the workforce, the industry, and the value system of company management. The HR department may take full responsibility for human resource activities in some companies, whereas in others it may share the roles and responsibilities with managers of other departments such as finance, operations, or information technology. In some companies the HR department advises top-level management; in others the HR department may make decisions regarding staffing, training, and compensation after top managers have decided relevant business issues.

One way to think about the roles and responsibilities of HR departments is to consider HR as a business within the company with three product lines. Figure 1.2 shows the three product lines of HR. The first product line, administrative services and

Figure 1.2

HR as a Business with Three Product Lines

| **Administrative Services and Transactions:** Compensation, hiring, and staffing • Emphasis: Resource efficiency and service quality | **Business Partner Services:** Developing effective HR systems and helping implement business plans, talent management • Emphasis: Knowing the business and exercising influence—problem solving, designing effective systems to ensure needed competencies | **Strategic Partner:** Contributing to business strategy based on considerations of human capital, business capabilities, readiness, and developing HR practices as strategic differentiators • Emphasis: Knowledge of HR and of the business, competition, the market, and business strategies |

SOURCE: Adapted from Figure 1, "HR Product Lines," in E. E. Lawler, "From Human Resource Management to Organizational Effectiveness," *Human Resource Management* 44 (2005), pp. 165–69.

transactions, is the traditional product that HR has historically provided. The newer HR products—business partner services and the strategic partner role—are the HR functions that top managers want HR to deliver.

To ensure that HR is business-focused, Walgreens HR professionals are paired with functional leaders.[4] The HR field organization works to develop strategic talent plans for each business and helps implement important initiatives such as succession planning, change management, organizational design, and culture and leadership development. The HR director at TAMKO Building Products Inc. helped align the company's HR function to business needs.[5] She noticed that inexperienced HR professionals were spending too much time on transactional duties such as payroll and benefits administration. She wanted them to focus on supplying managers with skilled, well-trained employees and meaningful data. She revised their training to ensure that they understood the industry and the skills that the company needed for continued success. She urged her staff to be proactive (rather than reactive) about offering HR solutions to help managers avoid or solve workplace problems. The team responded by identifying and implementing a new time-and-attendance tracking system, a virtual onboarding and orientation process, and a leadership development program.

Strategic Role of the HRM Function

The amount of time that the HRM function devotes to administrative tasks is decreasing, and its roles as a strategic business partner, change agent, and employee advocate are increasing.[6] HR managers face two important challenges: shifting their focus from current operations to strategies for the future and preparing non-HR managers to develop and implement human resource practices.[7] To ensure that human resources contributes to the company's competitive advantage many HR departments are organized on the basis of a shared service model. The shared service model can help control costs and improve the business relevance and timeliness of HR practices. A **shared service model** is a way to organize the HR function that includes centers of expertise or excellence, service centers, and business partners.[8] Centers of expertise or excellence include HR specialists in areas such as staffing or training who provide their services companywide. Service centers are a central place for administrative and transactional tasks such as enrolling in training programs or changing benefits that employees and managers can access online. Business partners are HR staff members who work with business-unit managers on strategic issues such as creating new compensation plans or development programs for preparing high-level managers. Walgreens provides employee relations, recruiting, and HR data services through a shared services team.[9] Walgreens introduced a website, myHR, that employees can access to get answers to their questions about benefits, HR policies, and talent management. It provides confidential personalized information that is easy for employees to access. We will discuss the shared service model in more detail in Chapter 16.

The role of HRM in administration is decreasing as technology is used for many administrative purposes, such as managing employee records and allowing employees to get information about and enroll in training, benefits, and other programs. The availability of the Internet has decreased the HRM role in maintaining records and providing self-service to employees.[10] **Self-service** refers to giving employees online access to, or apps which provide, information about HR issues such as training, benefits, compensation, and contracts; enrolling online in programs and services; and completing online attitude surveys. The shift to self-service means that HR can focus more time on

Shared Service Model
A way to organize the HR function that includes centers of expertise, service centers, and business partners.

Self-service
Giving employees online access to HR information.

consulting with managers on important employee issues and less time on day-to-day transactional tasks. For example, U.S. Bancorp implemented PeopleSoft 9.1 human capital management system, which allows managers to review or approve basic personnel actions such as terminations, relocations, and salary changes.[11] As managers became more comfortable with the system they were given control over transactions such as approving bonuses, reviewing resumes, and evaluating job candidates. Managers were initially resistant to taking on duties that previously were handled by HR, but they accepted the change because they saw it made it quicker to execute transactions and gave them more access to workforce data they could use for decision making. HR professionals now have more time to work with managers on ensuring the right employee development plans are in place, evaluating workforce needs due to retirements or growth, and ensuring their organizational structures are efficient and effective.

Outsourcing
The practice of having another company provide services.

Many companies are also contracting with human resource service providers to conduct important but administrative human resource functions such as payroll processing, as well as to provide expertise in strategically important practice areas such as recruiting. **Outsourcing** refers to the practice of having another company (a vendor, third party or consultant) provide services. The most commonly outsourced activities include those related to benefits administration (e.g., flexible spending accounts, health plan eligibility status), relocation, and payroll. The major reasons that company executives choose to outsource human resource practices include cost savings, increased ability to recruit and manage talent, improved HR service quality, and protection of the company from potential lawsuits by standardizing processes such as selection and recruitment.[12] ADP, Hewitt, IBM, and Accenture are examples of leading outsource providers.

Goodyear Tire and Rubber Company reenergized its recruitment and hiring practices through outsourcing recruiting practices.[13] The recruiting outsource provider worked with the company to understand its culture, history, and its employees' recruitment experiences. The recruiting outsourcing service provider was able to help Goodyear streamline the recruiting process through providing hiring managers with online access to create new job requisitions, providing interview feedback, scheduling interviews, generating customized job offer letters, and gaining a real-time perspective on job candidates' progress in the recruitment process. Goodyear recognized several benefits from outsourcing recruitment including improving the timeliness of job offers, diversity and quality of new hires, and reducing turnover.

Traditionally, the HRM department (also known as "Personnel" or "Employee Relations") was primarily an administrative expert and employee advocate. The department took care of employee problems, made sure employees were paid correctly, administered labor contracts, and avoided legal problems. The HRM department ensured that employee-related issues did not interfere with the manufacturing or sales of products or services. Human resource management was primarily reactive; that is, human resource issues were a concern only if they directly affected the business. That still remains the case in many companies that have yet to recognize the competitive value of human resource management, or among HR professionals who lack the competencies and skills or understanding needed to anticipate problems and contribute to the business strategy. However, other companies believe that HRM is important for business success and therefore have expanded the role of HRM as a change agent and strategic partner.

A discussion group of company HR directors and academic thought-leaders reported that increasingly HR is expected to lead efforts focused on talent management and performance management.[14] Also, HR should take the lead in helping companies attract, develop, and retain talent in order to create the global workforces that companies need to be successful. HR professionals have to be able to use and analyze data to make a business case for ideas and problem solutions. In many companies top HR managers report directly to the CEO, president, or board of directors to answer questions about how people strategies drive value for the company. For example, at Pitney Bowes, the executive vice president and chief human resources officer responsibilities include the development of HR business strategies, strategic talent management, succession planning, diversity, total rewards and analytics, employee relations, and shared professional and transactional services.[15] During Johnna Torsone's tenure she has been a trusted business partner to four CEOs and several senior leadership teams. She has helped guide the company through several leadership and business changes. Under her leadership the HR function has supported Pitney Bowes' business strategy while maintaining the company culture and valuing employees. Like other HR leaders Torsone's biggest challenge is having the right talent to meet business needs, especially during times of change requiring new and different skills.

Consider how HR has supported the business at Coeur Mining and MGM Resorts International.[16] HR at Coeur Mining helped support the company's transformation to an entrepreneurial business culture that allowed employees to make decisions that affected their daily performance. For example, engineers working at a mine in Nevada didn't need to ask for corporate approval to redesign roads that helped improve productivity. A new performance management process was introduced (a culture of achievement) that eliminates ratings and instead reinforces frequent conversations between managers and employees. Together they set goals and employees are held accountable for achieving them. This gives employees full responsibility for their performance.

At MGM Resorts International employees worldwide are encouraged to ask questions, challenge policies, and improve practices. HR works with both top-level executives and front-line employees to help generate ideas that generate additional revenue, save the company money, and improve customers' experiences. HR coordinates meetings once a month with directors and vice presidents in which topics such as operations and innovation are discussed. The executives work in teams brainstorming ideas, choosing one to work on, and presenting it to the company's chief operations officer. One team recommended stopping the practice of branding water bottles with individual property names and adopting the brand called M Life. This saved the company $400,000. HR has created focus groups of front-line employees to generate ideas which are communicated to property managers. Also, HR developed an employee directory containing the e-mail and phone numbers of all employees including senior leaders. This empowers employees to communicate directly with senior managers. As a result of these efforts valet employees at The Mirage resort implemented several ideas including calling guests by their names and making changes to more quickly retrieve cars. This resulted in an increase in guest services scores and in employee perceptions of trust and empowerment measured on employee opinion surveys.

Table 1.2 provides several questions that managers can use to determine if HRM is playing a strategic role in the business. If these questions have not been considered, it is highly unlikely that (1) the company is prepared to deal with competitive challenges or (2) human resources are being strategically used to help a company gain a competitive advantage. The bottom line for evaluating the relationship between human resource management and the business strategy is to consider this question: "What is HR doing to ensure that the right people with the right skills are doing the right things in the jobs that are important for the execution of the business strategy?"[17] We will discuss strategic human resource management in more detail in Chapter 2.

Some companies that want managers to have more accountability for employees, believe that traditional HR departments are unnecessary because they inhibit innovation

Table 1.2
Questions to
Ask: Are Human
Resources Playing
a Strategic Role in
the Business?

1. What is HR doing to provide value-added services to internal clients?
2. Do the actions of HR support and align with business priorities?
3. How are you measuring the effectiveness of HR?
4. How can we reinvest in employees?
5. What HR strategy will we use to get the business from point A to point B?
6. From an HR perspective, what should we be doing to improve our marketplace position?
7. What's the best change we can make to prepare for the future?
8. Do we react to business problems or anticipate them in advance?

SOURCES: Based on A. Halcrow, "Survey Shows HR in Transition," *Workforce,* June 1988, p. 74; P. Wright, *Human Resource Strategy: Adapting to the Age of Globalization* (Alexandria, VA: Society for Human Resource Management Foundation, 2008); J. Mundy, "Be a Strategic Performance Consultant," *HR Magazine,* March 2013, pp. 44–46.

through creating unnecessary and inefficient policies and procedures.[18] In these companies important payroll, benefits, and other HR processes are automated or outsourced. For example, managers at Ruppert Landscape with 900 employees working in different markets across the United States perform human resource responsibilities such as recruiting employees and explaining the company's retirement plan. Its managers spend about 5% of their time on human resources. The CEO feels that local managers are in a better position to understand and solve employee problems than an HR professional located in the company's Maryland headquarters. However, there are many advantages to having HR professionals and an HR department. Managers often lack the specialized knowledge necessary to understand employment laws, how to identify potential employees, determine skills and salaries for positions, and develop current employees. HR professionals can create systems to avoid legal liability, counsel employees, and coach managers how to identify, retain, and develop talent.

Consider the role of HR at Tesla Motors, an automotive company with all of the characteristics of a high-tech company.[19] Tesla builds cars, manufactures electric power trains for other car companies, operates car-charging stations around the world, and sells its cars directly to customers. The luxurious Model S has won numerous awards and Tesla plans to introduce a more affordable electric car soon. HR's role at Tesla is to support the business by finding and helping to retain the most talented employees and ensure they understand and believe in the company's fast-paced culture, which requires long workdays and constant change. They do this in several different ways. HR seeks talented employees who have a positive, self-starting attitude and have tried to improve processes in whatever areas they have worked in. To find talent to fill a robotics team the HR staffing team looked beyond the traditional sources, such as other automakers, and instead focused on robotics competitions at colleges and different industries such as biotechnology which employ robotic-programming specialists. HR worked with employees from legal, security, and environmental health and safety departments and a small group of employees from company stores and the factory to develop an employee handbook. The handbook, known as the "anti-handbook handbook," captures in just four pages written in a conversational style what Tesla stands for and what it is like to work there.

For example, the employee attendance policy emphasizes that employees should be the kind of person their work team can rely on. Emphasis is placed on employees being at work when they are supposed to be, because the team can't get things done if employees are absent. HR supports Tesla's emphasis on open communications through the "Answer Bar" at its Freemont, California, factory. At the "Answer Bar" employees can walk up to

HR staffers and ask questions they have about benefits or the company. Tesla does conduct employee surveys but they encourage employees to use the "Answer Bar" to provide personal feedback. This allows Tesla to quickly make changes when new employee programs are introduced. HR has developed training that meets company and employee needs for just-in-time learning that is meaningful, short, holds employees' attention, and is provided just-in-time. For example, factory employees can use their smartphones next to their workstations to scan codes which allow them to view short tutorial videos on job tasks.

HRM may be the most important lever for companies to gain a competitive advantage over both domestic and foreign competitors. We believe this is because HRM practices are directly related to companies' success in meeting competitive challenges. These challenges and their implications for HRM are discussed later in the chapter.

DEMONSTRATING THE STRATEGIC VALUE OF HR: HR ANALYTICS AND EVIDENCE-BASED HR

For HR to contribute to business goals there is increasing recognition that it is necessary to use data to answer questions such as "Which practices are effective?" "Which practices are cost effective?" and to project the outcomes of changes in practices on employees' attitudes, behavior, and company profits and costs. This helps show that time and money invested in HR programs are worthwhile and HR is as important to the business as finance, marketing, and accounting! **Evidence-based HR** refers to the demonstration that human resources practices have a positive influence on the company's bottom or key stakeholders (employees, customers, community, shareholders). Evidence-based HR requires the use of HR or workforce analytics. **HR or workforce analytics** refers to the practice of using quantitative methods and scientific methods to analyze big data.

Big data refers to information merged from human resource databases, corporate financial statements, employee surveys, and other data sources to make evidence-based human resource decisions and show that HR practices influence the organization's bottom line, including profits and costs.[20] Intermountain Healthcare used big data and analytics to help reduce turnover.[21] The company was able to correlate departments where employees had the fewest work hours and those that had the highest turnover rates. Analytics software provides "heat maps" or visualizations of relationships in the data. The correlation between these two items showed that the fewer hours employees worked the more likely they were to leave. This showed managers that turnover was not due to poor orientation or lack of training. Rather, the data suggested increasing the workers' hours, which has resulted in reduced turnover.

Big data and workforce analytics helped Johnson Controls access and understand data related to each business unit's talent.[22] Each business unit completes a "People Scorecard" that shows the flow of talent in, up, and out of the company. This includes data on headcount, retentions, terminations, new hires, and promotions. Managers can access this data on dashboards which make it easy to "see" the data. Different hiring, retention, and promotion scenarios can be modeled by each business unit to help make decisions regarding their workforce goals. For example, based on the modeling results goals for hiring and retaining employees in specific positions or women and minorities can be set. To analyze data about how learning contributed to the success of their sales force, SuccessFactors used data from three systems: customer relationship management, learning and performance management, and employee records.[23] Customer relations data include number and size of sales. Learning data included courses taken and self-evaluation of

Evidence-Based HR
Demonstrating that human resource practices have a positive influence on the company's bottom line or key stakeholders (employees, customers, community, shareholders).

HR or Workforce Analytics
The practice of using data from HR databases and other data sources to make evidence-based human resource decisions.

Big Data
Information merged from a variety of sources, including HR databases, corporate financial statements, and employee surveys, to make evidence-based HR decisions and show that HR practices can influence the organization's bottom line.

training effectiveness. Performance data included managers' performance ratings and learning plans. Employee records included sales experience and hire date. They analyzed the performance and number and value of sales made by employees who completed training with those who did not.

Because evidence-based HR and analytics are important for showing the value of HR practices and how they contribute to business strategy and goals, throughout each chapter of the book we provide examples of companies' use of workforce analytics to make evidenced-based HR decisions or to evaluate HR practices.

THE HRM PROFESSION: POSITIONS AND JOBS

There are many different types of jobs in the HRM profession. Table 1.3 shows various HRM positions and their salaries. A survey conducted by the Society of Human Resource Management to better understand what HR professionals do found that the primary activities of HR professionals are performing the HR generalist role (providing a wide range of HR services), with fewer involved in other activities such as the HR function at the executive level of the company, training and development, HR consulting, and administrative activities.[24] Projections suggest that overall employment in human resource–related positions is expected to grow by 21% between 2010 and 2020, much faster than the occupational average.[25]

Salaries for HR professionals vary according to position, level of experience, training, location, and firm size. As you can see from Table 1.3, some positions involve work in specialized areas of HRM like recruiting, training, or labor and industrial relations. HR generalists usually make between $39,000 and $63,500 depending on their experience and education level. HR generalists perform a wide range of activities including recruiting, selection, training, labor relations, and benefits administration. HR specialists work in one specific functional area such as training or compensation. Although HR generalists tend to be found in smaller companies, many mid- to large-size companies employ HR generalists at the plant or business levels and HR specialists at the corporate, product, or regional levels. Most HR professionals chose HR as a career because they found HR appealing as a career, they wanted to work with people, or they were asked by chance to perform HR tasks and responsibilities.[26]

Table 1.3
Median Salaries for
HRM Positions

POSITION	SALARY
Top HR Executive	$225,026
Global HR Manager	116,161
Management Development Manager	109,969
Health and Safety Manager	98,636
Employee Benefits Manager	92,121
HR Manager	90,865
Mid-level Labor Relations Specialist	75,329
Campus Recruiter	62,500
Entry-level HRIS Specialist	52,069
HR Generalist	50,985
Compensation Analyst	56,877
Entry-level Employee Training Specialist	47,680

SOURCE: Based on data from Salary Wizard, www.salary.com, accessed May 14, 2015.

EDUCATION AND EXPERIENCE

The HR profession will likely continue to be in transition in the near future.[27] A large number of HR professionals who will be retiring soon have held mainly administrative roles with little previous formal education in human resources. As is currently the case for many HR professionals, the new generation of HR professionals will likely have a four-year college degree and many will have completed a graduate HR degree. Business is typically the field of study (human resources or industrial relations) although some HR professionals have degrees in the social sciences (economics or psychology), the humanities, or law. Those who have completed graduate work have master's degrees in HR management, business management, industrial organizational psychology, or a similar field. Human resource professionals can be expected to have both strategic and tactical roles. For example, a senior HR role will likely involve developing and support-ing the company culture, employee recruitment, retention and engagement, succession planning, and designing the company's overall HR strategy. Junior HR roles will handle all of the transactions related to paperwork, benefits and payroll administration, answer-ing employee questions, and data management.

Professional certification in HRM is less common than membership in professional associations. A well-rounded educational background will likely serve a person well in an HRM position. As one HR professional noted, "One of the biggest misconceptions is that it is all warm and fuzzy communications with the workers. Or that it is creative and involved in making a more congenial atmosphere for people at work. Actually it is both of those some of the time, but most of the time it is a big mountain of paperwork which calls on a myriad of skills besides the 'people' type. It is law, accounting, philosophy, and logic as well as psychology, spirituality, tolerance, and humility."[28]

COMPETENCIES AND BEHAVIORS

Many experts acknowledge that top-level HR professionals are generalists who have expertise in benefits, compensation, and labor relations and focus on important issues such as employee engagement and managing company culture.[29] However, they lack business acumen, the expertise in relating HR to real-world business needs, that is, they don't know how key decisions are made, and are unable to determine why employees or parts of the company fail to meet performance goals. This is congruent with the belief of companies' top HR leaders that developing the skills of professionals working in HR is an urgent need.[30] Less than 10% of HR leaders believe that their functional teams have the skills needed to help companies meet their current competitive challenges. Consider the requirements that Netflix wanted when it was looking for a new HR director.[31] Net-flix wanted someone who puts business first, customer second, and talent third. It did not want a change agent, organizational development practitioner, a SHRM certificate, or a people person. HR professionals should consider themselves as business people, not morale boosters. They need to be able to consider key questions, such as, What's good for the company? How do we communicate that to employees? How can we help every employee understand what is meant by high performance?

HR professionals need to have the nine competencies shown in Figure 1.3. These are the most recent competencies developed by the Society for Human Resource Management (SHRM). SHRM developed the competencies based on a literature review, input from over 1,200 HR professionals, and a survey of over 32,000 respondents.[32] The full version of the competency model, which can be found on the SHRM website (**www.shrm.org**), provides more detailed information on each competency, behaviors, and standards for proficiency for HR professionals at entry, mid, senior, and executive

Figure 1.3

Competencies and Example Behaviors for HR Professionals

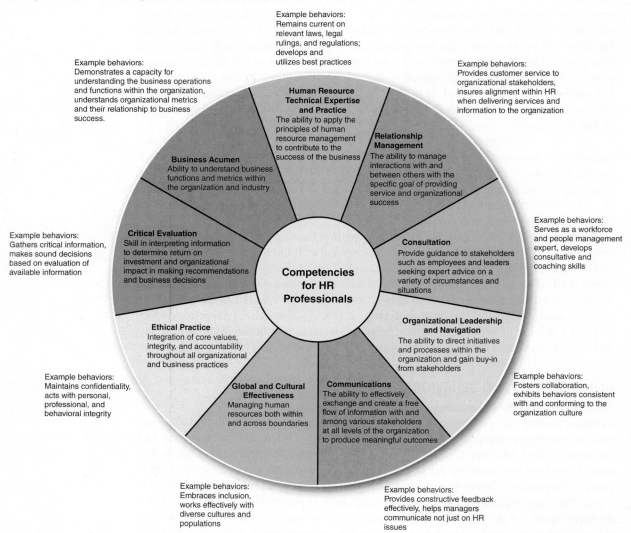

SOURCE: Based on SHRM Competency Model, Society for Human Resource Management, 2012, accessed from www.shrm.org, July 1, 2015.

career stages. Demonstrating these competencies can help HR professionals show managers that they are capable of helping the HR function create value, contribute to the business strategy, and shape the company culture. They also help the HR department effectively and efficiently provide the three HR products discussed earlier and shown in Figure 1.2. These competencies and behaviors show that although the level of expertise required may vary by career level, all HR professionals need to have a working knowledge of strategic business management, human resource planning, development, compensation and benefits, risk management (safety, quality, etc.), labor relations, HR technology, evidence-based decision making, and global human resources. HR professionals need to be able to interact and coach employees and managers, yet engage in ethical practice through maintaining confidentiality and acting with integrity. Providing support for the usefulness and validity of the SHRM competency model, research shows that HR professionals who have a higher level of proficiency on the SHRM competencies do perform better in their jobs.[33]

Many top-level managers and HR professionals believe that the best way to develop competencies of the future effective professionals needed in HR is to train employees or put them into experiences that help them understand the business and HR's role in contributing to it. For example, an HR leader at Rivermark Community Credit Union developed skills in reading and interpreting financial data by spending time with the Chief Financial Officer.[34] This has allowed her to make more contributions in senior-level leader meetings.

Consider how Google and Southwest Airlines are developing the right mix of HR skills and experience to best contribute to the business.[35] At Google, approximately one-third of the HR team's employees have HR backgrounds and expertise in specialty skill areas such as employment law, compensation, and benefits. Another one-third have little or no human resource experience and were recruited from consulting firms or within Google's engineering or sales functions. The final one-third is a workforce analytics group with employees who have doctorates in finance, statistics, and organizational psychology. Each group has its strengths. For example, HR staff who have limited HR experience are very skilled in problem solving and how the company works outside HR. To capitalize on the unique perspectives and skills that each group brings to working on human resource issues, the vice president of global people operations encourages interactions and knowledge sharing among the entire group of team members. Google develops human resources or key people operations staff through a year-long training program that includes HR specialist training, a business curriculum, and development of skills related to working with clients, communicating with senior executives, and solving business problems. The training is designed for HR employees with at least two years of experience and is taught by People Operations department employees. Google recruits top MBA program graduates, enticing them to consider HR because the opportunity to influence change in the company is greater than is common in other specialty areas and career advancement is faster.

The primary professional organization for HRM is the Society for Human Resource Management (SHRM). SHRM is the world's largest human resource management association with more than 250,000 professional and student members throughout the world. If you are interested in HR, you should join SHRM! SHRM provides education and information services, conferences and seminars, government and media representation, and online services and publications (such as *HR Magazine* and free videos and reports from the SHRM Foundation). You can visit SHRM's website to see their services at **www.shrm.org**.

Competitive Challenges Influencing Human Resource Management

Three competitive challenges that companies now face will increase the importance of human resource management practices: the challenge of sustainability, the global challenge, and the technology challenge. These challenges are shown in Figure 1.4.

As you will see in the following discussion, these competitive challenges are directly linked to the HR challenges that companies are facing including developing, attracting, and retaining talented employees, finding employees with the necessary skills, and breaking down cultural barriers to create a global company.[36]

Figure 1.4
Competitive
Challenges
Influencing U.S.
Companies

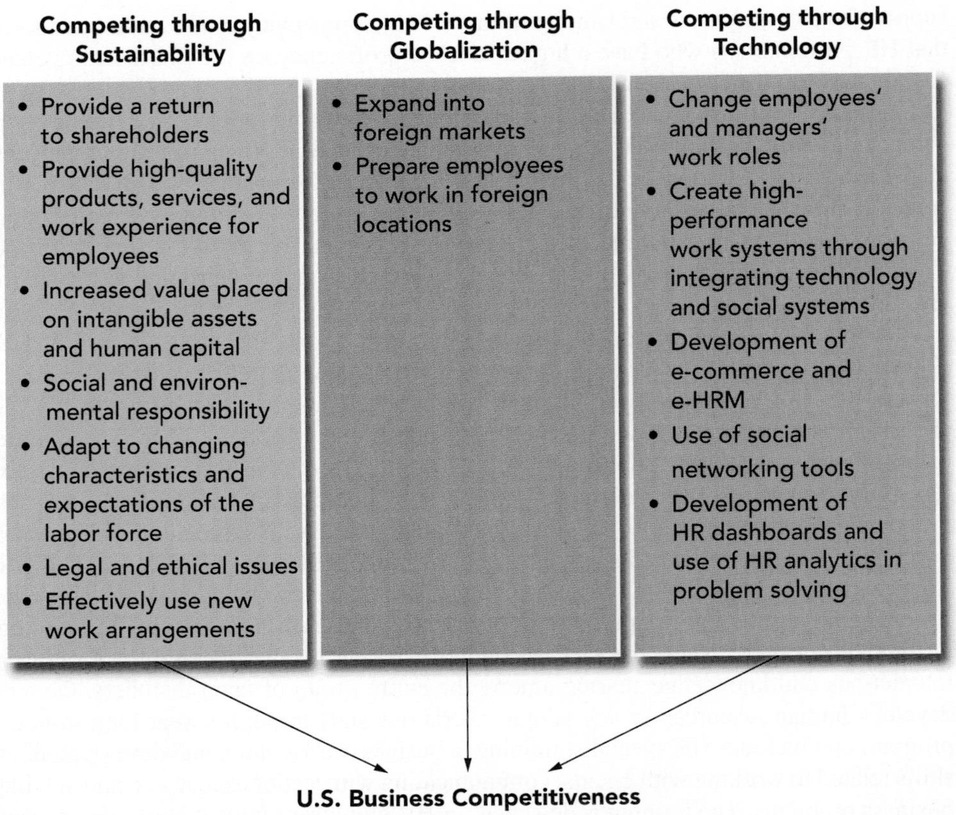

Competing through Sustainability	Competing through Globalization	Competing through Technology
• Provide a return to shareholders • Provide high-quality products, services, and work experience for employees • Increased value placed on intangible assets and human capital • Social and environmental responsibility • Adapt to changing characteristics and expectations of the labor force • Legal and ethical issues • Effectively use new work arrangements	• Expand into foreign markets • Prepare employees to work in foreign locations	• Change employees' and managers' work roles • Create high-performance work systems through integrating technology and social systems • Development of e-commerce and e-HRM • Use of social networking tools • Development of HR dashboards and use of HR analytics in problem solving

U.S. Business Competitiveness

THE SUSTAINABILITY CHALLENGE

Traditionally, sustainability has been viewed as one aspect of corporate social responsibility related to the impact of the business on the environment.[37] However, we take a broader view of sustainability. **Sustainability** refers to the company's ability to meet its needs without sacrificing the ability of future generations to meet their needs.[38] Organizations pursuing a sustainable strategy pursue the "triple bottom line": economic, social, and environmental benefits. Company success is based on how well the company meets the needs of its stakeholders. **Stakeholders** refers to shareholders, the community, customers, employees, and all of the other parties that have an interest in seeing that the company succeeds. Sustainability includes the ability to deal with economic and social changes, practice environmental responsibility, engage in responsible and ethical business practices, provide high-quality products and services, and put in place methods to determine if the company is meeting stakeholders' needs; that is, HR systems that create the skills, motivation, values, and culture that help the company achieve its "triple bottom line" and insure the long-term benefits for the organizations stakeholders.

The economy has important implications for human resource management. Some key statistics about the economy and the workforce are shown in Table 1.4. These include the structure of the economy, the development and spread of social networking, and growth in professional and service occupations. Growth in these occupations means that skill demands for jobs have changed, with knowledge becoming more valuable. Not only have skill demands changed, but remaining competitive in a global economy requires demanding work hours and changes in traditional employment patterns. The creation of new jobs, aging employees leaving the workforce, slow population growth, and a lack

Sustainability
A company's ability to meet its needs without sacrificing the ability of future generations to meet their needs.

Stakeholders
The various interest groups who have relationships with, and consequently, whose interests are tied to the organization (e.g., employees, suppliers, customers, shareholders, community).

LO 1-2
Discuss the implications of the economy, the makeup of the labor force, and ethics for company sustainability.

Table 1.4
Highlights of Employment Projections

- The labor force is expected to increase by 8 million, reaching 163 million by 2022.
- Today, 92% of U.S. jobs are nonagriculture wage and salary jobs; 12.5% of the jobs are in goods producing industries (mining, construction, manufacturing) and 79.7% are in service-providing industries. The distribution of jobs across industries is projected to be similar in 2020.
- 50.6 million job openings are expected by 2022 with more than two-thirds resulting from the need to replace workers who retire or leave an occupation.
- Health care and social assistant services are expected to generate more than one-third of the projected increase in total employment in 2022.
- Today, approximately 43% of jobs require a high school degree for entry, 16% a Bachelor's degree.
- The median age of the labor force will increase to 42.8 years old, the highest ever.

SOURCE: D. Sommers and J. Franklin, "Overview of Projections to 2020," *Monthly Labor Review,* January 2012, pp. 3–20; C. Lockard and M. Wolf, "Occupation Employment Projections to 2020," *Monthly Labor Review,* January 2012, pp. 84–108; Bureau of Labor Statistics, U.S. Department of Labor, "Employment Projections: 2012–2022," news release, www.bls.gov, accessed February 25, 2015.

of employees who have the skills needed to perform the high-demand jobs means that companies need to give more attention to HR practices that influence attracting and retaining employees.

Economic Cycles

Today, there are many positive signs that the U.S. economy is experiencing positive momentum.[39] Employers are adding jobs at the fastest rate since the late 1990s. The unemployment rate was 5.4% in April 2015, the lowest in seven years. Consumer spending benefited from steady job growth and lower gasoline prices and rose in the fourth quarter of 2014 at the fastest rate since the first quarter of 2006.[40] Growth in the Gross Domestic Product (GDP) was 2.4% higher than the increase in 2013, and U.S. manufacturing output moved past its prerecession levels. Surveys suggest that company CEOs are optimistic about the U.S. economy's growth prospects.[41] Hiring continues to be a priority for CEOs with two-thirds of them planning to add new employees in the next year.

However, there are several threats to continued economic growth.[42] Despite the low unemployment rate, employee pay is slowly increasing, which can ultimately result in reduced consumer spending. Broader measures of unemployment including the numbers of involuntary part-time employees and long-term unemployed were down during 2014 but still higher than before the recession. Over 6.6 million employees were in part-time jobs for economic reasons, such as their pay was cut or they couldn't find full-time work. Labor force participation has increased to approximately 63% but it is still close to its lowest level since the 1970s. Also, there are concerns that the Federal Reserve Bank will begin to raise the borrowing rate for federal funds, which has been near zero since the end of 2008. The lowest funds rate in history was provided as an emergency measure during the financial crisis several years ago, but the economy hasn't shown that it can grow without it. A fund rate hike could affect growth, inflation, and exchange rates throughout the world.

There are several implications of this economic period for human resource management. Despite companies looking to add new employees to expand operations, replace retiring employees, or keep up with increased demand for their products and services, many may be unable to find new employees with the skills they need.[43] Also, valuable high-performing employees may be looking to change jobs for higher wages or better career opportunities. As a result, companies are having problems attracting and retaining talented employees. Many are increasing wages, paying for benefits, and providing training as part of the solution. For example, Panera Bread, McDonald's, Walmart, Starbucks, Target, and Aetna all raised employees' pay recently.[44] M&M Manufacturing improved its benefits to attract and retain employees.[45] M&M increased coverage of employees health care premiums from 50 to 80%, and it started matching contributions to employees' retirement plans.

In addition to raising pay, Starbucks has focused on learning as a way to attract and retain employees and show it is committed to their success. Starbucks College Achievement Plan covers employees' tuition to earn an online bachelor's degree from Arizona State University.[46] Employees can choose from 50 different degree programs. The only requirements are that employees have to be working at least 20 hours each week, are U.S.-based working in support centers, plants, or at any of company-operated stores (including Teavana, La Boulange, Evolution Fresh, and Seattle's Best Coffee stores), and do not yet have a bachelor's degree. Employees have no commitment to remain at Starbucks after they graduate.

HR programs and the HR function are under pressure to relate to the business strategy and show a return on investment. Customer focus needs to be included in all HRM practices. New technology means that administrative and transactional HR activities will be delivered via technology, creating less need for HR professionals to provide these activities. The aging workforce combined with reduced immigration because of security concerns may lead employers to focus more on retraining employees or encouraging older, skilled workers to delay retirement or work part-time.[47]

Table 1.4 highlights 2012–2022 employment projections. Our discussion of employment projections is based on the work done by the U.S. Bureau of Labor Statistics.[48] Population is the most important factor in determining the size and composition of the labor force. The size of the labor force will increase but less than levels experienced over the previous 10 years. The median age of the workforce will be the highest ever. Because the U.S. population is expected to become increasingly diverse so is the workforce. Immigration is expected to add 1.5 million persons every year from 2012–2022 to the U.S. population. As a result every race and ethnicity will grow from 2012–2022 but the share of nonwhite Hispanics is expected to decline (we discuss the diversity and aging of the workforce in more detail later in this chapter).

The importance of the service sector in the U.S. economy is emphasized by considering industry and occupational employment rates and future projections. Almost 80% of jobs are in the service sector. Currently, the largest percentage of jobs are found in health care and social assistance, leisure and hospitality, state and local government, professional and business services, and retail trade. Most of the employment growth between 2012 and 2022 is expected to be in service-providing occupations.[49] Employment in construction is the second highest projected employment increase resulting in 1.6 million jobs between 2012 and 2022.

Table 1.5 provides examples of the largest percentage growth in jobs from 2012–2022. Of the 30 fastest-growing occupations, 14 are related to health care (such as personal care aides, home health aides, genetic counselors, and physical therapists) and 5 are related to construction (insulation workers, brickmasons and blockmasons, electrical, tile, and marble setter helpers). The growth in health care reflects the inpatient and outpatient medical care that is needed for the aging U.S. population. The growth in construction occupation is related to replacement needs, growth in the economy, and the need to repair the aging U.S. infrastructure.

| OCCUPATION | EMPLOYMENT CHANGE 2012–2022 | | MOST SIGNIFICANT EDUCATION OR TRAINING |
	NUMBER (IN THOUSANDS)	PERCENT	
Industrial-organizational psychologist	1	53	Master's degree
Personal care aides	581	49	Short-term, on-the-job training
Home health aides	424	49	Short-term, on-the-job training
Insulation workers	14	47	Apprenticeship
Interpreters and translators	29	46	Bachelor's degree
Diagnostic medical sonographers	27	46	Associate's degree
Helpers—brick masons, block and stone masons, tile and marble setters	11	43	Short-term, on-the-job training
Occupational therapy assistants	13	43	Associate's degree
Genetic counselors	1	41	Master's degree
Physical therapist assistants	29	41	Associate's degree

Table 1.5
Examples of the Occupations with the Largest Growth in Jobs

SOURCE: Based on Bureau of Labor Statistics, U.S. Department of Labor, "Employment Projections: 2012–2022," News Release, www.bls.gov, accessed February 25, 2015.

All major occupations are projected to gain jobs between 2012 and 2022 except farming, fishing, and forestry occupations. Six industries are projected to have decreases in employment—manufacturing; federal government; agriculture; forestry, fishing, and hunting; information; and utilities. This loss of jobs and workers is due to several factors including technological improvements, which means fewer workers are needed; foreign competition; industry consolidation; cost-cutting and more efficient work processes; and decrease in the number of workers who want to work in these occupations.

Education plays an important role in meeting occupational or job requirements and in employee earnings. Slightly less than two-thirds of the 30 fastest-growing occupations require education beyond high school—at least an associate degree or higher. Occupations requiring education beyond high school are expected to grow faster than those requiring a high school diploma or less (14% vs. 9%). The median annual wage for jobs requiring post-secondary education is $30,000 higher than jobs with no post-secondary education. Today the median annual wage for jobs requiring no post-secondary education is estimated to be approximately $27,670 compared to $35,170 for those with a high school diploma, $57,590 for an associate's degree, $67,140 for a bachelor's degree, and $96,420 for a doctorate degree. The discrepancy in earning is expected to continue in the future. Occupations that require an apprenticeship for training, including many construction jobs, are projected to grow approximately 22% between 2012 and 2022, which is faster than for jobs requiring any other type of on-the-job training. The median annual wage for jobs requiring an apprenticeship is $45,440, which is higher than for jobs requiring a high school diploma but less than for jobs requiring post-secondary education. Although they pay less than occupations requiring education beyond high school, occupations that do not typically require post-secondary education will continue to grow. They are projected to add 8.8 million jobs between 2012 and 2022—accounting for more than half of all new jobs.

Despite the availability of unemployed and underemployed workers and new high school and college graduates, companies are having a difficult time finding employees with the right skills. Several studies illustrate how the skills deficit is influencing companies and identify what skills are in short supply.[50] Although many businesses plan to hire new employees, they are concerned that they will not be able to find the talent needed to capitalize on investments they are making in new technology and other strategic capabilities. Skills deficits are not limited to any one business sector, industry or job. Nearly half of CEOs of U.S. businesses believe that a significant skills gap exists that will result in loss of business, revenue, decreased customer satisfaction, or a delay in new products or services. The Manufacturing Institute found that 80% of manufacturers report a moderate or serious shortage of qualified applicants for skilled and highly skilled production positions. The Organization for Economic Cooperation and Development found that the United States ranked 21 out of 23 countries in math and 17 out of 19 countries in problem solving. But skills deficits are not just a problem facing U.S. companies. They are occurring around the world. For example, in Italy and Spain nearly 3 out of 10 adults perform at or below the lowest proficiency level in literacy and numerical ability. One study found that regardless of their education level only half the companies surveyed rated new employees as adequately prepared for work. Companies' greatest basic skills needs were in reading, writing, and math. Many employers also feel that they are having a difficult time finding employees with the right "soft skills" such as work ethic, teamwork, and communications that they believe are more important for success on the job than job-specific or "hard skills" such as blueprint reading or writing. Interpersonal skills, the ability to learn, creativity, and problem solving are especially important in the service economy because employees have responsibility for the final product or service provided. There is especially a shortage of employees with skills in science, technology, engineering, and math (STEM skills).

Companies are partnering with unions, elementary and secondary schools, and colleges and universities to develop the necessary skills needed in today's workforce.[51] For example, an upturn in the construction industry following the recession has resulted in contractors having a difficult time finding the skilled workers they need. As result, local trade unions are advertising apprenticeship programs which can help train much-needed electricians, plumbers, iron workers, roofers, and pipefitters. The Greater Houston Partnership, which includes Exxon Mobil, Royal Dutch Shell PLC, and BP PLC, is working with pre-kindergarten classes to improve early childhood education. Siemens AG, an engineering company and manufacturer of medical equipment, wanted to expand its energy plant in Charlotte, North Carolina, which would require hiring an additional 1,500 employees. Although over 10,000 job applications were received, most did not have the required STEM skills. As a result, Siemens partnered with a community college in the area to develop a specialized course to prepare potential employees for jobs in the energy plant. Siemens put 3,500 of the 10,000 job applicants through the program. Four hundred were employed by Siemens and the others were encouraged to use their new STEM skills to find jobs with other companies.

Increased Value Placed on Intangible Assets and Human Capital. Today more and more companies are interested in using intangible assets and human capital as a way to gain an advantage over competitors. A company's value includes three types of assets that are critical for the company to provide goods and services: financial assets (cash and securities), physical assets (property, plant, equipment), and intangible assets. Table 1.6 provides examples of intangible assets. **Intangible assets** include human capital, customer capital, social capital, and intellectual capital. Intangible assets are equally or even more valuable than financial and physical assets but they are difficult to duplicate or imitate.[52] By one estimate, up to 75% of the source of value in a company is in intangible assets.[53]

Intangible assets have been shown to be responsible for a company's competitive advantage. Human resource management practices such as training, selection, performance management, and compensation have a direct influence on human and social capital through influencing customer service, work-related know-how and competence, and work relationships. Consider the effort that Macy's put into developing human capital, social capital, and customer capital.[54] Almost half of Macy's department store customer complaints are focused on interactions with sales associates. To cut costs to survive during the recession Macy's closed stores and invested in technology to improve efficiency which diverted attention away from customer service. But now Macy's is making a considerable investment in training its sales associates to provide better customer service. The new training program requires new sales associates to attend a three-hour training session and includes refresher courses and coaching from managers when they are working on the sales floor. The Magic Selling Program ("Magic" stands for meet and make a connection, ask questions and listen, give options and advice, inspire to buy, and celebrate the purchase) is designed to help sales associates make more personal connections with shoppers. Positive interactions with sales associates contribute to the number of

Intangible Assets
A type of company asset including human capital, customer capital, social capital, and intellectual capital.

Human capital
- Tacit knowledge
- Education
- Work-related know-how
- Work-related competence

Customer capital
- Customer relationships
- Brands
- Customer loyalty
- Distribution channels

Social capital
- Corporate culture
- Management philosophy
- Management practices
- Informal networking systems
- Coaching/mentoring relationships

Intellectual capital
- Patents
- Copyrights
- Trade secrets
- Intellectual property

Table 1.6
Examples of Intangible Assets

SOURCES: Based on L. Weatherly, *Human Capital: The Elusive Asset* (Alexandria, VA: 2003 SHRM Research Quarterly); E. Holton and S. Naquin, "New Metrics for Employee Development," *Performance Improvement Quarterly* 17 (2004), pp. 56–80; M. Huselid, B. Becker, and R. Beatty, *The Workforce Scorecard* (Boston: Harvard University Press, 2005).

items that a customer purchases and can help enhance Macy's service reputation as customers share experiences on social network sites such as Twitter and Facebook. Macy's effort has paid off in strong sales growth.

Intangible assets have been shown to be related to a company's financial performance, productivity, and innovation.[55] The American Society for Training and Development found that companies that invested the most in training and development had a shareholder return 86% higher than companies in the bottom half and 46% higher than the market average.

Knowledge Workers
Employees who own the intellectual means of producing a product or service.

One way companies try to increase intangible assets is through attracting, developing, and retaining knowledge workers. **Knowledge workers** are employees who contribute to the company not through manual labor, but through what they know about customers or a specialized body of knowledge. Employees cannot simply be ordered to perform tasks; they must share knowledge and collaborate on solutions. Knowledge workers contribute specialized knowledge that their managers may not have, such as information about customers. Managers depend on them to share information. Knowledge workers have many job opportunities. If they choose, they can leave a company and take their knowledge to a competitor. Knowledge workers are in demand because companies need their skills and jobs requiring them are growing (see Table 1.5).

Emphasis on Empowerment and Continuous Learning

Empowering
Giving employees responsibility and authority to make decisions.

To completely benefit from employees' knowledge requires a management style that focuses on developing and empowering employees. **Empowering** means giving employees responsibility and authority to make decisions regarding all aspects of product development or customer service.[56] Employees are then held accountable for products and services; in return, they share the rewards and losses of the results. For empowerment to be successful, managers must be trained to link employees to resources within and outside the company (people, websites, etc.), help employees interact with their fellow employees and managers throughout the company, and ensure that employees are updated on important issues and cooperate with each other. Employees must also be trained to understand how to use the Web, e-mail, and other tools for communicating, collecting, and sharing information.

Learning Organization
A culture of lifelong learning in which employees are continually trying to learn new things.

As more companies become knowledge-based, it's important that they promote continuous learning at the employee, team, and company levels. A **learning organization** embraces a culture of lifelong learning, enabling all employees to continually acquire and share knowledge. Improvements in product or service quality do not stop when formal training is completed.[57] Employees need to have the financial, time, and content resources (courses, experiences, development opportunities) available to increase their knowledge. Managers take an active role in identifying training needs and helping to ensure that employees use training in their work. Also, employees should be actively encouraged to identify problems, make decisions, continuously experiment, and improve.

At Cheesecake Factory Inc., which operates about 170 restaurants in the United States, the focus is on driving continuous learning related to guest satisfaction, perfect food, and execution of the many dishes on its menu.[58] To do so, the company is creating interactive learning content that employees access at work. Through the VideoCafe employees can upload and share short videos on topics such as customer greetings and food preparation. The company plans to develop interactive games including a simulation for building the perfect hamburger. Hands-on employee-driven learning is supported by managers observing employees and providing coaching and feedback to help them develop new skills and reinforce their use in the workplace.

Social collaboration and social networking technology are also contributing to the development of a learning organization.[59] CareSource uses Wikis, websites with content created by users, and discussion boards to encourage employees to engage in critical thinking and learn from each other by sharing ideas about how to apply skills that they have acquired in formal training programs. Coldwell Banker encourages its real estate professionals to develop and share videos of best sales techniques using the company's video portal. Coldwell Banker also uses communities of practice to encourage employees to share best practices and provide insights on how to best approach specific types of job assignments. inVentiv Health Inc. uses tools on Facebook to help sales employees share information and update lessons learned.

Need to Adapt to Change **Change** refers to the adoption of a new idea or behavior by a company. Technological advances, changes in the workforce or government regulations, globalization, and new competitors are among the many factors that require companies to change. Change is inevitable in companies as products, companies, and entire industries experience shorter life cycles.[60] This has played a major role in reshaping the employment relationship.[61] New or emergent business strategies that result from these changes cause companies to merge, acquire new companies, grow, and in some cases downsize and restructure. This has resulted in changes in the employment relationship. Companies demand excellent customer service and high productivity levels. Employees are expected to take more responsibility for their own careers, from seeking training to balancing work and family. In exchange for top performance and working longer hours without job security, employees want companies to provide flexible work schedules, comfortable working conditions, more autonomy in accomplishing work, training and development opportunities, and financial incentives based on how the company performs. Employees realize that companies cannot provide employment security, so they want employability—that is, they want their company to provide training and job experiences to help ensure that employees can find other employment opportunities. The human resource management challenge is how to build a committed, productive workforce in economic conditions that offer opportunity for financial success but can also quickly turn sour, making every employee expendable.

> **Change**
> The adoption of a new idea or behavior by a company.

For example, every aspect of Capital BlueCross is changing due to health care reform.[62] The company's leadership development curriculum helps prepare leaders at all levels of the company to deal with these changes. It includes providing each leader with a coach who reinforces what was learned in the curriculum and tailors it to the individual strengths and challenges of each learner. Each leader also shares what they learned with the employees who report to them. Hu-Friedy, a company that manufactures dental instruments, employs 750 employees.[63] Hu-Friedy is spending $60,000 on an apprenticeship program to develop its employees' skills. Many of the employees have worked on the factory floor making instruments for years but don't have the complex understanding of heat treatment, metallurgy, and metal composition necessary for making improvements to the company's products and production processes. Hu-Friedy hopes the apprenticeship program will help keep production work in the United States and keep the company competitive.

Concerns with Employee Engagement. **Employee engagement** refers to the degree to which employees are fully involved in their work and the strength of their commitment to their job and the company.[64] How do we know if an employee is engaged? An engaged employee is passionate about his or her work, is committed to the company and its mission, and works hard to contribute. Engagement survey results show that approximately 30% of U.S. employees are engaged in their work, 52% are not engaged, and 18% are

> **Employee Engagement**
> The degree to which employees are fully involved in their work and the strength of their job and company commitment.

actively disengaged.[65] Actively disengaged employees cost the United States billions of dollars every year in lost productivity.

Perhaps the best way to understand engagement is to consider how companies measure employee engagement. Companies measure employees' engagement levels with attitude or opinion surveys (we discuss these in detail in Chapter 10). Although the types of questions asked on these surveys vary from company to company, research suggests the questions generally measure 10 common themes shown in Table 1.7. As you probably realize after reviewing the themes shown in Table 1.7, employees' engagement is influenced by how managers treat employees as well as human resource practices such as recruiting, selection, training and development, performance management, work design, and compensation. For example, Bridgepoint Education recognizes that employee engagement is necessary for success.[66] To increase employee engagement the company uses events, celebrations, and a social learning platform to facilitate conversations among employees and employees and their managers. Company leaders host discussions with employees, communicate goals, and give employees a chance to ask questions. The results of Satellite Healthcare's engagement survey showed that the renal care provider's employees want more resources supporting their career development.[67] As a result, Satellite developed a Career Pyramid that defines the positions within a dialysis career category including the position titles from entry-level jobs to top management. The education, experience, and competencies for each position are listed. Standards for promotion and development to advance to each level on the pyramid are provided. The Career Pyramid is especially useful for employees in entry-level jobs such as patient care technicians because it provides a clear structure on possible career moves and the skills that employees need to develop. Employee engagement scores collected after the Career Pyramid was implemented have improved and 92% of employees report they expect to have a long-term career with Satellite.

Talent Management
A systematic planned strategic effort by a company to attract, retain, develop, and motivate highly skilled employees and managers.

Talent Management. **Talent management** refers to the systematic planned strategic effort by a company to use bundles of human resource management practices including acquiring and assessing employees, learning and development, performance management, and compensation to attract, retain, develop, and motivate highly skilled employees and managers. This means recognizing that all HR practices are inter-related, aligned with business needs, and help the organization manage talent to meet business goals. For example, at Qualcomm, a San Diego company, talent management is organized around core values that emphasize recruiting smart, motivated employees and creating a work

Table 1.7
Common Themes of Employee Engagement

Pride in employer
Satisfaction with employer
Satisfaction with the job
Opportunity to perform challenging work
Recognition and positive feedback from contributions
Personal support from manager
Effort above and beyond the minimum
Understanding the link between one's job and the company's mission
Prospects for future growth with the company
Intention to stay with the company

SOURCE: Based on R. Vance, *Employee Engagement and Commitment* (Alexandria, VA: Society for Human Resource Management, 2006).

environment that allows them to innovate, execute, partner, and lead.[68] When Qualcomm wanted to introduce technology for its performance management process, human resources generalists worked together with organizational development and information technology specialists to ensure that what employees were being evaluated on (performance management) and what employees were paid and rewarded for (compensation and rewards) were aligned. HR trained managers to use the performance management system and now focus on identifying employee skills gaps to identify opportunities to improve performance.

Survey results suggest that opportunities for career growth, learning, and development and performing exciting and challenging work are some of the most important factors in determining employees' engagement and commitment to their current employer.[69] As the economy improves, high-achieving employees may be looking to leave companies if they do not feel they have adequate opportunities to develop or move to positions in which they can best utilize their skills. For Cognizant, a global technology solutions company, business is based on knowledge, which depends on the skills of its workforce.[70] As a result, talent development is seen as a strategic business driver. To develop talent all employees have individual development plans that support their career goals. Learning at Cognizant focuses on building both technical and leadership talent to ensure employees help improve their clients' businesses. Cognizant has several programs to build talent. The Career Architecture program helps employees choose a career track that matches their interests and skills. It helps identify training courses and job rotations that can help employees move along their career track. The Emerging Partners program develops senior account managers and senior delivery managers. The program includes case studies, role plays, and simulations. More than 100 managers have completed the program and 45% have moved within six months into leadership roles involving interactions with clients.

Use of Alternative Work Arrangements. **Alternative work arrangements** include independent contractors, on-call workers, temporary workers, and contract company workers. The Bureau of Labor Statistics estimates that alternative work arrangements make up 11% of total employment.[71] There are 10.3 million independent contractors, 2.5 million on-call workers, 1.2 million temporary help agency workers, and approximately 813,000 workers employed by contract firms. Contingent workers, or workers who do not expect their jobs to last or who believe their jobs are temporary, account for approximately 2 to 4% of total employment.

More workers in alternative employment relationships are choosing these arrangements. Alternative work arrangements can benefit both individuals and employers. More and more individuals don't want to be attached to any one company. They want the flexibility to work when and where they choose. They may want to work fewer hours to effectively balance work and family responsibilities. Also, individuals who have been downsized may choose alternative work arrangements while they are seeking full-time employment. From the company perspective, it is easier to add temporary employees when they are needed and easier to terminate their employment when they are not needed. Part-time workers can be a valuable source of skills that current employees may not have and are needed for a specific project that has a set completion date. Part-time workers can be less expensive than permanent employees because they do not receive employer health benefits or participate in pension plans. Employing part-time workers such as interns allows the company to determine if the worker meets performance requirements and fits in with the company culture, and if so, to offer the employee a permanent position. For example, Verigy, a semiconductor manufacturer in California, employs only

Alternative Work Arrangements
Independent contractors, on-call workers, temporary workers, and contract company workers who are not employed full-time by the company.

a small number of permanent employees and nonessential jobs are outsourced. When demand for its products increases, engineers and other high-tech employees are hired through staffing companies or as independent contractors.[72] Alternative work arrangements have potential disadvantages. These include concerns about work quality, inability to maintain the company culture or team environment, and legal liability.[73]

Demanding Work, but with More Flexibility. The globalization of the world economy and the development of e-commerce have made the notion of a 40-hour work week obsolete. As a result, companies need to be staffed 24 hours a day, seven days a week. Employees in manufacturing environments and service call centers are being asked to move from 8- to 12-hour days or to work afternoon or midnight shifts. Similarly, professional employees face long hours and work demands that spill over into their personal lives. Notebook computers, smartphones, and smartwatches bombard employees with information and work demands. In the car, on vacation, on planes, and even in the bathroom, employees can be interrupted by work demands. More demanding work results in greater employee stress, less satisfied employees, loss of productivity, and higher turnover—all of which are costly for companies.

One study found that because of work demands 75% of employees report having not enough time for their children, and 61% report not having enough time for their husbands and wives. However, only half of employees in the United States strongly agree that they have the flexibility they need to successfully manage their work and personal or family lives.[74] Many companies are recognizing the benefits that can be gained by both the company and employees through providing flexible work schedules, allowing work-at-home arrangements, protecting employees' free time, and more productively using employees' work time.[75] The benefits include the ability to have an advantage in attracting and retaining talented employees, reduced stress resulting in healthier employees, and a rested workforce that can maximize the use of their skills. One estimate is that 9.5% or 13.4 million U.S. employees are working at home at least one day a week.[76] One in four home-based employees is working in management, business, and finance jobs and half are self-employed. Employees in health care and installation, maintenance and repair occupations are the least likely to work from home. Banana Republic, known for its stylish, yet affordable fashions, has implemented a results-oriented work environment (ROWE) at its San Francisco and New York headquarters offices. ROWE gives employees the opportunity to decide how and where they work according to the deliverables and results they are accountable for achieving.[77] At Medtronic, 150 of its 1,000 employees in Santa Bosa, California, are home-office workers.[78] They come into the office once or twice a week. Medtronic took several steps to ensure its program was successful. It allowed employees to work at home only if they had jobs in which most of their work was done by computer. This eliminated research and development jobs and other jobs requiring face-to-face social interaction. It provided both managers and employees with guidelines for telecommuting. These guidelines included emphasizing the importance of managers setting specific performance targets and requiring employees to respond to e-mails by the end of the day. Medtronic also provides rooms that home-office workers can use for meetings when they are in Santa Bosa. The program has saved Medtronic over $1 million dollars in office space costs and improves productivity. Also, it helps Medtronic attract employees from San Francisco (an hour away) who want to continue to live there but avoid commuting hassles and daycare expenses. Employees at Salesforce.com Inc. can work from home and use Chatter, a Facebook-type application, to coordinate projects.[79] Managers can monitor whether employees working at home have answered questions and finished reports.

The use of alternative work arrangements and work-at-home has resulted in the development of co-working sites where diverse workers such as designers, artists, freelancers, consultants, and other independent contractors pay a daily or monthly fee for a guaranteed work space.[80] Co-working sites are equipped with desks and wireless Internet and some provide access to copy machines, faxes, and conference rooms. Co-working sites help facilitate independent contractors and, employees working at home, traveling, or telecommuting, who have feelings of isolation, and give them the ability to collaborate and interact, provide a more professional working atmosphere than coffee shops, and help decrease traffic and pollution.

Meeting the Needs of Stakeholders, Shareholders, Customers, Employees, and Community

As we mentioned earlier, company effectiveness and competitiveness are determined by whether the company satisfies the needs of stakeholders. Stakeholders include stockholders (who want a return on their investment), customers (who want a high-quality product or service), and employees (who desire interesting work and reasonable compensation for their services). The community, which wants the company to contribute to activities and projects and minimize pollution of the environment, is also an important stakeholder.

Measuring Performance to Stakeholders: The Balanced Scorecard. The **balanced scorecard** gives managers an indication of the performance of a company based on the degree to which stakeholder needs are satisfied; it depicts the company from the perspective of internal and external customers, employees, and shareholders.[81] The balanced scorecard is important because it brings together most of the features that a company needs to focus on to be competitive. These include being customer-focused, improving quality, emphasizing teamwork, reducing new product and service development times, and managing for the long term.

The balanced scorecard differs from traditional measures of company performance by emphasizing that the critical indicators chosen are based on the company's business strategy and competitive demands. Companies need to customize their balanced scorecards based on different market situations, products, and competitive environments.

The balanced scorecard should be used to (1) link human resource management activities to the company's business strategy and (2) evaluate the extent to which the HRM function is helping the company meet its strategic objectives. Communicating the scorecard to employees gives them a framework that helps them see the goals and strategies of the company, how these goals and strategies are measured, and how they influence the critical indicators. Measures of HRM practices primarily relate to productivity, people, and process.[82] Productivity measures involve determining output per employee (such as revenue per employee). Measuring people includes assessing employees' behavior, attitudes, or knowledge. Process measures focus on assessing employees' satisfaction with people systems within the company. People systems can include the performance management system, the compensation and benefits system, and the development system. To show that HRM activities contribute to a company's competitive advantage, managers need to consider the questions shown in Table 1.8 and be able to identify critical indicators or metrics related to human resources. As shown in the last column of Table 1.8, critical indicators of HR practices primarily relate to people, productivity, and processes.

For example, at ConocoPhillips, the balanced scorecard for top executives includes costs, health and safety, production, and resource replacement.[83] ConocoPhillips has also developed scorecards for operational-level activity such as safety. Some physicians

Balanced Scorecard
A means of performance measurement that gives managers a chance to look at their company from the perspectives of internal and external customers, employees, and shareholders.

LO 1-3
Discuss how human resource management affects a company's balanced scorecard.

Table 1.8
The Balanced Scorecard

PERSPECTIVE	QUESTIONS ANSWERED	EXAMPLES OF CRITICAL BUSINESS INDICATORS	EXAMPLES OF CRITICAL HR INDICATORS
Customer	How do customers see us?	Time, quality, performance, service, cost	Employee satisfaction with HR department services Employee perceptions of the company as an employer
Internal	What must we excel at?	Processes that influence customer satisfaction, availability of information on service and/or manufacturing processes	Training costs per employee, turnover rates, time to fill open positions
Innovation and learning	Can we continue to improve and create value?	Improve operating efficiency, launch new products, continuous improvement, empowering of workforce, employee satisfaction	Employee/skills competency levels, engagement survey results, change management capability
Financial	How do we look to shareholders?	Profitability, growth, shareholder value	Compensation and benefits per employee, turnover costs, profits per employee, revenues per employee

SOURCE: Based on B. Becker, M. Huselid, and D. Ulrich, *The HR Scorecard: Linking People, Strategy, and Performance* (Boston: Harvard Business School Press, 2001).

employed by OhioHealth, a hospital system, receive up to 10% of their pay based on a balanced scorecard consisting of quality, service, financial performance, and employee engagement.[84]

Social Responsibility. Increasingly, companies are recognizing that social responsibility can help boost a company's image with customers, gain access to new markets, and help attract and retain talented employees. Companies thus try to meet shareholder and general public demands that they be more socially, ethically, and environmentally responsible. For example, Bill Gates, former chief executive officer and Microsoft Corporation founder, through personal involvement in a charitable foundation dedicated to bringing science and technology to improve lives around the world, has improved Microsoft's corporate reputation. Coke is applying its product development expertise along with its supply chain and distribution network to make essential nutrition accessible to people in need.[85] Coke offers a ready-to-drink fortified juice product, Nursha, that addresses micronutrient deficiencies in schoolchildren in Colombia and Ghana under the global trademark name Nurisha. Coke is also working to economically empower women. In the Philippines, women own or operate more than 86% of the small neighborhood stores that sell Coke products. Companies are realizing that helping to protect the planet can also save money.[86] International Paper, a global paper and packaging company, has focused on using less water and energy at its manufacturing operations. International Paper cut fossil fuel purchases by 21% by burning tree limbs and debris from tree processing. Dow Chemical has sustainability goals that include the use of sustainable chemistry, reducing energy usage, and publishing safety evaluations for all of its products.[87] American Express supports preservation of historic sites and has a mentoring program for nonprofits and social entrepreneurs around the world.

Socially Responsible Programs Help Improve the World

Sustainability is an important part of many companies' business strategy. Dow developed a new leadership development program, Leadership in Action, with its first location in Accra, Ghana, where the company had recently opened its first office. The program is part of Dow's approach to meeting the world's basic needs by matching its employees with organizations that need support for sustainable development projects, especially in business growth areas for Dow. Accra, the west African country's capital, was chosen because it provided a way to get potential leaders to understand a new business territory, develop a new market, and establish community relationships. High-potential employees organized into teams worked with a nongovernment organization on projects including determining where to grow plants that could provide medicine for malaria and working with a trade school to develop education, science, technology, engineering, and math curriculum.

The pharmaceutical company Novartis is actively involved in improving health care in Africa by helping the fight against infectious diseases that have made life expectancy in Africa 15 years less than the global average. Novartis worked with the World Health Organization to develop e-learning for managing childhood illnesses and provide 500 million free treatments. Merck has invested in a 10-year, $500 million dollar program, Mothers for Merck, which partners with nonprofit organizations worldwide to seek to reduce a drop in childbirth mortality rates. Merck provides top company employees with the opportunity for a three-month internship where they can work for global organizations who are affiliated with Mothers for Merck. Merck Gives Back is a website employees can access to learn about charitable opportunities they can get involved with.

DISCUSSION QUESTION

How do companies' sustainability efforts help a company attract, retain, and develop employees? Explain your answer.

SOURCES: Based on "Dow Chemical's New Formula for Global Leaders," *Chief Learning Officer,* April 2015, pp. 42–43, 49; company website, "Mission & Vision," www.dow.com, accessed April 14, 2015; company website, "Corporate Responsibility Performance Report 2013" and "Improving Healthcare in Africa," http://www.novartis.com, accessed April 22, 2015; and W. Bunch, "Doing the Right Thing," *Human Resource Executive,* October 2014, pp. 10–12.

The "Competing through Sustainability" box highlights the sustainable business practices of several companies.

Customer Service and Quality Emphasis

Companies' customers judge quality and performance. As a result, customer excellence requires attention to product and service features as well as to interactions with customers. Customer-driven excellence includes understanding what the customer wants and anticipating future needs. Customer-driven excellence includes reducing defects and errors, meeting specifications, and reducing complaints. How the company recovers from defects and errors is also important for retaining and attracting customers.

Due to increased availability of knowledge and competition, consumers are very knowledgeable and expect excellent service. This presents a challenge for employees who interact with customers. The way in which clerks, sales staff, front-desk personnel, and service providers interact with customers influences a company's reputation and financial performance. Employees need product knowledge and service skills, and they need to be clear about the types of decisions they can make when dealing with customers.

To compete in today's economy, whether on a local or global level, companies need to provide a quality product or service. If companies do not adhere to quality standards, their ability to sell their product or service to vendors, suppliers, or customers will be restricted. Some countries even have quality standards that companies must meet to conduct business there. **Total quality management (TQM)** is a companywide effort to continuously improve the ways people, machines, and systems accomplish work.[88] Core values of TQM include the following:[89]

Total Quality Management (TQM)
A cooperative form of doing business that relies on the talents and capabilities of both labor and management to continually improve quality and productivity.

- Methods and processes are designed to meet the needs of internal and external customers.
- Every employee in the company receives training in quality.
- Quality is designed into a product or service so that errors are prevented from occurring rather than being detected and corrected.
- The company promotes cooperation with vendors, suppliers, and customers to improve quality and hold down costs.
- Managers measure progress with feedback based on data.

One way that companies can improve the quality of their products or services is through competing for the **Malcolm Baldrige National Quality Award** or gaining certification in the **ISO 9000:2000** standards. The Baldrige award, created by public law, is the highest level of national recognition for quality that a U.S. company can receive. To become eligible for the Baldrige, a company must complete a detailed application that consists of basic information about the firm as well as an in-depth presentation of how it addresses specific criteria related to quality improvement.[90] The categories and point values for the Baldrige Award are found in Table 1.9. The award is not given for specific products or services. Organizations can compete for the Baldrige Award in one of several different categories, including: manufacturing, service, small business, education, health care and non-profit. The Baldrige Award is given annually in each of the categories with a total limit each year of 18 awards. All applicants for the Baldrige Award undergo a rigorous examination process that takes from 300 to 1,000 hours. Applications are reviewed by an independent board of about 400 examiners who come primarily from the private sector. One of the major benefits of applying for the Baldrige Award is the feedback report from the examining team noting the company's strengths and areas for improvement.[91]

Malcolm Baldrige National Quality Award
An award established in 1987 to promote quality awareness, to recognize quality achievements of U.S. companies, and to publicize successful quality strategies.

ISO 9000:2000
Quality standards adopted worldwide.

The Baldrige Award winners usually excel at human resource practices. For example, consider PricewaterhouseCoopers Public Sector Practice (PwC PSP), a 2014 award winner.[92] PwC PSP provides risk, management, and technology consulting to state, local, and federal governments. Contractor performance assessment reports have been nearly 100% "exceptional" or "very good" from 2010 to 2014. PwC PSP scores on a tool used to assess customer engagement and loyalty has been equal to or better than scores from other U.S. consulting companies. An important reason for its customer satisfaction and loyalty is that PwC PSP makes extensive use of knowledge management to help employees learn and to serve clients. It collects knowledge through the Knowledge Gateway where it is reviewed by knowledge management team members and content experts. The knowledge is then shared through a web-based tool designed to help employees collaborate with each other. Employees use this tool to share and find knowledge, exchange ideas, and seek developmental opportunities. Senior leaders at PwC PSP identify high-performing operations and invite them to present their practices at managing partner meeting. The practices are also shared on the Knowledge Gateway.

ISO (International Organization for Standardization), a network of national standards institutes including 160 countries with a central governing body in Geneva,

Leadership	**120**
The way senior executives create and sustain vision, values, and mission; promote legal and ethical behavior; create a sustainable company and communicate with and engage the workforce.	
Measurement, Analysis, and Knowledge Management	**90**
The way the company selects, gathers, analyzes, uses, manages, and improves its data, information, and knowledge assets	
Strategic Planning	**85**
The way the company sets strategic direction, how it determines action plans, how it changes strategy and action plans if required, and how it measures progress	
Workforce Focus	**85**
Company's efforts to develop and utilize the workforce to achieve high performance; how the company engages, manages, and develops the potential of the workforce in alignment with company goals	
Operations Focus	**85**
Design, management, and improvement of work systems and work processes to deliver customer value and achieve company success and sustainability	
Results	**450**
Company's performance and improvement in key business areas (product, service, and supply quality; productivity; operational effectiveness and related financial indicators; environmental, legal, and regulatory compliance); ethically and socially responsible	
Customer Focus	**85**
Company's knowledge of the customer, customer service systems, current and potential customer concerns, customer satisfaction and engagement	
Total Points	**1,000**

Table 1.9

Categories and Point Values for the Malcolm Baldrige National Quality Award Examination

SOURCE: Based on "2014–2015 Criteria for Performance Excellence" from the website for the National Institute of Standards and Technology, www.nist.gov/baldrige.

Switzerland, is the world's largest developer and publisher of international standards.[93] The ISO develops standards related to management, as well as a wide variety of other areas including education, music, ships, and even protecting children! ISO standards are voluntary but countries may decide to adopt ISO standards in their regulations and as a result they may become a requirement to compete in the market. The ISO 9000 is a family of standards related to quality (ISO 9000, 9001, 9004, and 10011). The ISO 9000 quality standards address what the company does to meet regulatory requirements and the customer's quality requirements while striving to improve customer satisfaction and continuous improvement. The standards represent an international consensus on quality management practices. ISO 9000:2000 has been adopted as the quality standard in nearly 100 counties around the world meaning that companies have to follow the standards to conduct business in those countries. The quality management standards of the ISO 9000 are based on eight quality management principles including customer focus, leadership, people involvement, a process approach, a systems approach to management, continuous improvement, using facts to make decisions, and establishing mutually beneficial relationships with suppliers. ISO 9001:2008 is the most comprehensive standard because it provides a set of requirements for a quality management system for all organizations both private and public. The ISO 9001:2008 has been implemented by over

1 million organizations in 176 countries. ISO 9004 provides a guide for companies that want to improve.

Why are standards useful? Customers may want to check that the product they ordered from a supplier meets the purpose for which it is required. One of the most efficient ways to do this is when the specifications of the product have been defined in an International Standard. That way, both supplier and customer are on the same wavelength, even if they are based in different countries, because they are both using the same references. Many products require testing for conformance with specifications or compliance with safety or other regulations before they can be put on many markets. In addition, national legislation may require such testing to be carried out by independent bodies, particularly when the products concerned have health or environmental implications. One example of an ISO standard is on the back cover of this book and nearly every other book. On the back cover is something called an ISBN. ISBN stands for International Standard Book Number. Publishers and booksellers are very familiar with ISBNs, because they are the method through which books are ordered and bought. Try buying a book on the Internet, and you will soon learn the value of the ISBN—there is a unique number for the book you want! And it is based on an ISO standard.

Six Sigma Process
System of measuring, analyzing, improving, and controlling processes once they meet quality standards.

In addition to competing for quality awards and seeking ISO certification, many companies are using the Six Sigma process and lean thinking. The **Six Sigma process** refers to a process of measuring, analyzing, improving, and then controlling processes once they have been brought within the narrow Six Sigma quality tolerances or standards. The objective of Six Sigma is to create a total business focus on serving the customer, that is, to deliver what customers really want when they want it. Six Sigma involves highly trained employees known as Champions, Master Black Belts, Black Belts, and Green Belts who lead and teach teams that are focusing on an ever-growing number of quality projects. The quality projects focus on improving efficiency and reducing errors in products and services. The Six Sigma quality initiative has produced more than $2 billion in benefits for GE. For example, at General Electric introducing the Six Sigma quality initiative meant going from approximately 35,000 defects per million operations—which is average for most companies, including GE—to fewer than four defects per million in every element of every process GE businesses perform—from manufacturing a locomotive part to servicing a credit card account to processing a mortgage application to answering a phone.[94]

Lean Thinking
A process used to determine how to use less effort, time, equipment, and space but still meet customers' requirements.

Training is an important component of quality programs because it teaches employees statistical process control and how to engage in "lean thinking." **Lean thinking** is a way to do more with less effort, time, equipment, and space, but still provide customers with what they need and want. Part of lean thinking includes training workers in new skills or how to apply old skills in new ways so they can quickly take over new responsibilities or use new skills to help fill customer orders. Baylor Health Care System wanted to decrease waste and improve patient satisfaction and outcomes through implementing lean thinking and process improvements in several of its hospitals.[95] This included training employees for how to make changes to work processes. Lean thinking and process improvement supported by training provided significant value. For example, the corporate supply management team eliminated two-thirds of the time for completing contracts, developed a decision tree for different types of projects, and reduced errors, saving $10 million dollars. A hospital re-admission team redesigned the patient discharge process to reduce the chances of patients returning within 30 days. They realized a 44% decrease in re-admissions over a six-month period, which improved the quality of life for patients and Baylor's ability to receive Medicare/Medicaid payments from the government.

In addition to developing products or providing services that meet customer needs, one of the most important ways to improve customer satisfaction is to improve the quality of employees' work experiences. Research shows that satisfied employees are more likely to provide high-quality customer service. Customers who receive high-quality service are more likely to be repeat customers. As Table 1.10 shows, companies that are recognized as providing elite customer service emphasize state-of-the-art human resource practices including rigorous employee selection, employee loyalty, training, and keeping employees satisfied by offering generous benefits.

Changing Demographics and Diversity of the Workforce

Company performance on the balanced scorecard is influenced by the characteristics of its labor force. The labor force of current employees is often referred to as the **internal labor force.** Employers identify and select new employees from the external labor market through recruiting and selection. The **external labor market** includes persons actively seeking employment. As a result, the skills and motivation of a company's internal labor

Internal Labor Force
Labor force of current employees.

External Labor Market
Persons outside the firm who are actively seeking employment.

Wegmans
Gives away $59 million in scholarships to 19,000 employees. Senior managers sit side-by-side with employees listening in on phones in the company's call center.

Asana
Gives employees a $10,000 dollar allowance for computers and office décor which employees can use to purchase mini-refrigerators, headphones, and ergonomic chairs. Asana also offers free yoga classes and in-house chefs.

Google
Provides employees with food service, fitness centers, bicycle repairs, and napping pods.

Unilever
Agile Working Program allows employees to work any hours, anywhere they want to. Office cubicles have been replaced with collaborative workspaces with small, shared work pods. The new work areas are designed to provide a comfortable environment by including televisions, foosball tables, and treadmills.

Delaware North Companies
Uses tests that assess job candidates' personality and work styles to ensure they have the friendliness, curiosity, and ability to multitask that are needed as customer service representatives to help customers plan vacations.

Cadillac
Performance of repair technicians is carefully monitored to ensure they are not repeating mistakes in repairs. Dealers who maintain good customer service ratings based on customer surveys receive cash rewards.

Starbucks
Entry-level baristas get 24 hours of training that prepares them to stay calm and courteous in busy times.

Publix Super Markets
Employees receive bonuses based on their unit's performance and share grants as part of their incentive plans.

Table 1.10
Examples of HR Practices That Enhance Customer Service

SOURCES: Based on L. Weber, "To Get a Job, New Hires Are Put to the Test," *The Wall Street Journal*, April 15, 2015, pp. A1, A10; R. Feintzeig, "Meet Silicon Valley's Little Elves," *The Wall Street Journal*, November 21, 2014, pp. A1, A10; W. Bunch, "Unleashing the Workforce," *Human Resource Executive*, November 2012, pp. 14–17; J. McGregor, "Customer Service Champs," *BusinessWeek*, March 5, 2007, pp. 52–64.

force are influenced by the composition of the available labor market (the external labor market). The skills and motivation of a company's internal labor force determine the need for training and development practices and the effectiveness of the company's compensation and reward systems.

Important changes in the demographics and diversity of the workforce are projected. First, the average age of the workforce will increase. Second, the workforce will become more diverse in terms of gender, race, and generations, and third, immigration will continue to affect the size and diversity of the workforce.

Aging of the Workforce. The labor force will continue to age and the number of workers age 55 or older will grow from 21 to 26% by 2022.[96] Figure 1.5 compares the projected distribution of the age of the workforce in 2012 and 2022. The labor force participation of those 55 years and older is expected to grow because older individuals are leading healthier and longer lives than in the past, providing the opportunity to work more years; the high cost of health insurance and decrease in health benefits causes many employees to keep working to keep their employer-based insurance or to return to work after retirement to obtain health insurance through their employer; and the trend toward pension plans based on individuals' contributions to them rather than years of service provides an incentive for older employees to continue working. The aging labor force means companies are likely to employ a growing share of older workers—many in their second or third career. Older people want to work and many say they plan a working retirement. Despite myths to the contrary, worker performance and learning are not adversely affected by aging.[97] Older employees are willing and able to learn new technology. An emerging trend is for qualified older workers to ask to work part-time or for only a few months at a time as a means to transition to retirement. Employees and companies are redefining the meaning of retirement to include second careers as well as part-time and temporary work assignments. An aging workforce means that employers will increasingly face HRM issues such as career plateauing, retirement planning, and retraining older workers to avoid skill obsolescence. Companies will struggle with how to control the rising costs of benefits and health care. Companies face competing challenges with older workers. Companies will have to ensure that older workers are not discriminated against in hiring, training, and workforce reduction decisions. At the same time companies will want to encourage retirement and make it financially and psychologically acceptable.

Many companies are offering special programs to capitalize on older employees' skills and accommodate their needs.[98] CVS/pharmacy has stores in every climate and region in the U.S. CVS created its Snowbirds Program to allow older employees to move

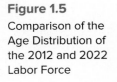

Figure 1.5

Comparison of the Age Distribution of the 2012 and 2022 Labor Force

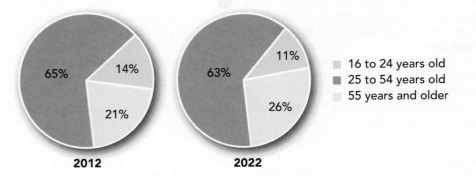

SOURCE: Bureau of Labor Statistics, "Employment Projections: 2012–2022," News Release, www.bls.gov, accessed February 25, 2015.

among locations according to their preferences. This is especially important for older employees who spend winters in the southern states and summer in the northern states. Over 1,000 employees including retail clerks, pharmacists, and managers have participated in the program.

At Herman Miller, the Michigan-based furniture manufacturer, employees can begin the retirement process two years ahead of their actual retirement date by working fewer hours. This helps ease their transition out of their job and workplace but provides them time to share their knowledge and help train other employees to take their job. National Institutes of Health (NIH) has two phased-retirement programs that allow employees to choose to gradually transition to retirement by reducing hours or a trial-retirement program that allows retirees to return to work within one year of retiring in case they decide they aren't ready to leave the workforce.

Generational Differences. Because employees are working longer the workforce now has five generations, each one with unique characteristics and characteristics similar to the others. In Table 1.11 the year born, nicknames, and ages of each generation are shown. Consider some of the attributes that are believed to characterize each generation.[99] For example, Millennials grew up with access to computers at home and school and access to the Internet. They grew up with diversity in their schools and were coached, praised, and encouraged for participation rather than accomplishment by their Baby Boomer parents. Millennials are characterized as being optimistic, willing to work and learn, eager to please, self-reliant, globally aware and as valuing diversity and teamwork. They are also believed to have high levels of self-esteem and narcissism. Generation Xers grew up during a time when the divorce rate doubled, the number of women working outside the home increased, and the personal computer was invented. They were often left to their own after school (latchkey kids). They value skepticism, informality, practicality, seek work/life balance, and dislike close supervision. They tend to be impatient and cynical. They have experienced change all of their lives (in terms of parents, homes, and cities). Baby Boomers, the "Me" generation, marched against the "establishment" for equal rights and an end to the Vietnam War. They value social conscientiousness and independence. They are competitive, hard working, and concerned with the fair treatment of all employees. They are often considered to be workaholics and rigid in conforming to rules. Traditionalists grew up during the Great Depression and lived during World War II. They tend to value frugality, are patriotic and loyal, adhere to rules, are loyal to employers, and take responsibility and sacrifice for the good of the company.

Members of each generation may have misperceptions of each other causing tensions and misunderstanding in the workplace.[100] For example, Millennials may think

YEAR BORN	GENERATION	AGES
1925–45	Traditionalists Silent Generation	>69
1946–64	Baby Boomers	51–69
1965–80	Generation X	35–50
1981–95	Millennials Generation Y Echo Boomers	20–34
1996	Generation Z Digital Natives	<20

Table 1.11
Generations in the Workforce

Generation X managers are bitter, jaded, abrasive, uninterested in them, and poor delegators. In turn, their Generation X managers consider Millennials too needy for attention, demanding, and overly self-confident. Millennials might believe that Baby Boomers are too rigid and follow company rules too closely. They believe employees in the older generations have been too slow in adopting social media tools and overvalue tenure rather than knowledge and performance. Traditionalists and Baby Boomers believe that Millennials don't have a strong work ethic because they are too concerned with work-life balance. Also, members of the younger generations may resent Baby Boomers and Traditionalists who are working longer before retiring, blocking promotions and career moves.

It is important to note that although generational differences likely exist, members of the same generation are no more alike than members of the same gender or race. This means that you should be cautious in attributing differences in employee behaviors and attitudes to generational differences or expecting all employees of a generation to have similar values. Research suggests that the generations of employees have similarities as well as differences.[101] Although differences in work ethic have been found among Baby Boomers, Generation Xers, and Millennials, Millennial employees are more similar than different from other generations in their work beliefs, job values, and gender beliefs. Most employees view work as a means to more fully use their skills and abilities, meet their interests, and allow them to live a desirable lifestyle. They also value work-life balance, meaning flexible work policies are necessary to allow them to choose where and when work is performed.

Consider what Dell Inc. does to alleviate misunderstandings and misperceptions of its multigenerational workforce.[102] Dell provides a course for all of their new managers that includes topics such as leading multigenerational teams and developing connections with the employees who report to them. The ability to relate to and motivate a multigenerational workforce, to lead teams to work together, and encourage an entrepreneurial spirit are required qualities that all successful managers at Dell must have regardless of what generation they come from. Dell also uses employee resource groups for employees to connect, build relationships, and network. For example, the resource group for Millennials is called "GenNext." Dell also encourages employees to participate in discussion with managers about new ways to consider where and how work gets done. This allows employees to choose to work remotely and telecommute, which helps them meet their personal needs, yet successfully complete their work.

Gender and Racial Composition of the Workforce. As Figure 1.6 shows, by 2022 the workforce is expected to be 78% white, 12% African American, 6% Asian, and 4% other

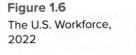

Figure 1.6
The U.S. Workforce,
2022

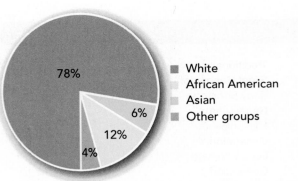

SOURCE: Bureau of Labor Statistics, "Employment Projections: 2012–2022," news release, www.bls.gov, accessed February 25, 2015.

groups, which includes individuals of multiple racial origin, American Indian, Alaskan Native or Native Hawaiian, and other Pacific Islanders.[103] The diversity of the workforce is expected to increase by 2022. As a result of different fertility rates and differences in immigration patterns, race and ethnic groups will show different trends in labor force growth.

Many U.S. industries, including meatpacking, construction, farming, and service, rely on immigrants from Mexico and other countries to perform short-term or labor-intensive jobs. Immigration contributes to the diversity of the U.S. population and workforce. More than 1 million immigrants come to the U.S. each year, and 6 out of 10 are relatives of U.S. citizens.[104] Another 14% come on work-related visas, some of which are available only for workers with exceptional qualifications in science, business, or the arts. The U.S. government also provides temporary visas to a limited number of highly educated workers, allowing them to work in the country for a set period of time but not to remain as immigrants. U.S. law requires employers to verify that any job candidate who is not a U.S. citizen has received permission to work in the United States as an immigrant or with a temporary permit. U.S. immigrants come from countries around the world but most come from Asia, the Americas, and Central America. Although a common belief is that immigrants have few skills, the percentage of highly skilled immigrants now exceeds the percentage of low–skilled immigrants. While the U.S. government is debating how to deal with illegal immigration, many companies would face a labor crisis if they were forced to terminate employment of illegal immigrants, many of whom have lived and worked in the United States for years but lack the work authorizations and visas needed to work legally in this country. However, in recent years Immigrations, Customs, and Enforcement has focused its efforts on auditing employers to insure they are not employing undocumented immigrants. For example, an oyster-processing operation in Maryland brings in workers from Mexico to perform the dirty and smelly work needed

Table 1.12
How Managing Cultural Diversity Can Provide Competitive Advantage

1. Cost argument	As organizations become more diverse, the cost of a poor job in integrating workers will increase. Those who handle this well will thus create cost advantages over those who don't.
2. Employee attraction and retention argument	Companies develop reputations on favorability as prospective employers for women and ethnic minorities. Those with the best reputations for managing diversity will win the competition for talent. As the labor pool shrinks and changes composition, this edge will become increasingly important.
3. Marketing argument	The insight and cultural sensitivity that diverse employees bring to the marketing effort should help the company enter new markets and develop products and services for diverse populations.
4. Creativity argument	Diversity of perspectives and less emphasis on conformity to norms of the past improves the level of creativity.
5. Problem-solving argument	Heterogeneity in decisions and problem-solving groups potentially produces better decisions through a wider range of perspectives and more thorough critical analysis of issues.
6. System flexibility argument	Greater flexibility to react to changes in customer preferences and tastes (i.e., reactions should be faster and cost less).

SOURCES: *Academy of Management Executive,* by T. H. Cox and S. Blake, 1991; N. Lockwood, *Workplace Diversity: Leveraging the Power of Difference for Competitive Advantage* (Alexandria, VA: Society for Human Resource Management, 2005).

to shuck oysters from October to February. The family-owned business has tried to hire U.S. workers but so far has had little success although the typical worker makes $12 per hour.[105] Many business owners believe the annual cap on visas is too low because they cannot find enough employees to fill their jobs.

The implications of the changing labor market for managing human resources are far-reaching. Managing diversity involves many different activities, including creating an organizational culture that values diversity, ensuring that HRM systems are bias-free, facilitating higher career involvement of women, promoting knowledge and acceptance of cultural differences, ensuring involvement in education both within and outside the company, and dealing with employees' resistance to diversity.[106] Table 1.12 presents ways that managing cultural diversity can provide a competitive advantage. How diversity issues are managed has implications for creativity, problem solving, retaining good employees, and developing markets for the firm's products and services. To successfully manage a diverse workforce, managers must develop a new set of skills, including:

1. Communicating effectively with employees from a wide variety of cultural backgrounds.
2. Coaching and developing employees of different ages, educational backgrounds, ethnicity, physical ability, and race.
3. Providing performance feedback that is based on objective outcomes rather than values and stereotypes that work against women, minorities, and handicapped persons by prejudging these persons' abilities and talents.
4. Creating a work environment that makes it comfortable for employees of all backgrounds to be creative and innovative.
5. Recognizing and responding to generational issues.[107]

Diversity is important for tapping all employees' creative, cultural, and communication skills and using those skills to provide competitive advantage as shown in Table 1.12. For example, the Latino Employee Network at Frito-Lay played a key role during the development of Doritos Guacamole Flavored Tortilla Chips.[108] The chips generated more than $500 million in sales during their first year, making this one of the most successful product launches in the company's history. Network members provided feedback on the taste and packaging to ensure that the product would be seen as authentic in the Latino community. Disabled workers can also be a source of competitive advantage. Innotrac provides contact-center support and packing services for a variety of global brands including Target, AT&T, Ferrari, Rodale's, and Groupon.[109] Over the past 30 years, Innotrac has hired employees with physical and mental disabilities, accommodated them, and partnered with organizations who help the disabled find work. For example, Innotrac contracted with a sign-interpreting firm to help a deaf maintenance employee communicate with his manager, allowed workers who have physical disabilities to sit down while packing products, and changed how mentally challenged workers who worked at a slower pace than nondisabled employees were paid (from hourly rate to pay by the piece). Innotrac believes that true diversity is hiring based on capabilities. They don't track the percentage of employees with disabilities because they don't want the emphasis to be on disabilities rather than abilities.

The bottom line is that to gain a competitive advantage, companies must harness the power of the diverse workforce. These practices are needed not only to meet employee needs but to reduce turnover costs and ensure that customers receive the best service possible. The implication of diversity for HRM practices will be highlighted throughout this book. For example, from a staffing perspective, it is important to ensure that tests used to select employees are not biased against minority groups. From a work design perspective, employees need flexible schedules that allow them to meet nonwork needs. From a training perspective, it is clear that all employees need to be made aware of the potential damaging effects of stereotypes. From a compensation perspective, new benefits such as elder care and day care need to be included in reward systems to accommodate the needs of a diverse workforce.

Legal Issues

There will likely be development and debate of new employment laws and regulations, as well as increased emphasis on enforcing specific aspects of current laws and regulations.[110] An emphasis on eliminating discrimination in recruitment and hiring will continue. The focus will likely be on pre-employment tests, criminal background screening, and online searches that might reveal the age of job applicants. Also, greater attention will be given to eliminating discrimination based on disability, pay rates, job category, family leave, religion (based on employee need to pray during work and wear religious clothing), and harassment. There are likely to be more challenges of sex and race discrimination because of lack of access to training and development opportunities that are needed for promotions to better paying jobs or higher level management positions. Eliminating discrimination against veterans and people with disabilities, especially among federal contractors, is likely. This is especially likely due to the expanded definition of disability under the Americans with Disabilities Act to include cancer, diabetes, epilepsy, and intellectual disabilities.

Workplace safety will get more attention as new regulations are considered, requiring companies to identify workplace hazards and either fix them or provide employees with protection. Companies in industries that are considered to be the most dangerous for employees will be asked to meet additional reporting and inspection requirements.

In their efforts to reduce employee health care insurance costs, companies are offering incentives for employees to participate in wellness programs and providing penalties if they do not. Wellness programs typically include smoking cessation, exercise, dieting, and submitting to biometric screening tests (e.g., blood tests) to detect illness or risk of illness such as heart attacks. However, wellness programs are coming under scrutiny. The Equal Employment Opportunity Commission has issued preliminary rules about when the penalties or rewards related to participating in wellness programs are too extreme and may violate the Americans with Disabilities Act.

Scrutiny of companies who employ unlawful immigrants or abuse laborers will continue to increase. Companies can face criminal charges if immigration and customs officials can show that they knowingly employed undocumented and illegal immigrants. The number of company audits conducted by the Immigration and Customs Enforcement (ICE) has increased over the past several years, resulting in over $10 million in fines.

The publication of classified documents by WikiLeaks and Wall Street insider trading probes have resulted in companies more carefully scrutinizing data-security practices and increased concerns about protecting intellectual property. This will likely influence human resource practices related to performance management such as the use of electronic monitoring and surveillance of knowledge workers. We may see more litigation related to employee privacy rights and intellectual property rights as a result of companies terminating employees or taking disciplinary action against them for data-security breaches, discussing employment practices using social media, or sharing or stealing intellectual property for personal gain. Also, issues regarding the confidentiality and security of employees' health care information will receive more attention as employees use wearables (such as Fitbits) and apps to track what they eat and drink, their heart rate, and physical activity. Employers who provide employees with wearables as part of wellness programs are not allowed by health privacy laws to view any single employee's health statistics.

Ethical Issues

Ethics
The fundamental principles of right and wrong by which employees and companies interact.

Many organizations have engaged in serious ethical misconduct, including General Motors (failure to fix and notify customers about faulty ignition switches), the Veterans Administration (concealed patient wait times), U.S. Secret Service (security breaches involving partying and prostitutes), and JPMorganChase (misrepresented mortgage-backed securities to the public). Many decisions related to managing human resources are characterized by uncertainty. **Ethics** can be considered the fundamental principles of right and wrong by which employees and companies interact.[111] These principles should be considered in making business decisions and interacting with clients and customers. Ethical, successful companies can be characterized by four principles shown in Figure 1.7.[112] First, in their relationships with customers, vendors, and clients, these companies emphasize mutual benefits. Second, employees assume responsibility for the actions of the company. Third, such companies have a sense of purpose or vision the employees value and use in their day-to-day work. Finally, they emphasize fairness; that is, another person's interests count as much as their own. HR and business decisions should be ethical but that is not always the case. A recent survey of employees found that 41% had witnessed some form of unethical conduct at their workplace.[113] This probably helps explain public perception of business ethics. Only 15% of Americans trust that business leaders are telling the truth and globally only 28% believe that businesses follow ethical practices.[114] It is important to note that ethics refers to behavior that is not clearly right or wrong. Compliance means that the company is not violating legal regulations. But a company can be compliant and still have employees engaging in unethical practices.

Sarbanes-Oxley Act of 2002
A congressional act passed in response to illegal and unethical behavior by managers and executives. The act sets stricter rules for business; especially accounting practices including requiring more open and consistent disclosure of financial data, CEOs' assurance that the data is completely accurate, and provisions that affect the employee–employer relationship (e.g., development of a code of conduct for senior financial officers).

The **Sarbanes-Oxley Act of 2002** sets strict rules for corporate behavior and sets heavy fines and prison terms for noncompliance: organizations are spending millions of dollars

Figure 1.7
Principles of Ethical Companies

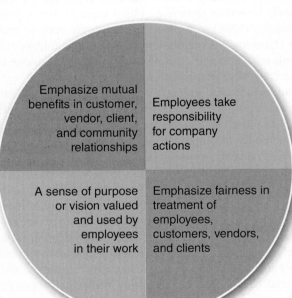

Emphasize mutual benefits in customer, vendor, client, and community relationships

Employees take responsibility for company actions

A sense of purpose or vision valued and used by employees in their work

Emphasize fairness in treatment of employees, customers, vendors, and clients each year to comply with regulations under the Sarbanes-Oxley Act, which imposes criminal penalties for corporate governing and accounting lapses, including retaliation against whistle-blowers reporting violations of Security and Exchange Commission rules.[115] Due to Sarbanes-Oxley and new Security and Exchange Commission regulations that impose stricter standards for disclosing executive pay, corporate boards are paying more attention to executive pay as well as issues like leadership development and succession planning.[116] This has resulted in an increase in the number of HR executives and individuals with HR expertise who are being asked to serve on corporate boards to provide data and analysis. For example, a CEO or chief financial officer (CFO) who falsely represents company finances may be fined up to $1 million and/or imprisoned for up to 10 years. The penalty for willful violations is up to $5 million and/or 20 years imprisonment. The law requires CEOs and CFOs to certify corporate financial reports, prohibits personal loans to officers and directors, and prohibits insider trading during pension fund blackout periods.[117] A "blackout" is any period of more than three consecutive business days during which the company temporarily stops 50% or more of company plan participants or beneficiaries from acquiring, selling, or transferring an interest in any of the company's equity securities in the pension plan. The law also requires retention of all documents relevant to a government investigation.

The law also has a number of provisions that directly affect the employer–employee relationship.[118] For example, the act prohibits retaliation against whistle-blowers (individuals who have turned in the company or one of its officers for an illegal act) and government informants. The act also requires that publically traded companies disclose whether they have a code of ethics.[119] Other federal guidelines such as the Federal Acquisition Regulation also require or provide incentives to encourage all businesses to adopt codes of conduct, train employees on these codes, and create effective ways to audit and report ethical and unethical behavior. This means that companies, with HR taking the lead, should develop codes of conduct that clearly define ethics and professional responsibility. HR professionals along with other top-level managers usually play a key role in helping conduct ethics audits, develop ethical codes of conduct, and respond to ethical violations. Guidelines for disciplinary actions for employees guilty of unethical behavior and conduct need to be developed. Managers and employees will need to be trained on ethics policies to ensure that business processes and procedures are correctly followed. HR professionals will need to document the fact that employees have received these policies and have attended training to ensure their compliance with the act. Because of the potential liability for retaliation in the context of discrimination and harassment, policies should include assurances that an employee will not be retaliated against for making a complaint or for serving as a witness. Executive compensation programs will need to be monitored to ensure that the program is in compliance with the no personal loans and no sales of pension funds during blackout period provisions.

Consider the policies and practices that companies are using to help ensure an ethical workplace.[120] Dimension Data's employees participate in a half-day ethics program discussing how they would respond to different ethical dilemmas that occur at work. Southern Company invited a convicted felon to speak to employees about how a good person can violate ethics. Before his conviction, which resulted in a five-year prison term, the felon was chief financial officer for a health care company. Eaton Corporation includes its ethics principles on its website. Examples of their principles include obeying the law, avoiding conflicts of interest, acting with integrity, protecting assets and information, and respecting human rights. Eaton Corporation's employees receive regular training on how to apply ethical principles to their daily work. The Global Ethics and Compliance Office provides ethics training programs and communications designed to ensure that Eaton's ethics and values are integrated into its business practices on a consistent basis around the

CEO Cuts Pay to Reduce Income Inequality

Gravity Payments, a credit-card payment processing company, was started by Dan Price in his dorm room at Seattle Pacific University with money from his older brother. Price, the CEO, pledged to make sure all of his employees make at least $70,000 annually in the next three years. The average salary at Gravity is $48,000. Under this pay plan, 30 employees will double their salaries. To achieve this, Price is cutting his $1 million salary to $70,000 and using approximately 80% of Gravity's annual $2 million in profits. There are several reasons why Price is instituting the new pay plan. First, he believes that Seattle's $15 an hour minimum wage law is insufficient. He had been hearing his employees talk about difficulties in finding housing and meeting their expenses

on their current salaries. Second, he feels that the new pay policy is a "moral imperative" that is necessary to reduce the large pay gap between his pay as CEO and other employees. Although he is a capitalist, he believes that the pay rates for CEOs compared to regular employees are absurd. Third, he believes the pay cut is necessary to make the company's more than 100 employees happy and build loyalty. When he told employees of the new pay policy at a meeting there was silence followed by applause and high-fives. The 50 employees who already earn more than $70,000 were as appreciative of the pay plan as their lower-paid peers. They are happy that the team members who helped them earn higher pay are going to be taken care of. Price, who feels

that reducing wage inequality was an issue he was in position to do something about as a business leader, is not raising customer prices or cutting back on service. Instead, he plans to keep his salary low until the company earns back the profits it had before the new pay plan.

DISCUSSION QUESTION
Money is not supposed to buy happiness (or love). In this situation will the new pay plan contribute to employee happiness and loyalty? Explain your answer.

SOURCES: Based on "CEO Cuts His Pay, Boosts Workers," *Columbus Dispatch,* April 16, 2015, p. A15; C. Isidore, "Gravity Payments CEO Takes 90% Pay Cut to Give Workers Huge Raise," April 14, 2015, from www.money.com; P. Cohen, "One Company's New Minimum Wage: $70,000 a Year," *The New York Times,* April 13, 2015, www.nytimes.com.

world. Xerox conducts regular ethics surveys, which ask employees if they have experienced an ethics violation. To receive promotions managers are expected to take an active role in supporting Xerox's ethics strategy. Managers review their previous year's performance, create action plans as to how they plan to improve the ethics policy (such as more training or better communications), and are expected to chair their local ethics committee. All employees are encouraged to report ethical violations or questions to the ethics office either face-to-face, using an ethics hotline, or sending them to an e-mail address. Xerox's high ethical standards have won it recognition as one of the world's most ethical companies. This has helped recruit high-quality employees especially in global locations where business decisions are not transparent to employees and ethics are frequently violated.

Human resource managers must satisfy three basic standards for their practices to be considered ethical.[121] First, HRM practices must result in the greatest good for the largest number of people. Second, employment practices must respect basic human rights of privacy, due process, consent, and free speech. Third, managers must treat employees and customers equitably and fairly.

To call attention to the important role of ethics in the workplace, throughout the book we include "Integrity in Action" boxes that highlight the good (and bad) decisions related to ethical HR practices made by company leaders and managers. The "Integrity in Action" box shows how the CEO of Gravity Payments introduced a new pay policy to help employees meet their expenses.

THE GLOBAL CHALLENGE

Companies are finding that to survive they must compete in international markets as well as fend off foreign corporations' attempts to gain ground in the United States. To meet these challenges, U.S. businesses must develop global markets, use their practices to improve global competitiveness, and better prepare employees for global assignments.

Every business must be prepared to deal with the global economy. Global business expansion has been made easier by technology. The Internet allows data and information to be instantly accessible and sent around the world. The Internet, e-mail, social networking, and video conferencing enable business deals to be completed between companies thousands of miles apart.

Globalization is not limited to any particular sector of the economy, product market, or company size.[122] Companies without international operations may buy or use goods that have been produced overseas, hire employees with diverse backgrounds, or compete with foreign-owned companies operating within the United States.

Businesses around the world are attempting to increase their competitiveness and value by increasing their global presence, often through mergers and acquisitions.

LO 1-4
Discuss what companies should do to compete in the global marketplace.

Entering International Markets

Many companies are entering international markets by exporting their products overseas, building manufacturing facilities or service centers in other countries, entering into alliances with foreign companies, and engaging in e-commerce. One estimate is that developing economies and emerging markets such as those found in the BRIC nations (Brazil, Russia, India, and China) are responsible for 19% of the world's economy.[123] Other countries such as Indonesia, Malaysia, Kenya, Colombia, and Poland have a growing middle class, strong infrastructure, business-friendly regulations, and stable governments and are likely new emerging markets. The importance of globalization is seen in recent hiring patterns of large U.S. multinational corporations that have increased their overseas workforce, particularly in Asia.[124] Markets in Brazil, China, and India have resulted in 60% of General Electric's business outside the United States with over half of its employees overseas. Clothing retailer Gap Inc. believes it needs to expand its international presence because the U.S. market is maturing and has many competitors. It opened its first company-owned store in China in 2010.[125] The retailer has stores in 48 countries including Asia, Australia, Eastern Europe, Latin America, the Middle East, and Africa. Banana Republic, a Gap Inc. company, recently expanded to important cities for fashions including Ginza, Paris, and Milan. The Coca-Cola Company operates in more than 200 countries. It recently opened its 43rd production facility in China and plans to invest $5 billion dollars in Africa over the next six years.[126] Coke also plans to open its first bottling plant in Myanmar, which will create thousands of jobs over the next five years. Yum! Brands, parent company of KFC, Pizza Hut, and Taco Bell, has over 6,200 stores in China contributing over 50% of the company's profits.[127]

Global companies are struggling both to find and retain talented employees, especially in emerging markets. Companies are moving into China, India, eastern Europe, the Middle East, Southeast Asia, and Latin America, but the demand for talented employees exceeds supply. Also, companies often place successful U.S. managers in charge of overseas operations, but these managers lack the cultural understanding necessary to attract, motivate, and retain talented employees. To cope with these problems, companies are taking actions to better prepare their managers and their families for overseas assignments and to ensure that training and development opportunities are available for global employees. Cross-cultural training prepares employees and their families to understand the culture and norms of the country they are being relocated to and to return to their home country after the assignment. Cross-cultural training is discussed in Chapter 7. For example, McDonald's continues to open new stores throughout the world.[128] It opened its first restaurant in Vietnam in 2014 and is planning to open a store in Kazakhstan in 2015. The Vietnam store is the 10,000th restaurant for McDonald's in Asia, the Pacific region, the Middle East, and Africa. Kazakhstan is McDonald's 120th global market! To train future managers in store operations, leadership, and staff management skills needed for global expansion to be successful, McDonald's has seven Hamburger Universities in the United States and abroad including campuses at Oak Brook, Illinois; Sydney; Munich; London; Tokyo; São Paulo; and Shanghai. All provide training materials and tools that can be used in different languages and cultures.

IBM obtains more than two-thirds of its revenue from outside the United States and is seeking to build team leadership in order to compete in emerging markets around the world. IBM's Corporate Service Program has donated the time and service of about 600 employees for over 1,000 projects in countries such as Turkey, Romania, Ghana, Vietnam, the Phillipines, and Tanzania.[129] The goal of the program is to develop a leadership team that learns about the needs and culture of these countries, at the same time providing valuable community service. For example, eight IBM employees from five countries traveled to Timisoara, Romania. Each employee was assigned to help a different company or nonprofit organization. One software-development manager helped GreenForest, a manufacturer of office, hotel, school, and industrial furniture, reach its goal of cutting costs and becoming more efficient by recommending computer equipment and systems needed to increase production and exports to western Europe. Another employee worked with a nonprofit organization that offers services to disabled adults. Besides benefiting the companies, the employees have also found that the experience has helped them understand cultural differences, improve their communication and teamwork skills, and gain insights on global marketing and strategy. The "Competing Through Globalization" box shows how several global companies are preparing employees for global assignments.

Offshoring & Reshoring

Offshoring
Exporting jobs from developed to less developed countries.

Offshoring refers to the exporting of jobs from developed countries, such as the United States, to countries where labor and other costs are lower. India, Canada, China, Russia, Ireland, Mexico, Brazil, and the Philippines are some of the destination countries for offshored jobs. Why are jobs offshored?[130] The reasons given for offshoring factory and other jobs often include lower labor costs and the availability of a skilled workforce with a strong work ethic. However, rather than offshoring work, **reshoring** is becoming more common. There are several reasons for this including higher product shipping costs, fear of supply chain disruptions due to natural disasters and political instability, quality concerns, and customer preference for U.S.-made products.[131] Also, rising labor costs in some countries, such as China, are becoming more comparable to those in the United States. Finally, some countries' local standards for safety, health, and working conditions may be substantially lower than those in the United States, resulting in negative publicity and turning off potential customers. For example, Hanesbrands has added workers to a plant in North Carolina.[132] The socks are knitted there and then sent to a plant in El Salvador that sews, dyes, and packages the socks. Although El Salvador has the advantage on labor costs, electricity costs in North Carolina are much less. Also, having plants in both places also provides a backup in case of problems. Peds Legwear also makes socks in North Carolina, allowing the company to avoid import taxes, cut shipping costs, and respond faster to shifts in demand. Plus, selling socks made in the United States was a major reason why Walmart contracted with the company.

Reshoring
Moving jobs from overseas to the U.S.

Effectiveness in Global Business Requires More Than Just a First-Class Ticket

For companies that conduct business around the world, employees need to go beyond just understanding cultural differences. Employees have to adapt and adjust their behavior to effectively work and live in the host culture. This means that employees and their families need to be prepared for international assignments. Iberdrola USA, a global company with 5,000 U.S. employees, is in the electricity transmission and generation business. Iberdrola sends U.S. employees to work at its locations in Mexico, Scotland, Brazil, and Britain and other European Union countries. Also, it brings employees to the United States to work for two to three years.

To prepare employees for international assignments, Iberdrola pays training consultants $1,500 to $3,000 per day to teach employees language and cultural basics, such as understanding preferences for personal space. The company also has an exchange program in which children of U.S. employees temporarily stay with host families overseas and vice versa.

SAP, the software company, is based in Germany but has locations in 130 countries. SAP provides cultural briefings that employees can access online. All SAP employees can take training that is customized based on the employees' overseas location and their specific skill needs. At Boeing, the aerospace company

with employees in 28 countries, employees and their families going on an international assignment are provided with one-on-one cultural sensitivity training and orientation. Boeing also provides "lunch and learn" cultural talks and rotation programs that allow overseas staff to work up to nine months in the United States.

DISCUSSION QUESTION

What topics should be included in training programs designed to prepare employees for global assignments? Why is it important for employees' families to receive training, too?

SOURCE: Based on R. Chebium, "A Common Language: Training Across Borders," *HR* Magazine, January/February 2015, pp. 52–58.

THE TECHNOLOGY CHALLENGE

Technology has reshaped the way we play, communicate, plan our lives, and where we work. Many companies' business models include e-commerce which allows consumers to purchase products and services online. The Internet is a global collection of computer networks that allows users to exchange data and information. Roughly 84% of U.S. households have a computer (desktop, laptop, tablet, or smartphone) and 75% have Internet access. Sixty percent visit Google during the week and 43% have a Facebook page.[133] Using Facebook, Twitter, LinkedIn, and other social networking tools available on the Internet accessed through smartphones, notebooks, or personal computers, companies can connect with job candidates and employers can connect with friends, family, and co-workers.

Social Networking

Advances in sophisticated technology along with reduced costs for the technology are changing many aspects of human resource management. Technological advances in electronics and communications software have made possible mobile technology such as personal digital assistants (PDAs), iPads, and iPods and enhanced the Internet through developing enhanced capability for social networking. **Social networking** refers to websites such as Facebook, Twitter, and LinkedIn, and wikis and blogs that facilitate interactions

LO 1-5
Identify how new technology, such as social networking, is influencing human resource management.

Social Networking
Websites, wikis, and blogs that facilitate interactions between people.

Table 1.13
Potential Uses of
Social Networking

ISSUES	USE
Loss of expert knowledge due to retirement	Knowledge sharing, capturing, and storing
Employee engagement	Collect employees' opinions, chat with employees
Identify and promote employee expertise	Create online expert communities
Promote innovation and creativity	Encourage participation in online discussions
Reinforce learning	Share best practices, applications, learning, points, links to articles and webinars
Employees need coaching and mentoring	Interact with mentors and coaching peers
Need to identify and connect with promising job candidates	Share job openings, respond to candidates' questions, cultivate a pool of potential employees

SOURCES: Based on D. Robb, "Cultivating Connections," *HR Magazine,* September 2014, pp. 65–66; M. McGraw, "Managing the Message," *Human Resource Executive,* December 2014, pp. 16–18; P. Brotherson, "Social Networks Enhance Employee Learning," *T + D,* April 2011, pp. 18–19; M. Derven, "Social Networking: A Frame for Development," *T + D,* July 2009, pp. 58–63; M. Weinstein, "Are You Linked In?" *Training,* September/October, 2010, pp. 30–33.

between people usually around shared interests. Table 1.13 shows some of the potential issues that can be addressed by using social networking.[134] In general, social networking facilitates communications, decentralized decision making, and collaboration. Social networking can be useful for connecting to customers and valuable for busy employees to share knowledge and ideas with their peers and managers with whom they may not have much time to interact face-to-face on a daily basis. Employees, especially young workers from the Millennial or Gen-Y generations have learned to use social networking tools such as Facebook throughout their lives and see them as valuable tools for both their work and nonwork lives.

Despite its potential advantages, many companies are uncertain as to whether they should embrace social networking.[135] They fear that social networking will result in employees wasting time or offending or harassing their co-workers. Other companies believe that the benefits of using social networking for HR practices and allowing employees to access social networks at work outweigh the risks. They trust employees to use social networking productively and are proactive in developing policies about personal use and training employees about privacy settings and social network etiquette. They realize that employees will likely check their Twitter, Facebook, or LinkedIn accounts but ignore it unless productivity is decreasing. In some ways, social networking has become the electronic substitute for daydreaming at one's desk or walking to the break room to socialize with co-workers!

Robotics, tracking systems, radio frequency identification, and nanotechnology are transforming work.[136] Technology has also made it easier to monitor environmental conditions and employees and operate equipment. Driverless cars, self-driving trucks at iron ore mines that need no human operators, and computers that perform legal research are recent advances in automation. But computing technology has been unable to replicate human skills and abilities used to fold laundry! Unlike humans, robots have been unable to make the distinctions between fabric types and weights and irregular clothes sizes that are needed to neatly fold clothes.

Amelia is a computer that learns from textbooks, transcriptions of conversations, e-mail chains, and other texts.[137] As long as the answer is in the data she receives, Amelia can solve problems. She also has the ability to learn. Programmers have tried to provide her with the human ability to think. Amelia is already being tested in customer call centers. Customer service depends on providing the right answer to the same question, regardless of who calls. Amelia can provide the correct answer because prior to working on her own she has worked alongside a human customer service rep listening to every support request received and the answers given. Amelia helps to automate tasks but she is not alive. However, she does have three emotional states, arousal, dominance, and pleasure, which are influenced by how customers communicate with her. These emotions affect her decision making in dealing with customers. Robots with artificial intelligence such as Amelia will likely increasingly provide performance support in the future or entirely replace employees in nonexpert repetitive jobs.

Wearables are just beginning to be developed and used for training and performance support solutions. Wearable Intelligence provides smart eyewear technology and camera technology that gives employees hands-free, voice-activated access to procedures and checklists, live access to experts using tablet computers which allows data and live video sharing, and the opportunity to review best practice videos before or during the performance of complex procedures and operations, and it provides real-time notifications and alerts.[138] For example, an operator who might be working on a remote oil rig or a surgeon in a sterile operating room can share live video with experts and get their advice needed to fix a broken valve or complete a medical procedure, while remaining focused on the equipment or patient. To understand whether personal interactions between employees made a difference, Bank of America asked call center employees to wear badges that contained sensors to record their movements and tone of their conversations.[139] The data showed that the most productive employees belonged to cohesive teams and they spoke frequently to their peers. To get employees to interact more the bank scheduled employees for group breaks. As a result productivity increased more than 10 percent.

Use of HRIS, Mobile Devices, Cloud Computing, and HR Dashboards

Companies continue to use human resource information systems to store large quantities of employee data including personal information, training records, skills, compensation rates, absence records, and benefits usages and costs. A **human resource information system (HRIS)** is a computer system used to acquire, store, retrieve, and distribute information related to a company's human resources.[140] An HRIS can support strategic decision making, help the company avoid lawsuits, provide data for evaluating policies and programs, and support day-to-day HR decisions. Hilton Worldwide is giving managers access to talent data so they can integrate it with business data to make more effective and strategic decisions about talent and performance.[141] This allows managers to perform workforce planning by seeing the gaps between workforce projections and available supply of staff or projected turnover and modeling different scenarios.

Mobile devices refer to smartphones and tablet computers. Mobile devices are increasingly being used to provide employees with anytime and anywhere access to HR applications and other work-related information. For example, at Rackspace, employees can check their pay stubs, bonus reports, time cards, and share knowledge.[142] At Biogen Idec, salespersons can access e-learning modules on their tablets. PepsiCo has a mobile-accessible career site. In the first year of using the recruitment app, the company found 150 job candidates who started an employment application each month. The "Competing Through Technology" box shows how Verizon is using social networking tools and

Human Resource Information System (HRIS)
A system used to acquire, store, manipulate, analyze, retrieve, and distribute HR information.

Mobile Devices
Equipment such as smartphones and tablet computers that provide employees with any-time, anywhere access to HR applications and other work-related information.

Connectiveness and Mobility Enhance HR Practices

Verizon uses social networking tools and mobile devices to train employees, interact with customers, and support new products and devices. Device Blog, Device Forum, and Learning Communities help insure that employees are ready to support customers when new products and devices are introduced to the market, engages Verizon's multigenerational workforce, and facilitates peer-to-peer learning. Device Blog makes available information and updates on wireless devices (such as DROID), FAQs (frequently asked questions), how-to-videos, and troubleshooting tips. Device Forums enable retail employees to learn from peers and product manufacturers. Employees can ask each other questions, share issues, post tips, make suggestions, and access product experts. Learning Communities are accessed through the Device Blog. They include video blogs, message boards, links to online training modules, and product demonstrations. In addition to these tools, employees have access to My Network for collaborating with their peers, knowledge and document sharing, and creating working groups. Some instructors also use it for posting supplemental content for learners use.

In 2013 Verizon implemented tablet computers for performance support and training of retail store employees. An app puts all the data that retail store employees need to learn about devices, service plans, promotions, and policies on the easy-to-use and readily accessible tablet computer. The app called SIMON (Simplified Information for the Moment of Need) runs on both Apple and Android devices and is designed to be used when interacting with a customer. Also, Verizon provided its field technicians with tablets. They can use the tablets to access product knowledge and fixes to service problems. Previously, each day local managers gave them handouts that contained this type of information.

DISCUSSION QUESTION

What are some of the potential disadvantages of using social networks and mobile devices for HR practices?

SOURCES: Based on J. Salopek, "Good Connections," *T + D*, October 2014, pp. 48–50; M. Weinstein, "Verizon Connects to Success," *Training*, January/February 2011, pp. 40–42.

---

mobile devices to support its products and provide customer service through employee training, collaboration, and performance support.

"Cloud computing" allows companies to lease software and hardware and employees don't even know the location of computers, databases, and applications they are using (they are in the "cloud"). **Cloud computing** refers to a computing system that provides information technology infrastructure over a network in a self-service, modifiable, and on-demand model.[143] Clouds can be delivered on-demand via the Internet (public cloud) or restricted to use by a single company (private cloud). Cloud computing gives companies and their employees access to applications and information from mobile devices rather than relying soley on personal computers. It also allows groups to work together in new ways, can make employees more productive by allowing them to more easily share documents and information, and provides greater access to large company databases. This means that tools for conducting workforce analytics using metrics on turnover, absenteeiem, and performance and social media and collaboration tools such as Twitter, blogs, Google documents, and YouTube videos will be more easily accessible and available for use. Cloud computing also can make it easier for employees to access training programs from a variety of vendors and educational institutions. Siemens has a cloud computing system for its more than 400,000 employees who work in 190 countries. This allowed Siemens to standardize its global recruitment and development processes into a single system using the cloud.[144]

Cloud Computing
A computing system that provides information technology infrastructure over a network in a self-service, modifiable, and on-demand model.

More sophisticated systems extend management applications to decision making in areas such as compensation and performance management. Managers can schedule job interviews or performance appraisals, guided by the system to provide the necessary information and follow every step called for by the procedure.[145] One of the most important uses of Internet technology is the development of HR dashboards. An **HR dashboard** is a series of indicators or metrics that managers and employees have access to on the company intranet or human resource information system. The HR dashboard provides access to important HR metrics for conducting workforce analytics. HR dashboards are important for determining the value of HR practices and how they contribute to business goals. As a result, the use of dashboards is critical for evidence-based HR discussed earlier in the chapter. For example, Cisco Systems views building talent as a priority so it has added to its dashboard of people measures a metric to track how many people move and the reasons why.[146] This allows Cisco to identify divisions that are developing new talent.

High-Performance Work Systems and Virtual Teams

New technology causes changes in skill requirements and work roles and often results in redesigning work structures (e.g., using work teams).[147] **High-performance work systems** maximize the fit between the company's social system (employees) and its technical system.[148] For example, computer-integrated manufacturing uses robots and computers to automate the manufacturing process. The computer allows the production of different products simply by reprogramming the computer. As a result, laborer, material handler, operator/assembler, and maintenance jobs may be merged into one position. Computer-integrated manufacturing requires employees to monitor equipment and troubleshoot problems with sophisticated equipment, share information with other employees, and understand the relationships between all components of the manufacturing process.[149]

Besides changing the way that products are built or services are provided within companies, technology has allowed companies to form partnerships with one or more other companies. **Virtual teams** refer to teams that are separated by time, geographic distance, culture, and/or organizational boundaries and that rely almost exclusively on technology (e-mail, Internet, videoconferencing) to interact and complete their projects. Virtual teams can be formed within one company whose facilities are scattered throughout the country or the world. A company may also use virtual teams in partnerships with suppliers or competitors to pull together the necessary talent to complete a project or speed the delivery of a product to the marketplace. For example, Art & Logic software developers all work remotely from across the U.S. and Canada from home offices, rented office space, or at a co-working facility.[150] Their clients represent a diverse set of industries, including education, aerospace, music technology, consumer electronics, entertainment, and financial services. The project teams work on the most unusual and difficult problems, which developers at other companies have failed to solve. Art & Logic tries to accommodate the unique schedule and work-style requirements of its developers, but its work is highly collaborative within project teams. Every project consists of at least a project manager/developer and has a maximum of five to seven developers. Teams use Google Apps for Business for sharing documents and communicating (both within the team and with clients).

Human resource management practices that support high-performance work systems are shown in Table 1.14. The HRM practices involved include employee selection, performance management, training, work design, and compensation. These practices are designed to give employees skills, incentives, knowledge, and autonomy. Research studies suggest that high-performance work practices are usually associated with increases

HR Dashboard
HR metrics such as productivity and absenteeism that are accessible by employees and managers through the company intranet or human resource information system.

High-Performance Work Systems
Work systems that maximize the fit between the company's social system and technical system.

LO 1-6
Discuss human resource management practices that support high-performance work systems.

Virtual Teams
Teams that are separated by time, geographic distance, culture and/or organizational boundaries and rely exclusively on technology for interaction between team members.

Table 1.14
How HRM Practices Support High-Performance Work Systems

Staffing	• Employees participate in selecting new employees, e.g., peer interviews.
Work Design	• Employees understand how their jobs contribute to the finished product or service. • Employees participate in planning changes in equipment, layout, and work methods. • Work may be organized in teams. • Job rotation used to develop skills. • Equipment and work processes are structured and technology is used to encourage flexibility and interaction between employees. • Work design allows employees to use a variety of skills. • Decentralized decision making, reduced status distinctions, information sharing. • Increased safety.
Training	• Ongoing training emphasized and rewarded. • Training in finance and quality control methods.
Compensation	• Team-based performance pay. • Part of compensation may be based on company or division financial performance.
Performance Management	• Employees receive performance feedback and are actively involved in the performance improvement process.

SOURCES: Based on K. Birdi, C. Clegy, M. Patterson, A. Robinson, C. Stride, T. Wall, and S. Wood, "The Impact of Human Resource and Operational Management Practices on Company Productivity: A Longitudinal Study," *Personnel Psychology* 61(2008), pp. 467–501; A. Zacharatos, J. Barling, and R. Iverson, "High Performance Work Systems and Occupational Safety," *Journal of Applied Psychology* 90 (2005), pp. 77–93; S. Way, "High Performance Work Systems and Intermediate Indicators of Performance within the U.S. Small Business Sector," *Journal of Management* 28 (2002), pp. 765–85; M. A. Huselid, "The Impact of Human Resource Management Practices on Turnover, Productivity, and Corporate Financial Performance," *Academy of Management Journal* 38 (1995), pp. 635–72.

in productivity and long-term financial performance.[151] Research also suggests that it is more effective to improve HRM practices as a whole, rather than focus on one or two isolated practices (such as the pay system or selection system).[152] There may be a best HRM system, but whatever the company does, the practices must be aligned with each other and be consistent with the system if they are to positively affect company performance.[153] We will discuss this alignment in more detail in Chapters 2 and 16.

Employees often have responsibility for hiring and firing team members and can make decisions that influence profits. As a result, employees must be trained in principles of employee selection, quality, and customer service. They need to understand financial data so they can see the link between their performance and company performance.

In high-performance work systems, previously established boundaries between managers and employees, employees and customers, employees and vendors, and the various functions within the company are abandoned. Employees, managers, vendors, customers, and suppliers work together to improve service and product quality and to create new products and services. Line employees are trained in multiple jobs, communicate directly with suppliers and customers, and interact frequently with engineers, quality experts, and employees from other functions.

Consider how human resource management practices support high-performance work systems at both small and large companies.[154] HindlePower is a manufacturer of battery chargers. Most of HindlePower's 75 employees work in the factory as assemblers. There is no time clock. Employees do not need to punch in or out and there are no rules for time off. Employees don't abuse the policy—hours in the factory consistently reach 97% to 100% of full time. Hindle established a program called the Professional

> ### EVIDENCE-BASED HR
>
> General Cable, one of the world's largest makers of wire and cable products, uses a high-performance work system at its Jackson, Tennessee, plant. Managers and employees worked together to determine how to exceed quality and safety expectations. They rearranged work into production cells, with employee teams making a completed product. Team members were responsible for their cell's safety, quality, and productivity. Employees were trained in new skills needed to work in cells. The move to a high-performance work system resulted in a 129% productivity increase, and 54% growth in first-pass yield, a measure of product quality. The Jackson plant also received *Industry Week*'s 2013 Best Plant Award.
>
> SOURCES: Based on A. Selko, "From Chopping Block to Award Banquet," *Industry Week*, January 2014, pp. 16–17; company website, "About Us" and "Careers," www.generalcable.com, accessed May 17, 2015.

Manufacturing Team, which pairs training with employee involvement in designing more efficient processes. The training includes 25 to 30 courses customized for each production line. Employees are responsible for completing all of the courses and when they do they are designated as a manufacturing professional. Employees are also involved in decisions that go beyond training. For example, employees redesigned a production line resulting in an additional 150,000 units produced per week. At Chrysler Dundee Engine plant, hourly employees rotate jobs and shifts, giving the company greater flexibility and employees more family time. The plant's culture emphasizes problem solving and the philosophy that anyone can do anything, anytime, anywhere. Every employee is either a team member or a team leader. Job candidates have to make it through a difficult screening process that includes testing, evaluation of how they perform in team activities, and interviews with managers and team leaders. Rotating jobs helps keep employees motivated and reduces injuries. Team leaders and engineers are expected on the shop floor as part of six-person teams. Large electronic screens hanging from the plant ceiling provide alerts of machinery parts that are ending their lifespan and need to be replaced before they malfunction. A performance management system, accessible on personal computers, alerts employees to delays or breakdowns in productivity. Employees are empowered to fix problems—not just managers or engineers.

Meeting Competitive Challenges through HRM Practices

We have discussed the global, stakeholder, new economy, and high-performance work system challenges U.S. companies are facing. We have emphasized that management of human resources plays a critical role in determining companies' success in meeting these challenges. HRM practices have not traditionally been seen as providing economic value to the company. Economic value is usually associated with equipment, technology, and facilities. However, HRM practices have been shown to be valuable. Compensation, staffing, training and development, performance management, and other HRM practices are investments that directly affect employees' motivation and ability to provide products and services that are valued by customers. Research has shown that companies that attempt to increase their competitiveness by investing in new technology and becoming involved in the quality movement also invest in state-of-the-art staffing, training, and compensation practices.[155] Figure 1.8 shows examples of human resource management practices that help companies

LO 1-7

Provide a brief description of human resource management practices.

Figure 1.8
Examples of How HRM Practices Can Help Companies Meet Competitive Challenges

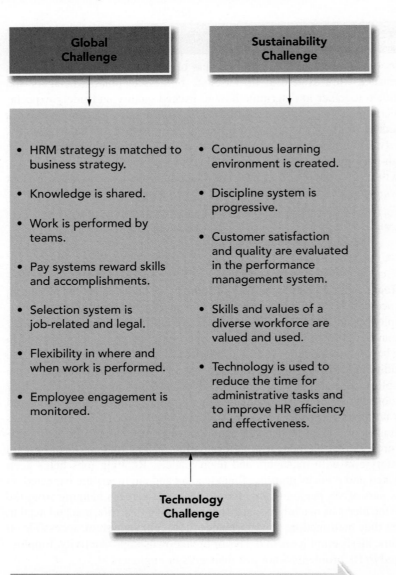

Figure 1.9
Major Dimensions of HRM Practices Contributing to Company Competitiveness

deal with the three challenges. For example, to meet the sustainability challenge, companies need to identify through their selection processes whether prospective employees value customer relations and have the levels of interpersonal skills necessary to work with fellow employees in teams. To meet all three challenges, companies need to capitalize on the diversity of values, abilities, and perspectives that employees bring to the workplace.

HRM practices that help companies deal with the competitive challenges can be grouped into the four dimensions shown in Figure 1.9. These dimensions include the human resource environment, acquiring and preparing human resources, assessment and development of human resources, and compensating human resources. In addition, some companies have special issues related to labor–management relations, international human resource management, and managing the human resource function.

Managing the Human Resource Environment

Managing internal and external environmental factors allows employees to make the greatest possible contribution to company productivity and competitiveness. Creating a positive environment for human resources involves

- Linking HRM practices to the company's business objectives—that is, strategic human resource management.
- Ensuring that HRM practices comply with federal, state, and local laws.
- Designing work that motivates and satisfies the employee as well as maximizes customer service, quality, and productivity.

Acquiring and Preparing Human Resources

Customer needs for new products or services influence the number and type of employees businesses need to be successful. Terminations, promotions, and retirements also influence human resource requirements. Managers need to predict the number and type of employees who are needed to meet customer demands for products and services. Managers must also identify current or potential employees who can successfully deliver products and services. This area of human resource management deals with

- Identifying human resource requirements—that is, human resource planning, recruiting employees, and selecting employees.
- Training employees to have the skills needed to perform their jobs.

Assessment and Development of Human Resources

Managers need to ensure that employees have the necessary skills to perform current and future jobs. As we discussed earlier, because of new technology and the quality movement, many companies are redesigning work so that it is performed by teams. As a result, managers and employees may need to develop new skills to succeed in a team environment. Companies need to create a work environment that supports employees' work and nonwork activities. This area of human resource management addresses

- Measuring employees' performance.
- Preparing employees for future work roles and identifying employees' work interests, goals, values, and other career issues.
- Creating an employment relationship and work environment that benefits both the company and the employee.

Compensating Human Resources

Besides interesting work, pay and benefits are the most important incentives that companies can offer employees in exchange for contributing to productivity, quality, and customer service. Also, pay and benefits are used to reward employees' membership in the company and attract new employees. The positive influence of new work designs, new technology, and the quality movement on productivity can be damaged if employees are not satisfied with the level of pay and benefits or believe pay and benefits are unfairly distributed. This area of human resource management includes

- Creating pay systems.
- Rewarding employee contributions.
- Providing employees with benefits.

Special Issues

In some companies, employees are represented by a labor union. Managing human resources in a union environment requires knowledge of specific laws, contract administration, and the collective bargaining process.

Many companies are globally expanding their business through joint ventures, mergers, acquisitions, and establishing new operations. Successful global expansion depends on the extent to which HRM practices are aligned with cultural factors as well as management of employees sent to work in another country. Human resource management practices must contribute to organizational effectiveness.

Human resource management practices of both managers and the human resource function must be aligned and contribute to the company's strategic goals. The final chapter of the book explains how to effectively integrate human resource management practices.

Organization of This Book

The topics in this book are organized according to the four areas of human resource management and special issues. Table 1.15 lists the chapters covered in the book.

Table 1.15

Topics Covered in This Book

The content of each chapter is based on academic research and examples of effective company practices. Each chapter includes examples of how the human resource management practice covered in the chapter helps a company gain a competitive advantage by addressing sustainability, global, and technological challenges. Also, each chapter includes an example of a company that demonstrates how HR practices add value (evidence-based HR).

A LOOK BACK

HRM at Marriott

One of Marriott's core values, "We Put People First," drives its management and human resources practices, which in turn lead to high levels of employee engagement, satisfied customers, and a positive "bottom line."

QUESTIONS

1. Which HR practices do you believe are the most critical for Marriott to maintain and grow its competitive advantage? Explain why.
2. Would Marriott have been successful without its current HR practices? Explain.
3. Can companies in other industries such as health care, manufacturing, or research and development adopt Marriott's value and practices and have similar success? Explain why or why not.
4. What other types of HR practices should Marriott consider adopting that would appeal to its growing number of Millennial employees?

SUMMARY

This chapter introduced the roles and activities of a company's human resource management function and emphasized that effective management of human resources can contribute to a company's business strategy and competitive advantage. HR can be viewed as having three product lines: administrative services, business partner services, and strategic services. To successfully manage human resources, individuals need personal credibility, business knowledge, understanding of the business strategy, technology knowledge, and the ability to deliver HR services. Human resource management practices should be evidence-based, that is, based on data showing the relationship between the practice and business outcomes related to key company stakeholders (customers, shareholders, employees, community). In addition to contributing to a company's business strategy, human resource practices are important for helping companies deal with sustainability, globalization, and technology challenges. The sustainability challenges are related to the economy, the characteristics and expectations of the labor force, how and where work is done, the value placed on intangible assets and human capital, and meeting stakeholder needs (ethical practices, high-quality

products and services, return to shareholders, and social responsibility). Global challenges include entering international markets, immigration, and offshoring. Technology challenges include using new technologies to support flexible and virtual work arrangements, high-performance work systems, and implementing and using social networks, wearables, human resource information systems, and mobile devices.

The chapter concludes by showing how the book is organized. The book includes four topical areas: the human resource environment (strategic HRM, legal, analysis and design of work), acquisition and preparation of human resources (HR planning and recruitment, selection, training), assessment and development of human resources (performance management, development, separation and retention), compensation of human resources (pay structures, recognizing employee contributions with pay, benefits), and special topics (collective bargaining and labor relations, managing human resources globally, and strategically managing the HR function). All of the topical areas are important for companies to deal with the competitive challenges and contribute to business strategy.

KEY TERMS

Competitiveness, 4
Human resource management
    (HRM), 4
Shared service model, 7
Self-service, 7
Outsourcing, 8
Evidence-based HR, 11
HR or workforce analytics, 11
Big data, 11
Sustainability, 16
Stakeholders, 16
Intangible assets, 21
Knowledge workers, 22
Empowering, 22

Learning organization, 22
Change, 23
Employee engagement, 23
Talent management, 24
Alternative work arrangements, 25
Balanced scorecard, 27
Total quality management (TQM), 30
Malcolm Baldrige National Quality
    Award, 30
ISO 9000:2000, 30
Six Sigma process, 32
Lean thinking, 32
Internal labor force, 33
External labor market, 33

Ethics, 40
Sarbanes-Oxley Act of 2002, 40
Offshoring, 44
Reshoring, 44
Social networking, 45
Human resource information system
    (HRIS), 47
Mobile devices, 47
Cloud computing, 48
HR dashboard, 49
High-performance work systems, 49
Virtual teams, 49

DISCUSSION QUESTIONS

1. Traditionally, human resource management practices were developed and administered by the company's human resource department. Some companies are abandoning or don't have HR departments. Why is this occurring? Is it a good idea for companies not to have an HR department or HR professionals? Explain your position.
2. Staffing, training, compensation, and performance management are important HRM functions. How can each of these functions help companies succeed in meeting the global challenge, the challenge of using new technology, and the sustainability challenge?
3. What are intangible assets? How are they influenced by human resource management practices?
4. What is "evidence-based HR"? Why might an HR department resist becoming evidence-based?
5. What types of big data would you collect and analyze to understand why an employer was experiencing a high turnover rate?
6. Which HR practices can benefit by the use of social collaboration tools like Twitter and Facebook? Identify the HR practices and explain the benefits gained.
7. Do you agree with the statement "Employee engagement is something companies should be concerned about only if they are making money"? Explain.
8. This book covers four human resource management practice areas: managing the human resource environment,

acquiring and preparing human resources, assessment and development of human resources, and compensating human resources. Which area do you believe contributes most to helping a company gain a competitive advantage? Which area do you believe contributes the least? Why?
9. What is the balanced scorecard? Identify the four perspectives included in the balanced scorecard. How can HRM practices influence the four perspectives?
10. Is HRM becoming more strategic? Explain your answer.
11. What is sustainability? How can HR practices help a company become more socially and environmentally conscious?
12. Explain the implications of each of the following labor force trends for HRM: (1) aging workforce, (2) diverse workforce, (3) skill deficiencies.
13. What role do HRM practices play in a business decision to expand internationally?
14. What might a quality goal and high-performance work systems have in common in terms of HRM practices?
15. What disadvantages might result from outsourcing HRM practices? From employee self-service? From increased line manager involvement in designing and using HR practices?
16. What factors should a company consider before reshoring? What are the advantages and disadvantages of reshoring?

SELF-ASSESSMENT EXERCISE

Do You Have What It Takes to Work in HR?

Instructions: Read each statement and circle *yes* or *no.*

Yes   No   1. I have leadership and management skills I have developed through prior job experiences, extracurricular activities, community service, or other noncourse activities.

Yes   No   2. I have excellent communications, dispute resolution, and interpersonal skills.

Yes   No   3. I can demonstrate an understanding of the fundamentals of running a business and making a profit.

Yes   No   4. I can use spreadsheets and the World Wide Web, and I am familiar with information systems technology.

Yes   No   5. I can work effectively with people of different cultural backgrounds.

Yes   No   6. I have expertise in more than one area of human resource management.

Yes   No   7. I have a willingness to learn.

Yes   No   8. I listen to issues before reacting with solutions.

Yes   No   9. I can collect and analyze data for business solutions.

Yes   No   10. I am a good team member.

Yes   No   11. I have knowledge of local and global economic trends.

Yes   No   12. I demonstrate accountability for my actions.

Scoring: The greater the number of yes answers, the better prepared you are to work as an HR professional. For questions you answered *no,* you should seek courses and experiences to change your answer to *yes*—and better prepare yourself for a career in HR!

SOURCE: Based on B. E. Kaufman, "What Companies Want from HR Graduates," *HR Magazine,* September 1994; SHRM Elements for HR Success Competency Model, 2012, from www.shrm.org, March 21, 2012.

EXERCISING STRATEGY

Zappos Faces Competitive Challenges

Zappos, based in Las Vegas, is an online retailer with the initial goal of trying to be the best website for buying shoes by offering a wide variety of brands, styles, colors, sizes, and widths. The zappos.com brand has grown to offer shoes, handbags, eyewear, watches, and accessories for online purchase. The company's goal is to provide the best service online, not just in shoes but in any product category. Zappos believes that the speed at which a customer receives an online purchase plays a critical role in how that customer thinks about shopping online again in the future, so they are focusing on making sure the items get delivered to our customers as quickly as possible.

Zappos CEO Tony Hsieh has shaped the company's customer-service focused culture, brand, and business strategy around 10 core values. They are:

Deliver WOW through service.
Embrace and drive change.
Create fun and a little weirdness.
Be adventurous, creative, and open-minded.
Pursue growth and learning.
Build open and honest relationships with communication.
Build a positive team and family spirit.
Do more with less.
Be passionate and determined.
Be humble.

Deliver WOW through Service means that call center employees need to provide excellent customer service. Call center employees encourage callers to order more than one size or color because shipping and return shipping is free. They are also encouraged to use their imaginations to meet customer needs.

Zappos has received many awards for its workplace culture and practices including being recognized as the 86th Best Company to Work for in *Fortune* magazine's 2014 ranking of the 100 Best Companies to Work For. HR's job at Zappos is more than just a rule enforcer. HR's job is to protect the culture and to educate employees. HR focuses on interactions with managers and employees to understand what they need from HR (HR is even invited to attend work teams' happy hours!). Zappos' employment practices help perpetuate its company culture. Only about one out of 100 applicants passes a hiring process that is equally weighted on job skills and on the potential to work in Zappos' culture. Some managers at Zappos believe that if you want to get a job the most important value to demonstrate is "be humble" including a focus on "we" instead of "I." Job candidates are interviewed for cultural fit and a willingness to change and learn. For example, they observe whether at lunch job candidates talk with others or just the person they think is making the hiring decision. The HR team uses unusual interview questions—such as, How weird are you? and What's your theme song?—to find employees who are creative and have strong individuality. Zappos provides free lunch in the cafeteria (cold cuts) and a full-time life coach (employees have to sit on a red velvet throne to complain), managers are encouraged to spend time with employees outside of the office, and any employee can reward another employee a $50 bonus for good performance. Call center employees can use an online scheduling tool that allows them to set their own hours and they can earn more pay if they work during hours with greater customer demand. Most of the 1,441 employees at Zappos are hourly. Every new hire undergoes four weeks of training, during which the company culture must be committed to memory, and spends two weeks dealing with customers by working the telephones. New recruits are offered $2,000 to leave the company during training to weed out individuals who will not be happy working at the company. Zappos provides free breakfast, lunch, snacks, coffee, tea, and vending machine snacks. Work is characterized by constant change, a loud, open office environment, and interacting in teams. Employees at Zappos move around. For example, in the call center employees can bid for different shifts every month.

To reinforce the importance of the 10 core values Zappos' performance management system asks managers to evaluate how well employees' behaviors demonstrate the core values such as being humble or expressing their personalities. To evaluate task performance managers are asked to regularly provide employees with status reports on such things as how much time they spend on the telephone with customers. The status reports and evaluations of the core values are informational or used to identify training needs. Zappos also believes in helping others understand what inspired the company culture. The company created the Zappos.com library which provides a collection of books about creating a passion for customer service, products, and local communities. These books can be found in the front lobby of Zappos offices and are widely read and discussed by company employees.

Corporate culture is more than a set of values, and it is maintained by a complex web of human interactions. At Zappos, the liberal use of social media including blogs and Twitter facilitates the network that links employees with one another and with the company's customers. Zappos takes the pulse of the organization monthly, measuring the health of the culture with a happiness survey. Employees respond to such unlikely questions as whether they believe that the company has a higher purpose than profits, whether their own role has meaning, whether they feel in control of their career path, whether they consider their co-workers to be like family and friends, and whether they are happy in their jobs. Results from the survey are broken down by department, and opportunities for development are identified and acted upon. For example, when it was clear from the survey that one department had veered off course and felt isolated from the rest of the organization, a program was instituted that

enabled individuals in the group to learn more about how integral their work was. To keep the vibrant company CEO Tony Hsieh spent $350 million to develop a neighborhood in downtown Las Vegas which is the home of Zappos.com's new headquarters. Hsieh wants to provide employees with a great place to work as well as to live and socialize. Recently, Zappos adopted a management philosophy, Holocracy, which eliminates managers and gives employees the freedom and responsibility to decide how to get their work done. Hsieh's intent was to allow employees to act more like entrepreneurs and help stimulate new ideas which would benefit the business. However, employees are finding the new management system confusing and requiring them to spend more time in meetings. Also, they wonder how they will earn raises and advance their career without management jobs. Two hundred ten employees found the new philosophy so dissatisfying that they took three months of severance pay and left the company.

Despite this setback, other companies are trying to learn from Zappos' practices. Zappos Insights is a department within Zappos created to share the Zappos culture with other companies. Zappos Insights provides programs about building a culture (3-Day Culture Camp), its WOW service philosophy (School of WOW), the power of a coaching-based culture (Coaching Event), how the human resources function protects the culture and how its programs support it (People Academy), and custom programs. The cost to attend these programs ranges from $2,000 to $6,000 for each attendee.

QUESTIONS

1. Zappos seems to be well-positioned to have a competitive advantage over other online retailers. What challenges discussed in Chapter 1 pose the biggest threat to Zappos' ability to maintain and enhance its competitive position? How can human resource management practices help Zappos meet these challenges?

2. Do you think that employees of Zappos have high levels of engagement? Why?

3. Which of Zappos' 10 core values do you believe that human resource practices can influence the most? The least? Why? For each of the core values, identify the HR practices that are related to it. Explain how each of the HR practice(s) you identified is related to the core values.

4. How might the change to the holocracy management style undermine the core values and cause employees to have lower levels of engagement?

SOURCES: Based on website for Zappos, www.zappos.com, accessed May 18, 2015; J. McGregor, "Zappos Gives Exit Prize If Its Culture Is a Turnoff," *The Columbus Dispatch,* April 6, 2015, p. C3; "Zappos Insights" from www.zapposinsights.com, accessed March 16, 2015; M. Moskowitz and R. Levering, "The 100 Best Companies to Work For," *Fortune,* March 15, 2015, pp. 140–154; D. Richard, "At Zappos, Culture Pays," *Strategy + Business,* August 2010, p. 60, www.strategybusiness.com, accessed March 25, 2013; K. Gurchick, "Delivering HR at Zappos," *HR Magazine,* June 2011; R. Pyrillis, "The Reviews Are In," *Workforce Management,* May 2011, pp. 20–25; J. O'Brien, "Zappos Knows How to Kick It," *Fortune,* February 2, 2009, pp. 55–66; R. Silverman, "Going Bossless Backfires at Zappos," *The Wall Street Journal,* May 21, 2015, pp. A1, A10.

MANAGING PEOPLE

Mars Incorporated: HR Practices Help Create Sweet Success

You may have enjoyed Mars Incorporated products if you have had M&Ms, Snickers, Lifesavers, Wrigley's Juicy Fruit, or Uncle Ben's Converted Rice. But are you aware that the "Ms" on M&Ms stand for Forrest Mars and R. Bruce Murrie, the son of the president of competitor Hershey's, which supplied Mars with chocolate when there was limited availability of cocoa during World War II? Mars is the third largest private company in the United States with 72,000 employees located in the U.S. and 72 other countries around the world. It operates in six business segments including food, drinks, pet care, chocolate, gum and confections, and symbioscience (a technology-based health and life sciences business focused on product development). Today, Mars includes eleven brands with revenues of $1 billion or more. Granted some of that success is attributed directly to the quality of and demand for the products that Mars offers consumers (who doesn't like M&Ms?). But a lot of the success is due to the HR practices that Mars uses to attract, motivate, and retain high-caliber employees. This has resulted in Mars ranking #95 on the 2013 Fortune 100 Best Companies to Work For.

It all starts with the Five Principles of Mars—Quality, Responsibility, Mutuality, Efficiency and Freedom—which are the foundation of the company culture and business approach. The Five Principles, found on the walls in its offices and manufacturing plants throughout the world, provide a common bond for all employees regardless of their business segment, location, national language, or generation. All employees are familiar with the Five Principles and they influence their daily work. Mars believes that *quality* work is *the* first ingredient of quality brands and the source of the company's reputation for high standards. All associates are asked to take direct *responsibility* for results, to exercise initiative and judgment, and to make decisions as required. *Mutuality* refers to the company's belief that all business relationships should be measured by the degree to which mutual benefits are created. The actions of Mars should never be at the expense, economic or otherwise, of others. *Efficiency* is seen as a strength of the company. It allows the company to organize physical, financial, and human assets for maximum productivity. It also contributes to making and delivering products and services with the highest quality, lowest possible costs, and lowest consumption of resources. Finally, Mars cherishes the *freedom* of being a privately held company, which allows it to make decisions free of short-term earnings reports and to be financially answerable to no one. This gives management and employees the ability to experiment with ideas and take the time to develop talents for longer-term gains.

Mars employees love the products they make but they also love the HR practices that help put the Five Principles into action. The turnover of non–sales force employees is only 5%. What is responsible for the low turnover as well as $33 billion in global revenue in 2012? Perhaps one reason is that Mars has an egalitarian workplace with no fancy offices or special perks for managers. Employees are officially called "associates" but because of the unifying value of the Five Principles, they often refer to themselves as Martians. Most employees have to "punch in" at their worksite every day, even the company president. Employees who are late are docked 10% of their pay. Also, the principle of Responsibility means that all employees, not just managers, have a "voice" and are expected to put themselves in the position of the consumer. They are encouraged to speak up rather than ever provide an inferior product or service.

Mars does not offer stock options or company pensions or game rooms or private chefs for its employees. It does provide vending machines that provide employees with free candy, and chewing Wrigley's gum at meetings is encouraged. Perhaps another reason for the low turnover and high revenues is that employees have many career and development opportunities both within their current business and in new ones. All new employees attend The Essence of Mars training program which introduces and reinforces the Five Principles. Mars also has a corporate university (Mars University) which offers online and classroom-based courses in functional topics as well as on leadership skills. Forty percent of associates have participated in a program offered by Mars University. Also, many employees have mentors, even executives who learn about social media from younger employees. Mars insures that all employees regardless of background have the opportunity to grow and advance. For example, Mars was ranked #25 in the 2012 World's Best Multinational Workplaces list, the world's first global workplace excellence ranking by Great Place to Work®, for its high percentage of women in executive and senior management positions.

Or, maybe turnover is low and revenues are high because of the bonuses that employees can earn which range from 10 to 20% of their salaries if their team performs well. Contributing to employees' motivation to earn their bonuses is the availability of performance data. Flat screens displays current financials including sales, earnings, cash flows, and factory efficiency. Mars also encourages community involvement, which gives employees opportunities to gain new insights and make meaningful contributions. The Mars Volunteer Initiative offers paid time off for associates to clean parks, teach courses, help pets find homes, work in medical clinics, and plant gardens. In 2012, employees devoted 50,000 hours to volunteering! The Mars Ambassadors is a select program in which employees spend six weeks working with Mars partners in developing areas of the world. In late 2012, seven Mars Drinks Associates traveled from all over the globe and met in Kenya. Their objective was to learn about the coffee farming process and about how Mars Drinks supports and improves the farming business through a partnership with Sustainable Management Services (SMS). During their week-long trip, that objective was met, and the experience became much more than a simple learning opportunity. As one Drinks Associate from France noted, "I realized that selling or buying coffee in Europe can have great repercussions in third world countries." Sustainability is not just a marketing operation but is a way of living and needs to be sponsored by everyone.

QUESTIONS

1. What HR practices do you believe are critical for Mars Incorporated to maintain the culture and product quality and growth it's known for?
2. Could Mars be successful without its current HR practices? Explain.
3. Do you think that Mars's culture and HR practices can also help the bottom line at companies in other industries such as health care, manufacturing, or research and development? Explain why or why not.
4. Mars is a privately held company and a family-owned business. What advantages (or disadvantages) can this provide for developing effective HR practices compared to a public company "owned" by its shareholders?

SOURCE: Based on D. Kaplan, "Inside Mars," *Fortune,* February 4, 2013, p. 82; www.mars.com, website for Mars Incorporated, accessed March 15, 2013.

HR IN SMALL BUSINESS

Managing HR at a Services Firm

Susan K. Dubin describes herself as someone who enjoys helping others and making her company a positive place to work. Those attitudes have provided a strong basis for her successful career in human resource management. In two different companies, Dubin took on responsibilities for payroll, training, and employee relations. As she built her experience, she established a strong working relationship with Danone Simpson, an insurance agent.

Dubin was impressed with what she saw as Simpson's "commitment to client services." So when Simpson prepared to open her own insurance services business, Dubin was interested in signing on. For several years now, Dubin has been HR director for Montage Insurance Solutions (formerly Danone Simpson Insurance Services), which operates from offices in Woodland Hills, California. She also answers questions from clients who call the agency's HR hotline.

Dubin sees herself as contributing to the fast growing company's success. For example, she looks for the best deals in benefits programs in order to have room in her budget for the little things that contribute to an employee-friendly workplace: monthly luncheons, raffle prizes, and break rooms. That's a priority, Dubin says, because employees who are "happy at work" are "more productive, so everybody wins." Simpson sees that balance between nurturing and practicality in Dubin. According to Simpson, Dubin is supportive but also firm in enforcing standards:

"She doesn't put up with any nonsense . . . but does it in a wonderful way."

Perhaps the Careers page of the company's website puts it best. Besides promoting the agency as an "honest and hardworking team," it says simply, "Please be advised that our organization cares about its employees."

QUESTIONS

1. Based on the description in this case, how well would you say Susan Dubin appreciates the scope of human resource management? What, if any, additional skills of an HR professional would you encourage her to develop?
2. Look up descriptions of HR jobs by searching under "human resources" in the latest edition of the Bureau of Labor Statistics' *Occupational Outlook Handbook* (available online at www.bls.gov/OCO/). What position in the handbook best matches Dubin's job, as described in this case?
3. How would you expect Dubin's job in a small services company to be different from a similar position in a large manufacturing company?

SOURCES: Montage Insurance Solutions corporate website, http://www.montageinsurance.com, accessed May 26, 2015; Mark R. Madler, "Valley's Top Human Resources Professionals: Susan K. Dubin," *San Fernando Valley Business Journal,* April 13, 2009, Business & Company Resource Center, http://galenet.galegroup.com.

NOTES

1. J. T. Delaney and M. A. Huselid, "The Impact of Human Resource Management Practices on Perceptions of Organizational Performance," *Academy of Management Journal* 39 (1996), pp. 949–69; R. E. Ployhart, J.A. Weekley, and J. Ramsey, "The Consequences of Human Resources Stocks and Flows: A Longitudinal Examination of Unit Service Orientation and Unit Effectiveness," *Academy of Management Journal* 52 (2009), pp. 996–1015; Y. Kim and R. E. Ployhart, "The Effects of Staffing and Training on Firm Productivity and Profit Growth Before, During, and After the Great Recession" *Journal of Applied Psychology* 99 (2014), pp. 361–389; R. Ployhart and T. Moliterno, "Emergence of the Human Capital Resource: A Multilevel Model," *Academy of Management Review* 36 (2011), pp. 127–150; B. Campbell, R. Coff, and D. Kryscynski, "Rethinking Sustained Competitive Advantage from Human Capital," *Academy of Management Review* 37 (2010), pp. 376–395; T. Crook, S. Todd, J. Combs, D. Woehr, and D. Ketchen, Jr., "Does Human Capital Matter? A Meta-Analysis of the Relationship between Human Capital and Firm Performance," *Journal of Applied Psychology* 96 (2011), pp. 443–456.

2. K. O'Leonard, "A Breed Apart," *Human Resource Executive,* January/February 2015, p. 38.

3. SHRM-BNA Survey No. 66, "Policy and Practice Forum: Human Resources Activities, Budgets, and Staffs: 2000–2001," Bulletin to Management, Bureau of National Affairs Policy and Practice Series, June 28, 2001 (Washington, DC: Bureau of National Affairs); Bureau of Labor Statistics, U.S. Department of Labor, *Occupational Outlook Handbook, 2012–13 Edition,* "Human Resources Specialists," www.bls.gov/ooh/business-and-financial/human-resources-specialists.htm, visited March 26, 2013.

4. G. Tucker, "HR at the Corner of People and Strategy," *HR Magazine,* May 2014, pp. 42–44.

5. R. Zeidner, "Rebuilding HR," *HR Magazine,* May 2015, pp. 26–34.

6. A. Halcrow, "Survey Shows HRM in Transition," *Workforce,* June 1998, pp. 73–80; J. Laabs, "Why HR Can't Win Today," *Workforce,* May 1998, pp. 62–74; C. Cole, "Kodak Snapshots," *Workforce,* June 2000, pp. 65–72; W. Ruona and S. Gibson, "The Making of Twenty-First Century HR: An Analysis of the Convergence of HRM, HRD, and OD," *Human Resource Management* 43 (2004), pp. 49–66.

7. J. Bersin, "What's in Store for HR in 2015," *HR Magazine,* January/February 2015, pp. 32–51; T. Starner, "An HR Exodus," *HR Executive,* May 2014, p. 13; T. Henneman, "Is HR at Its Breaking Point?" *Workforce Management,* April 2013, pp. 28–32; C. Gibson, I. Ziskin, and J. Boudreau, "What Is the Future of HR?" *Workforce,* January 2014, pp. 30–33, 48; M. McGraw, "What's Keeping HR Up at Night," *Human Resource Executive,* September 2013, pp. 32–36.

8. R. Grossman, "Saving Shared Services," *HR Magazine,* September 2010, pp. 26–31.

9. Tucker, "HR at the Corner of People and Strategy."

10. S. Greengard, "Building a Self-Service Culture That Works," *Workforce,* July 1998, pp. 60–64.

11. D. Zielinski, "Making the Most of Manager Self-Service," *HR Magazine,* December 2013, pp. 51–55.

12. K. Kramer, "Industrial-Organizational (I-O) Psychology's Contribution to Strategic Human Resources Outsourcing (HRO): How Can We Shape the Future of HR?" *The Industrial-Organizational Psychologist,* January 2011, pp. 13–20.

13. B. Roberts, "Outsourcing in Turbulent Times," *HR Magazine,* November 2009, pp. 42–47; The Right Thing, "The Goodyear Tire and Rubber Company Discovers Key to Successful Outsourcing Partnerships," *Workforce Management,* March 2011, p. S2.

14. SHRM Foundation Leadership Roundtable, "What's Next for HR?" November 12, 2010, www.shrm.org, accessed March 21, 2013.

15. K. Frasch, "The Most Powerful Women in HR," *Human Resource Executive,* March 2015, pp. 14–20.

16. C. Patton, "Leap of Faith," *HR Executive,* May 2014, pp. 14–16.

17. P. Wright, *Human Resource Strategy: Adapting to the Age of Globalization* (Alexandria, VA: Society for Human Resource Management Foundation, 2008).

18. L. Weber and R. Feintzeig, "Is It a Dream or a Drag? Companies without HR," *The Wall Street Journal,* March 9, 2014, pp. B1, B7; Henneman, "Is HR at Its Breaking Point?"

19. A. McIlvaine, "Powering a Revolution," *HR Executive,* July/August 2014, pp. 14–17.

20. E. Frauenheim, "Numbers Game," *Workforce Management,* March 2011, pp. 20–21; P. Gallagher, "Rethinking HR," *Human Resource Executive,* September 2, 2009, pp. 1, 18–23.

21. L. Stevens, "Taking Analytics Up a Notch," *Human Resource Executive,* May 2015, pp. 49–50.

22. M. McGraw, "The Data Detectives," *Human Resource Executive,* October 2014, pp. 24–26.

23. G. Dutton, "What's the Big Deal about Big Data?" *Training,* March/April 2014, pp. 16–19.

24. L. Claus and J. Collison, *The Maturing Profession of Human Resources: Worldwide and Regional View* (Alexandria, VA: Society for Human Resource Management, 2005).

25. Bureau of Labor Statistics, U.S. Department of Labor, *Occupational Outlook Handbook, 2012–13 Edition,* "Human Resources Specialists," www.bls.gov/ooh/business-and-financial/human-resources-specialists.htm, visited March 26, 2013.

26. Ibid; E. Krell, "Become a Master of Expertise and Credibility," *HR Magazine,* May 2010, pp. 53–63.

27. T. Starner, "An HR Exodus," *HR Executive,* May 2014, p. 13.

28. J. Wiscombe, "Your Wonderful, Terrible HR Life," *Workforce,* June 2001, pp. 32–38.

29. R. Charan, "It's Time to Split HR," *Harvard Business Review,* July–August 2014, p. 34; Henneman, "Is HR at its Breaking Point?"

30. D. Meinert, "Reskilling HR among Top Challenges Facing Companies," *HR Magazine,* May 2014, p. 18.

31. P. McCord, "How Netflix Reinvented HR," *Harvard Business Review,* January–February 2014, pp. 71–76; Henneman, "Is HR at Its Breaking Point?"

32. SHRM Elements for HR Success Competency Model, 2012, www.shrm.org, March 21, 2012; R. Zeidner, "Rebuilding HR," *HR Magazine,* May 2015, pp. 26–34.

33. K. Strobel, "Competency Proficiency Predicts Better Job Performance," *HR Magazine,* October 2014, p. 67.

34. Zeidner, "Rebuilding HR."

35. D. Zielinski, "Building a Better HR Team," *HR Magazine,* August 2010, pp. 65–68.

36. J. Bersin, "What's in Store for HR in 2015," *HR Magazine,* January/February 2015, pp. 32–51; M. McGraw, "It's (Still) All About Engagement," *Human Resource Executive,* July/August 2014, pp. 38–39; J. Boudreau, I. Ziskin, and C. Gibson, "What Is the Future of HR?" *Workforce,* January 2014, pp. 30–33, 48; McGraw, "What's Keeping HR Up at Night."

37. A. Jones, "Evolutionary Science, Work/Life Integration, and Corporate Responsibility," *Organizational Dynamics* 32 (2002), pp. 17–31; S. Ladika, "The Responsible Way," *Workforce Management,* July 2013, pp. 24–29.

38. E. Cohen, S. Taylor, and M. Muller-Camen, *HRM's Role in Corporate Social and Environmental Sustainability* (Alexandria, VA: SHRM Foundation, 2012); WCED, *Our Common Future,* (Oxford: Oxford University Press, 1987), A.A. Savitz, *The triple bottom line* (San Francisco: Jossey-Bass, 2006); S. Hart and S. Milstein, "Creating Sustainable Value," *Academy of Management Executive* 17 (2003), pp. 56–67.

39. U.S. Bureau of Labor Statistics, "Productivity and Costs, Fourth Quarter and Annual Averages 2014, Preliminary," February 5, 2015, http://data.bls.gov, accessed February 20, 2015; J. Sparshott, "Hiring Booms but Soft Wages Linger," *The Wall Street Journal,* January 10-11, 2015, pp. A1–2; E. Morath, "Brisk Jobs Growth Puts Fed on Notice," *The Wall Street Journal,* March 7–8, 2015, pp. A1–A2; J. Mitchell, "Job Market Rebounds after a Chill," *The Wall Street Journal,* Saturday/Sunday May 9–10, 2015, pp. A1–A2.

40. "Optimism about US Economy Driving Private-Company Expansion Plans, According to Latest PwC Survey," press release, www.pwc.com, accessed February 20, 2015.

41. "Good to Grow: 2014 US CEO Survey," www.pwc.com, accessed February 20, 2015.

42. U.S. Bureau of Labor Statistics, "Employment Situation Summary (February 6, 2015)," http://data.bls.gov, accessed February 20, 2015; P. Coy, "2015: A Users Guide," *Bloomberg Businessweek,* November 10, 2014–January 6, 2015, pp. 22–28; R. Neate, "US Growth Rate Slips to 2.6% Raising Doubts about the Strength of Economy," *The Guardian,* accessed February 20, 2015, www.theguardian.com.

43. "Good to Grow: 2014 US CEO Survey"; J. Mitchell, "Job Market Rebounds after a Chill."

44. B. Leubsdorf, "Wage Growth Shows Signs of Pickup," *The Wall Street Journal,* May 1, 2015, p. A2; P. Ziobro and E. Morath, "Wal-Mart Lifts Pay as Market Gets Tighter," *The Wall Street Journal,* February 20, 2015, pp. A1–A2.

45. J. Mitchell, "Job Market Rebounds after a Chill."

46. I. Brat, "Starbucks Expands School Aid for Workers," *The Wall Street Journal,* April 7, 2015, p. B6.

47. "Action Items: 42 Trends Affecting Benefits, Compensation, Training, Staffing, and Technology," *HR Magazine,* January 2013, pp. 33–35; "2015 State of Talent Management Research Report," *Human Resources Executive,* February 10, 2015, www.hreonline.com; *SHRM Workplace Forecast* (Alexandria, VA: Society for Human Resource Management, 2013).

48. Bureau of Labor Statistics, "Employment Projections: 2012–2022," News Release, www.bls.gov, accessed February 25, 2015; D. Sommers and J. Franklin, "Overview of projections to 2020," *Monthly Labor Review,* January 2012, pp. 3–20.

49. Bureau of Labor Statistics, "Employment projections: 2012–2022."

50. Organization for Economic Cooperation and Development (OECD), "Skilled for Life? Key Findings from the Survey of Adult Skills," http://skills.oecd.org, accessed February 20, 2015; "Good to Grow: 2014 US CEO Survey"; P. Gaul, "Nearly Half of U.S. Executives Are Concerned About Skills Gap," *T + D,* February 2014, p. 18; "2014 Accenture Manufacturing Skills & Training Study," www.themanufacturinginstitute.org, accessed March 2, 2015; "Survey of Adult Skills." M. Schoeff Jr., "Companies Report Difficulty Finding Qualified Employees," *Workforce Management,* October 19, 2009, p. 14; J. Casner-Lotto, E. Rosenblum, and M. Wright, *The Ill-Prepared U.S. Workforce* (New York: The Conference Board); P. Galagan, "Bridging the Skills Gap: New Factors Compound the Growing Skills Shortage," *T + D,* February 2010, pp. 44–49; K. Frasch, "The Talent-Job Mismatch," *Human Resource Executive,* March 2013, p. 10.

51. M. Lev-Ram, "The Business Case for STEM," *Fortune,* February 1, 2015, p. 20; J. Cook-Ramirez,"STEM-ing the Tide," *Human Resource Executive,* September 2014, pp. 27–31; A. Campoy, "Training Programs Target Skill Gaps," *The Wall Street Journal,* April 24, 2015, p. A3; S. Wartenberg, "No Snow Days," *Columbus Dispatch,* February 22, 2015, p. D3.

52. J. Barney, *Gaining and Sustaining a Competitive Advantage* (Upper Saddle River, NJ: Prentice Hall, 2002).

53. L. Weatherly, *Human Capital: The Elusive Asset* (Alexandria, VA: 2003 SHRM Research Quarterly).

54. R. Dodes, "At Macy's, a Makeover on Service," *The Wall Street Journal,* April 11, 2011, p. B10; K. Talley, "Macy's Strategy Paying Off," *Wall Street Journal,* February 27, 2013, p. B3.

55. L. Bassi, J. Ludwig, D. McMurrer, and M. Van Buren, *Profiting from Learning: Do Firms' Investments in Education and Training Pay Off?* (Alexandria, VA: American Society for Training and Development, September 2000); S. Sung and J. Choi, "Do Organizations Spend Wisely on Employees? Effects of Training and Development Investments on Learning and Innovation in Organizations," *Journal of Organizational Behavior* 35 (2014), pp. 393–412; H. Aguinis and K. Kraiger, "Benefits of Training and Development for Individuals, Teams, Organizations, and Society," *Annual Review of Psychology* 60 (2009), pp. 451–74.

56. T. J. Atchison, "The Employment Relationship: Untied or Re-Tied," *Academy of Management Executive* 5 (1991), pp. 52–62.

57. D. Senge, "The Learning Organization Made Plain and Simple," *Training and Development Journal,* October 1991, pp. 37–44.

58. G. Kranz, "More to Learn," *Workforce Management,* January 2011, pp. 27–30.

59. M. Weinstein, "Are You Linked In?" *Training,* September/October 2010, pp. 30–33.

60. *SHRM Workplace Forecast* (Alexandria, VA: Society for Human Resource Management, 2013).

61. J. O'Toole and E. Lawler III, *The New American Workplace* (New York: Palgrave McMillan, 2006); R. Hoffman, B. Casnocha, and C. Yeh, "Tours of Duty: The New Employer-Employee Compact," *Harvard Business Review,* June 2013, pp. 48–58.

62. M. Weinstein, "Capital BlueCross Rx for Change," *Training,* January/February 2014, pp. 44–46.

63. L. Weber, "Just Whose Job Is It to Train Workers," *The Wall Street Journal,* July 17, 2014, pp. B1, B5.

64. R. Vance, *Employee Engagement and Commitment* (Alexandria, VA: Society for Human Resource Management, 2006).

65. A. Adkins, "U.S. Employee Engagement Holds Steady at 31.7%," www.gallup.com, accessed May 15, 2015; *State of the American Workplace: Employee Engagement Insights for US Business Leaders* (Washington, DC: Gallup, Inc. 2013); "American Employees Hold Back Their Full Potential," *T + D,* September 2013, p.17.

66. "Bridgepoint Education," *T + D,* October 2014, p. 87.

67. B. Ware, "Stop the Gen Y Revolving Door," *T + D,* May 2014, pp. 58–63.

68. M. Ciccarelli, "Keeping the Keepers," *Human Resource Executive,* January/February 2011, pp. 1, 20–23.

69. P. Cappelli, "Talent Management for the Twenty-First Century," *Harvard Business Review,* March 2008, pp. 74–81; "Towers Watson 2014 Global Talent Management and Rewards Study," *HR Magazine,* April 2015, p. 54.

70. K. Fyfe-Mills, "Committed to Talent Development Excellence," *T + D,* October 2014, pp. 38–41.

71. Bureau of Labor Statistics, "Contingent and Alternative Employment Arrangements, February 2005," www.bls.gov, accessed January 21, 2009.

72. R. Zeidner, "Heady Debate," *HR Magazine,* February 2010, pp. 28–33.

73. E. Frauenheim, "Creating a New Contingent Culture," *Workforce Management,* August 2012, pp. 34–39.

74. C. Patton, "On the Frontier of Flexibility," *Human Resource Executive,* May 2, 2009, pp. 48–51.

75. A. Fox, "Achieving Integration," *HR Magazine,* April 2011, pp. 42–47; P. Marinova, "Who Works from Home and When," February 28, 2013, www.cnn.com; C. Suddath, "Work-from-home Truths, Half-truths, and Myths," *Bloomberg Businessweek,* March 4–March 10, 2013, p. 75; R. Silverman and Q. Fottrell, "The Home Office in the Spotlight," *The Wall Street Journal,* February 27, 2013, p. B6; N. Shah, "More Americans Working from Home Remotely," *The Wall Street Journal,* April 6, 2013, p. A3.

76. N. Shah, "More Americans Are Working Remotely," *The Wall Street Journal,* March 6, 2013, p. A3.

77. "Stop the Gen Y Revolving Door."

78. E. Frauenheim, "Reflecting Re: Flexing" *Workforce Management,* June 2013, pp. 28–37.

79. R. Silverman and Q. Fottrell, "The Home Office in the Spotlight," *Wall Street Journal,* February 27, 2013, p. B6.

80. A. Fox, "At Work in 2020," *HR Magazine,* January 2010, pp. 18–23.

81. R. S. Kaplan and D. P. Norton, "The Balanced Scorecard—Measures That Drive Performance," *Harvard Business Review,* January–February 1992, pp. 71–79; R. S. Kaplan and D. P. Norton, "Putting the Balanced Scorecard to Work," *Harvard Business Review,* September–October 1993, pp. 134–47.

82. S. Bates, "The Metrics Maze," *HR Magazine,* December 2003, pp. 50–55; D. Ulrich, "Measuring Human Resources: An Overview of Practice and a Prescription for Results," *Human Resource Management* 36 (1997), pp. 303–20.

83. SAS Institute, "Customer Success: SAS Helps ConocoPhillips Norway Focus on Performance and Control Costs," www.sas.com, accessed April 24, 2012.

84. B. Sutherly, "Doctor Pay Still Based on Volume," *The Columbus Dispatch,* March 24, 2013, pp. A1 and A9.

85. From Coca-Cola 2011–2012 Sustainability Report accessed March 22, 2013, from www.coca-colacompany.com/sustainabilityreport.

86. D. Stanford, "Sustainability Meets the Profit Motive," *Bloomberg Businessweek,* April 4–April 10, 2011, pp. 25–26.

87. Ladika, "The Responsible Way."

88. J. R. Jablonski, *Implementing Total Quality Management: An Overview* (San Diego: Pfeiffer, 1991).

89. R. Hodgetts, F. Luthans, and S. Lee, "New Paradigm Organizations: From Total Quality to Learning World-Class," *Organizational Dynamics,* Winter 1994, pp. 5–19.

90. National Institute of Standards and Technology (NIST), Baldrige Performance Excellence Program, "Baldrige Frequently Asked Questions," www.nist.gov/baldrige, accessed April 8, 2011.

91. A. Pomeroy, "Winners and Learners," *HR Magazine,* April 2006, pp. 62–67.

92. "Malcolm Baldrige National Quality Award 2014 Award Recipient, Service Category, PricewaterhouseCoopers Public Sector Practice," www.nist.gov, accessed February 24, 2015.

93. "ISO in One Page," "Quality Management Principles," "ISO 9000 Essentials," and "Management and Leadership Standards," International Organization for Standardization, www.iso.org, accessed April 9, 2011.

94. Company website, "What Is Six Sigma?" www.ge.com, accessed March 3, 2015; General Electric 1999 Annual Report, www.ge.com/annual99.

95. "Baylor Health Care System: Lean and Process Improvement Training," *Training,* January/February 2014, p. 106.

96. "Employment Projections: 2012–2022."

97. S. Milligan, "Wisdom of the Ages," *HR Magazine,* November 2014, pp. 22–27; C. Paullin, *The Aging Workforce: Leveraging the Talents of Mature Employees* (Alexandria, VA: The SHRM Foundation, 2014); N. Lockwood, *The Aging Workforce* (Alexandria, VA: Society for Human Resource Management, 2003).

98. Milligan, "Wisdom of the Ages"; V. Giang, "The Fifty Best Employers for Older Workers," *Business Insider,* accessed April 14, 2015, www.businessinsider.com; AARP website, www.aarp.org, "2009 AARP Best Employers for Workers over 50," accessed May 6, 2011; AARP website, www.aarp.org, S. Hewlett, L. Sherbin, and K. Sumberg, "How Gen Y & Boomers Will Reshape Your Agenda," *Harvard Business Review,* July–August 2009, pp. 71–76.

99. K. Tyler, "New Kids on the Block," *HR Magazine,* October 2013, pp. 35–40; Milligan, "Wisdom of the Ages"; Hewlett, Sherbin, and Sumberg, "How Gen Y & Boomers Will Reshape Your Agenda"; A. Fox, "Mixing It Up" *HR Magazine,* May 2011, pp. 22–27; K. Ball and G. Gotsill, *Surviving the Baby Boomer Exodus* (Boston, MA: Cengage, 2011).

100. J. Meriac, D. Woehr, and C. Banister, "Generational Differences in Work Ethic: An Examination of Measurement Equivalence across Three Cohorts," *Journal of Business and Psychology,* 25 (2010), pp. 315–24; K. Real, A. Mitnick, and W. Maloney, "More Similar than Different: Millennials in the U.S. Building Trades," *Journal of Business and Psychology,* 25 (2010), pp. 303–13.

101. S. Lyons and L. Kuron, "Generational Differences in the Workplace: A Review of the Evidence and Directions for Future Research," *Journal of Organizational Behavior* 35 (2013), pp. 139–57; J. Deal, D. Altman, and S. Rogelberg, "Millennials at Work: What We Know and What We Need to Do (if Anything)," *Journal of Business and Psychology,* 25 (2010), pp. 191–99.

102. A. McIlvaine, "Millennials in Charge," *Human Resource Executive,* January/February 2015, pp. 12–14.

103. "Employment Projections: 2012–2022."

104. R. Minger and J. Yankay, "US Legal Permanent Residents: 2012," *Annual Flow Report,* U.S. Department of Homeland Security, Office of Immigration Statistics, March 2013, http://www.dhs.gov; U.S. Citizenship and Immigration Services, "Green Card (Permanent Residence)," http://www.uscis.gov, last updated May 13, 2011; U.S. Department of State, "Temporary Work Visas," http://travel.state.gov, accessed April 14, 2014.

105. R. Zeidner, "Does the United States Need Foreign Workers?" *HR Magazine,* June 2009, pp. 42–47.

106. B. Groysberg and K. Connolly, "Great Leaders Who Make the Mix Work," *Harvard Business Review,* September 2013, pp. 68–76; K. Jones, E. King, J. Nelson, D. Geller, and L. Bowes-Sperry, "Beyond the Business Case: The Ethical Perspective on Diversity Training," *Human Resource Management,* January–February 2013, pp. 55–74; T. H. Cox and S. Blake, "Managing Cultural Diversity: Implications for Organizational Competitiveness," *The Executive* 5 (1991), pp. 45–56.

107. Groysberg and Connolly, "Great Leaders Who Make the Mix Work"; M. Loden and J. B. Rosener, *Workforce America!* (Homewood, IL: Business One Irwin, 1991); N. Lockwood, *Workplace Diversity: Leveraging the Power of Difference for Competitive Advantage* (Alexandria, VA: Society for Human Resource Management, 2005).

108. R. Rodriguez, "Diversity Finds Its Place," *HR Magazine,* August 2006, pp. 56–61.

109. J. Cook-Ramirez, "Ready and Able," *Human Resource Executive,* November 2013, pp. 44–47.

110. S. Sipek, "Wearing Your Health on Your Sleeve," *Workforce,* August 2014, p. 16; C. Donham, "Legal Considerations," *Workforce,* August 2014, p. 47; L. Weber, "EEOC Issues Proposal for Wellness Programs," *The Wall Street Journal,* April 17, 2015, p. B5; M. Mihelich, "Sacred Ground for Lawsuits," *Workforce,* April 2014, pp. 18–19; J. Hyman, "Any Headway on Headware?" *Workforce,* November 2013, p. 27; M. Mihelich, "The Expanded Definition of Disability," *Workforce,* February 2014, pp. 20–21; J. Palazzolo, "Family-Leave Lawsuits Take Off," *The Wall Street Journal,* August 9–10, 2014, p. A3; R. Grossman, "No Federal Regulatory Relief in Sight," *HR Magazine,* February 2013, pp. 24–25.

111. M. Pastin, *The Hard Problems of Management: Gaining the Ethics Edge* (San Francisco: Jossey-Bass, 1986); T. Thomas, J. Schermerhorn, Jr., and J. Dienhart, "Strategic Leadership of Ethical Behavior in Business," *Academy of Management Executive* 18 (2004), pp. 56–66.

112. Ibid.

113. D. Meinert, "Creating an Ethical Culture," *HR Magazine,* April 2014, pp. 22–27.

114. Ibid.

115. K. Gurchiek, "Sarbanes-Oxley Compliance Costs Rising," *HR Magazine,* January 2005, pp. 29, 33.

116. R. Grossman, "HR and the Board," *HR Magazine,* January 2007, pp. 52–58.

117. J. Segal, "The 'Joy' of Uncooking," *HR Magazine* 47 (11) (2002).

118. D. Buss, "Corporate Compasses," *HR Magazine* 49 (6) (2004), pp. 126–32.

119. E. Krell, "How to Conduct an Ethics Audit," *HR Magazine,* April 2010, pp. 48–50.

120. D. Meinert, "Creating an Ethical Culture," *HR Magazine,* April 2014, pp. 22–27; Ladika, "The Responsible Way"; "Ethics: The Power of Doing Business Right," www.eaton.com, accessed May 15, 2015; A. McIlvaine, "Ethical Champions," *Human Resource Executive,* November 2014, pp. 14–16.

121. G. F. Cavanaugh, D. Moberg, and M. Velasquez, "The Ethics of Organizational Politics," *Academy of Management Review* 6 (1981), pp. 363–74.

122. "Manufacturing: Engine of US Innovation," *National Association of Manufacturing,* October 4, 2006, www.nam.org, accessed January 21, 2009.

123. I. Bremmer, "The New World of Business," *Fortune,* February 1, 2015, pp. 86–92.

124. D. Wessel, "Big U.S. Firms Shift Hiring Abroad," *Wall Street Journal,* April 19, 2011, pp. B1, B2.

125. Company website, "Gap Inc. Has Continued to Grow Around the World," www.gapinc.com, accessed February 27, 2015.

126. Company website, "2013 Annual Review," www.coca-cola.com, accessed February 26, 2015; "Coca-Cola Invests an Additional US$5 Billion for Long-term Sustainable Growth in Africa," www.coca-cola.com, accessed February 26, 2015.

127. Company website, "2013 Yum! Brands Annual Report," www.yum.com, accessed February 27, 2015; A Gasparro, "Yum Sees Rise in International Earning," *Market Watch,* www.marketwatch.com, accessed February 27, 2015.

128. Company website, "McDonald's to Enter New Market of Kazakhstan in 2015; "McDonald's Announces Official Opening of First Restaurant in Vietnam," press release; and "Our Facility," www.mcdonalds.com, accessed February 27, 2015.

129. C. Hymowitz, "IBM Combines Volunteer Service, Teamwork to Cultivate Emerging Markets," *The Wall Street Journal,* August 4, 2008, p. B6.

130. J. Schramm, "Offshoring," *Workplace Visions* 2 (Alexandria, VA: Society for Human Resource Management, 2004); P. Babcock, "America's Newest Export: White Collar Jobs," *HR Magazine* 49 (4) 2004, pp. 50–57.

131. J. Hagerty and M. Magnier, "Companies Tiptoe Back Toward 'Made in America,'" *The Wall Street Journal,* January 14, 2015, pp. A1, A12.

132. J. Hagerty, "Decimated U.S. Industry Pulls Up Its Socks," *The Wall Street Journal,* December 26, 2014, p. B6.

133. Government website, "Census Bureau's American Community Survey Provides New State and Local Income, Poverty, Health Insurance Statistics," www.census.gov, accessed February 27, 2015; L. Morales, "Nearly Half of Americans Are Frequent Internet Users," January 2, 2009, www.gallup.com; L. Morales, "Google and Facebook Users, Skew Young, Affluent and Educated," February 17, 2011, www.gallup.com.

134. M. Derven, "Social Networking: A Frame for Development," *T + D,* July 2009, pp. 58–63; J. Arnold, "Twittering and Facebooking While They Work," *HR Magazine,* December 2009, pp. 53–55.

135. C. Goodman, "Employers Wrestle with Social-Media Policies," *The Columbus Dispatch,* January 30, 2011, p. D3.

136. G. Colvin, "In the Future, Will There Be Any Work Left for People to Do?" *Fortune,* June 2, 2014, accessed www.fortune.com, April 21, 2015; T. Aeppel, "Jobs and the Clever Robot," *The Wall Street Journal,* February 25, 2015, pp. A1, A10; I. Brat, "A Joy(stick) to Behold," *The Wall Street Journal,* June 23, 2008, p. R5.

137. C. Mims, "Amelia, a Machine, Thinks Like You," *The Wall Street Journal,* September 28, 2014, pp. B1–B2; M. Rundle, "Amelia: IPsoft's New Artificial Intelligence Can Think Like a Human and Wants Your Job," *Huffington Post UK,* accessed April 21, 2015, www.huffingtonpost.co.uk.

138. K. Everson, "Special Report: Learning Is All in the Wrist," *Chief Learning Officer,* accessed March 18, 2015, www.clomedia.com; company website, "About" and "Products," www.wearable-intelligence.com, the website for Wearable Intelligence, accessed April 21, 2015.

139. R. Silverman, "Tracking Sensors Invade the Workplace," *Wall Street Journal,* March 7, 2013, pp. B1, B2.

140. M. J. Kavanaugh, H. G. Guetal, and S. I. Tannenbaum, *Human Resource Information Systems: Development and Application* (Boston: PWS-Kent, 1990).

141. A. Abbatiello, "The Digital Override," *Workforce,* May 2014, pp. 36–39.

142. D. Zielinski, "The Mobilization of HR Tech," *HR Magazine,* February 2014, pp. 30–36.

143. A. McAfee, "What Every CEO Needs to Know about the Cloud," *Harvard Business Review,* November 2011, pp. 124–132; B. Roberts, "The Grand Convergence," *HR Magazine,* October 2011, pp. 39–46; M. Paino, "All Generations Learn in the Cloud," *Chief Learning Officer,* September 28, 2011, http://blog.clomedia.com, accessed October 11, 2011.

144. M. Charney, "Five Reasons Why Cloud Computing Matters for Recruitment and Hiring," *Monster.com,* http://hiring.monster.com, accessed May 17, 2015; D. Shane, "A Human Giant," *Information Age,* accessed May 17, 2015, http://www.information-age.com.

145. L. Weatherly, "HR Technology: Leveraging the Shift to Self-Service," *HR Magazine,* March 2005.

146. N. Lockwood, *Maximizing Human Capital: Demonstrating HR Value with Key Performance Indicators* (Alexandria, VA: SHRM Research Quarterly, 2006).

147. P. Choate and P. Linger, *The High-Flex Society* (New York: Knopf, 1986); P. B. Doeringer, *Turbulence in the American Workplace* (New York: Oxford University Press, 1991).

148. J. A. Neal and C. L. Tromley, "From Incremental Change to Retrofit: Creating High-Performance Work Systems," *Academy of Management Executive* 9 (1995), pp. 42–54.

149. K. A. Miller, *Retraining the American Workforce* (Reading, MA: Addison-Wesley, 1989).

150. B. Reynolds, "Twenty-six Companies That Thrive on Remote Work," *Flex Jobs,* www.flexjobs.com, accessed March 3, 2015; company website, www.artandlogic.com, accessed March 3, 2015. "Working at Art & Logic" from www.artandlogic.com/careers, accessed July 1, 2015.

151. M. A. Huselid, "The Impact of Human Resource Management Practices on Turnover, Productivity, and Corporate Financial Performance," *Academy of Management Journal* 38 (1995), pp. 635–72; U.S. Dept. of Labor, *High-Performance Work Practices and Firm Performance* (Washington, DC: U.S. Government Printing Office, 1993); J. Combs, Y. Liu, A. Hall, and D. Ketchen, "How Much Do High-Performance Work Practices Matter? A Meta-analysis of Their Effects on Organizational Performance," *Personnel Psychology* 59 (2006), pp. 501–28.

152. B. Becker and M. A. Huselid, "High-Performance Work Systems and Firm Performance: A Synthesis of Research and Managerial Implications," in *Research in Personnel and Human Resource Management* 16, ed. G. R. Ferris (Stamford, CT: JAI Press, 1998), pp. 53–101; A. Zacharatos, J. Barling, and R. Iverson, "High Performance Work Systems and Occupational Safety," *Journal of Applied Psychology* 90 (2005), pp. 77–93.

153. B. Becker and B. Gerhart, "The Impact of Human Resource Management on Organizational Performance: Progress and Prospects," *Academy of Management Journal* 39 (1996), pp. 779–801.

154. Company website, www.hindlepower.com, accessed May 17, 2015; P. Fehrenbach, "Hindle Power's Pro Shop: Greatness Within," *Industry Week,* June 3, 2014, ProQuest eLibrary, http://elibrary.bigchalk.com; J. Juski, "The Value of Labor," *Industry Week,* November 2013, pp. 24–26; A. Wlazelek, "HindlePower Inc.: Manufacturing Without a Time Clock," *Morning Call* (Lehigh Valley, PA), March 4, 2103, http://articles.mcall.com; Global Engineering Manufacturing Alliance website, www.gemaengine.com; company website, "Dundee Plant," www.media.chrysler.com, accessed March 3, 2015; J. Marquez, "Engine of Change," *Workforce Management,* July 2006, pp. 20–30.

155. S. A. Snell and J. W. Dean, "Integrated Manufacturing and Human Resource Management: A Human Capital Perspective," *Academy of Management Journal* 35 (1992), pp. 467–504; M. A. Youndt, S. Snell, J. W. Dean Jr., and D. P. Lepak, "Human Resource Management, Manufacturing Strategy, and Firm Performance," *Academy of Management Journal* 39 (1996), pp. 836–66.

PART ONE

Strategic Human Resource Management

2

C H A P T E R

LEARNING OBJECTIVES

After reading this chapter, you should be able to:

LO 2-1   Describe the differences between strategy formulation and strategy implementation. *page 70*

LO 2-2   List the components of the strategic management process. *page 72*

LO 2-3   Discuss the role of the HRM function in strategy formulation. *page 74*

LO 2-4   Describe the linkages between HRM and strategy formulation. *page 74*

LO 2-5   Discuss the more popular typologies of generic strategies and the various HRM practices associated with each. *page 80*

LO 2-6   Describe the different HRM issues and practices associated with various directional strategies. *page 88*

Southwest Airlines Hits Middle Age

Southwest Airlines has perennially been considered a model of how an innovative strategy combined with strong culture and a strong relationship between management and employees can lead to business success. The company was founded in 1967 and was built on low costs, labor harmony, simplicity, and rapid expansion. While labor strife seems endemic to the airline industry, Southwest always stood up for its workforce, which seemed unflinchingly committed to the company's success.

However, as the company has expanded and grown older, the original strategy seems to be in peril. Mergers among the major airlines such as American/US Airways, United/Continental, and Delta/Northwest have enabled them to reduce their cost structures and come closer to Southwest on price. In addition, ultra-discount airlines, such as Spirit Airlines, can undercut Southwest on price. Finally, airlines like JetBlue and Virgin America compete for Southwest's traditional middle-class customers.

While Southwest faces a number of competitive and technological challenges, its labor costs stand front and center. Because Southwest is not expanding as fast, the company cannot hire as many new employees at the lowest rungs of the wage scale. With 83% of its workforce unionized, Southwest now seeks to negotiate wage freezes and tighten rules on sick time. In addition, the airline wants to hire more

© rypson

part-time workers and has floated the idea of outsourcing a number of jobs.

Employees pine for the former CEO and co-founder, Herb Kelleher, who was beloved by employees. Says Randy Barnes, a union representative for the ramp workers, "Ever since Herb . . . left, this has been more of a corporation and less of a family."

This chapter explores how firms seek to align their human resources with strategy through a process called "strategic human resource management."

SOURCES: Based on T. Maxon, "Southwest Airlines Tops $1 Billion in Annual Profits for First Time," *Dallas Morning News,* January 22, 2015, http://aviationblog.dallasnews.com; J. Nicas and S. Carey, "Southwest Airlines, Once a Brassy Upstart, Is Showing Its Age," *The Wall Street Journal,* April 1, 2014, www.wsj.com.

Introduction

As the Southwest Airlines example just illustrated, business organizations exist in an environment of competition. They can use a number of resources to compete with other companies. These resources are physical (such as plant, equipment, technology, and geographic location), organizational (the structure, planning, controlling, and coordinating systems, and group relations), and human (the experience, skill, and intelligence of employees). It is these resources under the control of the company that provide competitive advantage.[1]

The goal of strategic management in an organization is to deploy and allocate resources in a way that gives it a competitive advantage. As you can see, two of the three classes of resources (organizational and human) are directly tied to the human resource management function. As Chapter 1 pointed out, the role of human resource management is to ensure that a company's human resources provide a competitive advantage. Chapter 1 also pointed out some of the major competitive challenges that companies face today. These challenges require companies to take a proactive, strategic approach in the marketplace.

To be maximally effective, the HRM function must be integrally involved in the company's strategic management process.[2] This means that human resource managers should (1) have input into the strategic plan, both in terms of people-related issues and in terms of the ability of the human resource pool to implement particular strategic alternatives; (2) have specific knowledge of the organization's strategic goals; (3) know what types of employee skills, behaviors, and attitudes are needed to support the strategic plan; and (4) develop programs to ensure that employees have those skills, behaviors, and attitudes.

We begin this chapter by discussing the concepts of business models and strategy and by depicting the strategic management process. Then, we discuss the levels of integration between the HRM function and the strategic management process in strategy formulation. Next, we review some of the more common strategic models and, within the context of these models, discuss the various types of employee skills, behaviors, and attitudes, and the ways HRM practices aid in implementing the strategic plan. Finally, we discuss the role of HR in creating competitive advantage.

What Is a Business Model?

A business model is a story of how the firm will create value for customers and, more important, how it will do so profitably. We often hear or read of companies that have "transformed their business model" in one way or another, but what that means is not always clear. To understand this, we need to grasp a few basic accounting concepts.

First, fixed costs are generally considered the costs that are incurred regardless of the number of units produced. For instance, if you are producing widgets in a factory, you have the rent you pay for the factory, depreciation of the machines, the utilities, the property taxes, and so on. In addition, you generally have a set number of employees who work a set number of hours with a specified level of benefits, and while you might be able to vary these over time, on a regular basis you pay the same total labor costs whether your factory runs at 70% capacity or 95% capacity.

Second, you have a number of variable costs, which are those costs that vary directly with the units produced. For instance, all of the materials that go into the widget might cost a total of $10, which means that you have to charge at least $10 per widget, or you cannot even cover the variable costs of production.

Third is the concept of "contribution margins," or margins. Margins are the difference between what you charge for your product and the variable costs of that product. They are called contribution margins because they are what contributes to your ability to cover your fixed costs. So, for instance, if you charged $15 for each widget, your contribution margin would be $5 ($15 price – $10 variable cost).

Fourth, the gross margin is the total amount of margin you made and is calculated as the number of units sold times the contribution margin. If you sold 1,000,000 units, your gross margin would then be $5,000,000. Did you make a profit? That depends. Profit refers to what is left after you have paid your variable costs and your fixed costs. If your gross margin was $5,000,000, and your fixed costs were $6,000,000, then you lost $1,000,000.

GM'S ATTEMPT TO SURVIVE

Let's look at how a business model plays out with the recent challenges faced by General Motors (GM). Critics of GM talk about the fact that GM has higher labor costs than their foreign competitors. This is true, but misleading. GM's average hourly wage for their existing workforce is reasonably competitive. However, the two aspects that make GM uncompetitive are their benefit costs (in particular, health care) and most important, the cost of their legacy workforce.

A legacy workforce describes the former workers (i.e., those no longer working for the company) to whom the firm still owes financial obligations. GM and the United Auto Workers (UAW) union have negotiated contracts over the years that provide substantial retirement benefits for former GM workers. In particular, retired GM workers have defined benefit plans that guarantee a certain percentage of their final (preretirement) salary as a pension payment as long as they live as well as having the company pay for their health insurance. In addition, the contract specifies that workers are entitled to retire at full pension after 30 years of service.

This might have seemed sustainable when the projections were that GM would continue growing its sales and margins. However, since the 1970s, foreign competitors have been eating away at GM's market share to the extent that GM's former 50% of the market has shrunk to closer to 20%. In addition, with the current economic crisis, the market itself has been shrinking, leaving GM with a decreasing percentage of a decreasing market. For instance, in December of 2005, GM sold 26% of the cars in the global market but by 2012 that market share had shrunk to 17.9%. Thus, in addition to the legacy workforce, they had a significant number of plants with thousands of employees that were completely unnecessary, given the volume of cars GM can produce and sell.[3,4]

If you look at Figure 2.1, you'll see that the solid lines represent the old GM business model, which was based on projections that GM would be able to sell 4 million units at a reasonably high margin, and thus completely cover its fixed costs to make a strong profit. However, the reality was that its products didn't sell at the higher prices, so to try to sell 4 million vehicles, GM offered discounts, which cut into its margins. When GM ended up selling only 3.5 million vehicles, and those were sold at a lower margin, the company could not cover its fixed costs, resulting in a $9 billion loss in 2008 (this is illustrated by the dotted blue line in the figure). So, when GM refers to the "redesigned business model," what it is referring to is a significant reduction in fixed costs (through closing plants and cutting workers) to get the fixed-cost base low enough (the dotted brown line) to be able to still be profitable selling fewer cars at lower margins (again, the dotted blue line).

One can easily see how, given the large component that labor costs are to most companies, reference to business models almost inevitably leads to discussions of labor costs. These can be the high cost associated with current unionized employees in developed countries within North America or Europe or, in some cases, the high costs associated

Figure 2.1

An Illustration of
a Business Model
for GM

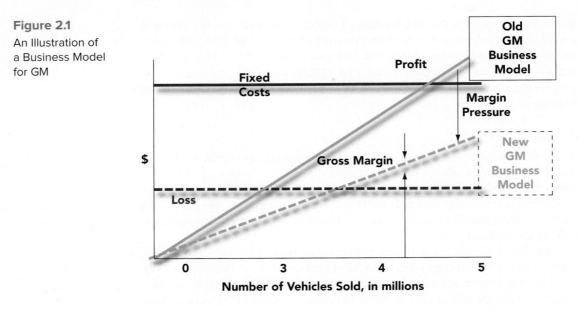

What Is Strategic Management?

LO 2-1

Describe the differ-
ences between strategy
formulation and strat-
egy implementation.

with a legacy workforce. For instance, the Big Three automakers have huge numbers of retired or laid-off workers for whom they still have the liability of paying pensions and health care benefits. This is a significant component of their fixed-cost base, which makes it difficult for them to compete with other automakers that either have fewer retirees to cover or have no comparable costs because their home governments provide pensions and health care. In fact, this changing business model at GM has driven them to locate more manufacturing outside of the United States. The "Competing through Globalization" box describes the challenges Facebook faces as it tries to meet the privacy protection requirements across the globe.

Many authors have noted that in today's competitive market, organizations must engage in strategic planning to survive and prosper. Strategy comes from the Greek word *strategos*, which has its roots in military language. It refers to a general's grand design behind a war or battle. In fact, *Webster's New American Dictionary* defines strategy as the "skillful employment and coordination of tactics" and as "artful planning and management."

Strategic management is a process, an approach to addressing the competitive challenges an organization faces. It can be thought of as managing the "pattern or plan that integrates an organization's major goals, policies, and action sequences into a cohesive whole."[5] These strategies can be either the generic approach to competing or the specific adjustments and actions taken to deal with a particular situation.

First, business organizations engage in generic strategies that often fit into some strategic type. One example is "cost, differentiation, or focus."[6] Another is "defender, analyzer, prospector, or reactor."[7] Different organizations within the same industry often have different generic strategies. These generic strategy types describe the consistent way the company attempts to position itself relative to competitors.

Facebook's European Privacy Policy Problems

As a student in the United States, you might not think twice about how Facebook uses data it gains from you when you are surfing the social media site. When you "like" or "share" something, you know you are publicly proclaiming something. However, in Europe, a number of regulators have questioned whether or not Facebook actually invades users' privacy. The Belgian Privacy Commission says Facebook is "in a unique position, since it can easily link its users' surfing behavior to their real identity, social network interactions, and sensitive data such as medical information and religious, sexual, and political preferences."

The regulator also seems frustrated by Facebook's suggestion that it only needs to adhere to regulators in Ireland, the home of Facebook's European headquarters. The Belgian regulator disagrees: "There is not a shadow of doubt on the applicability of the Belgian privacy legislation." Yet Facebook continues to refuse to recognize the application of Belgian law as well as the legitimacy of the Belgian Privacy Commission's questions.

DISCUSSION QUESTION
Is it possible for multinational firms to tailor their policies to each government's jurisdiction? How should they do so?

SOURCE: L. Fleisher and T. Fairless, "Belgian Watchdog Group Raps Facebook for Treating Personal Data 'with Contempt,'" *The Wall Street Journal,* May 15, 2015, www.wsj.com.

However, a generic strategy is only a small part of strategic management. The second aspect of strategic management is the process of developing strategies for achieving the company's goals in light of its current environment. Thus, business organizations engage in generic strategies, but they also make choices about such things as how to scare off competitors, how to keep competitors weaker, how to react to and influence pending legislation, how to deal with various stakeholders and special interest groups, how to lower production costs, how to raise revenues, what technology to implement, and how many and what types of people to employ. Each of these decisions may present competitive challenges that have to be considered.

Strategic management is more than a collection of strategic types. It is a process for analyzing a company's competitive situation, developing the company's strategic goals, and devising a plan of action and allocation of resources (human, organizational, and physical) that will increase the likelihood of achieving those goals. This kind of strategic approach should be emphasized in human resource management. HR managers should be trained to identify the competitive issues the company faces with regard to human resources and think strategically about how to respond.

Strategic human resource management (SHRM) can be thought of as "the pattern of planned human resource deployments and activities intended to enable an organization to achieve its goals."[8] For example, many firms have developed integrated manufacturing systems such as advanced manufacturing technology, just-in-time inventory control, and total quality management in an effort to increase their competitive position. However, these systems must be run by people. SHRM in these cases entails assessing the employee skills required to run these systems and engaging in HRM practices, such as selection and training, that develop these skills in employees.[9] To take a strategic approach to HRM, we must first understand the role of HRM in the strategic management process.

Strategic Human Resource Management (SHRM)
A pattern of planned human resource deployments and activities intended to enable an organization to achieve its goals.

COMPONENTS OF THE STRATEGIC MANAGEMENT PROCESS

LO 2-2
List the components of the strategic management process.

Strategy Formulation
The process of deciding on a strategic direction by defining a company's mission and goals, its external opportunities and threats, and its internal strengths and weaknesses.

Strategy Implementation
The process of devising structures and allocating resources to enact the strategy a company has chosen.

The strategic management process has two distinct yet interdependent phases: strategy formulation and strategy implementation. During **strategy formulation** the strategic planning groups decide on a strategic direction by defining the company's mission and goals, its external opportunities and threats, and its internal strengths and weaknesses. They then generate various strategic alternatives and compare those alternatives' ability to achieve the company's mission and goals. During **strategy implementation**, the organization follows through on the chosen strategy. This consists of structuring the organization, allocating resources, ensuring that the firm has skilled employees in place, and developing reward systems that align employee behavior with the organization's strategic goals. Both of these strategic management phases must be performed effectively. It is important to note that this process does not happen sequentially. As we will discuss later with regard to emergent strategies, this process entails a constant cycling of information and decision making. Figure 2.2 presents the strategic management process.

In recent years organizations have recognized that the success of the strategic management process depends largely on the extent to which the HRM function is involved.[10]

LINKAGE BETWEEN HRM AND THE STRATEGIC MANAGEMENT PROCESS

The strategic choice really consists of answering questions about competition—that is, how the firm will compete to achieve its missions and goals. These decisions consist of addressing the issues of where to compete, how to compete, and with what to compete, which are described in Figure 2.3.

Although these decisions are all important, strategic decision makers often pay less attention to the "with what will we compete" issue, resulting in poor strategic decisions. For example, PepsiCo in the 1980s acquired the fast-food chains of Kentucky Fried Chicken, Taco Bell, and Pizza Hut ("where to compete" decisions) in an effort to increase its customer base. However, it failed to adequately recognize the differences between its existing workforce (mostly professionals) and that of the fast-food industry (lower skilled people and high schoolers) as well as its ability to manage such a workforce. This was one reason that PepsiCo, in 1998, spun off the fast-food chains. In essence, it had made a decision about where to compete without fully understanding what resources would be needed to compete in that market.

Boeing illustrates how failing to address the "with what" issue resulted in problems in its "how to compete" decisions. When the aerospace firm's consumer products division entered into a price war with Airbus Industrie, it was forced to move away from its traditional customer service strategy toward emphasizing cost reduction.[11] The strategy was a success on the sales end as Boeing received large numbers of orders for aircraft from firms such as Delta, Continental, Southwest, and Singapore Airlines. However, it had recently gone through a large workforce reduction (thus, it didn't have enough people to fill the orders) and did not have the production technology to enable the necessary increase in productivity. The result of this failure to address "with what will we compete" in making a decision about how to compete resulted in the firm's inability to meet delivery deadlines and the ensuing penalties it had to pay to its customers. The end result is that after all the travails, for the first time in the history of the industry, Airbus sold more planes than Boeing in 2003. Luckily, Boeing was able to

Figure 2.2

A Model of the Strategic Management Process

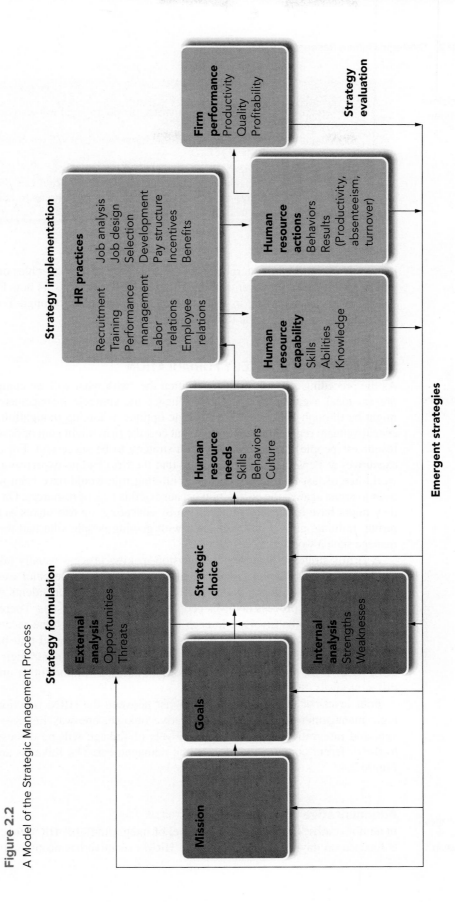

Figure 2.3

Strategy—Decisions about Competition

1. Where to compete?
    In what market or markets (industries, products, etc.) will we compete?
2. How to compete?
    On what criterion or differentiating characteristic(s) will we compete? Cost? Quality? Reliability? Delivery?
3. With what will we compete?
    What resources will allow us to beat our competition?
    How will we acquire, develop, and deploy those resources to compete?

overcome this stumble, in large part because of a number of stumbles on the part of its chief rival, Airbus. However, Boeing has faced difficulties as its new Dreamliner was grounded for fires starting in the wiring. The "Competing through Technology" box illustrates the increasing use of robotics in China.

ROLE OF HRM IN STRATEGY FORMULATION

LO 2-3

Discuss the role of the HRM function in strategy formulation.

As the preceding examples illustrate, often the "with what will we compete" questions present ideal avenues for HRM to influence the strategic management process. This might be through either limiting strategic options or forcing thoughtfulness among the executive team regarding how and at what cost the firm might gain or develop the human resources (people) necessary for such a strategy to be successful. For example, HRM executives at PepsiCo could have noted that the firm had no expertise in managing the workforce of fast-food restaurants. The limiting role would have been for these executives to argue against the acquisition because of this lack of resources. On the other hand, they might have influenced the decision by educating top executives as to the costs (of hiring, training, and so on) associated with gaining people who had the right skills to manage such a workforce.

A firm's strategic management decision-making process usually takes place at its top levels, with a strategic planning group consisting of the chief executive officer, the chief financial officer, the president, and various vice presidents. However, each component of the process involves people-related business issues. Therefore, the HRM function needs to be involved in each of those components. One recent study of 115 strategic business units within *Fortune* 500 corporations found that between 49 and 69% of the companies had some link between HRM and the strategic planning process.[12] However, the level of linkage varied, and it is important to understand these different levels.

Four levels of integration seem to exist between the HRM function and the strategic management function: administrative linkage, one-way linkage, two-way linkage, and integrative linkage.[13] These levels of linkage will be discussed in relation to the different components of strategic management. The linkages are illustrated in Figure 2.4.

LO 2-4

Describe the linkages between HRM and strategy formulation.

Administrative Linkage

In administrative linkage (the lowest level of integration), the HRM function's attention is focused on day-to-day activities. The HRM executive has no time or opportunity to

COMPETING THROUGH TECHNOLOGY

The Rise of the Robot in China

Much of China's economic growth can be traced to its low labor costs as a number of manufacturing firms entered the market to hire semi-skilled and skilled employees at a huge discount compared to the United States and Europe. However, with the growth in demand for such employees, labor costs have soared, leading a number of firms to replace the people with robots.

Sales of robots increased 54% from 2013 to 2014, and some suggest that by 2017 China will be the country with the most robots in the world. China is seen as the world's largest market for industrial robots because it has approximately 30 robots for every 10,000 factory workers, as compared to Germany which has 300 and Japan with 330.

Economists have always seen robots as a way to save on costly labor in developed economies, providing a rationale to maintain operations rather than offshore them. However, robots are increasingly seen as a way to manage costs in the developing world, with the risk that they may reduce the job creation that those economies seek.

DISCUSSION QUESTION
Can China afford to reduce job creation in this competitive environment by using more robots? Why or why not?

SOURCE: T. Aeppel, "Why China May Have the Most Factory Robots in the World by 2017," *The Wall Street Journal*, April 1, 2015, http://blogs.wsj.com.

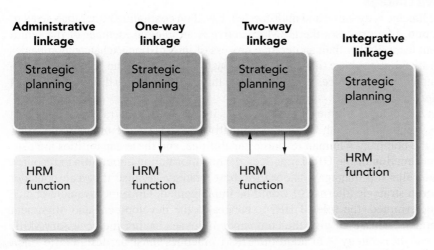

Figure 2.4
Linkages of Strategic Planning and HRM

SOURCE: Adapted from K. Golden and V. Ramanujam, "Between a Dream and a Nightmare: On the Integration of the Human Resource Function and the Strategic Business Planning Process," *Human Resource Management* 24 (1985), pp. 429–51.

take a strategic outlook toward HRM issues. The company's strategic business planning function exists without any input from the HRM department. Thus, in this level of integration, the HRM department is completely divorced from any component of the strategic management process in both strategy formulation and strategy implementation. The department simply engages in administrative work unrelated to the company's core business needs.

One-Way Linkage

In one-way linkage, the firm's strategic business planning function develops the strategic plan and then informs the HRM function of the plan. Many believe this level of integration constitutes strategic HRM—that is, the role of the HRM function is to design systems and/or programs that implement the strategic plan. Although one-way linkage does recognize the importance of human resources in implementing the strategic plan, it precludes the company from considering human resource issues while formulating the strategic plan. This level of integration often leads to strategic plans that the company cannot successfully implement.

Two-Way Linkage

Two-way linkage allows for consideration of human resource issues during the strategy formulation process. This integration occurs in three sequential steps. First, the strategic planning team informs the HRM function of the various strategies the company is considering. Then HRM executives analyze the human resource implications of the various strategies, presenting the results of this analysis to the strategic planning team. Finally, after the strategic decision has been made, the strategic plan is passed on to the HRM executive, who develops programs to implement it. The strategic planning function and the HRM function are interdependent in two-way linkage.

Integrative Linkage

Integrative linkage is dynamic and multifaceted, based on continuing rather than sequential interaction. In most cases the HRM executive is an integral member of the senior management team. Rather than an iterative process of information exchange, companies with integrative linkage have their HRM functions built right into the strategy formulation and implementation processes. It is this role that we will discuss throughout the rest of this chapter.

Thus, in strategic HRM, the HRM function is involved in both strategy formulation and strategy implementation. The HRM executive gives strategic planners information about the company's human resource capabilities, and these capabilities are usually a direct function of the HRM practices.[14] This information about human resource capabilities helps top managers choose the best strategy because they can consider how well each strategic alternative would be implemented. Once the strategic choice has been determined, the role of HRM changes to the development and alignment of HRM practices that will give the company employees having the necessary skills to implement the strategy.[15] In addition, HRM practices must be designed to elicit actions from employees in the company.[16] In the next two sections of this chapter we show how HRM can provide a competitive advantage in the strategic management process.

Strategy Formulation

Five major components of the strategic management process are relevant to strategy formulation.[17] These components are depicted in Figure 2.5. The first component is the organization's mission. The mission is a statement of the organization's reason for being; it usually specifies the customers served, the needs satisfied and/or the values received

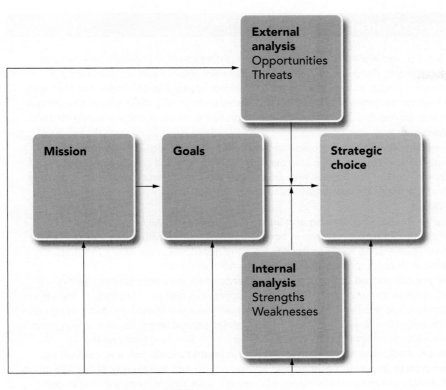

Figure 2.5
Strategy Formulation

HR input

SOURCE: Adapted from K. Golden and V. Ramanujam, "Between a Dream and a Nightmare," *Human Resource Management* 24 (1985), pp. 429–51.

by the customers, and the technology used. The mission statement is often accompanied by a statement of a company's vision and/or values. For example, Table 2.1 illustrates the mission and values of Merck & Co., Inc. In addition, the "Integrity in Action" box describes why 3M continues to be recognized as one of the world's most ethical companies.

An organization's **goals** are what it hopes to achieve in the medium- to long-term future; they reflect how the mission will be operationalized. The overarching goal of most profit-making companies in the United States is to maximize stockholder wealth. But companies have to set other long-term goals in order to maximize stockholder wealth.

External analysis consists of examining the organization's operating environment to identify the strategic opportunities and threats. Examples of opportunities are customer markets that are not being served, technological advances that can aid the company, and labor pools that have not been tapped. Threats include potential labor shortages, new competitors entering the market, pending legislation that might adversely affect the company, and competitors' technological innovations.

Internal analysis attempts to identify the organization's strengths and weaknesses. It focuses on the quantity and quality of resources available to the organization—financial, capital, technological, and human resources. Organizations have to honestly and accurately assess each resource to decide whether it is a strength or a weakness.

Goals
What an organization hopes to achieve in the medium- to long-term future.

External Analysis
Examining the organization's operating environment to identify strategic opportunities and threats.

Internal Analysis
The process of examining an organization's strengths and weaknesses.

Table 2.1
Merck & Co.'s
Mission and Values

MISSION STATEMENT
Merck & Co., Inc. is a leading research-driven pharmaceutical products and services company. Merck discovers, develops, manufactures and markets a broad range of innovative products to improve human and animal health. The Merck-Medco Managed Care Division manages pharmacy benefits for more than 40 million Americans, encouraging the appropriate use of medicines and providing disease management programs.
Our Mission
The mission of Merck is to provide society with superior products and services—innovations and solutions that improve the quality of life and satisfy customer needs—to provide employees with meaningful work and advancement opportunities and investors with a superior rate of return.
Our Values
1. **Our business is preserving and improving human life.** All of our actions must be measured by our success in achieving this goal. We value above all our ability to serve everyone who can benefit from the appropriate use of our products and services, thereby providing lasting consumer satisfaction.
2. **We are committed to the highest standards of ethics and integrity.** We are responsible to our customers, to Merck employees and their families, to the environments we inhabit, and to the societies we serve worldwide. In discharging our responsibilities, we do not take professional or ethical shortcuts. Our interactions with all segments of society must reflect the high standards we profess.
3. **We are dedicated to the highest level of scientific excellence and commit our research to improving human and animal health and the quality of life.** We strive to identify the most critical needs of consumers and customers; we devote our resources to meeting those needs.
4. **We expect profits, but only from work that satisfies customer needs and benefits humanity.** Our ability to meet our responsibilities depends on maintaining a financial position that invites investment in leading-edge research and that makes possible effective delivery of research results.
5. **We recognize that the ability to excel—to most competitively meet society's and customers' needs—depends on the integrity, knowledge, imagination, skill, diversity, and teamwork of employees, and we value these qualities most highly.** To this end, we strive to create an environment of mutual respect, encouragement, and teamwork—a working environment that rewards commitment and performance and is responsive to the needs of employees and their families.

SOURCE: Courtesy of Merck.

External analysis and internal analysis combined constitute what has come to be called the SWOT (strengths, weaknesses, opportunities, threats) analysis. Table 2.2 shows an example of a SWOT analysis for Google. After going through the SWOT analysis, the strategic planning team has all the information it needs to generate a number of strategic alternatives. The strategic managers compare these alternatives' ability to attain the organization's strategic goals; then they make their **strategic choice**. The strategic choice is the organization's strategy; it describes the ways the organization will attempt to fulfill its mission and achieve its long-term goals.

Many of the opportunities and threats in the external environment are people-related. With fewer and fewer highly qualified individuals entering the labor market, organizations compete not just for customers but for employees. It is HRM's role to keep close tabs on the external environment for human resource–related opportunities and threats,

Strategic Choice
The organization's strategy; the ways an organization will attempt to fulfill its mission and achieve its long-term goals.

3M Named One of World's Most Ethical Companies

One often hears jokes that the term "business ethics" is an oxymoron, but a number of firms prove that the joke is just that: only a joke. Ethisphere Institute, which seeks to lead the world in defining and advancing the standards of ethical business practices, develops a list of "the World's Most Ethical Companies." Ethisphere named 3M as one of the 2015 Most Ethical Companies, a recognition the company has gained for the second straight year.

"At 3M, living by our Code of Conduct is a team effort and responsibility we uphold for our customers, for our shareholders, and for each other," said Jim Zappa, 3M's chief compliance officer. "The commitment of our people to the highest ethical standard and to doing business the right way promotes trust with our customers and the quality of our products. Furthermore, it gives us confidence to grow our business anywhere in the world."

The CEO of Ethisphere, Timothy Erblich, stated, "The World's Most Ethical Companies embrace the correlation between ethical business practice and improved company performance. These companies use ethics as a means to further define their industry leadership and understand that creating an ethical culture . . . involves more than just an outward facing message or a handful of senior executives saying the right thing. Earning this recognition involves the collective action of a global workforce from the top down."

DISCUSSION QUESTION

Do you think 3M's recognition as one of the world's most ethical companies gives the company a competitive advantage? Why or why not?

SOURCE: Company website, "3M Named as a World's Most Ethical Company for Second Consecutive Year," http://news.3m.com, March 9, 2015.

STRENGTHS	WEAKNESSES
Expanding Liquidity	Issues with Chinese Government
Operational Efficiency	Dependence on Advertising Segment
Broad Range of Services Portfolio	Losses at YouTube

OPPORTUNITIES	THREATS
Growing Demand for Online Video	Weak Economic Outlook
Growth in Internet Advertising Market	Invalid Clicks
Inorganic Growth	Microsoft–Yahoo! Deal

Table 2.2
SWOT Analysis for Google, Inc.

SOURCE: GlobalData.

especially those directly related to the HRM function: potential labor shortages, competitor wage rates, government regulations affecting employment, and so on. For example, as discussed in Chapter 1, U.S. companies are finding that more and more high school graduates lack the basic skills needed to work, which is one source of the "human capital shortage."[18] However, not recognizing this environmental threat, many companies have encouraged the exit of older, more skilled workers while hiring less skilled younger workers who require basic skills training.[19]

An analysis of a company's internal strengths and weaknesses also requires input from the HRM function. Today companies are increasingly realizing that their human resources are one of their most important assets. In fact, one estimate is that over one-third of the total growth in U.S. gross national product (GNP) between 1943 and 1990 was the result of increases in human capital. A company's failure to consider the strengths and weaknesses of its workforce may result in its choosing strategies it is not capable of pursuing.[20] However, some research has demonstrated that few companies have achieved this level of linkage.[21] For example, one company chose a strategy of cost reduction through technological improvements. It built a plant designed around a computer-integrated manufacturing system with statistical process controls. Although this choice may seem like a good one, the company soon learned otherwise. It discovered that its employees could not operate the new equipment because 25% of the workforce was functionally illiterate.[22]

Thus, with an integrative linkage, strategic planners consider all the people-related business issues before making a strategic choice. These issues are identified with regard to the mission, goals, opportunities, threats, strengths, and weaknesses, leading the strategic planning team to make a more intelligent strategic choice. Although this process does not guarantee success, companies that address these issues are more likely to make choices that will ultimately succeed.

Recent research has supported the need to have HRM executives integrally involved in strategy formulation. One study of U.S. petrochemical refineries found that the level of HRM involvement was positively related to the refinery manager's evaluation of the effectiveness of the HRM function.[23] A second study of manufacturing firms found that HRM involvement was highest when top managers viewed employees as a strategic asset and associated them with reduced turnover.[24] However, both studies found that HRM involvement was unrelated to operating unit financial performance.

Research has indicated that few companies have fully integrated HRM into the strategy formulation process.[25] As we've mentioned before, companies are beginning to recognize that in an intensely competitive environment, managing human resources strategically can provide a competitive advantage. Thus, companies at the administrative linkage level will either become more integrated or face extinction. In addition, companies will move toward becoming integratively linked in an effort to manage human resources strategically.

It is of utmost importance that all people-related business issues be considered during strategy formulation. These issues are identified in the HRM function. Mechanisms or structures for integrating the HRM function into strategy formulation may help the strategic planning team make the most effective strategic choice. Once that strategic choice is determined, HRM must take an active role in implementing it. This role will be discussed in the next section.

Strategy Implementation

LO 2-5
Discuss the more popular typologies of generic strategies and the various HRM practices associated with each.

After an organization has chosen its strategy, it has to execute that strategy—make it come to life in its day-to-day workings. The strategy a company pursues dictates certain HR needs. For a company to have a good strategy foundation, certain tasks must be accomplished in pursuit of the company's goals, individuals must possess certain skills to perform those tasks, and these individuals must be motivated to perform their skills effectively.

The basic premise behind strategy implementation is that "an organization has a variety of structural forms and organizational processes to choose from when implementing a given strategy," and these choices make an economic difference.[26] Five important variables determine success in strategy implementation: organizational structure; task

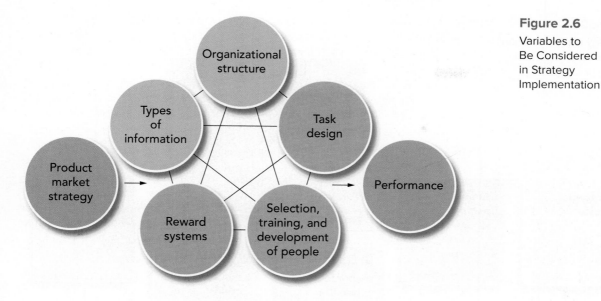

Figure 2.6
Variables to
Be Considered
in Strategy
Implementation

design; the selection, training, and development of people; reward systems; and types of information and information systems.

As we see in Figure 2.6, HRM has primary responsibility for three of these five implementation variables: task, people, and reward systems. In addition, HRM can directly affect the two remaining variables: structure and information and decision processes. First, for the strategy to be successfully implemented, the tasks must be designed and grouped into jobs in a way that is efficient and effective.[27] In Chapter 4 we will examine how this can be done through the processes of job analysis and job design. Second, the HRM function must ensure that the organization is staffed with people who have the necessary knowledge, skill, and ability to perform their part in implementing the strategy. This goal is achieved primarily through recruitment, selection and placement, training, development, and career management—topics covered in Chapters 5, 6, 7, and 9. In addition, the HRM function must develop performance management and reward systems that lead employees to work for and support the strategic plan. The specific types of performance management systems are covered in Chapter 8, and the many issues involved in developing reward systems are discussed in Chapters 11 through 13. In other words, the role of the HRM function becomes one of (1) ensuring that the company has the proper number of employees with the levels and types of skills required by the strategic plan[28] and (2) developing "control" systems that ensure that those employees are acting in ways that promote the achievement of the goals specified in the strategic plan.[29]

In essence, this is what has been referred to as the "vertical alignment" of HR with strategy. Vertical alignment means that the HR practices and processes are aimed at addressing the strategic needs of the business. But the link between strategy and HR practices is primarily through people. For instance, as IBM moved from being a manufacturer of personal computers to being a fully integrated service provider, the types of people it needed changed significantly. Instead of employing thousands of workers in manufacturing or assembly plants, IBM increasingly needed software engineers to help write new "middleware" programs, and an army of consultants who could help their corporate customers to implement these systems. In addition, as IBM increasingly differentiated itself as being the "integrated solutions" provider (meaning it could sell the

Figure 2.7

Strategy Implementation

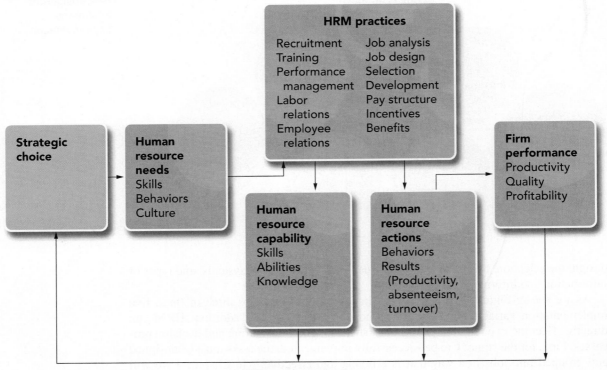

Emergent strategies

hardware, software, consulting, and service for a company's entire information technology needs), employees needed a new mindset which emphasized cooperating across different business divisions rather than running independently. Thus, the change in strategy required different kinds of skills, different kinds of employees, and different kinds of behaviors.

How does the HRM function implement strategy? As Figure 2.7 shows, it is through administering HRM practices: job analysis/design, recruitment, selection systems, training and development programs, performance management systems, reward systems, and labor relations programs. The details of each of these HRM practices are the focus of the rest of this book. However, at this point it is important to present a general overview of the HRM practices and their role in strategy implementation. We then discuss the various strategies companies pursue and the types of HRM systems congruent with those strategies. First we focus on how the strategic types are implemented; then we discuss the HRM practices associated with various directional strategies.

HRM PRACTICES

The HRM function can be thought of as having six menus of HRM practices, from which companies can choose the ones most appropriate for implementing their strategy. Each of these menus refers to a particular functional area of HRM: job analysis/design, recruitment/ selection, training and development, performance management, pay structure/incentives/ benefits, and labor–employee relations.[30] These menus are presented in Table 2.3.

Table 2.3
Menu of HRM
Practice Options

Job Analysis and Design

Few tasks	↔	Many tasks
Simple tasks	↔	Complex tasks
Few skills required	↔	Many skills required
Specific job descriptions	↔	General job descriptions

Recruitment and Selection

External sources	↔	Internal sources
Limited socialization	↔	Extensive socialization
Assessment of specific skills	↔	Assessment of general skills
Narrow career paths	↔	Broad career paths

Training and Development

Focus on current job skills	↔	Focus on future job skills
Individual orientation	↔	Group orientation
Train few employees	↔	Train all employees
Spontaneous, unplanned	↔	Planned, systematic

Performance Management

Behavioral criteria	↔	Results criteria
Developmental orientation	↔	Administrative orientation
Short-term criteria	↔	Long-term criteria
Individual orientation	↔	Group orientation

Pay Structure, Incentives, and Benefits

Pay weighted toward salary and benefits	↔	Pay weighted toward incentives
Short-term incentives	↔	Long-term incentives
Emphasis on internal equity	↔	Emphasis on external equity
Individual incentives	↔	Group incentives

Labor and Employee Relations

Collective bargaining	↔	Individual bargaining
Top-down decision making	↔	Participation in decision making
Formal due process	↔	No due process
View employees as expense	↔	View employees as assets

SOURCES: Adapted from R. S. Schuler and S. F. Jackson, "Linking Competitive Strategies with Human Resource Management Practices," *Academy of Management Executive* 1 (1987), pp. 207–19; and C. Fisher, L. Schoenfeldt, and B. Shaw, *Human Resource Management,* 2nd ed. (Boston: Houghton Mifflin, 1992).

Job Analysis and Design

Companies produce a given product or service (or set of products or services), and the manufacture of these products requires that a number of tasks be performed. These tasks are grouped together to form jobs. **Job analysis** is the process of getting detailed information about jobs. **Job design** addresses what tasks should be grouped into a particular job. The way that jobs are designed should have an important tie to the strategy of an organization because the strategy requires either new and different tasks or different ways of performing the same tasks. In addition, because many strategies entail the introduction of new technologies, this affects the way that work is performed.[31]

In general, jobs can vary from having a narrow range of tasks (most of which are simplified and require a limited range of skills) to having a broad array of complex tasks requiring multiple skills. In the past, the narrow design of jobs has been used to increase efficiency, while the broad design of jobs has been associated with efforts to increase

Job Analysis
The process of getting detailed information about jobs.

Job Design
The process of defining the way work will be performed and the tasks that will be required in a given job.

innovation. However, with the advent of total quality management methods and a variety of employee involvement programs such as quality circles, many jobs are moving toward the broader end of the spectrum.[32]

Employee Recruitment and Selection

Recruitment is the process through which the organization seeks applicants for potential employment. **Selection** refers to the process by which it attempts to identify applicants with the necessary knowledge, skills, abilities, and other characteristics that will help the company achieve its goals. Companies engaging in different strategies need different types and numbers of employees. Thus, the strategy a company is pursuing will have a direct impact on the types of employees that it seeks to recruit and select.[33]

Employee Training and Development

A number of skills are instilled in employees through training and development. **Training** refers to a planned effort to facilitate the learning of job-related knowledge, skills, and behavior by employees. **Development** involves acquiring knowledge, skills, and behavior that improve employees' ability to meet the challenges of a variety of existing jobs or jobs that do not yet exist. Changes in strategies often require changes in the types, levels, and mixes of skills. Thus, the acquisition of strategy-related skills is an essential element of the implementation of strategy. For example, many companies have recently emphasized quality in their products, engaging in total quality management programs. These programs require extensive training of all employees in the TQM philosophy, methods, and often other skills that ensure quality.[34]

Through recruitment, selection, training, and development, companies can obtain a pool of human resources capable of implementing a given strategy.[35]

Performance Management

Performance management is used to ensure that employees' activities and outcomes are congruent with the organization's objectives. It entails specifying those activities and outcomes that will result in the firm's successfully implementing the strategy. For example, companies that are "steady state" (not diversified) tend to have evaluation systems that call for subjective performance assessments of managers. This stems from the fact that those above the first-level managers in the hierarchy have extensive knowledge about how the work should be performed. On the other hand, diversified companies are more likely to use quantitative measures of performance to evaluate managers because top managers have less knowledge about how work should be performed by those below them in the hierarchy.[36]

Similarly, executives who have extensive knowledge of the behaviors that lead to effective performance use performance management systems that focus on the behaviors of their subordinate managers. However, when executives are unclear about the specific behaviors that lead to effective performance, they tend to focus on evaluating the objective performance results of their subordinate managers.[37]

An example of how performance management can be aligned with strategy is provided in Figure 2.8. This comes from a firm in the health care industry whose strategy consisted of five "strategic imperatives," or things that the company was trying to accomplish. In this company all individuals set performance objectives each year, and each of their objectives have to be tied to at least one of the strategic imperatives. The senior VP of HR used the firm's technology system to examine the extent to which each business unit or function was focused on each of the imperatives. The figure illustrates the percentage of objectives that were tied to each imperative across the different units. It

Figure 2.8

Percentage of Objectives Identified in Individual Performance Plans That Are Tied to Each Strategic Imperative

Strategic Imperative	Business A	Business B	International	Investment	Finance	Legal	IT	HR&S	Enterprise
Achieve superior medical performance	10.5%	12.5%	2.7%	7.6%	3.1%	2.7%	11.4%	2.1%	10.0%
Effectively serve our customers	24.7%	27.2%	36.7%	12.2%	10.3%	27.2%	18.9%	19.5%	23.7%
Create great products and services	5.6%	6.1%	10.1%	9.8%	5.0%	10.1%	15.3%	8.9%	6.9%
Create a winning environment	27.7%	29.7%	30.1%	29.9%	30.3%	33.7%	22.4%	39.4%	27.7%
Establish a cost advantage	31.5%	24.5%	20.5%	40.5%	51.3%	26.3%	32%	30.0%	31.7%
Total	100%	100%	100%	100%	100%	100%	100%	100%	100%

allows the company to determine if the mix of objectives is right enterprisewide as well as within each business unit or function.

Pay Structure, Incentives, and Benefits

The pay system has an important role in implementing strategies. First, a high level of pay and/or benefits relative to that of competitors can ensure that the company attracts and retains high-quality employees, but this might have a negative impact on the company's overall labor costs.[38] Second, by tying pay to performance, the company can elicit specific activities and levels of performance from employees.

In a study of how compensation practices are tied to strategies, researchers examined 33 high-tech and 72 traditional companies. They classified them by whether they were in a growth stage (greater than 20% inflation-adjusted increases in annual sales) or a maturity stage. They found that high-tech companies in the growth stage used compensation systems that were highly geared toward incentive pay, with a lower percentage of total pay devoted to salary and benefits. On the other hand, compensation systems among mature companies (both high-tech and traditional) devoted a lower percentage of total pay to incentives and a high percentage to benefits.[39]

Labor and Employee Relations

Whether companies are unionized or not, the general approach to relations with employees can strongly affect their potential for gaining competitive advantage.

Companies can choose to treat employees as an asset that requires investment of resources or as an expense to be minimized.[40] They have to make choices about how much employees can and should participate in decision making, what rights employees have, and what the company's responsibility is to them. The approach a company takes in making these decisions can result in it either successfully achieving its short- and long-term goals or ceasing to exist.

Recent research has begun to examine how companies develop sets of HRM practices that maximize performance and productivity. For example, one study of automobile assembly plants around the world found that plants that exhibited both high productivity and high quality used "HRM best practices," such as heavy emphasis on recruitment and hiring, compensation tied to performance, low levels of status differentiation, high levels of training for both new and experienced employees, and employee participation through structures such as work teams and problem-solving groups.[41] Another study found that HRM systems composed of selection testing, training, contingent pay, performance appraisal, attitude surveys, employee participation, and information sharing resulted in higher levels of productivity and corporate financial performance, as well as lower employee turnover.[42] Finally, a recent study found that companies identified as some of the "best places to work" had higher financial performances than a set of matched companies that did not make the list.[43] Similar results have also been observed in a number of other studies.[44]

In addition to the relationship between HR practices and performance in general, in today's fast-changing environment, businesses have to change quickly, requiring changes in employees' skills and behaviors. In one study the researchers found that the flexibility of HR practices, employee skills, and employee behaviors were all positively related to firm financial performance, but only the skill flexibility was related to cost efficiency.[45] While these relationships are promising, the causal direction has not yet been proven. For instance, while effective HR practices should help firms perform better, it is also true that highly profitable firms can invest more in HR practices.[46] The research seems to indicate that while the relationship between practices and performance is consistently positive, we should not go too far out on a limb arguing that increasing the use of HRM practices will automatically result in increased profitability.[47]

STRATEGIC TYPES

As we previously discussed, companies can be classified by the generic strategies they pursue. It is important to note that these generic "strategies" are not what we mean by a strategic plan. They are merely similarities in the ways companies seek to compete in their industries. Various typologies have been offered, but we focus on the two generic strategies proposed by Porter: cost and differentiation.[48]

According to Michael Porter of Harvard, competitive advantage stems from a company's being able to create value in its production process. Value can be created in one of two ways. First, value can be created by reducing costs. Second, value can be created by differentiating a product or service in such a way that it allows the company to charge a premium price relative to its competitors. This leads to two basic strategies. According to Porter, the "overall cost leadership" strategy focuses on becoming the lowest cost producer in an industry. This strategy is achieved by constructing efficient large-scale facilities, by reducing costs through capitalizing on the experience curve, and by controlling overhead costs and costs in such areas as research and development, service, sales force, and advertising. This strategy provides above-average returns within an industry, and it tends to bar other firms' entry into the industry because the firm can lower its prices below competitors' costs.

The "differentiation" strategy, according to Porter, attempts to create the impression that the company's product or service is different from that of others in the industry. The perceived differentiation can come from creating a brand image, from technology, from offering unique features, or from unique customer service. If a company succeeds in differentiating its product, it will achieve above-average returns, and the differentiation may protect it from price sensitivity. For instance, Dell Computer Company built its reputation on providing the lowest cost computers through leveraging its supply chain and direct selling model. However, recently they have seen share eroding as the consumer market grows and HP has offered more differentiated, stylish-looking computers sold through retail outlets where customers can touch and feel them. In addition, Apple has differentiated itself through its own operating system that integrates well with peripheral devices such as the iPad and iPhone. In both cases, these companies can charge a premium (albeit higher for Apple) over Dell's pricing.[49]

HRM NEEDS IN STRATEGIC TYPES

While all of the strategic types require competent people in a generic sense, each of the strategies also requires different types of employees with different types of behaviors and attitudes. As we noted earlier, different strategies require employees with specific skills and also require these employees to exhibit different "role behaviors."[50] **Role behaviors** are the behaviors required of an individual in his or her role as a jobholder in a social work environment. These role behaviors vary on a number of dimensions. Additionally, different role behaviors are required by the different strategies. For example, companies engaged in a cost strategy require employees to have a high concern for quantity and a short-term focus, to be comfortable with stability, and to be risk averse. These employees are expected to exhibit role behaviors that are relatively repetitive and performed independently or autonomously.

Thus, companies engaged in cost strategies, because of the focus on efficient production, tend to specifically define the skills they require and invest in training employees in these skill areas. They also rely on behavioral performance management systems with a large performance-based compensation component. These companies promote internally and develop internally consistent pay systems with high pay differentials between superiors and subordinates. They seek efficiency through worker participation, soliciting employees' ideas on how to achieve more efficient production.

On the other hand, employees in companies with a differentiation strategy need to be highly creative and cooperative; to have only a moderate concern for quantity, a long-term focus, and a tolerance for ambiguity; and to be risk takers. Employees in these companies are expected to exhibit role behaviors that include cooperating with others, developing new ideas, and taking a balanced approach to process and results.

Thus differentiation companies will seek to generate more creativity through broadly defined jobs with general job descriptions. They may recruit more from outside, engage in limited socialization of newcomers, and provide broader career paths. Training and development activities focus on cooperation. The compensation system is geared toward external equity, as it is heavily driven by recruiting needs. These companies develop results-based performance management system and divisional–corporate performance evaluations to encourage risk taking on the part of managers.[51]

> **Role Behaviors**
> Behaviors that are required of an individual in his or her role as a jobholder in a social work environment.

EVIDENCE-BASED HR

A study of HRM among steel minimills in the United States found that mills pursuing different strategies used different systems of HRM. Mills seeking cost leadership tended to use control-oriented HRM systems that were characterized by high centralization, low participation, low training, low wages, low benefits, and highly contingent pay, whereas differentiator mills used "commitment" HRM systems, characterized as the opposite on each of those dimensions. A later study from the same sample revealed that the mills with the commitment systems had higher productivity, lower scrap rates, and lower employee turnover than those with the control systems.

SOURCE: J. Arthur, "The Link between Business Strategy and Industrial Relations Systems in American Steel Mini-Mills," *Industrial and Labor Relations Review* 45 (1992), pp. 488–506.

DIRECTIONAL STRATEGIES

LO 2-6
Describe the different HRM issues and practices associated with various directional strategies.

As discussed earlier in this chapter, strategic typologies are useful for classifying the ways different organizations seek to compete within an industry. However, it is also necessary to understand how increasing size (growth) or decreasing it (downsizing) affects the HRM function. For example, the top management team might decide that they need to invest more in product development or to diversify as a means for growth. With these types of strategies, it is more useful for the HRM function to aid in evaluating the feasibility of the various alternatives and to develop programs that support the strategic choice.

Companies have used four possible categories of directional strategies to meet objectives.[52] Strategies emphasizing market share or operating costs are considered "concentration" strategies. With this type of strategy, a company attempts to focus on what it does best within its established markets and can be thought of as "sticking to its knitting." Strategies focusing on market development, product development, innovation, or joint ventures make up the "internal growth" strategy. Companies with an internal growth strategy channel their resources toward building on existing strengths. Those attempting to integrate vertically or horizontally or to diversify are exhibiting an **"external growth" strategy**, usually through mergers or acquisitions. This strategy attempts to expand a company's resources or to strengthen its market position through acquiring or creating new businesses. Finally, a "divestment," or downsizing, strategy is one made up of retrenchment, divestitures, or liquidation. These strategies are observed among companies facing serious economic difficulties and seeking to pare down their operations. The human resource implications of each of these strategies are quite different.

External Growth Strategy
An emphasis on acquiring vendors and suppliers or buying businesses that allow a company to expand into new markets.

Concentration Strategies

Concentration strategies require that the company maintain the current skills that exist in the organization. This requires that training programs provide a means of keeping those skills sharp among people in the organization and that compensation programs focus on retaining people who have those skills. Appraisals in this strategy tend to be more behavioral because the environment is more certain, and the behaviors necessary for effective performance tend to be established through extensive experience.

Concentration Strategy
A strategy focusing on increasing market share, reducing costs, or creating and maintaining a market niche for products and services.

Internal Growth Strategy
A focus on new market and product development, innovation, and joint ventures.

Internal Growth Strategies

Internal growth strategies present unique staffing problems. Growth requires that a company constantly hire, transfer, and promote individuals, and expansion into different markets may change the necessary skills that prospective employees must have. In addition, appraisals often consist of a combination of behaviors and results. The behavioral appraisal emphasis stems from the knowledge of effective behaviors in a particular product market, and the results appraisals focus on achieving growth goals. Compensation packages are heavily weighted toward incentives for achieving growth goals. Training needs differ depending on the way the company attempts to grow internally. For example, if the organization seeks to expand its markets, training will focus on knowledge of each market, particularly when the company is expanding into international markets. On the other hand, when the company is seeking innovation or product development, training will be of a more technical nature, as well as focusing on interpersonal skills such as team building. Joint ventures require extensive training in conflict resolution techniques because of the problems associated with combining people from two distinct organizational cultures.

Mergers and Acquisitions

Increasingly we see both consolidation within industries and mergers across industries. For example, Procter and Gamble's acquisition of Gillette represented a consolidation, or reduction in the number of firms within the industry. On the other hand, Citicorp's merger with Travelers Group to form Citigroup represented firms from different industries (pure financial services and insurance) combining to change the dynamics within both. Whatever the type, one thing is for sure—mergers and acquisitions are on the increase, and HRM needs to be involved.[53] In addition, these mergers more frequently consist of global megamergers, in spite of some warnings that these might not be effective.

According to a report by the Conference Board, "people issues" may be one of the major reasons that mergers do not always live up to expectations. Some companies now heavily weigh firm cultures before embarking on a merger or acquisition. For example, prior to acquiring ValueRx, executives at Express Scripts Inc. interviewed senior executives and middle managers at the potential target firm in order to get a sense of its culture.[54] In spite of this, fewer than one-third of the HRM executives surveyed said that they had a major influence in how mergers are planned, yet 80 percent of them said that people issues have a significant impact after the deals are finalized.[55]

In addition to the desirability of HRM playing a role in evaluating a merger opportunity, HRM certainly has a role in the actual implementation of a merger or acquisition. Training in conflict resolution is also necessary when companies engage in an external growth strategy. All the options for external growth consist of acquiring or developing new businesses, and these businesses often have distinct cultures. Thus many HRM programs face problems in integrating and standardizing practices across the company's businesses. The relative value of standardizing practices across businesses must be weighed against the unique environmental requirements of each business and the extent of desired integration of the two firms. For example, with regard to pay practices, a company may desire a consistent internal wage structure to maintain employee perceptions of equity in the larger organization. In a recent new business developed by IBM, the employees pressured the company to maintain the same wage structure as IBM's main operation. However, some businesses may function in environments where pay practices are driven heavily by market forces. Requiring these businesses to adhere to pay practices in other environments may result in an ineffective wage structure.

Downsizing

Of increasing importance to organizations in today's competitive environment is HRM's role in **downsizing** or "rightsizing." The number of organizations undergoing downsizing increased significantly from the third to the fourth quarter of 2008, and while this trend has slowed, layoffs are still significant (see Figure 2.9).[56] In fact, some of these layoffs are due to outright bankruptcies because firms simply did not have sustainable business models. For instance the "Competing through Sustainability" box describes how rather than laying off employees, Starbucks has begun offering to pay for their college degrees.

One would have great difficulty ignoring the massive "war for talent" that went on during the late 1990s, particularly with the notable dot-com craze. Firms during this time sought to become "employers of choice," to establish "employment brands," and to develop "employee value propositions" as ways to ensure that they would be able to attract and retain talented employees.

The current economic crisis means that one important question facing firms is, How can we develop a reputation as an employer of choice, and engage employees to the goals of the firm, while laying off a significant portion of our workforce? How firms answer this question will determine how they can compete by meeting the stakeholder needs of their employees.

In spite of the increasing frequency of downsizing, research reveals that it is far from universally successful for achieving the goals of increased productivity and increased

Downsizing
The planned elimination of large numbers of personnel, designed to enhance organizational effectiveness.

Starbucks Employees Go to School

As the U.S. economy recovers and the labor market tightens, employers have to do more to attract and retain talent. McDonald's Corp. will raise wages for many employees by more than 10%, Wal-Mart Stores Inc. is raising hourly pay to $10 for 500,000 workers next year, and Starbucks Corp. will pay for its employees' college tuition.

Starbucks' tuition program is the next step in a partnership with Arizona State University, in which it will reimburse employees who work at least 20 hours a week for their tuition expenses to receive an online bachelor's degree from ASU. The catch? Starbucks will only reimburse the cost of classes for which employees receive passing grades and can only be used to pay for the last two years of a bachelor's degree.

Starbucks expects that by 2025 this program will cost $250 million and have helped 25,000 employees receive their degrees. It hopes this program will help it to retain the 144,000 people it employs in the United States while also giving back to its employees. Individuals who participate may stop the program and/or terminate their employment with Starbucks at any time with no penalty. As the market improves for job seekers, companies must take action to become an employer of choice to retain their human talent.

DISCUSSION QUESTION

What traits help promote a company as an employer of choice?

SOURCE: I. Brat, "Starbucks to Pay Full Cost of Online Degree for Employees," *The Wall Street Journal,* April 6, 2015, www.wsj.com.

Figure 2.9

Layoff Events and Separations 2009–2013

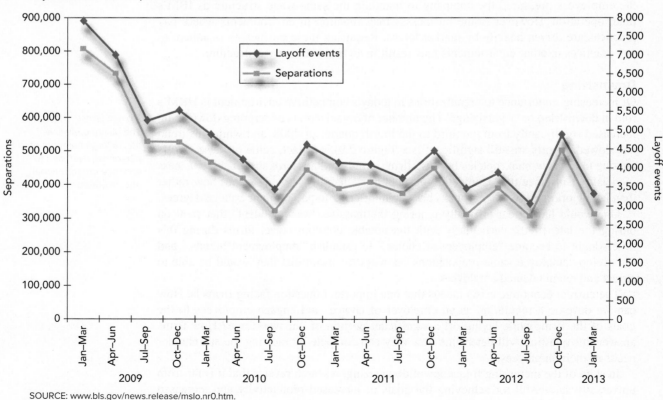

DESIRED OUTCOME	PERCENTAGE THAT ACHIEVED DESIRED RESULT
Reduced expenses	46%
Increased profits	32
Improved cash flow	24
Increased profits	22
Increased return on investment	21
Increased competitive advantage	19
Reduced bureaucracy	17
Improved decision making	14
Increased customer satisfaction	14
Increased sales	13
Increased market share	12
Improved product quality	9
Technological advances	9
Increased innovation	7
Avoidance of a takeover	6

Table 2.4
Effects of
Downsizing on
Desired Outcomes

SOURCE: From *Wall Street Journal* by News Corporation; Dow Jones & Co, June 6, 1991. Reproduced with permission of Dow Jones & Company via Copyright Clearance Center.

profitability. For example, Table 2.4 illustrates the results of a survey conducted by the American Management Association indicating that only about one-third of the companies that went through downsizings actually achieved their goal of increased profits. Another survey by the AMA found that over two-thirds of the companies that downsize repeat the effort a year later.[57] Also, research by the consulting firm Mitchell & Company found that companies that downsized during the 1980s lagged the industry average stock price in 1991.[58] Thus it is important to understand the best ways of managing downsizings, particularly from the standpoint of HRM.

Downsizing presents a number of challenges and opportunities for HRM.[59] In terms of challenges, the HRM function must "surgically" reduce the workforce by cutting only the workers who are less valuable in their performance. Achieving this is difficult because the best workers are most able (and often willing) to find alternative employment and may leave voluntarily prior to any layoff. For example, in 1992 General Motors and the United Auto Workers agreed to an early retirement program for individuals between the ages of 51 and 65 who had been employed for 10 or more years. The program provided those who agreed to retire their full pension benefits, even if they obtained employment elsewhere, and as much as $13,000 toward the purchase of a GM car.[60] As mentioned earlier in the chapter, this is part of GM's labor cost problem.

Early retirement programs, although humane, essentially reduce the workforce with a "grenade" approach. This type of reduction does not distinguish between good and poor performers but rather eliminates an entire group of employees. In fact, recent research indicates that when companies downsize by offering early retirement programs, they usually end up rehiring to replace essential talent within a year. Often the company does not achieve its cost-cutting goals because it spends 50 to 150% of the departing employee's salary in hiring and retraining new workers.[61]

Another HRM challenge is to boost the morale of employees who remain after the reduction; this is discussed in greater detail in Chapter 5. Survivors may feel guilt over keeping their jobs when their friends have been laid off, or they may envy their friends who have retired with attractive severance and pension benefits. Their reduced satisfaction with and commitment to the organization may interfere with work performance. Thus the HRM function must maintain open communication with remaining employees to build their trust and commitment rather than withholding information.[62] All employees should be informed of the purpose of the downsizing, the costs to be cut, the duration of the downsizing, and the strategies to be pursued. In addition, companies going through downsizing often develop compensation programs that tie the individual's compensation to the company's success. Employee ownership programs often result from downsizing, and gainsharing plans such as the Scanlon plan (discussed in Chapter 12) originated in companies facing economic difficulties.

In spite of these challenges, downsizing provides opportunities for HRM. First, it often allows the company to "get rid of dead wood" and make way for fresh ideas. In addition, downsizing is often a unique opportunity to change an organization's culture. In firms characterized by antagonistic labor–management relations, downsizing can force the parties to cooperate and to develop new, positive relationships.[63] Finally, downsizing can demonstrate to top-management decision makers the value of the company's human resources to its ultimate success. The role of HRM is to effectively manage the process in a way that makes this value undeniable. We discuss the implications of downsizing as a labor force management strategy in Chapter 5.

STRATEGY EVALUATION AND CONTROL

A final component to the strategic management process is that of strategy evaluation and control. Thus far we have focused on the planning and implementation of strategy. However, it is extremely important for the firm to constantly monitor the effectiveness of both the strategy and the implementation process. This monitoring makes it possible for the company to identify problem areas and either revise existing structures and strategies or devise new ones. In this process we see emergent strategies appear as well as the critical nature of human resources in competitive advantage.

The Role of Human Resources in Providing Strategic Competitive Advantage

Thus far we have presented the strategic management process as including a step-by-step procedure by which HRM issues are raised prior to deciding on a strategy and then HRM practices are developed to implement that strategy. However, we must note that human resources can provide a strategic competitive advantage in two additional ways: through emergent strategies and through enhancing competitiveness.

EMERGENT STRATEGIES

Having discussed the process of strategic management, we also must distinguish between intended strategies and emergent strategies. Most people think of strategies as being proactive, rational decisions aimed toward some predetermined goal. The view of strategy we have presented thus far in the chapter focuses on intended strategies. Intended strategies are the result of the rational decision-making process used by top managers as they develop a strategic plan. This is consistent with the definition of strategy as "the pattern or plan that integrates an organization's major goals, policies, and action sequences into a cohesive whole."[64] The idea of emergent strategies is evidenced by the feedback loop in Figure 2.2.

Most strategies that companies espouse are intended strategies. For example, when Howard Schultz founded Starbucks, he had the idea of creating a third place (between work and home) where people could enjoy traditional Italian-style coffee. He knew that the smell of the coffee and the deeper, darker, stronger taste would attract a new set of customers to enjoy coffee the way he thought it should be enjoyed. This worked, but as Starbucks grew, customers began asking if they could have non-fat milk in their lattes, or if they could get flavor shots in their coffees. Schultz swore that such things would essentially pollute the coffee and refused to offer them. Finally, after repeated requests from his store managers who kept hearing customers demanding such things, Schultz finally relented.[65]

Emergent strategies, on the other hand, consist of the strategies that evolve from the grassroots of the organization and can be thought of as what organizations actually do, as opposed to what they intend to do. Strategy can also be thought of as "a pattern in a stream of decisions or actions."[66] For example, when Honda Motor Company first entered the U.S. market with its 250-cc and 350-cc motorcycles in 1959, it believed that no market existed for its smaller 50-cc bike. However, the sales on the larger motorcycles were sluggish, and Japanese executives running errands around Los Angeles on Honda 50s attracted a lot of attention, including that of a buyer with Sears, Roebuck. Honda found a previously undiscovered market as well as a new distribution outlet (general retailers) that it had not planned on. This emergent strategy gave Honda a 50% market share by 1964.[67]

The distinction between intended and emergent strategies has important implications for human resource management.[68] The new focus on strategic HRM has tended to focus primarily on intended strategies. Thus HRM's role has been seen as identifying for top management the people-related business issues relevant to strategy formulation and then developing HRM systems that aid in the implementation of the strategic plan.

However, most emergent strategies are identified by those lower in the organizational hierarchy. It is often the rank-and-file employees who provide ideas for new markets, new products, and new strategies. HRM plays an important role in facilitating communication throughout the organization, and it is this communication that allows for effective emergent strategies to make their way up to top management. For example, Starbucks' Frappuccino was a drink invented by one of the store employees in California; Starbucks leaders (including Schultz) thought it was a terrible idea. They fought it in a number of meetings, but the employee kept getting more and more information supporting her case for how much customers seemed to like it. The leaders finally gave the go-ahead to begin producing it, and it has become a $1 billion a year product, and one that has contributed to the Starbucks brand.[69]

ENHANCING FIRM COMPETITIVENESS

A related way in which human resources can be a source of competitive advantage is through developing a human capital pool that gives the company the unique ability to adapt to an ever-changing environment. Recently managers have become interested in the idea of a "learning organization," in which people continually expand their capacity to achieve the results they desire.[70] This requires the company to be in a constant state of learning through monitoring the environment, assimilating information, making decisions, and flexibly restructuring to compete in that environment. Companies that develop such learning capability have a competitive advantage. Although certain organizational information-processing systems can be an aid, ultimately the people (human capital) who make up the company provide the raw materials in a learning organization.[71]

Thus, the role of human resources in competitive advantage should continue to increase because of the fast-paced change characterizing today's business environment. It is becoming increasingly clear that even as U.S. automakers have improved the quality of their cars to compete with the Japanese, these competitors have developed such flexible and adaptable manufacturing systems that they can respond to customer needs more quickly.[72] This flexibility of the manufacturing process allows the emergent strategy to come directly from the marketplace by determining and responding to the exact mix of customer desires. It requires, however, that the company have people in place who have the skills to similarly adapt quickly.[73] As Howard Schultz says, "If people relate to the company they work for, if they form an emotional tie to it and buy into its dreams, they will pour their heart into making it better. When employees have self-esteem and self-respect they can contribute so much more; to their company, to their family, to the world."[74] This statement exemplifies the increasing importance of human resources in developing and maintaining competitive advantage.[75]

A LOOK BACK

Southwest's Strategic HRM

Southwest Airlines' challenges face every company sooner or later. While firm success can be sustained for a number of years, at some point competition begins to take its toll. In addition, with changes in leadership (Herb Kelleher retired from the CEO role and handed it off to Gary Kelly in 2004), it is difficult to maintain the same strong culture. This has profound effects on how people must be managed to sustain success amid a changing competitive landscape.

In spite of these challenges, Southwest's performance remains strong. The airline made a record $1.1 billion in profits in 2014, almost twice as much as in 2013. In addition the airline will continue to expand internationally, providing new opportunities for revenue growth.

QUESTIONS

1. What do you think has made Southwest Airlines so successful?
2. What do you think are the major challenges facing Southwest?
3. How would a strategic approach to HRM help Southwest successfully address these challenges?

SUMMARY

A strategic approach to human resource management seeks to proactively provide a competitive advantage through the company's most important asset: its human resources. While human resources are the most important asset, they are also usually the single largest controllable cost within the firm's business model. The HRM function needs to be integrally involved in the formulation of strategy to identify the people-related business issues the company faces. Once the strategy has been determined, HRM has a profound impact on the implementation of the plan by developing and aligning HRM practices that ensure that the company has motivated employees with the necessary skills. Finally, the emerging strategic role of the HRM function requires that HR professionals in the future develop business, professional–technical, change management, and integration competencies. As you will see more clearly in later chapters, this strategic approach requires more than simply developing a valid selection procedure or state-of-the-art performance management systems. Only through these competencies can the HR professional take a strategic approach to human resource management.

KEY TERMS

Strategic human resource management (SHRM), 71
Strategy formulation, 72
Strategy implementation, 72

Goals, 77
External analysis, 77
Internal analysis, 77
Strategic choice, 78

Job analysis, 83
Job design, 83
Recruitment, 84
Selection, 84

DISCUSSION QUESTIONS

1. Pick one of your university's major sports teams (like football or basketball). How would you characterize that team's generic strategy? How does the composition of the team members (in terms of size, speed, ability, and so on) relate to that strategy? What are the strengths and weaknesses of the team? How do they dictate the team's generic strategy and its approach to a particular game?

2. Do you think that it is easier to tie human resources to the strategic management process in large or in small organizations? Why?

3. Consider one of the organizations you have been affiliated with. What are some examples of human resource practices that were consistent with that organization's strategy?

What are examples of practices that were inconsistent with its strategy?

4. How can strategic management within the HRM department ensure that HRM plays an effective role in the company's strategic management process?

5. What types of specific skills (such as knowledge of financial accounting methods) do you think HR professionals will need to have the business, professional-technical, change management, and integrative competencies necessary in the future? Where can you develop each of these skills?

6. What are some of the key environmental variables that you see changing in the business world today? What impact will those changes have on the HRM function in organizations?

SELF-ASSESSMENT EXERCISE

Mc Graw Hill Education **connect**
Additional assignable self-assessments available in Connect.

Think of a company you have worked for, or find an annual report for a company you are interested in working for. (Many companies post their annual reports online at their website.) Then answer the following questions.

QUESTIONS

1. How has the company been affected by the trends discussed in this chapter?

2. Does the company use the HR practices recommended in this chapter?

3. What else should the company do to deal with the challenges posed by the trends discussed in this chapter?

EXERCISING STRATEGY

Strategy and HRM at Delta Airlines

In 1994 top executives at Delta Air Lines faced a crucial strategic decision. Delta, which had established an unrivaled reputation within the industry for having highly committed employees who delivered the highest quality customer service, had lost more than $10 per share for two straight years. A large portion of its financial trouble was due to the $491 million acquisition of Pan Am in 1991, which was followed by the Gulf War (driving up fuel costs) and the early 1990s recession (causing people to fly less). Its cost per available seat mile (the cost to fly one passenger one mile) was 9.26 cents, among the highest in the industry. In addition, it was threatened by new discount competitors with significantly lower costs—in particular, Valujet, which flew out of Delta's Atlanta hub. How could Delta

survive and thrive in such an environment? Determining the strategy for doing so was the top executives' challenge.

Chairman and chief executive officer Ron Allen embarked upon the "Leadership 7.5" strategy, whose goal was to reduce the cost per available seat mile to 7.5 cents, comparable with Southwest Airlines. Implementing this strategy required a significant downsizing over the following three years, trimming 11,458 people from its 69,555-employee workforce (the latter number representing an 8% reduction from two years earlier). Many experienced customer service representatives were laid off and replaced with lower paid, inexperienced, part-time workers. Cleaning service of planes as well as baggage handling were outsourced, resulting in layoffs of long-term Delta employees. The numbers of maintenance workers and flight attendants were reduced substantially.

The results of the strategy were mixed as financial performance improved but operational performance plummeted. Since it began its cost cutting, its stock price more than doubled in just over two years and its debt was upgraded. On the other hand, customer complaints about dirty airplanes rose from 219 in 1993 to 358 in 1994 and 634 in 1995. On-time performance was so bad that passengers joked that Delta stands for "Doesn't Ever Leave The Airport." Delta slipped from fourth to seventh among the top 10 carriers in baggage handling. Employee morale hit an all-time low, and unions were beginning to make headway toward organizing some of Delta's employee groups. In 1996 CEO Allen was quoted as saying, "This has tested our people. There have been some morale problems. But so be it. You go back to the question of survival, and it makes the decision very easy."

Shortly after, employees began donning cynical "so be it" buttons. Delta's board saw union organizers stirring blue-collar discontent, employee morale destroyed, the customer service reputation in near shambles, and senior managers exiting the company in droves. Less than one year later, Allen was fired despite Delta's financial turnaround. His firing was "not because the company was going broke, but because its spirit was broken."

Delta's Leadership 7.5 strategy destroyed the firm's core competence of a highly experienced, highly skilled, and highly committed workforce that delivered the highest quality customer service in the industry. HRM might have affected the strategy by pointing out the negative impact that this strategy would have on the firm. Given the strategy and competitive environment, Delta might have sought to implement the cost cutting differently to reduce the cost structure but preserve its source of differentiation.

The present state of Delta provides further support to these conclusions. With the family atmosphere dissolved and the bond between management and rank-and-file employees broken, employees have begun to seek other ways to gain voice and security. By fall 2001 Delta had two union organizing drives under way with both the flight attendants and the mechanics. In addition, labor costs have been driven up as a result of the union activity. The pilots signed a lucrative five-year contract that will place them at the highest pay in the industry. In an effort to head off the organizing drive, the mechanics were recently given raises to similarly put them at the industry top. Now the flight attendants are seeking industry-leading pay regardless of, but certainly encouraged by, the union drive.[76]

The Delta Air Lines story provides a perfect example of the perils that can await firms that fail to adequately address human resource issues in the formulation and implementation of strategy.

QUESTIONS

1. How does the experience of Delta Air Lines illustrate the interdependence between strategic decisions of "how to compete" and "with what to compete"? Consider this with regard to both strategy formulation and strategy implementation.

2. If you were in charge of HRM for Delta Air Lines now, what would be your major priorities?

SOURCES: M. Brannigan and E. De Lisser, "Cost Cutting at Delta Raises the Stock Price but Lowers the Service," *The Wall Street Journal,* June 20, 1996, pp. A1, A8; M. Brannigan and J. White, "So Be It: Why Delta Air Lines Decided It Was Time for CEO to Take Off," *The Wall Street Journal,* May 30, 1997, p. A1.

MANAGING PEOPLE

Is Dell Too Big for Michael Dell?

He's back in charge—and he may have the toughest job in the computer business. Welcome back, Michael. Don't get too comfortable.

By returning to the top job at Dell Inc., replacing departing chief executive Kevin Rollins, founder Michael S. Dell takes on perhaps the toughest job in the computer industry. Since mid-2005 the PC maker has battled problems with customer service, quality, and the effectiveness of its direct-sales model. Lately, rivals Hewlett-Packard Co. and Apple Inc. have been gaining in sales and market share. On January 31, the day Rollins's departure was announced, the Round Rock (Texas) company disclosed that its fourth-quarter earnings and sales would fall short of analyst estimates. It's also under scrutiny by the Securities & Exchange Commission and a U.S. attorney for accounting irregularities.

As recently as last November, Dell insisted to *Business-Week* that Rollins's job was safe. Now, in an interview, he insists the decision to push Rollins out started with him. "I recommended to our board that I become the CEO," Dell says. For years, Dell and Rollins were held up as a prime example of the company's "two-in-a-box" management structure, in which two leaders worked together in lockstep. When Rollins was president, Michael Dell was CEO; when Rollins was promoted to CEO in 2004, Michael remained chairman. But financial performance has been deteriorating for a while now, and Michael Dell apparently ran out of patience in light of the latest disappointment. "People are looking forward to a change," said an analyst at one of Dell's largest institutional shareholders. Indeed, the company's share price jumped 3.6% in the couple of hours after the shift was announced.

But does Michael Dell have what it takes to turn the company around? It's been years since he shouldered day-to-day operational responsibility on his own. Since the early 1990s, Dell has always had a strong No. 2; back then, the company had less than $3 billion in yearly sales. Today it is a $60 billion company. But Dell says he has a clear plan. He believes the company's supply chain and manufacturing can be improved. "I think you're going to see a more streamlined organization, with a much clearer strategy."

But none of the paths to improve performance will be easy. Dell doesn't have the innovation DNA of an Apple or even an HP, should it want to overhaul its utilitarian products and services. Any effort to crank up R&D would crimp margins. Trying to win over more consumers, the fastest-growing part of the market, may well require a move away from its direct-sales model into retail. That could prove costly as well. Dell himself says he doesn't anticipate leaving the direct-sales model behind: "It's a significant strength of the company." Nor does a big acquisition seem to be an option, given that Dell has never done one in the past.

Slots to fill

But standing in place also looks hazardous, since Dell may now be slipping in its core corporate business, too. According to a January 30 study done by Goldman, Sachs & Co., Dell is losing share in business spending for PCs. (Hewlett-Packard is also losing share of spending, while Lenovo and Apple are gaining.) "Dell's troubles seem to be bleeding into its corporate business, which, up until now, had been a stronghold," the report said. Dell has also lost the top spot in the worldwide PC market-share rankings. In the fourth quarter, Hewlett-Packard's worldwide market share grew to 18.1%, while Dell's share dropped to 14.7%, according to market researcher IDC.

Dell also has several slots to fill in the executive suite; Rollins is only the latest departure among key managers. But for the first time in years, the tough choices will be solely in the lap of the man who started the company in his University of Texas dorm room back in 1984. "I'm not hiring a COO or a CEO," Dell says, "I'm going to be the CEO for the next several years." He adds: "We're going to fix this business."

QUESTIONS

1. How does the case describe Dell's transformed strategy over the years in terms of where to compete, how to compete, and with what to compete?
2. What are the major people issues that exist as Michael Dell retakes the reins at Dell?
3. How would HR help in addressing the issues that Dell faces?

SOURCE: From L. Lee and P. Burrows, "Is Dell Too Big for Michael Dell?" *BusinessWeek*, April 4, 2007. Used with permission of Bloomberg L. P. Copyright © 2013. All rights reserved.

HR IN SMALL BUSINESS

Radio Flyer Rolls Forward

The mid-2000s were a difficult time for Radio Flyer, a private business famous for its little red wagons. After spending hundreds of thousands of dollars to develop what they hoped was a hit, managers realized their idea wouldn't fly, so they killed it. And in the same year, management decided the company could no longer afford to build wagons in the United States.

First, the development flop: Thomas Schlegel, vice president for product development, thought he had a winner with an idea for a collapsible wagon to be called Fold 2 Go Wagon. It would be a fun product that parents could fold up and toss into the back of a minivan for a trip to the park or other outings. The problem was, a collapsing toy that children sit inside is difficult to make both functional and safe. The costs were excessive.

When Schlegel ended the project, he feared his reputation might suffer as well. But CEO Robert Pasin assured Schlegel that failure was acceptable as long as the company could learn from it. The value placed on learning became something that Schlegel capitalized on as his team applied what they learned to the development of a new success, the Twist Trike and a new model of its wagons called the Ultimate Family Wagon. Furthermore, Pasin expanded that one experience into a teaching opportunity. He invites new employees to join him for breakfasts, during which he recalls the incident as a way to reinforce the company's commitment to innovation and learning.

The story of Radio Flyer's need to outsource manufacturing has what some might see as a less-happy ending. Looking at the numbers, management determined that it would have to close its factory in Chicago and lay off about half of its workforce. Manufacturing moved to a factory in China. Pasin describes the effort as "an incredibly difficult time."

The company's effort with its remaining U.S. employees focused on building morale. These efforts include creating ideas for employees to have fun and pursue their passions, with events such as the Radio Flyer Olympics, during which employees compete in silly contests like tricycle races. More seriously, teams of employees tackle issues that they care about. The wellness committee put together a cash benefit that pays employees up to $300 for participating in health-related activities such as weight-loss counseling or running races. Another committee brought together employees concerned about the environment. They assembled a campaign aimed at persuading employees to reduce their carbon footprint.

In caring for the U.S. employees, Radio Flyer hasn't forgotten the ones in China. The company tries to maintain similar levels of benefits and engagement among the four dozen employees in its China office.

QUESTIONS

1. How could a human resource manager help Radio Flyer get the maximum benefit from the motivational efforts described in this case?
2. Do you think outsourcing would be harder on employees in a small company such as Radio Flyer than in a large corporation? Why or why not? How could HRM help to smooth the transition?
3. What additional developments described in this chapter could help Radio Flyer live out the high value it places on learning and innovation?

SOURCES: Company website, www.radioflyer.com, accessed May 24, 2015; "Best Places to Work 2015 in Chicago: #7 Radio Flyer," *Crain's Chicago Business,* www.chicagobusiness.com, accessed May 24, 2015; J. Scanlon, "Radio Flyer Learns from a Crash," *Bloomberg Businessweek,* www.businessweek.com, accessed May 24, 2015.

NOTES

1. J. Barney, "Firm Resources and Sustained Competitive Advantage," *Journal of Management* 17 (1991), pp. 99–120.
2. L. Dyer, "Strategic Human Resource Management and Planning," in *Research in Personnel and Human Resources Management,* ed. K. Rowland and G. Ferris (Greenwich, CT: JAI Press, 1985), pp. 1–30.
3. P. Ingrassia, "GM's Plan: Subsidize Our 48-Year-Old Retirees," *Wall Street Journal,* February 19, 2009, http://online.wsj.com/article/SB123500874299418721.html.
4. S. Terlep, and N. King, "Bondholders say GM's Plan Fails to Tackle Issues," *The Wall Street Journal,* February 19, 2009, http://online.wsj.com/article/SB123500467245718075.html?mod=testMod.
5. J. Quinn, *Strategies for Change: Logical Incrementalism* (Homewood, IL: Richard D. Irwin, 1980).
6. M. Porter, *Competitive Strategy: Techniques for Analyzing Industries and Competitors* (New York: Free Press, 1980).
7. R. Miles and C. Snow, *Organizational Strategy, Structure, and Process* (New York: McGraw-Hill, 1978).
8. P. Wright and G. McMahan, "Theoretical Perspectives for Strategic Human Resource Management," *Journal of Management* 18 (1992), pp. 295–320.
9. D. Guest, "Human Resource Management, Corporate Performance and Employee Well-Being: Building the Worker into HRM," *Journal of Industrial Relations* 44 (2002), pp. 335–58; B. Becker, M. Huselid, P. Pinckus, and M. Spratt, "HR as a Source of Shareholder Value: Research and Recommendations," *Human Resource Management* 36 (1997), pp. 39–47.
10. P. Boxall and J. Purcell, *Strategy and Human Resource Management* (Basingstoke, Hants, U.K.: Palgrave MacMillan, 2003).
11. F. Biddle and J. Helyar, "Behind Boeing's Woes: Chunky Assembly Line, Price War with Airbus," *The Wall Street Journal,* April 24, 1998, pp. A1, A16.
12. K. Martell and S. Carroll, "How Strategic Is HRM?" *Human Resource Management* 34 (1995), pp. 253–67.
13. K. Golden and V. Ramanujam, "Between a Dream and a Nightmare: On the Integration of the Human Resource Function and the Strategic Business Planning Process," *Human Resource Management* 24 (1985), pp. 429–51.
14. P. Wright, B. Dunford, and S. Snell, "Contributions of the Resource-Based View of the Firm to the Field of Strategic HRM: Convergence of Two Fields," *Journal of Management* 27 (2001), pp. 701–21.
15. J. Purcell, N. Kinnie, S. Hutchinson, B. Rayton, and J. Swart, *Understanding the People and Performance Link: Unlocking the Black Box* (London: CIPD, 2003).
16. P. M. Wright, T. Gardner, and L. Moynihan, "The Impact of Human Resource Practices on Business Unit Operating and Financial Performance," *Human Resource Management Journal* 13, no. 3 (2003), pp. 21–36.
17. C. Hill and G. Jones, *Strategic Management Theory: An Integrated Approach* (Boston: Houghton Mifflin, 1989).
18. W. Johnston and A. Packer, *Workforce 2000: Work and Workers for the Twenty-First Century* (Indianapolis, IN: Hudson Institute, 1987).
19. "Labor Letter," *The Wall Street Journal,* December 15, 1992, p. A1.
20. P. Wright, G. McMahan, and A. McWilliams, "Human Resources and Sustained Competitive Advantage: A Resource-Based Perspective," *International Journal of Human Resource Management* 5 (1994), pp. 301–26.
21. P. Buller, "Successful Partnerships: HR and Strategic Planning at Eight Top Firms," *Organizational Dynamics* 17 (1988), pp. 27–42.
22. M. Hitt, R. Hoskisson, and J. Harrison, "Strategic Competitiveness in the 1990s: Challenges and Opportunities for U.S. Executives," *The Executive* 5 (May 1991), pp. 7–22.
23. P. Wright, G. McMahan, B. McCormick, and S. Sherman, "Strategy, Core Competence, and HR Involvement as Determinants of HR Effectiveness and Refinery Performance." Paper presented at the 1996 International Federation of Scholarly Associations in Management, Paris, France.
24. N. Bennett, D. Ketchen, and E. Schultz, "Antecedents and Consequences of Human Resource Integration with Strategic Decision Making." Paper presented at the 1995 Academy of Management Meeting, Vancouver, BC, Canada.
25. Golden and Ramanujam, "Between a Dream and a Nightmare."
26. J. Galbraith and R. Kazanjian, *Strategy Implementation: Structure, Systems, and Process* (St. Paul, MN: West, 1986).
27. B. Schneider and A. Konz, "Strategic Job Analysis," *Human Resource Management* 27 (1989), pp. 51–64.
28. P. Wright and S. Snell, "Toward an Integrative View of Strategic Human Resource Management," *Human Resource Management Review* 1 (1991), pp. 203–25.
29. S. Snell, "Control Theory in Strategic Human Resource Management: The Mediating Effect of Administrative Information," *Academy of Management Journal* 35 (1992), pp. 292–327.
30. R. Schuler, "Personnel and Human Resource Management Choices and Organizational Strategy," in *Readings in Personnel and Human Resource Management,* 3rd ed., ed. R. Schuler, S. Youngblood, and V. Huber (St. Paul, MN: West, 1988).
31. J. Dean and S. Snell, "Integrated Manufacturing and Job Design: Moderating Effects of Organizational Inertia," *Academy of Management Journal* 34 (1991), pp. 776–804.
32. E. Lawler, *The Ultimate Advantage: Creating the High Involvement Organization* (San Francisco: Jossey-Bass, 1992).

33. J. Olian and S. Rynes, "Organizational Staffing: Integrating Practice with Strategy," *Industrial Relations* 23 (1984), pp. 170–83.

34. G. Smith, "Quality: Small and Midsize Companies Seize the Challenge—Not a Moment Too Soon," *BusinessWeek,* November 30, 1992, pp. 66–75.

35. J. Kerr and E. Jackofsky, "Aligning Managers with Strategies: Management Development versus Selection," *Strategic Management Journal* 10 (1989), pp. 157–70.

36. J. Kerr, "Strategic Control through Performance Appraisal and Rewards," *Human Resource Planning* 11 (1988), pp. 215–23.

37. Snell, "Control Theory in Strategic Human Resource Management."

38. B. Gerhart and G. Milkovich, "Employee Compensation: Research and Practice," in *Handbook of Industrial and Organizational Psychology,* 2nd ed., ed. M. Dunnette and L. Hough (Palo Alto, CA: Consulting Psychologists Press, 1992), pp. 481–569.

39. D. Balkin and L. Gomez-Mejia, "Toward a Contingency Theory of Compensation Strategy," *Strategic Management Journal* 8 (1987), pp. 169–82.

40. S. Cronshaw and R. Alexander, "One Answer to the Demand for Accountability: Selection Utility as an Investment Decision," *Organizational Behavior and Human Decision Processes* 35 (1986), pp. 102–18.

41. P. MacDuffie, "Human Resource Bundles and Manufacturing Performance: Organizational Logic and Flexible Production Systems in the World Auto Industry," *Industrial and Labor Relations Review* 48 (1995), pp. 197–221; P. McGraw, "A Hard Drive to the Top," *U.S. News & World Report* 118 (1995), pp. 43–44.

42. M. Huselid, "The Impact of Human Resource Management Practices on Turnover, Productivity, and Corporate Financial Performance," *Academy of Management Journal* 38 (1995), pp. 635–72.

43. B. Fulmer, B. Gerhart, and K. Scott, "Are the 100 Best Better? An Empirical Investigation of the Relationship between Being a 'Great Place to Work' and Firm Performance," *Personnel Psychology* 56 (2003), pp. 965–93.

44. J. E. Delery and D. H. Doty, "Modes of Theorizing in Strategic Human Resource Management: Tests of Universalistic, Contingency and Configurational Performance Predictions," *Academy of Management Journal* 39 (1996), pp. 802–83; D. Guest, J. Michie, N. Conway, and M. Sheehan, "Human Resource Management and Corporate Performance in the UK," *British Journal of Industrial Relations* 41 (2003), pp. 291–314; J. Guthrie, "High Involvement Work Practices, Turnover, and Productivity: Evidence from New Zealand," *Academy of Management Journal* 44 (2001), pp. 180–192; J. Harter, F. Schmidt, and T. Hayes, "Business-Unit-Level Relationship between Employee Satisfaction, Employee Engagement, and Business Outcomes: A Meta-analysis," *Journal of Applied Psychology* 87 (2002), pp. 268–79; Watson Wyatt, Worldwide, "Human Capital Index®: Human Capital as a Lead Indicator of Shareholder Value" (2002).

45. M. Bhattacharya, D. Gibson, and H. Doty, "The Effects of Flexibility in Employee Skills, Employee Behaviors, and Human Resource Practices on Firm Performance," *Journal of Management* 31 (2005), pp. 622–40.

46. D. Guest, J. Michie, N. Conway, and M. Sheehan, "Human Resource Management and Corporate Performance in the UK," *British Journal of Industrial Relations* 41 (2003), pp. 291–314; P. Wright, T. Gardner, L. Moynihan, and M. Allen, "The HR–Performance Relationship: Examining Causal Direction," *Personnel Psychology* 58 (2005), pp. 409–76.

47. P. Wright, *No Strategy: Adaptive to the Age of Globalization* (Arlington, VA: SHRM Foundation, 2008).

48. M. Porter, *Competitive Advantage* (New York: Free Press, 1985).

49. C. Lawton, "How HP Reclaimed Its PC Lead over Dell," June 2007; "Can Dell's Turnaround Strategy Keep HP at Bay?"

September 2007, *Knowledge@Wharton,* http://knowledge.wharton.upenn.edu/article.cfm?articleid51799.

50. R. Schuler and S. Jackson, "Linking Competitive Strategies with Human Resource Management Practices," *Academy of Management Executive* 1 (1987), pp. 207–19.

51. R. Miles and C. Snow, "Designing Strategic Human Resource Management Systems," *Organizational Dynamics* 13, no. 1 (1984), pp. 36–52.

52. A. Thompson and A. Strickland, *Strategy Formulation and Implementation: Tasks of the General Manager,* 3rd ed. (Plano, TX: BPI, 1986).

53. J. Schmidt, *Making Mergers Work: The Strategic Importance of People* (Arlington, VA: SHRM Foundation, 2003).

54. G. Fairclough, "Business Bulletin," *The Wall Street Journal,* March 5, 1998, p. A1.

55. P. Sebastian, "Business Bulletin," *The Wall Street Journal,* October 2, 1997, p. A1.

56. www.bls.gov/news.release/mslo.nro.gov.

57. S. Pearlstein, "Corporate Cutback Yet to Pay Off," *Washington Post,* January 4, 1994, p. B6.

58. K. Cameron, "Guest Editor's Note: Investigating Organizational Downsizing—Fundamental Issues," *Human Resource Management* 33 (1994), pp. 183–88.

59. W. Cascio, *Responsible Restructuring: Creative and Profitable Alternatives to Layoffs* (San Francisco: Berrett-Koehler, 2002).

60. N. Templin, "UAW to Unveil Pact on Slashing GM's Payroll," *The Wall Street Journal,* December 15, 1992, p. A3.

61. J. Lopez, "Managing: Early-Retirement Offers Lead to Renewed Hiring," *The Wall Street Journal,* January 26, 1993, p. B1.

62. A. Church, "Organizational Downsizing: What Is the Role of the Practitioner?" *Industrial–Organizational Psychologist* 33, no. 1 (1995), pp. 63–74.

63. N. Templin, "A Decisive Response to Crisis Brought Ford Enhanced Productivity," *The Wall Street Journal,* December 15, 1992, p. A1.

64. Quinn, *Strategies for Change.*

65. H. Schultz and D. Yang, *Pour Your Heart Into It* (New York: Hyperion, 1987).

66. R. Pascale, "Perspectives on Strategy: The Real Story behind Honda's Success," *California Management Review* 26 (1984), pp. 47–72.

67. Templin, "A Decisive Response to Crisis."

68. P. Wright and S. Snell, "Toward a Unifying Framework for Exploring Fit and Flexibility in Strategic Human Resource Management," *Academy of Management Review* 23, no. 4 (1998), pp. 756–72.

69. H. Behar, *It's Not about the Coffee: Lessons for Putting People First from a Life at Starbucks* (New York, NY: Penguin Group, 2007).

70. T. Stewart, "Brace for Japan's Hot New Strategy," *Fortune,* September 21, 1992, pp. 62–76.

71. B. Dunford, P. Wright, and S. Snell, "Contributions of the Resource-Based View of the Firm to the Field of Strategic HRM: Convergence of Two Fields," *Journal of Management* 27 (2001), pp. 701–21.

72. C. Snow and S. Snell, *Staffing as Strategy,* vol. 4 of *Personnel Selection* (San Francisco: Jossey-Bass, 1992).

73. T. Batten, "Education Key to Prosperity—Report," *Houston Chronicle,* September 7, 1992, p. 1B.

74. Schultz and Yang, *Pour Your Heart Into It.*

75. G. McMahan, University of Texas at Arlington, personal communications.

76. M. Brannigan, "Delta Lifts Mechanics' Pay to Top of Industry Amid Push by Union," *The Wall Street Journal Interactive,* August 16, 2001; M. Adams, "Delta May See Second Big Union," *USA Today,* August 27, 2001, p. 1B.

The Legal Environment: Equal Employment Opportunity and Safety

LEARNING OBJECTIVES

After reading this chapter, you should be able to:

LO 3-1 Identify the three branches of government and the role each plays in influencing the legal environment of human resource management. *page 102*

LO 3-2 List the major federal laws that require equal employment opportunity and the protections provided by each of these laws. *page 103*

LO 3-3 Discuss the roles, responsibilities, and requirements of the federal agencies responsible for enforcing equal employment opportunity laws. *page 111*

LO 3-4 Identify the three theories of discrimination under Title VII of the Civil Rights Act and apply these theories to different discrimination situations. *page 113*

LO 3-5 Identify behavior that constitutes sexual harassment, and list things that an organization can do to eliminate or minimize it. *page 125*

LO 3-6 Discuss the legal issues involved with preferential treatment programs. *page 128*

LO 3-7 Identify the major provisions of the Occupational Safety and Health Act (1970) and the rights of employees that are guaranteed by this act. *page 130*

Sexism at Kleiner Perkins?

Silicon Valley firms are notorious for their masculine cultures, and how they treat women has long been a sensitive issue. In fact, a 2014 Babson College study revealed that women comprise only 6% of venture capitalists. A recent discrimination case against venture capital firm Kleiner Perkins Caufield & Byers illustrates this problem.

Ellen Pao filed a $16 million discrimination suit against the firm, alleging sex discrimination and retaliation. She alleged that the firm's leaders failed to promote her and provide her with choice assignments following an affair with one of the firm's partners, Ajit Nazre, in 2006. She said that after the affair ended, Mr. Nazre made life difficult, alleging, "He would cut me out of e-mails, take me off e-mail threads. He would not invite me to meetings."

On the other hand, the firm paints a picture of a woman scorned. An attorney hired to examine her claims said that she was "not truthful about the relationship with Ajit Nazre" and suggested that the affair was consensual and that she had wanted a deeper relationship.

During the trial Ms. Pao testified that for Valentine's Day another male partner gave her a book of erotic poems. She told some of the partners that the firm would benefit from better human resources policy and training.

SOURCE: J. Elder, "Kleiner Accuser Testifies on Sexism," *The Wall Street Journal,* March 9, 2015, www.wsj.com.

Introduction

In the opening chapter, we discussed the environment of the HRM function, and we noted that several environmental factors affect an organization's HRM function. One is the legal environment, particularly the laws affecting the management of people. As the troubles at Kleiner Perkins suggests, legal issues can cause serious problems for a company's success and survival. In this chapter, we first present an overview of the U.S. legal system, noting the different legislative bodies, regulatory agencies, and judicial bodies that determine the legality of certain HRM practices. We then discuss the major laws and executive orders that govern these practices.

One point to make clear at the outset is that managers often want a list of "dos and don'ts" that will keep them out of legal trouble. They rely on rules such as "Don't ever ask a female applicant if she is married" without understanding the "why" behind these rules. Clearly, certain practices are illegal or inadvisable, and this chapter will provide some valuable tips for avoiding discrimination lawsuits. However, such lists are not compatible with a strategic approach to HRM and are certainly not the route to developing a competitive advantage. They are simply mechanical reactions to the situations. Our goal is to provide an understanding of how the legislative, regulatory, and judicial systems work to define equal employment opportunity law. Armed with this understanding, a manager is better prepared to manage people within the limits imposed by the legal system. Doing so effectively is a source of competitive advantage. Doing so ineffectively results in competitive disadvantage. Rather than viewing the legal system as a constraint, firms that embrace the concept of diversity can often find that they are able to leverage the differences among people as a tremendous competitive tool.

The Legal System in the United States

The foundation for the U.S. legal system is set forth in the U.S. Constitution, which affects HRM in two ways. First, it delineates a citizen's constitutional rights, on which the government cannot impinge.[1] Most individuals are aware of the Bill of Rights, the first 10 amendments to the Constitution; but other amendments, such as the Fourteenth Amendment, also influence HRM practices. The Fourteenth Amendment, called the equal protection clause, states that all individuals are entitled to equal protection under the law.

Second, the Constitution established three major governing bodies: the legislative, executive, and judicial branches. The Constitution explicitly defines the roles and responsibilities of each of these branches. Each branch has its own areas of authority, but these areas have often overlapped, and the borders between the branches are often blurred.

LEGISLATIVE BRANCH

The legislative branch of the federal government consists of the House of Representatives and the Senate. These bodies develop laws that govern many HRM activities. Most of the laws stem from a perceived societal need. For example, during the civil rights movement of the early 1960s, the legislative branch moved to ensure that various minority groups received equal opportunities in many areas of life. One of these areas was employment, and thus Congress enacted Title VII of the Civil Rights Act. Similar perceived societal needs have brought about labor laws such as the Occupational Safety and Health Act, the Employee Retirement Income Security Act, the Age Discrimination in Employment Act, and, more recently, the Americans with Disabilities Act of 1990 and the Civil Rights Act of 1991.

EXECUTIVE BRANCH

The executive branch consists of the president of the United States and the many regulatory agencies the president oversees. Although the legislative branch passes the laws, the executive branch affects these laws in many ways. First, the president can propose bills to Congress that, if passed, would become laws. Second, the president has the power to veto any law passed by Congress, thus ensuring that few laws are passed without presidential approval—which allows the president to influence how laws are written.

Third, the regulatory agencies, under the authority of the president, have responsibility for enforcing the laws. Thus, a president can influence what types of violations are pursued. For example, many laws affecting employment discrimination are enforced by the Equal Employment Opportunity Commission under the Department of Justice. During President Jimmy Carter's administration, the Department of Justice brought a lawsuit against Birmingham, Alabama's, fire department for not having enough black firefighters. This suit resulted in a consent decree that required blacks to receive preferential treatment in hiring and promotion decisions. Two years later, during Ronald Reagan's administration, the Department of Justice sided with white firefighters in a lawsuit against the city of Birmingham, alleging that the preferential treatment required by the consent decree discriminated against white firefighters.[2]

Fourth, the president can issue executive orders, which sometimes regulate the activities of organizations that have contracts with the federal government. For example, Executive Order 11246, signed by President Lyndon Johnson, required all federal contractors and subcontractors to engage in affirmative action programs designed to hire and promote women and minorities within their organizations. Fifth, the president can influence the Supreme Court to interpret laws in certain ways. When particularly sensitive cases come before the Court, the attorney general, representing the executive branch, argues for certain preferred outcomes. For example, one court case involved a white female schoolteacher who was laid off from her job in favor of retaining a black schoolteacher with equal seniority and performance with the reason given as "diversity." The white woman filed a lawsuit in federal court and the (first) Bush administration filed a brief on her behalf, arguing that diversity was not a legitimate reason to use race in decision making. She won in federal court, and the school district appealed. The Clinton administration, having been elected in the meantime, filed a brief on behalf of the school district, arguing that diversity was a legitimate defense.

Finally, the president appoints all the judges in the federal judicial system, subject to approval from the legislative branch. This affects the interpretation of many laws.

JUDICIAL BRANCH

The judicial branch consists of the federal court system, which is made up of three levels. The first level consists of the U.S. District Courts and quasi-judicial administrative agencies. The district courts hear cases involving alleged violations of federal laws. The quasi-judicial agencies, such as the National Labor Relations Board (or NLRB, which is actually an arm of the executive branch, but serves a judicial function), hear cases regarding their particular jurisdictions (in the NLRB's case, disputes between unions and management). If neither party to a suit is satisfied with the decision of the court at this level, the parties can appeal the decision to the U.S. Courts of Appeals. These courts were originally set up to ease the Supreme Court's caseload, so appeals generally go from the federal trial level to one of the 13 appellate courts before they can be heard by the highest level, the Supreme Court. The Supreme Court must grant certiorari before hearing an appealed case. However, this is not usually granted unless two appellate courts have come to differing decisions on the same point of law or if the case deals with an important interpretation of constitutional law.

The Supreme Court serves as the court of final appeal. Decisions made by the Supreme Court are binding; they can be overturned only through legislation. For example, Congress, dissatisfied with the Supreme Court's decisions in certain cases such as *Wards Cove Packing v. Atonio,* overturned those decisions through the Civil Rights Act of 1991.[3]

Having described the legal system that affects the management of HR, we now explore some laws that regulate HRM activities, particularly equal employment opportunity laws. We first discuss the major laws that mandate equal employment opportunity in the United States. Then we examine the agencies involved in enforcing these laws. This leads us into an examination of the four theories of discrimination, with a discussion of some relevant court cases. Finally, we explore some equal employment opportunity issues facing today's managers.

While laws are generally written to protect workers, sometimes workers do not want those protections. The "Competing through Globalization" box discusses how Uber faces a variety of regulatory challenges across different nations.

Equal Employment Opportunity

Equal employment opportunity (EEO) refers to the government's attempt to ensure that all individuals have an equal chance for employment, regardless of race, color, religion, sex, age, disability, or national origin. To accomplish this, the federal government has used constitutional amendments, legislation, and executive orders, as well as the court decisions that interpret these laws. (However, equal employment laws are not the same in all countries.) The major EEO laws we discuss are summarized in Table 3.1.

Equal Employment Opportunity (EEO)
The government's attempt to ensure that all individuals have an equal opportunity for employment, regardless of race, color, religion, sex, age, disability, or national origin.

LO 3-2
List the major federal laws that require equal employment opportunity and the protections provided by each of these laws.

Uber Faces Challenges in the EU

Founded in 2009, Uber is a car-sharing service that allows customers to hail and pay for rides using their smartphones. It has expanded quickly and globally, now operating in 19 EU countries with plans to be in 26 of the 28 by the summer of 2015. However, Uber's expansion has not been smooth sailing.

Uber has filed separate complaints with the European Commission against France, Germany, and Spain all in the past year. Although each member of the EU manages its own transportation policies, the EU treaties require them to provide "nondiscriminatory" open markets to new businesses.

Mark McGann, Uber's head of public policy for Europe, the Middle East, and Africa, says that the EU "is supposed to be a single market," but "what we're finding is that we're getting treated in completely different ways in different countries, and even within individual countries." Incumbent taxi operator groups have been their biggest opponents, filing lawsuits and holding protests—some of which have turned violent—against this disruptive new entrant.

An EU spokesman commented that "we don't close the doors to the possibilities offered by new technology but it needs to happen within a framework that brings current legislation together." The EU's transportation commission plans to launch a study of taxi-type services in the EU to better inform any future decisions.

DISCUSSION QUESTION

What are some of the implications of globalization for incumbent and expanding businesses?

SOURCE: T. Fairless, "Uber Files Complaints against European Governments over Bans," *The Wall Street Journal*, April 1, 2015, www.wsj.com.

CONSTITUTIONAL AMENDMENTS
Thirteenth Amendment

The Thirteenth Amendment of the Constitution abolished slavery in the United States. Though one might be hard-pressed to cite an example of race-based slavery in the United States today, the Thirteenth Amendment has been applied in cases where the discrimination involved the "badges" (symbols) and "incidents" of slavery.

Fourteenth Amendment

The Fourteenth Amendment forbids the states from taking life, liberty, or property without due process of law and prevents the states from denying equal protection of the laws. Passed immediately after the Civil War, this amendment originally applied only to discrimination against blacks. It was soon broadened to protect other groups such as aliens and Asian-Americans, and more recently it has been applied to the protection of whites in allegations of reverse discrimination. In *Bakke v. California Board of Regents,* Alan Bakke alleged that he had been discriminated against in the selection of entrants to the University of California at Davis medical school.[4] The university had set aside 16 of the available 100 places for "disadvantaged" applicants who were members of racial minority groups. Under this quota system, Bakke was able to compete for only 84 positions, whereas a minority applicant was able to compete for all 100. The court ruled in favor of Bakke, noting that this quota system had violated white individuals' right to equal protection under the law.

One important point regarding the Fourteenth Amendment is that it is applicable only to "state actions." This means that only the decisions or actions of the government or

Table 3.1
Summary of Major EEO Laws and Regulations

ACT	REQUIREMENTS	COVERS	ENFORCEMENT AGENCY
Thirteenth Amendment	Abolished slavery	All individuals	Court system
Fourteenth Amendment	Provides equal protection for all citizens and requires due process in state action	State actions (e.g., decisions of government organizations)	Court system
Civil Rights Acts (CRAs) of 1866 and 1871 (as amended)	Grants all citizens the right to make, perform, modify, and terminate contracts and enjoy all benefits, terms, and conditions of the contractual relationship	All individuals	Court system
Equal Pay Act of 1963	Requires that men and women performing equal jobs receive equal pay	Employers engaged in interstate commerce	EEOC
Title VII of CRA	Forbids discrimination based on race, color, religion, sex, or national origin	Employers with 15 or more employees working 20 or more weeks per year; labor unions; and employment agencies	EEOC
Age Discrimination in Employment Act of 1967	Prohibits discrimination in employment against individuals 40 years of age and older	Employers with 15 or more employees working 20 or more weeks per year; labor unions; employment agencies; federal government	EEOC
Rehabilitation Act of 1973	Requires affirmative action in the employment of individuals with disabilities	Government agencies; federal contractors and subcontractors with contracts greater than $2,500	OFCCP
Americans with Disabilities Act of 1990	Prohibits discrimination against individuals with disabilities	Employers with more than 15 employees	EEOC
Pregnancy Discrimination Act	Prohibits discrimination on the basis of pregnancy, childbirth, or related medical conditions	Employers with more than 15 employees	EEOC
Executive Order 11246	Requires affirmative action in hiring women and minorities	Federal contractors and subcontractors with contracts greater than $10,000	OFCCP
Civil Rights Act of 1991	Prohibits discrimination (same as Title VII)	Same as Title VII, plus applies Section 1981 to employment discrimination cases	EEOC

of private groups whose activities are deemed state actions can be construed as violations of the Fourteenth Amendment. Thus, one could file a claim under the Fourteenth Amendment if one were fired from a state university (a government organization) but not if one were fired by a private employer.

CONGRESSIONAL LEGISLATION

The Reconstruction Civil Rights Acts (1866 and 1871)

The Thirteenth Amendment eradicated slavery in the United States, and the Reconstruction Civil Rights Acts were attempts to further this goal. The Civil Rights Act passed in 1866 was later broken into two statutes. Section 1982 granted all persons the same property rights as white citizens. Section 1981 granted other rights, including the right to enter into and enforce contracts. Courts have interpreted Section 1981 as granting individuals the right to make and enforce employment contracts. The Civil Rights Act of 1871 granted all citizens the right to sue in federal court if they felt they had been deprived of some civil right. Although these laws might seem outdated, they are still used because they allow the plaintiff to recover both compensatory and punitive damages.

In fact, these laws came to the forefront in a Supreme Court case: *Patterson v. McClean Credit Union.*[5] The plaintiff had filed a discrimination complaint under Section 1981 for racial harassment. After being hired by McClean Credit Union, Patterson failed to receive any promotions or pay raises while she was employed there. She was also told that "blacks work slower than whites." Thus, she had grounds to prove discrimination and filed suit under Section 1981, arguing that she had been discriminated against in the making and enforcement of an employment contract. The Supreme Court ruled that this situation did not fall under Section 1981 because it did not involve the making and enforcement of contracts. However, the Civil Rights Act of 1991 amended this act to include the making, performance, modification, and termination of contracts, as well as all benefits, privileges, terms, and conditions of the contractual relationship.

The Equal Pay Act of 1963

The Equal Pay Act, an amendment to the Fair Labor Standards Act, requires that men and women in the same organization who are doing equal work must be paid equally. The act defines equal in terms of skill, effort, responsibility, and working conditions. However, the act allows for reasons why men and women performing the same job might be paid differently. If the pay differences are the result of differences in seniority, merit, quantity or quality of production, or any factor other than sex (such as shift differentials or training programs), then differences are legally allowable.

Title VII of the Civil Rights Act of 1964

This is the major legislation regulating equal employment opportunity in the United States. It was a direct result of the civil rights movement of the early 1960s, led by such individuals as Dr. Martin Luther King Jr. It was Dr. King's philosophy that people should "not be judged by the color of their skin but by the content of their character." To ensure that employment opportunities would be based on character or ability rather than on race, Congress wrote and passed Title VII, which President Lyndon Johnson signed into law.

Title VII states that it is illegal for an employer to "(1) fail or refuse to hire or discharge any individual, or otherwise discriminate against any individual with respect to his compensation, terms, conditions, or privileges of employment because of such individual's race, color, religion, sex, or national origin, or (2) to limit, segregate, or classify his employees or applicants for employment in any way that would deprive or tend to deprive any individual of employment opportunities or otherwise adversely affect his status as an employee because of such individual's race, color, religion, sex, or national origin." The act applies to organizations with 15 or more employees working 20 or more weeks a year that are involved in interstate commerce, as well as state and local governments, employment agencies, and labor organizations.

Age Discrimination in Employment Act (ADEA)

Passed in 1967 and amended in 1986, this act prohibits discrimination against employees over the age of 40. The act almost exactly mirrors Title VII in terms of its substantive provisions and the procedures to be followed in pursuing a case.[6] As with Title VII, the EEOC is responsible for enforcing this act.

The ADEA was designed to protect older employees when a firm reduces its workforce through layoffs. By targeting older employees, who tend to have higher pay, a firm can substantially cut labor costs. Recently, firms have often offered early retirement incentives, a possible violation of the act because of the focus on older employees. Early retirement incentives require employees to sign an agreement waiving their rights to sue under the ADEA. Courts have tended to uphold the use of early retirement incentives and waivers as long as the individuals were not coerced into signing the agreements, the agreements were presented in a way that the employees could understand, and the employees were given enough time to make a decision.[7]

However, age discrimination complaints make up a large percentage of the complaints filed with the Equal Employment Opportunity Commission, and the number of complaints continues to grow whenever the economy is slow. For example, as we see in Figure 3.1, the cases increased during the early 1990s when many firms were downsizing, but the number of cases decreased as the economy expanded. The number of charges increased again as the economy began slowing again in 2000 and again with the recession in 2008. This often stems from firms seeking to lay off older (and thus higher paid) employees when they are downsizing. These cases can be costly; most cases are settled out of court, but such settlements run from $50,000 to $400,000 per employee.[8] In one case, Schering-Plough fired 35-year employee Fred Maiorino after he twice failed to accept an early retirement offer made to all sales representatives. After hearing testimony that Maiorino's boss had plastered his file with negative paperwork aimed at

Figure 3.1

Age Discrimination Complaints, 1991–2014

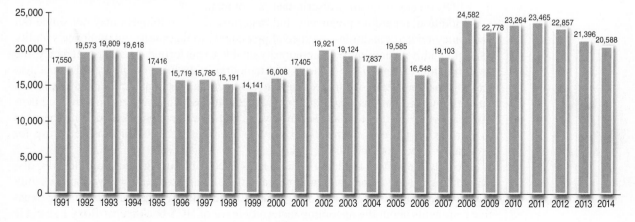

SOURCE: Equal Employment Opportunity Commission, at http://eeoc.gov/stats/adea.html.

firing him, rather than trying to help him improve his performance, the jurors unanimously decided he had been discriminated against because of his age. They awarded him $435,000 in compensatory damages and $8 million in punitive damages.[9]

The Vocational Rehabilitation Act of 1973

This act covers executive agencies and contractors and subcontractors that receive more than $2,500 annually from the federal government. It requires them to engage in affirmative action for individuals with disabilities. Congress designed this act to encourage employers to actively recruit qualified individuals with disabilities and to make reasonable accommodations to allow them to become active members of the labor market. The Employment Standards Administration of the Department of Labor enforces this act.

Vietnam Era Veteran's Readjustment Act of 1974

Similar to the Rehabilitation Act, this act requires federal contractors and subcontractors to take affirmative action toward employing Vietnam veterans (those serving between August 5, 1964, and May 7, 1975). The Office of Federal Contract Compliance Programs (OFCCP), discussed later in this chapter, has authority to enforce this act.

Pregnancy Discrimination Act

The Pregnancy Discrimination Act is an amendment to Title VII of the Civil Rights Act. It makes illegal discrimination on the basis of pregnancy, childbirth, or related medical conditions as a form of unlawful sex discrimination. An employer cannot refuse to hire a pregnant woman because of her pregnancy, a pregnancy-related condition, or the prejudices of co-workers, clients, or customers. For instance, in a recent court case, the retail store Motherhood Maternity, a Philadelphia-based maternity clothes retailer, settled a pregnancy discrimination and retaliation lawsuit brought by the Equal Employment Opportunity Commission (EEOC). The EEOC had charged that the company refused to hire qualified female applicants because they were pregnant. As a result of the settlement, Motherhood Maternity agreed to a three-year consent decree requiring them to pay plaintiffs $375,000, adopt and distribute an antidiscrimination policy specifically prohibiting discrimination on the basis of pregnancy, train its Florida employees on the new policy, post a notice of resolution of the lawsuit, and provide twice a year reports to the EEOC on any pregnancy discrimination complaints.[10]

In addition, regarding pregnancy and maternity leave, employers may not single out pregnancy-related conditions for special procedures to determine an employee's ability to work, and if an employee is temporarily unable to perform during her pregnancy, the employer must treat her the same as any temporarily disabled employees. The act also requires that any health insurance must cover expenses for pregnancy-related conditions on the same basis as costs for other medical conditions. Finally, pregnancy-related benefits cannot be limited to married employees, and if an employer provides any benefits to workers on leave, they must also provide the same benefits for those on leave for pregnancy-related conditions.

Recently the EEOC filed suit against HCS Medical Staffing, Inc., for allegedly discriminating against a pregnant employee and then firing her while she was on maternity leave. According to the EEOC's suit, owner Charles Sisson engaged in escalating negative comments about the upcoming maternity leave of HCS bookkeeper Roxy Leger. He allegedly insisted that Leger's pregnancy was a joke, described her maternity leave as "vacation," and insisted that maternity leave should be no longer than two days. Sisson then allegedly terminated Leger, who had no prior negative comments on her work performance, seven days after she gave birth by caesarean section.[11]

Civil Rights Act of 1991

The Civil Rights Act of 1991 (CRA 1991) amends Title VII of the Civil Rights Act of 1964, Section 1981 of the Civil Rights Act of 1866, the Americans with Disabilities Act, and the Age Discrimination in Employment Act of 1967. One major change in EEO law under CRA 1991 has been the addition of compensatory and punitive damages in cases of discrimination under Title VII and the Americans with Disabilities Act. Before CRA 1991, Title VII limited damage claims to equitable relief such as back pay, lost benefits, front pay in some cases, and attorneys' fees and costs. CRA 1991 allows compensatory and punitive damages when intentional or reckless discrimination is proven. Compensatory damages include such things as future pecuniary loss, emotional pain, suffering, and loss of enjoyment of life. Punitive damages are meant to discourage employers from discriminating by providing for payments to the plaintiff beyond the actual damages suffered.

Recognizing that one or a few discrimination cases could put an organization out of business, thus adversely affecting many innocent employees, Congress has put limits on the amount of punitive damages. Table 3.2 depicts these limits. As can be seen, damages range from $50,000 to $300,000 per violation, depending on the size of the organization. Punitive damages are available only if the employer intentionally discriminated against the plaintiff(s) or if the employer discriminated with malice or reckless indifference to the employee's federally protected rights. These damages are excluded for an employment practice held to be unlawful because of its disparate impact.[12]

The addition of damages to CRA 1991 has had two immediate effects. First, by increasing the potential payoff for a successful discrimination suit, it has increased the number of suits filed against businesses. Second, organizations are now more likely to grant all employees an equal opportunity for employment, regardless of their race, sex, religion, or national origin. Many organizations have felt the need to make the composition of their workforce mirror the general population to avoid costly lawsuits. This act adds a financial incentive for doing so.

Americans with Disabilities Act (ADA) of 1990

One of the most far-reaching acts concerning the management of human resources is the **Americans with Disabilities Act.** This act protects individuals with disabilities from being discriminated against in the workplace. It prohibits discrimination based on disability in all employment practices such as job application procedures, hiring, firing, promotions, compensation, and training—in addition to other employment activities such as advertising, recruitment, tenure, layoff, leave, and fringe benefits. Because this act is so new, we will cover its various stipulations individually.

Americans with Disabilities Act (ADA) of 1990
A 1990 act prohibiting individuals with disabilities from being discriminated against in the workplace.

EMPLOYER SIZE	DAMAGE LIMIT
14 to 100 employees	$ 50,000
101 to 200 employees	100,000
201 to 500 employees	200,000
More than 500 employees	300,000

Table 3.2
Maximum Punitive Damages Allowed under the Civil Rights Act of 1991

The ADA defines a disability as a physical or mental impairment that substantially limits one or more major life activities, a record of having such an impairment, or being regarded as having such an impairment. The first part of the definition refers to individuals who have serious disabilities—such as epilepsy, blindness, deafness, or paralysis—that affect their ability to perform major life activities such as walking, seeing, performing manual tasks, learning, caring for oneself, and working. The second part refers to individuals who have a history of disability, such as someone who has had cancer but is currently in remission, someone with a history of mental illness, and someone with a history of heart disease. The third part of the definition, "being regarded as having a disability," refers, for example, to an individual who is severely disfigured and is denied employment because an employer fears negative reactions from others.[13]

Thus the ADA covers specific physiological disabilities such as cosmetic disfigurement and anatomical loss affecting the neurological, musculoskeletal, sensory, respiratory, cardiovascular, reproductive, digestive, genitourinary, hemic, or lymphatic systems. In addition, it covers mental and psychological disorders such as mental retardation, organic brain syndrome, emotional or mental illness, and learning disabilities. However, conditions such as obesity, substance abuse, eye and hair color, and lefthandedness are not covered.[14]

In addition, the Americans with Disabilities Act Amendments Act (ADAAA), effective January 1, 2009, broadened the scope of who is considered to be an individual with a disability. It states that the definition of disability should be broadly construed and that the "question of whether an individual's impairment is a disability under the ADA should not demand extensive analysis." The Supreme Court had interpreted the term "substantially limited" in a major life activity to require the individual to be "significantly restricted," but the ADAAA states that this is too high a standard and directs the EEOC to revise its regulations to set a lower standard. Also, regarding the term "regarded as disabled," previously employers could avoid liability by showing that the impairment did not substantially limit a major life activity. However, the ADAAA states that an employee can prove he or she was subjected to an illegal act "because of an actual or perceived physical or mental impairment whether or not the impairment limits or is perceived to limit a major life activity." In fact, in response to the ADAAA, the EEOC has clarified and somewhat redefined "disability." According to their most recent guidelines, a disability is defined along three so-called "prongs": a physical or mental impairment that "substantially limits one or more major life activity," a record or past history of such an impairment; and/or being "regarded as" having a disability by an employer whether you have one or not, usually in terms of hiring, firing, or demotion. In essence, a person is considered disabled not only if he or she cannot DO something, but just because he or she has a medical condition whether or not it impairs functioning.[15]

EXECUTIVE ORDERS

Executive orders are directives issued and amended unilaterally by the president. These orders do not require congressional approval, yet they have the force of law. Two executive orders directly affect HRM.

Executive Order 11246

President Johnson issued this executive order, which prohibits discrimination based on race, color, religion, sex, and national origin. Unlike Title VII, this order applies only to federal contractors and subcontractors. Employers receiving more than $10,000 from the federal government must take affirmative action to ensure against discrimination, and those with contracts greater than $50,000 must develop a written affirmative action plan for each of their establishments within 120 days of the beginning of the contract. The Office of Federal Contract Compliance Programs enforces this executive order.

Executive Order 11478

President Richard M. Nixon issued this order, which requires the federal government to base all its employment policies on merit and fitness, and specifies that race, color, sex, religion, and national origin should not be considered. (The U.S. Office of Personnel Management is in charge of this.) The order also extends to all contractors and subcontractors doing $10,000 worth of business with the federal government. (The relevant government agencies have the responsibility to ensure that the contractors and subcontractors comply with the order.)

Enforcement of Equal Employment Opportunity

LO 3-3
Discuss the roles, responsibilities, and requirements of the federal agencies responsible for enforcing equal employment opportunity laws.

As discussed previously, the executive branch of the federal government bears most of the responsibility for enforcing all EEO laws passed by the legislative branch. In addition, the executive branch must enforce the executive orders issued by the president. The two agencies responsible for the enforcement of these laws and executive orders are the **Equal Employment Opportunity Commission** and the Office of Federal Contract Compliance Programs, respectively.

Equal Employment Opportunity Commission (EEOC)
The government commission to ensure that all individuals have an equal opportunity for employment, regardless of race, color, religion, sex, age, disability, or national origin.

EQUAL EMPLOYMENT OPPORTUNITY COMMISSION (EEOC)

An independent federal agency, the EEOC is responsible for enforcing most of the EEO laws, such as Title VII, the Equal Pay Act, and the Americans with Disabilities Act. The EEOC has three major responsibilities: investigating and resolving discrimination complaints, gathering information, and issuing guidelines.

Investigation and Resolution

Individuals who feel they have been discriminated against must file a complaint with the EEOC or a similar state agency within 180 days of the incident. Failure to file a complaint within the 180 days results in the case's being dismissed immediately, with certain exceptions, such as the enactment of a seniority system that has an intentionally discriminatory purpose. For instance, the recent Lilly Ledbetter Fair Pay Act signed by President Obama was crafted in direct response to the 180-day window. Ledbetter had been an area manager at the Goodyear Tire and Rubber plant in Alabama from 1979 to 1998, during which time she received lower raises than the males. The differences were such that by the end of her career she was making $6,700 less per year than her male counterparts, and because pension payments were related to the salary at the time of retirement, she received smaller pension payments. When she filed the lawsuit, the Supreme Court ruled that the illegal acts were the pay raise decisions themselves (which fell far outside the 180-day window); Ledbetter wanted to argue that every time she received a pension check lower than her peers it served as an act of discrimination. Thus, Congress passed the act specifying that an "illegal act" occurs when (1) a discriminatory compensation decision is adopted; (2) an employee becomes subject to the decision; or (3) an employee is affected by it application, including each time compensation is paid.

Once the complaint is filed, the EEOC takes responsibility for investigating the claim of discrimination. The complainant must give the EEOC 60 days to investigate the complaint. If the EEOC either does not believe the complaint to be valid or fails to complete the investigation, the complainant may sue in federal court. If the EEOC determines that discrimination has taken place, its representatives will attempt to provide a reconciliation between the two parties without burdening the court system with a lawsuit. Sometimes the EEOC enters into a consent decree with the discriminating organization. This decree is an agreement between the agency and the organization that the organization will cease certain discriminatory practices and possibly institute additional affirmative action practices to rectify its history of discrimination.

If the EEOC cannot come to an agreement with the organization, it has two options. First, it can issue a "right to sue" letter to the alleged victim, which certifies that the agency has investigated and found validity in the victim's allegations. Second, although less likely, the agency may aid the alleged victim in bringing suit in federal court.

Information Gathering

The EEOC also plays a role in monitoring the hiring practices of organizations. Each year organizations with 100 or more employees must file a report (EEO-1) with the EEOC that provides the number of women and minorities employed in nine different job categories. The EEOC computer analyzes these reports to identify patterns of discrimination that can then be attacked through class-action suits.

Issuance of Guidelines

A third responsibility of the EEOC is to issue guidelines that help employers determine when their decisions are violations of the laws enforced by the EEOC. These guidelines are not laws themselves, but the courts give great deference to them when hearing employment discrimination cases.

For example, the *Uniform Guidelines on Employee Selection Procedures* is a set of guidelines issued by the EEOC, the Department of Labor, the Department of Justice, and the U.S. Civil Service Commission.[16] This document provides guidance on the ways an organization should develop and administer selection systems so as not to violate Title VII. The courts often refer to the *Uniform Guidelines* to determine whether a company has engaged in discriminatory conduct or to determine the validity of the procedures it used to validate a selection system. Another example: Since the passage of the ADA, employers have been somewhat confused about the act's implications for their hiring procedures. Therefore, the EEOC issued guidelines in the *Federal Register* that provided more detailed information regarding what the agency will consider legal and illegal employment practices concerning disabled individuals. Although companies are well advised to follow these guidelines, it is possible that courts will interpret the ADA differently from the EEOC. Thus, through the issuance of guidelines the EEOC gives employers directions for making employment decisions that do not conflict with existing laws.

OFFICE OF FEDERAL CONTRACT COMPLIANCE PROGRAMS (OFCCP)

The OFCCP is the agency responsible for enforcing the executive orders that cover companies doing business with the federal government. Businesses with contracts for more than $50,000 cannot discriminate in employment based on race, color, religion, national origin, or sex, and they must have a written affirmative action plan on file.

These plans have three basic components.[17] First, the **utilization analysis** compares the race, sex, and ethnic composition of the employer's workforce with that of the available labor supply. For each job group, the employer must identify the percentage of its workforce with that characteristic (e.g., female) and identify the percentage of workers in the relevant labor market with that characteristic. If the percentage in the employer's workforce is much less than the percentage in the comparison group, then that minority group is considered to be "underutilized."

Second, the employer must develop specific **goals and timetables** for achieving balance in the workforce concerning these characteristics (particularly where underutilization exists). Goals and timetables specify the percentage of women and minorities that the employer seeks to have in each job group and the date by which that percentage is to be attained. These are not to be viewed as quotas, which entail setting aside a specific number of positions to be filled only by members of the protected class. Goals and timetables are much more flexible, requiring only that the employer have specific goals and take steps to achieve those goals. In fact, one study that examined companies with the goal of increasing black employment found that only 10% of them actually achieved their goals. Although this may sound discouragingly low, it is important to note that these companies increased their black employment more than companies that set no such goals.[18]

Third, employers with federal contracts must develop a list of **action steps** they will take toward attaining their goals to reduce underutilization. The company's CEO must make it clear to the entire organization that the company is committed to reducing underutilization, and all management levels must be involved in the planning process. For example, organizations can communicate job openings to women and minorities through publishing the company's affirmative action policy, recruiting at predominantly female or minority schools, participating in programs designed to increase employment opportunities for underemployed groups, and removing unnecessary barriers to employment. Organizations must also take affirmative steps toward hiring Vietnam veterans and individuals with disabilities.

The OFCCP annually audits government contractors to ensure that they actively pursue the goals in their plans. These audits consist of (1) examining the company's affirmative action plan and (2) conducting on-site visits to examine how individual employees perceive the company's affirmative action policies. If the OFCCP finds that the contractors or subcontractors are not complying with the executive order, then its representatives may notify the EEOC (if there is evidence that Title VII has been violated), advise the Department of Justice to institute criminal proceedings, request that the Secretary of Labor cancel or suspend any current contracts, and forbid the firm from bidding on future contracts. This last penalty, called debarment, is the OFCCP's most potent weapon.

Having discussed the major laws defining equal employment opportunity and the agencies that enforce these laws, we now address the various types of discrimination and the ways these forms of discrimination have been interpreted by the courts in a number of cases.

Types of Discrimination

How would you know if you had been discriminated against? Assume that you have applied for a job and were not hired. How do you know if the organization decided not to hire you because you are unqualified, because you are less qualified than the individual ultimately hired, or simply because the person in charge of the hiring decision "didn't like your type"? Discrimination is a multifaceted issue. It is often not easy to determine the extent to which unfair discrimination affects an employer's decisions.

Utilization Analysis
A comparison of the race, sex, and ethnic composition of an employer's workforce with that of the available labor supply.

Goals and Timetables
The part of a written affirmative action plan that specifies the percentage of women and minorities that an employer seeks to have in each job group and the date by which that percentage is to be attained.

Action Steps
The written affirmative action plan that specifies what an employer plans to do to reduce underutilization of protected groups.

LO 3-4
Identify the three theories of discrimination under Title VII of the Civil Rights Act and apply these theories to different discrimination situations.

Legal scholars have identified three theories of discrimination: disparate treatment, disparate impact, and reasonable accommodation. In addition, there is protection for those participating in discrimination cases or opposing discriminatory actions. In the act, these theories are stated in very general terms. However, the court system has defined and delineated these theories through the cases brought before it. A comparison of the theories of discrimination is given in Table 3.3.

DISPARATE TREATMENT

Disparate Treatment
A theory of discrimination based on different treatments given to individuals because of their race, color, religion, sex, national origin, age, or disability status.

Disparate treatment exists when individuals in similar situations are treated differently and the different treatment is based on the individual's race, color, religion, sex, national origin, age, or disability status. If two people with the same qualifications apply for a job and the employer decides whom to hire based on one individual's race, the individual not hired is a victim of disparate treatment. In the disparate treatment case the plaintiff must prove that there was a discriminatory motive—that is, that the employer intended to discriminate.

Whenever individuals are treated differently because of their race, sex, or the like, there is disparate treatment. For example, if a company fails to hire women with school-age children (claiming the women will be frequently absent) but hires men with school-age children, the applicants are being treated differently based on sex. Another example would be an employer who checks the references and investigates the conviction records of minority applicants but

Table 3.3
Comparison of Discrimination Theories

TYPES OF DISCRIMINATION	DISPARATE TREATMENT	DISPARATE IMPACT	REASONABLE ACCOMMODATION
Show intent?	Yes	No	Yes
Prima facie case	Individual is member of a protected group, was qualified for the job, and was turned down for the job, and the job remained open	Statistical disparity in the effects of a facially neutral employment practice	Individual has a belief or disability, provided the employer with notice (request to accommodate), and was adversely affected by a failure to be accommodated
Employer's defense	Produce a legitimate, non-discriminatory reason for the employment decision or show bona fide occupational qualification (BFOQ)	Prove that the employment practice bears a manifest relationship with job performance	Job-relatedness and business necessity, undue hardship, or direct threat to health or safety
Plaintiff's rebuttal	Reason offered was merely a "pretext" for discrimination	Alternative procedures exist that meet the employer's goal without having disparate impact	
Monetary damages	Compensatory and punitive damages	Equitable relief (e.g., back pay)	Compensatory and punitive damages (if discrimination was intentional or employer failed to show good faith efforts to accommodate)

does not do so for white applicants. Why are managers advised not to ask about marital status? Because in most cases, a manager will either ask only the female applicants or, if the manager asks both males and females, he or she will make different assumptions about females (such as "She will have to move if her husband gets a job elsewhere") and males (such as "He's very stable"). In all these examples, notice that (1) people are being treated differently and (2) there is an actual intent to treat them differently.[19]

For instance, The Timken Company agreed to a $120,000 settlement over a sex and disability discrimination suit. In 2007, Carmen Halloran applied for a full-time position at The Timken Company, after having worked at the facility as a part-time process associate for four years. The EEOC alleged that the company refused to hire Halloran because managers believed that Halloran, who is the mother of a disabled child, would be unable to work full-time and care for her disabled child. They also alleged that this decision was based on an unfounded gender stereotype that the mother of a disabled child would necessarily be the primary caregiver because they did hire men with disabled children. "The EEOC is committed to fighting discrimination in the workplace," said Lynette A. Barnes, regional attorney for the EEOC's Charlotte District Office. "Employers must be careful not to apply stereotypes against women based on perceptions that they must always be the primary caregivers and therefore are unreliable employees."[20]

To understand how disparate treatment is applied in the law, let's look at how an actual court case, filed under disparate treatment, would proceed.

The Plaintiff's Burden

As in any legal case, the plaintiff has the burden of proving that the defendant has committed an illegal act. This is the idea of a "prima facie" case. In a disparate treatment case, the plaintiff meets the prima facie burden by showing four things:

1. The plaintiff belongs to a protected group.
2. The plaintiff applied for and was qualified for the job.
3. Despite possessing the qualifications, the plaintiff was rejected.
4. After the plaintiff was rejected, the position remained open and the employer continued to seek applicants with similar qualifications, or the position was filled by someone with similar qualifications.

Although these four elements may seem easy to prove, it is important to note that what the court is trying to do is rule out the most obvious reasons for rejecting the plaintiff's claim (for example, the plaintiff did not apply or was not qualified, or the position was already filled or had been eliminated). If these alternative explanations are ruled out, the court assumes that the hiring decision was based on a discriminatory motive.

The Defendant's Rebuttal

Once the plaintiff has made the prima facie case for discrimination, the burden shifts to the defendant. The burden is different depending on whether the prima facie case presents only circumstantial evidence (there is no direct evidence of discrimination such as a formal policy to discriminate, but rather discriminatory intent must be inferred) or direct evidence (a formal policy of discrimination for some perceived legitimate reason). In cases of circumstantial evidence, the defendant simply must produce a legitimate, nondiscriminatory reason, such as that, although the plaintiff was qualified, the individual hired was more qualified.

Bona Fide Occupational Qualification (BFOQ)
A job qualification based on sex, religion, and so on, that an employer asserts is a necessary qualification for the job.

However, in cases where direct evidence exists, such as a formal policy of hiring only women for waitress jobs because the business is aimed at catering to male customers, then the defendant is more likely to offer a different defense. This defense argues that for this job, a factor such as sex or religion was a **bona fide occupational qualification (BFOQ).** For example, if one were hiring an individual to hand out towels in a women's locker room, being a woman might be a BFOQ. However, there are very few cases in which sex qualifies as a BFOQ, and in these cases it must be a necessary, rather than simply a preferred characteristic of the job.

UAW v. Johnson Controls, Inc., illustrates the difficulty in using a BFOQ as a defense.[21] Johnson Controls, a manufacturer of car batteries, had instituted a "fetal protection" policy that excluded women of childbearing age from a number of jobs in which they would be exposed to lead, which can cause birth defects in children. The company argued that sex was a BFOQ essential to maintaining a safe workplace. The Supreme Court did not uphold the company's policy, arguing that BFOQs are limited to policies that are directly related to a worker's ability to do the job.

Interestingly, some factors are by no means off-limits when it comes to discrimination. For instance, a recent survey by *Newsweek* of 202 hiring managers revealed that almost 60% said that qualified, yet unattractive, applicants face a harder time getting hired. In addition, two-thirds believe that managers hesitate before hiring qualified, but overweight, candidates.[22]

The Plaintiff's Rebuttal

If the defendant provides a legitimate, nondiscriminatory reason for its employment decision, the burden shifts back to the plaintiff. The plaintiff must now show that the reason offered by the defendant was not in fact the reason for its decision but merely a "pretext" or excuse for its actual discriminatory decision. This could entail providing evidence that white applicants with very similar qualifications to the plaintiff have often been hired while black applicants with very similar qualifications were all rejected. To illustrate disparate treatment, let's look at the first major case dealing with disparate treatment, *McDonnell Douglas Corp. v. Green.*

McDonnell Douglas Corp. v. Green. This Supreme Court case was the first to delineate the four criteria for a prima facie case of discrimination. From 1956 to 1964, Green had been an employee at McDonnell Douglas, a manufacturing plant in St. Louis, Missouri, that employed about 30,000 people. In 1964 he was laid off during a general workforce reduction. While unemployed, he participated in some activities that the company undoubtedly frowned upon: a "lock-in," where he and others placed a chain and padlock on the front door of a building to prevent the employees from leaving; and a "stall-in," where a group of employees stalled their cars at the gates of the plant so that no one could enter or leave the parking lot. About three weeks after the lock-in, McDonnell Douglas advertised for qualified mechanics, Green's trade, and he reapplied. When the company rejected his application, he sued, arguing that the company didn't hire him because of his race and because of his persistent involvement in the civil rights movement.

In making his prima facie case, Green had no problem showing that he was a member of a protected group, that he had applied for and was qualified for the job (having already worked in the job), that he was rejected, and that the company continued to advertise the position. The company's defense was that the plaintiff was not hired because he participated in the lock-in and the stall-in. In other words, the company was merely refusing to hire a troublemaker.

The plaintiff responded that the company's stated reason for not hiring him was a pretext for discrimination. He pointed out that white employees who had participated in the same activities (the lock-in and stall-in) were rehired, whereas he was not. The court found in favor of the plaintiff.

This case illustrates how similarly situated individuals (white and black) can be treated differently (whites were hired back whereas blacks were not) with the differences in treatment based on race. As we discuss later, most plaintiffs bring cases of sexual harassment under this theory of discrimination, sexual harassment being a situation where individuals are treated differently because of their sex.

Mixed-Motive Cases

In a mixed-motive case, the defendant acknowledges that some discriminatory motive existed but argues that the same hiring decision would have been reached even without the discriminatory motive. In *Hopkins v. Price Waterhouse,* Ann Hopkins was an accountant who had applied for partnership in her firm. Although she had brought in a large amount of business and had received high praise from her clients, she was turned down for a partnership on two separate occasions. In her performance reviews, she had been told to adopt more feminine dress and speech and received many other comments that suggested gender-based stereotypes. In court, the company admitted that a sex-based stereotype existed but argued that it would have come to the same decision (not promoted Hopkins) even if the stereotype had not existed.

One of the main questions that came out of this case was, Who has the burden of proof? Does the plaintiff have to prove that a different decision would have been made (that Hopkins would have been promoted) in the absence of the discriminatory motive? Or does the defendant have to prove that the same decision would have been made?

According to CRA 1991, if the plaintiff demonstrates that race, sex, color, religion, or national origin was a motivating factor for any employment practice, the prima facie burden has been met, and the burden of proof is on the employer to demonstrate that the same decision would have been made even if the discriminatory motive had not been present. If the employer can do this, the plaintiff cannot collect compensatory or punitive damages. However, the court may order the employer to quit using the discriminatory motive in its future employment decisions.

DISPARATE IMPACT

The second type of discrimination is called **disparate impact.** It occurs when a facially neutral employment practice disproportionately excludes a protected group from employment opportunities. A facially neutral employment practice is one that lacks obvious discriminatory content yet affects one group to a greater extent than other groups, such as an employment test. Although the Supreme Court inferred disparate impact from Title VII in the *Griggs v. Duke Power* case, it has since been codified into the Civil Rights Act of 1991.

There is an important distinction between disparate impact and disparate treatment discrimination. For there to be discrimination under disparate treatment, there has to be intentional discrimination. Under disparate impact, intent is irrelevant. The important criterion is that the consequences of the employment practice are discriminatory.

For example, if, for some practical reason, you hired individuals based on their height, you may not have intended to discriminate against anyone, and yet using height would have a disproportionate impact on certain protected groups. Women tend to be shorter than men, so fewer women will be hired. Certain ethnic groups, such as those of Asian

Disparate Impact
A theory of discrimination based on facially neutral employment practices that disproportionately exclude a protected group from employment opportunities.

ancestry, also tend to be shorter than those of European ancestry. Thus, your facially neutral employment practice will have a disparate impact on certain protected groups.

This is not to imply that simply because a selection practice has disparate impact, it is necessarily illegal. Some characteristics (such as height) are not equally distributed across race and gender groups; however, the important question is whether the characteristic is related to successful performance on the job. To help you understand how disparate impact works, let's look at a court proceeding involving a disparate impact claim.

The Plaintiff's Burden

In a disparate impact case, the plaintiff must make the prima facie case by showing that the employment practice in question disproportionately affects a protected group relative to the majority group. To illustrate this theory, let's assume that you are a manager who has 60 positions to fill. Your applicant pool has 80 white and 40 black applicants. You use a test that selects 48 of the white and 12 of the black applicants. Is this a disparate impact? Two alternative quantitative analyses are often used to determine whether a test has adverse impact.

Four-Fifths Rule
A rule that states that an employment test has disparate impact if the hiring rate for a minority group is less than four-fifths, or 80 percent, of the hiring rate for the majority group.

The **four-fifths rule** states that a test has disparate impact if the hiring rate for the minority group is less than four-fifths (or 80%) of the hiring rate for the majority group. Applying this analysis to the preceding example, we would first calculate the hiring rates for each group:

$$\text{Whites} = 48/80 = 60\%$$
$$\text{Blacks} = 12/40 = 30\%$$

Then we would compare the hiring rate of the minority group (30%) with that of the majority group (60%). Using the four-fifths rule, we would determine that the test has adverse impact if the hiring rate of the minority group is less than 80% of the hiring rate of the majority group. Because it is less (i.e., 30%/60% = 50%, which is less than 80%), we would conclude that the test has adverse impact. The four-fifths rule is used as a rule of thumb by the EEOC in determining adverse impact.

Standard Deviation Rule
A rule used to analyze employment tests to determine disparate impact; it uses the difference between the expected representation for minority groups and the actual representation to determine whether the difference between the two is greater than would occur by chance.

The **standard deviation rule** uses actual probability distributions to determine adverse impact. This analysis uses the difference between the expected representation (or hiring rates) for minority groups and the actual representation (or hiring rate) to determine whether the difference between these two values is greater than would occur by chance. Thus, in our example, 33% (40 of 120) of the applicants were blacks, so one would expect 33% (20 of 60) of those hired to be black. However, only 12 black applicants were hired. To determine if the difference between the expected representation and the actual representation is greater than we would expect by chance, we calculate the standard deviation (which, you might remember from your statistics class, is the standard deviation in a binomial distribution):

$$\sqrt{\text{Number hired} \times \frac{\text{Number of minority applicants}}{\text{Number of total applicants}} \times \frac{\text{Number of nonminority applicants}}{\text{Number of total applicants}}}$$

or in this case:

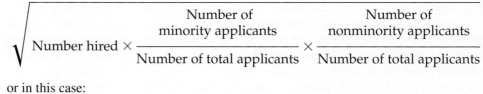

$$\sqrt{60 \times \frac{40}{120} \times \frac{80}{120}} = 3.6$$

If the difference between the actual representation and the expected representation ($20 - 12 = 8$ in this case) of blacks is greater than 2 standard deviations ($2 \times 3.6 = 7.2$ in this case), we would conclude that the test had adverse impact against blacks, because we would expect this result less than 1 time in 20 if the test were equally difficult for both whites and blacks.

The *Wards Cove Packing Co. v. Atonio* case involved an interesting use of statistics. The plaintiffs showed that the jobs in the cannery (lower paying jobs) were filled primarily with minority applicants (in this case, American Eskimos). However, only a small percentage of the noncannery jobs (those with higher pay) were filled by nonminorities. The plaintiffs argued that this statistical disparity in the racial makeup of the cannery and noncannery jobs was proof of discrimination. The federal district, appellate, and Supreme Courts all found for the defendant, stating that this disparity was not proof of discrimination.

Once the plaintiff has demonstrated adverse impact, he or she has met the burden of a prima facie case of discrimination.[23]

Defendant's Rebuttal

According to CRA 1991, once the plaintiff has made a prima facie case, the burden of proof shifts to the defendant, who must show that the employment practice is a "business necessity." This is accomplished by showing that the practice bears a relationship with some legitimate employer goal. With respect to job selection, this relationship is demonstrated by showing the job relatedness of the test, usually by reporting a validity study of some type, to be discussed in Chapter 6. For now, suffice it to say that the employer shows that the test scores are significantly correlated with measures of job performance.

Measures of job performance used in validation studies can include such things as objective measures of output, supervisor ratings of job performance, and success in training.[24] Normally, performance appraisal ratings are used, but these ratings must be valid for the court to accept the validation results. For example, in *Albermarle Paper v. Moody,* the employer demonstrated that the selection battery predicted performance (measured with supervisors' overall rankings of employees) in only some of the 13 occupational groups in which it was used. In this case, the court was especially critical of the supervisory ratings used as the measure of job performance. The court stated, "There is no way of knowing precisely what criteria of job performance the supervisors were considering."[25]

Plaintiff's Rebuttal

If the employer shows that the employment practice is the result of some business necessity, the plaintiff's last resort is to argue that other employment practices could sufficiently meet the employer's goal without adverse impact. Thus, if a plaintiff can demonstrate that selection tests other than the one used by the employer exist, do not have adverse impact, and correlate with job performance as highly as the employer's test, then the defendant can be found guilty of discrimination. Many cases deal with standardized tests of cognitive ability, so it is important to examine alternatives to these tests that have less adverse impact while still meeting the employer's goal. At least two separate studies reviewing alternative selection devices such as interviews, biographical data, assessment centers, and work sample tests have concluded that none of them met both criteria.[26] It seems that when the employment practice in question is a standardized test of cognitive ability, plaintiffs will have a difficult time rebutting the defendant's rebuttal.

Griggs v. Duke Power. To illustrate how this process works, let's look at the *Griggs v. Duke Power* case.[27] Following the passage of Title VII, Duke Power instituted a new system for making selection and promotion decisions. The system required either a high school diploma or a passing score on two professionally developed tests (the Wonderlic Personnel Test and the Bennett Mechanical Comprehension Test). A passing score was set so that it would be equal to the national median for high school graduates who had taken the tests.

The plaintiffs met their prima facie burden showing that both the high school diploma requirement and the test battery had adverse impacts on blacks. According to the 1960 census, 34% of white males had high school diplomas, compared with only 12% of black males. Similarly, 58% of white males passed the test battery, whereas only 6% of blacks passed.

Duke Power was unable to defend its use of these employment practices. A company vice president testified that the company had not studied the relationship between these employment practices and the employees' ability to perform the job. In addition, employees already on the job who did not have high school diplomas and had never taken the tests were performing satisfactorily. Thus, Duke Power lost the case.

It is interesting to note that the court recognized that the company had not intended to discriminate, mentioning that the company was making special efforts to help undereducated employees through financing two-thirds of the cost of tuition for high school training. This illustrates the importance of the consequences, as opposed to the motivation, in determining discrimination under the disparate impact theory.

PATTERN AND PRACTICE

In showing class action pattern and practice lawsuits, the plaintiffs attempt to show three things. First, they show some statistical disparities between the composition of some group within the company compared to some other relevant group. For instance, in a recent discrimination case brought against Walmart (Dukes v. Walmart), described how the plaintiff's lawyers pointed to two comparative statistics as evidence of discrimination. First, they compared the female representation in the non-managerial (63.4%) vs the managerial (33.6%) employee groups. They also compared the female representation in the managerial group (again, 33.6%) with that in their top 20 competitors (56.5%). They also calculated that hourly female workers were paid, on average, $1,100 less than men and salaried women received $14,500 less. However, Walmart disputes the list of comparison companies, arguing that if a broader group is used, reflecting Walmart's wide geographic footprint and variety of products offered, it does not differ from that group. It also claims that if it had claimed its highest-level hourly-wage supervisors as "managers" on its EEO-1 forms, as many of the comparison companies do, the entire disparity disappears. They also note that of the applicants for managerial positions, only 15% are female, and that of those promoted, 18% are female. Finally, regarding pay, Walmart's experts suggested that the plaintiff's pay comparisons did not account for crucial factors such as the number of hours worked or whether the work was night-shift work, which pays more. Their analyses suggested that when pay was compared at the department level, where pay decisions are determined, 92.8% of all stores showed no statistically significant pay disparities, and that of the remainder, 5.2% showed disparities favoring men while 2.0% showed disparities favoring women.

Second, the plaintiff tries to show that there are individual acts of intentional discrimination that suggest that the statistical disparity is a function of the larger culture. In the Dukes case, the plaintiffs argued that at Monday morning meetings of high-level Sam's Club executives, female store employees were referred to as "Janie Q's," and that this continued even after a woman executive complained that she found the term demeaning.

Finally, the plaintiff usually tries to make the case that the promotion and/or pay procedures leave too much discretion to managers, providing the avenue through which their unconscious biases can play a part. In the Dukes case the plaintiffs brought in expert witnesses to argue that the performance management processes were extremely subjective, and that male managers have subconscious tendencies to favor male over female employees.

REASONABLE ACCOMMODATION

Reasonable accommodation presents a relatively new theory of discrimination. It began with regard to religious discrimination, but has recently been both expanded and popularized with the passage of the ADA. Reasonable accommodation differs from these two theories in that rather than simply requiring an employer to refrain from some action, reasonable accommodation places a special obligation on an employer to affirmatively do something to accommodate an individual's disability or religion. This theory is violated when an employer fails to make reasonable accommodation, where that is required, to a qualified person with a disability or to a person's religious observation and/or practices.

> **Reasonable Accommodation**
> Making facilities readily accessible to and usable by individuals with disabilities.

Religion and Accommodation

Often individuals with strong religious beliefs find that some observations and practices of their religion come into direct conflict with their work duties. For example, some religions forbid individuals from working on the sabbath day when the employer schedules them for work. Others might have beliefs that preclude them from shaving, which might conflict with a company's dress code. Although Title VII forbids discrimination on the basis of religion just like race or sex, religion also receives special treatment requiring employers to exercise an affirmative duty to accommodate individuals' religious beliefs and practices. As Figure 3.2 shows, the number of religious discrimination charges has consistently dropped over the past few years.

In cases of religious discrimination, an employee's burden is to demonstrate that he or she has a legitimate religious belief and provided the employer with notice of the need to accommodate the religious practice, and that adverse consequences occurred due to the employer's failure to accommodate. In such cases, the employer's major defense is to assert that to accommodate the employee would require an undue hardship.

Examples of reasonably accommodating a person's religious obligations might include redesigning work schedules (most often accommodating those who cannot work on their sabbath), providing alternative testing dates for applicants, not requiring union membership and/or allowing payment of "charitable contributions" in lieu of union dues, or altering certain dress or grooming requirements. Note that although an employer is required to make a reasonable accommodation, it need not be the one that is requested by the employee.[28]

In one case, Walmart agreed to settle with a former employee who alleged that he was forced to quit in 1993 after refusing to work on Sunday. Walmart agreed to pay the former employee unspecified damages, to instruct managers on employees' rights to have their religious beliefs accommodated, and to prepare a computer-based manual describing employees' rights and religious harassment.[29]

Figure 3.2

Religious Discrimination Complaints, 1991–2014

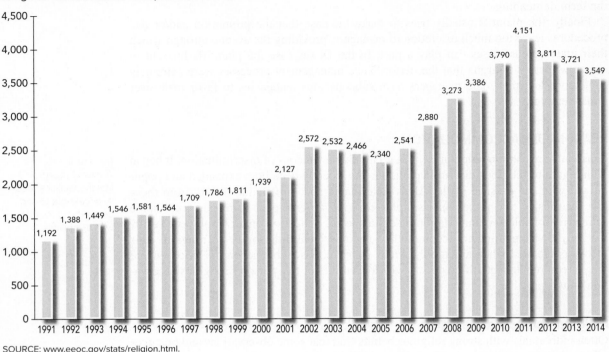

SOURCE: www.eeoc.gov/stats/religion.html.

Following the attack of 9/11, a number of cases sprang up with regard to discrimination against Muslims, partly accounting for the significant increase in religious discrimination complaints in 2002. In one case, the EEOC and Electrolux Group settled a religious accommodation case brought by Muslim workers from Somalia. The Islamic faith requires Muslims to offer five prayers a day, with two of these prayers offered within restricted time periods (early morning and sunset). Muslim employees alleged that they were disciplined for using an unscheduled break traditionally offered to line employees on an as-needed basis to observe their sunset prayer. Electrolux worked with the EEOC to respect the needs of its Muslim workers without creating a business hardship by affording them with an opportunity to observe their sunset prayer.[30]

Religion and accommodation also bring up the question as to what to do when different rights collide. For instance, John Nemecek had been a respected business professor at Spring Arbor University for 15 years. Spring Arbor is an evangelical college in Michigan which began to take issue with some of his behavior. After he began wearing earrings and makeup and asking friends to call him "Julie" he found himself demoted and fired because his womanly appearance violated "Christian behavior." In 2004 a doctor diagnosed Prof. Nemecek with a "gender-identity disorder," in which one's sexual identity differs from one's body. Soon after, the school began taking away some of his responsibilities, and then issued him a contract revoking his dean's post, reassigning him to a non-tenure-track role in which he would work from home, teaching online. It also required him to not wear any makeup or female clothing or to display any outward signs of femininity when visiting campus. Gayle Beebe, the university's president, said "We felt through a job reassignment we could give him the space to work on this issue."

Prof. Nemecek signed the contract but then violated it by showing up on campus with earrings and makeup on four separate occasions. The professor filed his complaint with the EEOC and the university then declined to renew his contract. Prof. Nemecek, whose Baptist church also asked him to leave the congregation, says of the university, "Essentially, they're saying they can define who is a Christian. I don't agree that our biology determines our gender."[31]

Disability and Accommodation

As previously discussed, the ADA made discrimination against individuals with disabilities illegal. However, the act itself states that the employer is obligated not just to refrain from discriminating, but to take affirmative steps to accommodate individuals who are protected under the act.

Under disability claims, the plaintiff must show that she or he is a qualified applicant with a disability and that adverse action was taken by a covered entity. The employer's defense then depends on whether the decision was made without regard to the disability or in light of the disability. For example, if the employer argues that the plaintiff is not qualified, then it has met the burden, and the question of reasonable accommodation becomes irrelevant.

If, however, the decision was made "in light of" the disability, then the question becomes one of whether the person could perform adequately with a reasonable accommodation. This leads to three potential defenses. First, the employer could allege job-relatedness or business necessity through demonstrating, for example, that it is using a test that assesses ability to perform essential job functions. However, then the question arises of whether the applicant could perform the essential job functions with a reasonable accommodation. Second, the employer could claim an undue hardship to accommodate the individual. In essence, this argues that the accommodation necessary is an action requiring significant difficulty or expense. Finally, the employer could argue that the individual with the disability might pose a direct threat to his own or others' health or safety in the workplace. This requires examining the duration of the risk, the nature and severity of potential harm, the probability of the harm occurring, and the imminence of the potential harm. For instance, Walmart was sued by one of its employees who was a fitting room attendant with cerebral palsy and confined to a wheelchair. The employee requested to use a grabber and a shopping cart to help her pick up and hold clothes. However, she was prevented from using both by the manager, who then implemented progressive discipline ending in the attendant's termination.[32]

What are some examples of reasonable accommodation with regard to disabilities? First is providing readily accessible facilities such as ramps and/or elevators for disabled individuals to enter the workplace. Second, job restructuring might include eliminating marginal tasks, shifting these tasks to other employees, redesigning job procedures, or altering work schedules. Third, an employer might reassign a disabled employee to a job with essential job functions he or she could perform. Fourth, an employer might accommodate applicants for employment who must take tests through providing alternative testing formats, providing readers, or providing additional time for taking the test. Fifth, readers, interpreters, or technology to offer reading assistance might be given to a disabled employee. Sixth, an employer could allow employees to provide their own accommodation such as bringing a guide dog to work.[33] Note that most accommodations are inexpensive. A study by Sears Roebuck & Co. found that 69% of all accommodations cost nothing, 29% cost less than $1,000, and only 3% cost more than $1,000.[34]

EVIDENCE-BASED HR

As information technology becomes more and more ubiquitous in the workplace, some have begun to explore the implications for people with disabilities. Researchers at the Employment and Disability Institute at Cornell University recently reviewed the accessibility of 10 job boards and 31 corporate e-recruiting websites using Bobby 3.2, a software program designed to check for errors that cause accessibility concerns. They found that none of the job boards and only a small minority of the e-recruiting sites met the Bobby standards.

In phase 2 of the study, they surveyed 813 HR professionals who were members of the Society for Human Resource Management (SHRM). Between 16 and 46% of the HR professionals were familiar with six of the most common assistive technologies to adapt computers for disabled individuals (screen magnifiers, speech recognitions software, video captioning, Braille readers/displays, screen readers, guidelines for web design). In addition, only 1 in 10 said they knew that their firm had evaluated the websites for accessibility to people with disabilities.

This study indicates that while firms may not have any intention of discriminating against people with disabilities, the rapid expansion of information technology combined with an inattention to and/or lack of education regarding accessibility issues may accidentally lead them to do so.

SOURCE: S. Bruyere, S. Erickson, and S. VanLooy, "Information Technology and the Workplace: Implications for Persons with Disabilities," *Disability Studies Quarterly* 25, no. 2 (Spring 2005), at www.dsq-sds.org.

Retaliation for Participation and Opposition

Suppose you overhear a supervisor in your workplace telling someone that he refuses to hire women because he knows they are just not cut out for the job. Believing this to be illegal discrimination, you face a dilemma. Should you come forward and report this statement? Or if someone else files a lawsuit for gender discrimination, should you testify on behalf of the plaintiff? What happens if your employer threatens to fire you if you do anything?

Title VII of the Civil Rights Act of 1964 protects you. It states that employers cannot retaliate against employees for either "opposing" a perceived illegal employment practice or "participating in a proceeding" related to an alleged illegal employment practice. Opposition refers to expressing to someone through proper channels that you believe that an illegal employment act has taken place or is taking place. Participation refers to actually testifying in an investigation, hearing, or court proceeding regarding an illegal employment act. Clearly, the purpose of this provision is to protect employees from employers' threats and other forms of intimidation aimed at discouraging the employees from bringing to light acts they believe to be illegal.

Recently the EEOC filed suit against Dillard's, a major department store chain, for firing a business manager as retaliation for filing a discrimination charge. In 2008, Shontel Mayfield filed a charge with the EEOC in which she alleged that Dillard's management had discriminated against her because of her race. She had begun working for Dillard's in July 2001, and earned a promotion to business manager of the Estee Lauder counter in 2006. However, in September 2008, Mayfield complied with a Jefferson County, Texas, mandatory evacuation order and evacuated the area in advance of Hurricane Ike. She returned to Jefferson County consistent with the directives of the county's "disaster declarations." After Mayfield returned to work she was told that she was being fired for the stated reason of "excessive absenteeism." On her termination paperwork, she was accused of having "failed to maintain verbal communication concerning her absences with either the store manager or the operations manager." Yet telephone records showed that Mayfield placed numerous calls to Dillard's "disaster recovery" number, as well as to the cellular telephones of the store manager and the operations manager during the evacuation period.[35]

These cases can be extremely costly for companies because they are alleging acts of intentional discrimination, and therefore plaintiffs are entitled to punitive damages. For example, a 41-year-old former Allstate employee who claimed that a company official told her that the company wanted a "younger and cuter" image was awarded $2.8 million in damages by an Oregon jury. The jury concluded that the employee was forced out of the company for opposing age discrimination against other employees.[36]

In one case, Target Corporation agreed to pay $775,000 to a group of black workers who charged that at one store, the company condoned a racially hostile work environment exemplified by inappropriate comments and verbal berating based on race. When one of the black employees objected to this treatment, he was allegedly retaliated against, forcing him to resign.[37]

This does not mean that employees have an unlimited right to talk about how racist or sexist their employers are. The courts tend to frown on employees whose activities result in a poor public image for the company unless those employees had attempted to use the organization's internal channels—approaching one's manager, raising the issue with the HRM department, and so on—before going public.

It is important to note that deciding when an employee has done something wrong is often difficult to both know and prove. The "Integrity In Action" box describes how the CEO of an Indian company, Satyam, was found guilty of fraud.

Current Issues Regarding Diversity and Equal Employment Opportunity

LO 3-5
Identify behavior that constitutes sexual harassment, and list things that an organization can do to eliminate or minimize it.

Because of recent changes in the labor market, most organizations' demographic compositions are becoming increasingly diverse. A study by the Hudson Institute projected that 85% of the new entrants into the U.S. labor force over the next decade will be females

Figure 3.3

Sexual Harassment Charges, 2010–2014

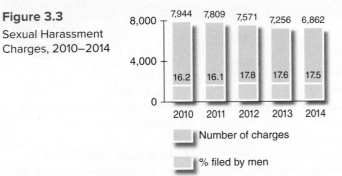

Number of charges

% filed by men

SOURCE: "U.S. Equal Employment Opportunity Commission, "Charges Alleging Sexual Harassment FY 2010-FY2014," www.eeoc.gov, accessed May 24, 2015.

and minorities.[38] Integrating these groups into organizations made up predominantly of able-bodied white males will bring attention to important issues like sexual harassment, affirmative action, and the "reasonable accommodation" of employees with disabilities.

SEXUAL HARASSMENT

Clarence Thomas's Supreme Court confirmation hearings in 1991 brought the issue of sexual harassment into increased prominence. Anita Hill, one of Thomas's former employees, alleged that he had sexually harassed her while she was working under his supervision at the Department of Education and the Equal Employment Opportunity Commission. Although the allegations were never substantiated, the hearing made many people more aware of how often employees are sexually harassed in the workplace and, combined with other events, resulted in a tremendous increase in the number of sexual harassment complaints being filed with the EEOC, as we see in Figure 3.3. In addition, after President Clinton took office and faced a sexual harassment lawsuit by Paula Corbin Jones for his alleged proposition to her in a Little Rock hotel room, the number of sexual harassment complaints took another jump from 1993 to 1994—again, potentially due to the tremendous amount of publicity regarding sexual harassment. However, the number of cases filed has actually decreased substantially since 2000.

Sexual harassment refers to unwelcome sexual advances (see Table 3.4). It can take place in two basic ways. "Quid pro quo" harassment occurs when some kind of benefit (or punishment) is made contingent on the employee's submitting (or not submitting) to sexual advances. For example, a male manager tells his female secretary that if she has

Table 3.4

EEOC Definition of Sexual Harassment

Unwelcome sexual advances, requests for sexual favors, and other verbal or physical contact of a sexual nature constitute sexual harassment when

1. Submission to such conduct is made either explicitly or implicitly a term or condition of an individual's employment,
2. Submission to or rejection of such conduct by an individual is used as the basis for employment decisions affecting such individual, or
3. Such conduct has the purpose or effect of unreasonably interfering with an individual's work performance or creating an intimidating, hostile, or offensive working environment.

SOURCE: EEOC guideline based on the Civil Rights Act of 1964, Title VII.

sex with him, he will help her get promoted, or he threatens to fire her if she fails to do so; these are clearly cases of quid pro quo sexual harassment.

The *Bundy v. Jackson* case illustrates quid pro quo sexual harassment.[39] Sandra Bundy was a personnel clerk with the District of Columbia Department of Corrections. She received repeated sexual propositions from Delbert Jackson, who was at the time a fellow employee (although he later became the director of the agency). She later began to receive propositions from two of her supervisors: Arthur Burton and James Gainey. When she raised the issue to their supervisor, Lawrence Swain, he dismissed her complaints, telling her that "any man in his right mind would want to rape you," and asked her to begin a sexual relationship with him. When Bundy became eligible for a promotion, she was passed over because of her "inadequate work performance," although she had never been told that her work performance was unsatisfactory. The U.S. Court of Appeals found that Bundy had been discriminated against because of her sex, thereby extending the idea of discrimination to sexual harassment.

A more subtle, and possibly more pervasive, form of sexual harassment is "hostile working environment." This occurs when someone's behavior in the workplace creates an environment that makes it difficult for someone of a particular sex to work. Many plaintiffs in sexual harassment lawsuits have alleged that men ran their fingers through the plaintiffs' hair, made suggestive remarks, and physically assaulted them by touching their intimate body parts. Other examples include having pictures of naked women posted in the workplace, using offensive sexually explicit language, or using sex-related jokes or innuendoes in conversations.[40]

Note that these types of behaviors are actionable under Title VII because they treat individuals differently based on their sex. In addition, although most harassment cases involve male-on-female harassment, any individual can be harassed. For example, male employees at Jenny Craig alleged that they were sexually harassed, and a federal jury found that a male employee had been sexually harassed by his male boss.[41]

In addition, Ron Clark Ford of Amarillo, Texas, agreed to pay $140,000 to six male plaintiffs who alleged that they and others were subjected to a sexually hostile work environment and different treatment because of their gender by male managers. Evidence gathered showed that the men were subjected to lewd, inappropriate comments of a sexual nature, and had their genitals and buttocks grabbed against their will by their male managers. The defendants argued that the conduct was "harmless horseplay."[42]

Finally, Babies 'R' Us agreed to pay $205,000 to resolve a same-sex suit. The lawsuit alleged that Andres Vasquez was subjected to a sexually hostile working environment and was the target of unwelcome and derogatory comments as well as behavior that mocked him because he did not conform to societal stereotypes of how a male should appear or behave.

Sexual harassment charge filings with the EEOC by men have increased to 16.4% of all filings in 2010, from 10% of filings in 1994. While the commission does not track same-sex, male-on-male charges, anecdotal evidence shows that most harassment allegations by men are against other men.[43]

There are three critical issues in these cases. First, the plaintiff cannot have "invited or incited" the advances. Often the plaintiff's sexual history, whether she or he wears provocative clothing, and whether she or he engages in sexually explicit conversations are used to prove or disprove that the advance was unwelcome. However, in the absence of substantial evidence that the plaintiff invited the behavior, courts usually lean toward assuming that sexual advances do not belong in the workplace and thus are unwelcome. In *Meritor Savings Bank v. Vinson,* Michelle Vinson claimed that during the four years she worked at a bank she was continually harassed by the bank's vice president, who repeatedly asked her to have sex with him (she eventually agreed) and sexually assaulted her.[44] The Supreme Court ruled that the victim's voluntary participation in sexual relations was not the major issue, saying that the focus of the case was on whether the vice president's advances were unwelcome.

A second critical issue is that the harassment must have been severe enough to alter the terms, conditions, and privileges of employment. Although it has not yet been consistently applied, many courts have used the "reasonable woman" standard in determining the severity or pervasiveness of the harassment. This consists of assessing whether a reasonable woman, faced with the same situation, would have reacted similarly. The reasonable woman standard recognizes that behavior that might be considered appropriate by a man (like off-color jokes) might not be considered appropriate by a woman.

The third issue is that the courts must determine whether the organization is liable for the actions of its employees. In doing so, the court usually examines two things. First, did the employer know about, or should he or she have known about, the harassment? Second, did the employer act to stop the behavior? If the employer knew about it and the behavior did not stop, the court usually decides that the employer did not act appropriately to stop it.

Sexual harassment suits can be quite costly for companies. For instance, Aaron's Inc., the furniture rental company, faced a sexual harassment suit filed by a female employee who claimed that her manager groped her, exposed himself to her, and sexually assaulted her. She contacted a company harassment hotline but was never called back. She also alleged that she was denied a promotion for complaining about the alleged assault. In 2011 a jury awarded the employee $95 million, a significant sum given that Aaron's profits had been $118 million the previous year.[45]

To ensure a workplace free from sexual harassment, organizations can follow some important steps. First, the organization can develop a policy statement that makes it very clear that sexual harassment will not be tolerated in the workplace. Second, all employees, new and old, can be trained to identify inappropriate workplace behavior. Third, the organization can develop a mechanism for reporting sexual harassment that encourages people to speak out. Fourth, management can prepare to take prompt disciplinary action against those who commit sexual harassment as well as appropriate action to protect the victims of sexual harassment.[46] The "Competing through Technology" box describes how e-mails helped to demonstrate how a leader was behaving inappropriately and possibly illegally at search firm Korn/Ferry.

AFFIRMATIVE ACTION AND REVERSE DISCRIMINATION

LO 3-6
Discuss the legal issues involved with preferential treatment programs.

Few would disagree that having a diverse workforce in terms of race and gender is a desirable goal, if all individuals have the necessary qualifications. In fact, many organizations today are concerned with developing and managing diversity. To eliminate discrimination in the workplace, many organizations have affirmative action programs to increase minority representation. Affirmative action was originally conceived as a way of taking extra effort to attract and retain minority employees. This was normally done by extensively recruiting minorities on college campuses, advertising in minority-oriented publications, and providing educational and training opportunities to minorities.[47] However, over the years, many organizations have resorted to quotalike hiring to ensure that their workforce composition mirrors that of the labor market. Sometimes these organizations act voluntarily; in other cases, the quotas are imposed by the courts or by the EEOC. Whatever the impetus for these hiring practices, many white and/or male individuals have fought against them, alleging what is called reverse discrimination.

Better Watch What You E-mail at Work

The world's largest executive search firm, Korn/Ferry, has found itself entangled in a messy legal dispute over its dismissal of a top executive, but e-mail may reveal an even messier set of details. Robert Damon, the company's former executive chairman of the Americas, says that he lost over $1.7 million in deferred compensation when he was fired in retaliation for complaining to the board of directors about how CEO Gary Burnison treated a number of female colleagues. An outside investigator who explored the allegations of Mr. Burnison's treatment of women did suggest to the directors that they hire a coach to teach him "how to lawfully behave in the workplace."

However, the company denies all the allegations. "Mr. Damon's complaint is an attempt to deflect the real reason for his termination," said Michael Distefano, Korn/Ferry's chief marketing officer. "He was terminated with cause of inappropriate personal behavior, flagrant violations of company policies, and material breaches of his own employment arrangements."

While the case has yet to be resolved, technology may point to a particular outcome. In a court filing, Korn/Ferry alleges Mr. Damon used his company e-mail "to solicit and arrange for meetings with at least 20 different call girls and escorts." In addition, Korn/Ferry says Mr. Damon used his company e-mail "to receive and distribute photographs of nude and semi-nude women."

DISCUSSION QUESTION

In this era of mobile technology and social media, should the fired senior executive have understood the implications of using his company e-mail account for inappropriate behavior?

SOURCES: J. S. Lublin, "Korn/Ferry Says It Fired Former Executive for Allegedly Soliciting Escorts," *The Wall Street Journal*, April 9, 2015, www.wsj.com; J. S. Lublin, "Former Korn/Ferry Executive Alleges Retaliation," *The Wall Street Journal*, April 1, 2015, www.wsj.com.

An example of an imposed quota program is found at the fire department in Birmingham, Alabama. Having admitted a history of discriminating against blacks, the department entered into a consent decree with the EEOC to hold 50% of positions at all levels in the fire department open for minorities even though minorities made up only 28% of the relevant labor market. The result was that some white applicants were denied employment or promotion in favor of black applicants who scored lower on a selection battery. The federal court found that the city's use of the inflexible hiring formula violated federal civil rights law and the constitutional guarantee of equal protection. The appellate court agreed, and the Supreme Court refused to hear the case, thus making the decision final.

Ricci v. DeStefano represents another recent case that has been appealed to the Supreme Court regarding the potential for reverse discrimination based on a situation in New Haven, Connecticut. In this case a professional consulting firm developed a firefighter test specifically eliminating questions that had adverse impact against minority members (based on pilot study testing). However, when the test was given, no blacks made the promotion list, so the city simply ignored the test and promoted no one. White and Hispanic firefighters who would have been on the promotion list sued, stating that the failure to use the test results discriminated against them because of their race. The district and appellate courts ruled that because no blacks were promoted either (because there were no promotions), there had been no discrimination.

The entire issue of affirmative action should evoke considerable attention and debate over the next few years. Although most individuals support the idea of diversity, few argue for the kinds of quotas that have to some extent resulted from the present legal climate. In fact, one recent survey revealed that only 16% of the respondents favored affirmative action with quotas, 46% favored it without quotas, and 28% opposed all affirmative action programs. One study found that people favor affirmative action when it is operationalized as recruitment, training, and attention to applicant qualifications but oppose it when it consists of discrimination, quotas, and preferential treatment.[48]

OUTCOMES OF THE AMERICANS WITH DISABILITIES ACT

The ADA was passed with the laudable goals of providing employment opportunities for the truly disabled who, in the absence of legislation, were unable to find employment. Certainly, some individuals with disabilities have found employment as a result of its passage. However, as often occurs with legislation, the impact is not necessarily what was intended. First, there has been increased litigation. The EEOC reports that more than 200,000 complaints have been filed since passage of the act. Approximately 50% of the complaints filed have been found to be without reasonable cause. For example, in one case a company fired an employee for stealing from other employees and bringing a loaded gun to work. The fired employee sued for reinstatement under the ADA, claiming that he was the victim of a mental illness and thus should be considered disabled.[49]

A second problem is that the kinds of cases being filed are not what Congress intended to protect. Although the act was passed because of the belief that discrimination against individuals with disabilities occurred in the failure to hire them, 52.2% of the claims deal with firings, 28.9% with failure to make reasonable accommodation, and 12.5% with harassment. Only 9.4% of the complaints allege a failure to hire or rehire.[50] In addition, although the act was passed to protect people with major disabilities such as blindness, deafness, lost limbs, or paralysis, these disabilities combined account for a small minority of the disabilities claimed. As we see in Table 3.5, the biggest disability category is "other," meaning that the plaintiff claims a disability that is not one of the 35 types of impairment listed in the EEOC charge data system. The second largest category is "being regarded as disabled" accounting for 13.4% of all charges, followed by "back impairment" claims at 8.8%. As an example, recently a fired employee sued IBM asking for $5 million in damages for violation of the Americans with Disabilities Act. The employee had been fired for spending hours at work visiting adult chat rooms on his computer. He alleged that his addiction to sex and the Internet stemmed from trauma experienced by seeing a friend killed in 1969 during an Army patrol in Vietnam.[51]

Finally, the act does not appear to have had its anticipated impact on the employment of Americans with disabilities. According to the National Organization on Disability, almost 20 years after the act was passed, 22 million of the 54 million disabled Americans are unemployed.[52]

For these reasons, Congress has explored the possibility of amending the act to more narrowly define the term disability.[53] The debate continues regarding the effectiveness of the ADA.

Employee Safety

LO 3-7
Identify the major provisions of the Occupational Safety and Health Act (1970) and the rights of employees that are guaranteed by this act.

In March 2005, officials at the BP refinery in Texas City, Texas, were aware of the fact that some repairs needed to be done on some of the equipment in an octane-boosting processing unit. On March 23, knowing that some of the key alarms were not working, managers authorized a start-up of the unit. The start-up resulted in the deadliest petrochemical accident in 15 years, killing 15 people and injuring an additional 170.[54]

Employee safety has become a great concern across a number of industries. The "Competing through Sustainability" box describes how Heineken has made safety one component of its global sustainability efforts.

Table 3.5

Sample of Complaints Filed under the ADA

	2000	2001	2002	2003	2004	2005	2006	2007	2008	2009	2010	2011	2012	2013	2014
Number of complaints	15,864	16,470	15,964	15,377	15,576	14,893	15,575	17,734	19,453	21,451	25,165	25,742	26,379	25,957	25,369
% dealing with*															
Asthma	2.0%	1.6%	1.6%	1.6%	1.5%	1.6%	1.7%	1.0%	1.7%	1.6%	1.7%	1.9%	1.6%	1.5%	1.4%
Back impairment	10.2	9.3	9.5	8.6	8.0	8.4	8.1	8.3	9.3	9.9	9.7	8.2	8.9	8.7	8.8
Cancer	2.7	2.8	2.9	2.9	2.8	2.7	3.2	3.3	3.6	3.7	3.9	4.4	4.4	4.7	4.4
Diabetes	4.1	4.3	4.7	4.8	4.7	4.5	4.8	5.1	5.6	5.5	5.4	4.6	4.2	4.7	5.0
Hearing	3.1	2.9	3.2	3.1	3.4	3.2	3.3	3.0	3.3	3.3	3.1	3.2	3.4	3.4	3.7
Vision	2.3	2.3	2.6	2.6	2.5	2.3	2.3	2.5	2.6	2.2	2.3	2.5	2.4	2.4	2.2
Heart	3.3	3.6	4.0	3.7	3.5	3.3	3.4	3.7	3.8	3.8	4.2	4.0	3.7	4.0	3.9
Regarded as disabled	13.7	12.8	13.7	16.8	18.2	17.4	17.2	17.7	16.7	14.1	12.8	13.0	13.1	13.8	13.4
Drug addiction	0.6	0.5	0.6	0.6	0.5	0.3	0.5	0.5	0.7	0.6	0.5	.5	.5	0.4	0.3
Anxiety	3.4	3.4	4.1	3.5	2.4	2.2	2.2	2.8	4.5	5.3	5.3	4.5	5.1	5.5	5.8
Depression	6.5	6.1	6.7	6.3	2.9	5.4	6.6	5.5	6.1	6.5	6.3	6.6	6.8	6.3	6.4
Other	22.2	22.3	23.7	18.1	12.3	14.7	15.7	16.4	20.2	24.4	26.3	29.8	30.3	29.0	32.1

*Not all complaints are listed.

SOURCE: EEOC, "ADA Charge Data by Impairment/Bases—Receipts," www.eeoc.gov, accessed May 26, 2015.

Global Beverage Giant Focuses on Safety and Sustainability

Heineken recently released its 2014 Sustainability Report, touting its sustainability performance in a number of areas. For instance, the company has reduced its water usage to 3.9 hectoliters for every hectoliter of beer produced, reduced its carbon emissions and electricity usage since 2008 by 30% and 20%, respectively, and invested over 25 million euros (more than $25 million U.S. dollars) in community development projects. In addition, the company developed a "Dance More, Drink Less" campaign to promote responsible drinking and added "Safety First" as a measured behavior in all of its performance reviews.

Sean O'Neill, Heineken's chief corporate relations officer, said, "Around the world 81,000 of our colleagues are engaged every day in building a successful, sustainable and responsible business. Our strong 2014 financial results coupled with the positive delivery of our Brewing a Better World commitments demonstrate that sustainability is increasingly integrated within our approach to doing business."

DISCUSSION QUESTION
What other sustainability efforts could Heineken undertake in an effort to reduce its environmental impact?

SOURCE: Company website, "2014 Sustainability Highlights," www.theheinekencompany.com, accessed May 24, 2015.

Like equal employment opportunity, employee safety is regulated by both the federal and state governments. However, to fully maximize the safety and health of workers, employers need to go well beyond the letter of the law and embrace its spirit. With this in mind, we first spell out the specific protections guaranteed by federal legislation and then discuss various kinds of safety awareness programs that attempt to reinforce these standards.

Occupational Safety and Health Act (OSHA)
The law that authorizes the federal government to establish and enforce occupational safety and health standards for all places of employment engaging in interstate commerce.

THE OCCUPATIONAL SAFETY AND HEALTH ACT (OSHA)

Although concern for worker safety would seem to be a universal societal goal, the **Occupational Safety and Health Act (OSHA)**—the most comprehensive legislation regarding worker safety—did not emerge in this country until the early 1970s. At that time, there were roughly 15,000 work-related fatalities every year.

OSHA authorized the federal government to establish and enforce occupational safety and health standards for all places of employment engaging in interstate commerce. The responsibility for inspecting employers, applying the standards, and levying fines was assigned to the Department of Labor. The Department of Health was assigned responsibility for conducting research to determine the criteria for specific operations or occupations and for training employers to comply with the act. Much of this research is conducted by the National Institute for Occupational Safety and Health (NIOSH).

General Duty Clause
The provision of the Occupational Safety and Health Act that states that an employer has an overall obligation to furnish employees with a place of employment free from recognized hazards.

Employee Rights under OSHA

The main provision of OSHA states that each employer has a general duty to furnish each employee a place of employment free from recognized hazards that cause or are likely to cause death or serious physical harm. This is referred to as the **general duty clause.** Some specific rights granted to workers under this act are listed in Table 3.6. The Department of Labor recognizes many specific types of hazards, and employers are required to comply with all the occupational safety and health standards published by NIOSH.

A recent example is the development of OSHA standards for occupational exposure to blood-borne pathogens such as the AIDS virus. These standards identify 24 affected

Employees have the right to
1. Request an inspection.
2. Have a representative present at an inspection.
3. Have dangerous substances identified.
4. Be promptly informed about exposure to hazards and be given access to accurate records regarding exposures.
5. Have employer violations posted at the work site.

Table 3.6
Rights Granted to Workers under the Occupational Safety and Health Act

industrial sectors, encompassing 500,000 establishments and 5.6 million workers. Among other features, these standards require employers to develop an exposure control plan (ECP). An ECP must include a list of jobs whose incumbents might be exposed to blood, methods for implementing precautions in these jobs, postexposure follow-up plans, and procedures for evaluating incidents in which workers are accidentally infected.

Although NIOSH publishes numerous standards, regulators clearly cannot anticipate all possible hazards that could occur in the workplace. Thus, the general duty clause requires employers to be constantly alert for potential sources of harm in the workplace (as defined by the standards of a reasonably prudent person) and to correct them. For example, managers at Amoco's Joliet, Illinois, plant realized that over the years some employees had created undocumented shortcuts and built them into their process for handling flammable materials. These changes appeared to be labor saving but created a problem: workers did not have uniform procedures for dealing with flammable products. This became an urgent issue because many of the experienced workers were reaching retirement age, and the plant was in danger of losing critical technical expertise. To solve this problem, the plant adopted a training program that met all the standards required by OSHA. That is, it conducted a needs analysis highlighting each task new employees had to learn and then documented these processes in written guidelines. New employees were given hands-on training with the new procedures and were then certified in writing by their supervisor. A computer tracking system was installed to monitor who was handling flammable materials, and this system immediately identified anyone who was not certified. The plant met requirements for both ISO 9000 standards and OSHA regulations and continues to use the same model for safety training in other areas of the plant.[55]

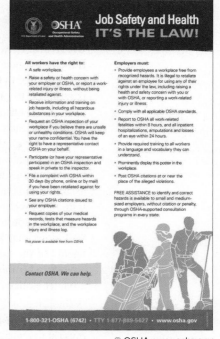

© OSHA, www.osha.gov

OSHA is responsible for inspecting businesses, applying safety and health standards, and levying fines for violations. OSHA regulations prohibit notifying employers of inspections in advance.

OSHA Inspections

OSHA inspections are conducted by specially trained agents of the Department of Labor called compliance officers. These inspections usually follow a tight "script." Typically, the compliance officer shows up unannounced. For obvious reasons, OSHA's regulations prohibit advance notice of inspections. The officer, after presenting credentials, tells the employer the reasons for the inspection and describes, in a general way, the procedures necessary to conduct the investigation.

An OSHA inspection has four major components. First, the compliance officer reviews the employer's records of deaths, injuries, and illnesses. OSHA requires this kind of record keeping from all firms with 11 or more full- or part-time employees. Second, the officer, typically accompanied by a representative of the employer (and perhaps by a representative of the employees), conducts a "walkaround" tour of the employer's premises. On this tour, the officer notes any conditions that may violate specific published standards or the less specific general duty clause. The third component of the inspection, employee interviews, may take place during the tour. At this time, any person who is aware of a violation can bring it to the attention of the officer. Finally, in a closing conference the compliance officer discusses the findings with the employer, noting any violations. The employer is given a reasonable time frame in which to correct these violations. If any violation represents imminent danger (that is, could cause serious injury or death before being eliminated through the normal enforcement procedures), the officer may, through the Department of Labor, seek a restraining order from a U.S. district court. Such an order compels the employer to correct the problem immediately.

Citations and Penalties

If a compliance officer believes that a violation has occurred, he or she issues a citation to the employer that specifies the exact practice or situation that violates the act. The employer is required to post this citation in a prominent place near the location of the violation—even if the employer intends to contest it. Nonserious violations may be assessed up to $7,000 for each incident, but this may be adjusted downward if the employer has no prior history of violations or if the employer has made a good-faith effort to comply with the act. Serious violations of the act or willful, repeated violations may be fined up to $70,000 per incident. Fines for safety violations are never levied against the employees themselves. The assumption is that safety is primarily the responsibility of the employer, who needs to work with employees to ensure that they use safe working procedures.

In addition to these civil penalties, criminal penalties may also be assessed for willful violations that kill an employee. Fines can go as high as $20,000, and the employer or agents of the employer can be imprisoned. Criminal charges can also be brought against anyone who falsifies records that are subject to OSHA inspection or anyone who gives advance notice of an OSHA inspection without permission from the Department of Labor.

The Effect of OSHA

OSHA has been unquestionably successful in raising the level of awareness of occupational safety. Table 3.7 presents recent data on occupational injuries and illnesses. Yet legislation alone cannot solve all the problems of work site safety.[56] Many industrial accidents are a product of unsafe behaviors, not unsafe working conditions. Because the act does not directly regulate employee behavior, little behavior change can be expected unless employees are convinced of the standards' importance.[57] This has been recognized by labor leaders. For example, Lynn Williams, president of the United Steelworkers of America, noted, "We can't count on government. We can't count on employers. We must rely on ourselves to bring about the safety and health of our workers."[58]

Because conforming to the statute alone does not necessarily guarantee safety, many employers go beyond the letter of the law. In the next section we examine various kinds of employer-initiated safety awareness programs that comply with OSHA requirements and, in some cases, exceed them.

Safety Awareness Programs
Employer programs that attempt to instill symbolic and substantive changes in the organization's emphasis on safety.

SAFETY AWARENESS PROGRAMS

Safety awareness programs go beyond compliance with OSHA and attempt to instill symbolic and substantive changes in the organization's emphasis on safety. These programs typically focus either on specific jobs and job elements or on specific types of injuries or disabilities. A safety awareness program has three primary components: identifying and communicating hazards, reinforcing safe practices, and promoting safety internationally.

NONFATAL INJURIES AND ILLNESSES, PRIVATE INDUSTRY	FATAL WORK-RELATED INJURIES
Total recordable cases: 3,007,300 in 2013	Total fatal injuries (all sectors): 4,585 in 2013
Cases involving days away from work: 917,100 in 2013	Roadway incidents (all sectors): 1,099 in 2013
Median days away from work: 8 in 2013	Falls, slips, trips (all sectors): 724 in 2013
Cases involving sprains, strains, tears: 327,060 in 2013	Homicides (all sectors): 404 in 2013
Cases involving injuries to the back: 170,450 in 2013	
Cases involving falls, slips, trips: 229,190 in 2013	

Table 3.7
Some of the Most Recent Statistics Provided by the Bureau of Labor Statistics Regarding Workplace Illnesses and Injuries

SOURCE: www.bls.gov.

Identifying and Communicating Job Hazards

Employees, supervisors, and other knowledgeable sources need to sit down and discuss potential problems related to safety. The **job hazard analysis technique** is one means of accomplishing this.[59] With this technique, each job is broken down into basic elements, and each of these is rated for its potential for harm or injury. If there is consensus that some job element has high hazard potential, this element is isolated and potential technological or behavioral changes are considered.

Another means of isolating unsafe job elements is to study past accidents. The **technic of operations review (TOR)** is an analysis methodology that helps managers determine which specific element of a job led to a past accident.[60] The first step in a TOR analysis is to establish the facts surrounding the incident. To accomplish this, all members of the work group involved in the accident give their initial impressions of what happened. The group must then, through group discussion, reach a consensus on the single, systematic failure that most contributed to the incident as well as two or three major secondary factors that contributed to it.

An analysis of jobs at Burger King, for example, revealed that certain jobs required employees to walk across wet or slippery surfaces, which led to many falls. Specific corrective action was taken based on analysis of where people were falling and what conditions led to these falls. Now Burger King provides mats at critical locations and has generally upgraded its floor maintenance. The company also makes slip-resistant shoes available to employees in certain job categories.[61]

Communication of an employee's risk should take advantage of several media. Direct verbal supervisory contact is important for its saliency and immediacy. Written memos are important because they help establish a "paper trail" that can later document a history of concern regarding the job hazard. Posters, especially those placed near the hazard, serve as a constant reminder, reinforcing other messages.

In communicating risk, it is important to recognize two distinct audiences. Sometimes relatively young or inexperienced workers need special attention. Research by the National Safety Council indicates that 40% of all accidents happen to individuals in the 20-to-29 age group and that 48% of all accidents happen to workers during their first year on the job.[62] The employer's primary concern with respect to this group is to inform them. However, the employer must not overlook experienced workers. Here the key concern is to remind them.

Job Hazard Analysis Technique
A breakdown of each job into basic elements, each of which is rated for its potential for harm or injury.

Technic of Operations Review (TOR)
Method of determining safety problems via an analysis of past accidents.

Research indicates that long-term exposure to and familiarity with a specific threat lead to complacency.[63] Experienced employees need retraining to jar them from complacency about the real dangers associated with their work. This is especially the case if the hazard in question poses a greater threat to older employees. For example, falling off a ladder is a greater threat to older workers than to younger ones. More than 20% of such falls lead to a fatality for workers in the 55-to-65 age group, compared with just 10% for all other workers.[64] While most of this discussion has focused on workplace safety, increasingly technology has enabled and encouraged workers to work at home off the clock.

Reinforcing Safe Practices

One common technique for reinforcing safe practices is implementing a safety incentive program to reward workers for their support and commitment to safety goals. Initially, programs are set up to focus on improving short-term monthly or quarterly goals or to encourage safety suggestions. These short-term goals are later expanded to include more wide-ranging, long-term goals. Prizes are typically distributed in highly public forums (like annual meetings or events). These prizes usually consist of merchandise rather than cash because merchandise represents a lasting symbol of achievement. A good deal of evidence suggests that such programs are effective in reducing injuries and their cost.[65]

Whereas the safety awareness programs just described focus primarily on the job, other programs focus on specific injuries or disabilities. Lower back disability (LBD), for example, is a major problem that afflicts many employees. LBD accounts for approximately 25% of all workdays lost, costing firms nearly $30 billion a year.[66] Human resource managers can take many steps to prevent LBD and rehabilitate those who are already afflicted. Eye injuries are another target of safety awareness programs. The National Society to Prevent Blindness estimates that 1,000 eye injuries occur every day in occupational settings.[67] A 10-step program to reduce eye injuries is outlined in Table 3.8. Similar guidelines can be found for everything from chemical burns to electrocution to injuries caused by boiler explosions.[68]

Promoting Safety Internationally

Given the increasing focus on international management, organizations also need to consider how to best ensure the safety of people regardless of the nation in which they operate. Cultural differences may make this more difficult than it seems. For example, a recent study examined the impact of one standardized corporationwide safety policy on employees in

Table 3.8
A 10-Step Program for Reducing Eye-Related Injuries

1. Conduct an eye hazard job analysis.
2. Test all employees' vision to establish a baseline.
3. Select protective eyewear designed for specific operations.
4. Establish a 100% behavioral compliance program for eyewear.
5. Ensure that eyewear is properly fitted.
6. Train employees in emergency procedures.
7. Conduct ongoing education programs regarding eye care.
8. Continually review accident prevention strategies.
9. Provide management support.
10. Establish written policies detailing sanctions and rewards for specific results.

SOURCE: From T. W. Turrif, "NSPB Suggests 10-Step Program to Prevent Eye Injury," *Occupational Health and Safety* 60 (1991), pp. 62–66. Copyright © Media Inc. Reprinted with permission.

three different countries: the United States, France, and Argentina. The results of this study indicated that the same policy was interpreted differently because of cultural differences. The individualistic, control-oriented culture of the United States stressed the role of top management in ensuring safety in a top-down fashion. However, this policy failed to work in Argentina, where the collectivist culture made employees feel that safety was everyone's joint concern; therefore, programs needed to be defined from the bottom up.[69]

At the beginning of this section we discussed a horrific accident at BP's Texas City refinery. After examining the causes of the explosion, the U.S. Chemical Safety and Hazard Investigation Board asked BP to set up an independent panel that would focus on oversee-ing radical changes in BP's safety procedures. This panel was tasked with investigating the safety culture at BP along with the procedures for inspecting equipment and reporting near-miss accidents. The panel's charter is not just to oversee the Texas City refinery, but also to look at the safety practices in refineries that BP has acquired over the years.[70]

A LOOK BACK

Did Kleiner Perkins Discriminate?

Ellen Pao lost her discrimination case against Kleiner Perkins. While her allegations carried credibility, the firm successfully argued that the decisions it took with regard to her were based on poor performance and poor relationships with co-workers. A number of witnesses described her as passive-aggressive, generally ineffective, and disloyal. In the trial Ms. Pao was accused of being both too aggressive and too timid. "You have this needle that you have to thread, and sometimes it feels like there's no hole in the needle," she said. "From what I've heard from women, they do feel like there's no way to win. They can't be aggressive and get this opportunity without being treated like they've done something wrong."

QUESTIONS

1. Do you think that all discrimination is overt and obvious, or does it often hap-pen due to implicit mindsets? Explain.
2. How can firms ensure that all employees have a fair chance at promotions and pay raises, and that these decisions are not determined by implicit discrimination?

SOURCE: J. Elder, "Ellen Pao Says Gender Issues Won't 'Go Away' after Kleiner Trial," *The Wall Street Journal,* April 6, 2015, www.wsj.com.

SUMMARY

Viewing employees as a source of competitive advantage results in dealing with them in ways that are ethical and legal as well as providing a safe workplace. An organiza-tion's legal environment—especially the laws regarding equal employment opportunity and safety—has a particu-larly strong effect on its HRM function. HRM is concerned with the management of people, and government is con-cerned with protecting individuals. One of HRM's major challenges, therefore, is to perform its function within the legal constraints imposed by the government. Given the multimillion-dollar settlements resulting from violations of EEO laws (and the moral requirement to treat people fairly regardless of their sex or race) as well as the penalties for violating OSHA, HR and line managers need a good under-standing of the legal requirements and prohibitions in order to manage their businesses in ways that are sound, both financially and ethically. Organizations that do so effectively will definitely have a competitive advantage.

KEY TERMS

Equal employment opportunity
(EEO), 103
Americans with Disabilities Act
(ADA) of 1990, 109
Equal Employment Opportunity
Commission (EEOC), 111
Utilization analysis, 113
Goals and timetables, 113

Action steps, 113
Disparate treatment, 114
Bona fide occupational qualification
(BFOQ), 116
Disparate impact, 117
Four-fifths rule, 118
Standard deviation rule, 118
Reasonable accommodation, 121

Occupational Safety and Health Act
(OSHA), 132
General duty clause, 132
Safety awareness programs, 134
Job hazard analysis technique, 135
Technic of operations review
(TOR), 135

DISCUSSION QUESTIONS

1. Disparate impact theory was originally created by the court in the *Griggs* case before finally being codified by Congress 20 years later in the Civil Rights Act of 1991. Given the system of law in the United States, from what branch of government should theories of discrimination develop?

2. Disparate impact analysis (the four-fifths rule, standard deviation analysis) is used in employment discrimination cases. The National Assessment of Education Progress conducted by the U.S. Department of Education found that among 21- to 25-year-olds (a) 60% of whites, 40% of Hispanics, and 25% of blacks could locate information in a news article or almanac; (b) 25% of whites, 7% of Hispanics, and 3% of blacks could decipher a bus schedule; and (c) 44% of whites, 20% of Hispanics, and 8% of blacks could correctly determine the change they were due from the purchase of a two-item restaurant meal. Do these tasks (locating information in a news article, deciphering a bus schedule, and determining correct change) have adverse impact? What are the implications?

3. Many companies have dress codes that require men to wear suits and women to wear dresses. Is this discriminatory according to disparate treatment theory? Why?

4. Cognitive ability tests seem to be the most valid selection devices available for hiring employees, yet they also have adverse impact against blacks and Hispanics. Given the validity and adverse impact, and considering that race norming is illegal under CRA 1991, what would you say in response to a recommendation that such tests be used for hiring?

5. How might the ADA's reasonable accommodation requirement affect workers such as law enforcement officers and firefighters?

6. The reasonable woman standard recognizes that women have different ideas than men of what constitutes appropriate behavior. What are the implications of this distinction? Do you think it is a good or bad idea to make this distinction?

7. Employers' major complaint about the ADA is that the costs of making reasonable accommodations will reduce their ability to compete with businesses (especially foreign ones) that do not face these requirements. Is this a legitimate concern? How should employers and society weigh the costs and benefits of the ADA?

8. Many have suggested that OSHA penalties are too weak and misdirected (aimed at employers rather than employees) to have any significant impact on employee safety. Do you think that OSHA-related sanctions need to be strengthened, or are existing penalties sufficient? Defend your answer.

SELF-ASSESSMENT EXERCISE

Additional assignable self-assessments available in Connect.

Take the following self-assessment quiz. For each statement, circle T if the statement is true or F if the statement is false.

WHAT DO YOU KNOW ABOUT SEXUAL HARASSMENT?

1. A man cannot be the victim of sexual harassment.
   T F
2. The harasser can only be the victim's manager or a manager in another work area.   T F
3. Sexual harassment charges can be filed only by the person who directly experiences the harassment.   T F

4. The best way to discourage sexual harassment is to have a policy that discourages employees from dating each other.   T F
5. Sexual harassment is not a form of sex discrimination.   T F
6. After receiving a sexual harassment complaint, the employer should let the situation cool off before investigating the complaint.   T F
7. Sexual harassment is illegal only if it results in the victim being laid off or receiving lower pay.   T F

EXERCISING STRATEGY

Home Depot's Bumpy Road to Equality

Home Depot is the largest home products firm selling home repair products and equipment for the "do-it-yourselfer." Founded 20 years ago, it now boasts 100,000 employees and more than 900 warehouse stores nationwide. The company's strategy for growth has focused mostly on one task: build more stores. In fact, an unwritten goal of Home Depot executives was to position a store within 30 minutes of every customer in the United States. They've almost made it. In addition, Home Depot has tried hard to implement a strategy of providing superior service to its customers. The company has prided itself on hiring people who are knowledgeable about home repair and who can teach customers how to do home repairs on their own. This strategy, along with blanketing the country with stores, has led to the firm's substantial advantage over competitors, including the now-defunct Home Quarters (HQ) and still-standing Lowe's.

But Home Depot has run into some legal problems. During the company's growth, a statistical anomaly has emerged. About 70% of the merchandise employees (those directly involved in selling lumber, electrical supplies, hardware, and so forth) are men, whereas about 70% of operations employees (cashiers, accountants, back office staff, and so forth) are women. Because of this difference, several years ago a lawsuit was filed on behalf of 17,000 current and former employees as well as up to 200,000 rejected applicants. Home Depot explained the disparity by noting that most female job applicants have experience as cashiers, so they are placed in cashier positions; most male applicants express an interest in or aptitude for home repair work such as carpentry or plumbing. However, attorneys argued that Home Depot was reinforcing gender stereotyping by hiring in this manner.

More recently, five former Home Depot employees sued the company, charging that it had discriminated against African American workers at two stores in southeast Florida. The five alleged that they were paid less than white workers, passed over for promotion, and given critical performance reviews based on race. "The company takes exception to the charges and believes they are without merit," said Home Depot spokesman Jerry Shields. The company has faced other racial discrimination suits as well, including one filed by the Michigan Department of Civil Rights.

To avoid such lawsuits in the future, Home Depot could resort to hiring and promoting by quota, ensuring an equal distribution of employees across all job categories—something that the company has wanted to avoid because it believes such action would undermine its competitive

advantage. However, the company has taken steps to broaden and strengthen its own nondiscrimination policy by adding sexual orientation to the written policy. In addition, company president and CEO Bob Nardelli announced in the fall of 2001 that Home Depot would take special steps to protect benefits for its more than 500 employees who serve in the Army reserves and had been activated. "We will make up any difference between their Home Depot pay and their military pay if it's lower," said Nardelli. "When they come home [from duty], their jobs and their orange aprons are waiting for them."

In settling the gender discrimination suit the company agreed to pay $65 million to women who had been steered to cashiers' jobs and had been denied promotions. In addition, the company promised that every applicant would get a "fair shot." Home Depot's solution to this has been to leverage technology to make better hiring decisions that ensure the company is able to maximize diversity.

Home Depot instituted its Job Preference Program, an automated hiring and promotion system, across its 900 stores at a cost of $10 million. It has set up kiosks where potential applicants can log on to a computer, complete an application, and undergo a set of prescreening tests. This process weeds out unqualified applicants. Then the system prints out test scores along with structured interview questions and examples of good and bad answers for the managers interviewing those who make it through the prescreening. In addition, the Home Depot system is used for promotions. Employees are asked to constantly update their skills and career aspirations so they can be considered for promotions at nearby stores.

The system has been an unarguable success. Managers love it because they are able to get high-quality applicants without having to sift through mounds of résumés. In addition, the system seems to have accomplished its main purpose. The number of female managers has increased 30% and the number of minority managers by 28% since the introduction of the system. In fact, David Borgen, the co-counsel for the plaintiffs in the original lawsuit, states, "No one can say it can't be done anymore, because Home Depot is doing it bigger and better than anyone I know."

QUESTIONS

1. If Home Depot was correct in that it was not discriminating, but simply filling positions consistent with those who applied for them (and very few women were applying for customer service positions), given your reading of this chapter, was the firm guilty of discrimination? If so, under what theory?

2. How does this case illustrate the application of new technology to solving issues that have never been tied to technology? Can you think of other ways technology might be used to address diversity/EEO/affirmative action issues?

SOURCES: "Home Depot Says Thanks to America's Military; Extends Associates/Reservists' Benefits, Announces Military Discount," company press release, October 9, 2001; S. Jaffe, "New Tricks in Home Depot's Toolbox?"

BusinessWeek Online, June 5, 2001, at www.businessweek.com; "HRC Lauds Home Depot for Adding Sexual Orientation to Its Non-discrimination Policy," Human Rights Campaign, May 14, 2001, at www.hrc.org; "Former Home Depot Employees File Racial Discrimination Lawsuit," Diversity at Work, June 2000, at www.diversityatwork.com; "Michigan Officials File Discrimination Suit against Home Depot," Diversity at Work, February 2000, at www.diversityatwork.com; M. Boot, "For Plaintiffs' Lawyers, There's No Place Like Home Depot," *The Wall Street Journal,* interactive edition, February 12, 1997.

MANAGING PEOPLE

Brown v. Board of Education: A Bittersweet Birthday

May 17 marks the 50th anniversary of *Brown v. Board of Education,* the landmark Supreme Court ruling that declared racially segregated "separate but equal" schools unconstitutional. The case is widely regarded as one of the court's most important decisions of the 20th century, but the birthday celebration will be something of a bittersweet occasion. There's no question that African Americans have made major strides since—economically, socially, and educationally. But starting in the late 1980s, political backlash brought racial progress to a halt. Since then, schools have slowly been resegregating, and the achievement gap between white and minority schoolchildren has been widening again. Can the United States ever achieve the great promise of integration? Some key questions follow.

What did the court strike down in 1954? Throughout the South and in border states such as Delaware, black and white children were officially assigned to separate schools. In Topeka, Kansas, the lead city in the famous case, there were 18 elementary schools for whites and just 4 for blacks, forcing many African American children to travel a long way to school. The idea that black schools were "equal" to those for whites was a cruel fiction, condemning most black kids to a grossly inferior education.

Surely we've come a long way since then? Yes, though change took a long time. Over 99% of Southern black children were still in segregated schools in 1963. The 1960s civil rights movement eventually brought aggressive federal policies such as busing and court orders that forced extensive integration, especially in the South. So by 1988, 44% of Southern black children were attending schools where a majority of students were white, up from 2% in 1964. "We cut school desegregation almost in half between 1968 and 1990," says John Logan, director of the Lewis Mumford Center for Comparative Urban and Regional Research at State University of New York at Albany.

What's the picture today? There have been some real gains. The share of blacks graduating from high school has nearly quadrupled since *Brown,* to 88% today, while the share of those ages 25 to 29 with a college degree has increased more than sixfold, to 18%.

Another important trend is in housing, which in turn helps determine the characteristics of school districts. Residential integration is improving, albeit at a glacial pace. There's still high housing segregation in major metropolitan areas, but it has fallen four percentage points, to 65%, on an index developed by the Mumford Center. Some of the gains are happening in fast-growing new suburbs where race lines aren't so fixed. A few big cities have improved, too. In Dallas, for example, black–white residential segregation fell from 78% in 1980 to 59% in 2000.

Why haven't schools continued to desegregate, too? The increased racial mixing in housing hasn't been nearly large enough to offset the sheer increase in the ranks of minority schoolchildren. While the number of white elementary school kids remained flat, at 15.3 million, between 1990 and 2000, the number of black children climbed by 800,000, to 4.6 million, while Hispanic kids jumped by 1.7 million, to 4.3 million. The result: Minorities now comprise 40% of public school kids, vs. 32% in 1990. And as the nonwhite population has expanded, so have minority neighborhoods—and schools.

So minorities have lost ground? Yes, in some respects. By age 17, black students are still more than three years behind their white counterparts in reading and math. And whites are twice as likely to graduate from college. Taken as a whole, U.S. schools have been resegregating for 15 years or so, according to studies by the Harvard University Civil Rights Project. "We're celebrating [Brown] at a time when schools in all regions are becoming increasingly segregated," says project co-director Gary Orfield.

What role has the political backlash against integration played? The courts and politicians have been pulling back from integration goals for quite a while. In 1974, the Supreme Court ruled that heavily black Detroit didn't have to integrate its schools with the surrounding white suburbs. Then, in the 1980s, the growing backlash against busing and race-based school assignment led politicians and the courts to all but give up on those remedies, too.

So what are the goals now? The approach has shifted dramatically. Instead of trying to force integration, the United States has moved toward equalizing education. In a growing number of states, the courts have been siding with lawsuits that seek equal or "adequate" funding for minority and low-income schools.

The No Child Left Behind Act goes even further. It says that all children will receive a "highly qualified" teacher by 2006 and will achieve proficiency in math and reading by 2014. It specifically requires schools to meet these goals for racial subgroups. Paradoxically, it sounds like separate but equal again. Both the equal-funding suits and No Child Left Behind aim to improve all schools, whatever their racial composition. Integration is no longer the explicit goal.

Can schools equalize without integrating?   It's possible in some cases, but probably not for the United States as a whole. The Education Trust, a nonprofit group in Washington, D.C., has identified a number of nearly all-black, low-income schools that have achieved exceptional test results. But such success requires outstanding leadership, good teachers, and a fervent commitment to high standards.

These qualities are far more difficult to achieve in large urban schools with many poor kids—the kind most black and Hispanic students attend. The average minority student goes to a school in which two-thirds of the students are low-income. By contrast, whites attend schools that are just 30% low-income.

So are black–white achievement gaps as much about poverty as race?   Yes, which is why closing them is difficult with or without racial integration. Studies show that middle-class students tend to have higher expectations, more engaged parents, and better teachers. Poor children, by contrast, often come to school with far more personal problems. Yet poor schools are more likely to get inferior teachers, such as those who didn't major in the subject they teach. Many poor schools also lose as many as 20% of their teachers each year, while most middle-class suburban schools have more stable teaching staffs. "Research suggests that when low-income students attend middle-class schools, they do substantially better," says Richard Kahlenberg, senior fellow at the Century Foundation, a public policy think tank in New York City.

Is it possible to achieve more economic integration?   There are a few shining examples, but they take enormous political commitment. One example that education-system reformers love to highlight is Wake County, N.C., whose 110,000-student school district includes Raleigh. In 2000, it adopted a plan to ensure that low-income students make up no more than 40% of any student body. It also capped those achieving under grade level at 25%. Moreover, it used magnet schools offering specialized programs, such as one for gifted children, to help attract middle-income children to low-income areas.

Already, 91% of the county's third- to eighth-graders work at grade level in math and reading, up from 84% in 1999. More impressive, 75% of low-income kids are reading at grade level, up from just 56% in 1999, as are 78% of black children, up from 61%. "The academic payoff has been pretty incredible," says Walter C. Sherlin, a 28-year Wake County schools veteran and interim director of the nonprofit Wake Education Partnership.

Could this serve as a national model?   For that to happen in many cities, school districts would have to merge with the surrounding suburbs. Wake County did this, but that was back in the 1970s and part of a long-term plan to bring about racial integration. In the metro Boston area, by contrast, students are balkanized into dozens of tiny districts, many of which are economically homogeneous. The result: Some 70% of white students attend schools that are over 90% white and overwhelmingly middle-class. Meanwhile, 97% of the schools that are over 90% minority are also high-poverty. Similar patterns exist in most major cities, but most affluent white suburbs aren't likely to swallow a move like Wake County's.

How important is funding equality within states?   It's critical, especially if segregation by income and race persists. Massachusetts, for instance, has nearly tripled state aid to schools since 1993, with over 90% of the money going to the poorest towns. That has helped make Massachusetts a national leader in raising academic achievement.

Nationally, though, there are still huge inequities in school spending, with the poorest districts receiving less money than the richest—even though low-income children are more expensive to educate. Fixing these imbalances would be costly. Even in Massachusetts, a lower court judge ruled on April 26 that the system still shortchanges students in the poorest towns. Nationally, it would cost more than $50 billion a year in extra funding to correct inequities enough to meet the goals of No Child, figures Anthony P. Carnevale, a vice president at Educational Testing Service.

If, somehow, the United States could achieve more economic integration, would racial integration still be necessary?   Proficiency on tests isn't the only aim. As the Supreme Court said last year in a landmark decision on affirmative action in higher education: "Effective participation by members of all racial and ethnic groups in the civic life of our nation is essential if the dream of one nation, indivisible, is to be realized." It's hard to see how students attending largely segregated schools, no matter how proficient, could be adequately prepared for life in an increasingly diverse country. In this sense, integrating America's educational system remains an essential, though still elusive, goal.

QUESTIONS

1. While segregation of public schools has been outlawed, the article notes that schools are not necessarily "desegregating" (i.e., there are still predominantly minority and predominantly nonminority schools). If students are to work in increasingly diverse workforces, is the current system failing them? Why or why not?
2. The black–white gap continues to exist with regard to reading, math, and graduation rates. What are the

implications of this on organizations' selection systems (i.e., disparate impact)?

3. Given the lack of a "diverse" educational experience for a large percentage of black children, and the gap between them and their white counterparts, what must organizations do to leverage diversity as a source of competitive advantage?

HR IN SMALL BUSINESS

Company Fails Fair-Employment Test

Companies have to comply with federal as well as state and local laws. One company that didn't was Professional Neurological Services (PNS), which was cited by the Chicago Commission on Human Relations when it discriminated against an employee because she is a parent. Chicago is one of a few cities that prohibit this type of discrimination.

The difficulties began with employee Dena Lockwood as soon as she was interviewing for a sales position with PNS. The interviewer noticed that Lockwood made a reference to her children, and he asked her if her responsibilities as a parent would "prevent her from working 70 hours a week." Lockwood said no, but the job offer she received suggests that the interviewer had his doubts. According to Lockwood's later complaint, female sales reps without children routinely were paid a $45,000 base salary plus a 10% commission. Lockwood was offered $25,000 plus the 10% commission. Lockwood negotiated and eventually accepted $45,000 plus 5%, with a promise to increase the commission rate to 10% when she reached sales of $300,000. She was also offered five vacation days a year; when she objected, she was told not to worry.

Lockwood worked hard and eventually reached her sales goal. Then the company raised the requirement for the higher commission rate, and the situation took a turn for the worse. Lockwood's daughter woke up one morning with pink-eye, a highly contagious ailment. Lockwood called in to reschedule a meeting for that day, but her manager told her not to bother; she was being fired. When Lockwood asked why, the manager said "it just wasn't working out."

She went to the Chicago Human Relations Commission for help. The commission investigated and could find no evidence of performance-related problems that would justify her dismissal. Instead, the commission found that Lockwood was a victim of "blatant" discrimination against employees with children and awarded her $213,000 plus attorney's fees—a hefty fine for a company with fewer than 50 employees. PNS stated that it would appeal the decision.

QUESTIONS

1. Why do you think "parental discrimination" was the grounds for this complaint instead of a federally protected class? Could you make a case for discrimination on the basis of sex? Why or why not?
2. How could Professional Neurological Services have avoided this problem?
3. Imagine that the company has called you in to help it hold down human resources costs, including costs of lawsuits such as this one. What advice would you give? How can the company avoid discrimination and still build an efficient workforce?

SOURCES: Courtney Rubin, "Single Mother Wins $200,000 in Job Bias Case," *Inc.,* January 25, 2010, www.inc.com; and Ameet Sachdev, "She Took a Day Off to Care for Sick Child, Got Fired," *Chicago Tribune,* January 24, 2010, NewsBank, http://infoweb.newsbank.com.

NOTES

1. J. Ledvinka, *Federal Regulation of Personnel and Human Resource Management* (Boston: Kent, 1982).
2. *Martin v. Wilks,* 49 FEP Cases 1641 (1989).
3. *Wards Cove Packing Co. v. Atonio,* FEPC 1519 (1989).
4. *Bakke v. Regents of the University of California,* 17 FEPC 1000 (1978).
5. *Patterson v. McLean Credit Union,* 49 FEPC 1814 (1987).
6. J. Friedman and G. Strickler, *The Law of Employment Discrimination: Cases and Materials,* 2nd ed. (Mineola, NY: Foundation Press, 1987).
7. "Labor Letter," *The Wall Street Journal,* August 25, 1987, p. 1.
8. J. Woo, "Ex-Workers Hit Back with Age-Bias Suits," *The Wall Street Journal,* December 8, 1992, p. B1.
9. W. Carley, "Salesman's Treatment Raises Bias Questions at Schering-Plough," *The Wall Street Journal,* May 31, 1995, p. A1.
10. www.eeoc.gov/press/1-8-07.html.
11. www.eeoc.gov/eeoc/newsroom/release/4-27-11b.cfm.
12. Special feature issue: "The New Civil Rights Act of 1991 and What It Means to Employers," *Employment Law Update* 6 (December 1991), pp. 1–12.
13. "ADA: The Final Regulations (Title I): A Lawyer's Dream/An Employer's Nightmare," *Employment Law Update* 16, no. 9 (1991), p. 1.

14. "ADA Supervisor Training Program: A Must for Any Supervisor Conducting a Legal Job Interview," *Employment Law Update* 7, no. 6 (1992), pp. 1–6.

15. www.hreonline.com/HRE/story.jsp?storyId=533335303.

16. Equal Employment Opportunity Commission, "Uniform Guidelines on Employee Selection Procedures," *Federal Register* 43 (1978), pp. 38290–315.

17. Ledvinka, *Federal Regulation.*

18. R. Pear, "The Cabinet Searches for Consensus on Affirmative Action," *The New York Times,* October 27, 1985, p. E5.

19. *McDonnell Douglas v. Green,* 411 U.S. 972 (1973).

20. www.eeoc.gov/eeoc/newsroom/release/4-29-11.cfm.

21. *UAW v. Johnson Controls, Inc.* (1991).

22. M. O'Brien, "Ugly People Need Not Apply?" *HR Executive,* September 16, 2010, p. 12.

23. Special feature issue: "The New Civil Rights Act of 1991," pp. 1–6.

24. *Washington v. Davis,* 12 FEP 1415 (1976).

25. *Albermarle Paper Company v. Moody,* 10 FEP 1181 (1975).

26. R. Reilly and G. Chao, "Validity and Fairness of Some Alternative Employee Selection Procedures," *Personnel Psychology* 35 (1982), pp. 1–63; J. Hunter and R. Hunter, "Validity and Utility of Alternative Predictors of Job Performance," *Psychological Bulletin* 96 (1984), pp. 72–98.

27. *Griggs v. Duke Power Company,* 401 U.S. 424 (1971).

28. B. Lindeman and P. Grossman, *Employment Discrimination Law* (Washington, DC: BNA Books, 1996).

29. M. Jacobs, "Workers' Religious Beliefs May Get New Attention," *The Wall Street Journal,* August 22, 1995, pp. B1, B8.

30. EEOC, "EEOC and Electrolux Reach Voluntary Resolution in Class Religious Accommodation Case," at www.eeoc.gov/press/9-24-03.

31. S. Sataline, "Who's Wrong When Rights Collide?" *The Wall Street Journal,* March 6, 2007, p. B1.

32. "Manager's Failure to Accommodate Creates Liability for Store," *Disability Compliance Bulletin,* January 15, 2009.

33. Lindeman and Grossman, *Employment Discrimination Law.*

34. J. Reno and D. Thornburgh, "ADA—Not a Disabling Mandate," *The Wall Street Journal,* July 26, 1995, p. A12.

35. www.eeoc.gov/eeoc/newsroom/release/4-28-11.cfm.

36. Woo, "Ex-Workers Hit Back."

37. EEOC, "Target Corp. to Pay $775,000 for Racial Harassment: EEC Settles Suit for Class of African American Employees; Remedial Relief Included," at www.eeoc.gov/press/1-26-07.html.

38. W. Johnston and A. Packer, *Workforce 2000* (Indianapolis, IN: Hudson Institute, 1987).

39. *Bundy v. Jackson,* 641 F.2d 934, 24 FEP 1155 (D.C. Cir., 1981).

40. L. A. Graf and M. Hemmasi, "Risqué Humor: How It Really Affects the Workplace," *HR Magazine,* November 1995, pp. 64–69.

41. B. Carton, "At Jenny Craig, Men Are Ones Who Claim Sex Discrimination," *The Wall Street Journal,* November 29, 1995, p. A1; "Male-on-Male Harassment Suit Won," *Houston Chronicle,* August 12, 1995, p. 21A.

42. EEOC, "Texas Car Dealership to Pay $140,000 to Settle Same-Sex Harassment Suit by EEOC," at www.eeoc.gov/press/10-28-02.

43. EEOC, "Babies 'R' Us to Pay $205,000, Implement Training Due to Same-Sex Harassment of Male Employee," at www.eeoc. gov/press/1-15-03.

44. *Meritor Savings Bank v. Vinson* (1986).

45. Source: Patrick, R. (June 10, 2011) Verdict: Jury awards $95 million in Fairview Heights sex harassment suit. www.stltoday.com/news/local/crime-and-courts/jury-awardsmil. . .icle_6f46fa47-3a8b-5266-b094-b95910d51c46.html

46. R. Paetzold and A. O'Leary-Kelly, "The Implications of U.S. Supreme Court and Circuit Court Decisions for Hostile Environment Sexual Harassment Cases," in *Sexual Harassment: Perspectives, Frontiers, and Strategies,* ed. M. Stockdale (Beverly Hills, CA: Sage); R. B. McAfee and D. L. Deadrick, "Teach Employees to Just Say 'No'!" *HR Magazine,* February 1996, pp. 586–89.

47. C. Murray, "The Legacy of the 60's," *Commentary,* July 1992, pp. 23–30.

48. D. Kravitz and J. Platania, "Attitudes and Beliefs about Affirmative Action: Effects of Target and of Respondent Sex and Ethnicity," *Journal of Applied Psychology* 78 (1993), pp. 928–38.

49. J. Mathews, "Rash of Unintended Lawsuits Follows Passage of Disabilities Act," *Houston Chronicle,* May 16, 1995, p. 15A.

50. C. Bell, "What the First ADA Cases Tell Us," *SHRM Legal Report* (Winter 1995), pp. 4–7.

51. J. Fitzgerald, "Chatty IBMer Booted," *New York Post,* February 18, 2007.

52. National Organization on Disability 2006 Annual Report at www.nod.org.

53. K. Mills, "Disabilities Act: A Help, or a Needless Hassle," *B/CS Eagle,* August 23, 1995, p. A7.

54. C. Cummins and T. Herrick, "Investigators Fault BP for More Lapses in Refinery Safety," *The Wall Street Journal,* August 18, 2005, p. A3.

55. V. F. Estrada, "Are Your Factory Workers Know-It-All?" *Personnel Journal,* September 1995, pp. 128–34.

56. R. L. Simison, "Safety Last," *The Wall Street Journal,* March 18, 1986, p. 1.

57. J. Roughton, "Managing a Safety Program through Job Hazard Analysis," *Professional Safety* 37 (1992), pp. 28–31.

58. M. A. Verespec, "OSHA Reform Fails Again," *Industry Week,* November 2, 1992, p. 36.

59. R. G. Hallock and D. A. Weaver, "Controlling Losses and Enhancing Management Systems with TOR Analysis," *Professional Safety* 35 (1990), pp. 24–26.

60. H. Herbstman, "Controlling Losses the Burger King Way," *Risk Management* 37 (1990), pp. 22–30.

61. L. Bryan, "An Ounce of Prevention for Workplace Accidents," *Training and Development Journal* 44 (1990), pp. 101–2.

62. J. F. Mangan, "Hazard Communications: Safety in Knowledge," *Best's Review* 92 (1991), pp. 84–88.

63. T. Markus, "How to Set Up a Safety Awareness Program," *Supervision* 51 (1990), pp. 14–16.

64. J. Agnew and A. J. Saruda, "Age and Fatal Work-Related Falls," *Human Factors* 35 (1994), pp. 731–36.

65. R. King, "Active Safety Programs, Education Can Help Prevent Back Injuries," *Occupational Health and Safety* 60 (1991), pp. 49–52.

66. J. R. Hollenbeck, D. R. Ilgen, and S. M. Crampton, "Lower Back Disability in Occupational Settings: A Review of the Literature from a Human Resource Management View," *Personnel Psychology* 45 (1992), pp. 247–78.

67. T. W. Turriff, "NSPB Suggests 10-Step Program to Prevent Eye Injury," *Occupational Health and Safety* 60 (1991), pp. 62–66.

68. D. Hanson, "Chemical Plant Safety: OSHA Rule Addresses Industry Concerns," *Chemical and Engineering News* 70 (1992), pp. 4–5; K. Broscheit and K. Sawyer, "Safety Exhibit Teaches Customers and Employees about Electricity," *Transmission and Distribution* 43 (1992), pp. 174–79; R. Schuch, "Good Training Is Key to Avoiding Boiler Explosions," *National Underwriter* 95 (1992), pp. 21–22.

69. M. Janssens, J. M. Brett, and F. J. Smith, "Confirmatory Cross-Cultural Research: Testing the Viability of a Corporation-wide Safety Policy," *Academy of Management Journal* 38 (1995), pp. 364–82.

70. Cummins and Herrick, "Investigators Fault BP."

The Analysis and Design of Work

CHAPTER 4

LEARNING OBJECTIVES

After reading this chapter, you should be able to:

LO 4-1 Analyze an organization's structure and work-flow process, identifying the output, activities, and inputs in the production of a product or service. *page 147*

LO 4-2 Understand the importance of job analysis in strategic human resource management. *page 161*

LO 4-3 Choose the right job analysis technique for a variety of human resource activities. *page 165*

LO 4-4 Identify the tasks performed and the skills required in a given job. *page 167*

LO 4-5 Understand the different approaches to job design. *page 167*

LO 4-6 Comprehend the trade-offs among the various approaches to designing jobs. *page 175*

Organizational Structure Contributes to GM's Major Recall

Organizations exist in order to allow people to accomplish goals and missions that would far outstrip what could ever be done by a single person working alone. Large complex missions have to be broken down into smaller parts that can be executed by individuals whose contributions can then be integrated together. Unfortunately, when the structure created by this process is ineffective, this means that organizations can also do more harm than could ever be done by a single person working alone. Nowhere was this more evident than in the 2014 recall of 2.7 million General Motor (GM) vehicles due to failures in the ignition system, which resulted in deaths and injuries to more than 500 customers, and financial losses of over $400 million.

There were two specific problems associated with GM's structure that helped contribute to the ignition system disaster. First, the structure created functional silos where people who worked on one aspect of the cars rarely spoke to people who worked in other functional areas. For example, the switch problem was, in part, a result of a single engineer who redesigned a faulty part but failed to renumber it. Because it was not renumbered, when the part moved down through the line through other divisions, those divisions all thought they were working on the original part. Then, when reports of cars stalling began rolling in, this was treated as a customer satisfaction problem, not a safety issue or a design flaw. Thus, the personnel monitoring customer satisfaction never talked to the personnel in design who were not even aware of the problem until it was too late.

A second problem with GM's structure was that it was not at all clear who had decision-making authority for different decisions, and people at lower levels of the organization were reluctant to take responsibility for problems or pass bad news up the organization chart. An external investigation of the incident conducted by the U.S. Attorney General's Office revealed that many people were aware of the problem as far back as 2001, but these individuals either said nothing or pointed the finger of blame at other units, and so no one actually did anything to solve the problem. In fact, when the U.S. Attorney General's Office asked a worker who knew about the problem if "fixing the problem was part of your job description," the person simply answered "No." The report from the Attorney General's Office specifically noted that "no single person owned any decision related to the ignition switch problem."

The ignition switch problem was one of the first to fall on the desk of GM's new CEO, Mary Barra, who vowed to fix the structural problems that contributed to this costly incident. Barra note that "we used to have an organizational structure built around parts—the body, the interior, the electrical structure, and unfortunately, that created a situation in which people were expert in this or that without recognizing people don't buy this or that—they buy a car and we've got to pull it together, and people have to talk." She also noted that GM was "going to restructure operations to prioritize safety." This was accomplished by creating a system of "czars" who have specific decision-making authority that cut across functional units and who all report to a single new Vice President of Global Safety.

SOURCES: R. Foroohar, "Mary Barra's Bumpy Ride," *Time Magazine*, October 6, 2014, pp. 33–38; T. Higgens and N. Summers, "GM Recalls: How General Motors Silenced a Whistle-Blower," *Bloomsberg Businessweek*, June 14, 2014, www.businessweek.com; P. Valdes-Dalpena and T. Yellin, "Steps to a Recall Nightmare," *CNNMoney*, May 21, 2014, http://money.cnn.com.

Introduction

In Chapter 2 we discussed the processes of strategy formulation and strategy implementation. Strategy formulation is the process by which a company decides how it will compete in the marketplace; this is often the energizing and guiding force for everything it does. Strategy implementation is the way the strategic plan gets carried out in activities of organizational members. We noted five important components in the strategy implementation process, three of which are directly related to the human resource management function and one of which we will discuss in this chapter: the task or job. For example, as we can see in the case of GM described in the opening vignette, the way the work was structured and the confusion regarding decision-making authority created conditions that led to a very costly recall.

Many central aspects of strategy formulation address how the work gets done, in terms of individual job design as well as the design of organizational structures that link individual jobs to each other and the organization as a whole. The way a firm competes can have a profound impact on the ways jobs are designed and how they are linked via organizational structure. In turn, the fit between the company's structure and environment can have a major impact on the firm's competitive success.

For example, if a company decides to compete on cost, and hence hire low-cost off-shore labor, the jobs have to be designed so that they can be performed by minimally skilled people who will require little training. The organization in this case needs to have a centralized structure so that low-level workers are not forced into making too many decisions and the workers should work independently to prevent errors from cascading through the system. In contrast, if the organization is going to compete by differentiating its product, and hence hiring high-wage labor, it has to design the jobs in a different way.

Throughout this chapter, we provide examples of the kinds of decisions that need to be made with regard to how organizations should be structured and to the jobs that exist within these organizations, so you can learn how these choices affect a number of outcomes. This includes not just quantity and quality of production, but also outcomes like coordination; innovation; and worker attraction, motivation, and retention. In many cases, there are trade-offs associated with the choices, and the more you know about these trade-offs, the better decisions you can make in terms of making your team or organization more competitive.

Thus, it should be clear from the outset of this chapter that there is no "one best way" to design jobs and structure organizations. The organization needs to create a fit between its environment, competitive strategy, and philosophy on the one hand, with its jobs and organizational design on the other. Failing to design effective organizations and jobs has important implications for competitiveness. Many years ago, some believed that the difference between U.S. auto producers and their foreign competitors could be traced to American workers; however, when companies like Toyota and Honda came into the United States and demonstrated clearly that they could run profitable car companies with American workers, the focus shifted to processes and organization. Although many U.S. automakers are now making a comeback, as we saw in our opening vignette, for some companies like GM, this is still an ongoing process.[1]

This chapter discusses the analysis and design of work and, in doing so, lays out some considerations that go into making informed decisions about how to create and link jobs. The chapter is divided into three sections, the first of which deals with "big-picture" issues related to work-flow analysis and organizational structure. The remaining two sections deal with more specific, lower-level issues related to job analysis and job design.

The fields of job analysis and job design have extensive overlap, yet in the past they have been treated differently.[2] Job analysis has focused on analyzing existing jobs to gather information for other human resource management practices such as selection, training, performance appraisal, and compensation. Job design, on the other hand, has focused on redesigning existing jobs to make them more efficient or more motivating to jobholders. Thus job design has had a more proactive orientation toward changing the job, whereas job analysis has had a passive, information-gathering orientation.

Work-Flow Analysis and Organization Structure

Work-flow design is the process of analyzing the tasks necessary for the production of a product or service, prior to allocating and assigning these tasks to a particular job category or person. Only after we thoroughly understand work-flow design can we make informed decisions regarding how to initially bundle various tasks into discrete jobs that can be executed by a single person.

Organization structure refers to the relatively stable and formal network of vertical and horizontal interconnections among jobs that constitute the organization. Only after we understand how one job relates to those above (supervisors), below (subordinates), and at the same level in different functional areas (marketing versus production) can we make informed decisions about how to redesign or improve jobs to benefit the entire organization.

Finally, work-flow design and organization structure have to be understood in the context of how an organization has decided to compete. Both work-flow design and organization structure can be leveraged to gain competitive advantage for the firm, but how one does this depends on the firm's strategy and its competitive environment.

LO 4-1
Analyze an organization's structure and work-flow process, identifying the output, activities, and inputs in the production of a product or service.

WORK-FLOW ANALYSIS

All organizations need to identify the outputs of work, to specify the quality and quantity standards for those outputs, and to analyze the processes and inputs necessary for producing outputs that meet the quality standards. This conception of the work-flow process is useful because it provides a means for the manager to understand all the tasks required to produce a number of high-quality products as well as the skills necessary to perform those tasks. This work-flow process is depicted in Figure 4.1.

Analyzing Work Outputs

Every work unit—whether a department, team, or individual—seeks to produce some output that others can use. An output is the product of a work unit and, within manufacturing realms like those discussed in our opening story, this is often an identifiable object such as a jet engine blade, a forklift, or a football jersey. However, an output can also be a service, such as the services provided by an airline that transports you to some destination, a housecleaning service that maintains your house, or a babysitter who watches over your children.

We often picture an organization only in terms of the product that it produces, and then we focus on that product as the output. Merely identifying an output or set of outputs is not sufficient. Once these outputs have been identified, it is necessary to specify standards for the quantity or quality of these outputs. In many cases, the number and

Figure 4.1

Developing a Work–Unit Activity Analysis

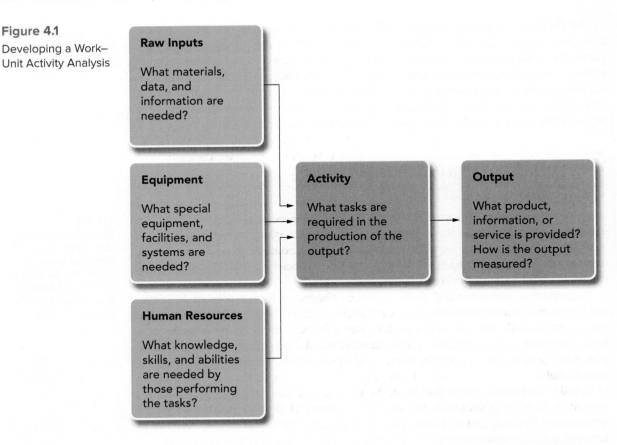

Raw Inputs

What materials, data, and information are needed?

Equipment

What special equipment, facilities, and systems are needed?

Human Resources

What knowledge, skills, and abilities are needed by those performing the tasks?

Activity

What tasks are required in the production of the output?

Output

What product, information, or service is provided? How is the output measured?

nature of the outputs chosen create challenges for how to efficiently process the inputs in order to generate the outputs. For example, recently McDonald's restaurants added many new items to its menus, including oatmeal, snack wraps, and lattes in order to appeal to a wider array of consumers. In fact, the number of menu items at McDonald's swelled to 121 items in 2014, compared to just 85 in 2007. Not surprisingly this results in slower service, and McDonald's also recorded its worst speed-of-performance metrics that same year. Managers often referred to the McWrap specifically as a "showstopper" that required many of the workers to look up a series of instructions in order to execute a single order. As one franchise owner stated, "We've recognized that we've overtaxed our restaurants and need to take a step back on that." Thus, this first step in deciding on the number of products or services offered is a critical step when it comes to structuring the work.[3]

Analyzing Work Processes

Once the outputs of the work unit have been identified, it is possible to examine the work processes used to generate the output. The work processes are the activities that members of a work unit engage in to produce a given output. Every process consists of operating procedures that specify how things should be done at each stage of the development of the product. These procedures include all the tasks that must be performed in the production of the output. The tasks are usually broken down into those performed by each person in the work unit. Of course, in many situations where the work that needs to be done is highly complex, no single individual is likely to have all the required skills. In these situations, the work may be assigned to a team, and team-based job design is becoming increasingly popular in contemporary organizations. In addition to providing a wider set of skills, team members can back each other up, share work when any member becomes overloaded, and catch each other's errors.

For example, in the field of medicine, team-based care is increasingly becoming the norm. Rather than a single one-on-one doctor–patient relationship, many medical services are delivered by a team that might include a nurse practitioner, physician's assistant, clinical pharmacist, and a variety of technicians who work alongside the primary physician. Part of this is a result of increased workload created by the new Affordable Care Act, as well as a reduction in the number of general practitioners minted by medical schools. As noted by Dr. Kirsten Meisinger, a supervising physician who oversees an 11-person team, "I can't possibly do everything that needs to be done for all of our patients as a single human being." The main challenge with team-based work design is to make sure that there is effective coordination and communication between team members to make sure patients do not fall through the cracks or miss some important treatment due to a weak "hand-off."[4]

Teams are not a panacea and for teams to be effective, it is essential that the level of task interdependence (how much they have to cooperate) matches the level of outcome interdependence (how much they share the reward for task accomplishment).[5] That is, if work is organized around teams, team bonuses rather than individual pay raises need to play a major role in terms of defining rewards. Teams also have to be given the autonomy to make their own decisions in order to maximize the flexible use of their skill and time and thus promote problem solving.[6] In addition, some members of teams may lean too much on the other team members and fail to develop their own skills or take responsibility for their own tasks, and so even in teams it is critical to establish individual accountability of behavior.[7]

There is a great deal of value in studying workflow processes and this is best illustrated when private equity groups come in and buy a failing company at a low price, revamp the workflow process, and then sell the company again at a higher price. Private equity groups employ efficiency experts who try to wring out every ounce of waste in production operations. When efficiency experts first come into a company, they are looking for three different kinds of waste: (1) movement that creates no value, (2) the overburdening of specific people or machines, and (3) inconsistent production that creates excessive inventories. Typically armed with stopwatches, clipboards, and flowcharts, efficiency experts prowl the manufacturing floor for waste that would not be detected by most managers. More often than not, this leads to a reduction in headcount because improved procedures dramatically streamline operations. As Justin Hillenbrand, an executive at Monomoy Capital Partners, notes, "You could have the best CEO in the world, but in a manufacturing company, profits are made on the floor."[8]

Organizations often work hard to minimize overstaffing via lean production techniques. Lean production refers to processes developed in Japan, but then adopted worldwide, emphasizing manufacturing goods with a minimum amount of time, materials, money—and most important—people. Lean production tries to leverage technology, along with small numbers of flexible, well-trained, and skilled personnel in order to produce more custom-based products at less cost. This can be contrasted with more traditional "batch work" methods, where large groups of low-skilled employees churn out long runs of identical mass products that are stored in inventories for later sale. In lean production systems, there are fewer employees to begin with, and the skill levels of

Photo by Andrew Ford/Courtesy of ConMed Corporation

This job may look tedious or possibly even uninteresting. Considering how to engage employees in seeing the benefits of their work outside of the lab is an important way to motivate them through their day.

those employees are so high that the opportunity to cuts costs by laying off employees is simply less viable.

Indeed, a paradox of the most recent recession in 2008–2009 was how small many of the layoffs in the manufacturing sector of the economy were given the huge drop in production levels. For example, 14 months into the recession of 2000, manufacturers cut 9.5% of their employees in response to a *2% cut* in production. In contrast, 14 months into the most recent recession, the same 9.5% of employees were laid off in response to a *12% cut* in production. If the same ratio of job cuts to production cuts from the year 2000 held in the year 2009, this would have resulted in an astounding layoff rate of over 50% of manufacturing employees. Many have attributed the lower "job cut" to a "production cut" ratio experienced in the most recent recession to the use of job redesign initiatives that emphasize lean production over more traditional approaches.

For example, at Parker Hannifan Corporation's plastics manufacturing plant in South Carolina, lean production techniques have cut the number of people required to run the plant to such a small number that permanently pulling one highly trained person off the line saves very little money, and yet makes it impossible to sustain production at all. In addition, the work has been restructured to create smaller production runs that result in reduced inventories, so that when a downturn hits, it is noticed more quickly and can be responded to more gradually. In the past, by the time a recession was detected, inventories had bulged to such a level that more employees had to be laid off more quickly and for longer time periods.[9]

Analyzing Work Inputs

The final stage in work-flow analysis is to identify the inputs used in the development of the work unit's product. As shown in Figure 4.1, these inputs can be broken down into the raw materials, equipment, and human skills needed to perform the tasks. *Raw materials* consist of the materials that will be converted into the work unit's product.

Organizations that try to increase efficiency via lean production techniques often try to minimize the stockpile of inputs via "just-in-time" inventory control procedures. Indeed, in some cases, inventories are being abandoned altogether, and companies at the edge of the lean production process do not even manufacture any products until customers actually place an order for them. For example, surgical device maker Conmed used to forecast demand for their products one to two months ahead, and when those forecasts turned out to be inaccurate they would either lose sales or stockpile inventories. Today, because the length of time it takes to produce their devices has decreased from 6 weeks to 48 hours, they do not even manufacture any products that are not already sold. The impact of this can be seen at Conmed's plant in Utica, New York, where a $93,000 inventory that used to take up 3,300 square feet on the factory floor has been all but

Orion and UPS: Plotting the Path to Efficiency and Savings

On average, one single UPS driver can log over 200 miles and make over 120 stops every day. When you multiply this times thousands of drivers who work 5 or 6 days a week for a year, then you begin to see how even very small improvements in efficiency can generate huge sums of money when it comes to saving on gas and vehicle wear and tear. As the company CEO says, "In our business, small things mean a lot. If you can reengineer the process, the gains will be greater than you think." In fact, UPS can save $50 million a year by just reducing the aggregated travel distance for its average driver just one mile.

This is critical to UPS because it competes directly with FedEx, but unlike FedEx, which employs a private contractor model and delivers mainly to businesses, UPS manages a high-wage union workforce that delivers mainly to widely scattered households. The problem with planning the best route each day, however, is that there are literally over a billion options. If one were to leave each driver to his or her own discretion in how to plan their route, there would be very wide variability in their decisions, and the odds that any one of them might come up with the optimal path, is for all intents and purposes zero.

This is where the computer program "Orion" comes in. Orion is a 1,000-page algorithm that tries to mathematically determine the optimal route for making those 120 stops every day for UPS drivers. Working like a GPS system on steroids, Orion constantly updates a driver's schedule and automatically vectors the vehicle based on two criteria: optimum efficiency and consistency. This latter criterion, consistency, is one of the features that make Orion different from most purely mathematical optimizing programs. The program recognizes that both human operators and customers place a great deal of value on consistency, and thus, sacrifices some degree of pure efficiency in order to create a comfortable routine in terms of delivery times and routes.

DISCUSSION QUESTION

Can you think of any other industries or jobs where a program like Orion might have value, and is this a product or service that you believe UPS could market to other companies?

SOURCES: S. Rosenbush and L. Stevens, "At UPS, the Algorithm Is the Driver," *The Wall Street Journal*, February 16, 2015, www.wsj.com; D. Zax, "Brown Down: UPS Drivers versus UPS Algorithms," *Fast Company*, January 3, 2013, www.fastcompany.com.

eliminated. This allowed the company to take back lost sales from Chinese competitors whom, despite their lower labor costs, face the costs of long lead times, inventory pile-ups, and quality problems and transportation costs. As David Johnson, Vice President for Global Operations at Conmed notes, "If more U.S. companies deploy these job design methods we can compete with anybody and still provide security to our workforce."[10]

However, there are also downsides to "just-in-time" inventory management practices. Specifically, the efficiency gained from maintaining an inventory measured in days rather than weeks creates a of lack of flexibility. An example of this can be seen in the aftermath of the earthquake that struck northern Japan in 2011. This region of Japan was home to a number of suppliers who had to unexpectedly halt all production overnight on March 22. This disruption rippled through the entire global economy that relied on "just-in-time" practices when organizations as varied as Boeing, General Motors, John Deere, Hewlett-Packard, and Dell had to halt their own production lines after running out of inputs. As one analyst noted, "If supply is disrupted in this situation, there's nowhere to get inputs."[11]

Equipment refers to the technology and machinery necessary to transform the raw materials into the product. Increasingly, as we see in the "Competing through

Technology" box, equipment refers to software programs that try to support human operators. Although most of the early software programs were designed to free human operators from many mundane tasks, such as an auto-pilot function on an airplane or computer-aided design program for an architect, increasingly new software is capable of analysis and decision making. Thus, rather than "up-skilling" the work, many programs "de-skill" the work, and over time, people who use it become less self-reliant. For example, one study found that the more pilots relied on auto-pilot when actually flying, the less able they were to react to emergencies in a training simulator. Some actually attributed the medical community's slow reaction to the Ebola breakout to medical diagnosing software that was not sensitive to detecting highly rare and complex events. As one physician noted, "medical software is no replacement for basic history-taking, examination skills, and critical thinking."[12] Still, as our Evidence-Based HR feature shows, there are cases in the field of medicine where electronic decision-making support can have a strong positive impact on efficiency.

In general, the amount of money that an organization invests in equipment is calculated in terms of the amount of "capital spending per worker," and some in the United States are concerned that this form of investment has not kept pace with what is needed to compete against international competition. For example, 2014 marked the fifth year in a row that the U.S. economy showed no growth in capital spending per worker, and

EVIDENCE-BASED HR

A key element of managing workflow efficiently is relying on the latest empirical evidence regarding best practices for certain routine tasks and then making sure every employee engages in standardized protocols. Sometimes this means not using equipment. In fact, nowhere is the push to develop standardized procedures more urgent than in the field of medicine, where spiraling costs in the United States—that do not seem to be related to patient outcomes—have been a major problem when it comes to affordable care. However, getting physicians who had wide latitude on making their own decisions to engage in standardized practices has been a challenge. Still, many different experiments have shown that if lone physician judgments were replaced by standard practices recommended by professional associations such as the American Heart Association (AHA), hospitals would be much better off.

For example, cardiac telemetry is performed with equipment that lets one monitor the heart for abnormal rhythms. At Christiana Care hospitals, administrators knew that this equipment was being used by many physicians, even when it was not considered necessary by the AHA. In order to reduce routine use of this machine, the electronic ordering system was redesigned so that this was not a multiple choice answer that could simply be checked. A physician could still override the system and "write it in," but he or she had to take this one extra step. The results a year later showed that use of telemetry fell by 70%, costs were reduced by over $13,000, and there was no negative effect on patients. Nader Najafi, a professor from the University of California–San Francisco who led the study, noted that "it is remarkable to achieve such a substantial reduction in the use of such a resource without significantly increased adverse outcomes."

SOURCE: J. Whalen, "Hospitals Cut Costs by Getting Doctors to Stick to Guidelines," *The Wall Street Journal*, September 22, 2014, www.wsj.com.

not coincidentally, this year also witnessed a severe drop in worker productivity. Even though profits are up, U.S. employers are not investing in equipment but instead are using their funds to pay stock dividends or support stock buyback programs. Thus, the average age of equipment in U.S. plants is 7.4 years old—the highest figure in 20 years.[13]

The final input in the work-flow process is the *human skills* and efforts necessary to perform the tasks. Obviously, the human skills consist of the workers available to the company. Generally speaking, in terms of human skills, work should be delegated to the lowest-cost employee who can do the work well, and in some cases this principle gets violated when too much emphasis is placed on reducing headcount. For example, between 2009 and 2011 the U.S. economy wiped out close to 1 million office and administrative support positions, and at one level, this might seem a reasonable place to cut costs. However, does it really make financial sense to have a C-level executive booking their own travel, typing up routine paperwork, loading toner into the copier and screening 500 e-mails a day when 400 of those are basically spam? For an executive making $1 million a year, an $80,000 assistant only needs to increase that person's productivity by 8% for the company to break even.[14]

ORGANIZATION STRUCTURE

Whereas work-flow design provides a longitudinal overview of the dynamic relationships by which inputs are converted into outputs, organization structure provides a cross-sectional overview of the static relationships between individuals and units that create the outputs. Organization structure is typically displayed via organizational charts that convey both vertical reporting relationships and horizontal functional responsibilities.

Dimensions of Structure

Two of the most critical dimensions of organization structure are centralization and departmentalization. **Centralization** refers to the degree to which decision-making authority resides at the top of the organizational chart as opposed to being distributed throughout lower levels (in which case authority is *decentralized*). **Departmentalization** refers to the degree to which work units are grouped based on functional similarity or similarity of work flow.

For example, a school of business could be organized around functional similarity so that there would be a marketing department, a finance department, and an accounting department, and faculty within these specialized departments would each teach their area of expertise to all kinds of students. Alternatively, one could organize the same school around work-flow similarity, so that there would be an undergraduate unit, a graduate unit, and an executive development unit. Each of these units would have its own marketing, finance, and accounting professors who taught only their own respective students and not those of the other units.

Structural Configurations

Although there are an infinite number of ways to combine centralization and departmentalization, two common configurations of organization structure tend to emerge in organizations. The first type, referred to as a *functional structure,* is shown in Figure 4.2. A functional structure, as the name implies, employs a functional departmentalization scheme with relatively high levels of centralization. High levels of centralization tend to go naturally with functional departmentalization because individual units in the

Centralization
Degree to which decision-making authority resides at the top of the organizational chart.

Departmentalization
Degree to which work units are grouped based on functional similarity or similarity of work flow.

Figure 4.2
The Functional Structure

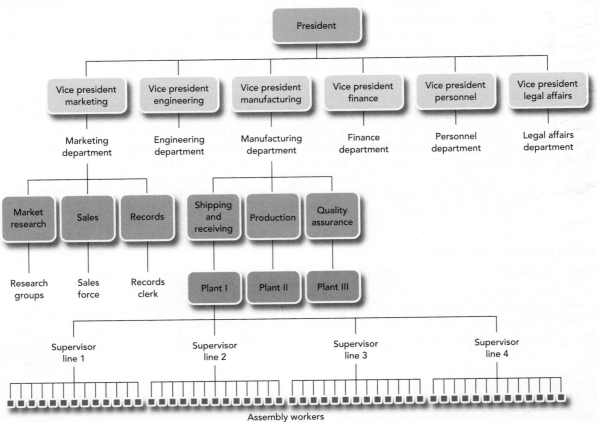

SOURCE: Adapted from J. A. Wagner and J. R. Hollenbeck, *Organizational Behavior: Securing Competitive Advantage,* 3rd ed. (New York: Prentice Hall, 1998).

structures are so specialized that members of the unit may have a weak conceptualization of the overall organization mission. Thus, they tend to identify with their department and cannot always be relied on to make decisions that are in the best interests of the organization as a whole. In addition, the opportunity for finger pointing and conflict between subunits that fundamentally do not understand the work that other subunits do creates the need for a centralized decision-making mechanism to manage potential disputes.[15]

For example, some believed that one of the major problems with the failed launch of the HealthCare.gov website that was meant to support the administration of the Affordable Care Act was that the structure of the system that employed highly functionalized groups for different elements of the website were not tightly linked to a centralized authority system. In testimony before the U.S. Congress, each contractor responsible for one part of the system pointed the finger of blame at some other contractor, and the central administration seemed unable to convey who they thought was accountable for what. At one point, the congressional committee became so frustrated with the lack of clarity on who in the central administration made key decisions that they forced people at the contracting agencies to name specifically who talked to whom on what date.[16] Note how the problems stated here are exactly the same issues that plagued General Motors in the vignette that opened this chapter.

COMPETING THROUGH GLOBALIZATION

Structuring a Global Terrorist Organization

Although one's stereotype of religiously based radical terrorist groups might be that they are loosely structured and impulsive in their actions, based upon a study of documents retrieved when U.S. forces helped allied forces retake Anbar Province, this is hardly the case when it comes to ISIS (i.e., the Islamic State in Iraq and Syria). These recovered documents detailed a very frightening but yet "very rational managerial approach" to organization that resembles many modern businesses, often referred to as an M-form.

Specifically, ISIS is structured as a set of geographically decentralized, semi-autonomous units that are responsible for day-to-day operations, but who report to a small central unit that is responsible for long-term strategy. The geographical subunits are for the most part self-funding, in the sense that they raise their own money through the sale of stolen goods, smuggling, kidnapping, extortion, and even oil production. The local divisions are then further broken down into functional specialties such as "mortars," "booby traps," "gas production," "tents," and "kitchens." At the lowest level of the organization are "suicide bombers," who typically are foreign fighters with no real skills and who cannot speak Arabic.

The subunits contribute a tax to the national treasury that is managed by the central authorities, and this treasury is used to help support strategic initiatives that may cross geographic boundaries or exploit rich local opportunities that are too expensive for any one geographic unit to support. This structure is highly resistant to external attacks from outside the organization, because lopping off the small head of the organization leaves most of the structure intact and operational. However, this structure is very vulnerable to internal exploitation since the lack of oversight makes it hard to control cheating on the tax or failing to report on side operations that generate revenue unknown to central authorities. Thus, as we have noted, there are strengths and liabilities associated with all forms of structure, even those directed at creating chaos.

DISCUSSION QUESTION

How does the structure that is employed by one's competitor affect one's own structure, and if one is trying to destroy an organization like ISIS, what type of structure would be best?

SOURCES: C. Simpson, "The Banality of Islamic State," *Bloomsberg Businessweek,* November 20, 2014, pp. 56–61; J. Opperman, "How ISIS Works," *The New York Times* September 16, 2014, www.nytimes.com.

Alternatively, a second common configuration is a *divisional structure,* three examples of which are shown in Figures 4.3, 4.4, and 4.5. Divisional structures combine a divisional departmentalization scheme with relatively low levels of centralization. Units in these structures act almost like separate, self-sufficient, semi-autonomous organizations. The organization shown in Figure 4.3 is divisionally organized around different products; the organization shown in Figure 4.4 is divisionally organized around geographic regions; and the organization shown in Figure 4.5 is divisionally organized around different clients. As you can see from the "Competing through Globalization" box, there are certain virtues to organizing divisionally by geographic region that make this particular form of structure a good fit for terrorist organizations.

Regardless of how subunits are formed, many organizations try to keep the size of each subunit small enough that people within the subunit feel like they can make a difference and feel connected to others. People within very large subunits experience reduced feelings of individual accountability and motivation, which hinders organizational performance. Research suggests that these types of problems start to manifest themselves once a group exceeds 150 people and hence many organizations try to limit subunits

Figure 4.3

Divisional Structure: Product Structure

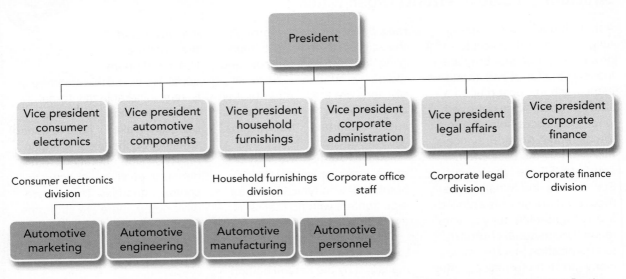

SOURCE: Adapted from J. A. Wagner and J. R. Hollenbeck, *Organizational Behavior: Securing Competitive Advantage,* 3rd ed. (New York: Prentice Hall, 1998).

to this specific size. For example, W.L. Gore and Associates, the company that makes Gore-Tex and other innovative materials, typically will break up a division once its size exceeds this number, splitting it in two and opening a new physical office.[17]

Because of their work-flow focus, their semi-autonomous nature, and their proximity to a homogeneous consumer base, divisional structures tend to be more flexible and innovative. They can detect and exploit opportunities in their respective consumer base faster than the more centralized functionally structured organizations. In fact, when highly functional structures that are really built for efficiency and cost containment try to compete via speed and flexibility, serious problems can ensue.

This is perfectly illustrated in the "fast fashion" industry. Historically, retailers launched new styles at the beginning of each season, and it often took a full year for

Figure 4.4

Divisional Structure: Geographic Structure

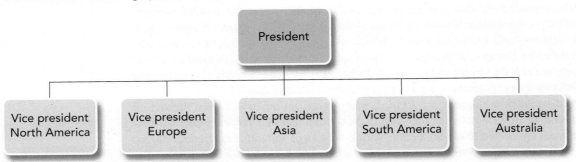

SOURCE: Adapted from J. A. Wagner and J. R. Hollenbeck, *Organizational Behavior: Securing Competitive Advantage,* 3rd ed. (New York: Prentice Hall, 1998).

Figure 4.5

Divisional Structure: Client Structure

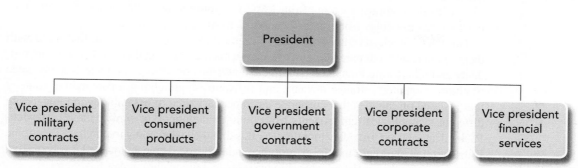

SOURCE: Adapted from J. A. Wagner and J. R. Hollenbeck, *Organizational Behavior: Securing Competitive Advantage*, 3rd ed. (New York: Prentice Hall, 1998).

a design concept to go from the drawing board to the store floor. Although last minute changes could be made, these were typically costly and cut into margins at a rate that offset the value of the change. However, chains such as H&M and Zara are rewriting the rules of the fashion industry and increasingly introducing new styles every month as part of the push for "fast fashion."[18] The only problem with this practice, however, is that many feel that it can only be accomplished via the exploitation of workers in small, emerging, third-world labor markets. It might not seem like such a major request to shift an order from 20,000 blue blouses to 10,000 blue blouses and 10,000 red blouses. However, quick shifts in operations like this, when not accompanied by changes in order delivery dates, cause plant managers in emerging economies to pump up worker hours and take short cuts with maintenance that create major safety issues.

These problems have surfaced most clearly in Bangladesh, a country that has been at the forefront of the fast fashion industry after surging wages in China sent retailers looking for cheaper and more accommodating manufacturers. In May 2013, 500 workers toiling away at the Rana Plaza garment factory died when the five-story building housing the operations collapsed. In all, over 1,000 garment workers in Bangladesh died between 2006 and 2013, most of whom were young women working 16-hour days for less than $40 a month.[19]

In some extreme cases, small divisions may not even be supervised by a formal manager, and the employees may self-manage. For example, Valve Corporation, a videogame producer located in Bellevue, Washington, touts itself as a "boss-free" company where decisions regarding hiring, firing, and pay are made by the employees themselves, who are organized into teams. The teams tend to vote on most decisions, or in some cases, due to experience or expertise, one or two people will emerge as leaders for specific projects. Typically this type of leadership emergence occurs in a way that is supported by the team. As one employee notes, "It absolutely is less efficient up front, but once you have the organization behind it, the buy-in and the execution happen quickly."[20]

A good example of the interplay of alternative structures can be seen in recent developments in the computer industry. Historically, the computer industry started with large and divisionally structured companies like IBM, that over time splintered off into increasingly smaller and functionally specialized organizations. Technology companies focused in narrowly on hardware *or* software *or* data storage *or* IT consulting services, but no one company was interested in providing all of these services. The thought was that specialization would boost efficiency and technical innovation. Indeed, as one analyst noted, "today, a typical corporate computer system might be assembled by Accenture PLC with data storage systems from EMC Corporation and computers from Hewlett-Packard that use chips from Intel Corporation to run Oracle software."

However, Oracle recently announced that they were going to reverse that trend with their announcement to purchase Sun Microsystems Inc., making them both a software producer and a hardware manufacturer. Oracle now plans on selling complete systems made of chips, computers, storage devices, and software—highlighting a competitive strategy that is based on the idea that corporate customers are tired of assembling and integrating different technological components from multiple suppliers. In similar moves, Hewlett-Packard announced just a few months after this that they were going to purchase Electronic Data Systems, thus entering the data storage industry and Apple announced it was making a move to enter the semiconductor chip business by buying chip maker P.A. Semi.

The temptation toward this type of "vertical integration" can be strong because one of the virtues of divisional structures is that they allow one to control all aspects of an entire business, making one's former supplier part of the team, as opposed to an unpredictable element of the business environment. Vertical integration also tends to generate large-scale operations that would not naturally evolve organically from smaller organizations, and with size comes some degree of power. Indeed, Oracle's CEO, Larry Ellison directly invoked the old 1960s IBM model by stating, "we want to be T. J. Watson's IBM, which was the greatest company in the history of enterprise in America because its hardware and software ran most companies."[21] Time will tell whether this strategy is effective, or like the old IBM, whether Oracle will learn that there are real limits associated with divisional structures as well.

Divisional structures are not very efficient because of the redundancy associated with each group carrying its own functional specialists. Also, divisional structures can "self-cannibalize" if the gains achieved in one unit come at the expense of another unit. For example, Kinko's stores are structured divisionally with highly decentralized control. Each manager can set his or her own price and has autonomy to make his or her own decisions. But the drawback to this is lack of coordination in the sense that "every Kinko's store considers every other Kinko's store a competitor; they vie against each other for work, they bid against each other competing on price."[22] These problems eventually led to the demise of the company when it was taken over by FedEx, restructured, and renamed FedEx Office and Print Shops.[23]

Lack of coordination caused by decentralized and divisional structures can be especially problematic with new and emerging organizations that do not have a great deal of history or firmly established culture. Higher levels of centralization and more functional design of work make it easier in this context to keep everyone on the same page while the business builds experience.[24] Decentralized and divisional structures can also create problems if the stand-alone divisions start making decisions that are overly risky or out of line with the organization's larger goals. For example, many analysts felt that many of the problems associated with the near bankruptcy of Citibank in 2009 were caused by excessive risk taking in several autonomous divisions that were not being closely monitored by any centralized authority. This was especially the case with the division that managed collateralized debt obligations (CDOs). Many conservative banking analysts warned that CDOs and other similar derivatives spread risk and uncertainty throughout the economy more widely and did little to reduce risk through diversification. This belief was validated in the 2008 recession, when the housing market crashed and thousands of people defaulted on their mortgages.[25]

Another example of this can be seen in the recent experiences at Procter and Gamble (P&G), where each separate division was given control over its own research and development budget. During tough economic times, each separate unit began to reduce expenditures on R&D resulting in an effort to tighten their budgets and meet short-term profit goals. The cumulative effect of all of these short-term independent decisions was that as a company, P&G was under investing in R&D, and a dearth of new and innovative products wound up harming long-term competitiveness. CEO Bob McDonald stepped in and centralized the R&D function so that the majority of researchers worked in a single unit and reported to a single authority, Jorge Mesquita. The hope was to leverage the research talent that was spread across the divisions and consolidate them into a single unit focused on more radical breakthroughs rather than incremental innovations.[26]

Alternatively, functional structures are very efficient, with little redundancy across units, and provide little opportunity for self-cannibalization or for rogue units running wild. Also, although the higher level of oversight in centralized structures tends to reduce the number of errors made by lower level workers, when errors do occur in overly centralized systems, they tend to cascade through the system as a whole more quickly and can, therefore, be more debilitating. Moreover, these structures tend to be inflexible and insensitive to subtle differences across products, regions, or clients.

Functional structures are most appropriate in stable, predictable environments, where demand for resources can be well anticipated and coordination requirements between jobs can be refined and standardized over consistent repetitions of activity. This type of structure also helps support organizations that compete on cost, because efficiency is central to making this strategy work. Divisional structures are most appropriate in unstable, unpredictable environments, where it is difficult to anticipate demands for resources, and coordination requirements between jobs are not consistent over time. This type of structure also helps support organizations that compete on differentiation or innovation, because flexible responsiveness is central to making this strategy work.

Of course, designing an organizational structure is not an either–or phenomenon, and some research suggests that "middle-of-the-road" options that combine functional and divisional elements are often best. For example, most organizations take a "mixed" approach to how they structure the Human Resource function within their organization. Typically, there is a subunit called a shared service center that is highly centralized and handles all the major routine transactional tasks such as payroll. There is also a center of excellence subunit that houses specialized expertise in the area of training or labor relations, which is centralized but separate from the shared service center. Finally, there is a third decentralized subunit that acts as business partner to other sub-unit leaders on talent management or succession planning. This three-pronged structure has elements that strive to achieve efficiency when it comes to routine tasks, specialization when it comes to complex tasks, and flexibility when it comes to supporting each separate business unit.[27]

Structure and the Nature of Jobs

Finally, moving from big-picture issues to lower-level specifics, the type of organization structure also has implications for the design of jobs. Jobs in functional structures need to be narrow and highly specialized. Workers in these structures (even middle managers) tend to have little decision-making authority or responsibility for managing coordination between themselves and others. For example, at Nucor Steel, production at its 30 minimill plants has doubled almost every two years and profit margins have pushed beyond 10% largely because of its flat, divisional structure. At Nucor, individual plant managers have wide autonomy in how to design work at their own mills. Nucor plants sometimes compete against each other, but the CEO makes sure that the competition is healthy and that best practices are distributed throughout the organization as fast as possible, preventing any long-term sustainable advantage to any one plant. Moreover, the profit-sharing plan that makes up the largest part of people's pay operates at the organizational level, which also promotes collaboration among managers who want to make sure that every plant is successful. Thus, after taking over a new mill for the first time, one new plant manager got a call or visit from every other manager, offering advice and assistance. As the new manager noted, "It wasn't idle politeness. I took them up on it. My performance impacted their paycheck."[28]

Nucor employs just four levels of management and operates a headquarters of just 66 people, compared to one of its competitors, U.S. Steel, which has over 20 levels and 1,200 people at its headquarters. This gives Nucor a long-term sustainable competitive advantage, which it has held for close to 15 years. Sales at Nucor grew from $4.5 billion in 2000 to over $13 billion in 2006. During the same period, U.S. Steel's volume decreased by 6%. This has translated into success for both investors (roughly 400% return on investment in the last five years) and workers, whose wages average $100,000 a year, compared to $70,000 a year at U.S. Steel. As one industry analyst notes, "In terms of a business model, Nucor has won this part of the world," and much of that victory can be explained by their superior structure and process for managing work.[29]

The choice of structure also has implications for people who would assume the jobs created in functional versus divisional structures. For example, managers of divisional structures often need to be more experienced or high in cognitive ability relative to managers of functional structures.[30] The relatively smaller scope and routine nature of jobs created in centralized and functional structures make them less sensitive to individual differences between workers. The nature of the structure also has implications for relationships, in the sense that in centralized and functional structures people tend to think of fairness in terms of rules and procedures, whereas in decentralized and divisional structures, they tend to think of fairness in terms of outcomes and how they are treated interpersonally.[31]

Taller structures also have implications for organizational culture in terms of ethics and accountability. For example, in a highly public scandal, Putnam Investments was fined $110 million for engaging in "market timing," that is, jumping quickly in and out of funds in order to take advantage of momentary market inefficiencies. This is considered an unethical practice within the industry because it increases fund expenses which, in turn, harms long-term investors. Many long-term investors left the organization, some of whom had more than $800 million being managed by Putnam.

According to Putnam insiders, the organization's tall and narrow organizational structure created a situation in which too many people were managing other people and telling them what they had to do to get promoted. Because the only way to earn more money at Putnam was to climb the corporate ladder, too much pressure was put on managers and employees alike to boost short-term results in order to attract the attention of those high above. The culture was one where people tended to ask "What is the fine for this?" instead of "What does this do to help my clients?" When new CEO Ed Haldeman was brought in to repair the damage, one of his first steps was to remove hundreds of salespeople, and then flatten the structure. The goal was to attract a different kind of employee, who would be less interested in short-term gains and hierarchical promotions handed out by others and more interested in establishing personal long-term relationships with customers and more collaborative relationships with colleagues. In Haldeman's words, "To retain and attract the best people, it's necessary to provide them with autonomy and independence to make their own decisions."[32]

In our next section, we cover specific approaches for analyzing and designing jobs. Although all of these approaches are viable, each focuses on a single, isolated job. These approaches do not necessarily consider how that single job fits into the overall work flow or structure of the organization. Whereas the Putnam Investments example shows how a firm moved from a functional structure to a divisional structure, Eli Lilly changed their structure in just the opposite direction, and this reinforces our general principle that there is no "one best way" when it comes to organizational structure. Without this big-picture appreciation, we might redesign a job in a way that might be good for that one job but out of line with the work flow, structure, or strategy of the organization.

For example, because patents for well-established drugs run out after a set time period, a company like Eli Lilly can only survive by inventing new products before the time bomb represented by their older drugs goes off. Faced with the prospect of losing the patent on its $5 billion a year schizophrenia pill, Zyprexa, this company restructured operations in a functional direction in order to create new products more quickly and efficiently. For example, all persons who were responsible for converting molecules into medicine were taken out of their home departments and placed under one roof in the new Development Center for Excellence.

This group of intensely focused specialists, who were all working together for the first time, came up with an innovative new method for launching and testing drugs. This group took a formerly sequential two-stage process for determining general effectiveness and then the optimal dosage, and converted it into a single-stage process where multiple dose levels were tested all at once and compared to each other. This process shaved 14 months off the process of developing a new drug for diabetes, and was then generalized to other therapeutic causes.[33]

Job Analysis

Job analysis refers to the process of getting detailed information about jobs. It is important for organizations to understand and match job requirements and people to achieve high-quality performance. This is particularly true in today's competitive marketplace.

THE IMPORTANCE OF JOB ANALYSIS

Job analysis is the building block of everything that human resource managers do. Almost every human resource management program requires some type of information that is gleaned from job analysis: selection, performance appraisal, training and development, job evaluation, career planning, work redesign, and human resource planning.

Work Redesign. As previously discussed, job analysis and job design are interrelated. Often a firm will seek to redesign work to make it more efficient or effective. To redesign the work, detailed information about the existing job(s) must be available. In addition, redesigning a job will, in fact, be similar to analyzing a job that does not yet exist.

Human Resource Planning. In human resource planning, managers analyze an organization's human resource needs in a dynamic environment and develop activities that enable a firm to adapt to change. This planning process requires accurate information about the levels of skill required in various jobs to ensure that enough individuals are available in the organization to meet the human resource needs of the strategic plan.

Selection. Human resource selection identifies the most qualified applicants for employment. To identify which applicants are most qualified, it is first necessary to determine the tasks that will be performed by the individual hired and the knowledge, skills, and abilities the individual must have to perform the job effectively. This information is gained through job analysis.

LO 4-2
Understand the importance of job analysis in strategic human resource management.

Job Analysis
The process of getting detailed information about jobs.

Training. Almost every employee hired by an organization will require training. Some training programs may be more extensive than others, but all require the trainer to have identified the tasks performed in the job to ensure that the training will prepare individuals to perform their jobs effectively.

Performance Appraisal. Performance appraisal deals with getting information about how well each employee is performing in order to reward those who are effective, improve the performance of those who are ineffective, or provide a written justification for why the poor performer should be disciplined. Through job analysis, the organization can identify the behaviors and results that distinguish effective performance from ineffective performance.

Career Planning. Career planning entails matching an individual's skills and aspirations with opportunities that are or may become available in the organization. This matching process requires that those in charge of career planning know the skill requirements of the various jobs. This allows them to guide individuals into jobs in which they will succeed and be satisfied.

Job Evaluation. The process of job evaluation involves assessing the relative dollar value of each job to the organization to set up internally equitable pay structures. If pay structures are not equitable, employees will be dissatisfied and quit, or they will not see the benefits of striving for promotions. To put dollar values on jobs, it is necessary to get information about different jobs to determine which jobs deserve higher pay than others.

THE IMPORTANCE OF JOB ANALYSIS TO LINE MANAGERS

Job analysis is clearly important to the HR department's various activities, but why it is important to line managers may not be as clear. There are many reasons. First, managers must have detailed information about all the jobs in their work group to understand the work-flow process. Second, managers need to understand the job requirements to make intelligent hiring decisions. Very seldom do employees get hired by the human resource department without a manager's input. Third, a manager is responsible for ensuring that each individual is performing satisfactorily (or better). This requires the manager to evaluate how well each person is performing and to provide feedback to those whose performance needs improvement. Finally, it is also the manager's responsibility to ensure that the work is being done safely, knowing where potential hazards might manifest themselves and creating a climate where people feel free to interrupt the production process if dangerous conditions exist.[34]

For example, some were shocked when Alcoa's new CEO Paul O'Neill's opening remarks at his first shareholders meeting were focused on pointing out the nearest emergency exits in the building. However, O'Neill's emphasis on safety and work processes actually wound up making him one of the best CEOs in history. After he took over at Alcoa, O'Neill changed reporting procedures so that any time an employee got hurt, the department head in that unit had to develop a plan detailing how work processes were going to be changed to make sure the same accident did not happen again. Executives who failed to embrace this new standard routine were fired. As a result of this new policy, each department head had to become intimately familiar with work processes which ultimately led to many conversations with lower level workers who had great ideas for not only shoring up safety, but also streamlining workflow. Eventually, even as safety was improving, costs came down, quality went up and productivity skyrocketed.[35]

Of course, one problem with trying to make job analysis fulfill so many different purposes is that the best job analysis for one objective may not be the best job analysis for another. For example, a job description that is based on a job analysis performed for recruitment purposes needs to be short and attract attention to applicants who may not spend a great deal of time reading an advertisement. In contrast, a job description that is based on a job analysis used as part of a performance management program needs to be detailed enough to tease out the strengths and weaknesses of a job incumbent who may have been observed over a full one year. Thus, a company may actually wind up performing multiple job analyses for a single job or derive multiple job descriptions from a single job analysis. Sodexo USA, a food and facilities management company, does exactly this and has "dual documents" for over 900 different jobs.[36]

JOB ANALYSIS INFORMATION
Nature of Information

Two types of information are most useful in job analysis: job descriptions and job specifications. A **job description** is a list of the tasks, duties, and responsibilities (TDRs) that a job entails. TDRs are observable actions. For example, a clerical job requires the jobholder to type. If you were to observe someone in that position for a day, you would certainly see some typing. When a manager attempts to evaluate job performance, it is most important to have detailed information about the work performed in the job (that is, the TDRs). This makes it possible to determine how well an individual is meeting each job requirement. Table 4.1 shows a sample job description. On the one hand, job descriptions need to be written broadly because overly restrictive descriptions make it easy for someone to claim that some important task, perhaps unforeseen, "is not my job." On the other hand, lack of specificity can also result in disagreement and conflict between people

Job Description
A list of the tasks, duties, and responsibilities (TDRs) that a job entails.

Table 4.1
A Sample Job Description

Job Title: Maintenance Mechanic

General Description of Job: General maintenance and repair of all equipment used in the operations of a particular district. Includes the servicing of company vehicles, shop equipment, and machinery used on job sites.

1. *Essential Duty (40%): Maintenance of Equipment*
   Tasks: Keep a log of all maintenance performed on equipment. Replace parts and fluids according to maintenance schedule. Regularly check gauges and loads for deviances that may indicate problems with equipment. Perform nonroutine maintenance as required. May involve limited supervision and training of operators performing maintenance.

2. *Essential Duty (40%): Repair of Equipment*
   Tasks: Requires inspection of equipment and a recommendation that a piece be scrapped or repaired. If equipment is to be repaired, mechanic will take whatever steps are necessary to return the piece to working order. This may include a partial or total rebuilding of the piece using various hand tools and equipment. Will primarily involve the overhaul and troubleshooting of diesel engines and hydraulic equipment.

3. *Essential Duty (10%): Testing and Approval*
   Tasks: Ensure that all required maintenance and repair has been performed and that it was performed according to manufacturer specifications. Approve or reject equipment as being ready for use on a job.

4. *Essential Duty (10%): Maintain Stock*
   Tasks: Maintain inventory of parts needed for the maintenance and repair of equipment. Responsible for ordering satisfactory parts and supplies at the lowest possible cost.

Nonessential Functions
Other duties as assigned.

about the essential elements of what the job entails.[37] Thus, it is critical to strike an effective balance between breadth and specificity when constructing job descriptions.

Job Specification
A list of the knowledge, skills, abilities, and other characteristics (KSAOs) that an individual must have to perform a job.

A **job specification** is a list of the knowledge, skills, abilities, and other characteristics (KSAOs) that an individual must have to perform the job. *Knowledge* refers to factual or procedural information that is necessary for successfully performing a task. A *skill* is an individual's level of proficiency at performing a particular task. *Ability* refers to a more general enduring capability that an individual possesses. Finally, *other characteristics* might be personality traits such as one's achievement motivation or persistence. Thus KSAOs are characteristics about people that are not directly observable; they are observable only when individuals are carrying out the TDRs of the job. If someone applied for the clerical job discussed, you could not simply look at the individual to determine whether he or she possessed typing skills. However, if you were to observe that individual typing something, you could assess the level of typing skill. When a manager is attempting to fill a position, it is important to have accurate information about the characteristics a successful jobholder must have. This requires focusing on the KSAOs of each applicant.

Sources of Job Analysis Information

In performing the job analysis, one question that often arises is, Who should be responsible for providing the job analysis information? Whatever job analysis method you choose, the process of job analysis entails obtaining information from people familiar with the job. We refer to these people as *subject-matter experts* because they possess deep knowledge of the job.

In general, it will be useful to go to the job incumbent to get the most accurate information about what is actually done on the job. This is especially the case when it is difficult to monitor the person who does the job. The ratings of multiple job incumbents that are doing the same job do not always agree, however, especially if the job is complex and does not involve standardized equipment or tight scripts for customer contact.[38] Thus, you will also want to ask others familiar with the job, such as supervisors, to look over the information generated by the job incumbent. This serves as a check to determine whether what is being done is congruent with what is supposed to be done in the job. Job incumbents are also useful when one is trying to assess the informal social network that exists within the formal organizational structure. That is, although the formal organizational structure suggests who *should* be talking to whom from a top-down normative perspective, an analysis of a company's social structure actually shows who really is talking to whom from a bottom-up descriptive perspective. In fact, one example of the growing field of business analytics deals with people analytic programs that show who is talking to whom on a day-to-day basis via self-report surveys or e-mail trails or from data derived from wearable sensors. In many cases, social networks develop due to limitations in the formal structure when people realize they need to interact with some person in a way that was not anticipated by a formal organizational designer. Once alerted to this need, formal planners may wish to reconfigure the formal structure to reflect the needs identified by the informal, emergent social structure.[39]

In contrast to cases where some communication link develops between people in order to meet a legitimate need to get the job done, a close examination of the social network in other cases uncovers individuals who overcommunicate for no good reason related to the work, and hence wind up wasting their time and the time of others. For example, one company that performed an analysis of its e-mail communications found one executive who generated so many e-mails that it took the equivalent of 10 people working full time just to read the e-mails sent by this one person. An analysis of these e-mails suggested that few of the people who were being sent the communications really needed e-mails from this person to do their job. An intervention directed at "fixing" this part of the social network wound up increasing the efficiency of a large number of people.[40]

One conclusion that can be drawn from this research is that incumbents may provide the most accurate estimates of the actual time spent performing job tasks. However, supervisors may be a more accurate source of information about the importance of job duties. Incumbents also seem more accurate in terms of assessing safety-related risk factors associated with various aspects of work, and in general the further one moves up the organizational hierarchy, the less accurate the risk assessments.[41] Although job incumbents and supervisors are the most obvious and frequently used sources of job analysis information, other sources, such as customers, can be helpful, particularly for service jobs. Finally, when it comes to analyzing skill levels, external job analysts who have more experience rating a wide range of jobs may be the best source.[42]

JOB ANALYSIS METHODS

LO 4-3
Choose the right job analysis technique for a variety of human resource activities.

There are various methods for analyzing jobs and no "one best way." In this section, we discuss two methods for analyzing jobs: the position analysis questionnaire and the Occupational Information Network (O*NET). Although most managers may not have time to use each of these techniques in the exact manner suggested, the two provide some anchors for thinking about broad approaches, task-focused approaches, and person-oriented approaches to conducting job analysis.

Position Analysis Questionnaire (PAQ)

We lead this section off with the PAQ because this is one of the broadest and most well-researched instruments for analyzing jobs. Moreover, its emphasis on inputs, processes, relationships, and outputs is consistent with the work-flow analysis approach that we used in leading off this chapter (Figure 4.1).

The PAQ is a standardized job analysis questionnaire containing 194 items.[43] These items represent work behaviors, work conditions, and job characteristics that can be generalized across a wide variety of jobs. They are organized into six sections:

1. *Information input*—Where and how a worker gets information needed to perform the job.
2. *Mental processes*—The reasoning, decision making, planning, and information processing activities that are involved in performing the job.
3. *Work output*—The physical activities, tools, and devices used by the worker to perform the job.
4. *Relationships with other persons*—The relationships with other people required in performing the job.
5. *Job context*—The physical and social contexts where the work is performed.
6. *Other characteristics*—The activities, conditions, and characteristics other than those previously described that are relevant to the job.

The job analyst is asked to determine whether each item applies to the job being analyzed. The analyst then rates the item on six scales: extent of use, amount of time, importance to the job, possibility of occurrence, applicability, and special code (special rating scales used with a particular item). These ratings are submitted to the PAQ headquarters, where a computer program generates a report regarding the job's scores on the job dimensions.

Research has indicated that the PAQ measures 12 overall dimensions of jobs (listed in Table 4.2) and that a given job's scores on these dimensions can be very useful. The significant database has linked scores on certain dimensions to scores on subtests of the General Aptitude Test Battery (GATB). Thus, knowing the dimension scores provides some guidance regarding the types of abilities that are necessary to perform the job. Obviously, this technique provides information about the work performed in a format that allows for comparisons across jobs, whether those jobs are similar or dissimilar. Another advantage of the PAQ is that it covers the work context as well as inputs, outputs, and processes.

Knowledge of work context is important because in many cases, one can predict absenteeism and turnover from the nature of the surroundings in which the work takes place, and some people are more resilient than others when it comes to dealing with adverse environments. In addition, if one knows that the job includes adverse working conditions, providing additional levels of peer support and supervisor support might be required to help people cope.[44] In contrast, work spaces that are designed in ways that people find pleasing can often help overcome other aspects of a job that are generally seen as less desirable.[45]

The Occupational Information Network (O*NET)

The *Dictionary of Occupational Titles* (DOT) was born during the 1930s and served as a vehicle for helping the new public employment system link the demand for skills and the supply of skills in the U.S. workforce. Although this system served the country well for more than 60 years, it became clear to officials at the U.S. Department of Labor that jobs in the new economy were so qualitatively different from jobs in the old economy, that the DOT no longer served its purpose. Technological changes in the nature of work, global competition, and a shift from stable, fixed manufacturing jobs to a more flexible, dynamic, service-based economy were quickly making the system obsolete.[46]

For all these reasons, the Department of Labor abandoned the DOT in 1998 and developed an entirely new system for classifying jobs referred to as the Occupational Information Network, or O*NET. Instead of relying on fixed job titles and narrow task descriptions, the O*NET uses a common language that generalizes across jobs to describe the abilities, work styles, work activities, and work context required for various

Table 4.2
Overall Dimensions of the Position Analysis Questionnaire

Decision/communication/general responsibilities
Clerical/related activities
Technical/related activities
Service/related activities
Regular day schedule versus other work schedules
Routine/repetitive work activities
Environmental awareness
General physical activities
Supervising/coordinating other personnel
Public/customer/related contact activities
Unpleasant/hazardous/demanding environment
Nontypical work schedules

occupations that are more broadly defined (e.g., instead of the 12,000 jobs in the DOT, the O*NET describes only 1,000 occupations).[47] Although it was developed to analyze jobs in the U.S. economy, research suggests that the ratings tend to be transportable across countries. That is, if one holds the job title constant (e.g., first-line supervisor, office clerk, computer programmer), the ratings of the job tend to be the same even if the job is located in a different country.[48]

The O*NET is being used by many employers and employment agencies. For example, after closing its Seattle-based headquarters, Boeing used the O*NET system to help find new jobs for the workers who were laid off because of the impending move.[49] The O*NET was also designed to help job seekers. For example, the O*NET seems particularly well suited to describing the literacy requirements associated with alternative jobs. Thus, individuals who want to improve their ability to find employment can obtain relatively accurate information about what jobs they are qualified for given their current literacy level from the O*NET. They can also see how much their literacy skills would have to improve if they wanted to apply for higher-level jobs characterized by higher levels of complexity.[50]

DYNAMIC ELEMENTS OF JOB ANALYSIS

LO 4-4
Identify the tasks performed and the skills required in a given job.

Although we tend to view jobs as static and stable, in fact, jobs tend to change and evolve over time. Those who occupy or manage the jobs often make minor, cumulative adjustments to the job that try to match either changing conditions in the environment or personal preferences for how to conduct the work.[51] Indeed, although there are numerous sources for error in the job analysis process,[52] most inaccuracy is likely to result from job descriptions simply being outdated. For this reason, in addition to statically defining the job, the job analysis process must also detect changes in the nature of jobs.

For example, in today's world of rapidly changing products and markets, some people have begun to question whether the concept of "the job" is simply a social artifact that has outlived its usefulness. Indeed, many researchers and practitioners are pointing to a trend referred to as "dejobbing" in organizations. This trend consists of viewing organizations as a field of work needing to be done rather than a set of discrete jobs held by specific individuals. For example, at Amazon.com, HR director Scott Pitasky notes, "Here, a person might be in the same 'job,' but three months later be doing completely different work."[53] This means Amazon.com puts more emphasis on broad worker specifications ("entrepreneurial and customer-focused") than on detailed job descriptions ("C++ programming") that may not be descriptive one year down the road.

Job Design

LO 4-5
Understand the different approaches to job design.

So far we have approached the issue of managing work in a passive way, focusing only on understanding what gets done, how it gets done, and the skills required to get it done. Although this is necessary, it is a very static view of jobs, in that jobs must already exist and that they are already assumed to be structured in the one best way. However, a manager may often be faced with a situation in which the work unit does not yet exist, requiring jobs within the work unit to be designed from scratch. Sometimes work loads within an existing work unit are increased, or work group size is decreased while the same work load is required. Finally, sometimes the work is not being performed in the most efficient manner. In these cases, a manager may decide to change the way that work is done in order for the work unit to perform more effectively and efficiently. This requires redesigning the existing jobs.

Job Design
The process of defining the way work will be performed and the tasks that will be required in a given job.

Job Redesign
The process of changing the tasks or the way work is performed in an existing job.

Job design is the process of defining how work will be performed and the tasks that will be required in a given job. **Job redesign** refers to changing the tasks or the way work is performed in an existing job. To effectively design jobs, one must thoroughly understand the job as it exists (through job analysis) and its place in the larger work unit's work-flow process (work-flow analysis). Having a detailed knowledge of the tasks performed in the work unit and in the job, a manager then has many alternative ways to design a job. This can be done most effectively through understanding the trade-offs between certain design approaches.

Research has identified four basic approaches that have been used among the various disciplines (such as psychology, management, engineering, and ergonomics) that have dealt with job design issues.[54] All jobs can be characterized in terms of how they fare according to each approach; thus a manager needs to understand the trade-offs of emphasizing one approach over another. Table 4.3 displays how jobs are characterized along each of these dimensions, and the Work Design Questionnaire (WDQ), a specific instrument that reliably measures these and other job design characteristics, is available for use by companies wishing to comprehensively assess their jobs on these dimensions.[55]

MECHANISTIC APPROACH

The mechanistic approach has roots in classical industrial engineering. The focus of the mechanistic approach is identifying the simplest way to structure work that maximizes efficiency. This most often entails reducing the complexity of the work to provide more human resource efficiency—that is, making the work so simple that anyone can be trained quickly and easily to perform it. This approach focuses on designing jobs around the concepts of task specialization, skill simplification, and repetition.

For example at Chili's Restaurants, cooks used to cut up vegetables, meats, and other ingredients as part of preparing a meal. In order to increase efficiency, however, the organization decided to break this job into two smaller parts: one job, called "prep cooks" who come in the morning and do all the cutting up, and the second job, "line cooks" who take these prepared ingredients and use them to assemble the final meal.[56]

Table 4.3
Major Elements of Various Approaches to Job Design

The mechanistic approach
  Specialization
  Skill variety
  Work methods autonomy
The motivational approach
  Decision-making autonomy
  Task significance
  Interdependence
The biological approach
  Physical demands
  Ergonomics
  Work conditions
The perceptual approach
  Job complexity
  Information processing
  Equipment use

SOURCE: From Michael A. Campion and Paul W. Thayer, "Job Design: Approaches, Outcomes, and Trade-Offs," *Organizational Dynamics,* Winter 1987, Vol. 15, No. 3. Reprinted with permission from Elsevier.

Scientific management was one of the earliest and best-known statements of the mechanistic approach.[57] According to this approach, productivity could be maximized by taking a scientific approach to the process of designing jobs. Scientific management first sought to identify the "one best way" to perform the job. Once the best way to perform the work is identified, workers should be selected based on their ability to do the job, they should be trained in the standard "one best way" to perform the job, and they should be offered monetary incentives to motivate them to work at their highest capacity.

The scientific management approach was built upon in later years, resulting in a mechanistic approach that calls for jobs to be designed so that they are very simple. By designing jobs in this way, the organization reduces its need for high-ability individuals and thus becomes less dependent on individual workers. Individuals are easily replaceable—that is, a new employee can be trained to perform the job quickly and inexpensively.

Many jobs structured this way are performed in developing countries where there is a large supply of low-skilled labor and relatively lax legal guidelines regarding safety standards. For example, manufacturing silicon chips involves a process that exposes workers to a large number of carcinogens that are less heavily regulated in Asia relative to what one would find in the United States, and hence chip production has largely moved overseas.[58] As one might expect, this includes a host of "low-tech" manufacturing and assembly jobs, but increasingly this also involves "digital factory jobs." For example, *ProQuest Historical Newspaper* provides a service where subscribers can access the contents of any article ever published by one of nine major U.S. newspapers simply by entering an author name, keyword, or image. You might wonder how all of this historical, nondigital information and text is entered into this digital database, and the answer would be found in Madras, India. Here workers take this material and enter the headline, author, major key words, and first paragraph of the work by hand into the database, and then run a program to attach a visual file to the rest of the article. This menial work is conducted by 850 workers, who comprise three 8-hour shifts that work 24 hours a day, 7 days a week.[59] It would be difficult, if not impossible to find workers in the United States willing to put up with work this boring.

In some cases, jobs designed via mechanistic practices result in work that is so simple that a child could do it, and this is exactly what can happen in some undeveloped countries. This can lead to a backlash against companies that benefit from this unethical practice, and increasingly, organizations are taking the lead in preventing these kinds of practices. For example, when it learned that Uzbekistan cotton growers were using child labor to pick their crops, Walmart used its power to force them to abandon this practice. Working with other large U.S. retailers, Walmart took the lead to create the first system for tracking where cotton came from and organized a boycott against Uzbekistan, which quickly acquiesced to the corporate giant's pressure, freeing the children to return to school.[60] At the time, almost everyone else perceived that Walmart was a corporate villain and bully, assaulting workers, the environment, and consumers. Over the course of his tenure as the Walmart CEO, H. Lee Scott dramatically reversed this perception, and now Walmart is routinely listed as one of the most sustainable and corporately responsible organizations in the United States.[61]

MOTIVATIONAL APPROACH

The motivational approach to job design has roots in organizational psychology and management literature and, in many ways, emerged as a reaction to mechanistic approaches to job design. It focuses on the job characteristics that affect psychological meaning and motivational potential, and it views attitudinal variables (such as satisfaction) as the most important outcomes of job design. The prescriptions of the motivational approach focus on increasing the meaningfulness of jobs through such interventions as job enlargement, job enrichment, and the construction of jobs around socio technical systems.[62]

A model of how job design affects employee reactions is the "Job Characteristics Model."[63] According to this model, jobs can be described in terms of five characteristics. *Skill variety* is the extent to which the job requires a variety of skills to carry out the tasks. *Task identity* is the degree to which a job requires completing a "whole" piece of work from beginning to end. *Autonomy* is the degree to which the job allows an individual to make decisions about the way the work will be carried out. *Feedback* is the extent to which a person receives clear information about performance effectiveness from the work itself. *Task significance* is the extent to which the job has an important impact on the lives of other people. Although all five characteristics are important, the belief that the task is significant because performing it well leads to outcomes one values may be the most critical motivational aspect of work.[64] This can often be enhanced by making it clear to the worker how his or her job affects other people, whether they be customers, co-workers or society in general.[65]

Job design interventions emphasizing the motivational approach tend to focus on increasing the meaningfulness of jobs. Much of the work on job enlargement (broadening the types of tasks performed), job enrichment (empowering workers by adding more decision-making authority to jobs), and self-managing work teams has its roots in the motivational approach to job design. Not all workers respond positively to enriched jobs like these because it requires some degree of flexibility and responsiveness to other people, but with the right workers, interventions such as these have been found to have dramatic effects on employee motivation.[66] Indeed, relatively elaborate theories have been developed that link specific personality traits to specific job characteristics and thus, to some degree, creating meaningful work requires matching the right type of person to the right type of task.[67]

In some cases, even work that may not be that interesting can be made significant by clarifying the link between what workers do and the outcomes of their work, perhaps far down the chain. For example, in medicine, a stent is an expandable wire form or perforated tube that is inserted into an artery to help promote blood flow after a heart operation. The actual work that goes into stent production is an assembly line process where each worker does a very small and, some might argue, boring task. To help increase the meaningfulness of this work, however, the company sponsors a party each year where line workers get to meet people whose lives were saved by the stents that were produced on that line. This is often a moving emotional experience for both parties and helps the employees see the impact of their work in a context where this would not naturally happen.[68] Indeed, one of the secrets behind effective transformational leaders is their ability to help workers see the larger meaning in what they are doing on a day-to-day basis.[69]

BIOLOGICAL APPROACH

Ergonomics
The interface between individuals' physiological characteristics and the physical work environment.

The biological approach to job design comes primarily from the sciences of biomechanics (i.e., the study of body movements), work physiology, and occupational medicine, and it is usually referred to as *ergonomics*. **Ergonomics** is concerned with examining the interface between individuals' physiological characteristics and the physical work environment. The goal of this approach is to minimize physical strain on the worker by structuring the physical work environment around the way the human body works. It therefore focuses on outcomes such as physical fatigue, aches and pains, and health complaints. Any job that creates a significant number of injuries is a target for ergonomic redesign.

The biological approach has been applied in redesigning equipment used in jobs that are physically demanding. Such redesign is often aimed at reducing the physical demands of certain jobs so that anyone can perform them. In addition, many biological interventions focus on redesigning machines and technology, such as adjusting the height of the computer keyboard to minimize occupational illnesses (like carpal tunnel syndrome). The design of chairs and desks to fit posture requirements is very important in many office jobs and is another example of the biological approach to job design. Although providing comfortable, ergonomically designed chairs is certainly laudable, recent research also suggests that getting employees out of their chairs is also critically important when it comes to health outcomes. That is, the evidence is becoming increasingly clear that merely sitting down for long periods can be damaging to employees. From an evolutionary perspective, the human body was designed to move and long stretches of sedentary behavior are at odds with this design. For example, people who are above the mean in "time spent sitting" are at a 24% greater risk to develop colon cancer, a 32% higher risk of endometrial cancer, and a 21% increased risk for lung cancer even when one controls for the amount of physical exercise that people get when they are not sitting. Thus, office redesign programs that involve the introduction of treadmill desks or stand-up desks are becoming increasingly common elements of design, and some organizations are trying to make standing, rather than sitting, as the default position for performing jobs.[70]

In addition to the direct effects of these kinds of interventions on worker well-being, these types of programs also have a positive psychological effect on workers by emphasizing an organizational climate that values safety and health.[71] That is, in addition to changes in design, some organizations try to instill a safety culture by giving each and every employee the power to report, or better yet, stop any worker who engages in unsafe behavior. At Chevron, for example, any worker within its headquarters office in Sam Ramon, California, can halt an activity he or she deems unsafe by taking out a small white "stop work" card. Thus, in terms of decision-making authority, each person has the power to identify and correct safety lapses regardless of where they reside on the formal organizational chart.[72] Indeed, in workplaces where safety is a major concern—such as working on a nuclear submarine—there may be hundreds of rules that new employees have to memorize prior to being able to start on the job.[73]

Often redesigning work to make it more worker-friendly also leads to increased efficiencies. For example, at International Truck and Engine Corporation, one of the most difficult aspects of truck production was pinning the axles to the truck frame. Traditionally, the frame was lowered onto the axle and a crew of six people, armed with oversized hammers and crowbars, forced the frame onto the axle. Because the workers could not see the bolts they had to tighten under the frame, the bolts were often not fastened properly, and many workers injured themselves in the process. After a brainstorming session, the workers and engineers figured that it would be better to flip the frame upside down and attach the axles from above instead of below. The result was a job that could be done twice as fast by half as many workers, who were much less likely to make mistakes or get injured.[74] Although in this case, designing for cost efficiency made the work more worker-friendly, as the "Competing through Sustainability" box shows, all too often, organizations that compete on cost and efficiency more often create jobs that do not promote employee well-being. The Occupational Safety and Health Organization is the primary agency for monitoring employer behavior with respect to safety, and as you can see from the "Integrity in Action" box, this organization often goes beyond the written law and regulations when it comes to forcing employers to engage in ethical behavior.

COMPETING THROUGH SUSTAINABILITY

Business Practices at Nail Salons May Be Cause for Concern

Although there may be nothing more fashionable than a fresh set of perfectly manicured nails, there has been increased scrutiny of how this service is traditionally delivered. Specifically, it is questionable whether current business practices are sustainable given the pressure on wages and working conditions that seem to go along with the current business model. Certainly, when it comes to barriers to entry, there are very few industries easier to get started into than this one. Setting up a new salon requires only a few thousand dollars for chairs, whirlpool baths, bottles of polish and wax, and some easily obtained (or easily ignored) licenses. Beyond this, it is just a matter of rent and employee wages and working conditions.

Perhaps because of the ease of entry, the number of salons that have opened up has skyrocketed. In New York City alone, the number of nail salons has increased five-fold between 2000 and 2015, and the oversupply of shops has put pressure on profits that now can often only be achieved by labor practices that border on slavery. Most low-level salon workers in New York City are illegal immigrants lacking basic English language skills. This is a workforce that is ripe for exploitation. New workers often have to pay up to $100 dollars just to join a salon and then work for up to three months with no pay. After this "apprenticeship" period, the workers, who are considered "tip workers," receive far less than the minimum wage. They also receive no health care coverage, despite the fact that many of the chemicals they work with for 12 hours a day are known carcinogens.

Recent crackdowns on owners of these salons by government bodies such as the New York Department of Labor (DOL) are beginning to change this picture. Indeed, many of the owners of the salons, like many of the customers, are highly affluent and have become rich on the backs of these poorly treated workers. However, progress toward reform is often hindered by the fact that workers will rarely cooperate with authorities. Many manicurists are unwilling or unable to speak to inspectors, and as one DOL agent noted, "they are totally running scared in this industry."

DISCUSSION QUESTION

Why is cost containment—the source of so many of these workers' problems—so essential to this industry, and what other industries are under similar pressures and respond the same way? What can be done to promote ethical behavior in these kinds of industries?

SOURCES: S. M. Nir, "Perfect Nails, Poisoned Workers," *The New York Times,* May 8, 2015, www.nytimes.com; S. M. Nir, "The Price of Nice Nails," *The New York Times,* May 7, 2015 www.nytimes.com.

PERCEPTUAL–MOTOR APPROACH

The perceptual–motor approach to job design has roots in human-factors literature. Whereas the biological approach focuses on physical capabilities and limitations, the perceptual–motor approach focuses on human mental capabilities and limitations. The goal is to design jobs in a way that ensures they do not exceed people's mental capabilities and limitations. This approach generally tries to improve reliability, safety, and user reactions by designing jobs to reduce their information-processing requirements. In designing jobs, one looks at the least capable worker and then constructs job requirements that an individual of that ability level could meet. Similar to the mechanistic approach, this approach generally decreases the job's cognitive demands.

Recent changes in technological capacities hold the promise of helping to reduce job demands and errors, but in some cases, these developments have actually made the

INTEGRITY IN ACTION

Policy Shift by OSHA May Help Pinpoint Unethical Business Activities

The difference between illegal behavior and unethical behavior is often a function of whether or not there is a valid and up-to-date statute, as well as the ability to monitor and enforce such statutes. The challenge that is often faced by OSHA in policing employers with respect to safety standards is that budget cuts have resulted in highly dated rules and a lack of resources when it comes to proving beyond a reasonable doubt that employers have violated the rules. In order to overcome these challenges, the agency has recently developed two new and controversial practices.

First, in order to overcome outdated rules, OSHA is now less focused on specific standards for exposure to toxic chemicals and instead targeting employers with the broader "general duty clause" that states that organizations must protect workers from known hazards. This is controversial because in some cases an employer may be well within the published standards for exposure but still found guilty. For example, even though an inspection found that levels of styrene at Fiberdome Inc. of Lake Mills, Wisconsin, were below the required threshold, the company was still fined $50,000 when a worker experienced respiratory bronchitis due to styrene.

Second, in January 2015, OSHA developed a new "name and shame" program that requires employers to notify the agency within 24 hours every time an employee loses an eye, suffers an amputation, or gets admitted to a hospital due to an injury incurred at work. The name of the employer is then placed on a public list that could be accessed by would-be job applicants when they are making decisions about where to accept employment. Note that in this case, there was no formal finding that the employer was engaged in any wrongful action, and yet, OSHA is suggesting to the world at large that where there is smoke, there is probably fire. Both of these new practices shift the focus from purely illegal activities to potentially unethical activities, but some question whether these practices themselves are ethical.

DISCUSSION QUESTION

Is it fair to hold employers liable for injuries that occur despite their being within the written regulations and without a formal finding of wrongdoing?

SOURCES: "Using the Web to Police Dangerous Workplaces," *Bloomberg Businessweek,* September 18, 2014, pp. 33–34; A. Berzon, "OSHA Uses New Way to Enforce Out-of-Date Rules," *The Wall Street Journal,* November 20, 2013, www.wsj.com.

---

problem worse. The term "absence presence" has been coined to refer to the reduced attentive state that one might experience when simultaneously interacting with multiple media. For example, someone might be talking on a cell phone while driving a car, or surfing the net while attending a business meeting, or checking e-mail while preparing a presentation. In all these cases, the new technology serves as a source of distraction from the primary task, reducing performance and increasing the opportunities for errors.[75] It is important to stress that in this case, the source of distraction is mental, not physical. Hence ergonomic interventions aimed at reducing physical barriers are likely to be largely ineffective. For example, holding a stressful conversation while driving in heavy traffic is dangerous regardless of whether one is using a "hands-free" device or not. It is the mental strain, not the physical challenge, that makes this a hazardous activity.[76] Research shows that on complex tasks, even very short interruptions can break one's train of thought and derail performance. Thus, e-mail servers that have a feature that signals the arrival of each incoming message might best be turned off if the job incumbent cannot resist the temptation this creates to interrupt ongoing activity.[77]

In addition to external disruptions, information processing errors are also increased in any context that requires a "handoff" of information from one person to another. Indeed, problems with handoffs have become a major concern in the field of medicine. As Mike Leonard, physician leader for patient safety at Kaiser Colorado Hospital, notes, "In almost all serious avoidable episodes of patient harm, communication failures play a central role." This would include information that fails to get handed off from nurses, doctors, and medical technicians to one another (e.g., the results of the most recent test that was handed to the attending doctor does not get handed to the attending nurse) or information that fails to get handed off from one work shift to another (e.g., a patient who has already received medication from one shift gets it again from the next shift). Problems between shifts are especially likely due to fatigue and burnout, which may be present at the end of a shift for workers in stressful jobs.[78]

Increasingly, hospitals are borrowing the "SBAR" method, originally developed in commercial and military aviation as a means to hand off an airplane moving through different people's airspace, to standardize communication protocols at the handoff point in medical contexts. SBAR stands for situation, background, assessment, and recommendation, which constitute the four components of every successful handoff. That is, in a few seconds, the person handing off the patient needs to get control of the situation by demanding the listener's attention (situation), then relay enough information to establish the context or the problem (background), then give an overall evaluation of the condition (assessment), and finally make a specific suggestion about the next best course of action (recommendation). At one hospital that introduced this procedure, the rate of adverse events (i.e., unexpected medical problems that cause harm) was reduced by more than half, from 90 to 40 for every 1,000 patients treated.[79]

As work design increasingly relies on teams to accomplish organizational objectives, studying the best way to manage "hand-offs" and other aspects of interdependence between jobs becomes more critical. Just as there are standardized instruments for assessing the nature of a job, there are also standardized frameworks for assessing the nature of teams. The three most critical dimensions needed to describe teams include (a) skill differentiation, the degree to which members have specialized knowledge or functional capacities that make it more or less difficult to substitute members, (b) authority differentiation, the degree to which decision-making responsibility is vested in individual members, subgroups of the team, or the collective as a whole, and (c) temporal stability, the degree to which team members are expected to work together for a long time.[80]

In many cases, team-based work design is a central component in terms of strategy and competitive advantage. In fact, even industries like apparel and clothing—where U.S. manufacturing was written off for dead—are experiencing a renaissance due to team-based work design. For example, Boathouse Sports, a manufacturer of jerseys, uniforms, and jackets in Philadelphia, Pennsylvania, relies on flexible manufacturing teams and finds its own unique competitive advantage in adaptively responding to small orders, and then delivering results with the kind of speed that simply cannot be matched by offshore producers. Even though Boathouse prices are 10–15% higher, they can deliver on most small orders in four weeks, compared to Chinese manufacturers who would take over eight weeks. Indeed, the high cost of shipping expenses due to the recent spike in oil prices is even cutting into the price differential. Thus, although some have suggested that global competition is eliminating high-wage manufacturing jobs where workers have a strong voice in how the work gets accomplished, in many corners of the economy, high-priced and empowered workers are more than earning their own way.[81]

TRADE-OFFS AMONG DIFFERENT APPROACHES TO JOB DESIGN

A great deal of research has aimed at understanding the trade-offs and implications of these different job design strategies.[82] For example, although the motivational and mechanistic approaches to job design do work against one another somewhat, at the same time there is not a tight, one-on-one correspondence between the two. Thus, not all efficiency-producing changes result in dissatisfying work, and not all changes that promote satisfaction create inevitable inefficiencies. By carefully and simultaneously attending to both efficiency and satisfaction aspects of job redesign, managers can sometimes achieve the best of both worlds.[83] For example, at the Indiana Heart Hospital in Indianapolis, much of the work was digitized in order to create a paperless organization. There are more than 600 computer terminals placed throughout the facility, and the doctors and staff directly enter or access information from these terminals as needed. This has eliminated the need for nurses' stations, chart racks, medical records departments, file storage rooms, and copiers and has cut down paperwork, resulting in an increase in efficiency, but also increased job satisfaction by eliminating bureaucracy, allowing the staff more immediate access to needed information. This has affected the bottom line by reducing the length of time a patient stays in the hospital from an average of five days at other hospitals to three days at Indiana Heart Hospital. This allows the hospital to process more patients per bed relative to the competition, giving them a direct source of competitive advantage.[84]

LO 4-6
Comprehend the trade-offs among the various approaches to designing jobs.

A LOOK BACK

Structural Problems at General Motors

This chapter opened with a vignette that illustrated how the workflow and organizational structure at General Motors contributed to a major disaster associated with an ignition switch failure that injured or killed a large number of people. We also showed throughout the chapter numerous methods and examples of how organizations can promote safety and still successfully compete via a more effective design for workflows, organizational structures, and individual jobs.

QUESTIONS

1. The analysis of workflow design traditionally starts at the end of the process, with the final product or service that is to be rendered. One then works back to determine the best process for this, and then the appropriate inputs. If an employer like GM wants to commit to processes that highlight the role of safety, how could the process of workflow design play out and how might the results be different than if the organization was committing to processes that were aimed at reducing costs?

2. Although there are advantages and disadvantages to different structural configurations, why might it be more difficult to change one's structure in some directions than others? Specifically, how are the HR challenges associated with moving from centralized and functional structures to decentralized and divisional different from the challenges of moving one's structure in the alternative direction?

3. Throughout this chapter we have seen that many ways of reducing the cost of getting jobs done often come at some price to workers who have to do those jobs. What can be done to promote a more just, fair, humane, and sustainable workforce in all corners of the world? Does the competitive nature of production or labor markets mean that "nice guys always finish last"?

SUMMARY

The analysis and design of work is one of the most important components to developing and maintaining a competitive advantage. Strategy implementation is virtually impossible without thorough attention devoted to work-flow analysis, job analysis, and job design. Managers need to understand the entire work-flow process in their work unit to ensure that the process maximizes efficiency and effectiveness. To understand this process, managers also must have clear, detailed information about the jobs that exist in the work unit, and the way to gain this information is through job analysis. Equipped with an understanding of the work-flow process and the existing job, managers can redesign jobs to ensure that the work unit is able to achieve its goals while individuals within the unit benefit from the various work outcome dimensions such as motivation, satisfaction, safety, health, and achievement. This is one key to competitive advantage.

KEY TERMS

Centralization, 153
Departmentalization, 153
Job analysis, 161

Job description, 163
Job specification, 164
Job design, 168

Job redesign, 168
Ergonomics, 170

DISCUSSION QUESTIONS

1. Assume you are the manager of a fast-food restaurant. What are the outputs of your work unit? What are the activities required to produce those outputs? What are the inputs?
2. Based on Question 1, consider the cashier's job. What are the outputs, activities, and inputs for that job?
3. Consider the "job" of college student. Perform a job analysis on this job. What are the tasks required in the job? What are the knowledge, skills, and abilities necessary to perform those tasks? What environmental trends or shocks (like computers) might change the job, and how would that change the skill requirements?
4. Discuss how the following trends are changing the skill requirements for managerial jobs in the United States: (a)

increasing use of computers, (b) increasing international competition.
5. Why is it important for a manager to be able to conduct a job analysis? What are the negative outcomes that would result from not understanding the jobs of those reporting to the manager?
6. What are the trade-offs between the different approaches to job design? Which approach do you think should be weighted most heavily when designing jobs?
7. For the cashier job in Question 2, which approach to job design was most influential in designing that job? In the context of the total work-flow process of the restaurant, how would you redesign the job to more heavily emphasize each of the other approaches?

SELF-ASSESSMENT EXERCISE

connect

Additional assignable self-assessments available in Connect.

The chapter described how the Department of Labor's Occupational Information Network (O*NET) can help employers. The system was also designed to help job seekers. To see if you think this new system meets the goal of promoting "the effective education, training, counseling, and employment needs of the American workforce," visit O*NET's website at http://online.onet-center.org/.

Look up the listing for your current job or dream job. List the skills identified for that job. For each skill, evaluate how well your own experiences and abilities enable you to match the job requirements.

EXERCISING STRATEGY

Safety as a Competitive Strategy

Even prior to the Upper Big Branch mine explosion that killed 29 workers, Massey Energy was notorious for putting coal miners at risk. In fact, according to a 2011 investigative report into the disaster, no United States coal company had a worse fatality record than Massey Energy, with over 50 deaths in the five years that led up to the fatal events at Upper Big Branch.

Many industry insiders attributed this record to an "organizational culture in which wrongdoing became acceptable, and where deviation was the norm." Under the leadership of CEO Donald Blankenship, Massey's competitive strategy was to push relentlessly for higher production and lower costs, and the organization largely turned a blind eye to worker safety. For example, government inspectors repeatedly shut down large stretches of the mine, but as one worker noted, "management never fully addressed the issues, they would fix it just good enough to fool the inspectors and get back to loading coal—that was just the Massey way."

Later in 2011, when Massey was acquired by Alpha Natural Resources, the new CEO, Kevin Crutchfield, vowed to change that culture, stating, "We're going to run this right and lead by example." One of Crutchfield's first moves was to initiate and promote the new "Running Right Program." The key component of this program was "observation cards" that workers were encouraged to anonymously submit to higher-level managers that identified unsafe practices or conditions anywhere in or around the mines. The "Running Right Program" is run by 18 staffers in central headquarters who process over 15,000 cards a month, and review these along with employee involvement groups that work at the sites.

The message sent by this program is quite a bit different from what the workers were used to under Blankenship's leadership. In one infamous memo, the previous CEO told all employees in writing that "if any of you have been asked by your group presidents, your supervisors, your engineers, or anyone else to do anything other than run coal, you need to ignore them and run coal. This memo is necessary only because we seem not to understand that coal pays the bills." Memos like this were one reason that despite residing in a region marked by chronically high unemployment, and where workers with nothing but a high school diploma could earn $70,000 a year, the turnover rate among coal miners at Massey was over 20% compared to their competitors who all had rates in the single digits. Crutchfield has vowed to get the turnover rate down to 5% in an effort to cut training costs and improve productivity. In the process he stresses, "I can assure you, I will not be sending any memos like that."

QUESTIONS

1. In what ways, other than higher than average turnover, does having an unsavory ethical reputation harm an organization's competitive advantage?
2. What role does the company's CEO play in establishing the competitive strategy and how does this "trickle down," when it comes to the organization's structure and culture?
3. What are some of the major difficulties associated with trying to change an unethical culture, and is it realistic for a new CEO to think he or she can change the culture without terminating a large number of upper-level managers?

SOURCES: P. M. Barrett, "Cleaning America's Dirtiest Coal Company," *Businessweek,* August 29, 2011; J. Raby, "Ex-CEO Implicated in Massey Coal Mine Disaster," *USA Today,* February 28, 2013, www.usatoday.com; H. Berkes, "Former Massey CEO Accused of Conspiracy in Court Hearing," *NPR,* February 28, 2013, www.npr.org.

MANAGING PEOPLE

Robots Attack Okun's Law

Okun's Law, named after economist Arthur Okun, states that there is a robust and steady relationship between productivity on the one hand, and unemployment rates on the other hand. In general, the formula expressed in this law suggests that every 3% gain in output should reduce the unemployment rate by 1%. Although the data fit this pattern extremely well in the time period between 1947 and 2005, more recently, this "law" does not even meet the criteria for a "rule of thumb." For example, if one applied this law to the five-year span from 2008 to 2012, then one would have expected to see an unemployment rate of around 1% in the U.S. economy—not nearly the 9% that was actually in place.

Some have suggested that the fundamental relationship between growth and unemployment has changed due to the increased use of robots in the workplace. In fact, the U.S. produces 25% more goods and services in 2012 than it did in 1999, but does so with almost the same number of workers. The difference can be traced to the substitution of technology for human labor, especially in the form of increasingly sophisticated robots. Although the traditional idea was that robots could do only simple jobs, and thus free humans up to do other work, this is less and less true.

For example, in the wake of the BP oil spill disaster where 11 workers died, a company called Robotic Drilling Systems designed a series of robots that did the work that was formerly done by deckhands and pipe handlers. The 10-foot-tall robot deckhand has a jointed arm that can extend 10 feet and has roughly a dozen interchangeable, three-fingered hands that allow it to pick up anything from a one-ton drill bit to an egg. Robots can now drive cars, fly airplanes, translate documents and speech from one language to another, search for legal precedents, and even write sports stories based solely on box scores. Labor economist David Autor has noted, "The era we're in is one in which the scope of tasks that can be automated is increasing rapidly and in the areas where we used to think those were our best skills—things that require thinking."

Still, others insist that rather than being job destroyers, robots will eventually become job creators in the sense that almost all new technologies spawn new jobs and business opportunities that could never have been imagined in prior times. For example, who would have thought that developing apps for smartphones would be a viable professional job a mere decade ago? Clearly, the productivity gains attributable to technological advancements need to be channeled back into education and training programs that make human workers and sophisticated robots valuable partners rather than direct competitors.

QUESTIONS

1. Can you think of some common jobs that exist today that would have been inconceivable to your parents or grandparents when they were your age?
2. Do these new lines of work require more or less of human beings when it comes to problem solving and critical thinking?
3. Are these new lines of work going to be relatively high-paying jobs or low-paying jobs, and what may determine one of these outcomes versus the other?

SOURCES: D. Lynch, "Did That Robot Take My Job?" *Businessweek,* January 9, 2012, pp. 15–16; D. Wethe, "Transformers on the Oil Patch," *Businessweek,* September 3, 2012, pp. 48–50; S. Grobart, "What Machines Can't Do," *Businessweek,* December 17, 2012, pp. 4–5.

HR IN SMALL BUSINESS

Inclusivity Defines BraunAbility's Products and Its Jobs

Ralph Braun built his company out of his creativity in meeting his own personal needs. Growing up in rural Indiana, Braun had difficulty climbing stairs, and doctors diagnosed him with spinal muscular atrophy. At age 14, Braun needed a wheelchair to get around. He was disappointed but developed his mechanical aptitude, honed by years of helping his uncles fix motorcycles and race cars, and used it to build himself a battery-powered scooter. With the scooter, Braun was able to navigate his way around a job at an automotive supply factory, where co-workers would ask him to build something similar for their family members and acquaintances. Later, for better transportation to and from the job, Braun figured out how to convert a Dodge van with a lift so he could enter the van on his scooter and drive it from there. Again, people saw the van and asked for something similar. Eventually, Braun took all his earnings from scooters and van conversions and started Save-A-Step Manufacturing, later named BraunAbility, which has become the world's largest maker of wheelchair-accessible vans and wheelchair lifts.

The passion and purposefulness of the company's founder are reflected in the structure of BraunAbility's jobs and work. Recruiting is inclusive, with an especially great appreciation for the potential of disabled workers. Cyndi Garnett, the company's director of human resources, notes that a person with a disability has to go through life solving accessibility problems creatively, so that person is likely to have become a great innovator. Wherever possible, work schedules are tailored to employees' needs. Many employees have flexible schedules, working their choice of eight hours between 7:00 A.M. and 6:00 P.M. Some employees telecommute full-time or part-time. Even production workers, who must coordinate their tasks as vans move from one work station to the next, have flexibility to negotiate arrangements that work for them as a group. They told the company that they wanted just a couple of short breaks during the day instead of a long lunch break, so they could leave earlier. BraunAbility went along with the idea.

As you might expect from a company founded by a creative man, innovation is valued over hierarchy at BraunAbility. Garnett says, "If anyone has an idea, that person is listened to." For example, an employee suggested that, rather than going through the process of safely disposing of leftover paint, workers use it to paint the vehicle floors under the carpet, for a little additional protection of the vehicle. The company readily adopted the suggestion.

Along with feeling respected, workers at Braun Ability feel their work matters to society. In Garnett's words, because the company's vans make it possible to travel independently, employees "know that they're changing the lives of people with disabilities with every product that goes out the door."

QUESTIONS

1. In what ways is work at BraunAbility motivating? What other features of motivating work might BraunAbility be able to offer its employees?

2. What place would efficient job design have in a company like BraunAbility? How could BraunAbil-ity improve job efficiency in a way that is consistent with the company's emphasis on inclusiveness and flexibility?

3. Imagine that you work with the HR director at BraunAbil-ity, and she has asked you to suggest some ways to

reinforce employees' sense that their jobs have an important positive impact on others. What would you suggest?

SOURCES: Company website, www.braunability.com, accessed May 14, 2014; "Collaboration, Inclusion Help Create That Small-Town' Feeling," white paper, HR.BLR.com, January 18, 2010, http://hr.blr.com; "How I Did It: Ralph Braun of BraunAbility," *Inc.,* December 1, 2009, www.inc.com; and "BraunAbility Launches EntervanXT to Accommodate Needs of Taller Wheelchair and Scooter Users," *Marketing Weekly News,* October 10, 2009, Business & Company Resource Center, http://galenet.galegroup.com.

NOTES

1. B. Snavely, "Fiat Chrysler Returns to $101.2 Million Profit in Q1," *USA Today,* April 29, 2015, www.usatoday.com.

2. D. Ilgen and J. Hollenbeck, "The Structure of Work: Job Design and Roles," in *Handbook of Industrial & Organizational Psychology,* 2nd ed., ed. M. Dunnette and L. Hough (Palo Alto, CA: Consulting Psychologists Press, 1991), pp. 165–208.

3. J. Jargon, "McDonald's Menu Problem: It's Supersized," *The Wall Street Journal,* December 3, 2014, www.wsj.com.

4. L. Landro, "The Doctor's Team Will See You Now," *The Wall Street Journal,* February 2014, www.wsj.com.

5. G. S. Van der Vegt, B. J. M. Emans, and E. Van de Vliert, "Patterns of Interdependence in Work Teams: A Two-Level Investigation of the Relations with Job and Team Satisfaction," *Personnel Psychology* 54 (2001), pp. 51–70.

6. F. P. Morgeson, M. D. Johnson, M. A. Campion, G. J. Medsker, and T. V. Mumford, "Understanding Reactions to Job Redesign: A Quasi-Experimental Investigation of the Moderating Effects of Organizational Context on Perceptions of Performance and Behavior," *Personnel Psychology* 59 (2006), pp. 333–63.

7. C. M. Barnes, J. R. Hollenbeck, D. T. Wagner, D. S. DeRue, J. D. Nahrgang, and K. M. Schwind, "Harmful Help: The Costs of Backing-up Behaviors in Teams," *Journal of Applied Psychology* 93 (2008), pp. 529–39.

8. B. Greeley, "We're from Private Equity and We're Here to Help," *Businessweek,* April 30, 2012, pp. 55–59.

9. T. Aeppel and J. Lahart, "Lean Factories Find It Hard to Cut Jobs Even in a Slump," *The Wall Street Journal,* March 9, 2009, pp. B2–B3.

10. P. Engardio, "Lean and Mean Gets Extreme," *Bloomberg Businessweek,* March 23, 2009, pp. 60–62.

11. T. Black, "Downsides of Just-in-Time Inventory," *Bloomberg Businessweek,* March 28, 2011, pp. 17–18.

12. N. Carr, "Automation Makes Us Dumb, *The Wall Street Journal,* November 21, 2014, www.wsj.com.

13. M. Phillips and P. Coy, "Choosing Profits over Productivity," *Bloomberg Businessweek,* May 19, 2014, pp. 12–13.

14. S. Kolhatkar, "Where Have All the Secretaries Gone?" *Businessweek,* April 8, 2013, pp. 67–69.

15. S. Grobart, "Hooray for Hierarchy," *Businessweek,* January 14, 2013, p. 74.

16. A. Schatz, "Contractors Point Fingers over Health Care Website," *The Wall Street Journal,* October 24, 2013, www.wsj.com.

17. D. Bennett, "The Dunbar Number," *Businessweek,* January 10, 2013, pp. 53–56.

18. K. Akter, "The Bloodshed Behind Our Cheap Clothes," *CNN,* May 3, 2013, www.cnn.com.

19. R. Dudley, A. Devanth, and M. Townsend, "The Hidden Cost of Fast Fashion," *Bloomberg Businessweek,* February 11, 2013, pp. 15–17.

20. R. E. Silverman, "Who's the Boss? There Isn't One," *The Wall Street Journal Online,* June 13, 2012.

21. B. Worthen, C. Tuna, and J. Scheck, "Companies More Prone to Go Vertical," *The Wall Street Journal* November 30, 2009, pp. A1 and A16.

22. T. Neff and J. Citrin, "You're in Charge: Now What?" *Fortune,* January 24, 2005, pp. 109–20.

23. P. Orfalea and A.Marsh, *Copy This!: How I Turned Dyslexia, ADHD, and 100 Square Feet into a Company Called Kinko's* (New York: Workman Publishing, 2007).

24. W. D. Sine, H. Mitsuhashi, and D. A. Kirsch, "Revisiting Burns and Stalker: Formal Structure and New Venture Performance in Emerging Economic Sectors," *Academy of Management Journal* 49 (2006), pp. 121–32.

25. J. Marquez, "Banking on a New Culture at Citibank," *Workforce Management,* May 19, 2008, pp. 1–3.

26. J. E. Ellis, "At P&G, the Innovation Well Runs Dry," *Businessweek,* September 12, 2012, pp. 24–26.

27. T. Henneman, "Is HR at Its Breaking Point," *Workforce Management,* April 2013, pp. 28–33.

28. P. Glader, "It's Not Easy Being Lean," *The Wall Street Journal,* June 19, 2006, pp. B1, B3.

29. N. Byrnes, "The Art of Motivation," *BusinessWeek,* May 1, 2006, pp. 57–62.

30. J. R. Hollenbeck, H. Moon, A. Ellis, B. West, D. R. Ilgen, L. Sheppard, C. O. Porter, and J. A. Wagner, "Structural Contingency Theory and Individual Differences: Examination of External and Internal Person–Team Fit," *Journal of Applied Psychology* 87 (2002), pp. 599–606.

31. M. L. Ambrose and M. Schminke, "Organization Structure as a Moderator of the Relationship between Procedural Justice, Interactional Justice, Perceived Organizational Support, and Supervisory Trust," *Journal of Applied Psychology* 88 (2003), pp. 295–305.

32. J. A. Marquez, "Taking a Longer View," *Workforce Management,* May 21, 2006, pp. 18–22.

33. A. Weintraub and M. Tirrell, "Eli Lilly's Drug Assembly Line," *Businessweek,* February 25, 2010, pp. 34–35.

34. D. A. Hofmann, F. P. Morgeson, and S. J. Gerras, "Climate as a Moderator of the Relationship between Leader–Member Exchange and Content-Specific Citizenship: Safety Climate as an Exemplar," *Journal of Applied Psychology* 88 (2003), pp. 170–78.

35. M. Rosenwald, "Bound by Habit," *Businessweek,* March 19, 2012, pp. 106–7.

36. L. Weber, "Help Wanted—on Writing Job Descriptions," *The Wall Street Journal,* October 2, 2013, www.wsj.com.

37. E. C. Dierdorf and F. P. Morgeson, "Effects of Descriptor Specificity and Observability on Incumbent Work Analysis Ratings," *Personnel Psychology* 62 (2009), pp. 601–28.

38. P. Lievens, J. I. Sanchez, D. Bartram, and A. Brown, "Lack of Consensus among Competency Ratings of the Same Occupation: Noise or Substance," *Journal of Applied Psychology* 95 (2010), pp. 562–71.

39. C. Mims, "In 'People Analytics,' You're Not a Human, You're a Data Point," *The Wall Street Journal,* February 16, 2015, www.wsj.com.

40. S. Shellenbarger, "Stop Wasting Everyone's Time," *The Wall Street Journal,* December 2, 2014, www.wsj.com.

41. A. K. Weyman, "Investigating the Influence of Organizational Role on Perceptions of Risk in Deep Coal Mines," *Journal of Applied Psychology* 88 (2003), pp. 404–12.

42. L. E. Baranowski and L. E. Anderson, "Examining Rater Source Variation in Work Behavior to KSA Linkages," *Personnel Psychology* 58 (2005), pp. 1041–54.

43. E. McCormick and R. Jeannerette, "The Position Analysis Questionnaire," in *The Job Analysis Handbook for Business, Industry, and Government,* pp. 880–901.

44. M. Biron and P. Bamberger, "Aversive Workplace Conditions and Abseteeism: Taking Referent Group Norms and Supervisor Support into Account," *Journal of Applied Psychology,* 97 (2012), pp. 901–12.

45. C. Coleman, "How to Create a Workplace People Never Want to Leave," *Businessweek,* April 11, 2013, p. 51.

46. N. G. Peterson, M. D. Mumford, W. C. Borman, P. R. Jeanneret, and E. A. Fleishman, *An Occupational Information System for the 21st Century: The Development of O*NET* (Washington, DC: American Psychological Association, 1999).

47. N. G. Peterson, M. D. Mumford, W. C. Borman, P. R. Jeanneret, E. A. Fleishman, K. Y. Levin, M. A. Campion, M. S. Mayfield, F. P. Morgenson, K. Pearlman, M. K. Gowing, A. R. Lancaster, M. B. Silver, and D. M. Dye, "Understanding Work Using the Occupational Information Network (O*NET): Implications for Practice and Research," *Personnel Psychology* 54 (2001), pp. 451–92.

48. P. J. Taylor, W. D. Li, K. Shi, and W. C. Borman, "The Transportability of Job Information Across Countries," *Personnel Psychology* 61 (2008), pp. 69–111.

49. S. Holmes, "Lots of Green Left in the Emerald City," *BusinessWeek Online* (March 28, 2000).

50. C. C. Lapolice, G. W. Carter, and J. W. Johnson, "Linking O*NET Descriptors to Occupational Literacy Requirements Using Job Component Validation," *Personnel Psychology* 61 (2008), pp. 405–441.

51. M. K. Lindell, C. S. Clause, C. J. Brandt, and R. S. Landis, "Relationship between Organizational Context and Job Analysis Ratings," *Journal of Applied Psychology* 83 (1998), pp. 769–76.

52. F. P. Morgeson and M. A. Campion, "Social and Cognitive Sources of Potential Inaccuracy in Job Analysis," *Journal of Applied Psychology* 82 (1997), pp. 627–55.

53. S. Caudron, "Jobs Disappear When Work Becomes More Important," *Workforce,* January 2000, pp. 30–32.

54. M. Campion and P. Thayer, "Development and Field Evaluation of an Interdisciplinary Measure of Job Design," *Journal of Applied Psychology* 70 (1985), pp. 29–34.

55. F. P. Morgeson and S. E. Humphrey, "The Work Design Questionnaire (WDQ): Developing and Validating a Comprehensive Measure for Assessing Job Design and the Nature of Work," *Journal of Applied Psychology* 91 (2006), pp. 1312–39.

56. J. Jargon, "Chili's Feels Heat to Pare Costs," *The Wall Street Journal,* January 28, 2011, pp. B.8.

57. F. Taylor, *The Principles of Scientific Management* (New York: W. W. Norton, 1967) (originally published in 1911 by Harper & Brothers).

58. Simpson, "Samsung's War at Home," *Bloomberg Businessweek,* April 10, 2014, pp. 60–65.

59. B. Helm, "Life on the Web's Factory Floor," *BusinessWeek,* May 22, 2006, pp. 70–71.

60. M. Gunther, "Wal-Mart: A Bully Benefactor," CNNMoney.com, December 5, 2008, p. 1.

61. L. Delevevigne, "Surprising Corporate Do-gooders," CNN. Money.com, January 20, 2009, p. 1.

62. R. Griffin and G. McMahan, "Motivation through Job Design," in *OB: The State of the Science,* ed. J. Greenberg (Hillsdale, NJ: Lawrence Erlbaum Associates, 1993).

63. R. Hackman and G. Oldham, *Work Redesign* (Boston: Addison-Wesley, 1980).

64. A. M. Grant, "The Significance of Task Significance," *Journal of Applied Psychology* 93 (2007), pp. 108–24.

65. A. M. Grant, E. M. Campbell, G. Chen, K. Cottone, D. Lapedia, and K. Lee, "Impact and Art of Motivation Maintenance: The Effects of Contact with Beneficiaries on Persistence Behavior," *Organizational Behavior and Human Decision Processes* 103 (2007), pp. 53–67.

66. F. W. Bond, P. E. Flaxman, and D. Bunce, "The Influence of Psychological Flexibility on Work Redesign: Mediated Moderation of a Work Reorganization Intervention," *Journal of Applied Psychology* 93 (2008), pp. 645–54.

67. M. R. Barrick, M. K. Mount, and N. Li, "The Theory of Purposeful Work Behavior: The Role of Personality, Higher-Order Goals,and Job Characteristics," *Academy of Management Review* 38 (2013), pp. 132–153.

68. W. E. Byrnes, "Making the Job Meaningful All the Way Down the Line," *BusinessWeek,* May 1, 2006, p. 60.

69. J. A. Colquitt and R. F. Piccalo, "Transformational Leadership and Job Behaviors: The Mediating Role of Core Job Characteristics," *Academy of Management Journal* 49 (2006), pp. 327–40.

70. A. Park, "Stand Up for Yourself," *Time Magazine,* September 8, 2014, pp. 22–23.

71. S. Mewman, M. A. Griffen, and C. Mason, "Safety in Work Vehicles: A Multilevel Study Linking Safety Values and Individual Predictors to Work-related Driving Crashes," *Journal of Applied Psychology* 93 (2008), pp. 632–44.

72. R. Feintzieg and A. Berzon, "Safety Cops Patrol the Office for High Heels," *The Wall Street Journal,* July 27, 2014, www.wsj.com.

73. J. E. Barnes, "Life on a Navy Sub Relies on Rules: Some Dead Serious, Others Completely Ridiculous," *The Wall Street Journal,* May 1, 2014, www.wsj.com.

74. S. F. Brown, "International's Better Way to Build Trucks," *Fortune,* February 19, 2001, pp. 210k–210v.

75. D. K. Berman, "Technology Has Us So Plugged into Data, We Have Turned Off," *The Wall Street Journal,* November 10, 2003, pp. A1–A2.

76. M. Beck, "What Cocktail Parties Teach Us," *The Wall Street Journal Online,* April 22, 2012.

77. J. Baker, "From Open Doors to Gated Communities," *Business-Week,* September 8, 2003, p. 36.

78. L. E. LaBlanc, J. J. Hox, W. B. Schaufell, T. W. Taris, and M. C. W. Peters, "Take Care! The Evaluation of a Team-Based Burnout Intervention Program for Oncology Health Care Providers," *Journal of Applied Psychology* 92 (2007), pp. 213–27.

79. L. Landro, "Hospitals Combat Errors at the 'Hand-Off,'" *The Wall Street Journal,* June 28, 2006, pp. D1, D2.

80. J. R. Hollenbeck, B. Beersma, and M. E. Schouten, "Beyond Team Types and Taxonomies: A Dimensional Scaling Approach for Team Description," *Academy of Management Review,* 37 (2012), pp. 82–108.

81. M. N. Leiber, "Suddenly, Made in the USA Looks like a Strategy," *Businessweek,* March 28, 2011, pp. 57–58.

82. J. R. Edwards, J. A. Scully, and M. D. Brteck, "The Nature and Outcomes of Work: A Replication and Extension of Interdisciplinary Work-Design Research," *Journal of Applied Psychology* 85 (2000), pp. 860–68.

83. F. P. Morgeson and M. A. Campion, "Minimizing Trade-Offs When Redesigning Work: Evidence from a Longitudinal Quasi-Experiment," *Personnel Psychology* 55 (2002), pp. 589–612.

84. E. Florian, "IT Takes on the ER," *Fortune,* November 24, 2003, pp. 193–200.

Human Resource Planning and Recruitment

PART TWO

5

CHAPTER

LEARNING OBJECTIVES

After reading this chapter, you should be able to:

LO 5-1   Discuss how to align a company's strategic direction with its human resource planning. *page 185*

LO 5-2   Determine the labor demand for workers in various job categories. *page 186*

LO 5-3   Discuss the advantages and disadvantages of various ways of eliminating a labor surplus and avoiding a labor shortage. *page 188*

LO 5-4   Describe the various recruitment policies that organizations adopt to make job vacancies more attractive. *page 204*

LO 5-5   List the various sources from which job applicants can be drawn, their relative advantages and disadvantages, and the methods for evaluating them. *page 206*

LO 5-6   Explain the recruiter's role in the recruitment process, the limits the recruiter faces, and the opportunities available. *page 212*

Is the Demand for On-Demand Labor about to Shift?

When they discuss their business model, representatives for Uber always focus on the software application that links would-be riders with would-be drivers, and hence, quickly and seamlessly connects a specific demand for labor with a specific supply of labor. The success of this business model is undeniable in the sense that even though it has only been existence for five years, the company has expanded to more than 300 cities and is now valued at over $50 billion. The number of people who drive for Uber all over the world is very difficult to estimate, but the company states that they have 26,000 drivers in New York City, 15,000 in London, 10,000 in Paris, and 20,000 in Chengdu, China alone.

Beyond the software application, though, a big part of Uber's success can also be attributed to the fact that all of the labor employed is low paid, has no job security, and is provided no benefits. In the United States, for example, many Uber drivers enjoy the flexibility that this work provides but the fact is that they are paid far less than the minimum wage, especially when one figures in expenses and vehicle depreciation. The company can get away with this because the drivers are classified as "independent contractors" rather than "traditional employees." This classification has been challenged in several instances, however, and in June 2015, the California Labor Commissioner's Office ruled that Uber drivers should be classified as traditional employees.

This finding has huge implications because Uber is just one of many "on-demand" companies that rely on this ever-increasing business model for managing workers. This is the same model that is employed by Uber's #1 rival, Lyft, as well as companies such as Instacart that delivers groceries, Handybook that provides cleaning services, TaskRabbit that does odd jobs, and Mechanical Turk that provides a broad range of services. Some have even suggested that this freelance model of employment is the next wave

© McGraw-Hill Education/Mark Dierker, photographer

of the future. As one labor economist noted, "The $40-an-hour-manufacturing job is not going to come back, but the $25 local services job represents a viable alternative."

Few of these jobs actually wind up paying at this rate, however, and the generally high level of worker discontent has made some of these companies reconsider their business model. For example, Instacart announced, ironically enough the week after the California ruling, that it was reclassifying its workers as employees. Instacart ran a trial experiment with this reclassification in Boston the year before and came to the conclusion that "this change improved the quality and efficiency of order picking and made for a better customer experience." Apparently, the customer services advantages of a more traditional supply of labor outweighed the cost savings associated with the on-demand labor supply.

SOURCES: S. A. O'Brien, "The Uber Effect: Instacart Shifts Away from Contract Workers," *CNN Money,* June 22, 2015, http://money.cnn.com; M. Isaac and N. Singer, "California Says Uber Driver Is Employee, Not a Contractor," *The New York Times,* June 17, 2015, www.nytimes.com; L. Weber and R.E. Silverman, "On-demand Workers: We Are Not Robots," *The Wall Street Journal,* January 27, 2015, www.wsj.com.

Introduction

Human resource managers are at the forefront of the worldwide war for competitive advantage. Organizations need to find the best set of workers for meeting their strategic objectives, attract those workers to their companies, and then get them to stay long enough to obtain some return on their investment. As our opening vignette shows, Uber was able to go from being worth zero to being worth $50 billion in just five years because of its unique business model that relies on an independent contracting model attached to a unique software application that matches the demand for a ride with the supply of a ride. Although some see this as the "wave of the future," other, more-established companies have used this same model as a source of competitive advantage. For example, Federal Express truck drivers also work as independent contractors, and this arrangement saves the company 30% of payroll costs, including the payroll tax, unemployment insurance, workers compensation, and state taxes versus a competitor such as UPS that treats workers as traditional employees. Both FedEx and UPS are committed to their business strategies, but they compete in different ways. UPS delivers mainly to far-flung individual residences and needs an experienced and committed workforce, whereas FedEx delivers mainly to businesses in urban environments and needs an efficient, but not necessarily engaged set of drivers.[1] Thus, there are advantages and disadvantages associated with different workforces, and organizations that survive and thrive find the best match between the workers they need and the strategy they employ to compete in the market.

The purpose of this chapter is to examine factors that influence the supply and demand for labor, and, in particular, focus on what human resources managers can do in terms of planning and executing human resource policies that give their firms competitive advantage in a dynamic environment. Although our focus in at the firm level, it is worth noting that nations also compete in labor markets, and when a country begins to see most of its human talent emigrate, this type of "brain drain" can have a devastating impact on national competitiveness. For example, in Iran, 40% of the top graduates in undergraduate science and technology programs leave the country to attend graduate school in Europe and the United States, and then, upon matriculation, 90% never return to Iran.[2] Two of the major ways that societal trends and events affect employers are through (1) consumer markets, which affect the demand for goods and services, and (2) labor markets, which affect the supply of people to produce goods and services. In some cases, the market might be characterized by a labor shortage. In other cases, the market may be characterized by a surplus of labor. Reconciling the difference between the supply and demand for labor presents a challenge for organizations, and how they address this will affect their overall competitiveness.

There are three keys to effectively utilizing labor markets to one's competitive advantage. First, companies must have a clear idea of their current configuration of human resources. In particular, they need to know the strengths and weaknesses of their present stock of employees. Second, organizations must know where they are going in the future and be aware of how their present configuration of human resources relates to the configuration that will be needed. Third, where there are discrepancies between the present configuration and the configuration required for the future, organizations need programs that will address these discrepancies.

This chapter looks at tools and technologies that can help an organization develop and implement effective strategies for leveraging labor market "threats" into opportunities to gain competitive advantage. In the first half of the chapter, we lay out the actual steps that go into developing and implementing a human resource plan. Through each section, we focus especially on recent trends and practices (like downsizing, employing temporary workers, and outsourcing) that can have a major impact on the firm's bottom line and overall reputation. In the second half of the chapter, we familiarize you with the process by which individuals find and choose jobs and the role of personnel recruitment in reaching these individuals and shaping their choices.

The Human Resource Planning Process

An overview of human resource planning is depicted in Figure 5.1. The process consists of forecasting, goal setting and strategic planning, and program implementation and evaluation. We discuss each of these stages in the next sections of this chapter.

LO 5-1
Discuss how to align a company's strategic direction with its human resource planning.

FORECASTING

The first step in the planning process is **forecasting,** as shown in the top portion of Figure 5.1. In personnel forecasting, the HR manager attempts to ascertain the supply of and demand for various types of human resources. The primary goal is to predict areas within the organization where there will be future labor shortages or surpluses.

Forecasting, on both the supply and demand sides, can use either statistical methods or judgmental methods. Statistical methods are excellent for capturing historic trends in a company's demand for labor, and under the right conditions they give predictions that are much more precise than those that could be achieved through subjective judgments of a human forecaster. On the other hand, many important events that occur in the labor market have no historical precedent; hence, statistical methods that work from historical trends are of little use in such cases. With no historical precedent, one must rely on the pooled subjective judgments of experts, and their "best guesses" might be the only source from which to make inferences about the future. Typically, because of the complementary strengths and weaknesses of the two methods, companies that engage in human resource planning use a balanced approach.

Forecasting
The attempts to determine the supply of and demand for various types of human resources to predict areas within the organization where there will be future labor shortages or surpluses.

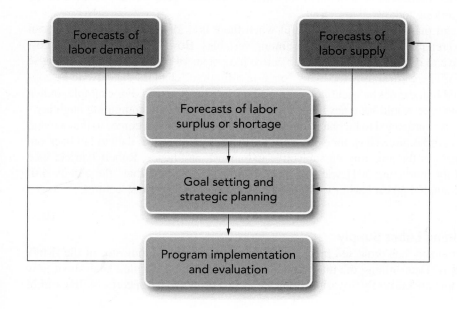

Figure 5.1

Overview of the Human Resource Planning Process

Determining Labor Demand

Typically, demand forecasts are developed around specific job categories or skill areas relevant to the organization's current and future state. Once the job categories or skills are identified, the planner needs to seek information that will help predict whether the need for people with those skills or in that job category will increase or decrease in the future. For example, due to the aging population in the United States, elder care is one of the fast-growing industries, and thus, there is likely to be a high demand for workers with skills that suit this work. In contrast, the advent of e-mail, the Internet, and text messaging means that the demand for postal carriers is headed in the opposite direction.[3] Organizations differ in the sophistication with which such forecasts are derived.

At the most sophisticated level, an organization might have statistical models that predict labor demand for the next year given relatively objective statistics on leading indicators from the previous year. A **leading indicator** is an objective measure that accurately predicts future labor demand. For example, in the cattle industry, the price of corn is closely related to the cost of beef. Hence, sharp increases in corn prices at Time 1 affect the price, and therefore the demand for cattle at Time 2. In turn, the demand for cattle affects the number of workers needed to staff slaughterhouses. Thus, when drought conditions in 2012 caused a spike in corn prices, this predictably meant that Cargill, a large beef processor, would need fewer workers in 2013. Thus, Cargill shut down a large plant in Plainview, Texas, well before the effects of the drought were even seen at the plant. Had the company not anticipated this drop in demand, as many as 2,000 workers would have had to be paid even though they had nothing to do.[4] In contrast, although the relationship between oil prices and demand for rig workers is well known, the drop in oil prices in 2015 attributed to the rapid growth of the fracking industry came as a surprise to many, and hence over 100,000 workers in this industry had to be laid off when confronted with an unanticipated change in demand.[5]

Similarly, the demand for welders can be predicted by the growth in the manufacturing sector of the economy. Thus, when the U.S. manufacturing sector grew for four straight years between 2010 and 2014, the demand for skilled welders increased. However, decades of slow manufacturing growth meant that many people left this field and few new people entered the field. Hence, the American Welding Society has estimated that by 2020 there will be a demand for close to 300,000 more welders relative to the number working today.[6]

Statistical planning models are useful when there is a long, stable history that can be used to reliably detect relationships among variables. However, these models almost always have to be complemented by subjective judgments of people who have expertise in the area. There are simply too many "once-in-a-lifetime" changes that have to be considered and that cannot be accurately captured in statistical models. For example, only a decade ago, one would have never even heard the job title "cloud computing engineer," and yet, this is projected to be one of the fast-growing areas when it comes to the demand for labor in the future. Thus, for a job like this, there is no historical data to fall back on. Still, experts in the area rely on subjective judgments, and hence, Robert Patrick, vice president for marketing at Hewlett-Packard, confidently predicts that "the clouds skill gap is the single biggest barrier to the future adoption of cloud infrastructures."[7]

Determining Labor Supply

Once a company has projected labor demand, it needs to get an indicator of the firm's labor supply. Determining the internal labor supply calls for a detailed analysis of how many people are currently in various job categories (or who have specific skills) within the company. This analysis is then modified to reflect changes in the near future caused by retirements, promotions, transfers, voluntary turnover, and terminations.

As in the case of labor demand, projections for labor supply can be derived either from historical statistical models or through judgmental techniques. One type of statistical procedure that can be employed for this purpose involves transitional matrices. **Transitional matrices** show the proportion (or number) of employees in different job categories at different times. Typically these matrices show how people move in one year from one state (outside the organization) or job category to another state or job category.

Table 5.1 shows a hypothetical transitional matrix for a hypothetical manufacturer, focusing on seven job categories. Although these matrices look imposing at first, you will see that they are easy to read and use in determining the internal labor supply. A matrix like the one in this table can be read in two ways. First, we can read the rows to answer the question "Where did people in this job category in 2013 go by 2016?" For example, 70% of those in the clerical job category (row 7) in 2013 were still in this job category in 2016, and the remaining 30% had left the organization. For the production assembler job category (row 6), 80% of those in this position in 2013 were still there in 2016. Of the remaining 20%, half (10%) were promoted to the production manager job category, and the other half (10%) left the organization. Finally, 75% of those in the production manager job category in 2013 were still there in 2016, while 10% were promoted to assistant plant manager and 15% left the organization.

Reading these kinds of matrices across rows makes it clear that there is a career progression within this firm from production assembler to production manager to assistant plant manager. Although we have not discussed rows 1 through 3, it might also be noted that there is a similar career progression from sales apprentice to sales representative to sales manager. In this organization, the clerical category is not part of any career progression. That is, this job category does not feed any other job categories listed in Table 5.1.

A transitional matrix can also be read from top to bottom (in the columns) to answer the question "Where did the people in this job category in 2016 come from (Where were they in 2013)?" Again, starting with the clerical job (column 7), 70% of the 2016 clerical positions were filled by people who were also in this position in 2013, and the remaining 30% were external hires (they were not part of the organization in 2013). In the production assembler job category (column 6), 80% of those occupying this job in 2016 occupied the same job in 2013, and the other 20% were external hires. The most diversely staffed job category seems to be that of production manager

Transitional Matrix
Matrix showing the proportion (or number) of employees in different job categories at different times.

Table 5.1
A Hypothetical Transitional Matrix for an Auto Parts Manufacturer

2013	2016							
	(1)	(2)	(3)	(4)	(5)	(6)	(7)	(8)
(1) Sales manager	.95							.05
(2) Sales representative	.05	.60						.35
(3) Sales apprentice		.20	.50					.30
(4) Assistant plant manager				.90	.05			.05
(5) Production manager				.10	.75			.15
(6) Production assembler					.10	.80		.10
(7) Clerical							.70	.30
(8) Not in organization	.00	.20	.50	.00	.10	.20	.30	

(column 5): 75% of those in this position in 2016 held the same position in 2013; however, 10% were former production assemblers who were promoted, 5% were former assistant plant managers who were demoted, and 10% were external hires who were not with the company in 2013.

Matrices such as these are extremely useful for charting historical trends in the company's supply of labor. More important, if conditions remain somewhat constant, they can also be used to plan for the future. For example, if we believe that we are going to have a surplus of labor in the production assembler job category in the next three years, we note that by simply initiating a freeze on external hires, the ranks of this position will be depleted by 20% on their own. Similarly, if we believe that we will have a labor shortage in the area of sales representatives, the matrix informs us that we may want to (1) decrease the amount of voluntary turnover in this position, since 35% of those in this category leave every three years, (2) speed the training of those in the sales apprentice job category so that they can be promoted more quickly than in the past, and/or (3) expand external recruitment of individuals for this job category, since the usual 20% of job incumbents drawn from this source may not be sufficient to meet future needs.

As with labor demand, historical precedents for labor supply may not always be reliable indicators of future trends. For example, it is typically the case that when unemployment is high, applications for any open positions increase dramatically compared to what might be experienced when the unemployment rate is low. However, in 2010, many employers who were posting open positions found that there were very few people actually applying for jobs. This was attributed to the fact that unemployment benefits had been extended to unprecedented lengths (99 weeks) and because the collapse of the housing market made it impossible for people to sell their homes, leaving them locked into their current location.[8] Similarly, in the nuclear energy field, the near meltdown of three nuclear power plants in Fukushima, Japan, following the earthquake and tsunami that rocked that region in 2011 had an immediate effect on students enrolling in nuclear engineering programs across the world. Many students stopped enrolling in those programs or switched to other fields of study, suggesting that in the future, the supply of young people with this set of skills is likely to be much lower than it is today.[9]

Determining Labor Surplus or Shortage

LO 5-3
Discuss the advantages and disadvantages of various ways of eliminating a labor surplus and avoiding a labor shortage.

Once forecasts for labor demand and supply are known, the planner can compare the figures to ascertain whether there will be a labor shortage or labor surplus for the respective job categories. When this is determined, the organization can determine what it is going to do about these potential problems. For example, in the construction industry in 2015, a shortage of skilled laborers meant that many real estate developers had to cut back on building plans or had these plans delayed an inordinate amount of time because of the inability to find workers with specific skills. In Denver, Shea Homes had plans and funding to build 325 homes but could not execute these plans because the company could not find workers to fit and install cabinets, as well as heating, ventilation, and air conditioning installers.[10] In contrast, the Bureau of Labor Statistics estimates that during the decade ending in 2020, the U.S. economy will create roughly 70,000 lawyer positions, while U.S. law schools are matriculating over 25,000 graduates a year. This translates into a labor surplus of 175,000 lawyers with little of nothing to do.[11] Clearly, the longer one has to adjust to these kinds of surpluses and shortages, the easier the adjustment, and thus forecasting is a critical strategic human resource activity.

GOAL SETTING AND STRATEGIC PLANNING

The second step in human resource planning is goal setting and strategic planning, as shown in the middle of Figure 5.1. The purpose of setting specific quantitative goals is to focus attention on the problem and provide a benchmark for determining the relative success of any programs aimed at redressing a pending labor shortage or surplus. The goals should come directly from the analysis of labor supply and demand and should include a specific figure for what should happen with the job category or skill area and a specific timetable for when results should be achieved.

The hypothetical manufacturer described in Table 5.1, for instance, might set a goal to reduce the number of individuals in the production assembler job category by 50% over the next three years. Similarly, the firm might set a goal to increase the number of individuals in the sales representative job category by 25% over the next three years.

Once these goals are established, the firm needs to choose from the many different strategies available for redressing labor shortages and surpluses. Table 5.2 shows some of the options for a human resource planner seeking to reduce a labor surplus. Table 5.3 shows some options available to the same planner intent on avoiding a labor shortage.

This stage is critical because the many options available to the planner differ widely in their expense, speed, effectiveness, amount of human suffering, and revocability (how easily the change can be undone). For example, if the organization can anticipate a labor surplus far enough in advance, it may be able to freeze hiring and then just let natural attrition adjust the size of the labor force. If successful, an organization may be able to avoid layoffs altogether, so that no one has to lose a job. Similarly, with enough advance warning, if an organization can anticipate a labor shortage for some job category like "welder," it might be able to work with a local community college to provide scholarships to students who are willing to learn those skills in return for committing to work for that employer in the future.

OPTION	SPEED	HUMAN SUFFERING
1. Downsizing	Fast	High
2. Pay reductions	Fast	High
3. Demotions	Fast	High
4. Transfers	Fast	Moderate
5. Work sharing	Fast	Moderate
6. Hiring freeze	Slow	Low
7. Natural attrition	Slow	Low
8. Early retirement	Slow	Low
9. Retraining	Slow	Low

Table 5.2
Options for Reducing an Expected Labor Surplus

OPTION	SPEED	REVOCABILITY
1. Overtime	Fast	High
2. Temporary employees	Fast	High
3. Outsourcing	Fast	High
4. Retrained transfers	Slow	High
5. Turnover reductions	Slow	Moderate
6. New external hires	Slow	Low
7. Technological innovation	Slow	Low

Table 5.3
Options for Avoiding an Expected Labor Shortage

Unfortunately for many workers, in the past decade the typical organizational response to a surplus of labor has been downsizing, which is fast but high in human suffering. The human suffering caused by downsizing has both an immediate and a long-term element. In the short term, the lack of pay, benefits, and meaningful work has negative implications for financial, physical, and psychological aspects of individuals, causing bankruptcies, illnesses, and depression. Then, even if one can survive these immediate problems, in the long term, an extended bout of unemployment (e.g., lasting over six months) can stigmatize the individual, thus reducing future opportunities. In particular, in job categories where skills are perishable and need to be constantly updated, many laid-off workers will take any work within their area—even unpaid volunteer work—in order to prevent a gap in their employment history.[12] However, after very long periods of unemployment, people may give up looking for work altogether. This can often create a confusing message as in 2014 when the unemployment rate improved, not because more people were finding work (and hence boosting the numerator of that index), but because instead, people stopped looking for work (and hence reduced the denominator of that index).[13] As our "Evidence-Based HR" feature shows, people often give up looking for work soon after their unemployment benefits run out. The typical organizational response to a labor shortage has been either hiring temporary employees or outsourcing, responses that are fast and high in revocability. Given the pervasiveness of these choices, we will devote special subsections of this chapter to each of these options.

Downsizing

Downsizing
The planned elimination of large numbers of personnel designed to enhance organizational effectiveness.

We define **downsizing** as the planned elimination of large numbers of personnel designed to enhance organizational effectiveness. Although one tends to think of downsizing as something that a company turns to in times of recession or when facing bouts of poor performance, in fact, many companies that are doing quite well still downsize their workforce regularly for strategic reasons. For example, although Microsoft was doing fine in 2014, it still laid off 18,000 workers in the phone and tablet divisions after the purchase of Nokia left the company with a surplus of workers in those areas.[14] Similarly, Hewlett-Packard cut 16,000 jobs that same year and used the roughly $1 billion in savings to invest more heavily in cloud computing services.[15]

Surveys indicate three major reasons that organizations engage in downsizing. First, many organizations are looking to reduce costs, and because labor costs represent a big part of a company's total costs, this is an attractive place to start. For example, in 2012, Yahoo cut 2,000 jobs, which amounted to 15% of their workforce. The company expects to see an annual savings of $375 million, although this is partially offset by an estimated $145 million onetime cost associated with paying employees severance pay.[16]

Second, in some organizations, the introduction of new technologies or robots reduces the need for a large number of employees. For example, at General Electric's new battery manufacturing plant in Schenectady, New York, the entire 200,000-square-foot facility requires only 370 workers, only 200 of which are actually on the shop floor. The plant manager runs the entire operation, including lights, heat, inventory, purchasing and maintenance from an iPad that is linked to wireless sensors embedded in the batteries themselves. As Prescott Logan, the general manager of the plant, states, "It is not about low cost labor but high technology. We are listening directly to what our batteries are telling us and then thinking about ways to monetize that."[17] In general, new technologies often displace workers, and in today's modern manufacturing plants, a small number of highly skilled workers can run a plant that in previous generations required hundreds of low-skilled laborers whose jobs will never come back.[18]

EVIDENCE-BASED HR

One constant question when it comes to public policy is whether unemployment benefits actually result in higher levels of unemployment because they reduce the level of motivation for people to go back to work. That is, even though that in order to obtain benefits, beneficiaries must be able to prove they are looking for work, many do not accept offers while they are still enjoying benefits. Thus, based upon this logic, some have argued that the duration of benefits should be reduced. This is exactly the opposite of recent policy, however, where the length of such benefits has been frequently extended.

A recent experiment in North Carolina provides some interesting new insights to this debate. In 2014, the Tarheel State cut back the duration of benefits for residents from 26 weeks, the standard in most states, to 12 weeks. Two facts quickly became clear after this move. First, the unemployment rate dropped from 8.8% to 7.4%, which at first glance sounds like good news. However, the second fact was that all of this was attributable to the fact that people stopped looking for work (and hence were dropped from the denominator of that ratio), not that people were obtaining work (the numerator of that ratio). In terms of motivation, unemployment benefits seem to keep people engaged in job search because they have to show they are searching in order to continue to receive benefits. When their unemployment benefits run out, however, they simply stop looking for work because benefits are no longer contingent upon searching; they just stop receiving benefits either way.

SOURCES: V. McGrane, "The Downside of Lower Unemployment," *The Wall Street Journal*, February 2, 2014, www.wsj.com; J. Green, "Unemployment Rate, Down, Unemployed People, Up," *Bloomberg Businessweek*, January 12, 2014.

A third reason for downsizing was that, for economic reasons, many firms changed the location of where they did business. Some of this shift was from one region of the United States to another—in particular, many organizations moved from the Northeast, the Midwest, and California to the South and the mountain regions of the West. In some cases, technology is employed to move work that one might think was not that mobile. For example, the McDonald's restaurant chain experimented with drive-up windows in Michigan that were staffed with lower-wage workers located in Fargo, North Dakota. What looked like a standard drive-up squawk box was actually a long-distance connection, where Michigan orders were taken down by a worker in North Dakota who then relayed the order information back to the Michigan staff.[19]

Although downsizing has an immediate effect on costs, much of the evidence suggests that it has negative effects on long-term organizational effectiveness, especially for some types of firms. Also, the negative effects of downsizing seem to be exacerbated in service industries characterized by high levels of customer contact. For example, in the five-year period between 2009 and 2013, Walmart added over 450 new stores to its portfolio, but at the same time, reduced headcount by over 20,000 people. The average number of employees per store dropped from 343 to 301 and this resulted in a workforce that was spread too thinly across the large stores. This in turn resulted in longer checkout lines, less support to customers who needed help, and difficulty keeping the shelves stocked. One former Walmart customer, Tim White, noted, "You wait 20, 25 minutes for someone to help you, and then, the person who comes was not trained in that area. And, even though the long checkout lines were irritating, the No. 1 reason I gave up on

Walmart was its prolonged, horrible, maddening inability to keep items in stock."[20] In addition, when downsizing efforts are not complemented by changes in the nature of work roles, then performance also tends to suffer.[21]

Still, many employers engage in this tactic and hence it is important to understand what goes into an effective versus ineffective downsizing campaign. There seem to be a number of reasons for the failure of most downsizing efforts to live up to expectations in terms of enhancing firm performance. First, although the initial cost savings are a short-term plus, the long-term effects of an improperly managed downsizing effort can be negative. Downsizing not only leads to a loss of talent, but in many cases it disrupts the social networks needed to promote creativity and flexibility.[22] For example, many have attributed the slow public health response to the Ebola outbreak in 2014 to cuts made at local agencies. City, county, and state health departments cut 60,000 jobs in the six-year period from 2008 to 2014, and thus, education programs—that might have prevented health care workers like those in Dallas from catching the disease from their own patients—were eliminated. Reversing this process in an area that relies on skilled employees is difficult. As one industry expert noted, "You may be able to buy equipment quickly but you can't buy trained personnel quickly."[23]

Second, many downsizing campaigns let go of people who turn out to be irreplaceable assets. In fact, one survey indicated that in 80% of the cases, firms wind up replacing some of the very people who were let go. In other cases, firms bring back the specific people who were let go, often at a higher salary. In fact, the term "boomerang employee" has been coined to refer to this increasingly used source of recruits. Several companies such as Procter and Gamble, J.C. Penney, Nike, PepsiCo, and Toys "R" Us have tapped former executives to lead their management team. These individuals come in knowing the company well, but they also bring a new perspective achieved by having success at some other venture. More than a traditional outsider, boomerang executives have a sense of what changes will and will not take hold at their old company.[24]

A third reason downsizing efforts often fail is that employees who survive the purges often become narrow-minded, self-absorbed, and risk-averse. Motivation levels drop off because any hope of future promotions—or even a future—with the company dies out. Many employees also start looking for alternative employment opportunities.[25] The negative publicity associated with a downsizing campaign can also hurt the company's image in the labor market, making it more difficult to recruit employees later. Especially in an age of blogs and text messaging, the once-private practice of laying off employees is becoming increasingly transparent, and any organizational mistake that gets made in the process is likely to become highly public.[26] The key to avoiding this kind of reputation damage is to ensure that the need for the layoff is well explained and that procedures for implementing the layoff are fair. Although this may seem like common sense, many employers execute layoffs in ways that make matters worse. For example, as we show in the "Competing through Technology" box, when business needs conflict with the personal needs of employees, heavy-handed practices involving layoffs can create a number of problems.

The key to a successful downsizing effort is to avoid indiscriminant across-the-board reductions, and instead perform surgical strategic cuts that not only reduce costs, but also improve the firm's competitive position. For example, at the State University of New York, $50 million was saved across the system via a series of cuts that consolidated many senior administrative positions. The same practice cut $70 million at the University of California at Berkeley, and $5 million at the University of Kansas. These cuts were specifically targeted at "administrative bloat" revealed by research that showed that the number of employees hired by colleges to administer people and programs rose 50% faster than the number of professors in the last 12 years. The size of the instructional and research staff was left as is, and the evidence suggests that student outcomes were not affected at all by such cuts.[27]

Early Retirement Programs and Buyouts

Another popular means of reducing a labor surplus is to offer an early retirement program. As shown in Figure 5.2, the average age of the U.S. workforce is increasing. But although many baby boomers are approaching traditional retirement age, early indications are that this group has no intention of retiring any time soon.[28] Several forces fuel the drawing out of older workers' careers. First, the improved health of older people in general, in combination with the decreased physical labor in many jobs, has made working longer a viable option. Second, this option is attractive for many workers because they fear Social Security will be cut, and many have skimpy employer-sponsored pensions that may not be able to cover their expenses. Third, age discrimination legislation and the outlawing of mandatory retirement ages have created constraints on organizations' ability to unilaterally deal with an aging workforce. Finally, many employers are increasingly concerned about losing the wealth of experience that older workers bring to their companies.

Although an older workforce has some clear advantages for employers in terms of experience and stability, it also poses problems. First, older workers are sometimes more costly than younger workers because of their higher seniority, higher medical costs, and higher pension contributions. For example, at Toyota's plant in Georgetown, Kentucky, veteran workers earn $26 an hour compared to $16 an hour for new hires. In an effort to shift the workforce from high-paid to low-paid workers, Toyota offered retirement incentives to 2,000 workers at the plant. Each worker could get a lump sum payment equal to two weeks of pay for every year of service, up to a maximum of 25 years, plus eight weeks additional pay. In return for taking the buyout, workers would agree to retire on a fixed schedule that prevents all the workers from retiring at once.[29] When the value of

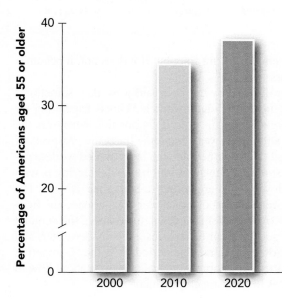

Figure 5.2

Aging of the U.S. Population, 2000–2020

COMPETING THROUGH TECHNOLOGY

You and Your Smartphone Are Both Fired!

Imagine you are at a restaurant enjoying dinner, and then all of a sudden, without warning, your smartphone powers off. Then, when you power it back up, you realize that everything you had on the device—your pictures, contacts, music, games, and e-mail were all erased. This is exactly what happened to one employee at AlphaCore the night that both he and his device were terminated in a process called "remote wiping." The worker was part of a work arrangement referred to as BYOD—"Bring Your Own Device"—and this is an ever-increasing policy and practice at many employers.

As the line between work and nonwork has blurred over the years, more and more workers are using their personal devices for work. At one time, employers used to provide such devices to employees themselves, but in order to reduce costs and avoid the complexities associated with the fact that every employee is likely to differ in their technological device needs, employers have migrated to a system whereby employees provide their own devices for work. This creates a situation where proprietary business information and personal information reside side-by-side, and when it becomes necessary for the company to erase one, it typically erases the other as well.

Most employees sign off on the practice when they accept an employment offer, but usually this is done as one of a number of "dialogue boxes" that employees check "yes" to but never really read. So when they are remotely wiped, it comes as a complete surprise. If you are aware that you are part of a BYOD system, you might want to make sure you back up your personal information to some other private device, but most companies also have rules that prevent you from copying business information from one of your devices to another. Thus, you need to be surgical in terms of what files that you back up at work and what files you do not copy. In contrast, your employer is probably going to be less than surgical when it comes to wiping out your device, in the sense that employers just sweep the whole device clean, including both business and personal data.

DISCUSSION QUESTIONS

1. Is it fair for employers to make employees provide their own technology in order to conduct business?
2. Can you think of other non-technological examples of how employees may have to pay their own way as part of an employment relationship?

SOURCES: C. Green, "Six Tips for Building a 2015-Proof BYOD Policy," *Information Age*, April 28, 2015, www.information-age.com; L. Weber, "BYOD: Leaving a Job Can Mean Losing Pictures of Grandma," *The Wall Street Journal*, January 21, 2014, www.wsj.com.

---

the experience offsets these costs, then employers are fine; but if it does not, it becomes difficult to pass these costs to consumers.

Second, because older workers typically occupy the best-paid jobs, they sometimes prevent the hiring or block the advancement of younger workers. This is frustrating for the younger workers and leaves the organization in a perilous position whenever the older workers decide to retire. Indeed, although a weak economy hurts the prospects of all workers, the impact is especially hard on young people who have limited work experience and skills. In many cases, the first place companies pull back when hiring is with entry-level jobs critical to young employees who are trying to start their careers. For example, the number of recruiters that require two or more years' experience for first-line management positions rose by 30% over the last five years. In addition, the demand for bottom-rung professional positions such as loan officer, insurance underwriter, and credit analyst has dropped substantially over the same time period.[30] As the "Competing through Sustainability" box shows, all these developments raise questions about how to best educate young people when it comes to securing employment.

COMPETING THROUGH SUSTAINABILITY

Underemployment: Is the Need for a Four-Year Degree Sustainable?

Although making the transition from college to the world of work has never been easy, recent studies suggest that this challenge is more difficult than it has ever been for recent U.S. college graduates. A staggering 56% of 22-year-old college graduates currently work in jobs that do not require a college degree, and in many cases, these jobs fail to provide enough income to support loans that might have been incurred in order to obtain such a degree.

Although this may make one question the wisdom of obtaining a college degree, especially if one has to go into debt to accomplish this, in fact, a lot depends upon the major one chooses in college. Students majoring in engineering, math, computers, health care, business, or education see a much higher return on their investment relative to students majoring in communications, liberal arts, and the social sciences. Also, although the picture for students with these majors is somewhat grim when it comes to underemployment, the picture looks a little better when it comes to unemployment. Indeed, in December 2014, among those who were older than 25, 7.7% of those without a college diploma were unemployed compared to just 3.3% of those with a college degree.

It appears that the demand for jobs that require "middle-level skills" accounts for a great deal of the underemployment rate for college graduates and the unemployment rate for those who never went to college. Many labor economists have argued the U.S. system of education would fare much better when it comes to employment by emphasizing two-year degrees and apprenticeship programs such as those popular in Germany. This would create a better, long-term sustainable fit between the supply and demand for labor when it comes to high- and middle-level skills.

DISCUSSION QUESTIONS

1. What are some of the reasons why it might be more difficult for college graduates to enter the workforce today versus 20 years ago?
2. In what ways are the limits associated with not attending college greater today than they were 20 years ago?

SOURCES: C. Gummer, "German-Style Training for American Factory Workers," *The Wall Street Journal,* September 9, 2014, www.wsj.com; D. Wessel, "For Recent Grads, Good Jobs Are Hard to Find," *The Wall Street Journal,* January 15, 2014, www.wsj.com; C. Porter, "Millennials Face Uphill Climb," *The Wall Street Journal,* September 30, 2013, www.wsj.com.

In fact, simply graduating into a bad economy can have lasting negative effects on workers. For example, one study found that for each percentage point rise in the unemployment rate, those who graduated during a recession earn 7% less in their first year on the job, and 3% less even 15 years later, relative to peers who just happened to graduate in better economic times.[31]

In the face of such demographic pressures, many employers try to induce voluntary attrition among their older workers through early retirement incentive programs. Although some research suggests that these programs do induce attrition among lower-performing older workers, to a large extent, such programs' success is contingent upon accurate forecasting. For example, in Japan, many workers continue to work well beyond the country's official retirement age of 60. Fortunately, Japan's private employers can force employees to retire at 60 if they wish, and workers often accept lower wages in order to stay on. Thus, Komatsu, the world's second largest construction equipment manufacturer, rehires 90% of its retirees at 40% of their past pay. In the United States, on the other hand, people cannot be forced into retirement and have to be coaxed out of the job with an incentive package.[32]

For example, the *Washington Post* offered workers roughly a year and a half in salary, and this offer seemed in line with what it generally takes to get people to leave voluntarily. Interestingly, while the *Post* was cutting the number of employees, the *New York Times* decided to reduce pay levels by roughly 3% and not lay off or buy out any employees. Rather than seeing size as a liability, Executive Editor Bill Keller saw it as a source of unique competitive advantage for the *Times* (in fact, the largest newsroom in the country), describing his current stock of employees as "the engine of our long term success."[33]

Pension plans often become extremely burdensome for companies, and hence, some large employers have recently tried to back away from their obligations. For example, in 2012, General Motors and Ford attempted to buy out the pensions of 140,000 salaried workers. Both companies were flush with cash after having recorded profit of $9 billion and $20 billion respectively in 2011, and saw this as a one-time opportunity to slash their pension liabilities with a mass buyout. Because pension funds are invested in securities, their values rise and fall unexpectedly, and hence removing these from the balance sheet is often a very desirable goal.[34]

Employing Temporary Workers

Whereas downsizing has been a popular method for reducing a labor surplus, hiring temporary workers and outsourcing has been the most widespread means of eliminating a labor shortage. The number of temporary employees in the United States swelled from 4.5 million in 1997 to 28 million in 2014.[35] Many expect this number to grow even larger with the passage of the Affordable Care Act because employers can avoid the mandate to provide health care to anyone who works less than 30 hours a week.[36] Temporary employment afforded firms the flexibility needed to operate efficiently in the face of swings in the demand for goods and services. In fact, a surge in temporary employment often preceded a jump in permanent hiring, and was often a leading indicator that the economy was expanding. However, that no longer seems to be the case. Employers today seem to appreciate the flexibility that comes with hiring temporary employees and like being able to match quick changes in consumer demands for products and services with quick changes in the supply of labor. As one CEO notes, "You need the flexibility in your manpower costs since sales can fluctuate more."[37]

In addition to flexibility, hiring temporary workers offers several other advantages:

- The use of temporary workers frees the firm from many administrative tasks and financial burdens associated with being the "employer of record."
- Small companies that cannot afford their own testing programs often get employees who have been tested by a temporary agency.
- Many temporary agencies train employees before sending them to employers, which reduces training costs and eases the transition for both the temporary worker and the company.
- Because the temporary worker has little experience in the host firm, the person brings an objective perspective to the organization's problems and procedures that is sometimes valuable.

Finally, although it may seem ironic, many employers wind up trying to hire excellent temporary workers for full-time jobs after some period of time. Note, however, that there is usually a fee that has to be paid for permanently "stealing" a temporary employee from a temp agency. Still, some temp agencies actually have "Temp-to-Full-Time programs" that actually try to promote this goal for some workers who want to be full-time employees. The client in this case is encouraged to make a job offer to the employee within a predetermined time period, should the match seem like a good one. According to the American Staffing Association, 74% of temporary workers actually decide to become temporary employees because it's a way to get a full-time job.[38]

Certain disadvantages to employing temporary workers need to be overcome to effectively use this source of labor. For example, in the service sector of the economy, low levels of commitment to the organization and its customers on the part of temporary employees often spills over and reduces the level of customer loyalty.[39] Instead of replacing long-term employees with temporary employees, many organizations try to buffer their "core employees" from wild swings in demand by supplementing their core staff with a small set of temporary workers. For example, in 2009, Boeing cut 1,500 temporary workers from one of its divisions, but retained all of its permanent workers. HR executive Jim Proulx noted that, "The first imperative was to reduce all of the contract and contingent labor that we possibly could to shield our regular employees."[40]

In addition, there is often tension between a firm's temporary employees and its full-time employees. If the organization is concerned about the reactions of full-time workers to the temporaries, it may want to go out of its way to hire "nonthreatening" temporaries. For example, although most temporary workers want their temporary assignments to turn into full-time work (75% of those surveyed expressed this hope), not all do. Some prefer the freedom of temporary arrangements. These workers are the ideal temporaries for a firm with fearful full-time workers.[41]

Outsourcing, Offshoring, and Immigration

Whereas a temporary employee can be brought in to manage a single job, in other cases a firm may be interested in getting a much broader set of services performed by an outside organization; this is called **outsourcing.** Outsourcing is a logical choice when a firm simply does not have certain expertise and is not willing to invest time and effort into developing it. For example, rather than hire an MBA full time, some companies may decide just to "rent one" for a short, specific project. In fact, a group of Harvard MBAs started a new firm called "HourlyNerd" to meet just this growing need. Businesses pay $75 to $100 an hour for specific one-time tasks like pricing a new product or valuating a business that requires a short dose of expertise.[42] Similarly, in the area of research and development, generic labs have sprung up that allow companies to perform experiments and product testing that may require expensive equipment that is better to rent than own. For example, Emerald Therapeutics provides these kinds of services for small pharmaceutical companies that may have big ideas but limited infrastructure to test such ideas. Emerald rents out both its expensive machinery and talented technicians, thus essentially creating a virtual research and development division for a small company that could never develop this capacity internally.[43]

Ironically, companies increasingly outsource many of their human resource management tasks to outside vendors who specialize in efficiently performing many of the more routine administrative tasks associated with this function. Figure 5.3 shows a forecast for growth rates in the human resource outsourcing (HRO) industry. Cost savings in this area are easily obtained because rather than purchase and maintain their own specialized hardware and software, as well as specialized staff to support such systems, companies can time-share the facilities and expertise of a firm that focuses

Outsourcing
An organization's use of an outside organization for a broad set of services.

Figure 5.3

U.S. Multiprocess HR Outsourcing Forecast

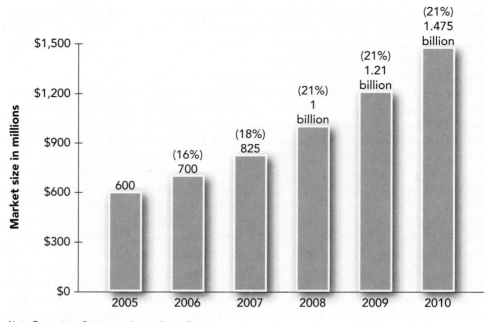

Note: Percentage 5 compound annual growth rate.

SOURCE: NelsonHall, "Multiple HR Outsourcing in the U.S.: Market Assessment," June 2006.

on this technology. The hope is also that this frees up HR managers to focus on more strategic issues. As Samuel Borgese, VP of HR for Catalina Restaurant Group, notes, "This allows us to keep strategic tasks in-house with tactical support from the outsourcing vendor. It's very difficult for a VP of HR to be a strategic player if he or she is managing the HR infrastructure."[44]

In other cases, outsourcing is aimed at simply reducing costs by hiring less expensive labor to do the work, and, more often than not, this means moving the work outside the country. **Offshoring** is a special case of outsourcing where the jobs that move actually leave one country and go to another. This kind of job migration has always taken place; however, rapid technological changes have made the current trends in this area historically unprecedented. Offshoring is controversial because close to 800,000 white-collar jobs have moved from the United States to India, eastern Europe, Southeast Asia, and China in the last 10 years.

Although initially many jobs that were outsourced were low scope and simple jobs, increasingly, higher skilled work is being done overseas. Indeed, the stereotype that "call center" staffing is the only type of work being offshored is increasingly invalid, as countries like China, India, and those in eastern Europe try to climb the skill ladder of available work. The growth in India is now in higher-paying contracts dealing with business process improvement, processing mortgages, handling insurance claims, overseeing payrolls, and reading X-rays and other medical tests.[45] Many of the simple call center jobs that moved to India are simply moving deeper into the rural Indian villages.[46] As the "Competing through Globalization" box highlights, there may be a new and close source for outsourcing high-skilled labor coming on line soon in the form of Cuba.

Although this may seem problematic for U.S. employers, in fact, if effectively managed, firms that offshore certain aspects of work gain an undeniable competitive advantage over

Offshoring

A special case of outsourcing where the jobs that move actually leave one country and go to another.

A Revolutionary Supply of High-Skilled Labor

In December 2014, President Obama announced plans to re-establish diplomatic ties between the United States and Cuba. Soon after this, the U.S. Chamber of Commerce, working on the behalf of employers, began lobbying Congress to formally lift the trade embargo on Cuba. The end goal of this effort was to help U.S. companies tap into the huge supply of high-skilled labor that has been locked away in that country for decades.

Although long characterized as a villain in the Unites States, one undeniable positive legacy of the Fidel Castro's regime was its emphasis on education. In the immediate wake of the revolution, Castro sent hundreds of teachers and college students to the Cuban countryside to eradicate illiteracy, which at the time was close to 50% of the population. The government also sponsored over 100,000 Cuban students to attend Russian and Ukrainian universities, and today,

80% of college-age Cubans are enrolled in postsecondary education. The emphasis of most of this education is on the hard sciences, engineering, and medicine, and the skilled nature of this labor force was critical to making the island nation sustainable after the Soviet Union withdrew its support in the 1990s. This history makes the current state of the labor pool in Cuba much more highly skilled relative to any other nation in the Caribbean region.

Given the gap between the high skills needed to support the U.S. economy and the skill base within the country, the opportunity to tap into a pool of high-skilled labor just a few hundred miles offshore is an opportunity that many find irresistible. This will not be a country where the economy is based simply on tourism or low-cost manufacturing. As Phillip Brenner, a professor of international relations notes, "No one in Cuba is talking

about a future scenario of making baseballs in sweatshops. They have people who will be adept at pharmaceuticals, computer engineering and advanced mechanical machinery."

DISCUSSION QUESTIONS

1. How would lifting the trade embargo on Cuba impact the regional economies of the Southeast portion of the United States?
2. How would lifting the trade embargo on Cuba impact other countries in the Caribbean region?
3. Who would be the economic winners and losers after such an event?

SOURCES: K. Vick, "Cuba on the Cusp," *Time Magazine,* March 26, 2015, http://time.com; A. S. Gomez and P. W. Hare, "How Education Shaped Communist Cuba," *The Atlantic Online,* February 26, 2015; A. Kurmanaev, E. Martin, and S. Valle, "Cuba's Highly Trained Workforce Beckons Foreign Investors," *Bloomberg Businessweek,* January 12, 2015, www.bloomberg.com.

their rivals. Ignoring this source of advantage is self-defeating, and akin to putting one's head in the sand. For example, Levi-Strauss tried for years to compete against other low-cost jeans manufacturers who offshored their labor. However, after years of one plant shutdown after another, the firm finally gave up and closed down all of its U.S. manufacturing plants. The move, which many saw as inevitable, was long overdue and had it been made earlier, the company might have been able to avoid losing over $20 million.

When making the decision to offshore some product or service, organizations should consider several critical factors. Many who failed to look before they leaped onto the offshoring bandwagon have been disappointed by their results. Quality control problems, security violations, and poor customer service experiences have in many cases wiped out all the cost savings attributed to lower wages and more. For example, in 2014, meat supplier OSI Group Inc., a main supplier of beef and chicken to restaurants such as McDonald's, Yum Brands, and Burger King, was fined when inspectors discovered that meat processed in Shanghai, China, was repackaged and sold long after the legally mandated sell-by dates. Sheldon Lavin, the CEO of the company, had to go public after this incident and stated, "I will not try to defend or explain it. It was terribly wrong, and I am appalled that it ever happened in a company that I own." This incident threatened the long-term relationship between OSI and the many restaurants that it supplied, and in some cases, those relationships came to an end.[47]

As another example, problems with the development of Boeing's 787 Dreamliner, a project that is three years overdue and billions of dollars over budget, have been attributed to both the amount and type of work that was offshored. With respect to the amount of outsourced work, the 787 had more foreign content (30%) than any plane Boeing ever built (where the average is 5%), and many of the component parts manufactured by far-flung suppliers did not fit together very well. In terms of the nature of the work, Boeing took on final assembly of the plane, but this is the activity that provided the least amount of value added.[48] Jim Albaugh, the company's chief of aviation, admitted that "We gave too much work to people that had never really done this before, and then we didn't provide the oversight that was necessary. In hindsight, we spent a lot more money than we ever would have spent if we tried to keep many of the key technologies closer to Boeing. The pendulum swung too far."[49]

These kinds of problems have led to a resurgence of outsourcing activity that keeps the work within the boundaries of the United States. For example, many rural areas of the United States that have been victims of lost manufacturing jobs have retooled themselves in an effort to attract work that is currently being shipped overseas. The value proposition offered by these firms is that "We cost less than cities on the East or West Coast, and we're easier to deal with than India."[50] Ironically, some of the growth in rural outsourcing has come from firms in India opening up U.S. facilities. For example, several of the large Indian outsourcing firms such as Tata, Wipro, and Infosys have opened up shop in rural Ohio using American workers. Privacy laws prevent certain data from being shipped overseas and hence being local allows these firms to do work with the U.S. government and health care providers that they could not do otherwise. Moreover, local workers have a more nuanced understanding of the language and culture that supports working on more complicated on-site business problems versus simply writing batch code.[51]

If one cannot take the work overseas, but still wishes to tap into less-expensive global talent to fill a labor shortage, then one might simply bring foreign workers into the country. Immigration has always been a vital part of the American economy, and many foreign workers are happy to leave their home and pursue their own American dream.[52] However, entrance of foreign workers into the United States to fill jobs is federally regulated, so there are limits to what can be accomplished here. Employers wishing to hire foreign workers need to help them secure work visas and show that there are no qualified Americans who could do the same work.[53]

The barriers that the U.S. government has put in place to limit visas—with the current ceiling of 85,000 a year—are designed to protect American jobs, but many believe this has actually had the opposite effect on the economy. Research suggests that every immigrant that is hired by a tech company actually winds up creating an additional five jobs.[54] Recognizing this fact, Canada has loosened its visa requirements and reached out to U.S. employers to move their operations north of the border. Many tech companies, including Microsoft, Amazon, Facebook, and Salesforce.com, have taken the Canadians up on this offer and are building spacious new facilities in Vancouver. As a representative for Microsoft stated, "The U.S. laws clearly did not meet our needs, and thus we have to look to other places."[55]

The limits on bringing foreign labor into the United States are particularly problematic for high-tech companies. The growth of these firms has not been matched by a growing number of students with the advanced skills in mathematics and the sciences that these firms need. Thus, employers like Mircrosoft and Oracle have aggressively lobbied the government to ease these restrictions.[56] These efforts paid off in 2013 when a new immigration bill was approved by the Senate Judiciary Committee. This new law provided access to a green card to any foreign worker with a job in the U.S. and an advanced degree in math, science, engineering or technology.[57] A green card allows a non-U.S. citizen to live and work in the U.S. on a permanent basis. Although many employers saw this as a step in the right direction, as we noted earlier, this did not stop companies from expanding their presence in Canada in 2014.

Altering Pay and Hours

Companies facing a shortage of labor may be reluctant to hire new full-time or part-time employees. Under some conditions, these firms may have the option of trying to garner more hours out of the existing labor force. Despite having to pay workers time-and-a-half for overtime production, employers see this as preferable to hiring and training new employees—especially if they are afraid that current demand for products or services may not extend to the future. Also, for a short time at least, many workers enjoy the added compensation. However, over extended periods, employees experience stress and frustration from being overworked in this manner.

In the face of a labor surplus, organizations can sometimes avoid layoffs if they can get their employees to take pay cuts. In general, wages tend to be "sticky" in the sense that employers are very reluctant to cut someone's pay, and the data suggests that this even holds true during economic recession and depressions.[58] Still, some employers have gone this route recently. For example, Hewlett-Packard cut salaries between 3% and 20% and reduced their contributions to 401(k) plans in the face of the last recession, and many other firms engaged in the same sort of practices.[59] Alternatively, one can avoid layoffs and hold the pay rate constant but reduce the number of hours of all the workers. For example, when business at the Bristol, Rhode Island, plastics manufacturer Saint Gobain slowed in 2102, none of the workers were laid off, but many had their hours cut by 40%. This would have resulted in a major cut in pay for the workers, except for a state government program that helped Saint Gobain pay 70% of the lost wages in return for the company keeping the workers on the payroll. The state would have wound up paying a similar amount in unemployment compensation, but this program allowed the company to hold on to experienced employees for when the economy turns around. These kinds of "work share" programs have always been popular in Europe but are now starting to be seen in the U.S.[60]

When a cut in hours is targeted at salaried workers rather than hourly workers, this is called a *furlough*. For example, at Arizona State University and the University of Maryland, professional workers were furloughed for between 9 to 15 days, saving the institutions roughly $25 million.[61] Furloughs are perceived as a good strategy to employ when the employer has an immediate need to conserve money and protect cash flow, but also believes that need will be short term and the employees involved have skills that make them hard to replace in the long term.[62]

Furloughs are controversial because, unlike most hourly workers who go home after the assembly line stops running, the work of most white-collar professionals simply piles up when they leave the office for extended periods of time. Indeed, at Arizona State and Maryland, most of the professional workers came to work anyway, meaning that the furloughs were actually pay cuts, not reductions in hours. Also furloughs are controversial because they hit higher-paid employees harder than lower-paid employees, and if these pay differences were a result of some type of pay-for-performance system, this means that the best employees take the biggest hit.

PROGRAM IMPLEMENTATION AND EVALUATION

The programs developed in the strategic-choice stage of the process are put into practice in the program-implementation stage, shown at the bottom of Figure 5.1. A critical aspect of program implementation is to make sure that some individual is held accountable for achieving the stated goals and has the necessary authority and resources to accomplish this goal. It is also important to have regular progress reports on the implementation to be sure that all programs are in place by specified times and that the early returns from these programs are in line with projections. The final step in the planning process is to evaluate the results.

THE SPECIAL CASE OF AFFIRMATIVE ACTION PLANNING

Human resource planning is an important function that should be applied to an organization's entire labor force. It is also important to plan for various subgroups within the labor force. For example, affirmative action plans forecast and monitor the proportion of various protected group members, such as women and minorities, that are in various job categories and career tracks. The proportion of workers in these subgroups can then be compared with the proportion that each subgroup represents in the relevant labor market. This type of comparison is called a **workforce utilization review.** This process can be used to determine whether there is any subgroup whose proportion in the relevant labor market is substantially different from the proportion in the job category.

Workforce Utilization Review
A comparison of the proportion of workers in protected subgroups with the proportion that each subgroup represents in the relevant labor market.

If such an analysis indicates that some group—for example, African Americans—makes up 35% of the relevant labor market for a job category but that this same group constitutes only 5% of the actual incumbents in that job category in that organization, then this is evidence of underutilization. Underutilization could come about because of problems in selection or from problems in internal movement, and this could be seen via the transitional matrices discussed earlier in this chapter. Interestingly, recent workforce utilization reviews with respect to women show that this subpopulation of the workforce has been faring well when it comes to employment. A record 67.5 million women were working in 2013 and whereas women regained all the jobs they lost in the last recession, the same was not true of men, whose labor force participation rates are at an all-time low. Much of this can be attributed to the fact that women work in industries with strong job growth and low wages, such as health care, education, hospitality and retail, whereas men tend to work in construction and manufacturing—industries that were struggling until very recently.[63]

These kinds of affirmative programs are often controversial because they are seen as unfair by many nonminorities.[64] Even some minorities feel that these kinds of programs unfairly stigmatize the most highly qualified minority applicants because of perceptions that their hiring was based on something other than their skills and abilities.[65] However, when the evidence provided from a workforce utilization review makes it clear that a specific minority group has been historically underrepresented because of past discrimination, and that increasing the level of representation will benefit workforce diversity and competitiveness, then these kinds of programs are easier to justify to all involved.[66] Organizations need to realize, however, that affirmative action plans need to be complemented with communication programs that clearly spell out the needs and benefits that these programs bring to the organization and the larger society.[67] For example, as the "Integrity in Action" box illustrates, creating an equal employment opportunity for members of all races is not just an ethical issue but also a matter of business necessity in work contexts that demand critical thinking and diverse opinions.

Beyond the Ethics of Representation:
The Business Case for Diversity at the CIA

One could definitely argue that there are ethical issues associated with any government agency where the representation of minorities is far below the proportion of those groups in the general set of citizens served by the agency. However, when it comes to the Central Intelligence Agency (CIA), the role of diversity is mission critical. Some outside critics blamed the agency's lack of preparedness for the 9/11 disaster on a lack of creative and "out-of-the-box" thinking on the part of staff at the agency that was mainly made up of older white Americans whose main experience dealt with fighting the Soviet Union. Even the agency's current director, John Brennan, notes that when it comes to a lack of diversity, "I think it has

not allowed us to optimize the capabilities we have and allows us to fall prey to groupthink."

When a recent 2015 workforce utilization review charged the agency with failure to recruit, hire, and promote African American employees, Brennan had to get out front of the agency and "make the business case for diversity." According to the utilization report, although non-whites make up 30% of the U.S. population, 90% of the agency's senior leadership positions are held by whites. Brennan, who is white, stressed that this problem goes well beyond the politics of this issue and has a direct impact on accomplishing the mission, emphasizing, "Individuals who look like me, they're not going to be able to operate clandestinely in many parts of the world."

In order to address this issue, the CIA set a goal to make sure that minorities would make up 30% of leadership positions at the agency within three years. Although the agency has made and broken this promise before, Brennan stated, "We're not kidding, this is real this time," and he backed up this statement with a formal plan that made it clear that the performance evaluations of senior managers were going to be based on how well they meet the diversity goals he set.

SOURCES: D. Paletta, "CIA Launches New Effort to Diversify Workforce," *The Wall Street Journal,* June 30, 2015, www.wsj.com; J. Donovan, "CIA Failing to Recruit and Promote Minorities, Study Finds," *The New York Times,* June 30, 2015, www.nytimes.com; E. Perez, "CIA Lagging in Recruiting, Promoting Minorities, Study Finds," *CNN,* June 30, 2015, www.cnn.com.

The Human Resource Recruitment Process

As the first half of this chapter shows, it is difficult to always anticipate exactly how many (if any) new employees will have to be hired in a given year in a given job category. The role of human resource recruitment is to build a supply of potential new hires that the organization can draw on if the need arises. Thus, **human resource recruitment** is defined as any practice or activity carried on by the organization with the primary purpose of identifying and attracting potential employees. It thus creates a buffer between planning and actual selection of new employees, which is the topic of our next chapter.

The goal of the recruiting is not simply to generate large numbers of applicants. If the process generates a sea of unqualified applicants, the organization will incur great expense in personnel selection, but few vacancies will actually be filled. This problem of generating too many applicants is often promulgated by the use of wide-reaching technologies like the Internet to reach people. For example, when Trend Micro was trying to fill a management position, it posted an advertisement on several online job boards, which resulted in a flood of nearly 1,000 resumes.[68]

Human Resource Recruitment
The practice or activity carried on by the organization with the primary purpose of identifying and attracting potential employees.

The goal of personnel recruitment is not to finely discriminate among reasonably qualified applicants either. Recruiting new personnel and selecting new personnel are both complex processes. Organizations explicitly trying to do both at the same time will probably not do either well. For example, research suggests that recruiters provide less information about the company when conducting dual-purpose interviews (interviews focused on both recruiting and selecting applicants).[69] Also, applicants apparently remember less information about the recruiting organization after dual-purpose interviews.[70]

In general as shown in Figure 5.4, all companies have to make decisions in three areas of recruiting: (1) personnel policies, which affect the kinds of jobs the company has to offer; (2) recruitment sources used to solicit applicants, which affect the kinds of people who apply; and (3) the characteristics and behaviors of the recruiter. These, in turn, influence both the nature of the vacancies and the nature of the people applying for jobs in a way that shapes job choice decisions.

LO 5-4

Describe the various recruitment policies that organizations adopt to make job vacancies more attractive.

PERSONNEL POLICIES

Personnel policies is a generic term we use to refer to organizational decisions that affect the nature of the vacancies for which people are recruited. If the research on recruitment makes one thing clear, it is that characteristics of the vacancy are more important than recruiters or recruiting sources when it comes to predicting job choice.

Internal versus External Recruiting: Job Security

One desirable feature of a vacancy is that it provides ample opportunity for advancement and promotion. One organizational policy that affects this is the degree to which the company "promotes from within"—that is, recruits for upper-level vacancies internally rather than externally. Indeed, a survey of MBA students found that this was their top consideration when evaluating a company.[71] Promote-from-within policies make it clear to applicants that there are opportunities for advancement within the company. These opportunities spring not just from the first vacancy but from the vacancy created when a person in the company fills that vacancy.

For example, Cisco Systems uses a program called "Talent Connection" to help identify internal candidates for jobs within the organization that have traditionally been staffed by outsiders. About half of Cisco's 65,000 employees have created profiles that

Figure 5.4

Overview of the Individual Job Choice—Organizational Recruitment Process

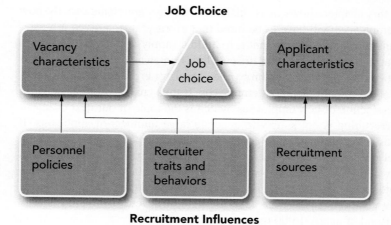

Job Choice

Vacancy characteristics → Job choice ← Applicant characteristics

Personnel policies | Recruiter traits and behaviors | Recruitment sources

Recruitment Influences

are stored in the program and these can be easily searched for matches when a new opening becomes available. Mark Hamberlin, Vice President for Global Staffing at Cisco, notes that the program has "saved the company millions of dollars in search firm fees and other recruiting costs while at the same time, employee satisfaction with career development has risen by 20%."A similar program called "Inside First," developed at Booz Allen Hamilton, helped increase internal staffing from 10% in 2008 to 30% in 2012. While these programs are very popular with employees because they increase job security and promotion opportunities, the only downside to this type of program is pushback from current managers of employees who are recruited away. Many of these employees are top performers in the current units and some managers bristle at the loss of these individuals.[72]

In addition to employing promote from within and internal recruiting sources, perceptions of job security and long-term commitment to the organization are also promoted by "due process policies." **Employment-at-will policies** state that either party in the employment relationship can terminate that relationship at any time, regardless of cause. Companies that do not have employment-at-will provisions typically have extensive due process policies. **Due process policies** formally lay out the steps an employee can take to appeal a termination decision. Organizational recruiting materials that emphasize due process, rights of appeal, and grievance mechanisms send a message that job security is high; employment-at-will policies suggest the opposite. Research indicates that job applicants find companies with due process policies more attractive than companies with employment-at-will policies.[73]

Extrinsic and Intrinsic Rewards

Because pay is an important job characteristic for almost all applicants, companies that take a "lead-the-market" approach to pay—that is, a policy of paying higher-than-current-market wages—have a distinct advantage in recruiting. For example, Matt Noon, owner of Noon Turf Care, a fast growing start-up with 50 employees and $4 million in revenue, struggled to find any experienced telemarketing employees when he was paying $25,000 per year for the position. When he changed that figure to $45,000 per year, he was able to hire four highly qualified individuals who more than made up for the pay difference when it came to generating additional revenue.[74] Pay can also make up for a job's less desirable features—for example, paying higher wages to employees who have to work midnight shifts. These kinds of specific shift differentials and other forms of more generic compensating differentials will be discussed in more detail in later chapters that focus on compensation strategies. We merely note here that "lead" policies make any given vacancy more attractive to applicants. For example, because the perception is that Walmart may not be the nation's best employer to work for, the company raised wages 24% for workers across the board in 2015 in order to help recruit new workers.[75]

There are limits to what can be done in terms of using pay to attract people to certain jobs, however. For example, the U.S. Army, because of the recent wars in Iraq and Afghanistan, struggled and failed to meet its recruiting goals for new soldiers, despite offering a $20,000 signing bonus and a $400 a month raise in base pay for infantry positions. As General Michael Rochelle, head of Army recruiting, notes, "We can't get started down a slippery slope where we are depending on money to lure people in. The reality is that while we have to remain at least competitive, we're never going to be able to pay as much as the private sector." To offset this disadvantage in extrinsic financial rewards, the Army has to rely on more intrinsic rewards related to patriotism and personal growth opportunities that people associate with military service. For example,

Employment-at-Will Policies
Policies which state that either an employer or an employee can terminate the employment relationship at any time, regardless of cause.

Due Process Policies
Policies by which a company formally lays out the steps an employee can take to appeal a termination decision.

Rochelle suggests that "the idea that being a soldier strengthens you for today and for tomorrow, for whatever you go on to do in life, that clearly resonates with them," and thus this serves as an alternative means of appealing to recruits.[76] The Army's Partnership for Youth Success Program uses this idea to match recruits with private-sector employers who are interested in hiring former soldiers who have received the skills and experiences that the Army provides.

Image Advertising

Organizations often advertise specific vacancies (discussed next in the section "Recruitment Sources"). Sometimes, however, organizations advertise just to promote themselves as a good place to work in general. Image advertising is particularly important for companies in highly competitive labor markets that perceive themselves as having a bad image. Indeed, research evidence suggests that the impact of company image on applicant reactions ranks second only to the nature of the work itself.[77]

For example, in a different context, in the wake of the Jerry Sandusky sex scandal at Pennsylvania State University, the school found it increasingly difficult to recruit out-of-state students. As one accepted student from Chicago noted, "The reputation of Penn State has taken a hit lately." Recruiting out-of-state students is critical to Penn State because it receives just 6% of its revenues from the state and nonresidents pay up to $12,000 more per year relative to Pennsylvanians. Thus, when out-of-state students' enrollments fell from 36% to 24% this was a major hit to revenue. In order to make up for this reputational damage, Penn State wound up lowering acceptance standards and sent out more than 4,000 acceptances for nonresidents relative to the years prior to the scandal.[78]

Even though it does not provide any information about any specific job, image advertising is often effective because job applicants develop ideas about the general reputation of the firm (i.e., its brand image) and then this spills over to influence their expectations about the nature of specific jobs or careers at the organization.[79] Research suggests that the language associated with the organization's brand image is often similar to personality trait descriptions that one might more commonly use to describe another person (such as innovative or competent or sincere).[80] These perceptions then influence the degree to which the person feels attracted to the organization, especially if there appears to be a good fit between the traits of the applicant and the traits that describe the organization.[81] Applicants seem particularly sensitive to issues of diversity and inclusion in these types of advertisements, and hence organizations that advertise their image need to go out of their way to ensure that the actors in their advertisements reflect the broad nature of the labor market constituencies that they are trying to appeal to in terms of race, gender, and culture.[82]

LO 5-5

List the various sources from which job applicants can be drawn, their relative advantages and disadvantages, and the methods for evaluating them.

RECRUITMENT SOURCES

The sources from which a company recruits potential employees are a critical aspect of its overall recruitment strategy. The type of person who is likely to respond to a job advertised on the Internet may be different from the type of person who responds to an ad in the classified section of a local newspaper. In this section we examine the different sources from which recruits can be drawn, highlighting the advantages and disadvantages of each.

Internal versus External Sources

We discussed internal versus external sources of recruits earlier in this chapter and focused on the positive effects that internal recruiting can have on recruits' perceptions of job security. We will now discuss this issue again, but with a focus on how using internal sources affects the kinds of people who are recruited.

In general, relying on internal sources offers a company several advantages. First, it generates a sample of applicants who are well known to the firm. Second, these applicants are relatively knowledgeable about the company's vacancies, which minimizes the possibility of inflated expectations about the job. Third, it is generally cheaper and faster to fill vacancies internally. Finally, inside hires often outperform outsiders, especially when it comes to filling jobs at the top end of the hierarchy. When one examines what happens at the top of the organization, the evidence is quite clear that outsiders often struggle to adapt to their new role. For example, when it comes to tenure, CEOs hired from outside the company average four years prior to departing compared to five years for insiders. In addition, when it comes to being forced out, 35% of outsider CEOs get ousted after less than three years compared to 19% for insiders. Finally, when it comes to return on investment, companies with an internally hired CEO outperformed those headed by an outsider by 4.4%.[83]

With all these advantages, you might ask why any organization would ever employ external recruiting methods. There are several good reasons why organizations might decide to recruit externally. First, for entry-level positions and perhaps even for some specialized upper-level positions, there may not be any internal recruits from which to draw. Second, bringing in outsiders may expose the organization to new ideas or new ways of doing business. Using only internal recruitment can result in a workforce whose members all think alike and who therefore may be poorly suited to innovation.

Finally, recruiting from outside sources is a good way to strengthen one's own company and weaken one's competitors at the same time. This strategy seems to be particularly effective during bad economic times, where "counter cyclical hiring" policies create once-in-a-lifetime opportunities for acquiring talent.[84] For example, during the most recent recession, many firms that were top performers—and hence able to weather the storm better than their lower-performing competitors—viewed this as an excellent opportunity to poach the highest-performing individuals within struggling companies.[85] Thus, for many organizations, times of crisis and turbulence are actually the best time for them to shine by leveraging their current talent and success to bring in more talent and achieve even greater success over the long term.[86]

In fact, having one's employees "poached" by another company can be so devastating that companies go to great lengths, perhaps even illegal or unethical lengths, to prevent this from happening. For example, in the constant war for talent in Silicon Valley, poaching the best programmers away from one's competition is a common strategy, and "cold calling" is the central tactic employed to execute that strategy. "Cold calling" refers to the practice where recruiters from one company call an employee of some other company who has the skills they need and try to get that person to switch sides. Thus, rather than search for new employees among those that do not have jobs and are looking for work, cold callers search the pool of people who have jobs and are not looking for work. Obviously, to move a person who is basically happy and not looking for work costs money, and this can lead to bidding wars that drive up salaries and employers' costs.

One tempting way for organizations to avoid this outcome is to come to agreements where they all refrain from trying to hire employees away from each other. For example, when an employee at Adobe (whose CEO at the time was Bruce Chizen) received a cold call from a recruiter at Apple, an Adobe HR executive sent an e-mail to the cold caller stating that "Bruce and Steve Jobs have an agreement that we are not to solicit ANY Apple employees and vice versa." In another e-mail, after receiving a telephone call from Jobs regarding a cold call to Apple originating at Google, CEO Eric Schmidt fired off an e-mail to his HR staff that stated "I believe we have a policy of no recruiting from Apple." Schmidt told his HR unit to "get this stopped and let me know why it is happening."[87]

As tempting as this kind of agreement might be, however, this way of "competing" is actually considered "anticompetitive," and the e-mails described above were at the center of an antitrust lawsuit filed against Apple, Google, Adobe, and Intel. The lawsuit charged these firms with colluding to restrict the free movement of labor and fix wages. These companies eventually agreed to an out-of-court settlement of $20 million to workers who were affected by this policy.[88]

Direct Applicants and Referrals

Direct Applicants
People who apply for a job vacancy without prompting from the organization.

Referrals
People who are prompted to apply for a job by someone within the organization.

Direct applicants are people who apply for a vacancy without prompting from the organization. **Referrals** are people who are prompted to apply by someone within the organization. These two sources of recruits share some characteristics that make them excellent sources from which to draw.

First, many direct applicants are to some extent already "sold" on the organization. Most of them have done some homework and concluded that there is enough fit between themselves and the vacancy to warrant their submitting an application. This process is called *self-selection*. A form of aided self-selection occurs with referrals. Many job seekers look to friends, relatives, and acquaintances to help find employment, and evoking these social networks can greatly aid the job search process for both the job seeker and the organization. Current employees (who are knowledgeable of both the vacancy and the person they are referring) do their homework and conclude that there is a fit between the person and the vacancy; they then sell the person on the job. These kinds of "word-of-mouth" endorsements from credible sources seem to have a particularly strong effect early in the recruitment process when people are still unfocused in their search process.[89]

In the war for talent, some employers who try to entice one new employee from a competitor will often try to leverage that one person to try to entice even more people away. The term "liftout" has been coined for this practice of trying to recruit a whole team of people. For example, when Mike Mertz was recruited as the new chief executive at Optimus, a computer servicing outfit, within hours of leaving his former employer, he in turn recruited seven other former colleagues to join Optimus. Liftouts are seen as valuable because in recruiting a whole intact group, as Mertz notes, "You get the dynamics of a functioning team without having to create that yourself."[90] The team chemistry and coordination that often takes years to build is already in place after a liftout, and this kind of speed provides competitive advantage. Of course, having a whole team lifted out of your organization is devastating, because customers are frequently next to leave, following the talent rather than standing pat, and hence firms have to work hard to make sure that they can retain their critical teams.

Advertisements in Newspapers and Periodicals

Advertisements to recruit personnel are ubiquitous, even though they typically generate less desirable recruits than direct applications or referrals—and do so at greater expense. However, because few employers can fill all their vacancies with direct applications and referrals, some form of advertising is usually needed. Moreover, an employer can take many steps to increase the effectiveness of this recruitment method.

The two most important questions to ask in designing a job advertisement are, What do we need to say? and To whom do we need to say it? With respect to the first question, many organizations fail to adequately communicate the specifics of the vacancy. Ideally, persons reading an ad should get enough information to evaluate the job and its requirements, allowing them to make a well-informed judgment regarding their qualifications. This could mean running long advertisements, which costs more. However, these additional costs should be evaluated against the costs of processing a huge number of applicants who are not reasonably qualified or who would not find the job acceptable once they learn more about it.

In terms of whom to reach with this message, the organization placing the advertisement has to decide which medium it will use. The classified section of local newspapers is the most common medium. It is a relatively inexpensive means of reaching many people within a specified geographic area who are currently looking for work (or at least interested enough to be reading the classifieds). On the downside, this medium does not allow an organization to target skill levels very well. Typically, classified ads are read by many people who are either over- or underqualified for the position. Moreover, people who are not looking for work rarely read the classifieds, and thus this is not the right medium for luring people away from their current employers. Specially targeted journals and periodicals may be better than general newspapers at reaching a specific part of the overall labor market. In addition, employers are increasingly using television—particularly cable television—as a reasonably priced way of reaching people.

Electronic Recruiting

The growth of the information superhighway has opened up new vistas for organizations trying to recruit talent. There are many ways to employ the Internet, and increasingly organizations are refining their use of this medium. Obviously, one of the easiest ways to get into "e-cruiting" is to simply use the organization's own web page to solicit applications. By using their own web page, organizations can highly tune their recruitment message and focus in on specific people. For example, the interactive nature of this medium allows individuals to fill out surveys that describe what they are looking for and what they have to offer the organizations. These surveys can be "graded" immediately and recruits can be given direct feedback about how well they are matched for the organization. Indeed, customizing e-recruiting sites to maximize their targeted potential for helping people effectively match their own values with the organization's values, and their skills with the demands of the job is probably their best feature.[91] The value of steering recruits to company websites is so high that many employers will pay to have their sites rise to the top of the list in certain search engines when certain terms are entered.

For example, PricewaterhouseCoopers (PwC) struck a deal with the career networking site LinkedIn so that if any student from one of the 60 schools it recruits does a search of accounting-related jobs, PwC pops up first and is listed as "the featured job." PwC also gets space on the page to promote the organization that includes videos of current employees extolling the virtues of working at that company.[92] Other companies pay LinkedIn roughly $8,000 a year for the opportunity to search among its 187 million profiles, and some, such as Adobe, fill roughly half of their jobs via LinkedIn alone.[93]

Of course, smaller and less well-known organizations may not attract any attention to their own websites, and thus for them this is not a good option. A second way for organizations to use the web is to interact with the large, well-known job sites such as Monster.com, HotJobs.com, or CareerBuilder.com. These sites attract a vast array of applicants, who submit standardized résumés that can be electronically searched using key terms. Applicants can also search for companies in a similar fashion. The biggest downside to these large sites, however, is their sheer size and lack of differentiation.

The growing use of iPods and iPads has also opened up a new and rich avenue to get information from employer to applicant via podcasts. A podcast is an audio or audio/

visual program that can be placed on the web by an employer and then downloaded for subsequent viewing. Podcasts are like e-mails in the sense that they can be used to reach out to a large number of people; however, the rich nature of the media—which employs color, sound, and video—is much more powerful than a simple text-only e-mail. "Podcasts really make the job description comes alive," notes Dan Finnigan, a general manager at HotJobs.com, and the ability to describe the organization's culture is so much more emotionally charged with this media relative to mere words on a page.[94]

Social networking sites such as Facebook and MySpace.com are yet another avenue for employers to reach out to younger workers in their own environments. Neither Facebook nor MySpace allow employers to create pages as members, but it does allow them to purchase pages in order to create what is called a "sponsored group." Ernst & Young's sponsored group page has been joined by more than 5,000 Facebook users, who can access information about Ernst & Young and chat with recruiters from the company in a blog-like manner.[95] Unlike more formal media, the conversations held here are very informal and serve as an easy first step for potential recruits to take in their relationship with the company. New entrants to this market like the site BranchOut take this informal format even further, and allow its members to rate other workers in a "Hot or Not" format. That is, users are shown the pictures of two of their Facebook friends and then asked to choose which one they would rather work with. Scores accumulate over time and founder Rick Marini suggests that "it provides a realistic, crowd sourced assessment of a candidate that recruiters might find hard to come by on their own."[96]

As with any new and developing technology, all of these approaches present some unique challenges. From an employer's perspective, the interactive, dynamic, and unpredictable nature of blogs and social networking sites means that sometimes people who have negative things to say about the organization join in on the conversations, and this can be difficult to control. The biggest liability from the applicant's perspective is the need to protect his or her identity, because this medium has also been a haven for identity thieves, who post false openings in the hope of getting some applicant to provide personal information.[97]

Public and Private Employment Agencies

The Social Security Act of 1935 requires that everyone receiving unemployment compensation be registered with a local state employment office. These state employment offices work with the U.S. Employment Service (USES) to try to ensure that unemployed individuals eventually get off state aid and back on employer payrolls. To accomplish this, agencies collect information from the unemployed about their skills and experiences.

Employers can register their job vacancies with their local state employment office, and the agency will attempt to find someone suitable using its computerized inventory of local unemployed individuals. The agency makes referrals to the organization at no charge, and these individuals can be interviewed or tested by the employer for potential vacancies. Because of certain legislative mandates, state unemployment offices often have specialized "desks" for minorities, handicapped individuals, and Vietnam-era veterans. Thus, this is an excellent source for employers who feel they are currently underutilizing any of these subgroups.

Public employment agencies serve primarily the blue-collar labor market; private employment agencies perform much the same service for the white-collar labor market. Unlike public agencies, however, private employment agencies charge the organization for the referrals. Another difference between private and public employment agencies is that one doesn't have to be unemployed to use a private employment agency. One special type of private employment agency is the so-called executive search firm (ESF). These agencies are often referred to as *headhunters* because, unlike the other sources we have examined, they operate almost exclusively with people who are currently employed. Dealing with executive search firms is sometimes a sensitive process because executives may not want to advertise their availability for fear of their current employer's reaction.

Many organizations have shifted away from private employment agencies in the last few years and focused more on using their own internal recruiters to staff openings. For example, Time Warner filled thousands of senior positions during the last seven years, but used an outside agency only once. Instead, like roughly 25% of the Fortune 500 companies, Times Warner has created a head of executive recruitment to do the work formerly done by private agencies. At Time Warner, this person oversees a 30-person team where each person handles 10–15 placements at a time. This unit saved Time Warner over $100 million in search firm fees and filled each job in roughly 100 days, compared to 170 days associated with a private agency.[98] Similarly, GE built an internal recruiting staff of around 500 people, and in 2012, helped by LinkedIn and other social networking sites, filled most of GE's 25,000 openings.[99] There is a general belief within these and other companies that internal recruiters have a better feel for the organization's culture and thus, in addition to filling positions faster and cheaper, those recruited are also a better fit for the company. Many have questioned whether the ESFs have a viable business model, given the recent changes in the economy and in technology.[100]

Colleges and Universities

Most colleges and universities have placement services that seek to help their graduates obtain employment. Indeed, on-campus interviewing is the most important source of recruits for entry-level professional and managerial vacancies. Organizations tend to focus especially on colleges that have strong reputations in areas for which they have critical needs (chemical engineering, public accounting, or the like).

Many employers have found that to effectively compete for the best students, they need to do more than just sign prospective graduates up for interview slots. One of the best ways to establish a stronger presence on a campus is with a college internship program. These kinds of programs allow an organization to get early access to potential applicants and to assess their capacities directly. These programs also allow applicants to gain firsthand experience with the employer, so that both parties can make well-informed choices about fit with relatively low costs and commitment.[101]

Another way of increasing one's presence on campus is to participate in university job fairs. In general, a job fair is a place where many employers gather for a short time to meet large numbers of potential job applicants. Although job fairs can be held anywhere (such as at a hotel or convention center), campuses are ideal locations because of the many well-educated, yet unemployed, individuals who live there. Job fairs are a rather inexpensive means of generating an on-campus presence and can even provide one-on-one dialogue with potential recruits—dialogue that could not be achieved through less interactive media like newspaper ads.

In some of the toughest labor markets, employers have bypassed colleges and gone straight to high schools. Online coding tutorials and collaborative web communities have made it possible for many high school students to develop their own applications well before they reach the age to go to college. If these apps become successful, then the coder who created them immediately draws attention from recruiters. For example, Facebook recruited Michael Saymen when he was just 16 years old after they learned that the game he built using Facebook's development tools had attracted more than 500,000 players.[102]

Evaluating the Quality of a Source

Because there are few rules about the quality of a given source for a given vacancy, it is generally a good idea for employers to monitor the quality of all their recruitment sources. One means of accomplishing this is to develop and compare yield ratios for each source. Yield ratios express the percentage of applicants who successfully move from one stage of the recruitment and selection process to the next. Comparing yield ratios for different sources helps determine which is best or most efficient for the type of vacancy being investigated.

Table 5.4 shows hypothetical yield ratios and cost-per-hire data for five recruitment sources. For the job vacancies generated by this company, the best two sources of recruits are local universities and employee referral programs. Newspaper ads generate the largest number of recruits, but relatively few of these are qualified for the position. Recruiting at nationally renowned universities generates highly qualified applicants, but relatively few of them ultimately accept positions. Finally, executive search firms generate a small list of highly qualified, interested applicants, but this is an expensive source compared with other alternatives.

LO 5-6

Explain the recruiter's role in the recruitment process, the limits the recruiter faces, and the opportunities available.

RECRUITERS

The last part of the model presented in Figure 5.4 that we will discuss is the recruiter. Moreover, many applicants approach the recruiter with some degree of skepticism. Knowing that it is the recruiter's job to sell them on a vacancy, some applicants may discount what the recruiter says relative to what they have heard from other sources (like friends, magazine articles, and professors). For these and other reasons, recruiters' characteristics and behaviors seem to have less impact on applicants' job choices than we might expect.

Table 5.4
Hypothetical Yield Ratios for Five Recruitment Sources

	RECRUITING SOURCE				
	LOCAL UNIVERSITY	RENOWNED UNIVERSITY	EMPLOYEE REFERRALS	NEWSPAPER AD	EXECUTIVE SEARCH FIRMS
Résumés generated	200	400	50	500	20
Interview offers accepted	175	100	45	400	20
Yield ratio	87%	25%	90%	80%	100%
Applicants judged acceptable	100	95	40	50	19
Yield ratio	57%	95%	89%	12%	95%
Accept employment offers	90	10	35	25	15
Yield ratio	90%	11%	88%	50%	79%
Cumulative yield ratio	90/200	10/400	35/50	25/500	15/20
	45%	3%	70%	5%	75%
Cost	$30,000	$50,000	$15,000	$20,000	$90,000
Cost per hire	$333	$5,000	$428	$800	$6,000

Recruiter's Functional Area. Most organizations must choose whether their recruiters are specialists in human resources or experts at particular jobs (supervisors or job incumbents). Some studies indicate that applicants find a job less attractive and the recruiter less credible when he is a personnel specialist.[103] This does not completely discount personnel specialists' role in recruiting, but it does indicate that such specialists need to take extra steps to ensure that applicants perceive them as knowledgeable and credible.

Recruiter's Traits. Two traits stand out when applicants' reactions to recruiters are examined. The first, which could be called "warmth," reflects the degree to which the recruiter seems to care about the applicant and is enthusiastic about her potential to contribute to the company. The second characteristic could be called "informativeness." In general, applicants respond more positively to recruiters who are perceived as warm and informative. These characteristics seem more important than such demographic characteristics as age, sex, or race, which have complex and inconsistent effects on applicant responses.[104] In addition, timing seems to play a role as well, in the sense that recruiters have a bigger impact early in the job search process, but then give way to job and organizational characteristics when it comes down to the applicant's final decision.[105]

Recruiter's Realism. Perhaps the most well-researched aspect of recruiting deals with the level of realism that the recruiter incorporates into his message. Because the recruiter's job is to attract candidates, there is some pressure to exaggerate the positive features of the vacancy while downplaying the negative features. Applicants are highly sensitive to negative information. On the other hand, if the recruiter goes too far in a positive direction, the candidate can be misled and lured into taking the job under false pretenses. This can lead to a serious case of unmet expectations and a high turnover rate. In fact, unrealistic descriptions of a job may even lead new job incumbents to believe that the employer is deceitful.[106]

Many studies have looked at the capacity of "realistic job previews" to circumvent this problem and help minimize early job turnover. On the whole, the research indicates that realistic job previews do lower expectations and can help reduce future turnover in the workforce.[107] Certainly, the idea that one can go overboard in selling a vacancy to a recruit has merit. However, the belief that informing people about the negative characteristics of the job will totally "inoculate" them to such characteristics seems unwarranted, based on the research conducted to date.[108] Thus we return to the conclusion that an organization's decisions about personnel policies that directly affect the job's attributes (pay, security, advancement opportunities, and so on) will probably be more important than recruiter traits and behaviors in affecting job choice.

Enhancing Recruiter Impact. Although research suggests that recruiters do not have much influence on job choice, this does not mean recruiters cannot have an impact. Organizations can take steps to increase the impact that recruiters have on those they recruit. First, recruiters can provide timely feedback. Applicants react very negatively to delays in feedback, often making unwarranted attributions for the delays (such as, the organization is uninterested in my application).[109] Second, recruiting can be done in teams rather than by individuals. As we have seen, applicants tend to view line personnel (job incumbents and supervisors) as more credible than personnel specialists, so these kinds of recruiters should be part of any team. On the other hand, personnel specialists have knowledge that is not shared by line personnel (who may perceive recruiting as a small part of their "real" jobs), so they should be included as well.

A LOOK BACK

Uber and the Traditional Employment Model

We opened this chapter with a story of how more and more jobholders are working as part of a local "independent contractor" model rather than a traditional employment model. We saw how this can create value for both employers and workers in some cases but also result in disgruntled workers who earn less than the minimum wage. We also saw how companies are shifting away from outsourcing and offshoring, and instead relying more on local talent to compete in today's fast-moving economy. Still there are advantages and disadvantages to recruiting workers from different sources, and we highlighted the strengths and weaknesses of alternative methods for addressing a labor shortage or a labor surplus.

QUESTIONS

1. Discuss the advantages and disadvantages of hiring local workers versus offshoring versus bringing in immigrant labor. How does the nature of the product market affect what you might do in the labor market?
2. Assume you are a well-established company facing a labor surplus in some job category. Why might it be in your best interest to use some method other than layoffs to reduce this surplus, and in what sense are your options here a function of how well you did in terms of forecasting labor demand and supply?
3. Discuss the advantages and disadvantages of promoting workers from within your own firm versus going outside the firm to bring in external hires. How does the nature of the business situation affect this decision?

SUMMARY

Human resource planning uses labor supply and demand forecasts to anticipate labor shortages and surpluses. It also entails programs that can be utilized to reduce a labor surplus (such as downsizing and early retirement programs) and eliminate a labor shortage (like bringing in temporary workers or expanding overtime). When done well, human resource planning can enhance the success of the organization while minimizing the human suffering resulting from poorly anticipated labor surpluses or shortages. Human resource recruiting is a buffer activity that creates an applicant pool that the organization can draw from in the event of a labor shortage that is to be filled with new hires.

Organizational recruitment programs affect applications through personnel policies (such as promote-from-within policies or due process provisions) that affect the attributes of the vacancies themselves. They can also impact the nature of people who apply for positions by using different recruitment sources (like recruiting from universities versus advertising in newspapers). Finally, organizations can use recruiters to influence individuals' perceptions of jobs (eliminating misconceptions, clarifying uncertainties) or perceptions of themselves (changing their valences for various work outcomes).

KEY TERMS

Forecasting, 185
Leading indicator, 186
Transitional matrix, 187
Downsizing, 190

Outsourcing, 197
Offshoring, 198
Workforce utilization review, 202
Human resource recruitment, 203

Employment-at-will policies, 205
Due process policies, 205
Direct applicants, 208
Referrals, 208

DISCUSSION QUESTIONS

1. Discuss the effects that an impending labor shortage might have on the following three subfunctions of human resource management: selection and placement, training and career development, and compensation and benefits. Which subfunction might be most heavily impacted? In what ways might these groups develop joint cooperative programs to avert a labor shortage?
2. Discuss the costs and benefits associated with statistical versus judgmental forecasts for labor demand and labor supply. Under what conditions might either of these techniques be infeasible? Under what conditions might both be feasible, but one more desirable than the other?
3. Some companies have detailed affirmative action plans, complete with goals and timetables, for women and minorities, and yet have no formal human resource plan for the organization as a whole. Why might this be the case? If you were a human resource specialist interviewing with this company for an open position, what would this practice imply for the role of the human resource manager in that company?
4. Recruiting people for jobs that entail international assignments is increasingly important for many companies. Where might one go to look for individuals interested in these types of assignments? How might recruiting practices aimed at these people differ from those one might apply to the "average" recruit?
5. Discuss the relative merits of internal versus external recruitment. What types of business strategies might best be supported by recruiting externally, and what types might call for internal recruitment? What factors might lead a firm to decide to switch from internal to external recruitment or vice versa?

SELF-ASSESSMENT EXERCISE

Mc Graw Hill Education **connect**

Additional assignable self-assessments available in Connect.

Most employers have to evaluate hundreds of résumés each week. If you want your résumé to have a good chance of being read by prospective employers, you must invest time and energy not only in its content, but also in its appearance. Review your résumé and answer yes or no to each of the following questions.

1. Does it avoid typos and grammatical errors?
2. Does it avoid using personal pronouns (such as I and me)?
3. Does it clearly identify what you have done and accomplished?
4. Does it highlight your accomplishments rather than your duties?
5. Does it exceed two pages in length?
6. Does it have correct contact information?
7. Does it have an employment objective that is specific and focuses on the employer's needs as well as your own?
8. Does it have at least one-inch margins?
9. Does it use a maximum of two typefaces or fonts?
10. Does it use bullet points to emphasize your skills and accomplishments?
11. Does it avoid use of underlining?
12. Is the presentation consistent? (Example: If you use all caps for the name of your most recent workplace, do you do that for previous workplaces as well?)

The more "yes" answers you gave, the more likely your résumé will attract an employer's attention and get you a job interview!

EXERCISING STRATEGY

Made in America: A Source of Competitive Advantage?

In the three-year period between 2010 and 2012, the United States created over a half million new jobs in the manufacturing sector, outpacing all other advanced countries. For example, Walmart, a pioneer in outsourcing, announced plans to shift $50 billion to American suppliers in 2013. At the same time, Apple, which has traditionally relied heavily on production in China, announced that it would build one of its new Mac computer lines in the United States. Airbus also announced that it would manufacture a new fleet of planes for JetBlue in Alabama, and Ashley Furniture targeted North Carolina as the site for a new $80 million plant. As Paul Ashworth, chief economist for research firm Capital Economics noted, "The offshoring boom has seemed to run its course."

Clearly, having once been written off for dead, U.S. manufacturing is staging a much-needed comeback. Although for most people, any kind of job creation is good job creation, there are special virtues to the creation of manufacturing jobs. For one, manufacturing represents 30% of the country's productivity growth and every $1.00 of manufacturing activity adds $1.48 to the economy as a whole. In addition, 67% of private-sector spending for research and development takes place in manufacturing companies. As Dow Chemical CEO Andrew Liveris states, "Innovation doesn't just happen in laboratories by researchers. It happens on the factory floor. The process of making stuff helps you experiment and produce new products. If everything is made in China, people there will gain the skills knowledge and experience to innovate. And we will be left behind."

There are several forces that have combined to rekindle interest in the United States for organizations that used to send manufacturing jobs overseas. Part of this is attributable to low energy costs that resulted from the oil and gas shale boon; however, the role of human capital in this reversal is also critical. U.S. workers are still highly paid relative to workers in other countries; however, in many cases, this gap is closing. Wage rates for Chinese workers have gone up 13% a year as that country has expanded, and the gap that still remains is often closed by the higher productivity rates of American workers who rely more heavily on technological advances that reduce the need for a vast army of workers.

In addition, unsafe and unethical practices in some underdeveloped countries make some employers afraid of the reputational damage caused by relying on third-world suppliers or worried about the theft of intellectual property. The stability and tight regulation of U.S. suppliers removes these concerns, and after years of sitting on the sidelines, many American workers have come back to manufacturing with a new set of skills and willingness to be flexible that cannot be matched by European competitors. This was one of the major reasons why German-based Volkswagen and French-based Michelin decided to open new facilities in the southern states rather than in their own countries. For these and a host of other reasons, as noted by Jeff Immelt, the CEO of General Electric, "We are probably the most competitive, on a global basis, than we've been in the past 30 years."

QUESTIONS

1. Competitive advantage is never a "once-and-for all" achievement, but instead, either countries cycle through leadership exchanging the lead or a one-time competitive nation just falls off the map forever. What might be the distinguishing factors between countries that merely cycle out of leadership for a time versus those that shine brightly for a moment and then fade out forever?

2. Do you think China is going to fade out forever as a competitive force or just cycle back to the top after a short period?

SOURCES: R. Foroohar and B. Shaparito, "Made in the U.S.A.," *Time Magazine,* April 22, 2013, http://business.time.com; J. Bussey, "U.S. Manufacturing: Denying Naysayers," *The Wall Street Journal,* April 19, 2012, www.wsj.com; F. Zakaria, "The Case for Making It in the USA," *Time Magazine,* February 6, 2012, p. 19; A. Ohnsman, "Surprise! Carmakers Are a Recovery Bright Spot," *Businessweek,* November 7, 2011, pp. 19–20.

MANAGING PEOPLE

Few Line Up for Jobs Abandoned by Immigrants

Randy Rhodes, the company president of Harvest Select, a food processing plant in Uniontown, Alabama, thought he was just having a nightmare. He simply could not believe it when he showed up at his plant one day only to find that all of his 160 workers were missing. He had 850,000 pounds of catfish that had to be skinned, gutted, and trimmed for sale, and it would not be a pretty sight (or smell) if he were unable to get that work done. Unfortunately this was not just a bad dream and this experience was not limited to his company. In plants, fields, hotels, and restaurants across the state of Alabama, chickens were going unprocessed, tomatoes were going unpicked, hotel beds were going unmade, and dishes were going unwashed as thousands of workers vanished, almost overnight.

The cause of this mass worker exodus was the passage of Alabama House Bill 56, which required police to question people they suspect might be in the country illegally and punish any business that hires them. The goal of this legislation was to free up jobs that Governor Robert Bentley said illegal immigrants "had stolen from recession-battered Americans," and it was true that the unemployment rate in Perry County where Harvest Select was located was just under 20%. Unfortunately, none of these unemployed native Alabamians had any interest in any of these jobs, and thus whereas the new law failed to put even a tiny dent in the unemployment rate, it totally devastated employers in the region. Indeed, the results in Alabama pretty much reflected what has been found in large-scale research studies from other regions of the country, where the presence of immigrant labor has had almost no effect on employment levels and wages. For the most part, few Americans compete for the jobs that are taken by immigrant workers due to the undesirable nature of those jobs.

It is easy to see why most people would be uninterested in the jobs at Harvest Select. People working at the plant perform manually difficult work slicing up smelly fish for ten hours a day in a cold, wet room for $7.25 an hour with virtually no benefits. Of course, the comeback to this argument is why anyone would think they should be able to get away with creating such terribly dissatisfying jobs in the first place, and then expect to be entitled to an endless supply of cheap labor. For example, Alabama's director of industrial relations, Tom Surtees, struck back at some of the local employers countering with "Don't tell me an Alabamian can't work out in the field picking produce because it's hot. Go into a steel mill. Go into a foundry. Go into numerous other occupations and tell them Alabamians won't do work where it's hot or requires manual labor. The difference being, jobs in Alabama's foundries and steel mills pay better and offer better benefits." The stakes of this battle are high in the sense that this is a fight over the basic business model that has been in these industries for decades. As Surtees notes, "Whether an employer in agriculture used migrant workers or whether it's another industry that used illegal immigrants, they had a business model and that business model is going to have to change."

Rhodes and other local employers claim they are stuck with the business model that they have now due to foreign competition that pays their workers even lower wages. Rhodes counters, "I'm sorry, but I can't pay those kids $13.00 per hour and then sell my product at a competitive price—it is just not realistic." Although it is difficult to predict how this conflict will all play out in the future, it is interesting to note that one of the major adaptations that employers made in the short term was to bring in refugee labor from war-torn countries of Africa and weather-devastated Haiti. Ironically, people admitted to the country as refugees are legally allowed to work the day they arrive, and hence, are not affected by House Bill 56. Republican State Senator Scott Beason, who sponsored the law, is very unhappy with this most recent development, but his hands are tied. He states, "We would prefer that the companies hire native Alabamians," but it is unclear that this is ever going to happen.

QUESTIONS

1. Is the inability to find traditional workers willing to perform the types of jobs described here a sign that the business model in some of these industries has to change?
2. Why do the laws of supply and demand not seem to hold within these industries when it comes to labor markets?

SOURCES: N. Shah, "Do Illegal Immigrants Depress Wages, Job Opportunities?" *The Wall Street Journal,* April 12, 2013, http://blogs.wsj.com; M. Newkirk and G. Doubon, "Legal Immigrants Wanted for Dirty Jobs," *Bloomberg Businessweek,* October 8, 2012, pp. 34–35; E. Dwoskin, "Do You Want This Job?" *Bloomberg Businessweek,* November 14, 2011, pp. 70–78.

HR IN SMALL BUSINESS

For Personal Financial Advisors, a Small Staffing Plan with a Big Impact

Robert J. Reed has been a financial planner since 1978 and received his Certified Financial Planner designation in 1981. In 1999, he hired Lucy Banquer, a former legal secretary, to work as his assistant and the only employee at his firm, Personal Financial Advisors LLC in Covington, Louisiana. At that point, human resource planning wasn't on Reed's radar at all.

But around 2005, Reed began to act on a desire to have a more complete plan for his firm's growth. He determined that he wanted the business to grow from about $400,000 in annual revenues to become a million-dollar firm by 2012. That was a realistic goal, but not one he could achieve with only the support of Banquer. Although Banquer does an excellent job of fielding client phone calls and answering questions, Reed needed to bring in more financial expertise to serve more clients.

Typically, a financial-planning firm like Reed's expands by hiring an entry-level advisor to handle routine tasks while learning on the job until he or she can take on clients independently. But Reed didn't simply take the usual path; he considered what role he wanted for himself in his firm as it grew. Reed realized that the part he excelled at and loved most was managing the investments, not the presentations to clients, and that he wanted the firm to grow in a way that would free more time for him to spend with his family, not expand his hours to supervise others. As Reed defined the scope of his own desired job, he clarified what he wanted from his next employee: a Certified Financial Planner who had experience plus an interest in all the planning and advising tasks *except* investment management.

With that strategy in mind, Reed began the search for another planner to work with him. After about eight months of recruiting, Reed met Lauren Gadkowski, who was running her own advisory firm in Boston but preparing to relocate to Baton Rouge to be with her future husband, Lee Lindsay. Reed wanted his new financial planner to operate independently, so he agreed to the idea of her office being in Baton Rouge, about a 45-minute drive from his, and he let her determine how often she would need to visit the Covington office.

Reed stuck to his plan: Lauren Lindsay quickly began working with Reed's larger clients and introduced herself as their main contact with the firm. After sitting in on a few meetings to satisfy himself that he had made a good hiring decision, Reed shifted his efforts to managing the investments. About 10% of the clients indicated they would prefer to maintain their working relationship with Reed. Lindsay took over the remaining 90% as well as the new clients she has brought into the firm since joining it.

Reed's decision to focus on investment management has paid off for Personal Financial Advisors, giving the firm better-than-average performance on its investments even as revenues have climbed. And with Lindsay on board to handle client contact, Reed became able to follow the more traditional path to further growth by hiring an associate financial planner, David Hutchinson, in 2008. In contrast to Lindsay, Hutchinson is still preparing to become a Certified Financial Planner, but he has an educational background in financial planning and experience as an investment broker.

QUESTIONS

1. Is a company ever too small to need to engage in human resource planning? Why or why not? Discuss whether you think Robert Reed planned his hiring strategy at an appropriate time in the firm's growth.
2. Using Table 5.3, review the options for avoiding a labor shortage, and discuss how well the options besides new hires could have worked as ways for Reed to reach his goals for growth. As you do so, consider qualities of a financial-planning business that might be relevant (for example, direct client contact and the need for confidentiality).
3. Suppose that when Reed was seeking to hire a certified financial planner, he asked you for advice on where to recruit this person. Which sources would you suggest, and why?

SOURCES: Angie Herbers, "Letting Go," *Investment Advisor,* June 2009, pp. 96–97; and Personal Financial Advisors, "Why Choose Us?" corporate website, http://www.mypfa.com, accessed June 26, 2015.

NOTES

1. J. Eidelson, "Designated Drivers," *Bloomberg Businessweek,* October 26, 2014, pp. 19–20.
2. G. Motevalli, "Iran's Latest Headache: A Brain Drain," *Bloomberg Businessweek,* May 18, 2014, pp. 18–19.
3. E. Morath, "Which Fields Hold Jobs of the Future? Low Paying Ones Mostly," *The Wall Street Journal,* January 9, 2014, www.wsj.com.
4. M. Phillips and S. Singh, "High Corn Prices Ripple Through Economy," *Businessweek,* February 4, 2013, pp. 13–14.
5. D. Molinski, "Oil Layoffs Hit 100,000 and Counting," *The Wall Street Journal* April 14, 2015, www.wsj.com.
6. M. Phillips, "Welders, America Needs You," *Bloomberg Businessweek,* April 6 2014, pp. 19–21.
7. G. Beach, "The Dog Fight for Tech Talent," *The Wall Street Journal,* August 18, 2014, http://blogs.wsj.com.
8. M. Whitehouse, "Some Firms Struggle to Hire Despite High Unemployment," *The Wall Street Journal,* August 9, 2010, pp. A1 and A7.
9. J. Johnsson, "A Labor Shortage for U.S. Nuclear Power Plants," *Businessweek,* July 11, 2013, pp. 50–51.
10. K. Hudson, "Labor Shortage Bests Home Builders," *The Wall Street Journal,* May 1, 2014, www.wsj.com.
11. P. M. Barrett, "Big Law: The Future," *Businessweek,* May 2, 2013, pp. 53–58.
12. T. R. Homan and Z. Tracer, "The Long-Term Jobless Are Being Left Behind," *Bloomberg Businessweek,* August 9, 2010, pp. 53–54.
13. G. Hubbard, "The Unemployment Puzzle: Where Have All the Workers Gone?" *The Wall Street Journal,* April 4, 2014, www.wsj.com.

14. S. Ovide, "Microsoft to Cut Up to 18,000 Jobs," *The Wall Street Journal,* July 17, 2014, www.wsj.com.

15. S.E. Ante, "H-P Slashes up to 16,000 More Jobs," *The Wall Street Journal,* May 22, 2014, www.wsj.com.

16. A. Efrati, "Yahoo Cuts 2,000 Jobs, Moves Forward with Restructuring," *The Wall Street Journal Online,* April 4, 2012.

17. R. Foroohar and B. Shaparito, "Made in the USA," *Time Magazine,* April 11, 2013, pp. 22–29.

18. C. Kenny, "Factory Jobs Are Gone, Get over It." *Bloomberg Businessweek,* February 2, 2014, pp. 12–13.

19. J. Schneider, "I'll Take a Big Mac, Fries and Hey How's the Weather in Fargo?" *Lansing State Journal,* January 15, 2009, p. B1.

20. R. Dudley, "What Good Are Low Prices If the Shelves Are Empty," *Businessweek,* April 1, 2013, pp. 23–24.

21. D. S. DeRue, J. R. Hollenbeck, M. D. Johnson, D. R. Ilgen, and D. K. Jundt, "How Different Team Downsizing Approaches Influence Team-level Adaptation and Performance," *Academy of Management Journal* 51 (2008), pp. 182–96.

22. P. P. Shaw, "Network Destruction: The Structural Implications of Downsizing," *Academy of Management Journal* 43 (2000), pp. 101–12.

23. J. Tozzi and B. Greeley, "Making It Up as We Go," *Bloomberg Businessweek,* October 26, 2014, pp. 27–28.

24. J.S. Lublin, "How to Be a Good Boss—The Second Time Around," *The Wall Street Journal,* January 9, 2014, www.wsj.com.

25. C. O. Trevor and A. J. Nyberg, "Keeping Your Headcount When All About You Are Losing Theirs: Downsizing, Voluntary Turnover Rates, and the Moderating Role of HR Practices," *Academy of Management Journal* 51 (2008), pp. 259–76.

26. E. Frauenheim, "Technology Forcing Firms to Shed More Light on Layoffs," *Workforce Management,* January 19, 2009, pp. 7–8.

27. D. Belkin, "Colleges Trim Staffing Bloat," *The Wall Street Journal,* December 25, 2013, www.wsj.com.

28. J. Marquez, "The Would-be Retirees," *Workforce Management,* November 3, 2008, pp. 24–28.

29. M. Ramsey, "Toyota Offers U.S. Workers Retirement Incentives," *The Wall Street Journal Online,* November 30, 2012.

30. L. Weber and M. Korn, "Where Did All the Entry Level Jobs Go?" *The Wall Street Journal,* August 5, 2014, www.wsj.com.

31. P. Coy, "The Lost Generation," *BusinessWeek,* October, 19, 2009, pp. 33–35.

32. K. Matsuyama, "In Japan, Retirees Go On Working," *Businessweek,* September 3, 2012, pp. 14–15.

33. R. Adams, "New York Times Will Cut Salaries; Washington Post to Offer Buyouts," *The Wall Street Journal,* March 26, 2009, p. C1.

34. K. Naughton, "U.S. Automakers Cut Retirees Loose," *Businessweek,* July 2, 2012, pp. 15–16.

35. M. Zuckerman, "The Full-Time Scandal of Part-Time America," *The Wall Street Journal,* July 13, 2014, www.wsj.com.

36. B. O'Connell, "Five Tips on Hiring Temporary Employees," *Forbes Online,* January 30, 2013.

37. E. E. Derez and M. Robinson, "Help Wanted—For Now," *Bloomberg Businessweek,* August 9, 2010, pp. 51–52.

38. B. Smith, "Hiring Temporary Employees," *Entrepreneur Online,* February 25, 2013.

39. S. A. Johnson and B. E. Ashforth, "Externalization of Employment in a Service Environment: The Role of Organizational and Customer Identification," *Journal of Organizational Behavior* 29 (2008), pp. 287–309.

40. P. Coy, M. Conlin, and M. Herbst, "The Disposable Worker," *Bloomberg Businessweek,* January 18, 2010, pp. 33–39.

41. J. Feife, R. Schook, B. Schyns, and B. Six, "Does the Form of Employment Make a Difference? Commitment of Traditional, Temporary, and Self-employed Workers," *Journal of Vocational Behavior* 72 (2008), pp. 81–94.

42. "Why Hire an MBA When You Can Rent One," *Bloomberg Businessweek,* October 24, 2013, pp. 60–62.

43. A. Vance, "Emerald Therapeutics: Biotech Lab for Hire," *Bloomberg Business,* July 3, 2014, www.bloomberg.com.

44. F. Hanson, "Special Report: Mid-market Outsourcing," *Workforce Management,* February 12, 2007, pp. 23–26.

45. M. Kripalani, "Call Center? That's so 2004," *BusinessWeek,* August 7, 2006, pp. 40–41.

46. S. Hamm, "Outsourcing Heads to the Outskirts," *BusinessWeek,* January 22, 2007, p. 56.

47. L. Burkitt and J. Bunge, "Meat Supplier's CEO Apologizes for China Unit," *The Wall Street Journal,* July 23, 2014, www.wsj.com.

48. M. Reitzig and S. Wagner, "The Hidden Costs of Outsourcing: Evidence from Patent Data," *Strategic Management Journal* 11 (2010), pp. 1183–1201.

49. M. Hiltzik, "787 Dreamliner Teaches Boeing a Costly Lesson on Outsourcing," *The Los Angeles Times,* February 15, 2013, p. B1.

50. N. Leiber, "Rural Outsources vs. Bangalore," *Bloomberg Businessweek,* September 27, 2010, pp. 51–52.

51. M. Srivastava and M. Herbst, "The Return of the Outsourced Job," *Bloomberg Businessweek,* January 11, 2010, pp. 16–17.

52. K. Weise, "Send Us Your Educated Masses," *Bloomberg Businessweek,* May 23, 2013, p. 30.

53. J. Light, "Labor Shortage Persists in Some Fields," *The Wall Street Journal,* February 7, 2013, p. C1.

54. M. L. Slaughter, "How America Loses a Job Every 43 Seconds," *The Wall Street Journal,* March 25, 2014, www.wsj.com.

55. K. Weise, "How to Hack a Visa Limit," *Bloomberg Businessweek,* June 1, 2014.

56. E. Dwoskin, "Want to Move a Worker to the U.S.? Good Luck," *Businessweek,* June 18, 2012, pp. 27–28.

57. E. Werner, "Unlimited Visas Could Boost Tech," *Lansing State Journal,* May 27, 2013, p. 5B.

58. B. Greeley, "The Incredible Stickiness of Wages," *Bloomberg Businessweek,* April 10, 2015.

59. C. Tuna, "Looking for More Tools to Trim Costs," *The Wall Street Journal,* February 23, 2013, p. B4.

60. L. Woellert, "Half the Hours, Most of the Pay," *Businessweek,* January 31, 2013, pp. 23–24.

61. D. Mattioli and S. Murray, "Employers Hit Salaried Staff with Furloughs," *The Wall Street Journal,* February 24, 2009, pp. C1–C3.

62. C. Tuna, "Weighing Furlough vs. Layoff," *The Wall Street Journal,* April 13, 2009, p. B6.

63. J. House, "Women Reach Milestone in Job Market," *The Wall Street Journal,* November 17, 2013, www.wsj.com.

64. G. Shteynberg, L. M. Leslie, A. P. Knight,, and D. M. Mayer, "But Affirmative Action Hurts Us! Race-Related Beliefs Shape Perceptions of White Disadvantage and Policy Unfairness," *Organizational Behavior and Human Decision Processes* 115 (2013), pp. 1–12.

65. R. Cropanzano, J. E. Slaughter, and P. D. Bachiochi, "Organizational Justice and Black Applicants Reactions to Affirmative Action," *Journal of Applied Psychology* 90 (2005), pp. 1168–84.

66. D. A. Harrison, D. A. Kravitz, D. M. Mayer, L. M. Leslie, and D. Lev-Arey, "Understanding Attitudes toward Affirmative Action Programs in Employment: Summary and Meta-analysis of 35 Years of Research," *Journal of Applied Psychology* 91 (2006), pp. 1013–36.

67. I. Hideg and J. L. Michela, "Overcoming Negative Reactions of Nonbeneficiaries of Employment Equity: The Effect of Participation in Policy Formulation," *Journal of Applied Psychology* 96 (2013), pp. 363–76.

68. M. Totty, "New Tools for Frazzled Recruiters," *The Wall Street Journal,* October 23, 2006, p. C11.

69. C. K. Stevens, "Antecedents of Interview Interactions, Interviewers' Ratings, and Applicants' Reactions," *Personnel Psychology* 51 (1998), pp. 55–85.

70. A. E. Barber, J. R. Hollenbeck, S. L. Tower, and J. M. Phillips, "The Effects of Interview Focus on Recruitment Effectiveness: A Field Experiment," *Journal of Applied Psychology* 79 (1994), pp. 886–96.

71. S. J. Marks, "After School," *Human Resources Executive,* June 15, 2001, pp. 49–51.

72. R. E. Silverman and L. Weber, "An Inside Job: More Firms Opt to Recruit from Within," *The Wall Street Journal Online,* May 29, 2012.

73. M. Magnus, "Recruitment Ads at Work," *Personnel Journal* 64 (1985), pp. 42–63.

74. E. Maltby and S. E. Needleman, "Small Firms Seek Skilled Workers but Can't Find Any," *The Wall Street Journal Online,* July 25, 2012.

75. P. Ziobro and M. Calia, "Wal-Mart Plans to Boost Pay of U.S. Workers," *The Wall Street Journal,* February 9, 2015, www.wsj.com.

76. P. J. Kiker, "Recruitment Battles," *Workforce Management,* October 24, 2005, pp. 20–31.

77. D. S. Chapman, K. L. Uggerslev, S. A. Carroll, K. A. Piasentin, and D. A. Jones, "Applicant Attraction to Organizations and Job Choice: A Meta-analytic Review of the Correlates of Recruiting Outcomes," *Journal of Applied Psychology* 90 (2005), pp. 928–44.

78. A. Athavaley, R. Bachman, K. Maher, and J. W. Miller, "Selling Students on Penn State," *The Wall Street Journal Online,* January 31, 2012.

79. C. Collins and C. K. Stevens, "The Relationship between Early Recruitment-Related Activities and the Application Decisions of New Labor Market Entrants: A Brand Equity Approach to Recruitment," *Journal of Applied Psychology* 87 (2002), pp. 1121–33.

80. F. Lievens and S. Highhouse, "The Relation of Instrumental and Symbolic Attributes to a Company's Attractiveness as an Employer," *Personnel Psychology* 56 (2003), pp. 75–102.

81. J. E. Slaughter, M. J. Zickar, S. Highhouse, and D. C. Mohr, "Personality Trait Inferences about Organizations: Development of a Measure and Assessment of Construct Validity," *Journal of Applied Psychology* 89 (2004), pp. 85–103.

82. D. R. Avery, "Reactions to Diversity in Recruitment Advertising—Are Differences Black and White?" *Journal of Applied Psychology* 88 (2003), pp. 672–79.

83. L. Kwoh, "Chief Executives Hired Internally Outlast, Outperform Their Rivals," *The Wall Street Journal,* May 29, 2012, www.wsj.com.

84. G. Colvin, "How to Manage Your Business in a Recession," *Fortune,* January 19, 2009, pp. 88–93.

85. M. Orey, "Hang the Recession, Let's Bulk Up," *BusinessWeek,* February 2, 2009, pp. 80–81.

86. J. Collins, "How Great Companies Turn Crisis into Opportunity," *Fortune,* February 2, 2009, p. 49.

87. S. Lynch, "Google and Apple Are Safe from an Anti-Poaching Lawsuit, But Maybe Not for Long," *Silicon Valley Business Journal,* April 5, 2013, www.bizjournals.com.

88. J. Elder, "Tech Companies Agree to Settle Wage Suit," *The Wall Street Journal,* April 24, 2014, www.wsj.com.

89. G. Van Hoye and F. Lievens, "Tapping the Grapevine: A Closer Look at Word-of-Mouth as a Recruitment Source," *Journal of Applied Psychology* 94 (2009), pp. 341–52.

90. J. McGregor, "I Can't Believe They Took the Whole Team," *BusinessWeek,* December 18, 2006, pp. 120–22.

91. B. Dineen and R. A. Noe, "Effects of Customization on Applicant Decisions and Applicant Pool Characteristics in a Web-based Recruiting Context," *Journal of Applied Psychology* 94 (2009), pp. 224–34.

92. "PwC Pays for Priority," *The Wall Street Journal,* October 4, 2010, p. B6.

93. O. Kharif, "Finding Job Candidates Who Aren't Looking," *Businessweek,* December 17, 2012, pp. 41–42.

94. A. Singh, "Podcasts Extend Recruiters Reach," *The Wall Street Journal,* April 24, 2006, p. B3.

95 E. White, "Ernst & Young Reaches Out to Recruits on Facebook," *The Wall Street Journal,* January 8, 2007, p. B5.

96. S. Berfield, "Dueling Your Facebook Friends for a New Job," *Bloomberg Businessweek,* March 7, 2013, pp. 35–36.

97. D. Mattioli, "Who's Reading On-Line Resumes? Identity Crooks," *The Wall Street Journal,* October 17, 2006, p B9.

98. J. S. Lublin, "More Executive Recruiting Shifts In-House," *The Wall Street Journal Online,* October 9, 2012.

99. C. Hymowitz and J. Green, "These Days, Anybody Can Headhunt," *Businessweek,* January 21, 2013, pp. 19–20.

100. A. McConnon, "A Headhunter Searches for a Second Life," *BusinessWeek,* January 26, 2009, pp. 80–81.

101. H. Zhao and R. C. Liden, "Internship: A Recruitment and Selection Perspective," *Journal of Applied Psychology* 96 (2011), pp. 221–229.

102. "OMG, Best Summer Ever," *Bloomberg Businessweek,* July 20, 2014, pp. 31–32.

103. M. S. Taylor and T. J. Bergman, "Organizational Recruitment Activities and Applicants' Reactions at Different Stages of the Recruitment Process," *Personnel Psychology* 40 (1984), pp. 261–85.

104. L. M. Graves and G. N. Powell, "The Effect of Sex Similarity on Recruiters' Evaluations of Actual Applicants: A Test of the Similarity–Attraction Paradigm," *Personnel Psychology* 48 (1995), pp. 85–98.

105. K. L. Uggerslev, N. E. Fassina, and D. Kraichy, "Recruiting Through the Stages: A Meta-Analytic Test of Predictors of

Applicant Attraction at Different Stages of the Recruiting Process," *Personnel Psychology, 65* (2012), pp. 597–660.

106. P. Hom, R. W. Griffeth, L. E. Palich, and J. S. Bracker, "An Exploratory Investigation into Theoretical Mechanisms Underlying Realistic Job Previews," *Personnel Psychology* 51 (1998), pp. 421–51.

107. J. M. Phillips, "The Effects of Realistic Job Previews on Multiple Organizational Outcomes: A Meta-analysis," *Academy of Management Journal* 41 (1998), pp. 673–90.

108. P. G. Irving and J. P. Meyer, "Reexamination of the Met-Expectations Hypothesis: A Longitudinal Analysis," *Journal of Applied Psychology* 79 (1995), pp. 937–49.

109. W. J. Becker, T. Connolly, and J. E. Slaughter, "The Effect of Job Offer Timing on Offer Acceptance, Performance, and Turnover," *Personnel Psychology* 63 (2010), pp. 223–41.

Selection and Placement

LEARNING OBJECTIVES

After reading this chapter, you should be able to:

LO 6-1 Establish the basic scientific properties of personnel selection methods, including reliability, validity, and generalizability. *page 224*

LO 6-2 Discuss how the particular characteristics of a job, organization, or applicant affect the utility of any test. *page 233*

LO 6-3 Describe the government's role in personnel selection decisions, particularly in the areas of constitutional law, federal laws, executive orders, and judicial precedent. *page 235*

LO 6-4 List the common methods used in selecting human resources. *page 239*

LO 6-5 Describe the degree to which each of the common methods used in selecting human resources meets the demands of reliability, validity, generalizability, utility, and legality. *page 239*

U.S. Supreme Court Makes a Fashion Statement

Samantha Elauf was a mere 17 years old when she began a journey that would take her all the way to the U.S. Supreme Court. Like many 17-year-olds, Samantha liked to spend her time hanging out at the local mall. She loved to shop, watch movies, and above all eat at her favorite sushi restaurant. Thus, when she needed money and decided to apply for a part-time job, she sought out employment within the mall at the local Abercrombie & Fitch clothing store. Everything seemed to go well in her interview, but in the end, Samantha was denied employment because of what she was wearing—a simple black head scarf. Samantha was a Muslim American and wearing such a scarf was required by her religious beliefs.

In terms of competitive advantage, Abercrombie & Fitch has tried to carve out a unique retail niche by promoting what it calls is a "classic East Coast collegiate style." Promoting this image is paramount to the company from top to bottom, and this includes young people who work on the sales floor. This is not a unique characteristic of Abercrombie & Fitch, and virtually all modern retailers maintain what is called a "looks policy" that is used to reinforce their brand image. The problem with some of these policies, however, is that the "looks" being reinforced are not nearly as diverse as the nation as a whole. Thus, in this case, a hijab, which is apparently not part of the "looks policy" at Abercrombie & Fitch, became a major if unstated issue, because avoiding an employee wearing a hijab put its brand image strategy in conflict with laws that prevent religious discrimination in hiring.

In general, there are three categories of religious discrimination in the workplace, and two of them are central parts of this case. First, it is illegal to make employment decisions based upon someone's faith or lack of faith. Second, it is illegal to harass someone at work because of their religion. Third, it is illegal to fail to make reasonable accommodations to meet an employee's religious beliefs, unless such accommodations create some undue hardship for the employer. Clearly in this case, both the first and third categories come into play; however, lawyers for Abercrombie & Fitch argued that Samantha never explicitly stated in the interview that she wore the hijab for religious reasons, and hence, "they had no idea that she was Muslim."

In the end, the Supreme Court sided with Samantha in an 8-1 ruling, and Judge Antonin Scalia, noted explicitly that, "This is really easy." Allowing Muslim employees to wear the hijab was considered a very reasonable accommodation, and not a factor that could be used to deny someone employment. Although this may have been an easy call in Samantha's favor in the United States, it should be noted that in other countries, this would have been an easy call for Abercrombie & Fitch. For example, in France, the laws actually prohibit people from wearing overt signs of religion, including the hijab, and hence Samantha would not have fared so well had the trial been held in France.

SOURCES: C. A. Liptak, "Muslim Denied Job over Head Scarf Wins in Supreme Court," *The Wall Street Journal*, June 1, 2015, www.wsj.com; "A Muslim Woman Beats Abercrombie and Fitch," *The Washington Post*, June 1, 2015, www.washingtonpost.com; J. Smith; "European Court Upholds French Full Veil Ban, *BBC News*, July 1, 2014, www.bbc.com.

Introduction

Any organization that intends to compete through people must take the utmost care with how it chooses organizational members. These decisions have a critical impact on the organization's ability to compete, as well as each and every job applicant's life. Organizations have to strive to make sure that the decisions they make with respect to who gets accepted or rejected for jobs promote the best interests of the company and are fair to all parties involved. Inaccurate and biased stereotypes like those alluded to in our opening vignette threaten the viability of organizations, especially in an increasingly diverse world.

This is as true at the level of individual firms, as it is with respect to competition between nations. The United States has always been a magnet for talent from other nations, and this country grew economically powerful through the contributions of many different people who emigrated here from other countries. Some have suggested the United States is losing its edge in this regard, however, and that "this is America's most serious long-term threat."[1] That is, social and economic inequality, racial and ethnic bias, growing political intolerance, and a failing educational system are contributing to a state of reverse migration, where highly trained professionals who came to this country are now leaving the United States in larger percentages than those coming in. Innovation and economic growth are fueled by people, and the firms or countries that bring in the best people will be the ones that compete most successfully.

The purpose of this chapter is to familiarize you with ways to minimize errors in employee selection and placement and, in doing so, improve your company's competitive position. The chapter first focuses on five standards that should be met by any selection method. The chapter then evaluates several common selection methods according to those standards.

Selection Method Standards

LO 6-1

Establish the basic scientific properties of personnel selection methods, including reliability, validity, and generalizability.

Personnel selection is the process by which companies decide who will or will not be allowed into organizations. Several generic standards should be met in any selection process. We focus on five: (1) reliability, (2) validity, (3) generalizability, (4) utility, and (5) legality. The first four build off each other in the sense that the preceding standard is often necessary but not sufficient for the one that follows. This is less the case with legal standards. However, a thorough understanding of the first four standards helps us understand the rationale underlying many legal standards.

RELIABILITY

Much of the work in personnel selection involves measuring characteristics of people to determine who will be accepted for job openings. For example, we might be interested in applicants' physical characteristics (like strength or endurance), their cognitive abilities (such as spatial memory or verbal reasoning), or aspects of their personality (like their decisiveness or integrity). Many people have inaccurate stereotypes about how these kinds of characteristics may be related to factors such as race, sex, age, or ethnic background, and therefore, we need to get past these stereotypes and measure the actual attributes directly. So for example, in the vignette that opened this chapter, one could see that Abercrombie & Fitch may have had stereotypes about Muslim workers that did not really apply to Samantha Elauf, who was a very traditional American teenager with perhaps one exception—the hijab. At the other end of the age spectrum, many people have stereotypes about older workers that no longer hold up to any type of scrutiny.[2]

One key standard for any measuring device is its reliability. We define **reliability** as the degree to which a measure is free from random error. If a measure of some supposedly stable characteristic such as intelligence is reliable, then the score a person receives based on that measure will be consistent over time and in different contexts.

Reliability
The consistency of a performance measure; the degree to which a performance measure is free from random error.

Estimating the Reliability of Measurement

Most measurement in personnel selection deals with complex characteristics like intelligence, integrity, and leadership ability. However, to appreciate some of the complexities in measuring people, we will consider something concrete in discussing these concepts: the measurement of height. For example, if we were measuring an applicant's height, we might start by using a 12-inch ruler. Let's say the first person we measure turns out to be 6 feet 1 and $^4/_{16}$ inches tall. It would not be surprising to find out that someone else measuring the same person a second time, perhaps an hour later, found this applicant's height to be 6 feet and $^{12}/_{16}$ inches. The same applicant, measured a third time, maybe the next day, might be measured at 6 feet 1 and $^8/_{16}$ inches tall.

As this example makes clear, even though the person's height is a stable characteristic, we get slightly different results each time he is assessed. This means that each time the person is assessed, we must be making slight errors. If we used a measure of height that was not as reliable as a ruler—for example, guessing someone's height after seeing her walk across the room—we might see an even greater amount of unreliability in the measure. Thus *reliability* refers to the measuring instrument (a ruler versus a visual guess) rather than to the characteristic itself.

We can estimate reliability in several different ways, however; and because most of these rely on computing a correlation coefficient, we will briefly describe and illustrate this statistic. The *correlation coefficient* is a measure of the degree to which two sets of numbers are related. The correlation coefficient expresses the strength of the relationship in numerical form. A perfect positive relationship (as one set of numbers goes up, so does the other) equals +1.0; a perfect negative relationship (as one goes up, the other goes down) equals –1.0. When there is no relationship between the sets of numbers, the correlation equals .00. Although the actual calculation of this statistic goes beyond the scope of this book, it will be useful for us to conceptually examine the nature of the correlation coefficient and what this means in personnel selection contexts.

When assessing the reliability of a measure, for example, we might be interested in knowing how scores on the measure at one time relate to scores on the same measure at another time. Obviously, if the characteristic we are measuring is supposedly stable (like intelligence or integrity) and the time lapse is short, this relationship should be strong. If it were weak, then the measure would be inconsistent—hence unreliable. This is called assessing *test–retest reliability*. Note that the time period between measurements is important when it comes to interpreting test–retest reliability. The assumption is that the characteristic being measured is not changing, and hence any change from Time 1 to Time 2 is treated as an error. When the time period becomes too long, this increases the opportunity that the characteristic is actually changing. For example, if one is measuring personality traits, the evidence suggests that people become more conscientious, more introverted, and more emotionally stable as they get older. These are not age stereotypes, but rather scientifically documented facts about the instability of certain personality traits over extended periods of time.[3]

Plotting the two sets of numbers on a two-dimensional graph often helps us to appreciate the meaning of various levels of the correlation coefficient. Figure 6.1, for example, examines the relationship between student scholastic aptitude in one's junior and senior years in high school, where aptitude for college is measured in three ways: (1) via the scores on the Scholastic Aptitude Test (SAT), (2) via ratings from a high school counselor on a 1-to-100 scale, and (3) via tossing dice. In this plot, each number on the graphs represents a person whose scholastic aptitude is assessed twice (in the junior and senior years), so in Figure 6.1a, 1_1 represents a person who scored 1580 on the SAT in the junior year and 1500 in the senior year; 20_{20} represents a person who scored 480 in the junior year and 620 in the senior year.

Figure 6.1a shows a very strong relationship between SAT scores across the two years. This relationship is not perfect in that the scores changed slightly from one year to the next, but not a great deal. Turning to Figure 6.1b, we see that the relationship between the high school counselors' ratings across the two years, while still positive, is not as strong. That is, the counselors' ratings of individual students' aptitudes for college are less consistent over the two years than their test scores. This might be attributable to the fact the counselor's rating during the junior year was based on a smaller number of observations relative to the ratings made during senior year. Finally, Figure 6.1c shows a worst-case scenario, where the students' aptitudes are assessed by tossing two six-sided dice. As you would expect, the random nature of the dice means that there is virtually no relationship between scores taken in one year and scores taken the next. Although no one would seriously consider tossing dice to be a measure of aptitude, it is worth noting that research shows that the correlation of overall ratings of job applicants' suitability for jobs based on unstructured interviews is very close to .00. Thus, one cannot assume a measure is reliable without actually checking this directly. Novices in measurement are often surprised at exactly how unreliable many human judgments turn out to be. Thus,

Figure 6.1a

Measurements of a Student's Aptitude

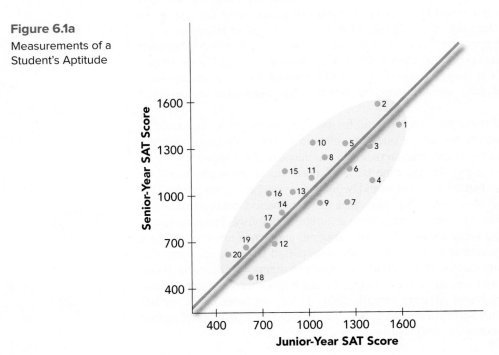

Figure 6.1b

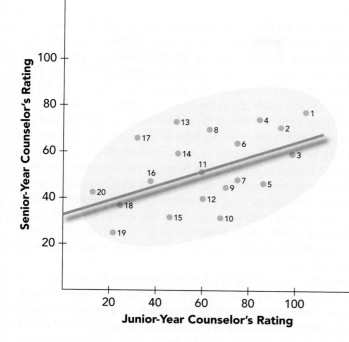

much of the science that deals with selection tries to go beyond subjective human judgments. So for example, if one wants to really know how extraverted someone is, a sociometric badge that records the number, length, and nature of this person's communication patterns across time is likely to provide more reliable test–retest data relative to the subjective perceptions of a former supervisor or interviewer who met the person just once.[4]

Figure 6.1c

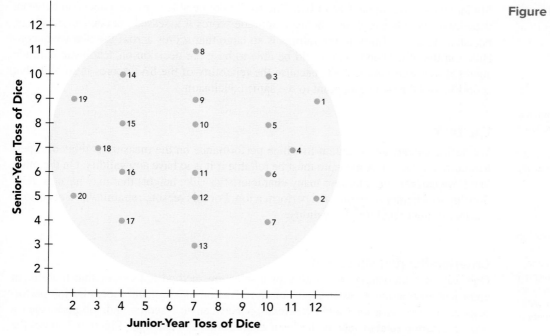

Standards for Reliability

Regardless of what characteristic we are measuring, we want highly reliable measures. Thus, in the previous example, when it comes to measuring students' aptitudes for college, the SAT is more reliable than counselor ratings, which in turn are more reliable than tossing dice. But in an absolute sense, how high is high enough—.50, .70, .90? This is a difficult question to answer specifically because the required reliability depends in part on the nature of the decision being made about the people being measured.

For example, let's assume some college admissions officer was considering several students depicted in Figures 6.1a and 6.1b. Turning first to Figure 6.1b, assume the admissions officer was deciding between Student 1 (1_1) and Student 20 (20_{20}). For this decision, the .50 reliability of the ratings is high enough because the difference between the two students is so large that one would make the same decision for admission regardless of the year in which the rating was taken. That is, Student 1 (with scores of 100 and 80 in the junior and senior year, respectively) is always admitted and Student 20 (with scores of 12 and 42 for junior and senior years, respectively) is always rejected. Thus, although the ratings in this case are not all that reliable in an absolute sense, their reliability is high enough for this decision.

On the other hand, let's assume the same college admissions officer was deciding between Student 1 (1_1) and Student 2 (2_2). Looking at Figure 6.1a, it is clear that even with the highly reliable SAT scores, the difference between these students is so small that one would make a different admission decision depending on what year one obtained the score. Student 1 would be selected over Student 2 if the junior-year score was used, but Student 2 would be chosen over Student 1 if the senior-year score was used. Thus, even though the reliability of the SAT exam is high in an absolute sense, it is not high enough for this decision. Under these conditions, the admissions officer needs to find some other basis for making the decision regarding these two students (like high school GPA or rank in graduating class).

Although these two scenarios clearly show that no specific value of reliability is always acceptable, they also demonstrate why, all else being equal, the more reliable a measure is, the better. For example, turning again to Figures 6.1a and 6.1b, consider Student 9 (9_9) and Student 14 (14_{14}). One would not be able to make a decision between these two students based on scholastic aptitude scores if assessed via counselor ratings, because the unreliability in the ratings is so large that scores across the two years conflict. On the other hand, one would be able to base the decision on scholastic aptitude scores if assessed via the SAT, because the reliability of the SAT scores is so high that scores across the two years point to the same conclusion.

VALIDITY

Validity
The extent to which a performance measure assesses all the relevant—and only the relevant—aspects of job performance.

We define **validity** as the extent to which performance on the measure is related to performance on the job. A measure must be reliable if it is to have any validity. On the other hand, we can reliably measure many characteristics (like height) that may have no relationship to whether someone can perform a job. For this reason, reliability is a necessary but insufficient condition for validity.

Criterion-Related Validation

Criterion-Related Validity
A method of establishing the validity of a personnel selection method by showing a substantial correlation between test scores and job-performance scores.

One way of establishing the validity of a selection method is to show that there is an empirical association between scores on the selection measure and scores for job performance. If there is a substantial correlation between test scores and job-performance scores, **criterion-related validity** has been established.[5] For example, Figure 6.2 shows the relationship between 2014 scores on the Scholastic Aptitude Test (SAT) and 2015 freshman grade point average (GPA). In this example, there is roughly a .50 correlation between the SAT and GPA. This .50 is referred to as a *validity coefficient.* Note that we have used the correlation coefficient to assess both reliability and validity, which may seem somewhat confusing. The key distinction is that the correlation reflects a reliability estimate when we are attempting to assess the same characteristic twice (such as SAT scores in the junior and senior years), but the correlation coefficient reflects a validity coefficient when we are attempting to relate one characteristic (SAT) to performance on some task (GPA).

Criterion-related validity studies come in two varieties. **Predictive validation** seeks to establish an empirical relationship between test scores taken *prior* to being hired and eventual performance on the job. Because of the time and effort required to conduct a predictive validation study, many employers are tempted to use a different design. **Concurrent validation** assesses the validity of a test by administering it to people already on the job and then correlating test scores with existing measures of each person's performance. For example, the testing company Infor measures 39 behavioral, cognitive, and cultural traits among job applicants and then compares their scores on those dimensions with the top performers in the company. The assumption is that if high performers in the company score high on any trait, then the company should use scores on this trait to screen new hires.[6] Figure 6.3 compares the two types of validation study.

Despite the extra effort and time needed for predictive validation, it is superior to concurrent validation for a number of reasons. First, job applicants (because they are seeking work) are typically more motivated to perform well on the tests than are current employees (who already have jobs). Thus, job applicants are more tempted to fake responses in order to look good relative to current job holders. Second, current employees have learned many things on the job that job applicants have not yet learned. Therefore, the correlation between test scores and job performance for current employees may not be the same as the correlation between test scores and job performance for less

Predictive Validation
A criterion-related validity study that seeks to establish an empirical relationship between applicants' test scores and their eventual performance on the job.

Concurrent Validation
A criterion-related validity study in which a test is administered to all the people currently in a job and then incumbents' scores are correlated with existing measures of their performance on the job.

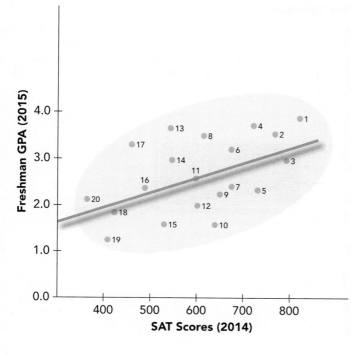

Figure 6.2

Relationship between 2014 SAT Scores and 2015 Freshman GPA

knowledgeable job applicants. Third, current employees tend to be homogeneous—that is, similar to each other on many characteristics. Thus, on many of the characteristics needed for success on the job, most current employees will show restriction in range. This restricted range makes it hard to detect a relationship between test scores and job-performance scores because few of the current employees will be very low on the characteristic you are trying to validate. For example, if emotional stability is required for a nursing career, it is quite likely that most nurses who have amassed five or six years' experience will score high on this characteristic. Yet to validate a test, you need both high test scorers (who should subsequently perform well on the job) and low test scorers (who should perform poorly on the job). Thus, although concurrent studies can sometimes help one anticipate the results of predictive studies, they do not serve as substitutes.

Obviously, we would like our measures to be high in validity; but as with the reliability standard, we must also ask, how high is high enough? When trying to determine how much validity is enough, one typically has to turn to tests of statistical significance. A test of statistical significance answers the question, "Assuming that there is no true

Figure 6.3

Graphic Depiction of Concurrent and Predictive Validation Designs

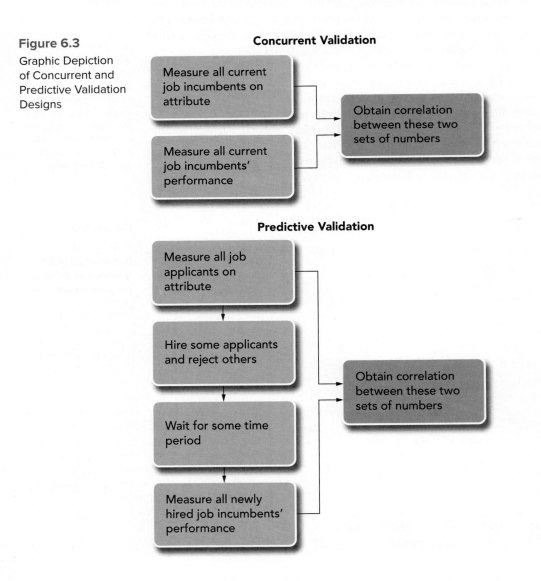

Concurrent Validation

Measure all current job incumbents on attribute

Measure all current job incumbents' performance

Obtain correlation between these two sets of numbers

Predictive Validation

Measure all job applicants on attribute

Hire some applicants and reject others

Wait for some time period

Measure all newly hired job incumbents' performance

Obtain correlation between these two sets of numbers

relationship between the predictor and the criterion, what are the odds of seeing a relationship this strong by chance alone?" If these odds are very low, then one might infer that the results from the test were in fact predicting future job performance.

Table 6.1 shows how big a correlation between a selection measure and a measure of job performance needs to be to achieve statistical significance at a level of .05 (that is, there is only a 5 out of 100 chance that one could get a correlation this big by chance alone). Although it is generally true that bigger correlations are better, the size of the sample on which the correlation is based plays a large role as well. Because many of the selection methods we examine in the second half of this chapter generate correlations in the .20s and .30s, we often need samples of 80 to 90 people. A validation study with a small sample (such as 20 people) is almost doomed to failure from the start. Fortunately, advances in the ability to process "big data" via cloud-based analytics is greatly expanding the ability to find valid predictors of future job performance. For example, in the old days, when it came to staffing its call centers, Xerox Corporation always looked for applicants who had done the job before. This seemed like a reasonable approach to take until one day, when they actually assessed the empirical relationship between experience, on the one hand, and performance and turnover on the other hand, they learned that experience did not matter at all. Instead, what really separated winners and losers in this occupation was their personality. People who were creative tended to perform well and stay on the job for a long time, whereas those who were inquisitive tended to struggle with the job and leave well before the company ever recouped its $5,000 investment in training.

Xerox now leaves all hiring for its nearly 500,000 call center jobs to a computer software algorithm that tirelessly looks for links between responses to personality items and a highly specific set of job outcomes. The program was developed by Evolv Incorporated, and rather than relying on interviewer judgments that might be subject to personal biases, the Evolv program puts applicants through a battery of tests and personality items, then tracks their outcomes at the company over time. The algorithm is constantly adjusting itself with the accumulation of ever more data, all in an effort to develop a statistical model that describes the ideal call center employee.[7]

Evolv is just one player in an expanding industry that seeks to use big data to help companies find and retain the best employees. Globally, spending on this sort of talent management software rose 15% in just one year to an estimated value of $3.8 billion and the competition for this business is intense. For example, in 2011 alone, IBM purchased Kenexa Corporation for $1.3 billion, Oracle acquired Taleo for $1.9 billion, and SAP bought SuccessFactors for $3.4 billion.[8]

Content Validation

When sample sizes are small, an alternative test validation strategy, content validation, can be used. **Content validation** is performed by demonstrating that the questions or

Content Validation
A test-validation strategy performed by demonstrating that the items, questions, or problems posed by a test are a representative sample of the kinds of situations or problems that occur on the job.

SAMPLE SIZE	REQUIRED CORRELATION
5	.75
10	.58
20	.42
40	.30
80	.21
100	.19

Table 6.1
Required Level of Correlation to Reach Statistical Significance as a Function of Sample Size

problems posed by the test are a representative sample of the kinds of situations or problems that occur on the job. A test that is content valid exposes the job applicant to situations that are likely to occur on the job, and then tests whether the applicant currently has sufficient knowledge, skill, or ability to handle such situations.

Many of the new simulations that organizations are using are essentially computer-based role-playing games, where applicants play the role of the job incumbent, confronting the exact types of people and problems real-live job incumbents would face. The simulations are just like traditional role-playing games (e.g., "The Sims"), and the applicant's reactions and behaviors are scored to see how well they match with what one would expect from the ideal employee. For example, if one is considering applicants for a wait staff job at a restaurant, the game *Wasabi Waiter,* designed by Knack.it, allows the employer to watch how the applicant responds to finicky customers, uppity receptionists, emotionally unstable chefs, and other predictably challenging situations that are likely to take place in a very busy establishment.[9] Because the content of these tests so closely parallels the content of the job, one can safely make inferences from one to the other. Although criterion-related validity is established by empirical means, content validity is achieved primarily through a process of expert judgment.

The ability to use content validation in small sample settings makes it generally more applicable than criterion-related validation. However, content validation has two limitations. First, one assumption behind content validation is that the person who is to be hired must have the knowledge, skills, or abilities at the time she is hired. Second, because subjective judgment plays such a large role in content validation, it is critical to minimize the amount of inference involved on the part of judges. Thus the judges' ratings need to be made with respect to relatively concrete and observable behaviors.

GENERALIZABILITY

Generalizability
The degree to which the validity of a selection method established in one context extends to other contexts.

Generalizability is defined as the degree to which the validity of a selection method established in one context extends to other contexts. Thus, the SAT may be a valid predictor of someone's performance (e.g., as a measure of someone's GPA in an undergraduate program), but, does this same test predict performance in graduate programs? If the test does not predict success in this other situation, then it does not "generalize" to this other context.

There are two primary "contexts" over which we might like to generalize: different situations (jobs or organizations) and different samples of people. Just as reliability is necessary but not sufficient for validity, validity is necessary but not sufficient for generalizability.

It was once believed, for example, that validity coefficients were situationally specific—that is, the level of correlation between test and performance varied as one went from one organization to another, even though the jobs studied seemed to be identical. Subsequent research has indicated that this is largely false. Rather, tests tend to show similar levels of correlation even across jobs that are only somewhat similar (at least for tests of intelligence and cognitive ability). Correlations with these kinds of tests change as one goes across widely different kinds of jobs, however. Specifically, the more complex the job, the higher the validity of many tests. It was also believed that tests showed differential subgroup validity, which meant that the validity coefficient for any test–job performance pair was different for people of different races or genders. This belief was also refuted by subsequent research, and, in general, one finds very similar levels of correlations across different groups of people.[10]

Because the evidence suggests that test validity often extends across situations and subgroups, *validity generalization* stands as an alternative for validating selection methods for companies that cannot employ criterion-related or content validation. Validity generalization is a three-step process. First, the company provides evidence from previous criterion-related validity studies conducted in other situations that shows that a specific test (such as a test of emotional stability) is a valid predictor for a specific job (like nurse at a large hospital). Second, the company provides evidence from job analysis to document that the job it is trying to fill (nurse at a small hospital) is similar in all major respects to the job validated elsewhere (nurse at a large hospital). Finally, if the company can show that it uses a test that is the same as or similar to that used in the validated setting, then one can "generalize" the validity from the first context (large hospital) to the new context (small hospital).

UTILITY

Utility is the degree to which the information provided by selection methods enhances the bottom-line effectiveness of the organization. In general, the more reliable, valid, and generalizable the selection method is, the more utility it will have. On the other hand, many characteristics of particular selection contexts enhance or detract from the usefulness of given selection methods, even when reliability, validity, and generalizability are held constant.

Figures 6.4a and 6.4b, for example, show two different scenarios where the correlation between a measure of extroversion and the amount of sales revenue generated by a sample of sales representatives is the same for two different companies: Company A and Company B. Although the correlation between the measure of extroversion and sales is the same, Company B derives much more utility or practical benefit from the measure. That is, as indicated by the arrows proceeding out of the boxes (which indicate the people selected), the average sales revenue of the three people selected by Company B (Figure 6.4b) is $850,000 compared to $780,000 from the three people selected by Company A (Figure 6.4a).

The major difference between these two companies is that Company B generated twice as many applicants as Company A. This means that the selection ratio (the percentage of

LO 6-2
Discuss how the particular characteristics of a job, organization, or applicant affect the utility of any test.

Utility
The degree to which the information provided by selection methods enhances the effectiveness of selecting personnel in real organizations.

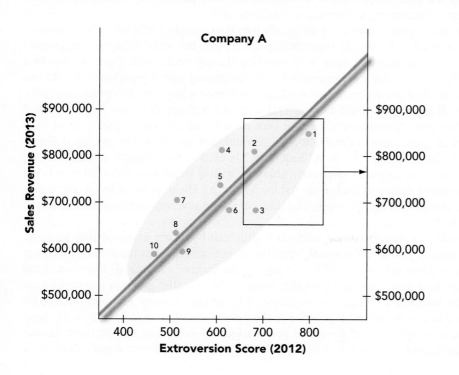

Figure 6.4a
Utility of Selecting on Extroversion Scores when Selection Ratio Is High

Figure 6.4b

Utility of Selecting on Extroversion Scores when Selection Ratio Is Low

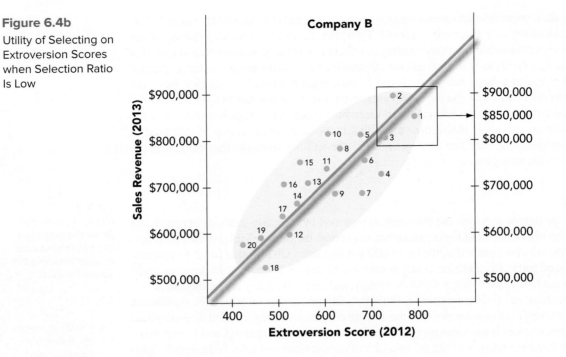

people selected relative to the total number of people tested) is quite low for Company B (3/20) relative to Company A (3/10). Thus, the people selected by Company B have higher amounts of extroversion than those selected by Company A; therefore, Company B takes better advantage of the relationship between extroversion and sales. Thus, the utility of any test generally increases as the selection ratio gets lower, so long as the additional costs of recruiting and testing are not excessive.

Many other factors relate to the utility of a test. For example, the value of the product or service produced by the job incumbent plays a role: the more valuable the product or service, the more value there is in selecting the top performers. For example, in a high-tech company, there is tremendous value associated with a great team of software engineers with a proven record of working productively together to create innovative products. If a company tried to hire total strangers without this kind of track record and build a team from scratch, it might take years to see any value from a set of individual hires. Thus, many organizations in this industry are willing to pay top dollar to hire entire intact teams. The term "acqui-hire" is used in this industry to describe this practice, and in some cases, large companies are willing to pay up to $5 million to bring an independent team into their fold. Ashley Vandy, an HR director at Facebook, notes, "We are always looking for talent, and these deals are one way to bring great teams to Facebook."[11]

The utility of hiring the best talent is highlighted by recent evidence that suggests, performance in jobs is not normally distributed, but instead takes the shape of a power law. That is, most individual differences take on the form of a normal distribution, in the sense that most people are in the middle, followed by a smaller group of people who are a little bit above or below the mean, followed by an even smaller group of outliers far above and below the mean. This belief in the normal distribution has traditionally been extended to people's belief about job performance as well, even though there has not been a great deal of evidence collected to test this belief. However, a study examining over 600,000 entertainers, politicians, amateur athletes, professional athletes, and scientists has challenged this idea and instead suggests that job performance follows a power law distribution. Figure 6.5 shows how a distribution that follows a power law differs dramatically from a normal distribution, in the sense that there are actually very few high performers and a large group of potentially poor performers. The implication of these new findings for utility analysis is important because it implies that the dollar value of a "highly productive worker" (e.g., someone who is one standard deviation above the mean, perhaps selected based upon a validated test) and an "average worker" (e.g., at the mean, perhaps selected at random) is much greater than one would expect if the distribution were normal.[12]

LEGALITY

The final standard that any selection method should adhere to is *legality*. All selection methods should conform to existing laws and existing legal precedents. So for example, as we saw in the vignette that opened this chapter, Abercrombie & Fitch was found to illegally discriminate based upon religion because they failed to make reasonable accommodations to Samantha Elauf. In a very similar case, Kentucky Fried Chicken, which requires its workers to wear slacks, was charged with discrimination when it refused to allow Sheila Silver, a Pentecostal Christian, to wear a long dress at work, which her religion required. These are hardly isolated incidents in the sense that cases based upon religious discrimination have skyrocketed recently. According to the EEOC, in 2013 alone, there were over 3,700 religious discrimination claims brought against employers.[13] Employers who are taken to court for illegal discrimination experience high costs associated with litigation, settlements, and awards, and also suffer potential damage to their social reputations as good employers, making recruitment more difficult. Moreover, although the threat of litigation is ever present, this is especially a problem during economic recessions, when it is difficult to find a job. The number of discrimination cases filed with the EEOC set a record of over 100,000 in 2011 alone.[14]

For example, a lawsuit leveled at Walmart sought damages of over $1 billion, and charged that the retailer discriminated against women via a set of subjective and decentralized interview processes that were rife with gender stereotypes that limited their advancement opportunties.[15] Although this case was eventually decided in Walmart's favor for a technical reason (the 1 million women plaintiffs failed to establish that they were common victims of a common policy), the reputational damage caused by all the testimony

LO 6-3

Describe the government's role in personnel selection decisions, particularly in the areas of constitutional law, federal laws, executive orders, and judicial precedent.

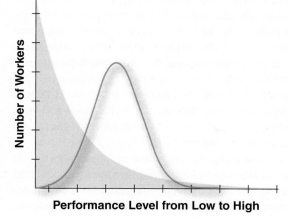

Figure 6.5

Comparing a Normal Distribution to a Power Law

seriously wounded the company. Supreme Court Justice Ruth Ginsberg noted, "The plaintiffs' evidence, including class members' tales of their own experiences suggests gender bias." This kind of reputational damage can only hurt an employer in the labor market, even if the employer prevails in court.[16] In addition, the negative reputational effects associated with being perceived as an employer who discriminates unfairly can even hurt the company in the product market. For example, if Walmart is perceived as treating women unfairly, this might be a turn-off for female customers some of whom may shop elsewhere.

This is exactly what was experienced by Chick-fil-A. Even though the firm had never been charged with any form of employment discrimination, when the president of the company made disparaging comments regarding gay marriage in 2012, there was an immediate negative backlash against "hate chicken" that harmed sales. Even worse, it threatened the company's expansion plans and strategy to move into northern and urban areas. The Mayor of Boston went so far as to send a letter to the company urging them to back down from plans to locate in Boston, and he was quoted in the *Boston Herald* saying that "he would make it very difficult" for the restaurant to come to town. Chicago Mayor Rahm Emanual chimed in and stated that "Chick-fil-A's values are not Chicago's values" and protest movements in New York and San Francisco were organized to oppose expansion into those areas. All of this despite the fact that no one ever presented any evidence or even charged the company with actual discrimination against gay customers or job applicants.[17]

Federal Legislation

Three primary federal laws form the basis for a majority of the suits filed by job applicants. First, the Civil Rights Act of 1991 (discussed in Chapter 3), an extension of the Civil Rights Act of 1964, protects individuals from discrimination based on race, color, sex, religion, and national origin with respect to hiring as well as compensation and working conditions. Thus, the religious statute was grounds for Samantha Elauf's lawsuit, but there are several other categories within this act that define other protected groups. The 1991 act differs from the 1964 act in three important areas.

First, it defines employers' explicit obligation to establish the business necessity of any neutral-appearing selection method that has had adverse impact on groups specified by the law. This is typically done by showing that the test has significant criterion-related or content validity. If the employer cannot show such a difference, which the research suggests will be difficult, then the process may be ruled illegal. Ironically, for example, the Consumer Finance Protection Bureau (CFPB) that was created as part of the Dodd-Frank Act, which regulates banks and financial institutions to specifically prevent discrimination in loan practices, recently discovered that its own promotion policies created adverse impact. An investigation into the CFPB's promotion policies found that 21% of the agency's white employees received the highest performance rating compared with just 10% of the African American employees and 9% of Hispanic employees. Since this rating was used to make promotion decisions, it became a neutral-appearing employment practice that created adverse impact, and thus, had to be justified.[18] Because adverse impact is determined for both races and ethnicities, as the "Evidence-Based HR" box shows, the subjective nature of the "ethnicity" categorization process sometimes makes determining adverse impact a complicated matter.

Second, the 1991 act allows the individual filing the complaint to have a jury decide whether he or she may recover punitive damages (in addition to lost wages and benefits) for emotional injuries caused by the discrimination. This can generate large financial settlements as well as poor public relations that can hinder the organization's ability to compete.

Finally, the 1991 act explicitly prohibits the granting of preferential treatment to minority groups. Preferential treatment is often attractive because many of the most valid methods for screening people, especially cognitive ability tests and work sample tests, often are high in adverse impact.[19] Thus, there is somewhat of a trade-off in terms of selecting the highest scorers on validated tests on the one hand and creating diversity in the workforce on the other hand.[20]

One potential way to "have your cake and eat it too" is to simply rank the scores of different races or gender groups within their own groups, and then taking perhaps the top 10% of scorers from each group, instead of the top 10% that would be obtained if one ignored race or gender. Many feel that this practice is justified because it levels the playing field in a context where bias works against African Americans. However, the 1991 act specifically outlaws this practice (sometimes referred to as *race norming*). The reason for this is that adjusting scores in this way has been found to have a number of negative effects, not only on the attitudes of white males who claim it causes reverse discrimination,[21] but on the proposed beneficiaries of such preferential treatment.

Two recent Supreme Court cases show that policies that may be construed as promoting preferential treatment will not stand up in court. In the first case, voters in the state of Michigan backed an initiative that made it illegal to engage in affirmative action for minorities when it came to admissions to Michigan colleges. Because the majority of voters in this state were white, this initiative was challenged because of legal precedents that protect minorities from being targeted for unfair treatment through the political process. That is, taken to an extreme, if a majority of members of a state were white, it would not be permissible to support a ballot that would prevent minorities from attending college at all, since this would be patently unfair. The challenge to the Michigan initiative claimed that the initiative was close to this, but this challenge was struck down by the Supreme Court, which decided that this is within the rights of the electorate.[22] The court did not necessarily say that affirmative action was illegal in this case, but rather it was fair for the general electorate to impose its will in this way, which leaves colleges trying to promote diversity scrambling for other alternatives, one of which took place at the University of Texas.[23]

EVIDENCE-BASED HR

Although race is an immutable characteristic for many white, black, and Asian Americans, this is much less clear-cut for Hispanic Americans. Hispanics do not constitute a race, and therefore, the U.S. Census asks two separate questions: one about ethnicity and one about race. The first question asks whether the person is of Hispanic or Latin origin, and the second asks about race. In the 2000 census data, 37% of Hispanics, apparently dissatisfied with the choice between white, black, and Asian, chose the category "Other." However, in the 2010 Census data, 7% of the 35 million Americans of Hispanic origin changed their race from "Other" to "White." This shift was mainly due to young Hispanics who either did not answer the questions for themselves in the 2000 survey or changed their self-image as they became older. For HR managers, this shows some of the complications of trying to make sure various selection procedures do not have adverse impact on various protected groups when the very concept of group status is dynamically changing over time.

SOURCE: N. Cohn, "More Hispanics Declaring Themselves White," *The New York Times,* May 21, 2014, www.nytimes.com.

The second recent Supreme Court case involved the University of Texas (UT) and illustrates how difficult it can be to achieve diversity goals while still upholding merit-based selection and avoiding perceptions of reverse discrimination. Specifically, in order to increase the percentage of African American and Hispanic students in the UT system, the school made it a policy to accept the top 10% of the graduating class of every high school. Because many high schools in Texas tend to be segregated by race and ethnicity, this policy worked somewhat like race norming in ensuring that members of every group found their way into college; so far, so good.[24] To push the diversity gains even further though, the admissions officers at UT noted that many African American students in affluent suburban schools often were rejected for admission, even though they had higher test scores than African American students from urban schools. When the school tried to reach out and accept those students, however, this policy was challenged and then struck down by the Supreme Court. The court reacted negatively to this policy because it meant that a white student at an affluent school who had the same test score as an African American at the same affluent school would be rejected whereas the African American student would be accepted. The court decided that this was a clear case of reverse discrimination based solely on race.[25]

Rather than employing race norming, employers can partially achieve both goals of maximizing predicted future performance and diversity in several ways. First, aggressive recruiting of members of protected groups allows an employer to generate a larger pool of protected group members, and, by being highly selective within this larger group, the scores of admitted applicants will more closely match those of all the other groups.[26] Second, as we see later in this chapter, different selection methods have different degrees of adverse impact, and multistage selection batteries that use different methods at different stages can also help.[27]

Finally, one common approach that does not seem to work is to abandon the kinds of compliance-driven, evidenced-based workforce utilization reviews that we discussed in our last chapter, in favor of softer, "inclusion" initiatives that express the generic value of diversity but fail to document goals and timetables statistically. Some organizations treat diversity more like a marketing campaign than an HR initiative, and it is not uncommon to see companies that won awards for their "inclusion programs" such as Texaco and Bank of America, also later convicted of illegal discrimination. Some observers have noted that there is an almost complete overlap of the lists of the top 50 companies for inclusion and the top 50 companies for advertising expenditures, and the need to complement style with substance cannot be overlooked in this critical area.[28] The simple truth is that best predictors of whether a firm becomes truly diverse and avoids litigation is whether (a) there is a specific person (e.g., a diversity compliance officer) whose sole job is to monitor hiring statistics, (b) this person has the power to change hiring practices, and (c) this person is held strictly accountable in their own performance appraisal for achieving quantifiable results.[29]

The Age Discrimination in Employment Act of 1967 is also widely used in personnel selection. Court interpretations of this act also mirror those of the Civil Rights Act, in the sense that if any neutral-appearing practice happens to have adverse impact on those over 40, the burden of proof shifts to the employer, who must show business necessity to avoid a guilty verdict.[30] The act does not protect younger workers (thus there is never a case for "reverse discrimination" here), and like the most recent civil rights act, it allows for jury trials and punitive damages. This act outlaws almost all "mandatory retirement" programs (company policies that dictate that everyone who reaches a set age must retire).

Finally, the Americans with Disabilities Act (ADA) of 1991 protects individuals with physical and mental disabilities (or with a history of the same), and requires that employers make "reasonable accommodation" to disabled individuals whose handicaps may prevent them from performing essential functions of the job as currently designed. "Reasonable accommodation" could include restructuring jobs, modifying work schedules, making facilities accessible, providing readers, or modifying equipment. The ADA does not require an organization to hire someone whose disability prevents him or her from performing either critical or routine aspects of the job nor does it require accommodations that would cause "undue hardship." Technological advancements in the area of accommodations, along with the general shift in jobs from those that are physically demanding to those that are more mentally challenging, is increasing the percentage of jobs that disabled workers can hold.[31]

There is also some degree of political pressure to increase the hiring of disabled workers, and in 2014, the Department of Labor issued new rules aimed at government contractors that decreed that they should set a goal of composing 7% of their workforce with disabled employees. Thus, if you are applying for a job with a government contractor you need to check a box that asks whether or not you are disabled. This ruling was controversial because many disabled workers, especially those with non-obvious physical impairments or mental impairments, are very unlikely to check that box. This means that some employers may actually be meeting the goals but not be able to show it due to employee reluctance to check the box.[32] Indeed, when it comes to boxes, as the "Competing through Sustainability" feature shows, the Department of Labor has strong opinions about what boxes should be added as well as dropped from job application forms.

Executive Orders

As noted in Chapter 3, the executive branch of the government also regulates hiring decisions through the use of executive orders. Executive Order 11246 parallels the protections provided by the Civil Rights Act of 1964 but goes beyond the 1964 act in two important ways. First, not only do the executive orders prohibit discrimination, they actually mandate that employers take affirmative action to hire qualified minority applicants.[33] Executive orders also allow the government to suspend all business with a contractor while an investigation is being conducted (rather than waiting for an actual finding), which puts a great deal of pressure on employers to comply with these orders.

Types of Selection Methods

The first half of this chapter laid out the five standards by which we can judge selection measures. In the second half of this chapter, we examine the common selection methods used in various organizations and discuss their advantages and disadvantages in terms of these standards.

INTERVIEWS

A selection interview has been defined as "a dialogue initiated by one or more persons to gather information and evaluate the qualifications of an applicant for

LO 6-4
List the common methods used in selecting human resources.

LO 6-5
Describe the degree to which each of the common methods used in selecting human resources meets the demands of reliability, validity, generalizability, utility, and legality.

Ban-the-Box Policies Attempt to Open Up Opportunities

A key to maintaining a sustainable workforce is to find some meaningful role for every member of society and to prevent it from becoming impossible for large numbers of people to find gainful employment. This becomes very difficult, however, when the person in question has a criminal record. Increased efficiency and widespread use of background checks have made arrests and convictions easier to identify, and publicized cases where employers were held liable for negligent hiring provide both the opportunity and motivation to simply avoid hiring anyone with a criminal background. In a labor market where there are often far more applicants than openings, the simple decision to not consider any person who has a criminal record for employment seems like an efficient screening system. Thus, one often sees a specific box on standard employment applications that asks the question, "Have you ever been convicted of a crime?"

This box has become the new "scarlet letter" that forever excludes a number of Americans from ever finding gainful employment, and regrettably, the number of people affected by this box is large and growing over time. According to the Federal Bureau of Investigation (FBI), three decades of tougher law enforcement and minimum sentence guidelines have created a situation where nearly 80 million Americans have criminal records. In 2012 alone, over 630,000 people were released from state and federal prisons, and then went looking for work. Moreover, the fact that there are race differences in incarceration rates only makes matters more complicated. The EEOC, in an effort to help create some opportunities for people with less than perfect records, recently issued formal guidance and recommendation to employers to strike that box from formal applications.

This ban-the-box movement does not mean that employers cannot ask such a question; however, the EEOC wants to push that question farther down the line in the employment process. Large employers like Target and Walmart have embraced this guidance and now only ask this question after there has been a conditional job offer made to the applicant. Tara Raddohl, an HR representative for Walmart notes that "the removal of the box does not eliminate the background check, but it offers those who have been previously incarcerated a chance to get their foot in the door."

DISCUSSION QUESTIONS

1. Is it fair to deny employment to all convicted felons, and if so, is this condemning such individuals to a permanent life of crime?
2. Is it fair to hold employers liable for any crimes committed by employees with known criminal backgrounds, and if so, is this also condemning such individuals to a permanent life of crime?

SOURCES: J. Smialek, "Putting Released Prisoners Back to Work," *Bloomberg Businessweek,* February 6, 2014, pp. 30–31; C. G. Koch and M. V. Holden, "The Danger of Putting So Many People in Prison," *Chicago Tribune,* January 28, 2015, www.chicagotribune.com; J. R. Emshwiller and G. Fields, "Decades Long Arrest Wave Vexes Employers," *The Wall Street Journal,* December 12, 2014, www.wsj.com.

employment." The selection interview is the most widespread selection method employed in organizations, and there have been literally hundreds of studies examining their effectiveness.[34]

Unfortunately, the long history of research on the employment interview suggests that, without proper care, it can be unreliable, low in validity, and biased against a number of different groups. Moreover, interviews are relatively costly because they require at least one person to interview another person, and these persons have to be brought to the same geographic location. Finally, in terms of legality, the subjectivity embodied in the process, as well as the opportunity for unconscious bias effects, often makes applicants upset, particularly if they fail to get a job after being asked apparently irrelevant questions. In the end, subjective selection methods like the interview must be validated by traditional criterion-related or content-validation procedures if they show any degree of adverse impact.

Fortunately, more recent research has pointed to a number of concrete steps that one can employ to increase the utility of the personnel selection interview. First, HR staff should keep the interview structured, standardized, and focused on accomplishing a small number of goals. That is, they should plan to come out of each interview with quantitative ratings on a small number of dimensions that are observable (like interpersonal style or ability to express oneself) and avoid ratings of abilities that may be better measured by tests (like intelligence). In addition to coming out of the interview with quantitative ratings, interviewers should also have a structured note-taking system that will aid recall when it comes to justifying the ratings.[35]

Second, interviewers should ask questions dealing with specific situations that are likely to arise on the job, and use these to determine what the person is likely to do in those situations. These types of **situational interview** items have been shown to have quite high predictive validity.[36] Situational judgment items come in two varieties, as shown in Table 6.2. Some items are "experience-based" and require the applicant to reveal an actual experience he or she had in the past when confronting the situation. Other items are "future-oriented" and ask what the person is likely to do when confronting a certain hypothetical situation in the future. Research suggests that these types of items can both show validity but that experience-based items often outperform future-oriented items. Experience-based items also appear to reduce some forms of impression management, such as ingratiation, better than future-oriented items.[37]

Situational Interview
An interview procedure where applicants are confronted with specific issues, questions, or problems that are likely to arise on the job.

Table 6.2
Examples of Experience-Based and Future-Oriented Situational Interview Items

Experience-based	
Motivating employees:	"Think about an instance when you had to motivate an employee to perform a task that he or she disliked but that you needed to have done. How did you handle that situation?"
Resolving conflict:	"What was the biggest difference of opinion you ever had with a co-worker? How did you resolve that situation?"
Overcoming resistance to change:	"What was the hardest change you ever had to bring about in a past job, and what did you do to get the people around you to change their thoughts or behaviors?"
Future-oriented	
Motivating employees:	"Suppose you were working with an employee who you knew greatly disliked performing a particular task. You needed to get this task completed, however, and this person was the only one available to do it. What would you do to motivate that person?"
Resolving conflict:	"Imagine that you and a co-worker disagree about the best way to handle an absenteeism problem with another member of your team. How would you resolve that situation?"
Overcoming resistance to change:	"Suppose you had an idea for change in work procedures that would enhance quality, but some members of your work group were hesitant to make the change. What would you do in that situation?"

© Digital Vision RF

When more than one person is able to interview a candidate for a position, there is significant advantage in removing any errors or biases that a single individual might make in choosing the correct person for the job. In today's technological world, it is becoming easier for multiple people to give their input in an interview by watching a video tape or listening via conference call if they cannot be there in person.

It is also important to use multiple interviewers who are trained to avoid many of the subjective errors that can result when one human being is asked to rate another. For example, at Google, there were definite concerns with demographic similarity bias in interviews, because their own analysis of local data was suggesting that managers were hiring people who seemed just like them. To eliminate this problem, Google now compiles elaborate files for each candidate, and then has all interviews conducted by groups rather than individuals. Laszlo Bock, vice president for Google's People Operations, notes that "we do everything to minimize the authority and power of the lone manager in making hiring decisions that are going to affect the entire company."[38] Many companies find that a good way to get "multiple eyes" on an applicant is to conduct digitally taped interviews, and then send the digitalized files (rather than the applicants) around from place to place.

This is seen by some as a cost-effective means of allowing numerous raters to evaluate the candidate under standard conditions. The use of video-based interviews began on college campuses, where technology resources were widely available. However, over time, private start-up companies began selling those same services to the general public.[39] Of course, many employers find that the lack of true interaction that can take place in videos limits their value somewhat and, hence, the use of face-to-face interactive technology like Skype is also on the rise.[40]

Regardless of the medium, anyone who will be conducting an employment interview needs to be trained, and a relatively small amount of money spent on training up front (in the $3,000 to $30,000 range) can save major expenses later in the process if it prevents a lawsuit or a poor hiring decision that harms the organization.[41] The goal of most training programs is to limit the subjectivity of the process and research suggests that it is best to ask interviewers to be "witnesses" of facts that can later be integrated via objective formulas, as opposed to being "judges" allowed to idiosyncratically weigh how various facts should be combined to form the final recommendation.[42]

In addition to being a witness, the interviewer sometimes has to be the prosecuting attorney, because in some cases the interviewees may be motivated to try to present an overly positive, if not outright false, picture of their qualifications. The role of interviewer as prosecutor has been greatly facilitated recently by social media sites that allow employers to gather a great deal of information on candidates just by looking them up online. As the "Competing through Technology" box shows, some of this search may even involve information that would be illegal to ask in an interview, and the evidence clearly suggests employers use everything they can obtain from social media to make decisions. Given the increasing role of social media in everyday life for most new entrants into the labor pool, the ability to go beyond the formal interview when obtaining information about applicants is only going to increase in the years ahead.[43]

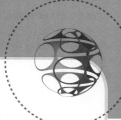

Facebook: Where Do Employers Go to Collect Illegal Information?

More than a third of U.S. employers admit to searching social networking sites to obtain information about job applicants. More often than not, these searches focus mainly on issues related to drug use, unprofessional behavior, or problems with previous employers or co-workers. This kind of information could clearly be job related and would be considered by most to be effective due diligence. However, social media sites contain all sorts of information that may not be job related, as well as information that employers would be strictly prohibited from collecting as part of the formal selection process. The question becomes: Do employers tap into social networks for information that they would not be legally allowed to collect in an interview?

In order to test this question, researchers from Carnegie-Mellon University sent out 4,000 fabricated résumés to 15 employers and then created Facebook sites for each of these fictitious persons. The Facebook sites provided religious information that made it clear that the person was Christian versus Muslim, but it was impossible to discern this in the résumé or the name attached to the résumé. On average, despite the fact that the résumé revealed no information regarding religion, only 2% of the applicants who appeared to be Muslim on Facebook received callbacks versus 17% for applicants who appeared to be Christian. Thus, it appears that employers can and do access information online that they would not be legally allowed to obtain in an interview.

Clearly, the legal landscape concerning the use of social media for screening purposes is evolving and changing quickly, and it is hard for regulators in the information age to keep up with all the new and different ways that employers can obtain information. From a job applicant's perspective, however, one might want to control what one can control, and hence it is wise to study your own Facebook page with at least as much scrutiny as some employer might.

DISCUSSION QUESTIONS

1. How might you become aware of the fact that an employer went above and beyond the materials you submitted when evaluating you for employment?
2. If you knew an employer searched information about you online, would this make you more or less attracted to work for that company?

SOURCES: R. Jacobson, "Facebook Snooping on Job Candidates May Backfire on Employers," *Scientific American,* January 13, 2014; J. Valentino-Devries, "Bosses May Use Social Media to Discriminate Against Job Seekers," *The Wall Street Journal,* November 20, 2013, www.wsj.com.

REFERENCES, APPLICATION BLANKS, AND BACKGROUND CHECKS

Just as few employers would think of hiring someone without an interview, nearly all employers also use some method for getting background information on applicants before an interview. This information can be solicited from the people who know the candidate through reference checks.

The evidence on the reliability and validity of reference checks suggests that these are, at best, weak predictors of future success on the job. The main reason for this low validity is that the evaluations supplied in most reference letters are so positive that it is hard to differentiate applicants. This problem with reference letters has two causes. First, the applicant usually gets to choose who writes the letter and can thus choose only those writers who think the highest of her abilities. Second, because letter writers can never be sure who will read the letters, they may justifiably fear that supplying damaging information about someone could come back to haunt them. Thus, it is clearly not in the past employers' interest to reveal too much information beyond job title and years of service. Another problem with reference checks is that applicants do not always tell the truth when it comes to listing their references. In fact, 30% of the companies that check references find false or misleading references on applications. Michael Erwin, a career advisor at Career Builder, notes, "For some reason, people think companies aren't going to check their references and therefore they think they can get away with all sorts of fabrications. In reality, 80% of companies do in fact check references prior to offering someone an interview or prior to making an offer.[44]

The evidence on the utility of biographical information collected directly from job applicants is much more positive, especially for certain outcomes like turnover.[45] The low cost of obtaining such information significantly enhances its utility, especially when the information is used in conjunction with a well-designed, follow-up interview that complements, rather than duplicates, the biographical information bank.

One of the most important elements of biographical information deals with educational background. In some cases, employers are looking for specialized educational backgrounds reflected in functional degrees such as business or nursing or engineering, but in other cases, employers are just looking for critical thinking and problem solving skills that might be associated with any college degree.[46] For example, Chip Kelly, the coach of the Philadelphia Eagles football team, places more emphasis on drafting players who have completed their college degrees than any other coach in the National Football League (NFL). At a time when more and more of the best players come out of college early, this may seem counterintuitive. Kelly feels that the complexity of his offensive and defensive schemes demands someone who has proven they can successfully "hit the books," whether those are playbooks or textbooks.[47] The evidence seems to back up this belief in the sense that of the four teams in the NFL with the most fifth-year seniors, three of them—Seattle, Denver, and New England—played in the Super Bowl in 2014 and 2015.

This focus on education is attributed to the nature of the economy, which increasingly demands people with high levels of education. Indeed, it is ironic that despite relatively high levels of employment, many employers find it impossible to find people with the skills they need.[48] The term "education gap" has been coined to capture the difference between the average years of education required in a job listing in a given area, and the average years of education in that same area. For the nation as a whole, the "education gap" runs at about 5%, but in some cities like Las Vegas the number exceeds 10%. Areas that have larger education gaps experience much higher rates of unemployment and are usually the last to show signs of job recovery during an economic expansion.[49]

Again, as with the interview, the biggest concern with the use of biographical data is that applicants who supply the information may be motivated to misrepresent themselves. Résumé fraud is on the rise and one survey indicated that roughly 45% of job applications that were audited contained some amount of inaccurate material. One recent and highly public example of this occurred at the Spokane chapter of the NAACP, which is described in the "Integrity in Action" box.

In order to prevent embarrassing episodes, many employers hire outside companies to do background checks on employees. For example, when Steve Masiello applied for a position coaching basketball at the University of South Florida, a routine background check revealed that he had lied on his application when he stated that he had earned a degree in communications from the University of Kentucky in 2000. This came as an embarrassment to Masiello's current employer, Manhattan College, which also required a college degree for any top coaching position, but apparently never checked on this when they hired Masiello.[50] A similar failure to conduct a routine background check was partially to blame for the 2015 jailbreak at the Clinton Correctional Facility in New York City, where an employee helped two convicted murderers escape.[51] An investigation in the wake of this incident revealed widespread lapses and failures to conduct adequate background checks at the prison.[52]

INTEGRITY IN ACTION

Race and Racial Identity: One and the Same?

The National Association for the Advancement of Colored People (NAACP) has never had a requirement that leaders within the organization had to be African American, and many white Americans have served the association with distinction in a variety of roles. However, in the summer of 2015, when it became clear that the head of the Spokane chapter of the NAACP had been pretending to be black when in fact, both of her parents were white, this sparked a national debate about what it means to be African American—specifically, whether or not "identifying as black" is the same as being black.

Rachel Dolezal went to great lengths to appear to be black. She attended Howard University, a traditional black college, taught African American studies at Eastern Washington University, and often publically referred to a black friend of hers as her father. In addition to serving as head of the Spokane NAACP, she was appointed by the city's mayor on a police oversight committee on race relations. On the application for that position, she checked the box "African American," and in an interview with Spokane's KERM television station, Dolezal stated that "if I was asked, I would definitely say that yes, I consider myself to be black."

However, the fact that both of her biological parents were 100% white means that checking the African American box on her employment application was a lie. The city of Spokane immediately launched an ethics commission to investigate the matter, and Dolezal eventually stepped down from her post at the NAACP. Although many within the NAACP recognized her valuable service to the association, as one member noted, "You just don't get to put on blackness like this season's trendy coat. You can always take it off and black people can't. . . there is a shared history and a shared common experience in the present that she can't authentically claim."

DISCUSSION QUESTIONS

1. What might motivate someone to claim identity to a racial or ethnic group in which he or she really does not belong?

2. In an age where people are increasingly of mixed parentage, does a single check-the-box categorization system for race still make sense?

SOURCES: C. Valdary, "What Ralph Ellison Could Tell Rachel Dolezal," *The Wall Street Journal,* June 17, 2015, www.wsj.com; G. Botelho, "Ex-NAACP Leader Rachel Dolezal: 'I Identify As Black,'" *CNN,* June 17, 2015, www.cnn.com; Z. Elinson, "Rachel Dolezal Resigns As Head of Spokane NAACP Chapter," *The Wall Street Journal,* June 15, 2015, www.wsj.com.

Although the use of background checks is increasingly common in the United States, they are rarely used in Europe. There are several reasons for these differences between Europe and the United States. First, in terms of values and culture, in Europe, the applicant's right to privacy trumps the organization's right to know. As noted by Andrew Boling, partner at Baker and McKenzie, a Chicago-based HR outsourcing firm, "outside the United States, individual privacy rights enjoy the same protections that we give to our First Amendment—in Europe what's private, stays private."[53] Thus, a U.S. firm that seeks an employee's consent to do a background check is likely to be denied in Europe, and performing the check without consent would be illegal in many countries.

Second, relative to the United States, one sees far fewer incidences of workplace violence in Europe, and the rates of theft and fraud are also much lower. Similarly, unlike Americans, Europeans tend to carry less debt, and hence background checks for credit problems rarely turn up applicants whose financial situations are so dire that one might be afraid of trusting them around money. At the height of the U.S. financial crisis, for example, over 40% of people who were screened on credit card balances would

Privacy and Public Safety Collide on Germanwings Flight 9525

Germanwings Flight 9525 was well on its journey from Barcelona, Spain, to Düsseldorf, Germany, when it crashed into the French Alps killing all 149 people on board. Although every plane crash is a tragedy, two facts stood out in this case that made it especially tragic. First, it became clear that the co-pilot, Andreas Lubitz, intentionally drove the plane into the mountains as part of a suicide attempt. Lubitz locked the cabin door after the pilot left the cockpit, and ignored pleas from the rest of the flight crew while he crashed the plane. Second, it also became clear that prior to being hired at Germanwings, Lubitz had been repeatedly treated for mental illness and suicidal tendencies.

News of these two facts spurred a major debate regarding the selection of pilots, especially as this relates to uncovering evidence of mental illness. In the United States, health professions are legally required to report on any patients who are likely to engage in conduct that would result in serious harm to themselves or others. However, in Germany, the law emphasizes privacy, and the laws of that country bar doctors from revealing any medical information about their patients. German laws place responsibility for reporting mental health problems on the individual, and the belief is that forcing mental health officials to "out" their patients merely drives mental illness underground. People with problems will not come forward for treatment for fear of losing their jobs if their condition is reported.

Clearly, this system broke down in the Andreas Lubitz case. In fact, investigators found a note in his apartment from a doctor that would have excused him from work for a time period that included the day of the fatal crash, but this note was never shared with his employer. Thus, Germanwings claims that they had no knowledge of his condition either before or after he was hired. The question becomes—should they have—and will regulators and consumers allow this to continue in the future or demand changes in how Europe balances privacy rights against the rights of public safety?

DISCUSSION QUESTION

German and U.S. laws clearly differ on the role of public reporting of mental illness. Which side do you think has the better argument, and, in your opinion, how should a society balance the rights to privacy and public safety?

SOURCES: S. Meichtry and R. Wall, "Germanwings Investigation to Focus on How Industry Vets Psychological Backgrounds of Pilots," *The Wall Street Journal,* March 31, 2015, www.wsj.com; N. Kulish and M. Eddy, "Germanwings Co-Pilot Was Treated for 'Suicidal Tendencies,' Authorities Say," *The New York Times,* March 30, 2015, www.nytimes.com; E. Goode, "Role of Illness in Germanwings Crash Raises Worry about Stigma," *The New York Times,* March 30, 2015, www.nytimes.com.

have been rejected as viable hires given most standards adopted by companies that do background checks. The percentage of similarly situated bad risks in Europe is simply much lower.[54]

Third, although the greater deference to individual privacy would seem to put the employer at a disadvantage, on the other side of the equation, the legal concept of negligent hiring is also largely unheard of in Europe. This reduces the need for employers to show copious amounts of due diligence in order to protect themselves legally. As in any country, individual employees in Europe may run afoul of the law or commit egregious acts; however, this is an issue between the offender and the law, and one's employing organization is rarely held legally responsible for their actions. As the "Competing Through Globalization" box shows, this view may be changing in Europe, however, due to the facts involving the crash of Germanwings Flight 9525 in 2015.

PHYSICAL ABILITY TESTS

Although automation and other advances in technology have eliminated or modified many physically demanding occupational tasks, many jobs still require certain physical abilities or psychomotor abilities. In these cases, tests of physical abilities may be relevant not only to predicting performance but to predicting occupational injuries and disabilities as well.[55] There are seven classes of tests in this area: ones that evaluate (1) muscular tension, (2) muscular power, (3) muscular endurance, (4) cardiovascular endurance, (5) flexibility, (6) balance, and (7) coordination.[56]

The criterion-related validities for these kinds of tests for certain jobs like firefighting are quite strong.[57] Unfortunately, these tests, particularly the strength tests, are likely to have an adverse impact on some applicants with disabilities and many female applicants. For example, roughly two-thirds of all males score higher than the highest-scoring female on muscular tension tests.[58]

Because of this there are two key questions to ask in deciding whether to use these kinds of tests. First, is the physical ability essential to performing the job and is it mentioned prominently enough in the job description? Neither the Civil Rights Act nor the ADA requires employers to hire individuals who cannot perform essential job functions, and both accept a written job description as evidence of the essential functions of the job. Second, is there a probability that failure to adequately perform the job would result in some risk to the safety or health of the applicant, co-workers, or clients? The "direct threat" clause of the ADA makes it clear that adverse impact against those with disabilities is warranted under such conditions.

Invoking this clause can sometimes cause controversy, as in 2014, when United Parcel Service (UPS) cited this clause to support the decision to fire a worker who got pregnant because she could not lift packages weighing more than 20 pounds. UPS was sued, because it routinely made accommodations for injured employees, and the same woman who was fired for being pregnant would have been accommodated had she thrown her back out. UPS eventually settled out of court and eliminated this policy, probably as much for public relations reasons as well as for any other factor related to business necessity.[59]

COGNITIVE ABILITY TESTS

Cognitive ability tests differentiate individuals based on their mental rather than physical capacities. Cognitive ability has many different facets, although we will focus only on three dominant ones. **Verbal comprehension** refers to a person's capacity to understand and use written and spoken language. **Quantitative ability** concerns the speed and accuracy with which one can solve arithmetic problems of all kinds. **Reasoning ability,** a broader concept, refers to a person's capacity to invent solutions to many diverse problems.

Some jobs require only one or two of these facets of cognitive ability. Under these conditions, maintaining the separation among the facets is appropriate. However, many jobs that are high in complexity require most, if not all, of the facets, and hence one general test is often as good as many tests of separate facets. Highly reliable commercial tests measuring these kinds of abilities are widely available, and they are generally valid predictors of job performance in many different kinds of contexts, including widely different countries.[60] The validity of these kinds of tests is related to the complexity of the job, however, in that one sees higher criterion-related validation for complex jobs than for simple jobs.

One of the major drawbacks to these tests is that they typically have adverse impact on some minority groups. Indeed, the size of the differences is so large that some have advocated abandoning these types of tests for making decisions regarding who will be accepted for certain schools or jobs. This is somewhat ironic in the sense that these

Cognitive Ability Tests
Tests that include three dimensions: verbal comprehension, quantitative ability and reasoning ability.

Verbal Comprehension
Refers to a person's capacity to understand and use written and spoken language.

Quantitative Ability
Concerns the speed and accuracy with which one can solve arithmetic problems of all kinds.

Reasoning Ability
Refers to a person's capacity to invent solutions to many diverse problems.

standardized tests were originally designed to be anti-elitist and to help identify talented individuals who may not be high in socioeconomic status but were still very bright by objective standards. However, over time, the tests have become a major hurdle to many disadvantaged groups by restricting their college opportunities, and thus are now perceived as elitist due to their adverse impact on minorities.[61]

The notion of race norming, alluded to earlier, was born of the desire to use these high-utility tests in a manner that avoided adverse impact. Although race norming was made illegal by the recent amendments to the Civil Rights Act, some have advocated the use of banding to both achieve the benefits of testing and minimize its adverse impact. The concept of *banding* suggests that similar groups of people whose scores differ by only a small amount all be treated as having the same score. Then, within any band, preferential treatment is given to minorities. Most observers feel preferential treatment of minorities is acceptable when scores are tied, and banding simply broadens the definition of what constitutes a tied score. Like race norming, banding is very controversial, especially if the bands are set too wide.[62]

As with all the selection measures we have seen so far, one is always concerned that applicants may be tempted to cheat in order to score well on whatever instrument is used to make selection decisions and that is also the case here. Cheating on tests is hardly a new phenomenon, however. What is new is the degree to which the use of computerized testing and social networking has changed the nature and scope of cheating. The term "question harvesting" has been coined to capture the process whereby test takers use advanced technology to download questions or capture images of questions with digital cameras or other devices while taking a test, and then transmit the content of the test wirelessly to people outside the testing facility who then post the questions for future test takers.[63] Cheating scandals such as these become particularly controversial when allegations are based on nationality. For example, the evidence of wrongdoing with respect to test scores reported from China and South Korea grew so large in 2014 that the Educational Testing Service withheld the scores for applicants from these countries until all the allegations could be sorted out.[64]

PERSONALITY INVENTORIES

While ability tests attempt to categorize individuals relative to what they can do, personality measures tend to categorize individuals by what they are like. The number of firms employing personality tests as screens has ballooned over the years, from just 26% in 2000 to just under 60% in 2014.[65] Research suggests that there are five major dimensions of personality, known as "the Big Five": (1) extroversion, (2) adjustment, (3) agreeableness, (4) conscientiousness, and (5) openness to experience. Table 6.3 lists each of these with a corresponding list of adjectives that fit each dimension.

Table 6.3
The Five Major Dimensions of Personality Inventories

1. Extroversion	Sociable, gregarious, assertive, talkative, expressive
2. Adjustment	Emotionally stable, nondepressed, secure, content
3. Agreeableness	Courteous, trusting, good-natured, tolerant, cooperative, forgiving
4. Conscientiousness	Dependable, organized, persevering, thorough, achievement-oriented
5. Openness to experience	Curious, imaginative, artistically sensitive, broad-minded, playful

Although it is possible to find reliable, commercially available measures of each of these traits, the evidence for their validity and generalizability is mixed at best.[66] For example, conscientiousness, which captures the concepts of self-regulation and self-motivation, is one of the few factors that displays any validity across a number of different job categories, and many real-world managers rate this as one of the most important characteristics they look for in employees. People who are high in conscientiousness tend to show very good self-control when pursuing work goals and are especially adept at overcoming challenges and obstacles relative to people low in this trait.[67]

Instead of showing strong direct and positive correlations with future performance across all jobs, the validity coefficients associated with personality measures tend to be job specific. For example, extroverts tend to excel in jobs likes sales or politics because these jobs demand gregariousness and assertiveness, two of the central features shared by all extroverts. In contrast, introverts are better at studying and working in isolation, and hence they are best at jobs like accountant or research scientist because these jobs demand patience and vigilance. Extroverts tend to enjoy working in team-oriented environments more than introverts, but this does not always spill over into performance differences for engaging in teamwork.[68] Both extroverts and introverts can become effective leaders, although they achieve effectiveness in different ways. Extroverts tend to be top-down, autocratic and charismatic leaders who motivate followers by getting them emotionally engaged. In contrast, effective introverted leaders tend to be more bottom-up, participative leaders who listen to empowered employees and then engineer reward structures so that people are working toward their own self-interests.[69]

One important element of staffing in team-based structures, however, relates to how the selection of one team member influences the requirements associated with other team members.[70] In some cases, organizations might try to select people who have very similar values and personality traits in order to create a strong team culture. When there is a strong team culture, everyone shares the same views and traits, promoting harmony and cohesiveness.[71]

In other cases, people putting together a team go out of their way to make sure that the people on the team have different values and personalities. The hope here is that a diversity of opinion promotes internal debate and creativity.[72] If one does take this approach to staffing a team, it is critical that one also takes steps to make sure that there are not strong "fault lines" within the group that create strong and opposing subgroups. Diversity can be built into a team, and subgrouping problems avoided with judicious selection. For example, imagine a four-person group comprised of two men and two women, two marketing experts and two engineers, and two people from the United States and two people from France. One way this diversity could configure itself is such that the two males were also both engineers and both from the United States, and the two women were both marketing experts from France. In this configuration, the group has a strong fault line because all three dimensions of diversity converge, and it is easy to predict how this group might break apart into two subgroups. In contrast, the same level of diversity could be configured in a group where one of the men was an engineer, but one of the women was an engineer also. Similarly, one of the marketing experts was a man and one was woman. Finally, one of the men was from France and one was from the United States. In this second configuration, there is no strong fault line, and it is harder to see how the group is likely to fall apart.[73]

The concept of "emotional intelligence" is also important in team contexts and has been used to describe people who are especially effective in fluid and socially intensive contexts. Emotional intelligence is traditionally conceived of having five aspects: (1) self-awareness (knowledge of one's strengths and weaknesses), (2) self-regulation (the ability to keep disruptive emotions in check), (3) self-motivation (how to motivate oneself and persevere in the face of obstacles), (4) empathy (the ability to sense and read emotions in others), and (5) social skills (the ability to manage the emotions of other people).[74] Relative to standard measures of ability and personality, there has not been a great deal of scientific research on emotional intelligence, and critics have raised both theoretical and empirical questions about the construct. Theoretically, some have argued that the construct is overly broad and confuses aspects of perception, ability, and temperament that are best conceptualized as separate processes.[75] Empirically, the data seem to suggest that if one holds scores on the variables captured by the five-factor model of personality and scores on tests of cognitive ability constant, there is very little, if any, added predictive power attributable to emotional intelligence.[76]

Regardless of the nature of the context, the validity for almost all of the Big Five factors in terms of predicting job performance also seems to be higher when the scores are not obtained from the applicant but are instead taken from other people.[77] The lower validity associated with self-reports of personality can be traced to three factors. First, people sometimes lack insight into what their own personalities are actually like (or how they are perceived by others), so their scores are inaccurate or unreliable. Second, people's personalities sometimes vary across different contexts. Thus, someone may be very conscientious when it comes to social activities such as planning a family wedding or a fraternity party, but less conscientious when it comes to doing a paid job. Thus, contextualized measures that add the term "at work" to standard personality items often perform better as predictors than standard noncontextualized measures. On average, "contextualizing" measures on personality tests in this manner can boost their average validity coefficient from around .10 to .25.[78] Third, with some traits like ability, validity coefficients are higher when one uses a curvilinear prediction instead of just a straight linear prediction. That is, with a trait like emotional stability, the best job performers often score in the middle range, and for a lot of jobs, both being too nervous and being too calm can be problematic.[79] This kind of curvilinear finding is rarely found with ability measures, in the sense that people who are "overqualified" on ability typically perform at the highest levels with evidence of a drop-off at extreme levels.[80]

Finally, one factor that also limits the validity of personality items is that, unlike cognitive ability scores, applicants find it easier to fake traits by providing socially desirable responses to questions. Research suggests that when people fill out these inventories when applying for a job, their scores on conscientiousness and emotional stability are much higher relative to when they are just filling out the same questionnaires anonymously for research purposes.[81] In addition to being "fake-able," some of the items that tap emotional stability start to get close to categories of mental illness that reflect protected groups according to the ADA, and some applicants have legally challenged these sorts of screening devices on that score.[82] Also, if people fail a personality test and then take the same test again in the future, their scores seem to drastically increase.[83] Several steps can be used to try to reduce faking. For example, if employers simply warn applicants that they are going to cross-check the applicants' self-ratings with other people, this seems to reduce faking.[84] Also, the degree to which people can fake various personality traits is enhanced with questionnaires, and one sees much less faking of traits when interviewers are assessing the characteristics.[85] All of this reinforces the idea that it is better to obtain this information from people other than the job applicant, and that it is better to use this information to reject low scorers but not necessarily hire all higher scorers on the basis of self-reports alone.[86]

WORK SAMPLES

Work-sample tests attempt to simulate the job in a prehiring context to observe how the applicant performs in the simulated job. The degree of fidelity in work samples can vary greatly. In some cases, applicants respond to a set of standardized hypothetical case studies and role play how they would react to certain situations.[87] Often these standardized role plays employ interactive video technology to create "virtual job auditions."[88] Simulations involving video-based role-plays seem to be more engaging and display higher levels of predictive validity relative to paper-and-pencil approaches.[89] In other cases, the job applicants are brought to the employers' location and actually perform the job for a short time period as part of a "job tryout."[90]

In some cases, employers will sponsor competitions where contestants (who at this point are not even considered job applicants) vie for attention by going head-to-head in solving certain job-related problems. These sorts of competitions have been common in some industries like architecture and fashion design, but their use is spreading across many other business contexts. These competitions tend to be cost effective in generating a lot of interest, and some have attracted as many as 1,000 contestants who bring their talents to bear on specific problems faced by the employing organization.[91] Competitions are particularly well-suited for assessing and "discovering" young people who may not have extended track records or portfolios to evaluate. For example, "hack-athons," that is, competitions between computer programmers, were once only held on campuses with college students. However, today these contests are increasingly being won by high school dropouts who bypassed college altogether to focus exclusively on programming and application development using web-based tools generally accessible to a wider audience.[92]

As part of its own fight in the war for talent, Google sponsors an event called "Google Code Jam," which attracts more than 10,000 contestants a year from all over the world. This one-day competition requires contestants work to solve some very difficult programming problems under relatively high levels of time pressure. For example, finalists have to develop software that would perform unique and difficult searches employing a minimum number of "clicks" or develop a complex interactive war game from scratch in under two hours. The winner of the contest receives $7,000 and a guaranteed job at Google's prestigious Research and Development Center, but, in fact, Google usually winds up hiring more than half of the 50 finalists each year (but that is not guaranteed). The finalists in this contest represent the best of the best in terms of the world's top programmers, and as Robert Hughes, director of the Code Jam, notes, "Wherever the best talent is, Google wants them."[93]

With all these advantages of work-sample tests come three drawbacks. First, by their very nature the tests are job-specific, so generalizability is low. Second, partly because a new test has to be developed for each job and partly because of their nonstandardized formats, these tests are relatively expensive to develop. It is much more cost-effective to purchase a commercially available cognitive ability test that can be used for a number of different job categories within the company than to develop a test for each job. Finally, at least with respect to work-sample tests developed as contests and competitions, these events tend to attract more male applicants than female applicants. In fact, for evening occupations where roughly 50% of the job incumbents are women, only 15% of the people who show up for competitions for such jobs are female, suggesting this is a practice that could easily lead to adverse impact if not carefully monitored.[94]

Assessment Center
A process in which multiple raters evaluate employees' performance on a number of exercises.

In the area of managerial selection, work-sample tests are typically the cornerstone in assessment centers. Generically, the term **assessment center** is used to describe a wide variety of specific selection programs that employ multiple selection methods to rate either applicants or job incumbents on their managerial potential. Someone attending an assessment center would typically experience work-sample tests such as an in-basket test and several tests of more general abilities and personality. Because assessment centers employ multiple selection methods, their criterion-related validity tends to be quite high. Assessment centers seem to tap a number of different characteristics, but "problem-solving ability" stands out as probably the most important skill tapped via this method.[95]

HONESTY TESTS AND DRUG TESTS

Many problems that confront society also exist within organizations, which has led to two new kinds of tests: honesty tests and drug-use tests. Many companies formerly employed polygraph tests, or lie detectors, to evaluate job applicants, but this changed with the passage of the Polygraph Act in 1988. This act banned the use of polygraphs in employment screening for most organizations. However, it did not eliminate the problem of theft by employees. As a result, the paper-and-pencil honesty testing industry was born.

Paper-and-pencil honesty tests come in a number of different forms. Some directly emphasize questions dealing with past theft admissions or associations with people who stole from employers. Other items are less direct and tap more basic traits such as social conformity, conscientiousness, or emotional stability.[96] A large-scale independent review of validity studies suggests they can predict both theft and other disruptive behaviors. However, the reported correlations tend to be much higher when the research studies were conducted by test publishers who market the tests relative to outside, objective parties with a less obvious conflict of interest. Thus, it is always a good idea for organizations to check the predictive accuracy of these kinds of tests for themselves and not rely solely on the results reported by test publishers.[97]

As is the case with measures of personality, some people are concerned that people confronting an honesty test can fake their way to a passing score. The evidence suggests that people instructed to fake their way to a high score (indicating honesty) can do so. However, it is not clear that this affects the validity of the predictions made using such tests. That is, it seems that despite this built-in bias, scores on the test still predict future theft. Thus, the effect of the faking bias is not large enough to detract from the test's validity.[98]

As with theft, there is a growing perception of the problems caused by drug use among employees. The major controversies surrounding drug tests involve not their reliability and validity but whether they represent an invasion of privacy, an unreasonable search and seizure, or a violation of due process. Urinalysis and blood tests are invasive procedures, and accusing someone of drug use is a serious matter. Employers considering the use of drug tests would be well advised to make sure that their drug-testing programs conform to some general rules. First, these tests should be administered systematically to all applicants for the same job. Second, testing seems more defensible for jobs that involve safety hazards associated with failure to perform.[99] Test results should be reported back to the applicant, who should be allowed an avenue of appeal (and perhaps retesting). Tests should be conducted in an environment that is as unintrusive as possible, and results from those tests should be held in strict confidence. Also, when testing current employees, the program should be part of a wider organizational program that provides rehabilitation counseling.[100] Finally, employers who employ drug testing also have to recognize the changing legal status for drugs like marijuana over time. Marijuana is legal for medicinal or recreational use in 23 states, and many employers are backing off requirements associated with marijuana. Ironically, one such employer is the Federal Bureau of Investigation (FBI), which noticed that many of the young applicants best skilled for tracking down cyber crimes also have a history of marijuana use. James Comey, the director of the FBI, suggested the agency may have to loosen its no-tolerance policy for marijuana in order to attract this talent. Comey notes, "I have to hire a great workforce to compete with cyber criminals and some of the best kids want to smoke weed on the way to the interview."[101] Thus, the quest for deriving competitive advantage from one's workforce sometimes takes some odd twists.

A LOOK BACK

Diversity and Discrimination at Abercrombie & Fitch

The decisions that organizations make regarding who is going to be part of the team and who is going to be turned away are some of the most important decisions that a firm will make in terms of gaining a competitive advantage. In addition, as we saw in our opening vignette, these decisions also have a major impact on the lives of individuals, and it may sometimes require flexibility to project a particular brand image and also employ a diverse workforce. The importance of these decisions means that they have to be based upon procedures that have been empirically validated and not left to idiosyncratic judgments of untrained individuals who may be subject to stereotyped biases. This chapter has summarized hundreds of years of research and demonstrated a large and varied set of tactics that firms can use to make the right hiring decisions when it comes to the selection process.

QUESTIONS

1. Based on this chapter, what are the best methods of obtaining information about job applicants?
2. What are the best characteristics to look for in applicants, and how does this depend on the nature of the job?
3. If you could use only two of the methods described in this chapter and could assess only two of the characteristics discussed, which would you choose, and why?

SUMMARY

In this chapter we examined the five critical standards with which all personnel selection methods should conform: reliability, validity, generalizability, utility, and legality. We also looked at nine different selection methods currently used in organizations and evaluated each with respect to these five standards. Table 6.4 summarizes these selection methods and can be used as a guide in deciding which test to use for a specific purpose. Although we discussed each type of test individually, it is important to note in closing that there is no need to use only one type of test for any one job. Indeed, managerial assessment centers use many different forms of tests over a two- or three-day period to learn as much as possible about candidates for important executive positions. As a result, highly accurate predictions are often made, and the validity associated with the judicious use of multiple tests is higher than for tests used in isolation.

Table 6.4
A Summary of Personnel Selection Methods

METHOD	RELIABILITY	VALIDITY	GENERALIZABILITY	UTILITY	LEGALITY
Interviews	Low when unstructured and when assessing nonobservable traits	Low if unstructured and nonbehavioral	Low	Low, especially because of expense	Low because of subjectivity and potential interviewer bias; also, lack of validity makes job-relatedness low
Reference checks	Low, especially when obtained from letters	Low because of lack of range in evaluations	Low	Low, although not expensive to obtain	Those writing letters may be concerned with charges of libel
Biographical information	High test–retest, especially for verifiable information	High criterion-related validity; low in content validity	Usually job-specific, but have been successfully developed for many job types	High; inexpensive way to collect vast amounts of potentially relevant data	May have adverse impact; thus often develop separate scoring keys based on sex or race
Physical ability tests	High	Moderate criterion-related validity; high content validity for some jobs	Low; pertain only to physically demanding jobs	Moderate for some physical jobs; may prevent expensive injuries and disability	Often have adverse impact on women and people with disabilities; need to establish job-relatedness
Cognitive ability tests	High	Moderate criterion-related validity; content validation inappropriate	High; predictive for most jobs, although best for complex jobs	High; low cost and wide application across diverse jobs in companies	Often have adverse impact on race, especially for African Americans, though decreasing over time
Personality inventories	High	Low to moderate criterion-related validity for most traits; content validation inappropriate	Low; few traits predictive for many jobs, except conscientiousness	Low, although inexpensive for jobs where specific traits are relevant	Low because of cultural and sex differences on most traits, and low job-relatedness in general
Work-sample tests	High	High criterion and content validity	Usually job-specific, but have been successfully developed for many job types	High, despite the relatively high cost to develop	High because of low adverse impact and high job-relatedness
Honesty tests	Insufficient independent evidence	Insufficient independent evidence	Insufficient independent evidence	Insufficient independent evidence	Insufficient history of litigation, but will undergo scrutiny
Drug tests	High	High	High	Expensive, but may yield high payoffs for health-related costs	May be challenged on invasion-of-privacy grounds

KEY TERMS

Reliability, 225
Validity, 228
Criterion-related validity, 228
Predictive validation, 229
Concurrent validation, 229

Content validation, 231
Generalizability, 232
Utility, 233
Situational interview, 241
Cognitive ability tests, 247

Verbal comprehension, 247
Quantitative ability, 247
Reasoning ability, 247
Assessment center, 252

DISCUSSION QUESTIONS

1. We examined nine different types of selection methods in this chapter. Assume that you were just rejected for a job based on one of these methods. Obviously, you might be disappointed and angry regardless of what method was used to make this decision, but can you think of two or three methods that might leave you most distressed? In general, why might the acceptability of the test to applicants be an important standard to add to the five we discussed in this chapter?

2. Videotaping applicants in interviews is becoming an increasingly popular means of getting multiple assessments of that individual from different perspectives. Can you think of some reasons why videotaping interviews might also be useful in evaluating the interviewer? What would you look for in an interviewer if you were evaluating one on videotape?

3. Distinguish between concurrent and predictive validation designs, discussing why the latter is preferred over the former. Examine each of the nine selection methods discussed in this chapter and determine which of these would have their validity most and least affected by the type of validation design employed.

4. Some have speculated that in addition to increasing the validity of decisions, employing rigorous selection methods has symbolic value for organizations. What message is sent to applicants about the organization through hiring practices, and how might this message be reinforced by recruitment programs that occur before selection and training programs that occur after selection?

SELF-ASSESSMENT EXERCISE

Additional assignable self-assessments available in Connect.

Reviews of research about personality have identified five common aspects of personality, referred to as the Big Five personality traits. Find out which are your most prominent traits. Read each of the following statements, marking "Yes" if it describes you and "No" if it does not.

1. In conversations I tend to do most of the talking.
2. Often people look to me to make decisions.
3. I am a very active person.
4. I usually seem to be in a hurry.
5. I am dominant, forceful, and assertive.
6. I have a very active imagination.
7. I have an active fantasy life.
8. How I feel about things is important to me.
9. I find it easy to feel myself what others are feeling.
10. I think it's interesting to learn and develop new hobbies.
11. My first reaction is to trust people.
12. I believe that most persons are basically well intentioned.
13. I'm not crafty or shy.
14. I'd rather not talk about myself and my accomplishments.
15. I'd rather praise others than be praised myself.
16. I come into situations being fully prepared.
17. I pride myself on my sound judgment.
18. I have a lot of self-discipline.
19. I try to do jobs carefully so they don't have to be done again.
20. I like to keep everything in place so I know where it is.
21. I enjoy performing under pressure.
22. I am seldom sad or depressed.
23. I'm an even-tempered person.
24. I am levelheaded in emergencies.
25. I feel I am capable of coping with most of my problems.

The statements are grouped into categories. Statements 1–5 describe extroversion, 6–10 openness to experience, 11–15 agreeableness, 16–20 conscientiousness, and 21–25 emotional stability. The more times you wrote "Yes" for the statements in a category, the more likely you are to have the associated trait.

EXERCISING STRATEGY

Pink Quotas Aim at Cultural Change

Although women constitute roughly half of Italy's population, as a group, they comprise only 6% of corporate board members in Italian companies. This is one of the lowest levels in Europe and can be traced to larger societal issues. For example, labor force participation rates for Italian women stand at 46%, which is the lowest rate in any major European country. This low rate can be attributed to rigid labor laws that make it difficult for women to work part time, and thus many women leave the labor market after having children, and never return. This attrition then "trickles up," creating a situation where few women have acquired the skills and experience necessary to hold corporate board positions.

In an effort to help reverse this trend, the Italian government passed a new law that required all Italian listed and state-owned companies to ensure that 33% of their board seats are held by women by 2014. This sort of law, often referred to as a "Pink Quota," is increasingly common in Europe, but the rate set by the Italian government is much more aggressive than rates set in France (20% by 2014) and the United Kingdom (25% by 2015). Also, unlike statutes in Sweden and the Netherlands that promote voluntary compliance, the Italian program establishes a mandate. As Joyce Bigio, a recently added member to the board at Fiat notes, "I have always been convinced of the need for affirmative action. It is the only way to break into certain areas and correct an imbalance."

Ironically, because this new demand for labor often runs up against a short supply of European candidates, many companies trying to come into compliance with these laws wind up bringing in American women to fill board positions. Women already occupy close to 20% of the corporate board positions in the United States and thus constitute an experienced pool of candidates from which to choose. In addition, many European companies compete in U.S. product markets, and thus, in addition to experience, American women bring an intuitive understanding of U.S. consumers that is not shared by many European women.

Recruiting American women for a European board is often difficult, however. Part of this is attributable to the time commitment and overseas travel required by such positions, but the very existence of the quota system itself is also a detriment. Helena Morrissey, a veteran of several U.S. boards, speaks for many when she notes, "I don't support the European plan to force female quotas on boards. I wouldn't want to be part of a board because I am filling a quota." Many Italian women share this feeling, but at the same time, see the need for change. Elisabetta Magistretti, who sits on three different Italian corporate boards, captures this sentiment when she states, "It's been disappointing for me as a woman to need a pitchfork to join a board, but without this new law companies would have never thought about us. Now it is up to women to demonstrate they're well-prepared for the job."

QUESTIONS

1. How does greater representation of women on corporate boards promote both societal goals and competiveness goals at the same time?
2. What long-term steps can be taken by countries and companies to eliminate the need for quotas over time?

SOURCES: D. Brady, "Hard Choices," *Bloomberg Businessweek,* October 1, 2012, p. 88; J. S. Lublin, "Pink Quotas Alter Europe's Boards," *The Wall Street Journal,* September 11, 2012, www.wsj.com; G. Zampano, "Italy to Push 'Pink Quotas,'" *The Wall Street Journal,* June 5, 2012, www.wsj.com.

MANAGING PEOPLE

When Do the Unemployed Become Unemployable?

In the spring of 2012, some statistics associated with the U.S. economy were definitely showing signs of improvement. Employers had stepped up hiring, layoffs had slowed, and the unemployment rate began to drop. One statistic that stubbornly refused to move, however, was the long-term unemployment rate, typically defined as someone who has been out of work for over six months. In 2012, over 5.5 million workers had been unemployed for over six months, and a staggering 4 million had been out of work for 12 months. This latter figure is important because research suggests that long-term bouts of unemployment can sometimes make people unemployable. This creates an entire subclass of citizens that can never be hired, harming the competitive interests of both employers and the larger society in which they are embedded.

There are three reasons why long-term unemployment can scar potential job applicants for years. First, over time, the nature of work changes and people who have been outside the workforce may no longer have the skills needed for current jobs. For example, Andrew Bricknell was an automotive designer for several years, prior to being laid off at General Motors (GM). Bricknell struggled to find design work after he was laid off and eventually took a bus-driving job to make ends meet. When GM's fortunes turned around in 2012, the company began hiring in many job categories, including designers. However, by that time, car design had migrated from drafting boards to more sophisticated computer platforms that Bricknell had never seen, and hence he was no longer qualified for his old job.

Second, even when the skills required for a job have not changed, some employers seem to believe that long-term unemployment implies a lack of skills. That is, instead of testing for skills, employers just make the assumption that anyone out of work for an extended period of time must lack skills. For example, Amy Grimmer, an HR staffing specialist for a sales company, states openly that when trying to fill sales positions, "We're not looking at the unemployment pool. We feel like the sales people who are talented enough would have already found positions."

Finally, some employers seem to believe that regardless of one's skill level, long-term unemployment reflects a lack of conscientiousness and ambition on the part of a job applicant. In particular, if someone applies for a job only after their unemployment benefits expire, some employers believe that the person is lazy and would actually prefer to

not work if they could get away with it. Thus, rather than trying to directly assess conscientiousness with a personality inventory or from references from past employers (who become increasingly difficult to contact over extended time periods) applicants are rejected based upon a presumption of guilt. In reality, many individuals who have experienced long-term unemployment want nothing more than to get back to meaningful employment, but they face a form of discrimination that is not covered by any type of law.

QUESTIONS

1. How might a systematic and comprehensive system of testing and reference checking help eliminate some sources of long-term unemployment?
2. On the other hand, in what sense does the solution to this problem go beyond hiring practices of employers?

SOURCES: D. Akst, "How Employers See Prolonged Joblessness (and Why)," *The Wall Street Journal,* September 27, 2012, http://blogs.wsj.com; B. Casselman, "Time Not on the Side of the Jobless," *The Wall Street Journal,* March 26, 2012, www.wsj.com; S. Murray and C. McWhirter, "Long-term Unemployment Ripples Through One Town," *The Wall Street Journal,* January 18, 2012; D. Bennett, "Do the Unemployed Get a Second Act?" *Bloomberg Businessweek,* September 19, 2011, pp. 64–70.

HR IN SMALL BUSINESS

Kinaxis Chooses Sales Reps with Personality

Kinaxis is a software company headquartered in Ottawa, Ontario, that sells to clients around the world. Its specialty is software for supply chain management—all the processes and relationships through which companies obtain supplies as needed and get their products to customers on time and at minimal cost. This is a sophisticated type of product, tailored to a company's specific needs. Therefore, Kinaxis depends on salespeople who understand how businesses work, who listen carefully to identify needs, and who provide excellent customer service to maintain long-term business relationships.

Recently, Bob Dolan, vice president for sales at Kinaxis, needed to hire a sales team to serve clients in North America. The company had just one salesperson serving the continent, and Dolan wanted to add four more. He received about 100 resumes and wanted to select from these. He started by reviewing the resumes against job requirements and selected 20 candidates for a first round of interviews. The interview process helped Dolan cut the list of candidates in half, so he needed another way to narrow his options.

Dolan decided his next step would be personality testing. He hired a firm called Opus Productivity Solutions to administer a test called PDP ProScan to the remaining 10 candidates. In addition, Dolan himself took the test and had his current sales rep do the same. The existing salesperson was doing an excellent job, so the results of his test

could help Dolan and Opus pinpoint the characteristics of someone likely to succeed in sales at Kinaxis. Based on analysis of all the results, Opus created a benchmark of traits associated with success in the job.

Representatives from Opus also discussed the test results with each candidate, giving each one a chance to disagree with the scores. No one did. Dolan observed that all the candidates scored high in assertiveness and extroversion—not surprising for people in sales. In addition, two of them scored above the benchmark in conformity and below the benchmark in dominance. Those results suggested to Dolan that these candidates might be so eager to please that they would be quick to give in to whatever customers requested—a pattern that could become costly for the company. Dolan eliminated those two candidates.

That meant Dolan still had eight candidates to fill four positions. He asked each one to give him the names of major accounts he or she had signed up in the previous two years. Four candidates were able to come up with three or four large clients. Those were the candidates Dolan hired.

Since then, Dolan says his experience with personality testing has only reinforced his belief that this selection method helps Kinaxis identify the best candidates. For example, one sales rep had scored low on "pace," indicating that the individual might lack the patience needed for the slow cycles required to close a sale of a complex software system. Dolan hoped the issue could be overcome if he provided enough coaching, but in fact, the sales rep sometimes behaved impatiently, annoying prospects. After three years of trying to help him grow into the job, Dolan laid him off.

The company's commitment to careful selection is expressed on its website: "As a growing and determined company, we're always looking for people eager to push the limits of each day of what's possible." Kinaxis was recently named one of Canada's top employers for young people.

QUESTIONS

1. What selection methods did Bob Dolan use for hiring salespeople? Did he go about using these methods in the best order? What, if anything, would you change about the order of the methods used?

2. What were the advantages to Kinaxis of using personality tests to help select sales representatives? What were the disadvantages?

3. Given the information gathered from the selection methods, what process did Dolan use to make his selection decision? What improvements can you recommend to this process for decisions to hire sales reps in the future?

SOURCES: Susan Greco, "Personality Testing for Sales Recruits," *Inc.*, March 1, 2009, www.inc.com; and Kinaxis website, Corporate Overview and Careers pages, www.kinaxis.com, accessed June 30, 2015.

NOTES

1. V. Wadhwa, "America's Immigrant Brain Drain," *BusinessWeek*, March 16, 2009, p. 68.
2. D. Nishi, "Tackling Stereotypes Before Your Job Interview," *The Wall Street Journal*, August 2, 2014, www.wsj.com.
3. E. Bernstein, "Personality Research Says Change in Major Traits Occurs Naturally," *The Wall Street Journal*, April 22, 2014, www.wsj.com.
4. B. Weber, "Gender Bias by the Numbers," *Bloomberg Businessweek*, January 30, 2014.
5. C. H. Van Iddekinge and R. E. Ployhart, "Developments in the Criterion-Related Validation of Selection Procedures: A Critical Review and Recommendations for Practice," *Personnel Psychology* 61 (2008), pp. 871–925.
6. E. Gray, "Do You Understand Why Stars Twinkle?" *Time Magazine*, June 22, 2015.
7. J. Walker, "Meet the New Boss: Big Data," *The Wall Street Journal*, September 20, 2012, www.wsj.com.
8. D. Cormier-Smith, "AkzoNobel Selects Oracle Talent Management Cloud Services for Its Recruiting Needs," *The Wall Street Journal*, April 10, 2013, www.wsj.com.
9. A. Ito, "Hiring in the Age of Big Data," *Bloomberg Businessweek*, November 13, 2013, pp. 40–41.
10. F. Schmidt, H. Le, I. S. Oh, and J. Shaffer, "General Mental Ability, Job Performance, and Red Herrings: Responses to Osterman, Hauser, and Schmitt," *Academy of Management Perspectives* 21 (2007), pp. 64–76.
11. S. E. Needleman, "Start-Ups Get Snapped Up for Their Talent," *The Wall Street Journal Online*, September 12, 2012.
12. E. O'Boyle and H. Aguinis, "The Best and the Rest: Revisiting the Norm of Normality of Individual Performance," *Personnel Psychology* 65 (2012), pp. 79–119.
13. M. Mihelich, "Sacred Grounds—for Lawsuits," *Workforce*, April 2014, pp. 18–19.
14. M. Trottman, "Charges of Bias at Work Hit Record," *Time Magazine*, January 29, 2012, p. 7.
15. O. Kinnander and K. McLaughlin, "Wal-Mart Faces the Big Box of Class Actions," *Bloomberg Businessweek*, March 28, 2011, pp. 31–34.
16. G. Stohr, "The Supreme Court Takes on Trial Lawyers," *Bloomberg Businessweek*, June 27, 2011, pp. 34–35.
17. D. Bennett, "Deep Fried Civil War," *Bloomberg Businessweek*, August 2, 2012, pp. 62–64.
18. R. L. Lubin, "When 'Disparate Impact' Bites Back," *The Wall Street Journal*, March 9, 2014, www.wsj.com.
19. P. Roth, P. Bobko, L. McFarland, and M. Buster, "Work Sample Tests in Personnel Selection: A Meta-analysis of Black-White Differences in Overall Exercise Scores," *Personnel Psychology* 61 (2008), pp. 637–61.
20. R. E. Ployhart and B. C. Holtz, "The Diversity-Validity Dilemma: Strategies for Reducing Racioethnic and Sex Group Differences and Adverse Impact in Selection," *Personnel Psychology* 61 (2008), pp. 153–72.
21. G. Flynn, "The Reverse Discrimination Trap," *Workforce*, June 2003, pp. 106–7.
22. J. Bravin, "Supreme Court Upholds Michigan's Affirmative Action Ban," *The Wall Street Journal*, April 22, 2014, www.wsj.com.
23. T. Lewin, "Colleges Seek New Paths to Diversity After Court Ruling," *The New York Times*, April 22, 2014, www.nytimes.com.
24. E. Zlomik, "An End Run Around Affirmative Action Bans," *Bloomberg Businessweek*, April 23, 2012, p. 52.
25. J. Bravin "Justices Clash on Affirmative Action," *The Wall Street Journal Online*, October 10, 2012.
26. D. A. Newman and J. S. Lyon, "Recruitment Efforts to Reduce Adverse Impact: Targeted Recruiting for Personality, Cognitive Ability and Diversity," *Journal of Applied Psychology* 94 (2009), pp. 298–317.
27. D. M. Finch, B. D. Edwards, and J. C. Wallace, "Multistage Selection Strategies: Simulating the Effects of Adverse Impact and Expected Performance for Various Predictor Combinations," *Journal of Applied Psychology* 94 (2009), pp. 318–40.
28. F. Hanson, "Diversity of a Different Color," *Workforce Management*, June 2010, pp. 21–24.
29. L. T. Cullen, "The Diversity Delusion," *Time*, May 2007, p. 45.
30. A. Gutman, "Smith versus City of Jackson: Adverse Impact in the ADEA (Well Sort Of)," *Industrial Psychologist*, July 2005, pp. 31–32.
31. J. Mullich, "Hiring without Limits," *Workforce*, June 2002, pp. 53–58.
32. L. Weber, "Are You Disabled? Your Boss Needs to Know," *The Wall Street Journal*, March 18, 2014, www.wsj.com.
33. L. T. Cullen, "The Diversity Delusion," *Time*, May 7, 2007, p. 45.
34. R. A. Posthuma, F. R. Morgeson, and M. A. Campion, "Beyond Employment Interview Validity: A Comprehensive Narrative

Review of Recent Research and Trends over Time," *Personnel Psychology* 55 (2002), pp. 1–81.

35. C. H. Middendorf and T. H. Macan, "Note-Taking in the Interview: Effects on Recall and Judgments," *Journal of Applied Psychology* 87 (2002), pp. 293–303.

36. M. A. McDaniel, F. P. Morgeson, E. B. Finnegan, M. A. Campion, and E. P. Braverman, "Use of Situational Judgment Tests to Predict Job Performance: A Clarification of the Literature," *Journal of Applied Psychology* 86 (2001), pp. 730–40.

37. A. P. J. Ellis, B. J. West, A. M. Ryan, and R. P. DeShon, "The Use of Impression Management Tactics in Structured Interviews: A Function of Question Type?" *Journal of Applied Psychology* 87 (2002), pp. 1200–8.

38. A. Bryant, "Google's Quest to Build a Better Boss," *The New York Times,* March 12, 2011, p. C1.

39. D. Middleton, "Non-Campus Recruiting," *The Wall Street Journal,* February 23, 2010, p. D4.

40. A. Dizik, "Wooing Job Recruiters with Video Resumes," *The Wall Street Journal,* May 2010, p. D4.

41. L. Weber, "Now Hiring? Tips for Conducting Interviews," *The Wall Street Journal Online,* December 4, 2012.

42. J. S. Lublin, "What Won't You Do for a Job," *The Wall Street Journal,* June 2, 2009, p. B1.

43. L. Weber, "Now Hiring? Tips for Conducting Interviews," *The Wall Street Journal Online,* December 4, 2012.

44. C. Suddath, "Imaginary Friends," *Bloomberg Businessweek,* January 21, 2013, p. 66.

45. M. R. Barrick and R. D. Zimmerman, "Reducing Voluntary Turnover through Selection," *Journal of Applied Psychology* 90 (2005), pp. 159–66.

46. M. Korn, "Wealth of Waste? Rethinking the Value of a Business Major," *The Wall Street Journal Online,* April 5, 2012.

47. K. Clark, "The Philadelphia Eagles' Personnel Strategy: Targeting College Grads," *The Wall Street Journal,* May 20, 2014, www.wsj.com.

48. V. L. Chien and J. Berman, "Companies Are Hiring, Just Not You," *Bloomberg Businessweek,* August 15, 2011, pp. 10–11.

49. C. Dougherty, "Gap Hurts Job Hunters," *The Wall Street Journal Online,* August 29, 2012.

50. K. Darcy, "Manhattan: Steve Masiello on Leave," *ESPN,* March 26, 2014, http://espn.go.com.

51. R. Sanchez, G. Botelho, and F. Karimi, "New York Prison Employee Arraigned for Allegedly Helping Killers Escape," *CNN,* June 12, 2015, www.cnn.com.

52. M. Schwirtz and M. Winerip, "Warning Signs Overlooked in Hiring for New York City Jails," *The New York Times,* January 15, 2015, www.nytimes.com.

53. F. Hanson, "Worker Screening Limited Overseas," *Workforce Management,* February 16, 2009, p. 37.

54. F. Hanson and G. Hernandez, "Caution amid the Credit Crunch," *Workforce Management,* February 16, 2009, pp. 35–36;

55. M. Barnekow-Bergkvist, U. Aasa, K. A. Angquist, and H. Johansson, "Prediction of Development of Fatigue during a Simulated Ambulance Work Task from Physical Performance Tests," *Ergonomics* 47 (2004), pp. 1238–50.

56. J. Hogan, "Structure of Physical Performance in Occupational Tasks," *Journal of Applied Psychology* 76 (1991), pp. 495–507.

57. N. D. Henderson, "Predicting Long-term Firefighter Performance from Measures of Cognitive Ability and Physical Ability Measures," *Personnel Psychology* 63 (2010), pp. 999–1039.

58. J. Hogan, "Physical Abilities," in *Handbook of Industrial & Organizational Psychology,* 2nd ed., ed. M. D. Dunnette and L. M. Hough (Palo Alto, CA: Consulting Psychologists Press, 1991).

59. Editorial Board, "Women Who Work," *The New York Times,* November 30, 2014, www.nytimes.com.

60. J. F. Salagado, N. Anderson, S. Moscoso, C. Bertua, and F. De Fruyt, "International Validity Generalization of GMA and Cognitive Abilities: A European Community Meta-Analysis," *Personnel Psychology* 56 (2003), pp. 573–605.

61. P. Coy, "The SAT Is Elitist, Unfair, Out of Date, or All of the Above," *Bloomberg Businessweek,* October 7, 2013.

62. M. A. Campion, J. L. Outtz, S. Zedeck, F. S. Schmidt, J. E. Kehoe, K. R. Murphy, and R. M. Guion, "The Controversy over Score Banding in Personnel Selection: Answers to 10 Key Questions," *Personnel Psychology* 54 (2001), pp. 149–85.

63. C. McWhirter, "High Tech Cheaters Pose Test Threat," *The Wall Street Journal Online,* June 10, 2013.

64. E. Barber, "Chinese and South Korean SAT Students Face Nervous Wait After Scores Delayed," *Time Magazine,* October 30, 2014, http://time.com.

65. L. Weber, "Today's Personality Tests Raise the Bar for Job Seekers," *The Wall Street Journal,* April 14, 2015, www.wsj.com.

66. F. P. Morgeson, M. A. Campion, R. L. Dipboye, J. R. Hollenbeck, K. R. Murphy, and N. Schmitt, "Reconsidering the Use of Personality Tests in Personnel Selection Contexts," *Personnel Psychology* 60 (2007), pp. 683–729.

67. L. Winerman, "What Sets High Achievers Apart?" *Monitor on Psychology,* December 2013, pp. 28–31.

68. R. Pyrillis, "Searching for Solace," *Workforce,* November, 2014, pp. 41–43.

69. B. Walsh, "The Upside of Being an Introvert (and Why Extroverts Are Over-rated)," *Time Magazine,* February 6, 2012, pp. 40–45.

70. S. E. Humphrey, J. R. Hollenbeck, C. J. Meyer, and D. R. Ilgen, "Trait Configurations in Self-managed Teams: A Conceptual Examination of the Use of Seeding for Maximizing and Minimizing Trait Variance in Teams," *Journal of Applied Psychology* 92 (2007), pp. 885–92.

71. A. Hedger, "Employee Screening: Common Challenges, Smart Solutions," *Workforce Management,* March 17, 2008, pp. 39–46.

72. J. Welch and S. Welch, "Team Building: Right and Wrong," *BusinessWeek,* November 24, 2008, p. 130.

73. A. C. Homan, D. van Knippenberg, G. A. van Kleff, and C. K. W. De Dreu, "Bridging Faultlines by Valuing Diversity: Diversity Beliefs, Information Elaboration, and Performance in Diverse Work Groups," *Journal of Applied Psychology* 92 (2007), pp. 1189–99.

74. D. Goleman, "Sometimes, EQ Is More Important than IQ," CNN.com, January 14, 2005, p. 1.

75. R. D. Roberts, G. Mathews, and M. Zeidner, "Emotional Intelligence: Muddling through Theory and Measurement," *Industrial and Organizational Psychology* 3 (2010), pp. 140–44.

76. D. L. Joseph and D. A. Newman, "Emotional Intelligence: An Integrative Meta-Analysis and Cascading Model," *Journal of Applied Psychology* 95 (2010), pp. 54–78.

77. J. M. Hunthausen, D. M. Truxillo, T. N. Bauer, and L. B. Hammer, "A Field Study of Frame of Reference Effects on Personality Test Validity," *Journal of Applied Psychology* 88 (2003), pp. 545–51.

78. J. A. Shaffer and J. E. Postlewaite, "A Matter of Context: A Meta-analytic Investigation of the Relative Validity of Contextualized and Non-contextualized Personality Measures," *Personnel Psychology,* 65 (2012), pp. 445–494.

79. H. Le, I. S. Oh, S. B. Robbins, R. Ilies, E. Holland, and P. Westrick, "Too Much of a Good Thing? Curvilinear Relationship

between Personality Traits and Job Performance," *Journal of Applied Psychology* 96 (2011), pp. 113–33.

80. B. Erdogan, T. N. Bauer, J. M. Peiro, and D. M. Truxillo, "Overqualified Employees: Making the Best of a Potentially Bad Situation for Individuals and Organizations," *Industrial and Organizational Psychology* 4 (2011), pp. 215–32.

81. S. A. Birkland, T. M. Manson, J. L. Kisamore, M. T. Brannick, and M. A. Smith, "Faking on Personality Measures," *International Journal of Selection and Assessment* 14 (December 2006), pp. 317–35.

82. L. Weber and E. Dwoskin, "Are Personality Tests Fair?" *The Wall Street Journal,* September 29, 2014, www.wsj.com.

83. J. P. Hausknecht, "Candidate Persistence and Personality Test Practice Effects: Implications for Staffing System Management," *Personnel Psychology* 63 (2010), pp. 299–324.

84. N. L. Vasilopoulos, J. M. Cucina, and J. M. McElreath, "Do Warnings of Response Verification Moderate the Relationship between Personality and Cognitive Ability?" *Journal of Applied Psychology* 90 (2005), pp. 306–22.

85. C. H. Van Iddekinge, P. H. Raymark, and P. L. Roth, "Assessing Personality with a Structured Employment Interview: Construct-Related Validity and Susceptibility to Response Inflation," *Journal of Applied Psychology* 90 (2005), pp. 536–52.

86. R. Mueller-Hanson, E. D. Heggestad, and G. C. Thornton, "Faking and Selection: Considering the Use of Personality from Select-In and Select-Out Perspectives," *Journal of Applied Psychology* 88 (2003), pp. 348–55.

87. C. Palmeri, "Putting Managers to the Test," *BusinessWeek,* November 20, 2006, p. 82.

88. C. Winkler, "Job Tryouts Go Virtual: Online Job Simulations Provide Sophisticated Candidate Assessments," *HR Magazine,* September 2006, pp. 10–15.

89. M. S. Christian, B. D. Edwards, and J. C. Bradley, "Situational Judgment Tests: Constructs Assessed and a Meta-Analysis of Their Criterion-Related Validities," *Personnel Psychology* 63 (2010), pp. 83–117.

90. E. White, "Walk a Mile in My Shoes," *The Wall Street Journal,* January 16, 2006, p. B3.

91. K. Maher, "Win in a Competition, Land on Square that Offers Job," *The Wall Street Journal,* June 1, 2004, p. B10.

92. S. Leckhart, "The Hackathon Fast Track, From Campus to Silicon Valley," *The New York Times,* April 6, 2015, www.nytimes.com.

93. J. Puliyenthuruthel, "How Google Searches—For Talent," *BusinessWeek,* April 11, 2005, pp. 32–34.

94. K. E. Klein, "Business Plan Contests: Where Are the Women?" *Bloomberg Businessweek,* February 14, 2011, pp. 48–49.

95. W. Arthur, E. A. Day, T. L. McNelly, and P. S. Edens, "Meta-Analysis of the Criterion-Related Validity of Assessment Center Dimensions," *Personnel Psychology* 56 (2003), pp. 125–54.

96. J. E. Wanek, P. R. Sackett, and D. S. Ones, "Toward an Understanding of Integrity Test Similarities and Differences: An Item-Level Analysis of Seven Tests," *Personnel Psychology* 56 (2003), pp. 873–94.

97. C. H. Van Iddekinge, P. L. Roth, P. H. Raymark, and H. N. Odle-Dusseau, "The Criterion-related Validity of Integrity Tests: An Updated Meta-analysis, *Journal of Applied Psychology,* 97 (2012), pp. 499–530.

98. M. R. Cunningham, D. T. Wong, and A. P. Barbee, "Self-Presentation Dynamics on Overt Integrity Tests: Experimental Studies of the Reid Report," *Journal of Applied Psychology* 79 (1994), pp. 643–58.

99. M. E. Paronto, D. M. Truxillo, T. N. Bauer, and M. C. Leo, "Drug Testing, Drug Treatment, and Marijuana Use: A Fairness Perspective," *Journal of Applied Psychology* 87 (2002), pp. 1159–66.

100. K. R. Murphy, G. C. Thornton, and D. H. Reynolds, "College Students' Attitudes toward Drug Testing Programs," *Personnel Psychology* 43 (1990), pp. 615–31.

101. C. Levinson, "Comey: FBI 'Grappling' with Hiring Policy Concerning Marijuana," *The Wall Street Journal,* May 20, 2014, www.wsj.com.

7

Training

Learning Helps Make the Sale at Keller Williams

At Keller Williams, the largest real estate franchise in North America, the vision is to be the real estate company of choice for agents, franchisees, and customers. Keller Williams strives to train its agents better than any other company in the world so they can delight customers, build their business, and have financial success. Just as location is a key factor in attracting buyers to purchase a home or commercial property, training is a reason for Keller Williams' ability to reach its business goals, which include adding 8,000 agents, increasing agents' commissions by 20%, and ensuring that over 90% of its franchise offices are profitable. Keller Williams' CEO believes that training is critical for the company to attract new agents because it helps them quickly become productive, resulting in sales and commissions. Training involves both online and classroom instruction where learning occurs through interacting with instructors and coaching and opportunities for agents to collaborate, which helps them learn from each other by sharing knowledge and practices. Keller Williams' commitment to training and its role in the success of the business was recognized by the top ranking it received in back-to-back years in *Training* magazine's Top 125. The company earned the distinction of being ranked #1 in 2015 and #2 in 2014.

Keller Williams has several different training programs that support agents and the business. Business Objective: A Life By Design (BOLD) is a seven-week training program during which agents are taught mindset exercises and language techniques, and in which they participate in lead generation activities. The course focuses on personal well-being as well as business skills. During some classes in the program agents engage in "real play," calling customers with instructors providing guidance and support. This allows the agents to generate business while learning. BOLD graduates have increased sales volumes by 80%, closed sales by 86%, and

increased commissions by 118% compared to agents who haven't taken the program.

Mega Agent Expansion (MAE) helps top-performing agents understand how and when to expand into new markets. MAE includes instructor-led classes, webinars, expert interviews, productivity resources, and coaching. The program helps participants understand all aspects of expanding their business including how to centralize lead generation and administration and develop a workable business plan. They have access to a social media network for learning and sharing as well as monthly opportunities to ask questions of Keller Williams' top expansion agents. Growth Initiative (GI) is a distant learning and consulting program that trains managers how to effectively recruit and retain agents. The program includes weekly one-hour seminars, requires managers to make two recruiting appointments each day, five days a week, and helps managers share best practices through an online community and a dedicated Facebook page. In addition to its training programs Keller Williams invested in building a training and education center at its corporate headquarters in Austin, Texas. The center manages all aspects of learning and develops new courses, learning tools, and videos. Recently, the center developed apps that provide short training opportunities that agents can access anytime and anywhere through their smartphone, laptop, or notebooks.

Keller Williams doesn't just invest time and money into training, it also takes steps to ensure its effectiveness. To keep training standards high and improve learning every trainer and instructor must take several "Train the Trainer" courses before they can teach any courses. Different types of evaluation data are collected and shared with agents and managers. Because all of training is voluntary, one measure of its value is participation. This includes tracking how

CONTINUED

much time employees spend in training (82 average per-person hours of formal, planned training) and the number of employees and franchisees trained each year in instructor-led courses (100,000) and online courses (26,000). The return on investment (ROI) of many courses is calculated. For example, BOLD costs $799 per student but the average agent who participated in the course earned an additional $55,000 for the year. Keller Williams also tracks metrics such as the average days a property is on the market. The average days on the market is lower than their competitors, providing evidence that training is helping agents close deals quicker and provide better service.

SOURCES: L. Freifeld, "Keller Williams Is at Home at No. 1," *Training*, January/February 2015, pp. 28–34; L. Freifeld, "Keller Williams Is on the Move," *Training*, January/February 2014, pp. 40–42.

Introduction

As the chapter opener shows, training contributes to Keller Williams' focus on its employees and customers. Training helps Keller Williams' employees develop skills they need to succeed in their current jobs and develop for future positions. From Keller Williams' perspective, training is strategic because it leads to consistent service that attracts and retains customers, high-quality agents, and positive revenues. Keller Williams recognizes that there is stiff competition for consumers' real estate business—success requires smart, motivated employees who can delight customers.

Why is the emphasis on strategic training important? Companies are in business to make money, and every business function is under pressure to show how it contributes to business success or face spending cuts and even outsourcing. To contribute to a company's success, training activities should help the company achieve its business strategy. (Consider how Keller Williams' training contributed to development of employees selling skills.)

There is both a direct and an indirect link between training and business strategy and goals. Training can help employees develop skills needed to perform their jobs, which directly affects the business. Giving employees opportunities to learn and develop creates a positive work environment, which supports the business strategy by attracting talented employees as well as motivating and retaining current employees.

Why do Keller Williams and many other companies believe that an investment in training can help them gain a competitive advantage? Training can

- Increase employees' knowledge of foreign competitors and cultures, which is critical for success in foreign markets.
- Help ensure that employees have the basic skills to work with new technology, such as robots and computer-assisted manufacturing processes.
- Help employees understand how to work effectively in teams to contribute to product and service quality.
- Ensure that the company's culture emphasizes innovation, creativity, and learning.
- Ensure employment security by providing new ways for employees to contribute to the company when their jobs change, their interests change, or their skills become obsolete.
- Prepare employees to accept and work more effectively with each other, particularly with minorities and women.[1]

In this chapter, we emphasize the conditions through which training practices can help companies gain competitive advantage and how managers can contribute to effective training and other learning intiatives. The chapter begins by discussing a systematic and effective approach to training design. Next we review training methods and training evaluation. The chapter concludes with a discussion of training issues including cross-cultural preparation, managing diversity, and socializing employees.

Training: Its Role in Continuous Learning and Competitive Advantage

As we discussed in Chapter 1, intangible assets including human capital, customer capital, social capital, and intellectual capital help companies gain competitive advantage. Recognizing that formal training, informal learning, and knowledge management are important for the development of intangible assets, many companies now consider training one part of a larger emphasis on continuous learning. Figure 7.1 shows that formal training and development, informal learning, and knowledge management are the key features of a continuous learning philosophy that focuses on performance and supports the business strategy. **Continuous learning** refers to a learning system that requires employees to understand the entire work system and they are expected to acquire new skills, apply them on the job, and share what they have learned with other employees.[2]

Training refers to a planned effort by a company to facilitate learning of job-related competencies, knowledge, skills, and behaviors by employees. The goal of training is for employees to master the knowledge, skills, and behaviors emphasized in training and apply them to their day-to-day activities. Traditionally, companies have relied on formal training through a course, program, or event to teach employees the knowledge, skills, and behaviors they need to successfully perform their jobs. **Formal training** refers to training and development programs, courses, and events that are developed and organized by the company. Typically employees are required to attend or complete these programs, which can include face-to-face training programs (such as instructor-led courses) as well as online programs. U.S. companies make substantial investments in formal training. One estimate is that U.S. organizations spend over $61 billion on formal employee training and development.[3] We will discuss development in Chapter 9, "Employee Development."

Despite companies' significant investments in formal training and development activities, informal learning is also important for facilitating knowledge and skill acquisition.[4]

LO 7-1
Discuss how training, informal learning, and knowledge management can contribute to continuous learning and companies' business strategy.

Continuous Learning
A learning system that requires employees to understand the entire work process and expects them to acquire new skills, apply them on the job, and share what they have learned with other employees.

Training
A planned effort to facilitate the learning of job-related knowledge, skills, and behavior by employees.

Formal Training
Training and development programs and courses that are developed and organized by the company.

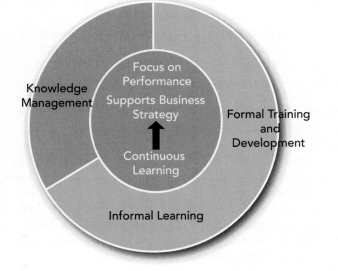

Figure 7.1
Key Features of Continuous Learning

Informal Learning
Learning that is learner initiated, involves action and doing, is motivated by an intent to develop, and does not occur in a formal learning setting.

Informal learning refers to learning that is learner initiated, involves action and doing, is motivated by an intent to develop, and does not occur in a formal learning setting.[5] Informal learning occurs without an instructor, and its breadth, depth, and timing are controlled by the employee. It occurs on an as-needed basis and may involve an employee learning alone or through face-to-face or technology-aided social interactions. Informal learning can occur through many different ways, including casual unplanned interactions with peers, e-mail, informal mentoring, or company-developed or publicly available social networking websites such as Twitter or Facebook. The application of social media from a marketing strategy to a learning strategy and the availability of Web 2.0 technologies such as social networks, microblogs, and wikis allow employees easy access to social learning through collaboration and sharing with one or two or more people.[6] One estimate is that informal learning may account for up to 75% of learning within organizations!

Both formal training and informal learning contribute to the development of intangible assets but especially human capital. Human capital includes knowledge (know what), advanced skills (know how), system understanding and creativity (know why), as well as motivation to deliver high-quality products and services (care why).[7] One reason why informal learning may be especially important is that it may lead to the effective development of *tacit* knowledge, which can be contrasted with *explicit* knowledge.[8] **Explicit knowledge** refers to knowledge that is well documented, easily articulated, and easily transferred from person to person. Examples of explicit knowledge include processes, checklists, flowcharts, formulas, and definitions. Explicit knowledge tends to be the primary focus of formal training. **Tacit knowledge** refers to personal knowledge based on individual experiences that make it difficult to codify. It is best acquired through informal learning. The characteristics of the formal training environment may limit the extent to which tacit knowledge can be acquired, such as the relatively short duration of classroom or online training and limited opportunities for practice. Thus, informal learning is central to the development of tacit knowledge. Well-designed formal training programs can help employees acquire explicit knowledge. But to acquire tacit knowledge employees need to interact with peers, colleagues, and experts and have learning experiences that are not usually found in formal training. Informal learning does not replace formal training. Formal training is still needed to prepare employees for their jobs and help them progress to future positions. Informal learning complements training by helping employees gain tacit knowledge that formal training cannot provide.

Explicit Knowledge
Knowledge that is well documented and easily transferred to other persons.

Tacit Knowledge
Knowledge based on personal experience that is difficult to codify.

Knowledge management refers to the process of enhancing company performance by designing and implementing tools, processes, systems, structures, and cultures to improve the creation, sharing, and use of knowledge.[9] Knowledge management contributes to informal learning. McAfee, a security company, uses a software program (Jive) which gives employees and customers the ability to access discussions, videos, and blogs.[10] The software recommends relevant content and identifies individuals who can help with specific issues. As a result, knowledge sharing has improved between customer support, sales, and research and development functions. Customer satisfaction ratings have improved 25% and call volume has decreased even as the company has added customers.

Knowledge Management
Process of enhancing company performance by using tools, processes, systems, and cultures to improve the creation, sharing, and use of knowledge.

It is important for all aspects of continuous learning, including training, knowledge management, and informal learning, to contribute to and support the business strategy. Continuous learning needs to address performance issues that lead to improved business results. To do so requires that the emphasis on continuous learning aligns with the business strategy, has visible support from senior managers and involves leaders as instructors and teachers, creates a culture or work environment that encourages learning, provides a wide range of learning opportunities including training, informal learning, knowledge management, and employee development, uses traditional methods and innovative technologies to design and deliver learning, and measures the effectiveness and overall business impact of learning.[11]

Consider how Jiffy Lube embraces a continuous learning philosophy that supports the business strategy.[12] Jiffy Lube's strategic goals focus on developing growth opportunities for franchisees and providing a world-class customer experience. Jiffy Lube's customer value proposition is that every driver deserves to be free from the anxiety of keeping his or her vehicle in excellent shape. This requires that service technicians are knowledgable about and able to provide high quality and necessary services to drivers. At Jiffy Lube this means that service technicians need to be trained and certified. Training is provided through Jiffy Lube University (JLU). One estimate is that employees participated in more than 2 million learning hours. Learning for employees and franchisees is offered using face-to-face and virtual instruction, as well as online self-paced modules. JLU evaluates the success of learning efforts many ways including learner feedback, franchisee surveys, the number of training courses completed, earned certifications, and customer service scores from mystery shoppers.

Jiffy Lube recognizes the value of continuous learning and informal learning. Recently, every employee, including the company president, was required to complete courses at JLU plus spend at least one day at a Jiffy Lube service center. The courses included orientation and safety and training for the Courtesy Technician, Upper Bay Technician, Customer Service Advisor, and Team Lead positions and products. Jiffy-Lube also has established partnerships with colleges to allow service center employees to transfer credits from courses earned through JLU to earn an undergrad certificate in Management Foundations. Learners and managers can access online a roadmap which shows how training is helping them advance their careers. Also, recognizing that its service center employees typically are 18- to 25-year-olds who are actively involved in social media, Jiffy-Lube provides video cameras so that store employees can capture best practices and ideas. These videos have focused on customer service, team building, operational excellence, and safety. Jiffy-Lube trainers edit the videos and make them available to all employees on YouTube.

Designing Effective Formal Training Activities

A key characteristic of training activities that contribute to competitiveness is that they are designed according to the instructional design process.[13] **Training design process** refers to a systematic approach for developing training programs. Instructional System Design (ISD) and the ADDIE model (analysis, design, development, implementation, evaluation) are two specific types of training design processes you may know. Figure 7.2 presents the six stages of this process, which emphasizes that effective training practices involve more than just choosing the most popular or colorful training method.

The first stage is to assess needs to determine if training is needed. The second stage involves ensuring employees have the readiness for training, and they have the motivation and basic skills to master training content. Stage 3 addresses whether the training session (or the learning environment) has the factors necessary for learning to occur. Stage 4 is to ensure that trainees apply the content of training to their jobs. This requires support from managers and peers for the use of training content on the job as well as

Training Design Process
A systematic approach for developing training programs.

LO 7-2
Explain the role of the manager in identifying training needs and supporting training on the job.

Figure 7.2
The Training Process

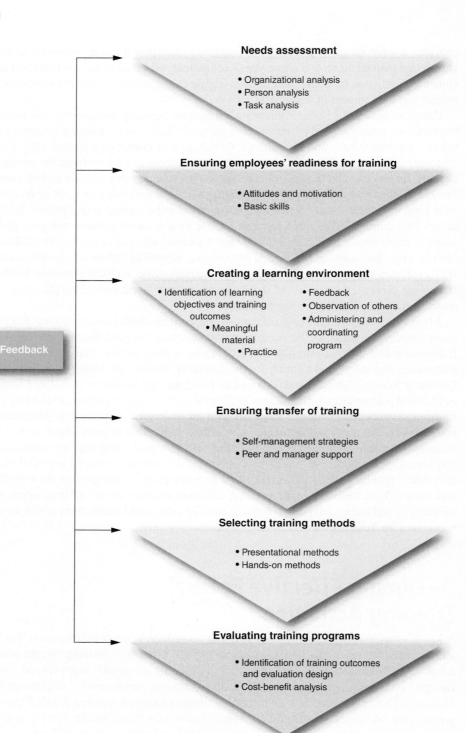

getting the employee to understand how to take personal responsibility for skill improvement. Stage 5 involves choosing a training method. As we shall see in this chapter, a variety of training methods are available ranging from traditional on-the-job training to newer technologies such as social media. The key is to choose a training method that will provide the appropriate learning environment to achieve the training objectives. Stage 6 is evaluation—that is, determining whether training achieved the desired learning outcomes and/or financial objectives.

The training design process should be systematic yet flexible enough to adapt to business needs. Different steps may be completed simultaneously. Also feedback from each stage in the training progress can be useful for the other stages. For example, if transfer of training is difficult, then the learning environment should overemphasize practice and feedback. Keep in mind that designing training unsystematically will reduce the benefits that can be realized. For example, choosing a training method before determining training needs or ensuring employees' readiness for training increases the risk that the method chosen will not be the most effective one for meeting training needs. Also, training may not even be necessary and may result in a waste of time and money! Employees may have the knowledge, skills, or behavior they need but simply not be motivated to use them. Next we will discuss important aspects of the training design process.

NEEDS ASSESSMENT

The first step in the instructional design process, **needs assessment**, refers to the process used to determine if training is necessary. Figure 7.3 shows the causes and outcomes resulting from needs assessment. As we see, many different "pressure points" suggest that training is necessary. These pressure points include performance problems, new technology, internal or external customer requests for training, job redesign, new legislation, changes in customer preferences, new products, or employees' lack of basic skills as well as support for the company's business strategy (e.g., growth, global business expansion). Note that these pressure points do not guarantee that training is the correct solution. Consider, for example, a delivery truck driver whose job is to deliver anesthetic gases to medical facilities. The driver mistakenly hooks up the supply line of a mild anesthetic to the supply line of a hospital's oxygen system, contaminating the hospital's oxygen supply. Why did the driver make this mistake, which is clearly a performance problem? The driver may have done this because of a lack of knowledge about the appropriate line hookup for the anesthetic, anger over a requested salary increase that his manager recently denied, or mislabeled valves for connecting the gas supply. Only the

LO 7-3
Conduct a needs assessment.

Needs Assessment
The process used to determine if training is necessary.

Figure 7.3
The Needs Assessment Process

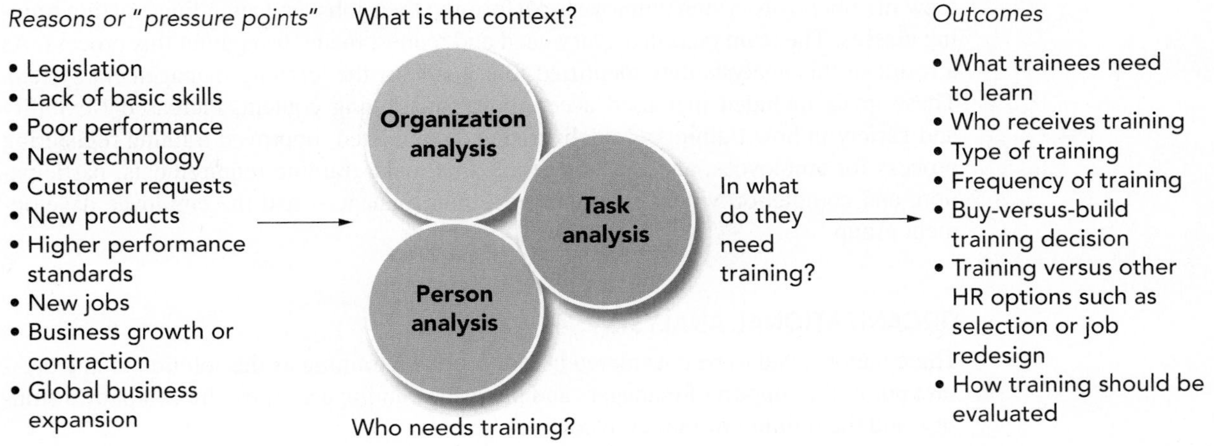

Reasons or "pressure points"

- Legislation
- Lack of basic skills
- Poor performance
- New technology
- Customer requests
- New products
- Higher performance standards
- New jobs
- Business growth or contraction
- Global business expansion

What is the context?

Organization analysis

Task analysis

Person analysis

Who needs training?

In what do they need training?

Outcomes

- What trainees need to learn
- Who receives training
- Type of training
- Frequency of training
- Buy-versus-build training decision
- Training versus other HR options such as selection or job redesign
- How training should be evaluated

lack of knowledge can be addressed by training. The other pressure points require addressing issues related to the consequence of good performance (pay system) or the design of the work environment.

Needs assessment typically involves organizational analysis, person analysis, and task analysis.[14] Organizational analysis considers the context in which training will occur. That is, **organizational analysis** involves determining the business appropriateness of training, given the company's business strategy, its resources available for training, and support by managers and peers for training activities.

Person analysis helps identify who needs training. **Person analysis** involves (1) determining whether performance deficiencies result from a lack of knowledge, skill, or ability (a training issue) or from a motivational or work-design problem; (2) identifying who needs training; and (3) determining employees' readiness for training. **Task analysis** includes identifying the important tasks and knowledge, skills, and behaviors that need to be emphasized in training for employees to complete their tasks.

In practice, organizational analysis, person analysis, and task analysis are usually not conducted in any specific order. However, because organizational analysis is concerned with identifying whether training fits with the company's strategic objectives and whether the company wants to devote time and money to training, it is usually conducted first. Person analysis and task analysis are often conducted at the same time because it is often difficult to determine whether performance deficiencies are a training problem without understanding the tasks and the work environment.

What outcomes result from a needs assessment? As shown in Figure 7.3, needs assessment shows who needs training and what trainees need to learn, including the tasks in which they need to be trained plus knowledge, skill, behavior, or other job requirements. Needs assessment helps determine whether the company will purchase training from a vendor or consultant or develop training using internal resources.

MasTec is a construction company that engineers, procures, constructs, and maintains the infrastructures for electric transmission and distribution, oil and natural gas pipelines, and communications companies.[15] The company wanted to develop an online learning management system through which employees could access training and development courses. MasTec conducted a needs assessment to identify questions such as what technology and functionality were needed to support new training programs and to identify unique employee needs. As a result, the development team started by conducting a shareholder analysis. This involved considering who would be involved in the process, understanding how to partner with them, and what type of information they could offer. This further involved meeting with safety team leaders, trainers, and construction crew members, observing employees performing their jobs, and attending existing training classes. The team recorded every need and request made throughout this process. As a result of this analysis they identified four goals for the learning management system. These goals included increased accessibility of training content, increased flexibility and variety in how training was delivered and completed, improved training registering process for employees, and reporting tools that make training requirements, participation, and completion visible to employees, their managers, and the employee development group.

ORGANIZATIONAL ANALYSIS

Three factors need to be considered before choosing training as the solution to any pressure point: the support of managers and peers for training activities, the company's strategy, and the training resources available.

Organizational Analysis
A process for determining the business appropriateness of training.

Person Analysis
A process for determining whether employees need training, who needs training, and whether employees are ready for training.

Task Analysis
The process of identifying the tasks, knowledge, skills, and behaviors that need to be emphasized in training.

Support of Managers and Peers

Various studies have found that peer and manager support for training is critical. The key factors to success are a positive attitude among peers and managers about participation in training activities; managers' and peers' willingness to tell trainees how they can more effectively use knowledge, skills, or behaviors learned in training on the job; and the availability of opportunities for the trainees to use training content in their jobs.[16] If peers' and managers' attitudes and behaviors are not supportive, employees are not likely to apply training content to their jobs.

Company Strategy

In Chapter 2 we discussed the importance of business strategy for a company to gain a competitive advantage and earlier in this chapter we discussed how Jiffy Lube relies on learning to support the company's mission and strategy. As Figure 7.1 highlights, training should help companies achieve the business strategy. Table 7.1 shows possible strategic initiatives and their implications for training practices.

It is important to identify the prevailing business strategy and goals to ensure that the company allocates enough of its budget to training, that employees receive training on relevant topics, and that employees get the right amount of training.[17] Umpqua

Table 7.1

Examples of Strategic Initiatives and Their Implications for Training Practices

STRATEGIC TRAINING AND DEVELOPMENT INITIATIVES	IMPLICATIONS
Improve Customer Service	• Ensure that employees have product and service knowledge • Ensure that employees have skills needed to interact with customers • Ensure that employees understand their roles and decision-making authority
Improve Employee Engagement	• Ensure that employees have opportunities to develop • Ensure that employees understand career opportunities and personal growth opportunities • Ensure that training and development addresses employees' needs in current job as well as growth opportunities
Enhance Innovation and Creativity	• Capture insight and information from knowledgeable employees • Logically organize and store information • Provide methods to make information available (e.g., resource guides, websites) • Dedicate physical space to encourage teamwork, collaboration, creativity, and knowledge sharing
Growth in Global Markets	• Prepare high potential managers to take over global leadership positions • Cross-cultural preparation of expatriates • Train local workforce in company culture

SOURCE: Based on S. Tannenbaum, "A Strategic View of Organizational Training and Learning," in *Creating, Implementing and Managing Effective Training and Development,* ed. K. Kraiger (San Francisco: Jossey-Bass, 2002), pp. 10–52.

INTEGRITY IN ACTION

Connecting Learning to Business Success

The STIHL Group develops, produces, and markets power tools including chain saws, blowers, trimmers, and edgers. The tools, which are distributed through 40,000 dealers in more than 160 countries, are used in forestry and landscape maintenance and construction by homeowners, lumberjacks, firefighters, and the military. Fred Whyte, president of STIHL Inc., recognizes that learning and development are necessary to help all of the company's stakeholders—employees, wholesale distributors, retailers, and consumers—work safely and productively.

At the retail level, STIHL provides training programs that help dealers understand how to sell and service the equipment. STIHL iCademy provides online programs covering topics such as troubleshooting, in-store marketing, selling skills, and customer service. Employees can attend Tooling University, an online program to develop their technical skills, and supervisor training and leadership development programs are used for developing effective managers. Consumers can access blogs and YouTube videos on the company's website to learn how to use STIHL's power tools.

Whyte believes that the "people make the business." When STIHL introduced automation and robots in its factory, Whyte decided to enhance employees' skills rather than resort to layoffs. Employees were trained to repair or operate robots or for other positions. During the recession, instead of layoffs, employees worked in different jobs around the factory. This cost more in the short term, but when business picked up after the recession STIHL had retained employees with the skill sets necessary to meet increased demands for its products and services. Whyte also believes that training and development programs aren't just for fun. They need to be meaningful with measurable results. He points to record sales in 20 out of the past 21 years and awards recognizing STIHL as one of the best manufacturing companies as evidence of training effectiveness.

DISCUSSION QUESTIONS

1. How is learning and training strategic at STIHL Group?
2. What did Fred Whyte do that was most important for sending the message that training was strategic at STIHL Group? Explain.

SOURCES: Based on T. Bingham and Pat Galagan, "Training Powers Up at STIHL," *T + D*, January 2014, pp. 29–33; C. Gambill, "Creating Learning Solutions to Satisfy Customers," *T + D*, January 2014, pp. 35–39.

Bank, a small Oregon regional bank, strives to provide a customer experience unlike any other bank.[18] Its concept of service is called "slow banking," which is about getting to know customers and building relationships with them. The physical layout of the banks encourages customers to take their time and bank associates to get to know and understand their customers. There are couches, free Wi-Fi, coffee, and interactive video screens showing community activities as well as highlighting the financial products the bank offers. Umpqua wants customers to be impressed by the relaxing surroundings and bank associates to be empowered to do whatever it takes to deliver a great customer experience. Training plays an important role in developing employees' service skills and reinforcing the company's service culture. New hires receive extensive training so they can perform every banking function. Associates receive regular training in courses in partnership with Ritz-Carlton Hotel, a model company for customer service. Courses include "Creating a Culture of Service Excellence" and "Radar On, Antenna Up," which focuses on fulfilling customers' unexpressed needs. Umpqua also sends employees out to other companies to experience how they are providing customer service and asks them to report back any practices that the bank isn't currently using to satisfy customers. The "Integrity in Action" box highlights what business leaders might reasonably expect from their training and development or learning function.

Training Resources

It is necessary to identify whether the company has the budget, time, and expertise for training. For example, if the company is installing computer-based manufacturing equipment in one of its plants, it has three possible strategies to have computer-literate employees. First, the company can use technical experts on staff to train all affected employees. Second, the company may decide that it is more cost-effective to identify computer-literate employees by using tests and work samples and replace or reassign employees who lack the necessary skills. Third, if it lacks time or expertise, the company may decide to purchase training from an outside consultant or organization.

Table 7.2 provides examples of questions to ask vendors and consultants to help evaluate whether they can meet the company's training needs.

PERSON ANALYSIS

Person analysis helps the manager identify whether training is appropriate and which employees need training. In certain situations, such as the introduction of a new technology or service, all employees may need training. However, when managers, customers, or employees identify a problem (usually as a result of a performance deficiency), it is often unclear whether training is the solution.

A major pressure point for training is poor or substandard performance—that is, a gap between employees' current performance and their expected performance. Poor performance is indicated by customer complaints, low performance ratings, or on-the-job accidents or unsafe behavior. Another potential indicator of the need for training is if the job changes so current performance levels need improvement or employees must complete new tasks.

From a manager's perspective, to determine if training is needed, for any performance problem you need to analyze characteristics of the performer, input, output, consequences, and feedback. How might this be done? You should ask several questions to determine if training is the likely solution to a performance problem.[19]

Assess whether

1. The performance problem is important and has the potential to cost the company a significant amount of money from lost productivity or customers.

Table 7.2
Questions to Ask Vendors and Consultants

How do your products and services fit our needs?
How much and what type of experience does your company have in designing and delivering training?
What are the qualifications and experiences of your staff?
Can you provide demonstrations or examples of training programs you have developed?
Can you provide references of clients for whom you worked?
What evidence do you have that your programs work?
How long will it take to develop the training program?
How much will your services cost?
What instructional design methods do you use?
What about recurring costs, such as costs related to administering, updating, and maintaining the training program?
Do you provide technical support?

SOURCES: Adapted from R. Zemke and J. Armstrong, "Evaluating Multimedia Developers," *Training Magazine*, November 1996, pp. 33–38; B. Chapman, "How to Create the Ideal RFP," *Training*, January 2004, pp. 40–43; M. Weinstein, "What Vendors Wished You Knew," *Training*, February 2010, pp. 122–125.

2. Employees do not know how to perform effectively. Perhaps they received little or no previous training or the training was ineffective (person characteristics).
3. Employees cannot demonstrate the correct knowledge or behavior. Perhaps they were trained but they infrequently or never used the training content (knowledge, skills, etc.) on the job (input problem).
4. Performance expectations are clear (input) and there are no obstacles to performance such as faulty tools or equipment (output).
5. There are positive consequences for good performance, whereas poor performance is not rewarded. For example, if employees are dissatisfied with their compensation, their peers or a union may encourage them to slow down their pace of work (consequences).
6. Employees receive timely, relevant, accurate, constructive, and specific feedback about their performance (feedback).
7. Other solutions such as job redesign or transferring employees to other jobs are too expensive or unrealistic.

If employees lack the knowledge and skill to perform and the other factors are satisfactory, training is likely the effective solution. If employees have the knowledge and skill to perform, but input, output, consequences, or feedback are inadequate, training may not be the best solution. For example, if poor performance results from faulty equipment, training cannot solve this problem, but repairing the equipment will! If poor performance results from lack of feedback, then employees may not need training, but their managers may need training on how to give performance feedback.

TASK ANALYSIS

A task analysis, which we defined earlier in the chapter, identifies the conditions in which tasks are performed. The conditions include identifying equipment and the environment the employee works in, time constraints (deadlines), safety considerations, or performance standards. Task analysis results in a description of work activities, including tasks performed by the employee and the knowledge, skills, and abilities required to successfully complete the tasks. A *job* is a specific position requiring the completion of specific tasks. A *task* is a statement of an employee's work activity in a specific job. The four steps in a task analysis include identifying the job(s) to be analyzed, developing a list of tasks performed on the job, validating or confirming the tasks, and identifying the knowledge, skills, abilities, and other factors (e.g., equipment, working conditions) needed to successfully perform each task.[20]

For example, consider how KLA-Tencor conducted a needs assessment for its service engineers.[21] KLA-Tencor supplies process controls and equipment to the semiconductor industry. KLA-Tencor service engineers need to diagnose and repair its customers' complex machines that use advanced laser, optical, and robotic technologies. The engineers need to main proficiency in their current skills as well as add new skills to keep pace with new technology used in the company's equipment. This is critical for KLA-Tencor to quickly solve equipment problems, which if unresolved, can result in millions of dollars of lost revenue for its customers. Providing effective service is critical for the company to keep current customers and develop new business. In fact, one of the company's values is "Indispensable" (the others values are Perseverance, Drive to Be Better, High Performance Teams, and Honest, Forthright, and Consistent).

KLA-Tencor uses a skills management process (the Right People, Right Knowledge process) to monitor its workforce skills and use this information to change its training programs. The process involves developing a task list, training on the task, practicing on-the-job training to gain certification, and conducting an annual skills assessment. To conduct the skills assessment a survey was sent to all of KLA-Tencor's more than 1,000 service engineers. For each task the engineers were asked to rate their capability of doing the task on a scale from "I don't know how" to "I can teach it to others." Also, they were asked to evaluate how frequently they performed the task from "Never" to "More than two times per year." Based on their responses, they were assigned a training task. More than 200 courses were created to train the engineers. To ensure that the training was completed, both engineers and their managers were held accountable. This helped achieve a 95% completion rate within one year after training was assigned. The skills assessment data was also used to identify gaps in current training, resulting in more than 2,000 changes in courses and certification programs. The skills assessment is done annually to ensure service engineers' skills keep up to date with new technology and products.

ENSURING EMPLOYEES' READINESS FOR TRAINING

The second step in the training design process is to evaluate whether employees are ready for training. **Readiness for training** refers to employee characteristics that provide employees with the desire, energy, and focus necessary to learn from training. The desire, energy, and focus is referred to as **motivation to learn**.[22] Various research studies have shown that motivation to learn is related to knowledge gain, behavior change, or skill acquisition in training programs.[23] Table 7.3 presents factors that influence motivation to learn and the actions that strength them. Motivation to learn influences mastery of all types of training content, including knowledge, behavior, and skills. Managers need to ensure that employees' motivation to learn is as high as possible. They can do this by ensuring employees' self-efficacy; understanding the benefits of training; being aware of training needs, career interests, and goals; understanding work environment characteristics; and ensuring employees' basic skill levels.

The "Competing through Sustainability" box shows efforts to develop the skills of the "hidden workforce" and in return get motivated and committed employees.

CREATING A LEARNING ENVIRONMENT

Learning permanently changes behavior. For employees to acquire knowledge and skills in the training program and apply this information in their jobs, the training program must include specific learning principles. Educational and industrial psychologists and instructional design specialists have identified several conditions under which employees learn best.[24] Table 7.4 shows the events that should take place for learning to occur in the training program and their implications for instruction.

Consider how several companies are creating a positive learning environment using a variety of training methods.[25] Feedback about a learning program at Mindtree Limited, a global information technology solutions company, suggested that trainees were not transferring learning to the job. The program was redesigned to ensure that employees would learn skills such as analyzing the impact of change and how to successfully integrate, review, and resolve coding problems. The new program includes four phases each with clear objectives and expected outcomes. Trainees are actively involved in learning through the use of project simulations in which they work in teams, under the supervision of a more experienced technical employee, to fix defects, address change requests, and implement new features. Trainees are evaluated and provided feedback throughout the program on their analysis, design, coding, and documentation skills, turnaround time, and collaboration skills. Nemours, a children's health system, emphasizes family-centered care. Nemours partners with parents and children to help deliver care in both

LO 7-4
Evaluate employees' readiness for training.

Readiness for Training
Employee characteristics that provide them with the desire, energy, and focus necessary to learn from training.

Motivation to Learn
The desire of the trainee to learn the content of a training program.

Table 7.3
Factors That Influence Motivation to Learn

FACTOR	DESCRIPTION	ACTIONS TO ENHANCE OR IMPROVE
Self-efficacy	Employee belief that they can successfully learn content of the training program.	Show employees training success of their peers. Communicate that purpose of training is to improve, not identify, area of incompetence. Communicate purpose and activities involved in training. Emphasize that learning is under their personal control.
Benefits or consequences of training	Job-related, personal, career benefits that can result from attending training.	Realistic communication about short- and long-term benefits from training.
Awareness of training needs	Knowledge of skill strengths and weaknesses.	Communicate why they were asked to attend training program. Share performance appraisal information. Encourage trainees to complete self-evaluation of all strengths and weaknesses. Allow employees to participate in choice of training to attend.
Work environment	Proper tools and equipment, materials, supplies, budget time. Managers' and peers' willingness to provide feedback and reinforce use of training content.	Give employees opportunities to practice and apply skills to their work. Encourage employees to provide feedback to each other. Encourage trainees to share training experiences and situations where use of training content was beneficial. Acknowledge use of training content in their work. Provide resources necessary for training content to be used in their work.
Basic skills	Cognitive ability, reading, and writing skills.	Ensure trainees have prerequisite skills needed for understanding and learning training content. Provide remedial training. Use video or other visual training methods. Modify training program to meet trainees' basic skill levels.
Goal orientation	Goals held by employees in a learning situation.	Create a learning goal orientation by deemphasizing competition between trainees, allowing trainees to make errors and to experiment with new knowledge, skills, behavior during training, and setting goals-based learning and experimenting.
Conscientiousness	Tendency to be reliable, hardworking, self-disciplined, and persistent.	Communicate need for learning.

SOURCES: Based on J. Colquitt, J. LePine, and R. Noe, "Toward an Integrative Theory of Training Motivation: A Meta-Analytic Path Analysis of 20 Years of Research," *Journal of Applied Psychology* 85 (2000), pp. 678–707; and R. Noe and J. Colquitt, "Planning for Impact Training: Principles of Training Effectiveness," in K. Kraiger (ed.), *Creating, Implementing, and Managing Effective Training and Development* (San Francisco: Jossey-Bass, 2002), pp. 53–79.

inpatient and outpatient settings, design facilities, educate staff, and develop and evaluate policies and programs. Nemours provides high-quality educational opportunities for associates, continuing medical education for physicians, nurses, and other allied health professionals through internships, residency programs, fellowship training, and graduate medical education. Its pediatric emergency medical skills course for first year fellows involves role playing. The role playing scenarios often involve patient and family interactions. These can be difficult because they can be emotionally complex such as when difficult news must be provided to patients' families. Experienced clinicians observe and mentor the fellows and provide feedback on their communications and interpersonal skills.

ENSURING TRANSFER OF TRAINING

Transfer of training refers to on-the-job use of knowledge, skills, and behaviors learned in training. As Figure 7.4 shows, transfer of training is influenced by manager support, peer support, opportunity to use learned capabilities, technology support, and self-management skills. As we discussed earlier, learning is influenced by the learning environment (such as meaningfulness of the material and opportunities for practice and feedback) and employees' readiness for training (for example, their self-efficacy and basic skill level). If no learning occurs in the training program, transfer is unlikely.

Transfer of Training
The use of knowledge, skills, and behaviors learned in training on the job.

Table 7.4
Conditions for Learning and Their Importance

CONDITIONS FOR LEARNING	IMPORTANCE AND APPLICATION TO TRAINING
Need to know why they should learn	Employees need to understand the purpose or objectives of the training program to help them understand why they need training and what they are expected to accomplish.
Meaningful training content	Motivation to learn is enhanced when training is related to helping learner (such as related to current job tasks, problems, enhancing skills, or dealing with jobs or company changes). The training context should be similar to the work environment.
Opportunities for practice	Trainees need to demonstrate what is learned (knowledge, skill, behavior) to become more comfortable using it and to commit it to memory. Let trainees choose their practice strategy.
Feedback	Feedback helps learner modify behavior, skill, or use knowledge to meet objectives. Videotape, other trainees, and the trainer are useful feedback sources.
Observe, experience, and interact with training content, other learners, and the instructor	Adults learn best by doing. Gain new perspectives and insights by working with others. Can learn by observing the actions of models or sharing experiences with each other in communities of practice or through social networking. Interact and manipulate content through reading or using tools that allow for building ideas and solving problems, such as worksheets and online interactions.
Good program coordination and administration	Eliminate distractions that could interfere with learning, such as cell-phone calls. Make sure the room is properly organized, comfortable, and appropriate for the training method (e.g., movable seating for team exercises). Trainees should receive announcements of the purpose of training, place, hour, and any pretraining materials such as cases or readings.
Commit training content to memory	Facilitate recall of training content after training. Examples include using concept maps showing relationships among ideas, using multiple types of review (writing, drawing, role-plays), teaching key words, providing a visual image, or asking trainees to reflect on what they learned. Limit instruction to manageable units or chunks that don't exceed memory limits; review and practice over multiple days (over-learning). Use short quizzes or other activities to help trainees retrieve what they learned and emphasize its importance.

SOURCES: Based on R. M. Gagne, "Learning Processes and Instruction," *Training Research Journal* 1 (1995/1996), pp. 17–28; M. Knowles, *The Adult Learner,* 4th ed. (Houston: Gulf, 1990); A. Bandura, *Social Foundations of Thought and Action* (Englewood Cliffs, NJ: Prentice Hall, 1986); E. A. Locke and G. D. Latham, *A Theory of Goal Setting and Task Performance* (Englewood Cliffs, NJ: Prentice Hall, 1990); B. Mager, *Preparing Instructional Objectives,* 2nd ed. (Belmont, CA: Lake, 1984); B.J. Smith and B. L. Delahaye, *How to Be an Effective Trainer,* 2nd ed. (New York: John Wiley and Sons, 1987); K. A. Smith-Jentsch, F. G. Jentsch, S. C. Payne, and E. Salas, "Can Pretraining Experience Explain Individual Differences in Learning?" *Journal of Applied Psychology* 81 (1996), pp. 110–16; and H. Nuriddin, "Building the Right Interaction," *T + D,* March 2011, pp. 32–35; R. Feloni, "This Simple Daily Exercise Boosts Employee Performance," *Business Insider India,* accessed July 29, 2014, www.businessinsider.in.com; G. Di Stefano, F. Gino, G. Pisano, and B. Staats, "Learning by Thinking: How Reflection Aids Performance," Harvard Business School Working Paper, 14-093 (March 25, 2014); M. Plater, "Three Trends Shaping Learning," *Chief Learning Officer,* June 2014, pp. 44–47; A. Kohn, "Use It or Lose It," *T + D,* February 2015, pp. 56–61; J. Karpicke and Henry Roediger III, "The Critical Importance of Retrieval for Learning" *Science,* February 2008, pp. 966–68.

Manager Support

Manager support refers to the degree to which trainees' managers (1) emphasize the importance of attending training programs and (2) stress the application of training content to the job. Table 7.5 shows what managers should do to support training.

Figure 7.4
Work Environment
Characteristics
Influencing Transfer
of Training

At Ingersoll Rand, to ensure that top managers understand and support the role that training and development can play in the company, a "ladder of engagement" model was created.[26] Top managers are engaged in training and development in many different ways, including providing input into learning program development, serving as trainers or co-trainers, visiting courses as an executive speaker, or serving as advisory council members for Ingersoll Rand's corporate university.

The greater the level of manager support, the more likely that transfer of training will occur.[27] The basic level of support that a manager should provide is acceptance, that is, allowing trainees to attend training. The highest level of support is to participate in training as an instructor (teaching in the program). Managers who serve as instructors are more likely to provide lower-level support functions such as reinforcing use of newly learned capabilities, discussing progress with trainees, and providing opportunities to practice. Managers can also facilitate transfer through use of action plans. An **action plan** is a written document that includes the steps that the trainee and manager will take to ensure that training transfers to the job. The action plan includes (1) a goal identifying what training content will be used and how it will be used (project, problem); (2) strategies for reaching the goal, including resources needed; (3) strategies for getting feedback

Manager Support
Degree to which trainees' managers emphasize the importance of attending training programs and stress the application of training content to the job.

Action Plan
Document summarizing what the trainee and manager will do to ensure that training transfers to the job.

Understand the content of the training.
Know how training relates to what you need employees to do.
In performance appraisals, evaluate employees on how they apply training to their jobs.
Support employees' use of training when they return to work.
Ensure that employees have the equipment and technology needed to use training.
Prior to training, discuss with employees how they plan to use training.
Recognize newly trained employees who use training content.
Give employees release time from their work to attend training.
Explain to employees why they have been asked to attend training.
Give employees feedback related to skills or behavior they are trying to develop.
If possible, be a trainer.

Table 7.5
How Managers Can
Support Training

SOURCES: Based on S. Bailey, "The Answer to Transfer," *Chief Learning Officer,* November 2014, pp. 33–41; R. Hewes, "Step by Step," *T + D,* February 2014, pp. 56–61; R. Bates, "Managers as Transfer Agents," in E. Holton III and T. Baldwin (eds.), *Improving Learning Transfer in Organizations* (San Francisco: Jossey-Bass, 2003), pp. 243–70; and A. Rossett, "That Was a Great Class, but . . ." *Training and Development,* July 1997, p. 21.

(such as meetings with the manager); and (4) expected outcome (what will be different?). The action plan includes a schedule of specific dates and times when the manager and trainee agree to meet to discuss the progress being made in using learned capabilities on the job. To help ensure learning and transfer of training, Spectrum Health, a nonprofit health system in Michigan uses a coaching guide to ensure skills are reinforced by a manager.[28] When an employee is scheduled to attend training his or her manager is sent a coaching guide describing the training objectives and questions that managers are supposed to ask employees, such as "What are you supposed to get out of the training?" In addition, after employees attend training, managers are asked to have another conversation with the employee to reinforce and apply what was learned.

At a minimum, special sessions should be scheduled with managers to explain the purpose of the training and set expectations that they will encourage attendance at the training session, provide practice opportunities, reinforce use of training, and follow up with employees to determine the progress in using newly acquired capabilities.

Peer Support

Support Network
Trainees who meet to discuss their progress in using learned capabilities on the job.

Transfer of training can also be enhanced by creating a support network among the trainees.[29] A **support network** is a group of two or more trainees who agree to meet and discuss their progress in using learned capabilities on the job. This could involve face-to-face meetings or communications via e-mail, Twitter, or other social networking tools. Trainees can share successful experiences in using training content on the job; they can also discuss how they obtained resources needed to use training content or how they coped with a work environment that interfered with use of training content.

Websites or newsletters might be used to show how trainees are dealing with transfer of training issues. Available to all trainees, the newsletter or website might feature interviews with trainees who were successful in using new skills or provide tips for using new skills. Managers may also provide trainees with a mentor—a more experienced employee who previously attended the same training program. The mentor, who may be a peer, can provide advice and support related to transfer of training issues (such as how to find opportunities to use the learned capabilities).

Opportunity to Use Learned Capabilities

Opportunity to Perform
Trainee is provided with or actively seeks experience using newly learned knowledge, skills, or behavior.

Opportunity to use learned capabilities (**opportunity to perform**) refers to the extent to which the trainee is provided with or actively seeks experience with newly learned knowledge, skill, and behaviors from the training program.[30] Opportunity to perform is influenced by both the work environment and trainee motivation. One way trainees can use learned capabilities is through assigned work experiences (problems or tasks) that require their use. The trainees' manager usually plays a key role in determining work assignments. Opportunity to perform is also influenced by the degree to which trainees take personal responsibility to actively seek out assignments that allow them to use newly acquired capabilities. Trainees given many opportunities to use training content on the job are more likely to maintain learned capabilities than trainees given few opportunities.[31]

Performance Support Systems
Computer applications that can provide (as requested) skills training, information access, and expert advice.

Technological Support: Performance Support and Knowledge Management Systems

Performance support systems are computer applications that can provide, as requested, skills training, information access, and expert advice.[32] Performance support may be used to enhance transfer of training by giving trainees an electronic information source that they can refer to as needed as they attempt to apply learned capabilities on the job.

Companies provide performance support in different ways.[33] Coca-Cola Sabo, a South African bottling company, provides on-demand learning materials using YouTube videos accessible on smartphones and tablet computers that focus on tasks such as the way to stack products correctly inside coolers. SNI, a company that supplies negotiations skills training, provides its clients with a checklist of seven negotiating tactics they can pull up on their smartphones. Although these tactics are covered in training, the checklist is available to aid clients' recall and transfer of skills to real negotiation situations. Rather than train employees on infrequently performed tasks, ADP provides employees with "Learning Bytes," two-minute learning solutions demonstrating how to perform these tasks. The Learning Bytes have helped to reduce calls into ADP's service center.

As we discussed earlier in the chapter, many companies are using knowledge management systems to improve the creation, sharing, and use of knowledge. NASA needs to manage knowledge to ensure its space missions are successful.[34] At NASA knowledge management means sharing solutions and expertise across employees, teams, projects, programs, centers, and missions. This includes scientific, engineering, and technical knowledge and business processes as well as know-how including techniques and procedures. To manage knowledge NASA uses online tools including collaboration sites, video and document libraries, search and tagging tools, case studies and publications, processes to identify and retain lessons learned, knowledge networks, and social exchanges such as forums and workshops.

Knowledge management systems often include communities of practice. **Communities of practice** are groups of employees who work together, learn from each other, and develop a common understanding of how to get work accomplished.

Communities of Practice
Groups of employees who work together, learn from each other, and develop a common understanding of how to get work accomplished.

Chicago-based Grant Thornton LLP, part of the Global Six accounting organizations, developed and deployed a knowledge management system known as "K-Source."[35] K-Source was designed to help meet key business goals of growing sales, improving customer service, supporting company values, and increasing efficiency of internal services. K-Source includes an online community of practice for every line of service offered by the company, industry group, and geographic area. Employees are encouraged to contribute to K-Source by a knowledge manager who solicits their participation as well as by including it as part of their performance evaluation goals. Using K-Source, employees can create personal profiles, set up personalized news feeds from financial websites, access courses, e-books and webcasts, and participate in online discussions.

Self-Management Skills

Training programs should prepare employees to self-manage their use of new skills and behaviors on the job.[36] Specifically, within the training program, trainees should set goals for using skills or behaviors on the job, identify conditions under which they might fail to use them, identify the positive and negative consequences of using them, and monitor their use of them. Also, trainees need to understand that it is natural to encounter difficulty in trying to use skills on the job; relapses into old behavior and skill patterns do not indicate that trainees should give up. Finally, because peers and supervisors on the job may be unable to reward trainees using new behaviors or to provide feedback automatically, trainees need to create their own reward system and ask peers and managers for feedback.

As you should have realized by now, learning and transfer of training are closely related. If training does not facilitate learning there is nothing to transfer to the job.

Similarly, if employees do learn, transfer of training will not occur if the work environment does not support or actively discourages applying what was learned. Consider how Verizon, the telecommunication company, facilitates both learning and transfer through its instructor-led virtual classrooms which bring training to many of its geographically dispersed employees.[37] Recognizing the importance of keeping learners actively involved with each other and the training content, Verizon has implemented a number of new learning strategies. The training which supports its business customer service billing process combines leader-led discussions with interactive assignments that participants complete in groups in virtual breakout rooms. Webinars include online polling to keep learners engaged. Its information technology classes include labs and simulated technical equipment for practice and instruction. For retail training, Verizon's Virtual Trainer (VT) brings the trainer to the retail store virtually with initial training provided by VT. VT is then supported by a document completed by the learner and used as a job aid to reinforce training, a discussion guide used by managers to discuss examples, ideas, content, and activities, and a scenario and coaching form that gives the learner the opportunity to apply skills after training.

SELECTING TRAINING METHODS

LO 7-5

Discuss the strengths and weaknesses of presentation, hands-on, and group training methods.

A number of different methods can help employees acquire new knowledge, skills, and behaviors. Figure 7.5 provides an overview of the use of training methods across all size companies. The instructor-led classroom still remains the most frequently used training method. However, it is important to note that the use of online learning, mobile learning, social learning, and use of blended learning, i.e., a combination of approaches, for training continues to increase. Expectations are that this trend with continue.

Figure 7.5

Overview of Use of Training Methods

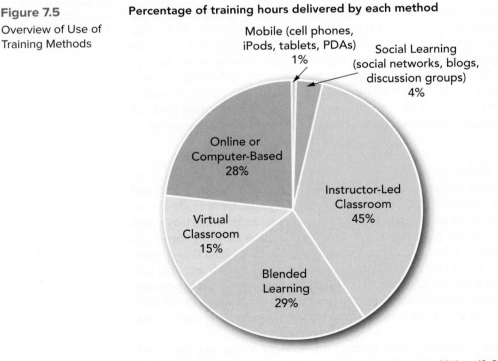

Percentage of training hours delivered by each method

SOURCE: Data from "2014 Industry Report," *Training,* November/December 2014, pp. 16–29.

Adopting Training Practices for Global Businesses

Consider how globalization has affected the training practices of Philips, Accenture, and Etihad Airways. Philips is the Dutch technology company that focuses on health care, lighting, and consumer lifestyle products. Philips' learning function has to serve employees in more than 100 different countries. As a result, the company has developed a standard global learning approach that is locally appropriate. Philips has global standards in place to ensure learning is high quality but each business unit is encouraged to tailor learning to match learners' needs at the location. For example, in India and China employees are encouraged to learn using one-on-one coaching, but in Europe employees are more receptive to learning delivered online. Accenture employs approximately 281,000 employees working in 200 cities and 56 countries around the world. To bring expertise to its multiple worldwide locations, Accenture has created a global network of virtual classrooms that can connect to each other. This means that experts located in one location can now share their skills with employees in locations around the world who need those skills. Training flight attendants to act as a team in an emergency is one of the biggest challenges facing global airlines. Etihad Airways, a Persian Gulf airline, operates in English, but it is the second language for almost all employees. As a result, Etihad revised its training program to include more visual learning for its employees, who come from 113 different countries. Interactive computer programs teach flight attendants how to set a business-class dinner table to the airline's standards by clicking and dragging pictures rather than reading instructions.

DISCUSSION QUESTIONS

1. What are the advantages and disadvantages of using virtual classrooms for training a global workforce? How would you overcome the disadvantages?
2. How might you have to adapt online or e-learning programs that include text, video, and discussion groups moderated by a trainer for a global audience?

SOURCES: Based on K. Kuehner-Hebert, "Philips: A Learning Organization Transformed," *Chief Learning Officer*, October 2014, pp. 22–25; F. Kalman, "Accenture: Staying Ahead of the Curve," *Chief Learning Officer*, June 2014, pp. 24–25; S. McCartney, "A Future Model for Flight Crews," *The Wall Street Journal*, December 4, 2014, pp. D1–D2.

One estimate is that nearly 40% of executives plan to use tablets such as the iPad in their new training and development initiatives.[38] These devices are expected to be used for learning and performance support but also for coaching and mentoring employees, mobile gaming, and microblogging (e.g., Twitter).

Regardless of the training method, for training to be effective it needs to be based on the training design model shown in Figure 7.2. Needs assessment, a positive learning environment, and transfer of training are critical for training program effectiveness. The "Competing through Globalization" box shows how globalization affects the choice of training methods.

Presentation Methods

Presentation methods refer to methods in which trainees are passive recipients of information. Presentation methods include traditional classroom instruction, distance learning, and audiovisual training. They can include the use of personal computers, smartphones, and tablet computers such as iPads. These methods ideal for presenting new facts, information, different philosophies, and alternative problem-solving solutions or processes.

Presentation Methods
Training methods in which trainees are passive recipients of information.

Instructor-Led Classroom Instruction. Classroom instruction typically involves having the trainer lecture a group. In many cases the lecture is supplemented with question-and-answer periods, discussion, or case studies. Classroom instruction remains a popular training method despite new technologies such as interactive video and computer-assisted instruction. Traditional classroom instruction is one of the least expensive, least time-consuming ways to present information on a specific topic to many trainees. The more active participation, job-related examples, and exercises that the instructor can build into traditional classroom instruction, the more likely trainees will learn and use the information presented on the job. For example, PPL Electric Utilities uses a classroom session to introduce its storm damage assessors to devices used to identify damage, patrolling techniques, and reporting.[39] Then the assessors participate in a simulation involving a downed power line and are asked to perform a patrol and provide a written assessment of the power line. Assessors are also invited to participate in an annual storm drill.

Distance learning is used by geographically dispersed companies to provide information about new products, policies, or procedures as well as skills training and expert lectures to field locations.[40] Distance learning features two-way communications between people.[41] First, it can include teleconferencing. **Teleconferencing** refers to synchronous exchange of audio, video, and/or text between two or more individuals or groups at two or more locations. Trainees attend training programs in training facilities in which they can communicate with trainers (who are at another location) and other trainees using the telephone or personal computer. Second, distance learning can include a virtual classroom. A third type of distance learning also includes individualized, personal-computer–based training.[42] Employees participate in training anywhere they have access to a personal computer. This can also include **webcasting**, which involves face-to-face instruction provided online through live broadcasts. Course material, including video, can be distributed using the company's intranet. Trainers and trainees interact using e-mail, bulletin boards, and conferencing systems. Distance learning can also allow trainees to respond to questions posed during the training program using a keypad.

Distance learning usually includes a link so that trainees viewing the presentation can call in questions and comments to the trainer. Also, satellite networks allow companies to link up with industry-specific and educational courses for which employees receive college credit and job certification. IBM, Digital Equipment, and Eastman Kodak are among the many firms that subscribe to the National Technological University, which broadcasts courses throughout the United States that technical employees need to obtain advanced degrees in engineering.[43]

An advantage of distance learning is that the company can save on travel costs. It also allows employees in geographically dispersed sites to receive training from experts who would not otherwise be available to visit each location.

The major disadvantage of distance learning is the potential for lack of interaction between the trainer and the audience. To help ensure distance learning is effective, a high degree of interaction between trainees and the trainer is necessary.[44] That's why establishing a communications link between employees and the trainer is important. Also, on-site instructors or facilitators should be available to answer questions and moderate question-and-answer sessions.

Audiovisual Training. *Audiovisual training* includes overheads, slides, and video. It has been used for improving communications skills, interviewing skills, and customer-service skills and for illustrating how procedures (such as welding) should be followed. Video is, however, rarely used alone. Learners may not be required to attend a class. They can work independently, using materials in workbooks, DVDs, or on the Internet.

Teleconferencing
Synchronous exchange of audio, video, or text between individuals or groups at two or more locations.

Webcasting
Classroom instruction provided online via live broadcasts.

PowerPoint or other presentational software and video or audio clips can also be used to show learning points, real-life experiences, and examples. Audiovisual training can easily be made available on desktop computers, smartphones, and tablet computers. These devices allow users to access the materials at any time or place. They also allow instruction to include video clips, podcasts, charts and diagrams, learning points, and lectures. This helps facilitate learning though appealing to a variety of the users' senses and both communicating and demonstrating knowledge, skills, and behaviors. For example, a restaurant called Flippin' Pizza provides training via an iPad app.[45] Trainees can use the app to link to a series of short videos each with a lesson in cooking or customer service.

© Jetta Productions/Getty Images

Mobile technology is useful not only for entertainment but can also be used for employees who travel and need to be in touch with the office. Smartphones, tablets, and other digital devices also give employees the ability to listen to and participate in training programs at their leisure.

Sales representatives at Coca-Cola Bottling Company Consolidated (CCBCC) are responsible for business development and customer relationships.[46] Most of their time is spent traveling to meet customer needs or visiting prospects for new business. To help sales reps better manage their workload and meet their sales quotas, CCBCC developed an online learning program. Sales reps can use an iPad to access an app that links to the program's content as well as videos on key concepts and action planning templates. The program's content covers how to get work done, how to work smart, and how to handle information overload. The app also includes editable PDF files that allow sales reps working with their managers during on-the-job coaching sessions to create and update action plans. The app is frequently used by sales reps, and its use has contributed to a 20% increase in daily sales calls.

The use of audio visual training has a number of advantages. First, users have control over the presentation. They can review, slow down, or speed up the lesson, which permits flexibility in customizing the session depending on trainees' expertise. Second, trainees can be exposed to equipment, problems, and events that cannot be easily demonstrated in a classroom. Another advantage is that learners get a consistent presentation.

Most problems from these methods result from having too much content for the trainee to learn, overuse of humor or music, and drama that distracts from the key learning points.[47]

Hands-on Methods

Hands-on methods are training methods that require the trainee to be actively involved in learning. Hands-on methods include on-the-job training, simulations, business games and case studies, behavior modeling, interactive video, and web-based training. These methods are ideal for developing specific skills, understanding how skills and behaviors can be transferred to the job, experiencing all aspects of completing a task, and dealing with interpersonal issues that arise on the job.

Hands-on Methods
Training methods that actively involve the trainee in learning.

ON-THE-JOB TRAINING (OJT)

On-the-job training (OJT) refers to new or inexperienced employees learning through observing peers or managers performing the job and trying to imitate their behavior. OJT can be useful for training newly hired employees, upgrading experienced employees' skills when new technology is introduced, cross-training employees within a department or work unit, and orienting transferred or promoted employees to their new jobs.

On-the-Job Training (OJT)
Peers or managers training new or inexperienced employees who learn the job by observation, understanding, and imitation.

OJT takes various forms, including apprenticeships and internships. (Both are discussed later in this section.) OJT is an attractive training method because, compared to other methods, it needs less investment in time or money for materials, trainer's salary, or instructional design. Managers or peers who are job knowledge experts are used as instructors. OJT must be structured to be effective. Table 7.6 shows the principles of structured OJT.

Apprenticeship is a work-study training method with both on-the-job training and classroom training. To qualify as a registered apprenticeship program under state or federal guidelines, at least 144 hours of classroom instruction and 2,000 hours, or one year, of on-the-job experience are required.[48] Apprenticeships can be sponsored by individual companies or by groups of companies cooperating with a union. The majority of apprenticeship programs are in the skilled trades, such as plumbing, carpentry, electrical work, and bricklaying.

The hours and weeks that must be devoted to completing specific skill units are clearly defined. OJT involves assisting a certified tradesperson (a journeyman) at the work site. The on-the-job training portion of the apprenticeship follows the guidelines for effective on-the-job training.[49]

A major advantage of apprenticeship programs is that learners can earn pay while they learn. This is important because programs can last several years. Learners' wages usually increase automatically as their skills improve. Also, apprenticeships are usually effective learning experiences because they involve learning why and how a task is performed in classroom instruction provided by local trade schools, high schools, or community colleges. Apprenticeships also usually result in full-time employment for trainees when the program is completed. From the company's perspective, apprenticeship programs meet specific business needs and help to attract talented employees.

At its manufacturing facility in Toledo, Ohio, Libbey Glass has apprenticeship programs in mold making, machine repair, millwrighting, and maintenance repair.[50] Each

Apprenticeship
A work-study training method with both on-the-job and classroom training.

Table 7.6
Principles of On-the-Job Training

PREPARING FOR INSTRUCTION	
1. Break down the job into important steps. 2. Prepare the necessary equipment, materials, and supplies.	3. Decide how much time you will devote to OJT and when you expect the employees to be competent in skill areas.

ACTUAL INSTRUCTION	
1. Tell the trainees the objective of the task and ask them to watch you demonstrate it. 2. Show the trainees how to do it without saying anything. 3. Explain the key points or behaviors. (Write out the key points for the trainees, if possible.) 4. Show the trainees how to do it again. 5. Have the trainees do one or more single parts of the task and praise them for correct reproduction (optional).	6. Have the trainees do the entire task and praise them for correct reproduction. 7. If mistakes are made, have the trainees practice until accurate reproduction is achieved. 8. Praise the trainees for their success in learning the task.

SOURCES: Based on W. J. Rothwell and H. C. Kazanas, "Planned OJT Is Productive OJT," *Training and Development Journal,* October 1990, pp. 53–55; P. J. Decker and B. R. Nathan, *Behavior Modeling Training* (New York: Praeger Scientific, 1985).

apprentice requires the support of a journeyman for each work assignment. The program also requires apprentices to be evaluated every 1,000 hours to meet Department of Labor standards. The reviews are conducted by a committee including representatives of management and department journeymen. The committee also develops tests and other evaluation materials. The committee members cannot perform their normal duties during the time they are reviewing apprentices so their workload has to be spread among other employees or rescheduled for some other time. The benefits of the program include the development of employees who are more receptive to change in the work environment, the ability to perform work at Libbey instead of having to outsource jobs to contract labor, and an edge for Libbey in attracting talented employees who like the idea that after completing an apprenticeship they are eligible for promotions to other positions in the company, including management positions. Also, the apprenticeship program helps Libbey tailor training and work experiences to meet specific needs in maintenance repair, which is necessary to create and repair production mold equipment used in making glass products.

One disadvantage of apprenticeship programs is that there is no guarantee that jobs will be available when the program is completed. Another disadvantage is that employers may not hire apprentices because they believe apprentices are narrowly trained in one occupation or with one company, and program graduates may have only company-specific skills and may be unable to acquire new skills or adapt their skills to changes in the workplace.

An **internship** is on-the-job learning sponsored by an educational institution or is part of an academic program. Students are placed in paid positions where they can gain experiences related to their area of study. For example, Ford, Whirlpool, and Rolls-Royce use interns in human resources and engineering positions. If they perform well many companies offer interns full-time positions after they complete their studies.

Internship
On-the-job learning sponsored by an educational institution, or part of an academic program.

Simulations. A **simulation** is a training method that represents a real-life situation, with trainees' decisions resulting in outcomes that mirror what would happen if the trainee were on the job. Simulations, which allow trainees to see the impact of their decisions in an artificial, risk-free environment, are used to teach production and process skills as well as management and interpersonal skills. Simulations are used for training pilots, cable installers, and call center employees.

Simulation
A training method that represents a real-life situation, allowing trainees to see the outcomes of their decisions in an artificial environment.

Flight simulators including full motion and high-resolution graphics are recent additions to pilot training in the commercial helicopter industry.[51] The simulators are intended to improve helicopters' safety record. On average more than one major helicopter accident occurs each day somewhere in the world. Training accidents using actual helicopters account for approximately one-fourth of all commercial crashes. Buying or leasing a simulator can cost millions of dollars while contracting costs range between $1,000 and $1,500 dollars per hour. But the cost is much less than the hourly cost of taking helicopters out of service to teach pilots. Also, in addition to cost savings the simulators allow pilots to focus on important safety issues and emergency procedures that are impossible to replicate in an actual helicopter.

Avatars refer to computer depictions of humans that are being used as imaginary coaches, co-workers, and customers in simulations.[52] Typically, trainees see the avatar who appears throughout the training course. For example, a sales training course at CDW Corporation, a technology products and service company, guides trainees through mock interviews with customers. The avatar introduces the customer situation, and the trainee hears the customer speaking in a simulated phone conversation. The trainee has to determine with help from the avatar what is happening in the sales process by reading the customer's voice.

Avatars
Computer depictions of humans that can be used as imaginary coaches, co-workers, and customers in simulations.

Virtual Reality
Computer-based technology that provides trainees with a three-dimensional learning experience. Trainees operate in a simulated environment that responds to their behaviors and reactions.

A way to enhance simulations is through virtual reality. **Virtual reality** is a computer-based technology that provides trainees with a three-dimensional learning experience. Using specialized equipment or viewing the virtual model on the computer screen, trainees move through the simulated environment and interact with its components.[53] Technology is used to stimulate multiple senses of the trainee.[54] Devices relay information from the environment to the senses. For example, audio interfaces, gloves that provide a sense of touch, treadmills, or motion platforms are used to create a realistic, artificial environment. Devices also communicate information about the trainee's movements to a computer. These devices allow the trainee to experience the perception of actually being in a particular environment.

PPD is a global contract research organization that is involved in drug discovery, development, lifecycle management, and laboratory services. PPD uses a virtual 3D learning environment to deliver its clinical foundations program.[55] PPD created a virtual doctor's office, reception, and training and conference rooms. Both trainees and instructors communicate and interact using avatars. Excel, PowerPoint, and video can also be used along with the virtual universe. PPD found that virtual training improved the cost-effectiveness, speed, and employees' accessibility to training. Eight percent of trainees who participated in virtual programs preferred it to classroom training and 95% believed they were more engaged than in traditional instruction.

As you can see from the example, simulations can be effective for several reasons.[56] First, trainees can use them on their desktop, eliminating the need to travel to a central training location. Second, simulations are meaningful, get trainees involved in learning, and are emotionally engaging (they can be fun!). This helps increase employees' willingness to practice, retain, and improve their skills. Third, simulators provide a consistent message of what needs to be learned; trainees can work at their own pace; and, compared to face-to-face instruction, simulators can incorporate more situations or problems that a trainee might encounter. Fourth, simulations can safely put employees in situations that would be dangerous in the real world. Fifth, simulations have been found to result in positive outcomes such as training being completed in a shorter time compared to traditional training courses, and providing a positive return on investment. Disadvantages of simulations include their cost and need for constant updating. This is because simulators must have identical elements found in the work environment. The simulator needs to respond exactly as the equipment (or customer) would under the conditioned response given by the trainee.[57]

Business Games and Case Studies. Situations that trainees study and discuss (case studies) and business games in which trainees must gather information, analyze it, and make decisions are used primarily for management skill development. There are many sources of case studies including Harvard Business School and the Darden Business School at University of Virginia.

Games stimulate learning because participants are actively involved and they mimic the competitive nature of business. The types of decisions that participants make in games include all aspects of management practice, including labor relations (such as agreement in contract negotiations), marketing (the price to charge for a new product), and finance (financing the purchase of new technology). A realistic game or case may stimulate more learning than presentation methods (such as classroom instruction) because it is more meaningful. KLA-Tencor uses case studies as part of a program known as "The Situation Room" to help managers learn how to deal with common leadership problems.[58] A group of between 8 and 20 managers get together face-to-face or virtually each month for one year and read one of twelve 350- to 400-word case studies. The case is based on a real situation or problem that occurred at KLA-Tencor. The situation needs to be broad enough for most managers to have experienced the situation, issue, or problem, but specific enough to be useful. After they read the case, the managers are given three minutes to write their response to the situation. Participants share their responses and their peers provide feedback. If a peer doesn't like the response they can provide an alternative. After all participants have shared their responses four teams are formed and they are given "homework." Between the first and next session, participants are expected to meet for an hour in their teams and review content, models, methodology, and or tools that they have been exposed to in prior courses. Based on this review they are asked to provide a response to the situation. During the second session each of the participants share their prepared responses and discuss them. Based on what they learned from both the first and second session, participants are asked to prepare a personal response focusing on how they will handle this situation if they encounter it on their job. The outcomes of the sessions are documented on the company's knowledge management system so practices can be shared with other managers facing similar challenges.

CMS Energy uses an online game (The Resolver) to teach employees about conflicts of interest.[59] For example, employees understand that accepting bribes is illegal, but they might not understand all of the different types of bribes. The Resolver begins with clinking champagne glasses and receiving tickets for a sporting event. In the game players interact with different characters and make decisions. Each decision they make affects different people including colleagues, friends, and family members. Those affected by each decision discuss how the player's decision affects them. Teams of five employees are formed to compete against each other. During game play, the team format facilitates conversations and questions among team members about ethics and conflicts of interest. When the competition ends team members can see how they rank against others on an electronic online leaderboard. This stimulates further employee conversations about how they responded to the scenarios and what they should have done differently to earn more points.

Cases may be especially appropriate for developing higher-order intellectual skills such as analysis, synthesis, and evaluation. These skills are often required by managers, physicians, and other professional employees. Cases also help trainees develop the willingness to take risks given uncertain outcomes, based on their analysis of the situation. To use cases effectively, the learning environment must let trainees prepare and discuss their case analyses. Also, face-to-face or electronic communication among trainees must be arranged. Because trainee involvement is critical for the effectiveness of the case method, learners must be willing and able to analyze the case and then communicate and defend their positions.

Behavior Modeling. Research suggests that behavior modeling is one of the most effective techniques for teaching interpersonal skills.[60] Each training session, which typically lasts four hours, focuses on one interpersonal skill, such as coaching or communicating ideas. Each session presents the rationale behind key behaviors, a DVD of a model performing key behaviors, practice opportunities using role-playing, evaluation of a model's performance in the videotape, and a planning session devoted to understanding how the key behaviors can be used on the job. In the practice sessions, trainees get feedback regarding how closely their behavior matches the key behaviors demonstrated by the model. The role-playing and modeled performance are based on actual incidents in the employment setting in which the trainee needs to demonstrate success.

E-Learning. **E-Learning**, *computer-based training (CBT), online learning,* and *web-based training* refer to instruction and delivery of training by computer through the Internet or the web.[61] To enhance learning all of these training methods can include and

LO 7-6
Explain the potential advantages of e-learning for training.

E-Learning
Instruction and delivery of training by computers through the Internet or company intranet.

integrate into instruction text, interaction using simulations and games, video, collaboration using blogs, wikis, and social networks, and hyperlinks to additional resources. In some types of CBT training content is provided standalone using software or DVDs with no connection to the Internet. Trainees can still interact with the training content, answer questions, and choose responses regarding how they would behave in certain situations, but they cannot collaborate with other learners. For example, Wipro Technologies developed a tool they call a Unified Learning Kit (ULK), a portable laptop programmable computer that enables new employees to experiment in engineering subjects.[62] One ULK can teach more than 10 different technical subjects related to hardware and software engineering.

Online learning, e-learning, and web-based training all include delivery of instruction using the Internet or web. The training program can be accessed using a password through the public Internet or the company's private intranet. There are many potential features that can be included in online learning to help trainees learn and transfer training to their jobs. For example, online programs that use video may make it an interactive experience for trainees. That is, trainees watch the video and have the opportunity to use the keyboard or touch the screen to answer questions, provide responses to how they would act in certain situations, or identify the steps they would take to solve a problem. Interactive video is especially valuable for helping trainees learn technical or interpersonal skills.

Greyhound Lines, the transportation company, has geographically dispersed employees including supervisors, field representatives, counter and customer service staff, and bus drivers who work around the clock every day of the year.[63] Greyhound uses e-learning to give employees access to leadership, business, and customer service skills courses when they need them.

Repurposing
Directly translating instructor-led training online.

Effective e-learning is grounded on a thorough needs assessment and complete learning objectives. **Repurposing** refers to directly translating an instructor-led, face-to-face training program online. Online learning that merely repurposes an ineffective training program will remain ineffective. Unfortunately, in their haste to develop online learning, many companies are repurposing bad training! The best e-learning combines the advantages of the Internet with the principles of a good learning environment. Effective online learning takes advantage of the web's dynamic nature and ability to use many positive learning features, including linking to other training sites and content through the use of hyperlinks, and allowing the trainee to collaborate with other learners. Online learning also gives learner control over the pace of learning, exercises, and use of links to other material and peer and expert networks. Online learning allows activities typically led by the instructor (presentation, visuals, slides), trainees (discussion, questions), and group interaction (discussion of application of training content) to be incorporated into training without trainees or the instructor having to be physically present in a training room. Effective online learning gives trainees meaningful content, relevant examples, and the ability to apply content to work problems and issues. Also, trainees can practice and receive feedback through problems, exercises, assignments, and tests.

Massive Open Online Courses (MOOCs)
Online learning designed to enroll large numbers of learners who have access to the Internet, and composed of interactive coursework including video lectures, discussion groups, wikis, and assessment quizzes.

Massive open online courses (MOOCs) are a new type of e-learning. **Massive open online courses (MOOCs)** is learning that is designed to enroll large number of learners (massive), is free and accessible to anyone with an internet connection (open), takes place online using videos of lectures, interactive course work including discussion groups, and wikis (online), and has specific start and completion dates, quizzes and assessment, and exams (courses).[64] MOOCs cover a wide variety of subject matter including chemistry, math, physics, computer science, philosophy, mythology, health policy, cardiac arrest and resuscitation, and even poetry. Popular providers of MOOCs include Coursera, edX (nonprofit founded by Harvard and MIT), and Udacity (a for-profit company founded by a Stanford University Research professor and founder of Google X Labs). The courses are often developed in partnership with colleges and universities, and recently, private companies. For example, edX is working with UPS, Procter & Gamble, and Walmart to design computer science and supply-chain management courses. Learners can take the course and complete a test that will earn them a certificate.[65]

MOOCs have several advantages and disadvantages.[66] Their low cost, accessibility, and wide range of topics make them attractive to learners. They include many features that facilitate learning and transfer: learning is interactive, learner-controlled, involves social interaction, and emphasizes application. Learning happens through engaging short lectures combined with interaction with course materials, interaction with other students and the instructor. It emphasizes applying knowledge and skills using role plays, cases, and projects. It is semi-synchronous meaning learners receive the same assignments, video lectures, readings, quizzes, and discussions, but they can complete the coursework on their own time. Also, many MOOCs offer college credit or certificates of completion which provide incentives for learning and formal acknowledgement. However, despite claims that MOOCs will revolutionize training and education, they have significant disadvantages. The interaction with the course of those who enroll in MOOCs tends to drop off after the first two weeks of the course, course completion rates are low (10–20%), and most students who complete the courses don't take the credential exam. MOOCs may also be inappropriate for courses where synchronous or real-time collaboration or interaction is needed.

Social Media. **Social media** refer to online and mobile technology used to create interactive communications allowing the creation and exchange of user-generated content.[67] They include blogs (a webpage where entries can be posted and readers can comment), wikis (a website with content created and edited by users), networks such as Facebook and LinkedIn, microsharing sites such as Twitter, and shared media such as YouTube. Many companies are considering using tablets such as the iPad for training because of their ease of use, colorful easy-to-read display, ability to connect to the web, access to social media, and availability of powerful apps. For example, Farmers Insurance Group supplies smartphones to its claim representatives.[68] They can use the smartphone to access product cards to learn about insurance policies, review requirements for settling atypical insurance claims, or learn about changes in policies. At Sonic, the fast-food restaurant, recipes and employee activities are constantly changing due to a rotating menu.[69] Sonic managers can use their smartphones to review food preparations with a team member, view a video, access store reports, contact experts, and post questions and answers to an online learning community. *Apps* refer to applications designed specifically for smartphones and tablet computers. Apps are primarily being used to supplement training, manage the path or sequence of training, and help employees maintain training records.[70] The "Competing through Technology" box highlights how social media and apps are being used for training.

Social Media
Online and mobile technology used to create interactive communications.

Blended Learning. Because of the limitations of e-learning related to technology (e.g., insufficient bandwidth, lack of high-speed web connections), because of trainee preference for face-to-face contact with instructors and other learners, and because of employees' inability to find unscheduled time during their workday to devote to learning from their desktops, many companies are moving to a hybrid, or blended, learning approach. **Blended learning** refers to combining technology methods, such as e-learning or social media, with face-to-face instruction, for delivery of learning content and instruction.

Blended Learning
Delivering content and instruction with a combination of technology-based and face-to-face methods.

Using Social Media and Apps for Learning

Evans Analytical Group (EAG), a high-tech analytical services company, is using social media to reduce the time it takes to locate subject matter experts and to connect its globally dispersed employees. Employees use Twitter, LinkedIn, or the company intranet to find and collaborate with subject matter experts, acquire and contribute knowledge, and discuss applications of knowledge and skills learned in training. Employees are encouraged to use blogs and wikis by linking their usage to their performance appraisals, publicly recognizing employees with the highest weekly usage rates, and CEO endorsements of their importance at company meetings. Training videos, tutorials, and frequently asked questions (FAQs) that employees can access on the intranet are provided to help employees understand how to use the tools and their value.

Sales representatives at Coca-Cola Bottling Company Consolidated (CCBCC) are responsible for business development and customer relationships. Most of their time is spent traveling to meet customer needs or visiting prospects for new business. To help sales reps better manage their workload and meet their sales quotas, CCBCC developed an online learning program. Sales reps can use an iPad to access an app that links to the program's content as well as videos on key concepts and action planning templates. The program's content covers how to get work done, how to work smart, and how to handle information overload. The app also includes editable PDF files that allow sales reps working with their managers during on-the-job coaching sessions to create and update action plans.

DISCUSSION QUESTION

As shown in Figure 7.1, continuous learning is supported by knowledge management, informal learning, and formal training and development. For which of these features of a continuous learning strategy are social learning and apps most effective? Explain why.

SOURCE: Based on J. Thomas, "At EAG, Learning's All About the Chatter," *Chief Learning Officer,* February 2015, pp. 42–43, 49; P. Harris, "Relying on Street Smarts," *T + D,* October 2014, pp. 92–94.

Farmers Insurance uses a blended learning approach to deliver effective learning to its multigenerational employees and insurance agents who are located across the country.[71] Farmers' training programs integrate face-to-face instruction, print, online, video, audio, virtual simulations, and coaching. Technology is used for delivering knowledge and instructor-led training is used for skill development.

Learning Management System (LMS)
Technology platform that automates the administration, development, and delivery of a company's training program.

Learning Management System. A **learning management system (LMS)** refers to a technology platform that can be used to automate the administration, development, and delivery of all of a company's training programs. An LMS can provide employees, managers, and trainers with the ability to manage, deliver, and track learning activities.[72] LMSs are becoming more popular for several reasons. An LMS can help companies reduce travel and other costs related to training, reduce time for program completion, increase employees' accessibility to training across the business, and provide administrative capabilities to track program completion and course enrollments. An LMS allows companies to track all of the learning activity in the business. MasTec's utility services group uses an LMS to help manage its training programs.[73] MasTec wanted to be able to make training content available to employees who work in rural areas as well as in cities. Also, they wanted to make it easier for employees to register for training and managers to approve their enrollment, and to see training requirements, participation rates, and training completion. Using MasTec's online LMS, employees can log in and view training courses and curriculum, access e-learning and videos, and schedule instructor-led courses. Employees can also access company safety bulletins and enroll in U.S. Department of Labor apprenticeship programs. Managers can request reports that show training requirements and which employees have met them. They can display course completion dates, training quiz scores, and expiration dates for compliance training that employees may have completed.

Group- or Team-Building Methods

Group- or team-building methods are training methods designed to improve team or group effectiveness. Training is directed at improving the trainees' skills as well as team effectiveness. In group-building methods, trainees share ideas and experiences, build group identity, understand the dynamics of interpersonal relationships, and get to know their own strengths and weaknesses and those of their co-workers. Group techniques focus on helping teams increase their skills for effective teamwork. All involve examination of feelings, perceptions, and beliefs about the functioning of the team; discussion; and development of plans to apply what was learned in training to the team's performance in the work setting. Group-building methods fall into three categories: experiential programs, team training, and action learning.

Experiential Programs. **Experiential programs** involve gaining conceptual knowledge and theory; taking part in a behavioral simulation or activity; analyzing the activity; and connecting the theory and activity with on-the-job or real-life situations.[74]

For experiential training programs to be successful, several guidelines should be followed. The program needs to tie in to a specific business problem. The trainees need to be moved outside their personal comfort zones but within limits so as not to reduce trainee motivation or ability to understand the purpose of the program. Multiple learning modes should be used, including audio, visual, and kinesthetic. When preparing activities for an experiential training program, trainers should ask trainees for input on the program goals. Clear expectations about the purpose, expected outcomes, and trainees' role in the program are important. Finally, training programs that include experiential learning should be linked to changes in employee attitudes, behaviors, and other business results.

DaVita Healthcare Partners provides kidney-related health care services such as dialysis.[75] DaVita contracted with a training provider to develop a three-hour experiential learning activity that would be collaborative, have a sense of purpose, and reinforce the company's values of teamwork, fulfillment, and fun. The goals of the program were to understand the importance or why of work, understand how team members relate to patients and to each other, and how to address challenges. The activity started with a discussion of the importance of communicating and collaborating for successful teamwork on the job. Employees were divided into three member teams and given the task of building prosthetic hands that would be donated to organizations serving amputees. Building the prostheses provided an opportunity for the achievement of the program's goals. The employees built more than 14,000 prostheses during the three-hour activity. The activity concluded with a discussion of ways to apply what they learned to their jobs at DaVita.

Adventure learning, a type of experiential program, develops teamwork and leadership skills using structured outdoor activities.[76] Adventure learning appears to be best suited for developing skills related to group effectiveness, such as self-awareness, problem solving, conflict management, and risk taking. Adventure learning may involve strenuous, challenging physical activities such as dogsledding or mountain climbing. It can also use structured individual and group outdoor activities such as climbing walls,

Group- or Team-Building Methods
Training techniques that help trainees share ideas and experiences, build group identity, understand the dynamics of interpersonal relationships, and get to know their own strengths and weaknesses and those of their co-workers.

Experiential Programs
Training programs in which trainees gain knowledge and theory, participate in behavioral simulations, analyze the activity, and connect the theory and activity with on-the-job situations

Adventure Learning
Learning focused on the development of teamwork and leadership skills by using structured outdoor activities.

going through rope courses, making trust falls, climbing ladders, and traveling from one tower to another using a device attached to a wire that connects the two towers.

To improve their leadership skills and teamwork, lawyers at Weil, Gotshal, & Manges in New York worked with New York City firefighters to learn how to hook up a fire hose, set the water pressure, and extinguish fires.[77] At the fire academy four-person teams rushed into burning buildings, rescued passengers in simulated subway accidents or other emergency drills. The FDNY program, Firefighter for a Day Team Challenge, was created to help teams develop decision-making and problem solving skills.

Adventure learning can also include demanding activities that require coordination and place less of a physical strain on team members. For example, Cookin' Up Change is one of many team-building courses offered around the United States by chefs, caterers, hotels, and cooking schools.[78] These courses have been used by companies such as Honda and Microsoft. The underlying idea is that cooking classes help strengthen communications and networking skills by requiring team members to work together to create a full-course meal (a culinary feast!). Each team has to decide who does what kitchen tasks (e.g., cooking, cutting, cleaning) and prepares the main course, salads, or dessert. Often team members are required to switch assignments in midpreparation to see how the team reacts to change.

For adventure learning programs to succeed, the exercises should be related to the types of skills that participants are expected to develop. Also, after the exercises, a skilled facilitator should lead a discussion about what happened in the exercise, what was learned, how the exercise relates to the job situation, and how to set goals and apply what was learned on the job.[79]

Does adventure learning work? Participants often report that they gained a greater understanding of themselves and the ways they interact with their co-workers. One key to the success of an adventure learning program may be the insistence that whole work groups participate together so that group dynamics that inhibit effectiveness can emerge and be discussed.

The physically demanding nature of adventure learning and the requirement that trainees often have to touch each other in the exercises may increase the company's risk for negligence claims due to personal injury, intentional infliction of emotional distress, and invasion of privacy. Also, the Americans with Disabilities Act (discussed in Chapter 3) raises questions about requiring employees with disabilities to participate in physically demanding training experiences.

Team Training. Team training coordinates the performance of individuals who work together to achieve a common goal. Such training is an important issue when information must be shared and individuals affect the overall performance of the group. For example, in the military as well as the private sector (think of nuclear power plants or commercial airlines), much work is performed by crews, groups, or teams. Success depends on coordination of individual activities to make decisions, team performance, and readiness to deal with potentially dangerous situations (like an overheating nuclear reactor).

Cross-Training
Team members understand and practice each other's skills.

Coordination Training
Trains the team in how to share information and decisions.

Team training strategies include cross-training and coordination training.[80] In **cross-training** team members understand and practice each other's skills so that members are prepared to step in and take another member's place. **Coordination training** trains the team in how to share information and decisions to maximize team performance. Coordination training is especially important for commercial aviation and surgical teams, who monitor different aspects of equipment and the environment but must share information to make the most effective decisions regarding patient care or aircraft safety and performance. **Team leader training** refers to training the team manager or facilitator. This may involve training the manager how to resolve conflict within the team or help the team coordinate activities or other team skills.

United Airlines (UAL) had its supervisors "lead" ramp employees in attending Pit Instruction & Training (Pit Crew U), which focuses on the preparation, practice, and teamwork of NASCAR pit crews. United used the training to develop standardized methods to safely and efficiently unload, load, and send off its airplanes.[81] Pit Instruction & Training, located outside of Charlotte, North Carolina, has a quarter-mile race track and a pit road with places for six cars. The school offers programs to train new racing pit crews, but most of its business comes from companies interested in having their teams work as safely, efficiently, and effectively as NASCAR pit crews. The training was part of a multimillion-dollar investment that includes updating equipment and providing luggage scanners. The purpose of the training is to reinforce the need for ramp teams to be orderly and communicate, to help standardize tasks of ramp team members, to help shorten the time an airplane is serviced at the gate, and to improve morale.

The keys for safety, speed, and efficiency for NASCAR pit crews is that each member knows what tasks to do (change tires, use air gun, add gasoline, clean up spills) and, when the crew has finished servicing the race car, moves new equipment into position anticipating the next pit stop. The training involved the ramp workers actually working as pit crews. They learn how to handle jacks, change tires, and fill fuel tanks on race cars. They are videotaped and timed just like real pit crews. They receive feedback from professional pit crew members who work on NASCAR teams and trainers. Also, the training requires them to deal with circumstances they might encounter on the job. For one pit stop, lug nuts had been sprinkled intentionally in the area where the car stops to see if the United employees would notice them and clean them up. On their jobs ramp employees are responsible for removing debris from the tarmac so it doesn't get sucked into jet engines or harm equipment. For another pit stop, teams had to work with fewer members, as sometimes occurs when ramp crews are understaffed due to absences.

Action Learning. In **action learning** teams or work groups get an actual business problem, work on solving it and commit to an action plan, and are accountable for carrying out the plan.[82] Typically, action learning involves between 6 and 30 employees; it may also include customers and vendors. There are several variations on the composition of the group. In one variation the group includes a single customer for the problem being dealt with. Sometimes the groups include cross-functional team members (members from different company departments) who all have a stake in the problem. Or the group may involve employees from multiple functions who all focus on their own functional problems, each contributing to helping solve the problems identified.

Consider how Sony and Kirin Brewery used action learning teams to provide solutions to urgent and complex business problems.[83] Sony was losing income because of sales revenue losses due to consumers' increased use of downloaded music such as iTunes. An action learning team of seven managers all from different countries met for a week in London, England, to identify ways to increase revenue. The solution they developed was a services contract in which Sony Music would distribute music and arrange artists' tours, market their merchandise, and help get their music placed in movies and television shows. This solution led to millions of dollars in revenue and helped Sony sign contracts with music artists from other record labels. Leaking beer cans and stale beer were examples of the types of quality problems that Kirin Brewery was experiencing, resulting in decreased sales and undermining of customer relationships. An action learning team with representatives from customer service, sales, manufacturing, and quality control was given the problem to develop a strategy for producing a higher quality can. The action learning team developed a redesigned beer can resulting in reduced manufacturing time, lower costs, and fewer customer complaints.

Action learning is often part of quality improvement processes such as Six Sigma training and Kaizen. Kaizen, the Japanese word for improvement, is one of the underlying principles of lean manufacturing and total quality management (we discussed lean thinking in Chapter 1). **Kaizen** refers to practices participated in by employees from all levels of the company that focus on continuous improvement of business processes.[84] Just Born, the company that makes Mike and Ikes and Peeps, uses the Wow . . . Now Improvement Process, a customized Kaizen process to improve business processes and results.[85] The Wow . . . Now Improvement Process includes training employees how to identify improvement opportunities, collect data, make improvements, measure results, and based on the results refine practices. As the Wow . . . Now Improvement Process illustrates, Kaizen involves considering a continuous cycle of activities including planning, doing, checking, and acting (PDCA). Statistical process controls such as cause-and-effect diagrams and scattergrams are used by employees to identify causes of problems and potential solutions.

Kaizen
Practices participated in by employees from all levels of the company that focus on continuous improvement of business processes.

Advice for Choosing a Training Method

LO 7-7
Design a training session to maximize learning.

Given the large number of training methods available to you, this task may seem difficult. One way to choose a training method is to compare methods. The first step in choosing a method is to identify the type of learning outcome that you want training to influence. These outcomes include verbal information, intellectual skills, cognitive strategies, attitudes, motor skills, or some combination. Training methods may influence one or several learning outcomes.

Also, you should take into account that, there is considerable overlap between learning outcomes across the training methods. Group-building methods are unique because they focus on individual as well as team learning (e.g., improving group processes). If you are interested in improving the effectiveness of groups or teams, you should choose one of the group-building methods (e.g., action learning, team training, adventure learning). Second, comparing the presentation methods to the hands-on methods illustrates that most hands-on methods provide a better learning environment and transfer of training than do the presentation methods. The presentation methods are also less effective than the hands-on methods. E-learning or blended learning can be an effective training method for geographically dispersed trainees. E-learning and other technology-driven training methods have higher development costs, but travel and housing cost savings will likely offset development costs over time. To take advantage of the positive features of both face-to-face and technology-based instruction, you should consider a blended learning approach. For example, Nationwide Mutual Insurance uses several different methods to train new agents.[86] An interactive game is used to help agents understand the lifecycle of an insurance policy. It includes an animated simulation using different customer profiles. New agents watch and listen to experienced agents interacting and communicating with customers both face-to-face and over the phone. They also engage in self-directed learning including calling competitors to get an insurance quote and evaluating their experience. A final but important consideration is the training budget. If you have a limited budget for developing new training methods, use structured on-the-job training—a relatively inexpensive yet effective hands-on method. If you have a larger budget, you might want to consider hands-on methods that facilitate transfer of training, such as simulators.

EVALUATING TRAINING PROGRAMS

Training evaluation can provide useful information including the program's strengths and weaknesses, identifying which learners benefited most and least from participating, determining the program's financial benefits and costs, and allowing the comparison of the benefits and costs of different programs.

Examining the outcomes of a program helps in evaluating its effectiveness. These outcomes should be related to the program objectives, which help trainees understand the purpose of the program. **Training outcomes** can be categorized as cognitive outcomes, skill-based outcomes, affective outcomes, results, and return on investment.[87] Table 7.7 shows the types of outcomes used in evaluating training programs and what is measured and how it is measured.

HCL Technologies, an IT consulting firm, grew during the last three years despite the economic recession and competition.[88] To be successful HCL employees must stay current on new tools and mobile and web technologies. To ensure that its employees' skills are up-to-date, HCL developed a technical academy that provides online learning, classroom instruction, on the job experiences, and mentoring. To facilitate employees' continuous improvement employees are encourage to complete technical certifications through taking courses and learning through virtual online labs which simulate real technical environments. Ninety percent of the learning programs are developed internally. HCL invested millions of dollars in learning and through this investment the company believes it can stay ahead of the competition and grow the business. HCL has found that employees who finish certification programs generate more billable hours, stay employed with the company longer, and are more satisfied.

LO 7-8
Choose appropriate evaluation design and training outcomes based on the training objectives and evaluation purpose.

Training Outcomes
A way to evaluate the effectiveness of a training program based on cognitive, skill-based, affective, and results outcomes.

Table 7.7
Outcomes Used in Evaluating Training Programs

OUTCOME	WHAT IS MEASURED	HOW MEASURED	EXAMPLE
Cognitive outcomes	• Acquisition of knowledge	• Pencil-and-paper tests • Work sample	• Safety rules • Electrical principles • Steps in appraisal interview
Skill-based outcomes	• Behavior • Skills	• Observation • Work sample • Ratings	• Jigsaw use • Listening skills • Coaching skills • Airplane landings
Affective outcomes	• Motivation • Reaction to program • Attitudes	• Interviews • Focus groups • Attitude surveys	• Satisfaction with training • Beliefs regarding other cultures
Results	• Company payoff	• Observation • Data from information system or performance records	• Absenteeism • Accidents • Patents
Return on investment	• Economic value of training	• Identification and comparison of costs and benefits of the program	• Dollars

Which training outcomes measure is best? The answer depends on the training objectives. For example, if the instructional objectives identified business-related outcomes such as increased customer service or product quality, then results outcomes should be included in the evaluation. Both reaction and cognitive outcomes are usually collected before the trainees leave the training site. As a result, these measures do not help determine the extent to which trainees actually use the training content in their jobs (transfer of training). Skill-based, affective, and results outcomes measured following training can be used to determine transfer of training—that is, the extent to which training has changed behavior, skills, or attitudes or directly influenced objective measures related to company effectiveness (such as sales).

Evaluation Designs

As shown in Table 7.8, a number of different evaluation designs can be applied to training programs. Table 7.8 compares each evaluation design on the basis of who is involved (trainees and/or a comparison group that does not receive training), when outcome measures are collected (pretraining, posttraining), the costs, the time needed to conduct the evaluation, and the strength of the design for ruling out alternative explanations for the results (e.g., are improvements due to factors other than the training?). In general, designs that use pretraining and posttraining measures of outcomes and include a comparison group reduce the risk that factors other than training itself are responsible for the evaluation results. This builds confidence to use the results to make decisions. The trade-off is that evaluations using these designs are more costly and time-consuming to conduct than evaluations not using pretraining or posttraining measures or comparison groups.

For example, if a manager is interested in determining how much employees' communications skills have changed as a result of a behavior-modeling training program, a pretest/posttest comparison group design is necessary. Trainees should be randomly assigned to training and no-training conditions. These evaluation design features give the manager a high degree of confidence that any communication skill change is the result of participating in the training program.[89] This type of evaluation design is also necessary if the manager wants to compare the effectiveness of two training programs.

Table 7.8
Comparison of Evaluation Designs

DESIGN	GROUPS	MEASURES PRETRAINING	POSTTRAINING	COST	TIME	STRENGTH
Posttest only	Trainees	No	Yes	Low	Low	Low
Pretest/posttest	Trainees	Yes	Yes	Low	Low	Medium
Posttest only with comparison group	Trainees and comparison	No	Yes	Medium	Medium	Medium
Pretest/posttest with comparison group	Trainees and comparison	Yes	Yes	Medium	Medium	High
Time series	Trainees	Yes	Yes, several	Medium	Medium	Medium

EVIDENCE-BASED HR

Sometimes naturally occurring comparison groups are available which provide the opportunity to use the pretest/posttest with comparison group or posttest with comparison group evaluation designs. This can occur because of the realities of scheduling employees to attend training (all employees cannot attend training at the same time) or when new training is implemented. For example, some employees may be scheduled to receive training later than others. The employees who do not initially receive training can be considered the comparison group. Outcomes can be measured and comparisons made between the employee group who received training and the employees who are waiting to receive the training. Consider how Mountain American Credit Union evaluated the effectiveness of a revised sales training program. Mountain American tracked the average monthly sales of 30 new employees during their first two months of employment. Ten of the 30 employees attended training before it was revised (they called this the Traditional Group). Twenty employees attended the program after it was revised (the Express Group). The revised program included more interactions with a variety of customers with different needs. Monthly sales were compared between the Express Group and the Traditional Group. Sales in the Express Group exceeded sales in the Traditional Group in both the first (11.4 versus 3.5 average sales) and second month (34.83 versus 5.5) of employment.

SOURCE: Based on "Mountain American Credit Union: Flow Philosophy Training," *Training*, January/February 2015, p. 103.

Many companies are interested in determining the financial benefits of learning, including training courses and programs and development activities (development activities are discussed in the next chapter). One way to do this is by determining return on investment (ROI). **Return on investment (ROI)** refers to the estimated dollar return from each dollar invested in learning. Keep in mind that ROI is not a substitute for outcomes that also provide an indication of the success or usefulness of learning such as trainees' reactions, knowledge acquisition, or behavior change. Also, ROI is best suited for outcomes that can be quantified such as quality, accidents, or turnover, otherwise you will have to make a well-considered educated guess about the value of the outcome (e.g., how do you value increased leadership skills?).

Return on Investment (ROI)
Refers to the estimated dollar return from each dollar invested in learning.

Determining the Financial Benefits of Learning
To make an ROI analysis follow these steps:[90]

1. Identify outcomes (e.g., quality, accidents).
2. Place a value on the outcomes.
3. Determine the change in performance after eliminating other potential influences on training results.
4. Obtain an annual amount of benefits (operational results) from training by comparing results after training to results before training (in dollars).
5. Determine the training costs (direct costs + indirect costs + development costs + overhead costs + compensation for trainees).
6. Calculate the total savings by subtracting the training costs from benefits (operational results).

7. Calculate the ROI by dividing benefits (operational results) by costs. The ROI gives an estimate of the dollar return expected from each dollar invested in training.

ROI can be measured and communicated based on a percentage or a ratio. For example, assume that a new safety training program results in a decline of 5% in a company's accident rate. This provides a total annual savings (the benefit) of $150,000 in terms of lost workdays, material and equipment damage, and workers' compensation costs. The training program costs $50,000 to implement (including both direct and indirect costs). To calculate the ROI you need to subtract the training costs from the benefits, divide by the costs, and multiply by 100. That is, ROI = [(150,000 − 50,000) ÷ 50,000] × 100% = 200%. The ROI for this program is 200%. Another way to think about ROI is to consider it as a ratio based on the return for every dollar spent. In this example, the company gained a net benefit of $2 for every dollar spent. This means the ROI is 2:1. Tata Consultancy Service LTD, a global information technology services company headquartered in India, measures ROI for its technology training programs.[91] To calculate the ROI, revenues earned as a result of training are calculated based on the billing rates of participants who attend the training and use the new skills. Then, training costs are subtracted from the revenues. ROI for the technical programs is 483%.

Special Training Issues

To meet the competitive challenges of sustainability, globalization, and technology discussed in Chapter 1, companies must successfully deal with several special training issues. The special training issues include preparing employees to work in different cultures abroad, managing workforce diversity, and socializing and orienting new employees.

CROSS-CULTURAL PREPARATION

Expatriate
Employee sent by his or her company to manage operations in a different country.

As we mentioned in Chapter 1, companies today are challenged to expand globally. Because of the increase in global operations, employees often work outside their country of origin or work with employees from other countries. An **expatriate** works in a country other than his or her country of origin. The most frequently selected locations for expatriate assignments include the United States, China, Africa, and India.[92] At Ernst & Young, about 2,600 of over 167,000 employees are on an international assignment at any one time including 270 Americans in 30 countries including Brazil, China, India, Russia, and South Africa.[93] Many U.S. companies are using expatriate assignments as a training tool. For example, employees who want top management positions, such as chief financial officer, need to understand how cultural norms and the political environment influence the movements in currencies and commodities in order to build effective global financial plans.[94]

Guardian Industries, a glass manufacturer in Michigan, has expats in 18 different countries.[95] Guardian's expat retention rate is close to 90% which is likely due to how it treats the expats during and after their assignments. Guardian values expat experience by looking at these employees first when considering whom to fill open positions. While on their assignments, Guardian stays in contact with the expats. Expat assignments can be of varying lengths depending on business needs. One former expat spent 13 years in Saudia Arabia and Thailand moving from department head to plant manager. The expat and his family asked to return to the U.S. but the company had no plant manager openings.

The expat was willing to take a lower-level position to learn things he didn't yet know about the business. When a plant manager position became available it was offered to him. We discuss international human resource management in detail in Chapter 15. Here the focus is on understanding how to prepare employees for expatriate assignments.

Cross-cultural preparation educates employees (expatriates) and their families who are to be sent to a foreign country. To successfully conduct business in the global marketplace, employees must understand the business practices and the cultural norms of different countries.

Cross-Cultural Preparation
The process of educating employees (and their families) who are given an assignment in a foreign country.

Steps in Cross-Cultural Preparation

To succeed overseas, expatriates (employees on foreign assignments) need to be

1. Competent in their areas of expertise.
2. Able to communicate verbally and nonverbally in the host country.
3. Flexible, tolerant of ambiguity, and sensitive to cultural differences.
4. Motivated to succeed, able to enjoy the challenge of working in other countries, and willing to learn about the host country's culture, language, and customs.
5. Supported by their families.[96]

One reason why U.S. expatriates' often fail is that companies place more emphasis on developing employees' technical skills than on preparing them to work in other cultures. This has resulted in failed overseas assignments which means companies don't fully capitalize on business opportunities and incur costs for replacing employees who leave the company after returning to the United States.[97] Cross-cultural preparation is especially important because North American companies plan to increase the length of expatriate assignments from two to five years.[98] Research suggests that the comfort of an expatriate's spouse and family is the most important determinant of whether the employee will complete the assignment.[99] Studies have also found that personality characteristics are related to expatriates' desire to terminate the assignment and performance in the assignment.[100] Expatriates who were extroverted (outgoing), agreeable (cooperative and tolerant), and conscientious (dependable, achievement oriented) were more likely to want to stay on the assignment and perform well. This suggests that cross-cultural training may be effective only when expatriates' personalities predispose them to be successful in assignments in other cultures.

The key to a successful foreign assignment is a combination of training and career management for the employee and family.

Predeparture Phase

Before departure, employees need to receive language training and an orientation to the new country's culture and customs. It is critical that the family be included in orientation programs.[101] Expatriates and their families need information about housing, schools, recreation, shopping, and health care facilities in the areas where they will live. Expatriates also must discuss with their managers how the foreign assignment fits into their career plans and what types of positions they can expect upon return.

Cross-cultural training methods include presentational techniques, such as lectures that expatriates and their families attend on the customs and culture of the host country, immersion experiences, or actual experiences in the home country in culturally diverse communities.[102] Experiential exercises, such as miniculture experiences, allow expatriates to spend time with a family in the United States from the ethnic group of the host country. For example, an Indian trainer took 20 managers from Advanced Micro Devices on a two-week immersion trip during which the group traveled to New Delhi, Bangalore, and Mumbai, meeting with business persons and government officials.[103] The program required six months of planning, including providing the executives with information on foods to eat, potential security issues, and how to interact in business meetings. For example, Indians prefer a relatively indirect way into business discussions, so the managers were advised to discuss current events and other subjects before talking business.

Research suggests that the degree of difference between the United States and the host country (cultural novelty), the amount of interaction with host country citizens and host nationals (interaction), and the familiarity with new job tasks and work environment (job novelty) all influence the "rigor" of the cross-cultural training method used.[104] Hands-on and group-building methods are most effective (and most needed) in assignments with a high level of cultural and job novelty that require a good deal of interpersonal interaction with host nationals.

On-Site Phase

On-site training involves continued orientation to the host country and its customs and cultures through formal programs or through a mentoring relationship. Expatriates should be encouraged to develop social relationships both inside and outside of the workplace.[105] Expatriates and their families may be paired with an employee from the host country who helps them understand the new, unfamiliar work environment and community.[106] Companies are also using the web to help employees on expatriate assignments get answers to questions.[107] Expatriates can use a website to get answers to questions such as, How do I conduct a meeting here? or What religious philosophy might have influenced today's negotiation behavior? Knowledge management software allows employees to contribute, organize, and access knowledge specific to their expatriate assignment.

A major reason that employees refuse expatriate assignments is that they can't afford to lose their spouse's income or are concerned that their spouse's career could be derailed by being out of the workforce for a few years.[108] Some "trailing" spouses decide to use the time to pursue educational activities that could contribute to their long-term career goals. But it is difficult to find these opportunities in an unfamiliar place. GlaxoSmithKline's International Service Center, which handles all of its relocations from or to the United States, offers a buddy system for spouses to connect with others who have lived in the area for the past several years.[109] General Motors offers career continuation services which reimburse spouses $2,500 each year during the expatriate assignment for maintaining professional licenses or certifications. The World Bank manages an Internet site dedicated for expatriates where spouses can post resumes and ask for job leads.

Repatriation Phase

Repatriation
The preparation of expatriates for return to the parent company and country from a foreign assignment.

Repatriation prepares expatriates for return to the parent company and country from the foreign assignment. Expatriates and their families are likely to experience high levels of stress and anxiety when they return because of the changes that have occurred since their departure. Employees should be encouraged to self-manage the repatriation process.[110] Before they go on the assignment they need to consider what skills they want to develop and the types of jobs that might be available in the company for an employee with those skills. Because the company changes and colleagues, peers, and managers may leave while the expatriate is on assignment, they need to maintain contact with key company and industry contacts. Otherwise, on return the employees' reentry shock will be heightened when they have to deal with new colleagues, a new job, and a company culture that may have changed. This includes providing expatriates with company newsletters and community newspapers and ensuring that they receive personal and work-related mail from the United States while they are on foreign assignment. It is also not uncommon for employees and their families to have to readjust to a lower standard of living in the United States than they had in the foreign country, where they may have enjoyed maid service, a limousine, private schools, and clubs. Salary and other compensation arrangements should be worked out well before employees return from overseas assignments.

Aside from reentry shock, many expatriates decide to leave the company because the assignments they are given upon returning to the United States have less responsibility, challenge, and status than their foreign assignments.[111] For example, after completing five overseas assignments in operations and human resources positions in Indonesia and China, a manager for Walmart Stores left the company because he missed the responsibility and authority he had in these assignments.[112] He couldn't find a similar position with Walmart when he completed his last international assignment. As a result, he took a job at Kimberly-Clark's international division as vice president of human resources. As noted earlier, career planning discussions need to be held before the employees leave the United States to ensure that they understand the positions they will be eligible for upon repatriation. At Xerox, expatriates are assigned a sponsor who helps ensure the assignment is a good fit and helps them transition back to the United States.[113]

Royal Dutch Shell, a joint Dutch and United Kingdom oil and gas company, has one of the world's largest expatriate workforces. To avoid expatriates who feel undervalued and leave the company, Royal Dutch gets involved with expatriates and their career. Resource planners track workers abroad, helping to identify their next assignment. Most expatriates know their next assignment three to six months before the move, and all begin the next assignment with a clear job description. Expatriates who have the potential to reach top-level management positions are placed in the home office every third assignment to increase their visibility to company executives. Expatriates are also assigned technical mentors who evaluate their skills and help them improve their skills through training at Royal Dutch's training center.

MANAGING WORKFORCE DIVERSITY AND INCLUSION

Diversity can be considered any dimension that differentiates a person from another.[114] For example at Verizon diversity means embracing differences and variety including age, ethnicity, education, sexual orientation, work style, race, gender, and more. **Inclusion** refers to creating an environment in which employees share a sense of belonging, mutual respect, and commitment from others so they can perform their best work.[115] Inclusion allows companies to capitalize not only on the diversity of their employees but also on their customers, suppliers, and community partners.

Diversity training refers to learning efforts that are designed to change employee attitudes about diversity and or/develop skills needed to work with a diverse workforce. However, training alone is insufficient to capitalize on the strengths of a diverse workforce.[116] **Managing diversity and inclusion** involves creating an environment that allows all employees to contribute to organizational goals and experience personal growth. This environment includes access to jobs as well as fair and positive treatment of all employees. The company must develop employees who are comfortable working with people from a wide variety of ethnic, racial, and religious backgrounds. Managing diversity may require changing the company culture. It includes the company's standards and

Inclusion
Refers to creating an environment in which employees share a sense of belonging, mutual respect, and commitment from others.

LO 7-10
Develop a program for effectively managing diversity.

Diversity Training
Refers to learning efforts that are designed to change employee attitudes about diversity and or/develop skills needed to work with a diverse workforce.

Managing Diversity and Inclusion
The process of creating an environment that allows all employees to contribute to organizational goals and experience personal growth.

norms about how employees are treated, competitiveness, results orientation, innovation, and risk taking. The value placed on diversity is grounded in the company culture.

For example, BAE Systems requires that middle managers and executives take a two-hour class on unconscious bias.[117] Unconscious bias means that based on their background and experiences, managers might unintentionally make employment decisions that give preference to individuals with certain characteristics such as the color of their skin, age, body type, or personality. Trainees watch videos, participate in exercises, and discuss research to help them understand why unconscious bias occurs and how to overcome it. In addition to this training BAE Systems also takes steps to manage diversity and inclusion.[118] For example, BAE has changed the composition of the interview panels used to hire middle managers. The interview panels now include women and people of color as well as white males. As a result, the number of women and people of color in managers' roles has increased about 10%.

Diversity may enhance performance when organizations have an environment that promotes learning from diversity. Research shows that diversity training has a small to medium effect on affective (attitudes), cognitive (acquiring knowledge), and behavioral outcomes.[119] There is no evidence to support the direct relationship between diversity and business.[120] Rather, a company will see the success of its diversity efforts only if it makes a long-term commitment to managing diversity. Successful diversity requires that it be viewed as an opportunity for employees to (1) learn from each other how to better accomplish their work, (2) be provided with a supportive and cooperative organizational culture, and (3) be taught leadership and process skills that can facilitate effective team functioning. Diversity is a reality in labor and customer markets and is a social expectation and value. Managers should focus on building an organizational environment, on human resource practices, and on managerial and team skills that all capitalize on diversity. As you will see in the discussion that follows, managing diversity requires difficult cultural change, not just slogans on the wall!

Consider Sodexo's diversity effort.[121] Sodexo is the leading food and facilities management company in the United States, Canada, and Mexico, daily serving 10 million customers. With employees in 80 countries representing 128 nationalities connecting with customers on a daily basis, a policy of inclusion is not an option or a choice—it is a business necessity. Sodexo is focused on gender representation, generational opportunities in the workplace, people with disabilities, and ethnic minority representation. As a result, diversity and inclusion are core elements of the business strategy. Sodexo believes that diversity and inclusion is a fundamental business objective focused on employees (e.g., work culture, recruitment, talent development, work life effectiveness), customers, clients, and shareholders (e.g., supplier diversity, cross-market diversity council, diversity consulting), and communities (e.g., Sodexo Foundation, Community Partners). For example, some of the objectives include understanding and living the business case for diversity and inclusion; increasing awareness of how diversity relates to business challenges; creating and fostering a diverse work environment by developing management practices that drive hiring, promotion, and retention of talent; engaging in relationship management and customer service to attract and retain diverse clients and customers; and partnering with women and minority businesses to deliver food and facility management services. Diversity and inclusion are core competencies at Sodexo. Diversity and inclusion are part of employees' training and managers' annual performance review; new employee orientation emphasizes Sodexo's values and expectations regarding diversity and inclusion.

Sodexo separates Equal Employment Opportunity (EEO) and legal compliance training from diversity training. At Sodexo, diversity training is part of the managing diversity strategy. Every three years, employees are required to take EEO and affirmative action refresher courses. Top management is also involved in and committed to managing diversity. The senior executives program includes ongoing classroom training that is reinforced with community involvement, sponsoring employee groups, and mentoring diverse employees. Executives are engaged in learning the business case for diversity and are personally held accountable for the company's diversity agenda. Every manager takes an eight-hour introductory class (Spirit of Diversity). Sodexo's diversity training involves learning labs focused on skill building and diversity awareness. Examples of these learning labs include Generations in the Workplace, Disability Awareness Training, Cross-Cultural Communications, and Improving Team Effectiveness through Inclusion. The company's learning and development team develops customized learning solutions for different functions and work teams. For example, a course related to selling to a diverse client base was developed and offered to the sales force, and a cross-cultural communications program was provided for recruiters.

In addition to diversity training activities, Sodexo has six employee network groups—such as the African American Leadership Forum, People Respecting Individuality, Diversity, and Equality (PRIDE), Honoring Our Nation's Finest with Opportunity and Respect (HONOR), and the Intergenerational Network Group (IGEN). These network groups provide forums for helping employees feel a sense of community, learning from each other, developing their careers, and sharing input and ideas to support the companys' diversity efforts. Sodexo's "Champions of Diversity" program rewards and recognizes employees who advance diversity and inclusion.

To emphasize the importance of diversity for the company, at Sodexo each manager has a diversity scorecard that evaluates their success in recruitment, retention, promotion, and development of all employees. The scorecard includes both quantitative goals as well as evaluation of behaviors such as participating in training, mentoring, and doing community outreach. A proportion of their pay bonuses is determined by success in these areas.

Sodexo has found that its diversity training and efforts to manage diversity are having a positive impact on business results. Its mentoring program has led to increased productivity, engagement, and retention of women and people of color. There was an estimated return on investment of $19 for every dollar spent on the program. Sodexo also has been awarded several new business contracts and retained clients because of its involvement in managing diversity. Sodexo has also been recognized for its diversity and inclusion efforts, which helps attract talented employees by signaling that the company cares about the well-being of all of its employees. Sodexo has been ranked number 2 on the 2012 DiversityInc Top 50 Companies for Diversity list. This marks the third consecutive year that Sodexo has been ranked number 2. Sodexo is also recognized as a top company for executive women and ranked among the top 10 companies for Latinos, blacks, global diversity, and people with disabilities. Most effective programs to manage diversity, such as Sodexo's diversity program, include the key components shown in Table 7.9.

As should be apparent from this discussion, successful diversity programs involve more than just an effective training program. They require an ongoing process of culture change that includes top management support, a position in charge of managing diversity (Chief Diversity Officer), as well as diversity policies and practices in the areas of recruitment and hiring, training and development, and administrative structures, such as conducting diversity surveys and evaluating managers' progress on diversity goals.[122] They also focus on enhancing diversity and inclusion with suppliers, vendors, and in the communities where the company conducts business. ABB North America recently

Table 7.9
Key Components of Effective Managing Diversity Programs

Top Management Support
- Make the business case for diversity.
- Include diversity as part of the business strategy and corporate goals.
- Participate in diversity programs, and encourage all managers to attend.
- Ensure that the composition of the executive management team mirrors the diversity of the workforce.

Recruitment and Hiring
- Ask search firms to identify wider arrays of candidates.
- Enhance the interviewing, selection, and hiring skills of managers.
- Expand college recruitment at historically minority colleges.

Identifying and Developing Talent
- Form a partnership with internship programs that target minority students for management careers.
- Establish a mentoring process.
- Refine the company's global succession planning system to improve identification of talent.
- Improve the selection and development of managers and leaders to help ensure that they are capable of maximizing team performance.
- Ensure that all employees, especially women and minorities, have access to management development and leadership programs.

Employee Support
- Form resource groups or employee network groups, including employees with common interests, and use them to help the company develop business goals and understand the issues they are concerned with (e.g., Asian Pacific employees, women, gays, lesbians, transgenders, Native Americans, veterans, Hispanics).
- Celebrate cultural traditions, festivities, and holidays.
- Make work/life balance initiatives (such as flextime, telecommuting, eldercare) available to all employees.

Ensuring Fair Treatment
- Conduct extensive diversity training.
- Implement an alternative dispute resolution process.
- Include women and minorities on all human resources committees throughout the company.

Holding Managers Accountable
- Link managers' compensation to their success in meeting diversity goals and creating openness and inclusion in the workplace.
- Use employee attitude or engagement surveys to track employees' attitudes such as inclusion, fairness, opportunities for development, work/life balance, and perceptions of the company culture.
- Implement 360-degree feedback for all managers and supervisors.

Improving Relationships with External Stakeholders
- Increase marketing to diverse communities.
- Provide customer service in different languages.
- Broaden the company's base of suppliers and vendors to include businesses owned by minorities and women.
- Provide scholarships and educational and neighborhood grants to diverse communities and their members.

SOURCES: Based on B. Groysberg and K. Connolly, "Great Leaders Who Make the Mix Work," *Harvard Business Review,* September 2013, pp. 68–76; K. Bezrvkova, K. Jehn, and C. Spell, "Reviewing Diversity Training: Where Have We Been and Where Should We Go?" *Academy of Management Learning & Education* 11 (2012), pp. 207–227; R. Anand and M. Winters, "A Retrospective View of Corporate Diversity Training from 1964 to the Present," *Academy of Management Learning & Education* 7 (2008), pp. 356–72; C. Chavez and J. Weisinger, "Beyond Diversity Training: A Social Infusion for Cultural Inclusion," *Human Resource Management* 47 (2008), pp. 331–50; V. Smith, "Texaco Outlines Comprehensive Initiatives," *Human Resource Executive,* February 1997, p. 13; "Diversity & Inclusion," Verizon's diversity program available at the company website, www.verizon.com.

created a chief diversity and inclusion officer position reporting directly to the CEO.[123] This sends a message that diversity is supported and creates a position responsible for managing diversity and inclusion and establishing metrics to track progress.

Onboarding and Socialization

Onboarding, or socialization, refers to the process of helping new hires adjust to social and performance aspects of their new jobs.[124] This is important to help employees adjust to their jobs by establishing relationships to increase satisfaction, clarifying goals and expectations to improve performance, and providing feedback, coaching, and follow-up activities to reduce turnover. There is wide variation in the types of onboarding programs across companies. However, effective onboarding involves the four steps shown in Figure 7.6. Effective onboarding does include understanding mundane tasks such as completing tax forms and knowing how to complete time sheets or travel reimbursement forms. But it goes beyond compliance to include enhancing new hires' self-confidence, their feeling socially comfortable and accepted by their peers and manager, understanding their role and job expectations, responsibilities, and performance requirements, and helping them "fit" into and understand the company culture. Effective onboarding is related to many important outcomes for the employee and the company including higher job satisfaction, organizational commitment, lower turnover, higher performance, reduced stress and career effectiveness.[125]

Table 7.10 shows the characteristics of effective onboarding programs. Effective onboarding programs actively involve the new employee. Several companies offer onboarding programs that include the characteristics shown in Table 7.10. New hires at Sierra Nevada Corporation, a company in the defense and aerospace industry, are contacted by the company's talent acquisition and training teams before orientation.[126] The program includes a review of the company's history, culture, vision, and values. New hires' first day on the job includes a meet-and-greet lunch date with their manager. Employees continue onboarding for 90 days, which includes e-learning, mentoring, on-the-job training, and a performance review. Booz Allen's onboarding programs involve face-to-face and online activities to enhance the effectiveness of their process. Booz Allen, a strategy and technology consulting company, revised their onboarding program to reduce the time it took for new employees to become productive, support

Onboarding
Refers to the process of helping new hires adjust to social and performance aspects of their new jobs.

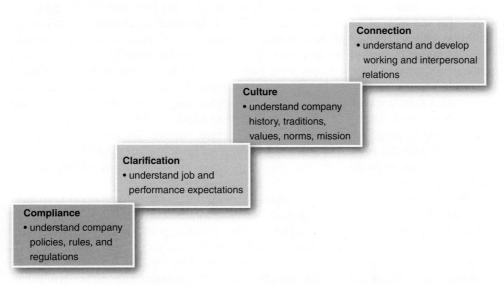

Figure 7.6

The Four Steps in Onboarding

Connection
• understand and develop working and interpersonal relations

Culture
• understand company history, traditions, values, norms, mission

Clarification
• understand job and performance expectations

Compliance
• understand company policies, rules, and regulations

SOURCE: Based on T. Bauer, "Onboarding New Employees: Maximizing Success" (Alexandria, VA: SHRM Foundation, 2010); G. Chao, A. O'Leary-Kelly, S. Wolf, H. Klein, and P. Gardner, "Organizational Socialization: Its Content and Consequences," *Journal of Applied Psychology* 79 (1994), pp. 730–743.

Table 7.10

Characteristics of
Effective Onboarding
Programs

Employees are encouraged to ask questions

Program includes information on both technical and social aspects of the job

The employee manager has some onboarding responsibility

Debasing or embarrassing new employees is avoided

Employees learn about the company culture, history, language, products, services, and customers

Follow-up of employee progress occurs at different points up to one year after joining the company

Program involves participation, active involvement, and formal and informal interaction between new hires and current employees

Relocation assistance is provided (such as house hunting or information sessions on the community for employees and their significant others)

their decision to join the company, and develop knowledge regarding the company culture and core values.[127] The new program, which spans 12 months, includes learning activities and events organized into three phases. The first phase, known as "Engage," is designed to motivate and prepare new hires for their first year. Engage spans two to three weeks. It includes learning activities that actively involve the new hires including working in cross-functional teams with members from different offices and levels. New hires can use their laptops to explore online resources for career planning and development. Teams of three new hires each begin to compete in a simulated year-long client project. They have access to an experienced employee who can provide insights and examples of how they have worked with clients during their career. Also, senior company leaders deliver welcome messages and lead discussions on how to succeed at the company. The second phase of the onboarding program, "Equip," begins the new hires' second week and continues through their first six months. "Equip" provides employees with the skills, behaviors, and tools they need for success at the company. It includes 30, 60, and 90 day meetings with their manager, a series of e-newsletters, and a detailed onboarding tool kit designed to reinforce and build on what they learned in the first phase of the program. The third and final phase, "Excel," emphasizes professional development, relationship building, and acceptance of the company's values. "Excel" involves the seven-month period through the end of the new hires' first year of employment. The employees' first annual performance review occurs at the end of "Excel." In addition to the three phases, new hires have access to and are encouraged to use the company's social media and knowledge management tool, known as the Onboarding Community, to discover and share information via blogs and take part in online activities and resources that support the onboarding program. As a result of the program, turnover for new employees who have been with the company six months or less has been reduced by 4%. Also, new employees' time to productivity has been reduced, saving the company millions of dollars in lost revenue.

Shape Corp. designs, engineers, manufactures, and tests metal and plastic products that absorb impact energy and protect vehicles, their occupants, and pedestrians.[128] Shape's employees work with cutting torches, welders, grinders, and other machinery. This makes it critical that Shape's orientation program focuses on safety as well as onboarding. Based on a needs assessment using employee focus groups, Shape found that many new employees had little experience working in manufacturing and had begun working prior to any training or orientation. As result, the orientation was changed from one day to four days for all new employees, followed by a six-day manufacturing technician training course for employees working in manufacturing. The new orientation includes speakers, plant tours, introduction to the company's mentoring program and the employee's mentor, web-based training, and instructor-led safety training. If employees fail the manufacturing technology training course they are not allowed to work in manufacturing and may be terminated. The orientation program has been implemented globally to 1,800 employees in their native languages. Shape constantly revises the program content based on focus groups who meet semi-annually. As a result of the new orientation program injury rates have decreased 75% among employees who have worked one year or less at Shape. The program provides employees with the knowledge they need to perform their jobs, improves their safety awareness, and helps them develop relationships at work that enhance their socialization.

A LOOK BACK

Keller Williams

The chapter opener highlights the different training methods that Keller Williams uses to support its business objectives.

QUESTIONS

1. What are the advantages and disadvantages of the blended learning approach used at Keller Williams?
2. Is Keller Williams' training strategic? Explain your answer.

SUMMARY

Technological innovations, new product markets, and a diverse workforce have increased the need for companies to reexamine how their training practices contribute to learning. In this chapter we discussed a systematic approach to training, including needs assessment, design of the learning environment, consideration of employee readiness for training, and transfer-of-training issues. We reviewed numerous training methods and stressed that the key to successful training was to choose a method that would best accomplish the objectives of training. We also emphasized how training can contribute to effectiveness through establishing a link with the company's strategic direction and demonstrating through cost–benefit analysis how training contributes to profitability. Managing diversity and cross-cultural preparation are two training issues that are relevant given company needs to capitalize on a diverse workforce and global markets.

KEY TERMS

Continuous learning, 265
Training, 265
Formal training, 265
Informal learning, 266
Explicit knowledge, 266
Tacit knowledge, 266
Knowledge management, 266
Training design process, 267
Needs assessment, 269

Organizational analysis, 270
Person analysis, 270
Task analysis, 270
Readiness for training, 275
Motivation to learn, 275
Transfer of training, 277
Manager support, 279
Action plan, 279
Support network, 280

Opportunity to perform, 280
Performance support systems, 280
Communities of practice, 281
Presentation methods, 283
Teleconferencing, 284
Webcasting, 284
Hands-on methods, 285
On-the-job training (OJT), 285
Apprenticeship, 286

DISCUSSION QUESTIONS

1. Noetron, a retail electronics store, recently invested a large amount of money to train sales staff to improve customer service. The skills emphasized in the program include how to greet customers, determine their needs, and demonstrate product convenience. The company wants to know whether the program is effective. What outcomes should it collect? What type of evaluation design should it use?

2. "Melinda," bellowed Toran, "I've got a problem and you've got to solve it. I can't get people in this plant to work together as a team. As if I don't have enough trouble with the competition and delinquent accounts, now I have to put up with running a zoo. It's your responsibility to see that the staff gets along with each other. I want a human relations training proposal on my desk by Monday." How would you determine the need for human relations training? How would you determine whether you actually had a training problem? What else could be responsible?

3. Assume you are general manager of a small seafood company. Most training is unstructured and occurs on the job. Currently, senior fish cleaners are responsible for teaching new employees how to perform the job. Your company has been profitable, but recently wholesale fish dealers that buy your product have been complaining about the poor quality of your fresh fish. For example, some fillets have not had all the scales removed and abdomen parts remain attached to the fillets. You have decided to change the on-the-job training received by the fish cleaners. How will you modify the training to improve the quality of the product delivered to the wholesalers?

4. A training needs analysis indicates that managers' productivity is inhibited because they are reluctant to delegate tasks to their subordinates. Suppose you had to decide between using adventure learning and a lecture using a virtual classroom for your training program. What are the strengths and weaknesses of each technique? Which would you choose? Why? What factors would influence your decision?

5. To improve product quality, a company is introducing a computer-assisted manufacturing process into one of its assembly plants. The new technology is likely to substantially modify jobs. Employees will also be required to learn statistical process control techniques. The new technology and push for quality will require employees to attend numerous training sessions. More than 50% of the employees who will be affected by the new technology completed their formal education more than 10 years ago. Only about 5% of the company's employees have used the tuition reimbursement benefit. How should management maximize employees' readiness for training?

6. A training course was offered for maintenance employees in which trainees were supposed to learn how to repair and operate a new, complex electronics system. On the job, maintenance employees were typically told about a symptom experienced by the machine operator and were asked to locate the trouble. During training, the trainer would pose various problems for the maintenance employees to solve. He would point out a component on an electrical diagram and ask, "What would happen if this component was faulty?" Trainees would then trace the circuitry on a blueprint to uncover the symptoms that would appear as a result of the problem. You are receiving complaints about poor troubleshooting from maintenance supervisors of employees who have completed the program. The trainees are highly motivated and have the necessary prerequisites. What is the problem with the training course? What recommendations do you have for fixing this course?

7. What factors contribute to the effectiveness of e-learning training programs?

8. Choose a job you are familiar with. Design a new employee onboarding program for that job. Explain how your program contributes to effective socialization.

9. Why might employees prefer blended learning to training using only iPads?

10. What learning condition do you think is most necessary for learning to occur? Which is least critical? Why?

11. What can companies do to encourage informal learning?

12. List and discuss the steps in cross-cultural preparation.

SELF-ASSESSMENT EXERCISE

Additional assignable self-assessments available in Connect.

In the chapter we discussed the need for learners to be motivated so that training will be effective. What is your motivation to learn? Find out by answering the following questions. Read each statement and indicate how much you agree with it, using the following scale:

5 = Strongly Agree
4 = Somewhat Agree
3 = Neutral
2 = Somewhat Disagree
1 = Strongly Disagree

1. I try to learn as much as I can from the courses I take.   5 4 3 2 1

2. I believe I tend to learn more from my courses than other students do.   5 4 3 2 1

3. When I'm involved in courses and can't understand something, I get so frustrated I stop trying to learn.   5 4 3 2 1

EXERCISING STRATEGY

IBM Offers Training (and Pay Cuts) to Employees to Learn New Technologies

Some employees in IBM's Global Technology Services group received e-mails from the company informing them that a recent evaluation had identified them as an employee who had not kept pace with acquiring the necessary skills and expertise needed to meet changing client needs, technology, and markets. As a result, IBM requires them to dedicate one day a week or up to 23 total days between October 2014 and March 2015 to focus on training. During this time, the employee will take a pay cut, receiving only 90% of their base salary. Once training is completed salaries will be restored in full. Employees can either take the training or look for job opportunities within IBM that better match their current skills set.

Employees have reacted negatively toward the program. Some feel the program with its pay cut is unfair because their work has received positive evaluations from their managers. Also, employees noted that all workers in their group were being assigned to the same training program regardless of their individual skill levels. A few employees believe that the training program is a cost-cutting exercise that is being presented as a training program. A spokesperson for IBM emphasized that the salary cut and retraining program was not standard practice across IBM but affected only a few hundred employees in the U.S. technology services

outsourcing business. The purpose of the program is to help employees develop key skills in areas such as cloud and mobile computing and advanced data analytics. Because the program can help employees in the long term to increase their billable hours with clients, IBM believes the salary cut is a co-investment cost shared by both the employees and the company. IBM calculated that it will lose one day of billing clients each week that the employees are in the training program, which matches the 20% of the compensation of the employees involved. So the 10% salary cut actually splits the difference.

QUESTIONS

1. Do you believe this program is strategic? Why or why not? Should employees' salaries be reduced for the time they attend training programs? Provide a rationale for your answer.

2. What other ways might IBM convince the affected employees to update and gain new skills?

SOURCES: P. Thibodeau, "IBM Cuts Pay by 10% for Workers Picked for Training," *Computerworld,* www.computerworld.com; accessed February 12, 2015, S. Lohr, "IBM Offers Workers Training and Pay Cuts," *The New York Times,* http://bits.blogs.nytimes.com; accessed February 12, 2015, P. Cappelli, "'Back to the Future' at IBM," *Human Resource Executive,* www.hreonline.com, accessed February 12, 2015.

MANAGING PEOPLE

Learning Opportunities for Employees Are No Accident at Farmers Insurance Group of Companies

Farmers Insurance Group of Companies is the third-largest insurer of auto and homeowners insurance in the United States and also provides other insurance and financial products. Farmers has 60,000 employees and exclusive and independent agents in every one of the 50 states. It processes millions of insurance quotes, new policies, renewals, and bills each year. In the insurance industry, legal requirements and the introduction of new products, processes and services make training and development critical for business success. At Farmers Insurance, learning professionals are rewarded based on the degree to which training programs change the behavior of employees and help the business meet its objectives. Learning is delivered based on the desired end result. No wonder that Farmers has been ranked in the Top 10 of *Training* magazine's Top 125 for the last four years and will be inducted into the Hall of Fame!

Farmers uses a blended learning approach to deliver effective learning to its multigenerational employees and agents who are located across the U.S. Farmers believes that rather than allowing learners to chose the type of training method that they believe best fits their style, a blended learning approach is more effective. As a result, its training programs integrate face-to-face instruction, print, online, video, audio, virtual simulations, and coaching. Technology is used for delivering knowledge and instructor-led training is used for skill development. In the past five years the amount of learning delivered through instructor-led classroom based training has dropped from 90 to 50%. The other 50% is online or informal learning. For example, Farmers is using various training methods to help its employees cope with the changes made in claims processing, ratings, billing and product systems in support of Farmers business strategy, which emphasizes customer experience, distribution, and product management excellence. For example, field managers were required to complete online training and webinars designed to provide the new knowledge they needed. Then the managers received instructor-led training, videos, and coaching guides. Farmers also revised its training program for new agents as a result of an increased failure rate of new agencies. The revised program includes more coaching, performance support aids, and multimedia methods. It also insures that new agents learn knowledge and skills when they are

relevant to their jobs rather than forcing them to learn everything at once and having them frustrated with being unable to recall the information when they need it later. As a result of the program revision, converting new agents to full-time status improved by 12%, sales results exceeded sales goals by 11%, and agency success rates increased 10%.

Recognizing that new technologies are potentially useful for training delivery and instruction, Farmers has started to use virtual classrooms, mobile learning, social networks, electronic tablets such as iPads, and learning simulations. While taking courses at the University of Farmers, learners can use electronic tablets to take notes, access websites and articles, and view videos. The video capabilities of the tablets allow instructors to use them to record the learners' practicing skills and then provide feedback and coaching. Also, the instructors can create learning materials such as iBooks with embedded videos. To encourage learning outside of a formal classroom environment, Farmers developed iFarmers apps for customers, sales agents, and employees. The iFarmers customer app helps customers learn about different insurance products. An iClaims app gives customers access to input and managing their insurance claims. The iAgent app provides business-focused learning for sales agents. Farmers has also been experimenting with social networking for employees to collaborate, create and share knowledge, and to provide performance support. Some training programs are using the social network for collaborative exercises. Farmers' "Agency Insider" program allows learners to specify whether they want to use Twitter, Facebook, e-mail, or an RSS feed.

QUESTIONS

1. Is Farmers' training strategic? Why? What information did you consider in determining your answer?
2. Does Farmers support informal learning? How? What else could the company do to facilitate informal learning?
3. How would Farmers determine if training, instead of some other reason, was responsible for the failure of new agents?

SOURCES: Based on www.farmers.com, website for Farmers Insurance; M. Weinstein, "Farmers' Comprehensive Training Policy," *Training* (January/February 2013), pp. 42–44; L. Freifeld, "Farmers' Premier Position," *Training* (January/February 2011), pp. 26–31; J. Salopek, "Thriving through Change, Cultivating Growth," *T + D* (October 2010), pp. 53–54.

HR IN SMALL BUSINESS

How Nick's Pizza Delivers Training Results

At first glance, Nick's Pizza & Pub sounds as ordinary as a company can be: a pizza restaurant with two locations, each

in one of Chicago's northwest suburbs. But when you take a look at the company's performance measures, something special seems to be going on. In an industry where 200% employee turnover and operating profits around 6.5% are normal, Nick's has to replace only 20% of its employees each year and enjoys operating profits of 14% or more. These results are amazing, especially for a business in which 4 out of 10 employees are high school students.

What makes the difference? It could be the culture at Nick's. Rather than hiring expert managers and laying down a lot of rules, Nick's is choosy about who gets hired for every position and then provides them with enough training to operate skillfully and exercise sound judgment. The whole training program emphasizes ways to develop trustworthy, dedicated employees.

Training at Nick's begins with a two-day orientation program. Trainees learn the company's purpose, values, and culture, and they participate in role-playing activities to practice those lessons. Then it's on to skills training, beginning with a course called simply 101. During that four-hour hands-on lesson in the kitchen, all the new employees—regardless of what their future job will be—learn to make a pizza. From there, the trainees divide into work groups for the next level of training. In 201, these groups of trainees embark on longer-term training to be certified in performing a particular job. For example, an employee might train in pizza making for a few weeks until he or she earns a certification as a pizza maker.

Class 201 ends the mandatory training, but Nick's provides incentives for further learning. An employee can participate in additional 201 courses to learn more jobs and earn a pay increase. An employee who earns two more certifications (say, one in salad making and one in sandwich preparation) enjoys a wage increase of 75 cents an hour—and the prestige of exchanging the uniform's tan hat for a red hat. Some employees earn nine certifications, after which their pay rises another $2 an hour, and they get to wear a black hat with their uniform.

Yet another level of training prepares employees to be trainers themselves. This level—301—prepares employees to earn a top skill rating in their areas of certification. Besides these task-oriented skills, the employees receive training in communication and leadership and study a book called *Mastery: The Keys to Success and Long-Term Fulfillment* by George Leonard. Employees who complete these requirements receive a Leadership 301 Passport, which includes a checklist of behaviors they are expected to model for the employees they lead. During the weeks that follow, they watch for situations in which they or others are exhibiting each behavior, jotting down descriptions of what they witnessed. When the listed behaviors have all been observed and noted, the participants take a course in training, and they finally are ready to be named trainers themselves.

Along with these formal training programs, Nick's provides further on-the-job learning through coaching by managers and trainers. The goal is to provide feedback in the moment, not waiting for performance appraisal meetings. For example, at the end of each shift, trainers will ask trainees to identify one thing they did well that day and one thing they would like to improve. In addition, managers are taught to observe employees' behavior on the job and ask themselves whether what they see would make them want to hire the employee. If yes, the manager is expected to give immediate positive feedback. If no, the manager is expected to coach the employee on how to do better.

QUESTIONS

1. To the extent that you can provide details from the information given and a visit to the Nick's Pizza website (www.nickspizzapub.com), prepare a needs assessment for training kitchen staff at Nick's. Remember to include organization, person, and task analyses.
2. How does the work environment support training at Nick's? In what additional ways, besides those described, could the work environment support training?
3. Do you think an outside contractor could provide training for Nick's as effectively as its current methods do? Why or why not? Are there some types or topics of training for which a contractor might be appropriate? If so, which ones?

SOURCES: Nick's Pizza & Pub corporate website, www.nickspizzapub.com, accessed May 18, 2015; and based on Bo Burlingham, "Lessons from a Blue-Collar Millionaire," *Inc.,* February 2010, www.inc.com.

NOTES

1. E. Salas and J. A. Cannon-Bowers, "The Science of Training: A Decade of Progress," *Annual Review of Psychology* 52 (2002), pp. 471–99; R. Noe, "Employee Training and Development," 7th ed. (New York: McGraw-Hill Irwin, 2015); H. Aguinis, and K. Kraiger, "Benefits of Training and Development for Individuals, Teams, Organizations, and Society," *Annual Review of Psychology, 60* (2009), pp. 451–474.

2. U. Sessa and M. London, *Continuous Learning in Organizations* (Mahwah, NJ: Lawrence Erlbaum, 2006); M. London, "Lifelong Learning: Introduction," in M. London (ed.), *The Oxford Handbook of Lifelong Learning* (New York, Oxford University Press, 2011), pp. 3–11.

3. "2014 Industry Report," *Training,* November/December 2014, pp. 16–29.

4. J. Roy, "Transforming Informal Learning into a Competitive Advantage," *T + D,* October 2010, pp. 23–25; P. Galagan, "Unformal, the New Normal," *T + D,* September 2010, pp. 29–31.

5. S. I. Tannenbaum, R. Beard, L. A. McNall, and E. Salas, "Informal Learning and Development in Organizations," in S. W. J. Kozlowski and E. Salas (eds.), *Learning, Training, and*

Development in Organizations (New York: Routledge, 2010), pp. 303–32; D. J. Bear, H. B. Tompson, C. L. Morrison, M. Vickers, A. Paradise, M. Czarnowsky, M. Soyars, and K. King, *Tapping the Potential of Informal Learning. An ASTD Research Study* (Alexandria, VA: American Society for Training and Development, 2008).

6. T. Bingham and M. Conner, *The New Social Learning* (Alexandria, VA: ASTD Press, 2010).

7. J. Quinn, P. Andersen, and S. Finkelstein, "Leveraging Intellect," *Academy of Management Executive* 10 (1996), pp. 7–39; R. Ployhart and T. Moliterno, "Emergence of the Human Capital Resource: A Multilevel Model," *Academy of Management Review* 36 (2011), pp. 127–50; B. Campbell, R. Coff, and D. Kryscynski, "Rethinking Sustained Competitive Advantage from Human Capital," *Academy of Management Review* 37 (2012), pp. 376–95; T. Crook, S. Todd, J. Combs, D. Woehr, and D. Ketchen, Jr., "Does Human Capital Matter? A Meta-Analysis of the Relationship between Human Capital and Firm Performance," *Journal of Applied Psychology* 96 (2011), pp. 443–56.

8. I. Nonaka and H. Takeuchi, *The Knowledge-Creating Company: How Japanese Companies Create the Dynamics of Innovation* (New York: Oxford University Press, 1995).

9. S. E. Jackson, M. A. Hitt, and A. S. Denisi, eds., *Managing Knowledge for Sustained Competitive Advantage: Designing Strategies for Effective Human Resource Management* (San Francisco: Jossey-Bass, 2003); A. Rossett, "Knowledge Management Meets Analysis," *Training and Development,* May 1999, pp. 63–68; R. Davenport, "Why Does Knowledge Management Still Matter?" *T + D* 59 (2005), pp. 19–23.

10. S. Ante, "Identifying Experts in the Company," *The Wall Street Journal,* September 16, 2013, p. R6.

11. M. Weinstein, "Long-Range Learning Plans," *Training,* November/December 2010, pp. 38–41; L. Miller, *2014 State of the Industry* (Alexandria, VA: American Society for Training & Development, 2014); "2014's Very Best Learning Organizations," *T + D,* October 2014, pp. 34–98.

12. L. Freifeld, "Jiffy Lube's Training Drive," *Training,* January/February 2013, pp. 34–37; M. Weinstein, "Jiffy-Lube Greases the Wheels of Success,", *Training,* January/February 2015, pp. 36–38; L. Freifeld, "Jiffy-Lube Revs Up to No. 1," *Training,* January/February 2014, pp. 30–38.

13. R. Noe, *Employee Training and Development,* 7th ed. (New York: Irwin/McGraw-Hill, 2015).

14. Ibid; E. A. Surface, "Training Needs Assessment: Aligning Learning and Capability with Performance Requirements and Organizational Objectives." In M. A. Wilson, W. Bennett, S. G. Gibson, & G. M. Alliger (Eds.), *The Handbook of Work Analysis: Methods, Systems, Applications and Science of Work Measurement in Organizations* (Routledge Academic, 2012), pp. 437–62.

15. J. Congemi, "MasTec Tackles the LMS," *Training,* July/August 2014, pp. 52–54.

16. J. B. Tracey, S. I. Tannenbaum, and M. J. Kavanaugh, "Applying Trained Skills on the Job: The Importance of the Work Environment," *Journal of Applied Psychology* 80 (1995), pp. 239–52; E. Holton, R. Bates, and W. Ruona, "Development of a Generalized Learning Transfer System Inventory," *Human Resource Development Quarterly* 11(2001), pp. 333–60; E. Helton III and T. Baldwin, eds., *Improving Learning Transfer in Organizations* (San Francisco: Jossey-Bass, 2003); J. S. Russell, J. R. Terborg, and M. L. Powers, "Organizational Performance and Organizational Level Training and Support," *Personnel Psychology* 38 (1985), pp. 849–63.

17. S. Tannenbaum, "A Strategic View of Organizational Training and Learning," in *Creating, Implementing, and Managing Effective Training and Development,* ed. K. Kraiger (San Francisco: Jossey-Bass, 2002), pp. 10–52.

18. A. McIlvaine, "Banking on Service," *HR Executive,* April 2014, pp. 14–16.

19. C. Reinhart, "How to Leap Over Barrier to Performance," *Training and Development,* January 2000, pp. 20–29; G. Rummter and K. Morrill, "The Results Chain," *T + D,* February 2005, pp. 27–35; O. Rummter, "In Search of the Holy Performance Grail," *Training and Development,* April 1996, pp. 26–31.

20. C. E. Schneier, J. P. Guthrie, and J. D. Olian, "A Practical Approach to Conducting and Using Training Needs Assessment," *Public Personnel Management,* Summer 1988, pp. 191–205; I. Goldstein, "Training in Organizations," in *Handbook of Industrial/Organizational Psychology,* 2nd ed., ed. M. D. Dunnette and L. M. Hough (Palo Alto, CA: Consulting Psychologists Press, 1991), vol. 2, pp. 507–619.

21. Company website, "Careers: About Us," www.kla-tencor.com, accessed February 25, 2015; "KLA-Tencor Corporation: Right People, Right Knowledge," *Training,* January/February 2015, pp. 56–57.

22. R. A. Noe, "Trainees' Attributes and Attitudes: Neglected Influences on Training Effectiveness," *Academy of Management Review* 11 (1986), pp. 736–49.

23. T. T. Baldwin, R. T. Magjuka, and B. T. Loher, "The Perils of Participation: Effects of Choice on Trainee Motivation and Learning," *Personnel Psychology* 44 (1991), pp. 51–66; S. I. Tannenbaum, J. E. Mathieu, E. Salas, and J. A. Cannon-Bowers, "Meeting Trainees' Expectations: The Influence of Training Fulfillment on the Development of Commitment, Self-Efficacy, and Motivation," *Journal of Applied Psychology* 76 (1991), pp. 759–69.

24. C. E. Schneier, "Training and Development Programs: What Learning Theory and Research Have to Offer," *Personnel Journal,* April 1974, pp. 288–93; M. Knowles, "Adult Learning," in *Training and Development Handbook,* 3rd ed., ed. R. L. Craig (New York: McGraw-Hill, 1987), pp. 168–79; R. Zemke and S. Zemke, "30 Things We Know for Sure about Adult Learning," *Training,* June 1981, pp. 45–52; B. J. Smith and B. L. Delahaye, *How to Be an Effective Trainer,* 2nd ed. (New York: John Wiley and Sons, 1987).

25. "Mindtree Limited," *T + D,* October 2014, p. 46; "Nemours," *T + D,* October 2013, p. 41.

26. R. Smith, "Aligning Learning with Business Strategy," *T + D* November 2008, pp. 40–43.

27. S. Bailey, "The Answer to Transfer," *Chief Learning Officer,* November 2014, pp. 33–41; R. Hewes, "Step by Step," *T + D,* February 2014, pp. 56–61; E. Holton III and T. Baldwin, eds, *Improving Learning Transfer in Organizations* (San Francisco: Jossey-Bass, 2003); J. M. Cusimano, "Managers as Facilitators," *Training and Development* 50 (1996), pp. 31–33.

28. F. Kalman, "Taking Control of On-the-Job Learning," *Chief Learning Officer,* August 2014, pp. 49–54.

29. C. M. Petrini, ed., "Bringing It Back to Work," *Training and Development Journal,* December 1990, pp. 15–21.

30. Ford, Quinones, Sego, and Sorra, "Factors Affecting the Opportunity to Perform Trained Tasks on the Job."

31. M. A. Quinones, J. K. Ford, D. J. Sego, and E. M. Smith, "The Effects of Individual and Transfer Environment Characteristics on the Opportunity to Perform Trained Tasks," *Training Research Journal* 1 (1995/96), pp. 29–48.

32. G. Stevens and E. Stevens, "The Truth about EPSS," *Training and Development* 50 (1996), pp. 59–61; J. Ford and T. Meyer, "Advances in Training Technology: Meeting the Workplace Challenges of Talent Development, Deep Specialization, and

Collaborative Learning," in M. Coovert and L. Thompson, eds., *The Psychology of Workplace Technology* (New York: Routledge, 2014), pp. 43–76.

33. P. Harris, "Relying on Street Smarts," *T + D,* October 2014, pp. 92–93; M. Weinstein, "Just-in-Time Technology Solutions," *Training,* September/October 2014, pp. 36–39.

34. E. Hoffman and J. Boyle, "Managing Mission Knowledge at NASA," *T + D,* July 2014, pp. 50–55.

35. "Grant Thornton LLP (USA)," *T + D,* October 2010, p. 74.

36. R. D. Marx, "Relapse Prevention for Managerial Training: A Model for Maintenance of Behavior Change," *Academy of Management Review* 7 (1982), pp. 433–41; G. P. Latham and C. A. Frayne, "Self-Management Training for Increasing Job Attendance: A Follow-up and Replication," *Journal of Applied Psychology* 74 (1989), pp. 411–16.

37. "Verizon," *Training,* January/February 2015, p. 58; M. Weinstein, "Verizon Connects to Success," *Training,* January/February 2011, pp. 40–42.

38. B. Mirza, "Social Media Tools Redefine Learning," *HR Magazine,* December 2010, p. 74; L. Patel, "The Rise of Social Media," *T + D,* July 2010, pp. 60–61; J. Meister, E. Kaganer, and R. Von Feldt, "2011: The Year of the Media Tablet as a Learning Tool," *T + D,* April 2011, pp. 28–31.

39. "PPL Electric Utilities," *Training,* January/February 2015, p. 101.

40. "Putting the Distance into Distance Learning," *Training,* October 1995, pp. 111–18.

41. D. Picard, "The Future Is Distance Training," *Training,* November 1996, pp. s3–s10.

42. A. F. Maydas, "On-line Networks Build the Savings into Employee Education," *HR Magazine,* October 1997, pp. 31–35.

43. J. M. Rosow and R. Zager, *Training: The Competitive Edge* (San Francisco: Jossey-Bass, 1988).

44. T. Byham and A. Lang, "Avoid These 10 Pitfalls of Virtual Classrooms," *Chief Learning Officer,* May 2014, pp. 18–21; C. Huggett, "Make Virtual Training a Success," *T + D,* January 2014, pp. 40–45.

45. "Flippin' Pizza training staff with new iPad app," *Pizza Market Place* (February 29, 2012). www.pizzamarketplace.com.

46. C. Tate, "Mobile Masters," *T + D,* April 2013, pp. 22–24.

47. R. B. Cohn, "How to Choose a Video Producer," *Training,* July 1996, pp. 58–61.

48. Commerce Clearing House, Inc., *Orientation–Training* (Chicago, IL: Personnel Practices Communications, Commerce Clearing House, 1981), pp. 501–905; K. Tyler, "The American Apprentice," *HR Magazine,* November 2013, pp. 33–36; S. Wartenberg, "No Snow Days," *The Columbus Dispatch,* February 22, 2015, pp. D1, D3; L. Weber, "Here's One Way to Solve the Skills Gap," *The Wall Street Journal,* April 28, 2014, p. R3.

49. A. H. Howard III, "Apprenticeships," in *The ASTD Training and Development Handbook,* pp. 803–13; Tyler, "The American Apprentice."

50. M. Rowh, "The Rise of the Apprentice," *Human Resource Executive,* January 2006, pp. 38–43.

51. A. Pasztor, "Chopper Simulators Take Off," *The Wall Street Journal,* July 12–13, 2014, p. B4.

52. J. Borzo, "Almost Human," *The Wall Street Journal,* May 24, 2004, pp. R1, R10; J. Hoff, "My Virtual Life," *BusinessWeek,* May 1, 2006, pp. 72–78.

53. N. Adams, "Lessons from the Virtual World," *Training,* June 1995, pp. 45–48.

54. Ibid.

55. P. Harris, "Avatars Rule," *T + D,* October 2013, pp. 60–61; company website for PPD: www.ppdi.com.

56. Cornell, "Better than the Real Thing?"; E. Frauenheim, "Can Video Games Win Points as Teaching Tools?" *Workforce Management,* April 10, 2006, pp. 12–14; S. Boehle, "Simulations: The Next Generation of e-Learning," *Training,* January 2005, pp. 22–31; Borzo, "Almost Human"; T. Sitzmann, "A Meta-Analytic Examination of the Instructional Effectiveness of Computer-Based Simulation Games," *Personnel Psychology* 64 (2011), pp. 489–528.

57. L. Freifeld, "Solid Sims," *Training,* October 2007, p. 48.

58. "KLA-Tencor: The Situation Room," *Training,* September/October 2014, pp. 60–61.

59. "CMS Energy: Tackling Conflicts with 'The Resolver,'" *Training,* September/October 2014, p. 46.

60. G. P. Latham and L. M. Saari, "Application of Social Learning Theory to Training Supervisors through Behavior Modeling," *Journal of Applied Psychology* 64 (1979), pp. 239–46.

61. M. Rosenberg, *E-learning Strategies for Delivering Knowledge in the Digital age* (New York: McGraw-Hill, 2001); "What Is Web-Based Training?" from www.clark.net/pub/nractive/ft.html; R. Johnson and H. Gueutal, *Transforming HR through Technology* (Alexandria, VA: SHRM Foundation, 2010).

62. P. Harris, "Where Innovative Learning Is the Norm," *T + D,* October 2011, pp. 61–62.

63. L. Freifeld, "Online versus In-Class Success," *Training,* September/October 2014, pp. 19–25.

64. S. Herring, "MOOCs Come of Age," *T + D,* January 2014, pp. 46–49.

65. D. Belkin and C. Porter, "Job Market Embraces Massive Online Courses," *The Wall Street Journal,* September 27, 2013, p. A3; C. Proulx, "You'll Never Guess Who's Disrupting Online Learning," *Forbes,* www.forbes.com, accessed December 10, 2013.

66. M. Weinstein, "Managing MOOCs," *Training,* September/October 2014, pp. 26–28; R. Grossman, "Are Massive Open Online Courses in Your Future?" *HR Magazine,* August 2013, pp. 30–36; J. Meister, "How MOOCs Will Revolutionize Corporate Learning and Development," *Forbes,* www.forbes.com, accessed August 20, 2013; C. Straumsheim, "MOOC Research Conference Confirms Commonly Held Beliefs About the Medium," from www.insidehighered.com, accessed January 3, 2014; K. Jordan, "MOOC Completion Rates: The Data," http://www.katyjordan.com/MOOCproject.html; M. Chafkin, "Uphill Climb," *Fast Company,* December 2013/January 2014, pp. 146–56.

67. M. Derven, "Social Networking a Force for Development," *T + D,* July 2009, pp. 58–63; A. Kaplan and M. Haenlein, "Users of the World Unite! The Challenges and Opportunities of Social Media," *Business Horizons,* 53 (2010), pp. 59–68.

68. K. Kuehner-Hebert, "Go Mobile?" *Chief Learning Officer,* March 2014, pp. 18–21.

69. B. Hall, "Go Slow, Quickly: Make the Move to Mobile," *Chief Learning Officer,* http://clomedia.com, accessed January 30, 2013.

70. G. Dutton, "There's an App for That!" *Training,* September/October 2011, pp. 36–37.

71. M. Weinstein, "Farmers' Comprehensive Training Policy," *Training,* January/February 2013, pp. 42–44.

72. "Learning Management Systems: An Executive Summary," *Training,* March 2002, p. 4; S. Castellano, "The Evolution of the LMS," *T + D,* November 2014, p. 14.

73. J. Congemi, "MasTec Tackles the LMS," *Training,* July/August 2014, pp. 52–54.

74. D. Brown and D. Harvey, *An Experiential Approach to Organizational Development* (Englewood Cliffs, NJ: Prentice Hall, 2000); J. Schettler, "Learning by Doing," *Training,* April 2002,

pp. 38–43; G. Kranz, "From Fire Drills to Funny Skills," *Workforce Management,* May 2011, pp. 28–32.

75. "Lending a Hand," *T + D,* December 2013, p. 72.

76. R. J. Wagner, T. T. Baldwin, and C. C. Rowland, "Outdoor Training: Revolution or Fad?" *Training and Development Journal,* March 1991, pp. 51–57; C. J. Cantoni, "Learning the Ropes of Teamwork," *The Wall Street Journal,* October 2, 1995, p. A14.

77. G. Kranz, "From Fire Drills to Funny Skills," *Workforce Management,* May 2011, pp. 28–32.

78. D. Mishev, "Cooking for the Company," *Cooking Light,* August 2004, pp. 142–47.

79. P. F. Buller, J. R. Cragun, and G. M. McEvoy, "Getting the Most Out of Outdoor Training," *Training and Development Journal,* March 1991, pp. 58–61.

80. J. Cannon-Bowers and C. Bowers, "Team Development and Functioning," in S. Zedeck (ed.), *APA Handbook of Industrial and Organizational Psychology* (Washington, DC: American Psychological Association, 2011), vol. 1, pp. 597–650. L. Delise, C. Gorman, A. Brooks, J. Rentsch, and D. Steele-Johnson, "The Effects of Team Training on Team Outcomes: A Meta-Analysis," *Performance Improvement Quarterly* 22 (2010), pp. 53–80.

81. S. Carey, "Racing to Improve," *The Wall Street Journal,* March 24, 2006, pp. B1, B6.

82. P. Froiland, "Action Learning," *Training,* January 1994, pp. 27–34.

83. M. Marquardt, "Action Learning Around the World," *T + D,* February 2015, pp. 44–49.

84. A. Brunet and S. New, "Kaizen in Japan: An Empirical Study," *International Journal of Production and Operations Management,* 23 (2003), pp. 1426–1446.

85. M. Sallie-Dosunmu, "Born to Grow," *TD,* May 2006, pp. 33–37.

86. "Nationwide Mutual Insurance Company: Fast-Start for Agents," *Training,* January/February 2015, p. 107.

87. K. Kraiger, J. K. Ford, and E. Salas, "Application of Cognitive, Skill-Based, and Affective Theories of Learning Outcomes to New Methods of Training Evaluation," *Journal of Applied Psychology* 78 (1993), pp. 311–28; J. J. Phillips, "ROI: The Search for Best Practices," *Training and Development,* February 1996, pp. 42–47; D. L. Kirkpatrick, "Evaluation of Training," in *Training and Development Handbook,* 2nd ed., ed. R. L. Craig (New York: McGraw-Hill, 1976), pp. 18-1 to 18–27.

88. J. Bersin, "Mastering the Skills Supply Chain Problem," *Chief Learning Officer,* April 2014, p. 14.

89. D. A. Grove and C. O. Ostroff, "Program Evaluation," in *Developing Human Resources,* ed. K. N. Wexley (Washington, DC: BNA Books, 1991), pp. 185–219.

90. J. J. Phillips, *Handbook of Training Evaluation and Measurement Methods* 2nd ed. (Houston, TX: Gulf Publishing, 1991); J. J. Phillips, "ROI: The Search for Best Practices," *Training and Development,* February 1996, pp. 42–47; J. Phillips and P. Phillips, "Moving from Evidence to Proof," *T + D,* August 2001, pp. 34–39.

91. P. Harris, "Short Can Be Oh, So Sweet," *T + D,* October 2013, pp. 66–69.

92. I. Speizer, "Rolling through the Downturn," *Workforce Management,* August 11, 2008, pp. 31–37.

93. S. Ladika, "Lost in Translation," *Workforce Management,* May 2013, pp. 30–33.

94. K. Johnson, "Career Booster for CFOs: A Stint Abroad," *The Wall Street Journal,* February 10, 2015, p. B7.

95. A. Andors, "Happy Returns," *HR Magazine,* March 2010, pp. 61–62.

96. W. A. Arthur Jr. and W. Bennett Jr., "The International Assignee: The Relative Importance of Factors Perceived to Contribute to Success," *Personnel Psychology* 48 (1995), pp. 99–114; G.

M. Spreitzer, M. W. McCall Jr., and Joan D. Mahoney, "Early Identification of International Executive Potential," *Journal of Applied Psychology* 82 (1997), pp. 6–29.

97. R. Feintzeig, "After Stints Abroad, Re-Entry Can Be Hard," *The Wall Street Journal,* September 18, 2013, p. B6.

98. Johnson, "Career Booster for CFOs."

99. J. S. Black and J. K. Stephens, "The Influence of the Spouse on American Expatriate Adjustment and Intent to Stay in Pacific Rim Overseas Assignments," *Journal of Management* 15 (1989), pp. 529–44; M. Shaffer and D. A. Harrison, "Forgotten Partners of International Assignments: Development and Test of a Model of Spouse Adjustment," *Journal of Applied Psychology* 86 (2001), pp. 238–54.

100. M. Shaffer, D. A. Harrison, H. Gregersen, J. S. Black, and L. A. Ferzandi, "You Can Take It with You: Individual Differences and Expatriate Effectiveness," *Journal of Applied Psychology* 91 (2006), pp. 109–25; P. Caligiuri, "The Big Five Personality Characteristics as Predictors of Expatriate's Desire to Terminate the Assignment and Supervisor-Rated Performance," *Personnel Psychology* 53 (2000), pp. 67–88.

101. E. Dunbar and A. Katcher, "Preparing Managers for Foreign Assignments," *Training and Development Journal,* September 1990, pp. 45–47.

102. J. S. Black and M. Mendenhall, "A Practical but Theory-Based Framework for Selecting Cross-Cultural Training Methods," in *Readings and Cases in International Human Resource Management,* ed. M. Mendenhall and G. Oddou (Boston: PWS-Kent, 1991), pp. 177–204.

103. P. Tam, "Culture Course," *The Wall Street Journal,* May 25, 2004, pp. B1, B12.

104. S. Ronen, "Training the International Assignee," in *Training and Development in Organizations,* ed. I. L. Goldstein (San Francisco: Jossey-Bass, 1989), pp. 417–53.

105. H. Ren, M. Shaffer, D. Harrison, C. Fu, and K. Fodchuk, "Reactive Adjustment or Proactive Embedding? Multistudy, Multiwave Evidence for Dual Pathways to Expatriate Retention," *Personnel Psychology* 67 (2014), pp. 203–39.

106. P. R. Harris and R. T. Moran, *Managing Cultural Differences* (Houston: Gulf, 1991).

107. J. Carter, "Globe Trotters," *Training,* August 2005, pp. 22–28.

108. C. Solomon, "Unhappy Trails," *Workforce,* August 2000, pp. 36–41.

109. C. Patton, "Coming to America," *Human Resource Executive,* January/February 2012, pp. 22, 26–29.

110. H. Lancaster, "Before Going Overseas, Smart Managers Plan Their Homecoming," *The Wall Street Journal,* September 28, 1999, p. B1; A. Halcrow, "Expats: The Squandered Resource," *Workforce,* April 1999, pp. 42–48.

111. Harris and Moran, *Managing Cultural Differences.*

112. Feintzeig, "After Stints Abroad, Re-Entry Can Be Hard.

113. Ibid.

114. H. Dolezalek, "The Path to Inclusion," *Training,* May 2008, pp. 52–54.

115. E. McKeown, "Quantifiable Inclusion Strategies," *T + D,* October 2010, p. 16.

116. S. E. Jackson and Associates, *Diversity in the Workplace: Human Resource Initiatives* (New York: Guilford Press, 1992).

117. J. Lublin, "Do You Know Your Hidden Work Biases?" *The Wall Street Journal,* January 10, 2014, pp. B1, B4.

118. Ibid.

119. Z. Kalinoski, D. Steele-Johnson, E. Payton, K. Leas, J. Steinke, and N. Bowling, "A Meta-Analytic Evaluation of Diversity Training Outcomes," *Journal of Organizational Behavior* 34 (2013), pp. 1076–1104.

120. T. Kochan, K. Bezrukova, R. Ely, S. Jackson, A. Joshi, K. Jehn, J. Leonard, D. Levine, and D. Thomas, "The Effects of Diversity on Business Performance: Report of the Diversity Research Network," *Human Resource Management* 42 (2003), pp. 8–21; F. Hansen, "Diversity's Business Case Just Doesn't Add Up," *Workforce*, June 2003, pp. 29–32; K. Jones, E. King, J. Nelson, D. Geller, and L. Bowes-Sperry, "Beyond the Business Case: The Ethical Perspective on Diversity Training," *Human Resource Management,* January–February 2013, pp. 55–74.

121. Company website, "Diversity & Inclusion," http://sodexousa. com, accessed April 13, 2015; M. Landel, "How We Did It . . . SODEXO's CEO on Smart Diversification," *Harvard Business Review,* March 2015, pp. 41–44; R. Emelo, "Peer Collaboration Enhances Diversity and Inclusion," *T + D,* December 2014, pp. 48–52. R. Anand and M. Winters, "A Retrospective View of Corporate Diversity Training from 1964 to the Present," *Academy of Management Learning & Education,* 7 (2008), pp. 356–72; Dolezalek, "The Path to Inclusion."

122. C. T. Schreiber, K. F. Price, and A. Morrison, "Workforce Diversity and the Glass Ceiling: Practices, Barriers, Possibilities," *Human Resource Planning* 16 (1994), pp. 51–69; K. Bezrvkova, K. Jehn, and C. Spell, "Reviewing Diversity Training: Where Have We Been and Where Should We Go?" *Academy of Management Learning and Education* 11 (2012), pp. 207–227. B. Groysberg and K. Connolly, "Great Leaders Who Make the Mix Work," *Harvard Business Review,* September 2013, pp. 68–76.

123. Groysberg and Connolly, "Great Leaders Who Make the Mix Work."

124. T. Bauer, "Onboarding New Employees: Maximizing Success" (Alexandria, VA: SHRM Foundation, 2010); T. Bauer and B. Erdogan, "Delineating and Reviewing the Role of Newcomer Capital in Organizational Socialization," *Annual Review of Organizational Psychology and Organizational Behavior* 1 (2014), pp. 439–57.

125. H. Klein and N. Weaver, "The Effectiveness of Organizational-level Orientation Program in the Socialization of New Hires," *Personnel Psychology* 23 (2000), pp. 47–66; C. Wanberg, J. Kammeyer-Mueller, "Predictors and Outcomes of Proactivity in the Socialization Process," *Journal of Applied Psychology* 85 (2000), pp. 373–385; T. Bauer, T. Bodner, B. Erdogan, D. Truxillo, and J. Tucker, "Newcomer Adjustment during Organizational Socialization: A Meta-analytic Review of Antecedents, Outcomes, and Methods," *Journal of Applied Psychology* 92 (2007), pp. 707–721; D. Allen, "Do Organizational Socialization Tactics Influence Newcomer Embeddedness and Turnover?" *Journal of Management* 32 (2006), pp. 237–256; J. Kammeyer-Mueller, C. Wanberg, A. Rubenstein, and Z. Song, "Support, Undermining, and Newcomer Socialization: Fitting in During the First 90 Days," *Academy of Management Journal* 56 (2013), pp. 1104–24.

126. "Training Top 125," *Training,* January/February 2011, p. 91.

127. D. Milliken, "Poised for Discovery," *T + D,* August 2011, pp. 70–71.

128. R. Weiss, "Inside Story: A New Orientation Program for New Employees," from the website for the Association for Talent Development, www.astd.org, accessed April 7, 2015.

Performance Management

8

LEARNING OBJECTIVES

After reading this chapter, you should be able to:

Reformatting Performance Evaluations

Many companies, such as Intel, Microsoft, and Gap Inc., have revamped their performance management systems to eliminate ratings they feel demoralize and threaten employees, take too long for managers to complete, and constrain performance discussions to formal reviews conducted one or two times each year. Adobe Systems Inc. provides multimedia and creativity software products including Photoshop, Adobe Acrobat, Adobe Reader, and the files we call pdfs, which stands for portable document format. Adobe was experiencing an increase in turnover which it discovered was related to employees' dissatisfaction with the performance review process, a lack of recognition, and the lack of regular feedback about their performance. Like other companies, Adobe's performance review included managers providing an overall rating of each employees on a 1 to 4 scale which was based on how their performance compared to other employees. This created a competitive rather than the collaborative work environment which Adobe values. Each year after employees received their reviews HR saw a spike in voluntary turnover which was especially concerning because Adobe was losing good employees.

To improve performance management Adobe decided to abandon annual ratings and introduced a new system called The Check-In. The Check-In emphasizes ongoing feedback. Instead of managers only discussing performance with employees during the formal performance review as tended to occur in the old system, Check-In encourages managers and employees to have informal performance discussions at least every other month. Managers are asked to focus performance discussions around employees' performance objectives or goals and what resources they need to succeed. Also, employees' career development needs are part of the conversations. Managers are given complete freedom to decide how often and in what ways they want to set goals and provide feedback. The discussion is future-focused. That is, both the employee and the manager consider what

to change to increase the likelihood that performance will be effective. Employees are evaluated on the basis of how they have performed against their goals rather than how they compare to other employees. More frequent performance feedback is especially important to Millennial employees who are used to real-time communications through texting and postings.

Managers no longer have to complete lengthy performance evaluation forms and submit them to HR. HR's role is to provide managers with consulting and tools to help with performance discussions rather than policing to see if reviews are completed or discussions have occurred. Both managers and employees can access a resource center that provides materials about coaching, giving feedback, and personal and professional development. For example, managers might use the resource center to help them with tough performance conversations such as those involving giving employees difficult feedback. HR relies on what is known as a skip-level process to insure that performance discussions are occurring throughout the year. This means that the manager's own boss holds them accountable for having performance discussions. The boss asks employees if discussions are occurring and if they have a development plan.

There are several indications that Check-In is effective. HR includes questions about performance management on its annual employee survey. Survey results show that 80% of employees responded that they had regular performance meetings with their managers and felt supported by them. Since Check-In was introduced voluntary turnover has decreased by 25%. Also, it is estimated that Check-In saves Adobe managers 80,000 hours each year that were previously spent completing employee performance evaluation forms.

SOURCES: Based on R. Feintzeig, "The Trouble with Grading Employees," *The Wall Street Journal,* April 22, 2015, pp. B1, B7; D. Meinert, "Reinventing Reviews," *HR Magazine,* April 2015, pp. 36–40; J. Ramirez, "Rethinking the Review," *Human Resource Executive,* July/August 2013, pp. 16–19.

Introduction

Companies that seek competitive advantage through employees must be able to manage the behavior and results of all employees. Traditionally, the formal performance appraisal system was viewed as the primary means for managing employee performance. Performance appraisal was an administrative duty performed by managers and was primarily the responsibility of the human resource function. Managers now view performance appraisal as an annual ritual—they quickly complete the form and use it to catalog all the negative information they have collected on an employee over the previous year. Because they may dislike confrontation and feel that they don't know how to give effective evaluations, some managers spend as little time as possible giving employees feedback. Not surprisingly, most managers and employees dislike performance appraisals. "Time-consuming," "frustrating," "dread," "burden," and "pain" are some of the words that come to employees' minds when giving or receiving performance reviews.[1] Some of the reasons include the lack of consistency of use of performance appraisals across the company; inability to differentiate among different performance levels; and the inability of the appraisal system to provide useful data for development, to help employees build their skills and competencies, or to build a high-performance culture.[2]

Some have argued that all performance appraisal systems are flawed to the point that they are manipulative, abusive, autocratic, and counterproductive. It is important to realize that the criticisms voiced about annual performance appraisals shown in Table 8.1 are not the result of evaluating employee performance. Rather, they result from how the performance management system is developed and used. If done correctly, performance appraisal can provide several valuable benefits to both employees and the company. An important part of appraising performance is to establish employee goals, which should be tied to the company's strategic goals. As the chapter opener illustrates, performance management should not occur just once or twice each year during a formal evaluation.

Table 8.1

Examples of Problems with Traditional Annual Performance Reviews

"Performance Management is an outdated concept. The entire conversation and mindset needs to change."   —VP of HR for Mozilla
"Over time the rating system has become a huge obstacle. The employee would see their rating first and then the whole review evolved into a discussion of Why this? Why not that? It was no longer driving performance."   —Executive VP for Global HR at Expedia
"There is a lot of pain in performance management."   —Senior Consultant for Towers Watson
". . . mainstream management is embedded in, and relies on, a culture of domination . . . the performance review is the biggest hammer management has."   —Samuel A. Culbert, author of *Get Rid of the Performance Review*
"In a traditional performance review, the employee listens until he hears the rating and then tunes out because he's doing the calculation in his head about how that will affect his bonus."   —Senior VP of Human Resources for Motorola Solutions

SOURCES: E. Goldberg, "Performance Management Gets Social," *HR Magazine,* August 2014, pp. 35–38; J. Ramirez, "Rethinking the Review," *Human Resource Executive,* July/August 2013, pp. 16–19; V. Liberman, "Performance Management: To Get Results Stop Measuring People by Them," *The Conference Board Review,* Summer 2013, pp. 57–63; S. Culbert, *Get Rid of the Performance Review* (New York: Business Plus, 2010).

The performance appraisal process tells top performers that they are valued by the company. It requires managers to at least annually communicate to employees their performance strengths and deficiencies. A good appraisal process ensures that all employees doing similar jobs are evaluated according to the same standards. The use of technology can reduce the administrative burden of performance appraisal, improve the accuracy of performance reviews, and ensure that employees get frequent feedback about their performance. Also, a properly conducted appraisal can help the company identify the strongest and weakest employees. It can help legally justify many HRM decisions such as promotions, salary increases, discipline, and layoffs.

We believe that performance appraisal is only one part of the broader process of performance management. We define **performance management** as the process through which managers ensure that employees' activities and outputs are congruent with the organization's goals. Performance management is central to gaining competitive advantage.

Our performance management system has three parts: defining performance, measuring performance, and feeding back performance information. First, a performance management system specifies which aspects of performance are relevant to the organization, primarily through job analysis (discussed in Chapter 4). Second, it measures those aspects of performance through **performance appraisal,** which is only one method for managing employee performance. Third, it provides feedback to employees through **performance feedback** sessions so they can adjust their performance to the organization's goals. Performance feedback is also fulfilled through tying rewards to performance via the compensation system (such as through merit increases or bonuses), a topic to be covered in Chapters 11 and 12.

In this chapter, we examine a variety of approaches to performance management. First we provide a brief summary of current performance management practices. Next, we present a model of performance that helps us examine the system's purposes. Then we discuss specific approaches to performance management and the strengths and weaknesses of each. We also look at various sources of performance information. The errors resulting from subjective assessments of performance are presented, as well as the means for reducing those errors. Then we discuss some effective components to performance feedback. Finally, we address components of a legally defensible performance management system.

Performance Management
The means through which managers ensure that employees' activities and outputs are congruent with the organization's goals.

Performance Appraisal
The process through which an organization gets information on how well an employee is doing his or her job.

Performance Feedback
The process of providing employees information regarding their performance effectiveness.

The Practice of Performance Management

Several recent surveys of human resource professionals suggest that most companies' performance management practices require annual paper-driven reviews that include both behaviors and business goals.[3] While many companies use performance management to manage employee performance and make pay decisions, less than 25% of the companies use performance management to help manage talent through identifying training needs and developing leadership talent. Sixty-six percent of companies used the same performance management system across all levels of the organization. Unfortunately, although performance management is a prevalent practice, it is often not valued or effectively used. Sixty-six percent of employees say that the performance review process interferes with their productivity and 65% believe it isn't relevant to their jobs. Many HR professionals don't believe that yearly performance evaluations are useful. More than one-half (53%) gave their organizations a grade of C+ to B, another one-fifth (21%) chose a C, and only 2% gave an A in performance management to their organizations.

Although almost one-half (46%) of HR professionals agreed with the statement that managers at their companies "did an effective job of differentiating between poor, average, and strong performers," about one-third (32%) had some level of disagreement with this statement. Similarly, although two-fifths (42%) agreed that managers at their organization were "willing to 'make the tough calls,'" another 38% disagreed.

The Process of Performance Management

LO 8-1

Identify the major parts of an effective performance management process.

As you may have already figured out from the chapter introduction and your own experiences, many employees and managers dislike the annual performance review. Although performance management does include the once or twice a year formal appraisal or evaluation meeting, effective performance management is a process, not an event. Figure 8.1 shows the performance management process. As shown in the process model, providing feedback and the formal performance evaluation are important but they are not the only important parts of an effective performance management process that contributes to the company's competitive advantage.[4] Also, visible CEO and senior management support

Figure 8.1

Model of the Effective Performance Management Process

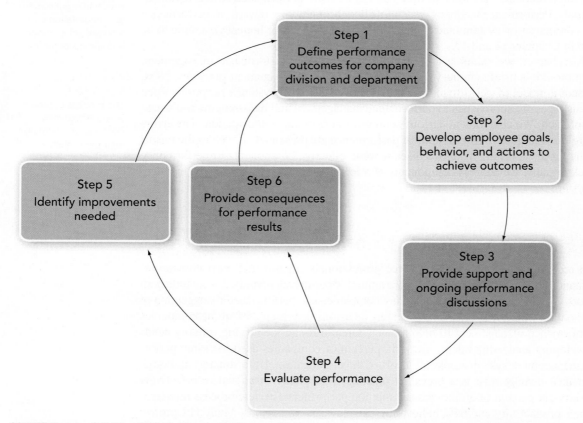

SOURCE: Based on E. Pulakos, R. Mueller-Hanson, R. O'Leary, and M. Meyrowitz, *Building a High-Performance Culture: A Fresh Look at Performance Management* (Alexandria, VA: SHRM Foundation, 2012); H. Aguinis, "An Expanded View of Performance Management," in J. W. Smith and M. London (eds.), *Performance Management* (San Francisco: Jossey-Bass, 2009), pp. 1–43; and J. Russell and L. Russell, "Talk Me through It: The Next Level of Performance Management," *T + D,* April 2010, pp. 42–48.

for the system are necessary. This ensures that the system is consistently used across the company, appraisals are completed on time, and giving and receiving performance feedback is an accepted part of the company culture. The first two steps of the performance management process involve identifying what the company is trying to accomplish (goals or objectives), a set of key performance dimensions that represent critical factors or drivers that influence the goals or objectives, and then develop performance measures for the key performance dimensions.[5] The first step in the performance management process starts with understanding and identifying important performance outcomes or results. Typically, these outcomes or results benefit customers, the employees' peers or team, and the organization itself. The company's and department or team's strategy, mission, and values play an important part in determining these outcomes. Chapter 2 pointed out that most companies pursue some type of strategy to reach revenue, profit, and market share goals. Divisions, departments, teams, and employees must align their goals and behaviors, and choose to engage in activities that help achieve the organization's strategy and goals. The second step of the process involves understanding the process (or how) to achieve the goals established in the first step. This includes identifying measurable goals, behaviors, and activities that will help the employee achieve the performance results. The goals, behaviors, and activities should be measurable so that the manager and employee can determine if they have been achieved. The goals, activities, and behaviors should be part of the employee's job description. Step three in the process, organizational support, involves providing employees with training, necessary resources and tools, and frequent feedback communication between the employee and manager focusing on accomplishments as well as issues and challenges influencing performance. For effective performance management managers and employees have to value feedback and regularly exchange it. Managers need to make time to provide feedback as well as train in how to give and receive it. Step four involves performance evaluation, that is, when the manager and employee discuss and compare the targeted performance goal and supporting behaviors with the actual results. This typically involves the annual or biannual formal performance review. As we will see later in the chapter there are many ways to help make this formal review more of a performance conversation designed to identify and discuss opportunities to improve and less of a one-way evaluation by the manager. One way to make the formal evaluation more effective is for managers to engage in frequent performance conversations with employees rather than wait for the formal annual review (step 3). The final steps of the performance management cycle involve the employee and manager identifying what the employee (with help from the manager) can do to capitalize on performance strengths and address weaknesses (step 5) and providing consequences for achieving (or failing to achieve) performance outcomes (step 6). This includes identifying training needs, adjusting the type or frequency of feedback the manager provides to the employee, clarifying, adjusting, or modifying performance outcomes, and discussions of behaviors or activities that need improvement or relate to new priorities based on changes or new areas of emphasis in organizational or department goals. Achieving performance results may relate to compensation (salary increases, cash bonuses), recognition, promotion, development opportunities, and continued employment. This depends on the purposes the company decides on for the performance management system (see our discussion in the section "Purposes of Performance Management"). Finally, it is important to realize that what employees accomplish (or fail to accomplish) and their consequences help shape changes in the organizational business strategy and performance goals and the ongoing performance management process. Evaluating the effectiveness of the performance management system is necessary to determine needed changes. This could include gathering comments about the managers' and employees' concerns about the system, analyzing rating data to determine if they are being affected by rating errors, reviewing objectives for their quality, and studying the relationship between employees meeting objectives and department and organizational results.

For example, Hilton Worldwide decided to develop a new performance management system from scratch to create a consistent process for helping its employees improve.[6] The new system is business-focused and easy to administer and use. The goal of the system is encouraging performance conversations between managers and employees outside of formal review meetings. The system focuses on what gets done and how it gets done by assessing behaviors and competencies. Managers set objectives at the beginning of the year and check in with employees at the middle of the year to discuss how they are performing. Managers enter comments on employees' performance directly into the online performance management system. Managers and employees can enter more comments about performance between the mid-year and end-of-year review. This encourages continuous feedback between managers and employees outside of the formal midyear and end of year review meetings. A recent survey showed that employee satisfaction with the new performance management process increased by 37% compared to the prior system. The "Integrity in Action" box shows how company leaders' behavior can help create a culture that encourages continuous improvement through performance feedback and recognition.

Purposes of Performance Management

LO 8-2
Discuss the three general purposes of performance management.

The purposes of performance management systems are of three kinds: strategic, administrative, and developmental.

STRATEGIC PURPOSE

First and foremost, a performance management system should link employee activities with the organization's goals. One of the primary ways strategies are implemented is through defining the results, behaviors, and, to some extent, employee characteristics that are necessary for carrying out those strategies, and then developing measurement and feedback systems that will maximize the extent to which employees exhibit the characteristics, engage in the behaviors, and produce the results.

Performance management is critical for companies to execute their talent management strategy, that is, to identify employees' strengths and weaknesses, drive employee engagement, link employees to appropriate training and development activity, and reward good performance with pay and other incentives. Also, performance management practices can relate positively to companies' financial success.[7] For example, among business executives who believe their companies are excellent or very good at performance management, 76% of their companies experienced a revenue increase. In contrast, 30% of companies that were less effective in performance management experienced a decline in revenues, and 20% performed more poorly than their competitors.

ADMINISTRATIVE PURPOSE

Organizations use performance management information (performance appraisals, in particular) in many administrative decisions: salary administration (pay raises), promotions, retention–termination, layoffs, and recognition of individual performance.[8] Despite the importance of these decisions, however, many managers, who are the source

Creating a Culture of Continuous Performance Improvement

Like other hospital groups, Kaiser Permanente follows the universal protocols and processes for patient care and buys and uses state-of-the-art medical equipment and technology. But George Halvorson, who recently retired as chairman and chief executive officer of Kaiser Permanente, believed that a culture of continuous improvement is what distinguishes his organizations from its competitors. During his tenure as CEO he helped to install a culture of continuous improvement that allowed employees to know it is acceptable to speak out about a way to do something better. Halvorson emphasized

that continuous improvement is a powerful, uniting value for an organization of over 180,000 staff members working with millions of patients. According to Halvorson, three conditions must exist to nurture a culture of continuous improvement. Employees must understand how small improvements snowball to make a big difference, they must love improving because they are passionate about their work, and they need confidence in their peers to believe that the organization is capable of making progress. As CEO, Halvorson reinforced these conditions through his actions. Every Friday afternoon

he wrote letters to all 180,000 employees celebrating a performance improvement, great research, or other rewards such as when Kaiser's hospitals were found to have the lowest number of pressure ulcers or when Kaiser received the top quality assurance score from a national health care accreditation organization.

DISCUSSION QUESTION

What other things can a company CEO do to create a culture of continuous improvement?

SOURCE: Based on G. Halvorson, "The Culture to Cultivate," *Harvard Business Review,* July–August 2013, p. 34.

---

of the information, see the performance appraisal process only as a necessary evil they must go through to fulfill their job requirements. They feel uncomfortable evaluating others and feeding those evaluations back to the employees. Thus, they tend to rate everyone high or at least rate them the same, making the performance appraisal information relatively useless. For example, one manager stated, "There is really no getting around the fact that whenever I evaluate one of my people, I stop and think about the impact—the ramifications of my decisions on my relationship with the guy and his future here. . . . Call it being politically minded, or using managerial discretion, or fine-tuning the guy's ratings, but in the end, I've got to live with him, and I'm not going to rate a guy without thinking about the fallout."[9]

© Stockbyte/Getty Images/RF

Performance management is critical for executing a talent management system and involves one-on-one contact with managers to ensure that proper training and development are taking place.

DEVELOPMENTAL PURPOSE

A third purpose of performance management is to develop employees. When employees are not performing as well as they should, performance management seeks to improve their performance. The feedback given during a performance evaluation process often pinpoints the employee's weaknesses. Ideally, however, the performance management system identifies not only any deficient aspects of the employee's performance but also the causes of these deficiencies—for example, a skill deficiency, a motivational problem, or some obstacle holding the employee back.

Managers are often uncomfortable confronting employees with their performance weaknesses. Such confrontations, although necessary to the effectiveness of the work group, often strain everyday working relationships. Giving high ratings to all employees enables a manager to minimize such conflicts, but then the developmental purpose of the performance management system is not fully achieved.[10] Development doesn't just focus on poor performers. Development also involves helping good performers get the training and other opportunities they need to enhance their skill set and advance their careers.

Texas Roadhouse revamped the performance management system for 500 employees at the company's corporate headquarters.[11] Under the previous system managers were having a hard time understanding the meaning of an overall rating of three on a five-point scale. For some managers a "three" meant that an employee was doing a good job while for others it meant that the employee was merely "average." The new system eliminated the rating and replaced it with a process called GPS, which stands for growth, plan, and support. The objective of GPS is to encourage managers to have frequent performance conversations with employees and for employees to take more responsibility for their performance and development. A month before the anniversary of their hiring date, employees are reminded to have GPS meetings with their managers to discuss their career goals and the resources they need to perform successfully. HR provides a discussion guide to help managers and employees have an effective conversation. Also, in the old performance management system managers tended to spend more time working with poor performers who represented less than 10% of employees. GPS emphasizes the need to spend similar amounts of time in performance conversations with good and high-performing employees. This means more frequent meetings with employees who need to improve but also having discussions with high performers, the top talent in the company, about how training and development opportunities can help them further develop their skills and reach their career goals.

An important step in performance management is to develop the measures by which performance will be evaluated. We next discuss the issues involved in developing and using different measures of performance.

Performance Measures Criteria

LO 8-3
Identify the five criteria for effective performance management systems.

In Chapter 4 we discussed how, through job analysis, one can analyze a job to determine exactly what constitutes effective performance. Once the company has determined, through job analysis and design, what kind of performance it expects from its employees, it needs to develop ways to measure that performance. This section presents the criteria underlying job performance measures. Later sections discuss approaches to performance measurement, sources of information, and errors.

Although people differ about criteria to use to evaluate performance management systems, we believe that five stand out: strategic congruence, validity, reliability, acceptability, and specificity.

STRATEGIC CONGRUENCE

Strategic Congruence
The extent to which the performance management system elicits job performance that is consistent with the organization's strategy, goals, and culture.

Strategic congruence is the extent to which a performance management system elicits job performance that is congruent with the organization's strategy, goals, and culture. If a company emphasizes customer service, then its performance management system should assess how well its employees are serving the company's customers. Strategic congruence emphasizes the need for the performance management system to guide employees in contributing to the organization's success. This requires systems flexible enough to adapt to changes in the company's strategic posture. The "Competing through Globalization" box shows the important role of performance management in developing a global business.

Many companies such as Brinker International, Federal Express, and Coca-Cola have introduced measures of critical success factors (CSFs) or key performance indicators (KPIs) into their performance management systems.[12] CSFs are factors in a company's business strategy that give it a competitive edge. Companies measure employee behavior that relates to attainment of CSFs, which increases the importance of these behaviors for employees. Employees can be held accountable and rewarded for behaviors that directly relate to the company attaining the CSFs.

Brinker International Inc., known for Chili's Restaurants, used to have 40 KPIs but employees were confused about what performance outcomes were expected. Brinker reduced the number of KPIs from 40 to 4. The focus on a smaller number of KPIs helped motivate and focus employees, resulting in a return of 20% to shareholders, lowered turnover, and increased employee engagement survey scores.

One challenge that companies face is how to measure customer loyalty, employee satisfaction, and other nonfinancial performance areas that affect profitability. To effectively use nonfinancial performance measures managers need to:[13]

- Develop a model of how nonfinancial performance measures link to the company's strategic goals. Identify the performance areas that are critical to success.
- Using already existing databases, identify data that exists on key performance measures (e.g., customer satisfaction, employee satisfaction surveys). If data are not available, identify a performance area that affects the company's strategy and performance. Develop measures for those performance areas.
- Use statistical and qualitative methods for testing the relationship between the performance measures and financial outcomes. Regression and correlation analysis as well as focus groups and interviews can be used. For example, studies show that employees' involvement, satisfaction, and enthusiasm for work are significantly related to business performance including customer satisfaction, productivity, and profitability.[14]
- Revisit the model to ensure that the nonfinancial performance measures are appropriate and determine whether new measures should be added. This is important to understand the drivers of financial performance and to ensure that the model is appropriate as the business strategy and economic conditions change.
- Act on conclusions that the model demonstrates. For example, Sears found that employee attitudes about the supervision they received and the work environment had a significant impact on customer satisfaction and shareholder results. As a result, Sears invested in managerial training to help managers do a better job of holding employees accountable for their jobs while giving them autonomy to perform their roles.[15]
- Audit whether the actions taken and the investments made produced the desired result.

Most companies' appraisal systems remain constant over a long time and through a variety of strategic emphases. However, when a company's strategy changes, its employees' behavior needs to change too.[16] The fact that appraisal systems often do not change may account for why many managers see performance appraisal systems as having little impact on a firm's effectiveness.

Timely and Future-Focused Feedback Helps Ensure Travel Customers Are Satisfied Around the World

Expedia Inc. is an online travel company with more than 140 travel websites in nearly 70 countries. Expedia wanted employees to receive more ongoing real-time feedback which they could use to change their performance rather than limiting performance conversations to the past-focused feedback they received during their formal performance review. The new emphasis in Expedia's Passport to Performance performance management program meant that managers were required to have weekly or at least bi-weekly conversations with employees that were focused on their performance, development, and career path along with completing a formal mid-year review. For this shift in focus to be effective, managers needed training on how to provide feedback in specific, behavior-based language that employees could understand.

Expedia's training consisted of providing managers with an overview of the new performance management system, helping them understand how to give feedback, and understanding the link between performance conversations and compensation decisions. Expedia also provided training for employees so they understood the new performance management system and how they could use it to benefit their development and career. For example, in the training focused on how to provide feedback, managers were told to stop using adjectives such as "be proactive" and instead use verbs to describe the behavior they wanted to see in employees such as "thinking through what could happen and planning before something becomes an emergency." Effective performance was now based on business goals and desired behaviors. Both managers and

employees feel the new performance management system is an improvement. For example, an employee survey found that over 40% reported that it had more focus on performance strengths and areas for improvement, 70% believed it had a good discussion of future-focused topics including business results and behaviors, and 61% felt the program improved how Expedia manages performance.

DISCUSSION QUESTION

One of the criteria used to evaluate a performance management system is development. How would you evaluate Expedia's Passport to Performance program according to this criterion? Explain your evaluation.

SOURCES: Based on K. Kuehner-Hubert, "Passport to Performance," *Chief Learning Officer,* July 2013, pp. 42–47; J. Ramirez, "Rethinking the Review," *Human Resource Executive,* July/August 2013, pp. 16–19.

VALIDITY

Validity
The extent to which a performance measure assesses all the relevant—and only the relevant—aspects of job performance.

Validity is the extent to which a performance measure assesses all the relevant—and only the relevant—aspects of performance. This is often referred to as "content validity." For a performance measure to be valid, it must not be deficient or contaminated. As you can see in Figure 8.2, one of the circles represents "true" job performance—all the aspects of performance relevant to success in the job. On the other hand, companies must use some measure of performance, such as a supervisory rating of performance on a set of dimensions or measures of the objective results on the job. Validity is concerned with maximizing the overlap between actual job performance and the measure of job performance (the green portion in the figure).

A performance measure is deficient if it does not measure all aspects of performance (the brown portion in the figure). An example is a system at a large university that assesses faculty members based more on research than teaching, thereby relatively ignoring a relevant aspect of performance.

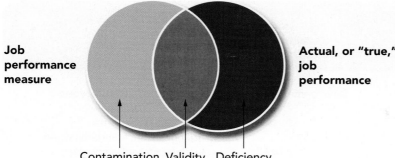

Figure 8.2
Contamination and
Deficiency of a
Job Performance
Measure

A contaminated measure evaluates irrelevant aspects of performance or aspects that are not job related (the gold portion in the figure). The performance measure should seek to minimize contamination, but its complete elimination is seldom possible. An example of a contaminated measure is the use of actual sales figures for evaluating salespersons across very different regional territories. Often sales are highly dependent upon the territory (number of potential customers, number of competitors, economic conditions) rather than the actual performance of the salesperson. A salesperson who works harder and better than others might not have the highest sales totals because the territory simply does not have as much sales potential as others. Thus, these figures alone would be a measure that is strongly affected by things beyond the control of the individual employee.

RELIABILITY

Reliability refers to the consistency of a performance measure. One important type of reliability is *interrater reliability:* the consistency among the individuals who evaluate the employee's performance. A performance measure has interrater reliability if two individuals give the same (or close to the same) evaluations of a person's job performance. Evidence seems to indicate that most subjective supervisory measures of job performance exhibit low reliability.[17] With some measures, the extent to which all the items rated are internally consistent is important (*internal consistency reliability*).

In addition, the measure should be reliable over time (*test–retest reliability*). A measure that results in drastically different ratings depending on when the measures are taken lacks test–retest reliability. For example, if salespeople are evaluated based on their actual sales volume during a given month, it would be important to consider their consistency of monthly sales across time. What if an evaluator in a department store examined sales only during May? Employees in the lawn and garden department would have high sales volumes, but those in the men's clothing department would have somewhat low sales volumes. Clothing sales in May are traditionally lower than other months. One needs to measure performance consistently across time.

ACCEPTABILITY

Acceptability refers to whether the people who use a performance measure accept it. Many elaborate performance measures are extremely valid and reliable, but they consume so much of managers' time that they refuse to use it. Alternatively, those being evaluated by a measure may not accept it.

Acceptability is affected by the extent to which employees believe the performance management system is fair. As Table 8.2 shows, there are three categories of perceived

Reliability
The consistency of a performance measure; the degree to which a performance measure is free from random error.

Acceptability
The extent to which a performance measure is deemed to be satisfactory or adequate by those who use it.

Table 8.2
Categories of
Perceived Fairness
and Implications
for Performance
Management
Systems

FAIRNESS CATEGORY	IMPORTANCE FOR PERFORMANCE MANAGEMENT SYSTEM	IMPLICATIONS
Procedural fairness	Development	• Give managers and employees opportunity to participate in development of system. • Ensure consistent standards when evaluating different employees. • Minimize rating errors and biases.
Interpersonal fairness	Use	• Give timely and complete feedback. • Allow employees to challenge the evaluation. • Provide feedback in an atmosphere of respect and courtesy.
Outcome fairness	Outcomes	• Communicate expectations regarding performance evaluations and standards. • Communicate expectations regarding rewards.

SOURCE: Adapted from S. W. Gilliland and J. C. Langdon, "Creating Performance Management Systems That Promote Perceptions of Fairness," in *Performance Appraisal: State of the Art in Practice,* ed. J. W. Smither. Copyright © 1998 by Jossey-Bass, Inc. This material is used by permission of John Wiley & Sons, Inc.

fairness: procedural, interpersonal, and outcome fairness. The table also shows specifically how the performance management system's development, use, and outcomes affect perceptions of fairness. In developing and using a performance management system, managers should take the steps shown in the column labeled "Implications" in Table 8.2 to ensure that the system is perceived as fair. Research suggests that performance management systems that are perceived as unfair are likely to be legally challenged, be used incorrectly, and decrease employee motivation to improve.[18]

SPECIFICITY

Specificity
The extent to which a performance measure gives detailed guidance to employees about what is expected of them and how they can meet these expectations.

Specificity is the extent to which a performance measure tells employees what is expected of them and how they can meet these expectations. Specificity is relevant to both the strategic and developmental purposes of performance management. If a measure does not specify what an employee must do to help the company achieve its strategic goals, it does not achieve its strategic purpose. Additionally, if the measure fails to point out employees' performance problems, it is almost impossible for the employees to correct their performance.

Deloitte's performance management system for its project teams meets most of the criteria for a good performance management system.[19] Deloitte's goals are to recognize, observe, and motivate performance through the annual compensation decision, the project performance snapshot, and the weekly performance conversations. Deloitte's client needs tend to involve both short- and long-term projects that are too complex for any one employee to have the expertise needed to carry them out. So to meet its clients' needs Deloitte relies on employee teams. These teams include a team leader and employees who each bring a different skill set. To evaluate each team member's performance Deloitte asks team leaders to answer four questions. These questions ask if the leader would award the person the highest possible compensation increase and bonus (measures overall performance and unique value to the organization), always want them on their team (measures ability to work well with others), and if the person is a risk for low performance (identifies problems that might harm the customer), and is ready for promotion today (measures potential). These four questions each represent a specific performance dimension (pay, teamwork, poor performance, promotion) that is relevant to Deloitte's project teams. The team leaders were chosen as the raters because they were in the best position to see the performance of team members and in their role must make subjective judgments. The questions were used after they were tested to see if they differentiated ineffective from effective team members and were correlated with other performance outcomes measured in other ways such as engagement surveys. For short-term projects, team member evaluations occur at the end of each project and longer-term project evaluations occur quarterly. To ensure that the evaluations are driving team performance and are accepted by team members, every team leader has to check in with each team member once each week. During these conversations team leaders discuss expectations, review priorities, and provide feedback on recent work. Team members are encouraged to initiate check-ins because team leaders may otherwise forget to have the discussions because they have many demands on their time. Once each quarter Deloitte's business leaders use the evaluations to review a group of employees, such as those with critical skills or who are eligible for promotion, to discuss the actions that need to be taken to develop that group. The questions provide input into compensation decisions made at the end of the year by business leaders who also consider the difficulty of project assignments and other contributions team members have made to Deloitte.

Approaches to Measuring Performance

An important part of effective performance management is establishing how we evaluate performance. This is difficult to do because performance is complex—it includes how employees perform their individual work tasks as well as contribute to teams and behave in ways that support their peers and the company.[20] What is considered effective performance and when and how it is measured likely varies across positions. For example, in sales positions results such as number of sales might be more important than behaviors while the opposite may be true in management positions. In this section we explore different ways to evaluate performance: the comparative approach, the attribute approach, the behavioral approach, the results approach, and the quality approach. We also evaluate these approaches against the criteria of strategic congruence, validity, reliability, acceptability, and specificity. As you will see, all of these approaches have strengths and weaknesses. As a result, many companies' performance evaluations use a combination of approaches. There is no one best approach for measuring performance. But to effectively contribute to organizational business strategy and goals, effective performance evaluation systems should measure both what gets accomplished (objectives) and how it gets accomplished (behaviors). Figure 8.3 shows an example of a performance management system that evaluates behavior and results. The results (project development) are linked to the goals of the business. The performance standards include behaviors that the employee must demonstrate to reach the results. The system provides feedback to the employee and holds both the employee and manager accountable for changing behavior.

LO 8-4

Discuss the four approaches to performance management, the specific techniques used in each approach, and the way these approaches compare with the criteria for effective performance management systems.

Figure 8.3

Example of a Performance Management System That Includes Behavior and Results

Accountabilities and Key Results	Performance Standards	Interim Feedback	Actual Results	Performance Rating	Areas for Development	Action
Key result areas that the employee will accomplish during the review period. Should align with company values, business goals, and job description.	How the key result area will be measured (quality, cost, quantity). Focus on work methods and accomplishments.	Employee and manager discuss performance on an ongoing basis.	Review actual performance for each key result.	Evaluate performance on each key result. 1 = Outstanding 2 = Highly effective 3 = Acceptable 4 = Unsatisfactory	Specific knowledge, skills, and behaviors to be developed that will help employee achieve key results.	What employee and manager will do to address development needs.
Project Development Manage the development of project scope, cost estimate studies, and schedules for approval.	Develop preliminary project material for approval within four weeks after receiving project scope. Eighty percent of new projects receive approval. Initial cost estimates are within 5% of final estimates.	Preliminary project materials are developed on time.	By end of year, approvals were at 75%, 5% less than standard.	3	Increase knowledge of project management software.	Read articles, research, and meet with software vendors.

THE COMPARATIVE APPROACH

The comparative approach to performance measurement requires the rater to compare an individual's performance with that of others. This approach usually uses some overall assessment of an individual's performance or worth and seeks to develop some ranking of the individuals within a work group. At least three techniques fall under the comparative approach: ranking, forced distribution, and paired comparison.

Ranking

Simple ranking requires managers to rank employees within their departments from highest performer to poorest performer (or best to worst). *Alternation ranking,* on the other hand, consists of a manager looking at a list of employees, deciding who is the best employee, and crossing that person's name off the list. From the remaining names, the manager decides who the worst employee is and crosses that name off the list—and so forth.

Ranking has received specific attention in the courts. As discussed in Chapter 3, in the *Albermarle v. Moody* case the validation of the selection system was conducted using employee rankings as the measure of performance. The court actually stated, "There is no way of knowing precisely what criteria of job performance that supervisors were considering, whether each supervisor was considering the same criteria—or whether, indeed, any of the supervisors actually applied a focused and stable body of criteria of any kind."[21]

Forced Distribution

The *forced distribution* method also uses a ranking format, but employees are ranked in groups. This technique requires the manager to put certain percentages of employees into predetermined categories. Most commonly, employees are grouped into three, four, or five categories usually of unequal size indicating the best workers, the worst workers, and one or more categories in between. The insurance company American International Group (AIG), is using a forced distribution system in which AIG employees are ranked on a scale of 1 to 4.[22] Using this system only 10% of employees receive the top ranking of "1," 20% of employees receive a ranking of "2," 50% of employees receive a ranking of "3," and 20% receive the lowest ranking of "4." Employees with higher rankings receive much more year-end incentive pay such as bonuses than those with lower rankings (employees ranked in the top 10% will get much greater bonuses compared to their peers). The CEO advocated the implementation of the forced distribution system to ensure that the company is paying the best people for their performance and to better differentiate poor from high performers. The company had previously used ranking systems but found that over half of employees were evaluated as high performers.

Advocates of these systems say that they are the best way to identify high-potential employees who should be given training, promotions, and financial rewards and to identify the poorest performers who should be helped or asked to leave. Top-level managers at many companies have observed that despite corporate performance and return to shareholders being flat or decreasing, compensation costs have continued to spiral upward and performance ratings continue to be high. They question how there can be such a disconnect between corporate performance and employees' evaluations and compensation. Forced distribution systems provide a mechanism to help align company performance and employee performance and compensation. Employees in the bottom 10% cause performance standards to be lowered, influence good employees to leave, and keep good employees from joining the company.

A forced distribution system helps managers tailor development activities to employees based on their performance. For example, as shown in Table 8.3, poor performers are given specific feedback about what they need to improve in their job and a timetable is set for their improvement. If they do not improve their performance, they are dismissed. Top performers are encouraged to participate in development activities such as job experiences, mentoring, and completion of leadership programs which will help prepare them for top management positions. The use of a forced distribution system is seen as a way for companies to increase performance, motivate employees, and open the door for new talent to join the company to replace poor performers.[23] Advocates say these systems force managers to make hard decisions about employee performance based on job-related criteria, rather than to be lenient in evaluating employees. Critics, on the other hand, say the systems in practice are arbitrary, erroneously assume that employees' performance can be best summarized by a normal distribution, may be illegal, and cause poor morale.[24] For example, one workgroup might have 20% poor performers while another might have only high performers, but the process mandates that 10% of employees be eliminated from both groups. Also, in many forced distribution systems an unintended consequence is the bottom category tends to consist of minorities, women, and people over 40 years of age, causing discrimination lawsuits (we discuss legal issues affecting performance management later in the chapter). Finally, it is difficult to rank employees into distinctive categories when criteria are subjective or when it is difficult to differentiate employees on the criteria (such as teamwork or communications skills). For example, Microsoft

Table 8.3
Performance and Development Based on Forced Distribution and Ranking

RANKING OR DISTRIBUTION CATEGORY	PERFORMANCE AND DEVELOPMENT PLAN
A Above average exceptional A1 performer	• Accelerate development through challenging job assignments • Provide mentor from leadership team • Recognize and reward contributions • Praise employee for strengths • Consider leadership potential • Nominate for leadership development programs
B Average meets expectations steady performer	• Offer feedback on how B can become a high performer • Encourage development of strengths and improvement of weaknesses • Recognize and reward employee contributions • Consider enlarging job
C Below expectations poor performance	• Give feedback and agree upon what specific skills, behavior, and/or results need to be improved with timetable for accomplishment • Move to job that better matches skills • Ask to leave the company

SOURCES: Based on B. Axelrod, H. Handfield-Jones, and E. Michaels, "A New Game Plan for C Players," *HBR*, January 2002, pp. 80–88; A. Walker, "Is Performance Management as Simple as ABC?" *T + D*, February 2007, pp. 54–57; T. De Long and V. Vijayaraghavan, "Let's Hear It for B Players," *HBR*, June 2003, pp. 96–102.

is no longer requiring its managers to evaluate its employees against one another and rank them on a one-to-five scale.[25] This system meant that a percentage of Microsoft's employees always had to be designated as poor performers. The system was abandoned because many employees complained that it resulted in unfair rankings, power struggles between managers over which of their employees could receive the more favorable rankings, and aggressive competition between employees. Also, the system was not consistent with Microsoft's new strategic emphasis on teamwork.

Research simulating different features of a forced system and other factors that influence company performance (e.g., voluntary turnover rate, validity of selection methods) suggests that forced distribution rating systems can improve the potential performance of a company's workforce.[26] Companies that have clear goals and management criteria, train evaluators, use the rankings along with other HR metrics, and reward good performance may find them useful. The majority of improvement appears to occur during the first several years the system is used, mainly because of the large number of poorly performing employees who are identified and fired. Keep in mind that despite the potential advantages of forced choice systems for improving a company's workforce performance, the potential negative side effects on morale, teamwork, recruiting, and shareholder perceptions should be considered before adopting such a system. Many companies have emphasized the linkage between employees' performance and their development plan without using a forced distribution or ranking system. Forced ranking is ethical as long as the system is clearly communicated, the system is part of a positive dimension of the organization culture (innovation, continuous improvement), and the employees have the chance to appeal decisions.

Paired Comparison

The *paired comparison* method requires managers to compare every employee with every other employee in the work group, giving an employee a score of 1 every time he or she is considered the higher performer. Once all the pairs have been compared, the manager computes the number of times each employee received the favorable decision (i.e., counts up the points), and this becomes the employee's performance score.

The paired comparison method tends to be time-consuming for managers and will become more so as organizations become flatter with an increased span of control. For example, a manager with 10 employees must make 45 (10 × $\frac{9}{2}$) comparisons. However, if the group increases to 15 employees, 105 comparisons must be made.

Evaluating the Comparative Approach

The comparative approach to performance measurement is an effective tool in differentiating employee performance; it virtually eliminates problems of leniency, central tendency, and strictness. This is especially valuable if the results of the measures are to be used in making administrative decisions such as pay raises and promotions. In addition, such systems are relatively easy to develop and in most cases easy to use; thus, they are often accepted by users.

One problem with these techniques, however, is their common failure to be linked to the strategic goals of the organization. Although raters can evaluate the extent to which individuals' performances support the strategy, this link is seldom made explicit. In addition, because of the subjective nature of the ratings, their actual validity and reliability depend on the raters themselves. Some firms use multiple evaluators to reduce the biases of any individual, but most do not. At best, we could conclude that their reliability and validity are modest.

These techniques lack specificity for feedback purposes. Based only on their relative rankings, individuals are completely unaware of what they must do differently to improve their ranking. This puts a heavy burden on the manager to provide specific feedback beyond that of the rating instrument itself. Finally, many employees and managers are less likely to accept evaluations based on comparative approaches. Evaluations depend on how employees' performance relates to other employees in a group, team, or department (normative standard) rather than on absolute standards of excellent, good, fair, and poor performance.

THE ATTRIBUTE APPROACH

The attribute approach to performance management focuses on the extent to which individuals have certain attributes (characteristics or traits) believed desirable for the company's success. The techniques that use this approach define a set of traits—such as initiative, leadership, and competitiveness—and evaluate individuals on them.

Graphic Rating Scales

The most common form that the attribute approach to performance management takes is the *graphic rating scale.* Table 8.4 shows a graphic rating scale used in a manufacturing company. As you can see, a list of traits is evaluated by a five-point (or some other number of points) rating scale. The manager considers one employee at a time, circling the number that signifies how much of that trait the individual has. Graphic rating scales can provide a number of different points (a discrete scale) or a continuum along which the rater simply places a check mark (a continuous scale).

Table 8.4
Example of a Graphic Rating Scale

The following areas of performance are significant to most positions. Indicate your assessment of performance on each dimension by circling the appropriate rating.

PERFORMANCE DIMENSION	RATING				
	DISTINGUISHED	EXCELLENT	COMMENDABLE	ADEQUATE	POOR
Knowledge	5	4	3	2	1
Communication	5	4	3	2	1
Judgment	5	4	3	2	1
Managerial skill	5	4	3	2	1
Quality performance	5	4	3	2	1
Teamwork	5	4	3	2	1
Interpersonal skills	5	4	3	2	1
Initiative	5	4	3	2	1
Creativity	5	4	3	2	1
Problem solving	5	4	3	2	1

The legal defensibility of graphic rating scales was questioned in the *Brito v. Zia* case. In this case, Spanish-speaking employees had been terminated as a result of their performance appraisals. These appraisals consisted of supervisors' rating subordinates on a number of undefined dimensions such as volume of work, quantity of work, job knowledge, dependability, and cooperation. The court criticized the subjective appraisals and stated that the company should have presented empirical data demonstrating that the appraisal was significantly related to actual work behavior.

Mixed-Standard Scales

Mixed-standard scales were developed to get around some of the problems with graphic rating scales. To create a mixed-standard scale, we define the relevant performance dimensions and then develop statements representing good, average, and poor performance along each dimension. These statements are then mixed with the statements from other dimensions on the actual rating instrument. An example of a mixed-standard scale is presented in Table 8.5.

As we see in the table, the rater is asked to complete the rating instrument by indicating whether the employee's performance is above (+), at (0), or below (–) the statement. A special scoring key is then used to score the employee's performance for each dimension. Thus, for example, an employee performing above all three statements receives a 7. If the employee is below the good statement, at the average statement, and above the poor statement, a score of 4 is assessed. An employee below all three statements is given a rating of 1. This scoring is applied to all the dimensions to determine an overall performance score.

Note that mixed-standard scales were originally developed as trait-oriented scales. However, this same technique has been applied to instruments using behavioral rather than trait-oriented statements as a means of reducing rating errors in performance appraisal.[27]

Evaluating the Attribute Approach

Attribute-based performance methods are the most popular methods in organizations. They are quite easy to develop and are generalizable across a variety of jobs, strategies, and organizations. In addition, if much attention is devoted to identifying those attributes relevant to job performance and carefully defining them on the rating instrument, they can be as reliable and valid as more elaborate measurement techniques.

However, these techniques fall short on several of the criteria for effective performance management. There is usually little congruence between the techniques and the company's strategy. These methods are used because of the ease in developing them and because the same method (list of traits, comparisons) is generalizable across any organization and any strategy. In addition, these methods usually have very vague performance standards that are open to different interpretations by different raters. Because of this, different raters often provide extremely different ratings and rankings. The result is that both the validity and reliability of these methods are usually low.

Virtually none of these techniques provides any specific guidance on how an employee can support the company's goals or correct performance deficiencies. In addition, when raters give feedback, these techniques tend to elicit defensiveness from employees. For example, how would you feel if you were told that on a five-point scale, you were rated a "2" in maturity? Certainly you might feel somewhat defensive and unwilling to accept that judgment, as well as any additional feedback. Also, being told you were rated a "2" in maturity doesn't tell you how to improve your rating.

Table 8.5

An Example of a Mixed-Standard Scale

Three traits being assessed:	Levels of performance in statements:
Initiative (INTV)	High (H)
Intelligence (INTG)	Medium (M)
Relations with others (RWO)	Low (L)

Instructions: Please indicate next to each statement whether the employee's performance is above (+), equal to (0), or below (–) the statement.

INTV	H	1. This employee is a real self-starter. The employee always takes the initiative and his/her superior never has to prod this individual.	+
INTG	M	2. While perhaps this employee is not a genius, s/he is a lot more intelligent than many people I know.	+
RWO	L	3. This employee has a tendency to get into unnecessary conflicts with other people.	0
INTV	M	4. While generally this employee shows initiative, occasionally his/her superior must prod him/her to complete work.	+
INTG	L	5. Although this employee is slower than some in understanding things, and may take a bit longer in learning new things, s/he is of average intelligence.	+
RWO	H	6. This employee is on good terms with everyone. S/he can get along with people even when s/he does not agree with them.	–
INTV	L	7. This employee has a bit of a tendency to sit around and wait for directions.	+
INTG	H	8. This employee is extremely intelligent, and s/he learns very rapidly.	–
RWO	M	9. This employee gets along with most people. Only very occasionally does s/he have conflicts with others on the job, and these are likely to be minor.	–

Scoring Key:

	STATEMENTS		SCORE
HIGH	MEDIUM	LOW	
+	+	+	7
0	+	+	6
–	+	+	5
–	0	+	4
–	–	+	3
–	–	0	2
–	–	–	1

Example score from preceding ratings:

	STATEMENTS		SCORE
	HIGH	MEDIUM	LOW	
Initiative	+	+	+	7
Intelligence	0	+	+	6
Relations with others	–	–	0	2

THE BEHAVIORAL APPROACH

The behavioral approach to performance management attempts to define the behaviors an employee must exhibit to be effective in the job. The various techniques define those behaviors and then require managers to assess the extent to which employees exhibit them. We discuss five techniques that rely on the behavioral approach.

Behaviorally Anchored Rating Scales

A *behaviorally anchored rating scale (BARS)* is designed to specifically define performance dimensions by developing behavioral anchors associated with different levels of performance.[28] An example of a BARS is presented in Figure 8.4. As you can see, the performance dimension has a number of examples of behaviors that indicate specific levels of performance along the dimension.

To develop a BARS, we first gather a large number of critical incidents that represent effective and ineffective performance on the job. These incidents are classified into performance dimensions, and the ones that experts agree clearly represent a particular level of performance are used as behavioral examples (or anchors) to guide the rater. The manager's task is to consider an employee's performance along each dimension and determine where on the dimension the employee's performance fits using the behavioral anchors as guides. This rating becomes the employee's score for that dimension.

Behavioral anchors have advantages and disadvantages. They can increase interrater reliability by providing a precise and complete definition of the performance dimension. A disadvantage is that they can bias information recall—that is, behavior that closely approximates the anchor is more easily recalled than other behavior.[29] Research has also demonstrated that managers and their subordinates do not make much of a distinction between BARS and trait scales.[30]

Behavioral Observation Scales

A *behavioral observation scale (BOS)* is a variation of a BARS. Like a BARS, a BOS is developed from critical incidents.[31] However, a BOS differs from a BARS in two basic ways. First, rather than discarding a large number of the behaviors that exemplify effective or ineffective performance, a BOS uses many of them to more specifically define all the behaviors that are necessary for effective performance (or that would be considered ineffective performance). Instead of using, say, 4 behaviors to define 4 levels of performance on a particular dimension, a BOS may use 15 behaviors. An example of a BOS is presented in Table 8.6.

A second difference is that rather than assessing which behavior best reflects an individual's performance, a BOS requires managers to rate the frequency with which the employee has exhibited each behavior during the rating period. These ratings are then averaged to compute an overall performance rating.

The major drawback of a BOS is that it may require more information than most managers can process or remember. A BOS can have 80 or more behaviors, and the manager must remember how frequently an employee exhibited each of these behaviors over a 6- or 12-month rating period. This is taxing enough for one employee, but managers often must rate 10 or more employees.

A direct comparison of BOS, BARS, and graphic rating scales found that both managers and employees prefer BOS for differentiating good from poor performers, maintaining objectivity, providing feedback, suggesting training needs, and being easy to use among managers and subordinates.[32]

Figure 8.4

Task-BARS Rating
Dimension: Patrol
Officer

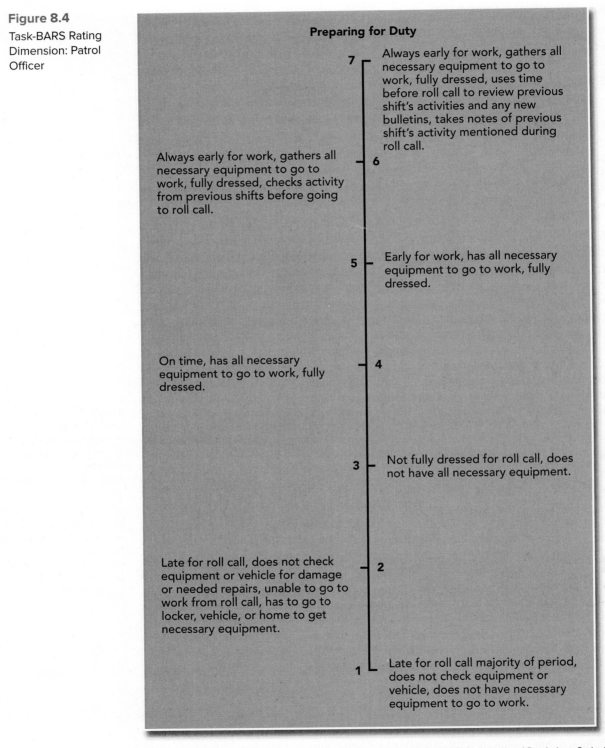

Preparing for Duty

7 — Always early for work, gathers all necessary equipment to go to work, fully dressed, uses time before roll call to review previous shift's activities and any new bulletins, takes notes of previous shift's activity mentioned during roll call.

Always early for work, gathers all necessary equipment to go to work, fully dressed, checks activity from previous shifts before going to roll call. — 6

5 — Early for work, has all necessary equipment to go to work, fully dressed.

On time, has all necessary equipment to go to work, fully dressed. — 4

3 — Not fully dressed for roll call, does not have all necessary equipment.

Late for roll call, does not check equipment or vehicle for damage or needed repairs, unable to go to work from roll call, has to go to locker, vehicle, or home to get necessary equipment. — 2

1 — Late for roll call majority of period, does not check equipment or vehicle, does not have necessary equipment to go to work.

SOURCE: Adapted from R. Harvey, "Job Analysis," in *Handbook of Industrial & Organizational Psychology,* 2nd ed., ed. M. Dunnette and L. Hough (Palo Alto, CA: Consulting Psychologists Press, 1991), p. 138.

Overcoming Resistance to Change						
(1) Describes the details of the change to subordinates.						
Almost Never	1	2	3	4	5	Almost Always
(2) Explains why the change is necessary.						
Almost Never	1	2	3	4	5	Almost Always
(3) Discusses how the change will affect the employee.						
Almost Never	1	2	3	4	5	Almost Always
(4) Listens to the employee's concerns.						
Almost Never	1	2	3	4	5	Almost Always
(5) Asks the employee for help in making the change work.						
Almost Never	1	2	3	4	5	Almost Always
(6) If necessary, specifies the date for a follow-up meeting to respond to the employee's concerns.						
Almost Never	1	2	3	4	5	Almost Always
Total = _____						

Below Adequate	Adequate	Full	Excellent	Superior
6–10	11–15	16–20	21–25	26–30

Table 8.6
An Example of a Behavioral Observation Scale (BOS) for Evaluating Job Performance

Scores are set by management.

SOURCE: From Gary Latham and Ken Wexley, *Increasing Productivity Through Performance Appraisal* (Prentice Hall Series in Human Resources), 2nd Edition © 1994. Reproduced by permission of Pearson Education, Inc., Upper Saddle River, New Jersey.

Competency Models

Competencies are sets of skills, knowledge, abilities, and personal characteristics that enable employees to successfully perform their jobs.[33] A **competency model** identifies and provides descriptions of competencies that are common for an entire occupation, organization, job family, or a specific job. Competency models can be used for performance management. However, one of the strengths of competency models is that they are useful for a variety of HR practices including recruiting, selection, training, and development. Competency models can be used to help identify the best employees to fill open positions, and as the foundation for development plans that allow the employee and manager to target specific strengths and development areas.

Table 8.7 shows the competency model that Luxottica Retail, known for premium, luxury, and sports eyewear sold through LensCrafters, Sunglass Hut, and Pearle Vision, developed for its associates in field and store positions.[34] The competency model includes leadership and managerial, functional, and foundational competencies. The goal was to define and identify competencies that managers could use for hiring, performance management, and training. Also, competencies would help associates identify and develop the skills they need to apply for different jobs. To effectively use competency models for performance evaluation they must be up-to-date, drive business performance, be job-related (valid), be relevant (or customized) for all of the company's business units, and provide sufficient detail to make an accurate assessment of employees' performance. At Luxottica Retail developing competencies started with meeting with business leaders to understand their current and future business strategies. Business drivers were identified and questionnaires, focus groups, and meetings with managers and associates were used to identify important competencies and examples of behaviors related to each. Competencies across business units and brands are reviewed every four or five years or whenever a major change in jobs or business strategy occurs to ensure they are relevant. Also, the weighting given to each set of competencies in the performance evaluation is

Competencies
Sets of skills, knowledge, abilities, and personal characteristics that enable employees to successfully perform their jobs.

Competency model
Identify and provide descriptions of competencies that are common for an occupation, organization, job family, or specific job.

Table 8.7
Luxottica Retail's
Competency Model

Leadership and Managerial
Leadership
Coach and develop others
Motivate others
Foster teamwork
Think strategically

Functional
Global perspective
Financial acumen
Business key performance indicators

Foundational
Critical thinking
Foster open communications
Build relationships and interpersonal skills
Develop and manage oneself
Adaptability and flexibility
Customer focus
Act with integrity
Diversity and multiculturalism
Drive and commitment

SOURCE: From C. Spicer, "Building a Competency Model," *HR Magazine,* April 2009, pp. 34–36. Reprinted with permission of Society for Human Resource Management.

reviewed to ensure that they are appropriate (e.g., what weights should be given to the functional skills). Depending on their relevance for a specific job, various combinations of these competencies are used for evaluating associates' performances. Associates are rated on a 1–5 scale for each competency with 5 meaning far exceeds expectations. HR, training and development, and operations teams worked together to define the levels of each competency, that is, what does it mean and what does the competency look like when an employee is rated "meets expectations" versus "below expectations"? This was necessary to ensure that managers are using a similar frame of reference when they evaluate associates using the competencies.

Evaluation of the Behavioral Approach

The behavioral approach can be very effective. It can link the company's strategy to the specific behavior necessary for implementing that strategy. It provides specific guidance and feedback for employees about the performance expected of them. Most of the techniques rely on in-depth job analysis, so the behaviors that are identified and measured are valid. Because those who will use the system develop the measures, the acceptability is also often high. Finally, with a substantial investment in training raters, the techniques are reasonably reliable.

The major weaknesses have to do with the organizational context of the system. Although the behavioral approach can be closely tied to a company's strategy, the behaviors and measures must be constantly monitored and revised to ensure that they are still linked to the strategic focus. This approach also assumes that there is "one best way" to do the job and that the behaviors that constitute this best way can be identified. One study found that managers seek to control behaviors when they perceive a clear relationship between behaviors and results. When this link is not clear, they tend to rely on managing results.[35] The behavioral approach might be best suited to less complex jobs (where the best way to achieve results is somewhat clear) and least suited to complex jobs (where there are multiple ways, or behaviors, to achieve success).

THE RESULTS APPROACH

The results approach focuses on managing the objective, measurable results of a job or work group. This approach assumes that subjectivity can be eliminated from the measurement process and that results are the closest indicator of one's contribution to organizational effectiveness.[36] We examine two performance management systems that use results: the balanced scorecard and the productivity measurement and evaluation system.

The Use of Objectives

The use of objectives is popular in both private and public organizations.[37] In a results-based system, the top management team first defines the company's strategic goals for the coming year. These goals are passed on to the next layer of management, and these managers define the goals they must achieve for the company to reach its goals. This goal-setting process cascades down the organization so that all managers set goals that help the company achieve its goals.[38] These goals are used as the standards by which an individual's performance is evaluated.[39]

Results-based systems have three common components.[40] They require setting effective goals. The most effective goals are SMART goals. That is, the goals are specific (clearly stated, define the result to be achieved), measurable (compared to a standard), attainable (difficult but achievable), relevant (link to organizational success factors or goals), and timely (measured in deadline, due dates, cycles, or schedules). Different types of measurements can be used for goals or objectives including timeliness (e.g., responds to requests within 12 hours), quality (report provided clear information with no revisions necessary), quantity (increased sales 25%), or financial metrics (e.g., reduced purchasing costs 10%). (An example of objectives used in a financial service firm is presented in Table 8.8.) The goals are not usually set unilaterally by management but with the managers' and subordinates' participation. And the manager gives objective feedback throughout the rating period to monitor progress toward the goals.

Research on objectives has revealed two important findings regarding their effectiveness.[41] Of 70 studies examined, 68 showed productivity gains, while only 2 showed productivity losses, suggesting that objectives usually increase productivity. Also, productivity gains tend to be highest when there is substantial commitment to the objectives program from top management: an average increase of 56% when commitment was high, 33% when commitment was moderate, and 6% when commitment was low.

KEY RESULT AREA	OBJECTIVE	% COMPLETE	ACTUAL PERFORMANCE
Loan portfolio management	Increase portfolio value by 10% over the next 12 months	90	Increased portfolio value by 9% over the past 12 months
Sales	Generate fee income of $30,000 over the next 12 months	150	Generated fee income of $45,000 over the past 12 months

Table 8.8
An Example of an Objectives Measure of Job Performance

Clearly, use of an objectives system can have a very positive effect on an organization's performance. Considering the process through which goals are set (involvement of staff in setting objectives), it is also likely that use of an objectives system effectively links individual employee performance with the firm's strategic goals. Evaluation of objectives, based on results or business-based metrics, removes the subjectivity from the evaluation process—employees either meet the objectives or they do not. For example, Long Island Jewish Medical Center implemented a computer-based performance management system that breaks the nurses' job description into measurable goals in order to keep infection rates for the unit low and patient-satisfaction scores high.[42]

Table 8.9 shows how to best use objectives or goals in performance management. Waiting for goals to cascade down from company leaders, to division, function, and their team, takes too much time and employees have a difficult time understanding how their goals are related to company goals (line of sight). As a result, employees should set goals that as much as possible are linked to organizational goals. It is important to make sure that goals are SMART but they also are meaningful.[43] Rewards and incentives are best for motivating employees to achieve performance goals in jobs in which the results are easily measured and under employees' control. It is also important to remember that goals typically focus just on results not on behaviors, values, or how things get done. If you want employees to behave in certain ways (or avoid behaving in certain ways) in achieving goals you need to also insure your performance management system includes evaluating behaviors. Otherwise, for example, a goal emphasis on sales might cause employees to mislead customers and poorly treat their peers.

Balanced Scorecard

Some companies use the balanced scorecard to measure performance (we discussed the use of the balanced scorecard in Chapter 1). The balanced scorecard includes four perspectives of performance including financial, customer, internal or operations, and learning and growth (see Table 1.8 in Chapter 1). The financial perspective focuses on creating sustainable growth in shareholder value, the customer perspective defines value for customers (e.g., service, quality), the internal or operations perspective focuses on processes that influence customer satisfaction, and the learning and growth perspective focuses on the company's capacity to innovate and continuously improve. Each of these perspectives are used to translate the business strategy into organizational,

Table 8.9
Best Practices in Goal Setting

1. Employees and managers should discuss and set no more than 3 to 5 goals.
2. Goals should be brief, meaningful, challenging, and include the results the employee is expected to achieve.
3. The time frame for goal achievement should be related to when they are expected to be accomplished.
4. The relationship between goals and rewards should be appropriate.
5. Goals should be "linked up" rather than "cascaded down". This means that functions, teams, and employees should set their own goals that are related to company goals.

SOURCES: Based on R. Hanson and E. Pulakos, *Putting the "Performance" Back in Performance Management* (Alexandria, VA: Society for Human Resource Management, 2015); R. Noe, and L. Inks, *It's About People: How Performance Management Helps Middle Market Companies Grow Faster* (Columbus, Ohio: National Center for the Middle Market, Ohio State University Fisher College of Business, GE Capital, 2014): D. Grote, *How to be Good at Performance Appraisals* (Boston, MA: Harvard University Press, 2011); A. Fox, "Put Plans into Action," *HR Magazine,* April 2013, pp. 27–31.

managerial, and employee objectives. Employee performance is linked with the business strategy through communicating and educating employees on the elements of the balanced scorecard, translating strategic objectives into measures for departments and employees, and linking rewards to performance measures.[44] Employees need to know the corporate objectives, how they translate into objectives for each business unit, and develop their own and team objectives that are consistent with the business unit and company objectives. Effective balanced scorecards allow employees to understand the business strategy by looking only at the scorecard and the strategy map (the cause-and-effect relationships among the measures). For example, for the customer perspective of the balanced scorecard an airline might have on-time performance as a critical success factor.[45] Gate agents, ground, maintenance, and scheduling represent groups of employees who impact on-time performance. Gate agents have four roles that can influence boarding speed including check-in timeliness, effectively dealing with connections, flight documentation, and the boarding process. Gate agents' performance in these four roles should be evaluated because they impact key performance indicators related to on-time performance including cost savings, customer satisfaction, customer losses, and operational costs.

Productivity Measurement and Evaluation System (ProMES)

The main goal of ProMES is to motivate employees to improve team or company-level productivity.[46] It is a means of measuring and feeding back productivity information to employees.

Team members try to map the relationship between specific outcomes and productivity and the relationships between effect and performance, performance and outcomes, and outcomes relationship to satisfaction of employee needs. ProMES consists of four steps. First, people in an organization identify the products, or the set of activities or objectives, the organization expects to accomplish. The organization's productivity depends on how well it produces these products. At a repair shop, for example, a product might be something like "quality of repair." Second, the staff defines indicators of the products. Indicators are measures of how well the products are being generated by the organization. Quality of repair could be indicated by (1) return rate (percentage of items returned that did not function immediately after repair) and (2) percentage of quality-control inspections passed. Third, the staff establishes the contingencies between the amount of the indicators and the level of evaluation associated with that amount. Fourth, a feedback system is developed that provides employees and work groups with information about their specific level of performance on each of the indicators. An overall productivity score can be computed by summing the effectiveness scores across the various indicators.

Research thus far strongly suggests this technique is effective in increasing productivity. (Figure 8.5 illustrates the productivity gains in the repair shop described previously.) The research also suggests the system is an effective feedback mechanism. However, users found it time-consuming to develop the initial system.

Evaluation of the Results Approach

The results approach minimizes subjectivity, relying on objective, quantifiable indicators of performance. Thus, it is usually highly acceptable to both managers and employees. Another advantage is that it links an individual's results with the organization's strategies and goals.

Figure 8.5

Increases in Productivity for a Repair Shop Using ProMES Measures

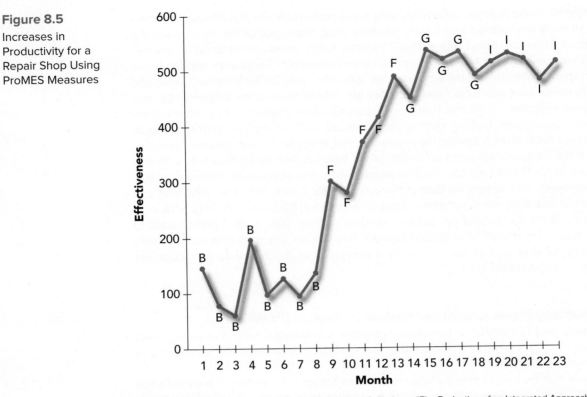

SOURCE: P. Pritchard, S. Jones, P. Roth, K. Stuebing, and S. Ekeberg, "The Evaluation of an Integrated Approach to Measuring Organizational Productivity," *Personnel Psychology*, 42, (1989), pp. 69–115. Used by permission.

However, there are a number of challenges in using objective performance measures. Objective measurements can be both contaminated and deficient—contaminated because they are affected by things that are not under the employee's control and deficient because not all the important aspects of job performance are amenable to objective measurement. For example, consider how an economic recession can influence sales goals or, for a teacher, parental support for studying can influence student's achievement test scores. Another disadvantage is that individuals may focus only on aspects of their performance that are measured, neglecting those that are not. For example, if the large majority of employees' goals relate to productivity, it is unlikely they will be concerned with customer service. One study found that objective performance goals led to higher performance but that they also led to helping co-workers less.[47] It is important to identify if goals should be set at the individual, team, or department level. Setting employees' objectives may not be appropriate if work is team-based. Individual objectives may undermine behaviors related to team success such as sharing information and collaboration. A final disadvantage is that, although results measures provide objective feedback, the feedback may not help employees learn how they need to change their behavior to increase their performance. If baseball players are in a hitting slump, simply telling them that their batting average is .190 may not motivate them to raise it. Feedback focusing on the exact behavior that needs to be changed (like taking one's eye off the ball or dropping one's shoulder) would be more helpful.[48]

John Deere takes specific actions to avoid these problems.[49] At the start of each fiscal year, managers and employees meet to discuss objectives for the year. A midyear review is then conducted to check on the employees' progress in meeting the goals. The year-end review meeting focuses on evaluating goal accomplishment. Goal achievement at the end of the year is linked to pay increases and other rewards. All company objectives are supported by division objectives that are available for employees to view online. Employees also have available a learning and activities courseware catalog they can use to help develop skills needed to achieve their performance objectives.

THE QUALITY APPROACH

Thus far we have examined the traditional approaches to measuring and evaluating employee performance. Fundamental characteristics of the quality approach include a customer orientation, a prevention approach to errors, and continous improvement. Improving customer satisfaction is the primary goal of the quality approach. Customers can be internal or external to the organization. A performance management system designed with a strong quality orientation can be expected to

- Emphasize an assessment of both person and system factors in the measurement system.
- Emphasize that managers and employees work together to solve performance problems.
- Involve both internal and external customers in setting standards and measuring performance.
- Use multiple sources to evaluate person and system factors.[50]

Based on this chapter's earlier discussion of the characteristics of an effective performance management system, it should be apparent to you that these characteristics are not just unique to the quality approach but are characteristics of an effective appraisal system!

Advocates of the quality approach believe that most U.S. companies' performance management systems are incompatible with the quality philosophy for a number of reasons:

1. Most existing systems measure performance in terms of quantity, not quality.
2. Employees are held accountable for good or bad results to which they contribute but do not completely control.
3. Companies do not share the financial rewards of successes with employees according to how much they have contributed to them.
4. Rewards are not connected to business results.[51]

Sales, profit margins, and behavioral ratings are often collected by managers to evaluate employees' performance. These are person-based outcomes. An assumption of using these types of outcomes is that the employee completely controls them. However, according to the quality approach, these types of outcomes should not be used to evaluate employees' performance because they do not have complete control over them (i.e., they are contaminated). For example, for salespersons, performance evaluations (and salary increases) are often based on attainment of a sales quota. Salespersons' abilities and motivation are assumed to be directly responsible for their performance. However, quality approach advocates argue that better determinants of whether a salesperson reaches the quota are "systems factors" (such as competitors' product price changes) and economic conditions (which are not under the salesperson's control).[52] Holding employees accountable for outcomes affected by systems factors is believed to result in dysfunctional behavior, such as falsifying sales reports, budgets, expense accounts, and other performance measures, as well as lowering employees' motivation for continuous improvement.

Quality advocates suggest that the major focus of performance evaluations should be to provide employees with feedback about areas in which they can improve. Two types of feedback are necessary: (1) subjective feedback from managers, peers, and customers about the personal qualities of the employee and (2) objective feedback based on the work process itself using statistical quality control methods.

At Just Born, the company that makes Peeps and Mike and Ike candy, the performance management process is designed with a strong quality orientation.[53] The performance management system is designed to facilitate employee improvement (a forward-looking approach) rather than focus entirely on what the employee has accomplished during the past year. Also, managers and employees are encouraged to work together to solve performance problems.

The performance management system is part of the company's broader people development system (PDS) which is designed to ensure that learning and development align with business strategy and drive business results while ensuring employees have the skills to succeed in their current and future jobs. The PDS includes the performance management process, learning and career development processes, and succession planning process. Information from each of these systems is shared to ensure that employees are developing the skills through training and on-the-job experiences needed for their current jobs as well as preparing for their future career interests. Just Born's performance management system starts with a planning meeting between the employee and their manager. At this meeting the employee's role and strategic goals of the department are discussed. The manager and employee agree on up to four personal objectives that will help the department meet its objectives and the employee achieve the specific deliverables described in the job description. Two competencies that the employee needs to deliver or improve on are identified. The manager and employee work together to develop a learning plan to help the employee gain the competencies. During the year, the employee and manager meet to discuss the progress in meeting the deliverables and improving the competencies. Pay decisions made at the end of each fiscal year are based on the achievement of performance objectives and learning goals.

Just Born also uses the Wow . . . Now improvement process, a customized Kaizen process to improve business processes and results. The Wow . . . Now improvement process includes teaching employees how to identify improvement opportunities, collect data, make improvements, measure results, and, based on the results, refine practices. Kaizen, the Japanese word for improvement, is one of the underlying principles of lean manufacturing and total quality management (we discussed lean thinking in Chapter 1). **Kaizen** refers to practices participated in by employees from all levels of the company that focus on continuous improvement of business processes.[54] As the Wow . . . Now improvement process illustrates, Kaizen involves considering a continuous cycle of activities including planning, doing, checking, and acting (PDCA). Statistical process control techniques are used by employees to identify causes of problems and potential solutions. They include process-flow analysis, cause-and-effect diagrams, control charts, histograms, and scattergrams.

Kaizen
Employee practices that emphasize continuous improvement of business processes.

Statistical process control techniques are very important in the quality approach. These techniques provide employees with an objective tool to identify causes of problems and potential solutions. These techniques include process-flow analysis, cause-and-effect diagrams, Pareto charts, control charts, histograms, and scattergrams. *Process-flow analysis* identifies each action and decision necessary to complete work, such as waiting on a customer or assembling a television set. Process-flow analysis is useful for identifying redundancy in processes that increase manufacturing or service time. In *cause-and-effect diagrams,* events or causes that result in undesirable outcomes are identified. Employees try to identify all possible causes of a problem. The feasibility of the causes is not evaluated, and as a result, cause-and-effect diagrams produce a large list of possible causes.

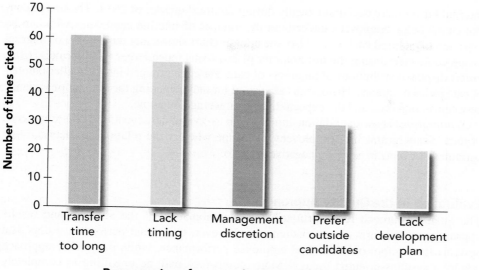

Figure 8.6
Pareto Chart

SOURCE: From Clara Carter, *HR Magazine*. Copyright 1992. Reprinted with permission of Society for Human Resource Management.

A *Pareto chart* highlights the most important cause of a problem. In a Pareto chart, causes are listed in decreasing order of importance, where *importance* is usually defined as the frequency with which that cause resulted in a problem. The assumption of Pareto analysis is that the majority of problems are the result of a small number of causes. Figure 8.6 shows a Pareto chart listing the reasons managers give for not selecting current employees for a job vacancy. *Control charts* involve collecting data at multiple points in time. By collecting data at different times, employees can identify what factors contribute to an outcome and when they tend to occur. Figure 8.7 shows the percentage of employees hired internally for a company for each quarter between 2013 and 2015.

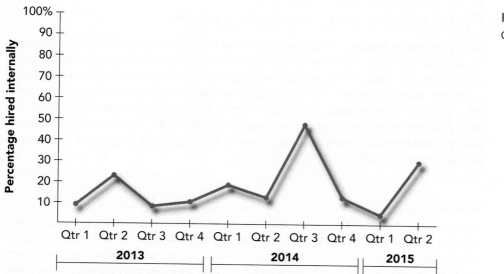

Figure 8.7
Control Chart

SOURCE: Based on Clara Carter, *HR Magazine*. Copyright 1992.

Internal hiring increased dramatically during the third quarter of 2014. The use of control charts helps employees understand the number of internal candidates who can be expected to be hired each year. Also, the control chart shows that the amount of internal hiring conducted during the third quarter of 2014 was much larger than normal. *Histograms* display distributions of large sets of data. Data are grouped into a smaller number of categories or classes. Histograms are useful for understanding the amount of variance between an outcome and the expected value or average outcome.

Scattergrams show the relationship between two variables, events, or different pieces of data. Scattergrams help employees determine whether the relationship between two variables or events is positive, negative, or zero.

LO 8-5
Choose the most effective approach to performance measurement for a given situation.

Evaluation of the Quality Approach

The quality approach relies primarily on a combination of the attribute and results approaches to performance measurement. However, traditional performance appraisal systems focus more on individual employee performance, while the quality approach adopts a systems-oriented focus.[55] Many companies may be unwilling to completely abandon their traditional performance management system because it serves as the basis for personnel selection validation, identification of training needs, or compensation decisions. Also, the quality approach advocates evaluation of personal traits (such as cooperation), which are difficult to relate to job performance unless the company has been structured into work teams.

In summary, organizations can take five approaches to measuring performance: comparative, attribute, behavioral, results, and quality. Table 8.10 summarizes the various approaches to measuring performance based on the criteria we set forth earlier and illustrates that each approach has strengths and weaknesses. As a result, effective performance evaluations involve a combination of approaches including assessment of objectives and behaviors.

Choosing a Source for Performance Information

LO 8-6
Discuss the advantages and disadvantages of the different sources of performance information.

Whatever approach to performance management is used, it is necessary to decide whom to use as the source of the performance measures. Each source has specific strengths and weaknesses. We discuss five primary sources: managers, peers, subordinates, self, and customers. Many companies include manager and self-assessment of performance. This helps facilitate a conversation about performance during the appraisal meeting and on a more frequent basis. The "Competing through Sustainability" box illustrates the importance of using multiple sources of performance information to ensure that the needs of all stakeholders are being met.

LO 8-7
Choose the most effective source(s) for performance information for any situation.

MANAGERS

Managers are the most frequently used source of performance information. It is usually safe to assume that supervisors have extensive knowledge of the job requirements and that they have had adequate opportunity to observe their employees—in other words, that they have the ability to rate their employees. In addition, because supervisors have something to gain from the employees' high performance and something to lose from

Table 8.10

Evaluation of Approaches to Performance Measurement

APPROACH	CRITERIA				
	STRATEGIC CONGRUENCE	**VALIDITY**	**RELIABILITY**	**ACCEPTABILITY**	**SPECIFICITY**
Comparative	Poor, unless manager takes time to make link	Can be high if ratings are done carefully	Depends on rater, but usually no measure of agreement used	Moderate; easy to develop and use but resistant to normative standard	Very low
Attribute	Usually low; requires manager to make link	Usually low; can be fine if developed carefully	Usually low; can be improved by specific definitions of attributes	High; easy to develop and use	Very low
Behavioral	Can be quite high	Usually high; minimizes contamination and deficiency	Usually high	Moderate; difficult to develop, but accepted well for use	Very high
Results	Very high	Usually high; can be both contaminated and deficient	High; main problem can be test–retest—depends on timing of measure	High; usually developed with input from those to be evaluated	High regarding results, but low regarding behaviors necessary to achieve them
Quality	Very high	High, but can be both contaminated and deficient	High	High; usually developed with input from those to be evaluated	High regarding results, but low regarding behaviors necessary to achieve them

low performance, they are motivated to make accurate ratings.[56] Finally, feedback from supervisors is strongly related to performance and to employee perceptions of the accuracy of the appraisal if managers attempt to observe employee behavior or discuss performance issues in the feedback session.[57]

Burlington Northern Santa Fe Corporation of Fort Worth, Texas, improved its performance management process by holding leaders accountable in setting annual goals, creating individual development plans, providing feedback and coaching to employees, and self-evaluation.[58] An online performance management system supports the process. The company's executive team creates the overall company objectives, which cascade down to each department and individual employees who can now see how they contribute to the company's success. The online system allows managers and employees to see how they and the department are progressing on the objectives. Required to be engaged in the performance management process, managers are more focused on the necessary communications, coaching, and giving feedback, and they are more inclined to seek out training to be sure that they have the necessary communications, feedback, and coaching skills. Managers' effectiveness is monitored by periodic employee surveys that ask questions about whether the manager discusses performance, whether the dialogue with the manager is two-way, and whether the employee receives ongoing feedback.

Connecticut Health Foundation Uses Goals to Ensure It Meets Mission and Objectives

The Connecticut Health Foundation (CHF) is a nonprofit organization whose mission is to improve the health status of people in Connecticut, specifically helping more people of color and underserved communities gain access to affordable and high-quality care. It provides funding for programs to improve health systems in Connecticut and helps Connecticut residents make informed decisions about health care and advocate for their health. Its strategic goals focus on health equity and oral health. For each need, the organization's leaders establish yearly objectives the agency should attain to fulfill its mission. Each employee collaborates with their supervisor to define the employee's performance objectives. Because the organization has already established and published yearly organization-level objectives, the supervisor has a sense of what his or her group needs to accomplish to support those objectives. This information enables the manager to support the employee in identifying SMART goals that will contribute to achieving the group's effort. In practice, setting and meeting these goals can be challenging. Some accomplishments are difficult to measure, and some appear unrelated to CHF's overall goals and mission related to promoting health. For example, it can be easier for employees to think about paying vendor bills on time than to focus on a broader purpose such as "maintaining the integrity of the foundation's financial information." Also, for the organization to succeed over the long term it's not enough to pay vendors accurately and on time if employees don't have a positive, customer-focused attitude.

DISCUSSION QUESTION

What source(s) for performance information do you think is best to use to determine whether employees are working toward the organization's long-term goals and mission, and ultimately its future? What performance outcomes (attributes, behaviors, competencies, objective results) would you assess?

SOURCES: Connecticut Health Foundation, "About Us" and "Our Strategic Plan," http://www.cthealth.org, accessed April 28, 2015; Carol Pollack, "Measuring Employee Performance: Easier Said Than Done!" *Connecticut Health Foundation blog,* January 3, 2012, http://www.cthealth.org; Carol Pollack, "Employee Performance: From Both an Inside and Outside View," *Connecticut Health Foundation blog,* January 5, 2012, http://www.cthealth.org.

Problems with using supervisors as the source of performance information can occur in particular situations. In some jobs, for example, the supervisor does not have an adequate opportunity to observe the employee performing his job duties. For example, in outside sales jobs, the supervisor does not have the opportunity to see the salesperson at work most of the time. This usually requires that the manager occasionally spend a day accompanying the salesperson on sales calls. However, on those occasions the employee will be on best behavior, so there is no assurance that performance that day accurately reflects performance when the manager is not around.

Also, some supervisors may be so biased against a particular employee that to use the supervisor as the sole source of information would result in less-than-accurate measures for that individual. Favoritism is a fact of organizational life, but it is one that must be minimized as much as possible in performance management.[59] Thus, the performance evaluation system should seek to minimize the opportunities for favoritism to affect ratings. One way to do this is not to rely on only a supervisor's evaluation of an employee's performance.

PEERS

Another source of performance information is the employee's co-workers. Peers are an excellent source of information in a job such as law enforcement, where the supervisor does not always observe the employee. Peers have expert knowledge of job requirements, and they often have the most opportunity to observe the employee in day-to-day activities. Also, peers are often in the best position to praise and recognize each other's performance on a daily basis. Peer evaluations can be even more motivating than managers' evaluations because, unlike managers, peers are not expected to provide feedback.

Google provides employees with Kudos, a peer-to-peer recognition program that lets employees send online thank-you notes and Peer Bonus, through which they can nominate their peers for $175 rewards.[60] At Colorado's Douglas County Libraries employees nominate colleagues for their accomplishment.[61] Each year a committee chooses employees or teams who will be recognized. For example, honored employees include librarians who created a storytime for special needs children and improved an inventory management process. The employees are honored during a recognition dinner, given one day off with pay, and are asked to choose a favorite book in which a label is placed acknowledging the award.

Peers also bring a different perspective to the evaluation process, which can be valuable in gaining an overall picture of the individual's performance. In fact, peers have been found to provide extremely valid assessments of performance in several different settings.[62]

One disadvantage of using peer ratings is the potential for friendship to bias ratings.[63] Little empirical evidence suggests that this is often a problem, however. Another disadvantage is that when the evaluations are made for administrative decisions, peers often find the situation of being both rater and ratee uncomfortable. When these ratings are used only for developmental purposes, however, peers react favorably.[64]

SUBORDINATES

Subordinates are an especially valuable source of performance information when managers are evaluated. Subordinates often have the best opportunity to evaluate how well a manager treats employees. **Upward feedback** refers to appraisals that involve collecting subordinates' evaluations of manager's behavior or skills. Dell Inc., the Texas-based computer company, recently took steps to focus not only on financial goals but also on making the company a great place to work to attract and keep talented employees.[65] To help develop what Dell calls a "winning culture," Dell added a people management component to its results-oriented performance management system. Managers are now rated by their employees on semiannual "Tell Dell" surveys. Managers who receive less than 50% favorable scores on five questions receive less favorable compensation, bonus, and promotion opportunities and are required to take additional training. Table 8.11 shows

Upward Feedback
Managerial performance appraisal that involves subordinates' evaluations of the manager's behavior or skills.

- Even if I were offered a comparable position with similar pay and benefits at another company, I would stay at Dell.
- I receive ongoing feedback that helps me to improve my performance.
- My manager/supervisor supports my efforts to balance my work and personal life.
- My manager/supervisor is effective at managing people.
- I can be successful at Dell and still retain my individuality.

Table 8.11
Example of Upward Feedback Survey Questions from "Tell Dell" Surveys

SOURCE: Based on A. Pomeroy, "Agent of Change," *HR Magazine,* May 2005, pp. 52–56.

the five questions. Managers are expected to work continuously to improve their scores. Their goal is to receive at least 75% favorable ratings from employees on the five questions. One study found that managers viewed receiving upward feedback more positively when receiving feedback from subordinates who were identified, but subordinates preferred to provide anonymous feedback. When subordinates were identified, they inflated their ratings of the manager.[66]

One problem with subordinate evaluations is that they give subordinates power over their managers, thus putting the manager in a difficult situation.[67] This can lead to managers' emphasizing employee satisfaction over productivity. However, this happens only when administrative decisions are made from these evaluations. As with peer evaluations, it is a good idea to use subordinate evaluations only for developmental purposes. To assure subordinates that they need not fear retribution from their managers, it is necessary to use anonymous evaluations and at least three subordinates for each manager.

SELF

Although self-ratings are not often used as the sole source of performance information, they can still be valuable.[68] Obviously, individuals have extensive opportunities to observe their own behavior, and they usually have access to information regarding their results on the job. The YMCA of Greater Rochester, New York, added employee self-evaluation as part of its performance review process to address concerns that employees had little input into the appraisal process. Its original performance management process didn't help facilitate conversation between employees and managers, and both parties dreaded formal appraisal meetings.[69] In the revamped process, self-evaluation allows employees to give examples of good performance and to request training to improve their weaknesses. Before they are finalized, performance ratings are based on a discussion between the manager and employee. Self-evaluations have lessened the fear and anxiety associated with the old appraisal process. Employees feel they have a voice and the opportunity to influence the appraisal process. Managers are relieved because the burden for evaluation is no longer completely their responsibility. Now, employees provide them with feedback and insight into their performance which help determine performance ratings.

One problem with self-ratings, however, is a tendency toward inflated assessments. Research has found that self-ratings for personal traits as well as overall performance ratings tend to be lenient compared to ratings from other sources.[70] This stems from two sources. If the ratings are going to be used for administrative decisions (like pay raises), it is in the employees' interests to inflate their ratings. And there is ample evidence in the social psychology literature that individuals attribute their poor performance to external causes, such as a co-worker who they think has not provided them with timely information. Although self-ratings are less inflated when supervisors provide frequent performance feedback, it is not advisable to use them for administrative purposes.[71] The best use of self-ratings is as a prelude to the performance feedback session to get employees thinking about their performance and to focus discussion on areas of disagreement.

CUSTOMERS

Many companies are involving customers in their evaluation systems. One writer has defined *services* this way: "Services is something which can be bought and sold but which you cannot drop on your foot."[72] Because of the unique nature of services—the product is often produced and consumed on the spot—supervisors, peers, and subordinates often do not have the opportunity to observe employee behavior. Instead, the customer is often the only person present to observe the employee's performance and thus is the best source of performance information.

Many companies in service industries have moved toward customer evaluations of employee performance. Marriott Corporation provides a customer satisfaction card in every room and mails surveys to a random sample of customers after their stay in a Marriott hotel. Whirlpool's Consumer Services Division conducts on-site (using the service technicians' handheld computers), mail, and telephone surveys of customers after factory service technicians have serviced their appliances. These surveys allow the company to evaluate an individual technician's customer-service behaviors while in the customer's home.

Using customer evaluations of employee performance is appropriate in two situations.[73] The first is when an employee's job requires direct service to the customer or linking the customer to other services within the company. Second, customer evaluations are appropriate when the company is interested in gathering information to determine what products and services the customer wants. That is, customer evaluations serve a strategic goal by integrating marketing strategies with human resource activities and policies. Customer evaluations collected for this purpose are useful for both evaluating the employee and helping to determine whether changes in other HRM activities (such as training or the compensation system) are needed to improve customer service.

The weakness of customer surveys is their expense, particularly if printing, postage, telephone, and labor are involved. On-site surveys completed using handheld computers help eliminate these expenses.

In conclusion, the best source of performance information often depends on the particular job. One should choose the source or sources that provide the best opportunity to observe employee behavior and results. Often, eliciting performance information from a variety of sources results in a performance management process that is accurate and effective. In fact, one recent popular trend in organizations is called **360-degree appraisal**.[74] This technique consists of having multiple raters (boss, peers, subordinates, customers) provide input into a manager's evaluation. The major advantage of the technique is that it provides a means for minimizing bias in an otherwise subjective evaluation technique. It has been used primarily for strategic and developmental purposes and is discussed in greater detail in Chapter 9.[75] Netflix doesn't use annual performance reviews but instead uses informal 360-degree reviews.[76] Employees are asked to identify things that their peers should start, stop, and continue doing. The reviews are not anonymous and many teams hold the reviews face-to-face. Netflix's use of 360-degree appraisals fits into the company's performance culture that emphasizes that performance should be discussed simply and honestly.

360-Degree Appraisal
A performance appraisal process for managers that includes evaluations from a wide range of persons who interact with the manager. The process includes self-evaluations as well as evaluations from the manager's boss, subordinates, peers, and customers.

Use of Technology in Performance Management

Technology is influencing performance management systems in four ways. First, many companies are moving to web-based online paperless performance management systems. These systems help companies ensure that performance goals across all levels of the organization are aligned, provide managers and employees with greater access to performance information, and tools for understanding and use of the performance management process.[77]

LO 8-8
Discuss the potential advantages of performance management, gamification, social performance management, and electronic monitoring.

Social Performance Management
Social media and microblogs similar to Facebook, LinkedIn, and Yammer that allow employees to quickly exchange information, talk to each other, provide coaching, and receive feedback and recognition in the form of electronic badges.

Second, social media tools similar to Facebook and Twitter are increasingly being used to deliver timely feedback. **Social performance management** refers to systems similar to Facebook, LinkedIn, and Yammer that allow employees to quickly exchange information, talk to each other, provide coaching, and receive recognition. Social performance management is especially valued by Milliennial generation employees who want more frequent feedback about their performance because they have grown up electronically connected to each other through social networking tools that enable personal and professional connections.[78] Although Baby Boomers may be more likely to believe that feedback involves judgment compared to younger generations who see feedback as an opportunity to learn, high performers of all ages across generations are likely to seek and value feedback. As emphasized in the effective performance management model (see Figure 8.1) performance feedback is a critical part of the performance management process that should not be limited to quarterly, midyear, or annual formal performance evaluations. Also sometimes peers and co-workers can give more timely and accurate feedback and recognition than busy managers. For example, Mozilla's social performance management system can be accessed by employees on their computers and smartphones.[79] Employees and managers can send each other colorful "badges" to recognize good performance. The badges include slogans such as "you rock" or "kicking butt." Also, employees can receive feedback and coaching from peers. Employees can post short questions about their performance such as "What did you think about my speech?" or "How can I handle angry customers better?" The questions are e-mailed to managers, peers, and anyone else from whom the employee wants to receive feedback. The responses are gathered together so they are anonymous and sent back to the employee, providing a quick and timely performance review.

Gamification
Game-based strategies applied to performance management to make it a fun, effective, transparent, and inclusive process for employees and managers.

Third, companies are starting to use gamification in performance management. **Gamification** means that game-based strategies are applied to performance management to make it a fun, effective, transparent, and inclusive process for employees and managers. The "Competing through Technology" box shows how gamification is being used by Persistent Systems.

Fourth, companies are relying on electronic tracking and monitoring systems to ensure that employees are working when and how they should be and to block access to visiting certain websites (such as those containing pornographic images). These systems include hand and fingerprint recognition systems, global positioning systems (GPS), and software that can track employees using smartphones and notebook computers.

For example, at the New York law firm Akin & Smith LLC, paralegals, receptionists, and clerks clock in by placing their finger on a sensor kept at a secretary's desk. The managing partners believe the system improves productivity and keeps everyone honest, holding them to their lunch times.[80]

In the trucking industry, drivers are constantly monitored.[81] An onboard computer records whether the driver is on or off duty, documents his gas mileage, and tells him where to get gas. If the truck stops while on duty the driver is asked to provide an explanation. The electronic monitoring system built in the computer tells him which route to follow and records even slight deviations from the route due to traffic or accidents. Plants, Inc., a company that provides interior landscaping services to homes and businesses, uses monitoring software installed on company-provided phones.[82] Managers can see employee location and any photo, text message, e-mail, and website visits made over the phones. However, managers only use the location-tracking feature in response to customer questions about when and if Plants' employees had provided service on the scheduled date and time.

Gamification Improves Performance Management

Persistent Systems, a global technology innovation and software solutions company, asked eMee to help develop a game-based approach to performance management. The game-based approach allows any employee to participate in performance management. In the system every employee has a virtual avatar. Managers and peers can present virtual gifts to employees for their achievements. The virtual gifts carry points which provide a measure of performance against key performance indicators (KPIs). The system is integrated with other business applications and information systems. Employees and managers can access all aspects of performance management including

KPIs, performance goals, training needs, and certifications. The new system has allowed performance management to provide just-in-time feedback from customers, peers, and managers, across teams and business functions. This is important because Persistent's work is project-driven, which means that employees often switch managers and projects many times each year. Last year, approximately 500,000 comments and citations were provided by managers and peers in the system. The company estimates it saved more than 28,000 hours by using the new system. Persistent believes that the new performance management system is directly responsible for a 5%

drop in turnover and increase in customer ratings and satisfaction scores.

DISCUSSION QUESTIONS

1. Consider the performance management process shown in Figure 8.1. On which step(s) in the process do you think that gamification of performance management can have the most positive influence?

2. Why did this performance management system result in lowering turnover? Increasing customer ratings and satisfaction?

SOURCE: Based on D. Zinger and S. Bhobe, "Game-changing Performance Management," *T + D,* January 2014, p. 80.

Memorial Care, a nonprofit hospital group, keeps detailed data on the extent to which doctors perform immunizations and mammograms and reduce the blood sugar levels of diabetes patients.[83] In its hospitals the company tracks the extent to which patients experience complications and hospital readmissions, as well as the cost of services. Doctors are graded as green, yellow, or red based on how well they are performing compared to their peers. The data collected is discussed with individual doctors as well as clinics. For example, at one clinic all of the numbers exceeded the standards except cervical cancer screenings. Some patients were getting pap smears more often than the recommended guideline of every three years. The clinic doctors discussed the results and identified that the high rate of pap smears was because some of the tests were ordered by gynecologists outside the groups who also saw Memorial care patients and some low cancer-risk patients' resistance to not getting annual pap smears. To persuade these patients and reduce the number of pap smears one doctor hung cervical cancer guidelines on the wall of the exam room.

Companies are using software that analyzes employees' computers and creates a profile.[84] Over time the software is able to create a baseline of normal behavior including where they log in, what programs are used, databases accessed, and external websites browsed. It also provides a score for users (a risk score) based on what dangers they may pose to the company such as stealing data or new product designs or viewing pornography. Software called Scout can be used to evaluate the content of employees e-mail and other communications. The software scans for variations in language usage in the e-mails such as an increase in the use of phrases such as "medical bills" or "missed payments" that may mean the employee is an increased risk for stealing.

Despite the potential increased productivity and efficiency benefits that can result from these systems, they still present privacy concerns.[85] Critics argue that these systems threaten to reduce the workplace to an electronic sweatshop in which employees are treated as robots that are monitored to maximize productivity for every second they are at work. Also, electronic monitoring systems threaten employees' rights and dignity to work without being monitored.

Some argue that electronic tracking systems are needlessly surveilling and tracking employees when there is no reason to believe that anything is wrong. Good managers know what their employees are doing, and electronic systems should not be a substitute for good management. Critics also argue that such systems result in less productivity and motivation, demoralize employees, and create unnecessary stress. A mentality is created that employees have to always be at their desks to be productive. However, these systems can ensure that time is not abused, they improve scheduling, and they help motivate workers and improve performance.[86] To avoid the potential negative effects of electronic monitoring, managers must communicate why employees are being monitored. Monitoring can also be used as a way for more experienced employees to coach less experienced employees.

REDUCING RATER ERRORS, POLITICS, AND INCREASING RELIABILITY AND VALIDITY OF RATINGS

LO 8-9
Distinguish types of rating errors, and explain how to minimize each in a performance evaluation.

Research consistently reveals that humans have tremendous limitations in processing information. Because we are so limited, we often use "heuristics," or simplifying mechanisms, to make judgments, whether about investments or about people.[87] These heuristics, which appear often in subjective measures of performance, can lead to rater errors. Performance evaluations may also be purposefully distorted to achieve personal or company goals (appraisal politics). Table 8.12 shows the different types of rating errors. *Similar to me* error is based on stereotypes the rater has about how individuals with certain characteristics are expected to perform.[88] Leniency, strictness, and central tendency are known as distributional errors because the rater tends to use only one part of the rating scale.

Appraisal Politics
A situation in which evaluators purposefully distort ratings to achieve personal or company goals.

Appraisal politics refer to evaluators purposefully distorting a rating to achieve personal or company goals. Research suggests that several factors promote appraisal politics. These factors are inherent in the appraisal system and the company culture. Appraisal politics are most likely to occur when raters are accountable to the employee being rated, there are competing rating goals, and a direct link exists between performance appraisal and highly desirable rewards. Also, appraisal politics are likely to occur if top executives tolerate distortion or are complacent toward it, and if distortion strategies are part of "company folklore" and are passed down from senior employees to new employees. For example, employees at King Pharmaceutical resisted development of a centralized performance system.[89] King Pharmaceutical is built from smaller acquired companies, each with a unique culture. Each department within the company had developed its own way of figuring out how to evaluate performance and link it to pay.

There are three approaches to reducing rating errors.[90] They include rater error training, frame-of-reference training, and calibration meetings. *Rater error training* attempts to make managers aware of rating errors and helps them develop strategies for minimizing those errors.[91] These programs consist of having the participants view videotaped vignettes designed to elicit rating errors such as "contrast." They then make their ratings and discuss how the error influenced the rating. Finally, they get

RATER ERROR	DESCRIPTION
Similar to me	Individuals who are similar to us in race, gender, background, interest, beliefs, etc., receive higher ratings than those who are not.
Contrast	Ratings influenced by comparison between individuals instead of an objective standard (e.g., employee receives lower than deserved rating because he/she is compared to outstanding peers).
Leniency	Rater gives high ratings to all employees regardless of their performance.
Strictness	Rater gives low ratings to all employees regardless of their performance.
Central tendency	Rater gives middle or average ratings to all employees despite their performance.
Halo	Rater gives employee high ratings on all aspects of performance because of their overall positive impression of the employee.
Horns	Rater gives employee low ratings on all aspects of performance because of an overall negative impression of the employee.

Table 8.12
Typical Rater Errors

tips to avoid committing those errors. This approach has been shown to be effective for reducing errors, but there is evidence that reducing rating errors can also reduce accuracy.[92]

Rater accuracy training, also called *frame-of-reference training,* attempts to emphasize the multidimensional nature of performance and to get raters to understand and use the same idea of high, medium, and low performance when making evaluations. This involves providing examples of performance for each dimension and then discussing the actual or "correct" level of performance that the example represents.[93] Accuracy training seems to increase accuracy, provided that in addition the raters are held accountable for ratings, job-related rating scales are used, and raters keep records of the behavior they observe.[94]

An important way to help ensure that performance is evaluated consistently across managers and to reduce the influence of rating errors and politics on appraisals is to hold calibration meetings.[95] **Calibration meetings** provide a way to discuss employees' performance with the goal of ensuring that similar standards are applied to their evaluations. These meeting include managers responsible for conducting performance appraisals and their managers and are facilitated by an internal HR representative or an external consultant. In the meetings, each employee's performance rating and the manager's reasons for the ratings are discussed. Managers have the opportunity to discuss the definition of each performance rating and ask questions. The calibration meetings help managers identify if their ratings are too positive or negative or tend to be based on employees' most recent performance. Managers are more likely to provide accurate evaluations that are well-documented when they know they may have to justify them in a calibration meeting. Calibration meetings can also help eliminate politics by discussing how performance ratings relate to business results. Also, in addition to rater training and calibration meetings, to minimize appraisal politics, managers should keep in mind

Calibration Meetings
Meetings attended by managers in which employee performance ratings are discussed and evidence supporting the ratings is provided. The purpose of the meetings is to reduce the influence of rating errors and politics on performance appraisals.

the characteristics of a fair appraisal system, shown earlier in Table 8.2. Thus, managers should also:

- Build top management support for the appraisal system and actively discourage distortion.
- Give raters some latitude to customize performance objectives and criteria for their ratees.
- Recognize employee accomplishments that are not self-promoted.
- Provide employees with access to information regarding which behaviors are desired and acceptable at work.
- Encourage employees to actively seek and use feedback to improve performance.
- Make sure constraints such as budget do not drive the process.
- Make sure appraisal processes are consistent across the company.
- Foster a climate of openness to encourage employees to be honest about weaknesses.[96]

Performance Feedback

LO 8-10
Conduct an effective performance feedback session.

Once the expected performance has been defined and employees' performances have been measured, it is necessary to feed that performance information back to the employees so they can correct any deficiencies. The performance feedback process is complex and provokes anxiety for both the manager and the employee.

Few of us feel comfortable sitting in judgment of others. The thought of confronting others with what we perceive to be their deficiencies causes most of us to shake in our shoes. If giving negative feedback is painful, receiving it can be excruciating—thus the importance of the performance feedback process.

THE MANAGER'S ROLE IN AN EFFECTIVE PERFORMANCE FEEDBACK PROCESS

If employees are not made aware of how their performance is not meeting expectations, their performance will almost certainly not improve. In fact, it may get worse. Effective managers provide specific performance feedback to employees in a way that elicits positive behavioral responses. Because of the importance of performance feedback for an effective performance management system, many companies are training managers on how to provide feedback. For example, Lubrizol Corporation, a chemical manufacturer based in Wickliffe, Ohio, requires that managers enroll in a two-day training course designed to help them provide meaningful feedback.[97] The company's goal is to become recognized as the best developer of people. The training course focuses on how managers give feedback, who they need help from, and how they can hold themselves accountable. To contribute to the effectiveness of a performance management system through providing effective feedback, managers should consider the following recommendations.[98]

Feedback Should Be Given Frequently, Not Once a Year. There are two reasons for this. First, managers have a responsibility to correct performance deficiencies immediately on becoming aware of them. If performance is subpar in January, waiting until December to appraise the performance could mean an 11-month productivity loss. Second, a major determinant of the effectiveness of a feedback session is the degree to which the subordinate is not surprised by the evaluation. An easy rule to follow is that employees should receive such frequent performance feedback that they already know almost exactly what their formal evaluation will be.

Survey results from several companies suggest that many employees, especially those in Generation Y (employees born after 1980), want more frequent and candid performance feedback from managers beyond what is provided once or twice a year during their formal performance review.[99] As a result, Ernst & Young LLC created an online "Feedback Zone" that prompts employees twice a year to request feedback but also allows them to request or submit feedback at any time.

Create the Right Context for the Discussion. Managers should choose a neutral location for the feedback session. The manager's office may not be the best place for a constructive feedback session because the employee may associate the office with unpleasant conversations. Managers should describe the meeting as an opportunity to discuss the role of the employee, the role of the manager, and the relationship between them. Managers should also acknowledge that they would like the meeting to be an open dialogue.

Ask the Employee to Rate His or Her Performance before the Session. Having employees complete a self-assessment before the feedback session can be very productive. It requires employees to think about their performance over the past rating period, and it encourages them to think about their weaknesses. Although self-ratings used for administrative decisions are often inflated, there is evidence that they may actually be lower than supervisors' ratings when done for developmental purposes. Another reason a self-assessment can be productive is that it can make the session go more smoothly by focusing discussion on areas where disagreement exists, resulting in a more efficient session. Finally, employees who have thought about past performance are more able to participate fully in the feedback session.

Encourage the Employee to Participate in the Session. Managers can take one of three approaches in performance feedback sessions. In the "tell-and-sell" approach, managers tell the employees how they have rated them and then justify these ratings. In the "tell-and-listen" approach, managers tell employees how they have rated them and then let the employees explain their side of the story. In the "problem-solving" approach, managers and employees work together to solve performance problems in an atmosphere of respect and encouragement. In spite of the research demonstrating the superiority of the problem-solving approach, most managers still rely on the tell-and-sell approach.

When employees participate in the feedback session, they are consistently satisfied with the process. (Recall our discussion of fairness earlier in this chapter.) Participation includes allowing employees to voice their opinions of the evaluation, as well as discuss performance goals. One study found that, other than satisfaction with one's supervisor, participation was the single most important predictor of satisfaction with the feedback session.[100]

Recognize Effective Performance through Praise. One usually thinks of performance feedback sessions as focusing on the employee's performance problems. This should never be the case. The purpose of the session is to give accurate performance feedback, which entails recognizing effective performance as well as poor performance. Praising effective performance provides reinforcement for that behavior. It also adds credibility to the feedback by making it clear that the manager is not just identifying performance problems.

Focus on Solving Problems. A common mistake that managers make in providing performance feedback is to try to use the session as a chance to punish poorly performing employees by telling them how utterly lousy their performance is. This only reduces the employees' self-esteem and increases defensiveness, neither of which will improve performance.

To improve poor performance, a manager must attempt to solve the problems causing it. This entails working with the employee to determine the actual cause and then agreeing on how to solve it. For example, a salesperson's failure to meet a sales goal may be the result of lack of a proper sales pitch, lack of product knowledge, or stolen sales by another salesperson. Each of these causes requires a different solution. Without a problem-solving approach, however, the correct solution might never be identified.

Focus Feedback on Behavior or Results, Not on the Person. One of the most important things to do when giving negative feedback is to avoid questioning the employee's worth as a person. This is best accomplished by focusing the discussion on the employee's behaviors or results, not on the employee. Saying "You're screwing up! You're just not motivated!" will bring about more defensiveness and ill feelings than stating "You did not meet the deadline that you agreed to because you spent too much time on another project."

Minimize Criticism. Obviously, if an individual's performance is below standard, some criticism must take place. However, an effective manager should resist the temptation to reel off a litany of offenses. Having been confronted with the performance problem, an employee often agrees that a change is in order. However, if the manager continues to come up with more and more examples of low performance, the employee may get defensive.

Agree to Specific Goals and Set a Date to Review Progress. The importance of goal setting cannot be overemphasized. It is one of the most effective motivators of performance.[101] Research has demonstrated that it results in increased satisfaction, motivation to improve, and performance improvement.[102] Besides setting goals, the manager must also set a specific follow-up date to review the employee's performance toward the goal. This provides an added incentive for the employee to take the goal seriously and work toward achieving it.

EVIDENCE-BASED HR

Like most businesses, Google had files of data about managers—results of performance reviews, surveys measuring employee attitudes, and nominations for management awards. Google used its expertise in analyzing large amounts of data to identify a profile of the kind of manager whose team is most successful. The company's people analytics group (which brings together psychologists, MBAs, and data mining experts) analyzed 10,000 observations about managers in terms of more than 100 variables, looking for patterns. The initial finding was a surprise to some at a company that had once operated without managers: teams with good managers outperform teams with bad managers. But what makes a good manager? Under the leadership of Google's HR vice president, the company distilled its findings into a list of the behaviors that get results:

1. Be a good coach.
2. Empower your team, and don't micromanage.
3. Express interest in team members' success and personal well-being.
4. Don't be a sissy: Be productive and results-oriented.
5. Be a good communicator, and listen to your team.
6. Help your employees with career development.
7. Have a clear vision and strategy for the team.
8. Have key technical skills so you can help advise the team.

By building performance measures including the eight behaviors, Google was able to evaluate its managers' performance and identify those who needed to improve in particular areas. It developed training programs in the eight types of desired behavior. Before and after providing performance appraisals, training, and coaching, Google conducted surveys to gauge managers' performance. It measured a significant improvement in manager quality for 75% of its lowest-performing managers.

SOURCES: L. Bock, *Work Rules! Insights from Inside Google That Will Transform How You Live and Lead* (New York: Grand Central Publishing, 2015); A. Bryant, "Google's Quest to Build a Better Boss," *The New York Times,* March 12, 2011, www.nytimes.com; Clara Byrne, "People Analytics: How Google Does HR by the Numbers," *VentureBeat,* September 20, 2011, http://venturebeat.com; P. Galagan, "Measure for Measure," *T + D,* May 2011, pp. 28–30.

What Managers Can Do to Diagnose Performance Problems and Manage Employees' Performance

As we emphasized in the previous discussion, employees need performance feedback to improve their current job performance. As we discuss in Chapter 9, "Employee Development," performance feedback is also needed for employees to develop their knowledge and skills for the future. In addition to understanding how to effectively give employees performance feedback, managers need to be able to diagnose the causes of performance problems and take actions to improve and maintain employee performance. For example, giving performance feedback to marginal employees may not be sufficient for improving their performance.

LO 8-11
Identify the cause of a performance problem.

DIAGNOSING THE CAUSES OF POOR PERFORMANCE

Many different reasons can cause an employee's poor performance. For example, poor performance can be due to lack of employee ability, misunderstanding of performance expectations, lack of feedback, or the need for training an employee who does not have the knowledge and skills needed to meet the performance standards. When diagnosing the causes of poor performance it is important to consider whether the poor performance is detrimental to the business. That is, is poor performance critical to completing the job and does it affect business results? If it is detrimental, then the next step is to conduct a performance analysis to determine the cause of poor performance. The different factors that should be considered in analyzing poor performance are shown in Figure 8.8. For example, if an employee understands the expected level of performance, has been given sufficient feedback, understands the consequences, but lacks the knowledge and skills needed to meet the performance standard, this suggests that the manager may want to consider training the employee to improve performance, moving the employee to a different job that better fits that person's skills, or discharging the employee and making sure that selection methods to find a new employee measure the level of knowledge and skills needed to perform the job.

After conducting the performance analysis, managers should meet with the employee to discuss the results, agree to the next steps that the manager and employee will take to

Figure 8.8

Factors to Consider
in Analyzing Poor
Performance

Input

> Does the employee recognize what he or she is supposed to do?
>
> Are the job flow and procedures logical?
>
> Do employees have the resources (tools, equipment, technology, time) needed for
> successful performance?
>
> Are other job demands interfering with good performance in this area?

Employee Characteristics

> Does the employee have the necessary skills and knowledge needed?
>
> Does the employee know why the desired performance level is important?
>
> Is the employee mentally, physically, and emotionally able to perform at the
> expected level?

Feedback

> Has the employee been given information about his or her performance?
>
> Is performance feedback relevant, timely, accurate, specific, and understandable?

Performance Standard/Goals

> Do performance standards exist?
>
> Does the employee know the desired level of expected performance?
>
> Does the employee believe she or he can reach the performance standard?

Consequences

> Are consequences (rewards, incentives) aligned with good performance?
>
> Are the consequences of performance valuable to the employee?
>
> Are performance consequences given in a timely manner?
>
> Do work group or team norms encourage employees not to meet
> performance standards?

SOURCES: Based on G. Rummler, "In Search of the Holy Performance Grail," *Training and Development,* April 1996,
pp. 26–31; C. Reinhart, "How to Leap over Barriers to Performance," *Training and Development,* January 2000,
pp. 20–24; F. Wilmouth, C. Prigmore, and M. Bray, "HPT Models: An Overview of the Major Models in the Field,"
Performance Improvement 41 (2002), pp. 14–21.

improve performance (e.g., training, providing resources, giving more feedback), discuss
the consequences of failing to improve performance, and set a time line for improvement. This type of discussion is most beneficial if it occurs more frequently than the
quarterly or yearly performance review, so performance issues can be quickly dealt with
before they have adverse consequences for the company (and the employee). Following,
we discuss the actions that should be considered for different types of employees.

ACTIONS FOR MANAGING EMPLOYEES' PERFORMANCE

Table 8.13 shows actions for the manager to take with four different types of employees. As the table highlights, managers need to take into account employees' ability, motivation, or both in considering ways to improve performance. To determine an employee's level of ability, a manager should consider if he or she has the knowledge, skills, and abilities needed to perform effectively. Lack of ability may be an issue if an employee is new or the job has recently changed. To determine employees' level of motivation, managers need to consider if employees are doing a job they want to do and if they feel they are being appropriately paid or rewarded. A sudden negative change in an employee's performance may indicate personal problems.

Employees with high ability and motivation include likely good and outstanding performers *(solid performers)*. Table 8.13 emphasizes that managers should not ignore employees with high ability and high motivation. Managers should provide development opportunities to keep them satisfied and effective. Some individuals who are outstanding or good performers may be candidates for leadership positions within the company. As a result they will need challenging development experiences and exposure to different aspects of the business. These employees would be considered "A players" (see Table 8.3). We discuss development experiences in Chapter 9. Other employees may

Table 8.13
Ways to Manage Employees' Performance

	ABILITY	
	HIGH	**LOW**
High	**Solid performers** • Reward good performance • Identify development opportunities • Provide honest, direct feedback	**Misdirected effort** • Coaching • Frequent performance feedback • Goal setting • Training or temporary assignment for skill development • Restructured job assignment
MOTIVATION	**Underutilizers** • Give honest, direct feedback • Provide counseling • Use team building and conflict resolution • Link rewards to performance outcomes • Offer training for needed knowledge or skills • Manage stress levels	**Deadwood** • Withholding pay increases • Demotion • Outplacement • Firing • Specific, direct feedback on performance problems
Low		

SOURCES: Based on M. London, *Job Feedback* (Mahwah, NJ: Lawrence Erlbaum Associates, 1997), pp. 96–97; H. Aguinis and E. O'Boyle, Jr., "Star Performers in the Twenty-First Century," *Personnel Psychology* 67 (2014), pp. 313–50; D. Grote, *How to Be Good at Performance Appraisals* (Boston: Harvard University Press, 2011).

not desire positions with managerial responsibility. These employees need development opportunities to help keep them engaged in their work and to avoid obsolescence. These employees would be considered B players in Table 8.3. Finally, there are different reasons why employees are considered poor performers (C players shown in Table 8.3). Poor performance resulting from lack of ability but not motivation *(misdirected effort)* may be improved by skill development activities such as training or temporary assignments. Managers with employees who have the ability but lack motivation *(underutilizers)* need to consider actions that focus on interpersonal problems or incentives. These actions include making sure that incentives or rewards that the employee values are linked to performance and making counseling available to help employees deal with personal problems or career or job dissatisfaction. Chronic poor performance by employees with low ability and motivation *(deadwood)* indicates that outplacement or firing may be the best solution.

Developing and Implementing a System That Follows Legal Guidelines

We now discuss the legal issues and constraints affecting performance management. Because performance measures play a central role in such administrative decisions as promotions, pay raises, and discipline, employees who sue an organization over these decisions ultimately attack the measurement systems on which the decisions were made. Two types of cases have dominated: discrimination and unjust dismissal.

In discrimination suits, the plaintiff often alleges that the performance measurement system unjustly discriminated against the plaintiff because of age, race, gender, or national origin. Many performance measures are subjective, and we have seen that individual biases can affect them, especially when those doing the measuring harbor racial or gender stereotypes.

In *Brito v. Zia,* the Supreme Court essentially equated performance measures with selection tests.[103] It ruled that the *Uniform Guidelines on Employee Selection Procedures* apply to evaluating the adequacy of a performance appraisal instrument. This ruling presents a challenge to those involved in developing performance measures, because a substantial body of research on race discrimination in performance rating has demonstrated that both white and black raters give higher ratings to members of their own racial group, even after rater training.[104] There is also evidence that the discriminatory biases in performance rating are worse when one group makes up a small percentage of the workgroup. When the vast majority of the group is male, females receive lower ratings; when the minority is male, males receive lower ratings.[105]

In the second type of suit, an unjust dismissal suit, the plaintiff claims that the dismissal was for reasons other than those the employer claims. For example, an employee who works for a defense contractor might blow the whistle on the company for defrauding the government. If the company fires the employee, claiming poor performance, the employee may argue that the firing was, in fact, because of blowing the whistle on the employer—in other words, that the dismissal was unjust. The court case will likely focus on the performance measurement system used as the basis for claiming the employee's performance was poor. Unjust dismissal also can result from terminating for poor performance an employee who has a history of favorable reviews and raises. This may occur especially when a new evaluation system is introduced that results in more experienced older employees receiving unsatisfactory reviews. Rewarding poor performers or giving poor performers positive evaluations because of an unwillingness to confront a performance issue undermines the credibility of any performance management system. This makes it difficult to defend termination decisions based on a performance appraisal system.

For example, Baltimore-based MRA Systems, Inc., a subsidiary of General Electric, paid $130,000 to settle an age discrimination lawsuit.[106] An employee received a lower performance rating, despite his successful job performance, because of his age, which was 61. In addition, MRA Systems had to provide at least two hours of mandatory training on federal laws prohibiting employment discrimination to all managers, supervisors and other employees who participate in the performance evaluation process or assignment decisions. The Equal Employment Opportunity Commission sued Wisconsin Plastics, Inc. (WPI), a metal and plastic products manufacturer, for violating federal law by firing several Hmong and Hispanic employees because of their national origin.[107] WPI fired the Hmong and Hispanic employees based on 10-minute observations that marked them down for their English skills even though those skills were not needed to perform their jobs. The fired employees had received satisfactory ratings on their annual performance evaluations.

Because of the potential costs of discrimination and unjust dismissal suits, an organization needs to determine exactly what the courts consider a legally defensible performance management system. Based on reviews of such court decisions, we offer the following characteristics of a system that will withstand legal scrutiny.[108]

1. The system should be developed by conducting a valid job analysis that ascertains the important aspects of job performance. The requirements for job success should be clearly communicated to employees.
2. The system should be based on either behaviors or results; evaluations of ambiguous traits should be avoided. Also, performance discussions should focus on work behavior and results other than questioning potential underlying reasons for behavior and results such as a physical or mental disability.
3. Raters should be trained in how to use the system rather than simply given the materials and left to interpret how to conduct the appraisal.
4. There should be some form of review by upper-level managers of all the performance ratings, and there should be a system for employees to appeal what they consider to be an unfair evaluation.
5. The organization should provide some form of performance counseling or corrective guidance to help poor performers improve their performance before being dismissed. Both short- and long-term performance goals should be included.
6. Multiple raters should be used, particularly if an employee's performance is unlikely to be seen by only one rating source such as manager or customer. At a minimum, employees should be asked to comment on their appraisals. There should be a dialogue between the manager and the employee.
7. Performance evaluations need to be documented.

A LOOK BACK

Adobe's Revised Performance Management System

The chapter opener discussed how Adobe revised their performance evaluation system to abandon ranking employees and instead focus on managers and employees having frequent performance discussions.

QUESTIONS

1. What steps should managers take to ensure that performance discussions are effective?
2. What are the benefits and potential disadvantages of more frequent performance discussions between managers and employees?
3. Which purpose of performance management will be more difficult to achieve for companies like Adobe that decide to abandon ranking or rating employee performance?

SUMMARY

Measuring and managing performance is a challenging enterprise and one of the keys to gaining competitive advantage. Performance management systems serve strategic, administrative, and developmental purposes—their importance cannot be overestimated. A performance measurement system should be evaluated against the criteria of strategic congruence, validity, reliability, acceptability, and specificity. Measured against these criteria, the comparative, attribute, behavioral, results, and quality approaches have different strengths and weaknesses. Thus, deciding which approach and which source of performance information are best depends on the job in question. Effective managers need to be aware of the issues involved in determining the best method or combination of methods for their particular situations. In addition, once performance has been measured, a major component of a manager's job is to provide frequent informal as well as formal feedback that is provided during performance evaluations in a way that results in improved performance rather than defensiveness and decreased motivation. Technologies can be potentially useful in streamlining the performance management process and providing employees with feedback and other information, which can motivate them to perform effectively. Managers should take action based on the causes for poor performance: ability, motivation, or both. Managers must be sure that their performance management system can meet legal scrutiny, especially if it is used to discipline or fire poor performers.

KEY TERMS

Performance management, 321
Performance appraisal, 321
Performance feedback, 321
Strategic congruence, 326
Validity, 328
Reliability, 329

Acceptability, 329
Specificity, 330
Competencies, 341
Competency model, 341
Kaizen, 348
Upward feedback, 353

360-degree appraisal, 355
Social performance
    management, 356
Gamification, 356
Appraisal politics, 358
Calibration meetings, 359

DISCUSSION QUESTIONS

1. What are examples of administrative decisions that might be made in managing the performance of professors? Developmental decisions?

2. What would you consider the strategy of your university (e.g., research, undergraduate teaching, graduate teaching, a combination)? How might the performance

management system for faculty members fulfill its strategic purpose of eliciting the types of behaviors and results required by this strategy?

3. What do you think is the most important step shown in the model of the effective performance management process? Justify your answer.

4. What sources of performance information would you use to evaluate faculty members' performance?

5. What are the advantages and disadvantages of a performance management system? Would such a grading system motivate your classroom performance? Explain.

6. Think of the last time you had a conflict with another person, either at work or at school. Using the guidelines for performance feedback, how would you provide effective performance feedback to that person?

7. Explain what fairness has to do with performance management.

8. Why might a manager intentionally distort appraisal results? What would you recommend to minimize this problem?

9. Can electronic monitoring of performance ever be acceptable to employees? Explain.

10. Customer satisfaction surveys completed after a service call show that a call center representative is having difficulty answering customers questions about their cell phone bills. How would you diagnose the cause of this performance problem? Explain.

11. How can the use of social media such as Facebook and Twitter-like applications benefit the performance management process?

SELF-ASSESSMENT EXERCISE

Mc Graw Hill Education **connect**

Additional assignable self-assessments available in Connect.

How do you like getting feedback? To test your attitudes toward feedback, take the following quiz. Read each statement, and write A next to each statement you agree with. If you disagree with the statement, write D.

_____ 1. I like being told how well I am doing on a project.

_____ 2. Even though I may think I have done a good job, I feel a lot more confident when someone else tells me so.

_____ 3. Even when I think I could have done something better, I feel good when other people think well of me for what I have done.

_____ 4. It is important for me to know what people think of my work.

_____ 5. I think my instructor would think worse of me if I asked him or her for feedback.

_____ 6. I would be nervous about asking my instructor how she or he evaluates my behavior in class.

_____ 7. It is not a good idea to ask my fellow students for feedback; they might think I am incompetent.

_____ 8. It is embarrassing to ask other students for their impression of how I am doing in class.

_____ 9. It would bother me to ask the instructor for feedback.

_____ 10. It is not a good idea to ask the instructor for feedback because he or she might think I am incompetent.

_____ 11. It is embarrassing to ask the instructor for feedback.

_____ 12. It is better to try to figure out how I am doing on my own, rather than to ask other students for feedback.

For statements 1–4, add the total number of As: _____
For statements 5–12, add the total number of As: _____
For statements 1–4, the greater the number of As, the greater your preference for and trust in feedback from others. For statements 5–12, the greater the number of As, the greater the risk you believe there is in asking for feedback.

How might this information be useful in understanding how you react to feedback in school or on the job?

SOURCES: Based on D. B. Fedor, R. B. Rensvold, and S. M. Adams, "An Investigation of Factors Expected to Affect Feedback Seeking: A Longitudinal Field Study," *Personnel Psychology* 45 (1992), pp. 779–805; S. J. Asford, "Feedback Seeking in Individual Adaptation: A Resource Perspective," *Academy of Management Journal* 29 (1986), pp. 465–87.

EXERCISING STRATEGY

Making Unnecessary Repairs

Progress Rail Services inspects railcars at Terminal Island in the port of Los Angeles where cargo is unloaded from ships and moved across the country. Over 10,000 railcars each month are found in the port and most are inspected by Progress Rail Services. When Progress Rail Services employees find problems they repair the railcars and charge the owners. The workers, known as car men, are paid between $15 and $29 per hour. The job includes late night shifts and often working in wind and rain. Car men need to work quickly, spending about two minutes looking at each rail car. Some car men have smashed brake parts with hammers, gouged wheels, and used chains to tear off handles to make repairs necessary. Also, car men make "green repairs," which means replacing parts that are not broken and hiding the old parts or throwing them in the ocean so that company auditors cannot find them.

Progress Rail Services, a subsidiary of Caterpillar Inc., is being investigated by a federal prosecutor for criminal charges stemming from allegation of unnecessary repair work. Caterpillar is cooperating with the investigation, which it considers serious because it suggests employees have not behaved in a way consistent with company values.

Workers blame their managers who say that they would lose their jobs and be replaced if they didn't produce sufficient repair revenue. Employees who identify large numbers of parts to replace don't receive extra pay but their supervisors tend to treat them more favorably and they often receive employee-of-the-month recognition.

QUESTIONS

1. How could performance management have stopped the car men from making bogus repairs?
2. Consider the different performance management approaches discussed in the chapter. Which approach do you recommend for ensuring only correct repairs are made in the future? Explain the reasons for the approach you recommend.
3. Using the factors to consider in analyzing poor performance shown in Figure 8.8 determine the cause for the faulty repairs.

SOURCE: Based on J. Haggerty and B. Tita, "Workers at Caterpillar Say Train Repairs Were Often Bogus," *The Wall Street Journal,* July 21, 2014, pp. B1, B6.

MANAGING PEOPLE

Performance Management Is About Work and How Work Gets Done

Most companies have a unique set of core values that they believe contribute to business success through distinguishing them from competitors and helping create a brand image in the eyes of customers, clients, employees, and the general public. For example, VivaKi Nerve Center in Chicago, the research, development, and production unit of the advertising and communications firm Publicis Groupe's VivaKi, has a set of core values called The Way We Work. These values include "work hard playfully," "develop disruptive innovate solutions," "count on infectious talent and radical thinking," and "believe change ignites new energy and conversations." Studies have shown that companies' fixation on hitting financial targets often works against producing sustainable growth. One study found that the highest financial returns were achieved at companies whose CEOs had challenging financial goals and communicated a vision of the company beyond making profits such as creating an innovative product, providing greater customer service, or improving the quality of life. Despite the importance of values, it is challenging to define them in behavioral terms so they can be measured and included as part of a performance management system. Also, the results of a Society for Human Resource Management survey on performance management highlight the complexity of values for performance management. Survey results showed that over 85% of HR professionals agree it is more difficult to manage employee behaviors underlying values than it is to manage job performance.

A number of companies are taking on the challenge of redesigning their performance management systems to ensure that they are evaluating not only *what* employees get accomplished but *how* they get it accomplished. Grange Insurance performance management system for its associates includes both job-relevant performance objectives and core values. Managers rate the extent to which employees engage in behaviors underlying the company's core values, which include candor, do the right thing, integrity, ownership, and teamwork. For example, the evaluation for candor includes considering whether the associate engages in behaviors such as openly sharing information, seeks honest and constructive feedback, delivers honest and constructive feedback, and addresses problems and issues even when they are unpleasant or sensitive. Eastern Idaho Regional Medical Center (EIRMC) in Idaho Falls evaluates employees on seven values and their underlying behavior. The values and example behavior in parentheses include accountability (works to achieve individual, department, and hospital goals), I am EIRMC and I CARE (demonstrates the use of the center's caring model with every patient and visitor), integrity (manages conflict appropriately), respect (respects co-workers by being on time), quality (identifies a potential problem and also potential solutions), loyalty (builds teamwork by being a good team member and not backbiting), and enjoyment (greets and welcomes each person with a smiling face and a kind word). EIRMC uses a five-point scale to rate employees on the values. The scale values range from 1 meaning the employee exceeds expectations to 5 meaning their performance is unacceptable.

Because values impact morale, patient satisfaction, turnover, and finances, confronting employees about behaviors that breach company values is crucial. Assessing and changing behaviors that are incongruent with company values means that at the end of the day the company stands for something and reinforces the culture and the way the company conducts its business. All employees, including top leaders, need to be held accountable for living the values. For example, at EIRMC a nurse was disciplined for yelling and swearing at another nurse during a procedure with a patient. The nurse believed he was showing his passion for patient care and demonstrating his willingness to protect them. HR had to help the nurse understand that he had violated EIRMC's respect and integrity values, despite his good intentions. After several meetings the nurse understood and accepted the violation and has since repaired the relationships he damaged.

QUESTIONS

1. Why might peer or co-worker evaluations be necessary to evaluate values?
2. Do you think evaluations of values should receive equal, more, or less weight than evaluation of objectives (or what the employee accomplishes) in employees' performance evaluation? Why?
3. Are values only important for organizations that have a sales force or provide some type of customer service? Explain your answer.

SOURCE: Based on K. Tyler, "Evaluating Values," *HR Magazine,* April 2011, pp. 57–62; R. Pyrillis, "The Reviews Are In," *Workforce Management,* May 2011, pp. 20–25; and C. Hymowitz, "When Meeting the Targets Becomes the Strategy, CEO Is on the Wrong Path," *The Wall Street Journal,* March 8, 2005, p. B1.

HR IN SMALL BUSINESS

Performance Management at Xactly

Xactly is a compensation consulting firm with 360 employees in England, India, and the United States. It has received numerous awards recognizing it as a desirable place to work including ranked #25 on the Best Small Workplaces by the Great Places to Work organization. Its intrinsic core values are customer success, accountability, respect, and excellence (CARE). Xactly Corporation is about motivating people, both in the software products it provides clients as well as its employees. Xactly gives all employees stock options, and most staffers have a bonus plan. But connectedness is key to the company success. Connectedness is built through XactlyOne, an employee-led philanthropic group which helps Xactly give back to the community and holds monthly all-hands meetings. At the all-hands meetings, the CEO communicates what is going on with the company as well as introduces new employees and hands out awards to employees who have performed above and beyond what their job requires. In its San Jose location a giant rubber ball made up of different colored and shaped rubber bands is displayed in its trophy case which helps employees see that everyone has differences but that they are all part of one team with one goal. HR checks to see if employees are connected to the company by asking them to explain the company's mission or vision. Different answers suggest that the company mission and vision needs to be better communicated.

Performance management also helps employees feel connected. Xactly links management objectives to performance by assigning employees quarterly objectives which help build employee engagement and positively influence profitability. Xactly managers keep close track of employee performance, which allows them to get employees training if needed or fire poor performers before they can cause headaches for good performers. The company encourages employees to expand their career opportunities through interdepartmental movement. They have rapid-progression programs for employees who are hired into first-level positions. Xactly provides training programs in hard skills such as project management to soft skills such as cross-cultural communication. Xactly also provides tuition reimbursement for employees who want to pursue formal education and certificate programs.

QUESTIONS

1. Based on the information given, discuss how well performance management at Xactly meets strategic, administrative, and developmental purposes.
2. What methods for measuring employee performance do you think would be most beneficial for Xactly? Explain why.
3. How could Xactly include an emphasis on its core values in the performance management system?

SOURCES: Company website, www.xactlycorp.com, accessed April 28, 2015; "#25: Xactly Corporation," www.greatplacestowork.com; C. Patton, "The Low-Performer Drag," *Human Resource Executive,* October 2013, pp. 26–29.

NOTES

1. A. Bradley, "Taking the Formality out of Performance Reviews," *T + D,* June 2010, p. 18; R. Pyrillis, "The Reviews Are In," *Workforce Management,* May 2011, pp. 20–25.
2. M. Laff, "Performance Management Gives a Shaky Performance," *T + D,* September 2007, p. 18; A. Fox, "Curing What Ails Performance Reviews," *HR Magazine,* January 2009, pp. 52–56.
3. A. Freedman, "Balancing Values, Results in Reviews," *Human Resource Executive,* August 2006, pp. 62–63; G. Ruiz, "Performance Management Underperforms," *Workforce Management,* December 2006, pp. 47–49; A. Fox, "Curing What Ails Performance Reviews," *HR Magazine,* January 2009; A. Bradley, "Taking the Formality out of Performance Reviews," *T + D,* June 2010, p. 18; E. Pulakos, *Performance Management* (Oxford, England: Wiley-Blackwell, 2009); D. Meinert, "Reinventing Reviews," *HR Magazine,* April 2015, pp. 36–40; J. Ramirez, "Rethinking the Review," *Human Resource Executive,* July/August 2013, pp. 16–19; "SHRM Survey Findings: HR Professionals' Perceptions about Performance Management Effectiveness," October 14, 2014, from www.shrm.org, accessed April 27, 2015.
4. E. Pulakos, *Performance Management* (Oxford, England: Wiley-Blackwell, 2009); H. Aguinis, "An Expanded View of Performance Management," in J. W. Smith and M. London (eds.), *Performance Management* (San Francisco: Jossey-Bass, 2009), pp. 1–43; J. Russell and L. Russell, "Talk Me Through It: The Next Level of Performance Management," *T + D,* April 2010, pp. 42–48; J. Dahling and A. O'Malley, "Supportive Feedback Environments Can Mend Broken Performance Management Systems," *Industrial and Organizational Psychology* 4 (2011), pp. 201–3; E. Pulakos and R. O'Leary, "Why Is Performance Management Broken?" *Industrial and Organizational Psychology* 4 (2011), pp. 146–64; E. Mone, C., Eisinger, K. Guggenheim, B. Price, and C. Stine, "Performance Management at the Wheel: Driving Employee Engagement in Organizations," *Journal of Business & Psychology* 26 (2011), pp. 205–12.
5. J. Harbour, "The Three 'Ds' of Successful Performance Measurement: Design, Data, and Display," *Performance Improvement* 50 (February 2011), pp. 5–12.
6. A. McIlvaine, "There's Got to Be a Better Way," *Human Resource Executive,* July/August 2012, pp. 14–17.
7. R. Noe and L. Inks, *It's About People: How Performance Management Helps Middle Market Companies Grow Faster* (Columbus, Ohio: National Center for the Middle Market, Ohio State University Fisher College of Business, GE Capital, 2014).
8. J. Cleveland, K. Murphy, and R. Williams, "Multiple Uses of Performance Appraisal: Prevalence and Correlates," *Journal of Applied Psychology* 74 (1989), pp. 130–35.
9. C. Longenecker, "Behind the Mask: The Politics of Employee Appraisal," *Academy of Management Executive* 1 (1987), p. 183.
10. M. Beer, "Note on Performance Appraisal," in *Readings in Human Resource Management,* ed. M. Beer and B. Spector (New York: Free Press, 1985).
11. D. Meinert, "Reinventing Reviews," *HR Magazine,* April 2015, pp. 36–40.
12. C. G. Banks and K. E. May, "Performance Management: The Real Glue in Organizations," in *Evolving Practices in Human Resource Management,* ed. A. Kraut and A. Korman (San Francisco: Jossey-Bass, 1999), pp. 118–45; R. Connors and T. Smith, "Want

Results? Fix Accountability," *Chief Learning Officer,* February 2015, pp. 44–46.
13. C. D. Ittner and D. F. Larcker, "Coming Up Short on Nonfinancial Performance Measurement," *Harvard Business Review,* December 2003, pp. 88–95.
14. J. K. Harter, F. Schmidt, and T. L. Hayes, "Business-Unit Level Relationships between Employee Satisfaction, Employee Engagement, and Business Outcomes: A Meta-Analysis," *Journal of Applied Psychology* 87 (2002), pp. 268–79.
15. A. J. Rucci, S. P. Kim, and R. T. Quinn, "The Employee-Customer-Profit Chain at Sears," *Harvard Business Review,* January–February 1998, pp. 82–97.
16. R. Schuler and S. Jackson, "Linking Competitive Strategies with Human Resource Practices," *Academy of Management Executive* 1 (1987), pp. 207–19.
17. L. King, J. Hunter, and F. Schmidt, "Halo in a Multidimensional Forced-Choice Performance Evaluation Scale," *Journal of Applied Psychology* 65 (1980), pp. 507–16.
18. B. R. Nathan, A. M. Mohrman, and J. Millman, "Interpersonal Relations as a Context for the Effects of Appraisal Interviews on Performance and Satisfaction: A Longitudinal Study," *Academy of Management Journal* 34 (1991), pp. 352–69; M. S. Taylor, K. B. Tracy, M. K. Renard, J. K. Harrison, and S. J. Carroll, "Due Process in Performance Appraisal: A Quasi-experiment in Procedural Justice," *Administrative Science Quarterly* 40 (1995), pp. 495–523; J. M. Werner and M. C. Bolino, "Explaining U.S. Courts of Appeals Decisions Involving Performance Appraisal: Accuracy, Fairness, and Validation," *Personnel Psychology* 50 (1997), pp. 1–24.
19. M. Buckingham and A. Goodall, "Reinventing Performance Management," *Harvard Business Review,* April 2015, pp. 40–50.
20. J. Campbell and B. Wiernik, "The Modeling and Assessment of Work Performance," *Annual Review of Organizational Psychology and Organizational Behavior* 2 (2015), pp. 47–74.
21. *Albermarle Paper Company v. Moody,* 10 FEP 1181 (1975).
22. S. Ng and J. Lublin, "AIG Pay Plan: Rank and Rile," *The Wall Street Journal,* February 11, 2010, p. R8.
23. S. Bates, "Forced Ranking," *HR Magazine,* June 2003, pp. 63–68; A. Meisler, "Deadman's Curve," *Workforce Management,* July 2003, pp. 44–49; M. Lowery, "Forcing the Issue," *Human Resource Executive* (October 16, 2003), pp. 26–29; J. Welch, "Rank and Yank, That's Not How It's Done," *The Wall Street Journal,* November 15, 2013, p. A15.
24. Ibid; E. O'Boyle, Jr. and H. Aguinis, "The Best and the Rest: Revisiting the Norm of Normality of Individual Performance," *Personnel Psychology* 65 (2010), pp. 79–119.
25. S. Ovide and R. Feintzeig, "Microsoft Abandons Dreaded 'Stack,'" *The Wall Street Journal,* November 13, 2013, pp. B1, B5.
26. S. Scullen, P. Bergey, and L. Aiman-Smith, "Forced Choice Distribution Systems and the Improvement of Workforce Potential: A Baseline Simulation," *Personnel Psychology* 58 (2005), pp. 1–32.
27. F. Blanz and E. Ghiselli, "The Mixed Standard Scale: A New Rating System," *Personnel Psychology* 25 (1973), pp. 185–99; K. Murphy and J. Constans, "Behavioral Anchors as a Source of Bias in Rating," *Journal of Applied Psychology* 72 (1987), pp. 573–77.
28. P. Smith and L. Kendall, "Retranslation of Expectations: An Approach to the Construction of Unambiguous Anchors for Rating Scales," *Journal of Applied Psychology* 47 (1963), pp. 149–55.
29. Murphy and Constans, "Behavioral Anchors"; M. Piotrowski, J. Barnes-Farrel, and F. Esrig, "Behaviorally Anchored Bias: A

Replication and Extension of Murphy and Constans," *Journal of Applied Psychology* 74 (1989), pp. 823–26.

30. U. Wiersma and G. Latham, "The Practicality of Behavioral Observation Scales, Behavioral Expectation Scales, and Trait Scales," *Personnel Psychology* 39 (1986), pp. 619–28.

31. G. Latham and K. Wexley, *Increasing Productivity through Performance Appraisal* (Boston: Addison-Wesley, 1981).

32. Wiersma and Latham, "The Practicality of Behavioral Observation Scales, Behavioral Expectation Scales, and Trait Scales." *Personnel Psychology* 39 (1986), pp. 619–28.

33. M. Campion, A. Fink, B. Ruggeberg, L. Carr, G. Phillips, and R. Odman, "Doing Competencies Well: Best Practices in Competency Modeling," *Personnel Psychology* 64 (2011), pp. 225–62; J. Shippmann, R. Ash, M. Battista, L. Carr, L. Eyde, B. Hesketh, J. Kehow, K. Pearlman, and J. Sanchez, "The Practice of Competency Modeling," *Personnel Psychology* 53 (2000), pp. 703–40; A. Lucia and R. Lepsinger, *The Art and Science of Competency Models* (San Francisco: Jossey-Bass, 1999).

34. C. Spicer, "Building a Competency Model," *HR Magazine*, April 2009, pp. 34–36.

35. S. Snell, "Control Theory in Strategic Human Resource Management: The Mediating Effect of Administrative Information," *Academy of Management Journal* 35 (1992), pp. 292–327.

36. T. Patten Jr., *A Manager's Guide to Performance Appraisal* (New York: Free Press, 1982).

37. M. O'Donnell and R. O'Donnell, "MBO—Is It Passe?" *Hospital and Health Services Administration* 28, no. 5 (1983), pp. 46–58; T. Poister and G. Streib, "Management Tools in Government: Trends over the Past Decade," *Public Administration Review* 49 (1989), pp. 240–48.

38. E. Locke and G. Latham, *A Theory of Goal Setting and Task Performance* (Englewood Cliffs, NJ: Prentice Hall, 1990).

39. S. Carroll and H. Tosi, *Management by Objectives* (New York: Macmillan, 1973).

40. G. Odiorne, *MBO II: A System of Managerial Leadership for the 80's* (Belmont, CA: Pitman, 1986); E. Pulakos, *Performance Management* (Oxford, England: Wiley-Blackwell, 2009).

41. R. Rodgers and J. Hunter, "Impact of Management by Objectives on Organizational Productivity," *Journal of Applied Psychology* 76 (1991), pp. 322–26.

42. J. Light, "Performance Reviews by Numbers," *The Wall Street Journal*, June 29, 2010, p. D4.

43. V. Liberman, "Performance Management: To Get Results Stop Measuring People by Them," *The Conference Board Review*, Summer 2013, pp. 57–63.

44. R. S. Kaplan and D. P. Norton, "Using the Balanced Scorecard as a Strategic Management System," *Harvard Business Review*, July–August 2007, pp. 150–161.

45. W. Schiemann, "Aligning Performance Management with Organizational Strategy, Values, and Goals," in J. W. Smither and M. London (eds.), *Performance Management* (San Francisco: Jossey-Bass, 2009), pp. 45–87.

46. R. Pritchard, S. Jones, P. Roth, K. Stuebing, and S. Ekeberg, "The Evaluation of an Integrated Approach to Measuring Organizational Productivity," *Personnel Psychology* 42 (1989), pp. 69–115; R. Pritchard, M. Harrell, D. DiazGranados, and M. Guzman, "The Productivity Measurement and Enhancement System: A Meta-Analysis," *Journal of Applied Psychology* 93 (2008), pp. 340–67.

47. P. Wright, J. George, S. Farnsworth, and G. McMahan, "Productivity and Extra-Role Behavior: The Effects of Goals and Incentives on Spontaneous Helping," *Journal of Applied Psychology* 78, no. 3 (1993), pp. 374–81.

48. Latham and Wexley, *Increasing Productivity through Performance Appraisal.*

49. J. Liedman, "The Ongoing Conversation," *Human Resource Executive*, November 2006, pp. 71–74; R. Davenport, "John Deere Champions Workforce Development," *TD*, April 2006, pp. 41–43.

50. R. L. Cardy, "Performance Appraisal in a Quality Context: A New Look at an Old Problem," in *Performance Appraisal: State of the Art in Practice*, ed. J. W. Smither (San Francisco: Jossey-Bass, 1998), pp. 132–62.

51. E. C. Huge, *Total Quality: An Executive's Guide for the 1990s* (Homewood, IL: Richard D. Irwin, 1990): see Chapter 5, "Measuring and Rewarding Performance," pp. 70–88; W. E. Deming, *Out of Crisis* (Cambridge, MA: MIT Center for Advanced Engineering Study, 1986).

52. M. Caroselli, *Total Quality Transformations* (Amherst, MA: Human Resource Development Press, 1991); Huge, *Total Quality.*

53. M. Sallie-Dosunmu, "Born to Grow," *T + D*, May 2006, pp. 33–37.

54. A. Brunet and S. New, "Kaizen in Japan: An Empirical Study," *International Journal of Production and Operations Management* 23 (2003), pp. 1426–46.

55. D. E. Bowen and E. E. Lawler III, "Total Quality-Oriented Human Resource Management," *Organizational Dynamics* 21 (1992), pp. 29–41.

56. R. Heneman, K. Wexley, and M. Moore, "Performance Rating Accuracy: A Critical Review," *Journal of Business Research* 15 (1987), pp. 431–48.

57. T. Becker and R. Klimoski, "A Field Study of the Relationship between the Organizational Feedback Environment and Performance," *Personnel Psychology* 42 (1989), pp. 343–58; H. M. Findley, W. F. Giles, and K. W. Mossholder, "Performance Appraisal and Systems Facets: Relationships with Contextual Performance," *Journal of Applied Psychology* 85 (2000), pp. 634–40.

58. K. Ellis, "Developing for Dollars," *Training*, May 2003, pp. 34–39.

59. L. Axline, "Performance Biased Evaluations," *Supervisory Management*, November 1991, p. 3.

60. C. Patton, "Greater Recognition," *Human Resource Executive*, October 2013, pp. 71–73.

61. T. Vranjes, "Held in High Regard," *HR Magazine*, November 2014, pp. 54–56.

62. K. Wexley and R. Klimoski, "Performance Appraisal: An Update," in *Research in Personnel and Human Resource Management* (vol. 2), ed. K. Rowland and G. Ferris (Greenwich, CT: JAI Press, 1984).

63. F. Landy and J. Farr, *The Measurement of Work Performance: Methods, Theory, and Applications* (New York: Academic Press, 1983).

64. G. McEvoy and P. Buller, "User Acceptance of Peer Appraisals in an Industrial Setting," *Personnel Psychology* 40 (1987), pp. 785–97.

65. A. Pomeroy, "Agent of Change," *HR Magazine*, May 2005, pp. 52–56.

66. D. Antonioni, "The Effects of Feedback Accountability on Upward Appraisal Ratings," *Personnel Psychology* 47 (1994), pp. 349–56.

67. K. Murphy and J. Cleveland, *Performance Appraisal: An Organizational Perspective* (Boston: Allyn & Bacon, 1991).

68. J. Bernardin and L. Klatt, "Managerial Appraisal Systems: Has Practice Caught Up with the State of the Art?" *Public Personnel Administrator*, November 1985, pp. 79–86.

69. A. Fox, "Curing What Ails Performance Reviews," *HR Magazine,* January 2009.

70. H. Heidemeier and K. Moser, "Self-Other Agreement in Job Performance Rating: A Meta-Analytic Test of a Process Model," *Journal of Applied Psychology* 94 (2008), pp. 353–70.

71. R. Steel and N. Ovalle, "Self-Appraisal Based on Supervisor Feedback," *Personnel Psychology* 37 (1984), pp. 667–85; L. E. Atwater, "The Advantages and Pitfalls of Self-Assessment in Organizations," in J. Smither (ed.) *Performance Appraisal: State of the Art in Practice* (San Francisco: Jossey-Bass, 1998) pp. 331–65.

72. E. Gummerson, "Lip Services—A Neglected Area of Service Marketing," *Journal of Services Marketing* 1 (1987), pp. 1–29.

73. J. Bernardin, B. Hagan, J. Kane, and P. Villanova, "Effective Performance Management: A Focus on Precision, Customers, and Situational Constraints," in *Performance Appraisal: State of the Art in Practice,* ed. J. W. Smither (San Francisco: Jossey-Bass, 1998), pp. 3–48.

74. R. Hoffman, "Ten Reasons You Should Be Using 360-Degree Feedback," *HR Magazine,* April 1995, pp. 82–84.

75. S. Sherman, "How Tomorrow's Best Leaders Are Learning Their Stuff," *Fortune,* November 27, 1995, pp. 90–104; W. W. Tornow, M. London, and Associates, *Maximizing the Value of 360-Degree Feedback* (San Francisco: Jossey-Bass, 1998); D. A. Waldman, L. E. Atwater, and D. Antonioni, "Has 360-Degree Feedback Gone Amok?" *Academy of Management Executive* 12 (1988), pp. 86–94.

76. P. McCord, "How Netflix Reinvented HR," *Harvard Business Review,* January–February 2014, pp. 71–76.

77. J. Farr, J. Fairchild and S. Cassidy, "Technology and Performance Appraisal," In M. Coovert and L. Thompson, eds., *The Psychology of Workplace Technology* (New York: Routledge, 2014), pp. 77–98.

78. A. Brown, "Crossing the Generational Divide," *Financial* Post, April 14, 2011, www.financialpost.com.

79. E. Goldberg, "Performance Management Gets Social," *HR* Magazine, August 2014, pp. 35–38, http://work.com, accessed April 28, 2015.

80. K. Maher, "Big Employer Is Watching," *The Wall Street Journal,* November 4, 2003, pp. B1 and B6.

81. B. Morris, "Meet the Truck Driver of 2013," *The Wall Street Journal,* November 14, 2013, pp. B1, B6.

82. S. Ante and L. Weber, "Memo to Workers: The Boss Is Watching," *The Wall Street Journal,* October 23, 2013, pp. B1, B6.

83. A. Mathews, "Big Data's New Prescription: Tracking Doctors at Work," *The Wall Street Journal,* July 12, 2013, pp. 11, A10.

84. D. Lawrence, "Tracking the Enemy Within," *Bloomberg BusinessWeek,* March 16–March 22, 2015, pp. 39–41.

85. "Should Companies Monitor Their Employees Social Media," *The Wall Street Journal,* May 12, 2014, pp. R1, R2.

86. D. Bhave, "The Invisible Eye? Electronic Performance Monitoring and Employee Job Performance," *Personnel Psychology* 67 (2014), pp. 605–635.

87. A. Tversky and D. Kahneman, "Availability: A Heuristic for Judging Frequency and Probability," *Cognitive Psychology* 5 (1973), pp. 207–32.

88. K. Wexley and W. Nemeroff, "Effects of Racial Prejudice, Race of Applicant, and Biographical Similarity on Interviewer Evaluations of Job Applicants," *Journal of Social and Behavioral Sciences* 20 (1974), pp. 66–78.

89. G. Ruiz, "Lessons from the Front Lines," *Workforce Management,* December 2006, pp. 50–52.

90. D. Smith, "Training Programs for Performance Appraisal: A Review," *Academy of Management Review* 11 (1986), pp. 22–40.

91. G. Latham, K. Wexley, and E. Pursell, "Training Managers to Minimize Rating Errors in the Observation of Behavior," *Journal of Applied Psychology* 60 (1975), pp. 550–55.

92. J. Bernardin and E. Pence, "Effects of Rater Training: Creating New Response Sets and Decreasing Accuracy," *Journal of Applied Psychology* 65 (1980), pp. 60–66.

93. E. Pulakos, "A Comparison of Rater Training Programs: Error Training and Accuracy Training," *Journal of Applied Psychology* 69 (1984), pp. 581–88; E. Dierdorff, E. Surface, and K. Brown, "Frame-of-Reference Training Effectiveness: Effects of Goal Orientation and Self-Efficacy on Affective, Cognitive, Skill-Based and Transfer Outcomes," *Journal of Applied Psychology* 95 (2010), pp. 1181–1191.

94. H. J. Bernardin, M. R. Buckley, C. L. Tyler, and D. S. Wiese, "A Reconsideration of Strategies in Rater Training," in G. R. Ferris (ed.), *Research in Personnel and Human Resource Management* (Greenwich, CT: JAI Press, 2000), vol. 18, pp. 221–74.

95. J. Sammer, "Calibrating Consistency," *HR Magazine,* January 2008, pp. 73–75.

96. S. W. J. Kozlowski, G. T. Chao, and R. F. Morrison, "Games Raters Play: Politics, Strategies, and Impression Management in Performance Appraisal," in *Performance Appraisal: State of the Art in Practice,* pp. 163–205; C. Rosen, P. Levy, and R. Hall, "Placing Perceptions of Politics in the Context of the Feedback Environment, Employee Attitudes, and Job Performance," *Journal of Applied Psychology* 91 (2006), pp. 211–20.

97. R. Pyrillis, "The Reviews Are In," *Workforce Management,* May 2011, pp. 20–25.

98. K. Wexley, V. Singh, and G. Yukl, "Subordinate Participation in Three Types of Appraisal Interviews," *Journal of Applied Psychology* 58 (1973), pp. 54–57; K. Wexley, "Appraisal Interview," in *Performance Assessment,* ed. R. A. Berk (Baltimore: Johns Hopkins University Press, 1986), pp. 167–85; D. Cederblom, "The Performance Appraisal Interview: A Review, Implications, and Suggestions," *Academy of Management Review* 7 (1982), pp. 219–27; B. D. Cawley, L. M. Keeping, and P. E. Levy, "Participation in the Performance Appraisal Process and Employee Reactions: A Meta-analytic Review of Field Investigations," *Journal of Applied Psychology* 83, no. 3 (1998), pp. 615–63; H. Aguinis, *Performance Management* (Upper Saddle River, NJ: Pearson Prentice Hall, 2007); C. Lee, "Feedback, Not Appraisal," *HR Magazine,* November 2006, pp. 111–14; R. Hanson and E. Pulakos, *Putting the 'Performance' Back in Performance Management* (Alexandria, VA: Society for Human Resource Management, 2015); M. Budworth, G. Latham, and L. Manroop, "Looking Forward to Performance Improvement: A Field Test of the Feedforward Interview for Performance Management," *Human Resource Management* 54 (2014), pp. 45–54; A. Kinicki, K. Jacobson, S. Peterson, and G. Prussia, "Development and Validation of the Performance Management Behavior Questionnaire," *Personnel Psychology* 66 (2013), pp. 1–45.

99. B. Hite, "Employers Rethink How They Give Feedback," *Wall Street Journal,* October 13, 2008, p. B5.

100. W. Giles and K. Mossholder, "Employee Reactions to Contextual and Session Components of Performance Appraisal," *Journal of Applied Psychology* 75 (1990), pp. 371–77.

101. E. Locke and G. Latham, *A Theory of Goal Setting and Task Performance* (Englewood Cliffs, NJ: Prentice Hall, 1990).

102. H. Klein, S. Snell, and K. Wexley, "A Systems Model of the Performance Appraisal Interview Process," *Industrial Relations* 26 (1987), pp. 267–80; C. Crossley, C. Cooper, and T. Wernsing, "Making Things Happen Through Challenging Goals: Leader Proactivity, Trust, and Business-Unit Performance," *Journal of Applied Psychology,* 98 (2103), pp. 540–49.

103. *Brito v. Zia Co.,* 478 F.2d 1200 (10th Cir 1973).

104. K. Kraiger and J. Ford, "A Meta-Analysis of Ratee Race Effects in Performance Rating," *Journal of Applied Psychology* 70 (1985), pp. 56–65; S. Needleman, "Monitoring the Monitors: Small Firms Increasingly Are Keeping Tabs on Their Workers, Keystroke by Keystroke," *The Wall Street Journal,* August 16, 2010, p. R8.

105. P. Sackett, C. DuBois, and A. Noe, "Tokenism in Performance Evaluation: The Effects of Work Groups Representation on Male–Female and White–Black Differences in Performance Ratings," *Journal of Applied Psychology* 76 (1991), pp. 263–67.

106. "GE Subsidiary MRA Systems to Pay $130,000 to Settle EEOC Age Discrimination Suit," June 3, 2010, news release from www.eeoc.gov, accessed April 29, 2015.

107. "EEOC Sues Wisconsin Plastics for Discrimination against Hmong and Hispanic Employees," June 9, 2014, news release from www.eeoc.gov, accessed April 29, 2015.

108. G. Barrett and M. Kernan, "Performance Appraisal and Terminations: A Review of Court Decisions since *Brito v. Zia* with Implications for Personnel Practices," *Personnel Psychology* 40 (1987), pp. 489–503; H. Field and W. Holley, "The Relationship of Performance Appraisal System Characteristics to Verdicts in Selected Employment Discrimination Cases," *Academy of Management Journal* 25 (1982), pp. 392–406; J. M. Werner and M. C. Bolino, "Explaining U.S. Courts of Appeals Decisions Involving Performance Appraisal: Accuracy, Fairness, and Validation," *Personnel Psychology* 50 (1997), pp. 1–24; J. Segal, "Performance Management Blunders," *HR Magazine,* November 2010, pp. 75–77.

Employee Development

CHAPTER

LEARNING OBJECTIVES

After reading this chapter, you should be able to:

LO 9-1 Explain how employee development contributes to strategies related to employee retention, developing intellectual capital, and business growth. *page 379*

LO 9-2 Discuss the steps in the development planning process. *page 381*

LO 9-3 Explain the employees' and company's responsibilities in planning development. *page 381*

LO 9-4 Discuss current trends in using formal education for development. *page 386*

LO 9-5 Relate how assessment of personality type, work behaviors, and job performance can be used for employee development. *page 389*

LO 9-6 Explain how job experiences can be used for skill development. *page 394*

LO 9-7 Develop successful mentoring programs. *page 400*

LO 9-8 Describe how to train managers to coach employees. *page 404*

LO 9-9 Discuss what companies are doing for melting the glass ceiling. *page 405*

LO 9-10 Use the 9-box grid for identifying where employees fit in a succession plan and construct appropriate development plans for them. *page 406*

Development Helps ESPN Remain a Sports Dynasty

Entertainment and Sports Programming Network, known as ESPN, is one of the leading companies in the global multimedia sports and entertainment business. Over 30 years ago ESPN became the first sports network to televise complete sports coverage. Today, ESPN, headquartered in Bristol, Connecticut, has over 7,000 employees and includes eight U.S. cable networks, over 300 radio affiliates, and other multimedia and business companies. Its businesses include television networks (ESPN), audio (ESPN Radio, ESPN Deportes Radio), digital (WatchESPN), publishing (ESPN The Magazine), event management (X games, ESPYs, college bowls and basketball games), locations (ESPN ZONE at Disney) and corporate outreach (The V Foundation for Cancer). It televises 65 sports in 16 languages in more than 200 countries. In 2014, ESPN produced more than 47,000 hours of live event/studio programming. In the past several years ESPN has reached significant industry milestones including ESPN OnDemand Audio being recognized as the most downloaded radio app (215.6 million downloads) and the opening of Digital Center2, the new home of SportsCenter and one of the most sophisticated production centers in the world.

To remain in its leadership role in the sports and entertainment business, ESPN needs to continue to provide the best live sports programming as well as expand and develop its digital presence through social media. To do so, ESPN recognizes the importance of creating exceptional employee experiences through its commitment to people, partnerships, culture, and excellence. Employee development plays a key role in helping to create exceptional employee experiences at ESPN. But employee development at ESPN faces several challenges. One challenge is the speed at which the global news, broadcasting, and entertainment business operates. This can make it difficult for employees to take the time away from activities such as producing and delivering programming to focus on development activities. Another challenge is that ESPN is growing its business in global markets such as Latin America. This adds a layer of complexity to building a development culture and career management tools because they must align with local culture and norms in order to be effective.

ESPN has taken several steps to ensure that its development efforts overcome these challenges and support employees' career interests and goals, enhance their skills, and grow top leadership talent. ESPN requires every employee to complete an individual development plan (IDP). The IDP helps employees consider where they currently are in their careers, their career goals, and how they plan to reach their career goals. The learning function at ESPN reviews and supports the IDP, which has been completed by over 95% of employees. Similar to other companies, ESPN uses the 70-20-10 approach to development. This means that most of employee development occurs on the job, while 20% comes from relationships and informal learning, and 10% from formal courses targeted at specific skills. For example, ESPN has a Leadership GPS, which is a tool used by employees to track their development progress. The Leadership GPS helps employees set development goals. It also provides advice on which types of development activities (such as courses, job shadowing, or experiences) are available and will help them meet their goals. ESPN The University offers courses related to different business areas, which are taught by executives and business leaders. This is important because its gets company leaders from different business areas involved in developing employees. It also helps to provide employees with a greater understanding of the different aspects of

CONTINUED

ESPN's business such as production, programming, and HR and how they fit together. ESPN Center Court is a development program targeted exclusively to high-potential employees who are on the fast-track to future leadership roles in the company. Center Court uses job rotations to give high-potential employees the opportunity to experience different aspects of the business. They also interact with the company's president and top executives. To facilitate development through relationships ESPN has a mentoring program known as Open Access that is available to all employees. The only requirements are that employees desire to learn from others and want to build relationships to achieve their development goals.

To ensure development activities support business needs, ESPN has a learning and advisory board which includes senior leaders and vice presidents from its different businesses. Every major initiative is reviewed and has to receive support from the board before it is implemented. Also, the Employee Learning Council, which includes employees from each of ESPNs business units, provides feedback and helps to plan development programs.

SOURCES: Based on F. Kalman, "ESPN's Top Play: Learning," *Chief Learning Officer,* March 2013, pp. 22–25, 47; "Learning and Development" at http://espncareers.com/working_here/learning_development, accessed April 2, 2015; "ESPN Inc. Fact Sheet," from http://espnmediazone.com/, accessed April 2, 2015.

Introduction

As the ESPN example illustrates, employee development is a key contributor to a company's competitive advantage by helping employees understand their strengths, weaknesses, and interests and by showing them how new jobs and expanded job responsibilities are available to them to meet their personal growth needs. This helps retain valuable managers who might otherwise leave to join clients or competitors. It is also important to emphasize that development is important for all employees, not just managers. Employee development is a necessary component of a company's efforts to compete in the new economy, to meet the challenges of global competition and social change, and to incorporate technological advances and changes in work design. Employee development is key to ensuring that employees have the competencies necessary to serve customers and create new products and customer solutions. Regardless of the business strategy, development is important for retaining talented employees. Also because companies (and their employees) must constantly learn and change to meet customer needs and compete in new markets, the emphasis placed on both training and development has increased. As we noted in Chapter 1, employee commitment and retention are directly related to how employees are treated by their managers.

Career development for employees is a key contributor to ESPN's continued success across many digital platforms.

This chapter begins by discussing the relationship between development, training, and careers. Choosing an approach is one part of development planning. Second, before employees choose development activities, the employee and the company must have an idea of the employee's development needs and the purpose of development. Identifying the needs and purpose of development is part of its planning. The second section of the chapter describes the steps of the development planning process. Employee and company responsibilities at each step of the process are emphasized. Third, we look at development approaches, including formal education, assessment, job experiences, and interpersonal relationships. The chapter emphasizes the types of skills, knowledge, and behaviors that are strengthened by each development method. The chapter concludes with a discussion of special issues in employee development, including succession planning and using development to help women and minorities move into upper-level management positions (referred to as "melting the glass ceiling").

The Relationship among Development, Training, and Careers

LO 9-1
Explain how employee development contributes to strategies related to employee retention, developing intellectual capital, and business growth.

DEVELOPMENT AND TRAINING

Development refers to formal education, job experiences, relationships, and assessment of personality and abilities that help employees prepare for the future. The ESPN example illustrates that although development can occur through participation in planned programs, it often results from performing different types of work. Because it is future-oriented, it involves learning that is not necessarily related to the employee's current job.[1] Table 9.1 shows the differences between training and development. Traditionally, training focuses on helping employees' performance in their current jobs. Development prepares them for other positions in the company and increases their ability to move into jobs that may not yet exist.[2] Development also helps employees prepare for changes in their current jobs that may result from new technology, work designs, new customers, or new product markets. Development is especially critical for talent management, particularly for senior managers and employees with leadership potential (recall our discussion of attracting and retaining talent in Chapter 1). Companies report that the most important talent management challenges they face include developing existing talent and attracting and retaining existing leadership talent.[3] Chapter 7 emphasized the strategic role of training. As training continues to become more strategic (that is, related to business goals), the distinction between training and development will blur. Both training and development will be required and will focus on current and future personal and company needs.

Development
The acquisition of knowledge, skills, and behaviors that improve an employee's ability to meet changes in job requirements and in client and customer demands.

DEVELOPMENT AND CAREERS

Today's careers are known as protean careers.[4] A **protean career** is based on self-direction with the goal of psychological success in one's work. Employees take major responsibility for managing their careers. For example, an engineer may decide to take a sabbatical from her position to work in management at the United Way Agency for a year. The purpose of this assignment could be to develop her managerial skills as well as help her personally evaluate if she likes managerial work more than engineering.

The protean career has several implications for employee development. The goal of the new career is **psychological success**: the feeling of pride and accomplishment that comes from achieving life goals that are not limited to achievements at work (such as raising a family and having good physical health). Psychological success is self-determined rather than solely determined through signals the employee receives from the company (like salary increase and promotion). For example, a 52-year-old woman co-managed a real estate business in California with her husband.[5] She always wanted to work in medicine or health care and took health science classes in college but decided to work in real estate because it provided a good income and flexibility when raising her

Protean Career
A career that is based on self-direction with the goal of psychological success in one's work.

Psychological Success
The feeling of pride and accomplishment that comes from achieving life goals.

	TRAINING	DEVELOPMENT
Focus	Current	Future
Use of work experiences	Low	High
Goal	Preparation for current job	Preparation for changes
Participation	Required	Voluntary

Table 9.1
Comparison between Training and Development

children. After working in real estate for 25 years she pursued her passion by taking prerequisite classes and applying to nursing school. Unfortunately, her husband suffered a debilitating stroke making her the sole provider for the family. She sold the real estate business, applied and was accepted to nursing school, and managed her husband's care. At age 57 she graduated from nursing school but was unable to find a job in California. She eventually found a job in a hospital in Oklahoma and moved there with her husband. After gaining valuable experience she moved back to California and now works in a facility for developmentally disabled adults. She is passionate about her new job despite its long and inflexible working hours, and the physical and emotional demands of staying on her feet all day and helping people with many needs.

Employees need to develop new skills rather than rely on a static knowledge base. This has resulted from companies' need to be more responsive to customers' service and product demands. As we emphasized in Chapter 7, "Training," learning is continuous, often informal, and involves creating and sharing knowledge.

The emphasis on continuous learning has altered the direction and frequency of movement within careers (career pattern).[6] Traditional career patterns consisted of a series of steps arranged in a linear hierarchy, with higher steps related to increased authority, responsibility, and compensation. Expert career patterns involve a lifelong commitment to a field or specialization (such as law, medicine, or management). These types of career patterns will not disappear. Rather, career patterns involving movement across specializations or disciplines (a spiral career pattern) will become more prevalent. These new career patterns mean that developing employees (as well as employees taking control of their own careers) will require providing them with the opportunity to (a) determine their interests, skill strengths, and weaknesses and (b) based on this information, seek appropriate development experiences that will likely involve job experiences and relationships as well as formal courses.

The most appropriate view of today's careers are that they are "boundaryless and often change."[7] It may include movement across several employers (job hopping) or even different occupations. Studies have found that by age 35, 25% of employees have held five jobs or more and for employees 55 and older, 20% have held 10 jobs or more.[8] One-third of employers expect job hopping to occur, especially among new college graduates, but 40% believe it becomes less acceptable when employees are in their mid-30s. The reality is that employees will be unlikely to stay at one company for their entire or even a significant part of their career. This means that companies and employees should add value to each other.[9] That is, regardless of how long employees stay, developing them can help the company adapt to changing business conditions and strategies by providing new skill sets and managerial talent. In turn, development can facilitate employee engagement by enhancing their employability. It reduces employees' job hopping because they feel less need to change employers to build their skill sets or gain valuable job experiences.

"Boundaryless" means that careers may involve identifying more with a job or profession than with the present employer. A career can also be considered boundaryless in the sense that career plans or goals are influenced by personal or family demands and values. One way that employees cope with changes in their personal lives as well as in employment relationships is to rearrange and shift their roles and responsibilities. Employees can change their careers throughout their life based on awareness of strengths and weaknesses, perceived need to balance work and life, and the need to find stimulating and exciting work.[10] Career success may not be tied to promotions but to achieving goals that are personally meaningful to the employee rather than those set by parents, peers, or the company. As we discuss later in the chapter, careers are best managed through partnerships between employees and their company that create a positive relationship through which employees are committed to the organization but can take personal control for managing their own careers to benefit themselves and the company.

As this discussion shows, to retain and motivate employees companies need to provide a system to identify and meet employees' development needs. This is especially important to retain good performers and employees who have potential for managerial positions. This system is often known as a **development planning** or **career management system**. We discuss these systems in the following section.

Development Planning Systems

Companies' development planning systems vary in the level of sophistication and the emphasis they place on different components of the process. Steps and responsibilities in the development planning system are shown in Figure 9.1.

Self-Assessment

Self-assessment refers to the use of information by employees to determine their career interests, values, aptitudes, and behavioral tendencies. It often involves psychological tests such as the Myers-Briggs Type Indicator (described later in the chapter), the Strong-Campbell Interest Inventory, and the Self-Directed Search. The Strong-Campbell helps employees identify their occupational and job interests; the Self-Directed Search identifies employees' preferences for working in different types of environments (like sales, counseling, landscaping, and so on). Tests may also help employees identify the relative values they place on work and leisure activities.

Through the assessment, a development need can be identified. This need can result from gaps between current skills and/or interests and the type of work or position the employee wants. For example, employees at PEMCO Mutual Insurance Company use online self-assessments to assess their current skills and identify the skills and

Figure 9.1

Steps and Responsibilities in the Career Management Process

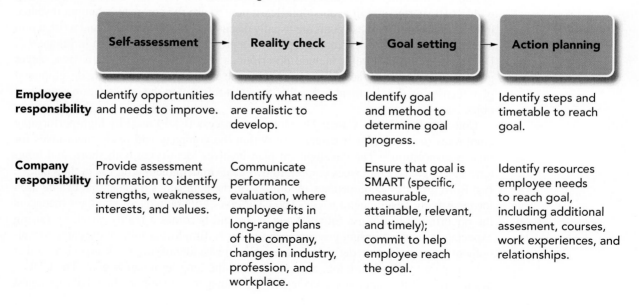

	Self-assessment	**Reality check**	**Goal setting**	**Action planning**
Employee responsibility	Identify opportunities and needs to improve.	Identify what needs are realistic to develop.	Identify goal and method to determine goal progress.	Identify steps and timetable to reach goal.
Company responsibility	Provide assessment information to identify strengths, weaknesses, interests, and values.	Communicate performance evaluation, where employee fits in long-range plans of the company, changes in industry, profession, and workplace.	Ensure that goal is SMART (specific, measurable, attainable, relevant, and timely); commit to help employee reach the goal.	Identify resources employee needs to reach goal, including additional assesment, courses, work experiences, and relationships.

competencies they want to acquire.[11] Employees use information obtained from this assessment to meet with managers of the departments that need the skill sets the employees intend to acquire to discuss how they will get the skills.

Reality Check

Reality check refers to the information employees receive about how the company evaluates their skills and knowledge and where they fit into the company's plans (potential promotion opportunities, lateral moves). Usually this information is provided by the employee's manager as part of performance appraisal. Some companies also use the 360-degree feedback assessment which involves employees completing a self-evaluation of their behaviors or competencies as well as managers, peers, direct reports, and even customers provide smaller evaluations. (360-degree feedback is discussed later in the chapter.) It is not uncommon in well-developed systems for the manager to hold separate performance appraisals and development discussions.

For example, at BKD, an accounting and consulting firm, employees frequently move between tax, auditing, and consulting projects.[12] They need a way to track their skills so that they can determine how to achieve their career goals such as moving from a generalist to becoming a tax expert for the health care industry. To provide feedback on their skills, project leaders use behavioral checklists, which provide ratings such as "exceptional," "needs improvement," or "developing." The checklists are given to employees who can then schedule a meeting with the project leader to get more specific feedback about the ratings as well as development recommendations. The development recommendations might include taking a course, seeking a coach or mentor, or networking with managers in areas in which the employee is interested in working.

Goal Setting

Goal setting refers to the process of employees developing short- and long-term development objectives. These goals usually relate to desired positions (such as becoming sales manager within three years), level of skill application (use one's budgeting skills to improve the unit's cash flow problems), work setting (move to corporate marketing within two years), or skill acquisition (learn how to use the company's human resource information system). These goals are usually discussed with the manager and written into a development plan. A development plan for a product manager is shown in Figure 9.2. Development plans usually include descriptions of strengths and weaknesses, career goals, and development activities for reaching the career goal. An effective development plan focuses on development needs that are most relevant to the organization's strategic objectives.

Consider Just Born's Career Development Process (CDP) used by high-performing employees to identify their career path within the company and ready themselves for their next position.[13] The development plan involves identifying both short- and long-term career goals. Employees commit to two goals to help them progress in their career. Just Born provides a competency dictionary on the company's intranet that can be used for identifying development needs. The CDP gives both employees and their managers the opportunity to discuss future career plans and becomes a reality check by raising expectations and increasing performance standards. Employees initiate the career development program by first defining future job interests, identifying work experiences that help prepare for the future job, and establishing the long-term career goal. The CDP is discussed with the employee's manager. The manager can support the CDP or suggest

Figure 9.2
Development Plan

Name: _____   **Title:** Project Manager   **Immediate Manager:** _____

Competencies
Please identify your three greatest strengths and areas for improvement.
Strengths
- Strategic thinking and execution (confidence, command skills, action orientation)
- Results orientation (competence, motivating others, perseverance)
- Spirit for winning (building team spirit, customer focus, respect colleagues)

Areas for Improvement
- Patience (tolerance of people or processes and sensitivity to pacing)
- Written communications (ability to write clearly and succinctly)
- Overly ambitious (too much focus on successful completion of projects rather than developing relationships with individuals involved in the projects)

Development Goals
Please describe your overall career goals.
- **Long-term:** Accept positions of increased responsibility to a level of general manager (or beyond). The areas of specific interest include but are not limited to product and brand management, technology and development, strategic planning, and marketing.
- **Short-term:** Continue to improve my skills in marketing and brand management while utilizing my skills in product management, strategic planning, and global relations.

Next Assignments
Identify potential next assignments (including timing) that would help you develop toward your goals.
- Manager or director level in planning, development, product, or brand management. Timing estimated to be Fall 2017.

Training and Development Needs
List both training and development activities that will either help you develop in your current assignment or provide overall development.
- Master's degree classes will allow me to practice and improve my written communications skills. The dynamics of my current position, teamwork, and reliance on other individuals allow me to practice patience and to focus on individual team members' needs along with the success of the projects.

Employee _____   **Date** _____
Immediate Manager _____   **Date** _____
Mentor _____   **Date** _____

---

changes. If employees' future job interests are outside their current department, the interests are communicated to the manager of that department.

Action Planning

During this phase, employees complete an action plan. An **action plan** is a written strategy that employees use to determine how they will achieve their short- and long-term career goals. Action plans may involve any one or combination of development approaches

Action Plan
Written strategy that employees use to determine how they will achieve their short- and long-term career goals.

discussed later the chapter (such as enrolling in courses and seminars, getting additional assessment, obtaining new job experiences, or finding a mentor or coach).[14] The development approach used depends on the needs and developmental goal.

Examples of Career Management and Development Systems

Effective career development systems include several important features (see Table 9.2). Several companies' development systems include one or more of these features. Consider career management and development systems at Xerox and General Mills.[15] Xerox Services University (XSU) provides an opportunity for employees to develop their skills. Those who enter the online website are presented with different schools, each of which provides a unique development path. Each development path provides recommendations about courses, experiences, and social learning (mentoring, peer coaching) which is facilitated through social media. The five XSU schools focus on creativity and innovation, operational excellence, leadership, people management, and business foundations. As employees use the system, provide their skill strengths and weaknesses and identify areas of interest, the social learning software generates personalized and specific recommendations for development opportunities. General Mills's development plan follows the process shown in Figure 9.2. Each employee completes a development plan that asks employees to consider four areas:

- *Professional goals and motivation:* What professional goals do I have? What excites me to grow professionally?
- *Talents or strengths:* What are my talents and strengths?
- *Development opportunities:* What development needs are important to improve?
- *Development objectives and action steps:* What will be my objective for this plan? What steps can I take to meet the objectives?

Every year managers and employees are expected to have a development discussion and create an individual development plan. Speakers, online tools, and workshops to help employees complete the development plan and prepare for a development discussion

Table 9.2
Design Factors of Effective Development Systems

1. System is positioned as a response to a business need or supports the business strategy.
2. Employees and managers participate in development of the system.
3. Employees are encouraged to take an active role in career management and development.
4. Evaluation is ongoing and used to improve the system.
5. Business units can customize the system for their own purposes (with some constraints).
6. Employees have access to development and career information sources (including advisors and positions available).
7. Senior management and the company culture support the development system.
8. The development system is linked to other human resource practices such as performance management, training, and recruiting systems.
9. A large, diverse talent pool is created.
10. Development plans and talent evaluation information are available and accessible to all managers.

SOURCE: Based on B. Baumann, J. Duncan, S. E. Former, and Z. Leibowitz, "Amoco Primes the Talent Pump," *Personnel Journal,* February 1996, pp. 79–84; D. Hall, *Careers In and Out of Organizations* (Thousand Oaks, CA: Sage, 2002).

with their manager increase the visibility and emphasize the importance of the development planning process. Evaluation data showed that more than 80% of employees report having an effective and motivating development plan. Also, annual survey results show that General Mills ranks 20% to 30% higher on continued improvement and impact of learning and growth compared to companies it is benchmarked against.

The "Competing through Technology" box shows how Genentech Inc. is using the web for development and career management.

Approaches to Employee Development

Four approaches are used to develop employees: formal education, assessment, job experiences, and interpersonal relationships.[16] Many companies use a combination of these approaches. In its Frontline Investment in Growing High-Potential Talent (FLIGHT) program, Asurion, a device insurance company, uses six-month rotational assignments to provide employees with an overall understanding of supply chain operations, mentoring and coaching opportunities with key leaders, and on-the-job and classroom training.[17] Figure 9.3 shows the frequency of use of different employee development practices. Larger companies are more likely to use leadership training and development planning more frequently than smaller companies.

Keep in mind that although much development activity is targeted at managers, all levels of employees may be involved in development. For example, most employees typically receive performance appraisal feedback (a development activity related to assessment) at least once per year. As we discussed in Chapter 8, as part of the appraisal process they are asked to complete individual development plans outlining (1) how they plan to change their weaknesses and (2) their future plans (including positions or

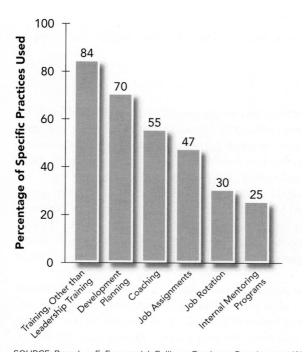

Figure 9.3

Frequency of Use of Employee Development Practices

SOURCE: Based on E. Esen and J. Collison, *Employee Development* (Alexandria, VA: SHRM Research, 2005).

CareerLab Is the Nucleus of Employee Development at Genentech

Genentech Inc., a biotechnology company, developed CareerLab to help employees perform well in their current job and provide opportunities for job enrichment and lateral career moves. CareerLab is a physical and virtual place where employees can consider their skill strengths and weaknesses, interests, and take ownership of their development. CareerLab provides several services. Career consultants are available to meet employees in-person, over the phone, or using Skype. LearningLabs are webinars and class sessions that cover different topics including networking for career growth, managing your personal brand, and leveraging strengths for

career growth. Mentoring Services help employees form mentorships. Employees can access online assessments that cover personal style, values, skills, strengths, and interests. Through CareerLab employees can access short videos designed to get employees to think about different career options, blogs written by career development experts, and animated podcasts. Genentech also offers employees three career development workshops (Growing Your Career, Growing Careers for Managers, and Personal Mastery: Developing Your Full Potential). CareerLab has helped Genentech maintain a lower than industry average turnover

rate (6.2%) and increased levels of employee engagement (17%) since CareerLab was introduced. Employees who have used CareerLab report they are more likely to remain with the company and are satisfied with the future of their careers.

DISCUSSION QUESTIONS

1. What design features of effective development systems are included in CareerLab?
2. What other design features might they consider including in CareerLab? Explain your recommendation.

SOURCES: Based on R. Emlo, "The Power of Discovery," *Chief Learning Officer*, January 2015, pp. 38–48; "Genentech, Inc.: Career Lab," *Training*, January/February 2015, pp. 102–3.

---

locations desired and education or experience needed). Next we explore each type of development approach.

FORMAL EDUCATION

LO 9-4
Discuss current trends in using formal education for development.

Formal Education Programs
Employee development programs, including short courses offered by consultants or universities, executive MBA programs, and university programs.

Formal education programs include off-site and on-site programs designed specifically for the company's employees, short courses offered by consultants or universities, executive MBA programs, and university programs in which participants actually live at the university while taking classes. These programs may involve lectures by business experts, business games and simulations, adventure learning, and meetings with customers.

Many companies such as McDonald's and General Electric rely primarily on in-house development programs offered by training and development centers or corporate universities, rather than sending employees to programs offered by universities.[18] Companies rely on in-house programs because they can be tied directly to business needs, can be easily evaluated using company metrics, and can get senior-level management involved.

The thousands of restaurant managers and owner-operators who attend McDonald's Hamburger University each year in Oak Brook, Illinois, get classroom training and participate in simulations on how to run a business that delivers consistent service, quality, and cleanliness. They also receive coaching and peer support face-to-face and online.

The company's highest-performing executives participate in a nine-month leadership institute at Hamburger U, where they tackle major issues facing the company.

General Electric (GE) has one of the oldest and most widely known management development centers in the world. GE invests approximately $1 billion each year for training and education programs for its employees.[19] Over the past 17 years, the 189 most senior executives in the company spent at least 12 months in training and professional development. GE develops managers at the John F. Welch Leadership Center at Crotonville, New York.[20] The facility has residence buildings where participants stay while attending programs as well as classrooms for courses, programs, and seminars. Each year GE employees chosen by their managers based on their performance and potential attend management development programs. The programs include professional skills development and specialized courses in areas such as risk analysis and loan structuring. All of the programs emphasize theory and practical application. Course time is spent discussing business issues facing GE. The programs are taught by in-house instructors, university faculty members, and even CEO Jeff Immelt. Examples of management development programs available at GE are shown in Table 9.3. As you can see, GE uses a combination of coursework and job experiences to develop entry-level and top levels of management. Other programs such as the Business Manager Course and the Executive Development Course involve action learning. Besides programs and courses for management development GE also holds seminars to better understand customer expectations and leadership conferences designed specifically for African Americans, women, or Hispanic managers to discuss leading and learning.

A number of institutions offering executive education in the United States and abroad include Harvard, the Wharton School of Business, the University of Michigan, INSEAD,

Table 9.3
Examples of Leadership Development Programs at General Electric

PROGRAM	SUMMARY	QUALIFICATIONS TO ATTEND
Early Career Program: Communications Leadership Development Program	Formal courses to develop leadership, communications, and business skills and techniques. Three eight-month rotations in one of GE's businesses. Challenging assignments in public relations and communications roles (marketing communications, employee communications, executive communications).	Bachelor's degree with communications-related coursework; minimum 3.0 GPA; prior internship or co-op experience, willingness to relocate.
Experienced Commercial Leadership Program (ECLP): Sales and Marketing	Receive at least six weeks of training to develop marketing and sales capabilities, strengthen leadership skills, foster ECLP culture. Three eight-month business rotations within a GE business; the rotations are marketing focused and sales focused. Every four months, review self-assessments and manager evaluations to identify accomplishments, development needs and career interests. Training includes classroom and online training and in-residence symposiums at the John F. Welch Learning Center.	MBA; 5–8 years marketing or sales experience; demonstrated achievement and leadership in sales or marketing communications, and analytical skills; willingness to relocate; expertise aligned with a GE business.

SOURCES: Based on http://www.ge.com/careers/culture/university-students/communications-leadership-development-program/united-states and http://www.ge.com/careers/culture/university-students/experienced-commercial-leadership-program/program-details#structure, both accessed April 3, 2015.

IMD, and the Center for Creative Leadership. At the University of Virginia, the Darden School of Business offers an executive MBA program in which students attend classes on campus once a month on Thursday through Saturday. The on-campus time provides opportunities for students to collaborate on presentations, simulations, and case studies. The school also brings executive MBA students to campus four times for leadership residencies. During each weeklong residency, the students use workshops, coaching, and reflection to get better at handling their everyday management challenges. Between the times on campus, the students continue their education with independent study, online classes, and tools for virtual meetings and online exams.[21]

Another trend in executive education is for employers and the education provider to create programs with content and experiences designed specifically for the audience. For example, Duke Corporate Education developed a custom program for Thomson Reuters to increase their managers' skills related to thinking innovatively to help the company grow.[22] The Thomson Reuters program sponsor encouraged each participant to identify an opportunity or problem with their business that would require innovative thinking. To help the managers develop innovative thinking Duke used an experiential exercise designed to help managers to consider how different global markets can impact their strategies and understand how consumers' tastes can shift according to where they are located. In the experiential exercise participants are immersed in a local market to learn how to think about and do business differently. Programs were offered in New York, London, and Shanghai and involved trips to neighborhoods, businesses, and museums and meetings with local leaders to understand the distinctive features of each business market. As a result, of the program participants increased their awareness of how they could be more innovative in their jobs and lead diverse teams. They also gained insights they could directly apply to their business such as how to use brainstorming techniques to quickly integrate knowledge and ideas.

Managers who attend the Center for Creative Leadership development program take psychological tests; receive feedback from managers, peers, and direct reports; participate in group-building activities (like adventure learning, discussed in Chapter 7); receive counseling; and set improvement goals and write development plans.[23]

Enrollment in executive education programs or MBA programs may be limited to managers or employees identified to have management potential. As a result, many companies also provide tuition reimbursement as a benefit for all employees to encourage them to develop. **Tuition reimbursement** refers to the practice of reimbursing employees' costs for college and university courses and degree programs. Companies that have evaluated tuition reimbursement programs have found that the programs increase employee retention rates, readiness for promotion, and improve job performance.[24] Verizon Wireless invests $26 million annually in tuition assistance program participated in by 23,000 of its employees.[25] Employees can receive tuition assistance for attending a university or college or for the costs of the company's on-site program conducted at call centers and corporate offices. The on-site program classes, taught by university faculty, help employees earn degrees by attending classes where they work and when they have free time in their work schedules. They are eligible for tuition reimbursement from the day they are hired and have to make no commitment to stay employed with the company. Their expenses are limited to $8,000 per year for full-time employees and $4,000 for part-time employees. This exceeds the $5,250 annual reimbursement limit that most companies use based on the tax-free maximum established by the IRS. To be eligible for reimbursement coursework has to relate to the employees' current job or career path within Verizon Wireless. Evaluation of the program has shown that it has resulted in increased morale and helped to attract new and retain current employees.

Tuition Reimbursement
The practice of reimbursing employees' costs for college and university courses and degree programs.

ASSESSMENT

Assessment involves collecting information and providing feedback to employees about their behavior, communication style, or skills.[26] The employees, their peers, managers, and customers may provide information. Assessments are used for several reasons. First, assessment is most frequently used to identify employees with managerial potential and to measure current managers' strengths and weaknesses. Assessment is also used to identify managers with the potential to move into higher-level executive positions, and it can be used with work teams to identify the strengths and weaknesses of individual team members and the decision processes or communication styles that inhibit the team's productivity. Assessments can help employees understand their tendencies, needs, the type of work environment they prefer, and the type of work they might prefer to do.[27] This information, along with the performance evaluations they receive from the company, can help employees decide what type of development goals might be most appropriate for them (e.g., leadership position, increase scope of their current position).

Companies vary in the methods and the sources of information they use in developmental assessment. Many companies use employee performance evaluations. Companies with sophisticated development systems use psychological tests to measure employees' skills, interests, personality types, and communication styles. Self, peer, and managers' ratings of employees' interpersonal styles and behaviors may also be collected. Popular assessment tools include personality tests, assessment center performance appraisal, and 360-degree feedback.

Personality Tests and Inventories

Tests are used to determine if employees have the personality characteristics necessary to be successful in specific managerial jobs or jobs involving international assignments. Personality tests typically measure five major dimensions: extraversion, adjustment, agreeableness, conscientiousness, and openness to experience (see Table 6.3 in Chapter 6).

The Myers-Briggs Type Inventory (MBTI)® refers to an assessment that is based on Carl Jung's personality type theory. This theory emphasizes that we have a fundamental personality type that shapes and influences how we understand the world, process information, and socialize. The assessment determines which one of 16 personality types fits best. The 16 unique personality types are based on preferences for introversion (I) or extraversion (E), sensing (S) or intuition (N), thinking (T) or feeling (F), and judging (J) or perceiving (P). The assessment tool identifies individuals' preferences for energy (introversion versus extraversion), information gathering (sensing versus intuition), decision making (thinking versus feeling), and lifestyle (judging versus perceiving).[28] Each personality type has implications for work habits and interpersonal relationships. For example, individuals who are introverted, sensing, thinking, and judging (known as ISTJs) tend to be serious, quiet, practical, orderly, and logical. These persons can organize tasks, be decisive, and follow through on plans and goals. ISTJs have several weaknesses because they do not tend to use the opposite preferences: extraversion, intuition, feeling, and perceiving. These weaknesses include problems dealing with unexpected opportunities, appearing too task-oriented or impersonal to colleagues, and making overly quick decisions. Visit the website www.cpp.com for more information on the personality types.

The DiSC measures personality and behavioral style including dominance (direct, strong-willed, forceful), influence (sociable, talkative), steadiness (gentle accommodating) and conscientiousness (private, analytical).[29] See www.discprofile.com for more information on DiSC.

LO 9-5
Relate how assessment of personality type, work behaviors, and job performance can be used for employee development.

Assessment
Collecting information and providing feedback to employees about their behavior, communication style, or skills.

Myers-Briggs Type Inventory (MBTI)®
A personality assessment tool used for team building and leadership development that identifies employees' preferences for energy, information gathering, decision making, and lifestyle.

For example, CareSource, a Medicaid-managed care provider in Dayton, Ohio, has a defined process for identifying and developing employees who have the potential to be strong leaders and effective managers.[30] Assessment of fit with the organizational values and culture which emphasize serving the underserved, begins with the recruiting process. The company uses multiple assessment tools to evaluate managers' competencies (recall our discussion of competencies in Chapter 8, "Performance Management"). These assessments include the Myers-Briggs Type Indicator; the Gallup's Strength Finder to identify managers' strengths and develop plans for using their strengths with their employee team; and the Leadership Practices Inventory, which provides managers with an idea of their leadership skills as evaluated by peers, their boss, and their own self-assessment, and is used to build a personal leadership development plan. Also twice a year, using the performance management system, they are evaluated on competencies and behavior that CareSource believes are characteristics of an effective leader and manager: a service orientation, organizational awareness, teamwork, communications, and organizational leadership. Based on the assessment results, managers with high leadership potential are encouraged to participate in a variety of development activities.

Assessment Center

Assessment Center
A process in which multiple raters evaluate employees' performance on a number of exercises.

At an **assessment center** multiple raters or evaluators (assessors) evaluate employees' performance on a number of exercises.[31] An assessment center is usually an off-site location such as a conference center. From 6 to 12 employees usually participate at one time. Assessment centers are primarily used to identify if employees have the personality characteristics, administrative skills, and interpersonal skills needed for managerial jobs. They are also increasingly being used to determine if employees have the necessary skills to work in teams.

Leaderless Group Discussion
Process in which a team of five to seven employees solves an assigned problem together within a certain time period.

The types of exercises used in assessment centers include leaderless group discussions, interviews, in-baskets, and role-plays.[32] In a **leaderless group discussion**, a team of five to seven employees is assigned a problem and must work together to solve it within a certain time period. The problem may involve buying and selling supplies, nominating a subordinate for an award, or assembling a product. In the **interview**, employees answer questions about their work and personal experiences, skill strengths and weaknesses, and career plans. An **in-basket** is a simulation of the administrative tasks of the manager's job. The exercise includes a variety of documents that may appear in the in-basket on a manager's desk. The participants read the materials and decide how to respond to them. Responses might include delegating tasks, scheduling meetings, writing replies, or completely ignoring the memo! **Role-plays** refer to the participant taking the part or role of a manager or other employee. For example, an assessment center participant may be asked to take the role of a manager who has to give a negative performance review to a subordinate. The participant is told about the subordinate's performance and is asked to prepare for and actually hold a 45-minute meeting with the subordinate to discuss the performance problems. The role of the subordinate is played by a manager or other member of the assessment center design team or company. The assessment center might also include interest and aptitude tests to evaluate an employee's vocabulary, general mental ability, and reasoning skills. Personality tests may be used to determine if employees can get along with others, their tolerance for ambiguity, and other traits related to success as a manager.

Interview
Employees are questioned about their work and personal experiences, skills, and career plans.

In-Basket
A simulation of the administrative tasks of a manager's job.

Role-Plays
A participant taking the part or role of a manager or other employee.

Assessment center exercises are designed to measure employees' administrative and interpersonal skills. Skills typically measured include leadership, oral and written communication, judgment, organizational ability, and stress tolerance. Table 9.4 shows an example of the skills measured by the assessment center. As we see, each exercise gives participating employees the opportunity to demonstrate several different skills. For example, the exercise requiring scheduling to meet production demands evaluates employees' administrative and problem-solving ability. The leaderless group discussion measures interpersonal skills such as sensitivity toward others, stress tolerance, and oral communication skills.

Managers are usually used as assessors. The managers are trained to look for employee behaviors that are related to the skills that will be assessed. Typically, each assessor observes and records one or two employees' behaviors in each exercise. The assessors review their notes and rate each employee's level of skills (for example, 5 = high level of leadership skills, 1 = low level of leadership skills). After all employees have completed the exercises, the assessors discuss their observations of each employee. They compare their ratings and try to agree on each employee's rating for each of the skills.

As we mentioned in Chapter 6, research suggests that assessment center ratings are related to performance, salary level, and career advancement.[33] Assessment centers may also be useful for development because employees who participate in the process receive feedback regarding their attitudes, skill strengths, and weaknesses.[34] For example, Steelcase, the office furniture manufacturer based in Grand Rapids, Michigan, uses assessment centers for first-level managers.[35] The assessment center exercises include in-basket, interview simulation, and a timed scheduling exercise requiring participants to fill positions created by absences. Managers are also required to confront an employee on a performance issue, getting the employee to commit to improve. Because the exercises relate closely to what managers are required to do at work, feedback given to managers

Table 9.4

Examples of Skills Measured by Assessment Center Exercises

		EXERCISES			
	IN-BASKET	SCHEDULING EXERCISE	LEADERLESS GROUP DISCUSSION	PERSONALITY TEST	ROLE-PLAY
SKILLS					
Leadership (Dominance, coaching, influence, resourcefulness)	X		X	X	X
Problem solving (Judgment)	X	X	X		X
Interpersonal (Sensitivity, conflict resolution, cooperation, oral communication)			X	X	X
Administrative (Organizing, planning, written communications)	X	X	X		
Personal (Stress tolerance, confidence)			X	X	X

X indicates skill measured by exercise.

based on their performance in the assessment center can target specific skills or competencies that they need to be successful managers.

Performance Appraisals and 360-Degree Feedback Systems

As we mentioned in Chapter 8, **performance appraisal** is the process of measuring employees' performance. Performance appraisal information can be useful for employee development under certain conditions.[36] The appraisal system must tell employees specifically about their performance problems and how they can improve their performance. This includes providing a clear understanding of the differences between current performance and expected performance, identifying causes of the performance discrepancy, and developing action plans to improve performance. Managers must be trained in frequent performance feedback. Managers also need to monitor employees' progress in carrying out action plans.

Recall our discussion in Chapter 8 of how Just Born uses performance appraisals for evaluation and development.[37] The appraisal starts with a planning meeting between employee and manager. The strategic initiatives of the department are discussed along with the employee's role. The employee and manager agree on four personal objectives that will help the department reach its goals as well as key performance outcomes related to the employee's job description. Competencies the employee needs to reach the personal objectives are identified. The manager and employee jointly develop a plan for improving or learning the competencies. During the year, the manager and employee monitor the progress toward reaching the performance and personal objectives and achievement of the learning plan. Pay decisions made at the end of each year are based on the achievement of both performance and learning objectives.

A recent trend in performance appraisals for management development is the use of upward feedback and 360-degree feedback. **Upward feedback** refers to appraisal that involves collecting subordinates' evaluations of managers' behaviors or skills. The 360-degree feedback process is a special case of upward feedback. In **360-degree feedback systems**, employees' behaviors or skills are evaluated not only by subordinates but by peers, customers, their bosses, and themselves. The raters complete a questionnaire asking them to rate the person on a number of different dimensions. Table 9.5 provides an example of the types of skills related to management success that are rated in a 360-degree feedback questionnaire. Typically, raters are asked to assess the manager's strength in a particular item or whether development is needed. Raters may also be asked to identify how frequently they observe a competency or skill (e.g., always, sometimes, seldom, never).

The results of a 360-degree feedback system show how the manager was rated on each item. The results also show how self-evaluations differ from evaluations from the other raters. Typically managers review their results, seek clarification from the raters, and set specific development goals based on the strengths and weaknesses identified.[38] Table 9.6 shows the type of activities involved in using 360-degree feedback for development.[39]

The benefits of 360-degree feedback include collecting multiple perspectives of managers' performance, allowing employees to compare their own personal evaluations with the views of others, and formalizing communications about behaviors and skills ratings between employees and their internal and external customers. Several studies have shown that performance improves and behavior changes as a result of participating in upward feedback and 360-degree feedback systems.[40] The most change occurs in individuals who receive lower ratings from others than they gave themselves (overraters).

Table 9.5
Skills Related to Managerial Success

Resourcefulness	Can think strategically, engage in flexible problem solving, and work effectively with higher management.
Doing whatever it takes	Has perseverance and focus in the face of obstacles.
Being a quick study	Quickly masters new technical and business knowledge.
Building and mending relationships	Knows how to build and maintain working relationships with co-workers and external parties.
Leading subordinates	Delegates to subordinates effectively, broadens their opportunities, and acts with fairness toward them.
Compassion and sensitivity	Shows genuine interest in others and sensitivity to subordinates' needs.
Straightforwardness and composure	Is honorable and steadfast.
Setting a developmental climate	Provides a challenging climate to encourage subordinates' development.
Confronting problem subordinates	Acts decisively and fairly when dealing with problem subordinates.
Team orientation	Accomplishes tasks through managing others.
Balance between personal life and work	Balances work priorities with personal life so that neither is neglected.
Decisiveness	Prefers quick and approximate actions to slow and precise ones in many management situations.
Self-awareness	Has an accurate picture of strengths and weaknesses and is willing to improve.
Hiring talented staff	Hires talented people for the team.
Putting people at ease	Displays warmth and a good sense of humor.
Acting with flexibility	Can behave in ways that are often seen as opposites.

SOURCE: Adapted with permission from C. D. McCauley, M. M. Lombardo, and C. J. Usher, "Diagnosing Management Development Needs: An Instrument Based on How Managers Develop," *Journal of Management* 15 (1989), pp. 389–403.

Table 9.6
Activities in Using 360-Degree Feedback for Development

1. **Understand strengths and weaknesses.**
   Review ratings for strengths and weaknesses.
   Identify skills or behaviors where self and others' (manager, peer, customer) ratings agree and disagree.
2. **Identify a development goal.**
   Choose a skill or behavior to develop.
   Set a clear, specific goal with a specified outcome.
3. **Identify a process for recognizing goal accomplishment.**
4. **Identify strategies for reaching the development goal.**
   Establish strategies such as reading, job experiences, courses, and relationships.
   Establish strategies for receiving feedback on progress.
   Establish strategies for reinforcing the new skill or behavior.

Potential limitations of 360-degree feedback include the time demands placed on the raters to complete the evaluations, managers seeking to identify and punish raters who provided negative information, the need to have a facilitator help interpret results, and companies' failure to provide ways that managers can act on the feedback they receive (development planning, meeting with raters, taking courses).

In effective 360-degree feedback systems, reliable or consistent ratings are provided, raters' confidentiality is maintained, the behaviors or skills assessed are job-related (valid), the system is easy to use, and managers receive and act on the feedback.[41]

Technology allows 360-degree questionnaires to be delivered online to the raters. This increases the number of completed questionnaires returned, makes it easier to process the information, and speeds feedback reports to managers.

Regardless of the assessment method used, the information must be shared with the employee for development to occur. Along with assessment information, the employee needs suggestions for correcting skill weaknesses and using skills already learned. These suggestions might be to participate in training courses or develop skills through new job experiences. Based on the assessment information and available development opportunities, employees should develop action plans to guide their self-improvement efforts.

At AlliedBarton Security Systems, its 360-degree feedback report maps onto the company's core values and what it calls its Leadership Non-Negotiables.[42] The process is linked to an online talent tool kit which gives managers leadership tips based on their 360-degree feedback. The CEO of Food4Less sought 360-degree feedback from his executive on his leadership skills.[43] After receiving the report of his results he met with his executive team to share what he learned, to thank them for their feedback, and to publicly commit to working on several key areas identified in the assessment. Following the CEO's lead, each member of his executive team also participated in a 360-degree assessment of their leadership skills. St. Joseph's Hospital and Medical Center is a nonprofit hospital that provides a wide range of health, social, and support services.[44] St. Joseph's has transitioned from a local community hospital to a research-based hospital with nationally recognized programs in selected fields of medicine. This meant recruiting and adding new physicians, some of whom have significant leadership responsibilities over departments, faculty, and resident physicians. St. Joseph's used 360-degree feedback to identify, measure, and emphasize those competencies necessary for these leaders. St. Joseph's developed the 360-degree assessment with a consulting firm. Based on the 360-degree assessments, one-on-one coaching was provided to give the hospital leaders insights into how to develop their competencies.

JOB EXPERIENCES

LO 9-6
Explain how job experiences can be used for skill development.

Job Experiences
The relationships, problems, demands, tasks, and other features that employees face in their jobs.

Most employee development occurs through **job experiences**:[45] relationships, problems, demands, tasks, or other features that employees face in their jobs. A major assumption of using job experiences for employee development is that development is most likely to occur when employees are given stretch assignments. **Stretch assignments** refer to assignments in which there is a mismatch between the employee's skills and past experiences and the skills required for success on the job. To succeed in their jobs, employees must stretch their skills—that is, they are forced to learn new skills, apply their skills and knowledge in a new way, and master new experiences.[46] New job assignments help take advantage of employees' existing skills, experiences, and contacts, while helping them develop new ones.[47] Job experiences are used for development in companies of all sizes but their type and availability vary.[48] Large companies such as HCA Inc. with 195,000 employees in the health care business have the ability to provide high potential employees with many different kinds of developmental experiences. For example, an administrator can begin working in a position in a smaller heath care facility, and then move to a larger facility including a hospital or heath care business. Smaller companies might not have the same type or number of development experiences at work, but can encourage employees to get relevant experiences outside of work. For example, the CEO at Pitney Bowes learned a lot about conflict management through his role as vice president of his homeowners association. Regardless of the size of the company, for job experiences to be an effective development activity they should be tailored to employees' development needs and goals.

Most of what we know about development through job experiences comes from a series of studies conducted by the Center for Creative Leadership.[49] Executives were asked to identify key career events that made a difference in their managerial styles and the lessons they learned from these experiences. The key events included those involving the job assignment (such as fixing a failing operation), those involving interpersonal relationships (getting along with supervisors), and the specific type of transition required (situations in which the executive did not have the necessary background). The job demands and what employees can learn from them are shown in Table 9.7.

One concern in the use of demanding job experiences for employee development is whether they are viewed as positive or negative stressors. Job experiences that are seen as positive stressors challenge employees to stimulate learning. Job challenges viewed as negative stressors create high levels of harmful stress for employees exposed to them. Recent research findings suggest that all of the job demands, with the exception of obstacles, are related to learning.[50] Managers reported that obstacles and job demands related to creating change were more likely to lead to negative stress than the other job demands. This suggests that companies should carefully weigh the potential negative consequences before placing employees in development assignments involving obstacles or creating change.

Stretch Assignments
Job assignments in which there is a mismatch between an employee's skills and past experiences and the skills required for success on the job.

Job Demands	What Employees Can Learn
Transitions	Handling responsibilities that are new, different, or broader than those in previous job
Change	Developing new strategic direction, reorganizing, growing or reducing staff, or responding to rapid change; dealing with poor performing employees
High Level of Responsibility	Making highly visible and important decisions that impact the business; managing multiple groups, functions, products, or departments; dealing with external stakeholders such as unions, government agencies, local politicians
Nonauthority Relationships	Getting work done by influencing persons over whom you have no direct authority such as peers, boss, and external stakeholders
Obstacles	Coping and succeeding despite adverse business conditions, a lack of top management or peer support and encouragement, or working with a boss who has poor management skills or a different management stylem

Table 9.7
Job Demands and What Employees Can Learn From Them

SOURCE: C. D. McCauley, L. J. Eastman, and J. Ohlott, "Linking Management Selection and Development through Stretch Assignments," *Human Resource Management* 84 (1995), pp. 93–115. Copyright © 1995 Wiley Periodicals, Inc., a Wiley Company.

Although the research on development through job experiences has focused on executives and managers, line employees can also learn from job experiences. As we noted earlier, for a work team to be successful, its members now need the kinds of skills that only managers were once thought to need (such as dealing directly with customers, analyzing data to determine product quality, and resolving conflict among team members). Besides the development that occurs when a team is formed, employees can further develop their skills by switching work roles within the team.

Figure 9.4 shows the various ways that job experiences can be used for employee development. These include enlarging the current job, job rotation, transfers, promotions, downward moves, and temporary assignments. For companies with global operations (multinationals), it is not uncommon for employee development to involve international assignments that require frequent travel or relocation. The "Competing through Sustainability" box describes how less-experienced lawyers are developing skills through pro bono work in the community.

Enlarging the Current Job

Job Enlargement
Adding challenges or new responsibilities to an employee's current job.

Job enlargement refers to adding challenges or new responsibilities to employees' current jobs. This could include special project assignments, switching roles within a work team, or researching new ways to serve clients and customers. For example, an engineering employee may join a task force developing new career paths for technical employees. Through this project work, the engineer may lead certain aspects of career path development (such as reviewing the company's career development process). As a result, the engineer not only learns about the company's career development system, but uses leadership and organizational skills to help the task force reach its goals. Some companies are enlarging jobs by giving two managers the same responsibilities and job title

Figure 9.4

How Job Experiences Are Used for Employee Development

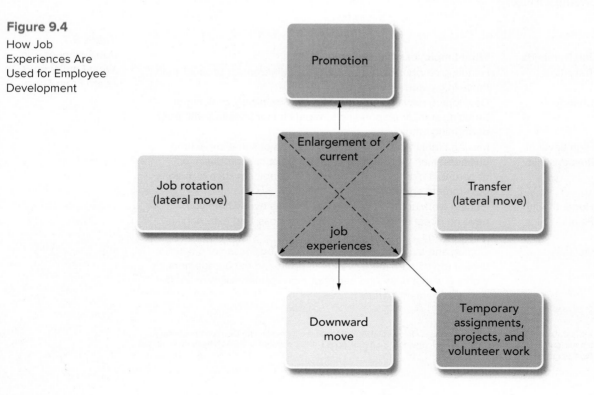

Legal Representation Benefits the Community and Associates' Skills

Like their counterparts at other legal firms, junior, less-experienced lawyers at Sidley Austin learn about the trial process through traditional development methods like reading books and cases, conducting mock depositions and trials, and observing more senior lawyers in the courtroom. But then they do pro bono work (work for no pay) in which they serve disadvantaged clients in one of the 18 communities where Sidley Austin has offices.

Pro bono work is especially valuable for developing the firm's associates because they get to work through an actual case from the beginning to the end, participating in each step. For example, junior associates can get experience putting witnesses on the stand or cross-examining them. Also, they can expand their personal network and the firm's knowledge by working on immigration or custody cases that the firm doesn't typically deal with in its for-profit business. The firm tracks each associate's skills and experiences regardless of whether they were developed in a pro bono case or a client paying regular fees. Besides developing skills, working on pro bono cases helps associates feel satisfied with their work because they have made a difference in their clients' lives, and the firm gets positive recognition for supporting the community. The pro bono casework often motivates associates to become board members or fundraisers for the community service organizations whose clients they represent.

DISCUSSION QUESTIONS

1. Job demands help employees stretch their skills. What job demands does pro bono work present to inexperienced lawyers?
2. What should Sidley Austin do to ensure that job demands are not too stressful and overwhelming for the junior lawyers?

SOURCE: Based on K. Everson, "Sidley Austin Harnesses Pro Bono Experience," *Chief Learning Officer*, December 2014, pp. 64–65.

and allowing them to divide the work (two-in-a-box).[51] This helps managers learn from a more experienced employee; helps companies fill jobs that require multiple skills; and, for positions requiring extensive travel, ensures that one employee is always on site to deal with work-related issues. For example, at Cisco Systems, the head of the Cisco routing group, who was trained as an engineer but now works in business development, shared a job with an engineer. Each employee was exposed to the other's skills, which has helped both perform their jobs better.

Job Rotation and Lateral Moves

Job rotation gives employees a series of job assignments in various functional areas of the company or movement among jobs in a single functional area or department. Job rotation involves a planned sequence of jobs that the employee is expected to hold, while lateral moves may not necessarily involve a predetermined sequence of jobs or positions. For example, at AT&T, 40% of the company's managers made a lateral move in 2013.[52] In her 11-year career at AT&T, one manager has held six different positions, and she never had the same title for more than three years. In her last position she was in charge of hiring, reporting to executives, and training and supporting all sellers located in her region. Now, she has taken a position as a director of call centers. This position has a greater scope and more responsibilities than her previous position (she oversees about 1,700 employees). At Stryker Orthopaedics the sales department allows employees the opportunity to experience five different functional

Job Rotation
The process of systematically moving a single individual from one job to another over the course of time. The job assignments may be in various functional areas of the company or movement may be between jobs in a single functional area or department.

areas with sales so that employees can decide which areas they might be most interested in working in.[53]

Job rotation helps employees gain an overall appreciation of the company's goals, increases their understanding of different company functions, develops a network of contacts, and increases their skills.[54] To attract and retain Millennials, General Motors uses internships and functional job rotation programs to give them responsibility for real jobs and projects and to help them explore career paths.[55] At TJX, retailer of off-price clothes and home fashions, buyers need to understand consumer and fashion trends and develop relationships with vendors.[56] Buyers' training includes classroom instruction on topics such as finance so they understand the results of their buying decisions and mentoring with more experienced buyers. After completing the training they spend time in the planning organization, which allocates merchandise to stores. The last step in becoming a buyer is to move between departments, brands, and locations, which exposes them to different parts of the business. The moves include both U.S. and international locations, which help them gain global experience. Working in different parts of the business helps the buyers develop their communications and negotiation skills and gain confidence in their buying decisions, which can involve hundreds or millions of items. Despite its advantages, there are several potential problems with job rotation for both the employee and the work unit. The rotation may cause employees to adopt a short-term perspective when problem-solving. Employees' satisfaction and motivation may be adversely affected because they find it difficult to develop functional specialties and they don't spend enough time in one position to receive a challenging assignment. Productivity losses and workload increases may be experienced by both the department gaining a rotating employee and the department losing the employee due to training demands and loss of a resource.

Transfers, Promotions, and Downward Moves

Transfer
The movement of an employee to a different job assignment in a different area of the company.

Upward, lateral, and downward mobility is available for development purposes in most companies.[57] In a **transfer**, an employee is assigned a job in a different area of the company. Transfers do not necessarily increase job responsibilities or compensation. They are likely lateral moves (a move to a job with similar responsibilities). **Promotions** are advancements into positions with greater challenges, more responsibility, and more authority than in the previous job. Promotions usually include pay increases.

Promotions
Advancement into positions with greater challenge, more responsibility, and more authority than the employee's previous job.

A **downward move** occurs when an employee is given less responsibility and authority.[58] This may involve a move to another position at the same level (lateral demotion), a temporary cross-functional move, or a demotion because of poor performance. Temporary cross-functional moves to lower-level positions, which give employees experience working in different functional areas, are most frequently used for employee development. For example, engineers who want to move into management often take lower-level positions (like shift supervisor) to develop their management skills.

Downward Move
A job change involving a reduction in an employee's level of responsibility and authority.

Because of the psychological and tangible rewards of promotions (such as increased feelings of self-worth, salary, and status in the company), employees are more willing to accept promotions than lateral or downward moves. Promotions are more readily available when a company is profitable and growing. When a company is restructuring or experiencing stable or declining profits'—especially if numerous employees are interested in promotions and the company tends to rely on the external labor market to staff higher-level positions—promotion opportunities may be limited.[59]

Transfers, job rotation, promotions, lateral moves, and downward moves may involve relocation within the United States or to another country. This can be stressful not only because the employee's work role changes, but if the employee is in a two-career family, the spouse must find new employment. Also, the family has to join a new community. Transfers disrupt employees' daily lives, interpersonal relationships, and work habits.[60] People have to find new housing, shopping, health care, and leisure facilities, and they may be many miles from the emotional support of friends and family. They also have to learn a new set of work norms and procedures; they must develop interpersonal relationships with their new managers and peers; and they are expected to be as productive in their new jobs as they were in their old jobs even though they may know little about the products, services, processes, or employees for whom they are responsible.

Because transfers can provoke anxiety, many companies have difficulty getting employees to accept them. Research has identified the employee characteristics associated with a willingness to accept transfers:[61] high career ambitions, a belief that one's future with the company is promising, and a belief that accepting a transfer is necessary for success in the company. Employees who are not married and not active in the community are generally most willing to accept transfers. Among married employees, the spouse's willingness to move is the most important influence on whether an employee will accept a transfer.

Unfortunately, many employees have difficulty associating transfers and downward moves with development. They see them as punishments rather than as opportunities to develop skills that will help them achieve long-term success with the company. Many employees decide to leave a company rather than accept a transfer. Companies need to successfully manage transfers not only because of the costs of replacing employees but because of the costs directly associated with them. For example, GTE spends approximately $60 million a year on home purchases and other relocation costs such as temporary housing and relocation allowances.[62] One challenge companies face is learning how to use transfers and downward moves as development opportunities—convincing employees that accepting these opportunities will result in long-term benefits for them.

To ensure that employees accept transfers, promotions, and downward moves as development opportunities, companies can provide

- Information about the content, challenges, and potential benefits of the new job and location.
- Involvement in the transfer decision by sending the employees to preview the new location and giving them information about the community.
- Clear performance objectives and early feedback about their job performance.
- A host at the new location to help them adjust to the new community and workplace.
- Information about how the job opportunity will affect their income, taxes, mortgage payments, and other expenses.
- Reimbursement and assistance in selling and purchasing or renting a place to live.
- An orientation program for the new location and job.
- Information on how the new job experiences will support the employee's career plans.
- Assistance for dependent family members, including identifying schools and child care and elder care options.
- Help for the spouse in identifying and marketing skills and finding employment.[63]

Temporary Assignments, Projects, Volunteer Work, and Sabbaticals

Temporary assignments refer to job tryouts such as employees taking on a position to help them determine if they are interested in working in a new role, employee exchanges, sabbaticals, and voluntary assignments. All temporary assignments have a predetermined ending

Temporary Assignments
Job tryouts such as employees taking on a position to help them determine if they are interested in working in a new role.

date after which the employees return to their permanent position. For example, Mondelez International, a snack company with 100,000 employees, wanted to help its managers learn about how to market its products using mobile devices. For several days, they sent their managers to nine small mobile-technology companies to help them gain an understanding of their entrepreneurial spirit and how quickly these companies generated ideas and built and tested prototypes of new marketing efforts.[64] An associate brand manager from PepsiCo's New York headquarters spent a week at Airbnb, a San Francisco–based start-up online travel rental business with only 200 employees. Managers from the two companies hoped to learn from each other's brand management practices. Both companies have casual, collaborative work environments. But compared to PepsiCo brand management, Airbnb's brand management is based more on instinct than on data analysis and the ideas of marketing agencies. Marketing managers at Airbnb were interested in learning about how PepsiCo built data sets of market research. To develop a broad understanding of the business, directors at Genentech Inc. spend 10% of their time over six to nine months in a different function working on special projects, participating in task forces, and shadowing business leaders.[65]

Employee exchange is another type of temporary assignment. Procter & Gamble (P&G) and Google have swapped employees.[66] Employees from the two companies participate in each other's training programs and attend meetings where business plans are discussed. Both companies hope to benefit from the employee swap. Procter & Gamble is trying to increase its understanding of how to market laundry detergent, toilet paper, and skin cream products to a new generation of consumers who spend more time online than watching television. Google wants to gain more ad revenue by persuading companies to shift from showcasing their brands on television to video-sharing sites such as YouTube.

Sabbatical
A leave of absence from the company for personal reflection, renewal, and skill development.

Temporary assignments can include a **sabbatical**. A sabbatical refers to a leave of absence from the company for personal reflection, renewal, and skill development. Employees on sabbatical often receive full pay and benefits. Sabbaticals let employees get away from the day-to-day stresses of their jobs and acquire new skills and perspectives. Sabbaticals also allow employees more time for personal pursuits such as writing a book or spending more time with young children. Sabbaticals are common in a variety of industries ranging from consulting firms to the fast-food industry.[67] They typically range from four to 10 weeks. Sabbaticals can involve travel, finishing a degree or other learning opportunities, donating time to charity, working on research or new product development, or working on a "green" cause. Birchbox Inc., an online beauty business, gives employees a three-week sabbatical after they work for the company for three years.[68] Birchbox employees have an unlimited vacation policy, but they were reluctant to take off work for more than one week. After taking the three week sabbatical employees returned to work refreshed, and less-experienced employees learned new skills filling in for them.

Volunteer assignments can also be used for development. Volunteer assignments may give employees opportunities to manage change, teach, have a high level of responsibility, and be exposed to other job demands shown earlier in Table 9.7. For General Mills, volunteer assignments and involvement with community projects is one of the ways the company lives its corporate values.[69] Employees work in a wide variety of charities, with duties ranging from serving meals to the homeless, painting child care center rooms, or serving as corporate board members. Besides providing valuable services to community organizations, General Mills believes volunteer assignments help employees improve team relationships and develop leadership and strategic thinking skills.

INTERPERSONAL RELATIONSHIPS

LO 9-7
Develop successful mentoring programs.

Employees can also develop skills and increase their knowledge about the company and its customers by interacting with a more experienced organization member. Mentoring and coaching are two types of interpersonal relationships that are used to develop employees.

Mentoring

A **mentor** is an experienced, productive senior employee who helps develop a less experienced employee (the protégé). Because of the lack of potential mentors, and recognizing that employees can benefit from relationships with peers and colleagues, some companies have initiated and supported group and peer mentoring.

Most mentoring relationships develop informally as a result of interests or values shared by the mentor and protégé. Research suggests that employees with certain personality characteristics (like emotional stability, the ability to adapt their behavior based on the situation, and high needs for power and achievement) are most likely to seek a mentor and be an attractive protégé for a mentor.[70] Mentoring relationships can also develop as part of a formal mentoring program, that is, a planned company effort to bring together successful senior employees with less experienced employees. Table 9.8 shows examples of how companies are using formal mentoring programs. Mentoring programs have many important purposes including socializing new employees, developing managers, and providing opportunities for women and minorities to share experiences and gain the exposure and skills needed to move into management positions.

Mentor
An experienced, productive senior employee who helps develop a less experienced employee.

Table 9.8
Examples of Mentoring Programs

SCC Soft Computer—Every new hire is assigned a mentor. The mentor creates a personalized learning passport including the new employee's photo and identifies the competency areas the new hire needs to develop. After identifying the competency the mentor is responsible for, the mentor follows up with the employee. When the employee's personal learning passport is complete they are eligible for advancement.

Microsoft—The mentoring program includes career development mentoring and peer mentoring. Career development mentoring focuses on career and professional development through structured, year-long cross-group mentoring. Peer mentoring is less structured and focuses on transfer of work-related knowledge among members of the same work team.

The Sacramento Municipal Utility District (SMUD)—Includes a one-year mentoring program in its Building Leadership Talent program. The program matches protégés with mentors who are outside their business unit. SMUD provides an orientation and half-day session for the mentors that includes skill building, role-playing, a process model for effective mentoring, templates for documenting goals and progress toward meeting the goals, skill practice, and web-based training.

Sodexo—Peer-to-peer mentoring is a program managed directly by Sodexo's Network Groups. Networks are organized around a common dimension of diversity and are created by employees who want to raise awareness in Sodexo of their identity groups. They include network groups based on national orientation, race, sexual preference, military service, and intergenerations. The Spirit of Mentoring Bridge Programs are informal divisional pairings in which newly hired and front-line managers come together to expand professional development opportunities and increase the depth and diversity of Sodexo's management.

Agilent Technologies—The Next Generation Leadership Program accelerates development for top talent by matching senior executives with high potential.

McDonald's—Offers a virtual online mentoring program that employees can use to build their skill sets and develop relationships.

Aditya Birla Minacs—The Altitude program is a career progression program designed to support front-line staff transition to a team leader role. Program outcomes include self-identified action items that the staff intends to complete to aid their career progression. Mentor Magic is a program in which successful supervisors based on their experience and performance mentor front-line staff on the action items.

SOURCES: Based on "Training Top 125: Aditya Birla Minacs," *Training,* January/February 2014, p. 101; www.sodexousa.com, website for Sodexo, Inc.; "Best Practices and Outstanding Initiatives," *Training,* January/February 2011, pp. 94–98; "Training Top 125," *Training,* January/February 2011, pp. 54–93; R. Emelo, "Conversations with Mentoring Leaders," *T + D,* June 2011, pp. 32–37.

Developing Successful Mentoring Programs. One major advantage of formalized mentoring programs is that they ensure access to mentors for all employees, regardless of gender or race. An additional advantage is that participants in the mentoring relationship know what is expected of them.[71] One limitation of formal mentoring programs is that mentors may not be able to provide counseling and coaching in a relationship that has been artificially created.[72] To overcome this limitation, it is important that mentors and protégés spend time discussing work styles, their personalities, and their backgrounds, which helps build the trust needed for both parties to be comfortable with their relationship.[73] Toshiba America Medical Systems doesn't have a formal mentoring program. However, Toshiba encourages informal mentoring from the first day employees are hired. Both managers and HR business partners take the time to help new employees meet their colleagues and show them around the workplace.[74]

Table 9.9 presents the characteristics of a successful formal mentoring program. Mentors should be chosen based on interpersonal and technical skills. They also need to be trained.[75] For mentors, protégés, and the company to get the most out of mentoring, tools and support are needed.[76] A key to successful mentoring programs is that the mentor and protégé are well-matched and can interact with each other face-to-face, virtually, or using social media.

EVIDENCE-BASED HR

A mentoring program for new regional sales managers at SAP, a global business software company, has many characteristics of a successful mentoring program. The mentoring program helps new sales managers understand company resources, identify experts to add to their sales network, assimilate into the company culture, and practice discovering clients, account plans, and presentations. Mentors track protégés' progress on sales plans, customer and prospective customer meetings, and closed deals. Mentors first interact with their protégés, new regional sales managers, when they accept their employment offer. The six-month mentoring program initially focuses on support for using sales tools and processes and learning the company culture. Next, territory planning, account prioritization, and internal and external network building are emphasized. Mentors are certified by the International Coaching Federation. They use a learning path designed to direct the new manager to training courses, job experience, and informal learning opportunities that match their needs. The mentors and new managers use social collaboration tools to share best practices, discuss challenges, and provide support to each other. Mentors use different types of data so they are prepared to meet each new manager's needs. They review their resume to determine the types of courses or personal support that may be helpful. Also, mentors review customer reports for each manager to track their progress and identify points of emphasis during their weekly discussions. A study comparing new sales managers who were mentored with those who were not found that mentored managers have more than a 300% improvement in closed sales deals, more than three times made quota, and turnover was down 80%.

SOURCE: Based on J. Dearborn, "Sinking Fast," *T + D*, December 2013, pp. 44–47.

Web-based matching systems are also available to help match mentors and protégés. Software is also available to track mentors' and protégés' work, help build development plans, and schedule mentor and protégé meetings.[77] For example, at Cartus, a relocation company,

Table 9.9
Characteristics of Successful Formal Mentoring Programs

1. Mentor and protégé participation is voluntary. Relationship can be ended at any time without fear of punishment.
2. The mentor–protégé matching process does not limit the ability of informal relationships to develop. For example, a mentor pool can be established to allow protégés to choose from a variety of qualified mentors.
3. Mentors are chosen on the basis of their past record in developing employees, willingness to serve as a mentor, and evidence of positive coaching, communication, and listening skills.
4. Mentor–protégé matching is based on how the mentor's skills can help meet the protégé's needs.
5. The purpose of the program is clearly understood. Projects and activities that the mentor and protégé are expected to complete are specified.
6. The length of the program is specified. Mentor and protégé are encouraged to pursue the relationship beyond the formal period.
7. A minimum level of contact between the mentor and protégé is specified. Mentors and protégés need to determine when they will meet, how often, and how they will communicate outside the meetings.
8. Protégés are encouraged to contact one another to discuss problems and share successes.
9. The mentor program is evaluated. Interviews with mentors and protégés give immediate feedback regarding specific areas of dissatisfaction. Surveys gather more detailed information regarding benefits received from participating in the program.
10. Employee development is rewarded, which signals to managers that mentoring and other development activities are worth their time and effort.

employees who are interested in being either a mentor or protégé can apply to participate in a mentoring program. Employees provide a profile of their interests, expertise, and experiences. Software matches mentors and protégés based on the profiles. Six months after the mentoring relationship is started, the software prompts them to report their progress.

Benefits of Mentoring Relationships. Both mentors and protégés can benefit from a mentoring relationship. Research suggests that mentors provide career and psycho-social support to their protégés. **Career support** includes coaching, protection, sponsorship, and providing challenging assignments, exposure, and visibility. **Psychosocial support** includes serving as a friend and a role model, providing positive regard and acceptance, and creating an outlet for the protégé to talk about anxieties and fears. Additional benefits for the protégé include higher rates of promotion, higher salaries, and greater organizational influence.[78]

Mentoring relationships provide opportunities for mentors to develop their interpersonal skills and increase their feelings of self-esteem and worth to the organization. For individuals in technical fields such as engineering or health services, the protégé may help them gain knowledge about important new scientific developments in their field (and therefore prevent them from becoming technically obsolete). Tamara Trummer summarizes some of the benefits she gained from mentoring relationships: "I found mentors in two of my earlier companies, both male and female managers who 'taught me the ropes' in an informal sense by giving me inside information about the company, certain executives—and even such practical things as how to conduct business travel and handle an expense account."[79] One mentor arranged for her to travel from the remote manufacturing plant where she worked to the corporate office and set up meetings to meet key employees she would have to work with. Her mentors have also included co-workers, peers, and even subordinates who have taught her computer software skills. As a result of her positive experiences as a protégé Trummer now mentors others employees.

Career Support
Coaching, protection, sponsorship, and providing challenging assignments, exposure, and visibility.

Psychosocial Support
Serving as a friend and role model, providing positive regard and acceptance, and creating an outlet for a protégé to talk about anxieties and fears.

Reverse Mentoring
Business situation in which younger employees mentor more senior employees.

Reverse mentoring refers to mentoring in which younger employees mentor more senior employees. For example, approximately 100 employees have been involved in reverse mentoring at MasterCard.[80] In one of the relationships, a 24-year-old with two years' experience in digital communications was paired as a mentor with a 50-year-old executive. The executive wanted to learn how to use social media to relate better to MasterCard's Millennial employees and customers and to refocus the company's image to a technology company rather than a credit card company. A reverse mentoring program at Hartford Financial Services Group led to benefits for mentors, protégés, and the company. The program led to changing rules to allow employees to use social media for work and more executives using an internal social network. Mentors filed a patent application on how online public safety data might be used by insurance underwriters to assess risks. Also, within a year of participating in the program, almost all of the mentors were promoted.

Mentoring can also occur between mentors and protégés from different organizations. Websites such as Everwise are available to help find online mentors. For example, Amy Dobler wanted to enhance her career at Jive Software so she went online and was matched with Edel Keville, a human resources vice president at Levi Strauss & Company.[81] Using Everwise, she completed an online questionnaire about her personality, education, career path, and personal goals. Both women had similar personalities and career paths in human resources and technology. After the online match, an Everwise relationship manager personally introduced the two women. The advice, guidance, and support that Dobler received from Keville in the mentoring relationship over a few months helped her gain confidence needed to present to senior managers, lead international training sessions, and improve her delegation skills.

Coaching

LO 9-8
Describe how to train managers to coach employees.

Coach
A peer or manager who works with an employee to motivate her, help her develop skills, and provide reinforcement and feedback.

A **coach** is a peer or manager who works with an employee to motivate him, help him develop skills, and provide reinforcement and feedback. There are three roles that a coach can play.[82] Part of coaching may be one-on-one with an employee (such as giving feedback). Another role is to help employees learn for themselves. This involves helping them find experts who can assist them with their concerns and teaching them how to obtain feedback from others. Third, coaching may involve providing resources such as mentors, courses, or job experiences that the employee may not be able to gain access to without the coach's help.

Consider how Walgreens, PwC, and University Hospitals use coaching.[83] Coaching sessions are part of Walgreens' executive development program. Executives meet for nine days of formal learning that includes face-to-face instruction, discussion, team building exercises, and action learning projects. They also are encouraged during and after the program to share ideas and get involved in discussions on Walgreens' social collaboration site. Each executive is involved in six coaching sessions, which reinforce learning and support their individual development. PwC's leadership development program "Discover" focuses on newly promoted senior associates increasing their skills in making effective decisions. Senior associates are typically struggling to balance careers with family, community and personal choices. The goals of the program are to help participants maximize their personal energy, clarify their values, identify their focus, and make conscious rather than reactive decisions. In the Explore phase of the program, participants complete pre-work assignments such as "Discover Your Values" and discuss the results with life coaches. Participants work with the coaches to create "Who Am I?" stories. At University Hospitals coaching is used as part of an executive development program designed for physician and functional leaders. The participants receive one-on-one coaching and also become certified coaches themselves. This allows them in the future to serve as formal coaches for other potential leaders. The one-on-one coaching they receive emphasizes discovering their ideal self, understanding their real self, creating a learning agenda, experimenting with new behaviors, and leveraging trusting relationships. It uses 360-feedback to help them recognize differences between their real self and ideal self and prepare a learning agenda to narrow this gap using new behaviors and personal relationships.

Research suggests that coaching helps managers improve by identifying areas for improvement and setting goals.[84] Getting results from a coaching relationship can take at least six months of weekly or monthly meetings. To be effective, a coach generally conducts an assessment, asks questions that challenge the employee to think deeply about his or her goals and motives, helps the employee create an action plan, and follows up regularly to help the employee stay on track. Employees contribute to the success of coaching when they persevere in practicing the behaviors identified in the action plan.[85]

Special Issues in Employee Development

MELTING THE GLASS CEILING

A major development issue facing companies today is how to get women and minorities into upper-level management positions—how to melt the **glass ceiling**. Surveys show that in Fortune 500 companies women represent less than 3% of CEOs and approximately 18% of executive officers.[86] Two-thirds of companies lack specific programs targeted at the needs of women leaders. Twenty-three percent of companies offer some activities or programs targeted to the needs of women. These activities include flexible scheduling, diversity recruiting, and coaching and mentoring. One of the dilemmas is that companies may be reluctant to treat women any differently than men from a leadership development perspective despite acknowledging that women lack executive sponsors or mentors, have insufficient experience, and need better work/life balance. This barrier may be due to stereotypes or company systems that adversely affect the development of women or minorities.[87] The glass ceiling is likely caused by lack of access to training programs, appropriate developmental job experiences, and developmental relationships (such as mentoring).[88] For example, Mary Barra made history when she became the first woman chief executive officer of global carmaker, General Motors.[89] Prior to becoming CEO, Barra was in a product development job, an operational job critical to the company's success. But 55% of women are in functional roles such as lawyers, chief of finance, or human resources, which may not put them in the career path needed to become a CEO. Women and minorities often have trouble finding mentors because of their lack of access to the "old boy network," managers' preference to interact with other managers of similar status rather than with line employees, and intentional exclusion by managers who have negative stereotypes about women's and minorities' abilities, motivation, and job preferences.[90] Research has found no gender differences in access to job experiences involving transitions or creating change.[91] However, male managers receive significantly more assignments involving high levels of responsibility (high stakes, managing business diversity, handling external pressure) and appreciation for their contributions than female managers of similar ability and managerial level. Also, female managers report experiencing more challenge due to lack of personal support (a type of job demand considered to be an obstacle that has been found to relate to harmful stress) and appreciation for their contributions than male managers. Career encouragement from peers and senior managers does help women advance to the higher

LO 9-9
Discuss what companies are doing for melting the glass ceiling.

Glass Ceiling
A barrier to advancement to higher-level jobs in the company that adversely affects women and minorities. The barrier may be due to lack of access to training programs, development experiences, or relationships (e.g., mentoring).

Table 9.10
Recommendations for Melting the Glass Ceiling

Make sure senior management supports and is involved in the program.
Make a business case for change.
Make the change public.
Gather data on problems causing the glass ceiling using task forces, focus groups, and questionnaires.
Create awareness of how gender attitudes affect the work environment.
Force accountability through reviews of promotion rates and assignment decisions.
Promote development for all employees.

SOURCES: Based on B. Groysberg and K. Connolly, "Great Leaders Who Make the Mix Work," *Harvard Business Review,* September 2013, pp. 68–76; D. McCracken, "Winning the Talent War for Women," *Harvard Business Review,* November–December 2000, pp. 159–67.

management levels.[92] Managers making developmental assignments need to carefully consider whether gender biases or stereotypes are influencing the types of assignments given to women versus men.

Many companies are making efforts to melt the glass ceiling.[93] AstraZeneca, a biopharmaceutical company, helps develop women leaders through providing workshops, formal mentoring programs, and leadership courses. In its commercial operations, an 18-month development program is available for mid-level employees. Fifty percent of those enrolled in the development program are female. Johnson & Johnson (J&J) has more than doubled women at the corporate executive level to 33% and seen a 29% increase in the number of women senior managers. J&J has taken steps to get women into important positions they need to grow and develop to meet their career goals and to position them for top management and executive positions. J&J is willing to take risks on employees wanting to develop skills and their careers through providing stretch assignments, mentoring, and coaching. For example, early in her career a woman who is now a vice president at J&J was sent to Switzerland as part of a team to launch a new business. She also spent nine years working in manufacturing, supply chain, and planning before switching to marketing based on the support of J&J's vice president for marketing who had recognized her skills and potential. J&J also supports women's career progress by allowing them to turn down an opportunity for a leadership position, promotion, or other opportunity if other priorities, such as family, are more important at that point in time in their career. Women are not seen as uninterested in their career as a result of turning down such opportunities but are considered again when they are available. Table 9.10 provides recommendations for melting the glass ceiling and helping retain talented women.

LO 9-10
Use the 9-box grid for identifying where employees fit in a succession plan and construct appropriate development plans for them.

Succession Planning
The identification and tracking of high-potential employees capable of filling higher-level managerial positions.

SUCCESSION PLANNING

Succession planning refers to the process of identifying and tracking high-potential employees who are capable of moving into different positions in the company resulting from planned or unplanned job openings due to turnover, promotion, or business growth. **Succession planning** is often discussed when considering company's managers or top leaders but it is an important consideration for any job. Succession planning helps organizations in several different ways.[94] It requires senior management to systematically review leadership talent in the company. It ensures that top-level managerial talent is available. It provides a set of development experiences that managers must complete to be considered for top management positions; this avoids premature promotion of managers who are not ready for upper management ranks. Succession planning systems also

1. Identify what positions are included in the plan.
2. Identify the employees who are included in the plan.
3. Develop standards to evaluate positions (e.g., competencies, desired experiences, desired knowledge, developmental value).
4. Determine how employee potential will be measured (e.g., current performance and potential performance).
5. Develop the succession planning review.
6. Link the succession planning system with other human resource systems, including training and development, compensation, performance management, and staffing systems.
7. Determine what feedback is provided to employees.
8. Measure the effectiveness of the succession plan.

Table 9.11
The Process of Developing a Succession Plan

SOURCES: Based on W. Rothwell, "The Future of Succession Planning," *T + D,* September 2010, pp. 51–54; B. Dowell, "Succession Planning," in *Implementing Organizational Interventions,* ed. J. Hedge and E. Pulaskos (San Francisco: Jossey-Bass, 2002), pp. 78–109; R. Barnett and S. Davis, "Creating Greater Success in Succession Planning," *Advances in Developing Human Resources* 10 (2008), pp. 721–39.

help attract and retain managerial employees by providing them with development opportunities that they can complete if upper management is a career goal for them. **High-potential employees** are those the company believes are capable of being successful in higher-level managerial positions such as general manager of a strategic business unit, functional director (such as director of marketing), or chief executive officer (CEO).[95] High-potential employees typically complete an individual development program that involves education, executive mentoring and coaching, and rotation through job assignments. Job assignments are based on the successful career paths of the managers whom the high-potential employees are being prepared to replace. High-potential employees may also receive special assignments, such as making presentations and serving on committees and task forces.

Despite the importance of succession planning, many companies do not do it well. A recent survey found that a approximately one-third of senior-level executives were satisfied or very satisfied with their company's succession planning programs and less than one-quarter believed their company had developed a strong pool of candidates ready to fill top leadership positions.[96] The dissatisfaction with succession planning may result from the tendency to focus only on managers at the vice president level or above, failing to identify successors because they don't want to risk potential leaders leaving the company because they are discouraged and disappointed, and a short-term focus rather than a long-term process designed to develop "bench strength." **Bench strength** refers to having a pool of talented employees who are ready when needed.

Table 9.11 shows the process used to develop a succession plan.[97] The first step is to identify what positions are included in the succession plan, such as all management positions or only certain levels of management. The second step is to identify which employees are part of the succession planning system. For example, in some companies only high-potential employees are included in the succession plan. Third, the company needs to identify how positions will be evaluated. For example, will the emphasis be on competencies needed for each position or on the experiences an individual needs to have before moving into the position? Fourth, the company should identify how employee potential will be measured. That is, will employees' performance in their current jobs as well as ratings of potential be used? Will employees' position interests and career goals be considered? Fifth, the succession planning review process needs to be developed.

High-Potential Employees
Employees the company believes are capable of being successful in high-level management positions.

Bench Strength
The business strategy of having a pool of talented employees who are ready when needed to step into a new position within the organization.

Typically, succession planning reviews first involve employees' managers and human resources. A talent review could also include an overall assessment of leadership talent in the company, an identification of high-potential employees, based on their performance and potential, and a discussion of plans to keep key managers from leaving the company. Many companies use the 9-box grid for conducting the succession planning review. The **9-box grid** is a three-by-three matrix used by groups of managers and executives to compare employees within one department, function, division, or the entire company.[98] The 9-box grid is used for analysis and discussion of talent, to help formulate effective development plans and activities, and to identify talented employees who can be groomed for top-level management positions in the company. As shown in Figure 9.5 one axis of the matrix is based on an assessment of job performance. The other axis is typically labeled "potential" or "promotability." Typically, managers' assessment of performance (based on the company's performance management system) and potential influences employees' development plans. For example, as shown in Figure 9.5, "Stars" should be developed for leadership positions in the company.

For example, CHG Healthcare Services' goal was to increase the number of company leaders by 15% and reduce leaders' turnover.[99] CHG used the 9-box to identify potential leaders and develop leadership bench strength. Employees were evaluated based on their performance and potential. Employees who were identified as high performers with high potential were selected to go through a 360-degree assessment of their skills. This assessment was used in a leadership program designed specifically to develop their potential and skills to ensure they were ready for promotion. The results have been positive. Leadership turnover has decreased by one-third, internal promotion rates for leaders have increased nearly 50%, and the leader-to-employee ratio has improved 24%.

Contrast the development plans of "Stars" with employees in the other areas of the grid. The development plans for "Poor Employees" emphasize performance improvement

9-box grid
A three-by-three matrix used by groups of managers and executives to compare employees within one department, function, division, or the entire company.

Figure 9.5
Example of a 9-Box Grid

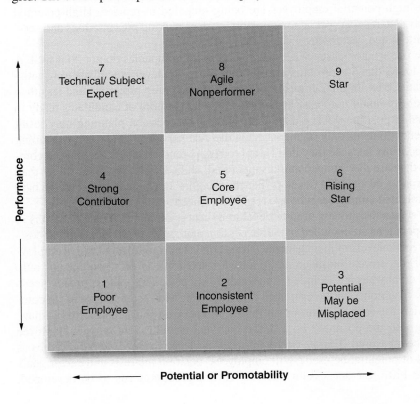

in their current position rather than getting them challenging new job experiences. If they do not improve in their current position they are likely to be fired. "Technical/Subject Experts" are outstanding performers but have low potential for leadership positions. Their development plans likely emphasize keeping their knowledge, skills, and competencies current and getting them experiences to continue to motivate them and facilitate creativity and innovation. "Potential May Be Misplaced" employees may have just taken a new position and haven't had the time to demonstrate high performance or these employees' knowledge, skills, or competencies might not match their job requirements. Their development plans might emphasize moving them to a position that best matches their skill set or if they have just moved to the job, insuring that they get the training and development opportunities and resources necessary to help them attain high performance levels. "Core Employees" are solid but not outstanding performers who have moderate potential. Development plans for these employees will include a mix of training and development designed to help insure their solid performance continues. Also, their development plans likely include some development experiences that can help grow their skills and determine their interest and ability to perform in positions requiring different skills and/or more responsibility.

Sixth, succession planning is dependent on other human resource systems, including compensation, training and development, and staffing. Incentives and bonuses may be linked to completion of development opportunities. Activities such as training courses, job experiences, mentors, and 360-degree feedback should be part of high-potential employees' development plans. Companies need to make decisions such as will they fill an open management position internally with a less-experienced employee who will improve in the role over time, or will they hire a manager from outside the company who can immediately deliver results. Seventh, employees need to be provided with feedback on future moves, expected career paths, and development goals and experiences. Finally, the succession planning process needs to be evaluated. This includes identifying and measuring appropriate results outcomes (such as reduced time to fill manager positions, increased use of internal promotions) as well as collecting measures of satisfaction with the process (reaction outcomes) from employees and managers. Also, modifications that will be made to the succession planning process need to be identified, discussed, and implemented. The "Competing through Globalization" box describes how Dow Chemical develops leaders by sending employees to work in unfamiliar environments.

Turnover is common in Valvoline Instant Oil Change's industry.[100] This means that succession planning and developing bench strength are critical for all employees. Each month managers rate all their employees on their readiness for promotion to their next job level and provide an overall evaluation of when they are ready such as "today" or "within six months." Managers work with employees on development plans designed to get them to be ready today. The development plans and evaluations are entered into an online system that allows higher-level managers to identify stores and areas where talent is not available in order to improve succession plans. Managers can identify employees, known as "blockers," who are not willing or able to develop further but are in positions that would be considered as a promotion for other employees. Succession planning has initiated a demand for training across the entire career path to ensure that assistant managers are developed as well as senior technicians who might take their jobs and new technicians who need to be ready to take on more responsibilities. Top-level managers use the online system to identify if talent is available to expand stores in a geographic area. Also, the company includes the number of managers available for promotion on their balanced scorecards, which measure company performance.

Blue Cross Blue Shield of Michigan (BCBSM) identifies and develops the company's next generation of leaders as well as talented employees.[101] Members of the executive

Dow Chemical Develops Leaders by Sending Them to Work in Unfamiliar Surroundings

As Dow Chemical expands its global presence, it needs employees who have the ability to network and develop relationships with local commercial and government leaders. Dow's leadership development program, Leadership in Action, is part of Dow's approach to meeting the world's basic needs by matching its employees with organizations that need support for sustainable development projects, especially in business growth areas for Dow. High-potential employees are organized in teams who work with nongovernment organizations on projects that meet community needs in Ethiopia, Ghana, and other countries where Dow is considering opening businesses. Some of the projects have included determining where to grow plants that could provide medicine for malaria and working with a trade school to develop education in science, technology, engineering, and math curricula.

Program participants spend five months virtually planning and collaborating from their home offices. This helps them develop their consulting skills and adapt to the unexpected such as the sudden loss of electricity or telephone service. After working virtually for five months the group travel to the host country to examine their finished projects. The team members develop skills in solving problems in a culture and community that are extremely different from the ones they are accustomed to experiencing. They focus on understanding social structures and values of the people in the communities to create meaningful, accepted, and useful solutions. They have represented Dow Chemical in news interviews, which enhanced their media relations skills and understanding of how to best represent the company.

DISCUSSION QUESTION

What are the advantages and disadvantages of the Leadership in Action program compared to more traditional ways of developing leaders such as formal courses (e.g., an MBA program) or giving them stretch assignments?

SOURCES: Based on K. Everson, "Dow Chemical's New Formula for Global Leaders," *Chief Learning Officer,* April 2015, pp. 42–43, 49; company website, "Mission & Vision" and "Leadership in Action: Ethiopia," www.dow .com, accessed April 14, 2015.

team have formal succession plans. BCBSM conducts companywide talent reviews to identify current and future skill strengths and weaknesses. BCBSM uses a 9-box grid to assess performance and potential. Management teams meet to discuss the 9-box results for their employees individually and as a group. Part of the meeting is devoted to ensuring that managers are using similar standards for evaluating employee performance and likelihood of future advancement. After the talent reviews are completed, BCBSM holds talent summits to ensure that managers across all divisions understand the company's talent, their development needs, and are aware of cross-division job openings and talent strengths and weaknesses. Supporting this process, BCBSM conducts an annual talent inventory. Employees are asked to identify their career interests and skills. This information is used in manager–employee discussions of BCBSM's talent needs, their individual development plans, career goals, and development activities.

Paychex bases succession planning on its leadership competency model.[102] Paychex uses the 9-box grid to identify leaders with high performance potential. Potential evaluations are based on agility, ability, and aspiration. Succession candidates participate in two leadership development programs. Each succession candidate develops an individual development plan. The individual development plans are designed to meet business needs and competency gaps through development activities known at Paychex as the 3Es: education, exposure, and experience. A dedicated "leadership developer" works with the employee and his or her manager to provide coaching, help with the individual development plan, and monitor progress. Last year, over 1,700 executives, senior executives, managers, and supervisors completed assessment of their leadership competencies, performance, and potential. The succession planning process has resulted in over 25% of senior managers, managers, and supervisors identified as ready for a promotion to the next level within one to two years, succession plans for all officer and senior manager positions at Paychex, and an increase of 18% in open senior management positions filled with internal candidates.

One of the important issues in succession planning is deciding whether to tell employees if they are on or off the list of potential candidates for higher-level manager positions.[103] There are several advantages and disadvantages that companies need to consider. One advantage to making a succession planning list public or telling employees who are on the list is that they are more likely to stay with the company because they understand they likely will have new career opportunities. Another is that high-potential employees who are not interested in other positions can communicate their intentions. This helps the company avoid investing costly development resources in them and allows the company to have a more accurate idea of its high-potential managerial talent. The disadvantages of identifying high-potential employees are those not on the list may become discouraged and leave the company or changes in business strategy or the employees' performance could take them off the list. Also, employees might not believe they have had a fair chance to compete for leadership positions if they already know that a list of potential candidates has been established. One way to avoid these problems is to let employees know they are on the list but not discuss a specific position they will likely reach. Another is to frequently review the list of candidates and clearly communicate plans and expectations. Managers at Midmark Corporation, a medical equipment manufacturer based in Versailles, Ohio, identify successors every six months as part of the company's performance review process and produce a potential list of candidates. Some employees are also labeled as high potential and others are identified as having high potential for leadership positions. Employees with high potential for leadership positions are considered for challenging development assignments involving overseas relocation. Using interviews the company determines if employees on the succession list are interested in and qualified for leadership positions.

A LOOK BACK

ESPN's Employee Development Programs

The chapter opener described ESPN's employee development programs.

QUESTIONS

1. ESPN requires all employees to complete an individual development plan (IDP). What should be included on an effective development plan?
2. How could ESPN identify employees with the potential for top leadership positions?
3. Why does most development occur at ESPN through experiences rather than by attending courses?

SUMMARY

This chapter emphasized the various development methods that companies use: formal education, assessment, job experiences, and interpersonal relationships. Most companies use one or more of these approaches to develop employees. Formal education involves enrolling employees in courses or seminars offered by the company or educational institutions. Assessment involves measuring the employee's performance, behavior, skills, or personality characteristics. Job experiences include job enlargement, rotating to a new job, promotions, or transfers. A more experienced, senior employee (a mentor) can help employees better understand the company and gain exposure and visibility to key persons in the organization. Part of a manager's job responsibility may be to coach employees. Regardless of the development approaches used, employees should have a development plan to identify (1) the type of development needed, (2) development goals, (3) the best approach for development, and (4) whether development goals have been reached. For development plans to be effective, both the employee and the company have responsibilities that need to be completed.

KEY TERMS

Development, 379
Protean career, 379
Psychological success, 379
Development planning system, 381
Action plan, 383
Formal education programs, 386
Tuition reimbursement, 388
Assessment, 389
Myers-Briggs Type Inventory
    (MBTI)®, 389
Assessment center, 390
Leaderless group discussion, 390
Interview, 390

In-basket, 390
Role-plays, 390
Performance appraisal, 392
Upward feedback, 392
360-degree feedback systems, 392
Job experiences, 394
Stretch assignments, 395
Job enlargement, 396
Job rotation, 397
Transfer, 398
Promotions, 398
Downward move, 398
Temporary assignment, 399

Sabbatical, 400
Mentor, 401
Career support, 403
Psychosocial support, 403
Reverse mentoring, 404
Coach, 404
Glass ceiling, 405
Succession planning, 406
High-potential employees, 407
Bench strength, 407
9-box grid, 408

DISCUSSION QUESTIONS

1. How could assessment be used to create a productive work team?
2. List and explain the characteristics of effective 360-degree feedback systems.
3. Why do companies develop formal mentoring programs? What are the potential benefits for the mentor? For the protégé?
4. Your boss is interested in hiring a consultant to help identify potential managers among current employees of a fast-food restaurant. The manager's job is to help wait on customers and prepare food during busy times, oversee all aspects of restaurant operations (including scheduling, maintenance, on-the-job training, and food purchase), and help motivate employees to provide high-quality service. The manager is also responsible for resolving disputes that might occur between employees. The position involves working under stress and coordinating several activities at one time. She asks you to outline the type of assessment program you believe would do the best job of identifying employees who will be successful managers. What will you tell her?
5. Many employees are unwilling to relocate because they like their current community, and spouses and children prefer not to move. Yet employees need to develop new skills, strengthen skill weaknesses, and be exposed to new aspects of the business to prepare for management positions. How could an employee's current job be changed to develop management skills?
6. What are some examples of sabbaticals and why are they beneficial?
7. What is coaching? Is there one type of coaching? Explain.
8. Why are many managers reluctant to coach their employees?

9. Why should companies be interested in helping employees plan their development? What benefits can companies gain? What are the risks?

10. What are the manager's roles in a development system? Which role do you think is most difficult for the typical manager? Which is the easiest role? List the reasons why managers might resist involvement in career management.

11. Draw the 9-box grid. How is it useful for succession planning?

12. Nationwide Financial, a 5,000-employee life insurance company based in Columbus, Ohio, found that its management development program contained four types of managers. One type, unknown leaders, have the right skills but their talents are unknown to top managers in the company. Another group, arrogant leaders, believe they have all the skills they need. What types of development program would you recommend for these managers?

SELF-ASSESSMENT EXERCISE

Mc Graw Hill Education **connect**

Additional assignable self-assessments available in Connect.

Go to www.keirsey.com. Complete the Keirsey Temperament Sorter. What did you learn about yourself? How could the instrument you completed be useful for employee development? What might be some disadvantages of using this instrument?

EXERCISING STRATEGY

Leadership Development at Raytheon

At Raytheon, a leader in the defense industry, leadership development focuses on high-potential early career leaders from different functional areas including information technology, human resources, supply chain, engineering, and business development. The program includes rotational assignments, and functional and cross-functional learning opportunities that are related to the company's competency model. The program includes more than 100 employees in each class. The learning environment is team-based and problem-focused to develop critical knowledge sharing, business acumen, and team leadership that are needed by Raytheon's managers. The capstone event for the program is a simulation that mirrors real market share and profit challenges faced by Raytheon's leaders. Twenty-five-person teams participate in the challenge. Each team has two engineers and the other three team members are from other business functions. The simulation is a test of how well the participants can apply what they learned in the program. To succeed in the simulation the teams have to be able to draw upon the functional expertise of all members. The simulation requires participants to use tools and processes that the company uses to manage costs, execute projects, and measure success. Teams need to balance both long- and short-term goals to insure they can successfully compete against each other. There are multiple rounds of competition with information provided on each team's effectiveness. This information is used for the next decisions the team needs to make.

QUESTIONS

1. What other types of development activities should Raytheon consider for its leadership development program? Provide a rationale for your recommendations.

2. What interpersonal skills could be improved by participating in the simulation? Explain how.

SOURCE: Based on M. Teeley, "Raytheon Challenges High-Tech Talent," *Training*, May/June 2014, pp. 12–13.

MANAGING PEOPLE

Employee Development Contributes to Winning the Battle Against Cancer

The American Cancer Society (ACS) is a nonprofit, nationwide, community-based voluntary health organization dedicated to creating a world without cancer. ACS strives to save lives by helping people stay well, and get well, by finding cures for cancer, and helping those who have cancer to fight the disease. ACS is headquartered in Atlanta, Georgia, and has regional and local offices throughout the United States that support 11 geographical divisions to ensure a presence in every community. The corporate office in Atlanta is responsible for overall strategic planning, corporate support services including training, development, and implementation of research programs, health programs, a 24-hour call center, and providing technical support and materials to regional and local offices. Regional and local offices deliver patient programs and services and engage in fundraising activities.

The philosophy of the talent development department is to provide "the right learning solution at the right time for the right person." One guiding principle is to support and drive the business through employee development and training. Another is that ACS wants employees to grow and develop, which is captured by the slogan "save lives, fulfill *yours*." Staff are encouraged to participate in leadership development, mentoring, coaching, and job-specific training classes. For staff interested in pursuing formal education, ACS has partnerships with online universities. Also, staff are encouraged to work with their manager to establish clear professional and development goals which map a path to career success.

At ACS it is important for training and development programs to be realistic in terms of taking into account budgetary constraints and job responsibilities. The programs need to be both efficient and effective and minimize the time that staff members are taken away from their primary responsibilities such as helping patients, working with community,

and planning and carrying out fundraising events. All delivered content is evaluated on the extent to which it is related to the job, staff member performance, and the organization's mission. The Nationwide Manager Development Program is designed to help build management strength for ACS. The program is marketed as an "adventure in management" and its design is intended to make training engaging, enjoyable, and enriching for the participants. The 18-month program helps participants learn management concepts using virtual discussion forums and e-learning. Also, participants are put into learning teams including members representing a diversity of thought, tenure, and experience. These teams engage in action learning, which focuses on developing management skills while developing solutions to business issues and problems facing ACS.

QUESTIONS

1. ACS uses a number of development activities to develop staff members' management and leadership skills. Explain how succession planning would be useful along with these activities for reviewing, preparing, and identifying leadership talent at ACS.

2. What can ACS do to ensure that women and minorities have a real potential to reach upper-level management positions?

SOURCES: Based on P. Harris, "Training as a Change Agent," *T + D*, October 2014, pp. 84–86; organization website, www.cancer.org, accessed May 26, 2015.

HR IN SMALL BUSINESS

Employee Sabbatical Benefits Others at Little Tokyo Service Center

The 100 full-time and 50 part-time employees of the Little Tokyo Service Center (LTSC) work to provide a range of social services targeting Asians and Pacific Islanders in Los Angeles County. The organization's focus is on the needs of people in financial difficulty, with physical disabilities, or struggling with language or cultural barriers. Services include counseling, transportation, translation, and consumer education. Emergency care is provided in several different Asian languages plus English and Spanish. LTSC also has sponsored the construction or renovation of community development projects including apartments and community facilities such as child care centers.

LTSC's executive director, Bill Watanabe, says he "really loves" his work, and no wonder, given the organization's importance to the community. Consequently, the thought of taking a sabbatical would not have occurred to him. But several years ago, Watanabe provided a professional reference to a colleague who had applied to the Durfee Foundation for a grant to fund a sabbatical. A staff member at the foundation suggested that Watanabe, too, might benefit from a sabbatical. His initial response was that he didn't need

one. After all, he wasn't burning out. But the staff member explained that a sabbatical could help LTSC's people learn to operate more independently. When Watanabe mentioned this to the board of directors, they encouraged him to apply.

With that backing, Watanabe took a three-month sabbatical from LTSC. The first two months were devoted to travel: a tour of Israel and Egypt, a vacation in Tahiti, and a road trip with his brother-in-law. After that, Watanabe stayed put long enough to write an autobiography.

Watanabe found that stepping away for a few months freshened his perspective on LTSC. When he returned, he applied his vision and renewed energy to restructure the agency through a merger of its community services center and its community development corporation, and he accelerated progress on a community organizing project. He also launched more vigorous advocacy to build a community gymnasium in the Little Tokyo neighborhood of Los Angeles, drawing positive attention from politicians and funding sources.

While Watanabe felt personally restored during his time away, he believes the agency benefited, too. In particular, he discovered that his absence provided developmental opportunities for others at LTSC. The agency's deputy director served as interim executive director while Watanabe was away, and two employees reporting to the deputy director shouldered the deputy's responsibilities. One of them has since been promoted. Building on these experiences, the second tier of management at LTSC has taken more direct control of the agency's day-to-day activities, freeing Watanabe to concentrate on broader strategy. Their greater preparation also amounts to a kind of succession planning. According to LTSC's board chairman, "If Bill were to leave tomorrow, the organization would be in very good hands."

QUESTIONS

1. Based on the information given, how well did Little Tokyo Service Center follow the career management process described in Figure 9.1 Which elements of that system, if any, were missing?

2. Imagine that LTSC has called you in as a consultant before Watanabe is to start his sabbatical. The agency has asked you to help obtain the maximum developmental benefit from the sabbatical arrangement. How would you recommend that Watanabe, the board of directors, and the second tier of management proceed?

3. Keeping in mind that an agency like LTSC would have funding and just a few senior managers, suggest two additional development activities that are likely to be most beneficial to the organization, and explain why you chose them.

SOURCES: Deborah S. Linnell and Tim Wolfred, *Creative Disruption: Sabbaticals for Capacity Building and Leadership Development in the Nonprofit Sector* (CompassPoint Nonprofit Services, 2009), p. 8; and Little Tokyo Service Center, "About LTSC," corporate website, www.ltsc.org, accessed May 26, 2015.

NOTES

1. D. Day, *Developing Leadership Talent* (Alexandria, VA: SHRM Foundation, 2007); M. London, *Managing the Training Enterprise* (San Francisco: Jossey-Bass, 1989); C. McCauley and S. Heslett, "Individual Development in the Workplace," in *Handbook of Industrial, Work, and Organizational Psychology,* Vol. 1, ed. N. Anderson, D. Ones, H. Sinangil, and C. Viswesveran (London: Sage Publications, 2001), pp. 313–35.

2. R. W. Pace, P. C. Smith, and G. E. Mills, *Human Resource Development* (Englewood Cliffs, NJ: Prentice Hall, 1991); W. Fitzgerald, "Training versus Development," *Training and Development Journal,* May 1992, pp. 81–84; R. A. Noe, S. L. Wilk, E. J. Mullen, and J. E. Wanek, "Employee Development: Issues in Construct Definition and Investigation of Antecedents," in *Improving Training Effectiveness in Work Organizations,* ed. J. K. Ford (Mahwah, NJ: Lawrence Erlbaum, 1997), pp. 153–89.

3. Company website, "Good to Grow: 2014 US CEO Survey," www.pwc.com, accessed February 20, 2015; "Action Items: 42 Trends Affecting Benefits, Compensation, Training, Staffing, and Technology," *HR Magazine,* January 2013, pp. 33–35; "Challenges Facing HR over the Next Ten Years," accessed from www.shrm.org, March 24, 2013.

4. M. Gubler, J. Arnold, and C. Coombs, "Reassessing the Protean Career Concept: Empirical Findings, Conceptual Components, and Measurement," *Journal of Organizational Behavior* 35 (2014), pp. 23–40; D. T. Hall, "Protean Careers of the 21st Century," *Academy of Management Executive* 11 (1996), pp. 8–16; D. Hall, *Careers In and Out of Organizations.* (Thousand Oaks, CA: Sage, 2002). J. Greenhaus, G. Callahan, and V. Godshalk, *Career Management,* 4th ed. (Thousand Oaks, CA: Sage, 2010).

5. K. Essick, "From a Job to a Calling," *The Wall Street Journal,* March 16, 2015, p. R4.

6. K. R. Brousseau, M. J. Driver, K. Eneroth, and R. Larsson, "Career Pandemonium: Realigning Organizations and Individuals," *Academy of Management Executive* 11 (1996), pp. 52–66.

7. M. B. Arthur, "The Boundaryless Career: A New Perspective of Organizational Inquiry," *Journal of Organization Behavior* 15 (1994), pp. 295–309; P. H. Mirvis and D. T. Hall, "Psychological Success and the Boundaryless Career," *Journal of Organization Behavior* 15 (1994), pp. 365–80; M. Lazarova and S. Taylor, "Boundaryless Careers, Social Capital, and Knowledge Management: Implications for Organizational Performance," *Journal of Organizational Behavior* 30 (2009), pp. 119–39; D. Feldman and T. Ng, "Careers: Mobility, Embeddedness, and Success," *Journal of Management* 33 (2007), pp. 350–77.

8. "Nearly One-Third of Employers Expect Workers to Job-Hop," *Career Builder,* www.careerbuilder.com, accessed April 2, 2015; "Is Job Hopping the New Normal?" *T + D,* August 2014, p. 20.

9. R. Hoffman, B. Casnocha, and C. Yeh, "Tours of Duty: The New Employer-Employee Compact," *Harvard Business Review,* June 2013, pp. 48–58.

10. L. Mainiero and S. Sullivan, "Kaleidoscope Careers: An Alternative Explanation for the 'Opt-Out' Revolution," *Academy of Management Executive* 19 (2005), pp. 106–23; S. Sullivan and L. Mainiero, "Benchmarking Ideas for Fostering Family-Friendly Workplaces," *Organizational Dynamics* 36 (2007), pp. 45–62.

11. L. Stevens, "Customizing Their Career," *Human Resource Executive,* November 2013, pp. 18–20.

12. Ibid.

13. M. Sallie-Dosunmu, "Born to Grow," *TD,* May 2006, pp. 34–37.

14. D. T. Jaffe and C. D. Scott, "Career Development for Empowerment in a Changing Work World," in *New Directions in Career Planning and the Workplace,* ed. J. M. Kummerow (Palo Alto, CA: Consulting Psychologists Press, 1991), pp. 33–60; L. Summers, "A Logical Approach to Development Planning," *Training and Development* 48 (1994), pp. 22–31; D. B. Peterson and M. D. Hicks, *Development First* (Minneapolis, MN: Personnel Decisions, 1995).

15. R. Emlo, "The Power of Discovery," *Chief Learning Officer,* January 2015, pp. 38–48; "Training Top 10 Hall of Fame," *Training,* 2010, pp. 60–62.

16. R. Noe, *Employee Training and Development,* 7th ed. (New York: McGraw-Hill, Irwin, 2015). K. O'Leonard and L. Loew,

"Investing in the Future," *Human Resource Executive,* July/August 2012, pp. 30–34.

17. "Leaders Take Flight," *T + D,* February 2014, p. 72.

18. C. Waxer, "Course Review," *Human Resource Executive,* December 2005, pp. 46–48. Pat Galagan, "90,000 Served: Hamburger University Turns 50," *T + D,* April 2011, pp. 46–51; Beth Kowitt, "Why McDonald's Wins in Any Economy," *Fortune,* September 5, 2011, EBSCOhost, http://web.ebscohost.com.

19. www.ge.com/company/culture/leaderhip_learning.html, April 18, 2013.

20. R. Knight, "GE's Corporate Boot Camp cum Talent Spotting Venue," *Financial Times Business Education,* March 20, 2006, p. 2; J. Durett, "GE Hones Its Leaders at Crotonville," *Training,* May 2006, pp. 25–27.

21. University of Virginia Darden School of Business, "MBA for Executives," www.darden.virginia.edu, accessed March 30, 2012.

22. Duke Corporate Education (2012), "Thomson Reuters Case Study: Innovation," http://www.dukece.com/clients/documents/ThomsonReutersCaseStudy.pdf, accessed April 3, 2015.

23. Center for Creative Leadership, "Develop a Pipeline of Successful Leaders at All Levels," http://www.ccl.org/leadership/pdf/programs/LDR.pdf, accessed April 3, 2015.

24. R. Johnson, "The Learning Curve: The Value of Tuition Reimbursement," *Training,* November 2005, pp. 30–33; G. Benson, D. Finegold, and S. Mohrman, "You Paid for the Skills, Now Keep Them: Tuition Reimbursement and Voluntary Turnover," *Academy of Management Journal* 47 (2004), pp. 315–331.

25. "Top 125 Hall of Fame: Verizon," *Training,* January/February 2014, pp. 58–59; company website, "Tuition Assistance," www.verizon.com, accessed April 3, 2015; P. Babcock, "Always More to Learn," *HR Magazine,* September 2009, pp. 51–56.

26. Day, *Developing Leadership Talent.*

27. M. Weinstein, "Personalities & Performance," *Training,* July/August 2008, pp. 36–40.

28. S. K. Hirsch, *MBTI Team Member's Guide* (Palo Alto, CA: Consulting Psychologists Press, 1992); A. L. Hammer, *Introduction to Type and Careers* (Palo Alto, CA: Consulting Psychologists Press, 1993); J. Llorens, "Taking Inventory of Myers-Briggs," *T + D,* April 2010, pp. 18–19.

29. From www.discprofile.com, website for DiSC, accessed February 1, 2012.

30. M. Weinstein, "The X Factor," *Training,* May/June 2011, pp. 65–67.

31. G. C. Thornton III and W. C. Byham, *Assessment Centers and Managerial Performance* (New York: Academic Press, 1982); L. F. Schoenfeldt and J. A. Steger, "Identification and Development of Management Talent," in *Research in Personnel and Human Resource Management,* ed. K. N. Rowland and G. Ferris (Greenwich, CT: JAI Press, 1989), vol. 7, pp. 151–81.

32. Thornton and Byham, *Assessment Centers and Managerial Performance.*

33. B. B. Gaugler, D. B. Rosenthal, G. C. Thornton III, and C. Bentson, "Metaanalysis of Assessment Center Validity," *Journal of Applied Psychology* 72 (1987), pp. 493–511; D. W. Bray, R. J. Campbell, and D. L. Grant, *Formative Years in Business: A Long-Term AT&T Study of Managerial Lives* (New York: Wiley, 1974).

34. R. G. Jones and M. D. Whitmore, "Evaluating Developmental Assessment Centers as Interventions," *Personnel Psychology* 48 (1995), pp. 377–88.

35. J. Schettler, "Building Bench Strength," *Training,* June 2002, pp. 55–58.

36. S. B. Silverman, "Individual Development through Performance Appraisal," in *Developing Human Resources,* pp. 5–120 to 5–151.

37. M. Sallie-Dosunmu, "Born to Grow," *TD,* May 2006, pp. 34–37.

38. J. S. Lublin, "Turning the Tables: Underlings Evaluate Bosses," *The Wall Street Journal,* October 4, 1994, pp. B1, B14; D. O'Reilly, "360-Degree Feedback Can Change Your Life," *Fortune,* October 17, 1994, pp. 93–100; J. F. Milliman, R. A. Zawacki, C. Norman, L. Powell, and J. Kirksey, "Companies Evaluate Employees from All Perspectives," *Personnel Journal,* November 1994, pp. 99–103.

39. Center for Creative Leadership, *Skillscope for Managers: Development Planning Guide* (Greensboro, NC: Center for Creative Leadership, 1992); G. Yukl and R. Lepsinger, "360-Degree Feedback," *Training,* December 1995, pp. 45–50.

40. L. Atwater, P. Roush, and A. Fischthal, "The Influence of Upward Feedback on Self- and Follower Ratings of Leadership," *Personnel Psychology* 48 (1995), pp. 35–59; J. F. Hazucha, S. A. Hezlett, and R. J. Schneider, "The Impact of 360-Degree Feedback on Management Skill Development," *Human Resource Management* 32 (1993), pp. 325–51; J. W. Smither, M. London, N. Vasilopoulos, R. R. Reilly, R. E. Millsap, and N. Salvemini, "An Examination of the Effects of an Upward Feedback Program over Time," *Personnel Psychology* 48 (1995), pp. 1–34; J. Smither and A. Walker, "Are the Characteristics of Narrative Comments Related to Improvements in Multirater Feedback Ratings over Time?" *Journal of Applied Psychology* 89 (2004), pp. 575–81; J. Smither, M. London, and R. Reilly, "Does Performance Improve Following Multisource Feedback? A Theoretical Model, Meta-analysis, and Review of Empirical Findings," *Personnel Psychology* 58 (2005), pp. 33–66.

41. D. Bracken, "Straight Talk about Multirater Feedback," *Training and Development,* September 1994, pp. 44–51; K. Nowack, J. Hartley, and W. Bradley, "How to Evaluate Your 360-Feedback Efforts," *Training and Development,* April 1999, pp. 48–52; M. Levine, "Taking the Burn out of the 360-Degree Hot Seat," *T + D,* August 2010, pp. 40–45.

42. "Training Top 125," *Training,* January/February 2011, pp. 54–93.

43. "Case Study: Seek Employee Feedback for Improvement Opportunities," http://www.talentsmart.com/case-studies/kroger.php, accessed April 3, 2015.

44. "St. Joseph's Medical Center Uses 360-Degree Feedback and Coaching to Develop Lead Physicians and Healthcare Leadership," https://www.decision-wise.com/case-study/360-feedback-and-coaching-for-physicians/, accessed April 3, 2015.

45. M. W. McCall Jr., M. M. Lombardo, and A. M. Morrison, *Lessons of Experience* (Lexington, MA: Lexington Books, 1988); L. Dragoni, P. Tesluk, J. Russell, and I. Oh, "Understanding Managerial Development: Integrating Developmental Assignments, Learning Orientation, and Access to Developmental Opportunities in Predicting Managerial Competencies," *Academy of Management Journal* 52 (2009), pp. 731–43.

46. R. S. Snell, "Congenial Ways of Learning: So Near yet So Far," *Journal of Management Development* 9 (1990), pp. 17–23.

47. R. Morrison, T. Erickson, and K. Dychtwald, "Managing Middlescence," *Harvard Business Review,* March 2006, pp. 78–86.

48. R. Grossman, "The Care and Feeding of High-potential Employees," *HR Magazine,* August 2011, pp. 34–39.

49. McCall, Lombardo, and Morrison, *Lessons of Experience;* M. W. McCall, "Developing Executives through Work Experiences," *Human Resource Planning* 11 (1988), pp. 1–11; M. N. Ruderman, P. J. Ohlott, and C. D. McCauley, "Assessing Opportunities for Leadership Development," in *Measures of Leadership,* pp. 547–62; C. D. McCauley, L. J. Estman, and P. J. Ohlott, "Linking Management Selection and Development through Stretch Assignments," *Human Resource Management* 34 (1995), pp. 93–115.

50. S. Courtright, A. Colbert, and D. Choi, "Fired Up or Burned Out? How Developmental Challenge Differentially Impacts Leader Behavior," *Journal of Applied Psychology* 99 (2014), pp. 681–96. C. D. McCauley, M. N. Ruderman, P. J. Ohlott, and J. E. Morrow, "Assessing the Developmental Components of Managerial Jobs," *Journal of Applied Psychology* 79 (1994), pp. 544–60; J. LePine, M. LePine, and C. Jackson, "Challenge and Hindrance Stress: Relationships with Exhaustion, Motivation to Learn, and Learning Performance," *Journal of Applied Psychology* 89 (2004) pp. 883–91.

51. S. Thurm, "Power-Sharing Prepares Managers,"*The Wall Street Journal,* December 5, 2005, p. B4.

52. E. Short, "Move Around before Moving Up," *Chief Learning Officer,* July 2014, pp. 19–21.

53. B. Ware, "Stop the Gen Y Revolving Door," *T + D,* May 2014, pp. 58–63.

54. M. London, *Developing Managers* (San Francisco: Jossey-Bass, 1985); M. A. Campion, L. Cheraskin, and M. J. Stevens, "Career-Related Antecedents and Outcomes of Job Rotation," *Academy of Management Journal* 37 (1994), pp. 1518–42; M. London, *Managing the Training Enterprise* (San Francisco: Jossey-Bass, 1989).

55. R. Hackett, "A Globe of Opportunity," *Fortune,* February 1, 2015, p. 22.

56. C. Meyrowitz, "The CEO of TJX on How to Train First-Class Buyers," *Harvard Business Review,* May 2014, pp. 45–48.

57. D. C. Feldman, *Managing Careers in Organizations* (Glenview, IL: Scott Foresman, 1988); D. Hall, *Careers In and Out of Organizations* (Thousand Oaks, CA: Sage, 2002).

58. D. T. Hall and L. A. Isabella, "Downward Moves and Career Development," *Organizational Dynamics* 14 (1985), pp. 5–23.

59. H. D. Dewirst, "Career Patterns: Mobility, Specialization, and Related Career Issues," in *Contemporary Career Development Issues,* ed. R. F. Morrison and J. Adams (Hillsdale, NJ: Lawrence Erlbaum, 1991), pp. 73–108.

60. J. M. Brett, L. K. Stroh, and A. H. Reilly, "Job Transfer," in *International Review of Industrial and Organizational Psychology: 1992,* ed. C. L. Cooper and I. T. Robinson (Chichester, England: John Wiley and Sons, 1992); D. C. Feldman and J. M. Brett, "Coping with New Jobs: A Comparative Study of New Hires and Job Changers," *Academy of Management Journal* 26 (1983), pp. 258–72.

61. R. A. Noe, B. D. Steffy, and A. E. Barber, "An Investigation of the Factors Influencing Employees' Willingness to Accept Mobility Opportunities," *Personnel Psychology* 41 (1988), pp. 559–80; S. Gould and L. E. Penley, "A Study of the Correlates of Willingness to Relocate," *Academy of Management Journal* 28 (1984), pp. 472–78; J. Landau and T. H. Hammer, "Clerical Employees' Perceptions of Intra-organizational Career Opportunities," *Academy of Management Journal* 29 (1986), pp. 385–405; R. P. Duncan and C. C. Perruci, "Dual Occupation Families and Migration," *American Sociological Review* 41 (1976), pp. 252–61; J. M. Brett and A. H. Reilly, "On the Road Again: Predicting the Job Transfer Decision," *Journal of Applied Psychology* 73 (1988), pp. 614–620.

62. N. C. Tompkins, "GTE Managers on the Move," *Personnel Journal,* August 1992, pp. 86–91.

63. J. M. Brett, "Job Transfer and Well-Being," *Journal of Applied Psychology* 67 (1992), pp. 450–63; F. J. Minor, L. A. Slade, and R. A. Myers, "Career Transitions in Changing Times," in *Contemporary Career Development Issues,* pp. 109–20; C. C. Pinder and K. G. Schroeder, "Time to Proficiency Following Job Transfers," *Academy of Management Journal* 30 (1987), pp. 336–53; G. Flynn, "Heck No—We Won't Go!" *Personnel Journal,* March 1996, pp. 37–43.

64. R. Silverman, "Field Trip: Learning from Startups," *The Wall Street Journal,* March 27, 2013, p. B8.

65. C. McCauley, "Make Experience Count," *Chief Learning Officer,* May 2014, p. 50.

66. E. Byron, "A New Odd Couple: Google, P&G Swap Workers to Spur Innovation," The *Wall Street Journal,* November 19, 2008, pp. A1, A18.

67. C. J. Bachler, "Workers Take Leave of Job Stress," *Personnel Journal,* January 1995, pp. 38–48. "Types of Sabbaticals" from www.yoursabbatical.com, accessed April 17, 2013.

68. R. Feintzeig, "A Cure for Office Burnout: Mini Sabbaticals," *The Wall Street Journal,* October 29, 2014, p. B7.

69. Company website, "Volunteerism," www.generalmills.com, accessed April 6, 2015; M. Weinstein, "Charity Begins @ Work," *Training,* May 2008, pp. 56–58; K. Ellis, "Pass It On," *Training,* June 2005, pp. 14–19.

70. D. B. Turban and T. W. Dougherty, "Role of Protégé Personality in Receipt of Mentoring and Career Success," *Academy of Management Journal* 37 (1994), pp. 688–702; E. A. Fagenson, "Mentoring: Who Needs It? A Comparison of Protégés' and Non-protégés' Needs for Power, Achievement, Affiliation, and Autonomy," *Journal of Vocational Behavior* 41 (1992), pp. 48–60.

71. A. H. Geiger, "Measures for Mentors," *Training and Development Journal,* February 1992, pp. 65–67.

72. K. E. Kram, *Mentoring at Work: Developmental Relationships in Organizational Life* (Glenview, IL: Scott Foresman, 1985); K. Kram, "Phases of the Mentoring Relationship," *Academy of Management Journal* 26 (1983), pp. 608–25; G. T. Chao, P. M. Walz, and P. D. Gardner, "Formal and Informal Mentorships: A Comparison of Mentoring Functions and Contrasts with Nonmentored Counterparts," *Personnel Psychology* 45 (1992), pp. 619–36; C. Wanberg, E. Welsh, and S. Hezlett, "Mentoring Research: A Review and Dynamic Process Model," in *Research in Personnel and Human Resources Management,* ed. J. Martocchio and G. Ferris (New York: Elsevier Science, 2003), pp. 39–124.

73. E. White, "Making Mentorships Work," *The Wall Street Journal,* October 23, 2007, p. B11; E. Holmes, "Career Mentors Today Seem Short on Advice but Give a Mean Tour," *The Wall Street Journal,* August 28, 2007, p. B1; J. Sandberg, "With Bad Mentors It's Better to Break Up than to Make Up," *The Wall Street Journal,* March 18, 2008, p. B1.

74. M. Weinstein, "Please Don't Go," *Training,* May/June 2011, pp. 28–34.

75. L. Eby, M. Butts, A. Lockwood, and A. Simon, "Protégés' Negative Mentoring Experiences: Construct Development and Nomological Validation," *Personnel Psychology* 57 (2004), pp. 411–47; M. Boyle, "Most Mentoring Programs Stink—but Yours Doesn't Have To," *Training,* August 2005, pp. 12–15.

76. R. Emelo, "Conversations with Mentoring Leaders," *T + D,* June 2011, pp. 32–37.

77. "Training Top 125: Cartus," *Training,* January/February 2015, p. 87; J. Alsever, " Looking for a Career Mentor You Love? Let Cold Data Be Your Guide, *Fast Company,* www.fastcompany.com, accessed July 22, 2014; M. Weinstein, "Tech Connects," *Training,* September 2008, pp. 58–59.

78. G. F. Dreher and R. A. Ash, "A Comparative Study of Mentoring among Men and Women in Managerial, Professional, and Technical Positions," *Journal of Applied Psychology* 75 (1990), pp. 539–46; T. D. Allen, L. T. Eby, M. L. Poteet, E. Lentz, and L. Lima, "Career Benefits Associated with Mentoring for Protégés: A Meta-Analysis," *Journal of Applied Psychology* 89 (2004), pp. 127–36; R. A. Noe, D. B. Greenberger, and S. Wang, "Mentoring: What We Know and Where We Might Go," in *Research in*

Personnel and Human Resources Management, ed. G. Ferris and J. Martucchio (New York: Elsevier Science, 2002), pp. 129–74; R. A. Noe, "An Investigation of the Determinants of Successful Assigned Mentoring Relationships," *Personnel Psychology* 41 (1988), pp. 457–79; B. J. Tepper, "Upward Maintenance Tactics in Supervisory Mentoring and Nonmentoring Relationships," *Academy of Management Journal* 38 (1995), pp. 1191–205; B. R. Ragins and T. A. Scandura, "Gender Differences in Expected Outcomes of Mentoring Relationships," *Academy of Management Journal* 37 (1994), pp. 957–71.

79. S. Wells, "Tending Talent," *HR Magazine,* May 2009, pp. 53–60.
80. S. Shellenbarger, "Tech-Impaired? Pair Up with a Younger Mentor," *The Wall Street Journal,* May 28, 2014, p. D3.
81. Alsever, "Looking for a Career Mentor You Love? Let Cold Data Be Your Guide."
82. D. B. Peterson and M. D. Hicks, *Leader as Coach* (Minneapolis, MN: Personnel Decisions, 1996).
83. "Walgreens: Leading Well at Walgreens," *Training,* January/February 2015, p. 104; "PwC: Discover," *Training,* January/February 2014, pp. 62–63; J. Marques, "Coaching," *Training,* May/June 2014, p. 76.
84. J. Smither, M. London, R. Flautt, Y. Vargas, and L. Kucine, "Can Working with an Executive Coach Improve Multisource Ratings over Time? A Quasiexperimental Field Study," *Personnel Psychology* 56 (2003), pp. 23–44.
85. A. Vorro, "Coaching Counsel," *Inside Counsel,* February 2012, Business & Company Resource Center, http://galenet.gale group.com.
86. P. Cappelli, M. Hamori, and R. Bonet, "Who's Got Those Top Jobs?" *Harvard Business Review,* March 2014, pp. 74–79. "Most Employers Lacking a Strategy for Developing Women Leaders," press release from October 25, 2010, at www.mercer.com, website of Mercer, a global provider of consulting, outsourcing, and investment services; R. Pyrillis, "Programs That Help Women Take the Lead," *Workforce Management,* January 2011, pp. 3–4.
87. U.S. Department of Labor, *A Report on the Glass Ceiling Initiative* (Washington, DC: U.S. Department of Labor, 1991).
88. B. Groysberg and K. Connolly, "Great Leaders Who Make the Mix Work," *Harvard Business Review,* September 2013, pp. 68–76; P. J. Ohlott, M. N. Ruderman, and C. D. McCauley, "Gender Differences in Managers' Developmental Job Experiences," *Academy of Management Journal* 37 (1994), pp. 46–67; D. Mattioli, "Programs to Promote Female Managers Win Citations," *The Wall Street Journal,* January 30, 2007, p. B7.
89. J. Green, "This Is Not a Trend," *Bloomberg Businessweek,* September 1–September 7, 2014, pp. 19–20.
90. U.S. Department of Labor, *A Report on the Glass Ceiling Initiative;* R. A. Noe, "Women and Mentoring: A Review and Research Agenda," *Academy of Management Review* 13 (1988), pp. 65–78; B. R. Ragins and J. L. Cotton, "Easier Said Than Done: Gender Differences in Perceived Barriers to Gaining a Mentor," *Academy of Management Journal* 34 (1991), pp. 939–51.
91. L. A. Mainiero, "Getting Anointed for Advancement: The Case of Executive Women," *Academy of Management Executive* 8 (1994), pp. 53–67; J. S. Lublin, "Women at Top Still Are Distant from CEO Jobs," *The Wall Street Journal,* February 28, 1995, pp. B1, B5; P. Tharenov, S. Latimer, and D. Conroy, "How Do You Make It to the Top? An Examination of Influences on Women's and Men's Managerial Advancement," *Academy of Management Journal* 37 (1994), pp. 899–931.
92. P. Tharenou, "Going Up? Do Traits and Informal Social Processes Predict Advancement in Management?" *Academy of Management Journal* 44 (2001), pp. 1005–17.
93. "The 2015 National Association for Female Executives Top 50 Companies for Executive Women: AstraZeneca," www.working mother.com, accessed April 13, 2015; K. Bowers, "Change the Ratio," www.workingmother.com, accessed April 13, 2015.
94. W. J. Rothwell, *Effective Succession Planning,* 4th ed. (New York: AMACOM, 2010).
95. C. B. Derr, C. Jones, and E. L. Toomey, "Managing High-Potential Employees: Current Practices in Thirty-Three U.S. Corporations," *Human Resource Management* 27 (1988), pp. 273–90.
96. "Comprehensive Global Korn/ Ferry Study Shows Only One Third of Executives Are Satisfied with Succession Management Outcomes," *Business Wire,* accessed April 7, 2015, www.business wire.com; B. Leonard, "Some Executives Doubtful Succession Plans Really Work," (February 18, 2015), from www.shrm.org, website for Society for Human Resource Management, accessed April 7, 2015.
97. D. Sims, "Five Ways to Increase Success in Succession Planning," *T + D,* August 2014, pp. 60–63; W.J. Rothwell, *Effective Succession Planning,* 4th ed. (New York: AMACOM, 2010); N. Davis and W. Pina-Ramirez, "Essential Continuity," *T + D,* March 2015, pp. 45–47.
98. K. Tyler, "On the Grid," *HR Magazine,* August 2011, pp. 67–69; D. Day, *Developing Leadership Talent* (Alexandria, VA: SHRM Foundation, 2007).
99. M. Weinstein, "The Heart of CHG Healthcare Services," *Training,* January/February 2015, pp. 44–48.
100. "Valvoline Instant Oil Change: Bench Planning," *Training,* January/February 2014, p. 108.
101. M. Weinstein, "BCBSM Empowers Employees," *Training,* January/February 2015, pp. 50–53.
102. J. Grenzer, "Succession Planning," *Training,* May/June 2014, pp. 74–75.
103. "Should You Tell Employees They're Part of a Succession Plan?" *HR Magazine,* January/February 2015, pp. 26–27. M. Steen, "Where to Draw the Line on Revealing Who's Next in Line," *Workforce Management,* June 2011, pp. 16–18.

Employee Separation and Retention

LEARNING OBJECTIVES

After reading this chapter, you should be able to:

LO 10-1 Distinguish between involuntary and voluntary turnover, and discuss how each of these forms of turnover can be leveraged for competitive advantage. *page 423*

LO 10-2 List the major elements that contribute to perceptions of justice and how to apply these in organizational contexts involving discipline and dismissal. *page 425*

LO 10-3 Specify the relationship between job satisfaction and various forms of job withdrawal, and identify the major sources of job satisfaction in work contexts. *page 437*

LO 10-4 Design a survey feedback intervention program, and use this to promote retention of key organizational personnel. *page 445*

Working at the Internal Revenues Service: A Taxing Experience

Dating all the way back to biblical times, being a tax collector has never been a popular occupation. However, one could argue that, at least when it comes to working for the Internal Revenue Service in the United States, the job has never been more difficult. The agency has faced five straight years of budget cuts, with the biggest of these—a $346 million cut—implemented in 2015. This last cut came as a result of congressional outrage when the agency was charged with politically mishandling requests for tax-exempt status from Tea Party and other Republican-leaning groups. One could argue that these historic cuts came at a time when the complexity of the work, due to the recent passage of the Affordable Care Act with its complicated set of tax subsidies, was higher than ever.

These cuts have certainly trickled down to the workforce where morale has never been lower. Salaries at the agency have risen only 2% the last five years, and the slashing of administrative support has left agents with a host of low-level clerical duties that cut into the more substantive parts of the job. Facilities have been allowed to decay, and the computers and software that agents work with are estimated to be three generations behind what one would find in the private sector. Office supplies are nowhere to be found, and workers have to provide their own pens, paper, and other basic necessities for performing their jobs. On top of all of this, worker safety is always an issue due to the crazed nature of some taxpayers who feel that the government is stealing their money. Several years ago, one such taxpayer flew a kamikaze mission with a single-engine plane into a Texas facility killing one worker and injuring many others.

Not surprisingly, all of this has led to a high rate of voluntary turnover within the worker ranks. Between the years 2010 and 2015, 15,000 employees quit their jobs, and this is just the tip of a demographic iceberg. The IRS has less than 2,000 employees who are under the age of 30, and half of those are part time. Over 50% of the workforce will be eligible to retire by 2019, and there is very little hope that many of the most experienced agents will stick around one day longer than they need to when it comes to retirement.

Clearly, no one enjoys paying their taxes, and thus, few are shedding any tears for these workers. However, the government does require money to operate, and many fear that employee turnover and morale problems are cutting into the agency's ability to accomplish their mission. Audits are at historically low levels, and many criminal investigations of known tax evaders have been delayed or placed on hold. As one IRS veteran noted in despair, "I shouldn't have to say this but the IRS brings in about 93% of the revenue in this country. We're not soldiers but we are serving our country."

SOURCES: D. F. Kettl, "Why the War on the IRS Makes No Cents," *Government Executive,* June 30, 2015, www.govexec.com; D. Leonard and R. Rubin, "The Taxman Bummeth," *Bloomberg Businessweek,* April 13, 2015, pp. 50–55; G. Korte, "IRS to Lose Tax Collectors, Do Fewer Audits in 2015," *USA Today,* January 13, 2015, www.usatoday.com.

Introduction

Every executive recognizes the need for satisfied, loyal customers. If the firm is publicly held, it is also safe to assume that every executive appreciates the need to have satisfied, loyal investors. Customers and investors provide the financial resources that allow the organization to survive. However, not every executive understands the need to generate satisfaction and loyalty among employees. For example, as we see in the opening vignette, dissatisfaction and turnover at the Internal Revenue Service (IRS) has threatened the ability of this agency to carry out its mission, and since this agency collects almost all the revenue that runs the United States, this could be considered a threat to national security. Job satisfaction is also critical to the missions of business organizations in the private sector of the economy. This may even be the deciding factor when it comes to who wins and who loses in the competitive market because retention rates among employees are related to retention rates among customers.[1] In fact, research has established a direct link between employee retention rates and sales growth and companies that are cited as one of the "100 Best Companies to Work For" routinely outperform their competition on many other financial indicators of performance. This is especially the case in the service industry where the direct contact between customers and employees enhances the relationship between employee satisfaction and customer satisfaction.

For example, Costco Wholesale is well-known throughout the retail industry for treating its employees better than most of its competitors. Costco pays its hourly workers over $20 an hour compared to the industry average of $12 an hour. Costco also provides company-sponsored health insurance to all employees, as well as tuition reimbursement programs that allow employees who start out at the lowest level of the shop floor to climb the corporate ladder. The result of this is that voluntary turnover within the organization is very low for the retail industry. The turnover rate among employees is less than 5% in a cut-throat industry where the average is closer to 30%. This feeds directly into Costco's business model and strategic plan where, due to their emphasis on low prices, 80% of their profit comes from membership fees. Despite the fact that their membership fees are 20% higher than Sam's Club, over 90% of customers renew each year, providing a stable and predictable source of income. CEO Craig Jelinek notes, "We know it's a lot more profitable in the long term to minimize employee turnover and maximize employee productivity, commitment and loyalty. If you treat consumers with respect and treat employees with respect, good things are going to happen to you."[2]

In addition to holding onto key personnel, another hallmark of successful firms is their ability and willingness to dismiss employees who are engaging in counterproductive behavior. It is somewhat ironic that one of the keys to retaining productive employees is ensuring that these people are not being made miserable by supervisors or co-workers who are engaging in unproductive, disruptive, or dangerous behavior. Unfortunately, surveys indicate that many managers—indeed as many as 70%—struggle to give frank and honest feedback to poorly performing subordinates, and then wind up experiencing and tolerating poor performance for very long periods.[3]

Thus, to compete effectively, organizations must take steps to ensure that good performers are motivated to stay with the organization, whereas chronically low performers are allowed, encouraged, or, if necessary, forced to leave. Retaining top performers is not always easy, however. Competing organizations are constantly looking to steal top performers, and "poaching talent" is becoming an increasingly common way for organizations to build themselves up, while at the same time, tearing their competitors down.[4] It is also not nearly as easy to fire employees as many people think. The increased willingness of people to sue their employer, combined with an unprecedented level of violence in the workplace, has made discharging employees who lack talent legally complicated and personally dangerous.[5] For example, in 2014, a former employee at United Parcel Services shot and killed two supervisors who he believed were responsible for his termination decision.[6]

The purpose of this chapter (the last in Part 3 of this book) is to focus on employee separation and retention. The material presented in Part 3's previous two chapters ("Performance Management" and "Employee Development") can be used to help establish who are the current effective performers as well as who is likely to respond well to future developmental opportunities. This chapter completes Part 3 by discussing what can be done to retain high-performing employees who warrant further development as well as managing the separation process for low-performing employees who have not responded well to developmental opportunities.

Since much of what needs to be done to retain employees involves compensation and benefits, this chapter also serves as a bridge to Part 4, which addresses these issues in more detail. The chapter is divided into two sections. The first examines **involuntary turnover**, that is, turnover initiated by the organization (often among people who would prefer to stay). The second deals with **voluntary turnover**, that is, turnover initiated by employees (often whom the company would prefer to keep). Although both types of turnover reflect employee separation, they are clearly different phenomena that need to be examined separately.

Managing Involuntary Turnover

Despite a company's best efforts in the area of personnel selection, training, and design of compensation systems, some employees will occasionally fail to meet performance requirements or will violate company policies while on the job. For example, in 2012, Secret Service members responsible for protecting the President of the United States on his upcoming trip to Colombia were caught bringing prostitutes to their hotel rooms. Secret Service work rules forbid bringing *any* foreign national, let alone prostitutes, to a security zone prior to a Presidential visit, and hence these employees had to be terminated.[7] However, problems at this agency persisted, and in 2015, the terminations climbed higher into the organizational ranks when four top Secret Service officers were also removed from their jobs following an incident where a man carrying a knife jumped the White House fence and managed to run all the way into the mansion before being caught. The new top official noted that "change is necessary to gain a fresh perspective on how we conduct business," and this is the rationale behind most such terminations.[8]

When events like this happen organizations need to invoke a discipline program that could ultimately lead to the individual's discharge. For a number of reasons, discharging employees can be a very difficult task that needs to be handled with the utmost care and attention to detail. First, legal aspects to this decision can have important repercussions for the organization. Historically, in the absence of a specified contract, either the employer or the employee could sever the employment relationship at any time. The severing of this relationship could be for "good cause," "no cause," or even "bad cause." Over time, this policy has been referred to as the **employment-at-will doctrine**. This employment-at-will doctrine has eroded significantly over time, however. Today employees who are fired sometimes sue their employers for wrongful discharge.

A wrongful discharge suit typically attempts to establish that the discharge either (1) violated an implied contract or covenant (that is, the employer acted unfairly) or (2) violated public policy (that is, the employee was terminated because he or she refused

Involuntary Turnover
Turnover initiated by the organization (often among people who would prefer to stay).

Voluntary Turnover
Turnover initiated by employees (often whom the company would prefer to keep).

LO 10-1
Distinguish between involuntary and voluntary turnover, and discuss how each of these forms of turnover can be leveraged for competitive advantage.

Employment-at-Will Doctrine
The doctrine that, in the absence of a specific contract, either an employer or employee could sever the employment relationship at any time.

to do something illegal, unethical, or unsafe). Wrongful discharge suits can also be filed as a civil rights infringement if the person discharged is a member of a protected group. For example, in 2015, 10 African American employees at McDonald's sued the company alleging that they were fired because of their race. In fact, the manager at the franchise was quoted as saying that he "needed to get the ghetto out of the store." McDonald's Corporation had no intention of defending this manager but tried to argue that this was an issue between the employees and the "franchisee" (i.e., the local manager) not the "franchiser" (i.e., the corporate entity). The National Labor Relations Board did not see it that way and ruled against the corporation.[9]

The number of such "protected groups" is large and includes racial minorities, women, older workers (over 40 years of age), homosexuals, disabled workers (including the obese), whistle-blowers, people who have filed workers compensation claims, and if one counts reverse discrimination claims—Caucasians. As noted by Lisa Cassilly, a defense attorney for the firm Alston and Bird, "It's difficult to find someone who doesn't have some capacity to claim protected status."[10] This means that in almost any instance when someone is fired for poor performance, the alternative possibility that this person was a victim of discrimination can be raised.

Not surprisingly, this has led to an increase in litigation. Although the research suggests that a plaintiff usually loses a wrongful termination case, the high cost of litigating the case makes some employers reluctant to fire employees, even when they are low performers. When this happens, the employer's short-term emphasis on staying out of court has come into conflict with the long-term need to develop a competitive workforce.

For example, one reaction to this dilemma is enduring long stretches of poor performance in order to create the extensive "paper trail" that would support a negative action. While HR professionals often point the finger of blame at supervisors who have not done a diligent job documenting past performance problems, supervisors often turn around and accuse HR of being "nervous Nellies" who never seem satisfied with the amount of evidence provided by supervisors. Moreover, keeping poor performers in their roles does not directly affect HR professionals every day, like it does supervisors, who have to watch helplessly as the morale of the rest of the workforce erodes. There is nothing more corrosive to team-based structures than wide variability in effort and performance between different members. As one member of a research team in a pharmaceutical firm noted with respect to the idea of "carrying" a poor performer for fear of litigation, "As a female and also of a minority race, I am appalled and saddened by this scenario as I must bear the weight of this constant underperformer."[11]

Another questionable reaction is to initiate punitive actions short of termination, in an effort to get the employee to quit on his or her own. This reaction is often a result of frustrated supervisors, who, unable to fire someone because of HR, resort to punishing the employee in other ways. This might include giving the person a low-level work assignment, a downsized office, or some other form of undesirable treatment. The problem with this approach, however, is that it might be construed as "retaliation," and the employer could be sued for this, even if the original discrimination suit is dismissed.

Finally, a third unsustainable reaction is to pay off the employee with thousands of dollars in excess severance pay in return for waiving their right to sue for wrongful dismissal. That is, even if the employer feels the case is unwarranted, in order to avoid litigation itself, the employer may offer the terminated employee $20,000 or more to waive their right to sue. The problem with this strategy is that it sets the expectation that all poor performers are entitled to compensation on their way out the door, and this eventually increases the amount of potential future litigation by rewarding frivolous charges. As defense attorney Mark Dichter notes, "I can design HR policies that can virtually eliminate your risk of facing employment claims, but you'll have a pretty lousy workforce. At the end of the day, you have to run your business."[12]

Zero tolerance for poor performers is a critical element of success, especially for new and small firms when there is a great deal on the line. For example, new start-ups are notorious for terminating workers ruthlessly in the early stages of their development, and firing people after just three days is not uncommon. Yammer, a social networking site for businesses, fired over 30% of its employees in its first few years of doing business. Adam Pisoni, the senior technical chief at Yammer, boasts, "We are just really good about eliminating people whose skills were lacking and brutally honest when it comes to evaluating newcomers."[13] Within this industry, where "failing fast" is considered a virtue, helping an employee move on from a situation where the fit is bad may result in that person moving on to a place where the fit is better. For example, Paul English was fired from one start-up, NetCentric Corporation, and this experience led him back to his roots as a coder, and this eventually led him to start his own business that he sold for millions of dollars. English's strategy with newcomers at his own start-up—not surprisingly—was equally tough. When it comes to poor performers, English notes, "You've got to cut that tumor out. If you can't fix it, you've got to get rid of it."[14]

© WIN-Initiative/Getty Images

Start-up companies are notorious for terminating employees in a ruthless manner in the early days of their development.

The costs associated with letting poor performers stay on within the organization cannot be discounted. Organizations that introduce forced distribution rating systems where low performers are systematically identified and, where necessary, eliminated from payrolls often experience quick improvement gains in the range of 40%.[15] Given the critical financial and personal risks associated with employee dismissal, it is easy to see why the development of a standardized, systematic approach to discipline and discharge is critical to all organizations. These decisions should not be left solely to the discretion of individual managers or supervisors. In the next section we explore aspects of an effective discipline and discharge policy.

PRINCIPLES OF JUSTICE

As we noted earlier in Chapter 8, **outcome fairness** refers to the judgment that people make with respect to the *outcomes received* relative to the outcomes received by other people with whom they identify (referent others). Clearly, a situation where one person is losing his or her job while others are not is conducive to perceptions of outcome unfairness on the part of the discharged employee. The only thing worse than losing one's job might be losing one's job and then being prevented from seeking a similar job elsewhere. Employers are increasingly asking would-be hires to sign noncompete clauses in their hiring paperwork. A noncompete clause means that if the employee is terminated or voluntarily leaves the job, this person cannot seek new employment at a firm in the same industry. Traditionally, these kinds of clauses were aimed at high-paid jobs such as top-level executives or senior technical personnel who, due to their positions, had access to critical proprietary knowledge about the company's strategy or technology. These contacts were jointly negotiated and were generally considered "fair." Today, however, these contracts have trickled down to low-paid, entry-level employees where there is little negotiation. For example, Jimmy Johns, the ubiquitous sandwich-making franchise,

LO 10-2
List the major elements that contribute to perceptions of justice and how to apply these in organizational contexts involving discipline and dismissal.

Outcome Fairness
The judgment that people make with respect to the outcomes received relative to the outcomes received by other people with whom they identify.

makes all employees sign a noncompete clause as a matter of standard business practice. Although the company has never tried to stop some minimum-wage employees from taking all their knowledge to Blimpie's or some other chain, the mere fact that they have the clause strikes many as unbalanced and unfair.[16]

Whereas outcome justice focuses on the ends, procedural and interactional justice focus on means. If methods and procedures used to arrive at and implement decisions that impact the employee negatively are seen as fair, the reaction is likely to be much more positive than if this is not the case. **Procedural justice** focuses specifically on the *methods used to determine the outcomes received.* Table 10.1 details six key principles that determine whether people perceive procedures as being fair. Even given all the negative ramifications of being dismissed from one's job, the person being dismissed may accept the decision with minimum anger if the procedures used to arrive at the decision are consistent, unbiased, accurate, correctable, representative, and ethical. When the procedures for the decisions are perceived in this fashion, the individual does not feel unfairly singled out, and this helps maintain his or her faith in the system as a whole, even if he or she is unhappy with the specific decision that was triggered by the system.[17]

Lack of bias and informational accuracy are the most critical features of the six, and the potential for subjective judgments to be biased means that employers often have to go beyond simple supervisor evaluations in most cases.[18] In an effort to ensure that they have an airtight case many employers have turned to private investigators to collect objective evidence where necessary. For example, when a Florida hospital suspected a worker who claimed she was out with the flu for three days was actually totally healthy, they hired a private investigator to look into the case. In fact, the woman had gone to Universal Studio theme parks those days and the investigation uncovered photos of her from three different roller coaster rides (which routinely photograph riders and then try to sell the pictures to them), as well as a video where she volunteered as part of an animal act—all time-stamped and dated. Needless to say, this led to a termination that the worker was not interested in challenging.[19]

Whereas procedural justice deals with how a decision was made, **interactional justice** refers to the *interpersonal nature of how the outcomes were implemented.* For example, in many documented cases, after giving employees the news of their termination, employers immediately have security guards whisk them out of the building with their various personal items haphazardly thrown together in cardboard boxes. This strips the

Procedural Justice
A concept of justice focusing on the methods used to determine the outcomes received.

Interactional Justice
A concept of justice referring to the interpersonal nature of how the outcomes were implemented.

Table 10.1
Six Determinants of Procedural Justice

(1) **Consistency.** The procedures are applied consistently across time and other persons.

(2) **Bias suppression.** The procedures are applied by a person who has no vested interest in the outcome and no prior prejudices regarding the individual.

(3) **Information accuracy.** The procedure is based on information that is perceived to be true.

(4) **Correctability.** The procedure has built-in safeguards that allow one to appeal mistakes or bad decisions.

(5) **Representativeness.** The procedure is informed by the concerns of all groups or stakeholders (co-workers, customers, owners) affected by the decision, including the individual being dismissed.

(6) **Ethicality.** The procedure is consistent with prevailing moral standards as they pertain to issues like invasion of privacy or deception.

(1) **Explanation.** Emphasize aspects of procedural fairness that justify the decision.
(2) **Social sensitivity.** Treat the person with dignity and respect.
(3) **Consideration.** Listen to the person's concerns.
(4) **Empathy.** Identify with the person's feelings.

Table 10.2
Four Determinants of Interactional Justice

person of their dignity, as well as their job, and employees who witness this happen to a co-worker show a drastically lower level of organizational commitment from that day forward.[20] Table 10.2 lists the four key determinants of interactional justice. When the decision is explained well and implemented in a fashion that is socially sensitive, considerate, and empathetic, this helps defuse some of the resentment that might come about from a decision to discharge an employee.

PROGRESSIVE DISCIPLINE AND ALTERNATIVE DISPUTE RESOLUTION

Except in the most extreme cases, employees should generally not be terminated for a first offense. However, as the "Integrity in Action" box illustrates, this cannot be avoided in some instances. Rather, termination should come about at the end of a systematic discipline program. Effective discipline programs have two central components: documentation (which includes specific publication of work rules and job descriptions that should be in place prior to administering discipline) and progressive punitive measures. Thus, as shown in Table 10.3, punitive measures should be taken in steps of increasing magnitude, and only after having been clearly documented. This may start with an unofficial warning for the first offense, followed by a written reprimand for additional offenses. At some point, later offenses may lead to a temporary suspension. Before a company suspends an employee, it may even want to issue a "last chance notification," indicating that the next offense will result in termination. Such procedures may seem exasperatingly slow, and they may fail to meet one's emotional need for quick and satisfying retribution. In the end, however, when problem employees are discharged, the chance that they can prove they were discharged for poor cause has been minimized.

At various points in the discipline process, the individual or the organization might want to bring in outside parties to help resolve discrepancies or conflicts. As a last resort, the individual might invoke the legal system to resolve these types of conflicts, but in

OFFENSE FREQUENCY	ORGANIZATIONAL RESPONSE	DOCUMENTATION
First offense	Unofficial verbal warning	Witness present
Second offense	Official written warning	Document filed
Third offense	Second official warning, with threat of temporary suspension	Document filed
Fourth offense	Temporary suspension and "last chance notification"	Document filed
Fifth offense	Termination (with right to go to arbitration)	Document filed

Table 10.3
An Example of a Progressive Discipline Program

Donald Trump Told: "You're Fired!"

When Donald Trump announced he was running for president in 2015 on the Republican ticket, he turned his stance on immigration reform to a vicious attack on Mexicans the likes of which has never been seen in U.S. politics. Trump declared, "When Mexico sends its people they're not sending their best. They're sending people that have a lot of problems and they're bringing those problems with them. They're bringing drugs. They're bringing crime. They're rapists. And some, I assume, are good people."

The backlash against these comments was immediate and intense, particularly within the Hispanic community. Univision, the largest Spanish-speaking broadcaster in the United States, quickly ended its relationship with Trump, canceling plans to air the Miss USA and Miss Universe pageants jointly owned by Trump and NBC. At first, NBC's reaction was more measured, and representatives for the company simply noted that "Mr. Trump's opinions do not represent those of NBC and we do not agree with his positions on a number of issues, including his recent comments on immigration."

However, after receiving a petition signed by over 200,000 people, as well as being lashed on social media, NBC hardened its position and severed all of its ties with Trump as well. The network said it would no longer air the two pageants and that the television shows "The Apprentice" and "Celebrity Apprentice" will go forward without Trump. A new statement was released noting, "At NBC, respect and dignity for all people are cornerstones of our values, and due to the recent derogatory comments by Donald Trump regarding immigrants, NBC is ending its business relationship with Mr. Trump."

DISCUSSION QUESTIONS

1. If you were training and preparing to be part of the Miss Universe Pageant and learned it would not be televised as a result of NBC's reaction to Trump's comments, should you be free to sue either NBC or Trump?

2. If a court injunction were issued, and NBC had to air the pageant, would you boycott the event if you were Miss Mexico?

SOURCES: S. Tareen, A. Rappeport, "NBC to Donald Trump: You're Fired," *The New York Times,* June 29, 2015, www.nytimes.com; K. Hagey, "NBC Cutting Ties with Donald Trump," *The Wall Street Journal,* June 29, 2015, www .wsj.com; A. Jones, "NBC Universal Cuts Ties with Donald Trump," *CNN,* June 29, 2015, www.cnn.com.

Alternative Dispute Resolution (ADR)
A method of resolving disputes that does not rely on the legal system. Often proceeds through the four stages of open door policy, peer review, mediation, and arbitration.

order to avoid this, more and more companies are turning to **alternative dispute resolution (ADR)**. Alternative dispute resolution can take on many different forms, but in general, ADR proceeds through the four stages shown in Table 10.4. Each stage reflects a somewhat broader involvement of different people, and the hope is that the conflict will be resolved at earlier steps. However, the last step may include binding arbitration, where an agreed upon neutral party resolves the conflict unilaterally if necessary. The use of ADR is growing rapidly among employers. In 2012, only 16% of employers required workers to sign away their legal rights to sue their employer in exchange for ADR procedures, but by 2014 this figure was up to 43%. Part of this was attributable to a 2011 Supreme Court ruling that upheld the legal status of pre-employment–required ADR sign-offs. Prior to this ruling, many lower courts were vacating or striking down ADR judgments, which meant that rather than staying out of court, ADR just added an additional layer to the process. The Supreme Court removed this layer and ruled that employees voluntarily signed the agreements. Thus they were bound to them, even though they could not have been hired had they not signed. This makes ADR very attractive to employers and litigation costs associated with class action suits dropped by roughly $150 million between 2011 and 2014.[21]

Stage 1: Open-door policy

The two people in conflict (e.g., supervisor and subordinate) attempt to arrive at a settlement together. If none can be reached, they proceed to

Stage 2: Peer review

A panel composed of representatives from the organization that are at the same level of those people in the dispute hears the case and attempts to help the parties arrive at a settlement. If none can be reached, they proceed to

Stage 3: Mediation

A neutral third party from outside the organization hears the case and, via a nonbinding process, tries to help the disputants arrive at a settlement. If none can be reached, the parties proceed to

Stage 4: Arbitration

A professional arbitrator from outside the organization hears the case and resolves it unilaterally by rendering a specific decision or award. Most arbitrators are experienced employment attorneys or retired judges.

Table 10.4
Stages in Alternative Dispute Resolution

Whereas ADR is effective in dealing with problems related to performance and interpersonal differences in the workplace, many of the problems that lead an organization to want to terminate an individual's employment relate to drug or alcohol abuse. In these cases, the organization's discipline and dismissal program should also incorporate an employee assistance program. Due to the increased prevalence of EAPs in organizations, we describe them in detail here.

EMPLOYEE ASSISTANCE AND WELLNESS PROGRAMS

An **employee assistance program (EAP)** is a referral service that supervisors or employees can use to seek professional treatment for various problems. EAPs vary widely, but most share some basic elements. First, the programs are usually identified in official documents published by the employer (such as employee handbooks). Supervisors (and union representatives, where relevant) are trained to use the referral service for employees whom they suspect of having health-related problems. Employees are also trained to use the system to make self-referrals when necessary.

Although originally targeted at the use of illegal drugs, many EAPs increasingly have had to deal with employees who have problems attributable to prescription drugs, especially painkillers. The percentage of workers who have tested positive for illegal drugs has decreased steadily from 14% in 1988 to just 3% in 2013. However, positive tests for painkillers such as Oxycontin and Vicodin rose 175% between 2005 and 2013 alone.[22] Obviously, just because the drug might be prescribed for the worker does not mean that this person, working under the drug's influence, is not a safety threat to other workers of customers. Thus, many organizations have zero tolerance policies for many prescription drugs that are just as strict as their EAP policies for illegal drugs.[23] Moreover, even if a painkiller is legal in one country where the firm operated, it may not be legal in another country. For example, in 2015, Julie Hamp, the most senior female executive at Toyota, was forced to resign when she was arrested for being in possession of oxycodone—another powerful painkiller—that just happened to be illegal in Japan.[24]

The key to the effectiveness of an EAP is striking the right balance between collecting information that can be used to promote employee health on the one hand and the employee's right to privacy on the other. Many employees are afraid to come forward

Employee Assistance Programs (EAPs)
Employer programs that attempt to ameliorate problems encountered by workers who are drug dependent, alcoholic, or psychologically troubled.

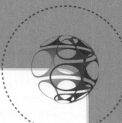

Wearable Sensors Make Employers' Hearts Race

It is not at all uncommon these days to see people donning wearable sensors like the Fitbit Charge, the Nike Fuelband, the Jawbone UP3, or the Microsoft Band. These wearable sensors allow people to track their daily activity levels, as well as health-related data such as body temperature, heart rate, and even blood pressure. Industry researchers note that in 2014, 42 million such devices were sold, up from 32 million in 2013. Clearly, people are increasingly health conscious, and this technology is a logical step in obtaining the kind of information people want to know about themselves.

However, due to the high cost of employee health care coverage, this information is also something that is generating the interest of employers. For example, one large health insurer, Cigna, launched a pilot program in 2014 where it distributed arm bands manufactured by Body Media to thousands of employees at one of its large customers. The devices were able to identify a number of workers who were on the verge of developing diabetes and got them on a path toward a healthier lifestyle. Similarly, at the oil company BP, the HR department gave 14,000 employees a free Fitbit if they would allow the company to monitor their physical activity. Employees who logged over a million steps within a specified time period were rewarded with lower premiums on their insurance.

Currently, most employer-sponsored wearable device programs have been voluntary and focused on rewards for healthy behavior, not compulsory and attached to punishments such as surcharges, but it is hard to anticipate what the future may hold. On the one hand, the ability of an employer to monitor the health of their employees just like the health of their stock price is tempting. On the other hand, many employees may react negatively and see this as an invasion of privacy. As Pam Dixon, executive director of the World Privacy Forum, states, "It is going to be very important that as we move towards the future we don't set up a system where people become pressured into wearing devices to monitor their health. That's a real problem. That's just not very free."

DISCUSSION QUESTIONS

1. If your employer were to give you a free Fitbit in return for the opportunity to download your data at the end of each day, would you sign up for this trade?
2. What kind of decisions should employers be able to make based on this data and what kind of decisions should be considered off base?

SOURCES: R. Pyrillis, "Collecting Health Data Is All in the Wrist for Some Employers," *Workforce*, February 24, 2015, www.workforce.com; B. Walsh, "The Doctor on Your Wrist," *Time Magazine*, November 14, 2014, pp. 35–38; P. Olson, "Wearable Tech Is Plugging into Health Insurance," *Forbes*, June 19, 2014, www.forbes.com.

with information that they think may damage their careers, and so it is in the employer's best interest to support people who do self-refer by keeping their information confidential, and then supporting them through counseling and rehabilitation.[25] However, rehabilitation rates for alcohol- and drug-addicted workers are far from 100%, and so the employer still has an obligation to monitor progress to make sure that these workers are not a safety threat to others. For example, the EEOC ruled in 2014 that if a worker is part of an EAP and being treated for alcoholism, a manager who knows this and sees this person drinking alcohol at an office party is obligated to report this to the EAP. Again, this may seem a violation of privacy, but this right has to be weighed against the other employees' right to a safe work place.[26]

Whereas EAPs deal with employees who have developed problems at work because of health-related issues, employee wellness programs take a proactive and preemptive focus on trying to prevent health-related problems in the first place. Employee wellness programs come in many different sizes and varieties, so it is very difficult to make general statements about their cost and effectiveness. Some companies just hand out pamphlets on how to maintain better health and call that a wellness program.[27] Other programs attach wearable sensors like Fitbit to their employees, monitor their health status continuously, provide company-sponsored facilities and medical staff to support better health, and then reward employees financially for accomplishing health-related goals.[28] Indeed, as the "Competing through Technology" box illustrates, wearable sensors are creating new and unprecedented opportunities to monitor employee health, but here too privacy concerns may arise.

Some organizations even reach beyond the employee and offer incentives to the worker's spouse and family. After all, if the organization is actually insuring everyone in the family, there are savings to be made by placing the focus on the whole family. For example, Aetna offers a $1,200 reward for employees who can get their spouse and children to sign up for its corporate wellness program. These kinds of financial incentives typically pay for themselves because research suggests that for large employers, every $1 spent on wellness results in a savings of $3.27 when it comes to costs.[29] Adding a social element to wellness programs often increases participation rates and effectiveness, and so some employers sponsor team-based competitions that pit various sub-units against each other in an effort to spike interest and motivation. It is one thing to let yourself down and not meet your exercise goals, but it is a different thing altogether when your failure results in the failure of your team. For example, when employees in city government in Charlotte, Virginia, were asked to participate in a six-week challenge where the only reward was bragging rights within the organization, participation rates doubled and the employees logged close to 9,000 hours of exercise.[30] Similar competitions have been successfully staged between various small businesses, who as a group tend to struggle when it comes to offering wellness programs.[31]

Not all employees will necessarily respond to positive incentives like this, however, and hence some companies take a more punitive approach to wellness. For example, Michelin Tire Company not only collects health-related data from employees but in addition punishes employees who fail to meet health goals. Michelin employees who have high blood pressure or whose waistlines exceed a certain limit (40 inches for men and 35 inches for women) are forced to pay an extra $1,000 for health care coverage. This might seem pretty strict for a company whose mascot is the "spare-tired" Michelin Man, but similar penalties have been levied by Miracle Gro, CVS Caremark, Honeywell, and General Electric. All of these companies have found that people react more strongly to threats of losses than promises of gains. Reward programs at these companies that offered incentives to get healthier simply did not seem to work; however, punishment-based programs definitely get people's attention. These companies have also found that roughly 80% of health care costs are generated by just 20% of the workers, and a staggering 1% of workers generate 33% of the costs. Targeting these specific individuals has proven to be an efficient way to get costs under control, but there are legal limits to how far employers can go with these sorts of penalties.[32]

One of the major determinants of how far employee wellness programs can push their employees is how central health is to effectively performing the work. In general, if one defines obese as having a body mass index (BMI) of 30 or higher, there is an obesity epidemic in the United States.[33] The obesity rate for Americans doubled between 1993 and 2012, and for some organizations, this is a threat to their ability to accomplish their mission. For example, the Federal Aviation Authority (FAA) passed a new rule in 2013 that any commercial or private pilot with a BMI of 40 or more has to be examined by a sleep specialist to confirm that they do not have sleep apnea. Sleep apnea is highly related to obesity, and the FAA identified over a half dozen incidents in 2012 where a pilot fell asleep in the cockpit. This included a well-publicized case where a Bombardier regional jet traveling to Hawaii overflew the airport where it was supposed to land by 30 miles after a 20-minute lapse in radio communication with the tower.[34]

Another organization that is highly concerned about obesity is the U.S. Federal Bureau of Investigation (FBI). In 2015, the director of the agency issued a new requirement that its agents pass a fitness test once a year and that failure to do so will be part of their annual performance evaluation and raise process. At one time, almost all members of the FBI worked in highly active jobs in the field where they were chasing and arresting criminals. However, the threats of terrorism, cyber security, and large-scale fraud have pushed many of the employees into offices where they sit behind computers for very long stretches of time. This has had the predictable effects on obesity rates in the agency, and in order to counter this, the agency now requires agents to be able to do 24 push-ups without stopping and 35 sit-ups in a minute. It also requires that agents be able to sprint 300 yards in less than a minute and run a mile in under 12 minutes.[35]

Although financial costs are often the driving force behind these programs, one should not lose sight of the fact that the quality of life enjoyed by employees both on and off the job is also affected. For example, while some employees were suing Miracle Gro over its program, another employee, Joe Pellegrini, was celebrating the fact that the very same program saved his life. Although physically fit, Pellegrini's health assessment indicated a high level of cholesterol, and the company forced him to see a physician. That trip to the doctor revealed a 95% blockage in a heart valve that would have probably killed him within five days. Obviously, Pellegrini has a different perception of Miracle Gro's policies than most employees, noting that when it came to his own life, "It was that close."[36]

OUTPLACEMENT COUNSELING

Outplacement Counseling
Counseling to help displaced employees manage the transition from one job to another.

The permanent nature of an employee termination not only leaves the person angry, it also leads to confusion as to how to react and in a quandary regarding what happens next. If the person feels there is nothing to lose and nowhere else to turn, the potential for violence or litigation is higher than most organizations are willing to tolerate. Therefore, many organizations provide **outplacement counseling**, which tries to help dismissed employees manage the transition from one job to another. There is a great deal of variability in the services offered via outplacement programs, typically including career counseling, job search support, résumé critiques, job interviewing training, and provision of networking opportunities. Increasingly, these programs are moving online both to reduce costs and in recognition that most job search activity now takes place online. Face-to-face meetings between counselors and clients are largely becoming a thing of the past, being replaced by web-based tools.[37]

Many have criticized the effectiveness of outplacement programs and charged that the companies that offer the service care more about avoiding litigation and bad public relations than getting former employees new jobs. Many programs take a "one-size-fits-all" approach with standardized training programs not tailored to the specific needs of clients and industries, as well as boilerplate resume services that wind up sending out almost identical documents for different workers. The evidence suggests that 40% of workers offered such services never show up, and another 30% quit after one or two sessions.[38] Still many employers are committed to these programs, and as you can see in the "Evidence-Based HR" box, there is evidence that supports the business case for this activity.

EVIDENCE-BASED HR

When it comes to outplacement activities, Bruce Williams, the executive director of Employee Relations at Procter and Gamble, notes, "We care about our employees and during times of change we offer outplacement services to those impacted to give them career guidance and support. What's more, employees that remain are assured of our company's commitment to our purpose and values knowing we are going to be responsible and respectful." All of this sounds good, but beyond sounding good, the evidence also seems to support the value of outplacement activities for a number of reasons according to a recent survey conducted by Right Management.

Specifically, when it comes to employee lawsuits, employers who offer outplacement activities stand a 10% reduced likelihood of litigation by prior employees relative to companies that fail to provide such services. In addition, in terms of pre- and post-evidence, roughly 20% of employers who engaged in outplacement activities reported that turnover among employees that remained went down after the initiation of such programs. Recruitment costs for new employees were also reported to be 24% lower for firms that provide this sort of employee assistance. Finally, 38% of employers that offered outplacement saw an increase in employee satisfaction one year after the downsizing event compared to just 14% for employers who did not offer such services.

SOURCE: B. Lowsky, "Inside Outplacement," *Workforce,* July 2014, pp. 37–38.

At the very least, though, outplacement counseling can help people realize that losing a job is not the end of the world and that other opportunities exist. For example, when John Morgridge was fired from his job as branch manager at Honeywell, it made him realize that his own assertiveness and need for independence were never going to cut it in a large, bureaucratic institution like Honeywell. Morgridge took his skills and went on to build computer network maker Cisco Systems, which is now worth more than $1 billion.[39] This is a success story for Morgridge, but the fact that a major corporation like Honeywell let his talent go certainly reflects a lost opportunity for the company. Retaining people who can make such contributions is a key to gaining and maintaining competitive advantage. The second half of this chapter is devoted to issues related to retention.

Managing Voluntary Turnover

In the first section of this chapter, our focus was on how to help employees who were not contributing to the organization's goal in a manner that protected the firm's ability to compete, and on how to support former employees' transition into alternative employment. In this second section, we focus on the other side of the separation equation—preventing employees who are highly valued by the organization from leaving (and perhaps even joining the competition). At the organizational level, turnover results in lowered work unit performance, which, in turn, harms the firm's financial performance.[40] This causal chain is especially strong when the organization is losing its top performers. Research suggests that some of the organization's top performers are up to 300% more productive than average employees, and retaining these workers is especially difficult.[41]

Moreover, if your organization has a reputation for being successful, you become an especially attractive target to external forces that may look to steal your talent.

For example, because of its positive reputation, Apple has always been a company that has had to work hard to hold onto its valued employees. Tesla Motors has hired over 150 former Apple executives, designers, and engineers in the last few years alone. Part of Tesla's competitive strategy is to exploit the fact that software has gone from providing 10% of the value of a car to 60%, and thus the skills and orientation of former Apple employees are a great fit for Tesla's business model.[42] Although this hiring pattern might be good news for Tesla, it is just the tip of the iceberg when it comes to losing valuable talent. As we saw in Chapter 5, stopping employee attrition was the driving factor behind an illegal anti-trust informal agreement between high tech companies to not recruit from each other—led by Steve Jobs, the CEO of Apple at that time.

There are many different reasons why one may be attached to his or her job, and employers need to recognize this in their efforts to retain workers. For example, pay and job security used to be the primary drivers of retention for older generations of workers, but this is not always the case today. The evidence seems to suggest that younger employees prefer benefits to cash, and generally want to work in an environment that is fun, collaborative and provides a great deal of immediate feedback and opportunities for development. This generation of employees has a lot to offer employers, including the fact that they are technically skilled, racially diverse, socially interconnected and collaborative. However, the annual rate of voluntary turnover among millennials tends to be higher than that associated with other generations, and this has led some to conclude that they are impatient and entitled. Still, as one experienced manager notes, "If they don't feel like they're making a contribution to a company quickly, they don't stay, but if you provide them with the right environment, they'll work forever—around the clock."[43] In this section of the chapter, we examine the job withdrawal process that characterizes voluntary employee turnover, and we illustrate the central role that job satisfaction plays in this process.

PROCESS OF JOB WITHDRAWAL

Job withdrawal is a set of behaviors that dissatisfied individuals enact to avoid the work situation. The right side of Figure 10.1 shows a model grouping the overall set of behaviors into three categories: behavior change, physical job withdrawal, and psychological job withdrawal.

Progression of Withdrawal
Theory that dissatisfied individuals enact a set of behaviors in succession to avoid their work situation.

We present the various forms of withdrawal in a progression, as if individuals try the next category only if the preceding is either unsuccessful or impossible to implement. This theory of **progression of withdrawal** has a long history and many adherents.[44] For example, someone who is dissatisfied with the job or organization might not be able to just jump to another job right away but will instead either disengage temporarily

Figure 10.1

An Overall Model of the Job Dissatisfaction–Job Withdrawal Process

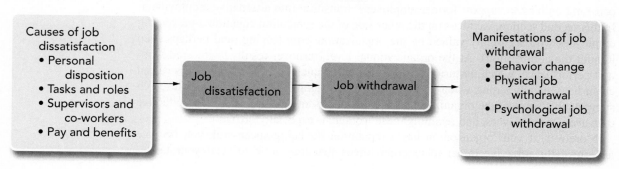

(through absenteeism or tardiness) or psychologically (through lower job involvement and organizational commitment) until the right opportunity comes along.[45] Others have suggested that there is no tight progression in that any one of the categories can compensate for another, and people choose the category that is most likely to redress the specific source of dissatisfaction.[46] Still other theories maintain that turnover is set up by a general level of persistent dissatisfaction that then is triggered abruptly by some single disruptive event at work that either pushes the employee away (such as a dispute with a supervisor or co-worker) or pulls the employee away (an alternative employment opportunity).[47] This model focuses on "the straw that breaks the camel's back" but shares with all the other theories an emphasis on job dissatisfaction as the necessary but insufficient cause of turnover. Regardless of what specific theory one endorses, there is a general consensus that withdrawal behaviors are clearly related to one another, and they are all at least partially caused by job dissatisfaction.[48]

Behavior Change

One might expect that an employee's first response to dissatisfaction would be to try to change the conditions that generate the dissatisfaction. This can lead to supervisor–subordinate confrontation, perhaps even conflict, as dissatisfied workers try to bring about changes in policy or upper-level personnel. Although at first this type of conflict can feel threatening to the manager, on closer inspection, this is really an opportunity for the manager to learn about and perhaps solve an important problem. When properly channeled by a secure and supportive leader, "voicing opportunities" for lower-level employees can often result in substantial organizational improvements and prevent turnover among highly engaged employees.[49]

Less constructively, employees can initiate change through **whistle-blowing** (making grievances public by going to the media).[50] Whistle-blowers are often dissatisfied individuals who cannot bring about internal change and, out of a sense of commitment or frustration, take their concerns to external constituencies. For example, regardless of what others thought of him, in his own mind Edward Snowden was doing the right thing. Concerned that the National Security Agency was increasingly spying on U.S. citizens by collecting information on over 10 million telephone calls, he went public with this information in June 2013. He felt he was doing his civic duty in trying to inspire a national debate on the "security–privacy" trade-off that seemed to be taking place in the United States at that time. He also knew the severity of his actions, noting, "I understand I will be made to suffer for my actions, but I will be satisfied if the federation of secret law, unequal pardon and irresistible executive powers that rule the world that I love are revealed for even an instant."[51]

In the eyes of many people within the U.S. government, Edward Snowden was a traitor. In the effort to thwart global terrorism, the program at the heart of this controversy merely captured data on who was talking to whom, and not the content of any of those conversations. The program was simply trying to lay out the social network of global terrorists, part of which resides within the country's borders. The data could be used to secure a legal warrant for tapping a phone, but no phone was ever tapped illegally. However, by making the program public, Snowden tipped off potential terrorists to heretofore unknown dangers, and thus aided and abetted them in the goal of avoiding detection.[52] Whether or not Edward Snowden is a whistle-blower or traitor will be for history to decide, but for ethicists, this example illustrates how the employee has to balance two central trusts: the trust of his employer, who pays him to do specific work under a specific contract he willingly signed; and the trust of the larger society in which he resides to protect its citizens from rogue companies or overreaching branches of government.[53]

Whistle-blowing
Making grievances public by going to the media or government.

Although this type of whistle-blowing activity has always taken place, the advent of websites like Wikileaks has provided a more obvious and convenient outlet for this activity. Wikileaks is most famous for collecting and publishing information provided by government and military sources, but it has also threatened private companies such as Bank of America.[54] This type of whistleblowing is also on the rise because of a provision of the 2010 Dodd-Franks regulatory overhaul that encourages this behavior by offering 30% of penalties collected by the government to individuals who help unearth illegal actions, in an effort to compensate them for the risks they take.[55] Because many of these settlements involve multi-million-dollar settlements, this specific incentive can be very powerful. For example, Floyd Landis, a former member of Lance Armstrong's cycling team, blew the whistle on an illegal doping scheme that Armstrong had denied for many years. Because Armstrong's team was funded by the U.S. Postal Service under a contract that prohibited the use of banned substances, the government sought $100 million in retribution from the team, 30% of which could go to Landis.[56]

Physical Job Withdrawal

If the job conditions cannot be changed, a dissatisfied worker may be able to solve the problem by leaving the job. This could take the form of an internal transfer if the dissatisfaction is job-specific (the result of an unfair supervisor or unpleasant working conditions). On the other hand, if the source of the dissatisfaction relates to organizationwide policies (lack of job security or below-market pay levels), organizational turnover is likely. As we indicated earlier, there is a negative relationship between turnover rates and organizational performance, and it is generally very costly to replace workers—especially high performers in skilled jobs.[57]

Another way of physically removing oneself from the dissatisfying work short of quitting altogether is to be absent. Although less financially disruptive relative to having an employee quit his or her job, absenteeism is still costly for many employers, especially very small companies where it is often harder to make up for a single person's absence. The direct cost of employee absenteeism has been estimated to represent roughly 2% of payroll; however, there are also indirect costs of absenteeism. For example, the employer may need to pay a replacement worker or pay other workers overtime to make up for the person who failed to show up. In addition, production might be reduced and customers may have to wait longer for services. When these indirect costs are added to the equation, absenteeism costs closer to 4% of payroll.[58]

Psychological Withdrawal

When dissatisfied employees are unable to change their situation or remove themselves physically from their jobs, they may psychologically disengage themselves from their jobs. Although they are physically on the job, their minds may be somewhere else.

Job Involvement
The degree to which people identify themselves with their jobs.

Organizational Commitment
The degree to which an employee identifies with the organization and is willing to put forth effort on its behalf.

This psychological disengagement can take several forms. First, if the primary dissatisfaction has to do with the job itself, the employee may display a very low level of job involvement. **Job involvement** is the degree to which people identify themselves with their jobs. People who are uninvolved with their jobs consider their work an unimportant aspect of their lives. A second form of psychological disengagement, which can occur when the dissatisfaction is with the employer as a whole, is a low level of organizational commitment. **Organizational commitment** is the degree to which an employee identifies with the organization and is willing to put forth effort on its behalf. Individuals who feel they have been unjustly treated by their employer often respond by reducing their level of commitment and are often looking for the first good chance to quit their jobs. In contrast, employees who are involved in their job and committed to their employer are much more likely to respond to problems by speaking up, voicing their concerns, and trying to change what they may consider a bad situation. Most whistle-blowers tend to be people committed to their jobs and organizations, not people who forget about their jobs the moment they leave the workplace.[59]

JOB SATISFACTION AND JOB WITHDRAWAL

As we saw in Figure 10.1, the key driving force behind all the different forms of job withdrawal is **job satisfaction**, which we will define as a pleasurable feeling that results from the perception that one's job fulfills or allows for the fulfillment of one's important job values.[60] This definition reflects three important aspects of job satisfaction. First, job satisfaction is a function of *values,* defined as "what a person consciously or unconsciously desires to obtain." Second, this definition emphasizes that different employees have different views of which values are important, and this is critical in determining the nature and degree of their job satisfaction. The third important aspect of job satisfaction is perception. An individual's perceptions may not be a completely accurate reflection of reality, and different people may view the same situation differently.

In particular, people's perceptions are often strongly influenced by their frame of reference. A **frame of reference** is a standard point that serves as a comparison for other points and thus provides meaning. For example, a nurse might compare her salary to the salaries of other nurses and her overall satisfaction with pay depends on this comparison as much as the absolute value of pay itself. A female nurse in 2011 made, on average, a little over $50,000 a year in salary. This is a healthy salary, and she might be satisfied with this salary until she learns that, on average, a male nurse doing the same work made slightly over $60,000 a year.[61] These kinds of frame-of-reference effects are powerful, and many companies try to reduce the impact of these kinds of social comparisons by making pay levels secret. However, as work becomes more collaborative and team-oriented, there is increasing demand for transparency about pay, and even team member input into pay decisions. Balancing team members' need-to-know with privacy concerns, as well as the need to mitigate conflict between team members who disagree about their relative worth is increasingly a struggle in many business contexts.[62]

SOURCES OF JOB DISSATISFACTION

Many aspects of people and organizations can cause dissatisfaction among employees. Managers and HR professionals need to be aware of these because they are the levers which can raise job satisfaction and reduce employee withdrawal.

Unsafe Working Conditions

Earlier in this chapter we discussed the employer's role in helping employees stay healthy via employee assistance programs for specific problems like drug addiction and alcohol dependency, as well as general wellness initiatives to promote health and reduce health care–related expenditures. Obviously, if employers care this much about the risk employees are exposed to off the job, there needs to be an even more important emphasis on risk exposure that occurs on the job.

Of course, each employee has a right to safe working conditions, and previously in this book (see Chapter 3) we reviewed the Occupational Safety and Health Act of 1970 (OSHA), which spells out those rights in a very detailed fashion. We also discussed in

LO 10-3
Specify the relationship between job satisfaction and various forms of job withdrawal, and identify the major sources of job satisfaction in work contexts.

Job Satisfaction
A pleasurable feeling that results from the perception that one's job fulfills or allows for the fulfillment of one's important job values.

Frame of Reference
A standard point that serves as a comparison for other points and thus provides meaning.

that chapter how to develop safety awareness programs that identify and communicate job hazards, as well as how to reinforce safe work practices that would allow one to pass an OSHA inspection. Although our emphasis in that chapter on safety was primarily directed at legal compliance, we need to revisit the topic in this chapter, because OSHA is not the only audience that is likely to evaluate the safety of jobs. The perception and reaction of the organization's own employees to working conditions has implications for satisfaction, retention, and competitive advantage that go well beyond merely meeting the legal requirements. That is, if applicants or job incumbents conclude that their health or lives are at risk because of the job, attracting and retaining workers will be impossible.

Not all jobs pose safety risks, but the nature of the work in a whole host of jobs makes managing safety-related perceptions critical. This includes jobs such as fishing boat operators, timber cutters, airline pilot/flight attendants, structural metal workers, garbage collectors, and taxi drivers/chauffeurs, which all have been identified as jobs where people are most likely to be involved in fatal accidents. In fact, in these job categories alone, close to 1,000 people die annually. Other jobs that rate low in terms of fatal accidents rate higher in nonfatal accidents, and this includes many jobs in eating establishments, hospitals, nursing homes, convenience stores, and the long-haul trucking industry. Still other jobs pose risks in terms of contracting occupational diseases due to exposure to chemicals. Finally, some jobs create health risks simply because of the long hours and high stress that are associated with them.[63] This was highlighted recently by several cases in the aviation industry where air traffic controllers who were working at night were found to be sleeping on the job because of extended hours. For example, in one case, a lone controller was working on less than two hours' sleep in the previous 24 hours, and this was a contributing factor in the crash of ComAir Flight 191 in Lexington, Kentucky.[64] In general, working at night runs counter to the basic physiology of the human body and disrupts one's natural circadian rhythm, which in turn causes a whole host of physical problems. Thus, working at night has to be considered a safety issue in any job that states this as a task requirement in the job description.[65]

Personal Dispositions

Because dissatisfaction is an emotion that ultimately resides within the person, it is not surprising that many who have studied these outcomes have focused on individual differences. For example, in Chapter 6, we described the Five Factor Model of Personality, and several of these traits have been linked to higher turnover intentions and actual turnover. In general, turnover is more likely to be an issue for employees who are low in emotional stability, low in conscientiousness, and low in agreeableness.[66]

Negative Affectivity
A dispositional dimension that reflects pervasive individual differences in satisfaction with any and all aspects of life.

Negative affectivity is a term used to describe a dispositional dimension that reflects pervasive individual differences in satisfaction with any and all aspects of life. Individuals who are high in negative affectivity report higher levels of aversive mood states, including anger, contempt, disgust, guilt, fear, and nervousness across all contexts (work and nonwork). People who are high in negative affectivity tend to focus extensively on the negative aspects of themselves and others. They also tend to persist in their negative attitudes even in the face of organizational interventions, such as increased pay levels, that generally increase the levels of satisfaction of other people.[67] All of this implies that some individuals tend to bring low satisfaction with them to work. Thus these people may be relatively dissatisfied regardless of what steps the organization or the manager takes. On the other hand, research suggests that people who are positive tend to work harder, are more likely to be committed to the organization, get paid more, and get promoted more often.[68] Like anything, however, one can get too much of a good thing, and if a work group is made up of people who are all high in positive affect, they are often overly optimistic and fail to engage in a sufficient level of critical thinking regarding what might go wrong with plans or projects. Thus, when it comes to team composition, a built-in "devil's advocate" can be a highly valuable member.[69]

The evidence on the linkage between these kinds of traits and job satisfaction suggests the importance of personnel selection as a way of raising overall levels of employee satisfaction. If job satisfaction remains relatively stable across time and jobs because of characteristics like negative affectivity, this suggests that transient changes in job satisfaction will be difficult to sustain in these individuals, who will typically revert to their "dispositional" or adaptation level over time. Thus, some employers actually try to screen for this when selecting job candidates. For example, at Zappos, the online retailer of shoes and apparel, CEO Tony Hsieh notes that "We do our best to hire positive people and put them where their positive thinking is reinforced."[70]

Tasks and Roles

As a predictor of job dissatisfaction, nothing surpasses the nature of the task itself. Many aspects of a task have been linked to dissatisfaction. Several elaborate theories relating task characteristics to worker reactions have been formulated and extensively tested. We discussed several of these in Chapter 4. In this section we focus on three primary aspects of tasks that affect job satisfaction: the complexity of the task, the amount of flexibility in where and when the work is done, and, finally, the value the employee puts on the task.[71]

With a few exceptions, there is a strong positive relationship between task complexity and job satisfaction. That is, the boredom generated by simple, repetitive jobs that do not mentally challenge the worker leads to frustration and dissatisfaction.[72] Many have attributed much of the recent labor unrest in China to this specific aspect of the work. For example, the Han Hoi riot started as a minor fracas between two young workers but soon escalated into a pitched battle that involved over 2,000 employees and 5,000 paramilitary forces. The two workers, who everyone agrees started the riot, were from different regions and had just finished a stressful 12-hour shift at the factory that makes iPod and iPads. The work was boring and low paid, and frustrations boiled over when a small argument turned into a shoving and pushing match. Witnesses claim that security workers at the plant overreacted to the incident and began brutally beating the two young people. At that point, hundreds of workers rushed the security personnel and returned the favor. Soon, more and more security personnel were called to the scene, followed by more and more restive workers. A major revolt was under way and when it was over, 40 people were hospitalized and the facility had to be shut down for days after fires and looting left many stretches of the campus that housed close to 80,000 workers gutted.[73] This instance of labor unrest received a great deal of national attention in China due to its severity, but as the "Competing through Globalization" box shows, labor unrest in China is hardly relegated to factories.

This riot was just one of many that put a spotlight on the tension between Chinese factories that base their business model on low cost-strategies that create low-scope jobs and unpleasant working conditions, and a new generation of Chinese workers who seem less willing to tolerate those conditions. Chinese authorities recognize this problem, and Han Hoi spokesman Louis Woo summed up the experience by noting, "We cannot argue that manufacturing jobs are exciting for workers. It's kind of boring and requires a lot of hard work, so we may have to change that rather than hoping the workers will change."[74]

Driven to Distraction: Chinese Taxi Drivers Protest Working Conditions

Worker strikes are common in Chinese factories as many young people rebel against long hours, low pay, and monotonously boring work. However, when it comes to government concern, the biggest fear is the increasing frequency and intensity of strikes by taxi drivers. As Wang Kan, a professor at the Chinese Institute of Industrial Relations, notes, "For factory strikes, no matter how big, the government can censor the news and usually no one knows about it because most are located outside the city. But with taxi strikes, everyone in the city feels it. This is bad for social stability."

The strikes are hardly a local phenomenon isolated in one city; instead demonstrations have broken out in 10 different cities in 2014 alone. In many cases, the drivers use social media to organize mass park-outs where they just stop their cars in the middle of the street, preventing the flow of any traffic. In one case in Nanjing, this practice resulted in violence when fights broke out between taxi drivers and other motorists who were viewed simply as collateral damage by the protestors.

As is often the case, the motivation driving this labor unrest is poor working conditions. The average city taxi driver works 13-hour days in congested and polluted traffic, earning roughly 3,000 yuan ($500) a month. Most drivers do not own their own cabs because government-issued licenses are scarce and costly, and thus, they have to pay high rental fees to use cars owned by others. Then, on top of all of this, the taxi drivers have to compete with "black cars"—that is, unregistered and unlicensed vehicles that use apps like Uber. The government, listening to these concerns, announced a ban on unregistered vehicles and ride-hailing apps in 2015, as well as a plan to reduce rental prices. Time will only tell if these moves will calm the situation, but clearly the meter is running on the need for change.

DISCUSSION QUESTIONS

1. Is the "collateral damage" incurred by nondisputants, that is, law-abiding innocent drivers who were affected by the taxi drivers' strike, "fair game" when it comes to winning a labor dispute such as this?
2. If you were part of the collateral damage in this case, whom would you blame more—the drivers or the government?

SOURCES: D. Roberts, "The Fury of the Chinese Cabbie," *Bloomberg Businessweek,* February 1, 2015; A. Jacobs, "Strikes by Taxi Drivers Spread Across China," *The New York Times,* January 14, 2015, www.nytimes.com; S. Yan, "Taxi Drivers Strike in China over Steep Fees and Uber," *CNN Money,* January 14, 2015, http://money.cnn.com.

One of the major interventions aimed at reducing job dissatisfaction by increasing job complexity is job enrichment. As the term suggests, this intervention is directed at jobs that are "impoverished" or boring because of their repetitive nature or low scope. Many job enrichment programs are based on the job characteristics theory discussed earlier in Chapter 4. For example, many job enrichment programs provide increased opportunities for workers to have input into important organizational decisions that involve their work, and this has been routinely found to reduce role conflict and ambiguity.

Job Rotation
The process of systematically moving a single individual from one job to another over the course of time. The job assignments may be in various functional areas of the company or movement may be between jobs in a single functional area or department.

Another task-based intervention is **job rotation**. This is a process of systematically moving a single individual from one job to another over the course of time. Although employees may not feel capable of putting up with the dissatisfying aspects of a particular job indefinitely, they often feel they can do so temporarily. Job rotation can do more than simply spread out the dissatisfying aspects of a particular job. It can increase work complexity for employees and provide valuable cross-training in jobs so that employees eventually understand many different jobs. This makes for a more flexible workforce and increases workers' appreciation of the other tasks that have to be accomplished for the organization to complete its mission.

Because of the degree to which nonwork roles often spill over and affect work roles, and vice versa, a second critical aspect of work that affects satisfaction and retention is the degree to which scheduling is flexible. To help employees manage their multiple roles, companies have turned to a number of family-friendly policies to both recruit new talent and hold onto the talent they already have. These policies may include provisions for child care, elder care, flexible work schedules, job sharing, telecommuting, and extended maternal and paternal leaves.[75] When it comes to maternity and paternity leave, however, most employers in the United States do far less than what one sees in the rest of the world. Although the Family Medical Leave Act does require employers to give parents 12 weeks of leave after having a child, this is an unpaid leave, and many employees cannot afford to go that long without pay—especially after just having a baby. In terms of international rankings, the United States ranks last, tied with Liberia, Papua New Guinea, and Suriname as one of the only four countries that does not offer paid leave for new parents.[76] In addition to the direct costs of taking time off to be with children, however, are the indirect costs that come about because of social norms in the United States that seem to punish both parents for taking time off. Research indicates that women who reduce their hours of work for family reasons incur a 10% penalty in lifetime earnings. This penalty is even larger for men—estimated at over 15%.[77] Although the family-friendly programs create some headaches for managers in terms of scheduling work and reporting requirements, they have a number of demonstrable benefits. First, the provision of these sorts of benefits is a recruitment aid that helps employers attract potential job applicants.[78] Second, once hired, flexible work arrangements result in reduced absenteeism. Third, over the long term, these programs result in higher levels of employee commitment to the organization.[79]

By far, the most important aspect of work in terms of generating satisfaction is the degree to which it is meaningfully related to core values of the worker. The term **prosocial motivation** is often used explicitly to capture the degree to which people are motivated to help other people. When people believe that their work has an important impact on other people, they are much more willing to work longer hours.[80] This prosocial motivation could be directed at co-workers and has been found to relate to helping behavior.[81] This form of motivation can also be triggered by recognizing that one's work has a positive impact on those who benefit from one's service, such as customers or clients.[82] In contrast, when one's social needs are thwarted, they often react negatively and in self-defeating ways that drive people further away from them.[83]

Prosocial Motivation
The degree to which people are energized to do their jobs because it helps other people.

In addition to prosocial motivation, work may have meaning for someone because they see it as a calling that gives their lives purpose. In this case, the exact tasks that go into the work may not even matter, but rather everything depends upon the outcome that results from that work. For example, Michael Pratt, a researcher who has studied meaning at work extensively often recounts a fable of bricklayers all working at the same site who are asked what they are doing. One sighs and states sadly that "I am putting one brick on top of another." A second says with indifference that that he is "making six pence an hour." The third responds excitedly exclaiming "I am building a cathedral!" All three workers are doing the same work, but one person finds meaning in it where others do not, and this makes all the difference when it comes to job satisfaction.[84]

Supervisors and Co-workers

The two primary sets of people in an organization who affect job satisfaction are co-workers and supervisors. A person may be satisfied with her supervisor for one of two reasons. First, the job incumbent may see her supervisor as having "warmth," that is, genuinely caring about the worker and respecting him or her as a person. Thus, being in a culture where people are generally civil and polite makes people feel their own

Lights Out for Late Night Workers

For many employees—and especially working parents—the best time of the day to really get some quality work done comes when they are out of the office and the kids are asleep. This is the new 9 to 11 PM work shift, and although the short-term benefits of leveraging these two hours for work may seem to be in the best interests of employers and employees, new evidence suggests that the long-term problems associated with this practice outweigh its benefits.

In particular, research shows that working right up until its "lights out for bed" is highly disruptive of sleep, which in turn harms employee engagement and performance the next day. Lack of performance on that next day then prompts even more late-night workload that creates a vicious cycle of sleep deprivation. Indeed, the mere practice

of looking at one's smartphone after 9 PM has demonstrable negative effects on sleeping patterns. The blue light emitted by a smartphone is the single most disruptive band of light when it comes to inhibiting the sleep-promoting chemical, melatonin. When one combines this chemical reaction with the chemical reaction caused by workplace stress experienced right before bedtime, as researcher Chris Barnes notes, "smartphones are almost perfectly designed to disrupt sleep."

The negative effects of sleep deprivation on employee performance and safety are well-known, and for some occupations, like airline pilots, there are strict rules that enforce sleep discipline. An airline will routinely ground flights for lack of crew rest, and although the safety and performance implications

for most jobs are not quite as critical as those associated with commercial aviation, if the job is worth doing right, it's worth doing right after a good night's sleep.

DISCUSSION QUESTIONS

1. Is it fair for an employer to ask people who already put in an 8-hour day to work 9 to 11 PM without overtime pay?
2. If an employer does not require this, but people do it anyway in order to get ahead, should the employer discourage or prevent it in order to promote long-term sustainability?

SOURCES: B. Stone, "The New Night Shift," *Bloomberg Businessweek,* August 7, 2014, pp. 87–89; R. Pyrillis, "Sleep Derailed," *Workforce,* July 2014, pp. 29–31; C. M. Barnes, K. Lanaj, and R. Johnson, "Research: Using a Smartphone After 9 PM Leaves Workers Disengaged," *Harvard Business Review,* January 15, 2014, https://hbr.org.

dignity and worth above and beyond their contributions to the work itself. Incivility causes stress and research shows that people who are treated rudely have a hard time focusing on the task, and instead, ruminate about their poor treatment and ways to perhaps get even.[85] Many employers recognize this fact and the tolerance that organizations once had for tough and cruel bosses is no longer accepted today. For example, in 2014, Jill Abramson, the editor of *The New York Times* was removed from her position because of "her arbitrary decision-making, a failure to consult and bring colleagues with her, inadequate communication, and mistreatment of colleagues."[86]

Second, as just mentioned, people may be satisfied with their supervisor because they provide support that helps them achieve their own goals. That is, although it is nice to have a supervisor and co-workers who are warm, it is also critical that these people are "competent" in terms of helping the worker and his or her team get the mission accomplished. In fact, when given a choice between a leader who was warm but incompetent or a leader who was cold but competent, 70% opted for the cold and competent leader.[87] Still, nothing beats that combination of high warmth and high competence in a leader, and employees led by a supervisor who is viewed as both supportive and competent will work longer hours and delay gratification in terms of rewards trusting that something good will eventually come to them from all their hard work. However, as the "Competing through Sustainability" box shows, a leader focused on long-term results may display both warmth and competence by limiting the number of hours his or her staff works.

Supervisors are not the only potential source of social warmth and support, and in many cases, abuse by co-workers can have an even more profound negative influence on one's job satisfaction. For example, one 2012 survey indicated that 35% of respondents reported being bullied by co-workers on the job. Workplace bullying is defined as repeated health-harming mistreatment by one or more perpetrators at work that takes the form of verbal abuse and offensive conduct that is threatening, humiliating or intimidating to the point where it prevents work from getting done. Unlike abusive bosses, who often let up once a specific task is accomplished, bullying by co-workers tends to be a constant, unrelenting process. Although it is common for high schools to adopt non-bullying rules, this has not been the case among employers, even though bullies rarely stop being bullies simply because they graduated from high school.[88]

Because a supportive environment reduces dissatisfaction, many organizations foster team building both on and off the job (such as via softball or bowling leagues). The idea is that group cohesiveness and support for individual group members will be increased through exposure and joint efforts. Although management certainly cannot ensure that each stressed employee develops friends, it can make it easier for employees to interact—a necessary condition for developing friendship and rapport. In fact, results of surveys indicate that endorsing the item "Most of my closest friendships are with people at work" is one of the most powerful tools for predicting turnover.[89]

Pay and Benefits

We should not discount the influence of the job incumbent, the job itself, and the surrounding people in terms of influencing job satisfaction, but for most people, work is their primary source of income and financial security. Pay is also seen as an indicator of status within the organization as well as in society at large. Thus, for many individuals, the standing of their pay relative to those within their organization, or the standing of their pay relative to others doing similar work for other employers, becomes even more important than the level of pay itself.[90] Thus, for some people, pay is a reflection of self-worth, so pay satisfaction takes on critical significance when it comes to retention.[91] The role of pay and benefits is so large that we devote the entire next part of this book to these topics. Within this chapter we focus primarily on satisfaction with two aspects of pay (pay levels and benefits) and how these are assessed within the organization. Methods for addressing these issues are discussed in Part 4 of this book.

One of the main dimensions of satisfaction with pay deals with pay levels relative to market wages. When it comes to retention, employees being recruited away from one organization by another are often lured with promises of higher pay levels. In fact, exit surveys of high-performing employees who have left their organization indicate "better pay" as the reason in over 70% of the cases compared to only 33% who indicate "better opportunity." Ironically, when the managers of those same workers are polled, 68% cite "better opportunity" versus 45% who indicate it was "better pay," suggesting quite a difference of opinion.[92] As labor markets started tightening up in 2015, many employers recognized the need to raise pay levels in order to stop attrition, even companies such as Walmart, which base their entire business model on cutting costs. Walmart boosted the pay of all their employees to $10 an hour in 2015, well above the minimum wage, in order to retain their most experienced personnel and reduce the need to hire and train new workers. Chief Executive Doug McMillon, who initiated the raises, noted, "We want associates who care about the company and are highly engaged about the business."[93]

Satisfaction with benefits is another important dimension of overall pay satisfaction. Because many individuals have a difficult time ascertaining the true dollar value of their benefits package, however, this dimension may not always be as salient to people as pay itself. To derive competitive advantage from benefits' expenditures, it is critical not only to make them highly salient to employees, however, but also link them to the organization's strategic direction. For example, Starbucks wanted to attract workers who were smart and valued education, but could not necessarily afford to hire people with college educations. As we discussed in Chapters 1 and 2, Starbucks started a tuition reimbursement program that would pay for employees who pursued their bachelor's degree at Arizona State University. The cost of program was roughly $45,000 per employee over the course of the four years, but the company saw this as a great way of attracting and retaining the kind of employee that fit their business model.[94]

MEASURING AND MONITORING JOB SATISFACTION

Most attempts to measure job satisfaction rely on workers' self-reports. There is a vast amount of data on the reliability and validity of many existing scales as well as a wealth of data from companies that have used these scales, allowing for comparisons across firms. Established scales are excellent places to begin if employers wish to assess the satisfaction levels of their employees. An employer would be foolish to "reinvent the wheel" by generating its own versions of measures of these broad constructs. Of course, in some cases, organizations want to measure their employees' satisfaction with aspects of their work that are specific to that organization (such as satisfaction with one particular health plan versus another). In these situations the organization may need to create its own scales, but this will be the exception rather than the rule.

One standardized, widely used measure of job satisfaction is the Job Descriptive Index (JDI). The JDI emphasizes various facets of satisfaction: pay, the work itself, supervision, co-workers, and promotions. Table 10.5 presents several items from the JDI scale. Other scales exist for those who want to get even more specific about

Table 10.5
Sample Items from a Standardized Job Satisfaction Scale (the JDI)

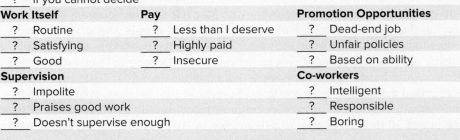

Instructions: Think of your present work. What is it like most of the time? In the blank beside each word given below, write

_Y_ for "Yes" if it describes your work

_N_ for "No" if it does NOT describe your work

_?_ if you cannot decide

Work Itself		Pay		Promotion Opportunities	
?	Routine	?	Less than I deserve	?	Dead-end job
?	Satisfying	?	Highly paid	?	Unfair policies
?	Good	?	Insecure	?	Based on ability
Supervision				**Co-workers**	
?	Impolite			?	Intelligent
?	Praises good work			?	Responsible
?	Doesn't supervise enough			?	Boring

SOURCE: W. K. Balzar, D. C. Smith, D. E. Kravitz, S. E. Lovell, K. B. Paul, B. A. Reilly, and C. E. Reilly, *User's Manual for the Job Descriptive Index (JDI)* (Bowling Green, OH: Bowling Green State University, 1990).

different facets of satisfaction. For example, although the JDI we just examined assesses satisfaction with pay, it does not break pay up into different dimensions.[95] The Pay Satisfaction Questionnaire (PSQ) focuses on these more specific dimensions (pay levels, benefits, pay structure, and pay raises); thus this measure gives a more detailed view of exactly what aspects of pay are most or least satisfying.[96]

Although satisfaction surveys used to be a once-a-year affair, increasingly technology is creating opportunities for firms and managers to get more rapid feedback. Pulse surveys are very short questionnaires that go out every day or once a week that focus on a small set of specific questions—perhaps even just one question—which the company wants to keep track of over time.[97] The idea behind these quick-fire polls is to uncover issues faster and as they develop rather than wait until the end of the year when the issue may have festered. Also, these surveys tend to avoid long-term memory problems that reduce the value of once-a-year questionnaires. Usually these surveys are anonymous in order to reduce fear of voicing one's opinions, and organizations try to show demonstrable actions taken soon after issues are raised.[98]

SURVEY-FEEDBACK INTERVENTIONS

Regardless of what measures are used or how many facets of satisfaction are assessed, a systematic, ongoing program of *employee survey research* should be a prominent part of any human resource strategy for a number of reasons. First, it allows the company to monitor trends over time and thus prevent problems in the area of voluntary turnover before they happen. For example, Figure 10.2 shows the average profile for different

LO 10-4

Design a survey feedback intervention program, and use this to promote retention of key organizational personnel.

Figure 10.2

Average Profile for Different Facets of Satisfaction over Time

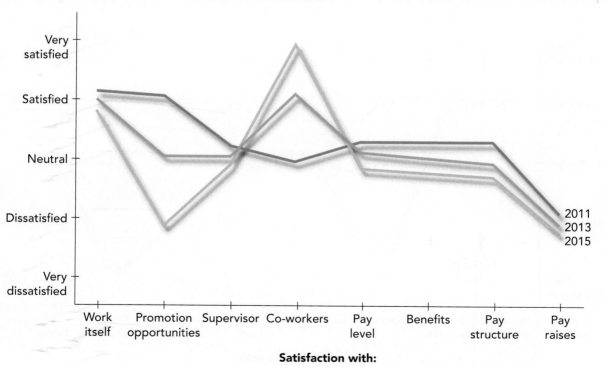

facets of satisfaction for a hypothetical company in 2011, 2013, and 2015. As the figure makes clear, the level of satisfaction with promotion opportunities in this company has eroded over time, whereas the satisfaction with co-workers has improved. If there was a strong relationship between satisfaction with promotion opportunities and voluntary turnover among high performers, this would constitute a threat that the organization might need to address via some of the techniques discussed in our previous chapter, "Employee Development."

A second reason for engaging in an ongoing program of employee satisfaction surveys is that it provides a means of empirically assessing the impact of changes in policy (such as introduction of a new performance appraisal system) or personnel (e.g., introduction of a new CEO) on worker attitudes. Figure 10.3 shows the average profile for different satisfaction facets for a hypothetical organization one year before and one year after a merger. An examination of the profile makes it clear that since the merger, satisfaction with supervision and pay structure has gone down dramatically, and this has not been offset by any increase in satisfaction along other dimensions. Again, this might point to the need for training programs for supervisors (like those discussed in Chapter 7) or changes in the pay system (like those discussed in Chapter 11). This was the exact pattern of results that was found by HCL Technologies, an India-based technology services provider. More specifically, the company learned from its survey that its variable pay-for-performance program was creating too many wild swings in the workers' paychecks, and many were leaving to take jobs with more stable month-to-month paychecks. The company responded by reducing the variable component in pay from 30% to just 10%. The result was an increase in customer satisfaction, a 140% growth in revenue, and a 50% reduction in turnover.[99]

Figure 10.3

Average Profile for Different Facets of Satisfaction before and after a Major Event

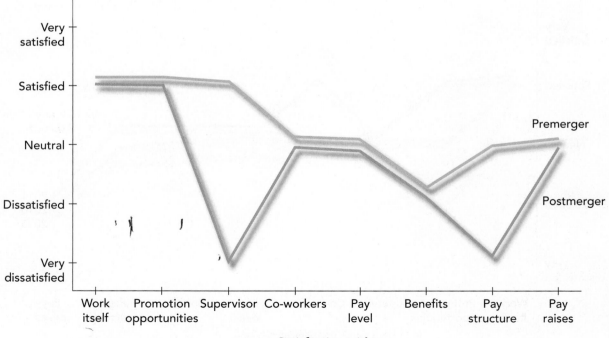

Third, when these surveys incorporate standardized scales like the JDI, they often allow the company to compare itself with others in the same industry along these dimensions. For example, Figure 10.4 shows the average profile for different satisfaction facets for a hypothetical organization and compares this to the industry average. Again, if we detect major differences between one organization and the industry as a whole (on overall pay levels, for example), this might allow the company to react and change its policies before there is a mass exodus of people moving to the competition.

According to Figure 10.4, the satisfaction with pay levels is low relative to the industry, but this is offset by higher-than-industry-average satisfaction with benefits and the work itself. As we showed in Chapter 6 ("Selection and Placement"), the organization might want to use this information to systematically screen people. That is, the fit between the person and the organization would be best if the company selected applicants who reported being most interested in the nature of the work itself and benefits, and rejected those applicants whose sole concern was with pay levels.

Within the organization, a systematic survey program also allows the company to check for differences between units and hence benchmark "best practices" that might be generalized across units. For example, Figure 10.5 shows the average profile for five different regional divisions of a hypothetical company. The figure shows that satisfaction with pay raises is much higher in one of the regions relative to the others. If the overall amount of money allocated to raises was equal through the entire company, this implies that the manner in which raises are allocated or communicated in the Midwest region might be something that the other regions should look into.

Figure 10.4

Average Profile for Different Facets of Satisfaction versus the Industry Average

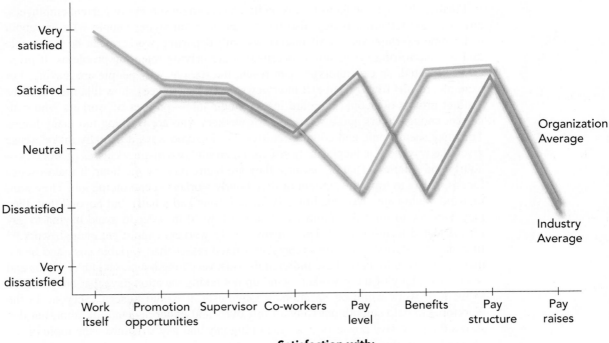

Figure 10.5

Average Profile for Different Facets of Satisfaction for Different Regional Divisions

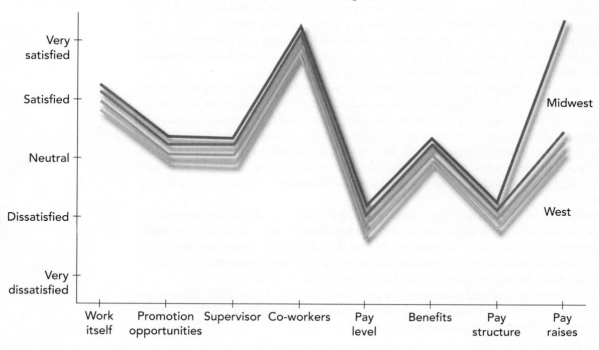

Finally, although the focus in this section has been on surveys of current employees, any strategic retention policy also has to consider surveying people who are about to become ex-employees. Exit interviews with departing workers can be a valuable tool for uncovering systematic concerns that are driving retention problems. If properly conducted, an exit interview can reveal the reasons why people are leaving. For example, results from recent exit interviews among employees show that there are two distinct groups of people who are leaving their jobs—one set of workers who cannot get enough hours and a second set of workers who are working too many hours. This may seem ironic and counterintuitive, but in some ways it actually makes sense given the way work is increasingly structured around two distinct classes of workers—hourly and salaried. That is, because they are being paid by the hour, it makes sense for employers to limit the amount of time hourly workers spend on the job. They want to avoid paying any overtime hours (valued at time and a half), but beyond that, they may even try to limit the number of hours below 30 in order to avoid having to pay for mandated health care.[100] Thus, many hourly workers cannot get enough work.[101] In contrast, salaried employees represent a fixed rather than variable cost, and hence there is pressure to make these individuals work very long hours, including nights and weekends. Many of these workers wind up not taking vacation days that are provided to them or work while on vacation.[102] Obviously, it would benefit everyone in the workforce to help smooth out some of this over- and under-demand for labor, but this shows the pervasive power of rules regarding pay and pay structure—the topic of the next section of this book.

A LOOK BACK

Job Satisfaction, Retention and the IRS

In the story that opened this chapter, we saw how recent cutbacks at the IRS, when combined with the traditional challenges associated with the job of tax collectors, created high levels of dissatisfaction and voluntary turnover rates among workers at the agency. A key factor influencing the ability of any organization to accomplish its mission is who is leaving and who is staying when it comes to turnover. Organizations need to have policies in place that make it easy and advantageous for low performers to leave (involuntary turnover) but make it difficult and costly for high performers to leave (voluntary turnover). Managing the "flow" of employees thus becomes a critical source of competitive advantage and is often the difference between survival and bankruptcy.

QUESTIONS

1. In what ways does an organizational crisis like that faced by the IRS make it easier for firms to manage involuntary turnover?
2. In what ways does an organizational crisis like that faced by the IRS make it more difficult for firms to manage voluntary turnover?
3. What role can employee attitude surveys play in maintaining a loyal and engaged workforce? What are some of the challenges associated with getting accurate and reliable information from employee surveys, and how can a survey process "backfire" in terms of harming, rather than helping, a firm's efforts?

SUMMARY

This chapter examined issues related to employee separation and retention. Involuntary turnover reflects a separation initiated by the organization, often when the individual would prefer to stay a member of the organization. Voluntary turnover reflects a separation initiated by the individual, often when the organization would prefer that the person stay a member. Organizations can gain competitive advantage by strategically managing the separation process so that involuntary turnover is implemented in a fashion that does not invite retaliation, and voluntary turnover among high performers is kept to a minimum. Retaliatory reactions to organizational discipline and dismissal decisions can be minimized by implementing these decisions in a manner that promotes feelings of procedural and interactive justice. Voluntary turnover can be minimized by measuring and monitoring employee levels of satisfaction with critical facets of job and organization, and then addressing any problems identified by such surveys.

KEY TERMS

Involuntary turnover, 423
Voluntary turnover, 423
Employment-at-will
  doctrine, 423
Outcome fairness, 425
Procedural justice, 426
Interactional justice, 426

Alternative dispute resolution
  (ADR), 428
Employee assistance programs
  (EAPs), 429
Outplacement counseling, 432
Progression of withdrawal, 434
Whistle-blowing, 435

Job involvement, 436
Organizational commitment, 436
Job satisfaction, 437
Frame of reference, 437
Negative affectivity, 438
Job rotation, 440
Prosocial motivation, 441

DISCUSSION QUESTIONS

1. The discipline and discharge procedures described in this chapter are systematic but rather slow. In your opinion, should some offenses lead to immediate dismissal? If so, how would you justify this to a court if you were sued for wrongful discharge?

2. Organizational turnover is generally considered a negative outcome, and many organizations spend a great deal of time and money trying to reduce it. What situations would indicate that an increase in turnover might be just what an organization needs? Given the difficulty of terminating employees, what organizational policies might be used to retain high-performing workers, and at the same time, increase attrition among low-performing workers?

3. Three popular interventions for enhancing worker satisfaction are job enrichment, job rotation, and role analysis.

What are the critical differences between these interventions, and under what conditions might one be preferable to the others?

4. If off-the-job stress and dissatisfaction begin to create on-the-job problems, what are the rights and responsibilities of the human resource manager in helping the employee to overcome these problems? Are intrusions into such areas an invasion of privacy, a benevolent and altruistic employer practice, or simply a prudent financial step taken to protect the firm's investment?

5. Discuss the advantages of using published, standardized measures in employee attitude surveys. Do employers ever need to develop their own measures for such surveys? Where would one turn to learn how to do this?

SELF-ASSESSMENT EXERCISE

connect

Additional assignable self-assessments available in Connect.

The characteristics of your job influence your overall satisfaction with the job. One way to be satisfied at work is to find a job with the characteristics that you find desirable. The following assessment is a look at what kind of job is likely to satisfy you.

The following phrases describe different job characteristics. Read each phrase, then circle a number to indicate how much of the job characteristic you would like. Use the following scale: 1 = very little; 2 = little; 3 = a moderate amount; 4 = much; 5 = very much.

1. The opportunity to perform a number of different activities each day   1 2 3 4 5

2. Contributing something significant to the company   1 2 3 4 5

3. The freedom to determine how to do my job   1 2 3 4 5

4. The ability to see projects or jobs through to completion, rather than performing only one piece of the job   1 2 3 4 5

5. Seeing the results of my work, so I can get an idea of how well I am doing the job   1 2 3 4 5

6. A feeling that the quality of my work is important to others in the company   1 2 3 4 5

7. The need to use a variety of complex skills   1 2 3 4 5

8. Responsibility to act and make decisions independently of managers or supervisors   1 2 3 4 5

9. Time and resources to do an entire piece of work from beginning to end   1 2 3 4 5

10. Getting feedback about my performance from the work itself   1 2 3 4 5

Add the scores for the pairs of items that measure each job characteristic. A higher score for a characteristic means that characteristic is more important to you.

Skill Variety: The degree to which a job requires you to use a variety of skills.

Item 1: _____ + Item 7: _____ = _____

Task Identity: The degree to which a job requires completion of a whole and identifiable piece of work.

Item 4: _____ + Item 9: _____ = _____

Task Significance: The degree to which a job has an impact on the lives or work of others.

Item 2: _____ + Item 6: _____ = _____

Autonomy: The degree to which a job provides freedom, empowerment, and discretion in scheduling the work and determining processes and procedures for completing the work.

Item 3: _____ + Item 8: _____ = _____

Feedback: The degree to which carrying out job-related tasks and activities provides you with direct and clear information about your effectiveness.

Item 5 _____ + Item 10: _____ = _____

SOURCE: Adapted from R. Daft and R. Noe, *Organizational Behavior* (New York: Harcourt, 2001).

EXERCISING STRATEGY

Churning About to Heat Up

Traditionally, the U.S. workforce has had one of the highest rates of voluntary turnover in the world, and this is actually considered a source of competitive advantage. Unlike layoffs that reduce the overall size of the economy, people who turn over voluntarily often have lined up better jobs already, and thus, create a new job opening for someone else after they leave. Thus, this kind of "churning" does not affect the size of the economy and results in a better person-job fit for many people. It also rewards good employers who can attract the best workers and punishes employers who fail to meet the needs of the workforce, thus "thinning the herd" at the firm level.

The churn rate for the U.S. economy, however, is not what is used to be, and many have pointed to this factor as one of the reasons for the weak nature of the most recent recovery. Many workers during the recession were very reluctant to leave their jobs, and this aversion to risk reduced the number of job openings over and above what might be attributable to the bad economy. One study suggested, for example, that 80% of the reduction in hiring during the 2007–2009 recession was due to a reduction in churn rather than a decline in job creation.

All of this seems to be changing, however. Turnover rates that stood at 9% in 2008 and 2009, jumped to 15% in 2010 and 2011. In addition, all signs pointed to even higher increases in 2012 and 2013. A national survey conducted by the Society of Human Resource Management indicated that job satisfaction, a leading indicator of voluntary turnover, was down over 80% in 2012, and a separate survey conducted by HR software vendor Cornerstone OnDemand estimated that 25% of employees were looking to change jobs in the 2013–2015 time period. Many of these workers suffered through years of increased workloads without increased pay during the recession and are looking to improve their situation as the economy continues to heat up.

For businesses, the cost of this churning is close to $2 trillion due to the need to recruit and train new workers. This cost is not distributed evenly across employers, however. Organizations that were not able to keep up employee morale are about to lose a large percentage of their most valued employees, whereas companies that met their employees' needs are likely to experience stability or growth. Thus, churning streamlines the economy and creates efficiency by eliminating weak competitors and strengthening the most competitive firms.

QUESTIONS

1. What are some of the steps organizations take to reduce and avoid turnover among employees?
2. How does an increase in churn rates create strategic opportunities for firms with strong reputations in the labor market?

SOURCES: D. Kanszak, "Turnover Rates Inching Up," *PR Web,* June 27, 2013, www.prweb.com; G. Kranz, "As Career Development Lags, Employees Are Going Places," *Workforce,* February 2013, p. 10; S. Halzack, "Worker Turnover Is Poised to Pick Up, Adding Urgency to Employers' Focus on Retention," *Washington Post,* January 22, 2013, www.washingtonpost.com; B. Casselman, "Little Room for New Workers," *The Wall Street Journal,* February 8, 2012, www.wsj.com.

MANAGING PEOPLE

Flextime: Has Its Time Come and Gone?

When Marissa Mayer was selected to be Yahoo's CEO in 2012, she became the 20th female CEO at a Fortune 500 company. Since she and her husband were expecting their first child when the news was announced, this made her the only pregnant CEO at a Fortune 500 company. Certain expectations come with being the only mother-to-be within the CEO ranks, but when Mayer announced that she was ending Yahoo's long-time policy allowing flextime at work, this was not one of them. Indeed, immediately after her announcement, another long-time provider of flexible work arrangements, Best Buy, followed her lead and ended its program. This left many wondering whether or not the time for flextime has come and gone.

In its defense, most research into the effects of flextime suggests that it has benefits, and many companies are standing by their policies. For example, Medtronic's operations in Santa Rosa, California designated 15% of its workforce as "home-office employees." Most of those workers telecommute from San Francisco, which is roughly one hour away by car. Medtronic swears by its program, noting that it saves over $1 million a year in office space and boosts its ability to attract top-level talent in the San Francisco area who are willing to commute one day a week, but not willing to move or commute every day.

However, managing flextime employees can be challenging for some managers because it forces them to manage outcomes and results, and not just employee face-time. Jody Thompson, the original architect of the Best Buy flextime program, notes that "Demanding face-time from employees is typically a sign that supervisors are unable to lead effectively. They don't know how to manage performance, so they manage people's time."

Mayer was quick to note that her decree was not meant to be a sweeping condemnation against flextime in general, but rather she was just saying that it was not right for Yahoo at this specific time. There were two issues that led to Mayer's somewhat controversial policy change. First, internal evidence from VPN logs showed that Yahoo's work-at-home staff did not seem to be working very hard when measured in terms of hours actually logged. The perception that some of the employees were abusing the privilege was widespread and created conflict with employees who were not abusing the privilege. Second, Mayer believed that Yahoo needed to come up with creative solutions to compete with Google and Facebook, which had siphoned

off users and advertisers from Yahoo over the years. Mayer stressed that "people are more productive when they are alone, but they are more collaborative and innovative when they're together." Thus, the decision was a strategic choice regarding how to best compete in that industry—no more, no less.

QUESTIONS

1. Discuss how the nature of a company's workers and the nature of the work itself might influence when and where flextime is a good policy and where it is a poor strategy.

2. Why might a "one-size-fits-all policy" for flextime be unrealistic?

SOURCES: E. Fraunheim, "Reflecting on Flexing," *Workforce Management,* June 2013, pp. 28–37; R. Bell, "Turning Their Backs on Telecommuting," *Workforce Management,* April 2013, p. 46; A.Efrati and J. Letzing, "Google's Mayer Takes Over as Yahoo Chief," *The Wall Street Journal,* July 17, 2012, www.wsj.com.

HR IN SMALL BUSINESS

Learning to Show Appreciation at Datotel

Datotel is a St. Louis company whose name explains what it does. The name combines the word *data* with the word *hotel,* and it uses its computers to safely store backups of its client companies' data. It's a fast-growing business, and for founder David Brown, one important challenge has been making sure employees know the company appreciates them even as everyone is scrambling to keep up with the demands of expanding a small business.

With about three dozen people to think about, Brown first tried a methodical approach: He created an employee-of-the-month program in which the lucky recipient would receive a thank-you e-mail message, a $25 gift card, and recognition for all employees to see on the company's intranet. Brown saw this program as one he could readily find the time to implement, and he hoped the reward and recognition would inspire high levels of job involvement and organizational commitment.

One advantage of a small company is that you can quickly see people's reactions to your efforts. Unfortunately, what Brown saw on people's faces and heard in their conversations was that recipients of the employee-of-the-month rewards were not exactly excited. The program was just too formulaic and impersonal. If Datotel was to keep employees engaged, it needed a different way to show that their efforts mattered.

So Brown tried a different approach, even though it requires more effort. He committed his eight managers to noticing and reporting employee accomplishments. To implement

this, he sets aside part of regular management meetings—part of each daily phone meeting and 15 minutes of each weekly in-person meeting—to discuss employee accomplishments. Whenever a manager notes that an employee has done something extraordinary, Brown asks for one of the managers besides the person's direct supervisor to thank the employee in person. Brown has also made a personal commitment to write thank-you notes. In fact, with e-mail the norm at his technology company, he makes some of the notes stand out by writing them by hand and mailing them to the employees at home.

One employee who thinks the extra effort matters is engineer Stephanie Lewis. One day Lewis returned home to find a note from Brown, observing that he had heard during management meetings that Lewis had done exceptionally well in working with a customer. Brown thanked her for the effort. Lewis's reaction: "It made me feel important to get something so personal and unique" from her company's busy leader.

Just as communicating "thank you" has helped with motivation, going the extra mile to communicate has helped Datotel's managers stay connected with one another and the company's mission. As the company grew and jobs became more specialized, Brown recognized that he would have to bring people together formally to share information about what was happening. He began to call meetings once a quarter, and so that the environment will be positive, he establishes a theme he thinks will get employees thinking and generate some fun. When the theme was "Rumble in the Jungle," the company leaders dressed as boxers, and when the theme was "Top Gun," they dressed as aviators and met in an airplane hangar.

The effort to allow for fun is interwoven with the company's core values: passion, integrity, fun, teamwork, "superior business value," and "improving the community in which we work." These aim to unite the employees in a commitment to customer service that gives the company an edge in the industry. The values are also meant to be an advantage for recruiting and retaining the best people. On Datotel's website, the "Inside Datotel" page lists 10 reasons for wanting to work at the company, and the top reason is the core values: "Our Core Values represent everything that we stand for, and we take pride in them."

QUESTIONS

1. Based on the information given, which sources of job satisfaction has Datotel addressed? What other sources might the company address, and how?

2. Suggest several measures Datotel could use to evaluate the success of its employee retention efforts. Be sure these are practical for a company of a few dozen employees.

3. In a company as small as Datotel, losing even one employee can present real difficulties. Suppose one of Datotel's managers begins to have performance problems and seems unwilling or unable to improve. Suggest how you, as an HR consultant, could help David Brown resolve this problem in a way that is fair to everyone involved and that keeps the company moving forward.

SOURCES: Datotel corporate website, www.datotel.com, accessed July 8, 2015; Nadine Heintz, "Building a Culture of Employee Appreciation," *Inc.,* September 2009, www.inc.com; Jeremy Nulik, "Never Stop Being a Student of Business," *Small Business Monthly (St. Louis),* July 2009, www.sbmon.com; Christopher Boyce, "Engineer Finds Solution to Business Problem," *St. Louis Post-Dispatch,* June 12, 2009, Business & Company Resource Center, http://galenet.galegroup.com.

NOTES

1. J. D. Shaw, M. K. Duffy, J. L. Johnson, and D. E. Lockhart, "Turnover, Social Capital Losses, and Performance," *Academy of Management Journal* 48 (2005), pp. 594–606.

2. B. Stone, "How Cheap Is Craig Jelinek?" *Bloomberg Businessweek,* June 6, 2013, pp. 55–60.

3. K. Sulkowicz, "Straight Talk at Review Time," *BusinessWeek,* September 10, 2007, p. 16.

4. F. Hanson, " 'Poaching' Can Be Pricey, but Benefits May Outweigh Costs," *Workforce Management,* January 30, 2006, pp. 37–39.

5. S. A. Feeney, "The High Cost of Employee Violence," *Workforce,* August 2003, pp. 23–24.

6. A. Campos-Flores and L. Stevens, "Ex-UPS Employee in Alabama Kills Two; Self," *The Wall Street Journal,* September 23, 2014, www.wsj.com.

7. E. Perez and D. Molinski, "More Firings at Secret Service," *The Wall Street Journal Online,* April 19, 2012.

8. A. Grossman, "Four Top Secret Service Officials to Be Removed from Posts," *The Wall Street Journal,* January 14, 2015, www.wsj.com.

9. J. Gershman, "McDonald's Wrongful Termination Lawsuit to Test NLRB Ruling," *The Wall Street Journal,* January 22, 2015, www.wsj.com.

10. M. Orey, "Fear of Firing," *BusinessWeek,* April 23, 2007, pp. 52–62.

11. G. Casellas, "Fired Up over Firing," *BusinessWeek,* May 14, 2007, p. 76.

12. Orey, "Fear of Firing."

13. S. Gleason and R. Feintzeig, "Startups Are Quick to Fire," *The Wall Street Journal,* December 12, 2013, www.wsj.com.

14. R. Feintzeig, "Once Fired, Now a Founder: How a Tech Leader Rebuilt His Career," *The Wall Street Journal,* December 13, 2013, www.wsj.com.

15. S. E. Scullen, P. K. Bergey, and L. Aimon-Smith, "Forced Distribution Rating Systems and the Improvement of Workforce Potential: A Baseline Simulation," *Personnel Psychology* 58 (2005), pp. 1–32.

16. N. Irwin, "When the Guy Making Your Sandwich Has a No-Compete Clause," *The New York Times,* October 14, 2014, www.nytimes.com.

17. C. M. Holmvall and D. R. Bobocel, "What Fair Procedures Say about Me: Self-Construals and Reactions to Procedural Fairness," *Organizational Behavior and Human Decision Processes* 105 (2008), pp. 147–68.

18. E. J. Castilla and S. Bernard, "The Paradox of Meritocracy in Organizations," *Administrative Science Quarterly* 55 (2010), pp. 543–76.

19. E. Spitznagel, "The Sick Day Bounty Hunters," *Bloomberg Businessweek,* December 6, 2010, pp. 93–95.

20. H. Y. Li, J. B. Bingham, and E. E. Umphress, "Fairness from the Top: Perceived Procedural Justice and Collaborative Problem Solving in New Product Development," *Organization Science* 18 (2007), pp. 200–16.

21. L. Weber, "More Companies Block Employees from Filing Suits," *The Wall Street Journal,* March 31, 2015, www.wsj.com.

22. L. Weber, "Drug Use on Decline at Work, Except Rx," *The Wall Street Journal,* November 18, 2014, www.wsj.com.

23. A. Campo-Flores, "Drug Use at Work Roils Firms," *The Wall Street Journal,* October 12, 2014, www.wsj.com.

24. Y. Kubota and E. Pfanner, "Arrested Toyota Managing Officer Resigns," *The Wall Street Journal,* July 1, 2015, www.wsj.com.

25. R. Pyrillis, "A Monumental Problem," *Workforce,* September 2014, pp. 45–47.

26. K. Everson, "Dealing with Demons and Deadlines," *Workforce,* April 2015, pp. 29–31.

27. S. Sipek, "Wondering about Wellness," *Workforce,* July 2014.

28. L. Weber, "Wellness Programs Get a Health Check," *The Wall Street Journal,* October 7, 2014, www.wsj.com.

29. "Your Boss to Your Kids: Slim Down," *Bloomberg Businessweek,* February 1, 2010, p. 67.

30. J. Tuzzi, "Let the Wellness Games Begin," *Bloomberg Businessweek,* July 23, 2012, pp. 43–44.

31. R. Veseley, "Small Business Adds a New Ingredient to Workforce Recipe: Wellness Training," *Workforce Management,* June 2013, p. 9.

32. L. Kwoh, "When Your Boss Makes You Pay for Being Fat," *The Wall Street Journal,* April 5, 2013, www.wsj.com.

33. S. Sipek, "Observations on Obesity in the Workforce," *Workforce,* September 2014, p. 18.

34. A. Pasztor, "FAA to Evaluate Obese Pilots for Sleep Disorder," *The Wall Street Journal,* November 20, 2013, www.wsj.com.

35. M.S. Schmidt, "Battling Crime and Calories at the FBI," *The New York Times,* April 5, 2015, www.nytimes.com.

36. V. Leo, "Wellness—Or Orwellness?" *BusinessWeek,* March 19, 2007, p. 82.

37. L. Weber and R. Feintzeig, "Assistance to Laid off Workers Gets Downsized," *The Wall Street Journal,* February 18, 2014, www.wsj.com.

38. P. Dvorack and J. S. Lublin, "Outplacement Firms Struggle to Do Job," *The Wall Street Journal Online,* August 20, 2009.

39. J. Jones, "How to Bounce Back if You're Bounced Out," *BusinessWeek,* January 27, 1998, pp. 22–23.

40. J. D. Shaw, N. Gupta, and J. E. Delery, "Alternative Conceptualizations of the Relationship between Voluntary Turnover and Organizational Performance," *Academy of Management Journal* 48 (2005), pp. 50–68.

41. J. Sullivan, "Not All Turnover Is Equal," *Workforce Management,* May 21, 2007, p. 42.

42. T. Higgins and D. Hull, "Apple Induction," *Bloomberg Businessweek,* February 15, 2015, pp. 36–37.

43. L. Kwoh, "More Firms Bow to Generation Y's Demands," *The Wall Street Journal Online,* August 21, 2012.

44. J. G. Rosse, "Relations among Lateness, Absence and Turnover: Is There a Progression of Withdrawal?" *Human Relations* 41 (1988), pp. 517–31.

45. E. R. Burris, J. R. Detert, and D. S. Chiaburu, "Quitting before Leaving: The Mediating Effects of Psychological Attachment and Detachment on Voice," *Journal of Applied Psychology* 93 (2008), pp. 912–22.

46. C. Hulin, "Adaptation, Persistence and Commitment in Organizations," in *Handbook of Industrial & Organizational Psychology* 2nd ed., ed. M. D. Dunnette and L. M. Hough (Palo Alto, CA: Consulting Psychologists Press, 1991), pp. 443–50.

47. C. Sablynski, T. Mitchell, T. Lee, J. Burton, and B. Holtom, "Turnover: An Integration of Lee and Mitchell's Unfolding Model and Job Embeddedness Construct and Hulin's Withdrawal Construct," in *The Psychology of Work,* ed. J. Brett and F. Drasgow (Mahwah, NJ: Lawrence Erlbaum Associates, 2002).

48. D. A. Harrison, D. A. Newman, and P. L. Roth, "How Important Are Job Attitudes? Meta-Analytic Comparisons of Integrative Behavioral Outcomes and Time Sequences," *Academy of Management Journal* 49 (2006), pp. 305–25.

49. E. J. McClean, E. R. Burris, and J. R. Detert, "When Does Voice Lead to Exit? It Depends on Leadership," *Academy of Management Review,* 56 (2013), pp. 525–548.

50. M. P. Miceli and J. P. Near, "Characteristics of Organizational Climate and Perceived Wrongdoing Associated with Whistle-Blowing Decisions," *Personnel Psychology* 38 (1985), pp. 525–44.

51. D. Barrett and D. Yadron, "Contractor Says He Is Source of NSA Leak," *The Wall Street Journal,* June 10, 2013, www.wsj.com.

52. M. Mukasey, "Leaking Secrets to Terrorists," *The Wall Street Journal,* June 9, 2013, www.wsj.com.

53. D. E. Wittkower, "Are You a Whistleblower or a Snitch?" *The Wall Street Journal,* June 17, 2013, www.wsj.com.

54. H. Son and A. Lee, "B of A was Unprepared for Wikileaks, Chief Moynihan Says," *Bloomberg Businessweek,* March 23, 2011, p. 23.

55. S. Patterson and J. Strasburg, "Source's Cover Blown by SEC," *The Wall Street Journal Online,* April 25, 2012.

56. R. Albergotti and V. O'Connell, "New Twist in Armstrong Saga," *The Wall Street Journal Online,* January 17, 2013.

57. T. Y. Park, and J. D. Shaw, "Turnover Rates and Organizational Performance: A Meta-analysis," *Journal of Applied Psychology,* 98 (2013), pp. 268–309.

58. S. E. Needleman, "Sick Time Rules Re-Emerge," *The New York Times,* March 1, 2012, www.wsj.com.

59. S. Shellenbarger, "When It Comes to Work, Can You Care Too Much?" *The Wall Street Journal,* April 29, 2014, www.wsj.com.

60. E. A. Locke, "The Nature and Causes of Job Dissatisfaction," in *The Handbook of Industrial & Organizational Psychology,* ed. M. D. Dunnette (Chicago: Rand McNally, 1976), pp. 901–69.

61. B. Casselman, "Male Nurses Make More Money," *The Wall Street Journal Online,* February 25, 2013.

62. R. E. Silverman, "Psst . . .. This is What Your Co-worker Is Paid," *The Wall Street Journal Online,* January 29, 2013.

63. F. Jones, D. B. O'Connor, M. Conner, B. McMillan, and E. Ferguson, "Impact of Daily Mood, Work Hours and Isostrain Variables on Self-Reported Health Behaviors," *Journal of Applied Psychology* 92 (2007), pp. 1731–40.

64. J. Jacoby, "Air Traffic Control Staffing under Scrutiny," CNN.com, March 25, 2011.

65. M. Price, "The Risks of Night Work," *Monitor on Psychology,* January 2011, pp. 39–41.

66. R. D. Zimmerman, "Understanding the Impact of Personality Traits on Individuals' Turnover Decisions: A Meta-analysis," *Personnel Psychology* 61 (2008), pp. 309–48.

67. T. Begley and C. Lee, "The Role of Negative Affectivity in Pay-at-Risk Reactions: A Longitudinal Study," *Journal of Applied Psychology,* 2005, pp. 382–88.

68. C. Kenny, "The Economic Power of Positive Thinking," *Bloomberg Businessweek,* January 10, 2015, pp. 8–9.

69. M. McCardle, "Why Negativity Is Really Awesome," *Bloomberg Businessweek,* February 20, 2014, pp. 6–7.

70. J. M. O'Brian, "Zappos Knows How to Kick It," *Fortune,* January 2, 2009, pp. 55–60.

71. E. F. Stone and H. G. Gueutal, "An Empirical Derivation of the Dimensions along Which Characteristics of Jobs Are Perceived," *Academy of Management Journal* 28 (1985), pp. 376–96.

72. L. W. Porter and R. M. Steers, "Organizational, Work and Personal Factors in Employee Absenteeism and Turnover," *Psychological Bulletin* 80 (1973), pp. 151–76.

73. P. Mozur and T. Orlink, "Hon Hoi Riot Undermines Squeeze on Chinese Manufacturers," *The Wall Street Journal,* September 24, 2012, www.wsj.com.

74. P. Mozur, "New Labor Attitudes Fed into China Riot," *The Wall Street Journal,* September 26, 2012, www.wsj.com.

75. E. C. Dierdorff and J. K. Ellington, "It's the Nature of the Work: Examining Behavior-based Sources of Work-Family Conflict," *Journal of Applied Psychology* 93 (2008), pp. 883–92.

76. L. Sandler, "How to Love Paid Family Leave," *The Wall Street Journal,* July 27, 2014, www.wsj.com.

77. D. Leonhardt, "Paternity Leave: The Rewards and Remaining Stigma," *The New York Times,* November 7, 2014, www.nytimes.com.

78. B. L. Rau and M. M. Hyland, "Role Conflict and Flexible Work Arrangements: The Effects on Applicant Attraction," *Personnel Psychology* 55 (2002), pp. 111–36.

79. G. Flynn, "The Legalities of Flextime," *Workforce,* October 2001, pp. 62–66.

80. A. M. Grant, "Relational Job Design and the Motivation to Make a Prosocial Difference," *Academy of Management Review* 32 (2007), pp. 393–417.

81. A. M. Grant, "Does Intrinsic Motivation Fuel the Prosocial Fire? Motivational Synergy in Predicting Persistence, Performance, and Productivity," *Journal of Applied Psychology* 93 (2007), pp. 48–58.

82. A. M. Grant, "The Significance of Task Significance," *Journal of Applied Psychology* 93 (2007), pp. 108–24.

83. A. M. Grant, E. M. Campbell, G. Chen, K. Cottone, D. Lapedia, and K. Lee, "Impact and Art of Motivation Maintenance: The Effects of Contact with Beneficiaries on Persistance Behavior," *Organizational Behavior and Human Decision Processes* 103 (2007), pp. 53–67.

84. K. Weir, "More Than Job Satisfaction," *Monitor on Psychology,* December 2013, pp. 39–43.

85. C. Porath, "No Time to Be Nice at Work," *The New York Times,* June 19, 2015, www.nytimes.com.

86. M. Korn and R. Feintzeig, "Is the Hard Nosed Boss Obsolete?" *The Wall Street Journal,* May 22, 2014, www.wsj.com.

87. S. Shellenbarger, "When the Boss Works Long Hours, Must We All? *The Wall Street Journal,* February 9, 2014, www.wsj.com.

88. D. Wescot, "Field Guide to Office Bullies," *Bloomberg Businessweek,* November 26, 2012, pp. 94–95.

89. G. C. Ganster, M. R. Fusiler, and B. T. Mayes, "Role of Social Support in the Experience of Stress at Work," *Journal of Applied Psychology* 71 (1986), pp. 102–11.

90. C. O. Trevor and D. L. Wazeter, "Contingent View of Reactions to Objective Pay Conditions: Interdependence among Pay Structure Characteristics and Pay Relative to Internal and External Referents," *Journal of Applied Psychology* 91 (2006), pp. 1260–75.

91. S. C. Currall, A. J. Towler, T. A. Judge, and L. Kohn, "Pay Satisfaction and Organizational Outcomes," *Personnel Psychology* 58 (2005), pp. 613–40.

92. E. White, "Opportunity Knocks, and It Pays a Lot Better," *The Wall Street Journal,* November 13, 2006, p. B3.

93. P. Ziobro and E. Morath, "Wal-Mart Raising Wages as Market Gets Tighter," *The Wall Street Journal,* February 19, 2015, www.wsj.com.

94. F. Wilkinson, "Starbuck's, Magna Cum Grande," *Bloomberg Businessweek,* June 19, 2014, p. 14.

95. H. G. Heneman and D. S. Schwab, "Pay Satisfaction: Its Multidimensional Nature and Measurement," *International Journal of Applied Psychology* 20 (1985), pp. 129–41.

96. T. Judge and T. Welbourne, "A Confirmatory Investigation of the Dimensionality of the Pay Satisfaction Questionnaire," *Journal of Applied Psychology* 79 (1994), pp. 461–66.

97. R. E. Silverman, "Are You Happy at Work? Bosses Push Weekly Polls," *The Wall Street Journal,* December 2, 2014, www.wsj.com.

98. C. Mims, "Bosses Use Anonymous Networks to Learn What Workers Really Think," *The Wall Street Journal,* June 21, 2015, www.wsj.com.

99. E. Frauenheim, "Tech Services Provider Sees Reduced Turnover and Explosive Revenue Growth After Making Employee Satisfaction Its Top Priority," *Workforce Management,* October 20, 2008, p. 25.

100. E. Maltby and S. E. Needleman, "Some Small Businesses Opt for the Health-Care Penalty," *The Wall Street Journal Online,* April 7, 2013.

101. S. J. Lambert, "When Flexibility Hurts," *The New York Times Online,* September 19, 2012.

102. P. Coy, "The Leisure Gap," *Bloomberg Businessweek,* July 23, 2012, pp. 8–9.

Pay Structure Decisions

11

CHAPTER

LEARNING OBJECTIVES

After reading this chapter, you should be able to:

Increasing Wages and Salaries: The Role of Labor Market Competition and Business Strategy

Many companies have recently raised wage and salary rates for their employees. Walmart, for example, has raised its lowest pay rate to $9/hour. (Previously, employees in some states could earn as little as $7.25/hour, the mandated federal minimum wage.) Other retailers like Target and Gap have made similar moves. McDonald's has also raised its wages. The reasons they have given vary. One reason is that it is a necessary response to the tightening of labor markets (i.e., more competition for workers). That makes it more challenging to compete to hire not only enough workers but also workers of the necessary quality. Employee wages and benefits are a major share of total costs at these companies, and they traditionally seek to keep a tight rein on such costs to keep their product prices low for consumers and to generate profits for shareholders.

Aetna, an insurance company, has a different business model that is somewhat less cost control oriented. Aetna recently raised its lowest pay rate to $16 (from roughly $12/hour previously) because it plans to move toward becoming a "much more consumer-oriented business" in the future. To execute that strategic change, the company says it will need "a better and more informed work force." So, competitive market forces play a role in pay level decisions. Companies with low wages, many employees, and high visibility, such as Walmart and McDonald's, have also faced pressure (including protests) to raise wages so that their employees have a better chance of being able to live on their wages. It is possible that such pressures, together with labor market tightening, have played a role in recent pay increases at such companies. Some companies such as Costco have long paid higher wages than competitors in the belief that doing so can be good for workers and good for the company, as long as the higher wages bring advantages in terms of objectives such as good employee relations, retention, productivity, quality, and/or innovation.

SOURCES: S. Strom, "McDonald's to Raise Pay at Outlets It Operates," *The New York Times*, April 2, 2015, p. B1; P. Zorro, "Target Says It Will Raise Wages, Too," *The Wall Street Journal*, March 19, 2015, p. B3; M. Krantz, "Walmart's Wages Get CEO's Attention," *USA Today*, March 2, 2015, p. 2B; A. Matthews and T. Francis, "Aetna Sets Wage Floor: $16 an Hour," *The Wall Street Journal*, January 13, 2015, p. B1.

Introduction

From the employer's point of view, pay is a powerful tool for furthering the organization's strategic goals. First, pay has a large impact on employee attitudes and behaviors. It influences the kind of employees who are attracted to (and remain with) the organization. In the chapter-opening story, Aetna decided to change its pay level in an effort to attract a workforce more in line with its future business strategy. Pay can also be a powerful motivational tool for aligning current employees' interests with those of the broader organization (an issue we address more fully in Chapter 12). Second, employee compensation is typically a significant organizational cost and thus requires close scrutiny. As Table 11.1 shows, total compensation (cash and benefits) accounts for 9% to 46% of revenues, depending on the industry.

LO 11-1

List the main decision areas and concepts in employee compensation management.

Table 11.1
Total Compensation as a Percentage of Revenues, Median by Industry

INDUSTRY	TOTAL COMPENSATION/REVENUES
Hospitals	46%
Manufacturing	19
Utilities	15
Insurance/health care	9
All industries	22

SOURCE: Data from PwC Saratoga's 2012/2013 U.S. Human Capital Effectiveness Report.

For Walmart and other companies, competing by keeping prices low for customers translates into paying low wages and raising them only when pressure from labor market competition (and perhaps from other sources, as we saw in the Chapter Opening) becomes sufficiently strong, such as now, with growth in the economy and lower unemployment rates. The economic cycle means economic activity and labor market competition will eventually slow. When things slow down for companies, they often cut labor costs by reducing headcount or reducing variable aspects of compensation (e.g., profit-sharing bonuses or 401k retirement-plan contributions). But every company should plan ahead for how they will have an efficient workforce in place and ready to go when the demand for their products picks up again. For example, when Toyota paused automobile assembly at U.S. plants due to slow sales, it did not lay off workers. It did offer a voluntary buyout plan under which workers signing up received 10 weeks of salary plus 2 weeks salary for every year worked. Workers who remained worked 36 hour rather than 40-hour weeks and reallocated their time to receive increased training and look for new ways to reduce costs.

From the employees' point of view, policies having to do with wages, salaries, and other earnings affect their overall income and thus their standard of living. Both the level of pay and its seeming fairness compared with others' pay are important. Pay is also often considered a sign of status and success. Employees attach great importance to pay decisions when they evaluate their relationship with the organization. Therefore, pay decisions must be carefully managed and communicated.

Total compensation, as noted, consists of cash compensation (salary, merit increases, bonuses, stock options, and other incentives) and benefits (e.g., health insurance, paid vacation, unemployment compensation). In the current chapter, we focus on salary levels. In Chapter 12, we address merit increase and incentive issues. In Chapter 13, we examine benefits decisions. Total rewards, total returns, and inducements are concepts that include not only total compensation, but also any other (nonmonetary) rewards (interesting or fulfilling work, good co-workers, development opportunities, recognition) that are associated with the employment relationship. These nonmonetary rewards are discussed in Chapters 4, 5, and 10. An organization must choose to what degree its total rewards strategy depends on monetary rewards (compensation) and what mix of compensation components will be used.

Pay Structure
The relative pay of different jobs (job structure) and how much they are paid (pay level).

Pay Level
The average pay, including wages, salaries, and bonuses, of jobs in an organization.

Job Structure
The relative pay of jobs in an organization.

Salary level decisions can be broken into two areas: pay structure and individual pay. In this chapter we focus on **pay structure**, which in turn entails a consideration of pay level and job structure. **Pay level** is defined here as the average pay (including wages, salaries, and bonuses) of jobs in an organization. (Benefits also matter, but these are discussed separately in Chapter 13.) **Job structure** refers to the relative pay of jobs in an organization. Consider the same two jobs in two different organizations. In Organization 1, jobs A and B are paid an annual average compensation of $40,000 and $60,000, respectively. In Organization 2, the pay rates are $45,000 and $55,000, respectively.

Organizations 1 and 2 have the same pay level ($50,000), but the job structures (relative rates of pay) differ.

Both pay level and job structure are characteristics of organizations and reflect decisions about jobs rather than about individual employees. This chapter's focus is on why and how organizations attach pay policies to jobs. In the next chapter we look within jobs to discuss the different approaches that can determine the pay of individual employees as well as the advantages and disadvantages of these different approaches.

Why is the focus on jobs in developing a pay structure? As the number of employees in an organization increases, so too does the number of human resource management decisions. In determining compensation, for example, each employee must be assigned a rate of pay that is acceptable in terms of external, internal, and individual equity (defined later) and in terms of the employer's cost. Although each employee is unique and thus requires some degree of individualized treatment, standardizing the treatment of similar employees (those with similar jobs) can help greatly to make compensation administration and decision making more manageable and more equitable. Thus pay policies are often attached to particular jobs rather than tailored entirely to individual employees.

Equity Theory and Fairness

In discussing the consequences of pay decisions, it is useful to keep in mind that employees often evaluate their pay relative to that of other employees. Equity theory suggests that people evaluate the fairness of their situations by comparing them with those of other people.[1] Equity is not equality. Equal pay for two workers with unequal contributions (inputs in equity theory) would likely be perceived as unfair if this information is known, especially by the worker making the stronger contributions to the organization. According to equity theory, a person (p) compares her own ratio of perceived outcomes O (pay, benefits, working conditions) to perceived inputs I (effort, ability, experience) to the ratio of a comparison other (o).

$$O_p/I_p <, >, \text{ or } = O_o/I_o?$$

If p's ratio (O_p/I_p) is smaller than the comparison other's ratio (O_o/I_o), underreward inequity results. If p's ratio is larger, overreward inequity results, although evidence suggests that this type of inequity is less likely to occur and less likely to be sustained because p may rationalize the situation by reevaluating her outcomes less favorably or inputs (self-worth) more favorably.[2]

The consequences of p's comparisons depend on whether equity is perceived. If equity is perceived, no change is expected in p's attitudes or behavior. In contrast, perceived inequity may cause p to restore equity. Some ways of restoring equity are counterproductive, including (1) reducing one's own inputs (not working as hard), (2) increasing one's outcomes (such as by theft), or (3) leaving the situation that generates perceived inequity (leaving the organization or refusing to work or cooperate with employees who are perceived as overrewarded).

Equity theory's main implication for managing employee compensation is that to an important extent, employees evaluate their pay by comparing it with what others get paid, and their work attitudes and behaviors are influenced by such comparisons. For example, consider the contract that shortstop Alex Rodriguez, now a New York Yankee (or perhaps we should say, *still* a New York Yankee), signed years ago with the Texas Rangers baseball team. One provision stated that during the the first several years of his contract, his base compensation had to be at least $2 million higher than any other short-stop in major league baseball. A second provision permitted Rodriguez to void seasons in the latter years of his contract unless his base compensation was at least $1 million higher than any position player in major league baseball. Otherwise, Rodriguez would be free to leave his current team. These provisions that pegged Rodriguez's pay to other players' pay provide a compelling example of the importance of being paid well in *relative* terms. (We later learned that "A-Rod" apparently felt compelled to break some rules in hopes of helping his on-field performance live up to his pay.)

Another implication is that employee perceptions are what determine their evaluation. The fact that management believes its employees are paid well compared with those of other companies does not necessarily translate into employees' beliefs. Employees may have different information or make different comparisons than management. For example, Toyota recently set a goal to move from using wages in the U.S. auto industry as the standard of comparison to using the (lower) prevailing wages in the state where each plant is located. To do so, however, Toyota recognizes its "challenge will be how to educate team members and managers . . . so they can understand and accept [this] change."

Two types of employee social comparisons of pay are especially relevant in making pay level and job structure decisions. (See Table 11.2.) First, *external equity* pay comparisons focus on what employees in other organizations are paid for doing the same general job. Such comparisons are likely to influence the decisions of applicants to accept job offers as well as the attitudes and decisions of employees about whether to stay with an organization or take a job elsewhere. (See Chapters 5 and 10.) The organization's choice of pay level influences its employees' external pay comparisons and their consequences. A market pay survey is the primary administrative tool organizations use in choosing a pay level.

Second, *internal equity* pay comparisons focus on what employees within the same organization, but in different jobs, are paid. Employees make comparisons with lower-level jobs, jobs at the same level (but perhaps in different skill areas or product divisions), and jobs at higher levels. These comparisons may influence general attitudes of employees; their willingness to transfer to other jobs within the organization; their willingness to accept promotions; their inclination to cooperate across jobs, functional areas, or product groups; and their commitment to the organization. The organization's choice

Table 11.2

Pay Structure Concepts and Consequences

PAY STRUCTURE DECISION AREA	ADMINISTRATIVE TOOL	FOCUS OF EMPLOYEE PAY COMPARISONS	CONSEQUENCES OF EQUITY PERCEPTIONS
Pay level	Market pay surveys	External equity	External employee movement (attraction and retention of quality employees); labor costs; employee attitudes
Job structure	Job evaluation	Internal equity	Internal employee movement (promotion, transfer, job rotation); cooperation among employees; employee attitudes

of job structure influences its employees' internal comparisons and their consequences. Job evaluation is the administrative tool organizations use to design job structures.

In addition, employees make internal equity pay comparisons with others performing the same job. Such comparisons are most relevant to the following chapter, which focuses on using pay to recognize individual contributions and differences.

We now turn to ways to choose and develop pay levels and pay structures, the consequences of such choices, and the ways two administrative tools—market pay surveys and job evaluation—help in making pay decisions.

Developing Pay Levels

MARKET PRESSURES

Any organization faces two important competitive market challenges in deciding what to pay its employees: product market competition and labor market competition.[3]

LO 11-2
Describe the major administrative tools used to manage employee compensation.

Product Market Competition

First, organizations must compete effectively in the product market. In other words, they must be able to sell their goods and services at a quantity and price that will bring a sufficient return on their investment. Organizations compete on multiple dimensions (quality, service, and so on), and price is one of the most important dimensions. An important influence on price is the cost of production.

An organization that has higher labor costs than its product market competitors will have to charge higher average prices for products of similar quality. Thus, for example, if labor costs are 30% of revenues at Company A and Company B, but Company A has labor costs that are 20% higher than those of Company B, we would expect Company A to have product prices that are higher by $(0.30 \times 0.20) = 6\%$. At some point, the higher price charged by Company A will contribute to a loss of its business to competing companies with lower prices (like Company B). Until recently, in the automobile industry, hourly labor cost (including not only wages, but also retiree and active worker benefits such as health care) in assembly plants averaged $75 for the U.S. Big Three (Chrysler, General Motors, Ford), compared to $52 for Toyota and Honda plants in the United States. On average, it takes roughly 30 hours to assemble a car. So, the labor cost per car for the Big Three was $30 \times \$75 = \$2,250$, compared to $30 \times \$52 = \$1,560$ for Toyota and Honda. That labor cost disadvantage had to have been offset by superior vehicle quality, performance, and so forth for the Big Three to make a profit. The bankruptcies at Chrysler and General Motors indicate that was not possible. More recently, the U.S. Big Three have reduced their labor costs to $49/hour at Chrysler and $59/hour at GM and Ford by hiring new workers at lower wages and by reducing benefits costs.[4] That is a major change, now putting them in the same range as Honda's and Toyota's $50/hour to $55/hour U.S. labor cost. As a result, the Big Three have become much more competitive and their financial performance has improved dramatically. Toyota's labor costs have risen over time in the United States due to the inevitable aging of its workforce and the associated increased health care and retiree benefits. In a sense, it is going through the same life cycle as the Big Three did. In contrast, a newly opened plant, such as the Volkswagen plant in Chattanooga, Tennessee, is estimated to have hourly labor costs of $27 initially.[5] That $27 per hour cost to build Volkswagen Passats in Tennessee is much lower than Volkswagen's hourly labor cost to build cars in Germany, which has been estimated as high as nearly $100 (when the euro was at its strongest against the U.S. dollar, but more recently is estimated to be about $38/hour).[6] Due to this labor cost saving (and due to lower costs for parts, transportation, and so forth), Volkswagen expected to be able to reduce the price of a Passat from $28,000 (when it was built in Germany) to $20,000 when it was first built in Tennessee. As we will see in the "Competing through Globalization" box later in the chapter, even lower labor costs can be found in Mexico (and even lower labor costs than in Mexico in other parts of the world). Audi, Honda, Mazda, and Nissan have all announced plans to open new North American plants, but in Mexico. Only recently, for the first time in many years, did an automobile company (Chinese-owned Volvo) announce plans to build a new plant in the United States.[7]

The cost of labor is directly reflected in the price of the car. Therefore, *product market competition* places an *upper bound* on labor costs and compensation. This upper bound is more constrictive when labor costs are a larger share of total costs and when demand for the product is affected by changes in price (i.e., when demand is *elastic*). Unless higher labor costs are offset by higher worker productivity or desirable product features that allow a higher product price, it will be difficult to sustain these relatively high costs in a competitive product market. As we have noted, Volkswagen will be able to lower the price of its Passat by producing it in the United States where its labor costs will be lower than in Germany and lower than those of U.S. competitors. The search for lower labor costs is a continuous process. As companies move production to low-wage countries, wages there eventually rise, sometimes causing companies to move production to countries with still lower wages.

What components make up labor costs? A major component is the average cost per employee. This is made up of both direct payments (such as wages, salaries, and bonuses) and indirect payments (such as health insurance, Social Security, and unemployment compensation). A second component of labor cost is the staffing level (number of employees). Not surprisingly, financially troubled organizations often seek to cut costs by focusing on one or both components. Staff reductions, hiring freezes, wage and salary freezes, and sharing benefits costs with employees are several ways of making the organization's labor costs more competitive in the product market.

Labor Market Competition

A second important competitive market challenge is *labor market competition,* which reflects the number of workers available relative to the number of jobs available. Shortages and surpluses influence pay levels. For example, as we saw in the chapter-opening story, a shortage of workers will put upward pressure on wages and salaries, as organizations must pay to compete against other companies that hire similar employees. These labor market competitors typically include not only companies that have similar products but also those in different product markets that hire similar types of employees. If an organization is not competitive in the labor market, it will fail to attract and retain employees of sufficient numbers and quality. For example, even if a computer manufacturer offers newly graduated electrical engineers the same pay as other computer manufacturers, if automobile manufacturers and other labor market competitors offer salaries $5,000 higher, the computer company may not be able to hire enough qualified electrical engineers. Labor market competition places a *lower bound* on pay levels.

EMPLOYEES AS A RESOURCE

Because organizations have to compete in the labor market, they should consider their employees not just as a cost but as a resource in which the organization has invested and from which it expects valuable returns.[8] Although controlling costs directly affects an organization's ability to compete in the product market, the organization's competitive position can be compromised if costs are kept low at the expense of employee productivity and quality. Having higher labor costs than your competitors is not necessarily a concern if you also have the best and most effective workforce, one that produces products more efficiently and with better quality.

Pay policies and programs are one of the most important human resource tools for encouraging desired employee behaviors and discouraging undesired behaviors. Therefore, they must be evaluated not just in terms of costs but in terms of the returns they generate—how they attract, retain, and motivate a high-quality workforce. For example, if the average revenue per employee in Company A is 20% higher than in Company B, it may not be important that the average pay in Company A is 10% higher than in Company B.

DECIDING WHAT TO PAY

Although organizations face important external labor and product market pressures in setting their pay levels, a range of discretion remains.[9] How large the range is depends on the particular competitive environment the organization faces. Where the range is broad, an important strategic decision is whether to pay above, at, or below the market average. The advantage of paying above the market average is the ability to attract and retain the top talent available and help generate positive job attitudes (e.g., satisfaction), all of which can translate into a highly effective and productive workforce. The disadvantage, however, is the added cost.[10]

Under what circumstances do the benefits of higher pay outweigh the higher costs? According to **efficiency wage theory**, one circumstance is when organizations have technologies or structures that depend on highly skilled employees. For example, organizations that emphasize decentralized decision making may need higher-caliber employees. Another circumstance where higher pay may be warranted is when an organization has difficulties observing and monitoring its employees' performance. It may therefore wish to provide an above-market pay rate to ensure the incentive to put forth maximum effort. The theory is that employees who are paid more than they would be paid elsewhere will be reluctant to shirk because they wish to retain their good jobs.[11] Interestingly, some companies have decided that it sometimes makes sense to pay employees to leave if they are staying only because of the money and despite being a better fit elsewhere. See the "Competing through Sustainability" box.

Efficiency Wage Theory
A theory stating that wages influence worker productivity.

MARKET PAY SURVEYS

To compete for talent, organizations use **benchmarking**, a procedure in which an organization compares its own practices against those of the competition. In compensation management, benchmarking against product market and labor market competitors is typically accomplished through the use of one or more pay surveys, which provide information on going rates of pay among competing organizations.

The use of pay surveys requires answers to several important questions:[12]

Benchmarking
Comparing an organization's practices against those of the competition.

1. Which employers should be included in the survey? Ideally, they would be the key labor market and product market competitors.
2. Which jobs are included in the survey? Because only a sample of jobs is ordinarily used, care must be taken that the jobs are representative in terms of level, functional area, and product market. Also, the job content must be sufficiently similar.

COMPETING THROUGH SUSTAINABILITY

Pay to Quit

Zappos, an online shoe sales company, recently made major changes to its management system. There are now supposed to be no job titles and traditional bosses. In place of hierarchical, command-control decision making, Zappos says it will have self-governed teams ("circles") in an effort to make the organization more innovative and faster moving by eliminating hierarchy and giving people more freedom to come up with new ideas and act on them. One problem with successfully implementing such a major change is that the people who fit a more hierarchical system may not fit the new self-management system. That lack of fit can generate resistance and poor execution. As one solution, Zappos will pay employees

to quit (up to 3 months of salary) if they don't like the new management system. Zappos also has an older program that pays new hires $2,000 to quit if they feel they made a mistake taking a job at Zappos. Amazon, which acquired Zappos several years ago, has also adopted a similar program, which it calls Pay to Quit. Amazon makes the offer once per year to workers in its "fulfillment centers" (warehouses). In employees' first year, they get paid $2,000 to quit, which goes up by $1,000/year to a maximum of $5,000. Jeff Bezos, the head of Amazon, has stated that Amazon wants "to encourage folks to take a moment and think about what they really want. In the long run, an employee staying

somewhere they don't want to be isn't healthy for the employee or the company."

DISCUSSION QUESTIONS
1. What is the business case or rationale for paying employees to quit?
2. Should more companies adopt such a program? Explain.
3. Have you ever had a job where you would have quit if there had been a "pay to quit" program? Why or why not?

SOURCES: J. McGregor, "Zappos to Employees: Get Behind Our 'No Bosses' Approach, or Leave with Severance," *The Washington Post*, March 31, 2015, www.washingtonpost.com; Kim Peterson, "Why Amazon Pays Employees $5,000 to Quit," *CBS Moneywatch*, accessed April 19, 2015, www.cbs.news.com.

3. If multiple surveys are used, how are all the rates of pay weighted and combined? Organizations often have to weight and combine pay rates because different surveys are often tailored toward particular employee groups (labor markets) or product markets. The organization must decide how much relative weight to give to its labor market and product market competitors in setting pay.

Several factors affect decisions on how to combine surveys.[13] Product market comparisons that focus on labor costs are likely to deserve greater weight when (1) labor costs represent a large share of total costs, (2) product demand is elastic (it changes in response to product price changes), (3) the supply of labor is inelastic, and (4) employee skills are specific to the product market (and will remain so). In contrast, labor market comparisons may be more important when (1) attracting and retaining qualified employees is difficult and (2) the costs (administrative, disruption, and so on) of recruiting replacements are high.

As this discussion suggests, knowing what other organizations are paying is only one part of the story. It is also necessary to know what those organizations are getting in return for their investment in employees. To find that out, some organizations examine ratios such as revenues/employees and revenues/labor cost. The first ratio includes the staffing component of employee cost but not the average cost per employee. The second ratio, however, includes both. Note that comparing these ratios across organizations requires caution. For example, different industries rely on different labor and capital resources. So comparing the ratio of revenues to labor costs of a petroleum company (capital intensive, high ratio) to a hospital (labor intensive, low ratio) would be like comparing apples and oranges. But within industries, such comparisons can be useful. Besides revenues, other return-on-investment data might include product quality, customer satisfaction, and potential workforce quality (such as average education and skill levels).

Rate Ranges

As the preceding discussion suggests, obtaining a single "going rate" of market pay is a complex task that involves a number of subjective decisions; it is both an art and a science. Once a market rate has been chosen, how is it incorporated into the pay structure? Typically—especially for white-collar jobs—it is used for setting the midpoint of pay ranges for either jobs or pay grades (discussed next). Market survey data are also often collected on minimum and maximum rates of pay as well. The use of **rate ranges** permits a company to recognize differences in employee performance, seniority, training, and so forth in setting individual pay (discussed in the next chapter). For some blue-collar jobs, however, particularly those covered by collective bargaining contracts, there may be a single rate of pay for all employees within the job.

Rate Ranges
Different employees in the same job may have different pay rates.

Key Jobs and Nonkey Jobs

In using pay surveys, it is necessary to make a distinction between two general types of jobs: key jobs (or benchmark jobs) and nonkey jobs. **Key jobs** (also known as benchmark jobs) have relatively stable content and—perhaps most important—are common to many organizations. Therefore, it is possible to obtain market pay survey data on them. Note, however, that to avoid too much of an administrative burden, organizations may not gather market pay data on all such jobs. In contrast to key jobs, **nonkey jobs** are, to an important extent, unique to organizations (and/or have content different from jobs in other organizations having the same title). Thus, by definition, they cannot be directly valued or compared through the use of market surveys. Therefore, they are treated differently in the pay-setting process.

Key Jobs
Benchmark jobs, used in pay surveys, that have relatively stable content and are common to many organizations.

Nonkey Jobs
Jobs that are unique to organizations and that cannot be directly valued or compared through the use of market surveys.

DEVELOPING A JOB STRUCTURE

Although external comparisons of the sort we have been discussing are important, employees also evaluate their pay using internal comparisons. So, for example, a vice president of marketing may expect to be paid roughly the same amount as a vice president of information systems because they are at the same organizational level, with similar levels of responsibility and similar impacts on the organization's performance. A job structure can be defined as the relative worth of various jobs in the organization, based on these types of internal comparisons. We now discuss how such decisions are made.

Job Evaluation

One typical way of measuring internal job worth is to use an administrative procedure called **job evaluation**. A job evaluation system is composed of compensable factors and a weighting scheme based on the importance of each **compensable factor** to the organization. Simply stated, compensable factors are the characteristics of jobs that an organization values and chooses to pay for. These characteristics may include job complexity, working conditions, required education, required experience, and responsibility.

Job Evaluation
An administrative procedure used to measure internal job worth.

Compensable Factors
The characteristics of jobs that an organization values and chooses to pay for.

Most job evaluation systems use several compensable factors. Job analysis (discussed in Chapter 4) provides basic descriptive information on job attributes, and the job evaluation process assigns values to these compensable factors.

Scores can be generated in a variety of ways, but they typically include input from a number of people. A job evaluation committee commonly generates ratings. Although there are numerous ways to evaluate jobs, the most widely used is the point-factor system, which yields job evaluation points for each compensable factor.[14]

The Point-Factor System

After generating scores for each compensable factor on each job, job evaluators often apply a weighting scheme to account for the differing importance of the compensable factors to the organization. Weights can be generated in two ways. First, *a priori* weights can be assigned, which means factors are weighted using expert judgments about the importance of each compensable factor. Second, weights can be derived empirically based on how important each factor seems in determining pay in the labor market. (Statistical methods such as multiple regression can be used for this purpose.) For the sake of simplicity, we assume in the following example that equal a priori weights are chosen, which means that the scores on the compensable factors can be simply summed.

Table 11.3 shows an example of a three-factor job evaluation system applied to three jobs. Note that the jobs differ in the levels of experience, education, and complexity required. Summing the scores on the three compensable factors provides an internally oriented assessment of relative job worth in the organization. In a sense, the Programmer Analyst job is worth 41% (155/110 − 1) more than the computer tech job, and the systems analyst job is worth 91% (210/110 − 1) more than the computer tech job. Whatever pay level is chosen (based on benchmarking and competitive strategy), we would expect the pay differentials to be somewhat similar to these percentages. The internal job evaluation and external survey-based measures of worth can, however, diverge.

DEVELOPING A PAY STRUCTURE

In the example provided in Table 11.4, there are 15 jobs, 10 of which are key jobs. For these key (also known as benchmark) jobs, both pay survey and job evaluation data are available. For the five nonkey jobs, by definition, no survey data are available, only job evaluation information. Note that, for simplicity's sake, we work with data from only two pay surveys and we use a weighted average that gives twice as much weight to survey 1. Also, our example works with a single structure. Many organizations have multiple structures that correspond to different job families (like clerical, technical, and professional) or product divisions.

How are the data in Table 11.4 combined to develop a pay structure? First, it is important to note that both internal and external comparisons must be considered in making compensation decisions. However, because the pay structures suggested by internal and

Table 11.3
Example of a Three-Factor Job Evaluation System

| JOB TITLE | COMPENSABLE FACTORS | | | |
	EXPERIENCE	EDUCATION	COMPLEXITY	TOTAL
Computer tech	40	30	40	110
Programmer analyst	40	50	65	155
Systems analyst	65	60	85	210

Table 11.4

Job Evaluation and Pay Survey Data

JOB	KEY JOB?	JOB TITLE	JOB EVALUATION	SURVEY 1 (S1)	SURVEY 2 (S2)	SURVEY COMPOSITE (2/3*S1 + 1/3*S2)
A	y	Computer tech	110	$3,219	$2,770	$3,070
B	y	Engineering tech I	115	3,530	3,053	3,370
C	y	Programmer analyst	155	4,666	4,142	4,491
D	n	Industrial engineer	165	—	—	—
E	n	Compensation analyst	170	—	—	—
F	y	Accountant	190	5,781	4,958	5,507
G	y	Systems analyst	210	6,840	6,166	6,614
H	n	Director of personal	225	—	—	—
I	y	Software engineer	245	7,971	7,210	7,717
J	y	System analyst—senior	255	8,328	6,832	7,829
K	y	Accounting manager	270	9,389	9,043	9,274
L	y	Electrical engineer—senior	275	8,794	7,670	8,419
M	n	Accounting director	315	—	—	—
N	y	Director of engineering	320	11,242	10,515	11,000
O	n	Chief scientist	330	—	—	—

SOURCES: Adapted from S. Rynes, B. Gerhart, G. T. Milkovich, and J. Boudreau, *Current Compensation Professional Institute* (Scottsdale, AZ: American Compensation Association, 1988); G. T. Milkovich and B. Gerhart, *Cases in Compensation,* Version 11.1e (2013). Reprinted with permission.

external comparisons do not necessarily converge, employers must carefully balance them. Studies suggest that employers may differ significantly in the degree to which they place priority on internal- or external-comparison data in developing pay structures.[15]

At least three pay-setting approaches, which differ according to their relative emphasis on external or internal comparisons, can be identified.[16]

MARKET SURVEY DATA

The approach with the greatest emphasis on external comparisons (market survey data) is achieved by directly basing pay on market surveys that cover as many key jobs as possible. For example, the rate of pay for job A in Table 11.5 would be $3,070; for job B, $3,370; and for job C, $4,491. For nonkey jobs (jobs D, E, H, M, and O), however, pay survey information is not available, and we must proceed differently. Basically, we develop a market **pay policy line** based on the key jobs (for which there are both job evaluation and market pay survey data available). As Figure 11.1 shows, the data can be plotted with a line of best fit estimated. This line can be generated using a statistical procedure (regression analysis). Regressing the data from the "Survey Composite" column in Table 11.4 on the data from the "Job Evaluation" column in Table 11.4 (using only rows without missing data) yields the equation

Pay Policy Line
Equation that describes the relationship between a job's pay and its job evaluation points.

$$-\$1,058 + \$36.30 \times \text{job evaluation points}$$

In other words, the predicted monthly salary (based on fitting a line to the key job data) is obtained by plugging the number of job evaluation points into this equation. Thus, for example, job M, a nonkey job, would have a predicted monthly salary of $-\$1058 + \$36.30 \times 315 = \$10,378$.

Table 11.5
Pay Midpoints under Different Approaches

JOB	KEY JOB?	JOB TITLE	JOB EVALUATION	(1) SURVEY + POLICY	(2) PAY POLICY	(3) GRADES
A	y	Computer tech	110	$3,070	$2,936	$3,480
B	y	Engineering tech I	115	3,370	3,117	3,480
C	y	Programmer analyst	155	4,491	4,570	5,296
D	n	Industrial engineer	165	4,933	4,933	5,296
E	n	Compensation analyst	170	5,114	5,114	5,296
F	y	Accountant	190	5,507	5,840	5,296
G	y	Systems analyst	210	6,614	6,566	7,110
H	n	Director of personnel	225	7,110	7,110	7,110
I	y	Software engineer	245	7,717	7,837	7,110
J	y	Systems analyst—senior	255	7,828	8,200	8,926
K	y	Accounting manager	270	9,274	8,744	8,926
L	y	Electrical engineer—senior	275	8,419	8,926	8,926
M	n	Accounting director	315	10,378	10,378	10,741
N	y	Director of engineering	320	11,000	10,560	10,741
O	n	Chief scientist	330	10,922	10,922	10,741

SOURCES: Adapted from S. Rynes, B. Gerhart, G. T. Milkovich, and J. Boudreau, *Current Compensation Professional Institute* (Scottsdale, AZ: American Compensation Association, 1988); G. T. Milkovich and B. Gerhart, *Cases in Compensation,* Version 11.1e (2013). Reprinted with permission.

As Figure 11.1 also indicates, it is not necessary to fit a straight line to the job evaluation and pay survey data. In some cases, a pay structure that provides increasing monetary rewards to higher-level jobs may be more consistent with the organization's goals or with the external market. For example, nonlinearity may be more appropriate

Figure 11.1

Pay Policy Lines, Linear and Natural Logarithmic Functions

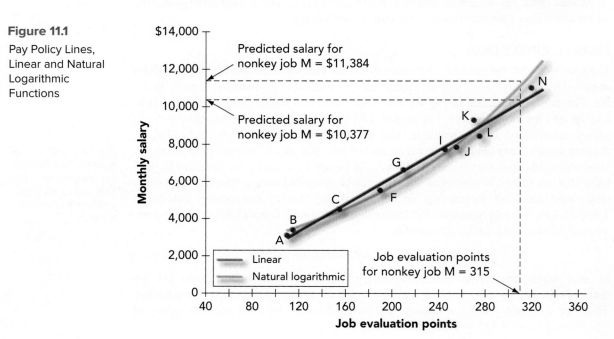

if higher-level jobs are especially valuable to organizations and the talent to perform such jobs is rare. The curvilinear function in Figure 11.1 is obtained in the same way as above, except that the salary survey data are first transformed using the natural logarithm (and then the equation result is transformed back, using for example the EXP function in Excel). The resulting equation is:

$$\text{Natural logarithm of pay} = \$7.446 + (0.006 \times \text{job evaluation points})$$

Pay Policy Line

A second pay-setting approach that combines information from external and internal comparisons is to use the pay policy line to derive pay rates for both key and nonkey jobs. This approach differs from the first approach in that actual market rates are no longer used for key jobs. This introduces a greater degree of internal consistency into the structure because the pay of all the jobs is directly linked to the number of job evaluation points.

Pay Grades

A third approach is to group jobs into a smaller number of pay classes, pay ranges, or **pay grades**. Table 11.6 (see also Table 11.5, last column), for example, demonstrates one possibility: a five-grade structure. Each job within a grade would have the same rate range (i.e., would be assigned the same midpoint, minimum, and maximum). The advantage of this approach is that the administrative burden of setting separate rates of pay for hundreds (even thousands) of different jobs is reduced. It also permits greater flexibility in moving employees from job to job without raising concerns about, for example, going from a job having 230 job evaluation points to a job with 215 job evaluation points. What might look like a demotion in a completely job-based system is often a nonissue in a grade-based system. Note that the **range spread** (the distance between the minimum and maximum) is larger at higher levels, in recognition of the fact that performance differences are likely to have more impact on the organization at higher job levels. (See Figure 11.2.)

The disadvantage of using grades is that some jobs will be underpaid and others overpaid. For example, job C and job F both fall within the same grade (Pay Grade 2). The midpoint for job C under a grade system is $5,296 per month, or about $700 to $800 or so more than under the two alternative pay-setting approaches in Table 11.5. Obviously, this will contribute to higher labor costs and potential difficulties in competing in the

Pay Grades
Jobs of similar worth or content grouped together for pay administration purposes.

Range Spread
The distance between the minimum and maximum amounts in a pay grade.

Table 11.6
Sample Pay Grade Structure

PAY GRADE	JOB EVALUATION POINTS RANGE		MONTHLY PAY RATE RANGE		
	MINIMUM	MAXIMUM	MINIMUM	MIDPOINT	MAXIMUM
1	100	150	$2,784	$3,480	$4,176
2	150	200	4,237	5,296	6,354
3	200	250	5,688	7,110	8,533
4	250	300	7,141	8,926	10,710
5	300	350	8,592	10,741	12,906

Figure 11.2

Sample Pay Grade Structure

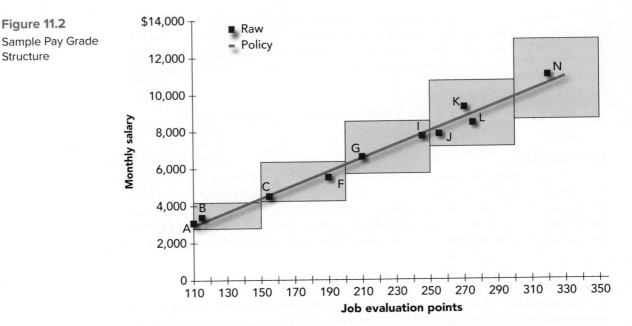

product market. Unless there is an expected return to this increased cost, the approach is questionable. Job F, on the other hand, is paid roughly $200 to $500 less per month under the grades system than it would be otherwise. Therefore, the company may find it more difficult to compete in the labor market.

CONFLICTS BETWEEN MARKET PAY SURVEYS AND JOB EVALUATION

LO 11-3

Explain the importance of competitive labor market and product market forces in compensation decisions.

An examination of Table 11.5 suggests that the relative worth of jobs is quite similar overall, whether based on job evaluation or pay survey data. However, some inconsistencies typically arise, and these are usually indicated by jobs whose average survey pay is significantly below or above the pay policy line. The closest case in Table 11.5 is job L, for which the average pay falls significantly below the policy line. One possible explanation is that a relatively plentiful supply of people in the labor market are capable of performing this job, so the pay needed to attract and retain them is lower than would be expected given the job evaluation points. Another kind of inconsistency occurs when market surveys show that a job is paid higher than the policy line (like job K). Again, this may reflect relative supply and demand, in this case driving pay higher.

How are conflicts between external and internal equity resolved, and what are the consequences? The example of the vice presidents of marketing and information technology may help illustrate the type of choice faced. The marketing VP job may receive the same number of job evaluation points, but market survey data may indicate that it typically pays less than the information technology VP job, perhaps because of tighter supply for the latter. Does the organization pay based on the market survey (external comparison) or on the job evaluation points (internal comparison)?

Emphasizing the internal comparison would suggest paying the two VPs the same. In doing so, however, either the VP of marketing would be "overpaid" or the VP of information technology would be "underpaid." The former drives up labor costs (product market problems); the latter may make it difficult to attract and retain a quality VP of information technology (labor market problems).

Another consideration has to do with the strategy of the organization. In some organizations (like Pepsi and Nike) the marketing function is critical to success. Thus, even though the market for marketing VPs is lower than that for information technology VPs, an organization may choose to be a pay leader for the marketing position (pay at the 90th percentile, for example) but only meet the market for the information technology position (perhaps pay at the 50th percentile). In other words, designing a pay structure requires careful consideration of which positions are most central to dealing with critical environmental challenges and opportunities in reaching the organization's goals.[17]

What about emphasizing external comparisons? Two potential problems arise. First, the marketing VP may be dissatisfied because she expects a job of similar rank and responsibility to that of the information technology VP to be paid similarly. Second, it becomes difficult to rotate people through different VP positions (for training and development) because going to the marketing VP position might appear as a demotion to the VP of information technology.

There is no one right solution to such dilemmas. Each organization must decide which objectives are most essential and choose the appropriate strategy. However, there has been a shift over time such that most organizations now emphasize external comparisons/market pricing, perhaps because of increasing competitive pressures over time.[18]

MONITORING COMPENSATION COSTS

Pay structure influences compensation costs in a number of ways. Most obviously, the pay level at which the structure is pegged influences these costs. However, this is only part of the story. The pay structure represents the organization's intended policy, but actual practice may not coincide with it. Take, for example, the pay grade structure presented earlier. The midpoint for grade 1 is $3,480, and the midpoint for grade 2 is $5,296. Now, consider the data on a group example of individual employees in Table 11.7. One frequently used index of the correspondence between actual and intended pay is the **compa-ratio**, computed as follows:

$$\text{Grade compa-ratio} = \text{Actual average pay for grade/Pay midpoint for grade}$$

The compa-ratio directly assesses the degree to which actual pay is consistent with the pay policy. A compa-ratio less than 1.00 suggests that actual pay is lagging behind the policy, whereas a compa-ratio greater than 1.00 indicates that pay (and costs) exceeds that of the policy. Although there may be good reasons for compa-ratios to differ from 1.00, managers should also consider whether the pay structure is allowing costs to get out of control.

Compa-Ratio
An index of the correspondence between actual and intended pay.

EMPLOYEE	JOB	PAY	MIDPOINT	EMPLOYEE COMPA-RATIOS	
	Grade 1				
1	Engineering tech I	$3,690	$3,480		1.06
2	Computer tech	3,306	3,480		.95
3	Engineering tech I	4,037	3,480		1.16
4	Engineering tech I	3,862	3,480		1.11
				Mean	**1.07**
	Grade 2				
5	Programmer analyst	6,250	5,296		1.18
6	Accountant	6,037	5,296		1.14
7	Accountant	5,878	5,296		1.11
				Mean	**1.15**

Table 11.7
Compa-Ratios for Two Grades

GLOBALIZATION, GEOGRAPHIC REGION, AND PAY STRUCTURES

As Figure 11.3 shows, market pay structures can differ substantially across countries both in terms of their level and in terms of the relative worth of jobs. Compared with cities in China, India, and Mexico the labor markets in U.S. and German cities provide much

Geographic location is an important factor for Human Resources to consider when establishing a pay structure. Living in New York City is more expensive than other places, and employers need to factor in living costs when deciding upon salaries in order to hire a strong workforce.

CREDIT: © Grant V Faint/Getty Images/RF

Figure 11.3

Net Earnings (After Taxes and Social Security Contributions) in Selected Occupations, Six World Cities

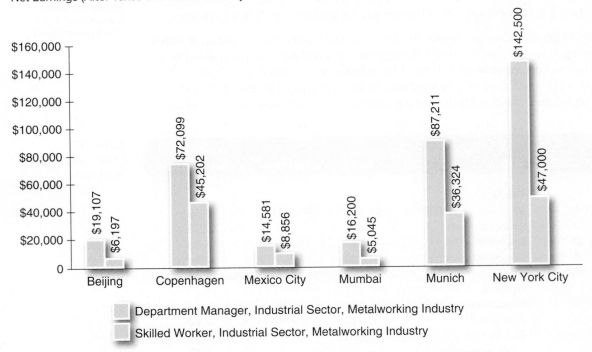

SOURCE: UBS, "Prices and Earnings 2015: A Comparison of Purchasing Power around the Globe," September 2015, Zurich, Switzerland.

lower levels of pay overall and also different payoffs to skill, education, and advancement. These differences create a dilemma for global companies. For example, should a German manager posted to Beijing be paid according to the standard in Germany or China? If the Germany standard is used, a sense of inequity is likely to exist among peers in Beijing. If the China market standard is used, it may be all but impossible to find a German engineer willing to accept an assignment in Beijing. Typically, expatriate pay and benefits (like housing allowance and tax equalization) continue to be linked more closely to the home country. However, this link appears to be slowly weakening and now depends more on the nature and length of the assignment.[19]

Within the United States, Runzheimer International reports that most companies have either a formal or an informal policy that provides for pay differentials based on geographic location.[20] These differentials are intended to prevent inequitable treatment of employees who work in more expensive parts of the country. For example, according to Salary.com the cost of living index for New York City is roughly 83% higher than in Madison, Wisconsin. Therefore, an employee receiving annual pay of $50,000 in Madison would require annual pay of $91,409 in New York City to retain the same purchasing power. The most common company approach is to move an employee higher in the pay structure to compensate for higher living costs. However, the drawback of this approach is that it may be difficult to adjust the salary downward if costs in that location fall or the employee moves to a lower-cost area. Thus, some percentage of the companies choose to pay an ongoing supplement that changes or disappears in the event of such changes.

EVIDENCE-BASED HR

Walmart is legendary for its attention to (some would say obsession with) cost control so that it can pass lower prices on to customers, making it difficult for other retailers to compete. The question, however, is whether this type of aggressive cost control makes sense when it comes to wages or is this a situation where "you get what you pay for"? Is it possible that a firm that pays its workers better can also do better? Costco pays higher wages, covers more of its employees with health insurance, requires them to pay smaller health insurance premiums, and contributes more to their retirement plans.

Major retailers in some cases experience 100% turnover each year, and when the associated costs (hiring, orienting, training, replacing) are considered, it can add up. One retailer with 50,000 employees found the annual turnover cost was more than $150 million per year. Thus, "saving money" by paying lower wages was maybe instead costing the company. At Walmart, some see a vicious cycle where low wages cut costs, but also harm service and customer satisfaction, ultimately harming profits. In the American Customer Satisfaction Index, Walmart is 15th and last in its category (department and discount stores). By contrast, Costco is first out of 20 in its category (specialty retail stores).

The Container Store, which sells shelving systems, storage containers, and other products to help organize the house and garage, pays front-line workers about $50,000 per year, even more than Costco pays workers with several years of experience (around $40,000 per year) and significantly more than Walmart pays such workers (around $25,000 per year). (Starting pay is much lower.) CEO and Container Store

CONTINUED

founder Kip Tindall explains their high wage this way: "One great person can easily do the business productivity of three good people," and that it is necessary to pay well "particularly if you are trying to attract and keep really good people."

QUESTIONS

1. What is the potential return on investment (ROI) to paying higher wages? Be specific about what objectives might be most positively affected by higher wages.
2. Under what conditions would high wages most likely generate a positive ROI?
3. Should Walmart pay wages more like those paid by Costco and the Container Store? Should Costco and the Container Store pay more like Walmart? Explain.

SOURCES: H. Tabuchi, "Walmart Lifts Its Wage Floor to $9 an Hour," *The New York Times,* February 20, 2015, p. A1; R. Feintzeig, "Container Store Bets on $50,000 Retail Worker," *The Wall Street Journal,* October 15, 2014, p. B6; C. DeRose and N. Tichy, "Are You Spending More by Paying Your Employees Less?" *Forbes,* April 29, 2013; W. F. Cascio, "The High Cost of Low Wages," *Harvard Business Review,* December 2006, p. 23.

The Importance of Process: Participation and Communication

LO 11-4

Discuss the significance of process issues such as communication in compensation management.

Compensation management has been criticized for following the simplistic belief that "if the right technology can be developed, the right answers will be found."[21] In reality, however, any given pay decision is rarely obvious to the diverse groups that make up organizations, regardless of the decision's technical merit or basis in theory. Of course, it is important when changing pay practices to decide which program or combination of programs makes most sense, but how such decisions are made and how they are communicated also matter.[22]

PARTICIPATION

Employee participation in compensation decision making can take many forms. For example, employees may serve on task forces charged with recommending and designing a pay program. They may also be asked to help communicate and explain its rationale. This is particularly true in the case of job evaluation as well as many of the programs discussed in the next chapter. To date, for what are perhaps obvious reasons, employee participation in pay level decisions remains fairly rare.

It is important to distinguish between participation by those affected by policies and those who must actually implement the policies. Managers are in the latter group (and often in the former group at the same time). As in other areas of human resource management, line managers are typically responsible for making policies work. Their intimate involvement in any change to existing pay practices is, of course, necessary.

COMMUNICATION

A dramatic example of the importance of communication was found in a study of how an organization communicated pay cuts to its employees and the effects on theft rates and perceived equity.[23] Two organization units received 15% across-the-board pay cuts. A third unit received no pay cut and served as a control group. The reasons for the pay cuts were communicated in different ways to the two pay-cut groups. In the "adequate explanation" pay-cut group, management provided a significant amount of information to explain its reasons for the pay cut and also expressed significant remorse. In contrast, the "inadequate explanation" group received much less information and no indication of remorse. The control group received no pay cut (and thus no explanation).

The control group and the two pay-cut groups began with the same theft rates and equity perceptions. After the pay cut, the theft rate was 54% higher in the "adequate explanation" group than in the control group. But in the "inadequate explanation" condition, the theft rate was 141% higher than in the control group. In this case communication had a large, independent effect on employees' attitudes and behaviors.

Communication is likely to have other important effects. We know, for example, as emphasized by equity theory that not only actual pay but the comparison standard influences employee attitudes.[24] Under two-tier wage plans, employees doing the same jobs are paid two different rates, depending on when they were hired. Moreover, the lower-paid employees do not necessarily move into the higher-paying tier. Common sense might suggest that the lower-paid employees would be less satisfied, but this is not necessarily true. In fact, a study by Peter Cappelli and Peter Sherer found that the lower-paid employees were more satisfied on average.[25] Apparently, those in the lower tier used different (lower) comparison standards than those in the higher tier. The lower-tier employees compared their jobs with unemployment or lower-paying jobs they had managed to avoid. As a result, they were more satisfied, despite being paid less money for the same work. This finding does not mean that two-tier wage plans are likely to be embraced by an organization's workforce. It does, however, support equity theory through its focus on the way employees compare their pay with other jobs and the need for managers to take this into consideration. Employees increasingly have access to salary survey information, which is likely to result in more comparisons and thus a greater need for effective communication.

Managers play the most crucial communication role because of their day-to-day interactions with their employees.[26] Therefore, they must be prepared to explain why the pay structure is designed as it is and to judge whether employee concerns about the structure need to be addressed with changes to the structure. One common issue is deciding when a job needs to be reclassified because of substantial changes in its content. If an employee takes on more responsibility, she will often ask the manager for assistance in making the case for increased pay for the job.

Challenges

PROBLEMS WITH JOB-BASED PAY STRUCTURES

The approach taken in this chapter, that of defining pay structures in terms of jobs and their associated responsibilities, remains the most widely used in practice. However, job-based pay structures have a number of potential limitations.[27] First, they may encourage bureaucracy. The job description sets out specific tasks and activities for which the incumbent is responsible and, by implication, those for which the incumbent is not responsible. Although this facilitates performance evaluation and control by the manager, it can also encourage a lack of flexibility and a lack of initiative on the part of employees: "Why should I do that? It's not in my job description." Second, the structure's hierarchical nature reinforces a top-down decision making and information flow as well as status differentials, which do not lend themselves to taking advantage of the skills and knowledge of those closest to production. Third, the bureaucracy required to generate and update job descriptions and job evaluations can become a barrier to change

LO 11-5

Describe new developments in the design of pay structures.

Table 11.8
Example of Pay Bands

TRADITIONAL STRUCTURE		BANDED STRUCTURE	
GRADE	TITLE	BAND	TITLE
10	Senior Engineer	5	Senior Engineer
8	Engineer II	4	Engineer
6	Engineer I		

because wholesale changes to job descriptions can involve a tremendous amount of time and cost. Fourth, the job-based pay structure may not reward desired behaviors, particularly in a rapidly changing environment where the knowledge, skills, and abilities needed yesterday may not be very helpful today and tomorrow. Fifth, the emphasis on job levels and status differentials encourages promotion-seeking behavior but may discourage lateral employee movement because employees are reluctant to accept jobs that are not promotions or that appear to be steps down.

RESPONSES TO PROBLEMS WITH JOB-BASED PAY STRUCTURES

Delayering and Banding

Delayering
Reducing the number of job levels within an organization.

In response to the problems caused by job-based pay structures, some organizations have implemented **delayering**, or reducing the number of job levels to achieve more flexibility in job assignments and in assigning merit increases. Pratt and Whitney, for example, changed from 11 pay grades and 3,000 job descriptions for entry-level through middle-management positions to 6 pay grades and several hundred job descriptions.[28] These broader groupings of jobs are also known as *broad bands*. Table 11.8 shows how banding might work for a small sample of jobs.

IBM greatly reduced the bureaucratic nature of the system, going from 5,000 job titles and 24 salary grades to a simpler 1,200 jobs and 10 bands. Within their broad bands, managers were given more discretion to reward high performers and to choose pay levels that were competitive in the market for talent.

One possible disadvantage of delayering and banding is a reduced opportunity for promotion. Therefore, organizations need to consider what they will offer employees instead. In addition, to the extent that there are separate ranges within bands, the new structure may not represent as dramatic a change as it might appear. These distinctions can easily become just as entrenched as they were under the old system. Broad bands, with their greater spread between pay minimums and maximums, can also lead to weaker budgetary control and rising labor costs. Alternatively, the greater spread can permit managers to better recognize high performers with high pay. It can also permit the organization to reward employees for learning.

Paying the Person: Pay for Skill, Knowledge, and Competency

A second, related response to job-based pay structure problems has been to move away from linking pay to jobs and toward building structures based on individual characteristics such as skill or knowledge.[29] Competency-based pay is similar but usually refers to a plan that covers exempt employees (such as managers). The basic idea is that if you want employees to learn more skills and become more flexible in the jobs they perform, you should pay them to do it. (See Chapter 7 for a discussion of the implications of skill-based pay systems on training.) According to Gerald Ledford, however, it is "a fundamental departure" because employees are now "paid for the skills they are capable of using, not for the job they are performing at a particular point in time."[30]

Skill-based pay systems seem to fit well with the increased breadth and depth of skill that changing technology continues to bring.[31] Indeed, research demonstrates that workforce flexibility is significantly increased under skill-based pay.[32] For example, in a production environment, workers might be expected not only to operate machines but also to take responsibility for maintenance and troubleshooting, quality control, even modifying computer programs.[33] Toyota concluded years ago that "none of the specialists [e.g., quality inspectors, many managers, and foremen] beyond the assembly worker was actually adding any value to the car. What's more . . . assembly workers could probably do most of the functions of specialists much better because of their direct acquaintance with conditions on the line."[34]

> **Skill-Based Pay**
> Pay based on the skills employees acquire and are capable of using.

In other words, an important potential advantage of skill-based pay is its contribution to increased worker flexibility, which in turn facilitates the decentralization of decision making to those who are most knowledgeable. It also provides the opportunity for leaner staffing levels because employee turnover or absenteeism can now be covered by current employees who are multiskilled.[35] In addition, multiskilled employees are important in cases where different products require different manufacturing processes or where supply shortages or other problems call for adaptive or flexible responses—characteristics typical, for example, of many newer so-called advanced manufacturing environments (like flexible manufacturing and just-in-time systems).[36] More generally, it has been suggested that skill-based plans also contribute to a climate of learning and adaptability and give employees a broader view of how the organization functions. Both changes should contribute to better use of employees' know-how and ideas. Consistent with the advantages just noted, a field study found that a change to a skill-based plan led to better quality and lower labor costs in a manufacturing plant.[37]

Of course, skill-based and competency-based approaches also have potential disadvantages.[38] First, although the plan will likely enhance skill acquisition, the organization may find it a challenge to use the new skills effectively. Without careful planning, it may find itself with large new labor costs but little payoff. In other words, if skills change, work design must change as quickly to take full advantage. Second, if pay growth is based entirely on skills, problems may arise if employees "top out" by acquiring all the skills too quickly, leaving no room for further pay growth. (Of course, this problem can also afflict job-based systems.) Third, and somewhat ironically, skill-based plans may generate a large bureaucracy—usually a criticism of job-based systems. Training programs need to be developed. Skills must be described, measured, and assigned monetary values. Certification tests must be developed to determine whether an employee has acquired a certain skill. Finally, as if the challenges in obtaining market rates under a job-based system were not enough, there is almost no body of knowledge regarding how to price combinations of skills (versus jobs) in the marketplace. Obtaining comparison data from other organizations will be difficult until skill-based plans become more widely used.

CAN THE U.S. LABOR FORCE COMPETE?

We often hear that U.S. labor costs are simply too high to allow U.S. companies to compete effectively with companies in other countries. The average hourly labor costs (cash and benefits) for manufacturing production workers in the United States and in other advanced industrialized and newly industrialized countries are given in Table 11.9 in U.S. dollars.

> **LO 11-6**
> Explain where the United States stands from an international perspective on pay issues.

Table 11.9
Average Hourly Labor Cost (Cash and Benefits) for Production Workers in Manufacturing by Country and Year

	1985	1990	1995	2000	2005	2010	2013
Industrialized							
Canada	$10.95	$15.95	$16.10	$16.04	$26.81	$34.60	$36.33
Czech Republic				2.83	7.28	11.61	12.17
Germany[a]	9.57	21.53	30.26	23.38	38.18	43.83	48.98
Japan	6.43	12.64	23.82	22.27	25.56	31.75	29.13
United States	13.01	14.91	17.19	19.76	29.74	34.81	36.34
Newly industrialized							
Brazil				4.38	5.05	11.08	10.69
China					0.62[b]	2.00[c]	3.38
Korea, Republic of	1.25	3.82	7.29	8.19	15.13	17.73	21.96
Mexico	1.60	1.80	1.51	2.08	5.36	6.14	6.83
Taiwan	1.49	3.90	5.85	7.30	7.93	8.37	9.37

[a] West Germany for 1985 and 1990 data.

[b] 2006.

[c] Most recent Conference Board data was $3.07 (in 2012) for China. The 2013 estimate was obtained by inflating the Conference Board estimates based on data from the National Bureau of Statistics of China.

SOURCES: Data from 1985–2010 are from the Bureau of Labor Statistics, U.S. Department of Labor, "International Comparisons of Hourly Compensation Costs in Manufacturing," various years. Data from 2013 are from the Conference Board, "International Comparisons of Hourly Compensation Costs in Manufacturing, 2013," December 2014.

As we have seen in Chapter 5 and the current chapter, companies, including Apple, continue to monitor labor costs and other factors in deciding where to locate production. Based solely on a cost approach, it would perhaps make sense to try to shift many types of production from a country like Germany to other countries, particularly the newly industrialized countries. Would this be a good idea? Not necessarily. There are several factors to consider.

Instability of Country Differences in Labor Costs

First, note that relative labor costs are very unstable over time. For example, in 1985, U.S. labor costs were (13.01/9.57) or 36% greater than those of (West) Germany. But by 1990, the situation was reversed, with (West) German labor costs exceeding those of the United States by (21.53/14.91), or 44%, and remaining higher. Did German employers suddenly become more generous while U.S. employers clamped down on pay growth? Not exactly. Because all our figures are expressed in U.S. dollars, currency exchange rates influence such comparisons, and these exchange rates often fluctuate significantly from year to year. For example, in 1985, when German labor costs were 74% of those in the United States, the U.S. dollar was worth 2.94 German marks. But in 1990 the U.S. dollar was worth 1.62 German marks. If the exchange rate in 1990 were still 1 to 2.94, the average German hourly wage in U.S. dollars would have been $11.80, or about 80% of the U.S. average rather than the actual $21.53, or 146% of the U.S. average. In any event, relative to countries like Germany, U.S. labor costs are now a bargain; this explains, in part, decisions by German companies like BMW, Mercedes-Benz, and Volkswagen to locate production facilities in South Carolina, Alabama, and Tennessee, respectively, where labor costs are lower than Germany's by a substantial amount. Proximity to the large U.S. market and currency exchange hedging are other factors. More recently, German automakers (and those from other countries) have been building new North American plants in Mexico for these reasons and for Mexico's low labor costs. (See the "Competing through Globalization" box.)

COMPETING THROUGH GLOBALIZATION

Manufacturing and Labor Costs

Toyota recently announced plans to build a new automobile assembly plant for the Corolla in Mexico (in the state of Guanajuato). In fact, almost all recently announced new automobile assembly plants in North America will be built in Mexico. One major reason is that wages and overall labor costs are lower in Mexico than in the United States. The Center for Automotive Research reports that the average hourly labor cost (wages and benefits) in the automobile industry (including both automakers and auto parts companies) is $7.79 in Mexico, compared to $37.38 in the United States. Labor costs differences are even larger if only automakers are compared, with the Big Three and Toyota having hourly labor costs of $48 to $58 versus perhaps $10 in Mexico. Even adjusting for productivity differences leaves a substantial advantage to Mexico in labor costs. Mexico is also close to the large U.S. product market and has a trade agreement with the United States (and many other

countries). Moving to the other side of the world, China has even lower labor costs than Mexico and the United States. In manufacturing overall, China's hourly labor costs are estimated to be about $3.38, compared to $6.82 in Mexico and $36.34 in the United States. Despite these low labor costs, some companies that used to manufacture in China have now decided that it is too expensive, given that as recently as 2005, hourly labor costs in China were less than $1 ($0.62) and given that hourly labor costs are much lower in other parts of Asia. For example, Japanese companies are building new plants in Laos, Cambodia, and Vietnam. The managing director at the Japanese-Lao joint venture that makes children's toys stated that their production costs, which are heavily influenced by labor costs, are "a third of that in China." In addition to labor costs, Japan is believed to see investments in these countries as a way also to spread its influence in that part of Asia as China has done.

DISCUSSION QUESTIONS

1. If a car takes 20 hours to assemble in both Mexico and the United States, how much per hour can be saved by assembling the car in Mexico versus the United States? (Ignore for now, of course, the cost of building the new plant and other associated costs.)

2. Why do you think that the Japanese toy company mentioned above entered into a joint venture agreement with a Lao company rather than building a wholly owned plant as the Japanese company Toyota plans to do in its new Mexico plant?

SOURCES: B. Woodall, "U.S. Autoworkers Face Threat as Car Makers Drawn to Mexico," *Reuters*, March 25, 2015, www.reuters.com; B. Woodall, "U.S. Auto Labor Cost Study Shows Impact of Two-Tier Wage System," *Reuters*, March 23, 2015, www.reuters.com; W. Chomchuen and M. Obe, "Japan Inc. Goes Deeper into Southeast Asia," *The Wall Street Journal*, September 30, 2014, p. B8; B. Snavely, "Free Trade, Lower Wages Drive Mexico's Automaking Boom," *Detroit Free Press*, March 2, 2014, http://archive.freep.com.

Skill Levels

Second, the quality and productivity of national labor forces can vary dramatically. This is an especially important consideration in comparisons between labor costs in industrialized countries like the United States and developing countries like Mexico. For example, the high school graduation rate in the United States is 77% versus 44% in Mexico.[39] Thus, lower labor costs may reflect the lower average skill level of the workforce; certain types of skilled labor may be less available in low–labor-cost countries. On the other hand, any given company needs only enough skilled employees for its own operations. Some companies have found that low labor costs do not necessarily preclude high quality.

As we have seen, many automakers have chosen Mexico for new plants to serve markets in North America. In Europe, countries such as Poland, Slovakia, and the Czech Republic have many skilled workers and lower labor costs than countries like Germany, which has resulted in the expansion of production there and/or a bargaining chip when seeking more productive work rules at home.

Productivity

Third, and most directly relevant, are data on comparative productivity and unit labor costs, essentially meaning labor cost per hour divided by productivity per hour worked. One indicator of productivity is gross domestic product (or total output of the economy) per person. On this measure, the United States fares well. (See Figure 11.4.) The combination of lower labor costs and higher productivity translates, at least on average, into lower unit labor costs in the United States than in Japan and western Europe.

Considerations Other Than Labor Cost

Fourth, any consideration of where to locate production cannot be based on labor cost considerations alone. For example, although the average hourly labor cost in Country A may be $15 versus $10 in Country B, if labor costs are 30% of total operating costs and nonlabor operating costs are roughly the same, then the total operating costs might be $65 (50 + 15) in Country A and $60 (50 + 10) in Country B. Although labor costs in Country B are 33% less, total operating costs are only 7.7% less. This may not be enough to compensate for differences in skills and productivity, customer wait time, transportation costs, taxes, and so on. Further, the direct labor component of many products, particularly high-tech products (such as electronic components), may often be 5% or less. Therefore, the effect on product price-competitiveness may be less significant.[40]

Figure 11.4

Gross Domestic Product (GDP) per Person, Adjusted for Purchasing Power Differences, U.S. dollars, 2013

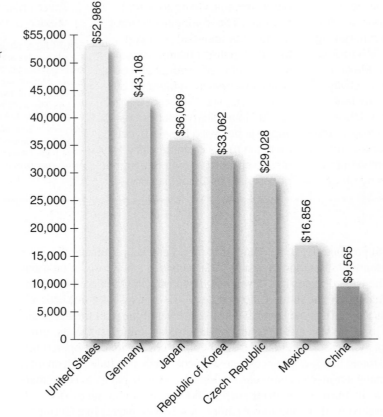

SOURCE: OECD, http://stats.oecd.org.

European Retailers Propose Higher Wages for Workers in Cambodia

Cambodia's $5.5 billion garment industry accounts for about 80% of its exports. Until 2014, the industry wage had been $80 per month. In November 2014, it was increased to $128 per month. In what has been described as "unprecedented" and as "recognition of the role they play," several European retail store companies, including Hennes & Mauritz AB ("H & M") and Zara parent Inditex, wrote to the Prime Minister of Cambodia pledging to pay more to owners of local Cambodian supplier factories so that they could in turn pay their workers more. However, there is a concern that the success in helping achieve higher pay for Cambodian workers could affect where the broader retail clothing industry decides to source its garments from. For example, the minimum wage is $68 per month in Bangladesh. So, there is a concern that paying Cambodian workers better so that they can be less impoverished risks losing even those jobs to other countries that have lower wages and thus can perhaps offer lower prices to foreign retail store buyers. Some evidence, however, suggests that foreign retailers can appeal better to their customer base by providing evidence that treatment of workers in their supplier factories meets some minimum set of standards. For example, Sri Lanka has a labor standard called "Garments without Guilt," and factories that meet these standards can market themselves as having met the standards, which may allow them to charge higher prices, and there is some evidence that such factories are also more efficient.

DISCUSSION QUESTIONS

1. Will the increased minimum wage for Cambodian garment workers improve their lives? What are the risks?
2. Did Zara and H & M do the right thing by saying that they would support paying higher prices for garments to support higher wages for garment workers? What else might they be able to do?
3. Do you think there would be a point at which Cambodian wage increases would lead Zara and H & M to buy garments elsewhere?
4. Can treating workers better in the low-cost garment industry be good for business? Explain.

SOURCES: M. Jayasinghe, "The Operational and Signaling Benefits of Voluntary Labor Code Adoption: Reconceptualizing the Scope of Human Resource Management in Emerging Economies," *Academy of Management Journal*, forthcoming. C. Larson, *Bloomberg Business*, February 5, 2015; T. Wright, "Stores Propose Higher Wages in Asia," *The Wall Street Journal*, October 15, 2014, p. B8; J. Hookway and S. Narin, "Cambodia Sets Minimum Wage Below Union Demands," *The Wall Street Journal*, November 12, 2014.

Thus, the decision on where to locate production depends on labor costs but also other factors. Being close to where customers are matters a great deal. Product development speed may be greater when manufacturing is physically close to the design group. Quick response to customers (like making a custom replacement product) is difficult when production facilities are on the other side of the world. Inventory levels can be dramatically reduced through the use of manufacturing methods like just-in-time production, but suppliers need to be in close physical proximity.

On the other hand, some firms are aggressively offshoring jobs (including professional or knowledge worker jobs) primarily to reduce labor costs. For example, financial services firms like Goldman Sachs and Citigroup now have significant numbers of employees in India doing statistical and research work at much lower pay levels.[41] As another example, IBM began to move thousands of programmer jobs overseas to countries like China where the hourly cost at the time was $12.50 an hour versus $56 an hour in the United States, potentially saving more than $100 million per year.[42] In some cases, companies using low-cost labor overseas have decided that those workers are paid too little and have decided to pay more than would be necessary to simply attract and retain enough workers. See the "Integrity in Action" box.

EXECUTIVE PAY

LO 11-7
Explain the reasons for the controversy over executive pay.

The issue of executive pay has been given widespread attention in the press. In a sense, the topic has received more coverage than it deserves because there are very few top executives and their compensation often accounts for a small share of an organization's total labor costs. On the other hand, top executives have a disproportionate ability to influence organization performance, so decisions about their compensation are critical. They can also be symbolic. During the Global Financial Crisis of several years ago the U.S. government, as part of the Troubled Asset Relief Program (TARP), decided it was appropriate to further regulate executive pay in firms receiving government "bailout" money. Top executives also help set the tone or culture of the organization. If, for example, the top executive's pay seems unrelated to the organization's performance, with pay staying high even when business is poor, employees may not understand why some of their own pay is at risk and fluctuates (not only up, but also down), depending on how the organization is performing.

How much do executives make? Table 11.10 provides some data. Long-term compensation, typically in the form of stock plans, is the major component of CEO pay, which means that CEO pay varies with the performance of the stock market (see the "change in S&P 500" column). Table 11.11 shows that some CEOs are paid well above the averages shown in Table 11.10.

Table 11.10
Realized CEO Compensation

	CEO PAY							
YEAR	SALARY PLUS BONUS	VALUE OF STOCK OPTIONS EXERCISED	VALUE OF STOCK GRANTS AND OTHER PAY***	TOTAL PAY	ANNUAL CHANGE IN CEO PAY	ANNUAL CHANGE IN S&P 500	WORKER PAY*	CEO PAY/ WORKER PAY**
2013	$4.1 million	$6.4 million	$6.4 million	$16.9 million	—	32%	$35,555	475
2012	$3.5 million	$3.2 million	$3.8 million	$10.5 million	11%	16%	$34,519	304
2011	$3.4 million	$2.8 million	$3.2 million	$9.4 million	10%	2%	$33,800	279
2010	$3.0 million	$3.0 million	$2.5 million	$8.5 million	−29%	15%	$33,119	258
2009	$3.0 million	$3.3 million	$5.8 million	$12.1 million	−14%	26%	$32,093	377
2008	$3.6 million	$3.6 million	$6.9 million	$14.1 million	−18%	−37%	$31,617	446
2007	$4.0 million	$4.9 million	$8.2 million	$17.1 million	34%	5%	$30,682	558
2006	$3.8 million	$2.4 million	$6.5 million	$12.7 million	3%	16%	$29,529	431
2005	$3.7 million	$2.1 million	$6.6 million	$12.4 million	—	—	$28,305	438
2000	$2.9 million	$4.5 million	$7.0 million	$14.3 million	—	—	$25,013	573
1995	$2.0 million	$0.7 million	$0.7 million	$3.3 million	—	—	$20,804	160
1990	$1.6 million	$0.3 million	$0.7 million	$2.6 million	—	—	$18,187	144

*Establishment survey data on earnings of production and nonsupervisory workers on private nonfarm payrolls, U.S. Bureau of Labor Statistics, "Establishment Data: Employment and Earnings."

**Ratio of CEO pay to hourly employee pay.

***In most cases, the value of stock grants accounts for most of pay in this category.

Note: Median total pay in 2013 was $9.9 million. That would yield a CEO pay/Worker pay ratio of 278.

SOURCES: Through 2012, CEO pay data from *Forbes* magazine. Through 1999, *Forbes* data pertain to the 800 largest companies. Beginning with year 2000, data pertain to the 500 largest U.S. companies. **Note:** 2013 CEO pay data based on 200 Standard & Poor's 500 companies that filed proxies with the Securities and Exchange Commission between January 1 and March 27, 2014. Original data from S&P Capital IQ; *USA Today* research as reported by B. Hansen and M. Hannan, "Millions by Millions, CEO Pay Goes Up," *USA Today,* April 4, 2014, www.usatoday.com.

Table 11.11
Highest-Paid CEOs

	TOTAL COMPENSATION
Satya Nadella, Microsoft	$84.3 million
Lawrence J. Ellison, Oracle Corp.	$67.3 million
Jon Feltheimer, Lions Gate Entertainment	$63.6 million
Steven M. Mollenkopf, Qualcomm Inc.	$60.7 million

Table 11.11
Highest-Paid CEOs

SOURCE: AFL-CIO, "Executive Paywatch: 100 Highest Paid CEOs, 2014," www.aflcio.org, accessed May 30, 2015.

Table 11.12
CEO Pay and Worker Pay (U.S. Dollars) and CEO/Worker Ratio, 2012, Selected Countries

COUNTRY	COMPANIES INCLUDED	CEO PAY	WORKER PAY	CEO/WORKER RATIO
USA	S & P 500	$12,259,894	$34,645	354
Germany	DAX (30 companies)	5,912,781	40,223	147
United Kingdom	FTSE 100	3,758,412	44,743	84
Japan	Nikkei 225	2,354,581	35,143	67

SOURCE: www.aflcio.org/Corporate-Watch/CEO-Pay-and-You/CEO-to-Worker-Pay-Gap-in-the-United-States/Pay-Gaps-in-the-World, accessed May 13, 2013.

As Table 11.12 shows, U.S. top executives are also the highest paid in the world. The fact that the differential between top-executive pay and that of an average manufacturing worker is so much higher in the United States than in some other countries has been described as creating a "trust gap"—that is, in employees' minds, a "frame of mind that mistrusts senior management's intentions, doubts its competence, and resents its self-congratulatory pay." The issue becomes more salient when many of the same companies with high executive pay simultaneously engage in layoffs or other forms of employment reduction. Employees might ask, "If the company needs to cut costs, why not cut executive pay rather than our jobs?"[43] The issue is one of perceived fairness. One study, in fact, reported that business units with higher pay differentials between executives and rank-and-file employees had lower customer satisfaction, which was speculated to result from employees' perceptions of inequity coming through in customer relations.[44] Perhaps more important than how much top executives are paid is how they are paid (i.e., whether performance-based). This is an issue we return to in the next chapter.

Government Regulation of Employee Compensation

We discuss equal employment opportunity, as well as minimum wage, overtime, and prevailing wage laws below. We additionally discuss regulation of executive compensation in Chapter 12.

EQUAL EMPLOYMENT OPPORTUNITY

Equal employment opportunity (EEO) regulation (such as Title VII of the Civil Rights Act) prohibits sex- and race-based differences in employment outcomes such as pay, unless justified by business necessity (like pay differences stemming from differences in job performance). In addition to regulatory pressures, organizations must deal with changing labor

LO 11-8
Describe the regulatory framework for employee compensation.

market and demographic realities. At least two trends are directly relevant in discussing EEO. First, women have gone from 33% of all employees in 1960 to 46% in 2014. Second, between 1960 and 2014, Whites have gone from 90% to 80% of all employees. White men now account for 43% of all U.S. employment and that percentage will probably continue to decline, making attention to EEO issues in compensation even more important.

Is there equality of treatment in pay determination? Typically, the popular press focuses on raw earnings ratios. For example, among full-time workers, the ratio of female-to-male weekly median earnings is .82, the ratio of Black-to-White earnings is .78, and the ratio of Hispanic–Latino-to-White earnings is .72.[45] These percentages have generally risen over the last two to three decades, but significant race and sex differences in pay clearly remain.[46] In contrast, Asian Americans earn 17% more than Whites. Among executives, women appear to have lower pay than men partly due to women being less likely to receive performance-based (e.g., stock and bonus-related) pay.[47]

The usefulness of raw percentages is limited, however, because some portion of earnings differences arises from differences in legitimate factors: education, labor market experience, and occupation. Adjusting for such factors reduces earnings differences based on race and sex, but significant differences remain. With few exceptions, such adjustments rarely account for more than half of the earnings differential.[48]

What aspects of pay determination are responsible for such differences? In the case of women, it is suggested that their work is undervalued. Another explanation rests on the "crowding" hypothesis, which argues that women were historically restricted to entering a small number of occupations. As a result, the supply of workers far exceeded demand, resulting in lower pay for such occupations. If so, market surveys would only perpetuate the situation.

Comparable Worth
A public policy that advocates remedies for any undervaluation of women's jobs (also called pay equity).

Comparable worth (or pay equity) is a public policy that advocates remedies for any undervaluation of women's jobs. The idea is to obtain equal pay, not just for jobs of equal content (already mandated by the Equal Pay Act of 1963) but for jobs of equal value or worth, on the basis of Title VII of the Civil Rights Act. Typically, job evaluation is used to measure worth. Table 11.13, which is based on Washington State data from one of the first comparable worth cases years ago, sought to compare measures of worth based on internal comparisons (job evaluation) and external comparisons (market surveys).[49] Disagreements between the two measures are apparent. Internal comparisons suggest that women's jobs are underpaid, whereas external comparisons are less supportive of

Table 11.13
Job Evaluation Points, Monthly Prevailing Market Pay Rates, and Proportion of Incumbents in Job Who Are Female

BENCHMARK JOB TITLE	JOB EVALUATION POINTS	MARKET PAY	MARKET PAY AS PERCENTAGE OF PREDICTED PAY	PERCENT FEMALE IN JOB
Warehouse worker	97	$1,286	109.1%	15.4%
Truck driver	97	1,493	126.6	13.6
Licensed practical nurse	173	1,030	75.3	89.5
Maintenance carpenter	197	1,707	118.9	2.3
Civil engineer	287	1,885	116.0	0.0
Registered nurse	348	1,368	76.3	92.2
Senior computer systems analyst	384	2,080	113.1	17.8

Note Predicted salary is based on regression of prevailing market rate on job evaluation points $2.43 × Job evaluation points + 936.19, r = 0.77.

this argument. For example, although the licensed practical nurse job receives 173 job evaluation points and the truck driver position receives 97 points, the market rate (and thus the state of Washington employer rate) for the truck driver position is $1,493 per month versus only $1,030 per month for the nurse. The truck driver is paid 26.6% more than the pay policy line would predict, whereas the nurse is paid only 75.3% of the pay policy line prediction. Based on job evaluation points, the value of the nurse is 78.3% (173/97 − 1) higher, not 31.0% (1 − $1,030/$1,493) lower as is seen in the market pay.

One potential problem with using job evaluation to establish worth independent of the market is that job evaluation procedures were never designed for this purpose.[50] Rather, as demonstrated earlier, their major use is in helping to capture the market pay policy and then applying that to nonkey jobs for which market data are not available. In other words, job evaluation has typically been used to help apply the market pay policy, quite the opposite of replacing the market in pay setting.

As with any regulation, there are also concerns that EEO regulation obstructs market forces, which, according to economic theory, provide the most efficient means of pricing and allocating people to jobs. In theory, moving away from a reliance on market forces would result in some jobs being paid too much and others too little, leading to an oversupply of workers for the former and an undersupply for the latter. In addition, some empirical evidence suggests that a comparable worth policy would not have much impact on the relative earnings of women in the private sector.[51] One limitation of such a policy is that it targets single employers, ignoring that men and women tend to work for different employers.[52] To the extent that segregation by employer contributes to pay differences between men and women, comparable worth would not be effective. In other words, to the extent that sex-based pay differences are the result of men and women working in different organizations with different pay levels, such policies will have little impact.

Perhaps most important, despite potential problems with market rates, the courts have consistently ruled that using the going market rates of pay is an acceptable defense in comparable worth litigation suits.[53] The rationale is that organizations face competitive labor and product markets. Paying less or more than the market rate will put the organization at a competitive disadvantage. Thus there is no comparable worth legal mandate in the U.S. private sector.

On the other hand, by the early 1990s, almost one-half of the states had begun or completed comparable worth adjustments to public-sector employees' pay. In addition, in 1988 the Canadian province of Ontario mandated comparable worth in both the private and public sectors. Further, although comparable worth is not mandated in the U.S. private sector, the Department of Labor (Office of Federal Contracts Compliance), which enforces Executive Order 11246, put into place enforcement standards and guidelines in 2006 that prohibit race or sex-based "systemic compensation discrimination," which it defines as a situation "where there are statistically significant compensation disparities (as established by a regression analysis) between similarly situated employees, after taking into account the legitimate factors which influence compensation, such as: education, prior work experience, performance, productivity, and time in the job."[54] Further, passage of the 2009 Lilly Ledbetter Fair Pay Act means that employers may face claims in situations where a discriminatory decision (e.g., too small of a pay raise) was made many years earlier, but the effect (lower pay) continues into the more current period.

Some work has focused on pinpointing where women's pay falls behind that of men. One finding is that the pay gap is wider where bonus and incentive payments (not just base salary) are examined. Other evidence indicates that women lose ground at the time they are hired and actually do better once they are employed for some time.[55] One interpretation is that when actual job performance (rather than the limited general qualification information available on applicants) is used in decisions, women may be less likely to encounter unequal treatment. If so, more attention needs to be devoted to ensuring fair treatment of applicants and new employees.[56] On the other hand, a "glass ceiling" is believed to exist in some organizations that allows women (and minorities) to come within sight of the top echelons of management, but not advance to them.

It is likely, however, that organizations will differ in terms of where women's earnings disadvantages arise. For example, advancement opportunities for women and other protected groups may be hindered by unequal access to the "old boy" or informal network. This, in turn, may be reflected in lower rates of pay. Mentoring programs have been suggested as one means of improving access. Indeed, one study found that mentoring was successful, having a significant positive effect on the pay of both men and women, with women receiving a greater payoff in percentage terms than men.[57]

MINIMUM WAGE, OVERTIME, AND PREVAILING WAGE LAWS

Fair Labor Standards Act (FLSA)
The 1938 law that established the minimum wage and overtime pay.

The 1938 **Fair Labor Standards Act (FLSA)** establishes a **minimum wage** for jobs, which new stands at $7.25 per hour. State laws may specify higher minimum wages. The FLSA also permits a subminimum training wage that is approximately 85% of the minimum wage, which employers are permitted to pay most employees under the age of 20 for a period of up to 90 days.

The FLSA also requires that employees be paid at a rate of one and a half times their hourly rate for each hour of overtime worked beyond 40 hours in a week. The hourly rate includes not only the base wage but also other components such as bonuses and piece-rate payments. The FLSA requires overtime pay for any hours beyond 40 in a week that an employer "suffers or permits" the employee to perform, regardless of whether the work is done at the workplace or whether the employer explicitly asked or expected the employee to do it. If the employer knows the employee is working overtime but neither moves to stop it nor pays time and a half, a violation of the FLSA may have occurred. A department store was the target of a lawsuit that claimed employees were "encouraged" to, among other things, write thank-you notes to customers outside of scheduled work hours but were not compensated for this work. Although the company denied encouraging this off-the-clock work, it reached an out-of-court settlement to pay between $15 million and $30 million in back pay (plus legal fees of $7.5 million) to approximately 85,000 sales representatives it employed over a three-year period.[58] As the "Competing through Technology" box shows, companies are wrestling with how to create a sustainable relationship with their workers in the era of the sharing economy.

Minimum Wage
The lowest amount that employers are legally allowed to pay; the 1990 amendment of the Fair Labor Standards Act permits a sub-minimum wage to workers under the age of 20 for a period of up to 90 days.

Exempt
Employees who are not covered by the Fair Labor Standards Act. Exempt employees are not eligible for overtime pay.

Executive, professional, administrative, outside sales, and certain "computer employees" occupations are **exempt** from FLSA coverage. *Nonexempt* occupations are covered and include most hourly jobs. Exempt status depends on job responsibilities and salary. All exemptions (except for outside sales) require that an employee be paid no less than $455 per week. Recently, the Wage and Hour Division has proposed increasing this salary "test" to $970 per week, which would greatly increase the number of U.S. employees who are nonexempt (i.e., covered by FLSA overtime provisions). Note also that the President has already issued an executive order to change the salary test amount and the only question that remains is whether the final salary test amount will be $970 exactly or something quite close to it.[59] The job responsibility criteria vary. For example, the executive exemption is based on whether two or more people are supervised, whether there is authority to hire and fire (or whether particular

Sharing Economy Exposes Gaps in Employment Law

Technology has helped create a sharing economy. With a touch of your smartphone, you can hail a car from Uber or schedule a housekeeper from Handybook to clean your home or fix something in it. Such companies often rely on workers they describe as micro-entrepreneurs, who have the flexibility to do only the jobs they want and when they want. Some workers find this model to be liberating. However, technology has also exposed gaps in employment law and raised challenges for workers and companies. Because these workers are often independent contractors, rather than employees, they are not covered by standard employment laws, such as the Fair Labor Standards Act (FLSA).

As discussed in this chapter, the FLSA requires that *employees* (but not independent contractors,

who are self-employed) be paid a minimum wage and overtime pay. Several sharing economy companies have faced FLSA-based lawsuits, especially by workers contending they should be treated as employees and that they ended up being paid less than the minimum wage. Although Uber's own study reported that its drivers make an average of $19/hour, that is before expenses. Drivers making less per hour may not reach the (federal) minimum wage of $7.25/hour, given that they supply their own vehicles and thus pay for expenses, including depreciation of their vehicles.

One company, Zirtual, which provides "remote personal assistants," has responded to this technology-related challenge by switching from using independent contractors to using employees, who are guaranteed a wage of at least $11/hour.

Zirtual reports that employee workers now stay longer with Zirtual. It says that although many workers initially like the flexibility of being a contractor, many eventually decide they need the security of a guaranteed paycheck and wage that they can live on.

DISCUSSION QUESTIONS

1. Why don't all companies follow Zirtual's lead in using employees rather than independent contractors? What are the advantages and disadvantages of this approach?
2. Should employment laws be revised to better cover workers in the sharing economy? Who would benefit? Would anyone lose?

SOURCE: Lauren Weber and Rachel Emma Silverman, "On-Demand Workers: 'We Are Not Robots,'" *The Wall Street Journal,* January 28, 2015, p. B1.

weight is given to the employee's recommendations), and whether the employee's primary duty is managing the enterprise, recognized department, or subdivision of the enterprise. The Wage and Hour Division, Employment Standards Administration (www.dol.gov/esa), U.S. Department of Labor, and its local offices can provide further information on these definitions. (The exemptions do *not* apply to police, firefighters, paramedics, and first responders.)

Two pieces of legislation—the 1931 Davis-Bacon Act and the 1936 Walsh-Healy Public Contracts Act—require federal contractors to pay employees no less than the prevailing wages in the area. Davis-Bacon covers construction contractors receiving federal money of more than $2,000. Typically, prevailing wages have been based on relevant union contracts, partly because only 30% of the local labor force is required to be used in establishing the prevailing rate. Walsh-Healy covers all government contractors receiving $10,000 or more in federal funds.

Finally, as we see in the Competing through Technology Box, employers must take care in deciding whether a person working on their premises is classified as an employee or independent contractor. We address this issue in Chapter 13.

A LOOK BACK

We began this chapter with examples of companies that have recently increased their pay levels. Although controlling compensation costs is important, it is especially important for some of these companies (e.g., Walmart) to allow them to compete on price in their product markets. They also felt they needed to pay more to compete in their labor markets, which have become more competitive in recent years as the economy has recovered and grown. Not doing so would make it more difficult to recruit and retain the quality of workforce needed. In at least one case (Aetna), a major increase in pay level was implemented because it was deemed necessary to raise workforce quality to support an upcoming change in business strategy. We also saw how companies (e.g., automakers) continue to use relative labor cost as an important decision in where they locate production plants. Thus, pay level and pay structure decisions influence the success of strategy execution by influencing not only labor costs but also workforce quality, as well as employee perceptions of equity. Different pay structures can also vary in the degree to which they provide flexibility and incentives for employees to learn and be productive.

QUESTIONS

1. What types of changes have the companies discussed in this chapter made to their pay levels and pay structures to support execution of their business strategies?
2. Would other companies seeking to better align their pay structures with their business strategies benefit from imitating the changes made at these companies?

SUMMARY

In this chapter we have discussed the nature of the pay structure and its component parts, the pay level, and the job structure. Equity theory suggests that social comparisons are an important influence on how employees evaluate their pay. Employees make external comparisons between their pay and the pay they believe is received by employees in other organizations. Such comparisons may have consequences for employee attitudes and retention. Employees also make internal comparisons between what they receive and what they perceive others within the organization are paid. These types of comparisons may have consequences for internal movement, cooperation, and attitudes (like organization commitment). Such comparisons play an important role in the controversy over executive pay, as illustrated by the focus of critics on the ratio of executive pay to that of lower-paid workers.

Pay benchmarking surveys and job evaluation are two administrative tools widely used in managing the pay level

and job structure components of the pay structure, which influence employee social comparisons. Pay surveys also permit organizations to benchmark their labor costs against other organizations. Globalization is increasing the need for organizations to be competitive in both their labor costs and productivity.

The nature of pay structures is undergoing a fundamental change in many organizations. One change is the move to fewer pay levels to reduce labor costs and bureaucracy. Second, some employers are shifting from paying employees for narrow jobs to giving them broader responsibilities and paying them to learn the necessary skills.

Finally, a theme that runs through this chapter and the next is the importance of process in managing employee compensation. How a new program is designed, decided on, implemented, and communicated is perhaps just as important as its core characteristics.

KEY TERMS

Pay structure, 458
Pay level, 458
Job structure, 458
Efficiency wage theory, 463
Benchmarking, 463
Rate ranges, 465
Key jobs, 465

Nonkey jobs, 465
Job evaluation, 465
Compensable factors, 465
Pay policy line, 467
Pay grades, 469
Range spread, 469
Compa-ratio, 471

Delayering, 476
Skill-based pay, 477
Comparable worth, 484
Fair Labor Standards Act
    (FLSA), 486
Minimum wage, 486
Exempt, 486

DISCUSSION QUESTIONS

1. You have been asked to evaluate whether your organization's current pay structure makes sense in view of what competing organizations are paying. How would you determine what organizations to compare your organization with? Why might your organization's pay structure differ from those in competing organizations? What are the potential consequences of having a pay structure that is out of line relative to those of your competitors?

2. Top management has decided that the organization is too bureaucratic and has too many layers of jobs to compete effectively. You have been asked to suggest innovative alternatives to the traditional "job-based" approach to employee compensation and to list the advantages and disadvantages of these new approaches.

3. If major changes of the type mentioned in Question 2 are to be made, what types of so-called process issues need to be considered? Of what relevance is equity theory in helping to understand how employees might react to changes in the pay structure?

4. Are executive pay levels unreasonable? Why or why not?

5. Your company plans to build a new manufacturing plant but is undecided where to locate it. What factors would you consider in choosing in which country (or state) to build the plant?

6. You have been asked to evaluate whether a company's pay structure is fair to women and minorities. How would you go about answering this question?

SELF-ASSESSMENT EXERCISE

McGraw Hill Education **connect**

Additional assignable self-assessments available in Connect.

Consider your current job or a job you had in the past. For each of the following pay characteristics, indicate your level of satisfaction by using the following scale: 1 = very dissatisfied; 2 = somewhat dissatisfied; 3 = neither satisfied nor dissatisfied; 4 = somewhat satisfied; 5 = very satisfied.

_____ 1. My take-home pay
_____ 2. My current pay
_____ 3. My overall level of pay
_____ 4. Size of my current salary
_____ 5. My benefit package
_____ 6. Amount the company pays toward my benefits
_____ 7. The value of my benefits
_____ 8. The number of benefits I receive
_____ 9. My most recent raise
_____ 10. Influence my manager has over my pay
_____ 11. The raises I have typically received in the past
_____ 12. The company's pay structure

_____ 13. Information the company gives about pay issues of concern to me
_____ 14. Pay of other jobs in the company
_____ 15. Consistency of the company's pay policies
_____ 16. How my raises are determined
_____ 17. Differences in pay among jobs in the company
_____ 18. The way the company administers pay

These 18 items measure four dimensions of pay satisfaction. Find your total score for each set of item numbers to measure your satisfaction with each dimension.

Pay Level
Total of items 1, 2, 3, 4, 9, 11: _____
Benefits
Total of items 5, 6, 7, 8: _____
Pay Structure and Administration
Total of items 12, 13, 14, 15, 17, 18: _____
Pay Raises
Total of items 10, 11, 16: _____

Considering the principles discussed in this chapter, how could your company improve (or how could it have improved) your satisfaction on each dimension?

SOURCE: Based on H. G. Heneman III and D. P. Schwab, "Pay Satisfaction: Its Multidimensional Nature and Measurement," *International Journal of Psychology* 20 (1985), pp. 129–41.

EXERCISING STRATEGY

U.S. Automakers Manufacture Parts Overseas to Contain Costs

U.S. automobile production has mounted a major comeback, but many of the parts used to assemble those cars increasingly come from other countries. In 2014, a record $138 billion in car parts were imported, equivalent to $12,135 of content in every vehicle built. That compares to $31.7 billion in parts imported in 1990 and $89 billion in parts imported in 2008. Why are more and more parts imported? Because parts can be made cheaper overseas. Mexico accounted for the largest single share (34%), followed by China (13%). To compete and survive, U.S. parts manufacturers have shifted production overseas. For example, Detroit-based American Axle has plants in low-wage countries such as Mexico, Brazil, Poland, China, and Thailand. American workers in the parts industry have seen their own wages fall by an inflation-adjusted 23% from a decade earlier to $19.91 today in the face of this low-wage competition. (Wages at U.S. assembly plants also declined during the same period by 22% to $27.83.) At one of American Axle's plants, wages start at $10 per hour, roughly what Walmart recently announced it will raise its starting wage to. At the Lear Corporation parts plant in Selma, Alabama, Denise Barnett works in a plant that supplies seats for a nearby Hyundai car assembly plant. Just recently, she received a 92% pay increase to bring her

hourly wage to $12.25. She tries to work as much overtime as she can to make ends meet, but the more overtime she works, the more day care she has to pay for. Thomas DiDonato, the chief human resources officer at Lear, says that the company pays competitive market wages. Indeed, he notes that "if our employees couldn't make ends meet, they would demonstrate their dissatisfaction with their feet" by leaving for a better job elsewhere. But, he notes, instead, employee turnover at Lear is only 2%.

QUESTIONS

1. As a consumer, what effect does the use of more foreign parts have when you look to purchase a new car?
2. How does globalization in the car parts industry affect U.S. workers? What about workers in parts plants in low-wage countries?
3. Do you agree with Thomas DiDonato that if workers could not make ends meet, they would leave Lear in greater numbers? Why or why not?
4. Should Lear and other automakers pay more? Why or why not?

SOURCE: J. R. Hagerty and J. Bennett, "Wages Drop as Foreign Parts Invade American Cars," *The Wall Street Journal*, March 24, 2015, p. A1.

MANAGING PEOPLE

Reporting the Ratio of Executive Pay to Worker Pay: Is it Worth the Trouble?

Section 953(b) of the 2010 Dodd-Frank Wall Street Reform and Consumer Protection Act requires covered companies to report the ratio of annual total compensation of the chief executive officer (or any equivalent position) to the median of the annual total compensation of all other employees.

Supporters of the rule, such as the AFL-CIO labor organization, argue that reporting the ratio will help rein in what it sees as exorbitant (and growing) levels of executive pay, especially when compared to what has happened to worker pay. According to a recent analysis of 248 public company CEOs by the *Wall Street Journal* and Hay Group, recent median CEO year pay stood at over $10 million. A separate analysis of the S&P 500 firms by the AFL-CIO reported that the ratio of CEO pay to typical U.S. worker pay rose from 42 in 1980 to 380 last year. At J.C. Penney,

Bloomberg computed the ratio to be 1,795 ($59.3 million for since departed CEO Ron Johnson versus an average salary of $29,668 for the average department store worker).

The AFL-CIO and other supporters of the rule hope it will also encourage Boards to consider whether worker pay, which has grown more slowly than inflation (and as indicated above, much more slowly than CEO pay), should be higher. The AFL-CIO also argues that research shows that larger pay differentials between CEOs and rank and file workers lead to poorer firm performance due to perceptions of inequity and the negative effects that has on worker morale and productivity. There is also a feeling that when CEOs get paid as much as they do, too much credit goes to them for a firm's success and not enough to other employees.

Many companies see things differently. David Hirschmann, head of the U.S. Chamber of Commerce's

Center for Capital Markets, says the ratio is not meaningful or helpful to investors and will instead be used as "a political tool to attack companies." Companies argue that with a global workforce and different payroll systems in different countries, computing the ratio is much more difficult than it would seem. For example, Accenture, a consulting firm has 246,000 employees in 120 countries and a variety of payroll systems (and definitions of pay in different countries). Jill Smart, head of human resources at Accenture, says that the work required to compute the ratio of CEO to worker pay would be "quite incredible."

Other companies, however, are already doing it and have done so for years. They say it is not that difficult or costly. Whole Foods, for example, put in place a cap (now 19x) on the ratio of executive to front-line worker pay about a decade ago. Mark Ehrnstein, a vice president there, says that it does not take months, but rather a few days, and that it does not cost "millions of dollars" to calculate the ratio.

After waiting several years to issue a proposed rule and then providing time for groups (like those above) to comment, the U.S. Securities and Exchange Commission (SEC) finally issued a final rule in August 2015. Rule details are provided in SEC press release 2015-160 available at its website, www.sec.gov.

QUESTIONS

1. Do you believe it is an undue burden on companies to compute and report the ratio of chief executive compensation to employee compensation?
2. Do you believe reporting this ratio will result in changes that benefit companies, employees, or society? Explain.

SOURCES: U.S. Securities and Exchange Commission. SEC Adopts Rule for Pay Ratio Disclosure. Press Release 2015-160. Washington D.C., Aug. 5, 2015. http://www.sec.gov/news/pressrelease/2015-160.html; G. Morgenson, "Despite Federal Regulation, C.E.O–Worker Pay Gap Data Remains Hidden," *The New York Times,* April 10, 2015, www.nytimes.com; Leslie Kwoh, "Firms Resist New Pay-Equity Rules," *Wall Street Journal,* June 26, 2012; Elliot Blair Smith and Phil Kuntz, "CEO Pay 1,795-to-1 Multiple of Wages Skirts U.S. Law," www.bloomberg.com, April 29, 2013, accessed May 9, 2013.

HR IN SMALL BUSINESS

Changing the Pay Level at Eight Crossings

Based in Sacramento, California, Eight Crossings provides medical transcription services for physicians, lawyers, hospitals, and authors. Its employees also answer phones, edit documents, and transcribe legal documents. The company's employees work either at the service center in Sacramento or in their homes, where they receive audio or text files via the Internet. In this way, Eight Crossings employees can work in their specialty as needed without tying up a doctor's or attorney's office space.

Initially, the ease of sending files electronically was an advantage that enabled Eight Crossings to grow at a tremendous pace. But it has also opened up the company to competition from similar services provided from low-wage locations such as India. In addition, as voice recognition software has improved, automation could take over some of the processes that have been handled by skilled, experienced transcribers.

In that situation, Eight Crossings CEO Patrick Maher felt the pressure when clients began to ask him for a lower rate. Most of the costs of running Eight Crossings are related to labor. Overhead and materials are minimal for this type of work. Consequently, for Maher to offer his clients a better price, he would have to cut what he paid employees or stop earning a profit.

The pay level at Eight Crossings had been about 5% about the average for the industry. Maher believed that this pay strategy gave his company an advantage in recruiting and keeping the best transcribers. Pay was calculated per line of text at a rate that varied according to the complexity of the material being transcribed. Depending on how many hours

they worked and how complex the jobs they took, each transcriber earned between $20,000 and $70,000 a year.

In looking for ways to trim expenses, Maher considered that part of most documents included sections of boilerplate text. These are generated automatically by transcribers' software but were included in the number of lines for which the transcribers were paid. Maher concluded these amounted to a 5% bonus paid for each assignment. Maher decided he could cut transcribers' pay by 5% and in effect still pay them the same rate for what they were actually transcribing (but without the "bonus").

That pay cut would bring pay levels at Eight Crossings down to the market rate. Would that mean employees would leave for greener pastures? Maher guessed not, considering that his company was receiving résumés from experienced transcribers looking for work.

Maher's next challenge was how to communicate the pay cut to employees working in 22 locations, many working from home and communicating with the office electronically. He began by discussing the situation with the company's eight supervisors, who check the transcribers' work for quality. This prepared them to address employees' concerns. Next, he sent an e-mail to the transcribers, explaining the reasons for the change and inviting questions.

Maher's fears about the pay cut were not realized. Employees expressed understanding of the move and appreciation for his commitment to continue sending work to U.S. workers. And because Eight Crossings is paying the market rate, moving to another company would not offer employees an advantage in terms of pay.

QUESTIONS

1. How did the change in pay level at Eight Crossings affect its ability to attract and retain a high-quality workforce?

2. Do you think the company's pay structure was better suited to its objectives before or after the reduction in pay level? Why?

3. How would you evaluate the company's method of communicating the change in pay level? What improvements to that process can you suggest?

SOURCES: Darren Dahl, "Special Financial Report: Employee Compensation," *Inc.*, July 2009, www.inc.com; Eight Crossings, corporate website, www.eightcrossings.com, accessed May 30, 2015, and "Company Profile: No. 609, Eight Crossings," Inc. 500/5000 (2000), www.inc.com.

NOTES

1. J. S. Adams, "Inequity in Social Exchange," in *Advances in Experimental Social Psychology,* ed. L. Berkowitz (New York: Academic Press, 1965); P. S. Goodman, "An Examination of Referents Used in the Evaluation of Pay," *Organizational Behavior and Human Performance* 12 (1974), pp. 170–95; C. O. Trevor and D. L. Wazeter, "A Contingent View of Reactions to Objective Pay Conditions: Interdependence among Pay Structure Characteristics and Pay Relative to Internal and External Referents," *Journal of Applied Psychology* 91 (2006), pp. 1260–1275; M. M. Harris, F. Anseel, and F. Lievens, "Keeping Up with the Joneses: A Field Study of the Relationships among Upward, Lateral, and Downward Comparisons and Pay Level Satisfaction," *Journal of Applied Psychology* 93, no. 3 (May 2008), pp. 665–73; and Gordon D. A. Brown, Jonathan Gardner, Andrew J. Oswald, Jing Qian, "Does Wage Rank Affect Employees' Well-being?" *Industrial Relations* 47, no. 3 (July 2008), p. 355; D. Card, M. Alexandre, E. Moretti, and E. Saez, "Inequality at Work: The Effect of Peer Salaries on Job Satisfaction," *American Economic Review* 102 (2012), pp. 2981–3003; E. Della Torre, M. Pelagatti, and L. Solari, "Internal and External Equity in Compensation Systems, Organizational Absenteeism, and the Role of the Explained Inequalities," *Human Relations* 68 (2015), pp. 409–40.

2. J. B. Miner, *Theories of Organizational Behavior* (Hinsdale, IL: Dryden Press, 1980); and B. Gerhart and S. L. Rynes, *Compensation: Theory, Evidence, and Strategic Implications* (Thousand Oaks, CA: Sage, 2003).

3. B. Gerhart and G. T. Milkovich, "Employee Compensation: Research and Practice," in *Handbook of Industrial and Organizational Psychology,* 2nd ed., ed. M. D. Dunnette and L. M. Hough (Palo Alto, CA: Consulting Psychologists Press, 1992); G. T. Milkovich, J. M. Newman, and B. Gerhart, *Compensation,* 11th ed. (New York: McGraw-Hill/Irwin, 2014).

4. D. Barkholz, "Can UAW Fix Tier 2 Disparity? Return to Pattern Bargaining Unlikely," *Automotive News,* March 8, 2015; K. Naughton, "Detroit Worker Bonuses Approach Records on Rising Profits," *Bloomberg Businessweek,* February 13, 2015.

5. Mike Ramsey, "VW Chops Labor Costs in U.S.," *The Wall Street Journal,* May 23, 2011, extracted June 2, 2011. http://online.wsj.com/article/SB10001424052748704083904576335501132396440.html; Mark Guarino, "Lower Wages Now at Big Three Automakers, But New Hires Aren't Whining," *Christian Science Monitor,* May 7, 2013.

6. J. D. Stoll, "Volvo to Open Plant in U.S., State to Be Chosen in a Month; Car Maker Says Labor Rates Are Just Part of It," *The Wall Street Journal,* March 30, 2015, www.wsj.com.

7. Ibid.

8. Wayne F. Cascio and John W. Boudreau, *Investing in People: Financial Impact of Human Resource Initiatives,* 2nd ed. (Upper Saddle River, NJ: Pearson Financial Times Press, 2010); I. S. Fulmer and R. E. Ployhart, "Our Most Important Asset: A Multidisciplinary/Multilevel Review of Human Capital Valuation for Research and Practice," *Journal of Management,* November 12, 2013; I. S. Fulmer, B. Gerhart, and K. S. Scott, "Are the 100 Best Better? An Empirical Investigation of the Relationship between Being a 'Great Place to Work' and Firm Performance," *Personnel Psychology* 56(2003), pp. 965–93; A. Edmans, "Does the Stock Market Fully Value Intangibles? Employee Satisfaction and Equity Prices," *Journal of Financial Economics* 101(3), pp. 621–40.

9. B. Gerhart and G. T. Milkovich, "Organizational Differences in Managerial Compensation and Financial Performance," *Academy of Management Journal* 33 (1990), pp. 663–91; E. L. Groshen, "Why Do Wages Vary among Employers?" *Economic Review* 24 (1988), pp. 19–38; Gerhart and Rynes, *Compensation.*

10. J. D. Shaw, "Pay Levels and Pay Changes," in *Handbook for Industrial, Work and Organizational Psychology* (forthcoming); A. L. Heavey, J. A. Holwerda, and J. P. Hausknecht, "Causes and Consequences of Collective Turnover: A Meta-Analytic Review," *Journal of Applied Psychology* 98, no. 3 (2013), p. 412; M. L. Williams, M. A. McDaniel, N. T. Nguyen, "A Meta-Analysis of the Antecedents and Consequences of Pay Level Satisfaction," *Journal of Applied Psychology* 91 (2006), pp. 392–413; M. C. Sturman, C. O. Trevor, J. W. Boudreau, and B. Gerhart, "Is It Worth It to Win the Talent War? Evaluating the Utility of Performance-Based Pay," *Personnel Psychology* 56 (2003), pp. 997–1035; B. Klaas and J. A. McClendon, "To Lead, Lag or Match: Estimating the Financial Impact of Pay Level Policies," *Personnel Psychology* 49 (1996), pp. 121–41; S. C. Currall, A. J. Towler, T. A. Judge, and L. Kohn, "Pay Satisfaction and Organizational Outcomes," *Personnel Psychology* 58 (2005), pp. 613–40; M. P. Brown, M. C. Sturman, and M. J. Simmering, "Compensation Policy and Organizational Performance: The Efficiency, Operational, and Financial Implications of Pay Levels and Pay Structures," *Academy of Management Journal* 46 (2003), pp. 752–62; Eric A. Verhoogen, Stephen V. Burks, and Jeffrey P. Carpenter, "Fairness and Freight-Handlers: Local Labor Market Conditions and Wage-Fairness Perceptions in a Trucking Firm," *Industrial & Labor Relations Review* 60, no. 4 (July 2007), p. 477; T. A. Judge, R. F. Piccolo, N. P. Podsakoff, J. C. Shaw, and B. L. Rich, "The Relationship between Pay and Job Satisfaction: A Meta-Analysis of the Literature," *Journal of Vocational Behavior* 77 (2010), pp. 157–67; M. Subramony, N. Krause, J. Norton, and G. N. Burns,

"The Relationship between Human Resource Investments and Organizational Performance: A Firm-Level Examination of Equilibrium Theory," *Journal of Applied Psychology* 93 (2008), pp. 778–88; J. P. Hausknecht and C. O. Trevor, "Collective Turnover at the Group, Unit, and Organizational Levels: Evidence, Issues, and Implications," *Journal of Management,* 37 (2011), pp. 352–388; A. L. Heavey, J. A. Holwerda, and J. P. Hausknecht, "Causes and Consequences of Collective Turnover: A Meta-Analytic Review," *Journal of Applied Psychology,* 98 (2013), pp. 412–453.

11. G. A. Akerlof, "Gift Exchange and Efficiency-Wage Theory: Four Views," *American Economic Review* 74 (1984), pp. 79–83; and J. L. Yellen, "Efficiency Wage Models of Unemployment," *American Economic Review* 74 (1984), pp. 200–5.

12. S. L. Rynes and G. T. Milkovich, "Wage Surveys: Dispelling Some Myths about the Market Wage," *Personnel Psychology* 39 (1986), pp. 71–90; R. J. Greene, "Compensation Surveys: The Rosetta Stones of Market Pricing," *World at Work,* 2014, 1st Quarter, pp. 23–31.

13. B. Gerhart and G. T. Milkovich, "Employee Compensation: Research and Practice," in *Handbook of Industrial and Organizational Psychology,* 2nd ed., ed. M. D. Dunnette and L. M. Hough (Palo Alto, CA: Consulting Psychologists Press, 1992).

14. G. T. Milkovich, J. M. Newman, and B. Gerhart, *Compensation,* 11th ed. (New York: McGraw-Hill/Irwin, 2014).

15. B. Gerhart, G. T. Milkovich, and B. Murray, "Pay, Performance, and Participation," in *Research Frontiers in Industrial Relations and Human Resources,* ed. D. Lewin, O. S. Mitchell, and P. D. Sherer (Madison, WI: IRRA, 1992).

16. C. H. Fay, "External Pay Relationships," in *Compensation and Benefits,* ed. L. R. Gomez-Mejia (Washington, DC: Bureau of National Affairs, 1989).

17. J. P. Pfeffer and A. Davis-Blake, "Understanding Organizational Wage Structures: A Resource Dependence Approach," *Academy of Management Journal* 30 (1987), pp. 437–55; and M. A. Carpenter and J. B. Wade, "Micro-Level Opportunity Structures as Determinants of Non-CEO Executive Pay," *Academy of Management Journal* 45 (2002), pp. 1085–1103.

18. M. Bidwell, F. Briscoe, I. Fernandez-Mateo, and A. Sterling, "The Employment Relationship and Inequality: How and Why Changes in Employment Practices Are Reshaping Rewards in Organizations," *Academy of Management Annals* 7, no. 1 (2013), pp. 61–121; G. E. Ledford, "The Changing Landscape of Employee Rewards: Observations and Prescriptions," *Organizational Dynamics* 43, no. 3 (2014), pp. 168–79; Milkovich, Newman, and Gerhart, *Compensation,* 11th ed.

19. C. M. Solomon, "Global Compensation: Learn the ABCs," *Personnel Journal,* July 1995, p. 70; and R. A. Swaak, " Expatriate Management: The Search for Best Practices," *Compensation and Benefits Review,* March–April 1995, p. 21.

20. *1997–1998 Survey of Geographic Pay Differential Policies and Practices* (Rochester, WI: Runzeimer International).

21. E. E. Lawler III, *Pay and Organizational Development* (Reading, MA: Addison-Wesley, 1981).

22. R. Folger and M. A. Konovsky, "Effects of Procedural and Distributive Justice on Reactions to Pay Raise Decisions," *Academy of Management Journal* 32 (1989), pp. 115–30; H. G. Heneman III and T. A. Judge, "Compensation Attitudes," in S. L. Rynes and B. Gerhart, eds., *Compensation in Organizations* (San Francisco: Jossey-Bass, 2002), pp. 61–103; J. Greenberg, "Determinants of Perceived Fairness of Performance Evaluations," *Journal of Applied Psychology* 71 (1986), pp. 340–42; and

H. G. Heneman III, "Pay Satisfaction," *Research in Personnel and Human Resource Management* 3 (1985), pp. 115–39.

23. J. Greenberg, "Employee Theft as a Reaction to Underpayment of Inequity: The Hidden Cost of Pay Cuts," *Journal of Applied Psychology* 75 (1990), pp. 561–68.

24. Adams, "Inequity in Social Exchange"; C. J. Berger, C. A. Olson, and J. W. Boudreau, "The Effect of Unionism on Job Satisfaction: The Role of Work-Related Values and Perceived Rewards," *Organizational Behavior and Human Performance* 32 (1983), pp. 284–324; P. Cappelli and P. D. Sherer, "Assessing Worker Attitudes under a Two-Tier Wage Plan," *Industrial and Labor Relations Review* 43 (1990), pp. 225–44; and R. W. Rice, S. M. Phillips, and D. B. McFarlin, "Multiple Discrepancies and Pay Satisfaction," *Journal of Applied Psychology* 75 (1990), pp. 386–93.

25. Cappelli and Sherer, "Assessing Worker Attitudes."

26. I. S. Fulmer and Y. Chen, "How Communication Affects Employee Knowledge of and Reactions to Compensation Systems," in V. Miller and M. Gordon, eds., *Meeting the Challenge of Human Resource Management: A Communication Perspective* (New York: Routledge/Taylor & Francis, 2014), pp. 167–178; I. Caron, A. K. Ben-Ayed, and C. Vandenberghe, "Collective Incentive Plans, Organizational Justice and Commitment," *Relations Industrielles/Industrial Relations* 68, no. 1 (2013).

27. R. M. Kanter, *When Giants Learn to Dance* (New York: Simon & Schuster, 1989); E. E. Lawler III, *Strategic Pay* (San Francisco: Jossey-Bass, 1990); "Farewell, Fast Track," *BusinessWeek,* December 10, 1990, pp. 192–200; and R. L. Heneman, G. E. Ledford, Jr., and M. T. Gresham, "The Changing Nature of Work and Its Effects on Compensation Design and Delivery," in S. L. Rynes and B. Gerhart, eds., *Compensation in Organizations.*

28. P. R. Eyers, "Realignment Ties Pay to Performance," *Personnel Journal,* January 1993, p. 74.

29. Lawler, *Strategic Pay;* G. Ledford, "3 Cases on Skill-Based Pay: An Overview," *Compensation and Benefits Review,* March–April 1991, pp. 11–23; G. E. Ledford, "Paying for the Skills, Knowledge, Competencies of Knowledge Workers," *Compensation and Benefits Review,* July–August 1995, p. 55; Heneman et al., "The Changing Nature of Work"; G. Ledford, "Factors Affecting the Long-term Success of Skill-based Pay," *WorldatWork Journal,* First Quarter (2008), pp. 6–18; J. Canavan, "Overcoming the Challenge of Aligning Skill-based Pay Levels to the External Market," *WorldatWork Journal,* First Quarter (2008), pp. 18–24; and E. C. Dierdorff and E. A. Surface, "If You Pay for Skills, Will They Learn? Skill Change and Maintenance Under a Skill-Based Pay System," *Journal of Management* 34 (2008), pp. 721–43.

30. Ledford, "3 Cases."

31. Heneman et al., "The Changing Nature of Work."

32. Atul Mitra, Nina Gupta, and Jason D. Shaw. "A Comparative Examination of Traditional and Skill-Based Pay Plans." *Journal of Managerial Psychology* 26 (2011): 278–296.

33. T. D. Wall, J. M. Corbett, R. Martin, C. W. Clegg, and P. R. Jackson, "Advanced Manufacturing Technology, Work Design, and Performance: A Change Study," *Journal of Applied Psychology* 75 (1990), pp. 691–97.

34. James P. Womack, Daniel T. Jones, Daniel Roos, and Donna S. Carpenter, *The Machine That Changed the World: Based on the Massachusetts Institute of Technology 5-Million Dollar 5-Year Study on the Future of the Automobile* (New York: Rawson Assoc., 1990), p. 56.

35. Lawler, *Strategic Pay.*

36. Ibid.; Gerhart and Milkovich, "Employee Compensation."

37. B. C. Murray and B. Gerhart, "An Empirical Analysis of a Skill-Based Pay Program and Plant Performance Outcomes," *Academy of Management Journal* 41, no. 1 (1998), pp. 68–78.

38. Ibid.; N. Gupta, D. Jenkins, and W. Curington, "Paying for Knowledge: Myths and Realities," *National Productivity Review,* Spring 1986, pp. 107–23; J. D. Shaw, N. Gupta, A. Mitra, and G. E. Ledford, "Success and Survival of Skill-Based Pay Plans," *Journal of Management* 31 (2005), pp. 28–49.

39. *Education at a Glance—OECD Indicators* 2010, www.OECD.org.

40. M. Hayes, "Precious Connection: Companies Thinking about Using Offshore Outsourcing Need to Consider More than Just Cost Savings," *Information Week Online,* www.information-week.com (October 20, 2003); Harold L. Sirkin et al., "Made in America Again," Boston Consulting Group, August 2011; K. Chu, "Not Made in China," *Wall Street Journal,* May 1, 2013; Y. Zhang, "China Begins to Lose Edge as World's Factory Floor," *Wall Street Journal,* January 17, 2013; A. Fox, "America, Inc.: More U.S. Manufacturers Are Making a U-turn on Offshoring," *HR Magazine,* May 2013, pp. 45–48.

41. Heather Timmons, "Cost-Cutting in New York, but a Boom in India," *New York Times,* August 12, 2008, p. C1. Reprinted with permission of PARS International.

42. William Bulkeley, "IBM Documents Give Rare Look at Sensitive Plans on 'Offshoring,'" *The Wall Street Journal,* January 19, 2004; David Wessel, "Big U.S. Firms Shift Hiring Abroad," *The Wall Street Journal,* April 19, 2011.

43. A. Farnham, "The Trust Gap," *Fortune,* December 4, 1989, pp. 56ff; and Scott McCartney, "AMR Unions Express Fury," *The Wall Street Journal,* April 17, 2003; AFL-CIO, "Dodd-Frank Section 953(b): Why CEO-to-Worker Pay Ratios Matter For Investors," www.aflcio.org/content/download/1090/9807/version/1/file/Why-CEO-to-Worker-Pay-Ratios-Matter-For-Investors.pdf, accessed May 16, 2013.

44. D. M. Cowherd and D. I. Levine, "Product Quality and Pay Equity between Lower-Level Employees and Top Management: An Investigation of Distributive Justice Theory," *Administrative Science Quarterly* 37 (1992), pp. 302–20.

45. U.S. Bureau of Labor Statistics, "Highlights of Women's Earnings in 2013," Report 1015, December 2014.

46. Ibid.

47. C. Kulich, G. Trojanowski, M. K. Ryan, S. A. Haslam, and L. D. R. Renneboog, "Who Gets the Carrot and Who Gets the Stick? Evidence of Gender Disparities in Executive Remuneration," *Strategic Management Journal* 32 (2011), pp. 301–21; and F. Munôz-Bullón, "Gender-Level Differences among High-Level Executives," *Industrial Relations* 49 (2010), pp. 346–70.

48. B. Gerhart, "Gender Differences in Current and Starting Salaries: The Role of Performance, College Major, and Job Title," *Industrial and Labor Relations Review* 43 (1990), pp. 418–33;

G. G. Cain, "The Economic Analysis of Labor-Market Discrimination: A Survey," in *Handbook of Labor Economics,* ed. O. Ashenfelter and R. Layard (New York: North-Holland, 1986), pp. 694–785; F. D. Blau and L. M. Kahn, "The Gender Pay Gap: Have Women Gone as Far as They Can?" *Academy of Management Perspectives,* February 2007, pp. 7–23.

49. Helen Remick, "The Comparable Worth Debate," *Public Personnel Management,* Winter 1981.

50. D. P. Schwab, "Job Evaluation and Pay-Setting: Concepts and Practices," in *Comparable Worth: Issues and Alternatives,* ed. E. R. Livemash (Washington, DC: Equal Employment Advisory Council, 1980).

51. B. Gerhart and N. El Cheikh, "Earnings and Percentage Female: A Longitudinal Study," *Industrial Relations* 30 (1991), pp. 62–78; R. S. Smith, "Comparable Worth: Limited Coverage and the Exacerbation of Inequality," *Industrial and Labor Relations Review* 61 (1988), pp. 227–39.

52. W. T. Bielby and J. N. Baron, "Men and Women at Work: Sex Segregation and Statistical Discrimination," *American Journal of Sociology* 91 (1986), pp. 759–99.

53. Rynes and Milkovich, "Wage Surveys"; and G. T. Milkovich, J. M. Newman, and B. Gerhart, *Compensation,* 10th ed. (New York: McGraw-Hill/Irwin, 2010).

54. U.S. Department of Labor website, at www.dol.gov/esa/regs/compliance/ofccp/faqs/comstrds.htm.

55. Gerhart, "Gender Differences in Current and Starting Salaries"; B. Gerhart and G. T. Milkovich, "Salaries, Salary Growth, and Promotions of Men and Women in a Large, Private Firm," in *Pay Equity: Empirical Inquiries,* ed. R. Michael, H. Hartmann, and B. O'Farrell (Washington, DC: National Academy Press, 1989); K. W. Chauvin and R. A. Ash, "Gender Earnings Differentials in Total Pay, Base Pay, and Contingent Pay," *Industrial and Labor Relations Review* 47 (1994), pp. 634–49; M. M. Elvira and M. E. Graham, "Not Just a Formality: Pay System Formalization and Sex-Related Earnings Effects," *Organization Science* 13 (2002), pp. 601–17.

56. Gerhart, "Gender Differences in Current and Starting Salaries"; B. Gerhart and S. Rynes, "Determinants and Consequences of Salary Negotiations by Graduating Male and Female MBAs," *Journal of Applied Psychology* 76 (1991), pp. 256–62.

57. G. F. Dreher and R. A. Ash, "A Comparative Study of Mentoring among Men and Women in Managerial, Professional, and Technical Positions," *Journal of Applied Psychology* 75 (1990), pp. 539–46.

58. G. A. Patterson, "Nordstrom Inc. Sets Back-Pay Accord on Suit Alleging 'Off-the-Clock' Work," *The Wall Street Journal,* January 12, 1993, p. A2; for additional information on overtime legal issues, see A. Weintraub and J. Kerstetter, "Revenge of the Overworked Nerds," *BusinessWeek Online,* www.businessweek.com (December 8, 2003).

59. http://www.dol.gov/whd/overtime/NPRM2015/factsheet.htm.

Recognizing Employee Contributions with Pay

LEARNING OBJECTIVES

After reading this chapter, you should be able to:

LO 12-1   Discuss how pay influences individual employees, and describe three theories that explain the effect of compensation on individuals. *page 498*

LO 12-2   Describe the fundamental pay programs for recognizing employees' contributions to the organization's success. *page 503*

LO 12-3   List the advantages and disadvantages of the pay programs. *page 505*

LO 12-4   Describe how organizations combine incentive plans in a balanced scorecard. *page 517*

LO 12-5   Discuss issues related to performance-based pay for executives. *page 518*

LO 12-6   Explain the importance of process issues such as communication in compensation management. *page 521*

LO 12-7   List the major factors to consider in matching the pay strategy to the organization's strategy. *page 524*

Employers Raise Pay, But Keep an Eye on Fixed Costs

According to the Employment Cost Index, U.S. Bureau of Labor Statistics, employer costs for wages and benefits grew at the fastest rate in 6 years—but that was still just 2.2%. Aon Hewitt reports, based on a survey of larger companies, that merit pay increases are expected to average 3.0% in 2015, larger than in recent years. The growth in pay reflects the tightening of labor markets that we discussed in Chapter 11. Aon Hewitt also found that in many of the companies it surveyed, merit bonuses, which unlike traditional merit salary/wage increases, do not become part of base salary, will be a much larger percentage of salary in 2015: as much as 12.7% in the companies that use them and for the employees they use them for. Ken Abosch of Aon Hewitt explains that "organizations are still very fixated on productivity and cost containment." Using bonuses, a form of variable pay, makes cost containment more possible in future years if business turns downward. In contrast, Barry Gerhart of the University of Wisconsin–Madison notes, "If you put the money into salary, it's there forever. If you give out money in terms of a bonus, people get it that year and have to re-earn it the following year." In this vein, the Big

Three U.S. automakers have moved to better control fixed labor costs by using profit-sharing payments, which are similar to bonuses, but often depend more on company performance and less on individual performance, in lieu of base pay increases in recent years. Another way that employers are keeping fixed costs under control is by maintaining strict control on the hiring of full-time employees, instead often relying on temporary workers or independent contractors. When asked what the explanation was for employers keeping tight control on hiring and on traditional merit increases, Jim Link, chief human resources officer at Randstad, an employee staffing company referred to "lessons learned from a tough recession."

SOURCES: Dorin Levin, "Automakers, Labor Union Face a Long, Hot Summer of Contract Talks," *Fortune,* April 7, 2015, www.fortune.com; Annie Baxter, "Wages and Benefits See Highest Bump in Six Years," *Market Watch,* January 30, 2015, www.marketplace.org; Jena McGregor, "The Likelihood of Getting a Raise in 2015," *The Washington Post,* January 9, 2015, www.washingtonpost.com; Rachel Feinsteig, "Bonuses Trickle Down," *The Wall Street Journal,* January 1, 2015, www.wsj.com; Dan Gorenstein, "Why You've Been Getting Bonuses, Not Raises, Lately," *Marketplace,* August 29, 2014, www.marketplace.org; Damian Paletta, "Temp Jobs Surge as Firms Contain Expenses," *The Wall Street Journal,* April 7, 2014, www.wsj.com; and Tracy Samilton, "Profit-Sharing Checks Replace Autoworkers Raises," *NPR,* January 30, 2013, www.npr.com.

Introduction

As the chapter opening illustrates, organizations must pay competitive salaries and benefits to compete in the labor market, which has tightened recently with unemployment rates dropping. At the same time, however, organizations must control labor costs (which influence product price) to compete in the product market. Employers have also learned to be especially careful about taking on fixed labor costs.

The preceding chapter discussed setting pay for jobs. In this chapter we focus on setting pay for individual employees. We examine how to use pay to recognize and reward employees' contributions to the organization's success. Employees' pay does not depend solely on the jobs they hold. Instead, differences in performance (individual, group, or organization), seniority, skills, and so forth are used as a basis for differentiating pay among employees.[1] In some cases, large amounts of compensation can be at stake.

Several key questions arise in evaluating different pay programs for recognizing contributions. First, what are the costs of the program? Second, what is the expected return (in terms of influences on attitudes and behaviors) from such investments? Third, does the program fit with the organization's human resource strategy and its overall business strategy? Fourth, what might go wrong with the plan in terms of unintended consequences? For example, will the plan encourage managers and employees to pay more attention to some objectives (e.g., short-term sales) than to some others (e.g., customer service, long-term customer satisfaction, and long-term sales)?

Organizations have a relatively large degree of discretion in deciding how to pay, especially compared with the pay level decisions discussed in the previous chapter. The same organizational pay level (or "compensation pie") can be distributed (shared) among employees in many ways. Whether each employee's share is based on individual performance, profits, seniority, or other factors (the "how" to pay decision), the size of the pie (and thus the cost to the organization, the "how much" to pay decision) can remain the same.

Regardless of cost differences, different pay programs can have very different consequences for productivity and return on investment. Indeed, a study of 150 organizations found not only that the largest differences between organizations had to do with how (rather than how much) they paid, but that these differences also resulted in different levels of profitability.[2]

How Does Pay Influence Individual Employees?

LO 12-1
Discuss how pay influences individual employees, and describe three theories that explain the effect of compensation on individuals.

Pay plans are typically used to energize, direct, sustain, or control the behavior of current employees. We refer to the effect of pay plans on current employees as an **incentive effect**. (Later, we will introduce the concept of a sorting effect, which is how pay influences employee behaviors by how pay shapes the composition of the workforce.) Equity theory, described in the previous chapter, is relevant here as well. Most employees compare their own pay with that of others, especially those in the same job. Perceptions of inequity may cause employees to take actions to restore equity. Unfortunately, some of these actions (like quitting, reduced effort, or lack of cooperation) may not help the organization.

Incentive Effect
The effect a pay plan has on the behaviors of current employees.

Three additional theories also help explain compensation's effects: reinforcement, expectancy, and agency theories.

REINFORCEMENT THEORY

E. L. Thorndike's Law of Effect states that a response followed by a reward is more likely to recur in the future. The implication for compensation management is that high employee performance followed by a monetary reward will make future high performance more likely. By the same token, high performance not followed by a reward will make it less likely in the future. The theory emphasizes the importance of a person's actual experience of a reward.

EXPECTANCY THEORY

Expectancy Theory
The theory that says motivation is a function of valence, instrumentality, and expectancy.

Although **expectancy theory** also focuses on the link between rewards and behaviors, it emphasizes expected (rather than experienced) rewards. In other words, it focuses on the effects of incentives. Behaviors (job performance) can be described as a function of ability and motivation. In turn, motivation is hypothesized to be a function of expectancy, instrumentality, and valence perceptions. Compensation systems differ according to their impact on these motivational components. Generally speaking, the main influence of compensation is on instrumentality: the perceived link between behaviors and pay. Valence of pay outcomes should remain the same under different pay systems. Expectancy perceptions (the perceived link between effort and performance) often have more to do with employee selection, job design and training than pay systems. A possible exception would be skill-based pay, which directly influences employee training and thus expectancy perceptions.

Intrinsic and Extrinsic Motivation

Although expectancy theory implies that linking an increased amount of rewards to performance will increase motivation and performance, some authors have used cognitive evaluation theory to question this assumption, arguing that monetary rewards may increase extrinsic motivation but decrease intrinsic motivation. Extrinsic motivation depends on rewards (such as pay and benefits) controlled by an external source, whereas intrinsic motivation depends on rewards that flow naturally from work itself (like performing interesting work).[3] In other words, the concern would be that paying a child to read books may diminish the child's natural interest (intrinsic motivation) in reading, and the child may in the future be less likely to read books unless there are monetary incentives. Although monetary incentives may reduce intrinsic motivation in some settings (such as education), the evidence suggests that such effects are small and probably not very relevant to most work settings, where monetary payment is the norm.[4] A meta-analytic review of field research found that intrinsic motivation was actually higher, not lower, when extrinsic incentives were in place. One reason that extrinsic incentives may not have an adverse effect on intrinsic motivation in the workplace is the sorting process (discussed shortly) in the labor market, which matches people, over time, to jobs that fit their preferences, including reward preferences (e.g., for intrinsic and/or extrinsic motivators).[5] Further, evidence indicates that incentive pay has significant positive effects on performance, which is a function of both intrinsic and extrinsic motivation.[6] Therefore, while it is important to keep in mind that money is not the only effective way to motivate behavior and that monetary rewards will not always be the answer to motivation problems, it does not appear that monetary rewards run much risk of compromising intrinsic motivation in most work settings. The "Competing through Technology" box provides an example of how monetary and nonmonetary rewards often go hand in hand.

AGENCY THEORY

This theory focuses on the divergent interests and goals of the organization's stakeholders and the ways that employee compensation can be used to align these interests and goals. We cover agency theory in some depth because it provides especially relevant implications for compensation design.

An important characteristic of the modern corporation is the separation of ownership from management (or control). Unlike the early stages of capitalism, where owner and manager were often the same, today, with some important exceptions (mostly smaller companies), most stockholders are far removed from the day-to-day operation of companies. Although this separation has important advantages (like mobility of financial capital and diversification of investment risk), it also creates agency costs—the interests of the **principals** (owners) and their **agents** (managers) may no longer converge. What is best for the agent, or manager, may not be best for the owner.

Principal
In agency theory, a person (e.g., an owner) who seeks to direct another person's behavior.

Agent
In agency theory, a person (e.g., a manager) who is expected to act on behalf of a principal (e.g., an owner).

Recruiting and Retaining Engineering Talent in China

China's economy has grown at a rapid pace, making it now the second largest economy in the world. Wages and salaries have risen as has consumption. For example, the number of automobiles sold in China, as well as their price points, continues to increase. Accordingly, foreign automakers increasingly produce and sell cars and increasingly expensive, higher end cars in China. Of course, consumers in China have some preferences that differ from other parts of the world. For example, Ford just introduced its Ford Taurus to China for the first time. But Ford announced that because second-row passengers are so important in China, "where the owner of the premium vehicle is often a passenger rather than the driver," the second row of the Taurus "has been designed with an emphasis on comfort." Specifically, the rear seat has more legroom and hip room than it would otherwise. Another design attribute tailored to the Chinese consumer is "more than 25 intelligent storage spaces," which include not just regular cupholders, but ones that can "securely hold different-sized tea bottles."

One challenge faced by Ford and other foreign automobile producers is the need to recruit engineers for their research and development centers, where, at a minimum, such tailoring of cars to Chinese consumers takes place. Ford's Nanjing product development center employed 300 people in 2007. Ford (like other companies) is investing hundreds of millions of dollars there in an effort to increase employment to 2,000 people by 2018. Mr. Ma, a Ford engineer from China, says in his current job, he and his team "mostly modifies existing Ford technology to fit Chinese market requirements." However, he has higher aspirations. He hopes that in the near future, Ford will give his group the opportunity to design new parts to be used globally by Ford. To keep the best engineers, Ford and other companies are starting to realize that they will need to not only be more competitive on pay and provide the opportunity to work in a leading global company, but also provide these sorts of career growth opportunities as China evolves to have a larger role in global product development.

A related challenge for Ford and other foreign companies is to take steps to avoid the perception that the top jobs are not open to local Chinese and to demonstrate that they will instead have more opportunities to work on higher level technical challenges and/or move into top research and development managerial roles in Chinese companies. Providing such opportunities for promotion and higher pay will likely be increasingly important in attracting/retaining the right number and quality of engineers needed to reach the goal of building a high level of engineering and product development capability in China.

DISCUSSION QUESTIONS

1. Why are foreign automakers increasing their research and development presence in China?
2. How do you think the growth and evolution of China's economy have influenced the aspirations of employees in China? What about engineers specifically?
3. What are the advantages and disadvantages foreign companies have in recruiting and retaining Chinese engineers? How might the employment "deal" offered by foreign companies need to change to be able to compete for this talent?

SOURCES: J. R. Healey, "Ford Shows Redone Taurus for China, not U.S.," *USA Today,* April 19, 2015, www.usatoday.com; C. Hetzner, "Mercedes Increases Emphasis on China in Bid to Pass BMW, Audi," *Automotive News Europe,* January 13, 2015; Colum Murphy, "In China, Engineers Are Hard to Keep," *The Wall Street Journal,* July 2, 2014, p. B1.

Agency costs can arise from two factors. First, principals and agents may have different goals (goal incongruence). Second, principals may have less than perfect information on the degree to which the agent is pursuing and achieving the principal's goals (information asymmetry).

Consider three examples of agency costs that can occur in managerial compensation.[7] First, although shareholders seek to maximize their wealth, management may spend money on things such as perquisites (corporate jets, for example) or "empire building" (making acquisitions that do not add value to the company but may enhance the manager's prestige or pay). Second, managers and shareholders may differ in their attitudes toward risk. Shareholders can diversify their investments (and thus their risks) more easily than managers (whose only major source of income may be their jobs), so managers are typically more averse to risk. They may be less likely to pursue projects or acquisitions with high potential payoff. It also suggests a preference on the part of managers for relatively little risk in their pay (high emphasis on base salary, low emphasis on uncertain bonuses or incentives). Indeed, research shows that managerial compensation in manager-controlled firms is more often designed in this manner.[8] Third, decision-making horizons may differ. For example, if managers change companies more than owners change ownership, managers may be more likely to maximize short-run performance (and pay), perhaps at the expense of long-term success.

Agency theory is also of value in the analysis and design of nonmanagers' compensation. In this case, interests may diverge between managers (now in the role of principals) and their employees (who take on the role of agents).

In designing either managerial or nonmanagerial compensation, the key question is, How can such agency costs be minimized? Agency theory says that the principal must choose a contracting scheme that helps align the interests of the agent with the principal's own interests (that is, it reduces agency costs). These contracts can be classified as either behavior-oriented (such as merit pay) or outcome-oriented (stock options, profit sharing, commissions, and so on).[9]

At first blush, outcome-oriented contracts seem to be the obvious solution. If profits are high, compensation goes up. If profits drop, compensation goes down. The interests of "the company" and employees are aligned. An important drawback, however, is that such contracts also increase the agent's risk. And because agents are averse to risk, they may require higher pay (a compensating wage differential) to make up for it.[10] Thus, there is a trade-off between risk and incentives that must be considered. Outcome-oriented contracts are, for example, typically a major component of executive compensation.[11]

Behavior-based contracts, on the other hand, do not transfer risk to the agent and thus do not require a compensating wage differential. However, the principal must be able to overcome the information asymmetry issue. To do so the principal must either invest in monitoring (e.g., add more supervisors) and information or else revert, at least in part, to structuring the contract so that pay is linked at least partly to outcomes.[12]

Which type of contract should an organization use? It depends partly on the following factors:[13]

- *Risk aversion.* Risk aversion among agents makes outcome-oriented contracts less likely.
- *Outcome uncertainty.* Profit is an example of an outcome. Agents are less willing to have their pay linked to profits to the extent that there is a risk of low profits. They would therefore prefer a behavior-oriented contract.
- *Job programmability.* As jobs become less programmable (less routine), outcome-oriented contracts become more likely because monitoring becomes more difficult.[14]
- *Measurable job outcomes.* When outcomes are more measurable, outcome-oriented contracts are more likely.[15]
- *Ability to pay.* Outcome-oriented contracts contribute to higher compensation costs because of the risk premium.
- *Tradition.* A tradition or custom of using (or not using) outcome-oriented contracts will make such contracts more (or less) likely.

In summary, the reinforcement, expectancy, and agency theories all focus on the fact that behavior–reward contingencies can shape behaviors. However, agency theory is of particular value in compensation management because of its emphasis on the risk–reward trade-off, an issue that needs close attention when companies consider variable pay plans, which can carry significant risk.

How Do Pay Sorting Effects Influence Labor Force Composition?

Traditionally, using pay to recognize employee contributions has been thought of as a way to influence the behaviors and attitudes of current employees, whereas pay level and benefits have been seen as a way to influence so-called membership behaviors: decisions about whether to join or remain with the organization. However, it is now recognized that individual pay programs may also affect the nature and composition of an organization's workforce.[16] For example, it is possible that an organization that links pay to performance may attract more high performers than an organization that does not link the two. There may be a similar effect with respect to job retention.[17] This effect on workforce composition is sometimes referred to as a **sorting effect**.

Sorting Effect
The effect a pay plan has on the composition of the current workforce (the types of employees attracted and retained).

Continuing the analysis, different pay systems appear to attract people with different personality traits and values.[18] Organizations that link pay to individual performance may be more likely to attract individualistic and risk-oriented employees, whereas organizations relying more heavily on team rewards are more likely to attract team-oriented employees. The implication is that the design of compensation programs needs to be carefully coordinated with the organization and human resource strategy. Increasingly, both in the United States and abroad, employers are seeking to establish stronger links between pay and performance.

Pay for Performance Programs

DIFFERENTIATION IN PERFORMANCE AND PAY

Many organizations seek to use pay to differentiate between employees (i.e., create pay dispersion) based on their performance, especially in jobs (e.g., higher job levels) where the consequences of good versus average versus poor performance become more important to organization performance.[19] Some evidence suggests that high performers can generate a disproportionate amount of value.[20] If so, paying high performers an amount they feel is equitable (see Chapter 11) to motivate them (i.e., achieve positive incentive effects), as well as attract and retain them (i.e., achieve positive sorting effects) becomes increasingly important. Conventional wisdom sometimes says that differentiation among individuals is ill-advised in certain contexts (e.g., teams, collectivistic cultures, where creativity/innovation are critical), but the evidence does not support such simple claims and, indeed, differentiation/pay for individual performance can be important for success in these contexts also.[21] What we can say is that employees will pay close attention to why different employees get paid differently and how fair those differences are, and their perceptions of fairness will drive their behaviors.[22]

DIFFERENTIATION STRENGTH/INCENTIVE INTENSITY: PROMISE AND PERIL

A key decision in designing pay for performance plans concerns incentive intensity, the strength of the relationship between performance and pay (i.e., how strongly we differentiate in performance and pay). For example, if I increase (decrease) my performance by 20%, by what percent will my pay increase (decrease)? The larger the change in pay, the stronger the incentive intensity. For jobs (sales, executives, stock brokers, investment bankers, investment portfolio managers, loan officers) where objective, results-based measures of performance are available, incentive intensity tends to be higher, compared to jobs (e.g., staff jobs in human resources, accounting) where more subjective, behavior-based (e.g., performance ratings) must be used. It is generally more of a challenge to credibly link big differences in pay to subjective measures. An important principle is that the stronger the incentive intensity, the stronger the motivation, but also the greater the chance that there will be unintended, undesirable consequences. We can link the pay of an automobile repair shop manager to sales and that will likely drive higher sales. Although we hope that higher sales result from efficiency and innovation in customer service, we have to recognize there is a risk that higher sales may be driven by fixing things on customers' cars that do not need fixing. Likewise, paying mortgage loan officers based on the mortgage revenue they create can generate more revenue, hopefully again through outstanding customer service, but the risk is that loans will be given to people who cannot afford them, which can come back to be a problem for the bank in the future. We can pay teachers partly based on how well their students perform on standardized tests. But we need to have safeguards in anticipation of the possibility that at least some teachers will look for ways to increase scores through means other than better teaching. If a financial institution's top executives believe the government will decide they are "too big to fail," they may be likely to take larger investment risks ("excessive risk taking" to the government that subsequently decides it must bail out the firm if the risks go bad and to the shareholders who lose if bankruptcy ensues). This is especially a risk if the executive does not have the same downside risk faced by shareholders. We will see other risks of pay for performance in this chapter as well and also steps (e.g., caps on bonuses, clawback provisions, balanced scorecards) companies and regulators have taken to avoid such risks. When one hears stories of what sometimes goes wrong with pay for performance, it is tempting to choose a weaker incentive intensity to avoid such problems. That may be wise in some cases. However, one must be careful not to weaken incentive intensity too much, else the reward for high performance can become too weak to motivate employees. And if a competitor provides a pay for performance environment with stronger incentive intensity, your strong performers may decide to work there instead (i.e., a negative sorting result). So, there is also a risk to weakening incentive intensity/pay for performance too much.

TYPES OF PAY FOR PERFORMANCE: AN OVERVIEW

LO 12-2
Describe the fundamental pay programs for recognizing employees' contributions to the organization's success.

Table 12.1 provides an overview of the programs for recognizing employee contributions. Each program shares a focus on paying for performance. The programs differ according to three design features: (1) payment method, (2) frequency of payout, and (3) ways of measuring performance. In a perhaps more speculative vein, the table also suggests the potential consequences of such programs for (1) performance motivation of employees, (2) attraction of employees, (3) organization culture, and (4) costs. Finally, there are two contingencies that may influence whether each pay program fits the situation: (1) management style and (2) type of work. We now discuss the different programs and some of their potential consequences in more depth.

In compensating employees, an organization does not have to choose one program over another. Instead, a combination of programs is often the best solution. For example, one program may foster teamwork and cooperation but not enough individual initiative.

Table 12.1
Programs for Recognizing Employee Contributions

	MERIT PAY	INCENTIVE PAY	PROFIT SHARING	OWNERSHIP	GAIN SHARING	SKILL-BASED
Design features						
Payment method	Changes in base pay	Bonus	Bonus	Equity changes	Bonus	Change in base pay
Frequency of payout	Annually	Weekly	Semiannually or annually	When stock sold	Monthly or quarterly	When skill or competency acquired
Performance measures	Supervisor's appraisal of individual performance	Individual output, productivity, sales	Company profit	Company stock returns	Production or controllable costs of stand-alone work unit	Skill or competency acquisition of individuals
Consequences						
Performance motivation	Relationship between pay and performance varies	Clear performance–reward connection	Stronger in smaller firms	Stronger in smaller firms	Stronger in smaller units	Encourages learning
Attraction	Over time pays better performers more	Pays higher performers more	Helps with all employees if plan pays out	Can help lock in employees	Helps with all employees if plan pays out	Attracts learning-oriented employees
Culture	Individual competition	Individual competition	Knowledge of business and cooperation	Sense of ownership and cooperation	Supports cooperation, problem solving	Learning and flexible organization
Costs	Requires well-developed performance appraisal system	Setting and maintaining acceptable standards	Relates costs to ability to pay	Relates costs to ability to pay	Setting and maintaining acceptable standards	Training and certification
Contingencies						
Management style	Some participation desirable	Control	Fits participation	Fits participation	Fits participation	Fits participation
Type of work	Individual unless group appraisals done	Stable, individual, easily measurable	All types	All types	All types	Significant skill depth or breadth

SOURCE: Adapted and modified from E. E. Lawler III, "Pay for Performance: A Strategic Analysis," in *Compensation and Benefits*, ed. L. R. Gomez-Mejia (Washington, DC: Bureau of National Affairs, 1989).

Another may do the opposite. Used in conjunction, a balance may be attained. Such balancing of objectives, combined with careful alignment with the organization and human resource strategy, may help increase the probability that a pay-for-performance program has its intended effects and reduce the probability of unintended consequences and problems.[23] The balanced scorecard, which we discuss in this chapter, is an example of a structured approach to balancing objectives. The fundamental principle is that we care about financial results, but we also care about HOW they are achieved and also how nonfinancial measures can be used, tracked, and influenced to achieve better future financial results. So, it also helps avoid too much short-term focus.[24]

LO 12-3
List the advantages and disadvantages of the pay programs.

Merit Pay

In traditional **merit pay** programs, annual base pay increases are usually linked to performance appraisal ratings. (See Chapter 8.) Some type of merit pay program exists in almost all organizations (although evidence on merit pay effectiveness is surprisingly scarce).[25] In some cases, employers have moved toward a form of merit pay that relies on bonuses rather than increases to base pay. One reason for the widespread use of merit pay, or **merit bonuses**, a form of variable pay, is its ability to define and reward a broad range of performance dimensions. (See Table 12.2 for an example.) Indeed, given the pervasiveness of merit pay programs, we devote a good deal of attention to them here.

Merit Pay
Traditional form of pay in which base pay is increased permanently.

Merit Bonus
Merit pay paid in the form of a bonus, instead of a salary increase.

Basic Features. Many merit pay programs work off of a **merit increase grid**. As Table 12.3 indicates, the size and frequency of pay increases are determined by two factors. The first factor is the individual's performance rating (better performers receive higher pay). The second factor is position in range (that is, an individual's compa-ratio). So, for example, an employee with a performance rating that exceeds expectations and a compa-ratio of 120 would receive a pay increase of roughly 3%. By comparison, an employee with a performance rating of exceeds expectations and a compa-ratio of 85 would receive an increase of around 7%. (Note that the general magnitude of increases in such a table is influenced by inflation rates.) One reason for factoring in the compa-ratio

Merit Increase Grid
A grid that combines an employee's performance rating with the employee's position in a pay range to determine the size and frequency of his or her pay increases.

1. Exercises good business judgment
2. Inspires enthusiasm, energy, understanding, loyalty for company goals
3. Attracts, grows, and retains outstanding talent
4. Shows initiative
5. Has position-specific knowledge
6. Delivers results
7. Builds internal good will

Table 12.2
Performance Dimensions for Lower to Midlevel Managers, Arrow Electronics

SOURCE: R. Riphahn (2011), Evidence on Incentive Effects of Subjective Performance Evaluations," Industrial and Labor Relations Review, 64.

Table 12.3
Merit Increase Grid

RECOMMENDED SALARY INCREASES BY PERFORMANCE RATING AND COMPA-RATIO		
COMPA-RATIO[a]		
80% TO 90%	91% TO 110%	111% TO 120%
Performance rating		
Exceeds expectations	7%	5%	3%
Meets expectations	4%	3%	2%
Below expectations	2%	0%	0%

[a]Employee salary/midpoint of their salary range.

Table 12.4
Performance Ratings
and Compa-Ratio
Targets

PERFORMANCE RATING	COMPA-RATIO TARGET
Exceeds expectations	111–120
Meets expectations	91–110
Below expectations	Below 91

is to control compensation costs and maintain the integrity of the pay structure. If a person with a compa-ratio of 120 received a merit increase of 7%, she would soon exceed the pay range maximum. Not factoring in the compa-ratio would also result in uncontrolled growth of compensation costs for employees who continue to perform the same job year after year. Instead, some organizations think in terms of assessing where the employee's pay is now and where it should be, given a particular performance level. Consider Table 12.4. An employee who consistently performs at the highest level is targeted to be paid at 111 to 120% of the market (that is, a compa-ratio of 111 to 120). To the extent that the employee is far from that pay level, larger and more frequent pay increases are necessary to move the employee to the correct position. On the other hand, if the employee is already at that pay level, smaller pay increases will be needed. The main objective in the latter case would be to provide pay increases that are sufficient to maintain the employee at the targeted compa-ratio.

In controlling compensation costs, another factor that requires close attention is the distribution of performance ratings. (See Chapter 8.) In many organizations, 60% to 70% of employees fall into the top two (out of four to five) performance rating categories.[26] This means tremendous growth in compensation costs because most employees will eventually be above the midpoint of the pay range, resulting in compa-ratios well over 100. To avoid this, some organizations provide guidelines regarding the percentage of employees who should fall into each performance category, usually limiting the percentage that can be placed in the top two categories. These guidelines are enforced differently, ranging from true guidelines to strict forced-distribution requirements.[27]

In general, merit pay programs have the following characteristics. First, they identify individual differences in performance, which are assumed to reflect differences in ability or motivation. By implication, system constraints on performance are not seen as significant. Second, the majority of information on individual performance is collected from the immediate supervisor. Peer and subordinate ratings are rare, and where they exist, they tend to receive less weight than supervisory ratings.[28] Third, there is a policy of linking pay increases to performance appraisal results.[29] Fourth, the feedback under such systems tends to occur infrequently, often once per year at the formal performance review session. Fifth, the flow of feedback tends to be largely unidirectional, from supervisor to subordinate.

Criticisms of Traditional Merit Pay Programs. Criticisms of this process have been raised. For example, W. Edwards Deming, a leader of the total quality management movement, argued that it is unfair to rate individual performance because "apparent differences between people arise almost entirely from the system that they work in, not from the people themselves."[30] Examples of system factors include co-workers, the job, materials, equipment, customers, management, supervision, and environmental conditions. These are believed to be largely outside the worker's control, instead falling under management's responsibility. Deming argued that the performance rating is essentially "the result of a lottery."[31] Although that may be true for some jobs, for others (attorneys, consultants, investment bankers, athletes, salespeople, managers), there can be major differences in individual performance.[32]

Deming also argued that the individual focus of merit pay discourages teamwork: "Everyone propels himself forward, or tries to, for his own good, on his own life preserver. The organization is the loser."[33] As an example, if people in the purchasing department are evaluated based on the number of contracts negotiated, they may have little interest in materials quality, even though manufacturing is having quality problems.

Deming's solution was to eliminate the link between individual performance and pay. This approach reflects a desire to move away from recognizing individual contributions. What are the consequences of such a move? It is possible that fewer employees with individual-achievement orientations would be attracted to and remain with the organization. One study of job retention found that the relationship between pay growth and individual performance over time was weaker at higher performance levels. As a consequence, the organization lost a disproportionate share of its top performers.[34] In other words, too little emphasis on individual performance may leave the organization with average and poor performers.[35]

Thus, although Deming's concerns about too much emphasis on individual performance are well taken, one must be careful not to replace one set of problems with another. Instead, there needs to be an appropriate balance between individual and group objectives. At the very least, ranking and forced-distribution performance-rating systems need to be considered with caution, lest they contribute to behavior that is too individualistic and competitive.

Another criticism of merit pay programs is the way they measure performance. If the performance measure is not perceived as being fair and accurate, the entire merit pay program can break down. One potential impediment to accuracy is the almost exclusive reliance on the supervisor for providing performance ratings, even though peers, subordinates, and customers (internal and external) often have information on a person's performance that is as good as or better than that of the supervisor. A 360-degree performance feedback approach (discussed in Chapter 9) gathers feedback from each of these sources. To date, however, organizations have mainly used such data for development purposes and have been reluctant to use these multisource data for making pay decisions.[36]

In general, process issues, including communication, expectation setting, and credibility/fairness, are important in administering merit pay and pay-for-performance in general.[37] In any situation where rewards are distributed, employees appear to assess fairness along two dimensions: distributive (based on how much they receive) and procedural (what process was used to decide how much).[38] Some of the most important aspects of procedural fairness, or justice, appear in Table 12.5. These items suggest that employees desire clear and consistent performance standards, as well as opportunities to provide input, discuss their performance, and appeal any decision they believe to be incorrect.

Perhaps the most basic criticism is that merit pay does not really exist. High performers, it is argued, are not paid significantly more than mediocre or even poor performers in most cases.[39] For example, consider the data in Table 12.6 from a WorldatWork survey. It shows that high performers received an average merit increase of 4.8%, compared to 2.6% for average performers. On a salary of $50,000 per year, that is a difference of $1,100 per year, or $21.15 per week (before taxes). Critics of merit pay point out that this difference is probably not significant enough to influence employee behaviors or attitudes. Indeed, as Table 12.7 indicates, the majority of employees do not believe there is much payoff to higher levels of performance in their organizations.

Table 12.5
Aspects of
Procedural Justice in
Pay Raise Decisions

Indicate the extent to which your supervisor did each of the following:
1. Was honest and ethical in dealing with you.
2. Gave you an opportunity to express your side.
3. Used consistent standards in evaluating your performance.
4. Considered your views regarding your performance.
5. Gave you feedback that helped you learn how well you were doing.
6. Was completely candid and frank with you.
7. Showed a real interest in trying to be fair.
8. Became thoroughly familiar with your performance.
9. Took into account factors beyond your control.
10. Got input from you before a recommendation.
11. Made clear what was expected of you.

Indicate how much of an opportunity existed, after the last raise decision, for you to do each of the following things:
12. Make an appeal about the size of a raise.
13. Express your feelings to your supervisor about the salary decision.
14. Discuss, with your supervisor, how your performance was evaluated.
15. Develop, with your supervisor, an action plan for future performance.

SOURCE: From R. Folger and M. A. Konovsky "Effects of Procedural and Distributive Justice on Reactions to Pay Raise Decisions," *Academy of Management Journal,* Volume 32, 1989, p. 115. Reproduced with permission of Academy of Management via Copyright Clearance Center.

Table 12.6
Distribution of
Performance Rating
and Average Base
Pay Increase as
a Function of
Performance
(United States)

	PERCENT OF WORKFORCE	AVERAGE BASE PAY INCREASE
Highest-rated	8%	4.8%
Next Highest-rated	28%	3.7%
Middle-rated	57%	2.6%
Low-rated	7%	0.9%
Lowest-rated	2%	0.1%

Note: Based on companies with a five-point rating scale.
SOURCE: Mercer, *2014/2015 US Compensation Planning Survey,* www.mercer.com.

Table 12.7
Pay and
Performance,
Employee
Perceptions

	% WHO AGREE
When I do a good job, my performance is rewarded.	40%
My organization does an adequate job of matching pay to performance.	46%

SOURCE: Mercer, "What's WorkingTM Survey, United States."

In fact, however, small differences in pay can accumulate into large differences over time. Consistently receiving 4.8% increases (versus 2.6%) over 30 years with a starting salary of $50,000 would translate into a career salary advantage (before taxes) of roughly $1,000,000 (net present value of roughly $600,000, assuming a discount rate of 2.5%).[40] Whether employees think in these terms is open to question. But even if they do not, nothing prevents an organization from explaining to employees that what may appear to be small differences in pay can add up to large differences over time.

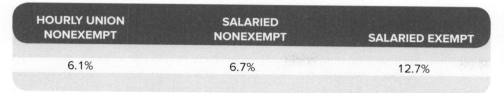

HOURLY UNION NONEXEMPT	SALARIED NONEXEMPT	SALARIED EXEMPT
6.1%	6.7%	12.7%

Table 12.8
Merit Bonus as a Percentage of Salary, by Employee Group

SOURCE: Company website, "New Aon Hewitt Survey Shows 2014 Variable Pay Spending Spikes to Record-High Level," http://aon.mediaroom.com, accessed May 3, 2015.

Of course, the accumulation effect just described can also be seen as a drawback if it contributes to an entitlement mentality. Here the concern is that a big merit increase given early in an employee's career remains part of base salary "forever." It does not have to be re-earned each year, and the cost to the organization grows over time, perhaps more than either the employee's performance or the organization's profitability would always warrant. Merit bonuses (payouts that do not become part of base salary, a form of variable pay), are thus increasingly used by organizations in lieu of or in addition to merit increases. In fact, merit bonuses (see Table 12.8), in the companies that use them and for the employee groups they use them for, are now larger than traditional pay increases. Preliminary evidence suggests that merit bonuses may have a larger positive impact (compared to traditional merit increases) on future performance.[41] If that result proves to be robust across organizations, it, together with the merit bonus advantage in terms of controlling fixed costs, likely goes far toward explaining the greater use of merit bonuses.

The payoff to high performance that comes from merit bonuses adds to the payoff from merit increases. Finally, high performing employees are also more likely to be promoted (into higher paying jobs) and are also more likely to have higher paying opportunities at alternative employers. All these factors can be communicated to employees to help them see the payoff to high performance.[42] And the higher the performance, the more likely it is one can keep the job (and salary).[43]

Individual Incentives

Like merit pay, individual incentives reward individual performance, but with two important differences. First, payments are not rolled into base pay. They must be continuously earned and re-earned. Second, performance is usually measured as physical output (such as number of water faucets produced) rather than by subjective ratings. Individual incentives have the potential to significantly increase performance. Locke and his colleagues found that monetary incentives increased production output by a median of 30%—more than any other motivational device studied.[44]

Nevertheless, individual incentives, at least in their purest form, are relatively rare for a variety of reasons.[45] Most jobs (like those of many managers and professionals) have, strictly speaking, no physical output measure. Instead, they involve what might be described as "knowledge work." There may or may not be alternative objective measures of performance available (e.g., financial and/or operational) which are needed to use individual incentives. The balanced scorecard gives a good flavor of what objective performance outcomes for managers often look like when they are available. Even in jobs where physical output measures are available, potential administrative problems (such as setting and maintaining acceptable standards) often prove intractable.[46] Third, individual incentives may do such a good job of motivating employees that they do whatever they get paid for and nothing else. (For example, one Dilbert cartoon showed employees celebrating when told they would be paid for every software error they found and fixed. The implication was that they would deliberately write errors into the software and then fix them to earn as much money as possible.) Fourth, as the name implies, individual incentives, again if used in their purest/simplest form, typically do not fit well with a team approach. Fifth, they may be inconsistent with the goals of acquiring multiple skills and proactive problem solving. Learning new skills often requires employees to slow or stop production. If the employees are paid based on production volume, they may not want to slow down or stop. Sixth, some incentive plans, if not carefully designed, reward output volume at the expense of quality or customer service.

Therefore, although individual incentives carry potential advantages, they are not likely to contribute to a flexible, proactive, quality-conscious problem-solving workforce unless they can be designed to avoid the potential pitfalls listed above. Incorporating a broader range of objectives beyond physical output alone is one common step toward that end.

Profit Sharing and Ownership

Profit Sharing
A compensation plan in which payments are based on a measure of organization performance (profits) and do not become part of the employees' base salary.

Profit Sharing. At the other end of the individual–group continuum are profit sharing and stock ownership plans. Under **profit sharing**, payments are based on a measure of organization performance (profits), and the payments do not become part of the base salary. Profit sharing has two potential advantages. First, it may encourage employees to think more like owners, taking a broad view of what needs to be done to make the organization more effective. Thus, the sort of narrow self-interest encouraged by individual incentive plans (and perhaps also by merit pay) is presumably less of an issue. Instead, increased cooperation and citizenship are expected. Second, because payments do not become part of base pay, but instead are variable pay, labor costs are automatically reduced during difficult economic times, and wealth is shared during good times. Consequently, organizations may not need to rely on layoffs as much to reduce costs during tough times.[47] The "Competing through Sustainability" box describes what General Motors did with its recent profit sharing plan payouts to strengthen its long-term relationship with its employees.

Does profit sharing contribute to better organization performance? The evidence is not clear. Although there is consistent support for a correlation between profit sharing payments and profits, questions have been raised about the direction of causality.[48] For example, Ford, Chrysler, and GM all have profit sharing plans in their contracts with the United Auto Workers (UAW). (See Table 12.9 for provisions of the GM–UAW plan.) Years ago, under an older profit sharing plan, the average profit sharing payment at Ford one year was $4,000 per worker versus an average of $550 per worker at GM and $8,000 at Chrysler. Given that the profit sharing plans used were very similar, it seems unlikely that the profit sharing plans (through their effects on worker motivation) caused Ford and Chrysler to be more profitable. Rather, it would appear that profits were higher at Ford for other reasons (e.g., better cars), resulting in higher profit sharing payments.

This example also helps illustrate the fundamental drawback of profit sharing. Why should automobile workers at GM receive profit sharing payments that are only 1/15 the size received by those doing the same type of work at Chrysler? Is it because Chrysler UAW members performed 15 times better than their counterparts at GM that year? Probably not. Rather, workers are likely to view top management decisions regarding

GM's Payout Strengthens Relationship with Workers

After spending nearly $3 billion to compensate victims and recall almost 30 million vehicles to address faulty ignition switches in some of its cars, General Motors' (GM) profits last year fell to $6.6 billion. Without the cost of the recalls, the company's profits would have been $9 billion. The profit-sharing plan in its contract with the United Auto Workers (UAW) pays out roughly $1,000 in profit sharing to workers for each $1 billion in GM profits. In the interest of supporting a positive and sustainable relationship with its blue-collar workers, and deciding that they should not be penalized for GM's mistakes in monitoring and acting on safety problems, GM decided to pay workers an average of $9,000 in profit-sharing, corresponding to the $9 billion profit figure, even though under its contract, it could have used the $6.6 billion figure. New UAW president Dennis Williams took the action in that spirit, stating that GM's action reflected the "strong, stable environment" that GM and the UAW had created together. GM's action and the goodwill it created may also prove helpful in its upcoming contract negotiations with the UAW.

DISCUSSION QUESTIONS

1. Did GM make the correct decision or should it have returned more money to its shareholders?

2. What was the rationale GM used to make a profit-sharing payment that was $2,000 per worker greater than the contract required? How would you go about assessing the return on investment that GM is likely to receive from its decision?

SOURCES: B. Vlasic, "Despite Recalls, GM Pays Workers Big Bonus," *The New York Times*, February 5, 2015, p. A1; J. D. Stoll, "UAW's Ranks Press to Close Pay Gap," *The Wall Street Journal*, March 23, 2015, p. B2.

products, engineering, pricing, and marketing as more important. As a result, with the exception of top (and perhaps some middle) managers or plans that cover a small number of employees (i.e., in small companies), most employees are unlikely to see a strong connection between what they do and what they earn under profit sharing. This means that performance motivation is likely to change very little under profit sharing. Consistent with expectancy theory, motivation depends on a strong link between behaviors and valued consequences such as pay (instrumentality perceptions).

Another factor that reduces the motivational impact of profit sharing plans is that most plans are of the deferred type. Roughly 16% of full-time employees in medium-size and large private establishments participate in profit sharing plans, but only 1% of employees overall (about 6% of those in profit sharing plans) are in cash plans where profits are paid to employees during the current time period.[49]

Not only may profit sharing fail to increase performance motivation, but employees may also react very negatively when they learn that such plans do not pay out during business downturns.[50] First, they may not feel they are to blame because they have been performing their jobs well. Other factors are beyond their control, so why should they be penalized? Second, what seems like a small amount of at-risk pay for a manager earning $80,000 per year can be very painful to someone earning $15,000 or $20,000.

Consider the case of the Du Pont Fibers Division, which had a plan that linked a portion of employees' pay to division profits.[51] After the plan's implementation, employees' base salary was about 4% lower than similar employees in other divisions unless 100% of the profit goal (a 4% increase over the previous year's profits) was reached. Thus, there was what might be called downside risk. However, there was also considerable upside opportunity: if 100% of the profit goal was exceeded, employees would earn

Table 12.9
Profit Sharing in the General Motors— United Auto Workers Contract

PROFITS $BILLIONS			MAXIMUM $PAYOUT	PROFITS $BILLIONS			MAXIMUM $PAYOUT
–	<	1.25	0	6.50	<	6.75	6,500
1.25	<	1.50	1,250	6.75	<	7.00	6,750
1.50	<	1.75	1,500	7.00	<	7.25	7,000
1.75	<	2.00	1,750	7.25	<	7.50	7,250
2.00	<	2.25	2,000	7.50	<	7.75	7,500
2.25	<	2.50	2,250	7.75	<	8.00	7,750
2.50	<	2.75	2,500	8.00	<	8.25	8,000
2.75	<	3.00	2,750	8.25	<	8.50	8,250
3.00	<	3.25	3,000	8.50	<	8.75	8,500
3.25	<	3.50	3,250	8.75	<	9.00	8,750
3.50	<	3.75	3,500	9.00	<	9.25	9,000
3.75	<	4.00	3,750	9.25	<	9.50	9,250
4.00	<	4.25	4,000	9.50	<	9.75	9,500
4.25	<	4.50	4,250	9.75	<	10.00	9,750
4.50	<	4.75	4,500	10.00	<	10.25	10,000
4.75	<	5.00	4,750	10.25	<	10.50	10,250
5.00	<	5.25	5,000	10.50	<	10.75	10,500
5.25	<	5.50	5,250	10.75	<	11.00	10,750
5.50	<	5.75	5,500	11.00	<	11.25	11,000
5.75	<	6.00	5,750	11.25	<	11.50	11,250
6.00	<	6.25	6,000	11.50	<	11.75	11,500
6.25	<	6.50	6,250	11.75	<	12.00	11,750
				>		= 12.0	12,000

Note: Employees working 1850 or more hours per year receive the maximum payout. Those working fewer hours receive a prorated payout based on their hours worked. Profits are defined as operating income (earnings before interest and taxes) for North America (only).
SOURCE: From www.uaw.org/content/new-lump-sum-payments-profit-sharing-quality-bonus.

more than similar employees in other divisions. For example, if the division reached 150% of the profit goal (6% growth in profits), employees would receive 12% more than comparable employees in other divisions.

Initially, the plan worked fine. The profit goal was exceeded, and employees earned slightly more than employees in other divisions. In the following year, however, profits were down 26%, and the profit goal was not met. Employees received no profit sharing bonus; instead, they earned 4% less than comparable employees in other divisions. Profit sharing was no longer seen as a very good idea. Du Pont management responded to employee concerns by eliminating the plan and returning to a system of fixed base salaries with no variable (or risk) component. This outcome is perhaps not surprising from an agency theory perspective, which suggests that employees must somehow be compensated to assume increased risk.

One solution some organizations choose is to design plans that have upside but not downside risk. In such cases, when a profit sharing plan is introduced, base pay is not reduced. Thus, when profits are high, employees share in the gain, but when profits are low, they are not penalized. Such plans largely eliminate what is purported to be a major advantage of profit sharing: reducing labor costs during business downturns. During business upturns, labor costs will increase. Given that the performance benefits of such plans are not assured, an organization runs the risk under such plans of increasing its labor costs with little return on its investment.

In summary, although profit sharing may be useful as one component of a compensation system (to enhance identification with broad organizational goals), it may need to be complemented with other pay programs that more closely link pay to outcomes that individuals or teams can control (or "own"), particularly in larger companies. In addition, profit sharing runs the risk of contributing to employee dissatisfaction or higher

EVIDENCE-BASED HR

Craig Durosko's remodeling company, Sun Design, was on the way to losing money. So, he turned to someone he thought could help—his employees. Sun Design now shares financial information (revenues and expenses, historical and projected) with its 50 employees, who gather each month for coffee, donuts, and a financial update. After revenues dropped to $6.4 million, they rebounded three years later to $8.7 million. A key reason is that, armed with new shared information, employees helped identify ways to reduce costs and increase revenues. More than 20 employees provided specific, detailed suggestions for how to do this.

The management approach, called open-book management, involves teaching employees to understand financial concepts and statements, asking them to become involved in developing and implementing cost reduction and revenue enhancement ideas, and rewarding them when they do.

A few years ago, Tasty Catering began to use open book management. Each week, its 49 full-time employees meet for lunch and review the previous week's profit and loss statement. Every employee takes responsibility for improving profits. Some ideas are simple. Keeping better maintenance logs for delivery trucks decreased repair costs by $16,000 per year. Charting gas prices by day and having drivers fill their tanks on the lower-cost days saved $20,000 per year. Paying more attention to recycling in the kitchen has allowed the company to stop paying another company to haul waste away, and instead Tasty now sells its recyclables each month, making about $3,600 per year. Salespeople are more careful as well. They are more selective about taking on events where they can make the most money. The net effect of these and other changes has been a rise in sales of 7% to $7 million and a much larger increase in profits of 75%. Importantly, when profits rise, employees share in them through a profit-sharing program. A Tasty manager notes that there were initial challenges. He says one mistake was initially limiting the meetings to only management. Also, he noted that it was necessary to teach employees how to read a profit and loss statement.

Many know open-book management from the book *The Great Game of Business,* written by Jack Stack about his experience at Springfield Remanufacturing (SRC). SRC purchased a failing division of International Harvester for $9 million, which rebuilt engines. The 119 employees learned to read financial statements, work as a team to improve costs and revenues, and earn cash bonuses for their successes. Currently, SRC employees are eligible for quarterly bonuses that depend on reaching a set of targets. Hourly workers can receive bonuses of up to 13% of their base pay, while salaried employees can receive bonuses of up to 18% of their base pay. Today, SRC has over 1,000 employees and $400 million in revenues.

The key to open-book management is sharing data to make evidence-based decisions. But a survey by Robert Half Associates reports that only 7% of private

CONTINUED

companies share financial information with all workers. Why? Many companies fear that information will fall into the hands of their competitors. Another concern is that some companies may not be prepared to give workers information that may lead them to question how management does certain things. (But of course, such questioning is just what may be needed for the company to improve.)

At Central States Manufacturing, located in Lowell, Arkansas, all new employees must take a Finance 101 course, as well as courses on steel basics, customer service, the company's values and mission, and its employee stock ownership plan. The company provides financial data, including very detailed measures. For example, Ladena Lambert, the Director of Human Resources, gives the example of scrap. "When they see that the amount of scrap they put out in one week costs about the same as we pay a person, it's no longer just 200 feet of scrap a day." She says they start thinking in terms of dollars.

SOURCES: L. Bertagnoli, "Getting Employees in the Profit Game: Tasty Catering Opens Its Books to Get All Involved in Cost Cuts," *Crain's Chicago Business*, August 11, 2014, p. 4; D. Meinert, "An Open Book," *HR Magazine*, April 2013.

labor costs, depending on how it is designed. However, moving beyond concerns about its motivation impact, profit sharing does have the major advantage of making labor costs more variable, a major advantage when sales and profits decline.

Ownership. Recent data show that in the neighborhood of 20 million Americans own stock in their company.[52] Employee ownership is similar to profit sharing in some key respects, such as encouraging employees to focus on the success of the organization as a whole. In fact, with ownership, this focus may be even stronger. Like profit sharing, ownership may be less motivational the larger the organization. And because employees may not realize any financial gain until they actually sell their stock (typically upon leaving the organization), the link between pay and performance may be even less obvious than under profit sharing. Thus, from a reinforcement theory standpoint (with its emphasis on actually experiencing rewards), the effect on performance motivation may be limited.

One way of achieving employee ownership is through **stock options**, which give employees the opportunity to buy stock at a fixed price. Say the employees receive options to purchase stock at $10 per share in 2016, and the stock price reaches $30 per share in 2021. They have the option of purchasing stock ("exercising" their stock options) at $10 per share in 2021, thus making a tidy return on investment if the shares are then sold. If the stock price goes down to $8 per share in the year 2021, however, there will be no financial gain. Therefore, employees are encouraged to act in ways that will benefit the organization.

For many years, stock options had typically been reserved for executives in larger, established companies. More recently, there was a trend toward pushing eligibility farther down in the organization.[53] In fact, many companies, including PepsiCo, Merck, McDonald's, Walmart, and Procter & Gamble, began granting stock options to employees at all levels. Among start-up companies like these in the technology sector, these broad-based stock option programs have long been popular and companies like Microsoft and Cisco Systems attribute much of their growth and success to these option plans. Some studies suggest that organization performance is higher when a large percentage of top and midlevel managers are eligible for long-term incentives

Stock Options
An employee ownership plan that gives employees the opportunity to buy the company's stock at a previously fixed price.

such as stock options, which is consistent with agency theory's focus on the problem of encouraging managers to think like owners.[54] However, it is not clear whether these findings would hold up for lower-level employees, particularly in larger companies, who may see much less opportunity to influence overall organization performance. Another issue with options is whether executives and employees place sufficient value on them, given their cost.[55]

The Golden Age of stock options has faded some. Investors have long questioned the historically favorable tax treatment of employee stock options. In 2004, the Financial Accounting Standards Board (FASB) issued SFAS 123R, a landmark change, requiring companies to expense options on their financial statements, which reduces reported net income, dramatically in some cases. Microsoft decided to eliminate stock options in favor of actual stock grants. This is partly in response to the new accounting standards and partly in recognition of the fact that Microsoft's stock price is not likely to grow as rapidly as it once did, making options less effective in recruiting, retaining, and motivating its employees. It appears that many companies are cutting back on stock options overall, and especially for nonexecutive employees.

Those companies that continue to use broad-based stock options have encountered difficulties in keeping employees motivated during years when there has been a steep decline in stock prices. For example, in 2009 Google's stock price dropped to $306, down from $741 in 2007, putting many employee stock options "underwater" (i.e., the stock price was under the option/exercise price), meaning that employees were not able to make any gain from exercising their options. Google's answer to this situation was an option exchange where employees turned in their underwater options in return for options having an exercise price equal to the current (lower) stock price. The hope was that employee motivation and retention would be reinvigorated.[56] As another example of the challenge in using stock-based compensation, one estimate was that (nonexecutive) employees of Facebook and of Zynga experienced declines in the value of their company stock and stock options of $7.2 billion and $1.4 billion, respectively, after initial public offerings of stock.[57] (Now, some years later, it seems like things have worked out OK for them!)

Employee stock ownership plans (ESOPs), under which employers give employees stock in the company, are the most common form of employee ownership, with the number of employees in such plans increasing from 4 million in 1980 to about 13.5 million in 2015 in the United States.[58] Including non-ESOP stock option, stock purchase, and stock-based retirement plans, it is estimated that about 28 million U.S. employees own some of their companies, controlling about 8% of U.S. corporate equity. In Japan, 91% of companies listed on Japanese stock markets have an ESOP, and these companies appear to have higher average productivity than non-ESOP companies.[59] ESOPs raise a number of unique issues. On the negative side, they can carry significant risk for employees. An ESOP must, by law, invest at least 51% of assets in its company's stock, resulting in less diversification of investment risk (in some cases, no diversification). Consequently, when employees buy out companies in poor financial condition to save their jobs, or when the ESOP is used to fund pensions, employees risk serious financial difficulties if the company does poorly.[60] This is not just a concern for employees, because, as agency theory suggests, employees may require higher pay to offset increased risks of this sort.

ESOPs can be attractive to organizations because they have tax and financing advantages and can serve as a takeover defense (under the assumption that employee owners will be "friendly" to management). ESOPs give employees the right to vote their securities (if registered on a national exchange).[61] As such, some degree of participation in a

Employee Stock Ownership Plan (ESOP)
An employee ownership plan that gives employers certain tax and financial advantages when stock is granted to employees.

select number of decisions is mandatory, but overall participation in decision making appears to vary significantly across organizations with ESOPs. Some studies suggest that the positive effects of ownership are larger in cases where employees have greater participation,[62] perhaps because the "employee–owner comes to psychologically experience his/her ownership in the organization."[63]

Gainsharing, Group Incentives, and Team Awards

Gainsharing
A form of compensation based on group or plant performance (rather than organizationwide profits) that does not become part of the employee's base salary.

Gainsharing. **Gainsharing** programs offer a means of sharing productivity gains with employees. Although sometimes confused with profit sharing plans, gainsharing differs in two key respects. First, instead of using an organization-level performance measure (profits), the programs measure group or plant performance, which is likely to be seen as more controllable by employees. Second, payouts are distributed more frequently and not deferred. In a sense, gainsharing programs represent an effort to combine the best features of organization-oriented plans like profit sharing and individual-oriented plans like merit pay and individual incentives. Like profit sharing, gainsharing encourages pursuit of broader goals than individual-oriented plans do. But, unlike profit sharing, gainsharing can motivate employees much as individual plans do because of the more controllable nature of the performance measure and the frequency of payouts. Studies indicate that gainsharing improves performance.[64]

One type of gainsharing, the Scanlon plan (developed in the 1930s by Joseph N. Scanlon, president of a local union at Empire Steel and Tin Plant in Mansfield, Ohio), provides a monetary bonus to employees (and the organization) if the ratio of labor costs to the sales value of production is kept below a certain standard. Table 12.10 shows a modified (i.e., costs in addition to labor are included) Scanlon plan. Because actual costs ($850,000) were less than allowable costs ($907,500) in the first and second periods, there is a gain of $57,500. The organization receives 45% of the savings, and the employees receive the other 55%, although part of the employees' share is set aside in the event that actual costs exceed the standard in upcoming months (as Table 12.10 shows did occur).

Gainsharing plans like the Scanlon plan and pay-for-performance plans in general often encompass more than just a monetary component. There is often a strong emphasis on taking advantage of employee know-how to improve the production process through problem-solving teams and suggestion systems.[65] A number of recommendations have been made about the organization conditions that should be in place for gainsharing to succeed. Commonly mentioned factors include (1) management commitment, (2) a need to change or a strong commitment to continuous improvement, (3) management's acceptance and encouragement of employee input, (4) high levels of cooperation and interaction, (5) employment security, (6) information sharing on productivity and costs, (7) goal setting, (8) commitment of all involved parties to the process of change and improvement, and (9) agreement on a performance standard and calculation that is understandable, seen as fair, and closely related to managerial objectives.[66]

Group Incentives and Team Awards. Whereas gainsharing plans are often plant-wide, group incentives and team awards typically pertain to a smaller work group.[67] Group incentives (like individual incentives) tend to measure performance in terms of physical output, whereas team award plans may use a broader range of performance measures (like cost savings, successful completion of product design, or meeting

ITEMS	AVERAGE OF 1ST AND 2ND PERIODS	AVERAGE OF 2ND AND 3RD PERIODS
1. Sales in dollars	$1,000,000	$1,000,000
2. Inventory change and work in process	100,000	100,000
3. Sales value of production	1,100,000	1,100,000
4. Allowable costs (82.5% × 3 above)	907,500	907,500
5. Actual costs	850,000	917,500
6. Gain (4–5 above)	57,500	–10,000
7. Employee share (55% of 6 above)	31,625	–5,500
8. Monthly reserve (20% of 7 above)	6,325	–5,500
*If no bonus, 100% of 7 above		
9. Bonus to be distributed (7–8)	25,300	0
10. Company share (45% of 6 above)	25,875	–4,500
11. Participating payroll	132,000	132,000
12. Bonus percentage (9/11)	19.2%	0.0%
13. Monthly reserve (8 above)	6,325	–5,500
14. Reserve at the end of last period	0	6,325
15. Year-end reserve to date	6,325	825

Table 12.10
Example of Gainsharing (Modified Scanlon Plan) Report

SOURCE: From *Gainsharing and Goalsharing: Aligning Pay and Strategic Goals,* by K. Mericle and D. O. Kim. Reproduced with permission of Greenwood Publishing Group via Copyright Clearance Center.

deadlines). As with individual incentive plans, these plans have a number of potential drawbacks. Competition between individuals may be reduced, but it may be replaced by competition between groups or teams. Also, consistent with our earlier discussion of pay effects on workforce composition, any plan that does not adequately recognize differences in individual performance risks demotivating top performers or losing them. Finally, as with any incentive plan, a standard-setting process must be developed that is seen as fair by employees, and these standards must not exclude important dimensions such as quality.

Balanced Scorecard

As the preceding discussion indicates, every pay program has advantages and disadvantages. Therefore, rather than choosing one program, some companies find it useful to design a mix of pay programs, one that has just the right chemistry for the situation at hand. Relying exclusively on merit pay or individual incentives may result in high levels of work motivation but unacceptable levels of individualistic and competitive behavior and too little concern for broader plant or organization goals. Relying too heavily on profit sharing and gainsharing plans may increase cooperation and concern for the welfare of the entire plant or organization, but it may reduce individual work motivation to unacceptable levels. However, a particular mix of merit pay, gainsharing, and profit sharing could contribute to acceptable performance on all these performance dimensions.

One approach that seeks to balance multiple objectives is the balanced scorecard (see Chapter 1), which Kaplan and Norton describe as a way for companies to "track financial results while simultaneously monitoring progress in building the capabilities and acquiring the intangible assets they would need for future growth."[68]

LO 12-4
Describe how organizations combine incentive plans in a balanced scorecard.

Table 12.11
Illustration of Balanced Scorecard Incentive Concept

| PERFORMANCE MEASURE | INCENTIVE SCHEDULE | | | ACTUAL PERFORMANCE | INCENTIVE EARNED |
	TARGET INCENTIVE	PERFORMANCE	% TARGET		
Financial • Return on capital employed	$100	20% + 16–20% 12–16% Below 12%	150% 100% 50% 0%	18%	$100
Customer • Product returns	$ 40	1 in: 1,000 + 900–999 800–899 Below 800	150% 100% 50% 0%	1 in 876	$ 20
Internal • Cycle time reduction (%)	$ 30	9% + 6–9% 3–6% 0–3%	150% 100% 50% 0%	11%	$ 45
Learning and growth • Voluntary employee turnover	$ 30	Below 5% 5–8% 8–12%	150% 100% 50%	7%	$ 30
Total	$200				$195

SOURCE: From F. C. McKenzie and M. P. Shilling, "Avoiding Performance Traps: Ensuring Effective Incentive Design and Implementation," *Compensation and Benefits Review,* July–August 1998, pp. 57–65. *Compensation and Benefits Review by American Management Association.* Reproduced with permission of Sage Publications, Inc. via Copyright Clearance Center.

Table 12.11 shows how a mix of measures might be used by a manufacturing firm to motivate improvements in a balanced set of key business drivers. We will also see shortly a scorecard used by Merck.

Managerial and Executive Pay

LO 12-5
Discuss issues related to performance-based pay for executives.

Because of their significant ability to influence organization performance, top managers and executives are a strategically important group whose compensation warrants special attention, including its competitiveness in the labor market.[69] In the previous chapter we discussed how much this group is paid. Here we focus on the issue of how their pay is determined.

Business magazines such as *Forbes* and *Bloomberg Businessweek* often publish lists of top executives who did the most for their pay and those who did the least. The latter group has been the impetus for much of the attention to executive pay. The problem seems to be that in some companies, top executive pay is high every year, regardless of profitability or stock market performance. One study, for example, found that CEO pay changes by $3.25 for every $1,000 change in shareholder wealth. Although this relationship was interpreted to mean that "the compensation of top executives is virtually independent of corporate performance," later work demonstrates, to the contrary, that executive pay, in most companies, is significantly aligned with shareholder return."[70]

	PREDICTED RETURN ON ASSETS		
BONUS/BASE RATIO	**LONG-TERM INCENTIVE ELIGIBILITY**	**%**	**$ª**
10%	28%	5.2%	$250 million
20	28	5.6	269 million
10	48	5.9	283 million
20	48	7.1	341 million

Table 12.12
The Relationship between Managerial Pay and Organization Return on Assets

ªBased on the assets of the average *Fortune* 500 company in 1990.

SOURCE: B. Gerhart and G. T. Milkovich, "Organizational Differences in Managerial Compensation and Financial Performance," *Academy of Management Journal* 33 (1990), pp. 663–91.

How can executive pay be linked to organization performance? From an agency theory perspective, the goal of owners (shareholders) is to encourage the agents (managers and executives) to act in the best interests of the owners. This may mean less emphasis on noncontingent pay, such as base salary, and more emphasis on outcome-oriented "contracts" that make some portion of executive pay contingent on the organization's profitability or stock performance.[71] Among midlevel and top managers, it is common to use both short-term bonus and long-term incentive plans to encourage the pursuit of both short- and long-term organization performance objectives. Indeed, the bulk of executive compensation comes from restricted stock, stock options, and other forms of long-term compensation. Putting pay "at risk" in this manner can be a strong incentive. However, agency theory suggests that while too little pay at risk may weaken the incentive effect, too much pay at risk can also be a problem if executives take too big of risks with firm assets.[72] The banking and mortgage industry problems of late provide an example.

Organizations use such pay-for-performance plans, and what are their consequences? Research suggests that organizations vary substantially in the extent to which they use both long-term and short-term incentive programs. Further, greater use of such plans among top and midlevel managers is associated with higher subsequent levels of profitability. As Table 12.12 indicates, greater reliance on short-term bonuses and long-term incentives (relative to base pay) resulted in substantial improvements in return on assets.[73] For top executives, aligning compensation with past shareholder return is associated with his or her future shareholder returns.[74]

Earlier, we saw how the balanced scorecard approach could be applied to paying manufacturing employees. It is also useful in designing executive pay. Table 12.13 shows how the choice of performance measures can be guided by a desire to balance shareholder, customer, and employee objectives. Sears sees financial results as a lagging indicator that tells the company how it has done in the past, whereas customer and employee metrics like those in Table 12.13, used by Merck, are leading indicators that tell the company how its financial results will be in the future. Importantly, Sears conducted empirical research to validate these presumed linkages.[75] Thus, Sears ties its executive compensation to achievement of objectives to "(1) drive profitable growth, (2) become customer-centric, (3) foster the development of a diverse, high-performance culture, and (4) focus on productivity and returns."[76]

As we saw in the Global Financial Crisis, a focus on only (aggressive) financial goals, without also considering how those goals are achieved, raises the danger executives and others will take too great a risk and/or engage in unethical behavior to

Table 12.13
Merck Performance (Balanced) Scorecard, Chief Executive Officer

	TARGET POINTS
Financial	60
Revenue vs. Plan	
Earnings Per Share vs. Plan	
Value of Growth (e.g., ROI vs. plan)	
Customer	14
Merck Customer Service Level (% orders delivered on time)	
Merck Trust & Value Customer Survey	
Key Business Drivers	16
Cost Structure (operating expense vs. plan)	
Revenue Growth in High Priority Areas	
Culture (high performance, sustainable)	10
Employee Culture Survey	
Total	100

SOURCE: Proxy Statement, Merck & Co., Inc., April 14, 2014, www.merck.com/finance/proxy/pr2014.pdf.

achieve those objectives, which can come back to do great harm to the company over time. Citibank's scorecard for its top 50 executives is weighted 70% toward financial objectives (profitability, expense management, use of capital, risk) and 30% toward nonfinancial (in the short-term) objectives (set strategic direction, strong risk and controls management, strong personnel management, enhance relations with external stakeholders, including shareholders). The highest possible performance score is 100%, while the lowest is minus 40%. The hope is that by linking pay incentives to this broader set of performance objectives, not just to financial goals as in the past, Citigroup will achieve better financial performance over time and achieve it in a less risky manner. Nobody wants to go through another financial industry meltdown and this is one part of the plan to avoid that. Similarly, but using more pointed language, Barclays has told its employees to act with integrity or leave. (See the Integrity in Action box.)

Finally, there is pressure from regulators and shareholders to better link pay and performance. The U.S. Securities and Exchange Commission (SEC) requires companies to report compensation levels for the five highest paid executives and the company's performance relative to that of competitors over a five-year period. In 2006, the SEC put additional rules into effect that require better disclosure of the value of executive perquisites and retirement benefits. In 2010, the Dodd-Frank Wall Street Reform and Consumer Protection Act was signed into law in the United States. Although its focus is primarily on financial institutions, Dodd-Frank added Section 14A to the Securities and Exchange, which added new requirements for public companies broadly.[77] For example, it requires that shareholders have a "say on pay," meaning that they have the right to a (nonbinding) vote on executive pay plans. Dodd-Frank also requires that firms disclose the ratio of the pay of the top executive to that of rank and file employees. Companies, under pressure from regulators and investors, have also increasingly adopted policies that allow them to "clawback" (i.e., "get back") compensation paid to executives who are later found to have increased their pay by engaging in behaviors detrimental to companies and the economy.

Barclays Tells Employees: Behave Ethically or Leave

A few years ago, Barclays was implicated in scandals, including rigging interest rates and selling insurance to mortgage borrowers that they did not need. The U.S. Securities and Exchange Commission concluded that there were cultural "deficiencies" at the bank. Since then, its leadership has been replaced. Its new chief executive, Antony Jenkins, announced that the bank's 140,000 employees would not only need to sign a new code of conduct, but also now be paid differently. Instead of being paid only based on their production as in the past, they will now, as Jenkins puts it, be paid based "not just on what we deliver, but on how we deliver it."

The how part will be based on an evaluation of how well the following five values were respected in achieving results: respect, integrity, service, excellence, and stewardship. Jenkins had a clear message for employees who did not accept the new Barclays: "Barclays is not the place for you." U.S. recruiters suggested that these changes have caused some brokers to heed Jenkins' advice and move to other firms and that recruiting new brokers could also become more of a challenge.

DISCUSSION QUESTIONS

1. What does Barclays hope to achieve by its new pay system where pay is based not only on results but on how those results are achieved? What do you think will be the actual results of the new system?

2. How serious of a concern do you think it is that the new pay system puts Barclays at risk of losing people who fit the old system better? Should Barclays take steps to retain those employees?

SOURCES: Corrie Driebusch, "Barclays Advisers' New Performance Metric: Their Behavior," *The Wall Street Journal,* February 13, 2014, p. C1; "Barclays Boss Tells Staff 'Sign Up' to Ethics or Leave," *BBC News,* January 17, 2013, www.bbc.com.

Regulators in a number of countries have also sought to limit the size of bonus payments in hopes of reducing the incentive to engage in behaviors such as excessive risk taking, which have proved detrimental in the past. See the "Competing through Globalization" box for an example from Europe.

Large retirement fund investors such as TIAA-CREF and CalPERS have proposed guidelines to better ensure that boards of directors act in shareholders' best interests when making executive pay decisions, rather than being beholden to management. Some of the governance practices believed to be related to director independence from management (Dodd-Frank has similar provisions) are shown in Table 12.14. More detailed analyses of board governance practices are available from Institutional Shareholder Services.[78] In addition, when a firm's future is at risk, the board may well need to demonstrate its independence from management by taking dramatic action, which may include removing the chief executive.

Process and Context Issues

In Chapter 11 we discussed the importance of process issues such as communication and employee participation. Earlier in the present chapter we discussed the importance of fairness, both distributive and procedural. Significant differences in how such issues are handled can be found both across and within organizations, suggesting that organizations have considerable discretion in this aspect of compensation management.[79] As such, it represents another strategic opportunity to distinguish one's organization from the competition.

LO 12-6

Explain the importance of process issues such as communication in compensation management.

COMPETING THROUGH GLOBALIZATION

European Banks Cope with Bonus Caps

The European Banking Authority has released new guidelines that would no longer exempt smaller banks and some large asset managers from caps on bonuses. These caps limit bonuses to no more than 100% of fixed pay (i.e., salaries). The intent of these caps is to reduce the incentive for banks and bankers to take unnecessary risks of the sort now seen as responsible for the Global Financial Crisis of a few years ago. Banks, however, have noted that such rules encourage banks to pay higher salaries, which not only increases their fixed costs (making them more prone to risk), but also limits their ability to recognize, incentivize, and reward employees for strong performance. There is also a fear that some banks could seek to avoid the caps by moving to countries outside of the European Union. In the United Kingdom, Europe's largest financial center, opposition to the codes is especially strong. The UK's largest five banks already cut bonus pools by over 1 billion pounds last year. Banks in the UK have been a frequent target of politicians with the *Financial Times* observing: "Competition between the political parties over who can be toughest on bankers has intensified ahead of [the upcoming] election." In the United States, while there were restrictions on pay following the Global Financial Crisis, there is now no widespread restriction on bonuses. However, regulators in the United States are aware of what Europe is doing.

DISCUSSION QUESTIONS

1. Are caps on bonuses good for banks, good for European economies, and good for consumers? Explain. Discuss both potential intended and unintended consequences.
2. Should the United States consider caps on bonuses in banks and related institutions?
3. What is the role of self-regulation by banks in responding to their risk-taking cultures? Consider the example of Barclays discussed in the "Integrity in Action" box in this chapter.

SOURCES: Laura Noonan, "UK's Top 5 Banks Slash Bonus Pools by more than £1 Billion," *Financial Times,* April 6, 2015, www.ft.com; David Wighton, "Many More EU Firms Face Caps on Bonuses," *The Wall Street Journal*, March 5, 2015, p. C3; Ben Moshinsky, "Too-Big-to-Fail May Lead to U.S. Bank Pay Rules: Hoenig," *Bloomberg Business*, December 9, 2014, www.bloomberg.com.

EMPLOYEE PARTICIPATION IN DECISION MAKING

Consider employee participation in decision making and its potential consequences. Involvement in the design and implementation of pay policies has been linked to higher pay satisfaction and job satisfaction, presumably because employees have a better understanding of and greater commitment to the policy when they are involved.[80]

What about the effects on productivity? Agency theory provides some insight. The delegation of decision making by a principal to an agent creates agency costs because employees may not act in the best interests of top management. In addition, the more agents there are, the higher the monitoring costs.[81] Together, these suggest that delegation of decision making can be very costly.

On the other hand, agency theory suggests that monitoring would be less costly and more effective if performed by employees because they have knowledge about the workplace and behavior of fellow employees that managers do not have. As such, the right compensation system might encourage self-monitoring and peer monitoring.[82]

Researchers have suggested that two general factors are critical to encouraging such monitoring: monetary incentives (outcome-oriented contracts in agency theory) and an environment that fosters trust and cooperation. This environment, in turn, is a function of employment security, group cohesiveness, and individual rights for employees—in other words, respect for and commitment to employees.[83]

Table 12.14
Guidelines for Board of Directors Independence and Leadership

1. **Majority of independent directors:** At a minimum, a majority of the board consists of directors who are independent. Boards should strive to obtain board composition made up of a substantial majority of independent directors.
2. **Independent executive session:** Independent directors meet periodically (at least once a year) alone in an executive session, without the CEO. The independent board chair or lead (or presiding) independent director should preside over this meeting.
3. **Independent director definition:** Each company should disclose in its annual proxy statement the definition of "independence" relied upon by its board.
4. **Independent board chairperson:** The board should be chaired by an independent director. The CEO and chair roles should only be combined in very limited circumstances; in these situations, the board should provide a written statement in the proxy materials discussing why the combined role is in the best interest of shareowners, and it should name a lead independent director to fulfill duties that are consistent with those provided in other company material.
5. **Examine separate chair/CEO positions:** When selecting a new chief executive officer, boards should reexamine the traditional combination of the "chief executive" and "chair" positions.
6. **Board role of retiring CEO:** Generally, a company's retiring CEO should not continue to serve as a director on the board and at the very least be prohibited from sitting on any of the board committees.
7. **Board access to management:** The board should have a process in place by which all directors can have access to senior management.
8. **Independent board committees:** Committees who perform the audit, director nomination, and executive compensation functions should consist entirely of independent directors.
9. **Board oversight:** The full board is responsible for the oversight function on behalf of shareowners. Should the board decide to have other committees (e.g., executive committee) in addition to those required by law, the duties and membership of such committees should be fully disclosed.
10. **Board resources:** The board, through its committees, should have access to adequate resources to provide independent counsel advice, or other tools that allow the board to effectively perform its duties on behalf of shareowners.

SOURCE: "Global Principles of Accountable Corporate Governance," The California Public Employees9 Retirement System, August 18, 2008.

In any case, a survey of organizations found that only 11% of employees always or often participated in compensation design teams. Participation by managers was better, but still the exception (32%).[84]

COMMUNICATION

Another important process issue is communication.[85] Earlier, we spoke of its importance in the administration of merit pay, both from the perspective of procedural fairness and as a means of obtaining the maximum impact from a merit pay program.[86] More generally, a change in any part of the compensation system is likely to give rise to employee concerns. Rumors and assumptions based on poor or incomplete information are always an issue in administering compensation, partly because of its importance to employee economic security and well-being. Therefore, in making any changes, it is crucial to determine how best to communicate reasons for the changes to employees. Some organizations rely on video messages from the chief executive officer to communicate the rationale for major changes. Brochures and/or websites that include scenarios for typical employees are sometimes used, as are focus group sessions where small groups of employees are interviewed to obtain feedback about concerns that can be addressed in later communication programs. Ultimately, however, most pay-related communications come through individual discussions with one's supervisor, still ahead of the company website, email, and discussions with the human resources department.[87]

PAY AND PROCESS: INTERTWINED EFFECTS

The preceding discussion treats process issues such as participation as factors that may facilitate the success of pay programs. At least one commentator, however, has described an even more important role for process factors in determining employee performance:

> Worker participation apparently helps make alternative compensation plans . . . work better—and also has beneficial effects of its own . . . . It appears that changing the way workers are treated may boost productivity more than changing the way they are paid.[88]

This suggestion raises a broader question: How important are pay decisions, per se, relative to other human resource practices? Although it may not be terribly useful to attempt to disentangle closely intertwined programs, it is important to reinforce the notion that human resource programs, even those as powerful as compensation systems, do not work alone.

Consider gainsharing programs. As described earlier, pay is often only one component of such programs. (See Table 12.10.) How important are the nonpay components?[89] There is ample evidence that gainsharing programs that rely almost exclusively on the monetary component can have substantial effects on productivity.[90] On the other hand, a study of an automotive parts plant found that adding a participation component (monthly meetings with management to discuss the gainsharing plan and ways to increase productivity) to a gainsharing pay incentive plan raised productivity. In a related study, employees were asked about the factors that motivated them to engage in active participation (such as suggestion systems). Employees reported that the desire to earn a monetary bonus was much less important than a number of nonpay factors, particularly the desire for influence and control in how their work was done.[91] A third study reported that productivity and profitability were both enhanced by the addition of employee participation in decisions, beyond the improvement derived from monetary incentives such as gainsharing.[92]

Organization Strategy and Compensation Strategy: A Question of Fit

LO 12-7
List the major factors to consider in matching the pay strategy to the organization's strategy.

Although much of our focus has been on the general, or average, effects of different pay programs, it is also useful to think in terms of matching pay strategies to organization strategies.[93] To take an example from medicine, using the same medical treatment regardless of the symptoms and diagnosis would be foolish. In choosing a pay strategy, one must consider how effectively it will further the organization's overall business strategy. Consider again the findings reported in Table 12.12. The average effect of moving from a pay strategy with below-average variability in pay to one with above-average variability is an increase in return on assets of almost two percentage points (from 5.2% to 7.1%). But in some organizations, the increase could be smaller. In fact, greater variability in pay could contribute to a lower return on assets in some organizations. In other organizations, greater variability in pay could contribute to increases in return on assets of greater than two percentage points. Obviously, being able to tell where variable pay works and where it does not could have substantial consequences.

In Chapter 2 we discussed directional business strategies, two of which were growth (internal or external) and concentration ("sticking to the knitting"). How should

PAY STRATEGY DIMENSIONS	ORGANIZATION STRATEGY	
	CONCENTRATION	GROWTH
Risk sharing (variable pay)	Low	High
Time orientation	Short-term	Long-term
Pay level (short run)	Above market	Below market
Pay level (long-run potential)	Below market	Above market
Benefits level	Above market	Below market
Centralization of pay decisions	Centralized	Decentralized
Pay unit of analysis	Job	Skills

Table 12.15
Matching Pay Strategy and Organization Strategy

SOURCES: Adapted from L. R. Gomez-Mejia and D. B. Balkin, *Compensation, Organizational Strategy, and Firm Performance* (Cincinnati: South-Western, 1992), Appendix 4b; and L. R. Gomez-Mejia, P. Berrone, and M. Franco-Santos. *Compensation and Organizational Performance* (Armonk, NY: M.E. Sharpe 2010), Appendix 3.2.

compensation strategies differ according to whether an organization follows a growth strategy or a concentration strategy? Table 12.15 provides some suggested matches. Basically, a growth strategy's emphasis on innovation, risk taking, and new markets is linked to a pay strategy that shares risk with employees but also gives them the opportunity for high future earnings by having them share in whatever success the organization has.[94] This means relatively low levels of fixed compensation in the short run but the use of bonuses and stock options, for example, that can pay off handsomely in the long run. Stock options have been described as the pay program "that built Silicon Valley," having been used by companies such as Apple, Microsoft, and others.[95] When such companies become successful, everyone from top managers to secretaries can become millionaires if they own stock. Growth organizations are also thought to benefit from a less bureaucratic orientation, in the sense of having more decentralization and flexibility in pay decisions and in recognizing individual skills, rather than being constrained by job or grade classification systems. On the other hand, concentration-oriented organizations are thought to require a very different set of pay practices by virtue of their lower rate of growth, more stable workforce, and greater need for consistency and standardization in pay decisions. As noted earlier, Microsoft has eliminated stock options in favor of stock grants to its employees, in part because it is not the growth company it once was.

A LOOK BACK

In this chapter, we discussed the potential advantages and disadvantages of different types of incentive or pay-for-performance plans. We also saw that these pay plans can have both intended and unintended consequences. Designing a pay-for-performance strategy typically seeks to balance the pros and cons of different plans and reduce the chance of unintended consequences. To an important degree, pay strategy will depend on the particular goals and strategy of the organization and its units. For example, Microsoft determined that its pay strategy needed to be revised (less emphasis on stock options, more on stock grants) to support a change in its business strategy and to recognize the slower-paced growth of its stock price. At the beginning of this chapter, we saw that many organizations are working to link pay to performance and reduce fixed labor costs.

QUESTIONS

1. Does money motivate? Use the theories and examples discussed in this chapter to address this question.
2. Think of a job that you have held. Design an incentive plan. What would be the potential advantages and disadvantages of your plan? If your money was invested in the company, would you adopt the plan?

SUMMARY

Our focus in this chapter has been on the design and administration of programs that recognize employee contributions to the organization's success. These programs vary as to whether they link pay to individual, group, or organization performance. Often, it is not so much a choice of one program or the other as it is a choice between different combinations of programs that seek to balance individual, group, and organization objectives.

Wages, bonuses, and other types of pay have an important influence on an employee's standard of living. This carries at least two important implications. First, pay can be a powerful motivator. An effective pay strategy can substantially promote an organization's success; conversely, a poorly conceived pay strategy can have detrimental effects. Second, the importance of pay means that employees care a great deal about the fairness of the pay process. A recurring theme is that pay programs must be explained and administered in such a way that employees understand their underlying rationale and believe it is fair.

The fact that organizations differ in their business and human resource strategies suggests that the most effective compensation strategy may differ from one organization to another. Although benchmarking programs against the competition is informative, what succeeds in some organizations may not be a good idea for others. The balanced scorecard suggests the need for organizations to decide what their key objectives are and use pay to support them.

KEY TERMS

Incentive effect, 498
Expectancy theory, 498
Principal, 499
Agent, 499
Sorting effect, 502

Merit pay, 505
Merit bonus, 505
Merit increase
   grid, 505
Profit sharing, 510

Stock options, 514
Employee stock ownership plan
   (ESOP), 515
Gainsharing, 516

DISCUSSION QUESTIONS

1. To compete more effectively, your organization is considering a profit sharing plan to increase employee effort and to encourage employees to think like owners. What are the potential advantages and disadvantages of such a plan? Would the profit sharing plan have the same impact on all types of employees? Is the size of your organization an important consideration? Why? What alternative pay programs should be considered?
2. Gainsharing plans have often been used in manufacturing settings but can also be applied in service organizations. How could performance standards be developed for gainsharing plans in hospitals, banks, insurance companies, and so forth?
3. Your organization has two business units. One unit is a long-established manufacturer of a product that competes on price and has not been subject to many technological innovations. The other business unit is just being started. It has no products yet, but it is working on developing a new technology for testing the effects of drugs on people via simulation instead of through lengthy clinical trials. Would you recommend that the two business units have the same pay programs for recognizing individual contributions? Why?

4. Throughout the chapter, we have seen many examples of companies making changes to how they pay for performance. Do you believe the changes at these companies make sense? What are the potential payoffs and pitfalls of their new pay strategies?

SELF-ASSESSMENT EXERCISE

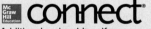

Additional assignable self-assessments available in Connect.

Pay is only one type of incentive that can motivate you to perform well and contribute to your satisfaction at work. This survey will help you understand what motivates you at work. Consider each aspect of work and rate its importance to you, using the following scale: 5 = very important, 4 = somewhat important, 3 = neutral, 2 = somewhat unimportant, 1 = very unimportant.

Salary or wages	1	2	3	4	5
Cash bonuses	1	2	3	4	5
Boss's management style	1	2	3	4	5
Location of workplace	1	2	3	4	5
Commute	1	2	3	4	5
Job security	1	2	3	4	5
Opportunity for advancement	1	2	3	4	5

Work environment	1	2	3	4	5
Level of independence in job	1	2	3	4	5
Level of teamwork required for job	1	2	3	4	5
Other (enter your own):					
_____	1	2	3	4	5
_____	1	2	3	4	5
_____	1	2	3	4	5

Which aspects of work received a score of 5? A score of 4? These are the ones you believe motivate you to perform well and make you happy in your job. Which aspects of work received a score of 1 or 2? These are least likely to motivate you. Is pay the only way to motivate you?

SOURCE: Based on the "Job Assessor" found at www.salarymonster.com, accessed August 2002.

EXERCISING STRATEGY

Pay for Performance for Educators

The Chinese government wished to reduce the number of accidental deaths in the country. It set a target of 2.5% of the population per year. Most of China's provinces adopted policies that linked career advancement among state officials in the provinces to meeting the 2.5% target. Eight years later, the accidental death rate was lower by one-half. However, upon closer inspection, there were troubling facts. For example, a death could be kept from being coded as accidental if the victim did not die within 7 days. So, keeping the person alive for 8 days or more was a focus. This and other facts led researchers evaluating the program to conclude that "manipulation" played a major role, meaning that actual improvements in safety were smaller than claimed. Similarly, in the United States, *Chicago Magazine* alleges that the Chicago police department reduces crime rates by re-classifying incidents as noncriminal. In education, many states now link educator evaluations and pay to student scores on standardized tests. Although how well such systems work depends on their design and execution, potential pitfalls clearly exist. For example, 11 educators in Atlanta were recently convicted of racketeering for their roles in manipulating test scores. In one school, for example, it was reported that a principal wore gloves while changing student answers to help them and the school district obtain higher scores.

QUESTIONS

1. Is it possible to successfully use pay for performance in education? What are the reasons to use it and what are the potential pitfalls? How can the latter be avoided?
2. Refer to the Integrity in Action box in this chapter, which describes Barclays' new pay for performance system. Also, refer to our discussion of measuring performance in terms of outcomes and/or behaviors. Apply these concepts and examples and suggest how pay for performance for educators might be better designed.

SOURCES: E. Porter, "Relying on Tests in Grading Teacher," *The New York Times,* March 25, 2015, p. B1; A. Blinder, "Atlanta Educators Are Convicted of Racketeering," *The New York Times,* April 2, 2015, p. A12.

MANAGING PEOPLE

ESOPs: Who Benefits?

Mandy Cabot wants to make sure the shoemaking business that she and her husband built over the past 20 years remains in good hands after they're gone. The 58-year-old co-founder of Dansko, a West Grove, PA, company with more than $150 million in annual sales, says she fears that selling to a competitor, or a private-equity firm, would result in layoffs or other cost-cutting measures.

So last February, the couple transferred ownership of the business to its 180 employees. By "keeping it in the family" and giving workers a real stake in its future, Ms. Cabot says she hopes the company will keep going strong for years to come. "This is our baby, but at some point we have to cease being parents and become grandparents," she adds.

Ms. Cabot, who launched Dansko in 1990 by selling shoes from the back of a Volvo station wagon, says the tax benefits associated with employee stock ownership enabled the S corporation to manage the long-term debt of buying out the couple's ownership stake. But, she adds, "It's not some tax dodge."

Known as employee stock-ownership plans, or ESOPs, the move is being embraced by smaller firms, especially those struggling to find buyers during the weak economy. Under typical plans, an owner's interest in a business is bought out, in part or in whole—often through a bank loan—with the stock being held in trust. Employees then cash in their shares as they retire.

Michael Keeling, president of the ESOP Association, a Washington lobby group, argues, "A company's success isn't just driven by the brilliance of the CEO, but also by its employees, and more owners feel [their employees] deserve something more for that."

This week, a bipartisan group of lawmakers introduced a bill to encourage employee-ownership plans. But critics of the plans say owners who are looking for an easy exit are simply spreading the risks of business ownership by convincing employees to gamble their retirement savings. Andrew Stumpff, University of Michigan, says it's bad enough to risk your retirement savings in a single company. But it's even worse if that company is your employer, he says. "If the company fails, you lose your savings and your job." That risk is very real, he adds, citing Enron, WorldCom and Lehman Brothers as examples of high-profile failures at shared-ownership companies, especially Enron Corp. where workers lost their savings.

The real attraction for owners, opponents say, is generous tax breaks that shelter capital gains and dividends tied to the plans.

As of 2011, there were an estimated 10,900 employee-owned businesses across the country, a 12% increase from 2007 and a record high dating back to the mid-1970s, when the plans first appeared, according to the National Center for Employee Ownership. Nearly all of the employee-owned businesses have fewer than 500 workers. Some 10 million employees are currently enrolled in these plans, representing more than $860 billion in assets, the group estimates.

Norman Stein, Drexel University, says employee ownership under the ESOP model causes more harm than good. Many of the plans are based on a bloated assessment of the value of the businesses. Many workers who are participating in the plans are left holding overvalued shares, long after the original owner has cashed out: "I'm not against employees owning some stock in their employer, but not if it's tied to a retirement plan," he says. "It's a troubling trend."

Separate studies by Harvard University and Rutgers, as well as by the National Bureau of Economic Research, have found that businesses with shared-ownership plans fared better during the recession than more traditionally structured firms, including fewer layoffs, higher productivity and stronger employee loyalty.

Dawn Huston, 31, started working at Dansko 11 years ago, sorting shoes for delivery. Now a warehouse processor, she says the idea of owning a piece of the company made her nervous at first—though she wasn't worried about her retirement savings, since the company offers a separate 401(k) plan, she adds. Over the past year, she's begun referring to Dansko as "our company." "I feel like they consider us family and it feels like a family," she says of the switch to employee ownership.

Adele Connors, 60, co-founder of Adworkshop, a Lake Placid, NY, marketing agency, says a move to employee ownership "really changed the culture of our company" with workers now being "more engaged." Kelly Frady, 43, an account supervisor at Adworkshop, says the agency's employee-ownership plan has fostered a team spirit among its staff. "Everyone knows that you do well and your stock will rise," she says. "It's a driving factor in making the company succeed in the long term."

Kim Jordan, who co-founded the New Belgium Brewing Co. with her husband in 1991, says employee ownership ensures that the company's values and culture will remain intact—including its commitment to sustainable farming and an environmentally friendly production process. In December, she extended full ownership of the Fort Collins, CO, brewery to its 480 employees.

"We've always tried to involve our people in the running of the business," she says. The goal, she says, isn't just to reward employees, but also to foster innovation by creating a company culture where workers think more like entrepreneurs.

QUESTIONS

1. Is an ESOP good for employees?
2. Does an ESOP motivate employees "better"?
3. What happens to employees' retirement income if they are at an ESOP company that runs into financial problems? What happens to the same employees, if instead, they work at a non-ESOP company that runs into financial problems?

SOURCE: Angus Loten, "Founders Cash Out, but Do Workers Gain?" *Wall Street Journal,* April 17, 2013.

HR IN SMALL BUSINESS

Employees Own Bob's Red Mill

Headquartered in Portland, Oregon, Bob's Red Mill Natural Foods sells a variety of whole-grain flours and mixes, specializing in gluten-free products. The "Bob" of the company's name is Bob Moore, the founder and president. In 2010, more than 30 years after he started the business, Moore called his 200 employees together and announced that he was giving them the company. As a retirement plan for them, he had set up an employee stock ownership plan, placing the company's stock in a trust fund. All employees who had been with the company at least three years were immediately fully vested in the plan. As employees retire, they will receive cash for their shares.

Watching the company's stock rise in their retirement plan is not the only financial incentive for employees of Bob's Red Mill. Fifteen years ago, the company established a profit-sharing plan. Chief financial officer John Wagner gives employees a weekly sales update, which they can use to estimate profits and determine their share.

The numbers have been mostly good during the past two decades. When Wagner joined the company in 1993, there were just 28 employees generating sales of $3.2 million. Under Wagner's guidance, the company began participating in trade shows, attracting the interest of health food stores, food distributors, and later on, supermarket chains. The company's market expanded from a few states to cover North America and some international markets. The company reports that its revenues have grown at rates between 20% and 30% in the years since 2004.

Along the way, Moore and his employees have been unwavering in their dedication to the company and its mission of providing foods that make America healthier. Ten years after the business started, a fire caused by arson destroyed the mill, but Moore had it rebuilt, and the company now runs a 15-acre production facility, operating in three shifts, six days a week.

Why did Moore give his company to his employees on his 81st birthday rather than selling it to one of the many parties who have expressed an interest in buying? For Moore, the answer is all about his employees and their commitment to the company. He told a reporter, "These people are far too good at their jobs for me to just sell [the business]." Employees return the praise. For example, Bo Thomas, maintenance superintendent, said, "It just shows how much faith and trust Bob has in us. For all of us, it's more than just a job."

QUESTIONS

1. Which types of incentive pay are described in this case? Are these based on individual, group, or company performance?

2. Would you expect the motivational impact of stock ownership or profit sharing to be different at a small company like Bob's Red Mill than in a large corporation? Explain.

3. Suppose Bob's Red Mill brought you in as a consultant to review the company's total compensation. Explain why you would or would not recommend that the company add other forms of incentive pay, and identify any additional forms of compensation you would recommend for the company's employees.

SOURCES: Corporate website, "About Us," www.bobsredmill.com, accessed June 7, 2015; Karen E. Klein, "ESOPs on the Rise among Small Businesses," *Bloomberg Businessweek,* April 26, 2010, www.businessweek.com; Dana Tims, "Founder of Bob's Red Mill Natural Foods Transfers Business to Employees," *Oregon Live,* February 16, 2010, http://blog.oregonlive.com; and Christine Brozyna, "American Heart: Owner of Multi-Million Dollar Company Hands Over Business to Employees," *ABC News,* February 18, 2010, http://abcnews.go.com.

NOTES

1. We draw freely in this chapter on several literature reviews: B. Gerhart and G. T. Milkovich, "Employee Compensation: Research and Practice," in *Handbook of Industrial and Organizational Psychology,* vol. 3, 2nd ed., ed. M. D. Dunnette and L. M. Hough (Palo Alto, CA: Consulting Psychologists Press, 1992); B. Gerhart and S. L. Rynes, *Compensation: Theory, Evidence, and Strategic Implications* (Thousand Oaks, CA: Sage, 2003); B. Gerhart, "Compensation Strategy and Organization Performance," in S. L. Rynes and B. Gerhart, eds., *Compensation in Organizations: Current Research and Practice* (San Francisco: Jossey-Bass, 2000), pp. 151–94; B. Gerhart, S. L. Rynes, and I. S. Fulmer, "Compensation," *Academy of Management Annals* 3 (2009); and Barry Gerhart and Meiyu Fang, "Pay for (Individual) Performance: Issues, Claims, Evidence and the Role of Sorting Effects," *Human Resource Management Review,* 24 (2014), pp. 41–52.

2. B. Gerhart and G. T. Milkovich, "Organizational Differences in Managerial Compensation and Financial Performance," *Academy of Management Journal* 33 (1990), pp. 663–91.

3. E. Deci and R. Ryan, *Intrinsic Motivation and Self-Determination in Human Behavior* (New York: Plenum, 1985); A. Kohn, "Why Incentive Plans Cannot Work," *Harvard Business Review,* September–October 1993.

4. B. Gerhart and M. Fang, "Pay, Intrinsic Motivation, Extrinsic Motivation, Performance, and Creativity in the Workplace: Revisiting Long-Held Beliefs," *Annual Review of Organizational Psychology and Organizational Behavior* 2 (2015), pp. 489–521; R. Eisenberger and J. Cameron, "Detrimental Effects of Reward: Reality or Myth?" *American Psychologist* 51 (1996), pp. 1153–66; S. L. Rynes, B. Gerhart, and L. Parks, "Personnel Psychology: Performance Evaluation and

Compensation," *Annual Review of Psychology* (2005); M. Fang and B. Gerhart, "Does Pay for Performance Diminish Intrinsic Interest? A Workplace Test Using Cognitive Evaluation Theory and the Attraction-Selection-Attrition Model," *International Journal of Human Resource Management*, 23 (2012), pp. 1176–1196; M. Gagné and E. L. Deci, "Self-Determination Theory and Work Motivation," Journal of Organizational Behavior 26, pp. 331–362; G. E. Ledford, Jr., M. Fang, and B. Gerhart, "Negative Effects of Extrinsic Rewards on Intrinsic Motivation: More Smoke than Fire," *World at Work Journal* (forthcoming); K. Byron, and S. Khazanchi, "Rewards and Creative Performance: A Meta-analytic Test of Theoretically Derived Hypotheses," *Psychological Bulletin,* 138 (2012), pp. 809–830.

5. P. C. Cerasoli, J. M. Nicklin, and M. T. Ford, "Intrinsic Motivation and Extrinsic Incentives Jointly Predict Performance: A 40-Year Meta-Analysis," *Psychological Bulletin* 140 (2014), pp. 980–1008; M. Fang and B. Gerhart, "Does Pay for Performance Diminish Intrinsic Interest? A Workplace Test Using Cognitive Evaluation Theory and the Attraction-Selection-Attrition Model," *International Journal of Human Resource Management* 23 (2012), pp. 1176–96; A. A. Grandey, N. W. Chi, and J. A. Diamond, "Show Me the Money! Do Financial Rewards for Performance Enhance or Undermine the Satisfaction from Emotional Labor?" *Personnel Psychology* 66, no. 3 (2013), pp. 569–612.

6. Y. Garbers and U. Konradt, "The Effect of Financial Incentives on Performance: A Quantitative Review of Individual and Team-Based Financial Incentives," *Journal of Occupational and Organizational Psychology* 87 (2014), pp. 102–37; D. G. Jenkins, Jr., A. Mitra, N. Gupta, and J. D. Shaw, "Are Financial Incentives Related to Performance? A Meta-analytic Review of Empirical Research," *Journal of Applied Psychology,* 83 (1998), pp. 777–787; Gerhart and Fang, "Pay for (Individual) Performance: Issues, Claims, Evidence and the Role of Sorting Effects."

7. D. R. Dalton, M. A. Hitt, S. T. Certo, and C. M. Dalton, "The Fundamental Agency Problem and Its Mitigation: Independence, Equity, and the Market for Corporate Control," Academy of Management Annals 1 (2007), pp. 1–64; R. A. Lambert and D. F. Larcker, "Executive Compensation, Corporate Decision Making, and Shareholder Wealth," in Executive Compensation, ed. F. Foulkes (Boston: Harvard Business School Press, 1989), pp. 287–309.

8. L. R. Gomez-Mejia, H. Tosi, and T. Hinkin, "Managerial Control, Performance, and Executive Compensation," *Academy of Management Journal* 30 (1987), pp. 51–70; H. L. Tosi Jr. and L. R. Gomez-Mejia, "The Decoupling of CEO Pay and Performance: An Agency Theory Perspective," *Administrative Science Quarterly* 34 (1989), pp. 169–89.

9. K. M. Eisenhardt, "Agency Theory: An Assessment and Review," *Academy of Management Review* 14 (1989), pp. 57–74.

10. R. E. Hoskisson, M. A. Hitt, and C. W. L. Hill, "Managerial Incentives and Investment in R&D in Large Multiproduct Firms," *Organizational Science* 4 (1993), pp. 325–41; M. Bloom and G. T. Milkovich, "Relationships among Risk, Incentive Pay, and Organizational Performance," *Academy of Management Journal* 41 (1998), pp. 283–97.

11. A. J. Nyberg, I. S. Fulmer, B. Gerhart, and M. A. Carpenter, "Agency Theory Revisited: CEO Return and Shareholder Interest Alignment," *Academy of Management Journal* 53 (2010), pp. 1029–49.

12. Eisenhardt, "Agency Theory."

13. Ibid.; E. J. Conlon and J. M. Parks, "Effects of Monitoring and Tradition on Compensation Arrangements: An Experiment with Principal–Agent Dyads," *Academy of Management Journal* 33 (1990), pp. 603–22; K. M. Eisenhardt, "Agency- and

Institutional-Theory Explanations: The Case of Retail Sales Compensation," *Academy of Management Journal* 31 (1988), pp. 488–511; Gerhart and Milkovich, "Employee Compensation."; J. Devaro and F. A. Kurtulus, "An Empirical Analysis of Risk, Incentives and the Delegation of Worker Authority," *Industrial and Labor Relations Review,* 63 (2010), pp. 641–661.

14. G. T. Milkovich, J. Hannon, and B. Gerhart, "The Effects of Research and Development Intensity on Managerial Compensation in Large Organizations," *Journal of High Technology Management Research* 2 (1991), pp. 133–50; J. Devaro and F. A. Kurtulus, "An Empirical Analysis of Risk, Incentives and the Delegation of Worker Authority," *Industrial and Labor Relations Review,* 63 (2010), pp. 641–661.

15. Vera Brenĉiĉ and John Brian Norris, "On-The-Job Tasks and Performance Pay: A Vacancy-Level Analysis," *Industrial and Labor Relations Review,* 63 (2010), pp. 511–544. See also the discussion of performance reliability in B. Gerhart and S.L. Rynes, *Compensation* (2003).

16. G. T. Milkovich and A. K. Wigdor, *Pay for Performance* (Washington, DC: National Academy Press, 1991); Gerhart and Milkovich, "Employee Compensation"; Gerhart and Rynes, *Compensation: Theory, Evidence, and Strategic Implications;* A. Nyberg, "Retaining Your High Performers: Moderators of the Performance-Job Satisfaction-Voluntary Turnover Relationship," *Journal of Applied Psychology* 95 (2010), pp. 440–53; C. O. Trevor, G. Reilly, and B. Gerhart, "Reconsidering Pay Dispersion's Effect on the Performance of Interdependent Work: Reconciling Sorting and Pay Inequality," *Academy of Management Journal* 55 (2012), pp. 585–610; S. Carnahan, R. Agarwal, and B. A. Campbell, "Heterogeneity in Turnover: The Effect of Relative Compensation Dispersion of Firms on the Mobility and Entrepreneurship of Extreme Performers," *Strategic Management Journal,* 33 (2012), pp. 1411–1430.

17. C. Trevor, B. Gerhart, and J. W. Boudreau, "Voluntary Turnover and Job Performance: Curvilinearity and the Moderating Influences of Salary Growth and Promotions," *Journal of Applied Psychology* 82 (1997), pp. 44–61; C. B. Cadsby, F. Song, and F. Tapon, "Sorting and Incentive Effects of Pay-for-Performance: An Experimental Investigation," *Academy of Management Journal* 50 (2007), pp. 387–405; A. Salamin and P. W. Hom, "In Search of the Elusive U-Shaped Performance-Turnover Relationship: Are High Performing Swiss Bankers More Liable to Quit?" *Journal of Applied Psychology* 90 (2005), pp. 1204–16; J. D. Shaw, and N. Gupta, "Pay System Characteristics and Quit Patterns of Good, Average, and Poor Performers," *Personnel Psychology* 60 (2007), pp. 903–28; J. D. Shaw, B. R. Dineen, R. Fang, R. F. Vellella, "Employee-Organization Exchange Relationships, HRM practices, and Quit Rates of Good and Poor Performers," *Academy of Management Journal,* 52 (2009), pp. 1016–1033.

18. B. D. Blume, R. S. Rubin, and T. T. Baldwin, "Who Is Attracted to an Organization Using a Forced Distribution Performance Management System?" *Human Resource Management Journal* 23, no. 4 (2013), pp. 360–78; T. Dohmen and A. Falk, "Performance Pay and Multidimensional Sorting: Productivity, Preferences, and Gender," *American Economic Review* 101, no. 2 (2011), pp. 556–90; R. D. Bretz, R. A. Ash, and G. F. Dreher, "Do People Make the Place? An Examination of the Attraction–Selection–Attrition Hypothesis," *Personnel Psychology* 42 (1989), pp. 561–81; T. A. Judge and R. D. Bretz, "Effect of Values on Job Choice Decisions," *Journal of Applied Psychology* 77 (1992), pp. 261–71; D. M. Cable and T. A. Judge, "Pay Performances and Job Search Decisions: A Person– Organization Fit Perspective," *Personnel Psychology* 47 (1994), pp. 317–48.

19. G. T. Milkovich, J. M. Newman, and B. Gerhart, *Compensation,* 11th ed. (New York: McGraw-Hill/Irwin, 2014); K. Abosch and B. Gerhart, "The Case for Differentiated Pay for Performance," World at Work Total Rewards Conference & Exhibition, 2013.

20. E. H. O'Boyle and H. Aguinis, "The Best and the Rest: Revisiting the Norm of Normality of Individual Performance," *Personnel Psychology* 65 (2012), pp. 79–119; H. Aguinis and E. O'Boyle, "Star Performers in Twenty-First Century Organizations," *Personnel Psychology* 67, no. 2 (2014), pp. 313–50; H. Aguinis, E. O'Boyle, E. Gonzalez-Mulé, and H. Joo, "Cumulative Advantage: Conductors and Insulators of Heavy-tailed Productivity Distributions and Productivity Stars," *Personnel Psychology,* 2014; K. F. Hallock, *Pay: Why People Earn What They Earn and What You Can Do Now to Make More* (Cambridge: Cambridge University Press, 2012). A key part of the argument is that performance is not normally distributed. For an alternative view of the evidence questioning whether the performance distribution is non-normal, see J. W. Beck, A. S. Beatty, and P. R. Sackett, "On the Distribution of Job Performance: The Role of Measurement Characteristics in Observed Departures from Normality," *Personnel Psychology* 67 (2014) pp. 531–66.

21. Gerhart and Fang, "Pay for (Individual) Performance: Issues, Claims, Evidence and the Role of Sorting Effects."

22. J. D. Shaw, "Pay Dispersion," *Annual Review of Organizational Psychology and Organizational Behavior* 1, no. 1 (2014), pp. 521–44; P. E. Downes and D. Choi, "Employee Reactions to Pay Dispersion: A Typology of Existing Research," *Human Resource Management Review* 24, no. 1 (2014), pp. 53–66; C. O. Trevor, G. Reilly, and B. Gerhart, "Reconsidering Pay Dispersion's Effect on the Performance of Interdependent Work: Reconciling Sorting and Pay Inequality," *Academy of Management Journal* 55 (2012), pp. 585–610; A. Bucciol, N. J. Foss, and M. Piovesan, "Pay Dispersion and Performance in Teams," PloS ONE 9(11): e112631, 2014.

23. E. E. Lawler III, *Strategic Pay* (San Francisco: Jossey-Bass, 1990); Gerhart and Milkovich, "Employee Compensation"; Gerhart and Rynes, *Compensation: Theory, Evidence, and Strategic Implications;* B. Gerhart, C. Trevor, and M. Graham, "New Directions in Employee Compensation Research" in G. R. Ferris (ed.), *Research in Personnel and Human Resources Management* (London: JAI Press, 1996), pp. 143–203; M. Beer and M. D. Cannon, "Promise and Peril in Implementing Pay-for-Performance," *Human Resource Management* 43 (2004), pp. 3–20.

24. In some cases, under exceptional circumstances, an organization may, at least temporarily, design an incentive plan to focus everyone's attention on one critical objective. For example, after the oil spill and worker fatalities in the Gulf of Mexico, BP temporarily revised its compensation program to make safety the sole factor in determining pay raises. (See G. Chazan and D. Mattioli, "BP Links Pay to Safety in Fourth Quarter," *The Wall Street Journal,* October 19, 2010.) But having a single objective is not typically advisable.

25. R. D. Bretz, G. T. Milkovich, and W. Read, "The Current State of Performance Appraisal Research and Practice," *Journal of Management* 18 (1992), pp. 321–52; R. L. Heneman, "Merit Pay Research," *Research in Personnel and Human Resource Management* 8 (1990), pp. 203–63; Milkovich and Wigdor, *Pay for Performance;* Rynes, Gerhart, and Parks, "Personnel Psychology: Performance Evaluation and Compensation." Some evidence suggests that merit pay may be more effective when reinforced by other aspects of the pay strategy and/or by leadership of supervisors. See J. H. Han, K. M. Bartol, and S. Kim, "Tightening Up the Performance–Pay Linkage: Roles of Contingent Reward

Leadership and Profit-Sharing in the Cross-Level Influence of Individual Pay-for-Performance," *Journal of Applied Psychology* 100 (2014), pp. 417–30. Other evidence suggests that merit pay may be more effective with certain employee personality profiles, consistent with our earlier discussion of sorting. See I. S. Fulmer and W. J. Walker, "More Bang for the Buck? Personality Traits as Moderators of Responsiveness to Pay-for-Performance," *Human Performance* 28, no. 1 (2015), pp. 40–65.

26. Bretz et al., "Current State of Performance Appraisal."

27. B. D. Blume, T. T. Baldwin, and R. S. Rubin, "Reactions to Different Types of Forced Distribution Performance Evaluation Systems," *Journal of Business and Psychology* 24 (2009), pp. 77–91.

28. Bretz et al., "Current State of Performance Appraisal."

29. Ibid.

30. W. E. Deming, *Out of the Crisis* (Cambridge, MA: Center for Advanced Engineering Study, Massachusetts Institute of Technology, 1986), p. 110.

31. Ibid.

32. E. O'Boyle Jr. and H. Aguinis, "The Best and The Rest: Revisiting The Norm of Normality of Individual Performance, *Personnel Psychology,* 65 (2012), pp. 79–119; C. O. Trevor, G. Reilly, and B. Gerhart, "Reconsidering Pay Dispersion's Effect on the Performance of Interdependent Work: Reconciling Sorting and Pay Inequality," *Academy of Management Journal,* 55 (2012), pp. 585–610.

33. Deming, *Out of Crisis.*

34. Trevor et al., "Voluntary Turnover."

35. Gerhart and Rynes, *Compensation: Theory, Evidence, and Strategic Implications.*

36. Rynes, Gerhart, and Parks, "Personnel Psychology: Performance Evaluation and Compensation."

37. J. Schaubroeck, J. D. Shaw, M. K. Duffy, "An Under-Met and Over-Met Expectations Model of Employee Reactions to Merit Raises," *Journal of Applied Psychology* 93 (2008) pp. 424–34; S. Kepes, J. Delery, and N. Gupta, "Contingencies in the Effects of Pay Range on Organizational Effectiveness," *Personnel Psychology* 62 (2009), pp. 497–531; M. S. Chien, J. S. Lawler, and J. F. Uen, "Performance-Based Pay, Procedural Justice and Job Performance for RD Professionals: Evidence from the Taiwanese High-Tech Sector" (2010), *International Journal of Human Resource Management* 21 (2010), pp. 2234–48; P. Bamberger and E. Belogolovsky, "The Impact of Pay Secrecy on Individual Task Performance," *Personnel Psychology* 63 (2010), pp. 965–96.

38. R. Folger and M. A. Konovsky, "Effects of Procedural and Distributive Justice on Reactions to Pay Raise Decisions," *Academy of Management Journal* 32 (1989), pp. 115–30; J. Greenberg, "Determinants of Perceived Fairness of Performance Evaluations," *Journal of Applied Psychology* 71 (1986), pp. 340–42.

39. Rynes, Gerhart, and Parks, "Personnel Psychology: Performance Evaluation and Compensation."

40. B. Gerhart and S. Rynes, "Determinants and Consequences of Salary Negotiations by Graduating Male and Female MBAs," *Journal of Applied Psychology* (1991), pp. 256–62; Gerhart and Rynes, *Compensation: Theory, Evidence, and Strategic Implications.*

41. A. J. Nyberg, J. R. Pieper, and C. O. Trevor, "Pay-for-Performance's Effect on Future Employee Performance Integrating Psychological and Economic Principles Toward a Contingency Perspective," *Journal of Management first published online December 19, 2013.* As we go to press, however, a different study reports no effect of merit bonuses, but does find a positive effect of merit pay on subsequent performance. See S. Park and M.C. Sturman, "Evaluating Form and Functionality of Pay-for-Performance Plans." Human Resource Management (published

online, 2015). Both the Nyberg et al. and Park and Sturman studies are of single organizations. Different pay-for-performance strategies may work in different organizations.

42. Gerhart and Fang, "Pay for (Individual) Performance: Issues, Claims, Evidence and the Role of Sorting Effects."

43. J. C. Dencker, "Why Do Firms Lay Off and Why?" *Industrial Relations,* 51 (2012), pp. 152–169.

44. E. A. Locke, D. B. Feren, V. M. McCaleb, K. N. Shaw, and A. T. Denny, "The Relative Effectiveness of Four Methods of Motivating Employee Performance," in *Changes in Working Life,* ed. K. D. Duncan, M. M. Gruenberg, and D. Wallis (New York: Wiley, 1980), pp. 363–88; D. G. Jenkins, Jr., A. Mitra, N. Gupta, and J. D. Shaw, "Are Financial Incentives Related to Performance? A Meta-analytic Review of Empirical Research," *Journal of Applied Psychology,* 83 (1998), pp. 777–787; for a summary of additional evidence, see also Gerhart and Rynes, *Compensation: Theory, Evidence, and Strategic Implications.*

45. Gerhart and Milkovich, "Employee Compensation."

46. D. Roy, "Quota Restriction and Goldbricking in a Machine Shop," *American Journal of Sociology* 57, no. 5 (1952), pp. 427–42.

47. This idea has been referred to as the "share economy." See M. L. Weitzman, "The Simple Macroeconomics of Profit Sharing," *American Economic Review* 75 (1985), pp. 937–53. For supportive empirical evidence, see the following studies: J. Chelius and R. S. Smith, "Profit Sharing and Employment Stability," *Industrial and Labor Relations Review* 43 (1990), pp. 256S–73S; B. Gerhart and L. O. Trevor, "Employment Stability under Different Managerial Compensation Systems," working paper 1995 (Cornell University: Center for Advanced Human Resource Studies); D. L. Kruse, "Profit Sharing and Employment Variability: Microeconomic Evidence on the Weitzman Theory," *Industrial and Labor Relations Review* 44 (1991), pp. 437–53.

48. Gerhart and Milkovich, "Employee Compensation"; M. L. Weitzman and D. L. Kruse, "Profit Sharing and Productivity," in *Paying for Productivity,* ed. A. S. Blinder (Washington, DC: Brookings Institution, 1990); D. L. Kruse, *Profit Sharing: Does It Make a Difference?* (Kalamazoo, MI: Upjohn Institute, 1993); M. Magnan and S. St-Onge, "The Impact of Profit Sharing on the Performance of Financial Services Firms," *Journal of Management Studies* 42 (2005), pp. 761–91.

49. "GM/UAW: The Battle Goes On," *Ward's Auto World* (May 1995), p. 40; E. M. Coates III, "Profit Sharing Today: Plans and Provisions," *Monthly Labor Review* (April 1991), pp. 19–25.

50. Gerhart and Rynes, *Compensation: Theory, Evidence, and Strategic Implications.*

51. American Management Association, *CompFlash,* April 1991, p. 3.

52. "New Data Show Widespread Employee Ownership in U.S.," National Center for Employee Ownership, www.nceo.org/library/widespread.html.

53. "Executive Compensation: Taking Stock," *Personnel* 67 (December 1990), pp. 7–8; "Another Day, Another Dollar Needs Another Look," *Personnel* 68 (January 1991), pp. 9–13; J. Blasi, D. Kruse, and A. Bernstein, *In the Company of Owners* (New York: Basic Books, 2003).

54. Gerhart and Milkovich, "Organizational Differences in Managerial Compensation."

55. K. F. Hallock, *Pay: What People Earn and What They Can Do to Earn More* (Cambridge: Cambridge University Press, 2012).

56. Scott Thurm, Joann S. Lublin, and Jessica E. Vascellaro, "Google's 'One-to-One' Exchange Could Prompt Others to Follow," *The Wall Street Journal,* January 23, 2009. Copyright © 2009 by Dow Jones & Co., Inc. Reproduced with permission of Dow Jones & Co., Inc. via Copyright Clearance Center.

57. S. Ovide and S. Thurm, "Silicon Valley's Stock Funk," *Wall Street Journal,* October 6–7, 2012.

58. www.esop.org/, accessed May 15, 2013.

59. D. Jones and T. Kato, "The Productivity Effects of Employee Stock Ownership Plans and Bonuses: Evidence from Japanese Panel Data," *American Economic Review* 185 (1995), pp. 391–414.

60. "Employees Left Holding the Bag," *Fortune* (May 20, 1991), pp. 83–93; M. A. Conte and J. Svejnar, "The Performance Effects of Employee Ownership Plans," in Blinder, *Paying for Productivity,* pp. 245–94.

61. Conte and Svejnar, "Performance Effects of Employee Ownership Plans."

62. Ibid.; T. H. Hammer, "New Developments in Profit Sharing, Gainsharing, and Employee Ownership," in *Productivity in Organizations,* ed. J. P. Campbell, R. J. Campbell and Associates (San Francisco: Jossey-Bass, 1988); K. J. Klein, "Employee Stock Ownership and Employee Attitudes: A Test of Three Models," *Journal of Applied Psychology* 72 (1987), pp. 319–32.

63. J. L. Pierce, S. Rubenfeld, and S. Morgan, "Employee Ownership: A Conceptual Model of Process and Effects," *Academy of Management Review* 16 (1991), pp. 121–44.

64. Derek C. Jones, Panu Kalmi, and Antti Kauhanen, "Teams, Incentive Pay, and Productive Efficiency: Evidence from a Food-Processing Plant," *Industrial and Labor Relations Review,* 63 (2010), pp. 606–626. R. T. Kaufman, "The Effects of Improshare on Productivity," *Industrial and Labor Relations Review* 45 (1992), pp. 311–22; M. H. Schuster, "The Scanlon Plan: A Longitudinal Analysis," *Journal of Applied Behavioral Science* 20 (1984), pp. 23–28; M. M. Petty, B. Singleton, and D. W. Connell, "An Experimental Evaluation of an Organizational Incentive Plan in the Electric Utility Industry," *Journal of Applied Psychology* 77 (1992), pp. 427–36; W. N. Cooke, "Employee Participation Programs, Group-Based Incentives, and Company Performance: A Union–Nonunion Comparison," *Industrial and Labor Relations Review* 47 (1994), pp. 594–609; J. B. Arthur and L. Aiman-Smith, "Gainsharing and Organizational Learning: An Analysis of Employee Suggestions over Time," *Academy of Management Journal* 44 (2001), pp. 737–54; J. B. Arthur and G. S. Jelf, "The Effects of Gainsharing on Grievance Rates and Absenteeism over Time," *Journal of Labor Research* 20 (1999), pp. 133–45.

65. Jerry L. McAdams, "Design, Implementation, and Results: Employee Involvement and Performance Reward Plans," *Compensation and Benefits Review,* March–April 1995, pp. 45–55.

66. T. L. Ross and R. A. Ross, "Gainsharing: Sharing Improved Performance," in *The Compensation Handbook,* 3rd ed., ed. M. L. Rock and L. A. Berger (New York: McGraw-Hill, 1991).

67. T. M. Welbourne and L. R. Gomez-Mejia, "Optimizing Team Incentives in the Workplace," in *The Compensation Handbook,* 3rd ed. (New York: McGraw-Hill, 2000), pp. 275–290; E. Siemsen, S. Balasubramanian, and A. V. Roth, "Incentives That Induce Task-Related Effort, Helping, and Knowledge Sharing in Workgroups," *Management Science* 10 (2007), pp. 1533–50.

68. R. S. Kaplan and D. P. Norton, "Using the Balanced Scorecard as a Strategic Management System," *Harvard Business Review,* January–February 1996, pp. 75–85.

69. I. S. Fulmer, "The Elephant in the Room: Labor Market Influences on CEO Compensation," *Personnel Psychology* 62 (2009), pp. 659–95.

70. M. C. Jensen and K. J. Murphy, "Performance Pay and Top-Management Incentives," *Journal of Political Economy* 98

(1990), pp. 225–64; A stronger relationship between CEO pay and performance was found by R. K. Aggarwal and A. A. Samwick, "The Other Side of the Trade-off: The Impact of Risk on Executive Compensation," *Journal of Political Economy* 107 (1999), pp. 65–105; A. J. Nyberg, I. S. Fulmer, B. Gerhart, and M. A. Carpenter, "Agency Theory Revisited: CEO Returns and Shareholder Interest Alignment, *Academy of Management Journal* 53 (2010), pp. 1029–49. Also, these observed relationships actually translate into significant changes in CEO pay in response to modest changes in financial performance of a company, as made clear by Gerhart and Rynes, *Compensation: Theory, Evidence, and Strategic Implications;* B. Gerhart, S. L. Rynes, and I. S. Fulmer, "Pay and Performance: Individuals, Groups, and Executives," *Academy of Management Annals* 3 (2009), pp. 251–315.

71. M. C. Jensen and K. J. Murphy, "CEO Incentives—It's Not How Much You Pay, but How," *Harvard Business Review* 68 (May–June 1990), pp. 138–53. The definitive resource on executive pay is B. R. Ellig, *The Complete Guide to Executive Compensation,* 2nd ed. (New York: McGraw-Hill); B. Gerhart, S. L. Rynes, and I. S. Fulmer, "Pay and Performance: Individuals, Groups, and Executives," *Academy of Management Annals* 3 (2009), pp. 251–315.

72. C. E. Devers, A. A. Cannella, G. P. Reilly, and M. E. Yoder, "Executive Compensation: A Multidisciplinary Review of Recent Developments," *Journal of Management* 33 (2007), pp. 1016–72; W. G. Sanders and D. C. Hambrick, "Swinging for the Fences: The Effects of CEO Stock Options on Company Risk Taking and Performance," *Academy of Management Journal* 50 (2007), pp. 1055–78; Genhart, Rynes, and Fulmer, "Pay and Performance."

73. Gerhart and Milkovich, "Organizational Differences in Managerial Compensation."

74. M. Hanlon, S. Rajgopal, and T. Shevlin, "Are Executive Stock Options Associated with Future Earnings?" *Journal of Accounting and Economics* 36 (2003), pp. 3–43; A. J. Nyberg, I. S. Fulmer, B. Gerhart, and M. Carpenter "Agency Theory Revisited: CEO Return and Shareholder Interest Alignment," *Academy of Management Journal* 53 (2010), pp. 1029–49.

75. See Anthony J. Rucci, Steven P. Kirn, and Richard T. Quinn, "The Employee-Customer-Profit Chain at Sears," *Harvard Business Review,* January-February 1998, pp. 82–97; Christopher D. Ittner and David F. Larcker, "Coming Up Short on Nonfinancial Performance Measurement," *Harvard Business Review,* November 2003, pp. 88–95.

76. Sears, Roebuck proxy statement to shareholders, March 22, 2004. Available at www.sec.gov.

77. J. E. Bachelder III, *New York Law Journal,* March 21, 2014.

78. http://www.issgovernance.com/file/files/ISSGovernanceQuick Score2.0.pdf.

79. J. Cutcher-Gershenfeld, "The Impact on Economic Performance of a Transformation in Workplace Relations," *Industrial and Labor Relations Review* 44 (1991), pp. 241–60; Irene Goll, "Environment, Corporate Ideology, and Involvement Programs," *Industrial Relations* 30 (1991), pp. 138–49.

80. L. R. Gomez-Mejia and D. B. Balkin, *Compensation, Organizational Strategy, and Firm Performance* (Cincinnati: South-Western, 1992); G. D. Jenkins and E. E. Lawler III, "Impact of Employee Participation in Pay Plan Development," *Organizational Behavior and Human Performance* 28 (1981), pp. 111–28.

81. D. I. Levine and L. D. Tyson, "Participation, Productivity, and the Firm's Environment," in Blinder, *Paying for Productivity.*

82. T. Welbourne, D. Balkin, and L. Gomez-Mejia, "Gainsharing and Mutual Monitoring: A Combined Agency–Organizational Justice Interpretation," *Academy of Management Journal* 38 (1995), pp. 881–99.

83. Ibid.

84. Dow Scott and Tom McMullen, "The Impact of Rewards Programs on Employee Engagement," *WorldatWork,* June 2010, Scottsdale, AZ.

85. I. S. Fulmer and Y. Chen, "How Communication Affects Employee Knowledge of and Reactions to Compensation Systems," in V. Miller and M. Gordon (eds.), *Meeting the Challenge of Human Resource Management: A Communication Perspective* (New York: Routledge/Taylor & Francis), in press.

86. A. Colella, R. L. Paetzold, A. Zardkoohi, and M. J. Wesson, "Exposing Pay Secrecy," *Academy of Management Review* 32 (2007), pp. 55–71; J. Schaubroeck et al., "An Under-Met and Over-Met Expectations Model of Employee Reactions to Merit Raises," *Journal of Applied Psychology* 93 (March 2008), pp. 424–34.

87. I. Caron, A. K. Ben-Ayed, and C. Vandenberghe, "Collective Incentive Plans, Organizational Justice and Commitment," *Relations Industrielles/Industrial Relations* 68, no. 1 (March 2013); "Compensation Programs and Practices 2012," *WorldatWork,* Scottsdale, AZ.

88. Blinder, *Paying for Productivity.*

89. Hammer, "New Developments in Profit Sharing"; Milkovich and Wigdor, *Pay for Performance;* D. J. B. Mitchell, D. Lewin, and E. E. Lawler III, "Alternative Pay Systems, Firm Performance and Productivity," in Blinder, *Paying for Productivity.*

90. Kaufman, "The Effects of Improshare on Productivity"; M. H. Schuster, "The Scanlon Plan: A Longitudinal Analysis," *Journal of Applied Behavioral Science* 20 (1984), pp. 23–28; J. A. Wagner III, P. Rubin, and T. J. Callahan, "Incentive Payment and Nonmanagerial Productivity: An Interrupted Time Series Analysis of Magnitude and Trend," *Organizational Behavior and Human Decision Processes* 42 (1988), pp. 47–74.

91. C. R. Gowen III and S. A. Jennings, "The Effects of Changes in Participation and Group Size on Gainsharing Success: A Case Study," *Journal of Organizational Behavior Management* 11 (1991), pp. 147–69.

92. L. Hatcher, T. L. Ross, and D. Collins, "Attributions for Participation and Nonparticipation in Gainsharing-Plan Involvement Systems," *Group and Organization Studies* 16 (1991), pp. 25–43; Mitchell et al., "Alternative Pay Systems."

93. L. R. Gomez-Mejia, P. Berrone, and M. Franco-Santos, *Compensation and Organizational Performance* (Armonk, NY: M. E. Sharpe, 2010).

94. B. R. Ellig, "Compensation Elements: Market Phase Determines the Mix," *Compensation and Benefits Review* 13 (3) (1981), pp. 30–38; L. R. Gomez-Mejia and D. B. Balkin, *Compensation, Organizational Strategy, and Firm Performance* (Cincinnati, Ohio: South-Western Publishing, 1992); M. K. Kroumova and J. C. Sesis, "Intellectual Capital, Monitoring, and Risk: What Predicts the Adoption of Employee Stock Options?" *Industrial Relations* 45 (2006), pp. 734–52; Y. Yanadori and J. H. Marler, "Compensation Strategy: Does Business Strategy Influence Compensation in High-Technology Firms?" *Strategic Management Journal* 27 (2006), pp. 559–70; B. Gerhart, "Compensation Strategy and Organizational Performance" in S. L. Rynes and B. Gerhart (eds.), *Compensation in Organizations* (San Francisco: Jossey-Bass, 2000).

95. A. J. Baker, "Stock Options—a Perk That Built Silicon Valley," *The Wall Street Journal,* June 23, 1993, p. A20.

Employee Benefits

LEARNING OBJECTIVES

After reading this chapter, you should be able to:

LO 13-1 Discuss the growth in benefits costs and the underlying reasons for that growth. *page 536*

LO 13-2 Explain the major provisions of employee benefits programs. *page 539*

LO 13-3 Discuss how employee benefits in the United States compare with those in other countries. *page 549*

LO 13-4 Describe the effects of benefits management on cost and workforce quality. *page 553*

LO 13-5 Explain the importance of effectively communicating the nature and value of benefits to employees. *page 562*

LO 13-6 Describe the regulatory constraints that affect the way employee benefits are designed and administered. *page 566*

Work (and Family?) in Silicon Valley

Recent statistics from the Organization for Economic Cooperation and Development show that the average annual hours actually worked per worker is 1,788 in the United States. By comparison, for the two largest economies in Europe, Germany and France, the corresponding numbers are 1,388 and 1,489. In other words, if the workweek is roughly 40 hours, workers in Germany and France work 7.5 to 10 weeks less per year than workers in the United States. Even in Japan, the largest developed economy in Asia (and second largest overall after China), which has wrestled with "death by overwork," workers work fewer hours per year (1,735) than those in the United States. The United States is sometimes referred to as "The no vacation nation." The United States is also one of the very few advanced economies that does not require paid sick leave or paid maternity leave.

The norm of working many hours is even more pronounced in certain parts of the U.S. economy, such as Silicon Valley. In a talk to aspiring entrepreneurs several years ago, Facebook co-founder and chief executive Mark Zuckerberg said, "We may not own a car. We may not have a family. Simplicity in life allows us to focus on what's important." Facebook has all-night hackathons. Google has laser-tag retreats on weekends. One of the first things Marissa Mayer did when she took over as Yahoo's chief executive, was to make it more difficult for employees to work from home. In a lawsuit against Facebook, a former employee claims she was admonished for volunteering one day per month at her child's school, even though this volunteering was part of (stated) company policy. Although one incident does not mean there is a systematic problem, former Facebook chief technology officer

Bret Taylor says, "The culture is not necessarily friendly to families" and that companies have not fully grasped that problem. But what happens as Silicon Valley's workforce ages and some workers have children? Facebook received a lot of attention for its egg-freezing employee benefit, which some interpreted as meaning Facebook was discouraging its employees from having children any time soon. (See the "Competing through Technology" box later in the chapter for a fuller range of viewpoints on that topic.)

At least some companies in the Valley have begun to focus on how to become more family-friendly as a way to recruit and retain valued employees. The Happy Home Company, a home repair start-up, focuses on recruiting parents because it feels they are overlooked by other start-ups for "not being a cultural fit," which is read by some to be code for too old, too female, too much of a parent, or too different. At Bret Taylor's new company, he says the founder group tells employees they have children of their own and that they leave each day at 5:30 p.m. If they have to work longer, they work from home to avoid employees' feeling pressure to stay late. Outside of the Valley, SAS Institute, a software company in North Carolina, has long had a policy of a 35-hour work week. Companies like Happy Home and SAS compete, in part, by being unique in the labor market. They offer an employment "deal" or relationship that allows them to recruit and retain high quality people who may not "fit" at competitors and they also have taken steps that allow employees to stay and contribute as they move through different phases of their lives.

SOURCE: C. C. Miller, "Silicon Valley's Struggle Adapting to Families," *The New York Times*, April 8, 2015, p. A3.

Introduction

If we think of benefits as a part of total employee compensation, many of the concepts discussed in the two previous chapters on employee compensation apply here as well. This means, for example, that both cost and behavioral objectives are important. The cost of benefits adds an average of 46.3% to every dollar of payroll, thus accounting for 31.6% of the total employee compensation package. Controlling labor costs is not possible without controlling benefits costs. Similarly, achieving the objective of labor costs being variable and moving in the same direction of revenues and profits (rather than being fixed costs) is also not possible without careful attention to benefits strategy. On the behavioral side, benefits seem to influence whether potential employees come to work for a company, whether they stay, when they retire—perhaps even how they perform (although the empirical evidence, especially for the latter point, is surprisingly limited).[1] Although employers continue to be focused on cost control, as the chapter-opening story indicates, different employees look for different types of benefits. Benefits can be used to differentiate an employer from competitors, allowing it to tap into what in some cases may be a valuable, but underutilized, part of the pool of human capital.

Although it makes sense to think of benefits as part of total compensation, benefits have unique aspects. First, there is the question of legal compliance. Although direct compensation is subject to government regulation, the scope and impact of regulation on benefits is far greater. Some benefits, such as Social Security, are mandated by law. Others, although not mandated, are subject to significant regulation or must meet certain criteria to achieve the most favorable tax treatment; these include pensions and savings plans. The heavy involvement of government in benefits decisions reflects the central role benefits play in maintaining economic security.

A second unique aspect of benefits is that organizations so typically offer them that they have come to be institutionalized. Providing medical and retirement benefits of some sort remains almost obligatory for many (e.g., large) employers. A large employer that did not offer such benefits to its full-time employees would be highly unusual, and the employer might well have trouble attracting and retaining a quality workforce.

A third unique aspect of benefits, compared with other forms of compensation, is their complexity. It is relatively easy to understand the value of a dollar as part of a salary, but not as part of a benefits package. The advantages and disadvantages of different types of medical coverage, pension provisions, disability insurance, and investment options for retirement funds are often difficult to grasp, and their value (beyond a general sense that they are good to have) is rarely as clear as the value of one's salary. Most fundamentally, employees may not even be aware of the benefits available to them; and if they are aware, they may not understand how to use them. When employers spend large sums of money on benefits but employees do not understand the benefits or attach much value to them, the return on employers' benefits investment will be fairly dismal.[2] One reason for giving more responsibility to employees for retirement planning and other benefits is to increase their understanding of the value of such benefits.

Reasons for Benefits Growth

LO 13-1
Discuss the growth in benefits costs and the underlying reasons for that growth.

In thinking about benefits as part of total compensation, a basic question arises: why do employers choose to channel a significant portion of the compensation dollar away from cash (wages and salaries) into benefits? Economic theory tells us that people prefer a dollar in cash over a dollar's worth of any specific commodity because the cash can be used to purchase the commodity or something else.[3] Cash is less restrictive. Several factors, however, have contributed to less emphasis on cash and more on benefits in compensation. To understand these factors, it is useful to examine the growth in benefits over time and the underlying reasons for that growth.

Figure 13.1 gives an indication of the overall growth in benefits. Note that in 1929, on the eve of the Great Depression, benefits added an average of only 3% to every dollar of payroll. By 1955 this figure had grown to 17%, and it has continued to grow, now accounting for 46.3 cents on top of every payroll dollar.

Many factors contributed to this tremendous growth.[4] First, during the 1930s several laws were passed as part of Franklin Roosevelt's New Deal, a legislative program aimed at buffering people from the devastating effects of the Great Depression. The Social Security Act and other legislation established legally required benefits (such as the Social Security retirement system) and modified the tax structure in such a way as to effectively make other benefits—such as workers' compensation (for work-related injuries) and unemployment insurance—mandatory. Second, wage and price controls instituted during World War II, combined with labor market shortages, forced employers to think of new ways to attract and retain employees. Because benefits were not covered

Figure 13.1

Growth of Employee Benefits, Percentage of Wages and Salaries and of Total Compensation, 1929–2015, Civilian Workers

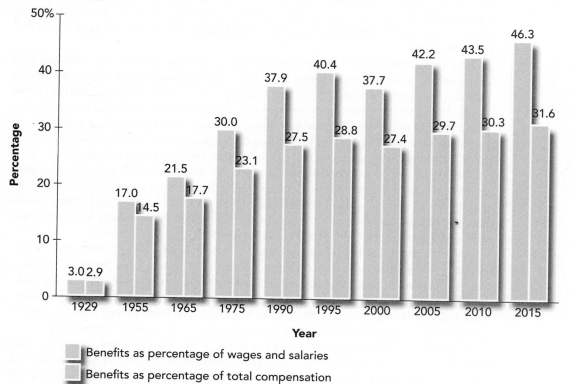

SOURCES: Data through 1990, U.S. Chamber of Commerce Research Center, *Employee Benefits 1990, Employee Benefits 1997, Employee Benefits 2000* (Washington, DC: U.S. Chamber of Commerce, 1991, 1997, and 2000). Data from 1995 onward, "Employer Costs for Employee Compensation," www.bls.gov.

Table 13.1
Example of Marginal
Tax Rates for an
Employee Salary of
$80,000

	NOMINAL TAX RATE	EFFECTIVE TAX RATE
Federal	25.00%	25.00%
State (New York)	6.65	4.99
City (New York)	3.59	2.69
Social Security	6.20	6.20
Medicare	1.45	1.45
Total tax rate	42.89	40.33

Note: State and city taxes are deductible on the federal tax return, reducing their effective tax rate.

Marginal Tax Rate
The percentage of an
additional dollar of
earnings that goes to
taxes.

by wage controls, employers channeled more resources in this direction. Once institutionalized, such benefits tended to remain even after wage and price controls were lifted.

Third, the tax treatment of benefits programs is often more favorable for employees than the tax treatment of wages and salaries, meaning that a dollar spent on benefits has the potential to generate more value for the employees than the same dollar spent on wages and salaries. The **marginal tax rate** is the percentage of additional earnings that goes to taxes. Consider the hypothetical employee in Table 13.1 and the effect on take-home pay of a $1,000 increase in salary. The total effective marginal tax rate is higher for higher-paid employees and also varies according to state and city. (New York State and New York City are among the highest.) A $1,000 annual raise for the employee earning $80,000 per year would increase net pay $596.70 ($1,000 × [1 − 0.4033]). In contrast, an extra $1,000 put into benefits would lead to an increase of $1,000 in "take-home benefits."

Employers, too, realize tax advantages from certain types of benefits. Although both cash compensation and most benefits are deductible as operating expenses, employers (like employees) pay Social Security and Medicare tax on salaries up to a limit ($118,500 for 2015) and Medicare tax on the entire salary, as well as other taxes like workers' compensation and unemployment compensation. However, no such taxes are paid on most employee benefits. The bottom line is that the employer may be able to provide more value to employees by spending the extra $1,000 on benefits instead of salary.

The tax advantage of benefits also takes another form. Deferring compensation until retirement allows the employee to receive cash, but at a time (retirement) when the employee's tax rate is sometimes lower because of a lower income level. More important, perhaps, is that investment returns on the deferred money typically accumulate tax free, resulting in much faster growth of the investment.

A fourth factor that has influenced benefits growth is the cost advantage that groups typically realize over individuals. Organizations that represent large groups of employees can purchase insurance (or self-insure) at a lower rate because of economies of scale, which spread fixed costs over more employees to reduce the cost per person. Insurance risks can be more easily pooled in large groups, and large groups can also achieve greater bargaining power in dealing with insurance carriers or medical providers.

A fifth factor influencing the growth of benefits was the growth of organized labor from the 1930s through the 1950s. This growth was partly a result of another piece of New Deal legislation, the National Labor Relations Act, which greatly enhanced trade unions' ability to organize workers and negotiate contracts with employers. Benefits were often a key negotiation objective. (Indeed, they still are. Benefits issues continue to be a common reason for work stoppages.) Unions were able to successfully pursue their

Table 13.2
Differentiating via
Benefits

Rooftop dog park	Zynga
$10,000 per employee allowance for computers and desk décor (e.g., refrigerators, headphones, custom-made chairs, rugs)	Pinterest
20 days of free backup care for 3- to 6-month-olds	Goldman Sachs
Paid week off for new grandparents	MBNA
Pregnant employees can take a paid month off before their due date	Eli Lilly
Use of the company plane for family emergencies	BE&K
Dinner with the president and CEO after 10 years	Cerner
A free stay at any company-run hotel. Six months to one year of service gets three free nights, while more than 10 years gets 20 nights	Four Seasons
Pet insurance	Timberland
$4 on-site haircuts	Worthington Industries
$10,000 total benefit for infertility treatments and adoption aid	CMP Media
10 paid hours a month for volunteer work	Fannie Mae
35 extra vacation days on 10th year and every fifth year after	Moog
1,200-acre camping and recreational area for employee use	Steelcase
Life Cycle account of $10,000 to help employees cross major thresholds such as buying first house or paying tuition	Xerox
Every four years, holds an international Olympics for its sports teams. The company covers the athletes' expenses and has an opening ceremony; most recent games were held in Budapest with over 70 countries participating.	Allianz

SOURCES: R. Feintzeig, "Lavish Perks Spawn New Job Category," *The Wall Street Journal,* November 20, 2014, www. wsj.com; "11 Top Perks from Best Companies," 100 Best Companies to Work For: 2013, *Fortune,* accessed May 22, 2013, http://archive.fortune.com; "Best Benefits: Unusual Perks," 100 Best Companies to Work For: 2012, *Fortune,* accessed May 22, 2013, http://archive.fortune.com; B. Ballou and N. H. Goodwin, "Quality of Work Life," *Strategic Finance,* October 2007, pp. 40–48.

members' interests in benefits, particularly when tax advantages provided an incentive for employers to shift money from cash to benefits. For unions, a new benefit such as medical coverage was a tangible success that could have more impact on prospective union members than a wage increase of equivalent value, which might have amounted to only a cent or two per hour. Also, many nonunion employers responded to the threat of unionization by implementing the same benefits for their own employees, thus contributing to benefits growth.

Finally, employers may also provide unique benefits as a means of differentiating themselves in the eyes of current or prospective employees. In this way, employers communicate key aspects of their culture that set them apart from the rest of the pack. Table 13.2 shows some examples. The "Competing through Sustainability" box describes how Patagonia uses benefits to help sustain its business strategy.

Benefits Programs

Most benefits fall into one of the following categories: social insurance, private group insurance, retirement, pay for time not worked, and family-friendly policies.[5] Table 13.3, based on Bureau of Labor Statistics (BLS) data, provides an overview of the prevalence of specific benefits programs. As Table 13.3 shows, the percentage of employees

LO 13-2

Explain the major provisions of employee benefits programs.

Company Benefits Help Sustain Patagonia's Business Strategy

Patagonia, an outdoor clothing company, prides itself on its commitment to the "triple bottom line": do well by shareholders, but also by employees and the community/environment. When it comes to shareholders and employees, Patagonia makes sure its employees get outside and test its gear. (To make that easier, they set their own hours.) That is something its employees enjoy and it also helps the company design and re-design products so that they are attractive to customers, which makes money for shareholders. It is only fitting for employees located in Ventura, California, that the title of founder Yvon Chouinard's memo is "Let My People Go Surfing."

Employees mix in a variety of activities in addition to surfing before, during, and after work hours, including climbing, biking, fly fishing, and kayaking. Retail marketing coordinator Danielle Egge pronounced that "I'm so much more productive when I get into the water every day" as she prepared to attend a meeting about Patagonia's new plant-based wetsuit. Employees are also eligible for two-month sabbaticals to pursue environmental projects. Patagonia was also one of the first companies to offer on-site child care. Overall, Patagonia wants its employees to live a full and balanced life because it feels it makes them happier and more invested in what they are doing and that it helps them bring an energy and enthusiasm that they can sustain over the course of their careers. Of course, it also provides a model that Patagonia hopes those outside the company will follow: enjoying the great outdoors and doing so in Patagonia gear.

DISCUSSION QUESTIONS

1. If you were a Patagonia share-holder, would you be pleased with the fact that employees can leave the office to surf, fish, climb, and kayak during work hours? Explain.

2. Think of an organization you know (e.g., where you are or were an employee). Describe why the Patagonia employment and benefits model would or would not work well at that organization.

SOURCES: J. Murphy, "At Patagonia, Trying New Outdoor Adventures Is a Job Requirement," *The Wall Street Journal*, March 9, 2015, www .wsj.com; B. Schulte, "A Company That Profits as It Pampers Workers," *The Washington Post*, October 25, 2014, www.washingtonpost.com.

---

covered by these benefits programs increases with establishment size. Likewise, as shown in Table 13.4, benefits (and total compensation) costs also increase with establishment size.

SOCIAL INSURANCE (LEGALLY REQUIRED)

Social Security

Among the most important provisions of the Social Security Act of 1935 was the establishment of old-age insurance and unemployment insurance. The act was later amended to add survivor's insurance (1939), disability insurance (1956), hospital insurance (Medicare Part A, 1965), and supplementary medical insurance (Medicare Part B, 1965) for the elderly. Together these provisions constitute the federal Old Age, Survivors, Disability, and Health Insurance (OASDHI) program. More than 90% of U.S. employees are covered by the program, the main exceptions being railroad and federal, state, and local government employees, who often have their own plans. Note, however, that an individual employee must meet certain eligibility requirements to receive benefits. To be fully insured typically requires 40 quarters of covered employment and minimum earnings of $1,160 per quarter in 2013. However, the eligibility rules for survivors' and disability benefits are somewhat different.

	ESTABLISHMENT SIZE		
	ALL	**1–99 EMPLOYEES**	**500 OR MORE EMPLOYEES**
Medical care	69%	57%	89%
Short-term disability insurance	40	29	62
Long-term disability insurance	34	22	61
All retirement	65	50	89
Defined benefit pension	19	8	46
Defined contribution plan	60	47	80
Life insurance	57	40	86
Paid Leave			
Sickness	61	52	81
Vacation	77	69	91
Personal	38	27	60
Family	12	8	21

Table 13.3
Percentage of Full-Time Workers in U.S. Private Industry with Access to Selected Benefits Programs, by Establishment Size

SOURCE: U.S. Bureau of Labor Statistics, *National Compensation Survey: Employee Benefits in the United States,* March 2014, Bulletin 2779, September 2014, www.bls.gov.

	ESTABLISHMENT SIZE		
	ALL	**1–99 EMPLOYEES**	**500 OR MORE EMPLOYEES**
Total compensation	$31.32	$26.23	$45.88
Wages and salaries	21.72	19.01	29.74
Benefits	9.60	7.01	16.14

Table 13.4
Total Hourly Compensation and Benefits Costs, U.S. Civilian Workers, by Establishment Size

SOURCE: *Employer Costs for Employee Compensation—December 2014,* USDL-15-0366, www.bls.gov.

Social Security retirement (old-age insurance) benefits for fully insured workers begin at age 65 years and 6 months (full benefits) or age 62 (at a permanent reduction in benefits) for those born in 1940. The full retirement age now rises with birth year, reaching age 67 for those born in 1960 or later. Although the amount of the benefit depends on one's earnings history, benefits do not go up after reaching a certain earnings level. Thus high earners help subsidize benefit payments to low earners. In 2015, the maximum annual benefit at full retirement age was $31,956. Cost-of-living increases are provided each year that the consumer price index increases. The age at which you retire matters. If retiring at age 62 (i.e., before full retirement age), the maximum annual benefit in 2015 was $24,300. But, if you waited until age 70, the maximum retirement benefit in 2015 was $42,012. There is no further benefit to retiring after age 70.

An important attribute of the Social Security retirement benefit is that for those at full retirement age, it is free from state tax in about half of the states and free from federal tax if no other income is received or if that other income falls below a certain level (recently, $25,000 for single tax return filers, $32,000 for married/joint filers. Additionally the federal tax code has an earnings test for those who are still earning wages (and not yet at full retirement age). In 2015, beneficiaries between age 62 and the full retirement age were allowed to make $15,720; in the year an individual reaches full retirement age, the earnings test is $41,880. If these amounts are exceeded, the Social Security benefit is reduced $1 for every $2 in excess earnings for those under the full retirement age and $1 for every $3 in the year a worker reaches the full retirement age. These provisions are important because of their effects on the work decisions of those between 62 and full retirement age. The earnings test increases a person's incentive to retire (otherwise full Social Security benefits are not received), and if she continues to work, the incentive to work part-time rather than full-time increases. A major change made in January 2000 is that there is no earnings test once full retirement age is reached. Therefore, these workers no longer incur any earnings penalty (and thus have no tax-related work disincentive).

How are retirement and other benefits financed? Both employers and employees are assessed a payroll tax of 7.65% (a total of 15.3%) on the first $118,500 (as of 2015) of the employee's earnings. Of the 7.65%, 6.2% funds OASDHI and 1.45% funds Medicare (Part A). Unlike the OASDHI tax, the 1.45% Medicare tax is assessed on all earnings. (Self-employed pay a 12.4% OASDHI tax plus a 2.9% Medicare tax.) In addition, as of 2013, the Affordable Care Act added what the Social Security Administration calls a High Income Tax and what the Internal Revenue Service calls the Additional Medicare Tax, which is 0.9% on adjusted gross income above $200,000 for single filers and $250,000 for married filers. This tax is paid only by individuals. Employers do not pay this tax.

What are the behavioral consequences of Social Security benefits? Because they are legally mandated, employers do not have discretion in designing this aspect of their benefits programs. However, Social Security does affect employees' retirement decisions. The eligibility age for benefits and any tax penalty for earnings influence retirement decisions. The elimination of the tax penalty on earnings for those at full retirement age should mean a larger pool of older workers in the labor force for employers to tap into.

Unemployment Insurance

Established by the 1935 Social Security Act, this program has four major objectives: (1) to offset lost income during involuntary unemployment, (2) to help unemployed workers find new jobs, (3) to provide an incentive for employers to stabilize employment, and (4) to preserve investments in worker skills by providing income during short-term layoffs (which allows workers to return to their employer rather than start over with another employer).

The unemployment insurance program is financed largely through federal and state taxes on employers. Although, strictly speaking, the decision to establish the program is left to each state, the Social Security Act created a tax incentive structure that quickly led every state to establish a program. The federal tax rate is currently 0.6% on the first $7,000 of wages. Many states have a higher rate or impose the tax on a greater share of earnings. Currently, Washington State has the maximum covered (taxable) earnings of any state at $42,100.[6]

A very important feature of the unemployment insurance program is that no state imposes the same tax on every employer. Instead, the size of the tax depends on the employer's experience rating. Employers that have a history of laying off a large share of their workforces pay higher taxes than those who do not. In some states, an employer that has had very few layoffs may pay no state tax. In contrast, an employer with a poor experience rating could pay a tax as high as 5% to 10%, depending on the state.[7]

Unemployed workers are eligible for benefits if they (1) have a prior attachment to the workforce (often 52 weeks or four quarters of work at a minimum level of pay); (2) are available for work; (3) are actively seeking work (including registering at the local unemployment office); and (4) were not discharged for cause (such as willful misconduct), did not quit voluntarily, and are not out of work because of a labor dispute.

Benefits also vary by state, but they are typically about 50% of a person's earnings and last for 26 weeks. Extended benefits for up to 13 weeks are also available. A state must, for example, pay extended benefits if the insured unemployment rate for the previous 13 weeks is at least 5% and is 120% of the rate for the same 13-week period in the two previous years.[8] Emergency extended (federal) benefits are also sometimes funded by Congress. All states have minimum and maximum weekly benefit levels. In contrast to Social Security retirement benefits, unemployment benefits are taxed as ordinary income.

Because unemployment insurance is, in effect, legally required, management's discretion is limited here, too. Management's main task is to keep its experience rating low by avoiding unnecessary workforce reductions (e.g., by relying, on the sorts of actions described in Chapter 5).

Workers' Compensation

Workers' compensation laws cover job-related injuries and death.[9] Prior to enactment of these laws, workers suffering work-related injuries or diseases could receive compensation only by suing for damages. Moreover, the common-law defenses available to employers meant that such lawsuits were not usually successful. In contrast, these laws operate under a principle of no-fault liability, meaning that an employee does not need to establish gross negligence by the employer. In return, employers receive immunity from lawsuits. (One exception is the employer who intentionally contributes to a dangerous workplace.) Employees are not covered when injuries are self-inflicted or stem from intoxication or "willful disregard of safety rules."[10] Approximately 90% of all U.S. workers are covered by state workers' compensation laws, although again there are differences among states, with coverage ranging from 70% to more than 95%.

Workers' compensation benefits fall into four major categories: (1) disability income, (2) medical care, (3) death benefits, and (4) rehabilitative services.

Disability income is typically two-thirds of predisability earnings, although each state has its own minimum and maximum. In contrast to unemployment insurance benefits, disability benefits are tax free. The system is financed differently by different states, some having a single state fund, most allowing employers to purchase coverage from private insurance companies. Self-funding by employers is also permitted in most states. The cost to the employer is based on three factors. The first factor is the nature of the occupations and the risk attached to each. Premiums for low-risk occupations may be less than 1% of payroll; the cost for some of the most hazardous occupations may be as high as 100% of payroll. The second factor is the state where work is located. For example, in the 50 U. S. states, the maximum compensation a worker can receive for loss of an arm averages $169,878, but it ranges from a minimum of $48,840 in Alabama to a maximum of $859,634 in Nevada.[11] The third factor is the employer's experience rating.

The experience rating system again provides an incentive for employers to make their workplaces safer. Dramatic injuries (like losing a finger or hand) are less prevalent than minor ones, such as sprains and strains. Back strain is the most expensive benign health condition in developed countries. Each year in the United States, 3 to 4% of the population is temporarily disabled and 1% is permanently and totally disabled.[12] Many actions can be taken to reduce workplace injuries, such as work redesign and training, and to speed the return to health, and thus to work (e.g., exercise).[13] Some changes can be fairly simple (such as permitting workers to sit instead of having them bend over). It is also important to hold managers accountable (in their performance evaluations) for making workplaces safer and getting employees back to work promptly following an injury. With the passage of the Americans with Disabilities Act, employers came under even greater pressure to deal effectively and fairly with workplace injuries. See the discussion in Chapter 3 on safety awareness programs for some of the ways employers and employees are striving to make the workplace safer.

One challenge is managing pain from workplace injuries effectively and efficiently and avoiding prescription painkiller abuse. Some firms and insurers have moved toward using data better to assess high-risk workers. In such cases, a case worker is assigned to the employee right from the start, who closely monitors the employee's situation. If, for example, a case worker sees that a worker with a broken ankle continues taking opioids longer than two weeks, an alert may be issued. The idea is to intervene so that a broken ankle or a minor lower-back injury does not turn into a lifetime problem with prescription painkiller addiction. Companies can also use analytics from Rising (Rising Medical Solutions) and similar companies to benchmark their workers' compensation cases against those of other companies in the same industry or geographical location as a way to compare the risk they face of fraud and abuse to that faced by other companies, which can help them decide how much of a problem they have.

PRIVATE GROUP INSURANCE

As we noted earlier, group insurance rates are typically lower than individual rates because of economies of scale, the ability to pool risks, and the greater bargaining power of a group. This cost advantage, together with tax considerations and a concern for employee security, helps explain the prevalence of employer-sponsored insurance plans. We discuss two major types: medical insurance and disability insurance. Note that these programs are not legally required; rather, they are offered at the discretion of employers.

Medical Insurance

Not surprisingly, public opinion surveys indicate that medical benefits are by far the most important benefit to the average person.[14] As Table 13.3 indicates, most full-time employees have medical insurance, especially in larger workplaces. Three basic types of medical expenses are typically covered: hospital expenses, surgical expenses, and physicians' visits. Other benefits that employers may offer include dental care, vision care, birthing centers, and prescription drug programs. Perhaps the most important issue in benefits management is the challenge of providing quality medical benefits while controlling costs, a subject we return to in a later section. We also discuss the Affordable Care Act in a later section.

The **Consolidated Omnibus Budget Reconciliation Act (COBRA)** of 1985 requires employers to permit employees to extend their health insurance coverage at group rates for up to 36 months following a "qualifying event" such as termination (except for gross misconduct), a reduction in hours that leads to the loss of health insurance, death, and other events. The beneficiary (whether the employee, spouse, or dependent) must have access to the same services as employees who have not lost their health insurance. Note that the beneficiaries do not get free coverage. Rather, they receive the advantage of purchasing coverage at the employer rather than the individual rate.

Consolidated Omnibus Budget Reconciliation Act (COBRA)
The 1985 act that requires employers to permit employees to extend their health insurance coverage at group rates for up to 36 months following a qualifying event, such as a layoff.

Disability Insurance

Two basic types of disability coverage exist.[15] As Table 13.3 indicates, only in larger workplaces are most employees covered by short-term and long-term disability insurance. Short-term plans typically provide benefits for six months or less, at which point long-term plans take over, potentially covering the person for life. The median and modal salary replacement rate is 60%, although short-term plans are sometimes higher. There are typically (in 88% of plans) caps on the amount (median = $8,000) that can be paid each month.[16]

Federal income taxation of disability benefits depends on the funding method. Where employee contributions completely fund the plan, there is no federal tax. Benefits based on employer contributions are taxed. Finally, disability benefits, especially long-term ones, need to be coordinated with other programs, such as Social Security disability benefits.

RETIREMENT

Earlier we discussed the old-age insurance part of Social Security, a legally required source of retirement income. This remains the largest single component of the elderly's overall retirement income (35%). Other sources of income are pensions (17%), earnings from assets (savings and other investments like stocks and bonds, 11%), earnings (34%) and other sources (3%).[17]

Employers have no legal obligation to offer private retirement plans, but many do. As we note later, if a private retirement plan is provided, it must meet certain standards set forth by the Employee Retirement Income Security Act.

Defined Benefit

A *defined benefit plan* guarantees ("defines") a specified retirement benefit level to employees based typically on a combination of years of service and age as well as on the employee's earnings level (e.g., the three to five highest earnings years). For instance, an organization might guarantee a monthly pension payment of $1,500 to an employee retiring at age 65 with 30 years of service and an average salary over the final 5 years of $40,000. As Table 13.3 indicates, full-time employees in 19% of all workplaces, 46% of large workplaces, are covered by such plans. (Defined benefit coverage has fallen by half since 1980.)[18]

Defined benefit plans insulate employees from investment risk, which is borne by the company. In the event of severe financial difficulties that force the company to terminate or reduce employee pension benefits, the **Pension Benefit Guaranty Corporation (PBGC)** provides some protection of benefits. Established by the **Employee Retirement Income Security Act (ERISA)** of 1974, the PBGC guarantees a basic benefit, not necessarily complete pension benefit replacement, for employees who were eligible for pensions at the time of termination. It insures the retirement benefits of 41 million workers in more than 24,000 plans. Since 1974, PBGC has become responsible for more than 1.5 million people in nearly 4,700 failed single-employer and multi-employer plans, making payments of $5.6 billion annually as of FY 2014.[19] The maximum annual benefit for single-employer plans is limited to the lesser of an employee's annual gross income during a PBGC-defined period or $60,136 at age 65 ($99,826 at age 70, $182,820 at age 75) for plans terminated in 2015. Thus, higher-paid employees, who would have received higher pensions under the company plan, can experience major cuts in pensions if the PBGC must take over the plan. Payouts are not adjusted for cost-of-living changes. The PBGC is funded by an annual contribution of $57 per (single-employer) plan participant in 2015 and $64 in 2016, plus an additional variable rate premium for underfunded plans.[20] Note that the PBGC does not guarantee health care benefits.

Defined Contribution

Unlike defined benefit plans, *defined contribution plans* do not promise a specific benefit level for employees upon retirement. Rather, an individual account is set up for each employee with a guaranteed size of contribution. The advantage of such plans for employers is that they shift investment risk to employees and present fewer administrative challenges because there is no need to calculate payments based on age and service and no need to make payments to the PBGC. As Table 13.3 indicates, defined contribution plans are especially preferred in smaller companies, perhaps because of small employers' desire to avoid long-term obligations or perhaps because small companies

Pension Benefit Guaranty Corporation (PBGC) The agency that guarantees to pay employees a basic retirement benefit in the event that financial difficulties force a company to terminate or reduce employee pension benefits.

Employee Retirement Income Security Act (ERISA) The 1974 act that increased the fiduciary responsibilities of pension plan trustees, established vesting rights and portability provisions, and established the Pension Benefit Guaranty Corporation (PBGC).

tend to be younger, often being founded since the trend toward defined contribution plans. Some companies have both defined benefit and defined contribution plans.

There is a wide variety of defined contribution plans, a few of which are briefly described here. One of the simplest is a money purchase plan, under which an employer specifies a level of annual contribution (such as 10% of salary). At retirement age, the employee is entitled to the contributions plus the investment returns. The term "money purchase" stems from the fact that employees often use the money to purchase an annuity rather than taking it as a lump sum. Profit sharing plans and employee stock ownership plans are also often used as retirement vehicles. Both permit contributions (cash and stock, respectively) to vary from year to year, thus allowing employers to avoid fixed obligations that may be burdensome in difficult financial times. Section 401(k) plans (named after the tax code section) permit employees to defer compensation on a pretax basis. Annual contributions in 2015 are limited to $18,000.[21] For those age 50 or over, an additional $6,000 per year in catch-up contributions is also permitted. Additionally, many employers (80%) match some portion (mean = 4.7%) of employee contributions.[22] A final incentive is tax based. For example, based on our earlier Table 13.1, $10,000 contributed to a 401(k) plan would only be worth $(1 - 0.4333) \times \$10,000 = \$5,667$ if taken in salary.

Defined contribution plans continue to grow in importance, while, as we saw earlier, defined benefit plans have become less common. An important implication is that defined contribution plans put the responsibility for wise investing squarely on the shoulders of the employee. Several factors affect the amount of income that will be available to an employee upon retirement. First, the earlier the age at which investments are made, the longer returns can accumulate. As Figure 13.2 shows, an annual investment of $3,000 made between ages 21 and 29 will be worth much more at age 65 than a similar investment made between ages 31 and 39. Second, different investments have different historical rates of return.

Figure 13.2

The Relationship of Retirement Savings to Age When Savings Begins and Type of Investment Portfolio

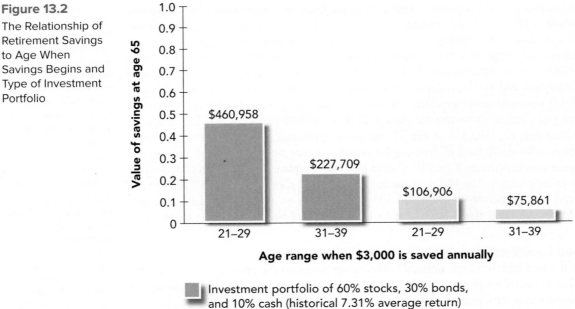

Note: Historical Rates of Return, Geometric Averages, 1928–2014: Stocks (S&P 500), 9.60%; Bonds 10-year U.S. Treasury Bond, 5.00%; Cash (3-month U.S. Treasury Bill), 3.49%.

SOURCE: http://people.stern.nyu.edu/adamodar/New_Home_Page/datafile/histretSP.html. Accessed June 8, 2015.

Between 1928 and 2014 the average annual return was 9.60% for stocks, 5.00% for bonds, and 3.49% for cash (e.g., short-term Treasury bills or bank savings accounts). As Figure 13.2 shows, IF historical rates of return were to continue, an investment in a mix of 60% stock, 30% bonds, and 10% cash between the ages of 21 and 29 would be worth about four times as much at age 65 as would the same amount kept in the form of cash. A third consideration is the need to counteract investment risk by diversification because stock and bond prices can be volatile in the short run. Although stocks have the greatest historical rate of return, that is no guarantee of future performance, particularly over shorter time periods. (This fact becomes painfully obvious during the dramatic drops in stock market values that are experienced every so often, most recently a drop of 38% in the S&P 500 in 2008.) Thus some investment advisers recommend a mix of stock, bonds, and cash, as shown in Figure 13.2, to reduce investment risk. Younger investors may wish to have more stock, while those closer to retirement age typically have less stock in their portfolios.

It's also important—indeed, extraordinarily important—not to invest too heavily in any single stock.[23] Some Enron employees had 100% of their 401(k) assets in Enron stock. When the price dropped from $90 to less than $1 and Enron entered bankruptcy their retirement money was gone. Risk is further compounded by risk of job loss when one's employer struggles financially. Employees at Bear Stearns, a storied Wall Street firm, also learned the hard way what can happen when you put all your eggs in one basket—company stock. When the stock price fell from its peak of $160 to $2 and Bear was purchased by JP Morgan Chase, the value of employee-owned shares fell from $6.3 billion to $79 million, a loss of 99%. So, repeat after me: *Always diversify* and don't put all your retirement eggs in one basket.[24]

The Pension Protection Act (PPA) of 2006 requires defined contribution plans holding publicly traded securities to provide employees with (1) the opportunity to divest employer securities and (2) at least three investment options other than employer securities. The PPA also allows employers to enroll workers in their 401(k) plan automatically and to increase a worker's 401(k) contribution automatically to coincide with a raise or a work anniversary. Workers can decline, but the onus is on them to do so. Since the PPA, automatic enrollment (50% of plans) and automatic escalation (44%) have become common, thus helping increase worker retirement contributions.[25]

According to the U.S. Department of Labor's Employee Benefits Security Administration, ERISA requires that employers "meet fiduciary responsibilities." That includes acting solely in the interest of plan participants in managing the retirement plan, carrying out these management duties prudently, following plan documents, diversifying plan investments, and paying only reasonable plan expenses. Companies can be sued for any breach of these fiduciary responsibility duties. As an example, Lockheed reached a $62 million settlement in 2015 of a lawsuit that alleged its 401(k) plan was not prudently managed (e.g., because it charged excessive fees to participants).

Cash Balance Plans

One way to combine the advantages of defined benefit plans and defined contribution plans is to use a **cash balance plan**. This type of retirement plan consists of individual accounts, as in a 401(k) plan. But in contrast to a 401(k), all the contributions come from the employer. Usually, the employer contributes a percentage of the employee's salary, say, 4% or 5%. The money in the cash balance plan earns interest according to a predetermined rate, such as the rate paid on U.S. Treasury bills. Employers guarantee this rate as in a defined benefit plan. This arrangement helps employers plan their contributions and helps employees predict their retirement benefits. If employees change jobs, they generally can roll over the balance into an individual retirement account.

Cash Balance Plan
Retirement plan in which the employer sets up an individual account for each employee and contributes a percentage of the employee's salary; the account earns interest at a predefined rate.

Organizations switching from traditional defined benefit plans to cash balance plans should consider the effects on employees as well as on the organization's bottom line. Defined benefit plans are most generous to older employees with many years of service, and cash balance plans are most generous to young employees who will have many years ahead in which to earn interest. For an organization with many experienced employees, switching from a defined benefit plan can produce great savings in pension benefits. In that case, the older workers are the greatest losers, unless the organization adjusts the program to retain their benefits.

Funding, Communication, and Vesting Requirements

ERISA does not require organizations to have pension plans, but those that are set up must meet certain requirements. In addition to the termination provisions discussed earlier, plans must meet certain guidelines on management and funding. For example, employers are required to make yearly contributions that are sufficient to cover future obligations. (As noted previously, underfunded plans require higher premiums.) ERISA also specifies a number of reporting and disclosure requirements involving the IRS, the Department of Labor, and employees.[26] Employees, for example, must receive within 90 days after entering a plan a **summary plan description (SPD)** that describes the plan's funding, eligibility requirements, risks, and so forth. Upon request, an employer must also make available to an employee an individual benefit statement, which describes the employee's vested and unvested benefits. Obviously, employers may wish to provide such information on a regular basis anyway as a means of increasing the understanding and value employees attach to their benefits.

Summary Plan Description (SPD)
A reporting requirement of the Employee Retirement Income Security Act (ERISA) that obligates employers to describe the plan's funding, eligibility requirements, risks, and so forth within 90 days after an employee has entered the plan.

ERISA guarantees employees that when they become participants in a pension plan and work a specified minimum number of years, they earn a right to a pension upon retirement. These are referred to as *vesting rights*.[27] Vested employees have the right to their pension at retirement age, regardless of whether they remain with the employer until that time. Employee contributions to their own plans are always completely vested. The vesting of employer-funded pension benefits must take place under one of two schedules. Employers may choose to vest employees after five years; until that time, employers can provide zero vesting if they choose. Alternatively, employers may vest employees over a three- to seven-year period, with at least 20% vesting in the third year and each year thereafter. These two schedules represent minimum requirements; employers are free to vest employees more quickly. These are the two choices relevant to the majority of employers. However, so-called top-heavy plans, where pension benefits for "key" employees (like highly paid top managers) exceed a certain share of total pension benefits, require faster vesting for nonkey employees. On the other hand, multiemployer pension plans need not provide vesting until after 10 years of employment.

These requirements were put in place to prevent companies from terminating employees before they reach retirement age or before they reach their length-of-service requirements in order to avoid paying pension benefits. It should also be noted that transferring employees or laying them off as a means of avoiding pension obligations is not legal either, even if such actions are motivated partly by business necessity.[28] On the other hand, employers are free to choose whichever of the two vesting schedules is most advantageous. For example, an employer that experiences high quit rates during the fourth and fifth years of employment may choose five-year vesting to minimize pension costs.

The traditional defined benefit pension plan discourages employee turnover or delays it until the employer can recoup the training investment in employees.[29] Even if an employee's pension benefit is vested, it is usually smaller if the employee changes employers, mainly because the size of the benefit depends on earnings in the final years with an employer. Consider an employee who earns $30,000 after 20 years and $60,000 after 40 years.[30]

The employer pays an annual retirement benefit equal to 1.5% of final earnings times the number of years of service. If the employee stays with the employer for 40 years, the annual benefit level upon retirement would be $36,000 ($0.015 \times \$60,000 \times 40$). If, instead, the employee changes employers after 20 years (and has the same earnings progression), the retirement benefit from the first employer would be $9,000 ($0.015 \times \$30,000 \times 20$). The annual benefit from the second employer would be $18,000 ($0.015 \times \$60,000 \times 20$). Therefore, staying with one employer for 40 years would yield an annual retirement benefit of $36,000, versus a combined annual retirement benefit of $27,000 ($9,000 + $18,000) if the employee changes employers once. It has also been suggested that pensions are designed to encourage long-service employees, whose earnings growth may eventually exceed their productivity growth, to retire. This is consistent with the fact that retirement benefits reach their maximum at retirement age.[31]

The fact that in recent years many employers have sought to reduce their workforces through early retirement programs is also consistent with the notion that pensions are used to retain certain employees while encouraging others to leave. One early retirement program approach is to adjust years-of-service credit upward for employees willing to retire, resulting in a higher retirement benefit for them (and less monetary incentive to work). These workforce reductions may also be one indication of a broader trend toward employees becoming less likely to spend their entire careers with a single employer.[32] On one hand, if more mobility across employers becomes necessary or desirable, the current pension system's incentives against (or penalties for) mobility may require modification. On the other hand, perhaps increased employee mobility will reinforce the continued trend toward defined contribution plans [like 401(k)s], which have greater portability (ease of transfer of funds) across employers.[33]

PAY FOR TIME NOT WORKED

At first blush, paid vacation, holidays, sick leave, and so forth may not seem to make economic sense. The employer pays the employee for time not spent working, receiving no tangible production value in return. Therefore, some employers may see little direct advantage. Perhaps for this reason, a minimum number of vacation days (20) is mandated by law in the European Community. As many as 30 days of vacation is not uncommon for relatively new employees in Europe. By contrast, there is no legal minimum in the United States, but 10 days is typical for large companies. U.S. workers must typically be with an employer for 20 to 25 years before they receive as much paid vacation as their western European counterparts.[34]

Sick leave programs in the United States, among employers that provide them, often provide full salary replacement for a limited period of time, usually not exceeding 26 weeks. The amount of sick leave is often based on length of service, accumulating with service (one day per month, for example). Sick leave policies need to be carefully structured to avoid providing employees with the wrong incentives. For example, if sick leave days disappear at the end of the year (rather than accumulate), a "use it or lose it" mentality may develop among employees, contributing to greater absenteeism. Organizations have developed a number of measures to counter this.[35] Some allow sick days to accumulate, then pay employees for the number of sick days when they retire or resign. Employers may also attempt to communicate to their employees that accumulated sick leave is better saved to use as a bridge to long-term disability, because the replacement rate (the ratio of sick leave or disability payments to normal salary) for the former is typically higher. Sick leave payments may equal 100% of usual salary, whereas the typical replacement ratio for long-term disability is 60%, so the more sick leave accumulated, the longer

LO 13-3
Discuss how employee benefits in the United States compare with those in other countries.

an employee can avoid dropping to 60% of usual pay when unable to work. As the "Integrity in Action" box shows, Microsoft recently required its contractors and vendors to provide paid sick leave for their employees. In 2015, President Obama signed an executive order requiring companies that contract with the federal government to provide paid sick leave. Other companies pay for time that employees devote to charity. For example, General Electric has a program where employees in its high potential program can be paid for a week doing charitable work. One recent example was volunteering with BuildOn, a charity that has built more than 660 schools in impoverished areas of the world.[36]

Although vacation and other paid leave programs help attract and retain employees, there is a cost to providing time off with pay, especially in a global economy. The fact that vacation and other paid leave practices differ across countries contributes to the differences in labor costs described in Chapter 11. Consider that, on average, in manufacturing, German workers work 400 fewer hours per year than their U.S. counterparts. (See Figure 13.3.) In other words, German workers are at work approximately 10 fewer weeks per year than their U.S. counterparts. It is perhaps not surprising then that German manufacturers have looked outside Germany for alternative production sites. (However, you might consider what you could do with the equivalent of an extra 10 weeks away from work. Hmm . . .)

FAMILY-FRIENDLY POLICIES

To ease employees' conflicts between work and nonwork, organizations may use *family-friendly policies* such as family leave policies and child care. Although the programs discussed here would seem to be targeted to a particular group of employees, these programs

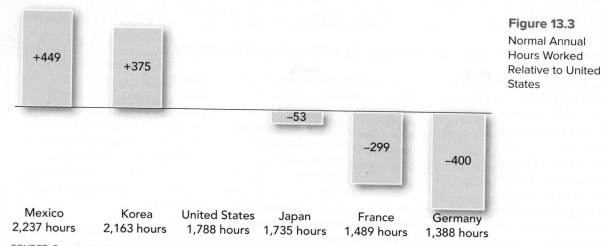

Figure 13.3
Normal Annual
Hours Worked
Relative to United
States

SOURCE: Organization for Economic Cooperation and Development. Data for 2013. http://stats.oecd.org/Index.aspx? Section on Labour, Subsection on Labour Force Statistics. Accessed May 4, 2015.

often have "spillover effects" on other employees, who see them as symbolizing a general corporate concern for human resources, thus promoting loyalty even among employee groups that do not use the programs and possibly resulting in improved organizational performance.[37] Evidence suggests that firms using family-friendly policies have better quality management practices overall that are positively associated with organization performance.[38]

Since 1993 the **Family and Medical Leave Act** requires organizations with 50 or more employees within a 75-mile radius to provide as much as 12 weeks of unpaid leave after childbirth or adoption; to care for a seriously ill child, spouse, or parent; or for an employee's own serious illness. Employees are guaranteed the same or a comparable job on their return to work. Employees with less than one year of service or who work under 25 hours per week or who are among the 10% highest paid are not covered.

Many employers had already taken steps to deal with this issue, partly to help attract and retain key employees. Less than 10% of American families fit the image of a husband working outside the home and a wife who stays home to take care of the children.[39]

The United States still offers significantly less unpaid leave than most western European countries and Japan. Moreover, paid family leave remains rare in the United States (12% of employees are eligible according to Table 13.3), in even sharper contrast to western Europe and Japan, where it is typically mandated by law.[40] Until the passage of the Americans with Disabilities Act, the only applicable law was the Pregnancy Discrimination Act of 1978, which requires employers that offer disability plans to treat pregnancy as they would any other disability.

Experience with the Family and Medical Leave Act suggests that a majority of those opting for this benefit fail to take the full allotment of time. This is especially the case among female executives. Many of these executives find they do not enjoy maternity leave as much as they expected they would and miss the challenges associated with their careers. Others fear that their careers would be damaged in the long run by missing out on opportunities that might arise while they are out on leave.[41] As the "Competing Through Technology" box demonstrates, "family friendly" can take many forms, with some debate over what is and what is not family friendly.

Child Care

U.S. companies increasingly provide some form of child care support to their employees. This support comes in several forms that vary in their degree of organizational

Family and Medical Leave Act
The 1993 act that requires employers with 50 or more employees to provide up to 12 weeks of unpaid leave after childbirth or adoption; to care for a seriously ill child, spouse, or parent; or for an employee's own serious illness.

"Family Friendly" Takes On a Whole New Meaning at Some Companies

Oocyte cryopreservation, more commonly known as egg freezing, is used in an attempt to allow women to preserve their eggs to have babies in the future. Apple and Facebook are among the companies that provide egg freezing as an employee benefit (i.e., they pay for the procedure). These companies came in for criticism for what some thought was their likely motive: discouraging women from interrupting their work at those companies to go on leave (either temporarily or permanently) to have a baby. As *Bloomberg Business* put it, this viewpoint was that the companies hoped for many "years of labor uninterrupted by soccer games and ballet recitals." Others worried that women would discount the risk that egg freezing would not work and/or the fact that fertility drops with age. Still others saw the egg-freezing benefit as a sign of all that is wrong with the Silicon Valley culture and what they see as its obsession with work

and its family (un)friendly nature. Rebecca Mead of *The New Yorker* argued, "The inclusion of egg freezing as an employee benefit partakes of the techno-utopian fantasy on which companies like Facebook and Apple subsist—the conviction that there must be a solution to every problem, an answer to every question, a response to every need, if only the right algorithm can be found."

As others have noted, however, it turns out that Facebook, the target of much of the criticism, actually offers very generous benefits to employees who *do* choose to have children. Facebook offers four months of paid parental leave. Only 15% of U.S. companies offer any paid leave at all. (Of course, in thinking about issues covered in the chapter opening, what we do not know is whether Facebook employees feel free to use this much leave or whether they feel pressure to return to work sooner than they might wish.) Facebook also

subsidizes daycare and has nursing rooms on its campus. Facebook also pays for alternative paths to pregnancy, including surrogacy agency fees, in-vitro fertilization, egg and sperm donor fees, and legal costs associated with adoption.

DISCUSSION QUESTIONS

1. What do you think is Facebook's motivation for offering egg freezing as a benefit? Do you think it matters?
2. Does Facebook sound like an environment that is open to its employees taking time off to have children or to spend time with their families? (As a further resource on this topic, please see: C. C. Miller, "Silicon Valley's Struggle Adapting to Families," *The New York Times,* April 8, 2015, p. A3.)

SOURCES: R. Mead, "Cold Comfort: Tech Jobs and Egg Freezing," *The New Yorker,* October 17, 2014; J. Brustein, "Facebook's Egg Freezing Policy Isn't an Evil Plot," *Bloomberg Business,* October 15, 2014, www.bloomberg.com.

© MCT via Getty Images

Toyota employees check in on their kids at the Georgetown location onsite child care.

involvement.[42] The lowest level of involvement, offered by 38% of companies, is when an organization supplies and helps employees collect information about the cost and quality of available child care. At the next level, organizations provide vouchers or discounts for employees to use at existing child care facilities (2% of companies). At the highest level, firms provide child care at or near their worksites (7% of companies). Toyota's Child Development Program provides 24-hours-a-day care for children of workers at its Georgetown, Kentucky, plant. This facility is designed to meet the needs of employees working evening and night shifts who want their children to be on the same schedule. In this facility, the children are kept awake all night. At the end of the night shift, the parents pick up their children and the whole family goes home to bed.[43]

An organization's decision to staff its own child care facility should not be taken lightly. It is typically a costly venture with important liability concerns. Moreover, the results, in terms of reducing absenteeism and enhancing productivity, are often mixed.[44] One reason for this is that many organizations are "jumping on the day care bandwagon" without giving much thought to the best form of assistance for their specific employees.

As an alternative example, Memphis-based First Tennessee Bank, which was losing 1,500 days of productivity a year because of child care problems, considered creating its own on-site day care center. Before acting, however, the company surveyed its employees. This survey indicated that the only real problem with day care occurred when the parents' regular day care provisions fell through because of sickness on the part of the child or provider. Based on these findings, the bank opted to establish a sick-child care center, which was less costly and smaller in scope than a full-time center and yet still solved the employees' major problem. As a result, absenteeism dropped so dramatically that the program paid for itself in the first nine months of operation.[45]

Managing Benefits: Employer Objectives and Strategies

Although the regulatory environment places some important constraints on benefits decisions, employers retain significant discretion and need to evaluate the payoff of such decisions.[46] As discussed earlier, however, this evaluation needs to recognize that employees have come to expect certain things from employers. Employers who do not meet these expectations run the risk of violating what has been called an "implicit contract" between the employer and its workers. If employees believe their employers feel little commitment to their welfare, they can hardly be expected to commit themselves to the company's success.

Clearly, there is much room for progress in the evaluation of benefits decisions.[47] Despite some of the obvious reasons for benefits—group discounts, regulation, and minimizing compensation-related taxes—organizations do not do as well as they could in spelling out what they want their benefits package to achieve and evaluating how well they are succeeding. Research suggests that most organizations do not have written benefits objectives.[48] Obviously, without clear objectives to measure progress, evaluation is difficult (and less likely to occur). Table 13.5 provides an example of one organization's written benefits objectives.

LO 13-4
Describe the effects of benefits management on cost and workforce quality.

SURVEYS AND BENCHMARKING

As with cash compensation, an important element of benefits management is knowing what the competition is doing. Survey information on benefits packages is available from private consultants, the U.S. Chamber of Commerce, and the Bureau of Labor Statistics (BLS).[49] BLS data of the sort in Table 13.3 and the more detailed information on programs and provisions available from consultants are useful in designing competitive benefits packages. To compete effectively in the product market, cost information is also necessary. A good source is again the BLS, which provides information on benefits costs for specific categories as well as breakdowns by industry, occupation, union status, and organization size. (See Figure 13.4.)

COST CONTROL

In thinking about cost control strategies, it is useful to consider several factors. First, the larger the cost of a benefit category, the greater the opportunity for savings. Second,

Table 13.5

Importance of Employee Benefits Objectives

OBJECTIVES	PERCENTAGE OF PLAN SPONSORS SAYING "VERY IMPORTANT"
Controlling health care-related costs	65%
Retaining employees	53
Reducing the cost of benefits administration	52
Increasing employee productivity	48
Attracting employees	41
Increasing employee satisfaction with the value of your overall benefits package	41
Helping employees make better benefits decisions	35
Addressing the diverse benefits needs of your employee population	28
Increasing enrollment in voluntary and/or optional plans	25

SOURCE: Prudential Group Insurance, "Sixth Annual Study of Employee Benefits: Today & Beyond: Insight into the Next Generation of Employee Benefits," 2011.

Figure 13.4

Employee Benefits Cost by Category, Private Sector Workers

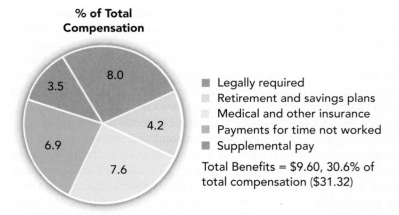

% of Total Compensation

- Legally required
- Retirement and savings plans
- Medical and other insurance
- Payments for time not worked
- Supplemental pay

Total Benefits = $9.60, 30.6% of total compensation ($31.32)

SOURCE: "Employer Costs for Employee Compensation," March 2015, www.bls.gov.

the growth trajectory of the benefit category is also important: even if costs are currently acceptable, the rate of growth may result in serious costs in the future. Third, cost containment efforts can only work to the extent that the employer has significant discretion in choosing how much to spend in a benefit category. Much of the cost of legally required benefits (like Social Security) is relatively fixed, which constrains cost reduction efforts. Even with legally required benefits, however, employers can take actions to limit costs because of "experience ratings," which impose higher taxes on employers with high rates of unemployment or workers' compensation claims.

One benefit—medical and other insurance—stands out as a target for cost control for two reasons. Costs are high and growth in costs has typically been high, even in the face of determined efforts to control the growth of costs. Second, employers have many options for attacking costs and improving quality, and the recent Affordable Care Act makes these issues even more salient for employers.

Health Care: Controlling Costs and Improving Quality

As Table 13.6 indicates, the United States spends more on health care than any other country in the world, which helps explain why there is so much focus on controlling health care costs. U.S. health care expenditures have gone from roughly 5% of gross domestic product (GDP) in 1960 (about $27 billion) to roughly 16% (about $2.7 trillion) more recently. Yet the percentage of full-time workers receiving job-related health benefits has declined over the same period, peaking at 16 to 17%, or almost 50 million uninsured (see Table 13.7).[50] As Table 13.6 also shows, the United States also trails Japan and western Europe on measures of life expectancy and infant mortality. Very recently, however, the United States has made progress on health insurance coverage (see Table 13.7), apparently due to the Affordable Care Act.[51]

Table 13.6

Health Care Costs and Outcomes in Various Countries

	LIFE EXPECTANCY AT BIRTH, FEMALE	INFANT MORTALITY RATE (PER 1,000)	HEALTH EXPENDITURES AS A PERCENTAGE OF GDP
Canada	84	5	10%
France	85	4	11
Germany	83	3	11
Japan	86	2	10
Korea	85	3	7
Mexico	77	13	6
United Kingdom	83	4	9
United States	81	6	16

SOURCES: Organization for Economic Cooperation and Development, *OECD Health Statistics 2014,* www.OECD.org and World Bank, http://data.worldbank.org/indicator/SP.DYN.IMRT.IN

YEAR	CENTERS FOR DISEASE CONTROL, ALL AGES		GALLUP–HEALTHWAYS, 18 AND OLDER
	MILLIONS	%	%
2000	41.3	14.9	
2005	41.2	14.2	
2010	48.6	16.0	16.4
2011	46.3	15.1	17.0
2012	45.5	14.7	16.8
2013	44.8	14.4	17.4
2014			14.0
2015 (1st Quarter)			11.9

Table 13.7
Number and Percentage of People without Health Insurance, United States

SOURCES: J. Levy, "In U.S., Uninsured Rate Dips to 11.9% in First Quarter," http://www.gallup.com/poll/182348/uninsured-rate-dips-first-quarter.aspx; J. S. Schiller, B. W. Ward, and G. Freeman, "Early Release of Selected Estimates Based on Data from the 2013 National Health Interview Survey," June 2014, Centers for Disease Control, http://www.cdc.gov/nchs/data/nhis/earlyrelease/earlyrelease201406.pdf.

Health Maintenance Organization (HMO)
A health care plan that provides benefits on a prepaid basis for employees who are required to use only HMO medical service providers.

Preferred Provider Organization (PPO)
A group of health care providers who contract with employers, insurance companies, and so forth to provide health care at a reduced fee.

Unlike workers in most western European countries, who have nationalized health systems, the majority of Americans receiving health insurance get it through their (or a family member's) employer.[52] Consequently, health insurance, like pensions, discourages employee turnover because not all employers provide health insurance benefits.[53]

One trend in plan design has been to shift costs to employees through the use of (higher) deductibles, coinsurance, exclusions and limitations, and maximum benefits.[54] These costs can be structured such that employees act on incentives to shift to less expensive plans.[55] Another trend has been to focus on reducing, rather than shifting, costs through such activities as preadmission testing and second surgical opinions. The use of alternative providers like **health maintenance organizations (HMOs)** and **preferred provider organizations (PPOs)** has also increased. HMOs differ from more traditional providers by focusing on preventive care and outpatient treatment, requiring employees to use only HMO services, and providing benefits on a prepaid basis. Many HMOs pay physicians and other health care workers a flat salary instead of using the traditional fee-for-service system, under which a physician's pay may depend on the number of patients seen. Paying on a salary basis is intended to reduce incentives for physicians to schedule more patient visits or medical procedures than might be necessary. (Of course, there is the risk that incentives will be reduced too much, resulting in inadequate access to medical procedures and specialists.) PPOs are essentially groups of health care providers that contract with employers, insurance companies, and so forth to provide health care at a reduced fee. They differ from HMOs in that they do not provide benefits on a prepaid basis and employees often are not required to use the preferred providers. Instead, employers may provide incentives for employees to choose, for example, a physician who participates in the plan. In general, PPOs seem to be less expensive than traditional delivery systems but more expensive than HMOs.[56]

Another trend in employers' attempts to control costs has been to vary required employee contributions based on the employee's health and risk factors rather than charging each employee the same premium. Some companies go further, refusing to employ people with certain risk factors such as smokers. See Exercising Strategy at the end of the chapter for more on this issue.

Some employers now offer a "Medical tourism" benefit, which means sending patients to other countries where medical procedures can sometimes be done much more cheaply. For example, under a program at Hannaford Brothers, a Maine-based grocery chain, the company would pay for an employee (and significant other) to travel to Singapore for a knee or hip replacement. Doing so saved the company roughly $30,000 to $40,000 and saved the employee about $3,000 in out-of-pocket costs (i.e., the deductible). And, the employee and travel companion get to experience another country.[57]

Employee Wellness Programs. Employee wellness programs (EWPs) focus on changing behaviors both on and off work time that could eventually lead to future health problems. EWPs are preventive in nature; they attempt to manage health care costs (and workers' compensation costs) by decreasing employees' needs for services. Typically, these programs aim at specific health risks such as high blood pressure, high cholesterol levels, smoking, and obesity. They also try to promote positive health influences such as physical exercise and good nutrition. Johnson & Johnson estimated a return of $2.71 for every $1.00 spent on employee wellness programs.[58]

EWPs are either passive or active. Passive programs use little or no outreach to individuals, nor do they provide ongoing support to motivate them to use the resources. Active wellness centers assume that behavior change requires not only awareness and opportunity but support and reinforcement.

EVIDENCE-BASED HR

Several years ago, Sloan Valve Company conducted research to identify the five most common medical conditions among its employees. They found that these medical conditions were all correlated with employee obesity. In response, Sloan designed and implemented a health and wellness program for the 500 employees at headquarters to address obesity in hopes of addressing the five medical conditions. Among its components were:

- Biometric screenings and health risk assessments. As an incentive, participating employees were able to enroll in a health plan with higher levels of coverage.
- A walking club was started to encourage employees to walk during their break times. For every mile walked, $1 was donated to the Juvenile Diabetes Research Foundation. Zumba and yoga classes were also offered onsite and participation was tracked.
- Biggest loser contest, smoking cessation classes, and wellness lunch and learns were also instituted.
- An onsite medical clinic was opened.

Sloan reports the following outcomes of their health and wellness program:

- More than 80 participants in the weight loss program lost a combined 1,040 pounds.
- Seven employees quit smoking.
- The walking club has 47 participants and recently walked 4,300 miles over a 20-week period.
- The number of employees classified as being high-risk in terms of their health has been decreased by 2.3%.

QUESTION

Do you feel the evidence on the outcomes of the Sloan plan's effectiveness is sufficient for you to evaluate its effectiveness? What about the "research design"? What other evidence or what other research/evaluation methods would you like to have or see used?

SOURCE: Margie Rodino. Case Study: *The Sloan Valve Co. Approach to Health & Wellness. Benefits & Work-Life Focus.* April 2015. WorldatWork. https://www.worldatwork.org/focus/benefits-focus.jsp

One example of a passive wellness program is a health education program, which aims to raise awareness of the importance of good health and how to achieve it. In these kinds of programs, a health educator usually conducts classes or lunchtime lectures (or coordinates outside speakers). The program may also have various promotions (like an annual mile run or a "smoke-out") and include a newsletter that reports on current health issues.

Another kind of passive employee wellness program is a fitness facility. In this kind of program, the company sets up a center for physical fitness equipped with aerobic and muscle-building exercise machines and staffed with certified athletic trainers. The facility is publicized within the organization, and employees are free to use it on their own time. Aetna, for example, has created five state-of-the-art health clubs that serve more than 7,500 workers.[59] Northwestern Mutual Life's fitness facilities are open 24 hours a day to its 3,300 employees.[60] Health education classes related to smoking cessation and weight loss may be offered in addition to the facilities.

One kind of active wellness center is the outreach and follow-up model. This type of wellness center contains all the features of a passive model, but it also has counselors who handle one-on-one outreach and provide tailored, individualized programs for employees. Typically, tailored programs obtain baseline measures on various indicators (weight, blood pressure, lung capacity, and so on) and measure individuals' progress relative to these indicators over time. The programs set goals and provide small, symbolic rewards to individuals who meet their goals. Of course, stronger incentives are available and these could be paired with a wellness program as well.

This encouragement needs to be particularly targeted to employees in high-risk categories (like those who smoke, are overweight, or have high blood pressure) for two reasons. First, a small percentage of employees create a disproportionate amount of health care costs; therefore, targeted interventions are more efficient. Second, research shows that those in high-risk categories are the most likely to perceive barriers (like family problems or work overload)[61] to participating in company-sponsored fitness programs. Thus untargeted interventions are likely to miss the people that most need to be included.

Research on these different types of wellness centers leads to several conclusions.[62] First, the costs of health education programs are significantly less than those associated with either fitness facility programs or the follow-up model. Second, all three models are effective in reducing the risk factors associated with cardiovascular disease (obesity, high blood pressure, smoking, and lack of exercise). However, the follow-up model is significantly better than the other two in reducing the risk factors.

Somewhat ironically, well-meaning employers sometimes do things that work at cross-purposes—for example, providing employees with easy access to good food, while also wanting employees to be fit. Google decided to keep its good food, but it also decided it needed to change the way it presented food to employees. Its research found that people tend to load up on the first food they see. So, Google changed the cafeteria line so that the first thing employees now see is something healthy: the salad bar. Desserts weren't taken away but were banished to the far corner of the cafeteria (and serving size reduced). Google also focused on communicating to employees which foods were low calories (green tags) and which ones (higher calorie) were best taken in smaller portions (red tags).[63]

Finally, unique employee health issues can arise for expatriates (and their families). The "Competing through Globalization" box provides an illustration.

Health Care Costs and Quality: Ongoing Challenges. In 2014, the average annual premium for family coverage was $16,834, with employers paying $12,011 (71%) and employees paying $4,843 (29%) on average.[64] (These numbers pertain only to employers that provide health care benefits.) Premiums for employer-sponsored health care (family coverage) continue to grow much faster than the overall inflation rate (2.4 times as fast from 2009 to 2014, 2.6 times as fast from 2004 to 2009, and 5.5 times as fast from 1999 to 2004). Thus, control of health care costs is an ongoing challenge.

Two important phenomena are often encountered in cost control efforts. First, piecemeal programs may not work well because steps to control one aspect (such as medical cost shifting) may lead employees to "migrate" to other programs that provide medical treatment at no cost to them (like workers' compensation). Second, there is often a so-called Pareto group, which refers to a small percentage (perhaps 20%) of employees being responsible for generating the majority (often 80%) of health care costs. Obviously, cost control efforts will be more successful to the extent that the costs generated by the Pareto group can be identified and managed effectively.[65]

Although cost control will continue to require a good deal of attention, there is a growing emphasis on monitoring health care quality, which has been described as "the

Air Quality in Beijing and Expatriate Recruiting Challenges

PM 2.5 refers to particulate matter 2.5 micrometers or smaller in diameter per cubic meter. When inhaled, PM 2.5 can interfere with gas exchange inside the lungs. Chronic exposure to PM particles contributes to the risk of developing cardiovascular and respiratory diseases, as well as of lung cancer. The World Health Organization recommends 24-hour exposure of no higher than 25 micrograms per cubic meter. In 2014, Beijing's average PM 2.5 was 85.9, and it had 45 days when PM 2.5 was 150 or higher. From February 2009 to December 2013, Beijing's worst one-day PM 2.5 reached 569, and it had 48 days where PM 2.5 exceeded 300. To put that in perspective, Los Angeles is considered to have the worst air pollution in the United States and is specifically third worst on PM 2.5, with an average level of 18. From February 2009 to December 2013, Beijing's worst one-day average reading was 569. In contrast, LA's worst PM 2.5 was 79. Over the same timeframe, Beijing had 48 days with a PM 2.5 above 300, which is considered to be "hazardous." The U.S. Embassy collects its own data on PM 2.5 levels in Beijing. It has recorded hourly readings as high as 886.

Not surprisingly, air pollution (or "Airpocalypse" as it is sometimes called) in Beijing and much of the rest of China is creating challenges for companies to recruit expatriates to work in the world's second largest economy and one of its fastest growing. As one possible indicator, UniGroup Relocation, which moves over 260,000 families per year worldwide for work, reports that twice as many people moved out of China than into the country in 2014. Global recruiters and companies report difficulties in attracting expatriates to China and keeping them there and companies have also reported that they are incurring added costs to do so. One cost is a recent return to offering hardship pay to compensate expatriates and their families for living with air pollution. For some expatriates, especially those with families, the added pay does not matter, as they are unwilling to put the health of their families at risk. Thus, recruiting mid-level and senior-level executives to China has become especially difficult.

Louie Cheng, president of Pure-Living China, which assists companies in improving indoor air, says installing air purifiers in an office space in China can cost $100,000 or more for larger offices. Some smaller companies are also buying air purifiers for their offices to provide employees with better air. For example, Qoros Auto Co., a joint Israeli–Chinese venture, spent about 150,000 yuan ($24,000) for purifiers at its offices. U.K. expatriate Robert Parkinson, who owns a 40-person executive search firm in Beijing, recently spent $6,000 to buy two air purifiers for his office. Simon Gleave heads KPMG's Asia-Pacific Financial Services Practice and is based in Beijing. He recently approved $4,000 for an air-quality monitor and $15,000 for air filters, and has an indoor virtual-reality biking system for days when the air is too bad for him to cycle outside. International schools, where the children of expatriates are often enrolled, have moved quickly to purchase sealed domes to cover playgrounds, so that children can play "outside" even when the air is not safe. For example, Dulwich College Beijing, an international school, recently paid $650,000 to install an 18,000-square-foot dome. Dulwich sends children into the dome, which has basketball courts and special lighting, rather than outside anytime the PM 2.5 index reaches 250.

As noted earlier, for some, these solutions are not enough. One family that decided to send the non-working spouse and children back to the United States put it this way: "It's not a way to live, to keep your baby inside with an air filter running."

DISCUSSION QUESTIONS

1. Would air quality concerns keep you from accepting an expatriate assignment in China?

CONTINUED

next battlefield." A major focus is on identifying best medical practices by measuring and monitoring the relative success of alternative treatment strategies using large-scale databases and research.[66] "Big data" can be used to move beyond intuition to make better decisions, including helping organizations to provide quality health care coverage for employees, while controlling costs. At Caesars Entertainment Corporation (which operates casinos), health-insurance claim data on its 65,000 employees and their covered family members is analyzed as part of meeting this challenge. Among the thousands of variables that can be tracked are how much different medical services are used, the degree to which employees use name-brand versus (less expensive) generic prescription drugs, and the number of emergency-room (ER) visits, which evidence shows costs over $1,200 on average (for outpatient visits). By contrast, a visit to the doctor's office or to an urgent care facility is much less expensive (e.g., between $100 and $200). As an example, when Caesars looked at its Harrah's property in Philadelphia, it discovered that only about 11% of emergencies were being treated at urgent care facilities versus 34% across all of Caesars. To encourage employees to use the less expensive urgent-care option more and emergency rooms less, Harrah's initiated a campaign to remind employees of how expensive ER visits are and provided them with a list of urgent-care and other alternative facilities that they were encouraged to use. Two years later, 17% of emergencies (up from 11%) were going to urgent care. Further, multiple ER visits by individual employees fell from 40% to 30%. Overall, on a companywide basis, in the first few years since beginning to track ER visits, Caesars reduced ER visits by 10,000, replacing them with less expensive alternatives, resulting in a savings of $4.5 million.[67] In addition, employers increasingly cooperate with one another to develop "report cards" on health care provider organizations to facilitate better choices by the employers and to receive improved health care. General Motors, Ford, and Chrysler, for example, have developed this type of system and made it web-accessible.[68]

When we come to the Affordable Care Act, we will see that the Act allows employers to use larger incentives (and penalties) than previously to encourage employee wellness and some companies are accordingly making changes. We have provided a number of examples in the current chapter of how employers use these tools. We now provide a few more. The State of Maryland will penalize employees as much as $450 per year for not undergoing required screenings or for not following up on treatment plans for chronic conditions. At pharmacy company CVS Health, an employee not completing the annual health assessment will have to pay $600 more per year for insurance coverage. (On the incentive side, JetBlue employees can receive as much as $400 per year in their health savings or reimbursement accounts for signing up for a variety of activities including smoking cessation.) Survey evidence indicates that most employees don't agree with such programs. Nevertheless, use seems to be increasing as employers seek to control health care costs.[69]

Staffing Responses to Control Benefits Cost Growth

Employers may change staffing practices to control benefits costs. First, because benefits costs are fixed (in that they do not usually go up with hours worked), the benefits cost per hour can be reduced by having employees work more hours. However, there are drawbacks to having employees work more hours. The Fair Labor Standards Act (FLSA), introduced in Chapter 11, requires that nonexempt employees be paid time-and-a-half for hours in excess of 40 per week. Yet the decline in U.S. work hours tapered off in the late 1940s; work hours have actually gone up since then. Thus, even with the time-and-a-half cost of overtime, it may be that employers prefer to work employees more hours, given their level of fixed benefits costs (and the fact that hiring additional workers would further increase fixed benefits costs, as well as recruiting and training costs).[70]

A second possible effect of FLSA regulations (although this is more speculative) is that organizations will try to have their employees classified as exempt whenever possible (although such attempts may run afoul of FLSA law). The growth in the number of salaried workers (many of whom are exempt) may also reflect an effort by organizations to limit the benefits cost per hour without having to pay overtime. A third potential effect is the growth in part-time employment and the use of temporary workers, which may be a response to rising benefits costs. Part-time workers are less likely to receive benefits than full-time workers although labor market shortages in recent years have reduced this difference.[71] Benefits for temporary workers are also usually quite limited.

Fourth, employers may be more likely to classify workers as independent contractors rather than employees, which eliminates the employer's obligation to provide legally required employee benefits. However, the Internal Revenue Service (IRS) scrutinizes such decisions carefully, as Microsoft and other companies have discovered. Microsoft was compelled to reclassify a group of workers as employees (rather than as independent contractors) and to grant them retroactive benefits. Uber, which competes with taxis by providing ride-sharing, is one of many companies currently facing legal action challenging its classification of workers (drivers in the Uber case) as contractors rather than as employees. The IRS looks at several factors, including the permanency of the relationship between employer and worker, how much control the employer exercises in directing the worker, and whether the worker offers services to only that employer. Permanency, control, and dealing with a single employer are viewed by the IRS as suggestive of an employment relationship.

NATURE OF THE WORKFORCE

Although general considerations such as cost control and "protection against the risks of old age, loss of health, and loss of life" (see Table 13.5) are important, employers must also consider the specific demographic composition and preferences of their current workforces in designing their benefits packages.

At a broad level, basic demographic factors such as age and sex can have important consequences for the types of benefits employees want. For example, an older workforce is more likely to be concerned about (and use) medical coverage, life insurance, and pensions. A workforce with a high percentage of women of childbearing age may care more about disability leave. Young, unmarried men and women often have less interest in benefits generally, preferring higher wages and salaries.

Although some general conclusions about employee preferences can be drawn based on demographics, more finely tuned assessments of employee benefit preferences need to be done. One approach is to use marketing research methods to assess employees' preferences the same way consumers' demands for products and services are assessed.[72] Methods include personal interviews, focus groups, and questionnaires. Relevant questions might include

- What benefits are most important to you?
- If you could choose one new benefit, what would it be?
- If you were given x dollars for benefits, how would you spend it?

As with surveys generally, care must be taken not to raise employee expectations regarding future changes. If the employer is not prepared to act on the employees' input, surveying may do more harm than good.

The preceding discussion may imply that the current makeup of the workforce is a given, but this is not the case. As discussed earlier, the benefits package may influence the composition of the workforce. For example, a benefits package that has strong medical benefits and pensions may be particularly attractive to older people or those with families. An attractive pension plan may be a way to attract workers who wish to make a long-term commitment to an organization. Where turnover costs are high, this type of strategy may have some appeal. On the other hand, a company that has very lucrative health care benefits may attract and retain people with high health care costs. Sick leave provisions may also affect the composition of the workforce. Organizations need to think about the signals their benefits packages send and the implications of these signals for workforce composition. In this vein, Table 13.8 shows the benefits used by Google, a company that regularly tops *Fortune*'s list of "100 Best Companies to Work For," to attract and retain its desired workforce.

COMMUNICATING WITH EMPLOYEES AND MAXIMIZING BENEFITS VALUE

Employees Typically Underestimate the Value of their Benefits

LO 13-5
Explain the importance of effectively communicating the nature and value of benefits to employees.

Effective communication of benefits information to employees is critical if employers are to realize sufficient returns on their benefits investments. Research makes it clear that current employees and job applicants often have a very poor idea of what benefits provisions are already in place and the cost or market value of those benefits. One study asked employees to estimate both the amount contributed by the employer to their medical insurance and

Table 13.8
Employee Benefits at Google

- Up to $8,000/year in tuition reimbursement
- On-site perks include medical and dental facilities; oil change and bike repair; valet parking; free washers and dryers; and free breakfast, lunch, and dinner on a daily basis at 11 gourmet restaurants
- Seven-acre sports complex, which includes a roller hockey rink; courts for basketball, bocce, and shuffle ball; and horseshoe pits
- Unlimited sick leave
- 27 days of paid time off after one year of employment
- Global Education Leave program enables employees to take a leave of absence to pursue further education for up to 5 years and $150,000 in reimbursement
- Free shuttles equipped with WiFi from locations around the Bay Area to headquarter offices
- Fuel-efficiency vehicle incentive program ($5,000 incentive to purchase a hybrid car)
- A climbing wall
- Classes on a variety of subjects from estate planning and home purchasing to foreign-language lessons in French, Spanish, Japanese, and Mandarin
- You can bring your dog to work
- When an employee dies, the spouse receives 50% of salary for 10 years and children each receive $12,000 per year until age 19 (age 23 if full-time students)
- Paid maternity (and paternity) leave: 5 months for mothers, 3 months for fathers

SOURCES: J. Bort, "These 18 Tech Companies Offer the Best Benefits, According to Employees," *Business Insider*, accessed May 5, 2015, www.businessinsider.com; J. D'Onfro and K. Smith, "Google Employees Reveal Their Favorite Perks about Working for the Company," *Business Insider*, accessed May 5, 2015, www.businessinsider.com; "100 Best Companies to Work For," *Fortune*, accessed May 5, 2015, http://fortune.com; The Great Place to Work® Institute, 2008, www.greatplacetowork.com.

what it would cost the employees to provide their own health insurance. Employees significantly underestimated both the cost and market value of their medical benefits. In the case of family coverage, employee estimates of what it costs their employer to provide coverage for them were, on average, 62% below the actual cost.[73] As we saw earlier, the average employer today providing health care benefits spends $12,011 per year for family coverage. In the absence of effective communication, the just-discussed study would imply that a typical employee today might credit employers with only providing a benefit worth $4,564 (0.38 × $12,011)—again, a very poor return on the employer's investment.

Research suggests that the situation with job applicants is no better. One study of MBAs found that 46% believed that benefits added 15% or less on top of direct payroll. Not surprisingly, perhaps, benefits were dead last on the applicants' priority lists in making job choices.[74] A study of undergraduate business majors found similar results, with benefits ranked 15th (out of 18) in importance in evaluating jobs. These results must be interpreted with caution, however. Some research suggests that job attributes can be ranked low in importance, not because they are unimportant per se, but because all employers are perceived to be about the same on that attribute. If some employers offered noticeably poorer benefits, the importance of benefits could become much greater.

Organizations can help remedy the problem of applicants' and employees' lack of knowledge about benefits. One study found that employees' awareness of benefits information was significantly increased through several media, including memoranda, question-and-answer meetings, and detailed brochures. The increased awareness, in turn, contributed to significant increases in benefits satisfaction. Another study suggests, however, that increased employee knowledge of benefits can have a positive or negative effect, depending on the nature of the benefits package. For example, there was a negative, or inverse, correlation between cost to the employee and benefits satisfaction overall, but the correlation was more strongly negative among employees with greater knowledge of their benefits.[75] The implication is that employees will be least satisfied with their benefits if their cost is high and they are well informed.

One thing an employer should consider with respect to written benefits communication is that it has been estimated that tens of millions of employees in the United States may be functionally illiterate. Of course, there are many alternative ways to communicate benefits information. (See Table 13.9.) Nevertheless, most organizations spend little to communicate information about benefits, and much of this is spent on general written communications. Considering that Bureau of Labor Statistics data cited earlier indicate that U.S. employers spend a very large amount of money on benefits ($9.60/hour or about $19,968/year) and that large employers spend even more ($16.14/hour or about $33,571/year), together with the complex nature of many benefits and the poor understanding of most employees, the typical communication effort may be inadequate.[76]

On a more positive note, organizations are increasingly using online tools to personalize and tailor communications to individual employees. Online tools have also enabled many organizations to eliminate benefits-related jobs now that employees can get answers to many benefits questions on their own. In addition, effective use of traditional approaches (e.g., booklets) can have a large effect on employee awareness.[77] Survey data (see Table 13.10) indicate that both traditional and online methods are seen as effective by employees, although one suspects that will continue to evolve over time.

Flexible Benefits Plans

Rather than a single standard benefits package for all employees, flexible benefit plans (flex-plans or cafeteria-style plans) permit employees to choose the types and amounts of benefits they want for themselves. The plans vary according to such things as whether

Table 13.9
Benefits
Communication
Methods Used by
Organizations

	PERCENTAGE
Enrollment materials (online or paper)	84%
Group employee benefits communications with an organizational representative	65
One-to-one employee benefits counseling with an organizational representative	51
Internet	48
Direct mail to home/residence	41
Newsletters (online or paper)	39
Benefit fairs	26
Virtual education	13
Social media	4
Group employee benefits communications with your vendor	3
Other	2

Note: Survey of 447 organizations.

SOURCE: Employee Benefits Communication Methods, Adapted from "SHRM Survey Findings: State of Employee Benefits in the Workplace—Communicating Benefits," © SHRM 2012 (series), p. 15. Reprinted with permission.

minimum levels of certain benefits (such as health care coverage) are prescribed and whether employees can receive money for having chosen a "light" benefits package (or have to pay extra for more benefits). One example is vacation, where some plans permit employees to give up vacation days for more salary or, alternatively, purchase extra vacation days through a salary reduction.

What are the potential advantages of such plans?[78] In the best case, almost all of the objectives discussed previously can be positively influenced. First, employees can gain a greater awareness and appreciation of what the employer provides them, particularly with plans that give employees a lump sum to allocate to benefits. Second, by permitting employee choice, there should be a better match between the benefits package and the employees' preferences. As just one example of heterogeneous employee preferences, one study looked at how much salary employees would be willing to give up to have certain benefits. In the case of work schedule flexibility, females, those above median pay, and those age 57 or older would give up 23%, 30%, and 28% more base pay (compared to other groups), respectively, for greater flexibility.[79] Matching benefits to different employee preferences should improve employee attitudes and retention and perhaps performance.[80] Third, employers may achieve overall cost reductions in their benefits programs. Cafeteria plans can be thought of as similar to defined contribution plans, whereas traditional plans are more like defined benefit plans. The employer can control the size of

Table 13.10
Percentage
of Employees
Preferring
Various Benefits
Communication
Methods

Work e-mail: 47%
Personal e-mail: 28%
Online avatar that recommends benefits to meet individual needs: 19%
Group meetings: 19%
Individual one-on-one meetings: 18%

Note: N = 1,000 employees, ages 22 or older, who work full time for a company with at least 25 employees.

SOURCE: Prudential Group Insurance, "Eighth Annual Study of Employee Benefits: Today & Beyond," http://research.prudential.com, 2014.

the contribution under the former, but not under the latter, because the cost and utilization of benefits is beyond the employer's control. Costs can also be controlled by designing the choices so that employees have an incentive to choose more efficient options. For example, in the case of a medical flex-plan, employees who do not wish to take advantage of the (presumably more cost-effective) HMO have to pay significant deductibles and other costs under the alternative plans. Choice and resulting better matches might also lower costs by reducing spending on benefits that few employees value.

One drawback of cafeteria-style plans is their administrative cost, especially in the initial design and start-up stages. However, software packages and standardized flex-plans developed by consultants offer some help in this regard. Another possible drawback to these plans is adverse selection. Employees are most likely to choose benefits that they expect to need the most. Someone in need of dental work would choose as much dental coverage as possible. As a result, employer costs can increase significantly as each employee chooses benefits based on their personal value. Another result of adverse selection is the difficulty in estimating benefits costs under such a plan, especially in small companies. Adverse selection can be controlled, however, by limiting coverage amounts, pricing benefits that are subject to adverse selection higher, or using a limited set of packaged options, which prevents employees from choosing too many benefits options that would be susceptible to adverse selection.

Flexible Spending Accounts

A flexible spending account permits pretax contributions to an employee account that can be drawn on to pay for uncovered health care expenses (like deductibles or copayments). A separate account of up to $2,500 per year is permitted for pretax contributions to cover dependent care expenses. The federal tax code requires that funds in the health care and dependent care accounts be earmarked in advance and spent during the plan year. Remaining funds revert to the employer. Therefore, the accounts work best to the extent that employees have predictable expenses. The major advantage of such plans is the increase in take-home pay that results from pretax payment of health and dependent care expenses. Consider again the hypothetical employee with an effective total marginal tax rate of 40.33% from Table 13.1. The take-home pay from an additional $10,000 in salary with and without a flexible dependent care account is as follows:

	NO FLEXIBLE SPENDING CARE ACCOUNT	FLEXIBLE SPENDING CARE ACCOUNT
Salary portion	$10,000	$10,000
Pretax dependent care contribution	0	−2,500
Taxable salary	10,000	7,500
Tax (40.33%)	−4,033	−3,025
Aftertax cost of dependent care	−2,500	0
Take-home pay	$ 3,467	$ 4,475

Therefore, the use of a flexible spending account saves the employee $1,000 ($4,475–$3,467) per year.

General Regulatory Issues

LO 13-6
Describe the regulatory constraints that affect the way employee benefits are designed and administered.

Although we have already discussed a number of regulatory issues, some additional ones require attention.

AFFORDABLE CARE ACT

The Affordable Care Act, signed into law in 2010, has several provisions that will have a major impact on employers as they are implemented through the year 2018. Table 13.11 summarizes key issues for employers.

NONDISCRIMINATION RULES, QUALIFIED PLANS, AND TAX TREATMENT

As a general rule, all benefits packages must meet certain rules to be classified as qualified plans. What are the advantages of a qualified plan? Basically, it receives more favorable tax treatment than a nonqualified plan. In the case of a qualified retirement plan, for example, these tax advantages include (1) an immediate tax deduction for employers for their contributions to retirement funds, (2) no tax liability for the employee at the time of the employer deduction, and (3) tax-free investment returns (from stocks, bonds, money markets, or the like) on the retirement funds.[81]

What rules must be satisfied for a plan to obtain qualified status? Each benefit area has different rules. It would be impossible to describe the various rules here, but some general observations are possible. Taking pensions as an example again, vesting requirements must be met. More generally, qualified plans must meet so-called nondiscrimination rules. Basically, this means that a benefit cannot discriminate in favor of "highly compensated employees." One rationale behind such rules is that the tax benefits of qualified benefits plans (and the corresponding loss of tax revenues for the U.S. government) should not go disproportionately to the wealthy.[82] Rather, the favorable tax treatment is designed to encourage employers to provide important benefits to a broad spectrum of employees. The nondiscrimination rules discourage owners or top managers from adopting plans that benefit them exclusively.

SEX, AGE, AND DISABILITY

Beyond the Pregnancy Discrimination Act's requirements that were discussed earlier in the chapter, a second area of concern for employers in ensuring legal treatment of men and women in the benefits area has to do with pension benefits. Women tend to live longer than men, meaning that pension benefits for women are more costly, all else being equal. However, in its 1978 *Manhart* ruling, the Supreme Court declared it illegal for employers to require women to contribute more to a defined benefit plan than men: Title VII protects individuals, and not all women outlive all men.[83]

Two major age-related issues have received attention under the Age Discrimination in Employment Act (ADEA) and later amendments such as the Older Workers Benefit Protection Act (OWBPA). First, employers must take care not to discriminate against workers over age 40 in the provision of pay or benefits. As one example, employers cannot generally cease accrual (stop the growth) of retirement benefits at some age (like 65) as a way of pressuring older employees to retire.[84] Second, early retirement incentive programs need to meet the following standards to avoid legal liability: (1) the employee is not coerced to accept the incentive and retire, (2) accurate information is provided regarding options, and (3) the employee is given adequate time (is not pressured) to make a decision.

Table 13.11

The Affordable Care Act: Impact on Employers

PENALTIES FOR NOT PROVIDING HEALTH BENEFITS

The health reform law does not require employers to provide health benefits. However, it does impose penalties in some cases on larger employers (those with 50 or more full-time workers or 50 or more full-time equivalents [FTE]) that do not provide insurance to their workers or that provide coverage that is unaffordable.

Larger employers that do not provide coverage are assessed a penalty if any one of their workers receives a tax credit when buying insurance on their own in a health insurance exchange. Workers with income up to 400% of the poverty level are eligible for tax credits. The employer penalty is equal to $2,000 multiplied by the number of workers in the business in excess of 30 workers (with the penalty amount increasing over time).

In some instances, larger employers that offer coverage could be subject to penalties as well. If the coverage does not have an actuarial value of at least 60%—meaning that on average it covers at least 60% of the cost of covered services for a typical population—or the premium for the coverage would exceed 9.5% of a worker's income, then the worker can obtain coverage in an exchange and be eligible for a tax credit. For each worker receiving a tax credit, the employer will pay a penalty up to a maximum of $2,000 times the number of workers in excess of 30 workers.

On the other hand, businesses with fewer than 25 full-time equivalents and average annual wages of less than $50,000 that pay at least half of the cost of health insurance for their employees are eligible for a tax credit.

TAXES*

The law increases the Medicare Hospital Insurance (Part A) payroll tax on earnings for higher-income taxpayers (more than $200,000/individual and $250,000/couple) by 0.9 percentage points from 1.45% to 2.35%. Employers will be responsible for withholding these taxes.

The law creates a new tax on so-called "Cadillac" insurance plans provided by employers. Beginning in 2018, plans valued at $10,200 or more for individual coverage or $27,500 or more for family policies will be subject to an excise tax of 40% on the value of the plan that exceeds these thresholds. The tax will be levied on insurers and self-insured employers, not directly on employees. The threshold amounts will be increased for inflation beginning in 2020, and may be adjusted upward if health care costs rise more than expected prior to implementation of the tax in 2018. The thresholds are also adjusted upward for retired individuals age 55 and older who are not eligible for Medicare, for employees engaged in high-risk professions, and for firms that may have higher health care costs because of the age or gender of their workers.

COVERAGE OF DEPENDENTS

The Affordable Care Act requires plans and issuers that offer dependent coverage to make the coverage available until a child reaches the age of 26. Both married and unmarried children qualify for this coverage. This rule applies to all plans in the individual market and to new employer plans. It also applies to existing employer plans unless the adult child has another offer of employer-based coverage (such as through his or her job). Children up to age 26 can stay on their parent's employer plan even if they have another offer of coverage through an employer.

WELLNESS PROGRAMS

Employers can provide rewards to employees of up to 30% of the total plan premium as part of a wellness program incentive, up from the previous limit of 20%. Under the law, the Secretary of Health and Human Services may increase this limit to 50% if deemed appropriate. Wellness programs must be "reasonably designed to promote health or prevent disease." The law also creates a five-year grant program to encourage small employers that do not currently have wellness programs to establish them. The program would offer $200 million in Fiscal Years 2011–2015 to employers with fewer than 100 employees who work 25 hours or more per week.

*Two new taxes do not directly involve employers. First, there is a 2.3% medical device excise tax on the sale of any taxable medical device by its manufacturer, producer or importer. Second, there is (another) additional Medicare payroll tax of 3.8% on investment income for singles earning $200,000 or more and couples earning $250,000 or more.

SOURCES: Internal Revenue Service, "Questions and Answers on Employer Shared Responsibility Provisions Under the Affordable Care Act," www.irs.gov, accessed May 5, 2015; The Henry J. Kaiser Family Foundation, http://kff.org/health-reform/faq/health-reform-frequently-asked-questions/ and http://kff.org/quiz/health-reform-quiz/, accessed May 22, 2013; UC-Berkeley Labor Center, "Affordable Care Act Summary of Provisions Affecting Employer-Sponsored Insurance," April 2013, http://laborcenter.berkeley.edu/healthpolicy/ppaca12.pdf, accessed May 22, 2013; National Association of Manufacturers, "Affordable Care Act Provisions Affecting Employers, 2013 and Beyond," www.nam.org/~/media/DB85A8CD0C174B6A8B-C9077850FE6AC9/AffordableCareActEmployers_11_2_12.pdf, accessed May 22, 2013; U.S. Department of Labor, Employee Benefits Security Administration, "Young Adults and the Affordable Care Act: Protecting Young Adults and Eliminating Burdens on Businesses and Families," www.dol.gov/ebsa/faqs/faq-dependentcoverage.html.

Employers also have to comply with the Americans with Disabilities Act (ADA), which went into effect in 1992. The ADA specifies that employees with disabilities must have "equal access to whatever health insurance coverage the employer provides other employees." However, the act also notes that the terms and conditions of health insurance can be based on risk factors as long as this is not a subterfuge for denying the benefit to those with disabilities. Employers with risk-based programs in place would be in a stronger position, however, than employers who make changes after hiring employees with disabilities.[85]

MONITORING FUTURE BENEFITS OBLIGATIONS

Financial Accounting Statement (FAS) 106
The rule issued by the Financial Accounting Standards Board in 1993 requiring companies to fund benefits provided after retirement on an accrual rather than a pay-as-you-go basis and to enter these future cost obligations on their financial statements.

Financial Accounting Statement (FAS) 106, issued by the Financial Accounting Standards Board, became effective in 1993. This rule requires that any benefits (excluding pensions) provided after retirement (the major one being health care) can no longer be funded on a pay-as-you-go basis. Rather, they must be paid on an accrual basis, and companies must enter these future cost obligations on their financial statements. The effect on financial statements can be substantial.

Increasing retiree health care costs (and the change in accounting standards) have also led some companies to require white-collar employees and retirees to pay insurance premiums for the first time in history and to increase copayments and deductibles. Survey data indicate that some companies are ending retiree health care benefits altogether. GM, for example, recently eliminated retiree health care benefits for white-collar workers. Union contracts prevented GM from eliminating the blue-collar plan.

However, as part of its bankruptcy proceeding it reached a settlement with the United Auto Workers union (UAW) to create a voluntary employee benefit association (VEBA) trust. GM agreed to contribute roughly $35 billion to fund the VEBA. Ford ($13.2 billion) and Chrysler ($7.1 billion) also reached agreements to set up VEBAs. By one estimate, the VEBAs moved $100 billion in retiree health care obligations off the financial statements of the three U.S. automakers, playing a major role in reducing labor cost per vehicle produced. Also, the VEBAs, like defined contribution plans, make the cost for the companies certain. After paying to set up the VEBAs, they have no future obligations to cover retiree health care. It is up to the UAW to administer the VEBA.[86]

Other companies have reduced benefits or increased retiree contributions. Obviously, such changes hit the elderly hard, especially those with relatively fixed incomes. Not surprisingly, legal challenges have arisen. The need to balance the interests of shareholders, current employees, and retirees in this area will be one of the most difficult challenges facing managers in the future.

Although use of defined benefit (pension) plans has declined significantly over time in the United States, there continue to be tens of millions covered by ongoing plans (and/or frozen plans—those not open to new participants). Two factors are about to make the cost of funding these plans significantly more expensive for organizations. First, the PBGC, which insures pensions, is raising its annual premium to $64/worker by 2016, up from $42/worker in 2014, a 53% increase in cost to employers. Second, the Society of Actuaries revised its mortality tables for the first time since 2000. Life expectancy for a 65-year-old has been revised upward from 85.2 to 88.8 for women and from 82.6 to 86.6 for men, again substantially increasing the cost obligation to employers.[87]

A LOOK BACK

We have seen that many organizations have become less paternalistic in their employee benefits strategies. Employees now have more responsibility, and sometimes more risk, regarding their benefits choices. One change has been in the area of retirement income plans, where employers have moved toward greater reliance on defined contribution plans. Such plans require employees to understand investing; otherwise, their retirement years may not be so happy. The risk to employees is especially great when defined contribution plans invest a substantial portion of their assets in company stock. One reason companies do this is because they wish to move away from an entitlement mentality and instead link benefits to company performance. However, if the company has financial problems, employees risk losing not only their jobs, but also their retirement money. Another change has been in the area of health care benefits. Employees are being asked to increase the proportion of costs that they pay and also to use data on health care quality to make better choices about health care. Of course, different companies have different benefits strategies. We saw at the beginning of the chapter (and later in the cases of Google and Patagonia) that tech companies, for example, are not in the mode of reducing benefits and/or passing on more costs to employees. Rather, they are looking for ways to make their benefits packages more attractive to help them compete in the labor market for valuable human capital.

QUESTIONS

1. Why do employers offer benefits? Is it because the law requires it, because it makes good business sense, or because it is the right thing to do? How much responsibility should employers have for the health and well-being of their employees? Take the perspective of both a shareholder and an employee in answering this question.
2. If you were advising a new company on how to design its health care plan, what would you recommend?

SUMMARY

Effective management of employee benefits is an important means by which organizations successfully compete. Benefits costs are substantial and continue to grow rapidly in some areas, most notably health care. Control of such costs is necessary to compete in the product market. At the same time, employers must offer a benefits package that permits them to compete in the labor market. Beyond investing more money in benefits, this attraction and retention of quality employees can be helped by better communication of the value of the benefits package and by allowing employees to tailor benefits to their own needs through flexible benefits plans.

Employers continue to be a major source of economic security for employees, often providing health insurance, retirement benefits, and so forth. Changes to benefits can have a tremendous impact on employees and retirees. Therefore, employers carry a significant social responsibility in making benefits decisions. At the same time, employees need to be aware that they will increasingly become responsible for their own economic security. Health care benefit design is changing to encourage employees to be more informed consumers, and retirement benefits will depend more and more on the financial investment decisions employees make on their own behalf.

KEY TERMS

Marginal tax rate, 538
Consolidated Omnibus Budget
   Reconciliation Act
   (COBRA), 544
Pension Benefit Guaranty Corporation
   (PBGC), 545

Employee Retirement Income Security
   Act (ERISA), 545
Cash balance plan, 547
Summary plan description
   (SPD), 548
Family and Medical Leave Act, 551

Health maintenance organization
   (HMO), 556
Preferred provider organization (PPO),
   556
Financial Accounting Statement (FAS)
   106, 568

DISCUSSION QUESTIONS

1. The chapter-opening story described how employers are shifting more employee health care costs to employees. What are the likely consequences of this change? Where does the social responsibility of employers end, and where does the need to operate more efficiently begin?
2. Your company, like many others, is experiencing double-digit percentage increases in health care costs. What suggestions can you offer that may reduce the rate of cost increases?
3. Why is communication so important in the employee benefits area? What sorts of programs can a company use to communicate more effectively? What are the potential positive consequences of more effective benefits communication?
4. What are the potential advantages of flexible benefits and flexible spending accounts? Are there any potential drawbacks?
5. Although benefits account for a large share of employee compensation, many feel there is little evidence on whether an employer receives an adequate return on the benefits investment. One suggestion has been to link benefits to individual, group, or organization performance. Explain why you would or would not recommend this strategy to an organization.

SELF-ASSESSMENT EXERCISE

connect

Additional assignable self-assessments available in Connect.

One way companies determine which types of benefits to provide is to use a survey asking employees which types of benefits are important to them. Read the following list of employee benefits. For each benefit, mark an X in the column that indicates whether it is important to you or not.

Benefit	Important to Have	Not Important to Have	% Employers Offering
Dependent-care flexible spending account			70%
Flextime			64
Ability to bring child to work in case of emergency			30
Elder-care referral services			21
Adoption assistance			21
On-site child care center			6
Gym subsidy			28
Vaccinations on site (e.g., flu shots)			61
On-site fitness center			26
Casual dress days (every day)			53
Organization-sponsored sports teams			39
Food services/subsidized cafeteria			29
Travel-planning services			27
Dry-cleaning services			15
Massage therapy services at work			12
Self-defense training			6
Concierge services			4

Compare your importance ratings for each benefit to the corresponding number in the right-hand column that indicates the percentage of employers that offer the benefit. Are you likely to find jobs that provide the benefits you want? Explain.

SOURCE: Based on Figure 2, "Percent of Employers Offering Work/Life Benefits (by Year)," in *Workplace Visions* 4 (2002), p. 3, published by the Society for Human Resource Management.

EXERCISING STRATEGY

Controlling Health Care Costs: Employers Turn to "Carrots and Sticks"

If you are a man with waist size 40 inches or more or a woman with waist size 35 inches or more, that "spare tire" will cost you some money this year if you work at tire-maker Michelin North America Inc. Employees may have to pay as much as an extra $1,000 in health insurance if their blood pressure, blood sugar, cholesterol or waist size exceeds targets.

As part of the plan to control increasing health care costs, companies are penalizing employees for not meeting health targets; and companies may also penalize employees if they decline to share personal health-related information like that discussed above (e.g., weight, blood pressure).

Companies say health-care costs cannot be controlled without changing workers' health-related lifestyles and habits. Large employers now pay an average of over $11,000 per worker per year in health care premiums. A Gallup survey and study estimated that overweight U.S. workers miss 450 million more days of work each year than other workers and that the lost productivity could exceed $153 million per year.

Employers like Michelin are using wellness plans and/or adding monetary consequences in hopes of more successfully getting employees to make healthier choices. Although framing the incentives in terms of rewards might seem like a more positive approach, it may be that framing them as penalties (instead of rewards) is more consistent with research from behavioral economics, which shows that people react more strongly to monetary losses than to monetary gains of the same dollar amount.

This approach gives rise to concerns among employee-rights advocates. Are such penalties for poor health a form of "legal discrimination"? Will workers with chronic conditions such as high blood pressure lose out on jobs? Are the penalties for those having costly health conditions anything other than lower pay for people with such conditions?

Under current law, companies can use health-contingent rewards or penalties, but they cannot exceed 20% of the cost of the employee's health coverage. Current law also requires employers to exempt employees from such penalties if they have conditions that make it impossible for them to meet the health care goals.

Honeywell International Inc. is another company that penalizes workers for some health care choices. The company used to provide an incentive to workers who got a second opinion before undergoing (expensive) elective surgeries such as knee replacement, hip replacement, and/or back surgery; but it looked at effectiveness data of using incentives in such cases and decided to re-frame the program as a penalty (of $1,000) that workers must pay if they do not comply. It reports that compliance with these steps went from under 20% to more than 90% as a result and that it is saving it at least $3 million more annually.

Companies also continue to increase their focus on smoking with some companies taking the step of no longer hiring smokers. For example, Arkansas Children's Hospital, which also has a new "Tobacco and Nicotine-Free Campus Policy," now requires applicants to take urine tests for nicotine after receiving a contingent offer of employment. If they fail, they are permitted to re-apply 90 days later. Health care costs are higher on average for smokers, and second-hand smoke is also a concern. Furthermore, a health care organization may feel that it should set an example for how to be healthier.

QUESTIONS

1. Does Title VII of the Civil Rights Act prohibit discrimination against smokers? Do you feel it is a wise business decision? Do you think it is unfair to smokers? Will not hiring smokers affect the quality of the workforce? How?

2. What are the reasons why companies are taking steps to improve the health of their employees? What is the nature of the expected return on this investment?

SOURCES: Associated Press, "Arkansas Children's Hospital to No Longer Hire Smokers," *The Washington Times,* April 1, 2015, www.washingtontimes.com; Leslie Kwoh, "When Your Boss Makes You Pay for Being Fat," *The Wall Street Journal,* April 5, 2013; The Henry J. Kaiser Family Foundation and Health Research and Educational Trust, "Survey of Employer Health Benefits 2012," www.kff.org.

MANAGING PEOPLE

The Affordable Care Act—How Will Small Employers Respond?

Sales at Automation Systems LLC, a parts-assembly factory in the Chicago suburbs, dropped 60% following the 2008 financial collapse. Owner Carl Schanstra was able to get the firm back on its feet by breaking into new markets, such as the auto industry. Sales are up 12% this year, and are likely to rise again next year, too.

But for the 34-year-old, the expected growth in sales brings a new concern. He is worried that as Automation Systems continues to expand, it will be subject to a provision in the health care overhaul that could damage its bottom line.

Mr. Schanstra is contemplating various strategies he can take next year in order to sidestep what he believes are significant burdens of complying with the law. In fact, he's considering whether he should split his manufacturing firm in two.

That is because his plant, with sales of about $1.6 million for 2012, currently employs 40 full-time workers, mostly low-paid employees who monitor the factory equipment. If sales were to continue to rise, the plant could, conceivably, employ 50 full-time workers in 2014. Under the new health care law, the Affordable Care Act, businesses with 50 or more full-time equivalent employees will be required, starting in that year, to offer workers health insurance or potentially pay a penalty.

The expense, says Mr. Schanstra, would drive up the cost of his labor. So he doesn't want to let employment at the factory reach that number. "I'll be hammered for having more people at work."

Splitting the business into two would be a "headache," he acknowledges. But with fewer than 50 full-time equivalent employees in each half of the business, he would hope to avoid paying the penalties that otherwise could amount to at least $40,000 a year. His firm hasn't offered health-insurance benefits since 2003, when premiums jumped 50%, bringing his yearly outlay for coverage for his staff of 20 people to about $40,000 total.

Experts say breaking up a firm—as Mr. Schanstra is contemplating—generally won't be a solution. According to the Internal Revenue Code, all workers who are employed by a common group of corporations or business partners must be treated as being employed by a single owner.

But an owner could potentially create a spinoff entity if his or her business has more than one revenue stream, and if there are different owners for each entity, says Peter Fleming, Wilke & Associates LLP. But, "the spinoff move is a big step," he says, because it requires surrendering a portion of the company over to someone else.

Exploring far-reaching strategies to dodge the employer mandate isn't uncommon, adds Katie Mahoney, executive director of health care policy at the U.S. Chamber of Commerce, because, for some business owners, "it's a matter of dollars and cents and they don't have it. They find a way around it or they close their business."

Some say they're likely to reduce their workers' hours or even lay off staff in order to remain below the thresholds established under the act. Under the law, firms with 50 or more full-time-equivalent employees will have to provide "minimum essential" and "affordable" coverage, or pay a penalty for each employee in excess of 30 full-time employees.

Sidney Brodsky, chief executive officer of James Gerard Foods, a gourmet food business in Phoenix with roughly 50 employees, says he is considering "weeding out" his weakest performers to reduce his firm's head count to below 50 full-time equivalents. He would then bring on contract workers, should he need more help.

Mr. Brodsky has offered health care benefits to his employees for the past 12 years, though he only contributes 50% toward their premiums. By hovering under the law's employee threshold, he can continue to offer health benefits to his employees without having to worry about meeting the "minimum essential" mandate. In order to avoid penalties, employers must offer a plan that covers at least 60% of the actuarial value of the cost of the benefits. In addition, employers must not charge the employee more than 9.5% of his or her household income toward the cost of health-insurance premiums.

Others plan to shift to part-time workers, because there are no penalties if part-time employees aren't offered coverage.

Mr. Schanstra says he is thinking of bringing in a partner to take over one-half of the business, should he divide it. He is also considering opening a factory in South America—and focus his growth there. "I want to see where the cards fall," he says. "Splitting the company is not off the table."

Mr. Schanstra is aware that dividing his business into two may not help him dodge the law's requirements. His backup plan, if he can't split his firm, is to keep his head count low or to invest in machinery that would replace workers. He also plans to raise prices as much as 20% starting in January to buffer any health care related costs he may incur in 2014.

Getting part-time staff is "not a really good functional way for us to operate our business," he says, because of how employees' shifts, which rotate 24 hours a day, are scheduled for optimal productivity.

"The unknown makes everyone stop spending and start saving," he says. "We will be more cautious and leaner and tighten up."

QUESTIONS

1. How do you feel about companies looking for ways to avoid coverage under the Affordable Care Act?
2. Do you feel that it is more understandable that small companies like these would look to avoid coverage, compared to larger companies?
3. What are the consequences for companies, workers, and society of companies avoiding coverage by the law?

HR IN SMALL BUSINESS

Babies Welcomed at T3

T3 is an independent advertising agency launched by Gay Warren Gaddis in Austin, Texas, in 1989. It has grown rapidly, thanks to Gaddis's ability to stay in front of tumultuous change in the advertising and marketing industry. Traditional agencies have approached their work by thinking about ads to be placed on the air or in newspapers and magazines. In contrast, Gaddis and her staff have specialized in developing integrated campaigns that harness all the ways to communicate about a brand, including communication via the Internet.

Innovation continues to be a company value. The company's careers web page says T3 looks for "Great thinkers. Individuals with curious, open minds. Relentless problem-solvers constantly looking for new, often unconventional, solutions." The company is structured without the boundaries that have traditionally separated functions in the advertising world, so that employees can bring their perspectives together to solve client problems.

That innovative spirit hasn't been limited to advertising. Gaddis also thinks creatively about managing her firm's human resources. Six years after starting T3, Gaddis observed that four of her key employees were all pregnant at about the same time. If they all proceeded in the traditional way, taking a few months' leave, Gaddis would be scrambling to keep her agency running without them. So Gaddis decided to try something unusual: she told the four employees they were welcome to bring their babies to work. While some big companies establish on-site day care, Gaddis simply counted on the employees to work flexibly in the presence of their children.

Many people would assume that babies at work would create a distracting environment, but in fact, the new program was a success. T3 kept the policy in place and even gave it a name: T3 and Under. So far, 80 babies have come to work at one point or another. Gaddis says parents are so appreciative that they try extra hard to make the arrangement work. One such parent, Emily Dalton, feels reassured by being able to just swivel her chair when she wants to check on her baby: "You're not worrying," she told a newspaper reporter, "You're being spit up on, but you're not . . . calling somewhere to check on your child." She admits that she has to be extra flexible when her baby, Annie, is awake but adds, "I powerhouse when she sleeps." When the babies reach nine months or start to crawl, the parents are expected to make arrangements for day care.

Bringing babies to work is, of course, only one employee benefit. T3, which now has offices in New York and San Francisco as well as the one in Austin, offers medical, dental, and vision insurance; various life insurance policies; disability insurance; a 401(k) plan; paid time for vacations, holidays, and sick leave; and discounts on gym memberships and cell phone plans. There are also some other unusual benefits: breakfast on Mondays, candy on Fridays, a book club, and a "bring your dog to work" policy. As for this last policy, the T3 website comments, "While we don't have hard metrics on what [dogs] do for our creativity or productivity, we do believe they play a part in adding balance to what can be a very unbalanced business."

Advertising may be an "unbalanced" business, but so far, T3 seems to be coping well enough. And T3's fearless leader, Gay Warren Gaddis, was recently named Ernst and Young's Entrepreneur of the Year for central Texas.

QUESTIONS

1. Of the employee benefits mentioned in this case, which of them do you think are important for keeping a creative workforce engaged at T3?

2. What are some of the advantages of the agency's T3 and Under policy? What are some of the risks? How can the company address those risks?

3. At what other kinds of companies, if any, do you think a "bring your baby to work" policy might be effective as an employee benefit? Why?

SOURCES: Josh Spiro, "Where Every Day Is Take Your Baby to Work Day," *Inc.*, December 9, 2009, www.inc.com; Eric Aasen, "Babies-at-Work Programs Let New Parents Stay Close to Their Kids," *Dallas Morning News*, March 26, 2008, Business & Company Resource Center, http://galenet.galegroup.com; and T3, "Careers" and "Company," corporate website, www.t-3.com, accessed July 21, 2014.

NOTES

1. James H. Dulebohn, Janice C. Molloy, Shaun M. Pichler, and Brian Murray, "Employee Benefits: Literature Review and Emerging Issues," *Human Resource Management Review* 19 (2009), pp. 86–103; Joseph J. Martocchio, *Employee Benefits*, 2nd ed. (New York: McGraw-Hill, 2006).

2. H. W. Hennessey, "Using Employee Benefits to Gain a Competitive Advantage," *Benefits Quarterly* 5, no. 1 (1989), pp. 51–57; B. Gerhart and G.T. Milkovich, "Employee Compensation: Research and Practice," in *Handbook of Industrial and Organizational Psychology*, vol. 3, 2nd ed., ed. M. D. Dunnette

and L. M. Hough (Palo Alto, CA: Consulting Psychologists Press, 1992); J. Swist, "Benefits Communications: Measuring Impact and Value," *Employee Benefit Plan Review*, September 2002, pp. 24–26.

3. R. Ehrenberg and R. S. Smith, *Modern Labor Economics: Theory and Public Policy*, 7th ed. (Upper Saddle River, NJ: Addison Wesley Longman, 2000).

4. B. T. Beam Jr. and J. J. McFadden, *Employee Benefits*, 6th ed. (Chicago: Dearborn Financial Publishing, 2000).

5. The organization and description in this section draws heavily on Beam and McFadden, *Employee Benefits*.

6. U.S. Department of Labor, Employment and Training Administration, "Comparison of State Unemployment Laws," http://workforcesecurity.doleta.gov/unemploy/comparison2012.asp; Employment Security Department, Washington State, "Taxable Wage Base," http://www.esd.wa.gov/uitax/taxreportsandrates/fileandpaytaxes/taxable-wage-base.php, accessed May 4, 2015.

7. J. A. Penczak, "Unemployment Benefit Plans," in *Employee Benefits Handbook,* 3rd ed., ed. J. D. Mamorsky (Boston: Warren, Gorham & Lamont, 1992).

8. U.S. Department of Labor, "Unemployment Compensation: Federal-State Partnership," Office of Unemployment Insurance, Division of Legislation, April 2013.

9. J. V. Nackley, *Primer on Workers' Compensation* (Washington, DC: Bureau of National Affairs, 1989).

10. Beam and McFadden, *Employee Benefits,* p. 81.

11. L. Groeger, M. Grabell, and C. Cotts, "Workers' Comp Benefits: How Much Is a Limb Worth?" *ProPublica,* accessed May 4, 2015, http://projects.propublica.org; see also: www.dol.gov/esa.

12. A. H. Wheeler, "Pathophysiology of Chronic Back Pain," www.emedicine.com (2002).

13. J. R. Hollenbeck, D. R. Ilgen, and S. M. Crampton, "Lower Back Disability in Occupational Settings: A Review of the Literature from a Human Resource Management View," *Personnel Psychology* 45 (1992), pp. 247–78; J. J. Martocchio, D. A. Harrison, and H. Berkson, "Connections between Lower Back Pain, Interventions, and Absence from Work: A Time-Based Meta-Analysis," *Personnel Psychology* (2000), p. 595.

14. Employee Benefit Research Institute, "Value of Employee Benefits Constant in a Changing World," www.ebri.org (March 28, 2002).

15. Beam and McFadden, *Employee Benefits.*

16. U. S. Bureau of Labor Statistics, *National Compensation Survey: Employee Benefits in the United States, 2014,* Bulletin 2779, September 2014, USDL-15-0386, www.bls.gov.

17. Social Security Administration, "Fast Facts and Figures about Social Security, 2014," published September 2014, http://www.ssa.gov/policy/docs/chartbooks/fast_facts/2014/fast_facts14.html#page5

18. Barbara A. Butrica, Howard M. Iams, Karen E. Smith, and Eric J. Toder, "The Disappearing Defined Benefit Pension and Its Potential Impact on the Retirement Incomes of Baby Boomers," U.S. Social Security Administration, Social Security Bulletin, Vol. 69, No. 3, 2009.

19. Pension Benefit Guaranty Corporation, *Annual Report, 2014,* www.pbgc.gov.

20. Ibid.

21. www.irs.gov. Those age 50 and over have higher contribution limits.

22. PSCA's *57th Annual Survey of Profit Sharing and 401(k) Plans,* 2014.

23. J. Fierman, "How Secure Is Your Nest Egg?" *Fortune,* August 12, 1991, pp. 50–54.

24. A. R. Sorking, "JP Morgan Pays $2 a Share for Bear Stearns," *The New York Times,* March 17, 2008; P. Lattman and J. Strasburg," We Are All in a Daze, Says One Employee, Life Savings Wiped Out, "*The Wall Street Journal,* March 18, 2008; D. Maxey, J. L. Pessin, and I. Salisbury, "The Job/Stock Double Whammy: Bear Saga Shows Perils of Loading Up on Employer Equity," *The Wall Street Journal,* March 18, 2008.

25. PSCA's *57th Annual Survey of Profit Sharing and 401(k) Plans.*

26. Beam and McFadden, *Employee Benefits.*

27. B. J. Coleman, *Primer on Employee Retirement Income Security Act,* 3rd ed. (Washington, DC: Bureau of National Affairs, 1989).

28. *Continental Can Company v. Gavalik,* summary in *Daily Labor Report* (December 8, 1987): "Supreme Court Lets Stand Third Circuit Ruling That Pension Avoidance Scheme Is ERISA Violation," No. 234, p. A-14.

29. A. L. Gustman, O. S. Mitchell, and T. L. Steinmeier, "The Role of Pensions in the Labor Market: A Survey of the Literature," *Industrial and Labor Relations* 47 (1994), pp. 417–38.

30. D. A. DeCenzo and S. J. Holoviak, *Employee Benefits* (Englewood Cliffs, NJ: Prentice Hall, 1990).

31. E. P. Lazear, "Why Is There Early Retirement?" *Journal of Political Economy* 87 (1979), pp. 1261–84; Gustman et al., "The Role of Pensions."

32. P. Cappelli, *The New Deal at Work: Managing the Market-Driven Workforce* (Boston: Harvard Business School Press, 1999).

33. S. Dorsey, "Pension Portability and Labor Market Efficiency," *Industrial and Labor Relations* 48, no. 5 (1995), pp. 276–92.

34. Commission of the European Communities, European Community Directive 93/104/EC, issued November 23, 1993, and amended June 22, 2000, by Directive 2000/34/EC, http://europa/eu.int/comm/index_en.htm.

35. DeCenzo and Holoviak, *Employee Benefits.*

36. N. Knox and M. Murphy, "Charity as a Recruiting Tool," *The Wall Street Journal,* September 2, 2014, p. B4.

37. S. L. Grover and K. J. Crooker, "Who Appreciates Family Responsive Human Resource Policies: The Impact of Family-Friendly Policies on the Organizational Attachment of Parents and Non-parents," *Personnel Psychology* 48 (1995), pp. 271–88; T. J. Rothausen, J. A. Gonzalez, N. E. Clarke, and L. L. O'Dell, "Family-Friendly Backlash: Fact or Fiction? The Case of Organizations' On-Site Child Care Centers," *Personnel Psychology* 51 (1998), p. 685; M. A. Arthur, "Share Price Reactions to Work–Family Initiatives: An Institutional Perspective," *Academy of Management Journal* 46 (2003), p. 497; J. E. Perry-Smith and T. Blum, "Work–Family Human Resource Bundles and Perceived Organizational Performance," *Academy of Management Journal* 43 (2000), pp. 1107–17.

38. N. Bloom, T. Kretschmer, and J. Van Reenen (2011), "Are Family-Friendly Workplace Practices a Valuable Firm Resource?" *Strategic Management Journal* 32 (2011), pp. 343–67.

39. "The Employer's Role in Helping Working Families." For examples of child care arrangements in some well-known companies (e.g., AT&T, Apple, Exxon, IBM, Merck), see "A Look at Child-Care Benefits," USA *Today,* March 14, 1989, p. 4B; U.S. Census Bureau, "America's Families and Living Arrangements," June 2001, www.census.gov.

40. J. Waldfogel, "International Policies toward Parental Leave and Child Care," *Future of Children* 11, no. 1 (2001), pp. 99–111.

41. P. Hardin, "Women Execs Should Feel at Ease about Taking Full Maternity Leave," *Personnel Journal,* September 1995, p. 19.

42. Families and Work Institute, "2012 National Study of Employers," http://familiesandwork.org/site/research/reports/main.html, accessed May 21, 2013. Nationally representative survey of 1,126 employers with 50 or more employees.

43. J. Fierman, "It's 2 a.m..: Let's Go to Work," *Fortune,* August 21, 1995, pp. 82–88.

44. E. E. Kossek, "Diversity in Child Care Assistance Needs: Employee Problems, Preferences, and Work-Related Outcomes," *Personnel Psychology* 43 (1990), pp. 769–91.

45. "A Bank Profits from Its Work/Life Program," *Workforce,* February 1997, p. 49.

46. R. Broderick and B. Gerhart, "Nonwage Compensation," in *The Human Resource Management Handbook,* ed. D. Lewin, D. J. B. Mitchell, and M. A. Zadi (San Francisco: JAI Press, 1996).

47. Dulabohn et al., "Employee Benefits."

48. Hennessey, "Using Employee Benefits to Gain a Competitive Advantage."

49. U.S. Bureau of Labor Statistics, "Employer Cost for Employee Compensation," www.bls.gov; U.S. Chamber of Commerce Research Center, Employee Benefits Study, annual (Washington, D.C.: U.S. Chamber of Commerce).

50. www.census.gov.

51. S. Armour, "Uninsured Rate Down Sharply Since Health Law Was Enacted," *The Wall Street Journal,* March 16, 2015, www.wsj.com.

52. Employee Benefit Research Institute, *EBRI's Fundamentals of Employee Benefit Programs,* ebri.org, 6th ed., 2009.

53. A. C. Monheit and P. F. Cooper, "Health Insurance and Job Mobility: The Effects of Public Policy on Job-Lock," *Industrial and Labor Relations Review* 48 (1994), pp. 86–102.

54. R. Lieber, "New Way to Curb Medical Costs: Make Employees Feel the Sting," *The Wall Street Journal,* June 23, 2004, p. A1.

55. M. Barringer and O. S. Mitchell, "Workers' Preferences among Company-Provided Health Insurance Plans," *Industrial and Labor Relations Review* 48 (1994), pp. 141–52.

56. Beam and McFadden, *Employee Benefits.*

57. Jared Shelly, "Transformation Vacation," *Human Resource Executive,* November 1, 2008.

58. Leonard Berry, Ann Mirabito, and William Baun, "What's the Hard Return on Employee Wellness Programs?" *Harvard Business Review,* December 2010, pp. 104–12.

59. S. Tully, "America's Healthiest Companies," *Fortune,* June 12, 1995, pp. 98–106.

60. G. Flynn, "Companies Make Wellness Work," *Personnel Journal,* February 1995, pp. 63–66.

61. D. A. Harrison and L. Z. Liska, "Promoting Regular Exercise in Organizational Fitness Programs: Health-Related Differences in Motivational Building Blocks," *Personnel Psychology* 47 (1994), pp. 47–71.

62. J. C. Erfurt, A. Foote, and M. A. Heirich, "The Cost-Effectiveness of Worksite Wellness Programs for Hypertension Control, Weight Loss, Smoking Cessation and Exercise," Personnel Psychology 45 (1992), pp. 5–27.

63. J. Chang and M. Marsh, "The Google Diet: Search Giant Overhauled Its Eating Options to 'Nudge' Healthy Choices," *ABC News,* accessed May 11, 2013, www.abc.com.

64. The Henry J. Kaiser Family Foundation, "Visualizing Health Policy: Recent Trends in Employer-Sponsored Insurance," http://kff.org, accessed May 5, 2015.

65. H. Gardner, unpublished manuscript (Cheyenne, WY: Options & Choices, 1995); The Henry J. Kaiser Family Foundation and Health Research and Educational Trust, http://kff.org/health-costs/slide/concentration-of-health-care-spending-in-the-u-s-population-2010/, accessed May 20, 2013.

66. H. B. Noble, "Quality Is Focus for Health Plans," *The New York Times,* July 3, 1995, p. A1; J. D. Klinke, "Medicine's Industrial Revolution," *The Wall Street Journal,* August 21, 1995, p. A8.

67. S. Rosenbush and M. Totty, "How Big Data Is Changing the Whole Equation for Business," *The Wall Street Journal,* March 8, 2013; S. Kliff, "An Average ER Visit Costs More than an Average Month's Rent," *The Washington Post,* March 2, 2013; A. W. Mathews, "Same Doctor Visit, Double the Cost," *The Wall Street Journal,* August 27, 2012.

68. J. B. White, "Business Plan," *The Wall Street Journal,* October 19, 1998, p. R18.

69. L. Weber, "A Health Check for Wellness Programs," *The Wall Street Journal,* October 8, 2014, p. B1.

70. J. Schor, *The Overworked American: The Unexpected Decline of Leisure* (New York: Basic Books, 1991); U.S. Bureau of Labor Statistics, "Workers Are on the Job More Hours over the Course of a Year," *Issues in Labor Statistics,* February 1997.

71. Hewitt Associates. www.hewitt.com.

72. Beam and McFadden, *Employee Benefits.*

73. M. Wilson, G. B. Northcraft, and M. Neale, "The Perceived Value of Fringe Benefits," *Personnel Psychology* 38 (1985), pp. 309–20.

74. R. Huseman, J. Hatfield, and R. Robinson, "The MBA and Fringe Benefits," *Personnel Administrator* 23, no. 7 (1978), pp. 57–60. See summary in H. W. Hennessey Jr., "Using Employee Benefits to Gain a Competitive Advantage," *Benefits Quarterly* 5, no. 1 (1989), pp. 51–57.

75. Hennessey et al., "Impact of Benefit Awareness"; the same study found no impact of the increased awareness and benefits satisfaction on overall job satisfaction. G. F. Dreher, R. A. Ash, and R. D. Bretz, "Benefit Coverage and Employee Cost: Critical Factors in Explaining Compensation Satisfaction," *Personnel Psychology* 41 (1988), pp. 237–54.

76. M. C. Giallourakis and G. S. Taylor, "An Evaluation of Benefit Communication Strategy," *Employee Benefits Journal* 15, no. 4 (1991), pp. 14–18; Employee Benefits Research Institute, "How Readable Are Summary Plan Descriptions for Health Care Plans," *EBRI Notes,* October 2006, ebri.org.

77. J. Abraham, R. Feldman, and C. Carlin, "Understanding Employee Awareness of Health Care Quality Information: How Can Employers Benefit?" *Health Services Research* 39 (2004), pp. 1799–1816; J. H. Marler, S. L. Fisher, and W. Ke, "Employee Self-Service Technology Acceptance: A Comparison of Pre-Implementation and Post-Implementation Relationships," *Personal Psychology* 62 (2009), pp. 327–58.

78. Beam and McFadden, *Employee Benefits;* M. W. Barringer and G. T. Milkovich, "A Theoretical Explanation of the Adoption and Design of Flexible Benefit Plans: A Case of Human Resource Innovation," *Academy of Management Review* 23 (1998), pp. 305–24.

79. T. Eriksson and N. Kristensen, "Wages or Fringes? Some Evidence on Trade-Offs and Sorting," *Journal of Labor Economics* 32, no. 4 (2014), pp. 899–928.

80. For supportive evidence, see A. E. Barber, R. B. Dunham, and R. A. Formisano, "The Impact of Flexible Benefits on Employee Satisfaction: A Field Study," *Personnel Psychology* 45 (1992), pp. 55–75; E. E. Lawler, *Pay and Organizational Development* (Reading, MA: Addison-Wesley, 1981); J. C. Dencker, A. Joshi, and J. J. Martocchio, "Employee Benefits as Context for Intergenerational Conflict," *Human Resource Management Review* 17 (2007), pp. 208–20; A. Caza, M. W. McCarter, and G. B. Northcraft, "Performance Benefits of Reward Choice: A Procedural Justice Perspective," *Human Resource Management Journal* 25 (2015), 184–199. Caza et al. also found a positive effect of benefits choice on performance in a library study where performance was measured by how well undergraduate students were able to combine words into compound words.

81. Beam and McFadden, *Employee Benefits.*

82. Ibid.

83. *Los Angeles Dept. of Water & Power v. Manhart,* 435 US SCt 702 (1978), 16 EPD, 8250.

84. S. K. Hoffman, "Discrimination Litigation Relating to Employee Benefits," *Labor Law Journal,* June 1992, pp. 362–81.

85. Ibid., p. 375.

86. S. J. Sacher and J. Day, "The New VEBAs," *BNA Pension and Benefits* blog, June 1, 2010. http://pblog.bna.com, extracted June 3, 2011; P. C. Borzi, "Retiree Health VEBAs: A New Twist on an Old Paradigm. Implications for Retirees, Unions, and Employers," The Henry J. Kaiser Family Foundation, March 2009.

87. V. Monga, "Pension Plans Brace for a One–Two Punch," *The Wall Street Journal,* March 25, 2014, p. B1.

PART FIVE

CHAPTER 14

Collective Bargaining and Labor Relations

LEARNING OBJECTIVES

After reading this chapter, you should be able to:

LO 14-1 Describe what is meant by collective bargaining and labor relations. *page 578*

LO 14-2 Identify the labor relations goals of management, labor unions, and society. *page 580*

LO 14-3 Explain the legal environment's impact on labor relations. *page 590*

LO 14-4 Describe the major labor–management interactions: organizing, contract negotiations, and contract administration. *page 594*

LO 14-5 Describe new, less adversarial approaches to labor–management relations. *page 609*

LO 14-6 Explain how changes in competitive challenges (e.g., product market competition and globalization) are influencing labor–management interactions. *page 616*

LO 14-7 Explain how labor relations in the public sector differ from labor relations in the private sector. *page 619*

Collective Action by Nonunion Workers and Supporters

The National Labor Relations Act protects "concerted action" (collectively discussing or taking action to address work conditions) by workers, whether they are represented by a union or not. Increasingly, low-wage, nonunion workers have taken concerted action to raise wages for themselves and others. A primary target has been McDonald's. A major goal is to create a national movement to raise hourly wages to $15/hour (the "Fight for 15") to help workers make ends meet.

Nonunion workers went out on strike a few years ago for a day in just one city, New York. But now, organizers believe they will soon have strikers and supporters out on the streets in 200 cities nationwide, with supporting actions in 35 other countries. A spokesman for McDonald's stated that such events were not strikes, but rather "organized rallies designed to garner media attention" and that "very few McDonald's employees have participated." According to *The New York Times,* the Service Employees International Union (SEIU) has contributed more than $15 million to support the movement. Some believe the SEIU has also coordinated with McDonald's European unions to bring pressure on the company there (e.g., accusing the company of tax avoidance in Europe).

Recently, McDonald's did increase its lowest wage rates to be at least $1 above the applicable minimum wage, which nationally is $7.25 and in New York, where the actions got their start, $8.75. Although protesters believed their actions played a major role, McDonald's did not attribute the wage increase to the protests, but rather said it was due to tightening labor market competition. (See the opening to Chapter 11.) Also, in reading the fine print of the announcement, only workers in stores owned by McDonald's (not franchisee-owned stores) will be covered, which accounts for only about 10% of McDonald's employees. And, of course, the new pay rates do not satisfy the goal of $15/hour. One activist stated, "We aren't going to stop until the service sector . . . becomes the next foundation for the American middle class."

SOURCES: R. L. Swarns, "McDonald's Workers, Vowing a Fight, Say Raises are Too Little for Too Few," *The New York Times,* April 6, 2015, www.nytimes; S. Greenhouse, "A Broader Strategy on Wages," *The New York Times,* March 31, 2015, www.nytimes.com.

Introduction

In the chapter opening, we see workers taking collective action to change collective terms and conditions of employment, but in this instance without any formal union representation and without being members of a union. The National Labor Relations Act protects such "concerted activity" for everyone, whether union members or not. In this case, workers and their supporters, similar to unionized workers, hope to bring pressure to bear on McDonald's (and others) to improve wages and other aspects of the job. Unions can help achieve important worker goals, including not only higher wages, but also worker protection, and giving workers a say in their workplaces. A main source of negotiating leverage for unions is the ability to strike, which interrupts production, sales, and profits. In the end, however, such conflicts must be balanced against the common interests that bind workers and companies together. Worker jobs and income, as well as company profits, depend on the two parties being able to cooperate to assure the ability of the company to be competitive and survive.

The Labor Relations Framework

LO 14-1

Describe what is meant by collective bargaining and labor relations.

John Dunlop, former secretary of labor and a leading industrial relations scholar, suggested in the book *Industrial Relations Systems* (1958) that a successful industrial relations system consists of four elements: (1) an environmental context (technology, market pressures, and the legal framework, especially as it affects bargaining power); (2) participants, including employees and their unions, management, and the government; (3) a "web of rules" (rules of the game) that describe the process by which labor and management interact and resolve disagreements (such as the steps followed in settling contract grievances); and (4) ideology.[1] For the industrial relations system to operate properly, the three participants must, to some degree, have a common ideology (e.g., acceptance of the capitalist system) and must accept the roles of the other participants. Acceptance does not translate into convergence of interests, however. To the contrary, some degree of worker–management conflict is inevitable because, although the interests of the two parties overlap (e.g., survival of the firm and thus survival of workers' jobs and investors' profits), they also diverge in key respects (such as how to divide the economic profits between workers and investors).[2]

Therefore, according to Dunlop and other U.S. scholars of like mind, an effective industrial relations system does not eliminate conflict. Rather, it provides institutions (and a "web of rules") that resolve conflict in a way that minimizes its costs to management, employees, and society. The collective bargaining system is one such institution, as are related mechanisms such as mediation, arbitration, and participation in decision making. These ideas formed the basis for the development in the 1940s of schools and departments of industrial and labor relations to train labor relations professionals who, working in both union and management positions, would have the skills to minimize costly forms of conflict such as strikes (which were reaching record levels at the time) and maximize integrative (win–win) solutions to such disagreements.

A more recent industrial relations model, developed by Harry Katz and Thomas Kochan, is particularly helpful in laying out the types of decisions management and unions make in their interactions and the consequences of such decisions for attainment of goals in areas such as wages and benefits, job security, and the rights and responsibilities of unions and managements.[3] According to Katz and Kochan, these choices occur at three levels.

First, at the strategic level, management makes basic choices such as whether to work with its union(s) or to devote its efforts to developing nonunion operations. Environmental factors (or competitive challenges) offer both constraints and opportunities in implementing strategies. For example, if public opinion toward labor unions becomes negative during a particular time period, some employers may see that as an opportunity to rid themselves of unions, whereas other employers may seek a better working relationship with their unions. Similarly, increased competition may dictate the need to increase productivity or reduce labor costs, but whether this is accomplished by shifting work to nonunion facilities or by working with unions to become more competitive is a strategic choice that management faces.

Although management has often been the initiator of change in recent years, unions face a similar choice between fighting changes to the status quo and being open to new labor–management relationships (like less adversarial forms of participation in decision making, such as labor–management teams).

Katz and Kochan suggest that labor and management choices at the strategic level in turn affect the labor–management interaction at a second level, the functional level, where contract negotiations and union organizing occur, and at the final workplace level, the arena in which the contract is administered. Although the relationships between labor and management at each of the three levels are somewhat interdependent, the relationship at the three levels may also differ. For example, while management may have a strategy of building an effective relationship with its unions at the strategic level, there may be significant day-to-day conflicts over work rules, grievances, and so forth at any given facility or bargaining unit (workplace level).

The labor relations framework depicted in Figure 14.1 incorporates many of the ideas discussed so far, including the important role of the environment (the competitive challenges); union, management, and societal goals; and a separation of union–management interactions into categories (union organizing, contract negotiation, contract administration) that can have important influences on one another but may also be analyzed somewhat independently. The model also highlights the important role that relative bargaining power plays in influencing goals, union–management interactions, and the degree to which each party achieves its goals. Relative bargaining power, in turn, is significantly influenced by the competitive environment (legal, social, quality, high-performance work systems, and globalization competitive challenges) and the size and depth of union membership.[4]

We now describe the components of this model in greater depth. The remainder of the chapter is organized into the following sections: the goals and strategies of society, management, and unions; union structure (including union administration and membership); the legal framework, perhaps the key aspect of the competitive environment for labor relations; union and management interactions (organizing, contract negotiation, contract administration); and goal attainment. Environmental factors (other than legal) and bargaining power are discussed in the context of these sections. In addition, two special topics, international comparisons and public sector labor relations, are discussed.

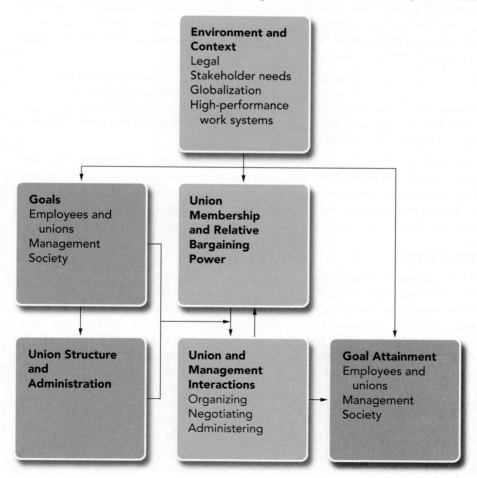

Figure 14.1

A Labor Relations Framework

Goals and Strategies

SOCIETY

In one sense, labor unions, with their emphasis on group action, do not fit well with the individualistic orientation of U.S. capitalism. However, industrial relations scholars such as Beatrice and Sidney Webb and John R. Commons argued in the late 1800s and early 1900s that individual workers' bargaining power was far smaller than that of employers, who were likely to have more financial resources and the ability to easily replace workers.[5] Effective institutions for worker representation (like labor unions) were therefore seen as a way to make bargaining power more equal.

Labor unions' major benefit to society is the institutionalization of industrial conflict, which is therefore resolved in the least costly way. Although disagreements between management and labor continue, it is better to resolve disputes through discussion (collective bargaining) than by battling in the streets. As an influential group of industrial relations scholars put it in describing the future of advanced industrial relations around the world, "Class warfare will be forgotten. The battles will be in the corridors instead of the streets, and memos will flow instead of blood."[6] In this sense, collective bargaining not only has the potential to reduce economic losses caused by strikes but may also contribute to societal stability. For this reason, industrial relations scholars have often viewed labor unions as an essential component of a democratic society.[7] These were some of the beliefs that contributed to the enactment of the National Labor Relations Act (NLRA) in 1935, which sought to provide an environment conducive to collective bargaining and has since regulated labor and management activities and interactions.

Even Senator Orrin Hatch, described by *Bloomberg BusinessWeek* as "labor's archrival on Capitol Hill," has spoken of the need for unions:

> There are always going to be people who take advantage of workers. Unions even that out, to their credit. We need them to level the field between labor and management. If you didn't have unions, it would be very difficult for even enlightened employers not to take advantage of workers on wages and working conditions, because of [competition from] rivals. I'm among the first to say I believe in unions.[8]

Although an industrial relations system based on collective bargaining has drawbacks, so too do the alternatives. Unilateral control by management sacrifices workers' rights. Extensive involvement of government and the courts can result in conflict resolution that is expensive, slow, and imposed by someone (a judge) with much less firsthand knowledge of the circumstances than either labor or management.

MANAGEMENT

One of management's most basic decisions is whether to encourage or discourage the unionization of its employees. It may discourage unions because it fears higher wage and benefit costs, the disruptions caused by strikes, and an adversarial relationship with its employees or, more generally, greater constraints placed on its decision-making flexibility and discretion. Historically, management has used two basic strategies to avoid unionization.[9] It may seek to provide employment terms and conditions that employees will perceive as sufficiently attractive and equitable so that they see little gain from union representation. Or it may aggressively oppose union representation, even where there is significant employee interest. Use of the latter strategy has increased significantly during the last 30 to 40 years.

If management voluntarily recognizes a union or if employees are already represented by a union, the focus is shifted from dealing with employees as individuals to employees as a group. Still, certain basic management objectives remain: controlling labor costs and increasing productivity (by keeping wages and benefits in check) and maintaining management prerogatives in important areas such as staffing levels and work rules. Of course, management always has the option of trying to decertify a union (that is, encouraging employees to vote out the union in a decertification election) if it believes that the majority of employees no longer wish to be represented by the union.

LABOR UNIONS

Labor unions seek, through collective action, to give workers a formal and independent voice in setting the terms and conditions of their work. Table 14.1 shows typical provisions negotiated by unions in collective bargaining contracts. Labor unions attempt to

Table 14.1

Typical Provisions in Collective Bargaining Contracts

Establishment and administration of the agreement	Wage determination and administration	Plant operations
Bargaining unit and plant supplements	General provisions	Work and shop rules
Contract duration and reopening and renegotiation provisions	Rate structure and wage differentials	Rest periods and other in-plant time allowances
Union security and the checkoff	Allowances	Safety and health
Special bargaining committees	Incentive systems and production bonus plans	Plant committees
Grievance procedures	Production standards and time studies	Hours of work and premium pay practices
Arbitration and mediation	Job classification and job evaluation	Shift operations
Strikes and lockouts	Individual wage adjustments	Hazardous work
Contract enforcement	General wage adjustments during the contract period	Discipline and discharge
Functions, rights, and responsibilities	**Job or income security**	**Paid and unpaid leave**
Management rights clauses	Hiring and transfer arrangements	Vacations and holidays
Plant removal	Employment and income guarantees	Sick leave
Subcontracting	Reporting and call-in pay	Funeral and personal leave
Union activities on company time and premises	Supplemental unemployment benefit plans	Military leave and jury duty
Union–management cooperation	Regulation of overtime, shift work, etc.	**Employee benefit plans**
Regulation of technological change	Reduction of hours to forestall layoffs	Health and insurance plans
Advance notice and consultation	Layoff procedures; seniority; recall	Pension plans
	Worksharing in lieu of layoff	Profit-sharing, stock purchase, and thrift plans
	Attrition arrangements	Bonus plans
	Promotion practices	**Special groups**
	Training and retraining	Apprentices and learners
	Relocation allowances	Workers with disabilities and older workers
	Severance pay and layoff benefit plans	Women
	Special funds and study committees	Veterans
		Union representatives
		Nondiscrimination clauses

SOURCE: From Harry Katz, Thomas Kochan, and Alexander Colvin, *An Introduction to Collective Bargaining and Industrial Relations* 4E, 2008. Reproduced with permission of The McGraw-Hill Companies, Inc.

The Alliance for Bangladesh Worker Safety

According to the website of the Alliance for Bangladesh Worker Safety, it was established to improve workplace safety in Bangladesh's garment factories in the aftermath of factory tragedies there such as the collapse of the Rana Plaza building. The Alliance reports that its accomplishments in its first year included:

- Developed and implemented Bangladesh's first integrated fire safety and structural integrity standard.

- Inspected all 587 factories used by Alliance members as sources for their garments.
- Provided fire safety training to roughly 1 million workers and managers employed in these factories.

The Alliance's first annual report also provided the following case study of its actions at a local company called RSI Apparels Limited. It reported that an inspection revealed a building structural problem that posed an immediate risk to worker safety. Production at the factory was stopped and safety upgrades made. The Alliance paid one-half of the salaries of workers who were not able to work during that time period and the owner of the factory paid the other half of employees salaries.

SOURCE: "Protecting the Lives and Livelihoods of Bangladesh's Garment Workers," *First Annual Report of the Alliance for Bangladesh Worker Safety,* July 2014, www.bangladeshworkersafety.org.

represent their members' interests in these decisions. Without adequate union representation, not only worker wages, but also their safety and welfare, are more likely to be put at risk. This is particularly true in low-wage economies where regulatory protection may also be lacking.

Just before more than 1,100 workers perished in the Rana Plaza eight-story factory building collapse in Bangladesh in April 2013, workers on the third floor were startled by what sounded like an explosion. They also saw cracks in the walls. An engineer was brought in to examine the cracks, and he found that they were structural. He recommended immediate evacuation of the building. Workers evacuated, but were ordered back to work. If they did not go back, they would lose their pay, which at $38 a month, they likely did not feel they could afford. The question was how could such a tragedy be prevented from happening again? One response has been for companies that buy from garment suppliers in Bangladesh to develop and enforce worker safety and treatment standards. (See the "Integrity in Action" box for more details on this effort.) Another response is: What if these workers at Rana Plaza had been represented by a labor union? Perhaps those workers, if unionized, could have refused to follow the order to return to work. As one response to the tragedy, the Bangladesh government stated that it would begin to allow the country's 4 million garment workers to form trade unions and do so without first obtaining prior permission from factory owners. Labor unions can provide protection for workers and also help negotiate higher wages for workers to give them a better standard of living. Of course, these potential advantages will be weighed against the potential consequence of higher labor costs and/or lost working time due to strikes (and thus less competitive product prices, which could reduce sales and employment). In the best case scenario, an effective labor–management relationship can bring more efficient organization of workers in the production process and higher wages can allow more selectivity in hiring and a more productive workforce.

A major goal of labor unions is bargaining effectiveness, because with it comes the power and influence to make the employees' voices heard and to effect changes in the workplace.[10] The right to strike is one important component of bargaining power. In turn, the success of a strike (actual or threatened) depends on the relative magnitude of the costs imposed on management versus those imposed on the union. A critical factor is the size of union membership. More members translate into a greater ability to halt or disrupt production and also into greater financial resources for continuing a strike in the face of lost wages.

Union Structure, Administration, and Membership

A necessary step in discussing labor–management interactions is a basic knowledge of how labor and management are organized and how they function. Management has been described throughout this book. We now focus on labor unions.

NATIONAL AND INTERNATIONAL UNIONS

Most union members belong to a national or international union. In turn, most national unions are composed of multiple local units, and most are affiliated with the American Federation of Labor and Congress of Industrial Organizations (AFL-CIO).

The largest national unions are listed in Table 14.2. The National Education Association, which is not affiliated with the AFL-CIO, is the largest union with almost 3 million

Table 14.2
Largest Labor Unions in the United States

ORGANIZATION	NUMBER OF MEMBERS
1. National Education Association	2,963,121
2. Service Employees International Union	1,893,775
3. American Federation of Teachers	1,597,140
4. American Federation of State, County, and Municipal Employees	1,337,126
5. International Brotherhood of Teamsters	1,305,773
6. United Food and Commercial Workers International Union	1,271,804
7. International Brotherhood of Electrical Workers	658,812
8. Communications Workers of America	623,020
9. United Steel, Paper and Forestry, Rubber, Manufacturing, Energy, Allied Industrial, and Service Workers International Union	589,907
10. International Association of Machinists and Aerospace Workers	569,373
11. Laborers	557,870
12. United Brotherhood of Carpenters and Joiners	412,278
13. United Automobile, Aerospace, and Agricultural Implement Workers of America International Union	403,466
14. International Union of Operating Engineers	374,521
15. United Association of Journeymen and Apprentices of the Plumbing and Pipe Fitting Industry of the United States and Canada	329,954

SOURCE: U.S. Department of Labor, Office of Labor-Management Standards, Public Disclosure Home, http://kcerds. dol-esa.gov/query/getOrgQry.do, accessed May 12, 2015.

members. An important characteristic of a union is whether it is a craft or industrial union. The electrical workers' and carpenters' unions are craft unions, meaning that the members all have a particular skill or occupation. Craft unions often are responsible for training their members (through apprenticeships) and for supplying craft workers to employers. Requests for carpenters, for example, would come to the union hiring hall, which would decide which carpenters to send out. Thus craft workers may work for many employers over time, their constant link being to the union. A craft union's bargaining power depends greatly on the control it can exercise over the supply of its workers.

In contrast, industrial unions are made up of members who are linked by their work in a particular industry (such as steelworkers and autoworkers). Typically they represent many different occupations. Membership in the union is a result of working for a particular employer in the industry. Changing employers is less common than it is among craft workers, and employees who change employers remain members of the same union only if they happen to move to other employers covered by that union. Whereas a craft union may restrict the number of, say, carpenters to maintain higher wages, industrial unions try to organize as many employees in as wide a range of skills as possible.

LOCAL UNIONS

Even when a national union plays the most critical role in negotiating terms of a collective bargaining contract, negotiation occurs at the local level as well as over work rules and other issues that are locally determined. In addition, administration of the contract is largely carried out at the local union level. Consequently, the bulk of day-to-day interaction between labor and management takes place at the local union level.

The local of an industrial-based union may correspond to a single large facility or to a number of small facilities. In a craft-oriented union, the local may cover a city or a region. The local union typically elects officers (like president, vice president, treasurer). Responsibility for contract negotiation may rest with the officers, or a bargaining committee may be formed for this purpose. Typically the national union provides assistance, ranging from background data about other settlements and technical advice to sending a representative to lead the negotiations.

Individual members' participation in local union meetings includes the election of union officials and strike votes. However, most union contact is with the shop steward, who is responsible for ensuring that the terms of the collective bargaining contract are enforced. The shop steward represents employees in contract grievances. Another union position, the business representative, performs some of the same functions, especially where the union deals with multiple employers, as is often the case with craft unions.

AMERICAN FEDERATION OF LABOR AND CONGRESS OF INDUSTRIAL ORGANIZATIONS (AFL-CIO)

The AFL-CIO is not a labor union but rather an association that seeks to advance the shared interests of its member unions at the national level, much as the Chamber of Commerce and the National Association of Manufacturers do for their member employers. As Figure 14.2 indicates, there are 56 affiliated national and international unions and thousands of locals. An important responsibility of the AFL-CIO is to represent labor's interests in public policy issues such as civil rights, economic policy, safety, and occupational health. It also provides information and analysis that member unions can use in their activities: organizing new members, negotiating new contracts, and administering contracts.

Figure 14.2
AFL-CIO
Organization Chart

**56 Affiliated
National Unions**

**Executive Council
55 Vice Presidents**

**President
Secretary-Treasurer
Executive Vice President**

AFL-CIO Departments
- Accounting
- Campaigns
- Civil, Human and Women's Rights
- Digital Strategies
- Facilities Management
- Government Affairs
- Human Resources
- Information Technology
- International
- Meetings and Travel
- Office of General Counsel
- Office of Investment
- Organizing
- Policy
- Political
- Public Affairs
- Support Services

**Trade and Industrial
Departments**
- Building and Construction Trades
- Maritime Trades
- Metal Trades
- Professional Employees
- Transportation Trades
- Union Label and Service Trades

Thousands of affiliated local
unions and 12.75 million
members

51 State Federations

SOURCE: AFL-CIO, www.aflcio.org, accessed May 13, 2015.

UNION SECURITY

The survival and security of a union depends on its ability to ensure a regular flow of new members and member dues to support the services it provides. Therefore, unions typically place high priority on negotiating two contract provisions with an employer that are critical to a union's security or viability: checkoff provisions and union membership or contribution. First, under a **checkoff provision**, the employer, on behalf of the union, automatically deducts union dues from employees' paychecks.

A second union security provision focuses on the flow of new members (and their dues). The strongest union security arrangement is a **closed shop**, under which a person must be a union member (and thus pay dues) before being hired. A closed shop is, however, illegal under the NLRA. A **union shop** requires a person to join the union within a certain amount of time (30 days) after beginning employment. An **agency shop** is similar to a union shop but does not require union membership, only that dues be paid. **Maintenance of membership** rules do not require union membership but do require that employees who choose to join must remain members for a certain period of time (such as the length of the contract).

Under the 1947 Taft–Hartley Act (an amendment to the NLRA), states may pass so-called **right-to-work laws**, which make union shops, maintenance of membership, and agency shops illegal. The idea behind such laws is that compulsory union membership (or making employees pay union dues) infringes on the employee's right to freedom of association. From the union perspective, a big concern is "free riders," employees who benefit from union activities without belonging to a union. By law, all members of a bargaining unit, whether union members or not, must be represented by the union. If the union is required to offer service to all bargaining unit members, even those who are not union members, it may lose its financial viability.

UNION MEMBERSHIP AND BARGAINING POWER

At the strategic level, management and unions meet head-on over the issue of union organizing. Increasingly, employers are actively resisting unionization in an attempt to control costs and maintain their flexibility. Unions, on the other hand, must organize new members and hold on to their current members to have the kind of bargaining power and financial resources needed to achieve their goals in future organizing and to negotiate and administer contracts with management. For this reason we now discuss trends in union membership and possible explanations for those trends.

Since the 1950s, when union membership rose to 35% of employment, membership has consistently declined as a percentage of employment. It now stands at 11.1% of all employment and 6.6% of private-sector employment.[11] As Figure 14.3 indicates, this decline shows no indication of reversing.[12]

What factors explain the decline in union membership? Several have been identified.[13]

Structural Changes in the Economy

At the risk of oversimplifying, we might say that unions have traditionally been strongest in urban workplaces (especially those outside the South) that employ middle-aged men in blue-collar jobs. However, much recent job growth has occurred among women and youth in the service sector (in contrast to the manufacturing sector) of the economy. Although unionizing such groups is possible, unions have so far not had much success organizing these groups in the private sector. Despite the importance of structural changes in the economy, studies show that they account for no more than one-quarter of the overall union membership decline.[14]

Checkoff Provision
A union contract provision that requires an employer to deduct union dues from employees' paychecks.

Closed Shop
A union security provision requiring a person to be a union member before being hired. Illegal under NLRA.

Union Shop
A union security provision that requires a person to join the union within a certain amount of time after being hired.

Agency Shop
A union security provision that requires an employee to pay union membership dues but not to join the union.

Maintenance of Membership
Union rules requiring members to remain members for a certain period of time (such as the length of the union contract).

Right-to-Work Laws
State laws that make union shops, maintenance of membership, and agency shops illegal.

Figure 14.3

Union Membership Density among U.S. Wage and Salary Workers, 1973–2014

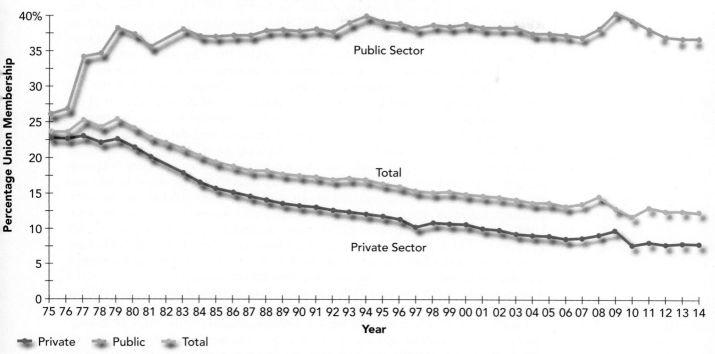

SOURCE: From B. T. Hirsch and D. A. MacPherson, *Union Membership and Earnings Data Book 2001* (Washington, DC: The Bureau of National Affairs, Inc., 2001). Reprinted with permission. Data for 2001 to 2014 obtained from U.S. Bureau of Labor Statistics, www.bls.gov.

Increased Employer Resistance

Almost one-half of large employers in a survey reported that their most important labor goal was to be union-free. This contrasts sharply with 60 years ago, when Jack Barbash wrote that "many tough bargainers [among employers] prefer the union to a situation where there is no union. Most of the employers in rubber, basic steel and the automobile industry fall in this category." The idea then was that an effective union could help assess and communicate the interests of employees to management, thus helping management make better decisions. But product-market pressures, such as foreign competition and deregulation (e.g., trucking, airlines, telecommunications), have contributed to increasing employer resistance to unions.[15] These changes in the competitive environment have contributed to a change in management's perspective and goals.[16]

In the absence of significant competition from foreign producers, unions were often able to organize entire industries. For example, the UAW organized all four major producers in the automobile industry (GM, Ford, Chrysler, and American Motors). The UAW usually sought and achieved the same union–management contract at each company. As a consequence, a negotiated wage increase in the industry could be passed on to the consumer in the form of higher prices. No company was undercut by its competitors because the labor cost of all major producers in the industry was determined by the same union–management contract, and the U.S. public had little option but to buy U.S.-made cars. However, the onset of foreign competition in the automobile market changed the competitive situation as well as the UAW's ability to organize the industry.[17] U.S. automakers were slow to recognize and respond to the competitive threat from foreign producers, resulting in a loss of market share and employment.

Competitive threats have contributed to increased employer resistance to union organizing and, in some cases, to an increased emphasis on ridding themselves of existing unions. Unionized workers receive, on average, 26% higher wages, and this advantage is still estimated to be 10% to 15% when observable characteristics of union and nonunion workers are equated. The compensation advantage is still larger if benefits are also included. Many employers have decided that they can no longer compete with these higher labor costs, and union membership has suffered as a result.[18] One measure of increased employer resistance is the dramatic increase in the late 1960s in the number of unfair employer labor practices (violations of sections of the NLRA such as section 8(a)(3), which prohibits firing employees for union organizing, as we discuss later) even though the number of elections held did not change much. (See Figure 14.4.) The use of remedies such as back pay for workers also grew, but the costs to employers of such penalties does not appear to have been sufficient to prevent the growth in employer unfair labor practices. Not surprisingly, the union victory rate in representation elections decreased from almost 59% in 1960 to below 50% by 1975. Although the union victory rate in elections during the two most recent years has actually been higher (64%), the number of elections has declined precipitously, from 7,422 in 1970 to 1,330 in 2013, a decrease of 82%. Moreover, decertification elections have come to represent a larger share of all elections in recent years.[19] Given the significant decline in both elections and union membership percentage (see Figure 14.3), the increases in the number of unfair labor practice charges and back pay awards is all the more notable.

Finally, even if a union wins the right to represent employees, its ability to successfully negotiate a contract with the employer is not guaranteed. Indeed, refusal to bargain by the employer is the unfair labor practice most frequently filed (over half of all charges) against employers. One study examined 22,000 organizing drives by unions in the United States over a six-year period. Only about one-seventh of these drives eventually resulted in a union contract, either because the election was lost (or challenged) or because after a win, a contract could not be obtained with the employer. Further, this success rate was lower still (by 30%) in cases where the employer filed an unfair labor practice against the union.[20]

At a personal level, some managers may face serious consequences if a union successfully organizes a new set of workers or mounts a serious organizing drive. One study indicated that 8% of the plant managers in companies with organizing drives were fired, and 10% of those in companies where the union was successful were fired (compared with 2% in a control group).[21] Furthermore, only 3% of the plant managers facing an organizing drive were promoted, and none of those ending up with a union contract were promoted (compared with 21% of the managers in the control group). Therefore, managers are often under intense pressure to oppose unionization attempts.

Substitution with HRM

A major study of the human resource management strategies and practices among large, nonunion employers found that union avoidance was often an important employee relations objective.[22] Top management's values in such companies drive specific policies such as promotion from within, an influential personnel–human resource department, and above-average pay and benefits. These policies, in turn, contribute to a number of desirable outcomes such as flexibility, positive employee attitudes, and responsive and committed employees, which ultimately lead to higher productivity and better employee relations. In other words, employers attempt to remain nonunion by offering most of the

Figure 14.4

Employer Resistance to Union Organizing, 1950–2013

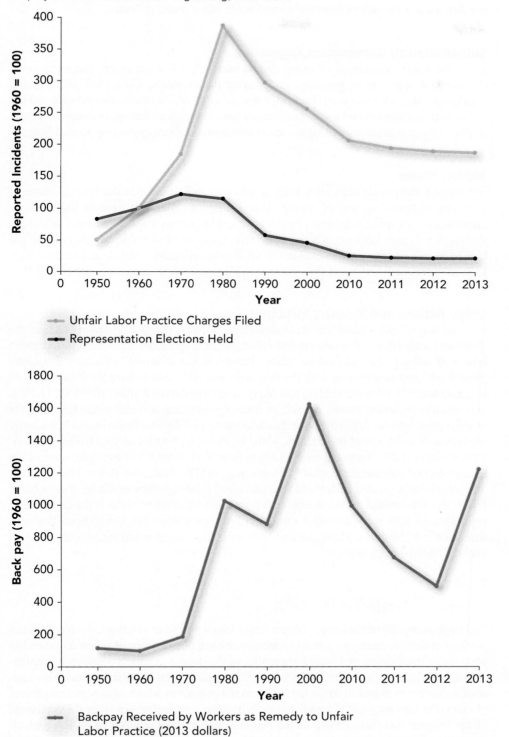

Unfair Labor Practice Charges Filed
Representation Elections Held

Backpay Received by Workers as Remedy to Unfair
Labor Practice (2013 dollars)

SOURCE: Adapted and updated from R. B. Freeman and J. L. Medoff, *What Do Unions Do?* (New York: Basic Books, 1984). Data for from www.nlrb.gov.

things a union can offer, and then some, while still maintaining a productivity advantage over their competitors. Of course, one aspect of union representation that employers cannot duplicate is the independent employee voice that a union provides.

Substitution by Government Regulation

Since the 1960s, regulation of many employment areas has increased, including equal employment opportunity, pensions, and worker displacement. Combined with existing regulations, this increase may result in fewer areas in which unions can provide worker rights or protection beyond those specified by law. Yet western European countries generally have more regulations and higher levels of union membership than the United States.[23]

Worker Views

Industrial relations scholars have long argued that the absence in the United States of a history of feudalism and of strong class distinctions found in western Europe have contributed to a more pragmatic, business-oriented (versus class-conscious) unionism. Although this may help explain the somewhat lower level of union membership in the United States, its relevance in explaining the downward trend is not clear. Further, when U.S. workers are asked about their interest in joining a union, interest is substantial.[24]

Union Actions and Industry Structure

In some ways, unions have hurt their own cause. First, corruption in unions such as the Teamsters may have had a detrimental effect. Second, questions have been raised about how well unions have adapted to recent changes in the economic structure. Employee groups and economic sectors with the fastest growth rates tend to have the lowest rates of unionization.[25] Women are slightly less likely to be in unions than men (10.5% vs. 11.7%.), and nonmanufacturing industries such as finance, insurance, and real estate have a lower union representation (2.0%) than does manufacturing (9.7%). The South is also less heavily organized than the rest of the country, with, for example, South Carolina having a unionization rate of 2.2%, compared with 24.6% in New York State.[26] For example, none of the foreign-owned automobile assembly plants (e.g., BMW, Mercedes-Benz, Toyota, Volkswagen, Nissan), located in the South are unionized (although they would be in their home countries). One reason for the smaller union presence in southern states is the existence of right-to-work laws (see our earlier discussion) in such states. (We should note, however, that since 2012, Indiana, Michigan, and Wisconsin, traditional union strongholds, have all become right-to-work states.)

Legal Framework

LO 14-3
Explain the legal environment's impact on labor relations.

Although competitive challenges have a major impact on labor relations, the legal framework of collective bargaining is an especially critical determinant of union membership and relative bargaining power and, therefore, of the degree to which employers, employees, and society are successful in achieving their goals. The legal framework also constrains union structure and administration and the manner in which unions and employers interact. Perhaps the most dramatic example of labor laws' influence is the 1935 passage of the Wagner Act (also known as the National Labor Relations Act or NLRA), which actively supported collective bargaining rather than impeding it. As a result, union membership nearly tripled, from 3 million in 1933 (7.7% of all employment) to 8.8 million

(19.2% of employment) by 1939.[27] With increased membership came greater union bargaining power and, consequently, more success in achieving union goals.

Before the 1930s, the legal system was generally hostile to unions. The courts generally viewed unions as coercive organizations that hindered free trade. Unions' focus on collective voice and collective action (strikes, boycotts) did not fit well with the U.S. emphasis on capitalism, individualism, freedom of contract, and property rights.[28]

The Great Depression of the 1930s, however, shifted public attitudes toward business and the free-enterprise system. Unemployment rates as high as 25% and a 30% drop in the gross national product between 1929 and 1933 focused attention on employee rights and on the shortcomings of the system as it existed then. The nation was in a crisis, and President Franklin Roosevelt responded with dramatic action, the New Deal. On the labor front, the 1935 NLRA ushered in a new era of public policy for labor unions, enshrining collective bargaining as the preferred mechanism for settling labor–management disputes.

The introduction to the NLRA states:

> It is in the national interest of the United States to maintain full production in its economy. Industrial strife among employees, employers, and labor organizations interferes with full production and is contrary to our national interest. Experience has shown that labor disputes can be lessened if the parties involved recognize the legitimate rights of each in their relations with one another. To establish these rights under the law, Congress enacted the National Labor Relations Act. Its purpose is to define and protect the rights of employees and employers, to encourage collective bargaining, and to eliminate certain practices on the part of labor and management that are harmful to the general welfare.[29]

The rights of employees are set out in Section 7 of the act, including the "right to self-organization, to form, join, or assist labor organizations, to bargain collectively through representatives of their own choosing, and to engage in other concerted activities for the purpose of collective bargaining. The act also gives employees the right to refrain from any or all of such activities except [in cases] requiring membership in a labor organization as a condition of employment."[30] Examples of protected activities include

- Union organizing.
- Joining a union, whether it is recognized by the employer or not.
- Going out on strike to secure better working conditions.
- Refraining from activity on behalf of the union.[31]

Although the NLRA has broad coverage in the private sector, Table 14.3 shows that there are some notable exclusions.

UNFAIR LABOR PRACTICES—EMPLOYERS

The NLRA prohibits certain activities by both employers and labor unions. Unfair labor practices by employers are listed in Section 8(a) of the NLRA. Section 8(a)(1) prohibits employers from interfering with, restraining, or coercing employees in exercising their rights to join or assist a labor organization or to refrain from such activities. Section 8(a)(2) prohibits employer domination of or interference with the formation or activities of a labor union. Section 8(a)(3) prohibits discrimination in any aspect of employment that attempts to encourage or discourage union-related activity. Section 8(a)(4) prohibits discrimination against employees for providing testimony relevant to enforcement of the NLRA. Section 8(a)(5) prohibits employers from refusing to bargain collectively with a labor organization that has standing under the act. Examples of employer unfair labor practices are listed in Table 14.4.

Table 14.3

Are You Excluded from the NLRA's Coverage?

The NLRA specifically excludes from its coverage individuals who are
- Employed as a supervisor.
- Employed by a parent or spouse.
- Employed as an independent contractor.
- Employed in the domestic service of any person or family in a home.
- Employed as agricultural laborers.
- Employed by an employer subject to the Railway Labor Act.
- Employed by a federal, state, or local government.
- Employed by any other person who is not an employer as defined in the NLRA.

SOURCE: www.nlrb.gov/publications/engulp.html.

Table 14.4

Examples of Employer Unfair Labor Practices

- Threatening employees with loss of their jobs or benefits if they join or vote for a union.
- Threatening to close down a plant if organized by a union.
- Questioning employees about their union membership or activities in a manner that restrains or coerces them.
- Spying or pretending to spy on union meetings.
- Granting wage increases that are timed to discourage employees from forming or joining a union.
- Taking an active part in organizing a union or committee to represent employees.
- Providing preferential treatment or aid to one of several unions trying to organize employees.
- Discharging employees for urging other employees to join a union or refusing to hire applicants because they are union members.
- Refusing to reinstate workers when job openings occur because the workers participated in a lawful strike.
- Ending operation at one plant and opening the same operation at another plant with new employees because employees at the first plant joined a union.
- Demoting or firing employees for filing an unfair labor practice or for testifying at an NLRB hearing.
- Refusing to meet with employees' representatives because the employees are on strike.
- Refusing to supply the employees' representative with cost and other data concerning a group insurance plan covering employees.
- Announcing a wage increase without consulting the employees' representative.
- Failing to bargain about the effects of a decision to close one of employer's plants.

SOURCE: National Labor Relations Board, *Basic Guide to the National Labor Relations Act* (Washington, DC: U.S. Government Printing Office, 1997). Available at www.nlrb.gov. Accessed May 13, 2015.

UNFAIR LABOR PRACTICES—LABOR UNIONS

Taft-Hartley Act
The 1947 act that outlawed unfair union labor practices.

Originally the NLRA did not list any union unfair labor practices. These were added through the 1947 **Taft-Hartley Act.** The 1959 *Landrum-Griffin Act* further regulated unions' actions and their internal affairs (like financial disclosure and conduct of elections). Section 8(b)(1)(a) of the NLRA states that a labor organization is not to "restrain or coerce employees in the exercise of the rights guaranteed in Section 7" (described earlier). Table 14.5 provides examples of union unfair labor practices.

ENFORCEMENT

Enforcement of the NLRA rests with the National Labor Relations Board, which is composed of a five-member board, the general counsel, and 33 regional offices. The basis

Table 14.5

Examples of Union Unfair Labor Practices

- Mass picketing in such numbers that nonstriking employees are physically barred from entering the plant.
- Acts of force or violence on the picket line or in connection with a strike.
- Threats to employees of bodily injury or that they will lose their jobs unless they support the union's activities.
- Fining or expelling members for crossing a picket line that is unlawful.
- Fining or expelling members for filing unfair labor practice charges or testifying before the NLRB.
- Insisting during contract negotiations that the employer agree to accept working conditions that will be determined by a group to which it does not belong.
- Fining or expelling union members for the way they apply the bargaining contract while carrying out their supervisory responsibilities.
- Causing an employer to discharge employees because they spoke out against a contract proposed by the union.
- Making a contract that requires an employer to hire only members of the union or employees "satisfactory" to the union.
- Insisting on the inclusion of illegal provisions in a contract.
- Terminating an existing contract and striking for a new one without notifying the employer, the Federal Mediation and Conciliation Service, and the state mediation service (where one exists).
- Attempting to compel a beer distributor to recognize a union (the union prevents the distributor from obtaining beer at a brewery by inducing the brewery's employees to refuse to fill the distributor's orders).
- Picketing an employer to force it to stop doing business with another employer who has refused to recognize the union (a "secondary boycott").

SOURCE: National Labor Relations Board, *A Guide to Basic Law and Procedures under the National Labor Relations Act* (Washington, DC: U.S. Government Printing Office, 1997). Available at www.nlrb.gov. Accessed May 13, 2015.

for the NLRA is the commerce clause of the U.S. Constitution. Therefore, the NLRB's jurisdiction is limited to employers whose operations affect commerce generally and interstate commerce in particular. In practice, only purely local firms are likely to fall outside the NLRB's jurisdiction. Specific jurisdictional standards (nearly 20) that vary by industry are applied. Two examples of businesses that are covered (and the standards) are retail businesses that had more than $500,000 in annual business and newspapers that had more than $200,000 in annual business.

The NLRB's two major functions are to conduct and certify representation elections and prevent unfair labor practices. In both realms, it does not initiate action. Rather, it responds to requests for action. The NLRB's role in representation elections is discussed in the next section. Here we discuss unfair labor practices.

Unfair labor practice cases begin with the filing of a charge, which is investigated by a regional office. A charge must be filed within six months of the alleged unfair practice, and copies must be served on all parties. (Registered mail is recommended.) If the NLRB finds the charge to have merit and issues a complaint, there are two possible actions. It may defer to a grievance procedure agreed on by the employer and union. Otherwise, a hearing is held before an administrative law judge. The judge makes a recommendation, which can be appealed by either party. The NLRB has the authority to issue cease-and-desist orders to halt unfair labor practices. It can also order reinstatement of employees, with or without back pay. In one recent year, for example, $110 million in back pay was awarded. Note, however, that the NLRA is not a criminal statute, and punitive damages are not available. If an employer or union refuses to comply with an NLRB order, the board has the authority to petition the U.S. Court of Appeals. The court can choose to enforce the order, remand it to the NLRB for modification, change it, or set it aside altogether.

Union and Management Interactions: Organizing

LO 14-4
Describe the major labor–management interactions: organizing, contract negotiations, and contract administration.

To this point we have discussed macro trends in union membership. Here we shift our focus to the more micro questions of why individual employees join unions and how the organizing process works at the workplace level.

WHY DO EMPLOYEES JOIN UNIONS?

Virtually every model of the decision to join a union focuses on two questions.[32] First, is there a gap between the pay, benefits, and other conditions of employment that employees actually receive versus what they believe they should receive? Second, if such a gap exists and is sufficiently large to motivate employees to try to remedy the situation, is union membership seen as the most effective or instrumental means of change? The outcome of an election campaign hinges on how the majority of employees answer these two questions.

THE PROCESS AND LEGAL FRAMEWORK OF ORGANIZING

The NLRB is responsible for ensuring that the organizing process follows certain steps. At the most general level, the NLRB holds a union representation election if at least 30% of employees in the bargaining unit sign authorization cards (see Figure 14.5). If more than 50% of the employees sign authorization cards, the union may request that the employer voluntarily recognize it. If 50% or fewer of the employees sign, or if the employer refuses to recognize the union voluntarily, the NLRB conducts a secret-ballot election. The union is certified by the NLRB as the exclusive representative of employees if more than 50% of employees vote for the union. If more than one union appears on the ballot and neither gains a simple majority, a runoff election is held. Once a union has been certified as the exclusive representative of a group of employees, no additional elections are permitted for one year. After the negotiation of a contract, an election

Figure 14.5
Authorization Card

YES, I WANT THE IAM

I, the undersigned employee of
(Company)
authorize the International Association of Machinists and Aerospace Workers (IAM) to act as my collective bargaining agent for wages, hours and working conditions. I agree that this card may be used either to support a demand for recognition or an NLRB election, at the discretion of the union.

Name (print)_____ Date _____

Home Address_____ Phone_____

City_____ State_____ Zip_____

Job Title_____ Dept._____ Shift_____

Sign Here X
_____

Note: This authorization to be SIGNED and DATED in employee's own handwriting. YOUR RIGHT TO SIGN THIS CARD IS PROTECTED BY FEDERAL LAW.

RECEIVED BY (Initial) _____

cannot be held for the contract's duration or for three years, whichever comes first. The parties to the contract may agree not to hold an election for longer than three years, but an outside party cannot be barred for more than three years.

As mentioned previously, union members' right to be represented by leaders of their own choosing was expanded under the Taft-Hartley Act to include the right to vote an existing union out—that is, to decertify it. The process follows the same steps as a representation election. A decertification election is not permitted when a contract is in effect. Research indicates that when decertification elections are held, unions typically do not fare well, losing the majority of the time.[33]

The NLRB also is responsible for determining the appropriate bargaining unit and the employees who are eligible to participate in organizing activities. A unit may cover employees in one facility or multiple facilities within a single employer, or the unit may cover multiple employers. In general, employees on the payroll just prior to the ordering of an election are eligible to vote, although this rule is modified in some cases where, for example, employment in the industry is irregular. Most employees who are on strike and who have been replaced by other employees are eligible to vote in an election (such as a decertification election) that occurs within 12 months of the onset of the strike.

As shown in Table 14.3, the following types of employees cannot be included in bargaining units: agricultural laborers, independent contractors, supervisors, and managers. Beyond this, the NLRB attempts to group together employees who have a community of interest in their wages, hours, and working conditions. In many cases this grouping will be sharply contested, with management and the union jockeying to include or exclude certain employee subgroups in the hope of influencing the outcome of the election.

In 2014 and 2015, the NLRB issued important new rulings. One ruling is designed to streamline and speed representation elections, presumably in hopes of helping unions be more successful in organizing new workers. Specific changes include allowing unions to file election petitions electronically rather than requiring they be submitted by mail, requiring businesses to give unions personal email addresses (in addition to telephone numbers) of workers if they have them on file (within two days), and making it more difficult for employers to challenge elections until after they are conducted. The changes are intended to shorten the time between the call for a vote and actual election to 25 days or less, nearly 2 weeks less than the current median of 38 days and 3.5 weeks less than the median of 59 days in cases where employers contest the holding or other aspects of an election.[34] A second ruling, which may have even larger ramifications, appears to make it more likely that in a case where Company A contracts with a staffing firm (Company B) to provide it with workers, Company A could be held responsible (depending on the amount of control it exercises over workers, directly and/or indirectly) as a joint employer (along with Company B) for employment practices, rather than such responsibility falling exclusively to Company B. As such, a union now has a better chance of being able to negotiate directly with Company A, making it more difficult for Company A to avoid dealing with the union.

Organizing Campaigns: Management and Union Strategies and Tactics

Tables 14.6 and 14.7 list common issues that arise during most campaigns.[35] Unions attempt to persuade employees that their wages, benefits, treatment by employers, and opportunity to influence workplace decisions are not sufficient and that the union will be effective in obtaining improvements. Management emphasizes that it has provided a good package of wages, benefits, and so on. It also argues that, whereas a union is unlikely to provide improvements in such areas, it will likely lead to certain costs for employees, such as union dues and the income loss resulting from strikes.

Table 14.6
Most Common Issues
Raised by Unions
in Representation
Election Campaigns

UNION ISSUES	PERCENTAGE OF CAMPAIGNS
Union will prevent unfairness and will set up a grievance procedure and seniority system.	82%
Union will improve unsatisfactory wages.	79
Union strength will give employees voice in wages, working conditions.	79
Union, not outsider, bargains for what employees want.	73
Union has obtained gains elsewhere.	70
Union will improve unsatisfactory sick leave and insurance.	64
Dues and initiation fees are reasonable.	64
Union will improve unsatisfactory vacations and holidays.	61
Union will improve unsatisfactory pensions.	61
Employer promises and good treatment may not be continued without union.	61
Employees choose union leaders.	55
Employer will seek to persuade or frighten employees to vote against union.	55
No strike without vote.	55
Union will improve unsatisfactory working conditions.	52
Employees have legal right to engage in union activity.	52

SOURCE: J. Getman, S. Goldberg, and J. B. Herman, *Union Representation Elections: Law and Reality* (New York: Russell Sage Foundation, 1976), Table 4–3; N = 33 representation election campaigns.

Table 14.7
Most Common
Issues Raised by
Companies in
Representation
Election Campaigns

COMPANY ISSUES	PERCENTAGE OF CAMPAIGNS
Improvements not dependent on unionization.	85%
Wages good, equal to, or better than under union contract.	82
Financial costs of union dues outweigh gains.	79
Union is outsider.	79
Get facts before deciding; employer will provide facts and accept employee decision.	76
If union wins, strike may follow.	70
Loss of benefits may follow union win.	67
Strikers will lose wages; lose more than gain.	67
Unions not concerned with employee welfare.	67
Strike may lead to loss of jobs.	64
Employer has treated employees fairly and/or well.	60
Employees should be certain to vote.	54

SOURCES: J. Fossum, *Labor Relations: Development, Structure and Processes,* 5th ed., 1992. Reprinted with permission of The McGraw-Hill Companies, Inc. Original data from J. Getman, S. Goldberg, and J. B. Herman, *Union Representation Elections: Law and Reality* (New York: Russell Sage Foundation, 1976), Table 4-2; N = 33 representation election campaigns.

As Table 14.8 indicates, employers use a variety of methods to oppose unions in organizing campaigns, some of which may go beyond what the law permits, especially in the eyes of union organizers. This perception is supported by our earlier discussion, which noted a significant increase in employer unfair labor practices since the late 1960s. (See Figure 14.4.)

Survey of employers	
Consultants used	41%
Unfair labor practice charges filed against employer	24
Survey of union organizers	
Consultants and/or lawyers used	70
Unfair labor practices by employer	
Charges filed	36
Discharges or discriminatory layoffs	42[a]
Company leaflets	80
Company letters	91
Captive audience speech	91[b]
Supervisor meetings with small groups of employees	92
Supervisor intensity in opposing union	
Low	14
Moderate	34
High	51

Table 14.8
Percentage of Firms Using Various Methods to Oppose Union Organizing Campaigns

[a]This percentage is larger than the figure for charges filed because it includes cases in which no unfair labor practice charge was actually filed against the employer.

[b]Refers to management's requiring employees to attend a session on company time at which the disadvantages of union membership are emphasized.

SOURCE: R. B. Freeman and M. M. Kleiner, "Employer Behavior in the Face of Union Organizing Drives," *Industrial and Labor Relations Review* 43, no. 4 (April 1990), pp. 351–65. © Cornell University.

Why would employers increasingly break the law? Fossum suggests that the consequences (like back pay and reinstatement of workers) of doing so are "slight."[36] His review of various studies suggests that discrimination against employees involved in union organizing decreases union organizing success significantly and that the cost of back pay to union activists reinstated in their jobs is far smaller than the costs that would be incurred if the union managed to organize and gain better wages, benefits, and so forth.

Still, the NLRB attempts to maintain a noncoercive atmosphere under which employees feel they can exercise free choice. It will set aside an election if it believes that either the union or the employer has created "an atmosphere of confusion or fear of reprisals."[37] Examples of conduct that may lead to an election result being set aside include

- Threats of loss of jobs or benefits by an employer or union to influence votes or organizing activities.
- A grant of benefits or a promise of benefits as a means of influencing votes or organizing activities.
- An employer or union making campaign speeches to assembled groups of employees on company time less than 24 hours before an election.
- The actual use or threat of physical force or violence to influence votes or organizing activities.[38]

Supervisors have the most direct contact with employees. Thus, as Table 14.9 indicates, it is critical that they be proactive in establishing good relationships with employees if the company wishes to avoid union organizing attempts. It is also important for supervisors to know what not to do (Threatening, Interrogating, Promising, Spying—TIPS) should a drive take place.

Table 14.9
What Supervisors Should and Should Not Do to Stay Union-Free

WHAT TO DO:

Report any direct or indirect signs of union activity to a core management group.

Deal with employees by carefully stating the company's response to pro-union arguments. These responses should be coordinated by the company to maintain consistency and to avoid threats or promises.

Take away union issues by following effective management practice all the time:

Deliver recognition and appreciation.

Solve employee problems.

Protect employees from harassment or humiliation.

Provide business-related information.

Be consistent in treatment of different employees.

Accommodate special circumstances where appropriate.

Ensure due process in performance management.

Treat all employees with dignity and respect.

WHAT TO AVOID:

Threatening employees with harsher terms and conditions of employment or employment loss if they engage in union activity.

Interrogating employees about pro-union or anti-union sentiments that they or others may have or reviewing union authorization cards or pro-union petitions.

Promising employees that they will receive favorable terms or conditions of employment if they forgo union activity.

Spying on employees known to be, or suspected of being, engaged in pro-union activities.

SOURCE: From J. A. Segal, *HR Magazine*. Reproduced with permission of Society for Human Resource Management (www.shrm.org), Alexandria, VA, publisher of *HR Magazine*.

Associate Union Membership
A form of union membership by which the union receives dues in exchange for services (e.g., health insurance, credit cards) but does not provide representation in collective bargaining.

Corporate Campaigns
Union activities designed to exert public, financial, or political pressure on employers during the union-organizing process.

In response to organizing difficulties, the union movement has tried alternative approaches. **Associate union membership** is not linked to an employee's workplace and does not provide representation in collective bargaining. Instead the union provides other services, such as discounts on health and life insurance or credit cards.[39] In return, the union receives membership dues and a broader base of support for its activities. Associate membership may be attractive to employees who wish to join a union but cannot because their workplace is not organized by a union. Supervisors and their employers must also recognize that social media is increasingly used as a tool in union organization drives and understand how to effectively and legally respond to such communications. See the "Competing through Technology" box for more on this point.

Corporate campaigns seek to bring public, financial, or political pressure on employers during the organizing (and negotiating) process.[40] For example, the Building and Construction Trades Department of the AFL-CIO successfully lobbied Congress to eliminate $100 million in tax breaks for a Toyota truck plant in Kentucky until Toyota agreed to use union construction workers and pay union wages.[41] The Amalgamated Clothing and Textile Workers Union (ACTWU) corporate campaign against J. P. Stevens during the late 1970s was one of the first and best known. The ACTWU organized a boycott of J. P. Stevens products and threatened to withdraw its pension funds from financial institutions where J. P. Stevens officers acted as directors. J. P. Stevens subsequently agreed to a contract with the ACTWU.[42]

Using Social Media for Union-Related Communications

The title of a recent blog posting was "Social Media: The New Big Tool for Union Organizing." No longer do workers need to go door to door to contact prospective union members and no longer do they need to find physical gathering places to discuss organizing strategies or to air grievances. That can now be done online via e-mail, Facebook, Twitter, and other social media platforms.

Employers need to be aware of how employee communications have changed to be able to respond effectively and legally. As noted in the opening to this chapter, the National Labor Relations Act has always protected concerted action by employees. One challenge is that when employees go online to criticize their company or supervisor, unlike when it was a discussion around the water cooler, such complaints can now reach millions of people, including customers and/or clients. Companies have sought to prevent such actions by developing policies for use of social media and to protect against disparagement. Such policies are likely to be less subject to challenge to the extent they are not overly broad (i.e., such that they prohibit almost any topics or any concerted action) and allow discussion of clearly legitimate topics such as wages, hours, and working conditions. Employers may (though it depends on the circumstances) prohibit the use of social media (for any purpose) by employees when they are scheduled to be working. Employers can also prohibit harassment of colleagues.

Employers also need to be aware that the National Labor Relations Board recently changed its rules on employee use of employer e-mail systems for the purpose of labor organizing. Its new rule states that use of e-mail for union-related communications must be permitted by employers in cases where employers allow employees general access to the employer's e-mail system. Although the Board said a total ban was possible, it also stated that "it will be the rare case." As such, in general, the Board stated that employees are permitted to use e-mail to engage in "statutorily protected discussions about the terms and conditions of their employment while on nonworking time." The Board also stated that employees had the right to use the employer e-mail system for "an initial organizational campaign" when attempting to form a union. Although technically this activity is not to be done during working time, as a practical matter, it may be difficult to tell whether an employee was on work time or break time when the e-mail was sent. Finally, it should be noted that an employer is typically permitted to monitor employee e-mail communications as long as it does not increase the intensity of such monitoring in response to union-related activity.

DISCUSSION QUESTIONS

1. From a union's perspective, what are some advantages of using social media for its communications?
2. From a company's perspective, what are some disadvantages of union-related communications being sent via social media?

SOURCES: W. Welkowitz, "Social Media: The New Big Tool for Union Organizing," Labor and Employment Blog, *Bloomberg BNA*, February 3, 2015, www.bna.com; T. Puckett, "NLRB Rulings Have Far-reaching Impact on Employers and Policies," *Oklahoma Employment Law Letter*, February 4, 2015, www.hrhero.com.

Unions also hope to use their financial assets to influence companies. Unions directly control billions in pension funds and share control with employers of billions more. All told, unions may have an influence over about $3 trillion in such investments.[43]

In some success stories unions have eschewed elections in favor of strikes and negative publicity to pressure corporations to accept a union. Several years ago, the Hotel Employees and Restaurant Employees (HERE) organized 9,000 workers, with 80%

of these memberships resulting from pressure on employers rather than a vote. The Union of Needletrade, Industrial, and Textile Employees (UNITE), also succeeded with this approach. After losing an election by just two votes among employees of Up-to-Date Laundry, which cleans linens for Baltimore hotels and hospitals, UNITE decided to try other tactics, including a corporate campaign. It called a strike to demand that Up-to-Date recognize the union. It also persuaded several major customers of the laundry to threaten to stop using the laundry's services, shared claims of racial and sexual harassment with state agencies and the National Association for the Advancement of Colored People (NAACP), and convinced the Baltimore city council to require testimony from Up-to-Date. Eventually, the company gave in, recognized the union, and negotiated a contract that raised the workers' $6-an-hour wages and gave them better benefits.

Another winning union organizing strategy is to negotiate employer neutrality and card-check provisions into a contract. Under a *neutrality provision,* the employer pledges not to oppose organizing attempts elsewhere in the company. A *card-check provision* is an agreement that if a certain percentage—by law, at least a majority—of employees sign an authorization card, the employer will recognize their union representation. An impartial outside agency, such as the American Arbitration Association, counts the cards. The Communication Workers of America negotiated these provisions in its dispute with Verizon. Evidence suggests that this strategy can be very effective for unions.

However, unions must avoid running afoul of the Racketeer Influenced and Corrupt Organizations Act (RICO). For example, the Service Employees International Union (SEIU) waged a corporate campaign beginning in 2009 against Sodexo, a French-owned food service company operating in the United States. The SEIU's campaign, "Clean Up Sodexo," focused on bringing to the public's attention food safety and other concerns at Sodexo, something that could damage its business. Sodex sued the SEIU, claiming the campaign was an attempt to conspire to extort Sodexo with the threat of financial damage unless Sodexo agreed to a card-check provision for recognizing the union (rather than requiring that workers vote in a secret-ballot election). Sodexo alleged that the SEIU engaged in blackmail, vandalism, and other prohibited actions in an effort to prevent Sodexo from winning food contracts. In 2011, a legal settlement was reached before trial, under which the SEIU agreed to end its campaign against Sodexo.[44]

Union and Management Interactions: Contract Negotiation

The majority of contract negotiations take place between unions and employers that have been through the process before. In most cases, management has come to accept the union as an organization that it must work with. But when the union has just been certified and is negotiating its first contract, the situation can be very different. In fact, unions are unable to negotiate a first contract in 27% to 37% of the cases.[45] As noted previously, more than half of all unfair labor practice charges filed against employers pertain to the refusal to negotiate.

Labor–management contracts differ in their bargaining structures—that is, the range of employees and employers that are covered. As Table 14.10 indicates, the contracts differ, first, according to whether narrow (craft) or broad (industrial) employee interests are covered. Second, they differ according to whether they cover multiple employers or

Table 14.10

Types and Examples of Bargaining Structures

EMPLOYEE INTERESTS COVERED	EMPLOYER INTERESTS COVERED		
	MULTIEMPLOYER (CENTRALIZED)	**SINGLE-EMPLOYER— MULTIPLANT**	**SINGLE-EMPLOYER— SINGLE PLANT (DECENTRALIZED)**
Craft (Narrow)	Construction trades Interstate trucking Longshoring Hospital association	Airline Teacher Police Firefighters Railroad	Craft union in small manufacturing plant Hospital
Industrial or Multiskill (Broad)	Coal mining (underground) Basic steel (pre-1986) Hotel association	Automobiles Steel (post-1986) Farm equipment State government Textile	Industrial union in small manufacturing plant

SOURCE: From H. C. Katz and T. A. Kochan, *An Introduction to Collective Bargaining and Industrial Relations* 4E, 2008. Reprinted with permission of The McGraw-Hill Companies, Inc.

multiple plants within a single employer. (A single employer may have multiple plants, some union and some nonunion.) Different structures have different implications for bargaining power and the number of interests that must be incorporated in reaching an agreement.

THE NEGOTIATION PROCESS

Richard Walton and Robert McKersie suggested that labor–management negotiations could be broken into four subprocesses: distributive bargaining, integrative bargaining, attitudinal structuring, and intraorganizational bargaining.[46] **Distributive bargaining** focuses on dividing a fixed economic "pie" between the two sides. A wage increase, for example, means that the union gets a larger share of the pie, management a smaller share. It is a win–lose situation. **Integrative bargaining** has a win–win focus; it seeks solutions beneficial to both sides. So if management needs to reduce labor costs, it could reach an agreement with the union to avoid layoffs in return for the union agreeing to changes in work rules that might enhance productivity.

Attitudinal structuring refers to the relationship and trust between labor and management negotiators. Where the relationship is poor, it may be difficult for the two sides to engage in integrative bargaining because each side hesitates to trust the other side to carry out its part of the deal. For example, the union may be reluctant to agree to productivity-enhancing work-rule changes to enhance job security if, in the past, it has made similar concessions but believes that management did not stick to its assurance of greater job security. Thus the long-term relationship between the two parties can have a very important impact on negotiations and their outcomes.

Intraorganizational bargaining reminds us that labor–management negotiations involve more than just two parties. Within management, and to an even greater extent within the union, different factions can have conflicting objectives. High-seniority workers, who are least likely to be laid off, may be more willing to accept a contract that

Distributive Bargaining
The part of the labor–management negotiation process that focuses on dividing a fixed economic "pie."

Integrative Bargaining
The part of the labor–management negotiation process that seeks solutions beneficial to both sides.

Attitudinal Structuring
The aspect of the labor–management negotiation process that refers to the relationship and level of trust between the negotiators.

Intraorganizational Bargaining
The part of the labor–management negotiation process that focuses on the conflicting objectives of factions within labor and management.

has layoffs (especially if it also offers a significant pay increase for those whose jobs are not at risk). Less senior workers would likely feel very differently. Thus negotiators and union leaders must simultaneously satisfy both the management side and their own internal constituencies. If they do not, they risk the union membership's rejecting the contract, or they risk being voted out of office in the next election. Management, too, is unlikely to be of one mind about how to approach negotiations. Some will focus more on long-term employee relations, others will focus on cost control, and still others will focus on what effect the contract will have on stockholders.

MANAGEMENT'S PREPARATION FOR NEGOTIATIONS

Clearly, the outcome of contract negotiations can have important consequences for labor costs and labor productivity and, therefore, for the company's ability to compete in the product market. Adapting Fossum's discussion, we can divide management preparation into the following seven areas, most of which have counterparts on the union side.[47]

1. *Establishing interdepartmental contract objectives:* The employer's industrial relations department needs to meet with the accounting, finance, production, marketing, and other departments and set contract goals that will permit each department to meet its responsibilities. As an example, finance may suggest a cost figure above which a contract settlement would seriously damage the company's financial health. The bargaining team needs to be constructed to take these various interests into account.

2. *Reviewing the old contract:* This step focuses on identifying provisions of the contract that might cause difficulties by hindering the company's productivity or flexibility or by leading to significant disagreements between management and the union.

3. *Preparing and analyzing data:* Information on labor costs and the productivity of competitors, as well as data the union may emphasize, needs to be prepared and analyzed. The union data might include cost-of-living changes and agreements reached by other unions that could serve as a target. Data on employee demographics and seniority are relevant for establishing the costs of such benefits as pensions, health insurance, and paid vacations. Finally, management needs to know how much it would be hurt by a strike. How long will its inventory allow it to keep meeting customer orders? To what extent are other companies positioned to step in and offer replacement products? How difficult would it be to find replacement workers if the company decided to continue operations during a strike?

4. *Anticipating union demands:* Recalling grievances over the previous contract, having ongoing discussions with union leaders, and becoming aware of settlements at other companies are ways of anticipating likely union demands and developing potential counterproposals.

5. *Establishing the cost of possible contract provisions:* Wages have not only a direct influence on labor costs but often an indirect effect on benefit costs (such as Social Security and paid vacation). Recall that benefits add about 46 cents to every dollar's worth of wages. Also, wage or benefit increases that seem manageable in the first year of a contract can accumulate to less manageable levels over time.

6. *Preparing for a strike:* If management intends to operate during a strike, it may need to line up replacement workers, increase its security, and figure out how to deal with incidents on the picket line and elsewhere. If management does not intend to operate during a strike (or if the company will not be operating at normal

levels), it needs to alert suppliers and customers and consider possible ways to avoid the loss of their business. This could even entail purchasing a competitor's product in order to have something to sell to customers.

7. *Determining strategy and logistics:* Decisions must be made about the amount of authority the negotiating team will have. What concessions can it make on its own, and which ones require it to check with top management? On which issues can it compromise, and on which can it not? Decisions regarding meeting places and times must also be made.

NEGOTIATION STAGES AND TACTICS

Negotiations go through various stages.[48] In the early stages, many more people are often present than in later stages. On the union side, this may give all the various internal interest groups a chance to participate and voice their goals. This, in turn, helps send a message to management about what the union feels it must do to satisfy its members, and it may also help the union achieve greater solidarity. Union negotiators often present an extensive list of proposals at this stage, partly to satisfy their constituents and partly to provide themselves with issues on which they can show flexibility later in the process. Management may or may not present proposals of its own; sometimes it prefers to react to the union's proposals.

During the middle stages, each side must make a series of decisions, even though the outcome is uncertain. How important is each issue to the other side? How likely is it that disagreement on particular issues will result in a strike? When and to what extent should one side signal its willingness to compromise on its position?

In the final stage, pressure for an agreement increases as the deadline for a strike approaches. Public negotiations may be only part of the process. Negotiators from each side may have one-on-one meetings or small-group meetings where public relations pressures are reduced. In addition, a neutral third party may become involved, someone who can act as a go-between or facilitator. In some cases, the only way for the parties to convince each other of their resolve (or to convince their own constituents of the other party's resolve) is to allow an impasse to occur.

Various books suggest how to avoid impasses by using mutual gains or integrative bargaining tactics. For example, *Getting to Yes*, by Roger Fisher and William Ury, describes four basic principles:[49]

1. Separate the people from the problem.
2. Focus on interests, not positions.
3. Generate a variety of possibilities before deciding what to do.
4. Insist that the results be based on some objective standard.

BARGAINING POWER, IMPASSES, AND IMPASSE RESOLUTION

Employers' and unions' conflicting goals are resolved through the negotiation process just described. An important determinant of the outcome of this process is the relative bargaining power of each party, which can be defined as the "ability of one party to achieve its goals when faced with opposition from some other party to the bargaining process."[50] In collective bargaining, an important element of power is the relative ability of each party to withstand a strike. Although strikes in the United States are rare, the threat of a strike often looms large in labor–management negotiations. The relative ability to take a strike, whether one occurs or not, is an important determinant of bargaining power and, therefore, of bargaining outcomes.

MANAGEMENT'S WILLINGNESS TO TAKE A STRIKE

Management's willingness to take a strike comes down to two questions:

1. *Can the company remain profitable over the long run if it agrees to the union's demands?* The answer is more likely to be yes to the extent that higher labor costs can be passed on to consumers without losing business. This, in turn, is most likely when the price increase is small because labor costs are a small fraction of total costs or there is little price competition in the industry. Low price competition can result from regulated prices, from competition based on quality (rather than price), or from the union's organizing all or most of the employers in the industry, which eliminates labor costs as a price factor.

   Unions share part of management's concern with long-term competitiveness because a decline in competitiveness can translate into a decline in employment levels. On the other hand, the majority of union members may prefer to have higher wages, despite employment declines, particularly if a minority of the members (those with low seniority) suffer more employment loss and the majority keep their employment with higher wages.

2. *Can the company continue to operate in the short run despite a strike?* Although "hanging tough" on its bargaining goals may pay off for management in the long run, the short-run concern is the loss of revenues and profits from production being disrupted. The cost to strikers is a loss of wages and possibly a permanent loss of jobs.

Under what conditions is management most able to take a strike? The following factors are important:[51]

1. *Product demand:* Management is less able to afford a strike when the demand for its product is strong because that is when more revenue and profits are lost.
2. *Product perishability:* A strike by certain kinds of employees (farm workers at harvest time, truckers transporting perishable food, airline employees at peak travel periods) will result in permanent losses of revenue, thus increasing the cost of the strike to management.
3. *Technology:* An organization that is capital intensive (versus labor intensive) is less dependent on its employees and more likely to be able to use supervisors or others as replacements. Telephone companies are typically able to operate through strikes, even though installing new equipment or services and repair work may take significantly longer than usual.
4. *Availability of replacement workers:* When jobs are scarce, replacement workers are more available and perhaps more willing to cross picket lines. Using replacement workers to operate during a strike raises the stakes considerably for strikers who may be permanently replaced. Most strikers are not entitled to reinstatement until there are job openings for which they qualify. If replacements were hired, such openings may not occur for some time (if at all). In some cases, companies can use managers to temporarily replace striking workers. For example, decades ago, the third author of this text recalls his father, a manager at Ohio Bell in Cleveland, going to New York Bell in New York State to cover for jobs left open by striking workers. (Years before that, he was walking the picket line on strike before he got promoted.) More recently, Caterpillar prepared for a possible strike by "training managerial and support staff for production jobs" at one of its plants.[52]

5. *Multiple production sites and staggered contracts:* Multiple sites and staggered contracts permit employers to shift production from the struck facility to facilities that, even if unionized, have contracts that expire at different times (so they are not able to strike at the same time).

6. *Integrated facilities:* When one facility produces something that other facilities need for their products, the employer is less able to take a strike because the disruption to production goes beyond that single facility. The just-in-time production system, which provides very little stockpiling of parts, further weakens management's ability to take a strike.

7. *Lack of substitutes for product:* A strike is more costly to the employer if customers have a readily available alternative source from which to purchase the goods or services the company provides.

As we see in the "Competing through Sustainability" box, Boeing has gone to great lengths to give itself the option of building aircraft in a nonunion plant and has used that capability as leverage in negotiations with its unions.

Bargaining outcomes also depend on the nature of the bargaining process and relationship, which includes the types of tactics used and the history of labor relations. The vast majority of labor–management negotiations do not result in a strike because a strike is typically not in the best interests of either party. Furthermore, both the union and management usually realize that if they wish to interact effectively in the future, the experience of a strike can be difficult to overcome. When strikes do occur, the conduct of each party during the strike can also have a lasting effect on labor–management relations. Violence by either side or threats of job loss by hiring replacements can make future relations difficult.

© McGraw-Hill Education/Andrew Resek, Photographer

Management has several factors to consider before taking a strike. Most negotiations do not result in a strike since it is often not in the best interests of either party.

IMPASSE RESOLUTION PROCEDURES: ALTERNATIVES TO STRIKES

Given the substantial costs of strikes to both parties, procedures that resolve conflicts without strikes have arisen in both the private and public sectors. Because many public sector employees do not have the right to strike, alternatives are particularly important in that arena.

Three often-used impasse resolution procedures are mediation, fact finding, and arbitration. All of them rely on the intervention of a neutral third party, most typically provided by the Federal Mediation and Conciliation Service (FMCS), which must be notified 60 days prior to contract expiration and 30 days prior to a planned change in contract terms (including a strike). **Mediation** is the least formal but most widely used of the procedures (in both the public and private sectors). One survey found it was used by nearly 40% of all large private sector bargaining units.[53] A mediator has no formal authority but, rather, acts as a facilitator and go-between in negotiations.

A **fact finder,** most commonly used in the public sector, typically reports on the reasons for the dispute, the views and arguments of both sides, and (in some cases) a

Mediation
A procedure for resolving collective bargaining impasses by which a mediator with no formal authority acts as a facilitator and go-between in the negotiations.

Fact Finder
A person who reports on the reasons for the labor–management dispute and the views and arguments of both sides and offers a nonbinding recommendation for settling the dispute.

COMPETING THROUGH SUSTAINABILITY

The Give and Take of Contract Negotiations

Boeing machinists in Seattle voted narrowly (51 % to 49%) to ratify an eight-year collective bargaining contract with the company. Boeing sought to control costs in the contract to enable it to compete in what it says is the "ultracompetitive world of selling jetliners." Under the contract, employees will take deep cuts to their health care and retirement benefits. The latter is the most controversial, as it will follow an economy wide trend in the United States over the past several decades by freezing its pension (defined benefit) plan and transferring workers to a 401(k) (defined contribution) plan.

Boeing was also successful in negotiating limited wage increases. It will provide a 1% pay increase every other year of the contract and further raises are possible as a function of changes in the cost of living. In return for these concessions that help the company control its costs, Boeing stopped searching for alternative locations to produce the 777X jetliner and promised it will produce it in Seattle, thus keeping worker jobs there. The jetliner is due to begin rolling off the line for delivery starting in the year 2020. Boeing some years ago opened its first nonunion plant in South Carolina, a state with very low unionization rates, and has used the plant as leverage in its negotiations with its union workers. Recently, it upgraded the production capabilities of the plant and will build its 787 Dreamliner aircraft exclusively there. So far, the machinists union (International Association of Machinists and Aerospace Workers) has made little headway in its efforts to organize that South Carolina plant.

DISCUSSION QUESTIONS

1. How do you think workers at Boeing feel about taking cuts to their health care and retirement? Why did they (narrowly) agree to the contract? What was their alternative?

2. Why did Boeing build the plant in South Carolina?

SOURCES: J. Ostrower, "Union Cancels Boeing Vote," *The Wall Street Journal,* April 18–19, 2015, p. B3; J. Ostrower, "New Dreamliner to Be Built at Nonunion Plant," *The Wall Street Journal,* July 31, 2014, www.wsj.com; J. Ostrower, "New Boeing Pact Wins Cost Controls," *The Wall Street Journal,* January 5, 2014, p. B3.

---

recommended settlement, which the parties are free to decline. That these recommendations are made public may give rise to public pressure for a settlement. Even if a fact finder's settlement is not accepted, the hope is that he or she will identify or frame issues in such a way as to facilitate an agreement. Sometimes, for the simple reason that fact finding takes time, the parties reach a settlement during the interim.

Arbitration
A procedure for resolving collective bargaining impasses by which an arbitrator chooses a solution to the dispute.

The most formal type of outside intervention is **arbitration,** under which a solution is actually chosen by an arbitrator (or arbitration board). In some instances the arbitrator can fashion a solution (conventional arbitration). In other cases the arbitrator must choose either the management's or union's final offer (final offer arbitration) on either the contract as a whole or on an issue-by-issue basis. Traditionally, arbitrating the enforcement or interpretation of contract terms (rights arbitration) has been widely accepted, whereas arbitrating the actual writing or setting of contract terms (interest arbitration, our focus here) has been reserved for special circumstances. These include some public sector negotiations, where strikes may be especially costly (such as those by police or firefighters) and a very few private-sector situations, where strikes have been especially debilitating to both sides (the steel industry in the 1970s).[54] One reason for avoiding greater use of interest arbitration is a strong belief that the parties closest to the situation (unions and management, not an arbitrator) are in the best position to effectively resolve their conflicts.

Union and Management Interactions: Contract Administration

GRIEVANCE PROCEDURE

Although the negotiation process (and the occasional resulting strike) receive the most publicity, the negotiation process typically occurs only about every three years, whereas contract administration goes on day after day, year after year. The two processes—negotiation and administration—are linked, of course. Vague or incomplete contract language developed in the negotiation process can make administration of the contract difficult. Such difficulties can, in turn, create conflict that can spill over into the next negotiation process.[55] Furthermore, events during the negotiation process—strikes, the use of replacement workers, or violence by either side—can lead to management and labor difficulties in working successfully under a contract.

A key influence on successful contract administration is the grievance procedure for resolving labor–management disputes over the interpretation and execution of the contract. During World War II, the War Labor Board helped institutionalize the use of arbitration as an alternative to strikes to settle disputes that arose during the term of the contract. The soon-to-follow Taft-Hartley Act further reinforced this preference. Today the great majority of grievance procedures have binding arbitration as a final step, and only a minority of strikes occur during the term of a contract. (Most occur during the negotiation stage.) Strikes during the term of a contract can be especially disruptive because they are more unpredictable than strikes during the negotiation phase, which occur only at regular intervals.

Beyond its ability to reduce strikes, a grievance procedure can be judged using three criteria.[56] First, how well are day-to-day contract questions resolved? Time delays and heavy use of the procedure may indicate problems. Second, how well does the grievance procedure adapt to changing circumstances? For example, if the company's business turns downward and the company needs to cut costs, how clear are the provisions relating to subcontracting of work, layoffs, and so forth? Third, in multiunit contracts, how well does the grievance procedure permit local contract issues (like work rules) to be included and resolved?[57]

From the employees' perspective, the grievance procedure is the key to fair treatment in the workplace, and its effectiveness rests both on the degree to which employees feel they can use it without fear of recrimination and whether they believe their case will be carried forward strongly enough by their union representative. The **duty of fair representation** is mandated by the NLRA and requires that all bargaining unit members, whether union members or not, have equal access to and representation by the union in the grievance procedure. Too many grievances may indicate a problem, but so may too few. A very low grievance rate may suggest a fear of filing a grievance, a belief that the system is not effective, or a belief that representation is not adequate.

As Table 14.11 suggests, most grievance procedures have several steps prior to arbitration. Moreover, the majority of grievances are settled during the earlier steps of the process, which is desirable both to reduce time delays and to avoid the costs of arbitration. If the grievance does reach arbitration, the arbitrator makes the final ruling in the matter. A series of Supreme Court decisions in 1960, commonly known as the Steelworkers' Trilogy, established that the courts should essentially refrain from reviewing the merits of arbitrators' decisions and, instead, limit judicial review to the question of whether the

Duty of Fair Representation
The National Labor Relations Act requirement that all bargaining unit members have equal access to and representation by the union.

Table 14.11

Steps in a Typical Grievance Procedure

Employee-initiated grievance

Step 1

a. Employee discusses grievance or problem orally with supervisor.

b. Union steward and employee may discuss problem orally with supervisor.

c. Union steward and employee decide (1) whether problem has been resolved or (2) if not resolved, whether a contract violation has occurred.

Step 2

a. Grievance is put in writing and submitted to production superintendent or other designated line manager.

b. Steward and management representative meet and discuss grievance. Management's response is put in writing. A member of the industrial relations staff may be consulted at this stage.

Step 3

a. Grievance is appealed to top line management and industrial relations staff representatives. Additional local or international union officers may become involved in discussions. Decision is put in writing.

Step 4

a. Union decides on whether to appeal unresolved grievance to arbitration according to procedures specified in its constitution and/or bylaws.

b. Grievance is appealed to arbitration for binding decision.

Discharge grievance

a. Procedure may begin at step 2 or step 3.

b. Time limits between steps may be shorter to expedite the process.

Union or group grievance

a. Union representative initiates grievance at step 1 or step 2 on behalf of affected class of workers or union representatives.

SOURCE: From H. C. Katz, T. A. Kochan, and A. J. S. Colvin, *An Introduction to Collective Bargaining and Industrial Relations,* 2008. Reprinted with permission of The McGraw-Hill Companies, Inc.

issue was subject to arbitration under the contract.[58] Furthermore, unless the contract explicitly states that an issue is not subject to arbitration, it will be assumed that arbitration is an appropriate means of deciding the issue. Giving further strength to the role of arbitration is the NLRB's general policy of deferring to arbitration.

What types of issues most commonly reach arbitration? Data from the FMCS on a total of 2,473 grievances show that discharge and disciplinary issues topped the list with 913 cases.[59] Other frequent issues include the use of seniority in promotion, layoffs, transfers, work assignments, and scheduling (309 cases); wages (178); and benefits (127).

What criteria do arbitrators use to reach a decision? In the most common case—discharge or discipline—the following due process questions are important:[60]

1. *Did the employee know what the rule or expectation was and what the consequences of not adhering to it were?*

2. *Was the rule applied in a consistent and predictable way?* In other words, are all employees treated the same?

3. *Are facts collected in a fair and systematic manner?* An important element of this principle is detailed record keeping. Both employee actions (such as tardiness) and management's response (verbal or written warnings) should be carefully documented.

4. *Does the employee have the right to question the facts and present a defense?* An example in a union setting is a hearing with a shop steward present.

5. *Does the employee have the right to appeal a decision?* An example is recourse to an impartial third party, such as an arbitrator.

6. *Is there progressive discipline?* Except perhaps for severe cases, an arbitrator will typically look for evidence that an employee was alerted as early as possible that behavior was inappropriate and the employee was given a chance to change prior to some form of severe discipline, such as discharge.

7. *Are there unique mitigating circumstances?* Although discipline must be consistent, individuals differ in terms of their prior service, performance, and discipline record. All of these factors may need to be considered.

COOPERATIVE LABOR–MANAGEMENT STRATEGIES

Jack Barbash described the nature of the traditional relationship between labor and management (during both the negotiation and administration phases) as follows:

> Bargaining is a love–hate, cooperation–conflict relationship. The parties have a common interest in maximizing the total revenue which finances their respective returns. But they take on adversarial postures in debating how the revenue shall be divided as between wages and profits. It is the adversarial posture which has historically set the tone of the relationship.[61]

LO 14-5

Describe new, less adversarial approaches to labor–management relations.

Although there had always been exceptions to the adversarial approach, one reading is that there has been a general trend toward less adversarial workplace relations (at least where the union's role is accepted by management).[62] This transformation has two basic objectives: (1) to increase the involvement of individuals and work groups in overcoming adversarial relations and increasing employee commitment, motivation, and problem solving and (2) to reorganize work so that work rules are minimized and flexibility in managing people is maximized. These objectives are especially important for companies that need to be able to shift production quickly in response to changes in markets and customer demands. The specific programs aimed at achieving these objectives include employee involvement in decision making, self-managing employee teams, labor–management problem-solving teams, broadly defined jobs, and sharing of financial gains and business information with employees. Examples include the labor–management relationships at Ford, Harley-Davidson, and Chrysler's engine plant in Dundee, Michigan.[63]

The Dundee engine plant is not only an example of a new approach to labor relations. It also has the blessing of the United Auto Workers (UAW). Why? According to the president of the UAW local, "It's a question of survival." Hourly workers at the plant are highly educated and skilled and rotate through different jobs to provide skill flexibility to support production flexibility, engage workers, and reduce repetitive motion injuries. Unlike a traditional plant where there can be scores of hourly job classifications/titles, the Dundee plant has only two: team member of team leader. There are no supervisors. Team leaders, rather than only observing, work alongside teams of six team members. The guiding principles are captured by what are called the "four As": "anyone can do anything anytime, anywhere." That is much different from the more typical idea of "if it's not in my job description, I don't have to do it, I won't do it, and if I did do it, I would probably get in trouble." The UAW was concerned at first with the "four As" approach because without narrow job descriptions, management has more discretion, workers less discretion, in what workers do each day. As the UAW put it, it could allow management to "pull out anybody, anytime." However, the need for flexibility in production is so central to the success of the plant in a global competitive environment and to Chrysler being willing to make future investments (the key to jobs) in the plant that the UAW leadership agreed. The team approach, job rotation, and flexibility expectations translate into higher skill and education requirements. Hourly workers at the plant must have a two-year technical degree, hold a skilled journeyman's card, or have had several years of experience in advanced manufacturing.[64]

Union resistance to such programs has often been substantial, precisely because the programs seek to change workplace relations and the role that unions play. Without the union's support, these programs are less likely to survive and less likely to be effective if they do survive.[65] Union leaders have often feared that such programs will weaken unions' role as an independent representative of employee interests. Indeed, according to the NLRA, to "dominate or interfere with the formation or administration of any labor organization or contribute financial or other support to it" is an unfair labor practice. An example of a prohibited practice is "taking an active part in organizing a union or committee to represent employees."[66]

One case that has received much attention is that of Electromation, a small electrical parts manufacturer. In 1992 the NLRB ruled that the company had violated Section 8(a)(2) of the NLRA by setting up worker–management committees (typically about six workers and one or two managers) to solve problems having to do with absenteeism and pay scales.[67] The original complaint was filed by the Teamsters union, which was trying to organize the (nonunion) company and felt that the committees were, in effect, illegally competing with them to be workers' representatives. Similarly, Polaroid dissolved an employee committee that had been in existence for over 40 years in response to the U.S. Department of Labor's claim that it violated the NLRA. The primary functions of the employee committee had been to represent employees in grievances and to advise senior management on issues such as pay and company rules and regulations. In a third case, the NLRB ruled in 1993 that seven worker–management safety committees at DuPont were illegal under the NLRB because they were dominated by management. The committee members were chosen by management and their decisions were subject to the approval of the management members of the committees. Finally, the committees made decisions about issues that were mandatory subjects of bargaining with the employees' elected representative—the chemical workers' union.[68] The impact of such cases will be felt both in nonunion companies, as union organizers move to fill the worker representation vacuum, and in unionized companies, as managers find they must deal more directly and effectively with their unions.

Employers must take care that employee involvement meets the legal test, but the NLRB has clearly supported the legality of involvement in important cases. For example, in a 2001 ruling, the NLRB found that the use of seven employee participation committees at a Crown Cork & Seal aluminum can manufacturing plant did not violate federal labor law. The committees in question make and implement decisions regarding a wide range of issues, including production, quality, training, safety, and certain types of worker discipline. The NLRB determined that these committees were not employer-dominated labor organizations, which would have violated federal labor law. Instead of "dealing with" management in a bilateral manner where proposals are made that are either rejected or accepted by management, the teams and committees exercise authority, delegated by management, to operate the plant within certain parameters. Indeed, the NLRB noted that rather than "dealing with management," the evidence indicated that within delegated areas of authority, the teams and committees "are management." This authority was found to be similar to that delegated to a first-line supervisor. Thus the charge that the teams and committees did not have final decision-making authority (and so were not acting in a management capacity) did not weigh heavily with the NLRB, which noted, "Few, if any, supervisors in a conventional plant have authority that is final

Table 14.12
When Teams May Be
Illegal

Primary factors to look for that could mean a team violates national labor law:	
Representation	Does the team address issues affecting nonteam employees? (Does it represent other workers?)
Subject matter	Do these issues involve matters such as wages, grievances, hours of work, and working conditions?
Management involvement	Does the team deal with any supervisors, managers, or executives on any issue?
Employer domination	Did the company create the team or decide what it would do and how it would function?

SOURCE: From *BusinessWeek*, January 25, 1993.

and absolute." Instead, it was noted that managers typically make recommendations that move up through "the chain of command."[69] (Table 14.12)

Although there are legal concerns to address, some evidence suggests that these new approaches to labor relations—incorporating greater employee participation in decisions, using employee teams, multiskilling, rotating jobs, and sharing financial gains—can contribute significantly to an organization's effectiveness,[70] as well as to workers' wages and job satisfaction.[71] Indeed, these practices are now often referred to as "high performance work practices" or systems. One study, for example, compared the features of traditional and transformational approaches to labor relations at Xerox.[72] As Table 14.13 indicates, the transformational approach was characterized by better conflict resolution, more shop-floor cooperation, and greater worker autonomy and feedback in decision making. Furthermore, compared with the traditional approach, transformational labor relations were found to be associated with lower costs, better product quality, and higher productivity. Several years ago, a presidential commission concluded that the evidence is "overwhelming that employee participation and labor–management partnerships are good for workers,

Table 14.13
Patterns in Labor–Management Relations Using Traditional and Transformational Approaches

DIMENSION	PATTERN	
	TRADITIONAL	TRANSFORMATIONAL
Conflict resolution		
Frequency of conflicts	High	Low
Speed of conflict resolution	Slow	Fast
Informal resolution of grievances	Low	High
Third- and fourth-step grievances	High	Low
Shop-floor cooperation		
Formal problem-solving groups (such as quality, reducing scrap, employment security)	Low	High
Informal problem-solving activity	Low	High
Worker autonomy and feedback		
Formal autonomous work groups	Low	High
Informal worker autonomous activity	Low	High
Worker-initiated changes in work design	Low	High
Feedback on cost, quality, and schedule	Low	High

SOURCE: Adapted from J. Cutcher-Gershenfeld, "The Impact on Economic Performance of a Transformation in Workplace Relations," *Industrial and Labor Relations Review* 44 (1991), pp. 241–60. Reprinted with permission.

firms, and the national economy." National survey data also indicate that most employees want more influence in workplace decisions and believe that such influence leads to more effective organizations.[73] Further evidence (see the Evidence-Based HR box) suggests that these "high performance work practices" work well across countries.

EVIDENCE-BASED HR

A recent study provided a review of the effect of "high performance work systems" (HPWSs) on business performance at the level of the plant and the firm. HPWSs are human resource practices (e.g., selective hiring, strong training/development, worker involvement in decision, pay for performance) that aim to increase worker contributions to business performance. Conventional wisdom is that these practices are best-suited to the United States or perhaps a few other countries (e.g., the United Kingdom) whose organizations are seen as having an "Anglo-Saxon" approach to management and are not likely to work as well in other countries due to the greater strength of unions, different legal frameworks, and/or cultural differences. However, many global companies globalize their employment policies despite these differences and feel that they can be successful. That is not to say that policies are executed in the exact same manner in all countries, but the broad policies are consistent. For example, a company may involve workers in decisions, but in Germany, it may be mandated in certain sectors of the economy, whereas in the United States it is not, but done according to the employer's choice. So, what does the evidence from the study say? The following table reports the mean correlation, mean r, between use of HPWSs and business performance, as well as the number of studies conducted in each country, K, and the number of firms/establishments included, N, in those k studies in each country. The 95% confidence interval is also reported. Results for the four countries with the largest k outside of the United States are reported separately.

COUNTRY OR REGION	K	N	MEAN r	95% CONFIDENCE INTERVAL FOR MEAN r
United States	48	11,309	.23	.20 to .26
Non-United States	108	24,458	.22	.18 to .26
China	16	3,692	.35	.26 to .43
Korea	8	1,899	.26	.17 to .36
Spain	13	3,430	.20	.14 to .26
United Kingdom	13	2,758	.16	.06 to .26

These countries differ significantly in terms of national culture (see Chapter 15) and in terms of union strength. (For example, in Spain, 70% of employees are covered by collective bargaining agreements versus 13% in the United States.) In looking at this pattern of results, ask yourself the following questions: (1) Is the mean r different in the United States versus outside the United States? (2) Is the mean r negative in any country? (3) Does the confidence interval include .00 for any country? Keeping in mind the caveat that policies can (and sometimes must) be implemented differently in different countries, what do these results say about the claim that policies must be tailored to the country?

SOURCE: T. Rabl, M. Jayasinghe, B. Gerhart, T. M. Kühlmann, "A Meta-Analysis of Country Differences in the High-Performance Work System–Business Performance Relationship: The Roles of National Culture and Managerial Discretion," *Journal of Applied Psychology* 99, no. 6 (2014), pp. 1011–41.

Labor Relations Outcomes

The effectiveness of labor relations can be evaluated from management, labor, and societal perspectives. Management seeks to control costs and enhance productivity and quality. Labor unions seek to raise wages and benefits and exercise control over how employees spend their time at work (such as through work rules). Each of the three parties typically seeks to avoid forms of conflict (like strikes) that impose significant costs on everyone. In this section we examine several outcomes.

STRIKES

Table 14.14 presents data on strikes in the United States that involved 1,000 or more employees. Of the 11 large strikes in 2014, five were in health care (nurses) and two were in education (teachers, professors). So most of the strikes involved white-collar employees. Because strikes are more likely in large units, the lack of data on smaller units is probably not a major concern, although such data would, of course, raise the figure on the estimated time lost to strikes. For example, for the 1960s, this estimate is 0.12% using data on strikes involving 1,000 or more employees versus 0.17% for all strikes. Although strikes impose significant costs on union members, employers, and society, it is clear from Table 14.14 that strikes are the exception rather than the rule. Very little working time is lost to strikes in the United States (with annual work hours of 1,800, less than 6 minutes per worker and less than one hour per unionized worker in 2014) and their frequency in recent years is generally low by historical standards. Does this mean that the industrial relations system is working well? Not necessarily. Some would view the low number of strikes as another sign of labor's weakness.

YEAR	STOPPAGES	NUMBER OF WORKERS (THOUSANDS)	PERCENTAGE OF TOTAL WORKING TIME
1950	424	1,698	0.26%
1955	363	2,055	0.16
1960	222	896	0.09
1965	268	999	0.10
1970	381	2,468	0.29
1975	235	965	0.09
1980	187	795	0.09
1985	54	324	0.03
1990	44	185	0.02
1995	31	192	0.02
2000	39	394	0.06
2005	22	100	<0.005
2010	11	45	<0.005
2011	19	113	<0.005
2012	19	148	<0.005
2013	15	55	<0.005
2014	11	34	<0.005

Table 14.14
Work Stoppages Involving 1,000 or More Workers

SOURCE: http://stats.bls.gov.

WAGES AND BENEFITS

Union workers receive higher wages and benefits. Table 14.15 provides a comparison of union members to nonunion members using both a survey of working individuals (CPS) and a survey of employers/establishments (NCS). In 2014, private-sector unionized workers received, on average, wages 26% higher than their nonunion counterparts.[74] The effect of unions on total compensation is even higher because of an even larger effect of unions on benefits.[75] However, these are raw differences. To assess the net effect of unions on wages more accurately, adjustments must be made.[76] We now briefly highlight a few of these.

The union wage effect is likely to be overestimated to the extent that unions can more easily organize workers who are already highly paid or who are more productive. The gap is likely to be underestimated to the extent that nonunion employers raise wages and benefits in response to the perceived "union threat" in the hope that their employees will then have less interest in union representation. When these and other factors are taken into account, the net union advantage in wages, though still substantial, is reduced by

Table 14.15

Compensation, Union versus Nonunion Employees, United States, Worker Survey and Employer Survey

| | | MEDIAN WEEKLY EARNINGS AND % IN UNION (WORKER SURVEY) | | |
| | | MEDIAN WEEKLY EARNINGS | | |
	% IN UNION	UNION REPRESENTED	NONUNION	UNION/ NONUNION
All	11.3	965	763	1.26
Men	11.9	1,013	840	1.21
Women	10.5	899	687	1.31
Occupation				
Management & Professional	11.9	1,132	1,139	0.99
Service	10.6	751	482	1.56
Sales & Office	6.6	788	654	1.20
Natural Resources, Construction, and Maintenance Operations	16.7	1,062	705	1.51
Production, Transportation, and Material Moving	15.1	830	614	1.35

| | WAGES/SALARIES, BENEFITS, AND TOTAL COMPENSATION (EMPLOYER SURVEY) | | |
	UNION MEMBERS	NONUNION	UNION/ NONUNION
Wages and Salaries	27.76	21.13	1.31
Benefits	18.74	8.70	2.15
Total Compensation	46.50	29.83	1.56

SOURCES: Median weekly earnings and percentages in union data are from U. S. Bureau of Labor Statistics, "Current Population Survey (CPS)," News Release USDL-15-0072: Union Members – 2014, www.bls.gov. Wages/salaries, benefits, and total compensation data are from U. S. Bureau of Labor Statistics, National Compensation Survey (NCS), "Employer Costs for Employee Compensation—December 2014," News Release USDL-15-0386. The worker survey includes civilian (private sector and public sector employees). The employer survey includes private sector employees only.

as much as one-half. The union benefits advantage is also reduced, but it remains larger than the union wage effect, and the union effect on total compensation is therefore larger than the wage effect alone.[77]

Beyond differences in pay and benefits, unions typically influence the way pay and promotions are determined. Whereas management often seeks to deal with employees as individuals, emphasizing performance differences in pay and promotion decisions, unions seek to build group solidarity and avoid the possibly arbitrary treatment of employees. To do so, unions focus on equal pay for equal work. Any differences among employees in pay or promotions, they say, should be based on seniority (an objective measure) rather than on performance (a subjective measure susceptible to favoritism). It is very common in union settings for there to be a single rate of pay for all employees in a particular job classification.

Although wages and benefits are higher for union members, job satisfaction is lower, on average.[78] Reasons include less positive perceptions of supervision, promotion opportunities, and the interest and discretion in their work.

PRODUCTIVITY

There has been much debate regarding the effects of unions on productivity.[79] Unions are believed to decrease productivity in at least three ways: (1) the union pay advantage causes employers to use less labor and more capital per worker than they would otherwise, which reduces efficiency across society; (2) union contract provisions may limit permissible workloads, restrict the tasks that particular workers are allowed to perform, and require employers to use more employees for certain jobs than they otherwise would; and (3) strikes, slowdowns, and working-to-rule (slowing down production by following every workplace rule to an extreme) result in lost production.[80]

On the other hand, unions can have positive effects on productivity.[81] Employees, whether members of a union or not, communicate to management regarding how good a job it is doing by either the "exit" or "voice" mechanisms. "Exit" refers to simply leaving the company to work for a better employer. "Voice" refers to communicating one's concerns to management without necessarily leaving the employer. Unions are believed to increase the operation and effectiveness of the voice mechanism.[82] This, in turn, is likely to reduce employee turnover and its associated costs. More broadly, voice can be seen as including the union's contribution to the success of labor–management cooperation programs that make use of employee suggestions and increased involvement in decisions. A second way that unions can increase productivity is (perhaps ironically) through their emphasis on the use of seniority in pay, promotion, and layoff decisions. Although management typically prefers to rely more heavily on performance in such decisions, using seniority has a potentially important advantage—namely, it reduces competition among workers. As a result, workers may be less reluctant to share their knowledge with less senior workers because they do not have to worry about less senior workers taking their jobs. Finally, the introduction of a union may have a "shock effect" on management, pressuring it into tightening standards and accountability and paying greater heed to employee input in the design and management of production.[83]

Although there is evidence that unions have both positive and negative effects on productivity, most studies have found that union workers are more productive than nonunion workers. Nevertheless, it is generally recognized that most of the findings on this issue are open to a number of alternative explanations, making any clear conclusions difficult. For example, if unions raise productivity, why has union representation of employees declined over time, even within industries?[84] A related concern is that unionized establishments are more likely to survive where there is some inherent productivity advantage unrelated to unionism that actually offsets a negative impact of unionism. If so, these establishments would be overrepresented, whereas establishments that did not survive the negative impact of unions would be underrepresented. Consequently, any negative impact of unions on productivity would be underestimated.

PROFITS AND STOCK PERFORMANCE

Even if unions do raise productivity, a company's profits and stock performance may still suffer if unions raise costs (such as wages) or decrease investment by a greater amount. Evidence shows that unions have a large negative effect on profits and that union coverage tends to decline more quickly in firms experiencing lower shareholder returns, suggesting that some firms become more competitive partly by reducing union strength.[85] Similarly, one study finds that each dollar of unexpected increase in collectively bargained labor costs results in a dollar reduction in shareholder wealth. Another study estimates that if policies were changed to encourage the unionization rate in the United States to double, the value of shareholder equity in newly organized firms would be decreased by 4.3%.[86] Other research suggests that investment in research and development is lower in unionized firms.[87] Strikes, although infrequent, lower shareholder returns in both the struck companies and firms (like suppliers) linked to those companies.[88] These research findings describe the average effects of unions. The consequences of more innovative union–management relationships for profits and stock performance are less clear.

The International Context

Except for China, Russia, and Ukraine, the United States has more union members than any other country. (If one were to include only countries where workers can freely elect union leaders of their own choosing, then the United States would arguably rank first in union membership.) Yet, as Table 14.16 indicates, aside from France and Korea, the United States has the lowest unionization rate (union density) of any country in the table. Even more striking are differences in union coverage, the percentage of employees whose terms and conditions of employment are governed by a union contract. (See Table 14.16.) In parts of western and northern Europe, it is not uncommon to have coverage rates of 80% to 90%, meaning that the influence of labor unions far outstrips what would be implied by their membership levels.[89] Why are the unionization rate and coverage comparatively low? One explanation is that the United States does not have as strong a history of deep class-based divisions in society as other countries do. For example, labor and social democratic political parties are commonplace in western Europe, and they are major players in the political process. Furthermore, the labor movement in western and northern Europe is broader than that in the United States. It extends not just to the workplace but—through its own or closely related political parties—directly into the national political process.

What is the trend in union membership rates and coverage? In the United States, we saw earlier that the trend is clearly downward, at least in the private sector. Although there have also been declines in membership rates in many other countries, coverage rates have stayed high in many of these countries. In the United States, deregulation and competition from foreign-owned companies have forced companies to become more efficient. Combined with the fact that the union wage premium in the United States is substantially larger than in other advanced industrialized countries, it is not surprising that management opposition would be higher in the United States than elsewhere.[90] This, in turn, may help explain why the decline in union influence has been especially steep in the United States.

COUNTRY	MEMBERSHIP PERCENTAGE OF EMPLOYMENT (DENSITY)[a]	COVERAGE PERCENTAGE OF EMPLOYMENT[d]
United States	10.8	13.3
Canada	27.2	31.5
Japan	17.8	—
Korea	9.9[b]	—
Germany	17.7	48.0
Australia	17.0	39.8
Netherlands	17.6	—
France	7.7[c]	97.7[e]
United Kingdom	25.4	34.6

Table 14.16
Union Membership and Union Coverage, Selected Countries

[a]Data from 2013, unless noted otherwise.

[b]2011.

[c]2012.

[d]Data from 2011, unless noted otherwise.

[e]2007.

SOURCES: OECD, *StatExtracts: Labour, Trade Union, Trade Union Density*, http://stats.oecd.org, extracted May 9, 2015; OECD, *Employment Outlook 2012: Trade Union Density and Collective Bargaining Coverage, 1990 and Latest Year*, http://stats.oecd.org, extracted May 9, 2015.

It seems likely that—with the growing globalization of markets—labor costs and productivity will continue to be key challenges. The European Union (EU) added 10 new member countries in 2004, 2 more in 2007, and 1 more in 2013, bringing its total to 28 countries and more than 500 million people, or about 63% larger than the United States. The newer EU countries (e.g., Bulgaria, Croatia, the Czech Republic, Poland, Romania, Slovakia) have much lower wages than the existing EU countries. Closer to home, we have the North American Free Trade Agreement among the United States, Canada, and Mexico. These common market agreements mean that goods, services, and production will continue to move more freely across international borders. Where substantial differences in wages, benefits, and other costs of doing business (such as regulation) exist, there will be a tendency to move to areas that are less costly, unless skills are unavailable or productivity is significantly lower there. Unless labor unions can increase their productivity sufficiently or organize new production facilities, union influence is likely to decline.

In addition to membership and coverage, the United States differs from western Europe in the degree of formal worker participation in decision making. Works' councils (joint labor–management decision-making institutions at the enterprise level) and worker representation on supervisory boards of directors (codetermination) are mandated by law in countries such as Germany. The Scandinavian countries, Austria, and Luxembourg have similar legislation. German works' councils make decisions about changes in work or the work environment, discipline, pay systems, safety, and other human resource issues. The degree of codetermination on supervisory boards depends on the size and industry of the company. For example, in German organizations having more than 2,000 employees, half of the board members must be worker representatives. (However, the chairman of the board, a management representative, can cast a tie-breaking vote.) In contrast, worker representation on boards of directors in the United States is still rare.[91]

The works' councils exist in part because collective bargaining agreements in countries such as Germany tend to be oriented toward industrywide or regional issues,

When in Germany, Do as the Germans Do?

The role of labor unions is much larger in Germany than in the United States. As Table 14.16 shows, unions cover 48% of employees in Germany versus 13% in the United States. German unions hold seats on the supervisory boards of major German companies. Thus, German unions are used to having a great deal of influence. On the other hand, Amazon, a U.S. company, has a goal of staying union free, whether it is in the United States or in Germany. This strategy has led to a clash of philosophies in Germany, Amazon's second largest market after the United States and where it employs more than 9,000 people.

Amazon has a works council (required by German law), and it deals with worker representatives "directly" (i.e., without the presence of a union). Verdi, a major German labor union, has been trying to change that, saying that Amazon has "a culture that we see as foreign." Amazon similarly says that, "Verdi and Amazon do not go together." Amazon and its "U.S. way of doing business" are sometimes referred to as using a "Wild West" approach to management.

(This is not meant as a compliment but rather indicates the belief that there is a lack of concern for worker welfare.)

McDonald's originally resisted unionization in Germany but eventually succumbed and now abides by industrywide wage agreements. Amazon, however, is different in some ways. For example, it opened warehouses in areas having high unemployment, making them perhaps more focused on having a job than on having a trade union represent them. Also, some say that as an Internet-based firm, Amazon is relatively invisible and more difficult to pressure using the usual tactics. Further, given the seasonal nature of its business, Amazon uses many temporary workers, who are more difficult to organize.

One standard union-organizing tactic being used (much as it is in the United States), is the use of strikes. Amazon says, however, they have not disrupted their operations because "the overwhelming majority of employees showed up for work as usual." One former union member, Ulrich Kleinschmidt, who works at Amazon, says the union he belonged to did nothing to help him when his previous company closed and "All I got were reminders to pay my [union] dues." He says "Verdi is striking itself to death" and that he enjoys working at Amazon. But he observes, "If you're anti-American, it might not be the right place to work."

DISCUSSION QUESTIONS

1. Do you think the Verdi trade union is anti-American? Do its goals for workers differ according to whether they are employed by an American or German company?

2. We often read that companies must adapt their management practices to the host country environment. Looking at Amazon's philosophy and its experience to date in Germany, comment on the degree to which that claim seems accurate.

3. Do you think that Amazon will eventually follow the path of McDonald's and agree to labor union representation for its employees in Germany?

SOURCE: S. Sloat, "In Germany, Amazon Keeps Unions at Bay," *The Wall Street Journal*, September 24, 2014, p. A1.

with less emphasis on local issues. However, competitive forces have led employers to increasingly opt out of centralized bargaining, even in the countries best known for centralized bargaining, like Sweden and Germany.[92]

What happens when a company from a country with low union strength operates in a country with high union strength? As the "Competing through Globalization" box describes, in the case of Amazon, an American company operating in Germany, the answer for now is that it is following its American strategy toward unions in Germany.

Another interesting example is Volkswagen, a German company operating an automobile production plant in Chattanooga, Tennessee, in the United States. It has a strong, formal relationship with unions in Germany, but has no union in the United States. Volkswagen has not actively opposed unionization at its U.S. plant (in contrast to the opposition unions would face from many U.S. companies). The United Auto Workers did not receive the necessary 50% + 1 votes in a recent representation election to become the sole representative of workers at VW's Chattanooga plant. More recently, Volkswagen, it is said under pressure from its unions in Germany, announced a new labor policy for its Chattanooga plant. Any labor group that receives (based on an independent outside audit) support from at least 15% of workers can have on-site space to post announcements and hold regular meetings with the plant's human resources department. Any group that receives support from at least 45% of workers would additionally be able to meet every two weeks with plant managers. Note that unlike in Germany, Volkswagen is thought to be unable to use a works council at the Chattanooga plant because under U.S. labor law, it might be deemed an employer-dominated labor organization. (See our earlier discussion of the Electromation case and the closely related Table 14.12.)[93]

China is now the world's second largest economy and one of its fastest growing. Workers increasingly want to share in economic growth through higher wages and more purchasing power. That means collective action can be expected to increase. Indeed, recent research finds that the level of strike activity and labor unrest has increased dramatically in China. Moreover, strikes, which were once predominantly defensive/reactive (to protect what workers already had), have become increasingly offensive/proactive (with the aim of achieving new gains for workers such as higher wages). In some sense, China, on its economic development path, may be now going through what the United States economy and labor relations went through many decades ago.[94]

The Public Sector

Unlike the private sector, union membership in the public sector grew in the 1960s and 1970s and remained fairly stable through the 1980s. As we saw earlier in Figure 14.3, in 2014 some 35.7% of government employees were union members. Like the NLRA in the private sector, changes in the legal framework contributed significantly to union growth in the public sector. One early step was the enactment in Wisconsin of collective bargaining legislation in 1959 for its state employees.[95] (However, things change. A few years ago, Wisconsin's governor signed a bill that stripped most state and local employees of most of their collective bargaining rights.) Executive Order 10988 provided collective bargaining rights for federal employees in 1962. By the end of the 1960s, most states had passed similar laws. The Civil Service Reform Act of 1978, Title VII, later established the Federal Labor Relations Authority (modeled after the NLRB). Many states have similar administrative agencies to administer their own laws.

An interesting aspect of public sector union growth is that much of it has occurred in the service industry and among white-collar employees—groups that have traditionally been viewed as difficult to organize. The American Federation of State, County, and Municipal Employees (AFSCME), with more than 1.6 million members, has several hundred thousand members in health care and in white-collar occupations.[96]

LO 14-7
Explain how labor relations in the public sector differ from labor relations in the private sector.

In contrast to the private sector, strikes are illegal at the federal level of the public sector and in most states. At the local level, all states prohibit strikes by police (Hawaii being a partial exception) and firefighters (Idaho being the exception). Teachers and state employees are somewhat more likely to have the right to strike, depending on the state. In 2012, of the 19 work stoppages involving 1,000 or more workers, four were in the public sector (local government—teachers, health care workers).

Nonunion Representation Systems

With unions now representing just 11.1% of U.S. workers, the question is to what degree are forms of nonunion representation operating to cover the remaining 88.9% of workers? Table 14.17 indicates that in one survey, about one-third (274 of 823) of nonunion workers were covered by a representation system established by management. In other words, more workers in this survey (274) were covered by nonunion representation systems than were covered by union-management collective bargaining contracts (170). In addition, the perceptions of workers regarding how strongly worker representatives "stand up" for them and how actively they consult with them about their ideas and concerns were remarkably similar under management-established systems to those covered under union collective bargaining agreements. That, of course, does not mean that a nonunion representation system, which ordinarily does not have the same independence and leverage as an elected labor union, is equivalent to having a collective bargaining agreement and union. But, clearly, nonunion representation systems play an important role in the workplace.[97]

Table 14.17
Worker Representation Systems, Union and Nonunion

	COLLECTIVE BARGAINING AGREEMENT (N = 170)	NO COLLECTIVE BARGAINING AGREEMENT (N = 823)	
		MANAGEMENT ESTABLISHED SYSTEM[a] (N = 274)	NO SYSTEM (N = 549)
Representatives can be counted on to stand up for workers, even if it means disagreeing with management[b]	84%	84%	NA
Representatives actively consult with workers about their ideas and concerns[b]	77%	89%	NA
Representatives actively consult with management over wages and benefits	100%[c]	77%	NA

N = 993 U.S. workers

[a]Covered by a "nonunion, management established system, where worker representatives meet with management."

[b]Sum of those responding either "To Some Extent" or "To a Great Extent."

[c]Estimated.

SOURCE: John Godard and Carola Frege, "Labor Unions, Alternative Forms of Representation, and the Exercise of Authority Relations in U.S. Workplaces," *Industrial and Labor Relations Review,* 6 (2013), pp. 142–168.

⌄⌄ A LOOK BACK

The membership rate, and thus influence, of labor unions in the United States and in many other long-industrialized countries has been on the decline in the private sector. However, even in the United States, there continue to be companies (e.g., automobiles, health care, education, airlines) where labor unions represent a large share of employees and thus play a major role in the operation and success of those companies. In each of these situations, effective labor relations are crucial for both companies and workers, as well as for society. Also, as we saw in the chapter opening, workers can take collective action without formal union representation as a possible means of improving their jobs.

QUESTIONS

1. many people picture labor union members as being men in blue-collar jobs in manufacturing plants. is that accurate? are there certain types of jobs where an employer can be fairly certain that employees will not join a union? Give examples.

2. why do people join labor unions? would you be interested in joining a labor union if given the opportunity? why or why not? As a manager, would you prefer to work with a union or would you prefer that employees be unrepresented by a union? Explain.

3. what led to a change in labor relations at Chrysler's Dundee engine plant? What was the nature of the change and do you think it is an important and sustainable change?

4. what role do (or can) labor unions play in low-wage countries such as Bangladesh?

SUMMARY

Labor unions seek to represent the interests of their members in the workplace. Although this may further the cause of industrial democracy, management often finds that unions increase labor costs while setting limits on the company's flexibility and discretion in decision making. As a result, the company may witness a diminished ability to compete effectively in a global economy. Not surprisingly, management in nonunion companies often feels compelled to actively resist the unionization of its employees. This, together with a host of economic, legal, and other factors, has contributed to union losses in membership and bargaining power in the private sector. There are some indications, however, that managements and unions are seeking new, more effective ways of working together to enhance competitiveness while giving employees a voice in how workplace decisions are made.

KEY TERMS

Checkoff provision, 586
Closed shop, 586
Union shop, 586
Agency shop, 586
Maintenance of membership, 586
Right-to-work laws, 586

Taft-Hartley Act, 592
Associate union membership, 598
Corporate campaigns, 598
Distributive bargaining, 601
Integrative bargaining, 601
Attitudinal structuring, 601

Intraorganizational bargaining, 601
Mediation, 605
Fact finder, 605
Arbitration, 606
Duty of fair representation, 607

DISCUSSION QUESTIONS

1. Why do employees join unions?
2. What has been the trend in union membership in the United States, and what are the underlying reasons for the trend?
3. What are the consequences for management and owners of having a union represent employees?
4. What are the general provisions of the National Labor Relations Act, and how does it affect labor–management interactions?
5. What are the features of traditional and nontraditional labor relations? What are the potential advantages of the "new" nontraditional approaches to labor relations?
6. How does the U.S. industrial and labor relations system compare with systems in other countries, such as those in western Europe?

SELF-ASSESSMENT EXERCISE

Mc Graw Hill Education connect

Additional assignable self-assessments available in Connect.

Would you join a union? Each of the following phrases expresses an opinion about the effects of a union on employees' jobs. For each phrase, circle a number on the scale to indicate whether you agree that a union would affect your job as described by the phrase.

Having a union would result in . . .	Strongly Disagree				Strongly Agree
1. Increased wages	1	2	3	4	5
2. Improved benefits	1	2	3	4	5
3. Protection from being fired	1	2	3	4	5
4. More promotions	1	2	3	4	5
5. Better work hours	1	2	3	4	5
6. Improved productivity	1	2	3	4	5
7. Better working conditions	1	2	3	4	5
8. Fewer accidents at work	1	2	3	4	5
9. More interesting work	1	2	3	4	5
10. Easier handling of employee problems	1	2	3	4	5
11. Increased work disruptions	5	4	3	2	1
12. More disagreements between employees and management	5	4	3	2	1
13. Work stoppages	5	4	3	2	1

Add up your total score. The highest score possible is 65, the lowest 13. The higher your score, the more you see value in unions, and the more likely you would be to join a union.

SOURCE: Based on S. A. Youngblood, A. S. DeNisi, J. L. Molleston, and W. H. Mobley, "The Impact of Work Environment, Instrumentality Beliefs, Perceived Union Image, and Subjective Norms on Union Voting Intentions," *Academy of Management Journal* 27 (1984), pp. 576–90.

EXERCISING STRATEGY

Board Rules That McDonald's Is a Joint Employer with Its Franchisees

As we have seen, workers at McDonald's and other fast food companies have been protesting to achieve a $15 minimum wage. We also saw that McDonald's, while not raising its minimum wage that high, did raise it to at least $1 above the prevailing local (national, state, or municipal) minimum wage. It said it did that in response to tightening labor conditions, not in response to the Fight for 15 protests. Some workers brought a complaint against McDonald's for retaliating against workers who went out on strike to join the protests. Importantly, the National Labor Relations Board (NLRB) ruled in the case that McDonald's, which owns only 10% of McDonald's stores, is a joint employer with its franchisees, which own, operate, and employ workers in the other 90% of stores. The NLRB stated that "through its franchise relationship and its use of tools, resources, and technology," McDonald's "engages in sufficient control over its franchisees' operations."

The ruling poses a threat to McDonald's and other companies that use a franchise model. McDonald's could become at least partly responsible (including for the cost of litigation-related expenses) for any labor and/or employment law violations committed by its franchisees and there are many (14,000) of them in far-flung places. The Service Employees International Union (SEIU) hopes the ruling will put pressure on large companies like McDonald's to take more responsibility for the actions of its franchisees, leading to better treatment of workers.

QUESTIONS

1. Have you worked in a franchise store at McDonald's or someplace similar? If so, what was your impression of the amount of control exercised over the franchisee by the parent company? How much coordination was there? Should the parent be deemed a joint employer?
2. Again, if you had such a job, what were the working conditions like? Were you satisfied with the job? Why or why not?

3. Would having a union have been attractive to you as a way to improve the work environment?
4. Why, if the workers in the case are nonunion, would they be bringing their case in front of the National Labor Relations Board, which enforces the National Labor Relations Act, the statute that gives employees the right to form and join unions of their own choosing?

SOURCES: "Obama's Union McDouble," (Editorial), *The Wall Street Journal*, December 22, 2014, www.wsj.com; M. Trottman and J. Jargon, "NLRB Names McDonald's as 'Joint-Employer' at Its Franchisees," *The Wall Street Journal*, December 19, 2014, www.wsj.com.

MANAGING PEOPLE

Twinkies, HoHos, and Ding Dongs: No Treat for Labor Unions

Let's talk about Twinkies, HoHos and Ding Dongs. They have long been found in the snack food aisle and have even been described as having "a legendary history" (!). One fun fact: The cream inside a Twinkie was banana flavored for many years. But when World War II brought rationing, including of bananas, Hostess changed the flavor of the cream to vanilla. OK, one more fun fact: Although there is an urban legend that Twinkies never go bad, it seems that the reality is they have a shelf life of about 25 days. That is considered quite a long shelf life for a baked good product. What is the secret? It may be that Twinkies lack any dairy products.

Unfortunately, whatever the flavor of the "cream" inside or the shelf life of a Twinkie, the company that makes them, Hostess Brands, recently declared bankruptcy. However, Metropoulos & Co. and Apollo Global, the new owners of Hostess Brands, will be reopening four bakery/plants, in hopes of getting snacks to Twinkie-deprived consumers shortly.

One thing Hostess will not do going forward after reopening plants is to use union workers. The 86-year-old company closed down and entered bankruptcy, in part, due to a nationwide strike by one of its unions. Chief Executive C. Dean Metropoulos said $60 million in capital investments will be spent on the plants and that the plan is to hire at least 1,500 workers. But Mr. Metropoulos in an interview made his views on the role of unions clear: There will be no role.

Hostess Brands Inc. once employed 19,000 workers. Of those, 15,000 were represented by unions. The Teamsters union, which represented the largest share of Hostess Brands workers, after difficult negotiations, agreed to a new collective bargaining contract following the bankruptcy trial in court. In contrast, the second-largest union, the Bakery, Confectionery, Tobacco Workers & Grain Millers International Union, began a nationwide work stoppage after failing to agree on a contract with the company, which led to the company imposing a new, less favorable contract on the union. The resulting strike,

according to the company, crippled its operations, ultimately leading the company to shut down.

The company and the Bakers union expressed different views on the importance of the unionized bakers. The president of the Bakers union, David Durkee, stated that because only members of the Bakers union knew how to run the equipment in the plants used to bake snacks, the Bakers union members would be hired back to work. In contrast, the new owners of Hostess have said that they will be able to find capable nonunion workers in the areas where plants are re-opening, which are all located in areas where unemployment is high. Prior to bankruptcy, Hostess plants had been running at less than 50% of capacity. Going forward, the plants are expected to run at 85% to 90% capacity, making production much more efficient and, presumably, allowing the company to make an adequate profit. Of course, if the nonunion workers to be used going forward are also less costly, that will further bring costs down and profits up. The caveat is that it remains to be seen whether new nonunion bakers can quickly learn how to efficiently do the work in the plants. To avoid hiring Teamsters as drivers, Hostess plans to outsource driving/delivery and related tasks. It will also outsource sales.

QUESTIONS

1. Why did Hostess Brands Inc. go into bankruptcy?
2. Did unions act in the best interests of the workers they represented? Did the two unions involved follow the same strategy?
3. Will the new company, Hostess Brands LLC, perform better? Why or why not?

SOURCE: Rachel Feintzeig, "New Twinkie Maker Shuns Union Labor," *Wall Street Journal*, April 24, 2013; www.huffingtonpost.com/2012/11/16/twinkie-facts-12-things_n_2144143.html, accessed July 2, 2013; www.snopes.com/food/ingredient/twinkies.asp, accessed July 2, 2013.

HR IN SMALL BUSINESS

Republic Gets Serious

When Serious Materials acquired Republic Windows and Doors, union–management relations got a much-needed breath of fresh air. Republic had nearly vanished amidst economic meltdown and accusations of mismanagement and corruption. Serious Materials, by contrast, is a firm with a high-minded business strategy and a commitment to fair-mindedness.

The problems became public when workers at Republic staged a six-day sit-in at the Chicago factory, which had been one of the largest window-glass factories in the United States. When orders from construction companies stopped coming in, management, after just three days' warning, closed the plant without granting workers any severance pay or giving the legally required 60 days' notice, and filed for bankruptcy. Bowing to public pressure, the company's lenders, including Bank of America, reached an agreement to give the workers $6,000 apiece in severance pay.

But that wasn't the end. The workers turned to the National Labor Relations Board with another complaint. They said Republic's owner, Richard Gillman, had secretly begun transferring the company's machinery to a (non-union) window-manufacturing facility he bought in Iowa just before closing the Chicago factory. In fact, all the equipment would have been gone, they said, except that their six-day occupation of the factory interfered with the plan—they wouldn't allow Gillman to enter. Employees also followed trucks carrying machinery to learn where it was being taken. The union demanded that the machinery be returned to the Chicago plant, so a new owner could operate it.

Meanwhile, a hero arrived on the scene: Kevin Surace, founder and chief executive of Serious Materials, a maker of eco-friendly building products, including energy-efficient windows. Surace saw acquisition of the Republic facility as a chance to expand into the Chicago region with a ready-made plant and equipment, not to mention trained people eager to work.

When he decided to make an offer, Surace did something unusual: instead of talking first to the firms' main creditors, he made his first visit to the employees' union, the United Electrical, Radio, and Machine Workers of America. He met with the union's president, Carl Rosen, as well as several Republic workers. Rosen recalled that Surace's reasoning was that for the deal to work, he needed a skilled workforce. The parties agreed that Serious Materials would make the facility a union shop, and employees would be paid their former salaries and receive credit for their seniority at Republic. Only then did Surace approach Bank of America. The bank initially wasn't interested, so Surace went to General Electric, owner of the lease on the equipment, and bought out the lease, a coup that convinced the bank to sell. Surace announced plans to reopen the plant and rehire all the 300 employees who had been laid off when Republic closed its doors. The resulting publicity quickly brought in inquiries and even some paying customers.

Since the acquisition, the Republic story may be nearing its end. County prosecutors brought charges against Gillman for looting the business and stealing machinery for the Iowa enterprise (which also failed, less than two months after it launched). Because Republic had been in bankruptcy, the equipment was not Gillman's but belonged to his creditor, GE. State's Attorney Anita Alvarez said, "Just two weeks before Christmas, in a dire economy, the company shut the doors of their business and deserted their workers and all of their families." Gillman denied the charges.

A sign of Surace's very different attitude toward his workforce came a few months after the acquisition by Serious Materials, when Vice President Joe Biden came to visit the Chicago facility. Biden was there to represent how the Obama administration's economic stimulus plan was supporting "green" initiatives. Surace noticed that onstage for the press conference were various dignitaries but no representatives of the workers. In spite of the Secret Service's reluctance to add last-minute guests, Surace insisted that workers have a face at the press conference. By the time the TV cameras were rolling, the cast of dignitaries included Armando Robles, a maintenance worker and the president of the employees' union.

QUESTIONS

1. Richard Gillman attempted to stay in business by transferring work to a nonunion facility, and Kevin Surace plans to make the operation profitable as a union shop. Do you think the decision to rely on union or nonunion labor spells the difference between the success and failure of this enterprise? Why or why not?
2. How (if at all) do you think Kevin Surace's initial approach to the union when acquiring the company will influence the business success of the window factory?
3. Imagine that Serious Materials has hired you as an HR consultant for the Chicago window factory. Suggest how the company can build on its initial goodwill with workers to create positive labor relations and a highly motivated workforce for the long run.

SOURCES: Robert Mitchum, "Republic Workers File Labor Charges," *Chicago Tribune*, January 7, 2009, NewsBank, http://infoweb.newsbank.com; Robert Mitchum, "Former Republic Workers Find Hope," *Chicago Tribune*, January 15, 2009, NewsBank, http://infoweb.newsbank.com; Annie Sweeney and Matthew Walberg, "Tables Turn on Man Who Shut Republic Windows," *Chicago Tribune*, September 11, 2009, NewsBank, http://infoweb.newsbank.com; and Leigh Buchanan, "Entrepreneur of the Year: Kevin Surace of Serious Materials," *Inc.*, December 2009, www.inc.com.

NOTES

1. J. T. Dunlop, *Industrial Relations Systems* (New York: Holt, 1958).

2. C. Kerr, "Industrial Conflict and Its Mediation," *American Journal of Sociology* 60 (1954), pp. 230–45.

3. T. A. Kochan, *Collective Bargaining and Industrial Relations* (Homewood, IL: Richard D. Irwin, 1980), p. 25; H. C. Katz and T. A. Kochan, *An Introduction to Collective Bargaining and Industrial Relations,* 3rd ed. (New York: McGraw-Hill, 2004).

4. Katz and Kochan, *An Introduction to Collective Bargaining.*

5. S. Webb and B. Webb, *Industrial Democracy* (London: Longmans, Green, 1897); J. R. Commons, *Institutional Economics* (New York: Macmillan, 1934).

6. C. Kerr, J. T. Dunlop, F. Harbison, and C. Myers, "Industrialism lnand World Society," *Harvard Business Review,* February 1961, pp. 113–26.

7. T. A. Kochan and K. R. Wever, "American Unions and the Future of Worker Representation," in *The State of the Unions,* ed. G. Strauss et al. (Madison, WI: Industrial Relations Research Association, 1991).

8. "Why America Needs Unions, but Not the Kind It Has Now," *BusinessWeek,* May 23, 1994, p. 70.

9. Katz and Kochan, *An Introduction to Collective Bargaining.*

10. J. Barbash, *The Elements of Industrial Relations* (Madison, WI: University of Wisconsin Press, 1984).

11. U.S. Bureau of Labor Statistics, www.bls.gov.

12. J. T. Bennett and B. E. Kaufman, *The Future of Private Sector Unionism in the United States* (Armonk, NY: M. E. Sharpe, 2002).

13. Katz and Kochan, *An Introduction to Collective Bargaining.* Katz and Kochan in turn build on work by J. Fiorito and C. L. Maranto, "The Contemporary Decline of Union Strength," *Contemporary Policy Issues* 3 (1987), pp. 12–27.

14. G. N. Chaison and J. Rose, "The Macrodeterminants of Union Growth and Decline," in *The State of the Unions,* George Strauss et al. (eds.) (Madison, WI: Industrial Relations Research Association, 1991).

15. D. L. Belman and K. A. Monaco, "The Effects of Deregulation, Deunionization, Technology, and Human Capital on the Work and Work Lives of Truck Drivers," *Industrial and Labor Relations Review* 54 (2001), pp. 502–24.

16. T. A. Kochan, R. B. McKersie, and J. Chalykoff, "The Effects of Corporate Strategy and Workplace Innovations in Union Representation," *Industrial and Labor Relations Review* 39 (1986), pp. 487–501; Chaison and Rose, "The Macrodeterminants of Union Growth"; J. Barbash, *Practice of Unionism* (New York: Harper, 1956), p. 210; W. N. Cooke and D. G. Meyer, "Structural and Market Predictors of Corporate Labor Relations Strategies," *Industrial and Labor Relations Review* 43 (1990), pp. 280–93; T. A. Kochan and P. Cappelli, "The Transformation of the Industrial Relations and Personnel Function," in *Internal Labor Markets,* ed. P. Osterman (Cambridge, MA: MIT Press, 1984); J. Logan, "The Union Avoidance Industry in the United States," *British Journal of Industrial Relations* 44 (2006), pp. 651–75.

17. Kochan and Cappelli, "The Transformation of the Industrial Relations and Personnel Function."

18. The 27% difference is based on 2012 data from www.bls.gov. S. B. Jarrell and T. D. Stanley, "A Meta-Analysis of the Union–Nonunion Wage Gap," *Industrial and Labor Relations Review* 44 (1990), pp. 54–67; P. D. Lineneman, M. L. Wachter, and W. H. Carter, "Evaluating the Evidence on Union Employment and Wages," *Industrial and Labor Relations Review* 44 (1990), pp. 34–53; L. Mischel and M. Walters, "How Unions Help All Workers," Economic Policy Institute Briefing Paper (2003).

19. National Labor Relations Board annual reports.

20. J. P. Ferguson, "The Eyes of the Needles: A Sequential Model of Union Organizing Drives, 1999–2004," *Industrial and Labor Relations Review* 62, no. 3 (2008), pp. 3–21.

21. R. B. Freeman and M. M. Kleiner, "Employer Behavior in the Face of Union Organizing Drives," *Industrial and Labor Relations Review* 43 (1990), pp. 351–65.

22. F. K. Foulkes, "Large Nonunionized Employers," in *U.S. Industrial Relations 1950–1980: A Critical Assessment,* eds. J. Steiber et al. (Madison, WI: Industrial Relations Research Association, 1981).

23. Katz and Kochan, *An Introduction to Collective Bargaining.*

24. R. B. Freeman and J. Rogers, *What Workers Want* (Ithaca, NY: Cornell University Press, 1999).

25. E. E. Herman, J. L. Schwarz, and A. Kuhn, *Collective Bargaining and Labor Relations* (Englewood Cliffs, NJ: Prentice Hall, 1992), p. 32.

26. www.bls.gov; AFL-CIO website.

27. Herman et al., *Collective Bargaining,* p. 33.

28. Kochan, *Collective Bargaining and Industrial Relations,* p. 61.

29. National Labor Relations Board, *A Guide to Basic Law and Procedures under the National Labor Relations Act* (Washington, DC: U.S. Government Printing Office, 1991).

30. Ibid.

31. Ibid.

32. H. N. Wheeler and J. A. McClendon, "The Individual Decision to Unionize," in *The State of the Unions.*

33. National Labor Relations Board annual reports, www.nlrb.gov.

34. M. Trottman, "New Rules Adopted for Union Elections," *The New York Times,* December 13–14, 2014, p. B4. Melanie Trottman. "Ruling Clears Way for Unions: Fast-food, construction to feel effects of labor board decision on temp and contract workers," *Wall Street Journal.* August 27, 2015.

35. J. G. Getman, S. B. Goldberg, and J. B. Herman, *Union Representation Elections: Law and Reality* (New York: Russell Sage Foundation, 1976).

36. J. A. Fossum, *Labor Relations,* 8th ed. (New York: McGraw-Hill, 2002), p. 149.

37. National Labor Relations Board, *A Guide to Basic Law,* p. 17.

38. Ibid.

39. Herman et al., *Collective Bargaining;* P. Jarley and J. Fiorito, "Associate Membership: Unionism or Consumerism?" *Industrial and Labor Relations Review* 43 (1990), pp. 209–24.

40. Katz and Kochan, *An Introduction to Collective Bargaining;* R. L. Rose, "Unions Hit Corporate Campaign Trail," *The Wall Street Journal,* March 8, 1993, p. B1.

41. P. Jarley and C. L. Maranto, "Union Corporate Campaigns: An Assessment," *Industrial and Labor Relations Review* 44 (1990), pp. 505–24.

42. Katz and Kochan, *An Introduction to Collective Bargaining.*

43. Atlee McFellin, "Labor Unions in the New Economy" *Common Dreams,* March 24, 2013, www.heartlandnetwork.org/newsroom/10-in-the-news/63-labor-unions-in-the-new-economy-2, accessed May 25, 2013.

44. Kris Maher, "SEIU to End Sodexo Campaign," *Wall Street Journal,* September 15, 2011.

45. Chaison and Rose, "The Macrodeterminants of Union Growth."

46. R. E. Walton and R. B. McKersie, *A Behavioral Theory of Negotiations* (New York: McGraw-Hill, 1965).

47. Fossum, *Labor Relations.* See also C. S. Loughran, *Negotiating a Labor Contract: A Management Handbook,* 2nd ed. (Washington, DC: Bureau of National Affairs, 1990).

48. C. M. Steven, *Strategy and Collective Bargaining Negotiations* (New York: McGraw-Hill, 1963); Katz and Kochan, *An Introduction to Collective Bargaining.*

49. Roger Fisher and William Ury, *Getting to Yes* (New York: Penguin Books, 1991).

50. Kochan, *Collective Bargaining and Industrial Relations.*

51. Fossum, *Labor Relations.*

52. J. R. Haggerty, "Caterpillar Girds for a Strike," *The Wall Street Journal,* March 2–3, 2013, p. B3.

53. Kochan, *Collective Bargaining and Industrial Relations,* p. 272.

54. Herman et al., *Collective Bargaining.*

55. Katz and Kochan, *An Introduction to Collective Bargaining.*

56. Kochan, *Collective Bargaining and Industrial Relations,* p. 386.

57. Alternative criteria would be efficiency, equity, and worker voice. John W. Budd and Alexander J. S. Colvin, "Improved Metrics for Workplace Dispute Resolution Procedures: Efficiency, Equity, and Voice," *Industrial Relations* 47, no. 3 (July 2008), p. 460.

58. *United Steelworkers v. American Manufacturing Co.,* 363 U.S. 564 (1960); *United Steelworkers v. Warrior Gulf and Navigation Co.,* 363 U.S. 574 (1960); *United Steelworkers v. Enterprise Wheel and Car Corp.,* 363 U.S. 593 (1960).

59. Original data from U.S. Federal Mediation and Conciliation Service, *Fiftieth Annual Report, Fiscal Year 2006* (Washington, DC: U.S. Government Printing Office, 2006); www.fmcs.gov.

60. J. R. Redecker, *Employee Discipline: Policies and Practices* (Washington, DC: Bureau of National Affairs, 1989).

61. Barbash, *The Elements of Industrial Relations,* p. 6.

62. T. A. Kochan, H. C. Katz, and R. B. McKersie, *The Transformation of American Industrial Relations* (New York: Basic Books, 1986), chap. 6.

63. J. B. Arthur, "The Link between Business Strategy and Industrial Relations Systems in American Steel Minimills," *Industrial and Labor Relations Review* 45 (1992), pp. 488–506; M. Schuster, "Union Management Cooperation," in *Employee and Labor Relations,* ed. J. A. Fossum (Washington, DC: Bureau of National Affairs, 1990); E. Cohen-Rosenthal and C. Burton, *Mutual Gains: A Guide to Union–Management Cooperation,* 2nd ed. (Ithaca, NY: ILR Press, 1993); T. A. Kochan and P. Osterman, *The Mutual Gains Enterprise* (Boston: Harvard Business School Press, 1994); E. Applebaum and R. Batt, *The New American Workplace* (Ithaca, NY: ILR Press, 1994). J. Marquez, "Streamlined Model: Engine of Change," *Workforce Management,* July 17, 2006, pp. 1, 20–30; B. Visnic, "Harbour—Topping Chrysler JV Engine Plant Attracting Foreign Attention," *Edmunds Auto Observer,* July 20, 2008, www.autoobserver.com.

64. J. McCracken, "Desperate to Cut Costs, Ford Gets Union's Help," *The Wall Street Journal,* March 2, 2007, p. A1; M. Oneal, "Model Partnership: Automakers, Labor Could Learn from Harley-Davidson's Kansas City Operation," *Columbus Dispatch,* May 27, 2006 (original article in *Chicago Tribune*).

65. A. E. Eaton, "Factors Contributing to the Survival of Employee Participation Programs in Unionized Settings," *Industrial and Labor Relations Review* 47, no. 3 (1994), pp. 371–89.

66. National Labor Relations Board, *A Guide to Basic Law.*

67. A. Bernstein, "Putting a Damper on That Old Team Spirit," *BusinessWeek,* May 4, 1992, p. 60.

68. Bureau of National Affairs, "Polaroid Dissolves Employee Committee in Response to Labor Department Ruling," *Daily Labor Report,* June 23, 1992, p. A3; K. G. Salwen, "DuPont Is Told It Must Disband Nonunion Panels," *The Wall Street Journal,* June 7, 1993, p. A2.

69. "NLRB 4-0 Approves Crown Cork & Seal's Use of Seven Employee Participation Committees," *HR News,* September 3, 2001.

70. Kochan and Osterman, *Mutual Gains;* J. P. MacDuffie, "Human Resource Bundles and Manufacturing Performance: Organizational Logic and Flexible Production Systems in the World Auto Industry," *Industrial and Labor Relations Review* 48, no. 2 (1995), pp. 197–221; W. N. Cooke, "Employee Participation Programs, Group-Based Incentives, and Company Performance: A Union–Nonunion Comparison," *Industrial and Labor Relations Review* 47, no. 4 (1994), pp. 594–609; C. Doucouliagos, "Worker Participation and Productivity in Labor-Managed and Participatory Capitalist Firms: A Meta-Analysis," *Industrial and Labor Relations Review* 49, no. 1 (1995), pp. 58–77; L. W. Hunter, J. P. MacDuffie, and L. Doucet, "What Makes Teams Take? Employee Reactions to Work Reforms," *Industrial and Labor Relations Review* 55 (2002), pp. 448–72; S. J. Deery and R. D. Iverson, "Labor-Management Cooperation: Antecedents and Impact on Organizational Performance," *Industrial and Labor Relations Review* 58 (2005), pp. 588–609; James Combs, Yongmei Liu, Angela Hall, and David Ketchen, "How Much Do High-Performance Work Practices Matter? A Meta-Analysis of Their Effects on Organizational Performance," *Personnel Psychology* 59, no. 3 (2006), pp. 501–28; T. Rabl, M. Jayasinghe, B. Gerhart, and T. M. Köhlmann, "How Much Does Country Matter? A Meta-Analysis of the HPWP Systems-Business Performance Relationship," *Academy of Management Annual Meeting Proceedings,* August 2011.

71. Robert D. Mohr and Cindy Zoghi, "High-Involvement Work Design and Job Satisfaction," *Industrial & Labor Relations Review* 61, no. 3 (April 2008), pp. 275–296; Paul Osterman, "The Wage Effects of High Performance Work Organization in Manufacturing," *Industrial and Labor Relations Review* 59 (2006), pp. 187–204.

72. J. Cutcher-Gershenfeld, "The Impact of Economic Performance of a Transformation in Workplace Relations," *Industrial and Labor Relations Review* 44 (1991), pp. 241–60.

73. R. B. Freeman and J. Rogers, *Proceedings of the Industrial Relations Research Association,* 1995. A survey of workers represented by the United Autoworkers at six Chrysler manufacturing plants found generally positive worker reactions to the implementation of work teams, streamlined job classifications, and skill-based pay. See L. W. Hunter, J. P. MacDuffie, and L. Doucet, "What Makes Teams Take? Employee Reactions to Work Reforms," *Industrial and Labor Relations Review* 55 (2002), p. 448. A study of the airline industry, moreover, concludes that relational factors, such as conflict and workplace culture, also play an important role in firm performance. See J. H. Gittell, A. vonNordenflycht, and T. A. Kochan, "Mutual Gains or Zero Sum? Labor Relations and Firm Performance in the Airline Industry," *Industrial and Labor Relations Review* 57 (2004), p. 163.

74. http://stats.bls.gov, Employer Costs for Employee Compensation (ECEC).

75. Ibid.

76. Mckinley L. Blackburn, "Are Union Wage Differentials in the United States Falling?" *Industrial Relations* 47, no. 3 (July 2008), p. 390.

77. Jarrell and Stanley, "A Meta-Analysis"; R. B. Freeman and J. Medoff, *What Do Unions Do?* (New York: Basic Books, 1984); L. Mishel and M. Walters, "How Unions Help All Workers," *Economic Policy Institute Briefing Paper,* August 2003, www.epinet.org.

78. T. H. Hammer and A. Augar, "The Impact of Unions on Job Satisfaction, Organizational Commitment, and Turnover," *Journal of Labor Research* 26 (2005), pp. 241–66; B. Artz "The Impact of Union Experience on Job Satisfaction," *Industrial Relations: A Journal of Economy and Society* 49 (2010), pp. 387–405.

79. J. T. Addison and B. T. Hirsch, "Union Effects on Productivity, Profits, and Growth: Has the Long Run Arrived?" *Journal of Labor Economics* 7 (1989), pp. 72–105.

80. R. B. Freeman and J. L. Medoff, "The Two Faces of Unionism," *Public Interest* 57 (Fall 1979), pp. 69–93.

81. Ibid.; L. Mishel and P. Voos, *Unions and Economic Competitiveness* (Armonk, NY: M. E. Sharpe, 1991); M. Ash and J. A. Seago, "The Effect of Registered Nurses' Unions on Heart-Attack Mortality," *Industrial and Labor Relations Review* 57 (2004), p. 422; C. Doucouliagos and P. Laroche, "What Do Unions Do to Productivity? A Meta-Analysis," *Industrial Relations* 42 (2003), pp. 650–91.

82. Freeman and Medoff, "Two Faces."

83. S. Slichter, J. Healy, and E. R. Livernash, *The Impact of Collective Bargaining on Management* (Washington, DC: Brookings Institution, 1960); Freeman and Medoff, "Two Faces."

84. Freeman and Medoff, What Do Unions Do?; Herman et al., R. B. Freeman J. L. Medoff 1984. *What Do Unions Do?* New York: Basic Books. *Collective Bargaining;* Addison and Hirsch, "Union Effects on Productivity"; Katz and Kochan, *An Introduction to Collective Bargaining;* Lineneman et al., "Evaluating the Evidence."

85. B. E. Becker and C. A. Olson, "Unions and Firm Profits," *Industrial Relations* 31, no. 3 (1992), pp. 395–415; B. T. Hirsch and B. A. Morgan, "Shareholder Risks and Returns in Union and Nonunion Firms," *Industrial and Labor Relations Review* 47, no. 2 (1994), pp. 302–18. Hristos Doucouliagos and Partice Laroche, "Unions and Profits: A Meta-Regression Analysis," *Industrial Relations* 48, no. 1 (January 2008), p. 146.

86. David S. Lee and Alexandre Mas, "Long-run Impacts of Unions on Firms: New Evidence from Financial Markets, 1961–1999," *Quarterly Journal of Economics,* 127 (2012), pp. 333–378.

87. Addison and Hirsch, "Union Effects on Productivity." See also B. T. Hirsch, *Labor Unions and the Economic Performance of Firms* (Kalamazoo, MI: W. E. Upjohn Institute, 1991); J. M. Abowd, "The Effect of Wage Bargains on the Stock Market Value of the Firm," *American Economic Review* 79 (1989), pp. 774–800; Hirsch, *Labor Unions.*

88. B. E. Becker, and C. A. Olson, "The Impact of Strikes on Shareholder Equity," *Industrial and Labor Relations Review* 39, no. 3 (1986), pp. 425–38; O. Persons, "The Effects of Automobile Strikes on the Stock Value of Steel Suppliers," *Industrial and Labor Relations Review* 49, no. 1 (1995), pp. 78–87.

89. C. Brewster, "Levels of Analysis in Strategic HRM: Questions Raised by Comparative Research," Conference on Research and Theory in HRM, Cornell University, October 1997.

90. C. Chang and C. Sorrentino, "Union Membership in 12 Countries," *Monthly Labor Review* 114, no. 12 (1991), pp. 46–53; D. G. Blanchflower and R. B. Freeman, "Going Different Ways: Unionism in the U.S. and Other Advanced O.E.C.D. Countries" (Symposium on the Future Role of Unions, Industry, and Government in Industrial Relations. University of Minnesota), cited in Chaison and Rose, "The Macrodeterminants of Union Growth," p. 23.

91. J. P. Begin and E. F. Beal, *The Practice of Collective Bargaining* (Homewood, IL: Richard D. Irwin, 1989); T. H. Hammer, S. C. Currall, and R. N. Stern, "Worker Representation on Boards of Directors: A Study of Competing Roles," *Industrial and Labor Relations Review* 44 (1991), pp. 661–80; Katz and Kochan, *An Introduction to Collective Bargaining;* H. Gunter and G. Leminsky, "The Federal Republic of Germany," in *Labor in the Twentieth Century,* ed. J. T. Dunlop and W. Galenson (New York: Academic Press, 1978), pp. 149–96.

92. "Adapt or Die," *The Economist,* July 1, 1995, p. 54; G. Steinmetz, "German Firms Sour on Stem That Keeps Peace with Workers: Centralized Bargaining, a Key to Postwar Gains, Inflates Costs, Companies Fear," *The Wall Street Journal,* October 17, 1995, p. A1; H. C. Katz, W. Lee, and J. Lee, *The New Structure of Labor Relations: Tripartism and Decentralization* (Ithaca, NY: ILR Press/Cornell University, 2004).

93. A. Young, "UAW Welcomes Volkswagen Policy Shift After Years of Failing to Gain Traction in Anti-Union South," *International Business Times,* accessed May 13, 2015, www.ibtimes.com.

94. M. Elfstrom and S. Kuruvilla, "The Changing Nature of Unrest in China," *Industrial and Labor Relations Review* April 2014, pp. 453–80.

95. J. F. Burton and T. Thomason, "The Extent of Collective Bargaining in the Public Sector," in *Public Sector Bargaining,* ed. B. Aaron, J. M. Najita, and J. L. Stern (Washington, DC: Bureau of National Affairs, 1988).

96. www.afscme.org.

97. John Godard and Carola Frege, "Labor Unions, Alternative Forms of Representation, and the Exercise of Authority Relations in U.S. Workplaces," *Industrial and Labor Relations Review,* 66 (2013), pp. 142–168; Paul J. Gollan and David Lewin, "Employee Representation in Non-Union Firms: An Overview," *Industrial Relations,* 52 (2013), pp. 173–193.

Managing Human Resources Globally

LEARNING OBJECTIVES

After reading this chapter, you should be able to:

LO 15-1 Identify the recent changes that have caused companies to expand into international markets. *page 631*

LO 15-2 Discuss the four factors that most strongly influence HRM in international markets. *page 633*

LO 15-3 List the different categories of international employees. *page 642*

LO 15-4 Identify the four levels of global participation and the HRM issues faced within each level. *page 642*

LO 15-5 Discuss the ways companies attempt to select, train, compensate, and reintegrate expatriate managers. *page 646*

Walmart's Global Strategy

Walmart's international division has an important job. With 80% of the retail industry's growth coming from outside of the United States, Wal-Mart international's $137 billion in sales in 2014, 29% of sales overall, is a key driver of overall revenue growth. In order to drive this performance, David Cheesewright, CEO of Wal-Mart's international division, is focusing on current operations in growth markets and e-commerce.

Shopping trends indicate that what customers buy is changing fast, and that they are quickly switching to online shopping platforms. After decades of work trying to develop a foundation in the Chinese market, Walmart is consolidating its portfolio of stores in that country, closing nonperforming retail stores and investing in successful ones. To enter the Chinese e-grocery market, Walmart holds a 51% stake in Yihaodian, which has posted triple-digit growth—twice the market rate.

The company's operations in Brazil and Mexico are experiencing slowing growth, in part a result of economic cycles and their brand's lifecycle, but they still offer the opportunity to develop strong, mature businesses.

© Bloomberg/Contributor

International expansion comes with country-specific challenges. After experiencing too many regulatory difficulties in India, Walmart canceled plans to open retail stores there. Instead, Walmart India is focusing on business-to-business sales.

SOURCE: S. Banjo, "Wal-Mart's Strategy to Jump Start Growth in China," *The Wall Street Journal,* August 5, 2014, www.wsj.com.

Introduction

The environment in which business competes is rapidly becoming globalized. More and more companies are entering international markets by exporting their products overseas, building plants in other countries, and entering into alliances with foreign companies. Back in the middle of the 1980s, 61 of the top 100 organizations had their headquarters in the United States. By 2004 that number had dropped to 35, and as you can see in Table 15.1, of the world's largest 25 organizations in 2014, only 7 were headquartered in the United States, with 10 in Europe and 7 in Asia. Of *Fortune* magazine's Global 500 (the 500 largest companies by revenues), 128 are headquartered in the United States, with 95 headquartered in China. In addition, in 2014 Toyota maintained its lead as the world's top automobile manufacturer, selling 10.23 million vehicles worldwide, closely followed by Volkswagen with 10.14 million vehicles, and General Motors with sales of 9.92 million vehicles.[1]

Forbes magazine lists its top 2000 global companies, and identifies a subset that exhibits exceptional growth rates which they dub "Global High Performers." In 2011, 69 of the 130 high-performer companies (those standing out from their peers in growth, return to investors, and future prospects) were headquartered outside of the United States.[2]

Table 15.1
2014 *Fortune*
Global 500

RANK	COMPANY	REVENUES ($ MILLIONS)	PROFITS ($ MILLIONS)
1	Wal-Mart Stores	476,294	16,022
2	Royal Dutch Shell	459,599	16,371
3	Sinopec Group	457,201	8,932
4	China National Petroleum	432,007	18,504
5	Exxon Mobil	407,666	32,580
6	BP	396,217	23,451
7	State Grid	333,386	7,982
8	Volkswagen	261,539	12,071
9	Toyota Motor	256,454	18,198
10	Glencore	232,694	−7402
11	Total	227,882	11,204
12	Chevron	220,356	21,423
13	Samsung Electronics	208,938	27,245
14	Berkshire Hathaway	182,150	19,476
15	Apple	170,910	37,037
16	AXA	165,893	5,950
17	Gazprom	165,016	35,769
18	E.ON	162,560	2,843
19	Phillips 66	161,175	3,726
20	Daimler	156,628	9,083
21	General Motors	155,427	5,346
22	ENI	154,108	6,850
23	Japan Post Holdings	152,125	4,782
24	EXOR Group	150,996	2,768
25	Industrial & Commercial Bank of China	148,802	42,718

SOURCE: From *Fortune.* © 2014 Time Inc. Used under license.

In addition, cross-border mergers (e.g., Merck/Schering-Plough, New York Stock Exchange/Deutche Bourse, etc.) are increasing. In fact, in 2011, 30% of all mergers were of companies headquartered in different countries, and the total value of cross-border mergers was up by 56%.[3]

Most organizations now function in the global economy. U.S. businesses are entering international markets at the same time foreign companies are entering the U.S. market.

What is behind the trend toward expansion into global markets? Companies are attempting to gain a competitive advantage, which can be provided by international expansion in a number of ways. First, these countries are new markets with large numbers of potential customers. For companies that are producing below their capacity, they provide a means of increasing sales and profits. Second, many companies are building production facilities in other countries as a means of capitalizing on those countries' lower labor costs for relatively unskilled jobs. For example, many of the *maquiladora* plants (foreign-owned plants located in Mexico that employ Mexican laborers) provide low-skilled labor at considerably lower cost than in the United States. In 2011 the average hourly compensation cost in Mexico was $6.48, versus $35.53 in the United States.[4] Third, the rapid increase in telecommunications and information technology enables work to be done more rapidly, efficiently, and effectively around the globe. With the best college graduates available

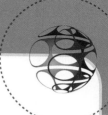
Staying Connected to Work 24/7: Good or Bad?

In order to better enable employees (particularly executives) to stay connected to the office, many companies have issued them smartphones. However, staying connected may make the blurring of work and nonwork problematic from a legal perspective. Some employees now claim that if they have to stay connected and do work via their phones, this is compensable time at work.

According to a Pew Research poll, about 44% of Internet users reported that they regularly performed work tasks outside of work hours, and 35% reported that this resulted in them working more hours.

Determining if the time requires compensation is neither easy nor cut and dried, particularly given how new the issue is. For instance, an hourly Verizon sales employee who frequently gets calls from customers asking for help during nonwork hours may be eligible for pay. On the other hand, an executive making $100,000 per year and working 70 hours a week probably does not need to be compensated for using her phone on work-related activities during nonwork hours.

Technology has changed the nature of work and is now changing the nature of work time. Companies face numerous challenges in managing this emerging trend.

DISCUSSION QUESTION

Do you think employees who have company-issued phones should be compensated when using them for work during nonwork hours? What if they are using their personal phones?

SOURCE: L. Weber, "Can You Sue the Boss for Making You Answer Late-Night Email?" *The Wall Street Journal,* May 20, 2015, www.wsj.com.

---

for $2.00 an hour in India versus $12–$18 an hour in the United States, companies can hire the best talent (resulting in better work) at a lower cost. And because their day is our night, work done in the United States can be handed off to those in India for a 24/7 work process.[5] The "Competing through Technology" box illustrates some of the pitfalls of the constant use of technology to stay linked to the workplace.

Deciding whether to enter foreign markets and whether to develop plants or other facilities in other countries, however, is no simple matter, and many human resource issues surface.

This chapter discusses the human resource issues that must be addressed to gain competitive advantage in a world of global competition. This is not a chapter on international human resource management (the specific HRM policies and programs companies use to manage human resources across international boundaries).[6] The chapter focuses instead on the key factors that must be addressed to strategically manage human resources in an international context. We discuss some of the important events that have increased the global nature of business over the past few years. We then identify some of the factors that are most important to HRM in global environments. Finally, we examine particular issues related to managing expatriate managers. These issues present unique opportunities for firms to gain competitive advantage.

Current Global Changes

Several recent social and political changes have accelerated the movement toward international competition. The effects of these changes have been profound and far-reaching. Many are still evolving. In this section we discuss the major developments that have

LO 15-1
Identify the recent changes that have caused companies to expand into international markets.

accentuated the need for organizations to gain a competitive advantage through effectively managing human resources in a global economy.

EUROPEAN UNION

European countries have managed their economies individually for years. Because of the countries' close geographic proximity, their economies have become intertwined. This created a number of problems for international businesses; for example, the regulations of one country, such as France, might be completely different from those of another country, such as Germany. In response, most of the European countries agreed to participate in the European Economic Community (EEC), which began in 1992. The EEC is a confederation of most of the European nations that agree to engage in free trade with one another, with commerce regulated by an overseeing body called the European Commission (EC). Under the EEC, legal regulation in the participating countries has become more, although not completely, uniform. Assuming the EEC's trend toward free trade among members continues, Europe has become one of the largest free markets in the world. In addition, as of 1999, all of the members of the European Economic Community share a common currency, the euro. This ties the members' economic fates even more closely with one another. In addition to the previous 15 EU states, as of May 1, 2004, 12 EU accession states—Bulgaria, Cyprus, the Czech Republic, Estonia, Hungary, Latvia, Lithuania, Malta, Poland, Romania, Slovakia, and Slovenia—were added to the EU, expanding the economic zone covered by the European Union. In 2013, Croatia was added to the EU, and Iceland, Montenegro, Serbia, Macedonia and Turkey are candidates to be admitted into the EU.

NORTH AMERICAN FREE TRADE AGREEMENT

The North American Free Trade Agreement (NAFTA) is an agreement among Canada, the United States, and Mexico that has created a free market even larger than the European Economic Community. The United States and Canada already had a free trade agreement since 1989, but NAFTA brought Mexico into the consortium. The agreement was prompted by Mexico's increasing willingness to open its markets and facilities in an effort to promote economic growth.[7] As previously discussed, the *maquiladora* plants exemplify this trend. In addition, some efforts have been made to expand the membership of NAFTA to other Latin American countries, such as Chile.

NAFTA has increased U.S. investment in Mexico because of Mexico's substantially lower labor costs for low-skilled employees. This has had two effects on employment in the United States. First, many low-skilled jobs went south, decreasing employment opportunities for U.S. citizens who lack higher-level skills. Second, it has increased employment opportunities for Americans with higher-level skills beyond those already being observed.[8]

THE GROWTH OF ASIA

An additional global market that is of economic consequence to many firms lies in Asia. Whereas Japan has been a dominant economic force for over 20 years, recently countries such as Singapore, Hong Kong, and Malaysia have become significant economic forces. In addition, China, with its population of more than 1 billion and trend toward opening its markets to foreign investors, presents a tremendous potential market for goods. In fact, a consortium of Singaporean companies and governmental agencies has jointly developed with China a huge industrial township in eastern China's Suzhou City that will consist of ready-made factories for sale to foreign companies.[9] While Asia has been affected by the recent recession, the main impact has only been to slow its rate of growth.

GENERAL AGREEMENT ON TARIFFS AND TRADE

The General Agreement on Tariffs and Trade (GATT) is an international framework of rules and principles for reducing trade barriers across countries around the world. It currently consists of more than 100 member-nations. The most recent round of GATT negotiations resulted in an agreement to cut tariffs (taxes on imports) by 40%, reduce government subsidies to businesses, expand protection of intellectual property such as copyrights and patents, and establish rules for investing and trading in services. It also established the World Trade Organization (WTO) to resolve disputes among GATT members.

These changes—the European Economic Community, NAFTA, the growth of Asia, and GATT—all exemplify events that are pushing companies to compete in a global economy. These developments are opening new markets and new sources of technology and labor in a way that has never been seen in history. However, this era of increasing international competition accentuates the need to manage human resources effectively to gain competitive advantage in a global marketplace. This requires understanding some of the factors that can determine the effectiveness of various HRM practices and approaches.

Factors Affecting HRM in Global Markets

Companies that enter global markets must recognize that these markets are not simply mirror images of their home country. Countries differ along a number of dimensions that influence the attractiveness of direct foreign investment in each country. These differences determine the economic viability of building an operation in a foreign location, and they have a particularly strong impact on HRM in that operation. Researchers in international management have identified a number of factors that can affect HRM in global markets, and we focus on four factors, as depicted in Figure 15.1: culture, education–human capital, the political–legal system, and the economic system.[10] The "Competing through Globalization" box provides an example of the kinds of things firms must address before deciding whether or not to set up operations in parts of Africa.

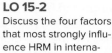

LO 15-2
Discuss the four factors that most strongly influence HRM in international markets.

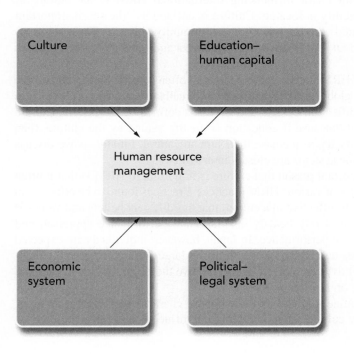

Figure 15.1

Factors Affecting Human Resource Management in International Markets

Risks and Rewards of Doing Business in Africa

One reason companies expand internationally is to escape the slowing economies of their home country and to capture some of the profits available in rapid-growth regions. Companies in Africa know this particularly well. Companies that have enjoyed the developed and wealthier economy of South Africa now complain of its slow (2.2%) GDP growth and seek opportunities in the faster-growing, less-developed countries of Nigeria (5.5%) and Angola (6.6%).

There are risks doing business in these regions, such as insurgent attacks by Boko Haram, and rapidly declining currencies. Nigeria, Africa's largest economy, is highly dependent on oil, so that when global oil prices dropped, so did its currency. A lack of existing infrastructure and the presence of militant groups make continued growth difficult and dangerous. Yet the old adage states, "more risk, more reward."

The search for this reward and the need for growth to power increased profitability is what has encouraged Nampak Ltd, a packaging company, to buy a $300 million factory in Nigeria and to build a $180 million factory in Angola. Africa's economy as a whole is growing at 5%, not far behind China and India. As more of the continent's population enters the middle class, they will demand and be able to afford more goods and services. With so much to gain, avoiding these countries may be the riskier option.

DISCUSSION QUESTION
What risks and opportunities should a company weigh when deciding whether it should expand into another country?

SOURCE: M. Stevis and P. McGroarty, "Businesses Seek Out New African Frontiers," *The Wall Street Journal*, March 31, 2015, www.wsj.com.

CULTURE

By far the most important factor influencing international HRM is the culture of the country in which a facility is located. Culture is defined as "the set of important assumptions (often unstated) that members of a community share."[11] These assumptions consist of beliefs about the world and how it works and the ideals that are worth striving for.[12]

Culture is important to HRM for two reasons. First, it often determines the other three factors affecting HRM in global markets. Culture can greatly affect a country's laws, in that laws are often the codification of right and wrong as defined by the culture. Culture also affects human capital, because if education is greatly valued by the culture, then members of the community try to increase their human capital. Finally, as we discuss later, cultures and economic systems are closely intertwined.[13]

However, the most important reason that culture is important to HRM is that it often determines the effectiveness of various HRM practices. Practices found to be effective in the United States may not be effective in a culture that has different beliefs and values.[14] For example, U.S. companies rely heavily on individual performance appraisal, and rewards are tied to individual performance. In Japan, however, individuals are expected to subordinate their wishes and desires to those of the larger group. Thus, individual-based evaluation and incentives are not nearly as effective there and, in fact, are seldom observed among Japanese organizations.[15]

In this section we examine a model that attempts to characterize different cultures. This model illustrates why culture can have a profound influence on HRM.

Hofstede's Cultural Dimensions

In a classic study of culture, Geert Hofstede identified four dimensions on which various cultures could be classified.[16] In a later study he added a fifth dimension that aids in characterizing cultures.[17] The relative scores for 10 major countries are provided in Table 15.2. **Individualism–collectivism** describes the strength of the relation between an individual and other individuals in the society—that is, the degree to which people act as individuals rather than as members of a group. In individualist cultures, such as the United States, Great Britain, and the Netherlands, people are expected to look after their own interests and the interests of their immediate families. The individual is expected to stand on her own two feet rather than be protected by the group. In collectivist cultures, such as Colombia, Pakistan, and Taiwan, people are expected to look after the interest of the larger community, which is expected to protect people when they are in trouble.

The second dimension, **power distance**, concerns how a culture deals with hierarchical power relationships—particularly the unequal distribution of power. It describes the degree of inequality among people that is considered to be normal. Cultures with small power distance, such as those of Denmark and Israel, seek to eliminate inequalities in power and wealth as much as possible, whereas countries with large power distances, such as India and the Philippines, seek to maintain those differences.

Differences in power distance often result in miscommunication and conflicts between people from different cultures. For example, in Mexico and Japan individuals are always addressed by their titles (Señor Smith or Smith-san, respectively). Individuals from the United States, however, often believe in minimizing power distances by using first names. Although this is perfectly normal, and possibly even advisable in the United States, it can be offensive and a sign of disrespect in other cultures.

The third dimension, **uncertainty avoidance**, describes how cultures seek to deal with the fact that the future is not perfectly predictable. It is defined as the degree to which people in a culture prefer structured over unstructured situations. Some cultures, such as those of Singapore and Jamaica, have weak uncertainty avoidance. They socialize individuals to accept this uncertainty and take each day as it comes. People from these cultures tend to be rather easygoing and flexible regarding different views. Other cultures, such as

Individualism–Collectivism
One of Hofstede's cultural dimensions; describes the strength of the relation between an individual and other individuals in a society.

Power Distance
One of Hofstede's cultural dimensions; describes how a culture deals with hierarchical power relationships.

Uncertainty Avoidance
One of Hofstede's cultural dimensions; describes how cultures seek to deal with an unpredictable future.

Table 15.2
Cultural Dimension Scores for 10 Countries

	PDᵃ	ID	MA	UA	LT
United States	40 Lᵇ	91 H	62 H	46 L	29 L
Germany	35 L	67 H	66 H	65 M	31 M
Japan	54 M	45 M	95 H	92 H	80 H
France	68 H	71 H	43 M	86 H	30ᶜ L
Netherlands	38 L	80 H	14 L	53 M	44 M
Hong Kong	68 H	25 L	57 H	29 L	96 H
Indonesia	78 H	14 L	46 M	48 L	25ᶜ L
West Africa	77 H	20 L	46 M	54 M	16 L
Russia	95ᶜ H	50ᶜ M	40ᶜ L	90ᶜ H	10ᶜ L
China	80ᶜ H	20ᶜ L	50ᶜ M	60ᶜ M	118 H

ᵃPD = power distance; ID = individualism; MA = masculinity; UA = uncertainty avoidance; LT = long-term orientation.
ᵇH = top third; M = medium third; L = bottom third (among 53 countries and regions for the first four dimensions; among 23 countries for the fifth).
ᶜEstimated.
SOURCE: From Geert Hofstede, "Cultural Constraints in Management Theories," *Academy of Management Executive*, February 1993, Vol. 7, No. 1, p. 91. Reproduced with permission of Academy of Management, via Copyright Clearance Center.

those of Greece and Portugal, socialize their people to seek security through technology, law, and religion. Thus these cultures provide clear rules as to how one should behave.

Masculinity–Femininity Dimension
One of Hofstede's cultural dimensions; describes the division of roles between the sexes within a society.

The **masculinity–femininity dimension** describes the division of roles between the sexes within a society. In "masculine" cultures, such as those of Germany and Japan, what are considered traditionally masculine values—showing off, achieving something visible, and making money—permeate the society. These societies stress assertiveness, performance, success, and competition. "Feminine" cultures, such as those of Sweden and Norway, promote values that have been traditionally regarded as feminine, such as putting relationships before money, helping others, and preserving the environment. These cultures stress service, care for the weak, and solidarity.

Long-Term–Short-Term Orientation
One of Hofstede's cultural dimensions; describes how a culture balances immediate benefits with future rewards.

Finally, the fifth dimension comes from the philosophy of the Far East and is referred to as the **long-term–short-term orientation**. Cultures high on the long-term orientation focus on the future and hold values in the present that will not necessarily provide an immediate benefit, such as thrift (saving) and persistence. Hofstede found that many Far Eastern countries such as Japan and China have a long-term orientation. Short-term orientations, on the other hand, are found in the United States, Russia, and West Africa. These cultures are oriented toward the past and present and promote respect for tradition and for fulfilling social obligations.

The current Japanese criticism of management practices in the United States illustrates the differences in long-term–short-term orientation. Japanese managers, traditionally exhibiting a long-term orientation, engage in 5- to 10-year planning. This leads them to criticize U.S. managers, who are traditionally much more short-term in orientation because their planning often consists of quarterly to yearly time horizons.

These five dimensions help us understand the potential problems of managing employees from different cultures. Later in this chapter we will explore how these cultural dimensions affect the acceptability and utility of various HRM practices. However, it is important to note that these differences can have a profound influence on whether a company chooses to enter a given country. One interesting finding of Hofstede's research was the impact of culture on a country's economic health. He found that countries with individualist cultures were more wealthy. Collectivist cultures with high power distance were all poor.[18] Cultures seem to affect a country's economy through their promotion of individual work ethics and incentives for individuals to increase their human capital.

Implications of Culture for HRM

Cultures have an important impact on approaches to managing people. As we discuss later, the culture can strongly affect the education–human capital of a country, the political–legal system, and the economic system. As Hofstede found, culture also has a profound impact on a country's economic health by promoting certain values that either aid or inhibit economic growth.

More important to this discussion, however, is that cultural characteristics influence the ways managers behave in relation to subordinates, as well as the perceptions of the appropriateness of various HRM practices. First, cultures differ strongly on such things as how subordinates expect leaders to lead, how decisions are handled within the hierarchy, and (most important) what motivates individuals. For example, in Germany, managers achieve their status by demonstrating technical skills, so employees look to them to assign their tasks and resolve technical problems. In the Netherlands, on the other hand, managers focus on seeking consensus among all parties and must engage in an open-ended exchange of views and balancing of interests.[19] Clearly, these methods have different implications for selecting and training managers in the different countries.

Second, cultures may influence the appropriateness of HRM practices. For example, as previously discussed, the extent to which a culture promotes an individualistic versus a collectivist orientation will impact the effectiveness of individually oriented human resource management systems. In the United States, companies often focus selection systems on assessing an individual's technical skill and, to a lesser extent, social skills. In collectivist cultures, on the other hand, companies focus more on assessing how well an individual will perform as a member of the work group.

Culture often influences how employees value certain aspects of their work environment. In an interesting study comparing call center workers in India (a collectivist culture) and the United States (an individualistic culture), researchers found that in the United States person–job fit was the stronger predictor of turnover relative to India, where person–organization fit, links to the organization, and links to the community were the stronger predictors of turnover.[20]

Similarly, cultures can influence compensation systems. Individualistic cultures such as those found in the United States often exhibit great differences between the highest- and lowest-paid individuals in an organization, with the highest-paid individual often receiving 200 times the salary of the lowest. Collectivist cultures, on the other hand, tend to have much flatter salary structures, with the top-paid individual receiving only about 20 times the overall pay of the lowest-paid one.

Cultural differences can affect the communication and coordination processes in organizations. Collectivist cultures, as well as those with less of an authoritarian orientation, value group decision making and participative management practices more highly than do individualistic cultures. When a person raised in an individualistic culture must work closely with those from a collectivist culture, communication problems and conflicts often appear. Much of the emphasis on "cultural diversity" programs in organizations focuses on understanding the cultures of others in order to better communicate with them.

EVIDENCE-BASED HR

While national culture is important, recent research also suggests that its importance may be overstated. Researchers reexamining Hofstede's original work found that while differences existed across nations, significant cultural differences also existed within nations. They further found that the differences in cultures across organizations within countries was larger than the differences across countries. Their results imply that while one cannot ignore national culture, one must not think that certain HR practices may not be effective simply based on a regard for national culture. People of varying cultural backgrounds within a nation will be drawn to organizations whose cultures better match their individual, as opposed to national, value systems.

In addition, many have suggested that the effectiveness of High Performance Work Systems (HPWS) depends upon the cultural or institutional constraints, such that they may be ineffective in cultures that exhibit high power distance and/or high collectivism. However, a recent meta-analysis revealed that the effects of HPWS on firm performance were positive in all cultures, and contrary to expectations, if anything, higher in the cultures where the cultural hypothesis suggested they would be lower.

SOURCES: T. Rable, M. Jayasinghe, B. Gerhart, and T. Kuhlmann, "A Meta-Analysis of Country Differences in the High-Performance Work System–Business Performance Relationship: The Roles of National Culture and Managerial Discretion," *Journal of Applied Psychology* 99, no. 6 (2014), pp. 1011–41; B. Gerhart and M. Fang, "National Culture and Human Resource Management Assumptions and Evidence," *International Journal of Human Resource Management* 16, no. 6 (June 2005), pp. 971–86.

EDUCATION–HUMAN CAPITAL

A company's potential to find and maintain a qualified workforce is an important consideration in any decision to expand into a foreign market. Thus a country's human capital resources can be an important HRM issue. *Human capital* refers to the productive capabilities of individuals—that is, the knowledge, skills, and experience that have economic value.[21]

A country's human capital is determined by a number of variables. A major variable is the educational opportunities available to the labor force. In the Netherlands, for instance, government funding of school systems allows students to go all the way through graduate school without paying.[22] Similarly, the free education provided to citizens in the former Soviet bloc resulted in high levels of human capital, in spite of the poor infrastructure and economy that resulted from the socialist economic systems. In contrast, some Third World countries, such as Nicaragua and Haiti, have relatively low levels of human capital because of a lack of investment in education.

A country's human capital may profoundly affect a foreign company's desire to locate there or enter that country's market. Countries with low human capital attract facilities that require low skills and low wage levels. This explains why U.S. companies desire to move their currently unionized low-skill–high-wage manufacturing and assembly jobs to Mexico, where they can obtain low-skilled workers for substantially lower wages. Similarly, Japan ships its messy, low-skill work to neighboring countries while maintaining its high-skill work at home.[23] Countries like Mexico, with relatively low levels of human capital, might not be as attractive for operations that consist of more high-skill jobs.

Countries with high human capital are attractive sites for direct foreign investment that creates high-skill jobs. In Ireland, for example, more than 25% of 18-year-olds attend college, a rate much higher than other European countries. In addition, Ireland's economy supports only 1.1 million jobs for a population of 3.5 million. The combination of high education levels, a strong work ethic, and high unemployment makes the country attractive for foreign firms because of the resulting high productivity and low turnover. The Met Life insurance company set up a facility for Irish workers to analyze medical insurance claims. It has found the high levels of human capital and the high work ethic provide such a competitive advantage that the company is currently looking for other work performed in the United States to be shipped to Ireland. Similarly, as already discussed, the skills of newly graduated technology workers in India are as high or higher than those found among their counterparts in the United States. In addition, because jobs are not as plentiful in India, the worker attitudes are better in many of these locations.[24]

POLITICAL–LEGAL SYSTEM

The regulations imposed by a country's legal system can strongly affect HRM. The political–legal system often dictates the requirements for certain HRM practices, such as training, compensation, hiring, firing, and layoffs. In large part, the legal system is an outgrowth of the culture in which it exists. Thus the laws of a particular country often reflect societal norms about what constitutes legitimate behavior.[25] The "Integrity in Action" box raises a question about U.S. airlines that profited from the government's temporary inability to collect airline transportation taxes.

For example, the United States has led the world in eliminating discrimination in the workplace. Because of the importance this has in our culture, we also have legal safeguards such as equal employment opportunity laws (discussed in Chapter 3) that strongly affect the hiring and firing practices of firms. As a society, we also have strong beliefs regarding the equity of pay systems; thus the Fair Labor Standards Act (discussed

Airlines Pocket Tax Money During Government Shutdown

When you buy an airline ticket, do you pay attention to all the parts that go into the price such as the fare itself, the fuel taxes, the airport taxes, etc.? If not, you might have overpaid for your tickets a few summers ago.

In the summer of 2011, a fight between Congress and President Obama resulted in a partial shutdown of the Federal Aviation Authority's (FAA) budget. During this time, the FAA was unable to collect the usual taxes on airline tickets, which should have meant that customers would save money when they bought tickets. However, airlines such as Delta, USAirways, Continental, and JetBlue immediately raised their ticket prices to make up the tax, thus pocketing the money themselves. On the other hand, airlines such as Virgin America, Spirit, and Alaska Air passed along the savings to their customers.

DISCUSSION QUESTION

Do you think the airlines that raised their rates were acting with integrity? Why or why not?

SOURCE: J. Martin, "FAA Shutdown to Continue as Congress Leaves," *USA Today,* accessed June 19, 2015, http://usatoday30. usatoday.com.

in Chapter 11), among other laws and regulations, sets the minimum wage for a variety of jobs. We have regulations that dictate much of the process for negotiation between unions and management. These regulations profoundly affect the ways human resources are managed in the United States.

Similarly, the legal regulations regarding HRM in other countries reflect their societal norms. For example, in Germany employees have a legal right to "codetermination" at the company, plant, and individual levels. At the company level, a firm's employees have direct influence on the important decisions that affect them, such as large investments or new strategies. This is brought about through having employee representatives on the supervisory council *(Aufsichtsrat).* At the plant level, codetermination exists through works councils. These councils have no rights in the economic management of the company, but they can influence HRM policies on such issues as working hours, payment methods, hirings, and transfers. Finally, at the individual level, employees have contractual rights, such as the right to read their personnel files and the right to be informed about how their pay is calculated.[26]

The EEC provides another example of the effects of the political–legal system on HRM. The EEC's Community Charter of December 9, 1989, provides for the fundamental social rights of workers. These rights include freedom of movement, freedom to choose one's occupation and be fairly compensated, guarantee of social protection via Social Security benefits, freedom of association and collective bargaining, equal treatment for men and women, and a safe and healthful work environment, among others.

ECONOMIC SYSTEM

A country's economic system influences HRM in a number of ways. As previously discussed, a country's culture is integrally tied to its economic system, and these systems provide many of the incentives for developing human capital. In socialist economic systems there are ample opportunities for developing human capital because the education system is free. However, under these systems, there is little economic incentive to develop human capital because there are no monetary rewards for increasing human capital. In addition, in former Soviet bloc countries, an individual's investment in human capital did not always result in a promotion. Rather, it was investment in the Communist Party that led to career advancements.

In capitalist systems the opposite situation exists. There is less opportunity to develop human capital without higher costs. (You have probably observed tuition increases at U.S. universities.) However, those who do invest in their individual human capital, particularly through education, are more able to reap monetary rewards, thus providing more incentive for such investment. In the United States, individuals' salaries usually reflect differences in human capital (high-skill workers receive higher compensation than low-skill workers). In fact, research estimates that an individual's wages increase by between 10% and 16% for each additional year of schooling.[27]

In addition to the effects of an economic system on HRM, the health of the system can have an important impact. For example, we referred earlier to lower labor costs in India. In developed countries with a high level of wealth, labor costs tend to be quite high relative to those in developing countries. While labor costs are related to the human capital of a country, they are not perfectly related, as shown by Figure 15.2. This chart provides a good example of the different hourly labor costs for manufacturing jobs in various countries.

An economic system also affects HRM directly through its taxes on compensation packages. Thus, the differential labor costs shown in Figure 15.2 do not always reflect the actual take-home pay of employees. Socialist systems are characterized by tax systems that redistribute wealth by taking a higher percentage of a person's income as she moves up the economic ladder. Capitalist systems attempt to reward individuals for their

Figure 15.2

Hourly Compensation Costs in Manufacturing, U.S. Dollars, 2012

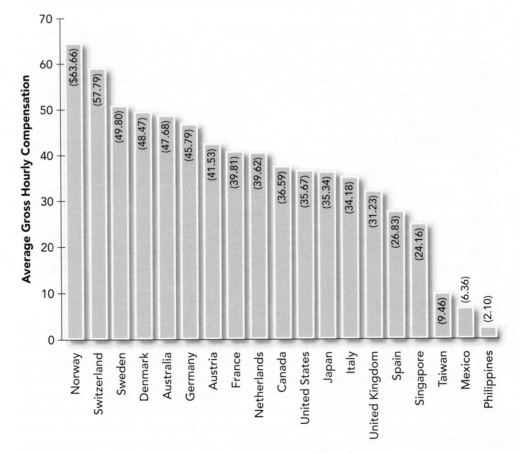

SOURCE: U.S. Bureau of Labor Statistics, www.bls.gov/news.release/pdf/ichcc.pdf.

Economic System Can Help Reduce Poverty

As Vietnam, China, and India have moved away from a state-controlled economy, the standard of living of their poor has improved. Over the last three decades, Vietnam has implemented free-market programs such as eliminating collective farming and reducing the number of state-controlled facilities. As a result, from 1993 to 2008, the percentage of its population living in poverty has decreased from 64% (of 70 million people) to 17% (of 85 million people), according to the World Bank.

In the 1980s, China began allowing farms to retain surplus crops and companies to retain profits above their quota. It also implemented the "General Principles of Civil Law," which outlined private-property ownership, creditor rights, and intellectual property rights. According to the World Bank, in 1981, 84% of China's population earned less than $1.25 a day. In 2011 that figure shrank to 6%.

The International Monetary Fund had to bail out India in the early 1990s. It required that India reduce tariffs, taxes, and regulation. Tariffs fell from 87% to 26% in six years. Most industries eliminated the requirement for licenses, encouraging new entrants, and India's capital markets opened themselves to foreign investment. India saw the percentage of its population that lived on less than $1.25 a day drop from 66% in 1979 to 24% in 2011. If a country wants to improve the lives of the poorest sections of its society, these three countries offer some lessons in the benefits of the free market.

DISCUSSION QUESTION

What steps can a government take to help improve the quality of life of its poorest citizens?

SOURCE: E. Lazear, "Want to Reduce Inequality? Consult China, Vietnam and India," *The Wall Street Journal,* March 31, 2015, www.wsj.com.

efforts by allowing them to keep more of their earnings. Companies that do business in other countries have to present compensation packages to expatriate managers that are competitive in take-home, rather than gross, pay. HRM responses to these issues affecting expatriate managers will be discussed in more detail later in this chapter.

These differences in economies can have a profound impact on pay systems, particularly among global companies seeking to develop an international compensation and reward system that maintains cost controls while enabling local operations to compete in the war for talent. One recent study examining how compensation managers design these systems indicates that they look at a number of factors including the global firm strategy, the local regulatory/political context, institutions and stakeholders, local markets, and national culture. While they try to learn from the best practices that exist globally, they balance these approaches with the constraints imposed by the local environment.[28] However, not just the hourly labor costs, but also the total cost of employees, affect decisions about where to locate workers. The "Competing through Sustainability" box explains how the economic system of a country can lift people out of poverty.

In conclusion, every country varies in terms of its culture, human capital, legal system, and economic system. These variations directly influence the types of HRM systems that must be developed to accommodate the particular situation. The extent to which these differences affect a company depends on how involved the company is in global markets. In the next sections we discuss important concepts of global business and various levels of global participation, particularly noting how these factors come into play.

Managing Employees in a Global Context

TYPES OF INTERNATIONAL EMPLOYEES

Before discussing the levels of global participation, we need to distinguish between parent countries, host countries, and third countries. A **parent country** is the country in which the company's corporate headquarters is located. For example, the United States is the parent country of General Motors. A **host country** is the country in which the parent country organization seeks to locate (or has already located) a facility. Thus Great Britain is a host country for General Motors because GM has operations there. A **third country** is a country other than the host country or parent country, and a company may or may not have a facility there.

There are also different categories of employees. **Expatriate** is the term generally used for employees sent by a company in one country to manage operations in a different country. With the increasing globalization of business, it is now important to distinguish among different types of expatriates. **Parent-country nationals (PCNs)** are employees who were born and live in the parent country. **Host-country nationals (HCNs)** are those employees who were born and raised in the host, as opposed to the parent, country. Finally, **third-country nationals (TCNs)** are employees born in a country other than the parent country and host country but who work in the host country. Thus, a manager born and raised in Brazil employed by an organization located in the United States and assigned to manage an operation in Thailand would be considered a TCN.

Research shows that countries differ in their use of various types of international employees. One study revealed that Japanese multinational firms have more ethnocentric HRM policies and practices (they tend to use Japanese expatriate managers more than local host-country nationals) than either European or U.S. firms. This study also found that the use of ethnocentric HRM practices is associated with more HRM problems.[29]

LEVELS OF GLOBAL PARTICIPATION

We often hear companies referred to as "multinational" or "international." However, it is important to understand the different levels of participation in international markets. This is especially important because as a company becomes more involved in international trade, different types of HRM problems arise. In this section we examine Nancy Adler's categorization of the various levels of international participation from which a company may choose.[30] Figure 15.3 depicts these levels of involvement.

Domestic

Most companies begin by operating within a domestic marketplace. For example, an entrepreneur may have an idea for a product that meets a need in the U.S. marketplace. This individual then obtains capital to build a facility that produces the product or service in a quantity that meets the needs of a small market niche. This requires recruiting, hiring, training, and compensating a number of individuals who will be involved in the production process, and these individuals are usually drawn from the local labor market. The focus of the selection and training programs is often on the employees' technical competence to perform job-related duties and to some extent on interpersonal skills. In addition, because the company is usually involved in only one labor market, determining the market rate of pay for various jobs is relatively easy.

As the product grows in popularity, the owner might choose to build additional facilities in different parts of the country to reduce the costs of transporting the product over

Figure 15.3

Levels of Global Participation

large distances. In deciding where to locate these facilities, the owner must consider the attractiveness of the local labor markets. Various parts of the country may have different cultures that make those areas more or less attractive according to the work ethics of the potential employees. Similarly, the human capital in the different areas may vary greatly because of differences in educational systems. Finally, local pay rates may differ. It is for these reasons that the U.S. economy in the past 10 years has experienced a movement of jobs from northern states, which are characterized by strong unions and high labor costs, to the Sunbelt states, which have lower labor costs and are less unionized.

Incidentally, even domestic companies face problems with cultural diversity. In the United States, for example, the representation of women and minorities is increasing within the workforce. These groups come to the workplace with worldviews that differ from those of the traditional white male. Thus, we are seeing more and more emphasis on developing systems for managing cultural diversity within single-country organizations, even though the diversity might be on a somewhat smaller scale than the diversity of cultures across national boundaries.[31]

In a recent meta-analysis of the effects of cultural diversity on the functioning of multicultural work groups, Stahl et al. (2010) found that cultural diversity leads to process losses through increased task conflict and decreased social integration. On the other hand, it leads to process gains through increasing creativity and satisfaction.[32]

It is important to note that companies functioning at the domestic level face an environment with very similar cultural, human capital, political–legal, and economic situations, although some variation might be observed across states and geographic areas.

International

As more competitors enter the domestic market, companies face the possibility of losing market share; thus they often seek other markets for their products. This usually requires entering international markets, initially by exporting products but ultimately by building production facilities in other countries. The decision to participate in international competition raises a host of human resource issues. All the problems regarding locating facilities are magnified. One must consider whether a particular location provides an environment where human resources can be successfully acquired and managed.

Now the company faces an entirely different situation with regard to culture, human capital, the political–legal system, and the economic system. For example, the availability of human capital is of utmost importance, and there is a substantially greater variability in human capital between the United States and other countries than there is among the various states in the United States.

A country's legal system may also present HRM problems. For example, France has a relatively high minimum wage, which drives labor costs up. In addition, regulations make it extremely difficult to fire or lay off an employee. In Germany companies are legally required to offer employees influence in the management of the firm. Companies that develop facilities in other countries have to adapt their HRM practices to conform to the host country's laws. This requires the company to gain expertise in the country's HRM legal requirements and knowledge about how to deal with the country's legal system, and it often requires the company to hire one or more HCNs. In fact, some countries legally require companies to hire a certain percentage of HCNs for any foreign-owned subsidiary.

Finally, cultures have to be considered. To the extent that the country's culture is vastly different from that of the parent organization, conflicts, communication problems, and morale problems may occur. Expatriate managers must be trained to identify these cultural differences, and they must be flexible enough to adapt their styles to those of their host country. This requires an extensive selection effort to identify individuals who are capable of adapting to new environments and an extensive training program to ensure that the culture shock is not devastating.

Multinational

Whereas international companies build one or a few facilities in another country, they become multinational when they build facilities in a number of different countries, attempting to capitalize on lower production and distribution costs in different locations. The lower production costs are gained by shifting production from higher-cost locations to lower-cost locations. For example, some of the major U.S. automakers have plants all over the world. They continue to shift their production from the United States, where labor unions have gained high wages for their members, to *maquiladora* facilities in Mexico, where the wages are substantially lower. Similarly, these companies minimize distribution and labor costs by locating facilities in central and eastern European countries such as Poland, Hungary, and the Slovak Republic for manufacturing and assembling automobiles to sell in the European market.

The HRM problems multinational companies face are similar to those international companies face, only magnified. Instead of having to consider only one or two countries' cultural, human capital, legal, and economic systems, the multinational company must address these differences for a large number of countries. This accentuates the need to select managers capable of functioning in a variety of settings, give them necessary training, and provide flexible compensation systems that take into account the different market pay rates, tax systems, and costs of living.

Multinational companies now employ many "inpatriates"—managers from different countries who become part of the corporate headquarters staff. This creates a need to integrate managers from different cultures into the culture of the parent company. In addition, multinational companies now take more expatriates from countries other than the parent country and place them in facilities of other countries. For example, a manager from Scotland, working for a U.S. company, might be assigned to run an operation in South Africa. This practice accentuates the need for cross-cultural training to provide managerial skills for interaction with individuals from different cultures.

Global

Many researchers now propose a fourth level of integration: global organizations. Global organizations compete on state-of-the-art, top-quality products and services and do so with the lowest costs possible. Whereas multinational companies attempt to develop identical products distributed worldwide, global companies increasingly emphasize flexibility and mass customization of products to meet the needs of particular clients. Multinational companies are usually driven to locate facilities in a country as a means of reaching that country's market or lowering production costs, and the company must deal with the differences across the countries. Global firms, on the other hand, choose to locate a facility based on the ability to effectively, efficiently, and flexibly produce a product or service and attempt to create synergy through the cultural differences.

This creates the need for HRM systems that encourage flexible production (thus presenting a host of HRM issues). These companies proactively consider the cultures, human capital, political–legal systems, and economic systems to determine where production facilities can be located to provide a competitive advantage. Global companies have multiple headquarters spread across the globe, resulting in less hierarchically structured organizations that emphasize decentralized decision making. This results in the need for human resource systems that recruit, develop, retain, and use managers and executives who are competent transnationally.

A transnational HRM system is characterized by three attributes.[33] **Transnational scope** refers to the fact that HRM decisions must be made from a global rather than a national or regional perspective. This creates the need to make decisions that balance the need for uniformity (to ensure fair treatment of all employees) with the need for flexibility (to meet the needs of employees in different countries). **Transnational representation** reflects the multinational composition of a company's managers. Global participation does not necessarily ensure that each country is providing managers to the company's ranks. This is a prerequisite if the company is to achieve the next attribute. **Transnational process** refers to the extent to which the company's planning and decision-making processes include representatives and ideas from a variety of cultures. This attribute allows for diverse viewpoints and knowledge associated with different cultures, increasing the quality of decision making.

These three characteristics are necessary for global companies to achieve cultural synergy. Rather than simply integrating foreigners into the domestic organization, a successful transnational company needs managers who will treat managers from other cultures as equals. This synergy can be accomplished only by combining selection, training, appraisal, and compensation systems in such a way that managers have a transnational rather than a parochial orientation. However, a survey of 50 companies in the United States and Canada found that global companies' HRM systems are far less transnational in scope, representation, and process than the companies' strategic planning systems and organizational structures.[34]

In conclusion, entry into international markets creates a host of HRM issues that must be addressed if a company is to gain competitive advantage. Once the choice has been made to compete in a global arena, companies must seek to manage employees who are sent to foreign countries (expatriates and third-country nationals). This causes the need to shift from focusing only on the culture, human capital, political–legal, and economic influences of the host country to examining ways to manage the expatriate managers who must be located there. Selection systems must be developed that allow the company to identify managers capable of functioning in a new culture. These managers must be trained to identify the important aspects of the new culture in which they will live as well as the relevant legal–political and economic systems. Finally, these managers must be compensated to offset the costs of uprooting themselves and their families to move to a new situation vastly different from their previous lives. In the next section we address issues regarding management of expatriates.

Transnational Scope
A company's ability to make HRM decisions from an international perspective.

Transnational Representation
Reflects the multinational composition of a company's managers.

Transnational Process
The extent to which a company's planning and decision-making processes include representatives and ideas from a variety of cultures.

MANAGING EXPATRIATES IN GLOBAL MARKETS

We have outlined the major macro-level factors that influence HRM in global markets. These factors can affect a company's decision whether to build facilities in a given country. In addition, if a company does develop such facilities, these factors strongly affect the HRM practices used. However, one important issue that has been recognized over the past few years is the set of problems inherent in selecting, training, compensating, and reintegrating expatriate managers.

According to a study by the National Foreign Trade Council (NFTC), there were 250,000 Americans on assignments overseas and that number was expected to increase. In addition, the NFTC estimates that the average one-time cost for relocating an expatriate is $60,000.[35] The importance to the company's profitability of making the right expatriate assignments should not be underestimated. Expatriate managers' average compensation package is approximately $250,000,[36] and the cost of an unsuccessful expatriate assignment (that is, a manager returning early) is approximately $100,000.[37] The failure rate for expatriate assignments among U.S. firms had been estimated at between 15% and 40%. However, more recent research suggests that the current figure is much lower. Some recent studies of European multinationals put the rate at 5% for most firms. While the failure rate is generally recognized as higher among U.S. multinationals, it is doubtful that the number reaches the 15% to 40% range.[38]

In the final section of the chapter, we discuss the major issues relevant to the management of expatriate managers. These issues cover the selection, training, compensation, and reacculturation of expatriates.

Selection of Expatriate Managers

One of the major problems in managing expatriate managers is determining which individuals in the organization are most capable of handling an assignment in a different culture. Expatriate managers must have technical competence in the area of operations; otherwise they will be unable to earn the respect of subordinates. However, technical competence has been almost the sole variable used in deciding who to send on overseas assignments, despite the fact that multiple skills are necessary for successful performance in these assignments.[39]

A successful expatriate manager must be sensitive to the country's cultural norms, flexible enough to adapt to those norms, and strong enough to make it through the inevitable culture shock. In addition, the manager's family must be similarly capable of adapting to the new culture. These adaptive skills have been categorized into three dimensions:[40] (1) the self dimension (the skills that enable a manager to maintain a positive self-image and psychological well-being), (2) the relationship dimension (the skills required to foster relationships with the host-country nationals), and (3) the perception dimension (those skills that enable a manager to accurately perceive and evaluate the host environment). One study of international assignees found that they considered the following five factors to be important in descending order of importance: family situation, flexibility and adaptability, job knowledge and motivation, relational skills, and extracultural openness.[41] Table 15.3 presents a series of considerations and questions to ask potential expatriate managers to assess their ability to adapt to a new cultural environment.

One construct that has been emerging in the expatriate literature is cultural intelligence (CQ). This characteristic refers to an individual's ability to adapt across cultures through sensing the different cues regarding appropriate behavior across cultural settings or in multicultural settings. In fact, one set of researchers found that CQ was related to cultural adjustment and task performance among a sample of international executives.[42]

Table 15.3

Select Topics for Assessing Candidates for Overseas Assignments

Motivation
- What are the candidate's reasons and degree of interest in wanting an overseas assignment?
- Does the candidate have a realistic understanding of what is required in working and living overseas?
- What is the spouse's attitude toward an overseas assignment?

Health
- Are there any health issues with the candidate or family members that might impact the success of the overseas assignment?

Language ability
- Does the candidate have the potential to learn a new language?
- Does the candidate's spouse have the ability to learn a new language?

Family considerations
- How many moves has the family made among different cities or parts of the United States? What problems were encountered?
- What is the spouse's goal in this move overseas?
- How many children are in the family and what are their ages? Will all the children move as part of the overseas assignment?
- Has divorce or its potential, or the death of a family member had a negative effect on the family's cohesiveness?
- Are there any adjustment problems the candidate would expect should the family move overseas?

Resourcefulness and initiative
- Is the candidate independent and capable of standing by his or her decisions?
- Is the candidate able to meet objectives and produce positive results with whatever human resources and facilities are available regardless of challenges that might arise in a foreign business environment?
- Can the candidate operate without a clear definition of responsibility and authority?
- Will the candidate be able to explain the goals of the company and its mission to local managers and workers?
- Does the candidate possess sufficient self-discipline and self-confidence to handle complex problems?
- Can the candidate operate effectively in a foreign country without normal communications and supporting services?

Adaptability
- Is the candidate cooperative, open to the opinions of others, and able to compromise?
- How does the candidate react to new situations and efforts to understand and appreciate cultural differences?
- How does the candidate react to criticism, constructive or otherwise?
- Will the candidate be able to make and develop contacts with peers in a foreign country?
- Does the candidate demonstrate patience when dealing with problems? Is he or she resilient and able to move forward after setbacks?

Career planning
- Does the candidate consider the assignment more than a temporary overseas trip?
- Is the overseas assignment consistent with the candidate's career development and one that was planned by the company?
- What is the candidate's overall attitude toward the company?
- Is there any history or indication of interpersonal problems with this candidate?

Financial
- Are there any current financial and/or legal considerations that might affect the assignment (e.g., house or car purchase, college expenses)?
- Will undue financial pressures be put upon the candidate and his or her family as a result of an overseas assignment?

SOURCES: P. Caligiuri, *Cultural Agility: Building a Pipeline of Successful Global Professionals* (San Francisco: Jossey-Bass, 2012); P. Caligiuri, D. Lepak, and J. Bonache, *Managing the Global Workforce* (West Sussex, United Kingdom: John Wiley & Sons, 2010); M. Shaffer, D. Harrison, H. Gregersen, S. Black, and L. Ferzandi, "You Can Take It with You: Individual Differences and Expatriate Effectiveness," *Journal of Applied Psychology* 91(2006), pp. 109–25; P. Caligiuri, "Developing Global Leaders," *Human Resource Management Review* 16 (2006), pp. 219–28; P. Caligiuri, M. Hyland, A. Joshi, and A. Bross, "Testing a Theoretical Model for Examining the Relationship between Family Adjustment and Expatriates' Work Adjustment," *Journal of Applied Psychology* 83(1998), pp. 598–614; David M. Noer, *Multinational People Management: A Guide for Organizations and Employees* (Arlington, VA: Bureau of National Affairs, 1975).

Little evidence suggests that U.S. companies have invested much effort in attempting to make correct expatriate selections. One researcher found that only 5% of the firms surveyed administered any tests to determine the degree to which expatriate candidates possessed cross-cultural skills.[43] More recent research reveals that only 35% of firms choose expatriates from multiple candidates and that those firms emphasize only technical job-related experience and skills in making these decisions.[44] These findings glaringly demonstrate that U.S. organizations need to improve their success rate in overseas assignments. As discussed in Chapter 6, the technology for assessing individuals' knowledge, skills, and abilities has advanced. The potential for selection testing to decrease the failure rate and productivity problems of U.S. expatriate managers seems promising. For instance, recent research has examined the "Big Five" personality dimensions as predictors of expatriate success (remember these from Chapter 6). For instance, one study distinguished between expatriate success as measured by not terminating the assignment and success as measured by supervisory evaluations of the expatriate. The researcher found that agreeableness, emotional stability, and extraversion were negatively related to the desire to terminate the assignment (i.e., they wanted to stay on the assignment longer), and conscientiousness was positively related to supervisory evaluations of the expatriate.[45]

A final issue with regard to expatriate selection is the use of women in expatriate assignments. For a long time U.S. firms believed that women would not be successful managers in countries where women have not traditionally been promoted to management positions (such as in Japan and other Asian countries). However, recent evidence indicates that this is not true. Robin Abrams, an expatriate manager for Apple Computer's Hong Kong office, states that nobody cares whether "you are wearing trousers or a skirt if you have demonstrated core competencies." In fact, some women believe that the novelty of their presence among a group of men increases their credibility with locals. In fact, some research suggests that male and female expatriates can perform equally well in international assignments, regardless of the country's cultural predispositions toward women in management. However, female expatriates self-rate their adjustment lower in countries that have few women in the workforce.[46] Also research has shown that female expatriates were perceived as being effective regardless of the cultural toughness of the host country.[47] And the fact is that female expatriates feel more strongly than their supervisors that prejudice does not limit women's ability to be successful.[48]

Training and Development of Expatriates

Once an expatriate manager has been selected, it is necessary to prepare that manager for the upcoming assignment. Because these individuals already have job-related skills, some firms have focused development efforts on cross-cultural training. A review of the cross-cultural training literature found support for the belief that cross-cultural training has an impact on effectiveness.[49] However, in spite of this, cross-cultural training is hardly universal. According to one 1995 survey, nearly 40% of the respondents offered no cross-cultural preparation to expatriates.[50]

What exactly is emphasized in cross-cultural training programs? The details regarding these programs were discussed in Chapter 7. However, for now, it is important to know that most attempt to create an appreciation of the host country's culture so that expatriates can behave appropriately.[51] This entails emphasizing a few aspects of cultural sensitivity. First, expatriates must be clear about their own cultural background, particularly as it is perceived by the host nationals. With an accurate cultural self-awareness, managers can modify their behavior to accentuate the effective characteristics while minimizing those that are dysfunctional.[52]

Second, expatriates must understand the particular aspects of culture in the new work environment. Although culture is an elusive, almost invisible phenomenon, astute expatriate managers must perceive the culture and adapt their behavior to it. This entails identifying the types of behaviors and interpersonal styles that are considered acceptable in both business meetings and social gatherings. For example, Germans value promptness for meetings to a much greater extent than do Latin Americans. Table 15.4 displays some ways body language conveys different messages in different countries.

Finally, expatriates must learn to communicate accurately in the new culture. Some firms attempt to use expatriates who speak the language of the host country, and a few

Table 15.4
International Body Language

COUNTRY	NONVERBAL MESSAGES
Argentina	If the waiter approaches pointing to the side of his head and making a spinning gesture with their finger, don't think they've lost it—they're trying to say you have a phone call.
Bangladesh	Bursting to go to the toilet? Hold it. It is considered very rude to excuse yourself from the table to use the bathroom.
Bolivia	Don't make "the sign of the fig" (thumb protruding between index and middle finger), historically a sign that you couldn't care less—it is very insulting.
Bulgaria	Bulgarians nod the head up and down to mean no, not yes. To say yes, a Bulgarian nods the head back and forth.
China	In Eastern culture, silence really can be golden. So don't panic if long periods of silence form part of your meeting with Chinese clients. It simply means they are considering your proposal carefully.
Egypt	As across the Arab world the left hand is unclean, use your right to accept business cards and to greet someone. Use only your right hand for eating.
Fiji	To show respect to your Fijian hosts when addressing them, stand with your arms folded behind your back.
France	The French don't like strong handshakes, preferring a short, light grip or air kissing. If your French colleague is seen to be playing an imaginary flute, however, it means he thinks you are not being truthful.
Germany	When Germans meet across a large conference table and it is awkward to reach over and shake hands, they will instead rap their knuckles lightly on the table by way of a greeting.
Greece	Beware of making the okay sign to Greek colleagues as it signifies bodily orifices. A safer bet is the thumbs-up sign. The thumbs-down, however, is the kind of gesture reserved for when a Greek motorist cuts you off on the highway.
Hong Kong	When trying to attract someone's attention, don't use your index finger with palm extended upward. This is how the Cantonese call their dogs.
India	Beware of whistling in public—it is the height of rudeness here.
Japan	Japan is a real minefield for Western businesspeople, but one that always gets to them is the way the Japanese heartily slurp their noodles at lunch. Far from being rude, it actually shows appreciation of the food in Japanese culture.
Jordan	No matter how hungry you are, it is customary to refuse seconds from your host twice before finally accepting a third time.
Lebanon	Itchy eyebrow? Don't scratch it. Licking your little finger and brushing it across your eyebrow is provocative.
Malaysia	If you find a Malaysian standing with hands on hips before you, you've clearly said something wrong. It means he's livid.
Mexico	Mexicans are very tactile and often perform a bizarre handshake whereby, after pressing together the palms, they will slide their hands upward to grasp each other's thumbs.

(continued)

Table 15.4

International Body Language (*concluded*)

COUNTRY	NONVERBAL MESSAGES
Netherlands	The Dutch may seem open-minded, but if Dutch people tap the underside of their elbow, it means they think you're unreliable.
Pakistan	The overt display of a closed fist is an incitement to war.
Philippines	The "Roger Moore" is a common greeting here—a quick flash of the eyebrows supersedes the need for handshakes.
Russia	The Russians are highly tactile meet and greeters, with bear hugs and kisses directly on the lips commonplace. Don't take this habit to nearby Uzbekistan, however. They'd probably shoot you.
Saudi Arabia	If a Saudi man takes another's hand on the street, it's a sign of mutual respect.
Samoa	When your new Samoan host offers you a cup of the traditional drink, kava, make sure to deliberately spill a few drops on the ground before taking your first sip.
Turkey	Be careful not to lean back on your chair and point the sole of your foot at anyone in a meeting in Istanbul. Pointing with the underside of the foot is highly insulting.

SOURCES: K. Elkins and M. Nudelman, "The Shocking Differences in Basic Body Language Around the World," *Business Insider,* March 17, 2015, www.businessinsider.com; www.businesstravelerusa.com/articles.php?articleID=490 Business Traveler Center; R. Axtell, *Gestures: The Dos and Taboos of Body Language Around the World,* (New York: John Wiley and Sons, 1991); P. Harris and R. Moran, *Managing Cultural Differences,* 3rd ed. (Houston, TX: Gulf Publishing Company, 1991); R. Linowes, "The Japanese Manager's Traumatic Entry into the United States: Understanding the American-Japanese Cultural Divide," *Academy of Management Executive* 7, no. 4 (1993), p. 26; D. Doke, "Perfect Strangers," *HR Magazine,* December 2004, pp. 62–68.

provide language training. However, most companies simply assume that the host-country nationals all speak the parent-country's language. Although this assumption might be true, seldom do these nationals speak the parent-country language fluently. Thus, expatriate managers must be trained to communicate with others when language barriers exist.

Effective cross-cultural training helps ease an expatriate's transition to the new work environment. It can also help avoid costly mistakes, such as the expatriate who attempted to bring two bottles of brandy into the Muslim country of Qatar. The brandy was discovered by customs; not only was the expatriate deported, the company was also "disinvited" from the country.[53]

Compensation of Expatriates

One of the more troublesome aspects of managing expatriates is determining the compensation package. As previously discussed, these packages average $250,000, but it is necessary to examine the exact breakdown of these packages. Most use a balance sheet approach to determine the total package level. This approach entails developing a total compensation package that equalizes the purchasing power of the expatriate manager with that of employees in similar positions in the home country and provides incentives to offset the inconveniences incurred in the location. Purchasing power includes all of the expenses associated with the expatriate assignment. Expenses include goods and services (food, personal care, clothing, recreation, and transportation), housing (for a principal residence), income taxes (paid to federal and local governments), reserve (savings, payments for benefits, pension contributions), and shipment and storage (costs associated with moving and/or storing personal belongings). A typical balance sheet is shown in Figure 15.4.

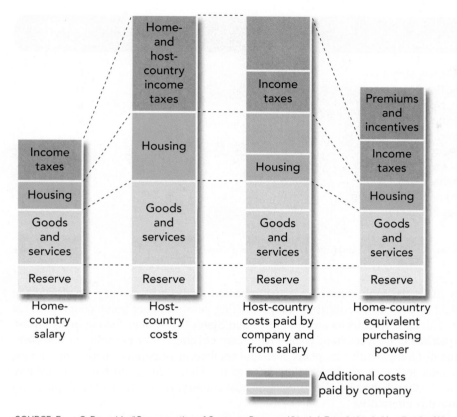

SOURCE: From C. Reynolds, "Compensation of Overseas Personnel," in J. J. Famulari, ed., *Handbook of Human Resource Administration,* 2nd ed., 1986. Copyright © 1986. Reproduced with permission of The McGraw-Hill Companies, Inc.

Figure 15.4
The Balance Sheet for Determining Expatriate Compensation

As you can see from this figure, the employee starts with a set of costs for taxes, housing, goods and services, and reserve. However, in the host country, these costs are significantly higher. Thus the company must make up the difference between costs in the home and those in the host country, and then provide a premium and/or incentive for the employee to go through the trouble of living in a different environment.

Total pay packages have four components. First, there is the base salary. Determining the base salary is not a simple matter, however. Fluctuating exchange rates between countries may make an offered salary a raise some of the time, a pay cut at other times. In addition, the base salary may be based on comparable pay in the parent country, or it may be based on the prevailing market rates for the job in the host country. Expatriates are often offered a salary premium beyond that of their present salary as an inducement to accept the expatriate assignment.

Tax equalization allowances are a second component. They are necessary because of countries' different taxation systems in high-tax countries. For example, a senior executive earning $100,000 in Belgium (with a maximum marginal tax rate of 70.8%) could cost a company almost $1 million in taxes over five to seven years.[54] Under most tax equalization plans, the company withholds the amount of tax to be paid in the home country, then pays all of the taxes accrued in the host country.

A third component, benefits, presents additional compensation problems. Most of the problems have to do with the transportability of the benefits. For example, if an expatriate contributing to a pension plan in the United States is moved to a different

Table 15.5
The 10 Most
Expensive Cities
(New York = 100)

CITY, COUNTRY	WCOL INDEX	RANK	RANK MOVEMENT (SINCE 2014)
Singapore, Singapore	129	1	0
Paris, France	126	2	0
Oslo, Norway	124	3	0
Zurich, Switzerland	121	4	0
Sydney, Australia	120	5	0
Melbourne, Australia	118	6	0
Geneva, Switzerland	116	7	−1
Copenhagen, Denmark	115	8	2
Hong Kong, Hong Kong	113	9	4
Seoul, South Korea	113	9	6

SOURCE: Economist Intelligence Unit (2015), "Worldwide Cost of Living 2015." www.eiu.com.

country, does the individual have a new pension in the host country, or should the individual be allowed to contribute to the existing pension in her home country? What about health care systems located in the United States? How does the company ensure that expatriate employees have equal health care coverage? For example, in one company, the different health care plans available resulted in situations where it might cost significantly less to have the employee fly to the United States to have a procedure performed rather than to have it done in the host country. However, the health plans did not allow this alternative.

Finally, allowances are often offered to make the expatriate assignment less unattractive. Cost-of-living allowances are payments that offset the differences in expenditures on day-to-day necessities between the host country and the parent country. For instance, Table 15.5 shows the differences in cost of living among some of the larger international cities. Housing allowances ensure that the expatriate can maintain the same home-country living standard. Education allowances reimburse expatriates for the expense of placing their children in private English-speaking schools. Relocation allowances cover all the expenses of making the actual move to a new country, including transportation to and from the new location, temporary living expenses, and shipping and/or storage of personal possessions. Figure 15.5 illustrates a typical summary sheet for an expatriate manager's compensation package.

The cost of a U.S. expatriate working in another country is approximately three to four times that of a comparable U.S. employee.[55] In addition, "about 38% of multinational companies surveyed by KPMG LLP for its 2006 Global Assignment Policies and Practices say overseas assignment programs are 'more generous than they need to be.' "[56] These two facts combined have put pressure on global organizations to rethink their tax equalization strategy and expatriate packages.

Reacculturation of Expatriates

A final issue of importance to managing expatriates is dealing with the reacculturation process when the managers reenter their home country. Reentry is no simple feat. Culture shock takes place in reverse. The individual has changed, the company has changed, and the culture has changed while the expatriate was overseas. According to

Figure 15.5
International
Assignment
Allowance Form

John H. Doe	1 October 2015
Name	**Effective date**

Singapore	Manager, SLS./Serv. AP/ME
Location of assignment	**Title**

Houston, Texas	1234	202	202
Home base	**Emp. no.**	**LCA code**	**Tax code**

Reason for Change: _____ International Assignment _____

	Old	**New**
Monthly base salary		$5,000.00
Living cost allowance		$1,291.00
Foreign service premium		$ 750.00
Area allowance		-0-
Gross monthly salary		$7,041.00
Housing deduction		$ 500.00
Hypothetical tax		$ 570.00
Other		
Net monthly salary		$5,971.00

_____	_____
Prepared by	**Date**

_____	_____
Vice President, Human Resources	**Date**

one source, 60% to 70% of expatriates did not know what their position would be upon their return, and 46% ended up with jobs that gave them reduced autonomy and authority.[57] Twenty percent of workers want to leave the company when they return from an overseas assignment, and this presents potentially serious morale and productivity problems.[58] In fact, the most recent estimates are that 25% of expatriate managers leave the company within one year of returning from their expatriate assignments.[59] If these repatriates leave, the company has virtually no way to recoup its substantial investment in human capital.[60]

Companies are increasingly making efforts to help expatriates through reacculturation. Two characteristics help in this transition process: communication and validation.[61] *Communication* refers to the extent to which the expatriate receives information and recognizes changes while abroad. The closer the contact with the home organization while abroad, the more proactive, effective, and satisfied the expatriate will be upon reentry. *Validation* refers to the amount of recognition received by the expatriate upon return home. Expatriates who receive recognition from their peers and their bosses for their foreign work and their future potential contribution to the company have fewer troubles with reentry compared with those who are treated as if they were "out of the loop." Given the tremendous investment that firms make in expatriate employees, usually aimed at providing global experience that will help the company, firms certainly do not want to lose expatriates after their assignments have concluded.

Finally, one research study noted the role of an expatriate manager's expectations about the expatriate assignment in determining repatriation adjustment and job performance. This study found that managers whose job expectations (constraints and demands in terms of volume and performance standards) and nonwork expectations (living and housing conditions) were met exhibited a greater degree of repatriation adjustment and higher levels of job performance.[62] Monsanto has an extensive repatriation program that begins long before the expatriate returns. The program entails providing extensive information regarding the potential culture shock of repatriation and information on how family members, friends, and the office environment might have changed. Then, a few months after returning, expatriate managers hold "debriefing" sessions with several colleagues to help work through difficulties. Monsanto believes that this program provides them with a source of competitive advantage in international assignments.[63]

In sum, a variety of HR practices can support effective expatriation. In general, the selection system must rigorously assess potential expatriates' skills and personalities and even focus on the candidate's spouse. Training should be conducted prior to and during the expatriate assignment, and the assignment itself should be viewed as a career development experience. Effective reward systems must go beyond salary and benefits, and while keeping the employee "whole" and even offering a monetary premium, should also provide access to career development and learning opportunities. Finally, serious efforts should be made to manage the repatriation process.[64] A summary of the key points is provided in Table 15.6.

A LOOK BACK

While Wal-Mart has successfully dominated the U.S. market, it has found that expanding its reach across the globe does not always fit with its strengths. In addition, navigating the variety of economic and regulatory requirements across different countries adds significant complexity to the company's operations. Finally, gaining access to and managing workforces with different values, cultures, and languages present tremendous challenges.

QUESTIONS

1. What criteria should a company use to determine which countries it should expand into?
2. How can a company assess how cultural and economic differences might impede its ability to succeed in different countries?
3. What things can companies do to manage a global workforce more effectively?

Table 15.6
Human Resource Practices That Support Effective Expatriation

Staffing and Selection

- Communicate the value of international assignments for the company's global mission.
- Ensure that those with the highest potential move internationally.
- Provide short-term assignments to increase the pool of employees with international experience.
- Recruit employees who have lived or who were educated abroad.

Training and Career Development

- Make international assignment planning a part of the career development process.
- Encourage early international experience.
- Create learning opportunities during the assignment.
- Use international assignments as a leadership development tool.

Performance Appraisal and Compensation

- Differentiate performance management based on expatriate roles.
- Align incentives with expatriation objectives.
- Tailor benefits to the expatriate's needs.
- Focus on equality of opportunities, not cash.
- Emphasize rewarding careers rather than short-term outcomes.

Expatriation and Repatriation Activities

- Involve the family in the orientation program at the beginning and the end of the assignment.
- Establish mentor relationships between expatriates and executives from the home location.
- Provide support for dual careers.
- Secure opportunities for the returning manager to use knowledge and skills learned while on the international assignment.

SOURCE: From P. Evans, V. Pucik and J. Barsoux, *The Global Challenge: Framework for International Human Resource Management,* 2002. Reproduced with permission of The McGraw-Hill Companies, Inc.

SUMMARY

Today's organizations are more involved in international commerce than ever before, and the trend will continue. Recent historic events such as the development of the EEC, NAFTA, the economic growth of Asia, and GATT have accelerated the movement toward a global market. Companies competing in the global marketplace require top-quality people to compete successfully. This requires that managers be aware of the many factors that significantly affect HRM in a global environment, such as culture, human capital, and the political–legal and economic systems, and that they understand how these factors come into play in the various levels of global participation. Finally, it requires that they be adept at developing HRM systems that maximize the effectiveness of all human resources, particularly with regard to expatriate managers. Managers cannot overestimate the importance of effectively managing human resources to gain competitive advantage in today's global marketplace.

KEY TERMS

Individualism–collectivism, 635
Power distance, 635
Uncertainty avoidance, 635
Masculinity–femininity dimension, 636
Long-term–short-term orientation, 636

Parent country, 642
Host country, 642
Third country, 642
Expatriate, 642
Parent-country nationals (PCNs), 642

Host-country nationals (HCNs), 642
Third-country nationals (TCNs), 642
Transnational scope, 645
Transnational representation, 645
Transnational process, 645

DISCUSSION QUESTIONS

1. What current trends and/or events (besides those mentioned at the outset of the chapter) are responsible for the increased internationalization of the marketplace?

2. According to Hofstede (in Table 15.2), the United States is low on power distance, high on individuality, high on masculinity, low on uncertainty avoidance, and low on long-term orientation. Russia, on the other hand, is high on power distance, moderate on individuality, low on masculinity, high on uncertainty avoidance, and low on long-term orientation. Many U.S. managers are transplanting their own HRM practices into Russia while companies seek to develop operations there. How acceptable and effective do you think the following practices will be and why? (a) Extensive assessments of individual abilities for selection? (b) Individually based appraisal systems? (c) Suggestion systems? (d) Self-managing work teams?

3. The chapter notes that political–legal and economic systems can reflect a country's culture. The former Eastern bloc countries seem to be changing their political–legal and economic systems. Is this change brought on by their cultures, or will culture have an impact on the ability to change these systems? Why?

4. Think of the different levels of global participation. What companies that you are familiar with exhibit the different levels of participation?

5. Think of a time when you had to function in another culture (on a vacation or job). What were the major obstacles you faced, and how did you deal with them? Was this a stressful experience? Why? How can companies help expatriate employees deal with stress?

6. What types of skills do you need to be able to manage in today's global marketplace? Where do you expect to get those skills? What classes and/or experiences will you need?

SELF-ASSESSMENT EXERCISE

Additional assignable self-assessments available in Connect.

The following list includes a number of qualities that have been identified as being associated with success in an expatriate assignment. Rate the degree to which you possess each quality, using the following scale:

1 = very low
2 = low
3 = moderate
4 = high
5 = very high

_____ Resourcefulness/resilience
_____ Adaptability/flexibility
_____ Emotional stability
_____ Ability to deal with ambiguity/uncertainty/differences
_____ Desire to work with people who are different

_____ Cultural empathy/sensitivity
_____ Tolerance of others' views, especially when they differ from your own
_____ Sensitivity to feelings and attitudes of others
_____ Good health and wellness

Add up your total score for the items. The higher your score, the greater your likelihood of success. Qualities that you rated low would be considered weaknesses for an expatriate assignment. Keep in mind that you will also need to be technically competent for the assignment, and your spouse and family (if applicable) must be adaptable and willing to live abroad.

SOURCE: Based on "Rating Scale on Successful Expatriate Qualities," from P. R. Harris and R. T. Moran, *Managing Cultural Differences,* 3rd ed. (Houston: Gulf, 1991), p. 569.

EXERCISING STRATEGY

Terrorism and Global Human Resource Management

Globalization has continued to increase as companies expand their operations in a number of countries, employing an increasingly global workforce. Although this process has resulted in a number of positive outcomes, it has also occasionally presented new types of problems for firms to face.

On September 11, 2001, terrorists with Middle Eastern roots (alleged to be part of Osama bin Laden's al Qaeda network) hijacked four U.S. planes, crashing two of them into the World Trade Center's twin towers and one into the Pentagon (a fourth was crashed in Pennsylvania in a scuffle with passengers). President George W. Bush and U.K. Prime Minister Tony Blair, after their demands that the Taliban government in Afghanistan turn over bin Laden and his leaders were ignored, began military action against that country on October 7, 2001. Both the terrorist acts and the subsequent war on terrorism have created a host of issues for multinational companies.

First, companies doing business overseas, particularly in Muslim-dominated countries such as the Arab states and Indonesia, must manage their expatriate workforce (particularly U.S. and British citizens) in what has the potential to become hostile territory. These employees fear for their security, and some have asked to return to their home countries.

Second, companies with global workforces must manage across what have become increasingly nationalistic boundaries. Those of us in the United States may view the terrorist attacks as an act of war and our response as being entirely justified. However, those in the Arab world, while not justifying the terrorist attacks, may similarly feel that the military response toward Afghanistan (and later Iraq) is hostile

aggression. One executive at a global oil company noted the difficulty in managing a workforce that is approximately 25% Arab. He stated that many of the Arab executives have said, "While we know that you are concerned about the events of September 11, you should know that we are equally concerned about the events of October 7 and since."

QUESTIONS

1. How can a global company manage the inevitable conflicts that will arise among individuals from different religious, racial, ethnic, and national groups who must work together within firms? How can these conflicts be overcome to create a productive work environment?
2. What will firms have to do differently in managing expatriates, particularly U.S. or British citizens who are asked to take assignments in predominantly Muslim countries?

MANAGING PEOPLE

The Toyota Way to No. 1

Toyota's top U.S. executive on how it managed to become the world's No. 1 carmaker and why the company can hang on to the top spot.

It happened. Toyota passed General Motors in worldwide sales globally in the first quarter. We knew it was coming. It's likely that the trend will continue and hold up for the entire year, and for years to come.

As the baton gets passed this year, there's a mix of opinions and perspectives in the auto industry about whether Toyota is succeeding fairly. Does its lack of health-care and pension responsibilities, which hobble GM, Ford, and DaimlerChrysler's Chrysler division, allow Toyota an advantage on an unlevel playing field? Does Japan's insular economy, which has made it so difficult for U.S. auto makers to achieve sales in Japan, offer an unfair advantage? Do charges that the Japanese government weakens the yen against the dollar to keep prices down and profit up abroad hold water?

Toyota isn't accepting the No. 1 position comfortably. It makes some of its executives nervous to be the chased, rather than the chaser. Yuki Funo is the chairman and CEO of Toyota Motor Sales USA—the top Japanese executive for Toyota in North America. He recently sat down with *BusinessWeek* Senior Correspondent David Kiley to discuss some of the issues confronting Toyota as it achieves top-dog status. Edited excerpts form their conversation follow:

Have you been talking among yourselves about protecting your culture, which could be vulnerable to change as you become the world's largest auto maker?
As far as Toyota culture goes . . . we regard ourselves as Japanese, but more important than the Japanese nature of our company is the "Toyota Way," which is embodied in our concepts and systems.

Toyota Way is more than just a Japanese Way. It's about constant improvement. If it was a Japanese Way only, then we wouldn't have Japanese companies that perform poorly or go into bankruptcy. Toyota doesn't monopolize this idea. And it has to translate beyond Japanese culture to be successful. We employ close to 400,000 worldwide, excluding dealers. If we include dealers, it might be about 1 million.

Of that, a significant number are Japanese. But there are people from every culture working for Toyota that share the concept and this way of doing business. From that viewpoint, growing larger doesn't suggest that we're stepping out of anything that's part of our culture.

Someone I know says Toyota really believes and nurtures the idea that the company should be able to build a car with no problems or flaws. When this person does business with Ford and GM, it's different, they tell me. Those companies strive to be better, but you don't get the idea they think a perfect car is possible.
With the Toyota Way . . . one of the key elements is *kaizen:* continuous improvement. There's no end to it. It's a never-ending journey. Respect for people is another important element. Employees. Customers. Suppliers. When it comes to consumers, they demand changes from time to time. We have to always keep watching what the consumer wants. If we base our business on what the customer wants, there's no end to the improvement we can achieve.

I remember a story related to me by a supplier company: They entered into a contract to supply axles for pickup trucks. It was the first contract his company had with Toyota. He said he was awarded the contract with no discussion of price. It was all based on whether his company's

processes and quality were acceptable to Toyota. He was flabbergasted. Is that a common way Toyota does business? Toyota's thinking based on the Toyota Way is teamwork with suppliers. This teamwork is going to be a long-lasting relationship. Price is only one element. Trust is a more important element. The relationship is a sharing concept, and should always be win–win. Price is important, too. But trust is perhaps more so. This is an idea that American business schools have come to preach. IBM, General Electric, and other companies talk about how important the mission of the company is. Toyota is only doing intelligently what the business schools are teaching.

In the church when you get married, the priest or minister doesn't ask each partner how much each will get from the other in terms of money. You're asked about how well you get along. What is your commitment to one another? Now, in real-life situations, some companies practice this, and some don't. Some practice this in the United States. Some don't. It's the same in Japan. So there are fantastic achievements in both countries, and there are bankruptcies in both countries. So, it isn't a Japanese issue or an American issue. It's a company-culture issue.

Growth comes from both new products and boosting volume of existing products. Will your sales growth come more from new products or from existing products in new geographic markets?
I think 15% global market share isn't low, but it's not that high either. There are a lot of opportunities for our product lineup as it is. But now that we have gone into full-size pickups with the new product, we fill in a significant segment.

I think we need to pursue more niches in the future. We had a car at the Detroit Auto Show that could be a replacement for the former Supra sports car. But what's more important is to keep improving the products we have. Like Camry—what consumers want out of Camry is always changing. That's my understanding of how to keep a product strong for the future. We will look after Camry customers by looking after Camry as a product. Same goes with RAV4 and others.

From time to time, a GM or Ford exec will complain about an uneven playing field: a health-care advantage for Toyota, or monetary policy that favors Japanese products. Do you and your colleagues read that and pay attention?
We always read the stuff in the newspapers. We know health care is a very difficult situation for the Big Three. It's a fact of life that they incur more costs. That's the political and economic history of the United States. A decision was made some years back on what they would give to workers. To some degree, the problem is of their own creation.

Not all the workers in every industry receive as high a medical benefit as in the auto industry. Who decided that? It's their management. They complain sometimes about the currency valuation. It's very difficult. For example, the biggest economy in the world is the United States. Bigger than Japan. It's the Big Three who have an advantage in operating in the biggest economy in the world. For myself, I invested in my English education. If you're born here, there's no need

to invest in that. So, that's not a level playing field. It's very difficult to define what a level playing field is.

You would think that GM and Ford execs, given the fact they all grew up here, should have a better idea of how to design and package a family sedan and minivan, yet these are two product segments where you and Honda have done especially well against the Big Three.
Increasingly, we're doing the development of our vehicles in the States. The Camry chief engineer is a Japanese man. Why the heck does he develop the most favorite car in the United States? That Camry car doesn't sell in Japan. It's a failure. Why? He applies himself to understanding what the customer wants. He visits here and learns things.

If we talk about the level playing field, what is it? He had to overcome such a big handicap being Japanese to create a car that's the top seller in America. It's very difficult to talk about what the level playing field is.

U.S. companies are saying that while they're improving manufacturing processes, costs, etc. they will never out-Toyota Toyota. They have decided the best way to outdo you as they close the gap on those things is by out-designing you. Do you feel a greater pressure to compete on expressive design than you once did?
Toyota, if you look at the history, our design hasn't been very expressive. If we aren't careful, design could fall into the dull category. Our designers have been seeing design as a critical challenge. If you look at the last 5 to 10 years, designers have done a great job of advancing here.

Look at the FJ Cruiser. People look at that and say, "Who designed that? Toyota? I can't believe it." Every organization has strengths and weaknesses. Twenty years ago, Toyota had no confidence in how we would operate manufacturing in the United States. That's why we regard the NUMMI joint-venture plant [where Toyota builds the Matrix and Corolla alongside the Pontiac Vibe] with GM as very beneficial. GM helped us a great deal.

The corporate advertising you have been running seems to be quite effective. Some of your Detroit rivals resent the fact that you're acting and talking like an American company.
We have a lot of dialogue about what should be the corporate message. That advertising is what we wanted to accomplish. We knew that many people didn't know what we have been doing in the United States for 50 years. In San Antonio, Texas, for example, we gave a lot of money to the local family-literacy program. We have been giving money to this organization nationally for 20 years. But we had never advertised it. People need to have a clearer and more correct image of Toyota.

Is your decision to advertise more aggressively a response to those kinds of remarks by people like Ford President of the Americas Mark Fields or GM Vice Chairman Bob Lutz?
More important than the political consideration, Toyota is known as a product. No one knows what Toyota is. Toyota is a faceless organization. It doesn't have a human element in the eyes of the consumer. Toyota is just a car.

Toyota is bigger than that though. It's people. We have some 40,000 people working for us in the United States. We need to have more of a face. That we are people. That's the most critical thing we have been trying to achieve.

Perhaps you would like to star in some ads yourself? DaimlerChrysler Chairman Dieter Zetsche did that last year as "Dr. Z." Do you want to be known as "Dr. T"?
No. We want to show everybody in the company. The heroes. Not one single person.

HR IN SMALL BUSINESS

Is Translating a Global Business?

One field in which small businesses have recently enjoyed rapid growth is in the business of providing translations. As barriers to international business continue to fall, more and more people are encountering language differences in the people they work with, sell to, and buy from. At the same time, advances in technology are providing avenues to deliver translations over the phone and over the Internet.

TransPerfect is one of the success stories. The company, based in New York, started out when founder Steve Iverson, a French teacher, began translating documents for clients. Satisfied customers returned, looking for translations of patents and annual reports—even for court reporting in foreign languages. The company now provides translations in over 170 languages. It has offices in more than 90 cities spread over six continents.

CETRA Language Solutions is headquartered in Elkins Park, Pennsylvania. It started with a lawsuit: while founder Jiri Stejskal was working on his doctorate degree in Slavic languages and literature, a Philadelphia law firm asked him to translate thousands of pages of documents related to a case. Stejskal brought in all the Czech translators he could find, and his company was born. Now CETRA's employees and hundreds of consultants serve the federal government plus companies involved in law, marketing research, and life sciences. The company's freelance translators and interpreters are located throughout the world.

LinguaLinx, based in Troy, New York, handles more than words. It converts documents, websites, and multimedia into almost 150 languages. The company not only has to find qualified translators, it needs experts in technology to make state-of-the-art presentations. To recruit employees, LinguaLinx emphasizes interesting work experiences, rather than fancy perks. The company's careers website describes opportunities to work with a diverse, multicultural group, including clients at leading corporations and nonprofit organizations.

QUESTIONS
1. What kinds of challenges would be involved in recruiting and selecting people to translate documents from Spanish, Polish, and French into English?
2. Would those challenges be easier to meet by recruiting within the United States or by looking for talent overseas? Explain.
3. Suppose a small translation business asked you to advise the company on how to overcome cultural barriers among a staff drawn from three countries. Suggest a few ways the company could use training and performance management to achieve this goal.

NOTES

1. "Global 500," *Fortune,* http://fortune.com, accessed June 19, 2015; T. Box, "Toyota Maintains Lead in World Sales in 2014," *Dallas Morning News,* January 21, 2015, http://bizbeatblog.dallasnews.org.
2. "The World's Biggest Companies," *Forbes,* April 26, 2011, www.wistv.com/Global/story.asp?S=14514970&clienttype=printable.
3. "For Mergers, It's a Small World after All," CNN Money.com, February 15, 2011, http://money.cnn.com/2011/02/15/markets/thebuzz/index.htm.
4. ftp://ftp.bls.gov/pub/suppl/ichcc.ichccaesuppt1_2.txt.
5. D. Kirkpatrick, "The Net Makes It All Easier—Including Exporting U.S. Jobs," *Fortune,* www.fortune.com/fortune/print/0,15935,450755,00.html (May 2003).

6. R. Schuler, "An Integrative Framework of Strategic International Human Resource Management," *Journal of Management* (1993), pp. 419–60.

7. L. Rubio, "The Rationale for NAFTA: Mexico's New 'Outward Looking' Strategy," *Business Economics* (1991), pp. 12–16.

8. H. Cooper, "Economic Impact of NAFTA: It's a Wash, Experts Say," *The Wall Street Journal,* interactive edition (June 17, 1997).

9. J. Mark, "Suzhou Factories Are Nearly Ready," *Asian Wall Street Journal,* August 14, 1995, p. 8.

10. R. Peiper, *Human Resource Management: An International Comparison* (Berlin: Walter de Gruyter, 1990).

11. V. Sathe, *Culture and Related Corporate Realities* (Homewood, IL: Richard D. Irwin, 1985).

12. M. Rokeach, *Beliefs, Attitudes, and Values* (San Francisco: Jossey-Bass, 1968).

13. L. Harrison, *Who Prospers? How Cultural Values Shape Economic and Political Success* (New York: Free Press, 1992).

14. N. Adler, *International Dimensions of Organizational Behavior,* 2nd ed. (Boston: PWS-Kent, 1991).

15. R. Yates, "Japanese Managers Say They're Adopting Some U.S. Ways," *Chicago Tribune,* February 29, 1992, p. B1.

16. G. Hofstede, "Dimensions of National Cultures in Fifty Countries and Three Regions," in *Expectations in Cross-Cultural Psychology,* eds. J. Deregowski, S. Dziurawiec, and R. C. Annis (Lisse, Netherlands: Swets and Zeitlinger, 1983).

17. G. Hofstede, "Cultural Constraints in Management Theories," *Academy of Management Executive* 7 (1993), pp. 81–90.

18. G. Hofstede, "The Cultural Relativity of Organizational Theories," *Journal of International Business Studies* 14 (1983), pp. 75–90.

19. G. Hofstede, "Cultural Constraints in Management Theories."

20. A. Ramesh, and M. Gelfland, "Will They Stay or Will They Go? The Role of Job Embeddedness in Predicting Turnover in Individualistic and Collectivistic Cultures," *Journal of Applied Psychology* 95, no. 5 (2010), pp. 807–23.

21. S. Snell and J. Dean, "Integrated Manufacturing and Human Resource Management: A Human Capital Perspective," *Academy of Management Journal* 35 (1992), pp. 467–504.

22. N. Adler and S. Bartholomew, "Managing Globally Competent People," *The Executive* 6 (1992), pp. 52–65.

23. B. O'Reilly, "Your New Global Workforce," *Fortune,* December 14, 1992, pp. 52–66.

24. A. Hoffman, "Are Technology Jobs Headed Offshore?" Monster. com, http://technology.monster.com/articles/offshore.

25. J. Ledvinka and V. Scardello, *Federal Employment Regulation in Human Resource Management* (Boston: PWS-Kent, 1991).

26. P. Conrad and R. Peiper, "Human Resource Management in the Federal Republic of Germany," in *Human Resource Management: An International Comparison,* ed. R. Peiper (Berlin: Walter de Gruyer, 1990).

27. R. Solow, "Growth with Equity through Investment in Human Capital," The George Seltzer Distinguished Lecture, University of Minnesota.

28. M. Bloom, G. Milkovich, and A. Mitra, "Toward a Model of International Compensation and Rewards: Learning from How Managers Respond to Variations in Local Host Contexts," working paper 00-14 (Center for Advance Human Resource Studies, Cornell University: 2000).

29. R. Kopp, "International Human Resource Policies and Practices in Japanese, European, and United States Multinationals," *Human Resource Management* 33 (1994), pp. 581–99.

30. Adler, *International Dimensions of Organizational Behavior.*

31. S. Jackson and Associates, *Diversity in the Workplace: Human Resource Initiatives* (New York: Guilford Press, 1991).

32. G. Stahl, M. Maznevski, A. Voight, and K. Jonsen, "Unraveling the Effects of Cultural Diversity in Teams: A Meta-Analysis of Research on Multicultural Work Groups," *Journal of International Business Studies* 41 (2010), pp. 690–709.

33. Adler and Bartholomew, "Managing Globally Competent People."

34. Ibid.

35. S. Dolianski, "Are Expats Getting Lost in the Translation?" *Workforce,* February 1997.

36. L. Copeland and L. Griggs, *Going International* (New York: Random House, 1985).

37. K. F. Misa and J. M. Fabricatore, "Return on Investments of Overseas Personnel," *Financial Executive* 47 (April 1979), pp. 42–46.

38. N. Forster, "The Persistent Myth of High Expatriate Failure Rates: A Reappraisal," *International Journal of Human Resource Management* 8, no. 4 (1997), pp. 414–34.

39. M. Mendenhall, E. Dunbar, and G. R. Oddou, "Expatriate Selection, Training, and Career-Pathing: A Review and Critique," *Human Resource Management* 26 (1987), pp. 331–45.

40. M. Mendenhall and G. Oddou, "The Dimensions of Expatriate Acculturation," *Academy of Management Review* 10 (1985), pp. 39–47.

41. W. Arthur and W. Bennett, "The International Assignee: The Relative Importance of Factors Perceived to Contribute to Success," *Personnel Psychology* 48 (1995), pp. 99–114.

42. K. Ng, and C. Earley, "Culture and Intelligence: Old Constructs, New Frontiers," *Group and Organization Management* 31 (2006), pp. 4–19; S. Ang, L. Van Dyne, C. Koh, K. Y. Ng, K. J. Templer, C. Tay, and N. A. Chandrasekar, "Cultural Intelligence: Its Measurement and Effects on Cultural Judgment and Decision Making, Cultural Adaptation, and Task Performance," *Management and Organization Review* 3 (2007), pp. 335–71.

43. R. Tung, "Selecting and Training of Personnel for Overseas Assignments," *Columbia Journal of World Business* 16, no. 2 (1981), pp. 68–78.

44. Moran, Stahl, and Boyer, Inc., *International Human Resource Management* (Boulder, CO: Moran, Stahl, & Boyer, 1987).

45. P. Caligiuri, "The Big Five Personality Characteristics as Predictors of Expatriates' Desire to Terminate the Assignment and Supervisor Rated Performance," *Personnel Psychology* 53 (2000), pp. 67–88.

46. P. Caligiuri and R. Tung, "Comparing the Success of Male and Female Expatriates from a U.S.-based Multinational Company," *International Journal of Human Resource Management* 10, no. 5 (1999), pp. 763–82.

47. L. Stroh, A. Varma, and S. Valy-Durbin, "Why Are Women Left at Home? Are They Unwilling to Go on International Assignments?" *Journal of World Business* 35, no. 3 (2000), pp. 241–55.

48. A. Harzing, *Managing the Multinationals: An International Study of Control Mechanisms* (Cheltenham: Edward Elgar, 1999).

49. J. S. Black and M. Mendenhall, "Cross-Cultural Training Effectiveness: A Review and Theoretical Framework for Future Research," *Academy of Management Review* 15 (1990), pp. 113–36.

50. B. Fitzgerald-Turner, "Myths of Expatriate Life," *HR Magazine* 42, no. 6 (June 1997), pp. 65–74.

51. P. Dowling and R. Schuler, *International Dimensions of Human Resource Management* (Boston: PWS-Kent, 1990).

52. Adler, *International Dimensions of Organizational Behavior.*

53. Dowling and Schuler, *International Dimensions of Human Resource Management.*

54. R. Schuler and P. Dowling, *Survey of ASPA/I Members* (New York: Stern School of Business, New York University, 1988).

55. C. Joinson, "No Returns: Localizing Expats Saves Companies Big Money and Can Be a Smooth Transition with a Little Due Diligence by HR," *HR Magazine* 11, no. 47 (2002), p. 70.

56. J. J. Smith, "Firms Say Expats Getting Too Costly, but Few Willing to Act" (2006), *SHRM Online,* retrieved March 9, 2007, www.shrm.org/global/library_published/subject/nonIC/CMS_018300.asp.

57. C. Solomon, "Repatriation: Up, Down, or Out?" *Personnel Journal* (1995), pp. 28–37.

58. "Workers Sent Overseas Have Adjustment Problems, a New Study Shows," *The Wall Street Journal,* June 19, 1984, p. 1.

59. J. S. Black, "Repatriation: A Comparison of Japanese and American Practices and Results," *Proceedings of the Eastern Academy of Management Bi-annual International Conference* (Hong Kong, 1989), pp. 45–49.

60. J. S. Black, "Coming Home: The Relationship of Expatriate Expectations with Repatriation Adjustment and Job Performance," *Human Relations* 45 (1992), pp. 177–92.

61. Adler, *International Dimensions of Organizational Behavior.*

62. Black, "Coming Home."

63. C. Solomon, "Repatriation: Up, Down, or Out?"

64. P. Evans, V. Pucik, and J. Barsoux, *The Global Challenge: International Human Resource Management* (New York: McGraw-Hill, 2002), p. 137.

Strategically Managing the HRM Function

LEARNING OBJECTIVES

After reading this chapter, you should be able to:

LO 16-1 Describe the roles that HRM plays in firms today and the categories of HRM activities. *page 664*

LO 16-2 Discuss how the HRM function can define its mission and market. *page 667*

LO 16-3 Explain the approaches to evaluating the effectiveness of HRM practices. *page 671*

LO 16-4 Describe the new structures for the HRM function. *page 676*

LO 16-5 Describe how outsourcing HRM activities can improve service delivery efficiency and effectiveness. *page 679*

LO 16-6 Relate how process reengineering is used to review and redesign HRM practices. *page 680*

LO 16-7 Discuss the types of new technologies that can improve the efficiency and effectiveness of HRM. *page 683*

LO 16-8 List the competencies the HRM executive needs to become a strategic partner in the company. *page 689*

The Need for HR at Tech Start-Ups

Marc Andreessen, one of Netscape's founders and a venture capitalist in the Silicon Valley, tweeted his version of the Top 10 ways that start-ups can damage themselves. One way was "Refuse to take HR seriously: allow terrible internal manager & employee behavior to catalyze into catastrophic ethical and legal crisis."

The San Francisco–based software start-up GitHub exemplifies this potential issue. On an anonymous messaging app, an unnamed user posted, "The self proclaimed Queen of GitHub is leaving her throne. The masses cheer." Julie Ann Horvath, the subject of the post, responded with a flurry of online allegations regarding gender harassment at the company. A month later, company president and co-founder Tom Preston-Werner stepped down, in spite of the fact that he was not associated with the post. He did acknowledge that he had made errors in judgment in how he handled the situation.

The situation exemplifies the problems that often plague a free-wheeling start-up company. The lack of rules and structure create a culture where people can innovate, but sometimes rules exist for a reason. An absence of rules combined with young people inexperienced in office politics and used to a say-whatever-you-want mindset with regard to social media can create a cauldron in which conflict brews.

The company brought in an investigator to explore the substance of the gender harassment and hostile work environment claims. The investigator found no evidence supporting the claims but did find that a culture that blurred personal and professional boundaries exacerbated the conflict between Mr. Preston-Werner and Ms. Horvath. In addition, with the lack of a substantive HR function, the company seemed ill-equipped to deal with the conflict.

SOURCE: E. Rusli, "Torment Claims Make GitHub Grow Up," *The Wall Street Journal*, July 17, 2014, www.wsj.com.

Introduction

Throughout this book we have emphasized how human resource management practices can help companies gain a competitive advantage. We identified specific practices related to managing the internal and external environment; designing work and measuring work outcomes; and acquiring, developing, and compensating human resources. We have also discussed the best of current research and practice to show how they may contribute to a company's competitive advantage.

As we said in Chapter 1, the role of the HRM function has been evolving over time. As we see in this chapter's opening story, it has now reached a crossroads. Although it began as a purely administrative function, most HR executives now see the function's major role as being much more strategic. However, this evolution has resulted in a misalignment between the skills and capabilities of members of the function and the new requirements placed on it. Virtually every HRM function in top companies is going through a transformation process to create a function that can play this new strategic role while successfully fulfilling its other roles. This transformation process is also going on globally. Managing this process is the subject of this chapter. First we discuss the various activities of the HRM function. Then we examine how to develop a market- or customer-oriented HRM function. We then describe the current structure of most HRM functions. Finally, we explore measurement approaches for assessing the effectiveness of the function.

Activities of HRM

LO 16-1
Describe the roles that HRM plays in firms today and the categories of HRM activities.

To understand the transformation going on in HRM, one must understand HRM activities in terms of their strategic value. One way of classifying these activities is depicted in Figure 16.1. Transactional activities (the day-to-day transactions such as benefits administration, record keeping, and employee services) are low in their strategic value. Traditional activities such as performance management, training, recruiting, selection, compensation, and employee relations are the nuts and bolts of HRM. These activities have moderate strategic value because they often form the practices and systems to ensure strategy execution. For instance, one role of HR is often to set policies regarding what are legitimate activities that salespeople can engage in to make sales in foreign countries. Transformational activities create long-term capability and adaptability for the firm. These activities include knowledge management, management development, cultural change, and strategic redirection and renewal. Obviously, these activities comprise the greatest strategic value for the firm.

As we see in the figure, most HRM functions spend the vast majority of their time on transactional activities, with substantially less on traditional and very little on transformational activities. However, virtually all HRM functions, in order to add value to the firm, must increase their efforts in the traditional and transformational activities. To do

Figure 16.1

Categories of HRM Activities and Percentages of Time Spent on Them

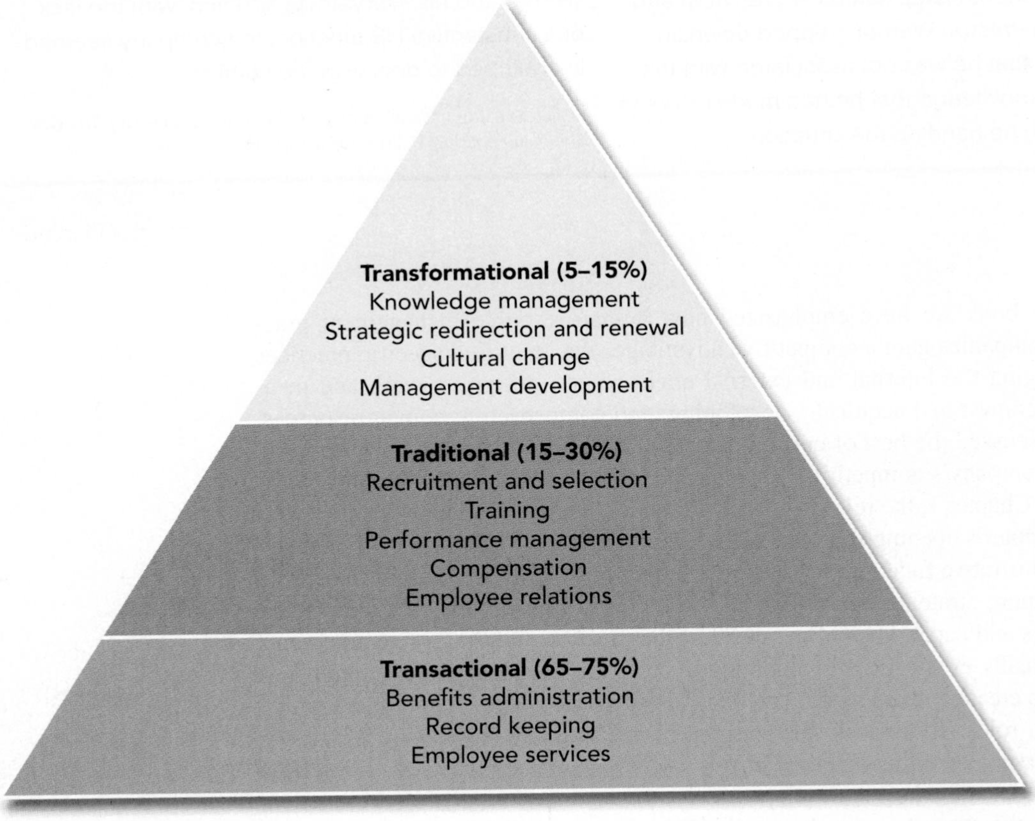

Transformational (5–15%)
Knowledge management
Strategic redirection and renewal
Cultural change
Management development

Traditional (15–30%)
Recruitment and selection
Training
Performance management
Compensation
Employee relations

Transactional (65–75%)
Benefits administration
Record keeping
Employee services

SOURCE: P. Wright, G. McMahan, S. Snell, and B. Gerhart, *Strategic Human Resource Management: Building Human Capital and Organizational Capability.* Technical report. Cornell University, 1998.

this, however, requires that HR executives (1) develop a strategy for the HRM function, (2) assess the current effectiveness of the HRM function, and (3) redesign, reengineer, or outsource HRM processes to improve efficiency and effectiveness. These issues will be discussed in the following sections.

Strategic Management of the HRM Function

In light of the various roles and activities of the HRM function, we can easily see that it is highly unlikely that any function can (or should) effectively deliver on all roles and all activities. Although this is a laudable goal, resource constraints in terms of time, money, and head count require that the HR executive make strategic choices about where and how to allocate these resources for maximum value to the firm.

Chapter 2 explained the strategic management process that takes place at the organization level and discussed the role of HRM in this process. HRM has been seen as a strategic partner that has input into the formulation of the company's strategy and develops and aligns HRM programs to help implement the strategy. However, for the HRM function to become truly strategic in its orientation, it must view itself as a separate business entity and engage in strategic management in an effort to effectively serve the various internal customers.

In this respect, one recent trend within the field of HRM, consistent with the total quality management philosophy, is for the HR executive to take a customer-oriented approach to implementing the function. In other words, the strategic planning process that takes place at the level of the business can also be performed with the HRM function. HR executives in more progressive U.S. companies have begun to view the HRM function as a strategic business unit and have tried to define that business in terms of their customer base, their customers' needs, and the technologies required to satisfy customers' needs (Figure 16.2). For example, Joe Ruocco, the Chief HR Officer at Goodyear,

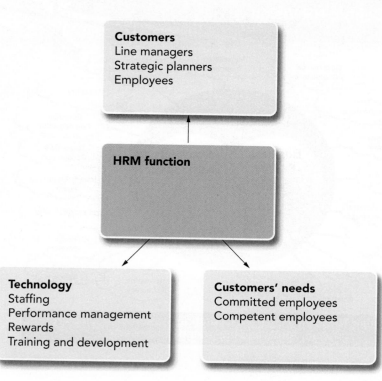

Figure 16.2

Customer-Oriented Perspective of the HRM Function

has encouraged his HR function to take a customer-centric approach. As you can see in Figure 16.3, they view the business (line clients) and the employees (associates) as their main customers. Then, they provide examples of the different tools and processes at their disposal to meet those customer needs.

A customer orientation is one of the most important changes in the HRM function's attempts to become strategic. It entails first identifying customers. The most obvious example of HRM customers are the line managers who require HRM services. In addition, the strategic planning team is a customer in the sense that it requires the identification, analysis, and recommendations regarding people-oriented business problems. Employees are also HRM customers because the rewards they receive from the employment relationship are determined and/or administered by the HRM department.

In addition, the products of the HRM department must be identified. Line managers want to have high-quality employees committed to the organization. The strategic planning team requires information and recommendations for the planning process as well as programs that support the strategic plan once it has been identified. Employees want compensation and benefit programs that are consistent, adequate, and equitable, and they want fair promotion decisions. At Southwest Airlines, the "People" department administers customer surveys to all clients as they leave the department to measure how well their needs have been satisfied.

Finally, the technologies through which HRM meets customer needs vary depending on the need being satisfied. Selection systems ensure that applicants selected for employment have the necessary knowledge, skills, and abilities to provide value to the organization. Training and development systems meet the needs of both line managers and employees by giving employees development opportunities to ensure they are constantly increasing their human capital and, thus, providing increased value to the company. Performance

Figure 16.3

Goodyear's Customer Centric View of HR

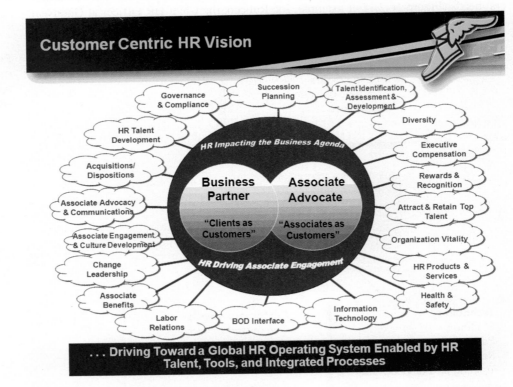

SOURCE: Courtesy of Goodyear Chief HR Officer Joe Ruocco.

management systems make clear to employees what is expected of them and assure line managers and strategic planners that employee behavior will be in line with the company's goals. Finally, reward systems similarly benefit all customers (line managers, strategic planners, and employees). These systems assure line managers that employees will use their skills for organizational benefit, and they provide strategic planners with ways to ensure that all employees are acting in ways that will support the strategic plan. Obviously, reward systems provide employees with an equitable return for their investment of skills and effort.

Building an HR Strategy

THE BASIC PROCESS

How do HR functions build their HR strategies? Recent research has examined how HR functions go about the process of building their HR strategies that should support the business strategies. Conducting case studies on 20 different companies, Wright and colleagues describe the generic approach as somewhat consistent with the process for developing a business strategy.[1]

LO 16-2
Discuss how the HRM function can define its mission and market.

As depicted in Figure 16.4, the function first scans the environment to determine the trends or events that might have an impact on the organization (e.g., future talent shortage, increasing immigrant population, aging of the workforce).

It then examines the strategic business issues or needs (e.g., is the company growing, expanding internationally, needing to develop new technologies?). For instance, Figure 16.5 displays Goodyear's major business strategy priorities. As can be seen in this example, a clear strategic priority is the attraction, motivation, and retention of talent.

From these issues, the HR strategy team needs to identify the specific people issues that will be critical to address in order for the business to succeed (a potential leadership vacuum, lack of technological expertise, lack of diversity, etc.). All of this information is used in designing the HR strategy, which provides a detailed plan regarding the major priorities and the programs, policies, and processes that must be developed or executed. Finally, this HR strategy is communicated to the relevant parties, both internal and external to the function. Again, Goodyear's talent management strategy, depicted in Figure 16.6, shows how Goodyear seeks to differentiate itself in the labor market as well as the major priority areas that the HR strategy seeks to address.

Thus, the HR strategy is a framework that guides individuals in HR by helping them understand where and how they will impact the company. At Google this four-pronged People Operations strategy consists of:

1. "Find them, Grow them, Keep them." The idea is to find great people to work for Google, grow and develop their skills, and do everything possible to keep them at Google.
2. "Put our users first." This goal echoes what Google does as a company, also illustrates how those in HR should think about the users of people operations, which are all the other Google employees.

Figure 16.4

Basic Process for HR Strategy

Scan the external environment → Identify strategic business issues → Identify people issues → Develop HR strategy → Communicate the HR strategy

Figure 16.5

Goodyear's Strategic Business Priorities

Figure 16.6

Goodyear's Global Talent Management Process

3. "Put on your own oxygen mask before assisting others." The thinking behind this goal is, in many organizations HR is doing all this work in the company for others and they forget to grow and develop their own people. Eventually this cripples the function's ability to serve the rest of the organization because the very best, most talented people get recruited out of HR to go be heads of HR at other companies.

4. "This space intentionally left blank." In Google's environment things change very, very quickly and that creates a lot of uncertainty. Uncertainty causes people to put less discretionary effort into their work, to be less satisfied, less collaborative, more competitive with fellow employees as well as making them more likely to leave the company. Hence, this goal is an attempt to explicitly recognize the dynamic nature of Google's internal and external environment.[2]

INVOLVING LINE EXECUTIVES

This generic process provides for the potential to involve line executives in a number of ways. Because the HR strategy seeks to address business issues, involving those in charge of running the business can increase the quality of information from which the HR strategy is created. This involvement can occur in a few ways. First, line executives could simply provide input, by either surveying or interviewing them regarding the business challenges and strategy. Second, they could be members of the team that actually develops the HR strategy. Third, once the strategy is developed, they could receive communications with the HR strategy information. Finally, they could have to formally approve the strategy, in essence "signing off" that the HR strategy fully supports the business strategy. The most progressive organizations use all four forms of involvement, asking a large group of executives for input, having one or two executives on the team, communicating the HR strategy broadly to executives, and having the senior executive team formally approve it.

CHARACTERIZING HR STRATEGIES

As you can see in Figure 16.7, the variety of ways that HR strategies can be generated results in various levels of linkage with the business. In general, four categories of this relationship can be identified.

First, at the most elementary level, "HR-focused" HR functions' articulation of people outcomes stems more from an analysis of what their functions currently do than from an understanding of how those people outcomes relate to the larger business. Second, "people-linked" functions have clearly identified, articulated, and aligned their HR activities around people issues and outcomes, but not business issues and outcomes. Third, "business-linked" HR functions begin with an assessment of what HR is doing, then identify the major people outcomes they should focus on, and, in a few cases, how those might translate into positive business outcomes. Finally, "business-driven" functions have fully developed HR strategies which begin by identifying the major business needs and issues, consider how people fit in and what people outcomes are necessary, and then build HR systems focused on meeting those needs. For example, as Kroger sought to develop a new strategy for competing in the retail grocery store market, it required a different approach to leadership. Figure 16.8 shows the leadership competencies necessary to execute the strategy. The larger focus is on leaders who have a passion for people and a passion for results, with a number of more specific competencies making up each.

Figure 16.7

Approaches to
Developing an HR
Strategy

An Outside-In Perspective

Business-Driven (5 cases)

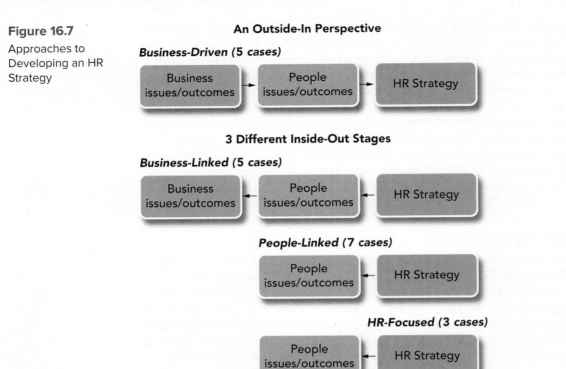

3 Different Inside-Out Stages

Business-Linked (5 cases)

People-Linked (7 cases)

HR-Focused (3 cases)

Figure 16.8

Kroger's Leadership
Model

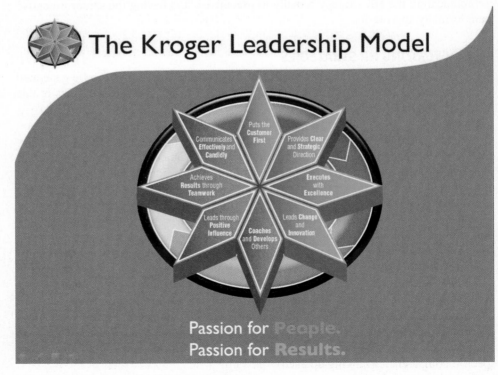

SOURCE: Courtesy of Kroger Chief HR Officer Katy Barclay.

The HR strategy must help address the issues that the business faces which will determine its success. As finding, attracting, and retaining talent has become a critical issue, virtually every HR function is addressing this as part of the HR strategy.

Measuring HRM Effectiveness

The strategic decision-making process for the HRM function requires that decision makers have a good sense of the effectiveness of the current HRM function. This information provides the foundation for decisions regarding which processes, systems, and skills of HR employees need improvement. Often HRM functions that have been heavily involved in transactional activities for a long time tend to lack systems, processes, and skills for delivering state-of-the-art traditional activities and are thoroughly unable to contribute in the transformational arena. Thus diagnosis of the effectiveness of the HRM function provides critical information for its strategic management.

In addition, having good measures of the function's effectiveness provides the following benefits:[3]

LO 16-3

Explain the approaches to evaluating the effectiveness of HRM practices.

- *Marketing the function:* Evaluation is a sign to other managers that the HRM function really cares about the organization as a whole and is trying to support operations, production, marketing, and other functions of the company. Information regarding cost savings and benefits is useful to prove to internal customers that HRM practices contribute to the bottom line. Such information is also useful for gaining additional business for the HRM function.
- *Providing accountability:* Evaluation helps determine whether the HRM function is meeting its objectives and effectively using its budget.

APPROACHES FOR EVALUATING EFFECTIVENESS

Two approaches are commonly used to evaluate the effectiveness of HRM practices: the audit approach and the analytic approach.

Audit Approach

The **audit approach** focuses on reviewing the various outcomes of the HRM functional areas. Both key indicators and customer satisfaction measures are typically collected. Table 16.1 lists examples of key indicators and customer satisfaction measures for staffing, equal employment opportunity, compensation, benefits, training, performance management, safety, labor relations, and succession planning. The development of electronic employee databases and information systems has made it much easier to collect, store, and analyze the functional key indicators (more on this later in the chapter) than in the past, when information was kept in file folders.

We previously discussed how HRM functions can become much more customer-oriented as part of the strategic management process. If, in fact, the function desires to be more customer-focused, then one important source of effectiveness data can be the customers. Just as firms often survey their customers to determine how effectively the customers feel they are being served, the HRM function can survey its internal customers.

One important internal customer is the employees of the firm. Employees often have both direct contact with the HRM function (through activities such as benefits administration and payroll) and indirect contact with the function through their involvement in activities such as receiving performance appraisals, pay raises, and training programs.

Audit Approach
Type of assessment of HRM effectiveness that involves review of customer satisfaction or key indicators (like turnover rate or average days to fill a position) related to an HRM functional area (such as recruiting or training).

Table 16.1
Examples of Key Indicators and Customer Satisfaction Measures for HRM Functions

KEY INDICATORS	CUSTOMER SATISFACTION MEASURES
Staffing Average days taken to fill open requisitions Ratio of acceptances to offers made Ratio of minority/women applicants to representation in local labor market Per capita requirement costs Average years of experience/education of hires per job family	Anticipation of personnel needs Timeliness of referring qualified workers to line supervisors Treatment of applicants Skill in handling terminations Adaptability to changing labor market conditions
Equal employment opportunity Ratio of EEO grievances to employee population Minority representation by EEO categories Minority turnover rate	Resolution of EEO grievances Day-to-day assistance provided by personnel department in implementing affirmative action plan Aggressive recruitment to identify qualified women and minority applicants
Compensation Per capita (average) merit increases Ratio of recommendations for reclassification to number of employees Percentage of overtime hours to straight time Ratio of average salary offers to average salary in community	Fairness of existing job evaluation system in assigning grades and salaries Competitiveness in local labor market Relationship between pay and performance Employee satisfaction with pay
Benefits Average unemployment compensation payment (UCP) Average workers' compensation payment (WCP) Benefit cost per payroll dollar Percentage of sick leave to total pay	Promptness in handling claims Fairness and consistency in the application of benefit policies Communication of benefits to employees Assistance provided to line managers in reducing potential for unnecessary claims
Training Percentage of employees participating in training programs per job family Percentage of employees receiving tuition refunds Training dollars per employee	Extent to which training programs meet the needs of employees and the company Communication to employees about available training opportunities Quality of introduction/orientation programs
Employee appraisal and development Distribution of performance appraisal ratings Appropriate psychometric properties of appraisal forms	Assistance in identifying management potential Organizational development activities provided by HRM department
Succession planning Ratio of promotions to number of employees Ratio of open requisitions filled internally to those filled externally	Extent to which promotions are made from within Assistance/counseling provided to employees in career planning
Safety Frequency/severity ratio of accidents Safety-related expenses per $1,000 of payroll Plant security losses per square foot (e.g., fires, burglaries)	Assistance to line managers in organizing safety programs Assistance to line managers in identifying potential safety hazards Assistance to line managers in providing a good working environment (lighting, cleanliness, heating, etc.)

KEY INDICATORS	CUSTOMER SATISFACTION MEASURES
Labor relations	
Ratio of grievances by pay plan to number of employees	Assistance provided to line managers in handling grievances
Frequency and duration of work stoppages	Efforts to promote a spirit of cooperation in plant
Percentage of grievances settled	Efforts to monitor the employee relations climate in plant
Overall effectiveness	
Ratio of personnel staff to employee population	Accuracy and clarity of information provided to managers and employees
Turnover rate	
Absenteeism rate	Competence and expertise of staff
Ratio of per capita revenues to per capita cost	Working relationship between organizations and HRM department
Net income per employee	

SOURCE: Reprinted with permission. Excerpts from Chapter 15, "Evaluating Human Resource Effectiveness," pp. 187–222, by Anne S. Tsui and Luis R. Gomez-Mejia, from *Human Resource Management: Evolving Roles and Responsibilities,* edited by Lee Dyer. Copyright © 1988 by The Bureau of National Affairs, Inc., Washington, DC, 20037. To order BNA publications call toll free 1-800-960-1220.

Many organizations such as AT&T, Motorola, and General Electric use their regular employee attitude survey as a way to assess the employees as users/customers of the HRM programs and practices.[4] However, the problem with assessing effectiveness only from the employees' perspective is that often they are responding not from the standpoint of the good of the firm, but, rather, from their own individual perspective. For example, employees notoriously and consistently express dissatisfaction with pay level (who doesn't want more money?), but to simply ratchet up pay across the board would put the firm at a serious labor cost disadvantage.

Thus, many firms have gone to surveys of top line executives as a better means of assessing the effectiveness of the HRM function. The top-level line executives can see how the systems and practices are impacting both employees and the overall effectiveness of the firm from a strategic standpoint. This can also be useful for determining how well HR employees' perceptions of their function's effectiveness align with the views of their line colleagues. For example, a study of 14 firms revealed that HR executives and line executives agreed on the relative effectiveness of HR's delivery of services such as staffing and training systems (that is, which were most and least effectively delivered) but not on the absolute level of effectiveness. As Figure 16.9 shows, HR executives' ratings of their effectiveness in different roles also diverged significantly from line executives'. In addition, line executives viewed HRM as being significantly less effective with regard to HRM's actual contributions to the firm's overall effectiveness, as we see in Figure 16.10.[5]

The Analytic Approach

The **analytic approach** focuses on either (1) determining whether the introduction of a program or practice (like a training program or a new compensation system) has the intended effect, (2) estimating the financial costs and benefits resulting from an HRM practice, or (3) using analytical data to increase organizational effectiveness. For example, in Chapter 7 we discussed how companies can determine a training program's impact on learning, behavior, and results. Evaluating a training program is one strategy for determining whether the program works. Typically, in an overall evaluation of effectiveness, we are interested in determining the degree of change associated with the program.

Analytic Approach
Type of assessment of HRM effectiveness that involves determining the impact of, or the financial cost and benefits of, a program or practice.

Figure 16.9

Comparing HR and Line Executives' Evaluations of the Effectiveness of HRM Roles

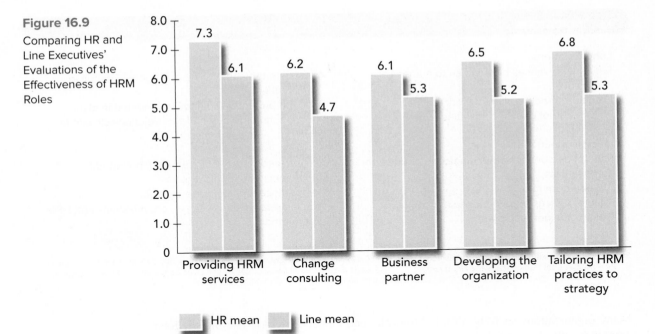

SOURCE: P. Wright, G. McMahan, S. Snell, and B. Gerhart, "Comparing Line and HR Executives' Perceptions of HR Effectiveness: Services, Roles, and Contributions," CAHRS (Center for Advanced Human Resource Studies) working paper 98-29, School of ILR, Cornell University, Ithaca, NY.

Figure 16.10

Comparing HR and Line Executives' Evaluations of the Effectiveness of HRM Contributions

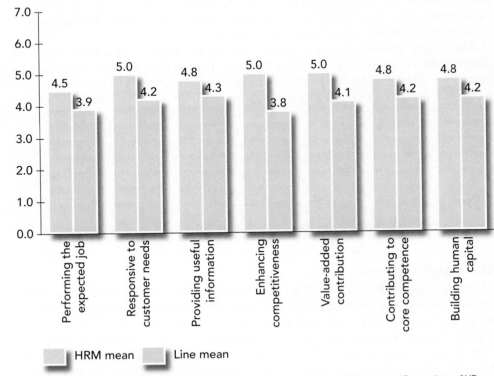

SOURCE: P. Wright, G. McMahan, S. Snell, and B. Gerhart, "Comparing Line and HR Executives' Perceptions of HR Effectiveness: Services, Roles, and Contributions," CAHRS (Center for Advanced Human Resource Studies) working paper 98-29, School of ILR, Cornell University, Ithaca, NY.

The second strategy involves determining the dollar value of the training program, taking into account all the costs associated with the program. Using this strategy, we are not concerned with how much change occurred but rather with the dollar value (costs versus benefits) of the program. Table 16.2 lists the various types of cost–benefit analyses that are done. The human resource accounting approach attempts to place a dollar value on human resources as if they were physical resources (like plant and equipment) or financial resources (like cash). Utility analysis attempts to estimate the financial impact of employee behaviors (such as absenteeism, turnover, job performance, and substance abuse).

For example, wellness programs are a popular HRM program for reducing health care costs through reducing employees' risk of heart disease and cancer. One study evaluated four different types of wellness programs. Part of the evaluation involved determining the costs and benefits associated with the four programs over a three-year period.[6] A different type of wellness program was implemented at each site. Site A instituted a program involving raising employees' awareness of health risks (distributing news articles, blood pressure testing, health education classes). Site B set up a physical fitness facility for employees. Site C raised awareness of health risks and followed up with employees who had identified health risks. Site D provided health education and follow-up counseling and promoted physical competition and health-related events. Table 16.3 shows the effectiveness and cost-effectiveness of the Site C and Site D wellness models.

The analytic approach is more demanding than the audit approach because it requires the detailed use of statistics and finance. A good example of the level of sophistication that can be required for cost–benefit analysis is shown in Table 16.4. This table shows the types of information needed to determine the dollar value of a new selection test for entry-level computer programmers.

Finally, HR analytics can be used by the function to increase the effectiveness of the firm. For instance, Google's analytical approach to HR has revealed which backgrounds and capabilities are correlated with high performance as well as the leading cause of attrition—an employee's feeling that he or she is underused at the company. It also discovered that the ideal number of recruiting interviews is 5, down from a previous average of 10.

In addition, Project Oxygen was aimed at developing great managers (named because good management, like oxygen, keeps the company alive). The analytics team poured through performance management scores, employee surveys, and other data to group managers based on two dimensions: their task performance and their people performance.

Table 16.2
Types of Cost–Benefit Analyses

Human resource accounting
- Capitalization of salary
- Net present value of expected wage payments
- Returns on human assets and human investments

Utility analysis
- Turnover costs
- Absenteeism and sick leave costs
- Gains from selection programs
- Impact of positive employee attitudes
- Financial gains of training programs

SOURCE: Based on A. S. Tsui and L. R. Gomez-Mejia, "Evaluating HR Effectiveness," in *Human Resource Management: Evolving Roles and Responsibilities,* ed. L. Dyer (Washington, DC: Bureau of National Affairs, 1988), pp. 1–196.

Table 16.3

Effectiveness and Cost-Effectiveness of Two Wellness Programs for Four Cardiovascular Disease Risk Factors

	SITE C	SITE D
Annual direct program costs, per employee per year	$30.96	$38.57
Percentage of cardiovascular disease risks[a] for which risk was moderately reduced or relapse prevented	48%	51%
Percentage of preceding entry per annual $1 spent per employee	1.55%	1.32%
Amount spent per 1% of risks reduced or relapse prevented	$.65	$.76

[a]High blood pressure, overweight, smoking, and lack of exercise.

SOURCE: J. C. Erfurt, A. Foote, and M. A. Heirich, "The Cost-Effectiveness of Worksite Wellness Programs," *Personnel Psychology* 45 (1992), p. 22.

Table 16.4

Example of Analysis Needed to Determine the Dollar Value of a Selection Test

Cost–benefit information

Current employment	4,404
Number separating	618
Number selected	618
Average tenure	9.69 years

Test information

Number of applicants	1,236
Testing cost per applicant	$10
Total test cost	$12,360
Average test score	0.80 SD
Test validity	0.76
SD$_y$ (per year)[a]	$10,413

Computation

Quantity = Average tenure × Applicants selected
= 9.69 years × 618 applicants
= 5,988 person-years

Quality = Average test score × Test validity × SD$_y$
= 0.80 × 0.76 × $10,413
= $6,331 per year

Utility = (Quantity × Quality) − Costs
= (5,988 person-year × $6,331 per year) − $12,360
= $37.9 million

[a]SD$_y$ = Dollar value of one standard difference in job performance. Approximately 40% of average salary.

SOURCES: From J. W. Boudreau, "Utility Analysis," in *Human Resource Management: Evolving Roles and Responsibilities,* ed. L. Dyer (Washington, DC: Bureau of National Affairs, 1988), p. 150; F. L. Schmidt, J. E. Hunter, R. C. McKenzie, and T. W. Muldrow, "Impact of Valid Selection Procedures on Work-Force Productivity," *Journal of Applied Psychology* 64 (1979), pp. 609–26.

They then conducted a double-blind study focusing on those who were top (or bottom) on both dimensions, in order to identify eight behaviors that characterized good managers.[7]

Improving HRM Effectiveness

LO 16-4

Describe the new structures for the HRM function.

Once a strategic direction has been established and HRM's effectiveness evaluated, leaders of the HRM function can explore how to improve its effectiveness in contributing to the firm's competitiveness. Returning briefly to Figure 16.1, which depicted the different activities of the HRM function, often the improvement focuses on two aspects of the pyramid. First, within each activity, HRM needs to improve both the efficiency and effectiveness in performing each of the activities. Second, often there is a push to eliminate as much of the transactional work as possible (and some of the traditional work) to free up time and resources to focus more on the higher-value-added transformational work. Redesign of the structure (reporting relationships) and processes (through outsourcing and information technology) enables the function to achieve these goals simultaneously. Figure 16.11 depicts this process.

RESTRUCTURING TO IMPROVE HRM EFFECTIVENESS

Traditional HRM functions were structured around the basic HRM subfunctions such as staffing, training, compensation, appraisal, and labor relations. Each of these areas had a director who reported to the VP of HRM, who often reported to a VP of finance and administration. However, for the HRM function to truly contribute strategically to firm effectiveness, the senior HR person must be part of the top management team (reporting directly to the chief executive officer), and there must be a different structural arrangement within the function itself.

A generic structure for the HRM function is depicted in Figure 16.12. As we see, the HRM function effectively is divided into three divisions: the centers for expertise,

Figure 16.11

Improving HRM Effectiveness

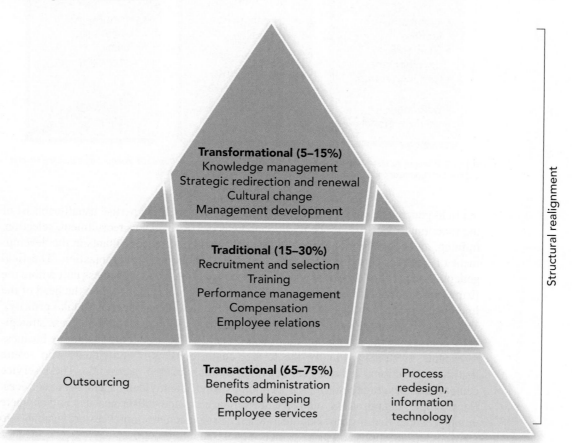

Figure 16.12

Old and New
Structures for the
HRM Organization

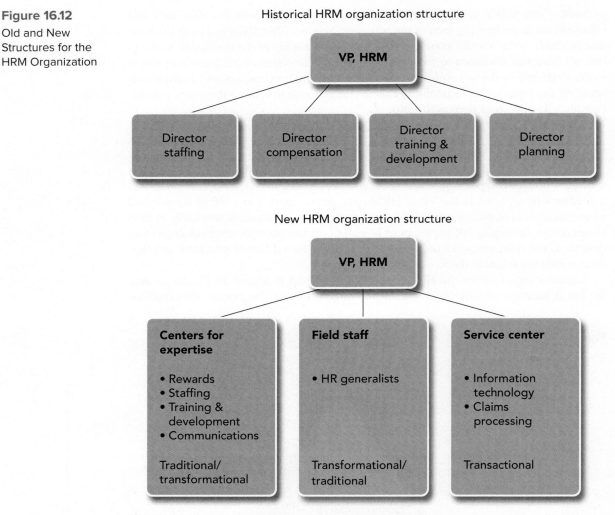

Historical HRM organization structure

VP, HRM

Director
staffing

Director
compensation

Director
training &
development

Director
planning

New HRM organization structure

VP, HRM

**Centers for
expertise**

• Rewards
• Staffing
• Training &
  development
• Communications

Traditional/
transformational

Field staff

• HR generalists

Transformational/
traditional

Service center

• Information
  technology
• Claims
  processing

Transactional

SOURCE: P. Wright, G. McMahan, S. Snell, and B. Gerhart, *Strategic Human Resource Management: Building Human Capital and Organizational Capability.* Technical report. Cornell University, 1998.

the field generalists, and the service center.[8] The centers for expertise usually consist of the functional specialists in the traditional areas of HRM such as recruitment, selection, training, and compensation. These individuals ideally act as consultants in the development of state-of-the-art systems and processes for use in the organization. The field generalists consist of the HRM generalists who are assigned to a business unit within the firm. These individuals usually have dual reporting relationships to both the head of the line business and the head of HRM (although the line business tends to take priority). They ideally take responsibility for helping the line executives in their business strategically address people issues, and they ensure that the HRM systems enable the business to execute its strategy. Finally, the service center consists of individuals who ensure that the transactional activities are delivered throughout the organization. These service centers often leverage information technology to efficiently deliver employee services. For example, organizations such as Chevron have created call-in service centers where employees can dial a central number where service center employees are available to answer their questions and process their requests and transactions.

Such structural arrangements improve service delivery through specialization. Center for expertise employees can develop current functional skills without being distracted by transactional activities, and generalists can focus on learning the business environment without having to maintain expertise in functional specializations. Finally, service center employees can focus on efficient delivery of basic services across business units.

OUTSOURCING TO IMPROVE HRM EFFECTIVENESS

Restructuring the internal HRM function and redesigning the processes represent internal approaches to improving HRM effectiveness. However, increasingly HR executives are seeking to improve the effectiveness of the systems, processes, and services the function delivers through outsourcing. **Outsourcing** entails contracting with an outside vendor to provide a product or service to the firm, as opposed to producing the product using employees within the firm.

Why would a firm outsource an HRM activity or service? Usually this is done for one of two reasons: either the outsourcing partner can provide the service more cheaply than it would cost to do it internally, or the partner can provide it more effectively than it can be performed internally. Early on, firms resorted to outsourcing for efficiency reasons. Why would using an outsourced provider be more efficient than having internal employees provide a service? Usually it is because outsourced providers are specialists who are able to develop extensive expertise that can be leveraged across a number of companies.

For example, consider a relatively small firm that seeks to develop a pension system for employees. To provide this service to employees, the HRM function would need to learn all of the basics of pension law. Then it would need to hire a person with specific expertise in administering a pension system in terms of making sure that employee contributions are withheld and that the correct payouts are made to retired employees. Then the company would have to hire someone with expertise in investing pension funds. If the firm is small, requirements of the pension fund might not fill the time (80 hours per week) of these two new hires. Assume that it takes only 20 total hours a week for these people to do their jobs. The firm would be wasting 60 hours of employee time each week. However, a firm that specializes in providing pension administration services to multiple firms could provide the 20 hours of required time to that firm and three other firms for the same cost as had the firm performed this activity internally. Thus the specialist firm could charge the focal firm 50% of what it would cost the small firm to do the pensions internally. Of that 50%, 25% (20 hours) would go to paying direct salaries and the other 25% would be profit. Here the focal firm would save 50% of its expenses while the provider would make money.

Now consider the aspect of effectiveness. Because the outsourced provider works for a number of firms and specializes in pensions, its employees develop state-of-the-art knowledge of running pension plans. They can learn unique innovations from one company and transfer that learning to a new company. In addition, employees can be more easily and efficiently trained because all of them will be trained in the same processes and procedures. Finally, with experience in providing constant pension services, the firm is able to develop a capability to perform these services that could never be developed by two individuals working 25% of the time on these services.

What kind of services are being outsourced? Firms primarily outsource transactional activities and services of HRM such as pension and benefits administration as well as payroll. However, a number of traditional and some transformational activities have been outsourced as well. The "Competing through Globalization" box shows how some firms that offshored some of their business activities have now begun reshoring them.

LO 16-5
Describe how outsourcing HRM activities can improve service delivery efficiency and effectiveness.

Outsourcing
An organization's use of an outside organization for a broad set of services.

Some U.S. Companies Bringing Jobs Back Home

United Technologies' Otis elevator company, the world's largest manufacturer and installer of elevators and escalators, is one of a growing number of manufacturing companies now "reshoring" their labor force to the United States. As the low overseas labor costs—which originally enticed companies to offshore their manufacturing facilities—rise, companies have begun taking advantage of the tax incentives and supply-chain and operations advantages of co- or near-locating their design facilities and manufacturing plants in the United States.

In 2012, Otis opened a 423,000-square-foot facility in Florence, South Carolina, estimating that the move would lower freight and logistic costs by 17% and reduce costs an additional 20% by co-locating design and production workers. At the same time, Otis closed facilities in Arizona and Indiana, transferring some of those workers to South Carolina.

Otis planned these factory moves with the intent to close its production factory in Nogales, Mexico. However, the company bit off more that it could chew, simultaneously updating computer systems and changing product offerings. It also struggled to find enough skilled workers in Florence. As demand for production continued to rise, delayed orders piled up and Otis had to postpone closing its Nogales factory five months in order to meet demand. These obstacles cost United Technologies $60 million in 2013 and $9 million in the first quarter of 2014.

DISCUSSION QUESTION

What challenges might a company face that plans to "reshore" its labor force?

SOURCE: T. Mann, "Otis Finds 'Reshoring' Manufacturing Is Not Easy," *The Wall Street Journal*, May 2, 2014, www.wsj.com.

IMPROVING HRM EFFECTIVENESS THROUGH PROCESS REDESIGN

LO 16-6
Relate how process reengineering is used to review and redesign HRM practices.

In addition to structural arrangements, process redesign enables the HRM function to more efficiently and effectively deliver HRM services. Process redesign often uses information technology, but information technology applications are not a requirement. Thus we will discuss the general issue of process reengineering and then explore information technology applications that have aided HRM in process redesign.

Reengineering
Review and redesign of work processes to make them more efficient and improve the quality of the end product or service.

Reengineering is a complete review of critical work processes and redesign to make them more efficient and able to deliver higher quality. Reengineering is especially critical to ensuring that the benefits of new technology can be realized. Applying new technology to an inefficient process will not improve efficiency or effectiveness. Instead, it will increase product or service costs related to the introduction of the new technology.

Reengineering can be used to review the HRM department functions and processes, or it can be used to review specific HRM practices such as work design or the performance management system. The reengineering process involves the four steps shown in Figure 16.13: identify the process to be reengineered, understand the process, redesign the process, and implement the new process.[9]

Identifying the Process

First, the company should identify the process they want to re-engineer and the individuals who are part of that process. Managers who control the process or are responsible for functions within the process (sometimes called "process owners") should be identified and asked to be part of the reengineering team. Team members should include employees involved in the process (to provide expertise) and those outside the process, as well as internal or external customers who see the outcome of the process.

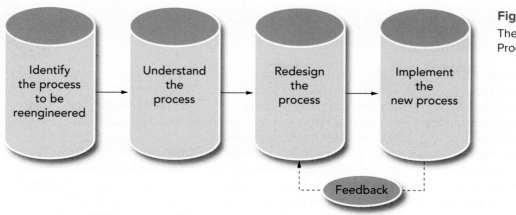

Figure 16.13
The Reengineering
Process

Understanding the Process

Several things need to be considered when evaluating a process:

- Can jobs be combined?
- Can employees be given more autonomy? Can decision making and control be built into the process through streamlining it?
- Are all the steps in the process necessary?
- Are data redundancy, unnecessary checks, and controls built into the process?
- How many special cases and exceptions have to be dealt with?
- Are the steps in the process arranged in their natural order?
- What is the desired outcome? Are all of the tasks necessary? What is the value of the process?

Various techniques are used to understand processes. Data-flow diagrams are useful to show the flow of data among departments. Figure 16.14 shows a data-flow diagram for payroll data and the steps in producing a paycheck. Information about the employee and department are sent to the general account. The payroll check is issued based on a payment voucher that is generated from the general accounting ledger. Data-entity relationship diagrams show the types of data used within a business function and the relationship among the different types of data. In scenario analysis, simulations of real-world issues are presented to data end users. The end users are asked to indicate how an information system could help address their particular situations and what data should be maintained to deal with those situations. Surveys and focus groups collect information about the data collected, used, and stored in a functional area, as well as information about time and information-processing requirements. Users may be asked to evaluate the importance, frequency, and criticality of automating specific tasks within a functional area. For example, how critical is it to have an applicant tracking system that maintains data on applicants' previous work experience? Cost–benefit analyses compare the costs of completing tasks with and without an automated system or software application. For example, the analysis should include the costs in terms of people, time, materials, and dollars; the anticipated costs of software and hardware; and labor, time, and material expenses.[10] The "Competing through Sustainability" box describes how IKEA has used the redesign of its products to reduce its costs, its customers' prices, and its carbon footprint.

Redesigning the Process

During the redesign phase, the team develops models, tests them, chooses a prototype, and determines how to integrate the prototype into the organization.

Figure 16.14

A Data-Flow Diagram for Payroll Data

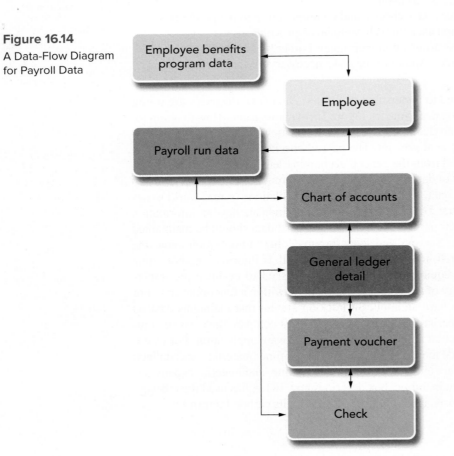

Implementing the Process

The company tries out the process by testing it in a limited, controlled setting before expanding companywide. For example, J. M. Huber Corporation, a New Jersey–based conglomerate that has several operating divisions scattered throughout the United States, used reengineering to avoid installing new software onto inefficient processes.[11] HR staff began by documenting and studying the existing work flow and creating a strategy for improving efficiency. Top management, midlevel managers, and human resources staff worked together to identify the processes that they most wanted to improve. They determined that the most critical issue was to develop a client–server system that could access data more easily than the mainframe computer they were currently using. Also, the client–server system could eliminate many of the requisitions needed to get access to data, which slowed down work. The HRM department's efforts have streamlined record-keeping functions, eliminated redundant steps, and automated manual processes. The fully automated client–server system allows employees to sign up and change benefits information using an interactive voice-response system that is connected to the company's database. In addition, managers have easier access to employees' salary history, job descriptions, and other data. If an employee is eligible for a salary increase and the manager requests a change and it is approved, the system will process it (without entry by a clerical worker), and the changes will be seen on the employee's paycheck. Results of the reengineering effort are impressive. The redesigned processes have reduced the number of problems that HRM has to give to other departments by 42%, cut work steps by 26%, and eliminated 20% of the original work. Although the company is spending more than $1 million to make the technology work, it estimates that the investment should pay for itself in five years.

IMPROVING HRM EFFECTIVENESS THROUGH USING NEW TECHNOLOGIES—HRM INFORMATION SYSTEMS

Several new and emerging technologies can help improve the effectiveness of the HRM function. **New technologies** are current applications of knowledge, procedures, and equipment that have not been used previously. New technology usually involves automation—that is, replacing human labor with equipment, information processing, or some combination of the two.

In HRM, technology has already been used for three broad functions: transaction processing, reporting, and tracking; decision support systems; and expert systems.[12] **Transaction processing** refers to computations and calculations used to review and document HRM decisions and practices. This includes documenting relocation, training expenses, and course enrollments and filling out government reporting requirements (such as EEO-1 reports, which require companies to report information to the government regarding employees' race and gender by job category). **Decision support systems** are designed to help managers solve problems. They usually include a "what if" feature that allows users to see how outcomes change when assumptions or data change. These systems are useful, for example, for helping companies determine the number of new hires needed based on different turnover rates or the availability of employees with a certain skill in the labor market. **Expert systems** are computer systems incorporating the decision rules of people deemed to have expertise in a certain area. The system recommends actions that the user can take based on the information provided by the user. The recommended actions are those that a human expert would take in a similar situation (such as a manager interviewing a job candidate).

LO 16-7
Discuss the types of new technologies that can improve the efficiency and effectiveness of HRM.

New Technologies
Current applications of knowledge, procedures, and equipment that have not been previously used. Usually involves replacing human labor with equipment, information processing, or some combination of the two.

Transaction Processing
Computations and calculations used to review and document HRM decisions and practices.

Decision Support Systems
Problem-solving systems which usually include a "what-if" feature that allows users to see how outcomes change when assumptions or data change.

Expert Systems
Computer systems incorporating the decision rules of people recognized as experts in a certain area.

Software Applications for HRM
IMPROVING HRM EFFECTIVENESS THROUGH NEW TECHNOLOGIES—E-HRM

Since the mid-1990s, as HRM functions sought to play a more strategic role in their organizations, the first task was to eliminate transactional tasks in order to free up time to focus on traditional and transformational activities. Part of building a strategic HR function requires moving much of the transactional work away from being done by people so that the people can have time available to work on strategic activities. Consequently, the use of technology can both make HR more strategic and by doing so increase the value that HR adds to the business.[13] As indicated in Figure 16.11, outsourcing of many of these activities provided one mechanism for reducing this burden. However, more relevant today is the focus on the use of information technology to handle these tasks. Early on this was achieved by the development and implementation of information systems that were run by the HRM function but more recently have evolved into systems that allow employees to serve themselves. For example, employees can access the system and make their benefit enrollment, changes, or claims online. Clearly, technology has freed HRM functions from transactional activities to focus on more strategic actions.

However, the speed requirements of e-business force HRM functions to explore how to leverage technology for the delivery of traditional and transformational HRM activities. This does not imply that over time all of HRM will be executed online, but that a number of HRM activities currently delivered via paper or face-to-face communications can be delivered electronically with no loss (and even gains) in effectiveness and efficiency. This is illustrated by Figure 16.15. We explore some examples next. The

Figure 16.15

Change in Delivery

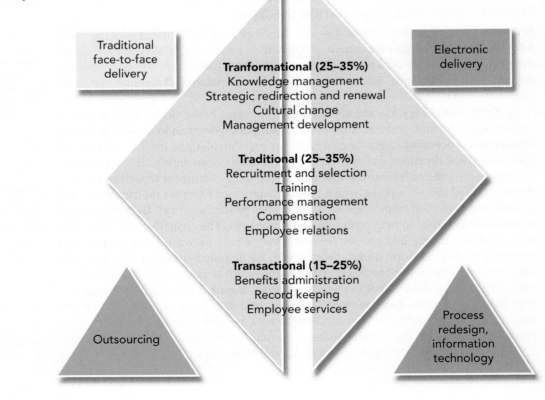

E-Enabled Delivery of HRM

Traditional face-to-face delivery

Electronic delivery

Tranformational (25–35%)
Knowledge management
Strategic redirection and renewal
Cultural change
Management development

Traditional (25–35%)
Recruitment and selection
Training
Performance management
Compensation
Employee relations

Transactional (15–25%)
Benefits administration
Record keeping
Employee services

Outsourcing

Process redesign, information technology

Improving Health through Technology

If you're a large health insurer who faces pressure from increasing medical costs, how can you encourage your customers to live healthier lifestyles? Multi-billion-dollar health insurer Humana has focused on using a team-based workplace design to produce applications that can help customers live better.

Humana's Digital Experience Center is located in Louisville, Kentucky, but presents a more Silicon Valley sort of structure and culture. The 11 designers and 4 remote workers end each morning's meeting with a hand clap, then go off to develop new apps that can be used by their customers. App designers work in pairs so that as one writes the code, the other can test it and make improvements.

These apps, such as HumanaVitality, allow customers to set health goals for themselves or challenge others to engage in healthy activities. For instance, they developed the "Step Challenge" encouraging customers to walk more during the day. The app has already been downloaded by over 135,000 customers and seems to be helping them increase their activity levels. This illustrates how technology and new forms of work design can provide companies with a competitive advantage.

DISCUSSION QUESTION

What other ways can you think of that companies might be able to leverage social media and mobile apps to better connect with their employees and customers?

SOURCE: T. Loftus, "Can You Put a Little Palo Alto into an Insurer in Louisville?" *The Wall Street Journal*, April 28, 2015, www.wsj.com.

"Competing through Technology" box illustrates how one health care company uses technology to improve customers' health.

In a world dominated by social media, companies like Google are now using it for internal purposes. Google developed "Grow," an internal platform that makes it easy for Googlers to find learning opportunities, jobs, one-on-one advice, and other development resources to suit their needs and interests. Grow unifies myriad learning, development, and job search tools into a one-stop shop for Googlers to manage and act on their development. It suggests courses, opportunities, advisors, and more based on what the company knows about the Googler (e.g., role, level, location) and the data a Googler provides within the tool (e.g., skills they want to develop). Not surprisingly given Google's search capability, this system allows employees to search for learning resources or jobs of interest.

Grow is an inherently social platform, and every Googler has a customizable profile that is visible to others. Figure 16.16 displays the Grow profile of Sunil Chandra, Google's VP of Staffing and Operations. As you can see, Googlers can tag skills they have (e.g., consulting, people management, and coaching for Sunil) and those they want to develop (e.g., entrepreneurship, and prioritization) in their profile. Skills listed in Grow help the system get to know the user and offer more personalized job recommendations. Googlers can also indicate if they would like to advise others on a particular skill. If Sunil tags himself as a "Skill Advisor" on a topic (e.g., leadership), he will appear in Grow's search results, and other Googlers can view his skills and contact him for advice. He can select the option to "teach other Googlers," as well, which would connect him to Google's g2g (or "Googlers-to-Googlers") program, an internal volunteer teaching network that allows employees to teach their peers on a variety of subjects.

As mentioned above, Grow also allows Googlers to list skills they would like to develop. They can add up to 10 skills, and Grow will use these inputs to further

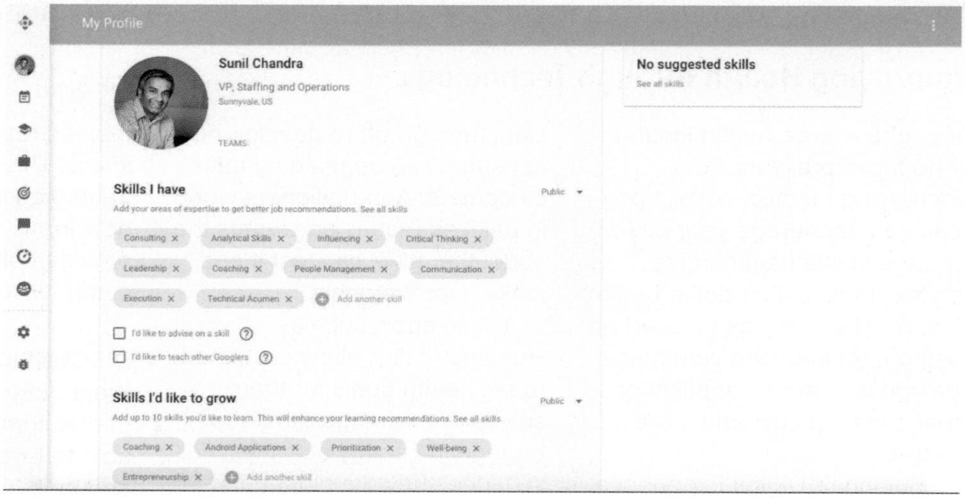

Figure 16.16

Personal Web Page
for Sunil Chandra

customize their learning recommendations. To help Googlers get started, Grow suggests a number of skills on the right-had side of the page (culled from a multi-year study of the skills that make Googlers effective in their roles). In Sunil's case, he has already added all of his suggested skills directly to his profile, hence why the tool reflects "no suggested skills." Sunil's profile also includes his picture, job title, location, and a link to his internal employee page to help his fellow Googlers get to know him.

In sum, Grow profiles are a great way for Googlers to teach the tool about their skills and development areas, and get better learning and job recommendations in the process. It also helps Googlers connect with their peers as advisors, mentors, or internal teachers, in addition to providing a host of other learning and development resources.

Recruitment and Selection

Traditional recruitment and selection processes have required considerable face-to-face communications with recruitment firms and potential employees, labor-intensive assessment devices, and significant monitoring of managerial decisions to ensure that hiring patterns and decisions do not run afoul of regulatory requirements. However, technology has transformed these processes.

For example, online recruiting accounts for one of every eight hires according to k-force.com's poll of 300 U.S. companies. IBM employees now fill out forms on the web to identify contract help they need, and that information is immediately sent to 14 temp agencies. Within an hour agencies respond with résumés for review, allowing IBM to cut hiring time from 10 days to 3 and save $3 million per year.

Finally, technology has enabled firms to monitor hiring processes to minimize the potential for discriminatory hiring decisions. For example, Home Depot was accused of forcing female applicants into cashier jobs while reserving the customer service jobs for males. While not admitting guilt, as part of their consent decree Home Depot uses technology to identify people who have skills for jobs they are not applying for based on key words in their résumés. In addition, the technology forces managers to interview diverse candidate sets before making decisions.

Compensation and Rewards

Compensation systems in organizations probably reflect the most pervasive form of bureaucracy within HRM. In spite of the critical role they play in attracting, motivating, and retaining employees, most systems consist of rigid, time-consuming, and ineffective processes. Managers fill out what they believe to be useless forms, ignore guidelines, and display a general disdain for the entire process.

Leveraging technology may allow firms to better achieve their compensation goals with considerably less effort. For example, one problem many merit or bonus pay plans face is that managers refuse to differentiate among performers, giving everyone similar pay increases. This allows them to spend less time thinking about how to manage (rate and review) performance as well as minimizes the potential conflict they might face. Thus, employees do not see linkages between performance and pay, resulting in lower motivation among all employees and higher turnover among top performers (and possibly lower turnover among bottom performers). To minimize this, Cypress Semiconductors requires managers to distinguish between equity and merit and forces distributions with regard to both concepts.[14] For example, equity means that the top-ranked performer in any group of peers should make 50% more than the lowest-ranked performer, and people with comparable performance should receive comparable salaries. With regard to merit, there must be at least a 7% spread between the lowest and highest pay raises (if the lowest raise is 3%, then the highest must be at least 10%). If ratings and raises are input into a system, the firm can monitor and control the rating process to ensure that adequate differentiations are made consistent with the policy.

Training and Development

Exploring different vehicles for delivering training (PC, video, and the like) certainly is not a new concept. In addition, a number of firms have begun delivering training via the web. Their experience suggests that some types of training can be done effectively via the Internet or an intranet, whereas others might not. For example, companies such as IBM and Dell both boast that they have developed Internet-based training for some parts of their workforce.

Interestingly, the challenge of speedy delivery of HRM services brings the concept of Internet-based training to the forefront. In today's competitive environment, firms compete to attract and retain both customers and talented employees. How well a firm develops and treats existing employees largely determines how well it achieves these outcomes. Yet the challenges of speed, project focus, and changing technology create environments that discourage managers from managing their people, resulting in a situation where employees may not feel respected or valued.

This presents a challenge to firms to provide both the incentive and the skills for managers to treat employees as assets rather than commodities. Consider how Internet-based training might facilitate this. Assume that you work for Widget.com, a fast-growing, fast-paced e-business. You arrive at work Monday morning, and your e-mail contains a high-priority message with either an attachment or a link to a URL. It is your Monday morning challenge from the CEO, and you know that the system will track whether you link and complete this challenge. When you link to it, you see a digital video of your CEO telling you how people are Widget.com's competitive advantage, and that when they don't feel valued, they leave. Thus his challenge to you is to make your employees feel valued today. To do so, you will in the next 10 minutes learn how to express appreciation to an employee. You receive six learning points; you observe a digitized video model performing the learning points; you review the learning points again and take a quiz. You then see the CEO giving you the final challenge: that in the next 15 minutes you are to take one of your employees aside and express your appreciation using the skill you just developed.

Notice the advantages of this process. First, it was not time-consuming like most three-day or one-week training programs. The entire process (training and demonstration with a real employee) took less than 30 minutes; you have developed a skill; and an employee now probably feels better about the organization. It communicated a real organizational value or necessary competency. It didn't require any travel expenses to a training facility. It did not overwhelm you with so much information that you would be lucky to remember 10% of what you were exposed to. Finally, it was a push, rather than pull, approach to training. The firm did not wait for you to realize you had a deficiency and then go search and sign up for training. It pushed the training to you.

Thus technology allows firms to deliver training and development for at least some skills or knowledge faster, more efficiently, and probably more effectively. It can quickly merge training, communication, and immediate response to strategic contingencies.

Creating and nurturing a committed workforce presents a tremendous challenge to firms today. According to a recent survey conducted by Monster.com, 61% of Americans consider themselves overworked and 86% are not satisfied with their jobs.[15] Such findings suggest that firms need to find ways to monitor commitment levels, identify potential obstacles to commitment, and respond quickly to eliminate those obstacles. In large part, attitude surveys have constituted the platform from which these activities were managed in the past.

Consider the traditional attitude survey. Surveys are administered to employees over a period of four to six weeks. The data are entered and analyzed, requiring another six to eight weeks. A group interprets the results to identify the major problem areas, and task forces are formed to develop recommendations; this process easily takes another four to six months. Finally, decisions must be made about implementing the task force recommendations. In the end, at best employees might see responses to their concerns 12 to 18 months after the survey—and then the survey administrators cannot understand why employees think that completing the survey is a waste of time.

Now consider how technology can shorten that cycle. E-pulse represents one attempt to create a platform for almost real-time attitude surveys. Developed by Theresa Welbourne at the University of Michigan, E-pulse is a scalable survey device administered online. Normally three questions are asked regarding how employees feel about work, but more questions can be added to get feedback on any specific issue. The survey goes out online, and when employees complete it, the data are immediately entered and analyzed. In essence, the part of the process that took four months in the past has been reduced to a day.

Next the firm can decide how it wants to use the information. For example, it could be broken down by business, site, or work unit, with the relevant information going to the leader of the chosen unit of analysis. In essence, a supervisor could receive almost immediate feedback about the attitudes of his or her work group, or a general manager about his or her business unit. The supervisor or manager can respond immediately, even if only to communicate that she or he realizes a problem exists and will take action soon.

One must recognize that although the technology provides for faster HRM, only a more systemic approach will ensure better and smarter HRM. For example, disseminating the information to the supervisors and managers may be faster, but unless those individuals possess good problem-solving and communication skills, they may either ignore the information or, worse yet, exacerbate the problem with inappropriate responses. As we noted with regard to training, this systemic approach requires knocking down traditional functional walls to deliver organizational solutions rather than functional programs. Thus the challenge is to get beyond viewing the technology as a panacea or even as a functional tool, but rather as a catalyst for transforming the HRM organization.

The Future for HR Professionals

The future for careers in the human resource profession seems brighter than ever. An increasing number of successful companies such as Microsoft have made the top HR job a member of the senior management team, reporting directly to the chief executive officer. CEOs recognize the importance of their workforce in driving competitive success. Firms need to seek the balance between attracting, motivating, and retaining the very best talent and keeping labor and administrative costs as low as possible. Finding such a balance requires HR leaders who have a deep knowledge of the business combined with a deep knowledge of HR issues, tools, processes, and technologies.

For a reader who is just getting a first glimpse of the HRM function, to portray what a vastly different role HRM must play today compared to 20 or even 10 years ago is impossible. As noted earlier, HRM has traditionally played a largely administrative role—simply processing paperwork plus developing and administering hiring, training, appraisal, compensation, and benefits systems—and all of this has been unrelated to the strategic direction of the firm. In the early 1980s HRM took on more of a one-way linkage role, helping to implement strategy. Now strategic decision makers are realizing the importance of people issues and so are calling for HRM to become the "source of people expertise" in the firm.[16] This requires that HR managers possess and use knowledge of how people can and do play a role in competitive advantage as well as the policies, programs, and practices that can leverage the firm's people as a source of competitive advantage. This leads to an entirely new set of competencies for today's strategic HR executive.[17]

In the future, HR professionals will need four basic competencies to become partners in the strategic management process.[18] First, they will need "business competence"—knowing the company's business and understanding its economic financial capabilities. This calls for making logical decisions that support the company's strategic plan based on the most accurate information possible. Because in almost all companies the effectiveness of decisions must be evaluated in terms of dollar values, the HR executive must be able to calculate the costs and benefits of each alternative in terms of its dollar impact.[19] In addition, it requires that the nonmonetary impact be considered. The HR executive must be fully capable of identifying the social and ethical issues attached to HRM practices. HR professionals must often act as the conscience of the organization in all aspects, and the "Integrity in Action" box shows how firms can sometimes border on unethical behavior when dealing with their customers.

Second, HR professionals will need "professional–technical knowledge" of state-of-the-art HRM practices in areas such as staffing, development, rewards, organizational design, and communication. New selection techniques, performance appraisal methods, training programs, and incentive plans are constantly being developed. Some of these programs can provide value whereas others may be no more than the products of today's HRM equivalent of snake oil. HR executives must be able to critically evaluate the new techniques offered as state-of-the-art HRM programs and use only those that will benefit the company.

Third, they must be skilled in the "management of change processes," such as diagnosing problems, implementing organizational changes, and evaluating results. Every time a company changes its strategy in even a minor way, the entire company has to

LO 16-8

List the competencies the HRM executive needs to become a strategic partner in the company.

change. These changes result in conflict, resistance, and confusion among the people who must implement the new plans or programs. The HR executive must have the skills to oversee the change in a way that ensures its success. In fact, one survey of Fortune 500 companies found that 87% of the companies had their organization development/change function as part of the HR department.[20]

Finally, these professionals must also have "integration competence," meaning the ability to integrate the three other competencies to increase the company's value. This requires that, although specialist knowledge is necessary, a generalist perspective must be taken in making decisions. This entails seeing how all the functions within the HRM area fit together to be effective and recognizing that changes in any one part of the HRM package are likely to require changes in other parts of the package.

Google has sought to achieve this integration with what they call the "three-thirds" staffing model. This consist of the following groups of people with complimentary skill sets:

1. One-third traditional HR people—subject matter experts in benefits, compensation, employee relations, learning, and recruiting. Their expertise, pattern recognition, and emotional intelligence serve as the foundation for developing the services and programs.
2. One-third consultants—high-end strategy experts with a background in management consulting who thrive on solving big, amorphous problems and bring a deliberate, business approach to people issues.
3. One-third analytics professionals—masters and doctoral-level folks who measure, analyze, and provide insight into all that the people operations function does, and to prove what really works. They have a healthy appetite for the impossible and drive experimentation to ensure that Google is as innovative on the people side as it is on the product side.

This staffing model has enabled Google to build the required skill base and integrate the various people to build a world-class HR organization.[21]

The Role of the Chief Human Resource Officer

Having discussed the increasing importance of HR and the new strategic role of HR professionals, in closing we examine the role of the leader of the HR function. These chief human resource officers (CHROs) bear the responsibility for leading the HR function as well as ensuring that HR systems and processes deliver value to the company. Only recently have researchers attempted to examine what these HR leaders do and how they affect the business.

A recent survey identified seven roles that CHROs have to play to one degree or another, and then asked Fortune 150 CHROs to identify how they spend their time across those roles. As can be seen in Figure 16.17, CHROs reported spending the second most time (21%) as a **strategic advisor** to the executive team. This role entails sharing the people expertise as part of the decision-making process, as well as shaping how the human capital of the firm fits into its strategy. This also was the role that was most frequently cited as having the greatest impact on the firm. One CHRO described the importance of the strategic advisor role as:

> HR is critical, but it's a tool in the firm's portfolio. First to truly impact the success of the firm, the CHRO needs to have a broad credibility that only comes from understanding every facet of the business at a level deep enough to be able to add business value in discussions with every leader. That means understanding the firm's economics, customer behavior, products, technology, etc. at a level deep enough to steer and shape decisions in these areas. From that flows the trust and credibility to counter the "conventional wisdom" on how best to manage people and shape the firm's talent agenda. Without this broader credibility, the CHRO can talk about talent, but risks not having sufficient context to make the right decisions. Second, from the CEO's perspective, the most useful thing is the integration of the people strategy with every other part of the firm's operations. The only way to truly integrate these areas is to be actively involved in the broader discussions as well.[22]

The role of **talent architect** also sees a significant portion of time spent (17%) and was also frequently cited as the role in which the CHRO has the greatest impact on

Strategic Advisor
A role of the CHRO that focuses on the formulation and implementation of the firm's strategy.

Talent Architect
A role of the CHRO that focuses on building and identifying the human capital critical to the present and future of the firm.

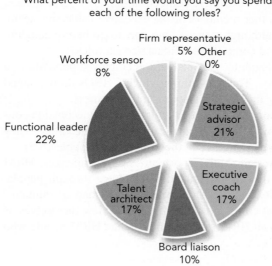

What percent of your time would you say you spend in each of the following roles?

- Firm representative 5%
- Other 0%
- Workforce sensor 8%
- Strategic advisor 21%
- Functional leader 22%
- Executive coach 17%
- Talent architect 17%
- Board liaison 10%

Figure 16.17

Percentage of Time CHROs Spend in Each Role

the business. Playing the role of talent architect requires that CHROs help the executive team see the importance of talent, identify present and future talent gaps, and come to own the talent agenda. One CHRO described the importance of this role this way:

> Keeping the senior team focused on the strategic talent needs of the business allows proper identification of talent gaps and future needs, thus allowing time to develop best talent and design appropriate experiential assignments.[23]

Counselor/Confidante/Coach
A role of the CHRO that focuses on counseling or coaching team members or resolving interpersonal or political conflicts among team members.

CHROs report spending as much time in the role of **counselor/confidante/coach** as they do in the talent architect role (17%), and a number of CHROs listed this role as one of the roles with the greatest impact. This role seemingly is a broad one, and it can entail anything from behavioral or performance counseling to being the personal sounding board for the CEO. Perhaps as pressure mounts on CEOs from investors and analysts, the CHRO is the most trusted advisor that can be counted on to give personal advice or simply to listen to the CEO's problems. One poignant comment regarding this role was:

> If I do my job right, I am the copper wire that connects all the outlets of the firm together effectively. This includes OD work (which some might put in the strategic advisor category), performance counseling and relationship building, business consulting and the strategic elements of talent acquisition and planning.[24]

Leader of the HR Function
A role of the CHRO that focuses on working with HR team members regarding the development, design, and delivery of HR services.

The **leader of the HR function** is the role in which CHROs spent the most time, but it is not seen as one that has the greatest impact. This role deals with ensuring that the HR function is aligning its activities and priorities toward the needs of the business, and it usually entails meeting with direct reports to provide guidance and check on progress. However, CHROs increasingly rely on their direct reports to design and deliver HR services while they shift their attention to advising and counseling the top executive team.

Often this counselor/confidante/coach role entails coaching senior leaders regarding their communications style, and particularly warning them when their messages might be misinterpreted by those lower in the organizations.

Liaison to the Board
A role of the CHRO that focuses on preparation for board meetings, phone calls with board members, and attendance at board meetings.

Liaison to the board entails all of the activities in which CHROs engage with the board of directors, including discussions of executive compensation, CEO performance, CEO succession, and performance of other members of the executive leadership team. This role is increasing in importance, although it has a long way to go before equaling the strategic advisor, talent architect, and counselor/confidante/coach roles.

Workforce Sensor
A role of the CHRO that focuses on identifying workforce morale issues or concerns.

The role of **workforce sensors** entails taking the pulse of the employee population to identify any morale or motivation issues. This is a role in which CHROs do not spend much time, and few viewed it as having the greatest impact on the business.

Finally, CHROs to some extent become the face of the organization to outside constituents such as labor unions, nongovernmental organizations, and the press. They spend the least amount of time in the **representative of the firm** role (see Table 16.5).

Representative of the Firm
A role of the CHRO that focuses on activities with external stakeholders, such as lobbying, speaking to outside groups, etc.

The new strategic role for HRM presents both opportunities and challenges. HRM has the chance to profoundly impact the way organizations compete through people. On the other hand, with this opportunity comes serious responsibility and accountability.[25] HRM functions of the future must consist of individuals who view themselves as businesspeople who happen to work in an HRM function, rather than HRM people who happen to work in a business.

Table 16.5
Roles of the CHRO

Strategic advisor to the executive team—activities focused specifically on the formulation and implementation of the firm's strategy.

Counselor/confidante/coach to the executive team—activities focused on counseling or coaching team members or resolving interpersonal or political conflicts among team members.

Liaison to the board of directors—preparation for board meetings, phone calls with board members, attendance at board meetings.

Talent architect—activities focused on building and identifying the human capital critical to the present and future of the firm.

Leader of the HR function—working with HR team members regarding the development, design, and delivery of HR services.

Workforce sensor—activities focused on identifying workforce morale issues or concerns.

Representative of the firm—activities with external stakeholders, such as lobbying, speaking to outside groups, etc.

A LOOK BACK

Tech start-up GitHub has been forced to grow up, and the 250-person company seems to have taken Mr. Andreessen's advice to heart when it comes to HR. The company now has almost a dozen people devoted to developing leadership training programs, organizational design, and conflict resolution. They also have an individual formally trained in conflict resolution. In addition, the company has begun developing a formal organizational structure with clear reporting relationships and distinct managerial predictions.

Start-up tech firms often resist such moves for fear that the rules, structures, and job descriptions will stifle innovation and cost too much money. However, as the GitHub story shows, often such costs serve as necessary investments to build a successful company over the long term.

QUESTIONS

1. Why is it important for start-ups to pay attention to people issues?
2. How can having a good HR function help start-ups to grow profitably?
3. How do you think HR differs in large companies like IBM or Goodyear compared to start-ups like GitHub?

SUMMARY

The roles required of the HRM function have changed as people have become recognized as a true source of competitive advantage. This has required a transformation of the HRM function from focusing solely on transactional activities to an increasing involvement in strategic activities. In fact, according to a recent study, 64% of HR executives said that their HRM function is in a process of transformation.[26] The strategic management of the HRM function will determine whether HRM will transform itself to a true strategic partner or simply be blown up.

In this chapter we have explored the various changing roles of the HRM function. HRM today must play roles as an administrative expert, employee advocate, change agent, and strategic partner. The function must also deliver transactional, traditional, and transformational services and activities to the firm, and it must be both efficient and effective. HR executives must strategically manage the HRM function just as the firm must be strategically managed. This requires that HRM develop measures of the function's performance through customer surveys and analytical methods. These measures can form the basis for planning ways to improve performance. HRM performance can increase through new structures for the function, through using reengineering and information technology, and through outsourcing.

KEY TERMS

Audit approach, 671

Analytic approach, 673

Outsourcing, 679

Reengineering, 680

New technologies, 683

Transaction processing, 683

Decision support systems, 683

Expert systems, 683

Strategic advisor, 691

Talent architect, 691

Counselor/confidante/coach, 692

Leader of the HR function, 692

Liaison to the board, 692

Workforce sensor, 692

Representative of the firm, 692

DISCUSSION QUESTIONS

1. Why have the roles and activities of the HRM function changed over the past 20 to 30 years? What has been driving this change? How effectively do you think HRM has responded?

2. How can the processes for strategic management discussed in Chapter 2 be transplanted to manage the HRM function?

3. Why do you think that few companies take the time to determine the effectiveness of HRM practices? Should a company be concerned about evaluating HRM practices? Why? What might people working in the HRM function gain by evaluating the function?

4. How might imaging technology be useful for recruitment? For training? For benefits administration? For performance management?

5. Employees in your company currently choose and enroll in benefits programs after reading communications

brochures, completing enrollment forms, and sending them to their HR rep. A temporary staff has to be hired to process the large amount of paperwork that is generated. Enrollment forms need to be checked, sorted, batched, sent to data entry, keypunched, returned, and filed. The process is slow and prone to errors. How could you use process reengineering to make benefits enrollment more efficient and effective?

6. Some argue that outsourcing an activity is bad because the activity is no longer a means of distinguishing the firm from competitors. (All competitors can buy the same service from the same provider, so it cannot be a source of competitive advantage.) Is this true? If so, why would a firm outsource any activity?

SELF-ASSESSMENT EXERCISE

Additional assignable self-assessments available in Connect.

How ethical are you? Read each of the following descriptions. For each, circle whether you believe the behavior described is ethical or unethical.

1. A company president found that a competitor had made an important scientific discovery that would sharply reduce the profits of his own company. The president hired a key employee of the competitor in an attempt to learn the details of the discovery.

    Ethical   Unethical

2. To increase profits, a general manager used a production process that exceeded legal limits for environmental pollution.

    Ethical   Unethical

3. Because of pressure from her brokerage firm, a stockbroker recommended a type of bond that she did not consider to be a good investment.

    Ethical   Unethical

4. A small business received one-fourth of its revenues in the form of cash. On the company's income tax forms, the owner reported only one-half of the cash receipts.

    Ethical   Unethical

5. A corporate executive promoted a loyal friend and competent manager to the position of divisional vice president in preference to a better qualified manager with whom she had no close ties.

    Ethical   Unethical

6. An employer received applications for a supervisor's position from two equally qualified applicants. The employer hired the male applicant because he thought some employees might resent being supervised by a female.

    Ethical   Unethical

7. An engineer discovered what he perceived to be a product design flaw that constituted a safety hazard. His company declined to correct the flaw. The engineer decided to keep quiet, rather than taking his complaint outside the company.

    Ethical   Unethical

8. A comptroller selected a legal method of financial reporting that concealed some embarrassing financial facts. Otherwise, those facts would have been public knowledge.
   Ethical
   Unethical

9. A company paid a $350,000 "consulting" fee to an official of a foreign country. In return, the official promised to help the company obtain a contract that should produce a $10 million profit for the company.
   Ethical
   Unethical

10. A member of a corporation's board of directors learned that his company intended to announce a stock split and increase its dividend. On the basis of this favorable information, the director bought additional shares of the company's stock. Following the announcement of the information, he sold the stock at a gain.
    Ethical
    Unethical

Now score your results. How many actions did you judge to be unethical?

All of these actions are unethical. The more of the actions you judged to be unethical, the better your understanding of ethical business behavior.

SOURCE: Based on S. Morris et al., "A Test of Environmental, Situational, and Personal Influences on the Ethical Intentions of CEOs," *Business and Society* 34 (1995), pp. 119–47.

EXERCISING STRATEGY

Transforming the Business and HR at Xerox

In 1958, Xerox launched the Xerox 914, the first automatic, plain-paper office copier. This product went on to become the top-selling industrial product of all time. Xerox's successful xerography technology gave it a sustainable competitive advantage that endured for years. However, all good things must come to an end, and in Xerox's case, that end was the late 1990s. By 2000, Xerox experienced its biggest slide in history, and the consensus among analysts within the industry was that Xerox was working with "an unsustainable business model," meaning unless things changed drastically, Xerox would soon cease to exist. In 2000 Xerox had $17.1 billion in debt, with only $154 million in cash on hand. By 2001, Xerox's stock, which had peaked at $63, fell to about $4—a loss of 90% of its market capitalization. And as if that was not enough, it also faced an accounting investigation by the Securities and Exchange Commission for how it accounted for its customer leases on copiers.

Enter new VP of HR Pat Nazemetz in 1999 and new CEO Anne Mulcahy in 2000 to try to right a sinking ship. Mulcahy put the company on a starvation diet. This entailed selling major operations in China and Hong Kong, reducing global headcount to 61,100 from 91,500 through selloffs, early retirements, and layoffs, and implementing drastic cost controls. While Mulcahy's strategy has brought Xerox back to life (2003 saw Xerox triple its net income to $360 million) as an organization, the HR function had to drive the change in the business while simultaneously transforming the function.

While many HR functions look to outsource, Xerox transformed its HR function largely internally. According to Nazemetz, outsourcing providers say " 'Let us in, let us take over your HR function and we can take 10% to 30% out of your cost base.' We began trimming down, finding synergies and opportunities to get more efficient. We found the savings ourselves."

The largest single savings came from consolidating and expanding the HR Service Center. The Center began with purely transactional work (e.g., address changes), then added web-based processes to handle routine work. The Center now conducts research and analysis to HR operations and handles employee-relations issues. This has enabled HR to reduce headcount without reducing levels of service.

Also, as with any organization that has shed 30% of its workforce, employee morale was and continues to be an issue. Even before the fall, HR had been taking the pulse of employees through their "hearts and minds" surveys. This intranet-based survey taps into a number of employee attitudes and seeks to identify the problem areas for HR and line executives to focus on. Employees have noted concerns with items like "Company supports risk-taking," "Company considers impact on employees," "Senior-management behavior is consistent with words," and "Trust level is high."

"People often ask me how Xerox has found success," says Mulcahy. "My answer is that you have to have a strategy and a plan, but [more importantly], what you really need is excellence of execution, and that starts and ends with a talented, motivated group of people aligned around a common set of goals. Our HR people came through with a series of alignment workshops and retention incentives just when we needed them [to] make Xerox the stronger, better company it is today."

QUESTIONS

1. After having gone through the massive downsizing, morale obviously has presented challenges. While Xerox employees seem to understand the need for change (minds), they may not emotionally embrace it (hearts). How can Xerox gain both "hearts" and "minds"?

2. Xerox's HR function focuses on three initiatives: (a) employee value proposition (what can employees expect from the company, and what can the company expect from employees?), (b) performance culture (how can the company develop a culture that encourages continuous improvement and high performance from all employees?), and (c) "three exceptional candidates" (how can HR deliver a pipeline of three-deep bench talent for every position within the organization?). From everything you have learned, how might Xerox address each of these issues?

MANAGING PEOPLE

Saving Starbucks' Soul

Chairman Howard Schultz is on a mission to take his company back to its roots. Oh, yeah—he also wants to triple sales in five years.

"A heady aroma of coffee reached out and drew me in. I stepped inside and saw what looked like a temple for the worship of coffee . . . it was my Mecca. I had arrived."—Howard Schultz on his first visit to Starbucks in 1981.

On April 3, Starbucks launches a pair of confections called Dulce de Leche Latte and Dulce de Leche Frappuccino. A 16-oz. Grande latte has a robust 440 calories (about the same as two packages of M&M's) and costs about $4.50 in New York City—or about three times as much as McDonald's most expensive premium coffee. Starbucks Corp. describes its latest concoctions, which took 18 months to perfect, this way: "Topped with whipped cream and a dusting of toffee sprinkles, Starbucks' version of this traditional delicacy is a luxurious tasty treat."

If you find yourself at Starbucks in the next few weeks, letting a Dulce de Leche Latte slide over your taste buds, you might wonder how this drink came to be. It's a tale worth hearing. On the surface it's a story about how the Starbucks marketing machine conjures and sells café romance to millions of people around the world. On a deeper level it's a story about how a company, along with its messianic leader, is struggling to hold on to its soul.

Ask Schultz for the key to Starbucks and he'll tell you it's all about storytelling. Starbucks is centered on two oft-repeated tales: Schultz's trip to Seattle in 1981, where he first enjoyed gourmet coffee, and a 1983 trip to Milan, where he discovered espresso bar culture. Not only are these journeys useful touchstones for recruits, they also provide the original marketing story for a company that prides itself on giving customers an authentic experience. "The one common thread to the success of these stories and the company itself," says Schultz, "is that they have to be true—and they have to be authentic."

TRUE BELIEVERS

Stories alone aren't enough, though, to fuel Starbucks' other obsession: to grow really, really big. By 2012, Schultz aims to nearly triple annual sales, to $23.3 billion. The company also plans to have 40,000 stores world wide, up from 13,500 today, not long after that, to hit its profit targets.

Starbucks has become expert at something that's decidedly unromantic—streamlining operations. Over the past 10 years the company has redesigned the space behind the counter to boost barista efficiency. Automatic espresso machines speed the time it takes to serve up a shot. Coffee is vacuum-sealed, making it easier to ship over long distances. To boost sales, the company sells everything from breath mints to CDs to notebooks. Add it up and you have an experience that's nothing like the worn wooden counters of the first store in Pike Place Market or an Italian espresso bar.

Somewhere along the way that disconnect began to gnaw at Schultz. Most recently it manifested itself in a note he wrote to his senior team. The Valentine's Day memo, which leaked to the web, cut to the heart of what he sees as the company's dilemma. "We have had to make a series of decisions," Schultz wrote, "that, in retrospect, have led to the watering down of the Starbucks experience, and what some might call the commoditization of our brand."

Now, Schultz is asking his lieutenants to redouble their efforts to return to their roots. "We're constantly—I don't want to say battling—but we don't want to be that big company that's corporate and slick," says Michelle Gass, senior vice-president and chief merchant for global products. "We don't. We still think about ourselves as a small entrepreneurial company." That's a tricky business when you have 150,000 employees in 39 countries. But keeping that coffee joie de vivre alive inside Starbucks is crucial to Schultz's entire philosophy. Who better to sell something than a true believer?

In 2004, Starbucks introduced something called the Coffee Master program for its employees. It's a kind of extra-credit course that teaches the staff how to discern the subtleties of regional flavor. Graduates (there are now 25,000) earn a special black apron and an insignia on their business cards. The highlight is the "cupping ceremony," a tasting ritual traditionally used by coffee traders. After the grounds have steeped in boiling water, tasters "crest" the mixture, penetrating the crust on top with a spoon and inhaling the aroma. As employees slurp the brew, a Starbucks Coffee Educator encourages them to taste a Kenyan coffee's "citrusy" notes or the "mushroomy" flavor of a Sumatran blend.

If the ritual reminds you of a wine tasting, that's intentional. Schultz has long wanted to emulate the wine business.

Winemakers, after all, command a premium by focusing on provenance: the region of origin, the vineyard, and, of course, the grape that gives the wine its particular notes—a story, in other words. Bringing wine's cachet to coffee would help take the brand upmarket and allow Starbucks to sell premium beans.

The product and marketing people call the strategy "Geography is a Flavor." And in 2005 they began selling this new story with whole-bean coffee. The company reorganized the menu behind the counter, grouping coffees by geography instead of by "smooth" or "bold." It replaced the colorful Starbucks coffee bags with clean white packages emblazoned with colored bands representing the region of origin. Later, for those connoisseurs willing to pay $28 a pound, Starbucks introduced single-origin beans called "Black Apron Exclusives."

The next step was to reach the masses who buy drinks in the stores. The team decided to launch a series of in-store promotions, each with a new set of drinks, that would communicate regional idiosyncrasies to customers. The first promotion, the team decided, would highlight Central and South America, where Starbucks buys more than 70% of its beans.

The sort of authenticity Schultz loves to talk about is hard to pull off when you're the size of Starbucks. Telling a story to a mass audience sometimes requires smoothing over inconvenient cultural nuances. Plus, the marketing folks have to work quickly to stay abreast of beverage trends, not to mention ahead of such rivals as Dunkin' Donuts and McDonald's. Diving deep is not an option.

A year ago, 10 Starbucks marketers and designers got on a plane and went looking for inspiration in Costa Rica. "It's being able to say: This is how and why this [drink] is made," says Angie McKenzie, who runs new product design. "Not because someone told us or we read it somewhere." The Starbucks team spent five days in Costa Rica, traveling on a minivan owned by TAM Tours. Later, a smaller group toured Mexico City and Oaxaca as well.

MADE IN CHINA

The mission was to find products that would evoke an authentic vibe in the United States. That's harder than it sounds. Philip Clark, a merchandising executive, wanted to sell traditional Costa Rican mugs. But the ones typically used to drink coffee were drab and brown; they wouldn't pop on store shelves. Plus, they broke easily. Then he found Cecilia de Figueres, who handpaints ceramic mugs in a mountainside studio an hour from the capital, San Jose. The artist favors bright floral patterns; they would pop nicely. Starbucks paid de Figueres a flat fee for her designs. Each mug will have a tag bearing her name and likeness; on the bottom it will say "Made in China."

Starbucks will weave artisans and other Costa Ricans into the in-store promotional campaign. Painter Eloy Zuñiga Guevara will appear on a poster with a decidedly homespun Latin aesthetic. (And if customers want some authenticity to take home with them, they can buy one of five paintings of Costa Rican farmers that Guevara produced for Starbucks. They will sell for $25 apiece.) A second poster will feature Costa Rican coffee farmers from whom Starbucks buys beans. A third will show a grandmotherly figure cooking up dulce de leche on a gas stove. (She's a paid model from Seattle.) Each poster will feature the tagline "I am Starbucks."

Having devised a story, Starbucks needed a drink that would say "Latin America." Beverage brainstorming takes place in the Liquid Lab, an airy space painted in Starbucks' familiar blue, green, and orange hues. The room features huge bulletin boards plastered with the latest beverage trends. In this case it didn't take an anthropologist to figure out which drink Starbucks should use to promote its Latin American theme.

Dulce de leche is a caramel-and-milk dessert enjoyed throughout much of the region. What's more, Häagen-Dazs introduced dulce de leche ice cream in 1998, and Starbucks followed suit with its own ice cream in 1999. So Americans are familiar with the flavor, says McKenzie, but "it still has a nice exotic edge to it." Besides, she adds, caramel and milk go great with coffee.

Even so, concocting a drink is never simple at Starbucks. The research-and-development department routinely tackles 70 beverage projects a year, with 8 of them leading to new drinks. A drink must not only appeal to a broad swath of coffee drinkers but also be easy for a barista to make quickly so as to maximize sales per store (hello, Wall Street). "The store . . . is a little manufacturing plant," says Gass, and yet it must seem as though the drink is being handcrafted specially for the customer (hello, Howard Schultz).

Creating the Dulce de Leche Latte and Frappuccino fell to Debbie Ismon, a 26-year-old beverage developer who holds a degree in food science and has worked at Starbucks for 2 1/2 years. In late June 2006, the design team brought her a small sample they'd whipped up that they felt embodied the right tastes, plus a written description of the characteristics they hoped to see. For the next four months, Ismon fiddled with various ratios of caramel, cooked milk, and sweetness "notes." After the design group decided which version tasted most "in-concept," Ismon mixed up three different flavors for the big taste test. One hundred or so random Starbucks employees filed in, sampled the drinks, and rated them on computer screens. The process was repeated two more times for each drink. Finally, 18 months after starting the process, Starbucks had its two latest premium beverages.

If previous drinks, such as Caramel Macchiato, are any guide, Starbucks' Dulce de Leche drinks will sell briskly. That should please Wall Street and perhaps even help perk up the stock, which is down 20% from its May 2006 high on worries that operating margins are falling and that Starbucks could miss its ambitious growth targets.

And as you wait in line for your Dulce de Leche Latte, you might ask yourself: Are you paying $4.50 for a caffeine jolt and caramel topping? Or have you simply been dazzled by Howard Schultz's storytelling magic?

QUESTIONS

1. What are some of the HRM issues inherent in Howard Schultz's concerns?

2. How would an effective strategic HRM function contribute to keeping Starbucks on track?

HR IN SMALL BUSINESS

Employees Make a Difference at Amy's Ice Creams

One of the bright spots for hungry people in Austin, Texas, is Amy's Ice Creams—its factory on Burnet Road or one of several Amy's stores. Founder Amy Miller, who dropped out of medical school to start the business, figures it is just another way to "make a difference in people's lives," offering customers a fun place to celebrate or cheer up.

Miller had been paying med school with a job at Steve's Ice Cream, but when the company was sold, she thought the new owners were too stodgy, so she opened her own ice cream shop. Given the motivation to strike out on her own, it's not surprising that her goal is to manage her employees in a different way, one that combines informal fun with care for others.

The spirit of fun is defined by the employee selection process Miller invented. When interviewing candidates, Miller hands them a white paper bag with the instruction to "make something creative" and show her later. One applicant used it to make a hot-air balloon. Another put food in a bag, gave it to a homeless person, took a photo of the gift, and put the photo in the bag to return as the creative offering.

Job design also plays up the fun. Amy's prized employees don't just scoop up ice cream but also come up with ways to create a playful atmosphere. The company encourages workers to juggle shakers or give away a scoop of ice cream to a customer who is willing to sing and dance.

While the two painted concrete cows that sit in front of the Amy's factory are an emblem of the company's commitment to fun, its commitment to caring has a more uplifting sign: Amy's Ice Creams funded the construction of a room in a local children's cancer care center. The room resembles an ice cream shop and includes freezers stocked with ice cream—a treat that patients can share with visiting family members.

Service to the community is also connected to employee engagement. At Amy's, the employees choose the charities the company will support. At a prom hosted by Amy's every year, the company selects a King and Queen to honor based on which employees did the most company-sponsored charitable work. In this way, employee rewards are tied to the company's value.

Fun and community service aren't just a way to be nice; they also have made Amy's Ice Creams a company ice cream lovers care to buy from. The company reaps millions of dollars in sales and has expanded the number of locations to meet growing demand in Austin as well as in Houston and San Antonio. Still, it's not just about the revenues. Co-owner (and Amy's husband) Steve Simmons told a reporter, "We never want to be a mega-company. When we don't know employees' names, there's a problem."

QUESTIONS

1. Which elements of a customer-oriented HRM perspective does Amy's Ice Creams seem to have? (See Figure 16.2.)
2. Suppose Amy's hired you as a consultant to evaluate whether the company has an effective HRM function. Which outcomes would you look for? How would you measure them?
3. Generally, a small ice cream shop such as Amy's cannot afford to pay store workers very high wages. How well do you think the company can achieve high employee satisfaction without high pay? What can it do to foster satisfaction besides the efforts described here? How could e-HRM support these efforts?

NOTES

1. P. Wright, S. Snell, and P. Jacobsen, "Current Approaches to HR Strategies: Inside-Out vs. Outside-In," *Human Resource Planning* 27 (2004), pp. 36–46.

2. Personal communication, June 2010.

3. A. S. Tsui and L. R. Gomez-Mejia, "Evaluating HR Effectiveness," in *Human Resource Management: Evolving Roles and*

Responsibilities, ed. L. Dyer (Washington, DC: Bureau of National Affairs, 1988), pp. 1-187–1-227.

4. D. Ulrich, "Measuring Human Resources: An Overview of Practice and a Prescription for Results," *Human Resource Management* 36, no. 3 (1997), pp. 303–20.

5. P. Wright, G. McMahan, S. Snell, and B. Gerhart, "Comparing Line and HR Executives' Perceptions of HR Effectiveness: Services, Roles, and Contributions," CAHRS (Center for Advanced Human Resource Studies) working paper 98-29, School of ILR, Cornell University, Ithaca, NY.

6. J. C. Erfurt, A. Foote, and M. A. Heirich, "The Cost-Effectiveness of Worksite Wellness Programs," *Personnel Psychology* 15 (1992), p. 22.

7. T. H. Davenport, J. Haris, and J. Shapiro, "Competing on Talent Analytics," *Harvard Business Review,* October 2010, pp. 52–59.

8. P. Wright, G. McMahan, S. Snell, and B. Gerhart, *Strategic HRM: Building Human Capital and Organizational Capability,* Technical report. Cornell University, Ithaca, NY, 1998.

9. T. B. Kinni, "A Reengineering Primer," *Quality Digest,* January 1994, pp. 26–30; "Reengineering Is Helping Health of Hospitals and Its Patients," *Total Quality Newsletter,* February 1994, p. 5; R. Recardo, "Process Reengineering in a Finance Division," *Journal for Quality and Participation,* June 1994, pp. 70–73.

10. L. Quillen, "Human Resource Computerization: A Dollar and Cents Approach," *Personnel Journal,* July 1989, pp. 74–77.

11. S. Greengard, "New Technology Is HR's Route to Reengineering," *Personnel Journal,* July 1994, pp. 32c–32o.

12. R. Broderick and J. W. Boudreau, "Human Resource Management, Information Technology, and the Competitive Edge," *Academy of Management Executive* 6 (1992), pp. 7–17.

13. S. Shrivastava and J. Shaw, "Liberating HR through Technology," *Human Resource Management* 42, no. 3 (2003), pp. 201–17.

14. C. O'Reilly and P. Caldwell, *Cypress Semiconductor (A): Vision, Values, and Killer Software* (Stanford University Case Study, HR-8A, 1998).

15. "61 Percent of Americans Consider Themselves Overworked and 86 Percent Are Not Satisfied with Their Job, According to Monster's 2004 Work/Life Balance Survey," *Business Wire,* August 3, 2004.

16. G. McMahan and R. Woodman, "The Current Practice of Organization Development within the Firm: A Survey of Large Industrial Corporations," *Group and Organization Studies* 17 (1992), pp. 117–34.

17. B. Becker, M. Huselid, and D. Ulrich, *The HR Scorecard: Linking People, Strategy, and Performance* (Cambridge, MA: HBS Press, 2001).

18. D. Ulrich and A. Yeung, "A Shared Mindset," *Personnel Administrator,* March 1989, pp. 38–45.

19. G. Jones and P. Wright, "An Economic Approach to Conceptualizing the Utility of Human Resource Management Practices," *Research in Personnel/Human Resources* 10 (1992), pp. 271–99.

20. R. Schuler and J. Walker, "Human Resources Strategy: Focusing on Issues and Actions," *Organizational Dynamics,* Summer 1990, pp. 5–19.

21. Company documents.

22. P. Wright, "Strategies and Challenges of the Chief Human Resource Officer: Results of the First Annual Cornell/CAHRS Survey of CHROs," Technical report, 2009.

23. Ibid.

24. Ibid.

25. J. Paauwe, *Human Resource Management and Performance: Unique Approaches for Achieving Long-Term Viability* (Oxford: Oxford University Press, 2004).

26. S. Csoka and B. Hackett, *Transforming the HR Function for Global Business Success* (New York: Conference Board, 1998), Report 1209-19RR.

GLOSSARY

9-box grid A three-by-three matrix used by groups of managers and executives to compare employees within one department, function, division, or the entire company.

Acceptability The extent to which a performance measure is deemed to be satisfactory or adequate by those who use it.

Action learning Teams work on an actual business problem, commit to an action plan, and are accountable for carrying out the plan.

Action plan Document summarizing what the trainee and manager will do to ensure that training transfers to the job.

Action steps The part of a written affirmative plan that specifies what an employer plans to do to reduce underutilization of protected groups.

Adventure learning Learning focused on the development of teamwork and leadership skills by using structured outdoor activities.

Agency shop A union security provision that requires an employee to pay union membership dues but not to join the union.

Agent In agency theory, a person (e.g., a manager) who is expected to act on behalf of a principal (e.g., an owner).

Alternative dispute resolution (ADR) A method of resolving disputes that does not rely on the legal system. Often proceeds through the four stages of open door policy, peer review, mediation, and arbitration.

Alternative work arrangements Independent contractors, on-call workers, temporary workers, and contract company workers who are not employed full-time by the company.

Americans with Disabilities Act (ADA) A 1990 act prohibiting individuals with disabilities from being discriminated against in the workplace.

Analytic approach Type of assessment of HRM effectiveness that involves determining the impact of, or the financial costs and benefits of, a program or practice.

Appraisal politics A situation in which evaluators purposefully distort a rating to achieve personal or company goals.

Apprenticeship A work-study training method with both on-the-job and classroom training.

Arbitration A procedure for resolving collective bargaining impasses by which an arbitrator chooses a solution to the dispute.

Assessment Collecting information and providing feedback to employees about their behavior, communication style, or skills.

Assessment center A process in which multiple raters evaluate employees' performance on a number of exercises.

Associate union membership A form of union membership by which the union receives dues in exchange for services (e.g., health insurance, credit cards) but does not provide representation in collective bargaining.

Attitudinal structuring The aspect of the labor–management negotiation process that refers to the relationship and level of trust between the negotiators.

Audit approach Type of assessment of HRM effectiveness that involves review of customer satisfaction or key indicators (e.g., turnover rate, average days to fill a position) related to an HRM functional area (e.g., recruiting, training).

Avatars Computer depictions of humans that can be used as imaginary coaches, co-workers, and customers in simulations.

Balanced scorecard A means of performance measurement that gives managers a chance to look at their company from the perspectives of internal and external customers, employees, and shareholders.

Bench strength The business strategy of having a pool of talented employees who are ready when needed to step into a new position within the organization.

Benchmarking Comparing an organization's practices against those of the competition.

Big data Information merged from a variety of sources, including HR databases, corporate financial statements, and employee surveys, to make evidence-based HR decisions and show that HR practices can influence the organization's bottom line.

Blended learning Delivering content and instruction with a combination of technology-based and face-to-face methods.

Bona fide occupational qualification (BFOQ) A job qualification based on race, sex, religion, and so on that an employer asserts is a necessary qualification for the job.

Calibration meetings A way to discuss employees' performance with the goal of ensuring that similar standards are applied to their evaluations.

Career support Coaching, protection, sponsorship, and providing challenging assignments, exposure, and visibility.

Cash balance plan Retirement plan in which the employer sets up an individual account for each employee and contributes a percentage of the employee's salary; the account earns interest at a predetermined rate.

Centralization Degree to which decision-making authority resides at the top of the organizational chart.

Change The adoption of a new idea or behavior by a company.

Checkoff provision A union contract provision that requires an employer to deduct union dues from employees' paychecks.

Closed shop A union security provision requiring a person to be a union member before being hired. Illegal under NLRA.

Cloud computing A computing system that provides information technology infrastructure over a network in a self-service, modifiable, and on-demand model.

Coach A peer or manager who works with an employee to motivate her, help her develop skills, and provide reinforcement and feedback.

Cognitive ability tests Tests that include three dimensions: verbal comprehension, quantitative ability, and reasoning ability.

Communities of practice Groups of employees who work together, learn from each other, and develop a common understanding of how to get work accomplished.

Comparable worth A public policy that advocates remedies for any undervaluation of women's jobs (also called *pay equity*).

Compa-ratio An index of the correspondence between actual and intended pay.

Compensable factors The characteristics of jobs that an organization values and chooses to pay for.

Competencies Sets of skills, knowledge, and abilities and personal characteristics that enable employees to perform their jobs.

Competency model Identifies and provides a description of competencies that are common for an entire occupation, organization, job family, or specific job.

Competitiveness A company's ability to maintain and gain market share in its industry.

Concentration strategy A strategy focusing on increasing market share, reducing costs, or creating and maintaining a market niche for products and services.

Concurrent validation A criterion-related validity study in which a test is administered to all the people currently in a job and then incumbents' scores are correlated with existing measures of their performance on the job.

Consolidated Omnibus Budget Reconciliation Act (COBRA) The 1985 act that requires employers to permit employees to extend their health insurance coverage at group rates for up to 36 months following a qualifying event, such as a layoff.

Content validation A test validation strategy performed by demonstrating that the items, questions, or problems posed by a test are a representative sample of the kinds of situations or problems that occur on the job.

Continuous learning A learning system that requires employees to understand the entire work process and expects them to acquire new skills, apply them on the job, and share what they have learned with other employees.

Coordination training Training a team in how to share information and decision-making responsibilities to maximize team performance.

Corporate campaigns Union activities designed to exert public, financial, or political pressure on employers during the union-organizing process.

Counselor/confidante/coach to the executive team A role of the CHRO that focuses on counseling or coaching team members or resolving interpersonal or political conflicts among team members.

Criterion-related validity A method of establishing the validity of a personnel selection method by showing a substantial correlation between test scores and job performance scores.

Cross-cultural preparation The process of educating employees (and their families) who are given an assignment in a foreign country.

Cross-training Training in which team members understand and practice each other's skills so that members are prepared to step in and take another member's place should he or she temporarily or permanently leave the team.

Decision support systems Problem-solving systems that usually include a "what-if" feature that allows users to see how outcomes change when assumptions or data change.

Delayering Reducing the number of job levels within an organization.

Departmentalization Degree to which work units are grouped based on functional similarity or similarity of workflow.

Development The acquisition of knowledge, skills, and behaviors that improve an employee's ability to meet changes in job requirements and in client and customer demands.

Development planning system A system to retain and motivate employees by identifying and meeting their development needs (also called *career management systems*).

Direct applicants People who apply for a job vacancy without prompting from the organization.

Disparate impact A theory of discrimination based on facially neutral employment practices that disproportionately exclude a protected group from employment opportunities.

Disparate treatment A theory of discrimination based on different treatment given to individuals because of their race, color, religion, sex, national origin, age, or disability status.

Distributive bargaining The part of the labor–management negotiation process that focuses on dividing a fixed economic "pie."

Diversity training Refers to learning efforts that are designed to change employees' attitudes about diversity and/or develop skills needed to work with a diverse workforce.

Downsizing The planned elimination of large numbers of personnel, designed to enhance organizational effectiveness.

Downward move A job change involving a reduction in an employee's level of responsibility and authority.

Due process policies Policies by which a company formally lays out the steps an employee can take to appeal a termination decision.

Duty of fair representation The National Labor Relations Act requirement that all bargaining unit members have equal access to and representation by the union.

Efficiency wage theory A theory stating that wage influences worker productivity.

E-learning Instruction and delivery of training by computers through the Internet or company intranet.

Employee assistance programs (EAPs) Employer programs that attempt to ameliorate problems encountered by workers who are drug dependent, alcoholic, or psychologically troubled.

Employee engagement The degree to which employees are fully involved in their work and the strength of their job and company commitment.

Employee Retirement Income Security Act (ERISA) The 1974 act that increased the fiduciary responsibilities of pension plan trustees, established vesting rights and portability provisions, and established the Pension Benefit Guaranty Corporation (PBGC).

Employee stock ownership plan (ESOP) An employee ownership plan that provides employers certain tax and financial advantages when stock is granted to employees.

Employment-at-will doctrine The doctrine that, in the absence of a specific contract, either an employer or employee could sever the employment relationship at any time.

Empowering Giving employees the responsibility and authority to make decisions.

Equal employment opportunity (EEO) The government's attempt to ensure that all individuals have an equal opportunity for employment, regardless of race, color, religion, sex, age, disability, or national origin.

Equal Employment Opportunity Commission (EEOC) The government commission established to ensure that all individuals have an equal opportunity for employment, regardless of race, color, religion, sex, age, disability, or national origin.

Ergonomics The interface between individuals' physiological characteristics and the physical work environment.

Ethics The fundamental principles of right and wrong by which employees and companies interact.

Evidence-based HR Demonstrating that human resource practices have a positive influence on the company's bottom line or key stakeholders (employees, customers, community, shareholders).

Exempt Employees who are not covered by the Fair Labor Standards Act. Exempt employees are not eligible for overtime pay.

Expatriate Employee sent by his or her company to manage operations in a different country.

Expectancy theory The theory that says motivation is a function of valence, instrumentality, and expectancy.

Experiential learning Training programs in which trainees gain knowledge and theory, participate in behavioral simulations, analyze the activity, and connect the theory and activity with on-the-job situations.

Expert systems Computer systems incorporating the decision rules of people recognized as experts in a certain area.

Explicit knowledge Knowledge that is well-documented and easily transferred to other persons.

External analysis Examining the organization's operating environment to identify strategic opportunities and threats.

External growth strategy An emphasis on acquiring vendors and suppliers or buying businesses that allow a company to expand into new markets.

External labor market Persons outside the firm who are actively seeking employment.

Fact finder A person who reports on the reasons for a labor–management dispute, the views and arguments of both sides, and a nonbinding recommendation for settling the dispute.

Fair Labor Standards Act (FLSA)   The 1938 law that established the minimum wage and overtime pay.

Family and Medical Leave Act   The 1993 act that requires employers with 50 or more employees to provide up to 12 weeks of unpaid leave after childbirth or adoption; to care for a seriously ill child, spouse, or parent; or for an employee's own serious illness.

Financial Accounting Statement (FAS) 106   The rule issued by the Financial Accounting Standards Board in 1993 requiring companies to fund benefits provided after retirement on an accrual rather than a pay-as-you-go basis and to enter these future cost obligations on their financial statements.

Forecasting   The attempts to determine the supply of and demand for various types of human resources to predict areas within the organization where there will be future labor shortages or surpluses.

Formal education programs   Employee development programs, including short courses offered by consultants or universities, executive MBA programs, and university programs.

Formal training   Training and development programs and courses that are developed and organized by the company.

Four-fifths rule   A rule that states that an employment test has disparate impact if the hiring rate for a minority group is less than four-fifths, or 80 %, of the hiring rate for the majority group.

Frame of reference   A standard point that serves as a comparison for other points and thus provides meaning.

Gamification   Game-based strategies applied to performance management to make it a fun, effective, transparent, and inclusive process for employees and managers.

Gainsharing   A form of group compensation based on group or plant performance (rather than organizationwide profits) that does not become part of the employee's base salary.

General duty clause   The provision of the Occupational Safety and Health Act that states an employer has an overall obligation to furnish employees with a place of employment free from recognized hazards.

Generalizability   The degree to which the validity of a selection method established in one context extends to other contexts.

Glass ceiling   A barrier to advancement to higher-level jobs in the company that adversely affects women and minorities. The barrier may be due to lack of access to training programs, development experiences, or relationships (e.g., mentoring).

Goals   What an organization hopes to achieve in the medium- to long-term future.

Goals and timetables   The part of a written affirmative action plan that specifies the percentage of women and minorities that an employer seeks to have in each job group and the date by which that percentage is to be attained.

Group mentoring program   A program pairing a successful senior employee with a group of four to six less experienced protégés.

Group- or team-building methods   Training methods that help trainees share ideas and experiences, build group identity, understand the dynamics of interpersonal relationships, and get to know their own strengths and weaknesses and those of their co-workers.

Hands-on methods   Training methods that require the trainee to be actively involved in learning.

Health maintenance organization (HMO)   A health care plan that provides benefits on a prepaid basis for employees who are required to use only HMO medical service providers.

High-performance work systems   Work systems that maximize the fit between employees and technology.

High-potential employees   Employees the company believes are capable of being successful in high-level management positions.

Host country   The country in which the parent-country organization seeks to locate or has already located a facility.

Host-country nationals (HCNs)   Employees born and raised in a host, not parent, country.

HR or workforce analytics   The practice of using data from HR databases and other data sources to make evidence-based human resource decisions.

HR dashboard   HR metrics (such as productivity and absenteeism) that are accessible by employees and managers through the company intranet or human resource information system.

Human resource information system (HRIS)   A system used to acquire, store, manipulate, analyze, retrieve, and distribute information related to human resources.

Human resource management (HRM)   The policies, practices, and systems that influence employees' behavior, attitudes, and performances.

Human resource recruitment   The practice or activity carried on by the organization with the primary purpose of identifying and attracting potential employees.

In-basket   A simulation of the administrative tasks of a manager's job.

Incentive effect The effect a pay plan has on the behaviors of current employees.

Inclusion Creating an environment in which employees share a sense of belonging, mutual respect, and commitment with others so they can perform their best work.

Individualism–collectivism One of Hofstede's cultural dimensions; describes the strength of the relation between an individual and other individuals in a society.

Informal learning Learning that is learner initiated, involves action and doing, is motivated by an intent to develop, and does not occur in a formal learning setting.

Intangible assets A type of company asset including human capital, customer capital, social capital, and intellectual capital.

Integrative bargaining The part of the labor–management negotiation process that seeks solutions beneficial to both sides.

Interactional justice A concept of justice referring to the interpersonal nature of how the outcomes were implemented.

Internal analysis The process of examining an organization's strengths and weaknesses.

Internal growth strategy A focus on new market and product development, innovation, and joint ventures.

Internal labor force Labor force of current employees.

Internship On-the-job learning sponsored by an educational institution, or part of an academic program.

Interview Employees are questioned about their work and personal experiences, skills, and career plans.

Intraorganizational bargaining The part of the labor–management negotiation process that focuses on the conflicting objectives of factions within labor and management.

Involuntary turnover Turnover initiated by the organization (often among people who would prefer to stay).

ISO 9000:2000 A series of quality assurance standards developed by the International Organization for Standardization in Switzerland and adopted worldwide.

Job analysis The process of getting detailed information about jobs.

Job description A list of the tasks, duties, and responsibilities that a job entails.

Job design The process of defining the way work will be performed and the tasks that will be required in a given job.

Job enlargement Adding challenges or new responsibilities to an employee's current job.

Job evaluation An administrative procedure used to measure internal job worth.

Job experience The relationships, problems, demands, tasks, and other features that employees face in their jobs.

Job hazard analysis technique A breakdown of each job into basic elements, each of which is rated for its potential for harm or injury.

Job involvement The degree to which people identify themselves with their jobs.

Job redesign The process of changing the tasks or the way work is performed in an existing job.

Job rotation The process of systematically moving a single individual from one job to another over the course of time. The job assignments may be in various functional areas of the company or movement may be between jobs in a single functional area or department.

Job satisfaction A pleasurable feeling that results from the perception that one's job fulfills or allows for the fulfillment of one's important job values.

Job specification A list of the knowledge, skills, abilities, and other characteristics (KSAOs) that an individual must have to perform a job.

Job structure The relative pay of jobs in an organization.

Kaizen Practices participated by employees from all levels of the company that focus on continuous improvement of business processes.

Key jobs Benchmark jobs, used in pay surveys, that have relatively stable content and are common to many organizations.

Knowledge management Process of enhancing company performance by designing and using tools, systems, and cultures to improve creation, sharing, and use of knowledge.

Knowledge workers Employees who own the intellectual means of producing a product or service.

Leader of the HR function A role of the CHRO that focuses on working with HR team members regarding the development, design, and delivery of HR services.

Leaderless group discussion Process in which a team of five to seven employees solves an assigned problem within a certain time period.

Leading indicator An objective measure that accurately predicts future labor demand.

Lean thinking A way to do more with less effort, equipment, space, and time, but providing customers with what they need and want.

Learning management system (LMS) Technology platform that automates the administration, development, and delivery of a company's training program.

Learning organization An organization whose employees are continuously attempting to learn new things and apply what they have learned to improve product or service quality.

Liaison to the board of directors A role of the CHRO that focuses on preparation for board meetings, phone calls with board members, and attendance at board meetings.

Long-term–short-term orientation One of Hofstede's cultural dimensions; describes how a culture balances immediate benefits with future rewards.

Maintenance of membership Union rules requiring members to remain members for a certain period of time (e.g., the length of the union contract).

Malcolm Baldrige National Quality Award An award established in 1987 to promote quality awareness, to recognize quality achievements of U.S. companies, and to publicize successful quality strategies.

Manager support Degree to which trainees' managers emphasize the importance of attending training programs and stress the application of training content to the job.

Managing diversity The process of creating an environment that allows all employees to contribute to organizational goals and experience personal growth.

Marginal tax rate The percentage of an additional dollar of earnings that goes to taxes.

Masculinity–femininity dimension One of Hofstede's cultural dimensions; describes the division of roles between the sexes within a society.

Massive Open Online Courses (MOOCs) Online learning designed to enroll large numbers of learners who have access to the Internet and composed of interactive coursework including video lectures, discussion groups, wikis, and assessment quizzes.

Mediation A procedure for resolving collective bargaining impasses by which a mediator with no formal authority acts as a facilitator and go-between in the negotiations.

Mentor An experienced, productive senior employee who helps develop a less experienced employee.

Merit bonus Merit pay paid in the form of a bonus, instead of a salary increase.

Merit increase grid A grid that combines an employee's performance rating with his or her position in a pay range to determine the size and frequency of his or her pay increases.

Merit pay Traditional form of pay in which base pay is increased permanently.

Minimum wage The lowest amount that employers are legally allowed to pay; the 1990 amendment of the Fair Labor Standards Act permits a subminimum wage to workers under the age of 20 for a period of up to 90 days.

Mobile devices Equipment such as smartphones and tablet computers that provide employees with anytime, anywhere access to HR applications and other work-related information.

Motivation to learn The desire of the trainee to learn the content of a training program.

Myers-Briggs Type Inventory (MBTI)® A psychological test used for team building and leadership development that identifies employees' preferences for energy, information gathering, decision making, and lifestyle.

Needs assessment The process used to determine if training is necessary.

Negative affectivity A dispositional dimension that reflects pervasive individual differences in satisfaction with any and all aspects of life.

New technologies Current applications of knowledge, procedures, and equipment that have not been previously used. Usually involves replacing human labor with equipment, information processing, or some combination of the two.

Nonkey jobs Jobs that are unique to organizations and that cannot be directly valued or compared through the use of market surveys.

Occupational Safety and Health Act (OSHA) The 1970 law that authorizes the federal government to establish and enforce occupational safety and health standards for all places of employment engaging in interstate commerce.

Offshoring A special case of outsourcing where the jobs that move actually leave one country and go to another.

Onboarding Refers to the process of helping new hires adjust to social and performance aspects of their new jobs.

On-the-job training (OJT) Peers or managers training new or inexperienced employees who learn the job by observation, understanding, and imitation.

Opportunity to perform The trainee is provided with or actively seeks experience using newly learned knowledge, skills, or behavior.

Organizational analysis A process for determining the business appropriateness of training.

Organizational commitment The degree to which an employee identifies with the organization and is willing to put forth effort on its behalf.

Outcome fairness The judgment that people make with respect to the outcomes received relative to the outcomes received by other people with whom they identify.

Outplacement counseling Counseling to help displaced employees manage the transition from one job to another.

Output A job's performance standards.

Outsourcing An organization's use of an outside organization for a broad set of services.

Parent country The country in which a company's corporate headquarters is located.

Parent-country nationals (PCNs) Employees who were born and live in a parent country.

Pay grades Jobs of similar worth or content grouped together for pay administration purposes.

Pay level The average pay, including wages, salaries, and bonuses, of jobs in an organization.

Pay policy line A mathematical expression that describes the relationship between a job's pay and its job evaluation points.

Pay structure The relative pay of different jobs (job structure) and how much they are paid (pay level).

Pension Benefit Guaranty Corporation (PBGC) The agency that guarantees to pay employees a basic retirement benefit in the event that financial difficulties force a company to terminate or reduce employee pension benefits.

Performance appraisal The process through which an organization gets information on how well an employee is doing his or her job.

Performance feedback The process of providing employees information regarding their performance effectiveness.

Performance management The means through which managers ensure that employees' activities and outputs are congruent with the organization's goals.

Performance support systems Computer applications that can provide (as requested) skills training, information access, and expert advice.

Person analysis A process for determining whether employees need training, who needs training, and whether employees are ready for training.

Power distance One of Hofstede's cultural dimensions; concerns how a culture deals with hierarchical power relationships—particularly the unequal distribution of power.

Predictive validation A criterion-related validity study that seeks to establish an empirical relationship between applicants' test scores and their eventual performance on the job.

Preferred provider organization (PPO) A group of health care providers who contract with employers, insurance companies, and so forth to provide health care at a reduced fee.

Presentation methods Training methods in which trainees are passive recipients of information.

Principal In agency theory, a person (e.g., the owner) who seeks to direct another person's behavior.

Procedural justice A concept of justice focusing on the methods used to determine the outcomes received.

Profit sharing A compensation plan in which payments are based on a measure of organization performance (profits) and do not become part of the employees' base salary.

Progression of withdrawal Theory that dissatisfied individuals enact a set of behaviors to avoid the work situation.

Promotions Advances into positions with greater challenge, more responsibility, and more authority than the employee's previous job.

Prosocial motivation The degree to which people are motivated to help other people.

Protean career A career that is frequently changing due to both changes in the person's interests, abilities, and values and changes in the work environment.

Psychological success The feeling of pride and accomplishment that comes from achieving life goals.

Psychosocial support Serving as a friend and role model, providing positive regard and acceptance, and creating an outlet for a protégé to talk about anxieties and fears.

Quantitative ability Concerns the speed and accuracy with which one can solve arithmetic problems of all kinds.

Range spread The distance between the minimum and maximum amounts in a pay grade.

Rate ranges Different employees in the same job may have different pay rates.

Readiness for training Employee characteristics that provide them with the desire, energy, and focus necessary to learn from training.

Reasonable accommodation Making facilities readily accessible to and usable by individuals with disabilities.

Reasoning ability Refers to a person's capacity to invent solutions to many diverse problems.

Recruitment The process of seeking applicants for potential employment.

Reengineering Review and redesign of work processes to make them more efficient and improve the quality of the end product or service.

Referrals People who are prompted to apply for a job by someone within the organization.

Reliability The consistency of a performance measure; the degree to which a performance measure is free from random error.

Repatriation The preparation of expatriates for return to the parent company and country from a foreign assignment.

Representative of the firm A role of the CHRO that focuses on activities with external stakeholders, such as lobbying, speaking to outside groups, etc.

Repurposing Directly translating instructor-led training online.

Reshoring Moving jobs from overseas to the U.S.

Return on investment Refers to the estimated dollar return from each dollar invested in learning.

Reverse mentoring Business situation in which younger employees mentor more senior employees.

Right-to-work laws State laws that make union shops, maintenance of membership, and agency shops illegal.

Role behaviors Behaviors that are required of an individual in his or her role as a job holder in a social work environment.

Role-play A participant taking the part or role of a manager or other employee.

Sabbatical A leave of absence from the company to renew or develop skills.

Safety awareness programs Employer programs that attempt to instill symbolic and substantive changes in the organization's emphasis on safety.

Sarbanes-Oxley Act of 2002 A congressional act passed in response to illegal and unethical behavior by managers and executives. The act sets stricter rules for business, especially accounting practices including requiring more open and consistent disclosure of financial data, CEOs' assurance that data are completely accurate, and provisions that affect the employee–employer relationship (e.g., development of a code of conduct for senior financial officers).

Selection The process by which an organization attempts to identify applicants with the necessary knowledge, skills, abilities, and other characteristics that will help it achieve its goals.

Self-service Giving employees online access to human resources information.

Shared service model A way to organize the HR function that includes centers of expertise or excellence, service centers, and business partners.

Simulation A training method that represents a real-life situation, allowing trainees to see the outcomes of their decisions in an artificial environment.

Situational interview An interview procedure where applicants are confronted with specific issues, questions, or problems that are likely to arise on the job.

Six Sigma process System of measuring, analyzing, improving, and controlling processes once they meet quality standards.

Skill-based pay Pay based on the skills employees acquire and are capable of using.

Social media Online and mobile technology used to create interactive communications.

Social networking Websites and blogs that facilitate interactions between people.

Social performance management Social media and microblogs similar to Facebook, LinkedIn, and Yammer that allow employees to quickly exchange information, talk to each other, provide coaching, and receive feedback and recognition in the form of electronic badges.

Sorting effect The effect a pay plan has on the composition of the current workforce (the types of employees attracted and retained).

Specificity The extent to which a performance measure gives detailed guidance to employees about what is expected of them and how they can meet these expectations.

Stakeholders The various interest groups who have relationships with and, consequently, whose interests are tied to the organization (e.g., employees, suppliers, customers, shareholders, community).

Standard deviation rule A rule used to analyze employment tests to determine disparate impact; it uses the difference between the expected representation for minority groups and the actual representation to determine whether the difference between the two is greater than would occur by chance.

Stock options An employee ownership plan that gives employees the opportunity to buy the company's stock at a previously fixed price.

Strategic advisor to the executive team A role of the CHRO that focuses on the formulation and implementation of the firm's strategy.

Strategic choice The organization's strategy; the ways an organization will attempt to fulfill its mission and achieve its long-term goals.

Strategic congruence The extent to which the performance management system elicits job performance that is consistent with the organization's strategy, goals, and culture.

Strategic human resource management (SHRM) A pattern of planned human resource deployments and activities intended to enable an organization to achieve its goals.

Strategy formulation The process of deciding on a strategic direction by defining a company's mission and goals, its external opportunities and threats, and its internal strengths and weaknesses.

Strategy implementation The process of devising structures and allocating resources to enact the strategy a company has chosen.

Stretch assignments Job assignments in which there is a mismatch between an employee's skills and past experiences and the skills required for success on the job.

Succession planning The identification and tracking of high-potential employees capable of filling higher-level managerial positions.

Summary plan description (SPD) A reporting requirement of the Employee Retirement Income Security Act (ERISA) that obligates employers to describe the plan's funding, eligibility requirements, risks, and so forth within 90 days after an employee has entered the plan.

Support network Trainees who meet to discuss their progress in using learned capabilities on the job.

Sustainability The ability of a company to make a profit without sacrificing the resources of its employees, the community, or the environment. Based on an approach to organizational decision making that considers the long-term impact of strategies on stakeholders (e.g., employees, shareholders, suppliers, community).

Tacit knowledge Knowledge based on personal experience that is difficult to codify.

Taft-Hartley Act The 1947 act that outlawed unfair union labor practices.

Talent architect A role of the CHRO that focuses on building and identifying the human capital critical to the present and future of the firm.

Talent management Attracting, retaining, developing, and motivating highly skilled employees and managers.

Task analysis The process of identifying the tasks, knowledge, skills, and behaviors that need to be emphasized in training.

Team leader training Training of the team manager or facilitator.

Technic of operations review (TOR) Method of determining safety problems via an analysis of past accidents.

Teleconferencing Synchronous exchange of audio, video, or text between individuals or groups at two or more locations.

Temporary assignment Job tryouts such as employees taking on a position to help them determine if they are interested in working in a new role.

Third country A country other than a host or parent country.

Third-country nationals (TCNs) Employees born in a country other than a parent or host country.

360-degree appraisal (feedback systems) A performance appraisal process for managers that includes evaluations from a wide range of persons who interact with the manager.

The process includes self-evaluations as well as evaluations from the manager's boss, subordinates, peers, and customers.

Total quality management (TQM) A cooperative form of doing business that relies on the talents and capabilities of both labor and management to continually improve quality and productivity.

Training A planned effort to facilitate the learning of job-related knowledge, skills, and behavior by employees.

Training design process A systematic approach for developing training programs.

Training outcomes A way to evaluate the effectiveness of a training program based on cognitive, skill-based, affective, and results outcomes.

Transaction processing Computations and calculations used to review and document HRM decisions and practices.

Transfer The movement of an employee to a different job assignment in a different area of the company.

Transfer of training The use of knowledge, skills, and behaviors learned in training on the job.

Transitional matrix Matrix showing the proportion or number of employees in different job categories at different times.

Transnational process The extent to which a company's planning and decision-making processes include representatives and ideas from a variety of cultures.

Transnational representation Reflects the multinational composition of a company's managers.

Transnational scope A company's ability to make HRM decisions from an international perspective.

Tuition reimbursement The practice of reimbursing employees' costs for college and university courses and degree programs.

Uncertainty avoidance One of Hofstede's cultural dimensions; describes how cultures seek to deal with an unpredictable future.

Union shop A union security provision that requires a person to join the union within a certain amount of time after being hired.

Upward feedback A performance appraisal process for managers that includes subordinates' evaluations.

Utility The degree to which the information provided by selection methods enhances the effectiveness of selecting personnel in real organizations.

Utilization analysis A comparison of the race, sex, and ethnic composition of an employer's workforce with that of the available labor supply.

Validity The extent to which a performance measure assesses all the relevant—and only the relevant—aspects of job performance.

Verbal comprehension Refers to a person's capacity to understand and use written and spoken language.

Virtual reality Computer-based technology that provides trainees with a three-dimensional learning experience. Trainees operate in a simulated environment that responds to their behaviors and reactions.

Virtual teams Teams that are separated by time, geographic distance, culture and/or organizational boundaries and rely exclusively on technology for interaction between team members.

Voluntary turnover Turnover initiated by employees (often whom the company would prefer to keep).

Webcasting Classroom instruction provided online via live broadcasts.

Whistle-blowing Making grievances public by going to the media or government.

Workforce sensor A role of the CHRO that focuses on identifying workforce morale issues or concerns.

Workforce utilization review A comparison of the proportion of workers in protected subgroups with the proportion that each subgroup represents in the relevant labor market.

NAME AND COMPANY INDEX

Hotel Employees and Restaurant Employees (HERE), 599–600
HotJobs.com, 209
Hough, L., 340
HourlyNerd, 197
Hsieh, Tony, 439
Hudson Institute, 125–126
Hu-Friedy, 23
Hughes, Robert, 251
Humana, 685
Hunter, J. E., 676
Huselid, M., 21, 28, 50
Hyland, M., 647

Iberdrola USA, 45
IBM, 8, 44, 81–82, 89, 130, 157, 158, 231, 284, 476, 481, 686, 687
IKEA, 681–682
Immelt, Jeff, 387
Immigrations, Customs, and Enforcement (ICE), 37, 39
Indiana Heart Hospital, 175
Inditex, 481
Industrial & Commercial Bank of China, 630
Infosys, 200
Ingersoll Rand, 279
Inks, L., 344
Innotrac, 38
Instacart, 183
Intel Corporation, 158, 208, 319
Intermountain Healthcare, 11
Internal Revenue Service (IRS), 421, 422, 542, 548, 561
International Association of Machinists and Aerospace Workers, 606
International Coaching Federation, 402
International Harvester, 513
International Paper, 28
International Truck and Engine Corporation, 171
Isaac, M., 183
Isidore, C., 42
ISO (International Organization for Standardization), 30–31
Iverson, R., 50

J. M. Huber Corporation, 683
J. P. Stevens, 598
Jackson, Delbert, 127
Jackson, S. F., 83
Jacobs, A., 440
Jacobson, R., 243
J&J. *see* Johnson & Johnson
Japan Post Holdings, 630
Jawbone, 430
Jayasinghe, M., 481, 612, 637
J.C. Penney, 192
Jehn, K., 306
Jelinek, Craig, 422
Jenkins, Antony, 521
Jenny Craig, 127
Jentsch, F. G., 278
JetBlue, 67, 639
Jiffy Lube, 267
Jimmy Johns, 425–426
Jinran, Z., 560
Jive Software, 404
Jobs, Steve, 207–208, 434
John Deere, 151, 346–347
Johnson, David, 151
Johnson, Lyndon, 102, 106, 110
Johnson, R., 442
Johnson & Johnson (J&J), 406, 556

Johnson Controls, Inc., 11, 116
Jones, A., 428
Jones, Paula Corbin, 126
Jones, S., 346
Joshi, A., 647
JPMorganChase, 40, 547
Jung, Carl, 389
Just Born, 296, 348, 382, 392
Juvenile Diabetes Research Foundation, 557

Kaiser Permanente, 325
Kalman, F., 283, 378
Kan, Wang, 440
Kaplan, R. S., 517
Karpicke, J., 278
Katz, H. C., 601, 608
Katz, Harry, 578, 581
Kazanas, H. C., 286
Kelleher, Herb, 67
Keller, Bill, 196
Keller Williams, 263–264
Kelly, Chip, 244
Kenexa Corporation, 231
Kentucky Fried Chicken, 72, 235
KERM television, 245
Kettl, D. F., 421
Keville, Edel, 404
KFC, 43
Kim. D. O., 517
Kimberly-Clark, 303
King, Martin Luther, Jr., 106
King Pharmaceutical, 358
Kinko's, 158
Kirin Brewery, 295
KLA-Tencor, 274–275, 288–289
Klein, H., 307
Kleiner, M. M., 597
Kleiner Perkins Caufield & Byers, 101
Kleinschmidt, Ulrich, 618
Knack.it, 232
Knowles, M., 278
Koch, C. G., 240
Kochan, T. A., 578, 581, 601, 608
Kohn, A., 278
Komatsu, 195
Konovsky, M. A., 508
Korn/Ferry, 128, 129
Korte, G., 421
KPMG, 559, 652
Kraiger, K., 271, 276
Krantz, M., 457
Kravitz, D. E., 444
Kroger, 669–670
Kuehner-Hebert, K., 283, 328
Kühlmann, T., 612, 637
Kulish, N., 246
Kurmanaev, A., 199

La Boulange, 18
Lambert, Ladena, 514
Lanaj, K., 442
Landis, Floyd, 436
Langdon, J. C., 330
Larson, C., 481
Latham, G. D., 278
Latham, Gary, 341

SUBJECT INDEX